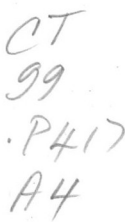

Made in United States of America

Published by The Geological Society of America
New York, New York

Printed by Waverly Press, Inc.
Baltimore, Maryland

LIFE AND LETTERS

OF

R. A. F. Penrose, Jr.

BY

HELEN R. FAIRBANKS
AND
CHARLES P. BERKEY

NEW YORK
November 15, 1952

Contents

Chapter	Page
1. A Man's Vision and His Bequest	1
2. From These Roots	7
3. School Days	41
4. Nathaniel Southgate Shaler Points the Way	77
5. Texas in the Early Days	107
6. J. C. Branner and the Arkansas Survey	141
7. Cripple Creek and Other Ventures	163
8. Mining in Arizona Territory	193
9. Adventures in Eurasia	211
10. A Harvard Alumnus	293
11. Beginnings of Utah Copper	305
12. Alaska in 1903	321
13. Trip to the Antipodes	335
14. Africa and its Gold Fields	377
15. Around South America in 1907	415
16. T. C. Chamberlin and the University of Chicago	493
17. Era of World War I	513
18. Beginnings of the Society of Economic Geologists	549
19. Philadelphia in the Nineteen-Twenties	599
20. Relations with the Geological Society	683
21. Relations with the American Philosophical Society	717
22. Search for an Heir	729
A Twenty-year Summary. By H. R. Aldrich	755

Illustrations

R. A. F. Penrose, Jr.	Frontispiece
	Facing page
Hanna Boies Penrose and her son Dick	54
Dr. R. A. F. Penrose	55
Dick Penrose as a student at Harvard	86
Nathaniel Southgate Shaler	87
Dick Penrose as a young man	118
Edward T. Dumble	119
Dick Penrose as a member of the Arkansas Survey	150
J. C. Branner	151
Cripple Creek, Colorado	182
Boies, Charles, and Spencer Penrose	183
Dick Penrose as a member of the University of Chicago faculty	502
Thomas Chrowder Chamberlin	503
John M. Clarke	694
Penrose Medal of The Geological Society of America	695
The Aitkin bust of Penrose	702

Foreword

WHEN, in the summer of 1931, Richard Alexander Fullerton Penrose, Jr., died in Philadelphia, he left his personally acquired fortune, amounting to approximately ten million dollars, to be divided equally between The Geological Society of America and the American Philosophical Society. As a memorial to its benefactor and as a picture of a period in the history of American geological science, this volume has been prepared by The Geological Society of America.

Beginning with notebooks, diaries, and letters in the possession of the Society, and adding thereunto material slowly accumulated from his family, his friends, his associates, and acquaintances, the story of his life has been pieced together.

Probably a volume such as this, which has been prepared as a memorial tribute of a grateful organization to the man who has endowed it with a large trust fund, needs no explanation of how and why it was written. If the reader will bear this fact in mind, he will understand more clearly why much has been included in this volume that might not otherwise be used.

Much of the material that seems to be repetitious was included for the precise reason that only by noting this trait and the discipline to which Penrose subjected himself can one understand what manner of man he was. From his school-boy letters to his father to the last one he wrote, Penrose never failed in courtesy to his reader, never failed to explain fully. This very courtesy is a measure of the man himself, an indication of the modest nature which never assumed that others would remember details concerning himself without having them freshly brought to mind.

For members of Penrose's profession, the geologists, this account of his life should have particular interest, for it presents a picture of a period which is gone forever, a picture of conditions under which the early investigators in geology and the mineral industry labored and brought forth the principles and methods of later days, methods more scientific, perhaps, but, nevertheless, methods founded upon the efforts of those pioneers. If one is inclined to smile at the picture of the young man of the 1880's sitting on a bluff above a Texas river, confronted with the problem of making a survey without knowing how to go about it, let him ask himself what he would have done, similarly unequipped and in hitherto unknown territory. Let the geologist of today, with his carefully prepared field equipment, ask himself just how well he would like to look forward to "living off the country," as Penrose did in the early days in Arkansas. It speaks volumes for the stamina of any man to be able to confront uncomfortable conditions with the nonchalance which Penrose displayed. And how much more to his credit this is, when a man is endowed by birth, position, and economic security so that he need never have left the comforts of urban living in Philadelphia.

That he accepted such conditions as a matter of course, that he refused to allow them to turn him from his chosen course, and that in the end he was able to surmount every difficulty as master of the situation is the measure of his character and stature.

We have tried to give a full picture of the man just as he was. Some parts of the story may be more interesting and some more suggestive than others, but all are needed, we think, to show what manner of man he was. It appears that outstanding was his ability to decide for himself upon a goal and then to stick to that objective, regardless of all hardships and attempts to dissuade him. Whether or not all his choices were wise is not an easy matter to decide, and perhaps not for us to say, for no one is wise enough to say what an alternative course could have accomplished. The one he followed finally gave to science in America much-needed financial support through a large bequest to the American Philosophical Society, and like permanent support to his own field of geology by lifting the Geological Society of America, at one stroke, into a position of outstanding opportunity and independence. It is more than doubtful whether any other course would have accomplished as much.

In many places, the story itself, as told in the letters, is commonplace. The men involved are outstanding, but the picture they create, in their assembled correspondence, is not very exciting. But that is as it should be; it is more true to life than the dramatized version. The ordinary development of trends is not very spectacular as seen by outsiders, even though there may be critical situations and decisions for the individual to face that have dynamite in them.

In places the story covers developments that are of interest to many people. It adds greatly to the historical background of an important era in the development of geological science in America. The persons who cross the stage are those who have controlled the course of organized geological association. Their individual characteristics crop out in normal exhibits, and the picture is eminently satisfying.

Through it all, despite the fact that Penrose was heavily involved from the very beginning in specialistic development, his interest in the broader field represented by the whole of geologic science is obvious. His vision remained clear, and when it came to the final disposition of his accumulated wealth he still maintained the broad views of earlier years. He was more deeply moved by the vision of the philosopher and the prophet than by specialistic genius. So he gave his bequests to all knowledge, reserving only the privilege of being more generous to Geologic Science than to other fields.

How much of this breadth of interest was born in him and how much grew out of his association with such great men in the geologic field as Dumble and Branner and such great teachers as Chamberlin and Shaler, and out of the fundamental training given him by his remarkable father, no one can determine. But he never lost sight of the greater goals these men inspired and never lost an opportunity to emphasize the superiority of their claims.

HELEN R. FAIRBANKS
and
CHARLES P. BERKEY

Preface

IN APRIL, 1938, the Council of The Geological Society of America authorized me to undertake the preparation of a biography of the late R. A. F. Penrose, Jr. The actual work was to be done by Helen R. Fairbanks, for six years managing editor of the publications of the Society. It was in that capacity that she came across the notebooks and diaries of Dr. Penrose, which are the property of the Society, and became convinced that within their pages lay the nucleus for a story of his life. It was largely due to her conviction upon that point that I was persuaded to present the matter to the Council, where it was promptly approved and the work was begun.

Since that time, however, many unexpected things have happened, some of which have greatly impeded and delayed the consummation of this work. The chief of these has been the World War II which, with its after-service, has claimed an unforeseen amount of time. Miss Fairbanks spent five years as head of the Department of Journalism at Saint Mary's College at South Bend, one year as head of American Red Cross service for women of the Armed Forces in the Military District of Washington, three years of active service as a lieutenant-commander in the WAVES, and is now with the Navy Department in Washington as historian for the Bureau of Yards and Docks.

Most of the actual collecting of data, however, was done at once. In the summer of 1938, Miss Fairbanks and I went together to see Dr. Penrose's brother, Spencer Penrose, at Colorado Springs. We found him much interested in the project and he put at our disposal all the material—literally trunksful—left in his hands. Miss Fairbanks spent some time there, going over and sorting a vast amount of material pertaining to the family, including many of the letters in this volume. She also visited Cripple Creek and Denver, and interviewed men who had known Penrose in his active days. Subsequently the same steps were taken with his close friends and relatives in Philadelphia and particularly his cousin, Ellen Penrose of Carlisle, Pennsylvania.

Literally hundreds of letters were written to those whose relations with Penrose, as indicated by the correspondence available, might have something of value to contribute to the picture.

From Charles Schuchert, late professor of paleontology at Yale University, we received valuable information concerning Penrose's early study of the problem of endowment with a portion of the fortune he had created. From Daniel C. Jackling, the man who saw the possibilities in low-grade copper, came a fine tribute and valuable other aid as given in the chapter on Utah copper. Dr. Edwin G. Conklin, longtime Secretary and three times President of the American Philosophical Society, contributed the material on that organization. Former

President Herbert Hoover not only loaned his files on Penrose, but also read and commented on the chapters which referred to his relationship with Penrose.

"From his diaries and letters, particularly those to his father," Miss Fairbanks wrote to me at the end of the summer's work in 1939, "I have been able to obtain a thoroughly interesting picture of a man who succeeded, a man who won the goals which he had set up for himself, and I am sure that he will be shown to be a much more interesting person than those who knew him only in the dignified austerity of his later years might have suspected."

Miss Fairbanks devoted five summer vacations and such time during the school year as could be spared from her teaching duties to the manuscript, which was turned over to me for submission in June, 1943. During all that work I was in constant touch with her by letter and through conference, reading manuscript and making suggestions, chapter by chapter. Then when the war made its immediate publication impracticable, the manuscript was set aside, to be rechecked before its final submission to the Society.

Much time has gone by, but nothing of value has been lost. The story of his life, like the growth of his fortune and the conviction as to its ultimate use, has grown slowly to its present form. We have endeavored to keep in mind that this book will be read by many who could not have known Penrose or his story. For those, we have made the picture as well rounded as we could. We have also sought to present the man as he was, to the best of our ability. The work is intended as a memorial to a human being and not as a best seller on an imaginary character. Neither is it devoted to the "debunking", nor to the "glorification" of a man. We have found him tremendously human, with faults, like the rest of us, but, also like the rest of us, with redeeming traits that make him particularly likable. In many ways, it appears, his very success defeated his inmost longings. In his closing years he was a lonely soul. In this atmosphere, when the end drew near, he gave away the fortune he had made to the interests he most valued in the world—the advancement of knowledge and the development of geologic science. Thus it happened that new and far-reaching opportunity came to the American Philosophical Society of Philadelphia, his home city, and The Geological Society of America, representing the future of his own life-time field.

So we present Richard Penrose as he was, neither a popular hero nor a plundering villain, but an earnest, intelligent, hard-working, ambitious, and self-reliant man who made his millions honestly out of the abundance of the Earth itself, as the fruit of his scientific and technical knowledge and skill, and whose life story is a part of the history of a stage in our country's growth the like of which we shall not see again.

CHARLES P. BERKEY

New York, April 1950

Acknowledgments

In any biography, acknowledgments are essential. This work is no exception; it has been completed only with the generous assistance of many individuals and institutions. As far as possible, acknowledgment of such assistance has been recorded at the appropriate place in the text. To each and every one, I hereby express my grateful appreciation.

There are also various individuals to whom I am particularly indebted.

In addition to those whose help and cooperation is acknowledged in the *Preface*, I am deeply grateful to various members of the Penrose family for aid in rounding out the portrait. My obligation is great to Mrs. Spencer Penrose, who graciously aided in the collection of family photographs, including the miniature of Hannah Boies Penrose. Boies Penrose, nephew, and Dr. Stephen B. L. Penrose, cousin, of Richard Penrose, were particularly generous in furnishing otherwise inaccessible material.

The entire manuscript has been read and criticized with cordial severity by Dr. Edward G. Conklin and John Stokes Adams. To each of these kindly critics I am especially indebted for helpful suggestions.

I wish also to express my sincere appreciation of the time and effort generously given out of their busy lives by those who read various chapters of this book and gave me the benefit of their frank and carefully considered criticism. In addition to former President Herbert Hoover and Daniel C. Jackling, the list includes Sydney H. Ball, Charles H. Behre, Marland Billings, George C. Branner, Rollin T. Chamberlin, Thomas S. Gates, L. C. Graton, Miriam F. Howells, Ina R. Marvin, Charles Palache, E. H. Sellards, J. Edward Spurr.

My obligation is great to all those who furnished information or granted me access to material. Especially am I indebted to George Saltonstall Mumford, Franklin Remington, and Dr. Arthur Pierce Butler for information concerning Penrose as a Harvard student.

Thanks are also due to those men who remembered the early days in Colorado and the part Dick Penrose played in the development of the mining industry, and willingly answered my questions with zeal and good humor. Their names include those of the Hon. Edward P. Arthur, Jr., Norris Eads, Ben Hill, Berne Hopkins, Charles Howbert, W. H. Leonard, Harry J. Newton, Etienne A. Ritter, Charles Searles, Gustav Sessinghaus, and Thomas B. Stearns.

Long is the list of those with whom I corresponded, too long to record at this point, but I particularly wish to thank Percy E. Barbour, Dr. William S. Bryant, Frederick Ehrenfeld, Nevin M. Fenneman, Edmund J. Farris, F. Lynwood Garrison, Robert T. Hill, Harriette E. Hills, Waldemar Lindgren, Edward W. Mumford, Morris L. Parrish, Thomas Ridgway, E. J. Sellers, Edmund Lowber Stokes, John Wagner, and John E. Wolff.

Acknowledgment is also gratefully made to J. Stanley-Brown, whose pioneer efforts in the writing of the Penrose memorial for the *Proceedings* of The Geological Society of America provided the original nucleus for this work.

And, finally, I am indebted beyond the possibility of adequate acknowledgment to Dr. Charles P. Berkey, to whose unfailing encouragement and counsel this work owes more than can be told.

HELEN R. FAIRBANKS

CHAPTER I

A Man's Vision and His Bequest

ON THE last day of July in the year one thousand nine hundred thirty-one, a man died in a hotel in Philadelphia—a man who had houses but no home, a family but no wife or child, many acquaintances and friends but no intimates to whom he confided everything. He was sixty-seven years of age, a man of fine physique and commanding presence, who had travelled widely over the world and who had observed much of the ways of nature and of other men. He was a college graduate and came of a family long prominent among the socially elite of Philadelphia, his native city. He was a geologist by profession, and in that field he had attained wealth and honor beyond that of most men. In short, he enjoyed in this life more than falls to the lot of most men; yet he lacked much that most men enjoy. His name was Richard Alexander Fullerton Penrose, Junior, but to his family and his intimates he was known as Dick. And to avoid any possible ambiguity or the cumbersome use of the term, Junior, he is designated as Dick in this book.

Early in life he manifested the poise and self-sufficiency which belong only to those who have learned to rely upon their own resources, who enjoy the society of their fellowmen but are not dependent upon them, and who are not encompassed by financial limitations. This self-reliance increased with the passing years, and thus, in the course of time, he became a somewhat mysterious figure in the social and professional worlds in which he moved.

But however different from most men he may have seemed to those who knew him only in later life, he would undoubtedly have soon become merely another name, to be quickly forgotten by a new generation, had it not been for his remarkable bequest, by which, in the lack of a child of his own, he made all men of science his heirs through two great societies—The Geological Society of America and the American Philosophical Society. As long as these organizations continue to function, the name of Penrose will be invoked whenever a grant-in-aid is sought.

Although many persons knew that Penrose was well supplied with this world's goods, very few, if any except his brother Spencer, who had been close to him in his investment program, had any idea of the extent of his wealth. He lived unostentatiously but comfortably in a spacious suite at the Hotel Bellevue-Stratford in Philadelphia; he maintained the old family residence at 1331 Spruce Street, fully staffed, just as it had been during the life of his father; he had a suite of offices in the Bullitt Building in Philadelphia, and also quarters at the University and the Harvard Clubs and at a hotel in New York. For the rest, he lived quietly among his books. One need not be tremendously wealthy to do all this. Most of his friends conceded that he must be a millionaire; nevertheless, when the will was made public and it was discovered that he had, in addition to several minor bequests, left approximately ten million dollars to be divided equally between his two principal scientific beneficiaries, every one was astonished.

And all this money had been earned by this man through his own efforts and through the application of his knowledge as a geologist. For although Dick Penrose came of a family socially and financially well placed, the family fortune was in the form of a trust, the income from which he shared with his brothers, but he could dispose of no part of the principal. The millions which he gave away were his own, earned by his knowledge and foresight.

Here was a story to be told in superlatives, and the newspapers told it in their own way:

"The largest public gifts by a Philadelphian, not even excluding the gifts of Stephen Girard to the City, which at the time of his death was about $6,000,000," declared the *Philadelphia Inquirer* of September 26, 1931.

"Richard's gift of $10,000,000 to two scientific bodies makes one of the largest benefactions in the world for such a purpose," the same paper stated in its issue of February 20, 1932.

"Dr. Penrose's public bequests exceed any in the history of the city," said the *Philadelphia Evening Bulletin* of September 26, 1931. And in the *Washington (D. C.) Star* of November 15, 1931, Frederick William Wile wrote:

"Thanks to the munificent bequests of the late Richard A. F. Penrose of Philadelphia, a brother of the former Senator Boies Penrose of Pennsylvania, American scientific development is scheduled for one of the greatest 'booms' in its history. Mr. Penrose, who passed away last Summer, left the bulk of his large estate to two of the country's foremost learned bodies—the Geological Society of America and the American Philosophical Society.

"For the particular purpose to which the funds are to be put," continues the Wile article, "the Penrose will is believed to establish a precedent. Never before have struggling American organizations of a scientific character—and the existence of most of them is a perpetual struggle—been so handsomely caparisoned with cash to carry out long-cherished plans."

One other surprise connected with this bequest was the fact that Dick Penrose left such a large proportion of cash—more than three million dollars—"the largest amount ever left in cash by an American," according to the *Philadelphia Ledger* of April 2, 1932. "The money was distributed in five banks or brokerage houses in Philadelphia, three in New York, two in Denver, and one in London. It included a large amount of foreign coinage, evidently for his use whenever he saw fit to travel."

Evidently, Dick Penrose had taken thoroughly to heart the old adage about not keeping all the eggs in one basket. However, it should be remembered that this was 1931, a time of great financial stress, when every one doubted the stability of many things financial—including investments and securities—and sought to protect themselves with good hard cash stored in safe places. And in view of what actually happened in the financial world, he evidenced that far-sighted and objective thinking which had made him outstanding throughout his life.

That same far-sightedness was evidenced in the manner in which he made his bequests, establishing trust funds from which the income only can be used but placing no strings upon the kind of use that should be made.

Except among the members of his own profession, Dick was probably the least widely known of the four remarkable sons of the equally remarkable Richard Alexander Fullerton Penrose, noted professor of medicine at the University of Pennsylvania for twenty-six years, and Sarah Hannah Boies Penrose. Most people knew Dick's eldest brother, Boies, long prominent in Pennsylvania politics and for years an outstanding figure in the nation's capital as the Senator from his native State. To the people of Colorado in particular and to the West in general, as well as to financial circles of the East, his youngest brother, Spencer, was a familiar figure, from the days of the Cripple Creek gold rush in 1891 until his death in 1939. Charles, between Boies and Dick in age, won like prominence in his own profession of medicine. Few families can show a more outstanding record of accomplishment in diverse fields.

The truth, of course, is that they had ability of a high order; their success did not "just happen." Fine flowering is ever the result of sturdy roots, careful training, and fortuitous circumstances.

"We are told that the Penroses were people of consequence and accomplishment, long established and deeply rooted in the soils and industries of old Cornwall," said Charles P. Berkey, Secretary of The Geological Society of America, in the course of his formal address before the Society in 1935 on the occasion of the unveiling of the Penrose bust, executed by Robert I. Aitken, which now stands in the headquarters of the Society in New York.

"Peering further into the family records, it appears that from this Cornish family sprang a man, Bartholomew Penrose, presumably one of the most venturesome and most courageous of his line," continued Berkey, "who came to America in the year 1700 and settled in Philadelphia, where he engaged in useful and profitable enterprise and founded the prominent American family of Penrose. To this family in the seventh generation, Richard Alexander Fullerton Penrose, Jr., belonged.

"After carefully supervised schooling in his own city, he was sent with his two elder brothers to Harvard, where they all finished advanced training with high honors; one, Boies Penrose, becoming in due time an outstanding political leader in his native state of Pennsylvania; the other, Charles, becoming a noted surgeon. A younger brother, Spencer, a prosperous mine operator and investor, is the only surviving member of this remarkable quartet.

"At Harvard, Richard came under the influence of that master inspirer of young men, Nathaniel Southgate Shaler, whose teaching and example undoubtedly shaped the remaining years of his life. It is an incidental matter that he became the first candidate for the degree of Doctor of Philosophy in geologic science in that institution. Much more important is the fact that thenceforth he devoted his whole energy to the field of geology and finally, at the end of a long and productive life, devised a way of his own to insure continuance of the search for truth that he had undertaken at the hand of Shaler.

"It is more than an accident, of course, that he became a member of several state geological surveys, that he came to be intensely interested in mineral deposits and contributed materially to their better understanding, that he enjoyed a period of university teaching, that at various times he was engaged in mine operating and management, and that he was unusually successful as an advisory engineer and investor in mines. Through many years, he was exceedingly active, finally extending his professional travels to every quarter of the earth in his search for new scientific adventure and economic opportunity.

"But Penrose was more than an intellectual machine, no matter how perfect or effective it might be. As a man among men, he was equally conspicuous for his fine human quality, although, even in his more sympathetic moods, one still felt something of the reserve that belongs by good right to the man of genuine worth. He was a staunch friend to those who found entrance to his inner circle. To all, he was a courtly gentleman, self-contained, dignified, serious-minded, and purposeful. For reasons or circumstances known only to himself, he did not establish a family of his own, and, denied that outlet for his generous spirit, he seems to have turned with increasing devotion to the scientific urgings and dreams of earlier days.

"Finally, in his later years, as the fires of his youth burned lower, and his financial cares and other interests grew to real burdens, some of his earlier ambition may have been smothered. But his keen interest was never quenched, and to his last day much of his concern had to do with new plans or revival of earlier ones.

"It was not my intention, however, to present a biographical survey of his life or a record of his accomplishments. . . . Neither have I come to deliver a eulogy. Men who probably knew him more intimately have paid such tribute. What I should like to do, if I could, would be to analyze his character and discover the elements of his fine faith in his fellow men and in the worthwhileness of organized science. His forward-looking plan embraced chiefly the physical problems of the Earth, and a certain restlessness seems to have developed with increasing appreciation of the enormous amount of work yet to be done. Always there was something to be done, something more pretentious or more comprehensive than he had ever attempted before or farther beyond the borders of the known.

"I know, of course, that the common explanation given for such journeys into the far corners of the earth as those of his maturer years would be more materialistic than I am now picturing. But I wonder, after all, how a great vision is created or discovered or snatched out of the surrounding somewhere. It must be, after all, an experience vouchsafed only to an occasional favored one, as if such gods as there be had marked him for special favor. Perhaps that is the way, deep devotions of men are aroused and great visions are gathered out of the elemental mists that surround us human beings.

"It must have been somewhere in this period of re-adjustments and gropings of later maturity that he sought new contact with the Geological Society of America. I recall vividly his many visits to the then-headquarters of the Society. As President, he was a persistent visitor. No other superior officer within my experience gave nearly so much time or appeared to be so deeply concerned about the future of the Society. And the approach was always the same; always an anxious peering into the future, as if somewhere in the distance there might be discerned the outlines of a more effective organic structure or the beginnings of a great adventure or accomplishment; always wondering what could be done that would be more worthwhile, and what the first steps should be.

"When he first came, the entire equipment of the Society's headquarters, insofar as the Secretary's office then represented it, was a gloomy roll-top desk standing in the far corner of a private office constantly used for other purposes, a noisy typewriter, and a typist three times a week. When he returned to his own office that first day, he wrote out a check for five hundred dollars to be applied to improvement of secretarial equipment and service. Thus, the subsidies that have continued in one form or another from that day, were begun. The wildest dreamer could not have read much into such an episode; but, perhaps it is true, also, that this is the substance on which visions grow.

"After finishing his presidential year, which he always spoke of as his greatest honor, his interest continued, taking even more practical turns. He once remarked that no society could impress even its own members with its dignity, without having a home of its own. How such advantages were to be afforded he would not discuss. Of course, one can see now that his plans were forming through that period, but no one other than he ever knew a word of it. Only a few months before his death, he had asked me to look up a possible location for such a home, and this search was in progress when the word came that seemed to end it all. But, instead of the end, it was only a new beginning, for the Penrose Bequest was his response, and it has opened a new world to the Geological Society.

"Through the later years, as time wore on, it must have become increasingly clear to him that the dreams he had, of continuing personal researches, could never be realized. A less persistent man, or a less confident and hopeful one, would have let it pass; he would have embraced the opportunity to devote both leisure and fortune to more immediate satisfactions. But not so Penrose. With him, it led only to the invention of a better solution. Instead of a new personal adventure based on his own effort, he became content at last to pass the responsibility over to the great brotherhood of searchers after truth to which he belonged. So he has provided a princely fortune to serve as a physical background for continuing programs of progress of geologic science....

"It seems only yesterday that he was a living presence. Today, he is but a memory. A few days more and, all too soon, he will become a tradition, and for generations to come, elders will tell the story of this lover of geologic science, who by one master stroke took the whole geological fraternity into permanent partnership. Thus do the physical elements of man perish and return as dust to dust, while his spiritual creations live after him."

CHAPTER 2

From These Roots

"MEN DO not gather grapes of thorns or figs of thistles."
Thus, did Dick Penrose preface a typewritten manuscript entitled *Early Life and Ancestral Sketch of Boies Penrose*, which he dictated May 6, less than three months before his death in Philadelphia, July 31, 1931.

Boies and Dick were two of the seven sons of Richard Alexander Fullerton Penrose and his wife, Sarah Hannah Boies, and what was written of Boies might with equal truth be applied to Dick.:

"Probably no man in public life ever felt more strongly than did Senator Penrose that his accomplishments should be based on his own efforts and that his fame should not depend on his ancestry. At the same time, he naturally took pride in what had been done by those from whom he was descended, though he never mentioned the matter without saying that 'a man should stand on his own feet or fall by the wayside.' No one ever carried out this conception of man's duty more completely and successfully than Boies Penrose. The writer, however, feels that it is only proper to introduce here a brief sketch of his family in Colonial days and subsequent times.

"He was descended from some of the oldest and best Colonial families of Pennsylvania, New England, and Maryland; his ancestors were men highly esteemed and honored in the times and communities in which they lived. The first member of the Penrose family to come to America was Bartholomew Penrose, who came to Philadelphia about 1700 and engaged with William Penn, William Penn, Jr., James Logan, and William Trent in shipbuilding and in operating lines of vessels to Jamaica and other places. Their ship, the *'Diligence,'* was the pride of the Colonial merchant marine of its day. Bartholomew Penrose had emigrated from Bristol, England, where his family had resided for a long time as ship-builders and leading citizens after they had left their original ancestral home in Cornwall."

According to Dr. Josiah Granville Leach, who wrote the *History of the Penrose Family of Philadelphia*, "it is from a quaint couplet, formed by a number of Cornish words, that the home of the Penrose family is learned:

> By Tre, Ros, Pol, Caer and Pen
> You may know most of the Cornish men.

"The word Penrose is of Cornu-British origin, and, according to the *Parochial History of the County of Cornwall*, an elaborate and careful work compiled from ancient authorities, is derived as a surname from the Manor of Penrose, in the parish of Sithney, County Cornwall, which manor gave dwelling to the very ancient family seated in that place, it is said, before William the Conqueror landed in Britain. The manor was charmingly situated near Helston, on the banks of the Loo-Pool, which partly belonged to it.

"At the time that William Borlase (1695–1722) was preparing his *Antiquities Historical and Monumental of Cornwall*, there was in the parish church of Sithney a tablet to the memory of Bernard Penrose, Prior to St. John's Hospital, who died in 1532, and in the east window of the south aisle, the Penrose arms were to be seen in the stained glass."

The arms of the Penrose family, as Dr. Leach points out, are: "Argent, three bands sable, each charged with as many roses of the field. Crest—a Loo troup naiant or.

"The roses in the Penrose coat-armor," he continued, "were probably suggested by a play on the last syllable of the name, a custom quite common in early heraldry; and a tradition in the family makes the Cornish Penroses adherents of the house of York in its famous feud with the rival house of Lancaster. . . . The fish in the crest of the Cornish family—a Loo trout naiant or—is, as were fishes in general, an emblem of chastity. It is supposed that fish were regarded with special favor as heraldic charges in the middle ages, from the belief that they were the first living things created by God, and from the fact that in early Christian times it was used as a symbol of Christ."

A Richard Penrose, of Sithney, was Sheriff of Cornwall in 1526, and an even earlier mention is of Godfrey de Penrose and Richard de Penrose, who were living at the manor in 1283.

Bartholomew Penrose and Dorothy Lancaster
(English generation)

Bartholomew Penrose, the emigrant, was the son of Bartholomew Penrose of Saint Stephen's Parish, Bristol, England, and his wife, Dorothy Lancaster, daughter of William Lancaster. According to the records of that parish, the son was baptised there January 21, 1674.

George H. Penrose, colonel in the United States Army, who published *A Geneological Chart of the Penrose Family* as a supplement to the Leach work, records that Bartholomew Penrose and Dorothy Lancaster, widow of one Pett, were married September 30, 1666, at Bristol, and that "the records of the Town Clerk of the City of Bristol and sworn to by him state—

"Bartholomew Penrose, shipwright, was admitted to the Liberties of that City on April 26th, 1670, for the purpose of marrying Dorothy, daughter of William Lancaster; that their son, James, was admitted to the Liberties of the same City, February 20th, 1689; that their son, Thomas, was admitted to the Liberties of the City, June 3rd, 1693; that their son, Bartholomew the emigrant, was engaged in ship building in Bristol in 1690."

Bartholomew Penrose and Esther Leech

(Emigrant generation)

Of Bartholomew Penrose, the emigrant, Dr. Leach writes that he "was engaged with his brother, Thomas Penrose, in the ship-building business at Bristol, Gloucestershire, before coming to America. Much of the early trading between England and Philadelphia was carried on from Bristol, and from that port sailed many of the ships which brought the early colonists to Pennsylvania. Bartholomew Penrose witnessed the departure and return of some of these ships, and from his intercourse with out- and in-going passengers and sea-captains, and possibly William Penn himself (with whom he was no doubt personally acquainted), he came to possess much information concerning Penn's rising province in the New World. Availing himself of such information, and being young, enthusiastic, and of an adventurous spirit, he finally determined to quit Old England, and to emigrate to Pennsylvania, whither he came about A. D. 1700, making his settlement in Philadelphia.

"Mr. Penrose doubtless came well provided with letters of recommendation and introduction, and with means, since he is found marrying, two or three years later (1703) the daughter of a wealthy and prominent citizen, and acquiring landed possessions."

The "wealthy and prominent citizen" was Tobias Leech, styled a "tanner" in

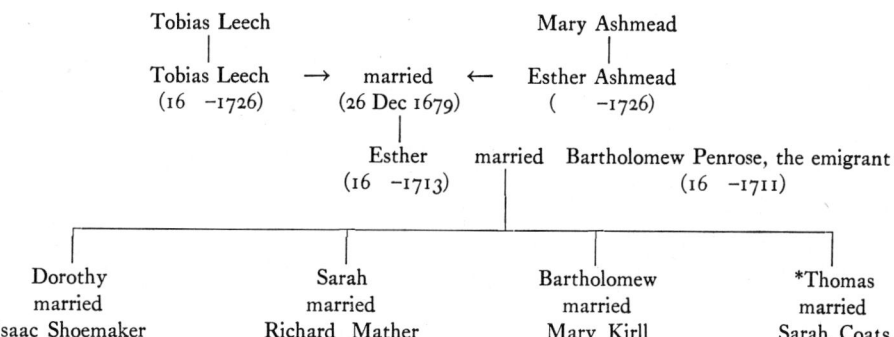

the early deeds of Pennsylvania. He had been born son of Tobias Leech, of Cheltenham, England, where he was baptized 1 January 1652. On 26 December 1679 he had married Esther Ashmead, and three years later (1682) had emigrated to the Pennsylvania colony, accompanied by his family and that of his mother-in-law, Mrs. Mary Ashmead. Family tradition says that he came with Penn in the ship, *Welcome*, and this may very well be, for, according to Dr. Leach, "in less than a month after Penn's arrival, Mr. Leech is known to have been in Philadelphia, and to have then purchased from Penn two hundred and fifty acres of land. The tract so secured was located in what became Cheltenham township, and there Mr. Leech settled, the Ashmeads locating on an adjoining tract of equal

---

* Ancestor of Dick Penrose.

size, the township deriving its name in honor of the English home of the Leeches and Ashmeads.

"Mr. Leech was one of the substantial men among the early colonists, and he came to be one of the largest landed proprietors in the province. Upon his home plantation he erected a corn and fulling mill, the first constructed in that part of the province, and he there carried on the milling business in conjunction with farming. His first mansion house was destroyed by fire in 1700, and the one built to take its place is still standing on Church Road east of the Old York Road, near the present (1903) Elkins Station, North Pennsylvania Railroad, and is one of the oldest houses in Pennsylvania. In 1713 he was elected a representative from Philadelphia County in the Provincial Assembly, and re-elected in 1714–1715, 1717, and 1719. Although his marriage was in Friends' Meeting, in later life, probably through the Keithian movement, he became an Episcopalian, and doubtless a founder of Trinity Church, Oxford, in the ancient graveyard of which he and his wife, and many of their descendants, are buried.

"Mr. Leech was possessed of a large estate at his death, and by his will disposed of twenty-seven hundred acres of land, six hundred of which composed his home plantation. Besides two other plantations, of five hundred acres each, in Philadelphia County, he owned one of five hundred acres in Chester County, and one of six hundred acres in New Castle County, Delaware. He also owned a number of slaves, eight of whom are named in his will."

Bartholomew Penrose and Esther Leech had four children—Dorothy, who married Isaac Shoemaker; Sarah, who married Richard Mather; Bartholomew, Jr., who married Mary Kirll; and Thomas Penrose (ancestor of Dick Penrose), born February 1709/10, married Sarah Coats, and died 17 November 1757.

That Bartholomew Penrose became a man of property soon after his arrival in the New World is evidenced by the fact, recorded by Dr. Leach, that "in 1705 he conveyed to Giles Green land on Front Street, where the most valuable real estate was situated, and which was described in the conveyance as bounded by other land belonging to Mr. Penrose. In March following (1706) he purchased of Edward Smout, merchant, a lot of land, containing in breadth one hundred and eight feet and in depth two hundred and fifty feet, situated on the street commonly called King Street, and on the banks of the Delaware River. In other words, a property at what is now Delaware Avenue and Market Street. For this property he paid two hundred and thirty pounds. Here he subsequently resided and carried on his business; and here, it is said, occurred a fire in which were lost, not only his own personal and family records, but much valuable property. The estate so purchased remained in his family until 19 August 1731, when his children sold and conveyed it to William Parsons, describing it as one hundred and eight feet in front, and depth two hundred and fifty feet to the river."

Bartholomew Penrose died at Philadelphia, and was buried 19 November 1711 in Christ Church ground. In 1917, the old tombstone, almost obliterated by weathering, was replaced by Dick's brother Charles with one of Knoxville marble, great pains being taken to retain the character of the original lettering.

After the death of her husband, Mrs. Penrose married Nathaniel Poole, also a ship-builder, but she lived only a short time, being buried in the Christ Church grounds 1 April 1713.

In his will, dated December 1709, Bartholomew Penrose did "bequeath to my Brother Thos Penrose in ye Kingdom of England shipwright Six Shillings." The will of Thomas, older than Bartholomew by five years, was dated 17 March 1721. After disposing of various properties to his wife and children and giving his brother James ten pounds, the will stated that "I not only forgive and release to the heirs and executors of my late brother Bartholomew Penrose lately residing in 'Pensilvana' all the money he owed me, but I also give to his children £5 when they shall come and demand same."

Thomas Penrose and Sarah Coats
(First American generation)

Thomas followed in his father's footsteps, being a ship-builder and shipping merchant, trading with foreign ports in ships of which he was part owner. His will disposed of real estate, interest in ships, merchandise, moneys, and personal property.

To his son, James (Dick's ancestor), he gave "all that Messuage or Tenement wherein I now dwell, Wharf & Lot of Ground Containing in Breadth on Delaware River fifty-six feet or thereabouts and extending Westward from Delaware River to the East side of Front Street Continued Southward beyond the City of Philada., & Together with the Kitchen, Edifaces, Buildings & appurtenances thereunto Belonging, Excepting & for Ever reserving thereto an Alley or Passage of Ten feet and a half wide on the North Side thereof, and to Extend from the East side of Swanson Street down as far Eastward as my New Stores & as much farther as will be Convenient to turn a Cart & Horse, which Alley or Passage Shall be & remain for the Common Use & Benefit of my sd Son James & my two Sons, Isaac & Samuel, their Heirs & Assigns for Ever, . . . And as for & concerning the Rest & Residue of my Lands in Wiccacoe or Moyamensing Township, which I purchased in Common with Philip Hulbeart, & since devided, my five acres of land in Passyunck, which I purchased of Isaac Roberts, And all other my Real Estate Whatsoever or Wheresoever, my mind & Will is, that the Same shall be equally divided between my sd five sons, their Respective Heirs & Assigns for Ever, when & as soon, but not before, as my Son Isaac Shall attain the age of twenty-one years. . . . And my Mind, Will, Order & Desire is that by from or out of my timber Stuff Shipwrights Stock, Utensils, Impliments & appurtenances belonging to my Trade, and by & from the Services & Labour of my apprentices & Negrows, and out of the profits arising by The vessel I am now Building or any other Vessel that may be set up, during the Minority of my Son James who shall Carry on my Trade until his full age, my Executors hereinafter named, or the Survivors or Survivor of them Shall in the first Place run out & Extend a pier or Wharf at the South East end of sd Son Samuel's lot of Twenty-eight feet in breadth by eighty-five or ninety feet into Delaware for the Use of him my sd Son Samuel And in the Next Place Shall Erect & Build, if my Wife

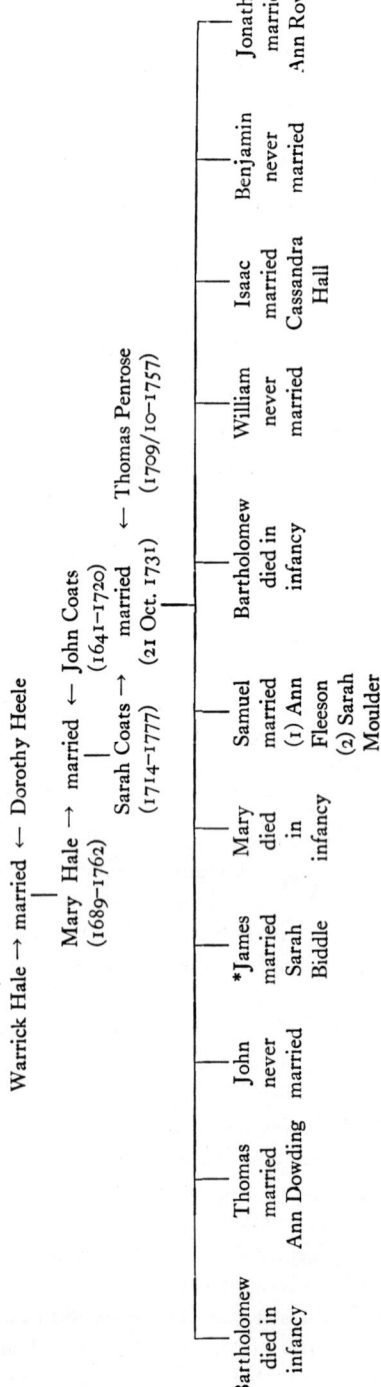

* Great-great-grandfather of Dick Penrose.

Desires it, the Tenement aforesd on my sd Son Jonathan's Lot, for her to Live in, And the overplus, if any, arising from my Trade when my Son James attain Twenty-one years, to go to & be divided in the same manner as the residuary part of my Personal Estate is herein after Directed. By when my Son James attains that Age, he shall have my Negro Man Peter, and then my Son Thomas shall have my Negro Man named Abraham, And I Nominate constitute & appoint my sd Wife Sarah, my Trusty faithful & esteemed friend Joseph Richardson of the City of Philada., Merchant, & my two Sons, Thomas & James to be Executors of this my Last Will & Testament. . . . To put & place out Twelve hundred and fifty pounds part thereof, at Interest upon Land Security in the City and County of Philada., and the Interest thereof yearly to pay unto my sd Wife, Sarah, for & During the term of her Natural Life and after her Decease to pay & divide the sd Principal sum of twelve hundred and fifty pounds unto & among my sd five sons part & share alike, And . . . pay the following Legacies, to wit: Unto my Son Thomas, Four Hundred pounds; unto my Son James, Four hundred pounds; unto my Son, Samuel, Five hundred and Seventy-five pounds, and unto my son Jonathan, Eight hundred and Twenty-five Pounds, to be paid unto them Severally & respectively, as they severally & respectively attain the age of Twenty one years."

Thomas Penrose signed the petition to the Penns, asking for a lot of ground on which to build St. Peter's Church, the second Episcopal church in Philadelphia, and when the lot, at Third and Pine streets, was granted for that purpose, he was named in the deed of grant as one of the trustees.

On October 21, 1731, he married Sarah Coats. She was the daughter of John Coats, a brick manufacturer of Philadelphia, who died there March 16, 1720, aged 76 years, and his wife, Mary, daughter of Warwick and Dorothy (Heele) Hale, who died September 10, 1752, aged 63 years. After the death of her husband, in 1757, Sarah Coats Penrose married March 1, 1763, Captain Lester Falkner, who died August 8, 1766. She then married, April 24, 1770, Anthony Duche. She died July 7, 1777, aged 63 years.

James Penrose and Sarah Biddle

(Second American generation)

James Penrose, heir to his father's trade, was born at Philadelphia, February 23, 1737/38, and died there September 7, 1771. His death was noted in the *Pennsylvania Gazette* of September 12, 1771, as follows:

"On Saturday last—died, in the 34th year of his age, Mr. JAMES PENROSE, an eminent Ship-builder. A man of great Ingenuity and abilities in his Profession, of universal Esteem among all that knew him, and particularly respected by all who were intimate with him. His remains, attended by a vast concourse of respectable inhabitants, of all Denominations, were Interred on Sunday evening in Friend's Burying Ground."

James Penrose was a contributor to the Pennsylvania Hospital, and, with his brother, Thomas, was a signer of the "Non-Importation Agreement." His grand-niece, Miss Annie Eliza Pennock, wrote of him:

"He was a very handsome man, with courtly manners of the 'old school,' fond of society, hospitable and generous, hot-tempered, but very popular, and always retained the good-will of friends and neighbors, notwithstanding frequent outbursts of temper."

On March 15, 1766, James Penrose married Sarah Biddle, by whom he had two children—John Penrose, who lived only fifteen months, and Clement Biddle Penrose, who, born February 20, 1771, was less than seven months old when his father died.

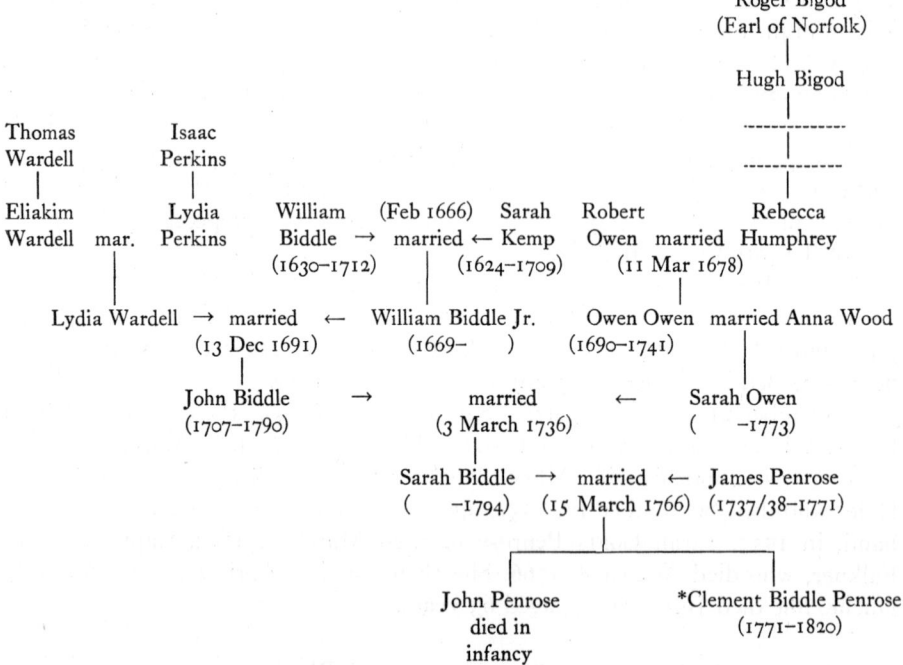

Mrs. Penrose was the daughter of John and Sarah (Owen) Biddle, and great-granddaughter of William Biddle, one of the original proprietors created by the English government in early Colonial days to take possession of what was then known as "West Jersey," now the State of New Jersey. He was born in England about 1630, and in 1681 emigrated to America.

"He was a Quaker, and was persecuted in England on account of his religious faith," says Dr. Leach. "At the time he emigrated he was a resident of London, and on his arrival in America he settled at what is now Kingora, about midway between Burlington and Bordentown, New Jersey, where he took up a plantation of five hundred acres on the mainland, and two hundred and seventy-eight acres, the area of an adjacent island, which has since borne the name of Biddle's Island. To this plantation Mr. Biddle gave the name of 'Mount Hope.' "

* Great-grandfather of Dick Penrose.

[Burlington and Bordentown are both on the Delaware River.]

"Mr. Biddle was one of the leading men in the early public affairs of the province," continues Dr. Leach, "and, in 1682, at the organization of the first governor's council, he became a member of that body, and was also commissioned one of the justices of the peace of Burlington County, and a member of the board of Land Commissioners. He was re-elected to the Council in 1683, 1684, and 1685, and again, in 1701, and during the years 1683, 1684, 1685, 1687, and 1697, he was a member of the Assembly. He was, also, re-commissioned a justice of the peace in 1683, and many years thereafter.

"At a meeting of the proprietors of West Jersey, held 14 February 1687, it was decided to appoint eleven of their number 'Commissioners and Trustees' to conduct the business of the proprietors. Mr. Biddle was chosen a member of this board, called the 'Council of the proprietors,' and was annually re-elected for many years, being the president of the Council in 1706 and 1707.

"In 1703, the provinces of East and West Jersey were united under the name and style of New Jersey, and Mr. Biddle was elected a member of the first Assembly under the government thus formed.

"He married in London, England, in February, 1666, Sarah Kemp, who died at her husband's seat, 'Mount Hope,' 27 April, 1709, in the seventy-fifth year of her age. Mr. Biddle died there in the early part of 1712, leaving two children: William and Sarah. . . . By his will, Mr. Biddle disposed of over fourteen hundred and seventy-eight acres of land, he being one of the largest landed proprietors in the Province.

"William Biddle, Jr., son of Honorable William Biddle by his wife Sarah Kemp, was born in London, England, 4 December 1669, and came to America with his parents in 1681. Under his father's will he acquired 'Mount Hope' and there resided until his death. He appears neither to have sought nor held public office, except that in 1703 he was one of the commissioners chosen by the Council of Proprietors of West Jersey 'to secure a survey and deed from the Indians of land above the Falls,' which land had been purchased from the latter. He married, 13 December, 1691, Lydia Wardell, of Shrewsbury, New Jersey, the ceremony being performed by Lewis Morris, Esq., a justice of the court of Monmouth County, New Jersey. She was a daughter of Eliakim Wardell by his wife Lydia Perkins, and a granddaughter of Thomas Wardell, who was living in Boston, Massachusetts, as early as 1634, subsequently removing to Piscataqua, New Hampshire, where he was commissioned a magistrate in 1643, under the Massachusetts government. By his wife, Lydia Wardell, William Biddle, Jr., had six children, to wit: William, Elizabeth, Sarah, Penelope, Joseph, and John."

Dick Penrose traced his ancestry back to William Biddle, Jr., through two lines: (1) through his paternal grandmother, who was Valeria Fullerton Biddle, great-granddaughter of the oldest child, William, and (2) through his paternal great-grandfather, Clement Biddle Penrose, who was the grandson of John Biddle, the youngest child. He also traced his lineage through two lines back to Eliakim Wardell and Lydia Perkins: (1) through the Biddle line, as already shown, and (2) through the Spencer line of his father's maternal grandmother.

In his *Spencer Fullerton Baird; a biography*, William Healey Dall speaks of Thomas Wardell and Isaac Perkins as "among the first comers to the colony of Massachusetts Bay. According to Professor Goode, they became disciples of Ann Hutchinson in the Antinomian controversy of 1636, were banished from the colony in company with the Rev. John Wheelwright, and assisted in founding the town of Exeter in New Hampshire. Their children, Eliakim Wardell and Lydia Perkins, married in 1659, joined the Society of Friends and on account of religious persecution removed in 1663 to Long Island, and in 1666 to Shrewsbury, East Jersey."

Footnotes in the Dall volume state that from one member of the family he learned that "Thomas Wardell, father of Eliakim, was one of the victims of the witchcraft delusion at Salem, Massachusetts, in 1692. Eliakim was a deputy to the General Assembly from 1667 to 1688; magistrate of Shrewsbury, New Jersey, in 1678, and High Sheriff from 1683 to 1685.

"Isaac Perkins, father of Lydia, who came from Hampton, Massachusetts, is described as a wealthy merchant of Boston and founder of the well-known Boston family of that name. The result of an attempt to force his daughter Lydia to attend orthodox religious services in Salem is thus described by her descendant, Jonathan Dickinson Sergeant, of Philadelphia:

" 'She was several times commanded to go to church and heavy fines imposed, because being of a different faith she would not. At last finding it impossible to escape, this high tempered young woman, who was also a remarkably beautiful one, appeared in church as God made her, saying that she thus bore testimony to the nakedness of the faith of her enemies.' "

John Biddle, the youngest son of William Biddle, Jr., was born, says Dr. Leach, "in 1707, and in early life settled in Philadelphia, where he died in 1790, and where he married, 3 March 1736, Sarah, daughter of Owen Owen, Esq., high sheriff of Philadelphia County from 1726 until 1729, and coroner of that county from 1729 until 1741. Mrs. Biddle died at Philadelphia, 1 January, 1773."

According to the researches of Colonel George H. Penrose, Owen Owen (1690–1741), who married Anna Wood, was the son of Robert Owen of Fron-goch Farm, near Bala, in Merionetshire, who moved to the "Welsh Farm Tract" near Philadelphia in 1690, and in 1695 erected a stone house on Montgomery Avenue, which was still standing "a few years ago." He was a justice of the peace for Merion Township, Pennsylvania, and a member of the Governor's Council.

Robert Owen married, March 11, 1678, Rebecca Humphrey, through whom the Penroses claim descent from Hugh Bigod, third Earl of Norfolk, son of Roger Bigod, Earl of Norfolk, both sureties for the Magna Charta.

Sarah Owen and John Biddle had five children: Owen, Clement, Sarah, Ann, and Lydia.

Colonel Owen Biddle, the older son, was prominent during the Revolution, being a member of the Committee of Safety, the Pennsylvania Board of War, and Commissary-General of Forage. He was for more than forty years a member of the American Philosophical Society, serving nine years as its Secretary, and seventeen years as a councillor. Colonel Clement Biddle, the younger son, served as deputy-quartermaster-general of the Continental Army during the Revolution, and was appointed by President Washington the first Marshal of the United States in Pennsylvania. His daughter, Mary, married General Thomas Cadwalader. Sarah married James Penrose. Ann married General James Wilkinson, who at one time commanded the army of the United States, and Lydia, the youngest, married Dr. James Hutchinson, a noted surgeon of the Revolutionary army.

After the death of her husband, Sarah Biddle Penrose married (1) John Shaw, August 15, 1776, and (2) November 16, 1784, Rudolph Tillier, a native of Berne, Switzerland. He was evidently a man of means, having invested largely in lands in various parts of America. In 1788, he went to Europe to visit his relatives, taking his wife and stepson, Clement Biddle Penrose, then seventeen years old, with him. In the Penrose family archives are several interesting letters concerning this European sojourn.

Extracts from a Letter from Sarah Penrose Tillier to her family, dated Berne, Switzerland, January 19th, 1789

We had a very agreeable passage of 29 days from Landsend to the Lizard Pt. ... We saw fresh sail every day, one that we thought was an Algerine which chased us 24 hours, the night before I had dreamed that we were taken by an Algerin ship which Alarm'd Mr. Abercrombe extremely but Clem behaved like man of true Courage as he did the whole passage ... I was astonished that I never was allarm'd nor one moment sick the whole passage ... The day before we made land a cutter came along side & informed us they were sent to conduct in to Plymouth the Swedish fleet that there had been an Engagement with the Russian and Swedish fleet & that the Sweeds had the worst of the Battle ... My beloved Tillier & Clem wanted to go to London, my desire was as strong as theirs to see this great & Celebrated Metropolis but our finances whispered us, it is most prudent to hurry on to your family, we attended to the voice of prudence, and boarded our small Cutter & proceeded to France to prevent landing twice, double Custome House expence & trouble.

Our intention was to have landed at Calais but the Wind proving more fare for Bologne Sur Mer we made for that port, found the tide against our landing, flat bottomed boats came to our assistance & here begins a Curious Scene. The boys that managed our fourth embarkation run us aground, we perceived running down to the shore great numbers of Women and Girls. I could not imagine the reason of such numbers of women receiving us, they tied their short petticoats round their middle & entered the sea, which was above the knees of the tallest of them we were soon surrounded and a dispute began who should have the honor of carrying us ashore. The Contest was ended by an old woman telling me to put a leg on each side and take her round the neck, not a pleasing task for me I'll assure you but necessity Obliged me to Comply, another took my Tillier & Clem in the same manner, also Goffs—being prepared we marched on in Indian file to make Our Grand entra en France, my fears for my husband tempt'd me to look round, but such figures I never beheld notwithstanding my situation my legs in the water Could not help laughing heartily, in this manner we were landed & found two Kings officers ready to receive us & take charge of our baggage, allso an Englishman to Conduct us to the most Elligant Engl's Hotel, kept by a Mr. Knowles whose Charriot Conducted us to the Hotel wet and driping as we were found it filled with French & English Nobility going to the Camp at St Omus where there was to be a grand review . . .

Our Journey through Picardie was delightful but it would take a quire of paper to give a just description of all the Villages and Country we passed, the principle towns were Amiens & Abbeville the first pleased me most being a better situation and more regerlarly built. . . . The third day arrived in Paris . . . Madam G & Madam Grand the daughter treated me with great attention as did all our friends. His Excellency Mr. Jefferson was very polite.

Letter from Sarah Tillier to her father and her aunt, Mary Biddle, dated Berne, Switzerland, 20 January 1789

I refer my much lov'd and Honored Father to my general letter for an account of our voyage & the reception our family gave us, which was as affectionate as we could wish, & indeed we have had more attention from every body than was agreeable to either of us.

We viewed everything—to satisfie Clement—that Mr. Tillier thought most curious & our short stay would admit. What pleased me most, was the Gobeling, the Hospital of Invalids & the building of the former Military school for Noblemen, begun by Lewis the 14th. At the Gobelins they are weaving Tapestry for the King's Palace. The Shades are equal to any painting in the world. The figures as large as life. One apartment is the History of Queen Hester, the others are Roman pieces. They have been three years at work on this & it is not half finish'd, but will exceed anything of the kind when compleated. The same day visited the Hospital; the structure of the dome in the chapel, is superb & magnificient beyond description of my feeble pen. The silence that reigned in this spacious building, four or five old soldiers at private prayer, the grandeur of the architecture & painting, struck us with reverential awe, of the great ruler of the universe, that poor lame mortals were addressing. The Military School is beautifully situated, a very grand building and paintings; The stairs ornamented with the statues of the greatest men of different ages. I was taken ill of an epidemic disorder that raged in Paris, & insisted on setting off, being sure that fresh air was the only thing to restore me & prevent my belov'd husband & son taking the same disorder, but it was too late, they had recd the infection & was ill a few days after. Notwithstanding there are so many grand edifices gardens and everything you can wish for but pure air, Paris is the dirtiest place in the world. The streets are narrow in general, the houses 4 & 5 stories high & the streets constantly muddy. I will do justice to its inhabitants in saying I never saw people behave at a public place with so much delicacy & true politeness as the Parisianers.

Clem was very ill on our journey, but as I recovered & could let him lay on my lap, & he was better when travelling, we concluded to proceed on our journey.

Mr. T. had the disorder lighter than either of us. We travelled through France in the height of the vintage. The roads were crowded with people loaded with grapes, & each one wore a face of contentment & plenty. Some were gathering, others loading waggons & baskets, singing, bowing and curtesying to us for three hundred miles through Champagne, Burgundy and part of French Compt. The roads are paved like our street, trees on each side through Champagne, handsomely trimm'd & vineyards on the side of the road. The fields are not enclosed, except Gentlemens seats with a hedge round the houses. Shepherds keep their flock, & tho not of the Arcadian kind, I wish'd, sick as I was, very much lov'd aunt for your pen to do justice to the countries I pass'd through.

We now approached the mountains. That of Saline was the first. I thought when near the top that it was too high to be inhabited but found a large well built Town, where the principal Salt Works of France are carried on. In travelling through France you see a great number of thach'd villages as well as well built Towns. We travelled for half a day between two ridges of mountains; had at the same time the view of a dozen ridges inhabited on the sides & many castles on the tops of the mountains, which appeared inaccessible. The road is cut in the side of the mountains wide enough for two carriages to pass. If you look up it is perpindicular five hundred feet, and cast your eyes below on the steep descent it is twice the highth of the Minesink by Reading, & terrifying to behold. Here I was certain of no Inhabitants, but after Assending six Miles found several farms on the very Sumit of the Mountain. We traveled from Mountain to Mountain till we reached the borders of Switzerland, here our name was known at every Inn & great respect paid us, but we soon found the difference of the French & Swiss Public House, the one very dirty & bad entertainment except at large Town, the Swiss were clean a good dish of tea Excellent provision & beds. Clem recovered as soon as he smelt the Air of Switzerland, which pleased his Papa very much. We remained two days at New Chattel. This place is call'd Switzerland, but is only in Alliome. It belongs to the King Pruss with liberty to form their own laws. The Town is built on several eminenc's. The buildings are handsome, and a place of great Trade. It is situated on the side of a large Lake, the best Vine Country we saw. Berne is a very beautiful situation, a kind of Peninsula. The River R runs on the north & south side, this river is about the width of Grey's Ferry, but a more rapid stream. It is a fortified Town, has four entries with double Gates and Centinals constantly at them. Their uniform Red & blue & Red twin'd up with black, which gives them the appearance of British. The streets are broad, extremely Clean with fountains in the Middle of each street & a stream of water running through them. The houses are built of stone, the second story projects over the first & is supported by arches, that you may allways walk dry. There are at the end of the East principal Public Walks that are laid out in grass plots, with trees & green seats, the shape of sofas. It is built on a hill which is wal'd & below the walls are hanging gardens. On the bank of the R it appears another Town. We are so much higher there. The washer women, hatters, diers, &c. live. From the south side we have a full view of the glassiers & neighboring hills which are a great distance off. The most noble sight the imagination can paint is the

Glasiers appearing above the Clouds. The sun will shine at the top when they are covered with thick Clouds half way down. How often my belov'd Father & aunt do I wish you at this place. My Father was form'd for it. The Old Gentlemen go to the Coffe house at 3 oc. play a part at cards, have the best of eating, return to supper at 8 oclock, dine at one, & we never have the house wash'd. This would be the very thing for my Belov'd Father. I must instruct you how to clean floors, rub them with soft stone cutters stone dry, sweep it off & take wet saw dust rub it on with a hard broom & sweep that off. I never saw such beautiful white floors as we have & this is the Method of Cleaning them. Dont know the use of a house Cloth. If water is spilt, they throw saw dust on it & sweep it off. My hand is so numb'd I can hardly hold my pen, therefor must leave off & request my Father to send this letter to aunt Biddle. With affc love to my dear Cousin L.M.P.B.W.B. & all the family, shall write soon to them all. My afft love to L. Spencer, the Miss Cliftons, & Mrs. Beach. Intend writing to them all. Adieu my much lov'd Father and Aunt. May Heavin continue you as blessing to your Family, & may you not forget the Child & neice that loves you sincerely tho distant Hills & seas divide us, her heart is with you. My brother often asks me to tell you he will bring us to pay you & my lov'd much lov'd sister & brother Wilkinson a visit. Tho I write in extreme pain cannot leave off. May you injoy health to answer our letters is my fervent prayer.

Yr   sincere afft child & neice
Sarah Tillier

Berne, Jan 20th
If there can be found at any rate the Biddle, Wardels, or Owen Coat of Arms pray send them let them cost what they will, as my brother is anxious to have them placed with the Women of the family. I have heard Aunt Tallman say the Biddles was three Bishops. It was on her Tankard. Will give you the Customs & Laws of Berne in my next letter.

Extracts from a letter by Sarah Tillier to the folks at home, dated Berne, Switzerland, May 4, 1789

I begin to be extremely anxious about my dear family it is nigh a year since I left my native home & have heard but twice from them in that long time ... I begin to return my numerous visits which are all in the highest stile, but not that sweett sociability that enlivens our agreeable societies in America the Ladies of Berne are an example for Economists to all the world, you have no Idea of Management in Comparison of the Swiss, in the Habiliment they are much as we are following the Fashions of England & France & with an addition of their own the liveing is very different, they Cook much better than we do, will make half a doz dishes out of one of our, nothwithstanding that I often long for bit of Bread & Butter, a flannel or Buckwheat Cake, Butter is looked upon here as extremely unwholesome except in cooking & my good brother will not let my beloved Tillier & self touch it. . . .

Tell my dear Lydia Spencer her letter gave us both great pleasure & that we request her to write by every Oportunity & tell me all the new & everything relative to herself & the family for which we have the most sincere regard, dear girl, I wish she was with us I miss her agreeable friendly visits very much indeed send for her and read all my letters to her & tell her my next letter will be much longer than the present to her.

[This same Lydia Spencer's daughter Valeria married Sarah Tillier's grandson, Charles Bingham Penrose, grandfather of Richard, the subject of this biography.]

Extracts from a letter by Rudolph Tillier to Owen Biddle, dated Berne, Switzerland, 21 October 1789

I wrote you fully dear Brother the 28 July last under cover of Mr. E. Lawrence. Since we have been deprived of Letters from America which should give us some uneasiness if we did not attribute it to the convulsed state of France, which may have occasioned their miscarriage, our health is prity well restablished. Clement grows very hearty. I send enclosed the duplicate of my last letter to Mr. Sam'l Morris by which he wuld see the reason of Clement's recall from Lausanne he has since some time begun lesons in Lattin, Mathematics and drawing we intend he shall take some other this Winter.

We had several of the first class of refugees from France here as Comte d'Artois, Pa. Conde, the Polliquais, etc., the Pays de Vaud is full of them. And more are expected since the revolution that brough the King from Versailles to Paris of which you will be informed by the English papers. My Brother in the Gurds has been an actor in the most critical event he protected the Archbishop of paris, when he was assualted by the mob, at the grand tumult or revolt, he was at the Halle Aux bles after he was emploid in the delicate commission abt. the retreat of the troops at the Champs de Mars which prevented the bloodshed of many, which all he managed with the approbation of the Marq. Lafayette & his Superiors but not without the most imminent danger of his Life, at the last tumult at Versaille the outside gate was consigned to him which he opend to Mrq. De Lafayette conditionaly that he allone with 2 others should enter to speak to the King, upon which the King ordered no resistance should be made and that all the avenues should be opened, many lost their Lives in the affray. You may judge from all this that the Democratic party has the uperhand & that they will have the freest constitution they have some great difficulty yett to overcome & one of the principal is to regulate & provide for their finances which are notwithstanding all that has been done in a bad situation relative particularly of the Debts I mentioned you from the begin of my arival in Europe how much people here and Geneva were interested If a Banqueroutcy should take place many would be reduced from Afluence to nothing in such circumstance it would have been follishness to think of proposing any privat business at any other time I am sure I should have succeeded to sell Lands. Considering our situation here I think to return with Sallie next Spring if possible to America....

The Russians & Austrians have been successful this year against the Sweedes & Turcs, I hope peace will be made between them this Winter.

Extracts from a letter from Sarah Tillier to her family, dated October 25, 1789

My beloved father sisters Brother & friends will smile when I tell them Motives of Economy deprives me the pleasure of writing them long letters each packet has cost us two louis & we are now like Misers hoarding up every farthing to pay our voyage to my dear native Country should Heaven favor us in guarding us through the dangers of the Seas and the Algerines. . . .

My Tillier tells our reasons for returning, he has every post of honor he can possibly have but can have none of profit until his affairs are in better train, besides Cenetor he has been chosen member of a board of the Chamber of Lords to try all cases of difuculty. . . .

My Clem is studying with the best professors to advantage & this winter is to attend cours of Natural Laws he has his Uncle's Library filled with the best authors in french Latin & German at command & reads History three or four Hours every evening that he can spare; thanks to the great ruler of the Univers his health has been better since we are in Berne than ever I knew it continue thy goodness to us in the blessing of health great God, we all enjoy at present. I often walk these mild afternoon which will surprise & show you that I am much stronger than I was I am so much of a Femme de Swiss that I fear I am getting a goitre in my throat which will not be very agreeable in America though thought nothing of here. . . .

Our eldest brother as well as all the world with us is deeply interested in the French funds that you may be sure we are well informed of what passes should it be sufficiently Peaseable we mean in March to set out for one of the ports of France, but shall write before that. . . .

Remember me to Mrs. & Mr. Luke & Saml Morris & thank the latter for me for his attention to my son & his good advice to him, you cannot form an idea how he has improved; his master of Mathematics says he never meet with a head so Clear and ready at that branch of learning.

Excerpts from undated letter from Sarah Tillier to the folks at home

The Rheumatism has prevented my writing to my beloved sister and brother oftener than I have heretofore, am at present much better, my Clem paid us a visit at Easter which is a great day with us . . . I cannot help remarking the beauty of the flowers of this place, the Carnation and many others that are unknown to me more Elligant than anything I have seen of that kind. . . .

My beloved boy has every advantage he can, his father is extremely fond of him, has given him all his fine Cloaths & lent him his watch as he feared he would not be allowed a proper one for him, he learns everything with great facility, fences very well tho I would not let him learn as I thought it was dangerous, but I am told he has such a taste for it must let him have a few lessons, it forms his shoulders & strengthens the breat while growing, he is as tall as his papa & begins to spread. . . . Do not be uneasy if our letters should not come to hand regular. Some of yours sent from America to Berne has been 12 months on the way, when others have arrived in two months. Clem has wrote all his cousins but my dear John's is the longest letter, his studies will not admit of much spare time to write to you, therefore you must excuse him as every moment is precious, he has lost so much from ill health. I hope my dear sister will remember my very dear friends the two Miss Cliftons & Lydia Spencer, she cannot imagine half how kind they were to us nor half their Merrit My T. thinks few women equal to them in Excellence.

The correspondence shows that in October, 1793, Sarah Tillier had returned to Philadelphia and that her husband was in Berne endeavoring to interest prospective buyers in Pennsylvania real estate west of Philadelphia. In writing to him concerning the matter, his brother-in-law, Owen Biddle, says:

"It will be necessary that [thou] should be allowed a liberty to enter into such terms as these and then and there thou will be in no danger of incurring a loss of thy good name and if thee can be allowed to dispose of only 40,000 Acres I should prefer confining our agency to that quantity, however flattering it may be our natural thirst after wealth to have large agencies and great Commissions yet persuaded I am that they would be a great interruption of our Advancement in virtue and solid happiness, let us my dear brother moderate our desire after greatly worldly possession and contract our views within such limits as to pursue happiness on rational principles."

Mrs. Tillier died the following year (October 24, 1794).

Clement Biddle Penrose and Anna Howard Bingham
(Third American generation)

Clement Biddle Penrose, only surviving child of James Penrose and Sarah Biddle [Tillier], had been brought up amid scenes of the American Revolution, having been selected as one of two youthful standard bearers to one of the first companies raised in Philadelphia.

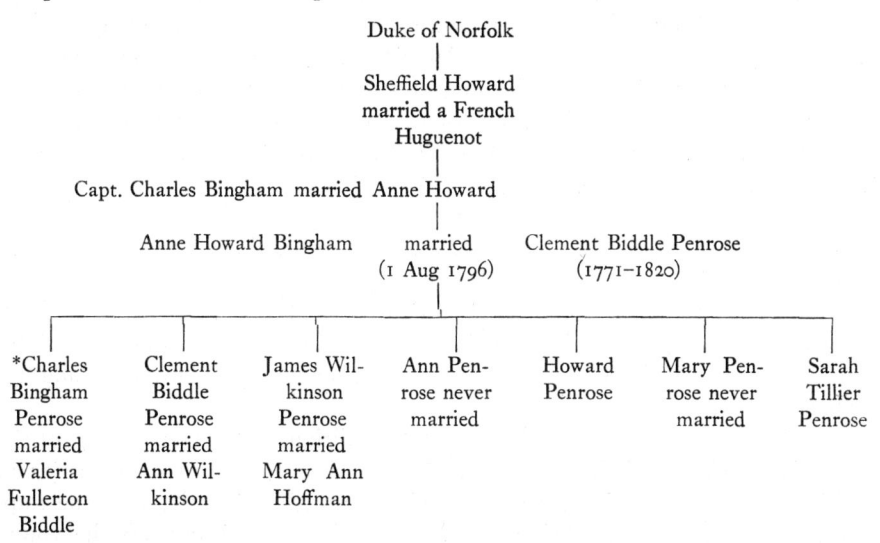

```
                        Duke of Norfolk
                               |
                        Sheffield Howard
                        married a French
                            Huguenot
                               |
        Capt. Charles Bingham married Anne Howard
                               |
    Anne Howard Bingham      married      Clement Biddle Penrose
                          (1 Aug 1796)        (1771-1820)
                               |
```

| *Charles Bingham Penrose married Valeria Fullerton Biddle | Clement Biddle Penrose married Ann Wilkinson | James Wilkinson Penrose married Mary Ann Hoffman | Ann Penrose never married | Howard Penrose | Mary Penrose never married | Sarah Tillier Penrose |

* Grandfather of Dick Penrose.

"Driven from Philadelphia when that city fell into the hands of the invading foe," his son, Charles Bingham Penrose said in March, 1839, in the course of an address made before the Senate of Pennsylvania, "he accompanied his widowed mother and an honored uncle (Colonel Clement Biddle), an officer high in the confidence of the great chief who led our armies to battle, to the Valley Forge; and though but a child, witnessed and shared in the sufferings of that terrible winter—one of the most gloomy periods of the revolution."

Returning to Philadelphia after his European sojourn, he was commissioned by Governor Mifflin an ensign of a company of light infantry in the seventh battalion of the City and Liberties Militia. In 1803 he was a candidate for Congress on the Democratic-Republican ticket, but failed of election. In 1805 he was commissioned by President Jefferson one of the two Land Commissioners of the Louisiana Territory, the other being John B. C. Lucas. The official document reads:

"In pursuance of the act of Congress proposed on the 2nd day of March, 1805 entitled 'An Act for ascertaining and adjusting the titles and claims of Land, within the Territory of Orleans and the District of Louisiana' and reposing special Trust and Confidence in the Integrity, Diligence and Discretion of John B. C. Lucas and Clement B. Penrose, both of Pennsylvania, I do appoint them Commissioners under the act aforesaid in the Territory of Louisiana for the purpose of ascertaining therein the rights of persons claiming Lands under any french or Spanish grant, conformably with the provisions of the said act; and to authorize and empower them to execute and fulfil the duties of their said offices, according to law; and to Have and to Hold the same with all the rights and emoluments thereunto legally appertaining during the pleasure of the President of the United States for the time being."

Clement Biddle Penrose accordingly moved his family to St. Louis, then headquarters for the Louisiana Territory, and there he lived for the remainder of his life, dying in 1820, aged 49 years. On August 21, 1813, he was among those appointed commissioners to raise the sum of $100,000 for the purpose of forming the Territorial Bank of St. Louis, the others being the aforementioned Mr. Lucas, August Chouteau, Moses Austin, Bernard Pratt, Manual Liza, Thomas Brady, B. Berthold, Samuel Hammon, Rufus Easton, Robert Simpson. Christian Wilt, and R. H. Price. The war interfered with the organization of the bank, and it was not until July 13, 1816, that the stock was fully subscribed. The bank was unsuccessful, and closed its doors in March, 1818.

On August 1, 1796, Clement Biddle Penrose had been married at Trinity Church, New York, by the Reverend Benjamin Moore, to Anne Howard Bingham, daughter of Major Charles Bingham and his wife, Anne Howard, daughter of Sheffield Howard.

Sheffield Howard, according to the family tradition, was a younger son of the Duke of Norfolk. He fell in love with his tutor's sister and wanted to marry her, but his father sternly forbade it and had him confined in a castle, in the best approved romantic manner. Opportunely, his godfather died and left the young man a sizable legacy, so he took the money and eloped with the young lady to

America, settling in New York, where he became a merchant. His first wife dying childless, he later married a French Huguenot lady who bore him two children, a son and a daughter. His business affairs prospered and he acquired a large fortune, which, however, was lost during the struggle between the Colonies and the Mother Country. As a son of the Duke of Norfolk, he "necessarily" sided with the Royalists and was accordingly "persecuted" by the Americans. His son became aide-de-camp on the staff of Lord Rawdon and was killed in one of the battles in New Jersey. His daughter, Anne, following her father's example, eloped with Captain Charles Bingham, a young British officer stationed in New York. He was a kinsman of Charles Bingham, the first Earl of Lucan, and December 25, 1776, had been commissioned an ensign in the 35th Regiment of Foot, British Army, under Colonel H. Fletcher Campbell. On March 21, 1782, he was commissioned Captain-Lieutenant and Captain in the 105th Regiment of Foot, under Francis, Lord Rawdon, Colonel Commanding. Later, he became a Major.

Upon the death of Major Bingham, his widow married Sir Thomas Hay, which fact is recorded in Burke's Peerage, as follows:

"Sir Thomas Hay, eldest son of Alexander Hay, married, 27 Aug., 1793, Anne, widow of Major Bingham, and daughter of Sheffield Howard, Esq., of New York, a scion of the noble house of Norfolk, and a loyalist, who lost large possessions during the War for Independence in America."

Anne Howard, daughter of Major and Mrs. Bingham, did not elope with Clement Biddle Penrose, but she also is the subject of a romantic tale. While traveling from Europe to New York, the vessel on which she was a passenger was hailed by a pirate ship. All the male passengers handed their valuables and watches to Mrs. Penrose, who was the only woman on board, and she secreted these possessions about her body. Soon after boarding, the pirate captain saw another ship approaching and made haste with his looting. Mrs. Penrose, noticing his perturbation, invited him into the captain's cabin for a glass of wine. The pirate captain was in a great hurry to get off and obviously did not wish to tarry, but he was not proof against a woman's wiles. She kept him in conversation, begging him not to hurry, and, calling his attention to the ship now not far away, mockingly suggested that if he tarried he might enjoy other society. The pirate, however, bade them all a hasty adieu and with all sails set hurried from the scene. Mrs. Penrose had saved all the valuables by her bravery and self-possession, but is said to have collapsed with fright after the ordeal was over.

Clement Biddle Penrose and Anne Howard Bingham had seven children, the eldest being Charles Bingham Penrose, who was born October 6, 1798 at his father's country seat, near Frankford, Philadelphia, and died at Harrisburg, Pennsylvania, April 6, 1857.

Charles Bingham Penrose and Valeria Fullerton Biddle
(Fourth American generation)

Most of Charles Bingham Penrose's boyhood was spent in St. Louis. He enlisted in one of the volunteer companies during the War of 1812, but his organization was not called into active service. As a young man he went to Philadel-

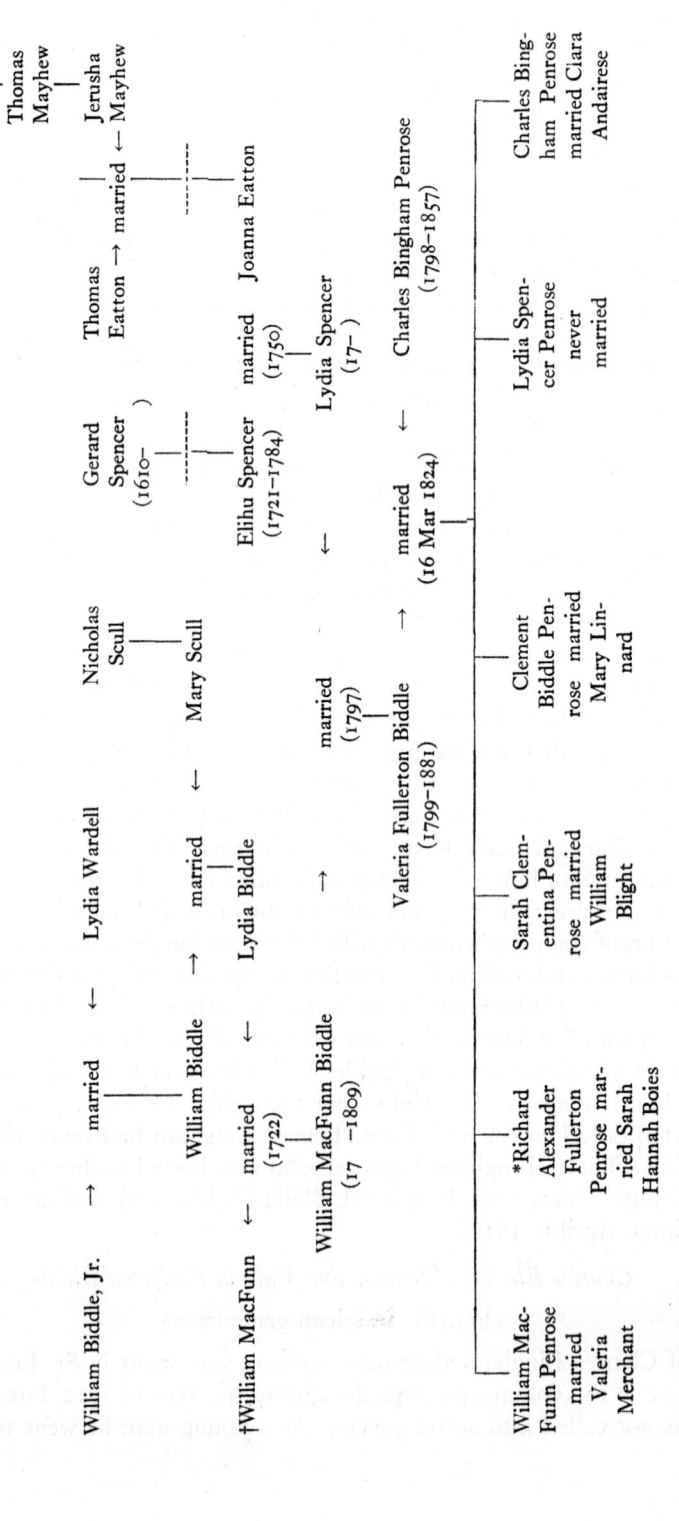

```
William Biddle, Jr. → married                                                                    Thomas
                                  ─────────────┐                                                 Mayhew
                                               ↓                                                    │
                                        Lydia Wardell                                            Thomas
                                               │                                                 Mayhew
                                               ↓                                                    │
                                        William Biddle                              Gerard      Jerusha
                                               │                                    Spencer  ← Mayhew
                                               ↓                                    (1610– )
†William MacFunn  ← married  → Lydia Biddle                                             │
                    (1722)                    │                                         ↓
                    ───────────────┐          ↓                          Elihu Spencer  married  Joanna Eatton
                                   ↓                                     (1721–1784)    (1750)
                          William MacFunn Biddle                                │                   │
                              (17 –1809)                                        ↓           Thomas
                                   │                             Nicholas    Lydia Spencer ← Eatton → married
                                   ↓                             Scull       (17– )
                          Valeria Fullerton Biddle                  │               │
                              (1799–1881)                           ↓               ↓
                                   │                             Mary Scull    Charles Bingham Penrose
                                   ↓                                │              (1798–1857)
                                   married ←───────────────────────────────────────┘
                                   (16 Mar 1824)
        ┌──────────────────────┬──────────────────────┬──────────────────────┐
        │                      │                      │                      │
William Mac-            *Richard              Sarah Clem-         Clement          Lydia Spen-    Charles Bing-
Funn Penrose            Alexander             entina Pen-         Biddle Pen-      cer Penrose    ham Penrose
married                 Fullerton             rose married        rose married     never          married Clara
Valeria                 Penrose mar-          William             Mary Lin-        married        Andairese
Merchant                ried Sarah            Blight              nard
                        Hannah Boies

* Father of Dick Penrose.
† See text for change of surname.
```

phia to study law under Samuel Ewing, and on May 9, 1821, he was admitted to the bar in that city. Shortly thereafter he removed to Carlisle, Pennsylvania, where he settled in the practice of his profession and rapidly rose to a foremost place. He took a leading part in many of the public movements of the day, and in 1833 was elected a member of the Senate of Pennsylvania, being re-elected in 1837. For four of the eight years during which he was a member of the Senate, he occupied the post of Speaker, or, as it was known in those days, President of the Senate.

"A remarkable political condition prevailed in his senatorial districts during the period he represented them in the Senate," said his son, Richard Alexander Fullerton Penrose, in discussing his father's political views. "He was originally elected as a Jackson Democrat from his district, a strongly Democratic one. When General Jackson removed the United States deposits from the Bank of the United States and declared he would destroy the Bank, Senator Penrose became member of the Whig party. At the next election for state senator, he was elected by an overwhelming majority as a Whig and an enemy of the Jackson democracy."

As the result of this change of party, Senator Penrose was violently assailed, and in March, 1839, replied before the Pennsylvania Senate in a speech which occupied three days in its delivery. He claimed that not he but Mr. Jackson had changed principles.

"The history of General Jackson will present the most remarkable instance of numerous promises, professions and principles, no doubt at the time honestly made and avowed, but violated and abandoned in succession under the influence of the venal flattery of the designing parasites who surround him," said Senator Penrose. "Instead of independent opinion, party discipline has substituted the will of the leaders of the party, and that will, however contradictory and capricious, must be obeyed.... President Jackson in his inaugural address declared, as Jefferson had done, that the patronage of the General Government had been brought into conflict with elections, and he promised to restore the Government to the simplicity of the early ages of the Republic. He promised reform of abuses, and he emphatically declared that this reform was inscribed by the people among the first of its duties. But instead of reform, abuses increased—instead of a return to the purity and simplicity of democratic principles, every day produced some new and wider departure from it—instead of restraining the mighty power of the executive arm, it was everywhere felt; and absolute submission claimed to the executive will ... The provisions of the constitution were disregarded, and all powers resolved into the will of the executive, fenced in by flatterers, and above all control and beyond all check.... This, sir, is the history of the latter days of the party, which has driven from its ranks the honest Democrats who were once its bone and sinew, and it has now nothing left of democracy but the much honored and long abused name."

On March 13, 1841, Senator Penrose resigned as Speaker and six days later resigned as member of the Senate in order to accept the position of Solicitor of the United States Treasury under William Henry Harrison, newly elected President of the United States. Mr. Penrose had been a member of the Whig national convention held in 1840, when General Harrison was nominated as the candidate for President to run against Van Buren, who was a candidate for a second term as President on the Democratic ticket. Mr. Penrose held his Treasury post until the close of the Tyler administration. He then returned to Pennsylvania and resumed the practice of law at Lancaster, but removed from that city to Philadelphia in 1847. In 1849 he was appointed Assistant Secretary of the Treasury, but soon resigned this post, and returned once more to Philadelphia.

In 1856 he was for the third time elected to the Pennsylvania State Senate, this time from Philadelphia and as a candidate of the People's, or Republican, Party. He was occupying this position at the time of his death, which was caused by pneumonia, brought on by exposure in a railroad accident which happened as he was returning to his post at Harrisburg after a short visit to his family in Philadelphia.

Mr. Penrose was one of the compilers of Penrose & Watt's three volumes of *Reports of Cases in the Supreme Court of Pennsylvania* (1831–1832). For some years he was a trustee of Dickinson College and for four years was secretary of the Board of Trustees. He was also the projector of the Cumberland Valley Railroad and served for some time as its president.

In *Men of Mark in Cumberland Valley, Pennsylvania*, Alfred Nevin says of Charles Bingham Penrose:

"The character of Mr. Penrose was distinguished by many strong and prominent points. He was emphatically self-reliant, depending on his own resources in the accomplishment of his plans and purposes. Whatever his hand found to do, he did it with all his might. Such was the enthusiasm of his nature, that it kindled a warm sympathy on all sides in his favor, and greatly aided him in carrying forward his life work. To selfishness he was an entire stranger.... Benevolence beamed in his countenance, and often found expression, not in good wishes merely, but in acts of delicate but seasonable kindness. His life was simple and frugal. Everything like ostentation was shunned by him, and he abhorred self-indulgence of all sorts. His generosity was apparent to everybody, amounting almost to a fault. His manner, which was highly cultivated, was gentle, courteous, and genial, offensive to none, attractive to all. Especially was he gracious to his inferiors, careful of their rights, and considerate of their feelings."

On March 16, 1824, Charles Bingham Penrose married Valeria Fullerton, daughter of William MacFunn Biddle by his wife, Lydia Spencer. Mrs. Penrose was born at Philadelphia in January, 1799, and died there November 15, 1881.

According to Dr. Leach, "William MacFunn Biddle was born MacFunn, but added Biddle to his surname by an act of the Legislature, to enable him to inherit an estate from his uncle, Honorable Edward Biddle. He was a son of Captain William MacFunn, an officer in the British Navy, by his wife Lydia Biddle, daughter of William Biddle by his wife Mary, a daughter of Nicholas Scull, the eminent Surveyor-General of Pennsylvania."

Scull was a member of the Junto, the little group which Benjamin Franklin brought together and which was the precursor of the larger group which he contrived to bind together in the beginnings of the American Philosophical Society. In his *Autobiography*, Franklin says of Scull that he was "a surveyor, afterwards surveyor-general, who loved books and sometimes made a few verses." Later, when the Junto decided to club their books into a library which they invited the other citizens of Philadelphia to join, the initial fee being forty shillings and the annual dues ten shillings, the initial meeting of the board of directors was held at Scull's house on November 8, 1731.

"William MacFunn, a bluff and hearty English seaman of the old heroic type, was an officer of the British navy, present with the British fleet at the siege of Quebec," declares William Healey Dall in his biography of Spencer Fullerton Baird. "While stationed on the Delaware in 1752, he won the hand of Lydia Biddle, then a young belle in Philadelphia society. He was ordered to duty at Antigua, and there became a victim of a tropical disease, of which he died at Philadelphia in 1769, leaving a son, William Biddle MacFunn.

"One of the maternal uncles of this son, having lost his own children, left a handsome fortune to young MacFunn on condition that he should change his surname to Biddle. Accepting this condition he was later known as William MacFunn Biddle. He was an accomplished musician, a banker, a friend of Robert Morris, and was drawn into some of the speculations in which the financiers of the Revolution were engaged in the early days of the Republic. In 1797 he married Lydia Spencer, of distinguished colonial lineage. . . .

"William MacFunn Biddle suffered as so many did from the collapse of the speculation in land. At one time reckoned the richest young man in Philadelphia, within a year he went with Robert Morris to a debtor's prison, where he remained until released by the passage of the first United States bankrupt law in 1800. He died in 1809."

William MacFunn Biddle married the Lydia Spencer mentioned by Sarah Penrose Tillier in her letters from Switzerland. She had been a bridesmaid to Anne Howard Bingham when she married Mrs. Tillier's son, Clement Biddle Penrose, and her great grandson, Dick Penrose, treasured the letter written from one gay laughing girl to another, asking her to act in that capacity.

She was the mother of three daughters and two sons, William and Edward. The eldest daughter, Lydia MacFunn Biddle, married Samuel Baird; the second, Valeria Fullerton Biddle, became Mrs. Charles Bingham Penrose; the third marries Major William Blaney, an officer of the Engineer Corps of the Army.

Lydia Spencer was the daughter of the Reverend Elihu Spencer, who was born in East Haddam, Connecticut, February 12, 1721, and died in Trenton, New Jersey, December 27, 1784. He was graduated at Yale in 1746, and, with a view to becoming a missionary to the Indians of the Six Nations, studied their dialect and prepared himself for his office under the Reverends John Brainer and Johnathan Edwards, accompanying the latter to the Indian Conference at Albany in 1748.

He was ordained September 14, 1748, and, after spending some time in western New York, was appointed pastor of the Presbyterian Church in Elizabeth, New Jersey, in 1750, which charge he held until 1756, when he was called to the Presbyterian Church of Jamaica, Long Island. About 1758 he was appointed by Governor James DeLancey, chaplain of the New York troops formed for service in the French war, at the close of which he returned to New Jersey, holding posts in Shrewsbury, Middletown Point, Shark River, and Amboy. From 1769 until his death he was pastor of the Presbyterian church in Trenton. He became a chaplain in the Revolutionary Army and took so active a part in the contest that the British government set a price on his head. When the British took possession of Trenton, according to family tradition, they burned his home and very valuable library to the ground. On October 20, 1777, Congress elected him chaplain for the hospitals of the Middle Department of the Continental Army.

From 1752 until his death he was a trustee of Princeton College. In 1782 the University of Pennsylvania gave him the degree of doctor of divinity.

Elihu Spencer was descended from Gerard, or Jared, Spencer, born 1610, who lived in 1638 at Lynn, Massachusetts, and in 1660 was one of the first settlers of East Haddam.

Dall tells the story that "when Aaron Burr was sent to college his father consigned him to the care and general superintendence of his friend Elihu Spencer, in whose family the youth was intimate at that period. Another family anecdote is that Burr, being in Philadelphia after the duel with Hamilton, called upon Mrs. MacFunn Biddle, whom he had known at Trenton as Lydia Spencer. The Biddles were intimate friends of Hamilton and possessed a fine marble bust of him which still remains in the family. After Burr had been there a short time he looked up and recognized the bust, turned very pale, took his leave in a few moments, and never called again."

Elihu Spencer married Joanna Eatton in 1750. She was descended from Thomas Eatton, who came to Rhode Island in 1660 and there married Jerusha Mayhew, widow of Joseph Wing. She was, according to Leach, "a descendent of the Rev. Thomas Mayhew, missionary to the Indians and son of Thomas Mayhew, first governor and patentee of Martha's Vineyard, Nantucket, and the Elizabeth Islands, Massachusetts. The missionary is said to have been much loved by his Indian flock. Called with his father by royal mandate to England, to give an account of the condition of the colony and their work among the aborigines, they were lost at sea, on their way in 1679."

Lydia Spencer's aunt, Valeria Eatton, married Pierre LeConte, M.D., from whom were descended John and Joseph LeConte, both professors at the University of California, and John L. LeConte, the distinguished entomologist of Philadelphia.

In the Baird book by Dall, Lucy Hunter Baird, only child of Spencer Fullerton Baird, second secretary of the Smithsonian Institution of Washington, and organizer and first commissioner of the United States Commission of Fish and Fisheries, presents the following picture of Lydia Spencer Biddle:

"My great-grandmother, Lydia Spencer Biddle, was a woman of great decision and energy of character. After the disastrous failures of the land speculations in which her husband and Robert Morris with many others were engaged, and which caused their imprisonment for debt, his business never recovered, and he died a poor man, leaving his widow and young family destitute. Her relatives offered to do all in their power, but she was a woman of independent spirit and put her own shoulder to the wheel in a manner more like that expected of women at the end rather than at the beginning of the nineteenth century. By a successful business venture in which she embarked, and aided by an unexpected windfall from another quarter, she was enabled not only to educate her children but at last to find herself the possessor of what was in those days a competency. After the marriage of her second daughter, Mrs. Penrose, she removed to Carlisle, where she built a comfortable house and passed the remainder of her life, dying at the age of ninety-two. She was very active up to the close of her life and was a person of very proud and independent spirit. She had no fear whatever of disregarding the smaller conventionalities in anything which she herself deemed right and dignified. Her granddaughters would sometimes object to wearing some garments, which she considered suitable, on the ground that it was not the fashion, and would be met with the crushing reply, 'When I was young anything that Miss Spencer wore *was* the fashion.' "

Included in the Dall volume is a letter from Mrs. Charles Bingham Penrose in Reading, Pa., to her mother, Mrs. Lydia Spencer Biddle, in Philadelphia. It is dated February 4, 1823, and reads as follows:

Dear Mamma,

I can readily imagine how delighted you will be to hear of the arrival of another grandson yesterday about half past twelve in the morning. It was about ten days sooner than Lydia expected, but she was, and still is so uncommonly well, we do not regret its having come so soon. She was not very sick more than an hour or an hour and a half, and I sent for cousin Betsey Eckert, who was the only person with her besides the doctor. We had no bustle or confusion, everything went on charmingly, and after the child was born, I was so fortunate as to get a pretty good nurse, who will stay until Mrs. Scott arrives, which I suppose will be on Thursday.

Lydia expects you on Saturday or Tuesday, and I suppose if you do not come she will have a complete chill. She says she never felt half so well in any of her confinements, and I hope if you come up for a week or two, to take good care of her, she will soon be quite well. I almost forgot to tell you what a fine baby it is, very large though not very fat, and looks a good deal like Will only it has dark hair. They talk of calling it Spencer Fullerton [this was Spencer Fullerton Baird] but I think it had better be Elihu Spencer. I suppose you will decide when you come. Will and Sam are delighted with it. I am afraid they will kill it with kindness, they are so rough. Will catches hold of it as it it were wood or stone.

Lydia says she has a long message to send you. She is now asleep but I suppose I must leave room for it. Love to all.

Yours affectionately,
Valeria

P.S. Lydia wants to know whether you think Aunt F. would like her to call the baby Spencer F. She is afraid perhaps it may give Aunty some dislike, or rather recall disagreeable recollections to her mind.* If you think that will be the case, she will call it Elihu Spencer. She likewise wants a box of tapers, which I forgot to bring, a bottle of lavender, and some raisins for cake. I believe this is all her important message, except that I must tell you she is uncommonly well.

V.F.P.

N.B. Please give my compliments to Mr. H. Hall and request him to send me a few books, some entertaining ones for Lydia and some improving ones for myself. I leave it to him to select, as I have such entire confidence in the goodness of his judgment. Lydia wants a few smoked herring.

V.

P.P.S.
Dear Mother,

I observe by the city papers that the puerperal fever prevails in the city. As this is a disease which is peculiar to ladies during their confinement, almost invariably proves fatal, and as it is believed that the infection is conveyed from one sick chamber to another in the clothes of nurses, should Nurse Scott have attended any lady who has been sick with it, it would be advisable that she should leave the garments she wore at the time, in the city. I have heard of no case of the kind in this neighborhood this season.

V.P.

On the outside of the folded letter is this note: "Jacob Heevener will please carry this letter round to Mrs. Biddle's as soon as he gets into the city, as she may wish to come up with him in the stage the next morning."

Heevener was evidently a carrier or local expressman between Reading and Philadelphia, who, in addition to packages, took charge of letters and delivered them, probably at a lower cost than the 25 cents then demanded by the U. S. postoffice.

Another interesting letter from Valeria Fullerton Penrose is dated Washington, February 27th, 1849, at the time when her husband was Assistant Secretary of the Treasury. It is addressed to her youngest child, Charles Bingham Penrose, who was born in 1838 and died in 1895.

My dear Charley

I was delighted to receive your letter this morning, by cousin Vally and to hear you were making out so well without me. The weather has been so unpleasant I have not been able to go out much, and very few of my friends have been able to come and see me. It has rained every day, and yesterday it rained all day. It is still very cloudy and damp, but I hope it will clear by twelve o'clock for I am afraid I shall leave Washington without seeing any of my old friends and neighbors.

Last evening we had a very pleasant party, given by the ladies of the house— each subscribed, and had the privilege of inviting two guests. I invited your Aunt

---

* Owing to the recent death of the cousin so named.

Blaney who arrived yesterday morning and is staying at old Dr. Brown's. She came and seemed to enjoy herself very much. We had cakes and lemonade, ice cream, pickled oysters and chicken salad, and plenty of good music. There was a Miss Stewart from Detroit who played splendidly—I think the finest female performance I ever heard. I have not yet been to see General Taylor and his ladies—it has been too wet and muddy to turn out—but your father called yesterday and seemed very much delighted with them. There was scarcely any one there, so that he had an opportunity of a long conversation with the President elect. Tonight Mr. Polk has his last levee—Tomorrow Gen. Taylor and his family dine at the White House and on Saturday they—the Polks—take their final departure. We want to go this evening, if the weather will permit, for it is the only place I intend to go to. I received my invitation to the Inauguration ball the day I arrived, and I wish Beck and Sal were here to attend it, in my place. On Friday there is to be another assembly; if the girls were here they could be as dissipated as they wished. Lent does not seem to make any difference, the Penitentes will all have to get absolution.

Mrs. Wise and the boys regret very much I did not bring you and Lyd. They speak of it every day and wish you were here. But it has been such bad weather, it would have been very dull for you, for you could not have gone out, and the children are at school all day. Warry has grown to be a nice pretty little gentle thing, and Willy Ames can read Plato and French, have grown a great deal, and are very good boys, attend to their lessons and give their mother very little trouble. Johnny Ames is also here, and has grown quite a big boy.

Tell Sal the next letter I write will be to her, by that time I shall have seen some persons and have heard some news. Tell her Mrs. Bache has got off another of her ugly daughters, who is to be married tomorrow evening to Lieut. Wainwright of the Navy.

Mr. Chase is not any better than when he left Phila. The Dr. here thinks very badly of his case—says one lung is entirely gone and the other much diseased, of course has no hope of his recovery. Give my love to your grandmother, I am glad to hear she is so much better, and hope she takes care of herself this damp weather. Love to Alice, Clem and all the girls, including Rosy and Maria. I hope you and Lyd will be good children until I return, and I shall hear good accounts of you.

Some of you must write almost every day. Your Aunt Blaney told me Will would leave Carlisle today for Washington so we will expect him tomorrow. Mrs. Wise will accommodate him, and I think he will find it very pleasant to be here now. I almost forgot to tell you that Jeannie Graham has a baby—a son—five weeks old. I saw Mr. Graham who seems perfectly delighted. Tell Sal Miss Eglantine Cochran is married, and the other Miss Latimer—Julia Latimer—is a widow with two children.

I must close my letter ready for the mail.

Your affectionate Mother
V. F. Penrose

The Sal referred to is her older daughter, Sarah Clementina Penrose, who married William Sergeant Blight; Lyd is the younger daughter, Lydia Spencer Penrose, who never married. Besides Charley, there were three other sons—William MacFunn, Richard Alexander Fullerton, and Clement Biddle. All the children were born at Carlisle, Pennsylvania.

Richard Alexander Fullerton Penrose and Sarah Hannah Boies
(Fifth American generation)

Richard Alexander Fullerton Penrose, second son and second child of Charles Bingham Penrose and Valeria Fullerton Biddle, was born March 24, 1827 and died December 1908. After graduating from Dickinson College (at Carlisle) in 1846, he entered upon the study of medicine at the Medical Department of the

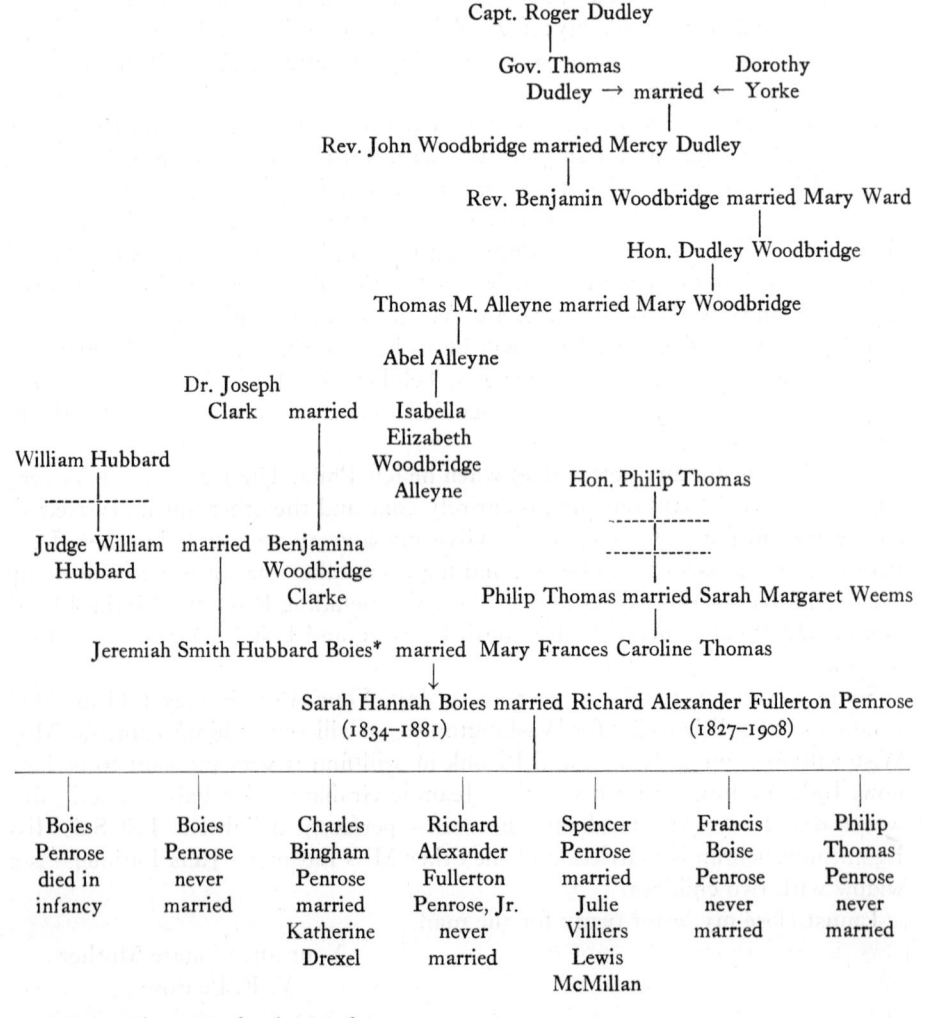

```
                          Capt. Roger Dudley
                                 |
                          Gov. Thomas          Dorothy
                          Dudley  → married ←  Yorke
                                         |
                    Rev. John Woodbridge married Mercy Dudley
                                                    |
                                Rev. Benjamin Woodbridge married Mary Ward
                                                                    |
                                            Hon. Dudley Woodbridge
                                                    |
                          Thomas M. Alleyne married Mary Woodbridge
                                            |
                                      Abel Alleyne
                            Dr. Joseph       |
                              Clark  married  Isabella
                                              Elizabeth
    William Hubbard                           Woodbridge
           |                                   Alleyne         Hon. Philip Thomas
    -------|-------                               |                    |
           |                                                     ------|------
    Judge William married Benjamina                                    |
      Hubbard            Woodbridge                              -----|------
                           Clarke                                     |
                             |              Philip Thomas married Sarah Margaret Weems
              Jeremiah Smith Hubbard Boies* married Mary Frances Caroline Thomas
                                              ↓
                       Sarah Hannah Boies married Richard Alexander Fullerton Penrose
                            (1834–1881)                        (1827–1908)
```

| Boies Penrose died in infancy | Boies Penrose never married | Charles Bingham Penrose married Katherine Drexel | Richard Alexander Fullerton Penrose, Jr. never married | Spencer Penrose married Julie Villiers Lewis McMillan | Francis Boise Penrose never married | Philip Thomas Penrose never married |

* *See* text for reason for change of surname.

University of Pennsylvania, from which he was graduated in 1849. From 1851 to 1853 he was resident physician at the Pennsylvania Hospital. In 1853 he became physician to the Southern Home for Children, and in 1854 consulting physician of the Philadelphia Hospital, where he delivered clinical lectures on diseases of women and children. He was one of the founders of the Children's Hospital in 1856, and contributed to its success much of his time, energy, and pecuniary resources. He was for a number of years a successful private teacher of medicine, his course of lectures being largely attended.

During the Civil War, he served as a surgeon at the Satterlee Hospital, one of the largest of the army hospitals in Philadelphia.

In 1863 the trustees of the University of Pennsylvania elected him to the professorship of obstetrics and diseases of women and children, which chair he filled with great distinction until 1889, when he retired from the position and from the practice of medicine. In 1854 he became a member of the College of Physicians, and he was one of the founders of the Hospital of the University of Pennsylvania, as well as of the Gynaecean Hospital of Philadelphia.

Dr. Penrose was a general favorite among his students, as is shown by the following resolutions adopted by his classes when there was a rumor of his resignation in 1885:

"*Whereas*, We the First Year Class of the Medical Department have received the assurance of the imminent resignation of Dr. Penrose from the Faculty of the University of Pennsylvania:

"And *Whereas*, The promise of instruction from so eminent and distinguished an authority both at home and abroad constituted one of the prime considerations that attracted us all to the institution to whose renown his name has contributed so largely; and

"*Whereas*, We are deeply impressed that his resignation would be an irreparable calamity both to ourselves and the University.

"Therefore, be it resolved,

That we present a memorial earnestly and unanimously requesting that he reconsider his determination, and remain at least for the term of the present classes enrolled;

"And be it further resolved,

That a copy of these resolutions be presented to Dr. Penrose, and to the Trustees, and the original to the Faculty."

To this was attached a second set of resolutions:

"*Whereas*, it has come to the knowledge of the Medical Classes of the University of Pennsylvania that Dr. R. A. F. Penrose, Professor of Obstetrics, anticipates tendering his resignation at the close of the present session, and

"*Whereas*, by such a course the classes now under his instruction would be deprived of the completion of his most valuable and highly appreciated lectures, and knowing that the best interests of the institution demand his retaining his present position, therefore, be it,

"*Resolved*, that the undersigned members of the Second Year class request that the esteemed professor reconsider and defer his action at least until all of the classes now in the Medical Department shall have terminated their studies, and, be it further,

"*Resolved*, that the original of these resolutions and signatures be sent to the Faculty of the said department of the University, and a copy to Professor Penrose and the Trustees of the University."

Not to be outdone, the graduating class likewise offered resolutions:

"Inasmuch as Dr. R. A. F. Penrose, Professor of Obstetrics, anticipates tendering his resignation at the close of the present course of lectures, be it

"*Resolved*, that we, the undersigned members of the Graduating Class, do sincerely regret the action of this great teacher, and heartily endorse the action taken by the first and second year students in their efforts to retain him as their instructor."

To each set of resolutions, which were carefully written out in long hand, were appended long lists of students.

Among those who studied under Professor Penrose was Barton C. Hirst, who wrote the memorial to his teacher which appeared in the *Proceedings* of the American Philosophical Society, of which Dr. Penrose had long been a distinguished member.

"He was one of those who secured the opening of wards of the hospital for instruction," wrote Dr. Hirst. "Medical education in America was in a stage of development so different in his time from the present that it is difficult even for those of us who have witnessed its evolution, to realize its crudity and provincialism. Our medical schools were mainly proprietary institutions conducted for financial profit. Laboratory facilities, clinical material and individual instruction were either lacking altogether or were just beginning to be provided.... It was under these conditions that Dr. Penrose was obliged to teach.... But of this means he availed himself with consummate ability ...

"It is no exaggeration to say that none of his contemporaries made his lectures at the same time so instructive, entertaining, amusing and useful. The most admirable quality of his art was the vivid and lasting impression made upon his auditors....

"His personal dignity, penetrating but kindly voice, exquisitely keen sense of humor, poetic fancy and eloquence were inimitable.... He fairly radiated kindliness. A harsh, unkind or ungenerous thought was absolutely foreign to his nature. He was affable, courteous, cordial to all degrees of men; but a consciousness of distinction in birth, connections and position gave him an innate dignity which forbade undue familiarity or lack of respect.

"He had some odd and whimsical views on men and things, giving his conversation a fascinating piquancy. In one of his amiable foibles, he was like that most lovable character in fiction, Colonel Newcome. His friends were perfection itself. He could see no fault in them....

"An incident in our association illustrates what I mean. He had determined to do all in his power to make me his successor. As the first step in that direction he told me to prepare a lecture as carefully as I could and to commit it to memory. When it was ready I was given a letter dated two days later, ostensibly received just before his lecture hour, and reading, 'I am unexpectedly detained. Please inform the class. If they care to stop and listen to you, you may use my hour.' I was instructed to enter the room in apparent confusion, making the open letter in my hand to tremble; to mount the rostrum and after giving the class Dr. Penrose's message, to say in a hesitating voice, 'If you are willing to stay and hear me, I have a word or two to say on an interesting subject.' 'They will stop to hear you,' said Dr. Penrose, 'in the expectation of seeing you make an exhibition of yourself.' His little plot carried out exactly as he had planned it. My lecture was well received and Penrose was hugely delighted at its success.

"I could give many more examples of characteristic generosity to younger men whom he befriended with a bounteous generosity that knew no stint."

In writing to his son Dick years later (in a letter dated June 9, 1925), his niece Ellen, daughter of his older brother, said:

"It has always been one of the things I most loved to do when I am in Phila. to go to your home. I loved to see Uncle Alex and have him tell me about his brothers and himself, the life they lived up here in Carlisle when they were all boys together, the house they had at Middlesex where they hunted and fished, then of the interesting books he had been reading. I always went after these talks and got something to read he had told me of.

"I think he was one of the most interesting people I ever knew. Now I love to come and see you. You make me think of Uncle Alex."

Those who knew the son and read this tribute by Dr. Hirst to the father, will have no difficulty in understanding why the niece felt as she did.

Another, whose life the elder Penrose touched with lasting effects, was H. L. Martin, who wrote to Dick, from New York, under date of May 17, 1924:

"For many years as a youngster in Seal Harbor, Maine, I was a semi-protege of your father's. I say 'semi-protege' for lack of a better expression. I did little errands for him, for which I was financially well paid, which was the beginning of our relationship. From that time until his death his interest in my welfare seemingly never abated. His suggestions as to what studies I should take in school, his insistence upon a certain very definite code of conduct and his gifts from time to time of worthwhile books on which he afterward questioned me, were acts that I now see were of inestimable [value] to the country boy. After I took up commercial work and could no longer do the little jobs he desired done he usually invited me for fifteen minutes each Sunday morning and talked to me on such topics as he felt I needed instruction at that particular time. For clarity of expression, knowledge of the subject, and his subjects were many and varied, and a final summary that embraced the points he wished to drive home, these talks have never been equalled in my experience."

On September 28, 1858, Dr. Penrose married Sarah Hannah Boies, daughter of Jeremiah Smith Hubbard Boies by his wife, Mary Frances Caroline Thomas. Mrs. Penrose was born at "Rockland," Cecil County, Maryland, March 31, 1834, and died of pneumonia at Philadelphia, March 30, 1881.

"Mrs. Penrose was a woman of rare culture and refinement, of unusual intelligence and phenomenal and magnificent beauty," says Leach. "She became the mother of seven sons. At a very early period of her married life she abandoned entirely society and devoted herself exclusively to the education of her children, and this she kept up until her death in 1881—a few months before her two eldest sons graduated from Harvard University with highest honors, honors due, in a great measure, to their mother's untiring devotion to them."

After the death of his wife left him with six* boys—the oldest, twenty; the youngest, just three weeks past his twelfth birthday—Dr. Penrose devoted himself to the upbringing of those sons with such effectiveness that each of the four who lived to enter a profession made for himself a name in his own right, and each in a separate profession. And of those boys none was closer to him in thought and example than his namesake.

Before he died, this remarkable man left explicit directions concerning the disposal of his body. He ordered that it should "be viewed by none save officials (doctors) and by my children, sister and brother, and no one else." The body was to lie eight days "in my front bath room where I kept the body of your mother for eight days after her death." Furthermore, there was to be no funeral unless one were necessary "for social reasons," and even then there was to be "no inspection of the body by any one under any pretext ... no sort or kind of religious services, no address, no prayer, *no anything, no flowers*." After eight days the body was to be cremated at night and the ashes to be placed in the vault of his wife.

Mrs. Penrose came of a lineage no less distinguished than that of her husband, tracing her forebears from among the best families of Massachusetts and Maryland. Her father was Jeremiah Smith Hubbard, son of Judge William Hubbard, who added Boies to his name after he was adopted by an uncle, Jeremiah Smith Boies, a prominent and wealthy merchant of Boston. Judge Hubbard had married Benjamina Woodbridge Clarke, daughter of Dr. Joseph Clark, by his wife Isabella Elizabeth Woodbridge Alleyne, daughter of Abel Alleyne, of Quincy, Massachusetts, and granddaughter of Thomas Alleyne, by his wife Mary, daughter of the Honorable Dudley Woodbridge, who was graduated at Harvard College in 1696, and became the director-general of the Royal Asciento Company of England, and agent of the South Sea Company in Barbadoes, and also judge-advocate-general of that island.

Dudley Woodbridge was the son of the Reverend Benjamin Woodbridge, who married Mary Ward, June 3, 1672, and the grandson of the Reverend John Woodbridge, who, bred at Oxford, came to America in 1634, and was ordained minister of the church at Andover, Massachusetts, in 1635. Later he became a member of the Governor's Council of Massachusetts. Reverend John Woodbridge married Mercy, daughter of Thomas Dudley, eminent among the early Massachusetts colonists.

Thomas, son of Captain Roger Dudley, of the English Army, descended from the Barons of Dudley, was born in Northampton, England, in 1576; at twenty was commissioned captain by Queen Elizabeth, and led his company "of the Northampton gallants over to the siege of Amiens, in Picardy." He became a

---

* The seventh and oldest died in infancy.

zealous Puritan, and was for many years the steware of the fourth Earl of Lincoln. In 1630 he was chosen deputy-governor of Massachusetts and came with Governor Winthrop to the colony that same year. In 1634, and again in 1640, 1645, and 1650, he was elected governor, and in 1644 was chosen commander-in-chief of the military forces of the colony, with the title of major-general. From the time of his arrival in Massachusetts, until his death, December 31, 1653, when not governor, he served either as deputy-governor or as a member of the Governor's Council of Assistants. He married Dorothy Yorke, April 25, 1603.

Judge Hubbard was a descendant of William Hubbard, who was a member of the first class graduated from Harvard College in 1642.

Mrs. Penrose's mother, Mary Frances Caroline Thomas, was a daughter of Philip Thomas, Jr., by his wife, Sarah Margaret Weems, and the great-great-great-granddaughter of the Honorable Philip Thomas, private secretary to Lord Baltimore, founder of the State of Maryland, and a member of the Governor's Council of the Province of Maryland. On that same Council was Colonel Samuel Chew, another ancestor of Mrs. Penrose.

From such roots sprang the subject of this volume, for to Dr. and Mrs. Penrose were born seven sons, all at Philadelphia, as follows:

Boies Penrose; died in infancy.

Boies Penrose, born November 1, 1860; died at Washington, D. C., December 31, 1921. Never married.

Charles Bingham Penrose, born February 1, 1862; married Katherine Drexel, November 17, 1892; died on the train, en route from Aiken, S. C., to Philadelphia, February 27, 1925.

Richard Alexander Fullerton Penrose, Jr., born December 17, 1863; died at Philadelphia, July 31, 1931. Never married.

Spencer Penrose, born November 2, 1865; married Julie V. McMillan, 1906; died at Colorado Springs, December 7, 1939.

Francis Boies Penrose, born August 2, 1867. Never married.

Philip Thomas Penrose, born March 10, 1869; died at El Paso, Texas, June 8, 1901. Never married.

CHAPTER 3

School Days

"AS A SMALL child I went to a school kept by three old ladies called the Misses Hough, just across the street from our house in Philadelphia, where I received the usual education given to children of that age," wrote Dick Penrose, in a typewritten manuscript, found among his effects. It is entitled "Memoirs" and at the top of the first page, in his handwriting, is penciled "(Rough draft) one copy. Notes dictated at odd times."

"Later," he continues, "I went to the Episcopal Academy, which was at that time located at Juniper and Locust Streets, and was presided over by Doctor Edward Robins, one of the kindest, most sympathetic, and at the same time learned heads of a school for older boys whom I have ever met. Though I greatly respected Doctor Robins, my main recollection of the Episcopal Academy was when we boys used to start in a body around the back streets between Juniper and 13th Streets to make raids on the boys at Doctor Fairies' school on 13th Street. These were real events to us and were more important with their bruises and blows than the serious studies and prayers at the Episcopal Academy."

That he was a good student, however, and kept his "mischief" for the hours after school is indicated by a document preserved among the family treasures which reads:

"I hereby Certify, that Richard A. F. Penrose, Jr., having attained an Average Standing of 9.10 in Scholarship and 9.92 in Conduct, is entitled to be ranked among those Commended with Honour, at the opening of the Christmas Holidays 1875. [Signed] James W. Robins, Head Master."

Another family treasure is a copy of THE RECORD of December 22, 1871, evidently "published" by Boies Penrose, at that time aged eleven. It is written on a sheet of notepaper and is ruled to form three narrow columns, the items being separated from each other by spaces and lines in approved newspaper fashion, but its editor seems to have had no use for punctuation. It is indeed a "record" of those six little boys. Charlie, known as Tal, was nine; Dick was eight; Spencer, or "Speck", was six; Francis, familiarly known as "Friday", was four; and Philip was two and a half.

   C Penrose commed for correcting a mesteak in Dictation
   The little chick is lame   it got run over by the goat   the goat is all well and so are the rabbits
   Mr Dicks flower is dead
   C B P is not well

B P has got 89 cents and wants 10 more to make a dollar
C B P has a dollar and 15 cents
D R et F P has 32 cents
S P has 18 cents
F P has 13 cents
P P has none but he wants some
A good show at 2 o clock and 3 o clock on any day   come and see children 1 men & women 2¢
R a F is very happy because he has 32¢
they have not found the hat at school
to day we get out at 10 or 11 o clock at school
New mediaen S 314 Spruce
Felter's Arithmetic the best in the world
a house [rude drawing of a house] to rent at 213 Walnut street Phia Pa
New things for sale at 314 18 street

The last four items are evidently intended as advertisements. The *Record* closes with a picture of "the owner of this paper" and the words "the end."

What a merry household that must have been at 1331 Spruce Street, near Broad, in the Eighth Ward of Philadelphia. The house was of brick, three stories in height, with wide hallways and generous-sized rooms, which echoed and re-echoed to the childish laughter and woes of six little boys.

After Dick's death, Henry S. Musser wrote an article which appeared in the *Philadelphia Record* of August 6, 1931, in the column "Mostly Personal" by Robert Reiss. Under the title, "1331 Spruce Street", Mr. Musser said:

"With deep regret I learned of the passing of R. A. F. Penrose, Jr., a patrician and thorough sportsman. Last winter I covered the world's figure skating championship in Madison Square Garden, and before sunset found time to take a brisk walk up 5th Ave.

"There, just afront St. Patrick's Cathedral I met Richard Penrose—he rarely used his degree, Doctor. We talked of weather, politics, Russia particularly, and then of 1331 Spruce st., where he and his brothers Boies, Charlie and Spencer, were born and raised in real American fashion; how some of the window glass, in strange fashion, had turned amethystine.

"Like the old yellow Dundas Lippincott mansion, for many years at Broad and Walnut, which first the Forrest Theater, and now the towering Fidelity-Philadelphia supplanted, '1331'—to use the vernacular of the politician in the salad days of the powerful Boies Penrose regime—remains unsullied, well-kept throughout the years. Senator Boies, Dr. Charles, and later Dick, as he was lovingly known to his friends, saw to that. And now only Spencer survives, the leading citizen of Colorado.

"Big physically and mentally, those four brothers were all big game sportsmen who roamed the Rockies as the average Philadelphian strolls Sunday through Fairmount Park.

"And it was Richard, star stroke oarsman at Harvard in '83 and '84, crews famous in Crimson tradition by virtue of victories over the eights of old Eli, that brought the four brothers to the Rockies and gave them their taste for big game hunting.

"Down on Spruce st., at '1331', you'll find the home filled with trophies of the chase. Grizzlies, moose, elk, black bear, Rocky Mountain sheep and goats, antelopes, all fell before the aim of the brothers four.

"After Richard graduated with high honors at Harvard in 1884 he turned his energies to geology with success such as had won him renown as an oarsman on the Charles, and then went West, a la Horace Greeley. For a time geologist at the University of Chicago, and later Leland Stanford, President Hoover's alma mater, his summers were spent in the Rockies along the Continental Divide, where he combined profession and sport with eminent success.

....

"In short, he mixed exact geological knowledge with a sporting chance—and gloriously won out. He knew his Rockies.

....

"And now the thread of fraternal combination is nearly severed on this mortal sphere. Boies and Dr. Charles, Dick and Spencer—the first two won fame in the East; the latter pair placed the Penrose star high in the Western firmament. What marvelous memories Spencer, the sole survivor, must treasure."

Both father and mother believed firmly in the doctrine of self-reliance, discipline, self-control, and the now seemingly obsolete virtues of courtesy and thoughtful consideration of others. They also believed that children should early be taught the value of money, and the sons were required to earn what spending money they had. When he had provided his children with a good education, the father told his sons, he would consider his duty to them was accomplished. For the rest, they must take care of themselves.

The *Record* sold for "2" (evidently two cents), and the notice of shows at two and three o'clock for paid admission gives evidence that some one stood to make a little pocket money.

Until his death, Spencer Penrose had, hanging in his bedroom at his beautiful estate, El Pomar, at Colorado Springs, the carefully framed printed "receipt" which shows that he was paid a dollar and thirty-five cents for binding the first copies of *Harper's Magazine* for his father. In that same room, those same bound volumes show that the youngster did a very creditable piece of work as a bookbinder and that he was not paid beyond his just desserts.

Philip's tastes were evidently in a different direction, for a receipt, dated "Philadelphia, Feb. the 15th, 1882," when he was eleven years old, shows that some one bought of "P. T. Penrose, dealer in squabs and pigeons, Office 1331 Spruce, $\frac{1}{2}$ a pair of squabs 15 cts."

That the sons profited from this training is also shown in the careful accounting which Dick gives his father in his letters from Harvard. If the sons of this wise father made money, it may have been because he had early taught them its value.

Another souvenir of that period in the life of young Penrose is a map of the southern United States, Mexico, and central America, to which is attached the penciled memorandum, "Map made by R. A. F. Penrose, Jr., when 10 yrs. old. Treasured by his father." The map shows evidence that, even at this early age, the care and precision which marked the work of Dick Penrose throughout his life, was already thoroughly ingrained in his character.

"Somewhat later," continue the *Memoirs*, "I went to Doctor Chase's school at 16th and Spruce Streets, over Mr. Gray's grocery store. Doctor Chase was a graduate of Harvard, and like Doctor Robins, was a very kind and learned man. He did his best to control a somewhat boisterous collection of boys, and to aid in this matter he employed an assistant instructor, Mr. McCarg from Scotland—big, brawny, and bald. The boys treated Doctor Chase with a semblance of respect, but their principal delight during the noon hour was to get Mr. McCarg started. Their usual method was to throw something at him, then climb out of the second-story window and slide down the posts of the awning in front of Mr. Gray's grocery store. Mr. Gray was generally sympathetic with us because we bought our lunch at his store, so that Mr. McCarg chasing us with a big, long, flat ruler, rarely caught us.

"Later I studied under a private tutor at 1331 Spruce Street, named William S. Roney, who was a very learned and excellent man, and under whom I was prepared for Harvard, where I passed the preliminary entrance examinations in the spring of 1879, and the final entrance examinations in 1880 at the age of 16 years."

By this time, young Dick had evidently formed those studious habits which were to mark the remainder of his life, for a letter from Francis—apparently the pencil artist of the family—written to his mother in the summer of 1880, from Atlantic City, shows "a picture of Dick" with his feet on a table, reading a book.

The envelope is addressed to "Mrs. R. A. F. Penrose at Miss Uphams, 17 Kirkland St., Cambridge, Mass.," and must have given the postmen along the way much amusement, for it is decorated, in front with the heads of two ferocious-looking men, and on the back, where the stamp is in the lower right-hand corner, with two "gentlemen" in high silk hats, one of whom is hitting the other in the jaw, the while he says "Down you go," whereat the victim says fiercely "Oh!!".

Within the envelope are letters from three of the boys and one from Charlotte E. Ward, who was in charge during Mrs. Penrose's absence. Miss Ward writes:

Friday evening

My dear Mrs. Penrose

Mrs. Taylor called with her daughter just as the dinner-bell was ringing, which frightened them away. I have not had time to go there.

Margaret and Isabella coo together like doves and all the servants overwhelm me with attentions which the boys think blind me to their countless short-comings. We have been fishing today.

Every evening we put on our cloth coats and walk an hour on the beach, which has obliged me to postpone bed-time till 8.15 or thereabouts.

Francis contributed a letter, as well as the envelope decorations. His is dated Thursday, June 25. He says:

My dear Mother

I had to use this paper because we forgot to get some yesterday   this morning we went to the wagon bridge to fish   at first we caught two   you kneed not get scary for the wagon bridge has railing on both side and we lean over them to fish   altogether we caught nine   I caught one black fish the rest were sea bass   we had them for dinner   they were hanged good but Ann burnt my black fish   they were about six inches long   Norris is fixing the roof   he said the leak in the dining-room came down through the roof   there used to be some slates under the house but when we went to get them for Norris they were not there   I am going to take a bath on Sunday this is the poorest paper I ever wrote on   my pen sticks at every letter
F B Penrose
important!!
this morning I could not sleep and Philip said he had a headache and all the entry smelt

The second letter was from Philip, at that time eleven years old.

My dear Mother

The hunny suckets that I got under the house are begining to sprout   we went fishing to day with Miss war   we drove to the wagon bridg and Speck drove the carriage home and Jona came for us at one o clock   we caught eight sea bass and one black fish and we had them for dinner   Why I wright on this good paper is because the other paper has run out and Miss ward is goeing to get some common paper today   Jona has begun to cut the grass
Philip Thomas Penrose

The third letter is signed "Penrose" and presumably is from "Speck." He writes in woeful tones:

Dear mother

I got your letter yesterday. Mearket makes all the second floor stink so bad, that it is exactly like a old nasty lard factory, that is every room is full of flies. This morning I had to go down stairs and bring up a fly fan to keep them from bothering me. Philip said that their were so many flies that he could not sleep. So both Friday and Philip had to come in to my bed to get under the fly catcher.

Isabella has not done any thing for two or three days but shell peas and always eating out of a big pan full of fried potatoes, ham, bread and butter. I wanted another pair of clean breeches one pair dont last me more than four or five days   they get devlish dirty going riding and it is to much bother changing them and I would not have a clean pair to put on if I wanted. She said she would wash them the next time she washed.

We had fish for breakfast. Jonas got them but they were not worth a cent. For dinner we had one chicken and a ham   no body eats any thing but myself so one chicken is a little to much.

There is no hint as to what Mrs. Penrose was doing in Cambridge, but it is a safe conjecture that her visit was not unmixed with some details as to the comfort of her sons' college life.

In speaking of these arrangements, Dick said in his *Memoirs:*
"For the first year at Harvard I lived with my two elder brothers, Boies Penrose and Charles B. Penrose, at a house which our parents had bought for us on Gerry Street, and which was kept for us by our maiden cousin, Sarah Beck, of somewhat advanced years but of a very kindly disposition, and with all the pride and prejudices of a descendant of those who landed at Plymouth Rock in the early Colonial days of Massachusetts.

"My two brothers graduated in 1881, and as it did not seem worth while to keep the house going for one student, I got rooms nearby on Appian Way, and left the house for the use and comfort of our cousin, Miss Beck, who had taken care of it and us so efficiently and in spite of many aggravating circumstances for over four years. She was allowed to have the house as a residence for her and her sister until the end of her days, some twenty years later. Even this was but small reward for some of the activities and irregular habits of her young cousins, for whom she felt always a great responsibility."*

Boies and Charles entered Harvard in 1877, and with them they took the following "Rules" presented by their father under date of October 1, 1877:

Rules

R. A. F. Penrose requests his sons Boies and Charley to observe the following rules while at college

Miss Beck, possessing the affection and entire confidence of your Father and Mother, should be treated with the greatest respect, and her advice and suggestions should be received respectfully, and, as a rule, followed.

Be particular and neat about your dress—keep your shoes clean and well blackened—wash hands, brush hair before going to meals, and endeavor always to be ready when the meal is served.

Never retire for the night after studying all evening, without first going to Miss Beck, having a little social conversation with her, and bidding her good night.

Let ten o'clock be your latest hour for going to bed, if possible go earlier, never later.

Twice a week take a soap bath—the best time for this bath I think would be before going to bed.

* His letters show that he lived with Miss Beck in 1881–1882 and the beginning of the Fall term at least, in 1882. *See* letters dated Oct. 21, 1882; Nov. 15, 1882; Dec. 3, 1882.

Take from two to three hours, daily, active exercise—about five days in the week, go to the gymnasium for about an hour a day—while there never attempt to excell or do any difficult or unusual feat—walk an hour or two every day—box daily, or frequently.

Be careful in changing wet shoes, stockings and cloths. Put on winter flannels when the thermometer gets about 32°. At all times, accept Miss Beck's advice about clothing.

Avoid constipation of the bowels, by exercise, bathing, eating fruit and vegetables, and especially, by taking some *fixed* time, as after breakfast, invariably, to give them an opportunity to act. If two days pass without a movement take a podophillar or Anderson's pill at bed time, or two teaspoonsful (more or less) of crab orchard salt in a whole tumblerful of water immediately on rising in the morning.

Always go to church on Sunday morning—preferably, with Miss Beck, if not with her, to the college chapel.

When invited out to dinner or tea be careful about dress, etc. If offered wine or cigars, quietly decline, by saying you never smoke or use wine, and, at all times, give the same answer, no matter where or by whom offered.

Form at first no intimacies—afterwards, only with quiet, hard working students. Avoid all "swell" fellows. And, by all means, join no secret society or club until the sophomore or Junior year.

Presumably, these same rules were passed on to the younger boys as they entered college. Several of them became part and parcel of their subsequent lives, notably those concerning personal appearance, exercise, courtesy, and intimacies.

Mr. and Mrs. Penrose carefully thought out every detail of the life they wished their sons to live at college. Charles W. Eliot was then president of Harvard, and in a letter to Boies Penrose, dated Asticou, Maine, September 28, 1921, he wrote concerning those early days:

"I was trying to refresh my memories this morning, with some help from Mrs. Eliot, concerning the arrangements your father and mother made for you and your brother Charles B., in regard to lodgings in Cambridge when you first entered Harvard College. I had had two interviews with your parents about the education of their boys before you came to Cambridge at all. They impressed me very much with their intelligence and solicitude with regard to the education of their boys. Although neither of their families had had any connection with Harvard University, unless possibly your mother in Jeremiah Smith Boies, A.B. 1763 [1793?], both were bent on educating all their sons at Harvard College. I thought at one time that your father selected Harvard College because of the interest he took in reforms in the Harvard Medical School, which took place between 1870 and 1875; but of this I am not sure. Can you tell me what his motive was in the selection of Harvard?

"Having studied the College dormitories and their management, and made themselves acquainted with the mode of life of Harvard students in general, your father and mother bought a small house on Gerry Street, and established there two ladies, one elderly and the other perhaps about thirty years old, and required you and your brother Charles B. to live in that house all through your college course. When your brother R. A. F. reached Cambridge in 1880, he went to the same house, and lived there throughout his college course. Your brother Spencer lived in the same house during his Freshman year; but then moved into Matthews Hall for his last three years. Your brother Francis B. lived one year in the house at Gerry Street; but during his second Freshman year, that is, in '84–'85, he joined your brother Spencer in Matthews. His college career was confined to two Freshman years.*

"Mrs Eliot and I were married in October '77. We both have very pleasant recollections of the two ladies who kept that house in Gerry Street for you; but we cannot recall their name. Please give it to me. They continued to live in the house belonging to your father and mother on Gerry Street for several years after the Penrose boys ceased to live there. The elder one died; and the younger one married a rather unbusinesslike person who undertook to make a living for himself and his wife by breeding pigeons for the market. Mrs Eliot maintained pleasant relations with the two for several years; but she thought them wholly unsuccessful as a restraining influence on you and your brother Charles B. So did I. Your younger brothers, Alexander F. and Spencer, did not seem to need so much restraint. Your three brothers, Charles B., R. A. F., Jr., and Spencer, became distinguished students of science, and had eminent careers in their various lines. Of the career of your brother Francis B. I have no knowledge. You turned to politics within three years of your graduation at Harvard, and have had a conspicuous career as a politician. Your home address seems to be now the same as that of your brother Francis B.

"From these five sons of Dr. Richard Alexander Fullerton Penrose no descendant has ever come to Harvard College. From my point of view as President of Harvard for forty years and from the point of view of any person interested in eugenics, this is a very peculiar family history. Can you give me any light upon it?†

"I am not writing an autobiography or even my reminiscences, and do not propose to write anything of the sort, although often urged to do so by publishers and other acquaintances."

Boies and Charlie graduated in 1881, Charlie at the head of a class of more than two hundred, and Boies, second. The latter was one of five selected by the faculty to deliver orations at the commencement exercises. He chose as his subject "Martin Van Buren as a Politician."

After graduation, Boies began the study of law with the Honorable Wayne McVeagh and George Tucker Bispham and was admitted to the Philadelphia bar in 1883. Charles entered upon the study of medicine at the University of Pennsylvania, and, as if this were not sufficient to keep any one busy, he also

* Francis suffered from a sudden and severe attack of brain fever in 1885 from which he never fully recovered.

† Boies Penrose 2nd, son of Charles, was graduated from Harvard in 1925. He was the only male issue.

continued his studies in mathematics and physics at Harvard, where, by special permission of the University Council, he was allowed to try for the degree of doctor of philosophy, on condition that he should spend two months of each yearly term at Harvard. He received the degree of doctor of medicine from the University of Pennsylvania and the degree of doctor of philosophy in physics from Harvard, both in the spring of 1884.

Here is a peculiar situation. Why did Charles prepare himself in two lines of endeavor? Did he prefer physics and his father wish him to follow in his own distinguished footsteps? The following letter, also written by President Eliot of Harvard to the young student's father, is of peculiar interest in the light of subsequent events:

> Harvard University,
> Cambridge, Mass.
> 13 Apr. 1883

My dear Sir:

Your son Charles has a very decided capacity for physics. His interest in medicine is relatively weak. May I suggest that he ought to devote himself to physics from this moment? If he gets his M.D. next year, he will still need a year or two in hospitals and Europe before he begins practice. To my mind it is a waste for him to give any more time to medicine. His bent being strong and his capacity unquestionable, the best economy is complete devotion to his favorite subject. The best chance of happiness for him also lies in the same decision.

I know that he can earn more money in medicine than in physics; but this is not a determining consideration in his case. He can earn a modest livelihood in physics. We have a small appointment for next year in which he could begin.

Believe me, with great regard,

> Very truly yours
> Charles W. Eliot

Dr. R. A. F. Penrose

But the full piquancy of their honors was lost to the two young college graduates in 1881, for the mother who had been the idol of her husband and her sons had died the previous March, the day before her forty-seventh birthday. Her stricken husband from that time strove to be both father and mother to his sons, the oldest of whom was twenty and the youngest just past his twelfth birthday.

This loss was more than just that of the devoted and beloved mother; it was the entire removal from the lives of those six boys of any feminine influence, a fact which undoubtedly affected their entire lives. Only two of those boys married, one when he was thirty and the other at forty-one.

It has been a matter of frequent speculation why neither Boies nor Dick ever married. They were fine-looking men and popular with men and women alike. Part of the reason may lie in the fact that they were both extremely interested in the fields where lay their life's work, but part of it was surely due to that lack of feminine contact in their life, and may be explained as an attitude similar to that discussed by young Francis in two letters, addressed to his father from Quogue. The first is dated August 19 (no year):

Dear father
I have got very little to tell you. I shall be very glad to get away from Quogue; it is a dry place, very little to do; I get tired of boating in shallow muddy "bays." Now and then I dance but I am tired of it. A sojourn in the Pennsylvania mountains sounds very good. I must admit that I am not very popular with the girls. I find that I am rather bashful, not exactly bashful, but a little sheepish. When I dance, I have learnt several dances, I am all right but when I stand still for a minute I wish that I was alone; I know that it is very foolish and I try to overcome it; I have partly succeeded; I suppose it arises from the fact that I saw so little of girls in Philadelphia. I will have to stop as Philip is complaining from his bed that I do not get undressed.

F. B. Penrose

The second letter is written about ten days later, for the writer himself is uncertain about the date, heading his letter "Wednesday, August 29th or 30th":

Dear father
We received your letter today. It is now half past eight. I have just come up from the parlor. First we had dancing, then it ran into *games*. I played "dum crambo" which was bad enough, but when it came to "clumps" I left. The complete seperation from girls in town, in which I have lived, has told very much on me this summer; I do not know how to approach a girl, much less to amuse her.

If I walk with a girl I do not like to stalk by her side in silence but my conversation does not seem to suit her.

The fact of the matter is that girls under 17 years talk, at least relish best to hear, a kind of nonsense in which, at present, I am not very proficient.

In spite of the difficulties under which I labor I am gradually conquering what might be called my bashfulness.

There are plenty of fine enough girls in Quogue but the one whom I like best has dark hair, usually an objection with me, and hazel eyes; at first sight she seemed to me quite ordinary as far as beauty was concerned but she has completely won me; St. John's feeling agrees with mine entirely. St. John tried for something more than her *chaste* love but in vain; my feelings revolted from this, as I consider it a mean and dishonorable act to take from a girl *in decent society* about the only thing which she has, her virtue.

F. B. Penrose

Among the great mass of family letters only one deals with the first year which Dick spent at college. It is from his mother and is dated at Philadelphia, November 18, 1880:

My dear Dick—

Your Father thinks that you ought to take some pains to get your marks in Geometry changed. He says to go yourself to Briggs and ask him politely to look over your paper again; tell him that you feel sure you did all that was given you. I want you to get a good grade and also to have a "Detin" [?] next year. What did you select for a speech? Let me know all about it.

You are right to wear your good clothes except in rainy or stormy weather; then you can wear that suit of Charlie's which he thought did not fit him. They looked very well on you. Be very careful always to change your pantaloons when you get wet. I think it is cold enough now for you to put on your winter flannels.

I am glad you enjoy the preserves. I have plenty, so use as many as you want, and if there is anything else you would like to have, let me know, for you well know what pleasure it will be to me to send it to you.

You may do as you choose about the dancing class. If they are boys that you like in it and they want you to join I would be glad to have you do so.

I imagine that Wyeth and Harrison are very swelly; they are just the kind that would be. Let them swell, they will burst some day.

I am glad to find you go regularly to Church with Cousin Sarah and I feel sure that you will pass through your college course without one censure mark.

Good night to you all my darling boys

S H B P

I sent stamps in Charlie's letter.

In the summer of 1881, following the death of his mother, Dick made his first trip to Europe, presumably in the company of his father. They visited England, Scotland, Belgium, Holland, Germany, France, and Switzerland, stopping in the principal cities and other places of interest, including some of the larger glaciers of Switzerland. That they visited the art galleries and all the usual tourist cultural spots is evidenced in some of his later letters, where he speaks of having done all these things.

Of his college days, much can be gleaned from the letters which father and son preserved. The letters of the father are addressed to "My dear Son" and close "Your affectionate father, R. A. F. Penrose." The letters of the son invariably begin "Dear Father" and, as invariably, close "Your affectionate son, R. A. F. Penrose, Jr." This form of closing the son kept up throughout his father's life, never departing from its stately courtesy to use the more familiar "Dick," which, from his father's salutations, can be seen was the regular manner of address among members of the family.

These letters are reproduced in toto, and while they might gain in dramatic effect by a more thorough editing, they would thereby lose something of their significance, for the thoroughness and careful attention to detail which were genuine factors in Dick's success in life are already obvious in the youth. He never seems to tire of being specific and accurate. The persistence and regularity of his writing and the attention to exact formula and detail which never failed to give precisely the information his correspondent would need for easy and exact reading, showed not only an orderly and exact mind but also extreme consideration for his reader. These same characteristics continued throughout his life, as the reader will notice if he looks with attention at the letters reproduced in this volume. One can hardly fail to be impressed with the meticulous care with which he deals with every situation and the pains he takes, however repetitious, to make every point clear.

This correspondence between the young college student and his father is significant also in that it shows clearly the close and sympathetic interest which the father took in all the small intimate details and problems which made up the life of his boys. How many fathers of the present day could, and would, keep up this regular detailed correspondence with six sons in addition to their regular duties?

Finally, this correspondence is of interest as the picture of college life now gone as completely as though a hundred years, rather than only a few decades, had intervened.

Letter from Dr. Penrose to his son Dick, dated 1331 Spruce St., Friday, Oct. 21, 1881

I shall mail this letter so late that I fear you will not receive it before Monday. Your letter reached me safely on Tuesday. I am glad to know that you have got all of your courses fixed to your satisfaction and that you have been able to arrange for Calculus.

You should make sure that J. C. White makes the proper correction in your trigonometry mark, as it is his carelessness places you lower in the published rank list than you ought to have been and this unfortunately is an error that cannot be corrected. I think Kollock's father was a classmate of mine when I was a medical student.

I was glad to learn by your letter that you have picked up some good fellows. Keep at it and make the acquaintance of all the *nice* fellows you can. Recollect, too, how you hold your head up! and how you look right down into a fellow's brain!

We are all well except Boies who has an attack of intermittent fever and is miserable. He has been in the house now for several days and looks miserable.

Tal is hard at work at medicine, and his play is going to his study and getting himself up in Quaternions. I think I would keep up your society, and if there are no nice fellows in it, try and have some elected as new members. But, by all means, don't shut yourself up—but keep yourself stirred up all the time.

Your letter was very good. I am sure your style of composition is improving rapidly. After you finish deQuincy's Caesars, read some others of his essays; you cannot go wrong as they are all excellent and you might read them all if you have time. I sent you no mutton this week as it was so warm I thought it might not keep.

Letter from Dr. Penrose to his son Dick, dated 1331 Spruce St., October 27, 1881

Your letter reached me on Wednesday, and was very satisfactory. It indicates marked improvement in stile in every way. Your theme I returned the same day I received it. I thought you handled a difficult subject very well. I think you ought to receive a high mark for it. We sent you yesterday, butter, mutton and coffee which, I have no doubt you received to-day. I enclose to-day a notice which came to the house a few days after you left. I have some idea there was another paper, but if there were I cannot find it. Tell S. B. that I have been so busy that I have really had not time to answer her letter but will answer her next as soon as received so as not to miss it a second time. Boies seems to have pretty much recovered, and begins to eat well again and look something like himself. The other boys are all well. I am glad to find you have plenty of companions. Cultivate all the nice fellows you find. *Recollect*—head up! nose at 45°, eyes looking straight into a fellow's brain!

Your bundle came all right. I smoked one of your cigars last night, but the knocking about that it had received had in a great measure destroyed its excellency.

I am each day getting more and more busy—much to my regret, as I should prefer this winte to have little or nothing to do. But I must work to be able to help you all along when you come to practice medicine.

My regards to Cousin Sarah.

Letter from Dick to his father, dated Cambridge, October 30, 1881

The butter and mutton came all right on Thursday. The mutton lasted for three days, and was better than any we have had since you sent the last leg. The coffee came all right with the butter and mutton.

I am glad to hear that Boies is well again.

That notice you sent was a list of the fellows in my class, who got over 70 percent. for an average. The one you sent was incorrect, but another has been gotten out in which I have been put one or two fellows higher. It is all the fault of that scoundrel C. J. White that I am so low. He was not contented with cheating me out of my right mark in Algebra, by giving me 55, but he had to *try* to give me 0, instead of 95, in Trigonometry, in which, however, he was unsuccessful, and I guess he will not attempt it again. I think it is a mean trick for White to give a fellow as low a mark as he can in the mathematics he teaches, first so as to spoil the mark he gets in the mathematics he does not teach. I intend that he shall be sorry for the way he has cheated me before I get out of college.

My theme came all right on Wednesday afternoon. I copied it off, making all the corrections you had advised, and gave it in on Thursday. The subject for the next theme has not yet been given out. I would have sent my last one sooner, but the subject was not given out until late, and I could not, at first, think of any thing to write.

Last Thursday it was very cold here, and the gutters and puddles were covered with ice, but today it is as warm as midsummer, and we have all the windows open.

I go to the gymnasium regularly almost every morning, and take a walk in the afternoon.

I spend five or six hours a week in the chemical laboratory, and though I have to work harder than in any of my other courses in it, I like it the best.

I am going to box with Reed and Kollock tomorrow in the gymnasium. The gymnasium is not a very good place for it, since a lot of miserable Freshmen stand around with their mouths wide open, as if they never saw any one boxing before. I don't see how I ever could have been a Freshman.

I took a long walk this afternoon with Reed and Kollock. It has been foggy all day, but this afternoon it got so thick that we could hardly see where we were walking, and, by the time we got home, we were dripping wet.

Letter from Dick to his brother Charles, dated Cambridge, October 30, 1881

Dear Tal

I will go into Boston tomorrow and get your books. Trowbridge has not said anything to me about your papers, but if he does not brace up I will go to see him again, and will certainly tell him that you are so deeply interested in the exciting study of Quaternions that your family have had to send you into the country, so as to divert your mind.

I sent the boxing gloves to you because Kollock has a pair which we are going to use.

I put a two cent stamp on the Scientific American because the beautiful Venus at the post-office told me it needed it.

I do not need your notes in Chemistry before the examination. Though Jackson lectures mighty fast I have now got used to him and can follow him pretty well.

I will go to see Notman this week about your pictures.

I hope you enjoy looking ["squinting" is crossed out] through your microscope at man's pis, bugs, etc.

I have not seen Hough this year, and do not know where he is, but if I see him I will give him your message. I intend to box with Blodget sometime, but as he has about twenty-five hours a week this year to make up conditions he does not have much time.

I have got Reed's experiment book in Chemistry I, which he says is copied off yours. It is very useful since any experiment I cannot make come right I find all done in it.

Cordeiro was out here last Wednesday. He is in the medical school here. He says that Chapman, the fellow with whom he got in a row last spring and whom he gave a black eye, went to Eliot and told him a lot of yarns about him and that this was the reason that Eliot took his fellowship away from him.

[The rest of the letter is missing.]

Letter from Dick to his father, dated Cambridge, November 6, 1881

The butter and mutton came all right on Thursday.

A lot of Frenchmen, who had been at Yorktown, at the celebration of the battle there, came out here last Wednesday. They came in a lot of four-horsed carriages with about a hundred soldiers on horseback. I do not know whether there were any big fellows among them, but I guess there must have been, for Eliot went around and made a great fuss with them. One of them was a great-nephew, or some relation, of Lafayette.

Hannah Boies Penrose
(Miniature loaned by Mrs. Spencer Penrose)

Dick Penrose at five months of age

Dick Penrose, aged three

Dick Penrose, aged nine

Dr. R. A. F. Penrose

Some Germans, who had also been at Yorktown, came to Boston but did not come out here.

It poured here from last Friday week until yesterday, during which it was so foggy most of the time that you could hardly see where you were going. It cleared off on Saturday, and in the morning the puddles were covered with ice, but today it is as hot as midsummer.

The next theme is due on December the second, and I will try to get it done this week or next and send it to you.

I run a mile in Jarvis field with Reed or Kollock or both almost every day after dark. I can run a mile with my shoes on in $7\frac{1}{2}$ minutes. Kollock is too fat to run fast: he is about an inch taller than I am and weighs about 185 pounds.

I have an examination in Calculus this week, or next, and I have been busy all day studying it up. Some fiend in the house opposite here has been playing hymns on a fiddle all morning. It was enough to drive any one crazy, and I was just about to go over and try to stop him, when he stopped of his own accord.

I have just returned from my run. I find it makes me sleep a great deal better, and feel much better, to take a run of a mile after I have been studying all evening. I do most of my studying in the evening as I find it impossible for me to get asleep before about eleven o'clock.

I have four hours of laboratory work a week in Chemistry and it is the most interesting thing I have.

My French and German are not very interesting, especially the French, but they seem so necessary that I do not regret having taken them. In French we have to commit to memory about seventeen lines of prose twice a week, which we are expected to remember at the examination in February. I have become so used to it that it does not take me more than about a half an hour to commit the seventeen or twenty lines to memory.

I find all my courses so easy that I would take some more as extras, but I I spend all my spare time in the laboratory, since there is always plenty to do. We are given a book full of experiments, a certain number of which we have to do, while others we can do or not as we please. I do as many as I can because I think the better I know the Chemistry I take this year, the more good I will get out of any courses I may take next year.

[These are words of wisdom surely, but somehow they seem quite unlike those of the average seventeen-year-old college boy—at least, those of today.]

Letter from Dr. Penrose to his son Dick, dated 1331 Spruce St., November 11, 1881

Your letter reached me, as usual, on Tuesday; it was very satisfactory; I see a constant improvement in your stile, etc., etc.

I am glad your work is so interesting and so easy for you. I highly approve of your French memorizing and your German studies; our experiences this summer have taught us how useful a facility in expression in both is for us.

Read up for your theme, if you can, before writing it and if possible let me have it at least a week before you have to hand it in. *Cultivate* all your instructors and professors. It certainly will secure for you better marks, as well as present and future good will, and all may prove of value to you some time or other. Go on with your gymnastics, but never forget my direction "Nose at angle 45°, head up, shoulders back, chest out, stomach in, and look right down to the bottom of a fellow's eyes." Even though you never intend to be a soldier you may possess a military bearing. We are all well. Our weather has been as changeable as yours—for some days past too warm for any fire. Last night we started the library fire, which had been out for almost a week.

Your butter and mutton went, as usual, on Wednesday.

Letter from Dick to his father, dated Cambridge, Nov. 13, 1881

The butter and mutton came all right on Thursday. I got your letter yesterday.

I got my theme back on Thursday and I enclose what he wrote on the back. My next theme is due on 2nd December. There are four subjects: "Addison's Prose compared with Macauly's," "The Intellectual Character of Swift as displayed in the Tale of a Tub, Battle of the Books or Gulliver's Travels," "Was Macauly's effort to obtain clearness excessive?", "the objects to be obtained by a course of Sophomore prescribed Rhetoric." I am going to take the first or second. I have been reading up for both.

I have been all morning and most of the afternoon trying to understand a hard part in Calculus—Maximum and Minimum—and I was just about to give it up, when I suddenly saw it all, and it seemed so easy that I could not think why I had had so much trouble getting it through my head.

Hill, the professor of English, is giving us a lot of lectures on the English authors, and he gives us so much to read from Dryden, Pope, Addison, etc., that I do not have much time to read DeQuincy.

I go to the gymnasium every day, except Saturday, when it is a haunt of no body but Freshmen. I run a mile every day with Reed and Kollock in Jarvis field. Kollock is so fat that it almost kills him to run a mile, but when he gets started he does not like to stop until the rest do.

I translate my German every other day with a fellow next door, named Bunker. Though he is a mucker, he is a nice enough fellow, and I find I can do my German better with two fellows than by myself. He is twenty-four years old and is tenth in the class. The only trouble I have in studying with other fellows is that they are so slow; I translate a sentence, or do a problem or whatever it may be, while they are thinking about it. I find the same difficulty with whomever I study.

Letter from Dick to his brother Charles, dated Cambridge, November 13, 1881

Dear Tal

I have been into Schoenhof's again, but he had not been able to find your book, Wand's "Potential Theory," so I told him to send again for it, and it will be here in five or six weeks.

I have not yet been able to find out whether J. W. Whites has published his book of root words; but if I can find out no other way I will go and see him. If he has not published it yet I will send those lists of root words which you gave me before my entrance examination.

That was a vile slander which Reed wrote to you about me; he told me he had written something of the kind and he thought it was a mighty fine joke.

If you have *no use at all* for your old laboratory book you might as well send it, but if you want it at all do not send it because I have Reed's, which he says is copied from yours and which is plenty good enough.

I am gradually becoming used to Jackson's fast lecturing and can now take pretty good notes.

I have been wrestling all day with Maximum and Minimum—in Calculus—and have at last got it down to a pretty fine point, though at first it was mighty hard. B. O. Pierce lectures as fast if not faster than Jackson.

There are several of your German books here, and some other book bristling with blood-thirsty-looking formulas—I think it is a calculus—it is printed with purple ink by one of those things you used to have to print the notices for the Rumford Club, if you want them write me word and I will send them.

I run a mile every day in Jarvis field with Reed and Kollock. I can run it now without any exertion in 6 min. 10 sec.

Your old rowing tights are here, if you want them I will send them.

R. A. F. Penrose, Jr.

Letter from Dr. Penrose to his son Dick, dated 1331 Spruce St., November 16, 1881

Your grandmother died yesterday morning; she had been getting more and more feeble, but sat up until eleven o'clock Monday night, and slept well afterwards, about eight o'clock she got out of bed, was seized with an attack of oppression. Your aunt Lyd sent for me immediately. I reached her in a short time and found her very weak. She died about three quarters of an hour after—gently and calmly as if going to sleep. At the time she died, I was lying beside her and holding her hand.

I thought I had suffered enough, and had my heart crushed so completely at the time of your mother's death that I could never feel anything else, no matter how grievous, but this was too much for me. I had to go home after it was all over and go to bed; had a raging headache all day and all night, could not eat, and, indeed, concluded that I was going to be ill. Today, however, I am better.

The boys are all well. Boies says "For a mighty fine analysis of Swift, see Taine's Hist. of Eng. Lit., Bk. 3, chapter 5." I think the criticism on the back of your theme complimentary. I am sure your theme was the best sent in on that subject. I approve of Hill's plan of making you read so extensively and, even, if you make but little progress in DeQuincy, now, you can keep him for a future opportunity.

I have no doubt Bunker is a good friend for you to have, his age is a great advantage; *so is his "Mucker"*, if he is a good student and a good fellow. I congratulate you on your victory over your Calculus. It is worth a dozen successes secured through another fellow's head.

Letter from Dick to his father, dated Cambridge, November 19, 1881

I was very sorry to hear, by your letter, of grandmother's death, and I was very much surprised, for I had thought that she was better than when we got home, in October.

I send you my theme! I do not have to hand it in until 1st December, so that if I get it on 30th of November it will be plenty soon enough.

I got "Taine's History of English Literature," which you said Boies advised, and read his analysis of Swift. I collected all I knew about him and put it down, though I do not know whether I have done it well enough or not. S. P. said to tell you she had received your letter.

I have been working pretty hard on my Chemistry all week! We have a recitation in it about every three or four weeks, which includes all the lectures and laboratory work of the three or four weeks previous, so that it is almost as bad as an examination. We had such a recitation this week. There is a fellow who is going to print some notes he took in chemistry last year or the year before, since there is no text book for the course, but I don't think I will get them for he wants $6 for them and I don't see why I can't take as good notes as he did.

It has been pouring all day. Last night it was so warm that I had to have my window wide open while I was studying.

We have been able to run our mile almost every night.

Reed and Kollock go to Dedham every Saturday and Sunday, so that if I want to run on those days I have to do it with Bunker.

I am going to have an examination on the 1st, 2nd, and 20th of December, and perhaps more, so that I will be pretty busy for the next month.

Do you know of any way for me to keep myself from getting so fat! I have gained 17 pounds since we left the Ohio: I weighed 136 then and now I weigh 153? No matter how much I run I keep on steadily increasing.

Letter from Dick to his father, dated Cambridge, November 27, 1881

I received your letter with my theme yesterday. I will rewrite it with your corrections and hand it in on Thursday. The mutton and butter came all right on Friday.

S. B. had Frederic Beck's family and Anne Beck out here on Thanksgiving! It was not very pleasant for me, but as I saw there was no getting out of it, I submitted like a Stoic, and displayed my displeasure only in a few inward curses.

About two or three inches of snow fell here on Wednesday, and it has not melted much till today, when it is as warm as in summer. Last Tuesday morning the thermometer was down to 14 degrees.

I have an examination in calculus on next Friday, and I have been all day studying it. I don't like it much.

I like Chemistry I and think I get more out of it than any other course I have. I would like to spend most of my time on it if I had not other things to do.

I have been reading lately a good deal of Pope, Dryden, Swift, etc., which is required in Rhetoric.

Since the snow has been on the ground we have not been able to run out in

Jarvis field, but I run a mile every day, except Saturday and Sunday, in the gymnasium.

We are going to have a French text-book in History, in four or five weeks. I guess it will not be very hard, since I find all the French I have this year almost as easy as English. We are now using Lewis' History of Germany. The French book we are going to have is a history of Italy. We are going to have an examination in the French we have been committing to memory, a week from tomorrow. I find I have been able to commit to memory seven pages without the slightest trouble, and can say it all off without using the book.

A somewhat different version of that same Thanksgiving Day is given by Sarah Beck in a letter to Dick's father, dated Cambridge, November 30, 1881, showing that even at the age of seventeen the youth had so well learned the lesson of perfect courtesy that he could successfully mask his feelings even from one who knew him as well as Miss Beck:

Dear Dr. Penrose,

I was glad to have your letter yesterday and to learn that all were well; and we also are the same. Your butter and mutton reached here on Friday noon in excellent order, for which we thank you.

Our Thanksgiving Day passed off pleasantly. Frederick and his family and Anna came. We had dinner earlier to enable F. to get home before dark. Annie and Catharine stayed all night, so we had a game of whist in the evening. I had an oyster soup, roast turkey, chicken pie—for dessert ice cream and a cup of coffee—no puddings or pies. Dick seemed to enjoy himself and was a great help to me.

My earliest associations of the day go back to those which we always passed at your wife's grandfather's, and they were to my youthful mind, times of high festivals! They had a large dinner company of family and friends—all the Holbrook, Gardner, and Dincy [?] families. I can now see the long table elegantly supplied and can hear Uncle Boies' voice giving the never omitted toast "to absent friends." Very few now remain who can join me in memory of those days! But I like to think them over. Yesterday, in cleaning up my writing desk I found some lines written by my father addressed to Uncle and Aunt Boies upon this annual dinner, humourously noticing the feast and the guests.

Dick says he shall be a happy man on Friday—his examinations for this term will be over. He has been pretty busy, and I hope he will get through well. Reed dined with him yesterday. Some friends of mine called today to invite him to join a class of dancing. I did not suppose he would care to go, but I gave him the invitation, and was pleased he had the attention, for it was to be composed of the best young society in Cambridge.

I have been getting in the rest of my winter supply of coal. I engaged it in Sept; but our cellar will not accommodate it all at once. I had 5 tons of cooking stove coal at $6.50 per ton, 2 tons of soft coal for parlour and study $12.25 per ton, 7 tons of furnace coal at $6.50 per ton, all paid for, and some kindling wood

$3.10. It all came to $105.60. Groceries, meats and vegetables and servant's wages with some little personal expenses brings me near the close of my cheques. I owe for nothing; anytime when it is convenient I would like a little more money. We have everything as usual only in smaller supply as the family is smaller. My girl is very economical and satisfactory, and has much improved. We move on smoothly, regularly, and Dick seems to be doing well. He is very considerate and pleasant. Reed seems to find him companionable and I hear he says "he likes him very much."

Give my love to the boys. Tell Charles I should not object to seeing his handwriting. I know he is busy all the time, so I do not urge it, but hope he may find a chance for a line to me some day. Love to Spencer and Friday and Phillip.

With best regards to yourself from

Sarah P. Beck

Letter from Dick to his father, dated Cambridge, December 11, 1881

I received your letter yesterday. The mutton and butter came all right on Friday.

My holiday begins December 23 and lasts until January 2. I may be able to come on December 22, but I don't think I can, because my theme comes in that day; but if I can get Drennan, the Rhetoric man, to give it to me before, I can come on the 22nd. I will write next Sunday what day I will come.

I got between 90 and 100 in the examination in Calculus, he does not tell us our exact marks: but I think I got 100 because Pierce told me, a few days before the examination, when I was asking him a question, that he kept a red crayon to mark any fellow's book who got 100, and he marked my book with his red crayon. It is the first time I ever got 100, and I think it shows that Pierce, the fellow who teaches Calculus, is going to be a great man. I thought, when he lent me a German chemistry a week or two ago, that he was getting mighty sweet on me.

I had my examination in French on Monday; it was mighty easy, but I do not know yet what I got in it. I have an examination in Rhetoric on December 20.

I saw Dyer last Wednesday; he was mighty sweet on me and told me to come and see him; though I do not have anything under him I think I will go, because I think he looks over some of the entrance Greek examination papers, and therefore he may be of use to Speck. I am not sure whether he will examine Speck's papers or not but I will find out before his examination. Calculus begins to be much more attractive after I have gotten 100 in it than it did before.

Hill, the man who gives the lectures in English literature, gives so much to read that it is impossible to read it all; last week he gave us to read during the *one* week, "The Sentimental Journey," the "Vicar of Wakefield," and six of Goldsmith's essays. It would be well enough to read all these if a fellow had nothing else to do, but with all the other work it is impossible, so I only read what I have time to do.

I have been most of today reading DeQuincy's Caesars; and Mignet's French

Revolution, which though it is written in French is very easy; I can read on an average of about 18 pages an hour of it.

I am making some crystals of potassic nitrate by the method you sent me; it succeeds mighty well and I have already made some almost two inches long. I keep the secret to myself as you advised me to do, and consequently my crystals are always larger than those of most the other fellows.

Letter from Dick to his father, dated Cambridge, December 18, 1881

I received your letter on Friday. The butter and mutton came all right on Thursday.

I got my theme last Thursday and therefore can leave next Thursday. If I leave Boston at 8.30 a.m. I get to New York at 4.22, in time to get the five o'clock train for Philadelphia.

I have an examination in Rhetoric next Tuesday and have been all day studying it. I got out of the library Van Laun's translation of Taine's English Literature, which Boies told me about, and am reading it for the examination.

There has been skating for two days during the last week, but it is so warm today that I guess it is almost all melted.

I am making some mighty fine crystals of ferrous sulphate by the method you sent me; they are already almost as large as a chestnut and very clear. If they are large enough by the time I come home I will bring some to show you.

We have been reading in German, the life of Charles James Fox, by a fellow named Althaus; we finished it last week and are now reading the life of Robespierre.

Nannie Thomas' address is 73 Courtland St., Baltimore, Md.

I will telegraph to you when I start on Thursday morning.

Letter from Dick to his father, dated Cambridge, January 8, 1882

I arrived in Cambridge at about 12 o'clock on Tuesday. The train, as usual, was three hours late.

The train from Philadelphia to New York was very crowded, but from New York to Boston I had two seats to myself almost all the time.

It had snowed much more here than at Philadelphia.

The skating has been very good until the day before yesterday when it was very warm. On Wednesday and Thursday it was very cold here; the thermometer was 2 degrees below zero on Thursday morning at eight o'clock.

I went skating with Kollock on Wednesday night; the ice was nearly a $\frac{1}{2}$ foot thick.

My examinations begin on January 27.

I got Taine's English Literature in Boston yesterday for 75 cents and have begun to read it.

The butter and mutton came all right on Thursday. The butter tasted mighty good after the nasty stuff S. P. had been having which tasted like salted lard.

It has been drizzling rain almost all day and is so warm that I have been studying all evening with my window wide open. I have been all day reading Taine, the magazines and doing problems in calculus.

I have begun my running and going to the gymnasium regularly.

I have finished my theme and will give it in on Thursday. I guess I will be the only fellow who has anything about Dolbear's Telephone.

Letter from Dick to his father, dated Cambridge, January 15, 1882

I received your letter on Friday. The butter and mutton came all right on Thursday.

I do not know what delayed the train coming on, but I guess it was the snow since there was a great deal of it.

Your rolls and sausages were mighty good and I had eaten them almost all before I got to Boston.

It snowed here all day Wednesday and Friday so that all the skating is spoiled.

S. P. had Annie Beck and the Harris crowd here to dinner yesterday so that I had to have dinner with four New England old maids, all of whose mustaches would have excited Tal's envy, and whose little tufts of yellow hair coming out of moles on the sides of their faces and chins would have driven Boies mad with jealousy.

My examinations do not come in very good order; I have three of them on three consecutive days, so that I have to prepare them a good while beforehand. I have been all day getting the French ready; I have read a hundred pages of it since yesterday afternoon.

I have made a single alum crystal which is now so large that it will hardly fit in a tumbler, which I keep full of a solution of alum so as to get the crystal larger. I do your way of keeping a piece of alum hung in the top of the solution so as to be sure to have it always strong enough.

Letter from Dick to his father, dated Cambridge, January 22, 1882

I received your letter yesterday. The butter and mutton came all right on Thursday.

Miss Hedge came here on Wednesday to invite me to a party at their house: I was not home, and she told S. P. she wanted to know right away whether I would come. S. P. had seen that I had been grinding pretty hard, so she told her that she did not think I would have time to go. I am glad she did so, for I did not want to go, and had no time to waste.

I have been all day studying calculus. Pierce, the fellow who teaches it, let us vote last Friday whether we would bring our text books into the examination room and have a hard examination, or not bring our books and have an easier examination. I wanted to bring the text book in, because, without it, a long list of formulas have to be committed to memory; but there were only four or five other fellows who voted the same as I did so that we cannot bring in our books.

The examination in Rhetoric comes on next Friday, but I do not expect to get much on it, because Drennan, the fellow who teaches it, is such a fool that he has not sense enough to tell a good paper from a bad one, but marks fellows high who write in big round letters like a ten year old baby. He also marks on the cleanness of the paper, the way it is folded and other such little-minded things.

I go to the gymnasium every morning! Kollock does not go at the same time, since he has joined the crew and rows in the gymnasium in the afternoon. Reed goes in the morning at the same time I do.

Letter from Dick to his father, dated Cambridge, January 29, 1882

I received your letter on Friday. The butter and mutton came all right on Thursday.

I had my examination in Rhetoric on Friday: it was an easy enough paper but a fellow cannot write a theme worth anything in an hour. I have an examination in Calculus on Tuesday, and have been all day studying it. It is the only one I have this week, but the next week I have four.

It was very cold here on Monday and Tuesday. The newspaper said it was colder on Monday than it had been for eleven years; the thermometer, out of my window, was fifteen degrees below zero. But it soon got warm, and on Wednesday it was very warm and all the ice was melting.

Recitations have stopped, so that there is nothing to do but grind for exaimnations, but I would rather have fifty recitations than one examination.

I have been taking the quinine, and it makes my head a great deal clearer than it would otherwise be.

I send you the Rhetoric examination paper.

Letter from Dick to his father, dated Cambridge, February 5, 1882

I received your letter on Wednesday. The butter and mutton came all right on Thursday.

I had my Calculus examination on Tuesday. The paper would have been easy enough, but he said he would not ask us any such questions as the last three, so that hardly any one had taken the time to get them up, and therefore hardly any one could answer them; but I guess that when the fellow finds that his cheating will not work he will not count them.

I have an examination in German tomorrow, and one on next Thursday, Friday and Saturday, so that I will be very busy all week.

There was a heavy snow here last Tuesday. It has snowed twice since then, and last night so much fell that it almost covered the fences.

It was almost impossible to get along this morning, and when I went to take a walk at twelve o'clock I had to walk in snow over my knees.

There was a big fire here on Friday night. It was a barrel factory on the Charles river. Nothing but a pile of ashes was left after it had been burning about an hour, though it was a very large place and 14 sheds full of barrel staves were burned with it.

My next theme is on "Dryden's Prose and Poetry Compared." I will send it to you after the examinations are over.

I enclose the Calculus examination paper. It is the only examination I have had this week.

Letter from Dick to his father, dated Cambridge, February 12, 1882

I received your letter all right on Thursday.

S. B. said she received the cheques after she had sent her letter, but she said that she had written to you the day I got your letter, so I did not send a postal card.

I finished my last examination yesterday after having had four last week. They were all pretty easy papers, especially the history. We had to write the French examination, except the translation, in French. I don't know how well I did it though I guess I did it as well as most fellows.

It has been very warm here this week so that the piles of snow have begun to melt, and flood the pavements and roads, making the walking very bad, and in some places it is almost impossible to get along without going into water almost up to your knees.

I am going to the slaughter house on Wednesday, the day they slaughter, with Reed to get some blood to crystalize by a method Tal told me about. I have tried to entice several fellows to box and get some blood by giving a bloody nose but I can't get anyone to do it.

I will send you my theme this week. It is due on the 23rd Feb. and I would have sent it before,

[The rest is missing.]

Letter from Dick to his father, dated Cambridge, February 19, 1882

I sent you my theme last week: I had to write it in such a hurry that I could not think of any thing worth writing.

I got a letter last Wednesday from Mrs. Wolcott, from New York, saying that she and her husband were staying a few days in Boston and would be glad to see me. I did not want to go, but I did not see how I could get out of it, so I went in to Boston yesterday. Luckily, however, they were out, so that I left a card with my name scribbled on it.

We have begun to use Zeller's History of Italy in my history course. It is in French, but is very easy to translate.

With this French history and my French course I have almost a hundred pages a week of French to read, so that I can now read it almost as easily as English.

According to the newspaper last Thursday was the warmest day of the winter here. The thermometer was 66°; but on Friday night it went down almost to zero so that everything is frozen up again.

The boat house will be opened in a week or two, so that we will soon begin to row.

Drennan, the theme man, thought my theme on the Telephone was mighty fine. He made so few corrections that I do not have to copy it over as most themes have to be.

Letter from Dick to his father, dated Cambridge, February 26, 1882

I received your letter and my theme last week. I recopied my theme with your corrections and handed it in on Thursday.

The fellow in Calculus does not give us our exact marks but I got somewhere between 85 and 100.

I got 93 in French, which was higher than any other fellow in the course got. There are about 75 fellows in the course.

I got a note from Mrs. Wolcott on Monday saying she was sorry not to have seen me on Saturday, etc., and that she was going away the middle of the week; so that I had no chance to go in again.

Jackson, the professor of Chemistry, saw some of my crystals last Tuesday and thought they were so fine that he asked me to make him some for the college collection. He used to show a broken crystal of a double salt of iron and ammonia in the class, and thought it was so fine that he kept it in cotton, in a box with a glass cover; but I have just made some whole crystals of the same salt and these were what he thought so fine.

I do not know any more of my marks but I guess I will get some this week.

It has been very warm this week, and almost all the snow is melted.

Letter from Dick to his father, dated Cambridge, March 5, 1882

I received your letter on Thursday. The butter and mutton came all right on Thursday night.

I have not yet gotten any more of my marks but I guess I will get some this week. My next theme is due on the 23rd March. I will send it this week or next.

It has been very warm here this week. It rained all day Thursday so that all the snow is melted.

Reed and I ran in Jarvis field on Friday for the first time since last fall.

Gummere, one of the theme men, from Philadelphia, has left and gone back to Phila., because he was getting some brain disease.

The boat house is going to be opened in about a week or two. Kollock is trying for the crew so that we will have to get two other fellows. Reed is going to get a fellow from the law school and I am going to get a fellow from my class named Keep. There are no good boats in the boat-house except those with four seats, so that we have to have four fellows to row.

Letter from R. A. F. Penrose to his son Dick, dated 1331 Spruce St., March 8, 1882

Your letter came yesterday, as usual. It found us well.

I sent the butter last week in old vegetable tin cans in order to save the return charge on the tin bucket; I shall do the same to-day. In your next letter tell me how it comes. Of course the cans are worthless and you may throw them in the ash pile. The boys said last week, "Dick will be fool enough to send the old cans back." I replied "Dick is a level headed fellow and knows what he is about" and "he will not send them back." The result is as I expected.

Yesterday Boies and Charley went to the Schuylkill to row from the new club boat house. They reported having a good time. I took a long ride with Spencer, the first I had taken for about two years. When I got home I was pretty sore and stiff, and am somewhat so to-day, yet much less so than I had anticipated. To-day the weather is quite cold.

Letter from Dick to his father, dated Cambridge, March 12, 1882

Your letter came all right on Thursday. The butter comes just as well in the small cans as it used to in the large one. S. P. had not sense enough to know how to take it out at first and therefore she wrote you that they were not good; but now that she has learned how to get it out they do just as well as the big can.

I got 91 in History. Emerton, who teaches it, is one of the hardest markers, so that it was a good mark to get from him. It was one of the highest in the course.

I will send my next theme this week. The subject is the "Story of Fort Sumter." It is due on the 23rd March.

They had the athletic games here yesterday. Biddle, the fellow from Philadelphia, was beaten in the boxing. When he was done the blood was running down his back and his left ear was about six times as large as the other and almost knocked off.

Several other fellows got their backs all cut up from wrestling, and most of them had bloody noses or eyes so swollen up that they could not see.

I run a mile and a half or two miles every day. We are going to row when the boat-house man has got the boats ready.

Letter from R. A. F. Penrose to his son Dick, dated 1331 Spruce St., March 11, 1882

Your letter reached me yesterday. I congratulate you on your high marks, and hope to learn that you stand head in Calculus or even in French.

Keep your secret about the big crystals to yourself—explain your success by your great care and watchfulness, etc., etc. The "ignotum" is that only which is worshipped by all, the noisest, as well as the most ignorant, here bow side by side at the same altar; he who professes the knowledge of it is esteemed only so long as he keeps his knowledge to himself.

We are all well today in the midst of a hard and warm rain. I am busy this week with my University examinations. Next week I shall be free, and shall be very ready to take a little rest.

P. S. The paper you signed has just arrived and I will send the boys with it down to Guillon.

Letter from Dick to his father, dated Cambridge, March 19, 1882

I got your letter on Thursday. The butter and mutton came all right.

It has not yet been given out when the spring holiday begins, but it is usually about the first of April; so I guess it will begin in about two weeks. There is a night train by the Boston & Albany railway, which is much better than the New York & New England, because it is always on time, while the New York & New England is always two or three hours late. The Boston & Albany is also a dollar cheaper than the other; so that don't you think I had better come by the Boston

& Albany, or else by one of the Long Island Sound boats? The boats are much cheaper than the railroad and just as good.

I got 90 in the Chemistry examination.

It was very cold here the beginning of the week but today it is as warm as midsummer.

I sent you my theme on Thursday. I could not write much of a theme on such a subject.

I have been elected vice-president of the Beta Omicron Pi, but as there are only about twenty fellows in it, it is not much to blow about.

Letter from R. A. F. Penrose to his son Dick, dated 1331 Spruce St., March 21, 1882

Your letter reached me this morning.

Tal thinks your mark of 90 in Chemistry is excellent. The paper was by no means an easy one.

We are all well. The two big boys and Friday (to steer) have gone to row on the Schuylkill. They find their new boat club a most valuable institution for them. Yesterday Boies rowed in a shell by himself. To-day, they row together.

I think I prefer that you should not come home in one of the Sound boats. The point of economy is of not any consequence. You can enquire about the trains on the B. & A. road. Perhaps you had better send me the time tables of all the roads—also which you yourself would prefer or which there are any of the fellows coming on at the same time. The members of the BOΠ are wise fellows to select their officers with so much judgment as your election to the vice-presidency displays. I congratulate them on their choice.

Letter from Dick to his father, dated Cambridge, March 26, 1882

I received your letter on Thursday. The spring holiday begins April 5, so that I can leave here on the night of Tuesday, April 4. I could come on Monday night but I have an examination in Rhetoric on Tuesday.

I send you the time-tables out of the news-paper for the N. Y. & N. E. and the Boston & Albany railroads.

I could come in the Boston & Albany train which leaves Boston at 10.30 P.M. and gets to New York at about 7.30 in the morning. It just wastes a whole day coming in the day time. The B. & A. is the road I came by last Christmas. There is a fellow in my class named Keep who is coming to Philadelphia for the holiday and will come by whatever road I do. A fellow named Hall is also going to Washington at the same time. If you would rather have me come by the N. Y. & N. E. or in the day time I will do so. There is no day train on the N. Y. & N. E. I have over $10 left, so that I have plenty to pay my fare.

The Zuni Indians were out here yesterday. They went about with bows, clubs, shields, etc., and were mighty fierce looking fellows. In the afternoon they came to the athletic meeting in the gymnasium. Every time any one did anything they liked they jumped up, clapped their hands and yelled. I believe they have come from New Mexico with a fellow named Cushing, who is a white man that they have adopted into their race. They danced a war dance in the middle of the gymnasium.

We are going to begin to row on the river tomorrow.

In the summer vacation of 1882, Dick made a trip on horseback from Philadelphia to Niagara and return, presumably with his brother Boies, who was very fond of horseback riding. He does not specify the route taken, but as the two places are about 375 miles apart, this would indicate a horseback trip of at least 750 miles.

Of one of those summer vacations while Dick was still in college, his cousin, Ellen Williams Penrose, living in 1942 at Carlisle, Pennsylvania, told an interesting anecdote.

"The boys were staying with us," she said, "and their father was staying at Mount Airey, a short distance south of here. There was a young girl about their age, who was staying in town, and one day when we all walked over to Mount Airey to see Uncle Aleck, I noticed that Dick was very careful to stay close to the young lady and pay her every attention.

"I was somewhat alarmed, for I did not consider her nice enough for Dick, and I spoke of the matter to Charley.

"'Do you think that there is any possibility of Dick falling in love with her?' I asked him.

"'Falling in love,' laughed Charley, 'I should say not. I don't like her and I told Dick that if he didn't stick to her and keep her away from me, I'd punch him.'

"Dick, with that beautiful courtesy that marked him throughout life, was doing all that he could to keep the girl from finding out how much the others disliked her," concluded Miss Penrose.

"He was always so gentle," she continued after a pause. "His father always called him 'my girl.'"

When Dick returned to Harvard in the fall of 1882, he was accompanied by Spencer and the next younger brother, Francis, familiarly known as Friday, who was placed in a preparatory school at Quincy, Massachusetts. His letters from that time on contain reports of his two younger brothers.

Letter from Dick to his father, dated Cambridge, October 11, 1882

The checks came all right last Saturday. Saturday was Piggy Everet's birthday so Friday had a holiday. He came out here on Saturday morning and stayed till Sunday afternoon.

Speck seems to be getting on very well; and don't seem to have to work especially hard. He goes to Howell every afternoon from three to four and I think he gets a good deal of benefit from him.

We have been rowing this afternoon for the first time this fall.

All my courses are very easy though my Chemistry occupies a great deal of time. I have been tonight to see Jackson, the Chemistry man, for whom I am going to write three theses. The first is to find whether Mendelejeff's classification can be applied to the rarer inorganic salts. The second is the Manufacture of Iron, and the third is the "Overthrow of the Phlogiston and the establishment of the Atomic Theory." He was mighty sweet on me: he gave me a book to read on Liebig's experiments. He also gave me some minerals which he said he thought I might like to have, and told me if I wanted any books to look up the subject of my theses in he would let me use his library. I spend all Tuesday and Thursday in the laboratory and generally manage to get most of my work done in those two days.

Letter from Francis to his father, dated Quincy, October 21, 1882

Dear father

I received your letter on the twentieth. I also received your other letter with Piggy's the last I destroyed according to your directions.

Our school played a match in foot ball with the Roxbury Latin School; we beat them badly much to the chagrin of a crowd of the Roxbury Latin fellows who came to Quincy to see the match.

On account of the match which lasted from three to five, I did not get out to Cambridge until after dinner when I got something to eat; by the time the match was done I was so hoarse from cheering that I could hardly speak.

Our athletic sports come on the Monday after next; I think that I shall go in for the $\frac{1}{4}$ mile, 100 yards, and hurdle race, though I have not the least hope of gaining any of them.

There does not seem to be much rowing at Quincy though I have no doubt that I could get a boat if I wanted to do so; I think that I shall keep my rowing for the spring.

On Thursday I spoke the speech of Marcullus which Philip spoke last year; the maximum mark for speaking is twenty. I got fifteen.

I would have done much better if I had not almost sunken beneath a load of abominable and inexcusable bashfullness or, as Piggy calls it "Being afraid of one's shadow." There were only four fellows out of twenty who got higher marks than mine.

When I got into the room a cold sweat broke out over me then, when my turn came near, I became burning hot and when I rose to speak I was almost freezing. I expect to do very much better the next time. I will spend more time studying my piece.

Dick has filled 2 Gerry St. with blocks, wheels and plans of machines; almost always when I go to Cambridge I find him tinkering at a machine.

F. B. Penrose

P. S. I do not think that I shall want the bycicle until spring.

Here is a strange Dick. Evidently his taste for mechanics was short-lived, for no subsequent mention is made of such leanings. This trait, however undeveloped, may have been of service to him in his ultimate experiences on state surveys and in the West, where ingeniousness was a necessary adjunct to success.

Letter from Dick to his father, dated Cambridge, October 25, 1882

Your letter came all right with Speck's bond.

I have begun to write one of my theses—on the manufacture of iron—and if you don't mind the trouble of looking over a dry uninteresting thing of twenty pages I will send it to you to criticize. None of my subjects for theses this year are ones in which I can put anything original, so that is not probable that any will be published.

Until this week we have been rowing almost every day but it is now getting a little too cold for it.

Speck is getting along all right and don't have to work especially hard. I think Howell does him a great deal of good especially in his mathematics.

I have been analysing some of those crystals I found this summer. I found that most of them were not carbonate of lime—as we had thought—but that they were dolomite.

I went with some fellows last Saturady to a place called Somerville, near Cambridge, to get minerals for my mineralogy course; and am going next Saturday to a place called Chelmsford—about twenty miles from here—where we expect to get some very rare minerals.

[P.S.] Speck lost his other deed and told me to send this one to you to sign.

Letter from Dick to his father, dated Cambridge, November 1, 1882

Your letter came all right on Monday with Speck's bond.

I send you my theme on the "Origin of the Title of Marquis." It didn't amount to much because I have been so busy lately that I have not had much time to spend on it. It is due on the 7th Nov. so that if possible I would like to have it by the 6th.

Speck is getting along all right. Howell comes every afternoon and spends an hour or more going over the next day's lesson with him. He don't have much trouble in learning anything, and even seems to like his Greek.

Friday comes out here on Saturday evening and stays till Sunday afternoon. He seems to like Quincy very well and to have gotten over all his laziness of last year.

I have been having an examination today in mineralogy, on which I got a hundred. I like mineralogy better than any of my other courses and have already got enough minerals to cover five shelves of a book-case.

[P.S.] Tal's essay came all right, and I gave it to the Dean on Tuesday.

Letter from Dick to his father, dated Cambridge, November 15, 1882

Your letter came all right yesterday.

I send you my thesis on "Cast Iron." I am in no special hurry to get it back—any time within the next two weeks will do. I would like to have as many corrections as you, Boies or Tal can make.

We are getting along all right.

Speck wrote to you about the room; it is in Thayer on the fourth floor; facing north East. It is a very good room though the building is not especially swell. The fellow wants $125 for it and give in with it a ton of coal. I think we could get it from him for $100. There is another room in Weld facing south west, on the second floor. It is slightly larger than the other and is $250. I don't think it is worth so much more than the Thayer room though the building is a little more swell.

Speck had an examination in Latin today in which I think he passed pretty well.

It is getting too cold to row now. The thermometer has been below freezing the last two nights and it is beginning to feel very wintery.

Speck has not got to know many fellows yet, though he knows a few and I think is inclined to make friends.

Friday seems to be getting on all right.

[P.S.] It is so late that I have not time to copy off my thesis, so I will send it tomorrow or the next day.

Letter from Dick to his father, dated Cambridge, November 21, 1882

Your letter came all right this morning.

I have not had time to get my thesis ready to send until tonight, but I send it now in the same mail as this letter. It is only a rough copy and it does not matter how much you mark it up.

We are getting along all right. Speck has an examination in Greek tomorrow and I think he ought to do pretty well on it as he has been studying hard for it all evening.

Friday was out on Sunday. One of the teachers would not let him come on Saturday because he said he did not want "him to get too used to coming every Saturday."

I have had two examinations later in crystalography, in both of which I got a hundred.

Speck wrote to you about the money. It seemed to go mighty fast; but when we added it up we could account for it all, though it seemed a great deal. Speck's dentist bill, which I think was extortionate, took a large part of it; and his clothes and paying Howell took most of the rest.

Letter from Dick to his father, dated Cambridge, November 30, 1882

Your letter came all right last Monday.

The cheque came all right. We got it cashed and payed Howell all we owed him. We were going to take our boxing lessons from the regular man at the gymnasium but we have just heard of a niger prize fighter who lives in Cambridge and who, for 25 cents a lesson, will teach you how to slug a fellow, including tripping up, smashing in a man's head, etc., etc., and I guess we will go to him.

Friday came out here yesterday afternoon and is going to stay till tonight or tomorrow morning. He seems to be getting on all right though he has a good deal of trouble with his mathematics. He spends all his time on Latin and can spout Cicero from morning till night.

I don't know when our Christmas holiday begins but I suppose it will begin somewhere about the 20th of December.

Speck is getting along all right and I guess he will pass his Christmas examinations without much trouble, though I don't think he could do much without Howell.

I hope to have my second thesis on wrought iron and steel ready sometime next week. I want to get them all done as soon as possible so as to get them off my hands.

Jackson makes his whole course—which is one of the largest in college and sometimes has 150 fellows in it—use our method of making crystals. Cooke asked me to make him some crystals of one kind stuff, and Jackson has got me to make him some of a different substance, so that I have a good deal of extra work on my hands.

If you direct the butter tub to me it will come for 3 cents cheaper though I don't know whether S.B. would have sense enough to show the cooperative card to the express man. But if you think it is worth while you might try it.

Letter from Spencer to his father, dated Cambridge, December 3rd (1882)

My dear Father,

I received your letter with the butter and mutton last Friday—I don't know if C. S. wants more than one leg or not—I would go down and ask her now if she wanted more than one leg but there is another vergin of over sixty years in the parlor and they are so busy chatterin I am afraid she would not be able to tell. I will find out and let you know by my next letter. I have another examination in Geometry next Thursday I will try to pass it better than I did my last Geometry examination since Byerly said I did not pass very well. The Greek class has been divided into five sections according to the marks the fellows got the last examination—I am in the fourth section—I passed well enough to be in the second but Dyer, the Greek fellow, don't agree with me, and this is the reason I am in the fourth. The Latin fellow has not told us our marks—I will ask him next recitation if he will let me [know] how I passed.

We have not joined the boxing class yet, Dick has changed his mind and don't want to join—I don't believe I will join until after Christmas. Dick intends to take lessons from a big nigger, who teaches tricky ways of knocking fellows down, etc. He knows a fellow in his class, who takes lessons from him. The price is 25 cts a lesson. I have forgotten to say that the preserves came alright, they are bully. We have been having some very good preserves, which S.B. bought, but they are not as good as these.

The thernenter is now 10° above zero, so I should think we would have skating in a day or so. Friday has been skating two or three times but there has not been any around here. There was a hevy snow storm Wenesday night, about a foot deep. I showeled snow for two hours Friday afternoon and for a hour yesterday morning, in helping to clear the foot ball field for the game yesterday afternoon. Our Freshmen played the Yale freshmen, the game was tie.

Speck

Letter from Dick to his father, dated Cambridge, December 6, 1882

My thesis came all right in the butter-tub last Friday. The mutton came all right, and tasted mighty good after that we got around here.

I got a letter from Farlow last Monday saying that I had been elected a member of the "Natural History Society." I don't suppose it is any very great honor to be elected, but as a good many professors belong to it, it might do me some good. I thought I would ask you about it before I joined. The only thing I dislike about it is that every fellow is made to read a paper at some meeting soon after his election.

Speck and Friday are getting on all right. Friday's holiday begins on the 21st December and our begins about the 23rd. If you don't want Friday to come home alone he could come out here and wait for us.

Friday had a little cold when he left here last Sunday, so I went out to Quincy to see him on Tuesday. He did not seem to be in especially good spirits, so I went out again today. He had been to a doctor who had given him something for his cold. Though he is now almost well of his cold, yet he don't seem to be in an especially good condition and says he cannot sleep at night. I write to you about it so that you can send him some medicine if you think necessary.

I began this letter last night but kept it over until today so as to tell you about Friday, after I had seen him.

Your letter with the butter and mutton came all right this afternoon.

We have paid Howell all we owe him, and have $55 left. By Christmas time Speck will owe Howell $20, which will leave us $35, and this will be plenty to bring us home. We will not have to buy any more books this fall so we will have a full $35 to come home with.

We have had to get three pairs of shoes half-soled, and I have had to get two books in the last week, but we will not have to get anything else before we come home.

Letter from Dick to his father, dated Cambridge, December 14, 1882

Your letter came all right on Monday.

Friday was out here on Saturday; he is entirely well of his cold and seems to be in as good a condition as ever.

Speck's examinations begin next Friday and he is now hard at work preparing them.

Our holiday begins on December 23rd, so if you would just as soon have us come at night we can come on the night of Dec. 22 by the Boston and Albany or by the New York and New England. There is a Boston and Albany train which leaves Boston at 10.30 p.m. and which would get us to Phila in time for breakfast.

I will send my second thesis—on wrought iron and steel—tomorrow. I would like to have it as soon as you can conveniently correct it, since I would like to give it to Jackson before Christmas.

I told Jackson the other day of a method I had thought of for keeping a thing at a constant temperature. He thought it was a mighty fine idea; and said that, though there were some practical difficulties about it, he thought these could be overcome and a good thing made out of it. He is going to help me to arrange it in a practicable form.

Cooke lent me a big brass goniometer which must have cost $15 or $20 to take to my room to determine crystals with.

I have succeeded in getting a room down in the cellar of Boylston Hall where the temperature is almost constant and which therefore is an excellent place for making crystals.

Howell has been all evening with Speck tutoring him for his examinations. I guess he will get through all right as he has lately begun to make a big brace.

In the summer vacation between his junior and senior years at college, Dick took a trip from Philadelphia to Montreal, Ottawa, and Quebec, where he embarked for a trip down the St. Lawrence River to Tadusac, thence up the Saguenay to Chicoutimi and return.

There are no letters concerning his senior year in college except that in which he announces with justifiable pride what have been his goals and how he has met them. The letter is addressed to his father and is dated Cambridge, June 20, 1884. It reads as follows:

Dear Father

Your letter came all right the day before yesterday, with the check, for which I am much obliged. I will not get the check cashed until I know whether we will need it to get home. I think we may possibly need some of it, as Speck has to pay his janitor $15 for the care of his room. Tal got your letter yesterday with the check for the college bills, which we will pay as soon as possible.

I had my honor examination last Tuesday, and succeeded in getting highest honors in Chemistry. Another fellow and I both got highest honors. It is the first time Highest Honors in chemistry have been given for six years, and only the third time they have been given, since they have been giving honors, in the history of Harvard College.

The four goals of my college ambition have been (1) to get into the Phi Beta Kappa, (2) to row on a victorious crew, (3) to get highest honors in Chemistry, (4) to get a summa cum laude degree. All these goals I have successfully arrived at. The summa cum laude especially pleases me, as I have got it by steadily raising my rank, every year more than the year before, ever since I was a freshman. I also get honorable mention in Natural History.

We will go to Philadelphia the day after commencement, stopping on the way for a few hours at New London to see the boat race with Yale.

Friday is going home tomorrow, as he wants to go to Atlantic City.

Barringer is coming up with Boies, and as he is going to N.F. with us, we will decide then when we will start. I will write next week, and tell you all about our arrangements.

Your affectionate son
R. A. F. Penrose, Jr.

I will send you all the commencement literature as soon as I can get it.

In the summer of 1884, after graduating from Harvard, Dick accompanied his brothers Boies and Charley and, according to the letter of June 20th, presumably Daniel Moreau Barringer, with whom he later became associated as a business partner. It may have been that summer of 1884 which Penrose had in mind when he said, in a memorial to Barringer, written for the Boone and Crockett Club in 1930, that "his energy and ambition for adventure soon led him to the Rocky Mountains, which were then im many parts a wild country, primeval in character, abounding in game and only sparsely settled. His first trip there was in 1882, but he made numerous later trips in association with some of his friends, among whom the writer was one. These trips were designed and carried out for the pure delight of the chase, and in these early days we never took guides, cooks, packers, or any other employees. We acted as our own guides, because we knew the country as well as anyone else; we made our own camps, and packed and unpacked our own horses. Each man of the party had his special duty in preparing meals. There was no tenderfoot element in these expeditions, for each man had a knowledge of woodcraft, camp life and hunting; each was a woodsman devoted to the call of the forests and its denizens."

This seems to have been a real vacation trip in every sense of the word, probably the last one he ever took without having a more or less professional interest in what he saw. During the remainder of his life, his trips were made largely for the purpose of securing information regarding ores and mines, for in the fall of 1884 he began his life's study and work as a geologist.

One other glimpse of those student days is given in the following letter from Miss Beck to R. A. F. Penrose, dated Cambridge, Mass., January 1, 1899, which throws further light on Dick as a student and upon his associations:

Dear Dr. Penrose

I feel like wishing you and yours "A Happy New Year." I have mailed to Boies and to Charles (to your care not knowing Charles' address) the Boston Transcript containing the address of Mayor Quincy on the opening of the great railroad station here. Now, this is my story which I think will interest you.

One afternoon while your sons were in college, young Quincy called upon them and myself, at the suggestion of his aunt, Miss Susan Quincy, with whom I was long and well acquainted. I think Quincy was not a class-mate, but a year before your sons in college. I was thinking yesterday what honorable worldly distinction each had attained—Boies, United States Senator; Charles, a distinguished Physician; Quincy, Mayor of the city of Boston, third in succession of his family. His Grandfather, the honorable Josiah Quincy, President of Harvard University and once Mayor of Boston. He and his family were old and valued friends of my Father and his family. If you should ask my brother Frederick for what old Bostonian he had the greatest respect, he would say the elder Quincy; he did so much for the wealth and good of Boston. His Father was a Revolutionary Patriot who died in the service of his country and left a young widow and this little boy Josiah a few years old. We have always known the family, in years back when the elder ones were living, I can well say I have enjoyed great pleasure and benefit from their society. All that generation is gone now, but the youngest daughter of the Hon. Josiah, Mrs. R. C. Waterston, who lives in Boston, much advanced in years and quite an invalid. I have outlived all the friends of my girlhood. There is no one living with whom I can talk over past times, but it is all right. I do not feel useless in the world and I enjoy good health and the blessing of many beautiful reminiscences, which well repay me.

Frederick and his family are well; he is a very devoted kind brother and gets out often to see me when the weather is good. He always sends kind remembrances to you.

I hope I have not tired you with my long story, but I thought it might interest you. This anniversary brings to mind a host of friends, who gathered around Uncle and Aunt Boies' supper table to celebrate her birth-day. I am glad little Sarah Hannah Boies is so beautiful a child. The name has been handled down with great distinctness. My Mother was the first to be named for her, and now your little grand-daughter bears the same name, not for her but for your dear wife.

My niece Alice is very well and I take much pleasure in having my nephew and his wife living here with me this winter.

Please remember me kindly to each of your sons as you write to them, and with very kind regards for yourself, from your

Affectionate cousin
Sarah P. Beck

CHAPTER 4

Nathaniel Southgate Shaler Points the Way

NEITHER in his *Memoirs* nor in any of the accounts prepared by himself for general publication does Dick Penrose give a clue as to why he turned to geology for his life's work. In the letter to his father, November 1, 1882 (quoted in the previous chapter) he says: "I like mineralogy better than any of my other courses and have already got enough minerals to cover five shelves of a book-case."

Undoubtedly, he had come to know and admire Nathaniel Southgate Shaler, one of the best-known and best-loved geologists of his time, whose work as a teacher was attracting many young men to Harvard for graduate study. In any event, Shaler became the first of three great geologists who exerted tremendous influence on the life of young Penrose. The other two were John Casper Branner and Thomas Chrowder Chamberlin. The friendship of the young Philadelphian with all three was life-lasting. Nor was it in any case a one-sided affair. Shaler, Branner, and Chamberlin responded enthusiastically throughout their lives. To have won the intimate friendship of three such leaders is, indeed, a mark of distinction in itself and one which tells much for the sincerity and evident worth of the younger man.

Whatever may have been the reason for his choice, Dick Penrose again returned to Harvard in the fall of 1884 and spent that year and the one following in graduate study under the direction of Shaler. In June 1886 he received the degrees of master of arts and doctor of philosophy in natural history, the first Ph.D. in geology not being given at Harvard until 1897.

"During my college course I devoted myself earnestly to acquiring what knowledge was available at such an institution, for I realized that it was a rare opportunity for that purpose," Penrose says in the *Memoirs*. "I graduated in 1884 with a Summa Cum Laude degree and highest honors in chemistry, and in consideration of this accomplishment I was, in accordance with custom, promptly elected a member of the Phi Beta Kappa Society. I returned to Harvard in 1884, 1885, and 1886.

"During the latter part of my college career I took more or less interest in athletics, and managed on one occasion to win the silver medal for a mile foot race. In 1884 I rowed on our Class Crew on the Charles River, which won the race of that year. Later on I rowed as a stroke of the Harvard University at New London in 1885 and 1886. I had been warned by the college doctor before I rowed at all that I had a very bad heart and that I would probably die before I could finish a two-mile race. After rowing this race, however, without dying, I rowed several other two-mile races, and several four-mile races at New London, and I am still living."

Among his "treasures" were two clippings, one from the *New York Herald* the other from the *Boston Journal*, concerning the historic race at New London, in June, 1885, when the Harvard crew gained its "famous victory" over Yale. Here is the scene as described by the *Herald:*

"At the crimson cottage down stream [from the Yale crew quarters] the men of Harvard likewise rested—confidently, quietly, peacefully. Coach Faulkner guarded the boat ... Graduates of years gone back flitted from point to point, filled with important thought and on important business. Mr. R. C. Watson, Mr. L. E. Sexton and Mr. R. L. McCook, radiant in the distinguishing colors of Cambridge, talked and smiled. It was the smile of satisfaction and no mistake. Then crimson whispered to crimson on that gentle slope, with its rich blanket of emeralds, as if armies were soon to meet in deadly combat, and acted as if some invisible telephone would waft the secrets of the day to the brown bearded hermit of Bartlett's point, miles away across the river ... Stroke Penrose, against whom a verbal protest had been entered by Yale, was reading a book and seemingly as cool and composed as if his standing in the university had not been questioned. Dignity and calmness marked this six feet of muscular manhood. This was about nine o'clock [in the morning] ....

"Robert C. Cornell, Columbia '74, came from New York in the night train, and shortly after breakfast went to Harvard's quarters in his official capacity as referee to settle the disputed point about the alleged disability of Penrose, of the crimson shell.

"There the stroke's ironclad affidavit was exhibited, and, in addition, a letter from a member of the Harvard faculty was shown, asserting that Penrose was a student in the university and in a department that conferred a degree. The referee decided Penrose eligible. There was a shout in response that struck the cat tails growing on Bolles Flat across the river as would a squall.

"'Penrose all right! Burgess O.K.! [Burgess had had trouble with his knee.] —That settles it' was the exultant cry of an old crimson oar....

"... Another whistle and there was a stir at the crimson quarters. The crew walked slowly to their boathouse, and looking back to the cottage, as if wondering whether good luck would follow them. Then picking up their shell—the same in which they sat in the winning race with Columbia—they marched down the float and launched it. This was at two minutes past eleven o'clock. .. Never did college oarsmen look better. They were like peas in a pod, and their oars entered the water and left it with a motion and unison that was marvelous. They were fit to row for a man's life. Confidence was stamped upon every man's face ... The blues were heavier than the crimsons, but they lacked that firmness of flesh, clearness of skin, brightness of eye and glow of perfect health marking their antagonists. The big bodies of the Yale men swung together and looked dangerous, and he fact that seven of the men were in the 1884 crew, which easily defeated Harvard, wasn't a pleasant reflection for Yale's opponents....

"The two shells shot away as one. There were vim and determination in the stroke. Thirty-six sweeps to the minute was Yale's effort, and Harvard set them with thirty-seven.... Harvard increased her lead inch by inch at every stroke ... Harvard increased her stroke to thirty-eight after passing the half-mile ... The Cambridge boys were as parts of a machine.... Harvard again dropped her stroke to 36 in the bubble of a sea, but she never lost her advantage ... although Yale men shouted until they were nearly as blue in the face as their colors, Harvard continued to open the gap between them with that clean, extraordinary stroke....

"The journey was half over, and the second half was a repetition of the first. The big men of Yale tugged and tugged, the symmetrical eight of Harvard continued their easy and effective sweep ... Harvard, with a rhythmic 36, shot by the three mile flag in 18 m. $53\frac{1}{2}$ s., retaining her glorious form and clean stroke, pulled all the way from stroke to finish....

"Harvard sent her shell spinning by the finish flag fifteen lengths in front.... Harvard finished in good shape and could have gone a greater distance..."

According to the *Boston Journal* account, "Up to a week ago both sides were confident of victory. Then Harvard rowed her university race with Columbia, and the Yale men had a chance to see what she could do. What they saw astonished them: the stroke, the speed, the way the boat drove through the water, everything was far beyond what they had any reason to expect, and from that time out they began to lose their confidence, while, as their hopes went down, those of Harvard rose correspondingly.

"The race was witnessed by a larger gathering than any since the first of the series in 1876.... The crimson boat began to feel the powerful strokes of its crew, as they worked with a long sweep, using arms, body and legs, in marked contrast to the short, quick movement of Yale."

George Saltonstall Mumford, member of that historic 1885 crew, and captain of the 1886 crew, author of *Twenty Harvard Crews* and of the chapter on rowing in *The H Book of Harvard Athletics*, coach of several Harvard University crews, member of the Crew Rowing Committee for many years, prepared the following statement concerning Penrose. In his letter of transmittal, Mumford, who in 1942 was chairman of the board of Calumet and Hecla Consolidated Copper Company, declared that he had "endeavored to make it clear that Penrose was the outstanding performer on the first crew that was rigged and boated as eight-oar crews in this country are at the present time, and that as an oarsman his appearance in the boat would be exactly like that of any present-day member of an eight-oar American crew.

"Early in April, 1885, the Harvard University Crew in preparation for its four-mile races the following June was at work on the Charles River in Cambridge with much determination but little enthusiam. James Jackson Storrow, a senior, was the captain and the sole member of the squad who had what could be really regarded as any experience in four-mile racing, although one other of the candidates, also a senior, did row at bow in the race against Yale the year before after only four days practice in the boat. The rest of the squad, including this writer [Mumford], consisted of one Senior who had had no previous rowing experience and some Sophomores selected from the Freshman crew of the previous June.

"The worst of the situation was that they had no coach. The Faculty had forbidden the hiring of a coach and no competent unpaid volunteer was in sight among the old oarsmen.

"Storrow turned to George Faulkner, who worked on a nearby coal dock and who had been in his day a professional oarsman with considerable experience in teaching other professionals how to handle their boats. After the situation had been explained to him he agreed to give what time he could to work on the crew without any pay, an extraordinary example of enthusiasm for a sport for its own sake. Almost immediately Faulkner suggested that Richard Penrose be asked to join the squad. This suggestion Penrose promptly agreed to and immediately began rowing with the crew.

"Penrose had graduated the previous June and had recently returned to Cambridge to take a special two-years course of study in geology in the Graduate Department in preparation for writing an essay required to obtain a degree of Ph.D. At that time a student regularly entered in any department of instruction was deemed eligible for University teams or crews.

"The men on the crew squad remembered Penrose very well as a member of his Senior Class crew a year previously in the class races of the spring of 1884 and heartily welcomed his reappearance.

"He had entered college in 1880 from his home in Philadelphia. To his classmates he appeared to be a shy, unassuming man, not given to making friendships easily but always polite and perhaps self-effacing. He was credited with having an excellent mind, more interested in talking on geological subjects with instructors and professors, especially Professor Shaler, than in creating intimacies with classmates. He was a well built active man, but made little gesture toward taking part in organized athletics and never, previous to his senior year, seems to have shown a desire to enter into competition for membership on any football teams or crews. Members of the University crews were generally men who had rowed on their Freshman crews and those without that background had comparatively little chance to be recognized as promising material in selecting University Crews.

"If Penrose had previous rowing ambitions, he had certainly been successful in hiding them although he did appear on the river occasionally in the middle of his college carreer, but only in a single scull. In some way at that time he came under the eye of George Faulkner who was always watching men on the river in crews or in singles.

"It so happened in Penrose's senior year that the senior class of '84 crew was coached for a time by Faulkner in defiance of the Faculty order that no professional could coach, and during that brief period Faulkner advised the '84 senior class crew captain to try Penrose on the crew. He proved at once to be a valuable acquisition and soon was placed at No. 6 in the boat. The Class Races were won easily by this '84 senior crew in that spring of 1884.

"At this period there were no intercollegiate boat races between many colleges such as had previously been held at Springfield and on Saratoga Lake and were afterward revived and are still held at Poughkeepsie. Harvard and Columbia held a four-mile race at New London about six days before the Harvard-Yale race. These three eights rowed either as they supposed the English University crews rowed, with ten-inch or twelve-inch slides and a carefully attempted control of the recover or else, as with Yale for two or three years, in professional sculler style, with long slides and complete disregard of rushing the recover, leading frequently to a very high stroke. It is now recognized that both of these styles were half right and half wrong. Clearly, a professional in his single scull cannot achieve anything like the headway of an eight-oar boat which, with nine men, oars, outriggers, etc., weighs approximately a ton. To stop and start such a weight each stroke becomes a very great strain on the endurance of the oarsmen, while to a single sculler this is of slight consequence. Up to 1885 all amateur coaches had put chief emphasis on the recover and little on the leg drive, which, anyhow, really did not amount to much with such short slides, while professionals in coaching confined themselves to teaching the oarsman to copy Edward Hanlon as closely as possible in the drive and let the other half of the stroke take care of itself.

"And now the Harvard '85 University Crew with Penrose seated at stroke and Captain Storrow behind him at No. 7 was henceforth to be jointly directed by Faulkner and Storrow, the one to see to it that the men should drive the boat as a professional sculler does and Storrow to see to it that the recover should be deliberate and under control as taught in England, where eight-oared rowing was more general than sculling in singles.

"The slides were lengthened to eighteen and twenty inches, which after all these years is still the accepted length, and the men took lessons in applying their power by rowing in very light pair oars with the professional Faulkner. Penrose proved to be the most apt pupil of all. His form was identical with that of the best strokes of the present day and the other men in the boat began to wonder whether the smooth progress of their boat through the water really meant that they were fast.

"Shortly after their arrival at New London they raced Columbia. Expecting a close contest they put every ounce of their power into the first few strokes, with the result that they had clear water on their rival in four strokes and soon after, easing down to what was called hard paddling, Harvard won the race by nearly half a mile, at least so the newspapers recorded it.

"Bob Cooke was coach of the Yale Crew. His connection with Yale rowing began as an undergraduate in 1872 and lasted for twenty-five years. Except for two or three years in the early eighties, his authority was supreme. There is no doubt that in rowing matters he was a very wise man. However, he never showed any interest in the Harvard '85 crew previous to the Columbia race and was reported to have said that Harvard this year not only had a weak crew physically, but one that had failed even to master the professional stroke Faulkner attempted to teach.

"With the Columbia race there came a decided change. He immediately proceeded to take advantage of every opportunity to follow the Harvard crew closely in its practice, and the Harvard men could hear him explaining to members of the Yale crew who accompanied him on the Yale launch what he regarded as improvements over older styles of rowing as here exemplified. He constantly referred to Penrose by name. He would say, 'I want you to row the way Penrose does, watch him. Do you see how firmly his blade takes hold of the water at the catch? Watch his legs. That man is the most perfect oarsman I ever saw. You men, if you row the way he does, can lick that crew which is weak physically. Probably if you press them in the early part of the race they will begin to give out in spite of Penrose. He can't row the whole boat.'

"At the same time he made an attempt to have Penrose removed from the boat on the ground that he was not an enrolled member of any department in Harvard University. This necessitated a quick trip to Cambridge by a crew substitute to secure a certificate from the Head of the Harvard Geological Department that Penrose was an actual student in a Graduate Division of the University. He made an equally useless and more pointless attempt to have Faulkner sent home. It was grounded on a statement that he was a paid coach in defiance of a Faculty prohibition. The Harvard Faculty sent down two of its members to investigate, and they reported there was no ground for action as they believed Faulkner received no pay whatever and the only gift they could trace was a box of cigars presented to his employer in recognition of his willingness to allow Faulkner so much time off from his regular duties on the Cambridge coal dock.

"The race with Yale turned out to be almost as complete a walkover as the race of the previous week, although Yale did succeed in clinging to Harvard fairly well for the first 100 yards.

"In 1886 there were to be the same two four-mile races for Harvard, but both Storrow and Penrose declared that they would not row. The writer [Mumford] was the captain, and Faulkner agreed, after he had consulted his employer, to do what coaching was asked of him, and again without pay.

"Another change concerned the two opponents, Yale and Columbia. They both made no secret of their intention to have crews at New London rowing and rigged exactly like the Harvard '85 crew, and Yale adopted what they called the Penrose style of stroke. Their chief problem lay in the way to teach it, which in fact has always been the difficulty in developing eight-oared crews. Any intelligent man could tell whether a crew controlled its recover and see to it that the men were properly rigged, but the real difficulty was to determine and direct their effectiveness in pulling the oar through the water.

"The Harvard '86 crew was fast at the end of May in spite of the absence of Penrose and Storrow from the boat, faster in the opinion of the men than the year before and the oarsmen more rugged and stronger.

"And now Penrose decided that he wanted to join the crew. It is probable that this was a mistake because of the short time left before the New London races.

However, he returned to his old position at stroke, and the whole crew was rearranged and almost immediately left for New London, there again to meet Columbia and Yale in two separate races.

"This time both Columbia and Yale were vastly different from their respective '85 crews, and that they had both diligently labored to row as Harvard did was very apparent.

"The race with Columbia again came first, on the Saturday before the Yale race. After rowing one mile Harvard was leading by a length and a half when the courses of the two crews, which were perfectly straight lines, led Columbia through fast water in the channel and Harvard over flats with shallow water. This difference, in theory, would have enabled Columbia to catch Harvard and put the two crews on about even terms when Harvard had again returned to the channel, but in this race the Harvard men on again reaching the channel were actually nine lengths astern of their rivals. Harvard did make up some of this and lost the race eventually by about six lengths.

"The strain on Penrose was terrific. It was his duty to drive the crew to catch its rival, which for some seemingly inexplicable reason had suddenly disappeared. He had been rowing only two or three weeks and could not possibly have been in proper physical condition to stand the strain. He did it, however, and his appearance after the race and during the rest of the stay at New London clearly demonstrated the tremendous pressure he had put upon his nerve and vitality. No man ever gave a greater display of courage under hostile physical conditions than he did in this race.

"After the race the coxswain stated that mass of drift wood and tree tops had caught on the flats in front of the Harvard boat, making it necessary to turn in shore to get around it. Obviously, he should have steered into Columbia's course even at the risk of censure from the referee and possible collision with the rival boat. The only other possible witness was the Referee, who followed the race in a fast steam launch, and this was the only boat anywhere near that part of the course at the time. The Harvard oarsmen were busy rowing, had their backs turned to any obstruction, and could hardly detect any deviation from the course by the coxswain.

"The Harvard Crew became greatly demoralized both physically and mentally by this defeat, and both Penrose and the seven men behind him in the race against Yale that took place six days later were entitled to great praise for holding a good Yale Crew down to a four-lengths victory.

"At Yale this poor record of the Harvard '86 crew had no effect on their admiration of Penrose. It seemed to be agreed that his appearance in the boat this second year was unfortunate for him because he took his seat too late to get into proper physical condition.

"This good Yale Crew became the first of a series of Yale University crews for eight or ten years which were coached by Robert J. Cooke, and during that time Yale stood at the top of eight-oared college rowing, with an almost constant succession of victories, and both Cooke and his assistant coaches frequently told Harvard men that it was Penrose that started Yale on this career of success. It was not until 1896 that Courtney, the Cornell coach, began to develop fast crews, for it was in that year that he, too, finally came to realize the necessity for practicing a deliberate well-controlled recover in eight-oar rowing.

"At Harvard the only immediate influence left by Penrose was a realization that a hard four-mile race within a week of the Yale race was too much of a risk, with the result that the race with Columbia was permanently abandoned after Harvard's victory over Columbia in 1887, when they repeated their experience of the year before in becoming over-exhausted in their race with a fast Columbia crew. The record of more recent years has pretty conclusively proved that after a close four-mile race, an interval of a couple of weeks is required to restore a crew to full vigor. The unfairness of that second mile also became generally recognized, and Harvard and Yale agree to row that part of the course on a curve so as to enable both crews to enjoy like conditions of tide and deep water at the same point in the race.

"At this time at Harvard, membership in the University Crew meant that the eight men were together at all meals, in the dressing rooms and in the boat while in Cambridge, and during nearly three weeks at New London they lived together in the same building, with sleeping quarters on the second floor fitted up with small alcoves, with bed and bureau in each for single occupants. There were some examinations and considerable studying and reading when not out practicing on the water. Penrose was especially popular, always genial and sociable. It was 'Hello, Dick, how do you feel today?' or, 'Hi,! Pen, listen to this.' It is true it was different after the unfortunate Columbia race of 1886, for none of the men felt like chaffing but sat around bewildered and in silence and they could not but observe the tired appearance Penrose presented. He had always contributed more to the general gaiety by his appreciation of the wit of others than by his own relation of anecdotes or stories, but his position as a good fellow and a good companion was thoroughly established.

"These men who were his close companions were many of them to attain prominence in later life. Storrow became head of the banking house of Lee, Higginson and Company and at his death left a fortune of many millions. Henry W. Keyes for eighteen years represented New Hampshire in the United States Senate in Washington. William A. Brooks became a prominent Boston surgeon. J. R. Yocum was a prominent physician on the Pacific Coast. T. P. Burgess (Bill) created a fortune for himself through manufacturing sulphite-fibre and retired satisfied at the age of forty years. Franklin Remington organized the Foundation Company, and under his presidency made it one of the largest contracting and construction companies in the world."

Remington, writing of Penrose, said, in a letter dated September 12, 1942: "He was one of the most modest men I ever knew, and while excelling in everything he undertook, one would have to know him well and be in personal contact with him very frequently to realize what lay beneath the retiring front he showed to the world. He had an amazing amount of personal charm and was one of the most entertaining and delightful companions a man could have. I only saw him once or twice after graduating, but I retain an indelible impression of him as a man you could rely on absolutely to stick by you in any kind of an emergency and to literally and figuratively pull his oar in any enterprise that he might be connected with, whether in sports such as rowing in which he excelled or in the more serious affairs of after life. Dick Penrose was perfectly fearless and accepted anything that came along in a cool calm matter-of-fact sort of way. He had a great sense of humor of a whimsical order. Looking back over fifty years of an active life which has taken me to many parts of the world, where I have mixed with all sorts and conditions of men, I do not know of anyone who has left a more delightful impression on my memory than Dick Penrose."

In the *Harvard Alumni Bulletin* of May 23, 1929, there appeared a picture of "The 1886 University Crew," a group of solemn-looking young men (Penrose was twenty-one at the time), most of them with mustaches, two of them with what were once termed "stocking caps," and all of them with sweaters that modestly covered the upper arm. They were T. P. Burgess, H. W. Keyes, W. A. Brooks, J. W. Wood, A. P. Butler, Franklin Remington, J. R. Yocum, G. S. Mumford, R. A. F. Penrose, Jr., J. J. Colony, J. Q. Browne, and C. F. Adams.

According to the story accompanying the picture, the group "is noteworthy, among many reasons, because in the right-hand lower corner is the present Secretary of the United States Navy (C. F. Adams), who according to the 'H Book of Harvard Athletics' is entitled to the rowing 'H' because of his connection with the 1886 crew . . . Mumford, captain of the crew, is a well known banker in Boston. Keyes is a United States Senator from New Hampshire. Remington has been president and is now chairman of the board of the Foundation Co., one of the leading construction corporations in New York City. Penrose is an eminent geologist in Philadelphia. Colony is a manufacturer in Keene, N. H. Butler has retired, but was for a long time associated with his classmates, J. Q. Browne and F. C. Woodman, in the Morristown School. Wood is a banker in New York City. Four of the men in the group are dead: Yocum, who practised medicine in the Northwest; Burgess, who was a manufacturer of wood pulp; Brooks, who was a prominent surgeon in Boston; and Browne, who was a schoolmaster."

In the *Harvard Graduates Magazine* for September, 1926, in an article concerning James Jackson Storrow, captain of the Harvard University crew of 1885, there is another reference to that famous race: "The men whom Storrow had selected for the crew, though physically below the previous standard, had been chosen by him partly for those abilities likely to make them successful in after life; and their subsequent career, from Penrose, the brilliant geologist, at stroke, to Keyes, future United States senator, at bow, has amply justified his judgment. This method of making his selection was peculiar and consisted largely in walking trips on which he took the several candidates—trying them against the background of his mountains

. . . .

"Then there arose a crisis which would have tried the nerve of any captain. Less than a week before the race Yale entered a formal protest to the referee that Penrose, the Harvard stroke, was not a bona fide student—that he had registered in the spring as a graduate student solely in order to stroke the crew. Storrow kept the seriousness of the situation to himself. He sent one of the substitutes to Cambridge and obtained a written statement from the responsible professor of Penrose's regular position as a student and affidavits to his good faith as such. The referee ruled that the intent was the real question and decided the case in Harvard's favor, and few of the crew realized that for several days the fate of their whole year's work had been hanging in the balance.

"Then came the race, and every Harvard man and every Yale man knows what happened. Harvard won by twenty-two lengths."

Even after he left Harvard and was working in Canada on his first job, the urge to row for Harvard was continued, as is evidenced in the following letter from H. W. Keyes, the New Hampshire Senator, his fellow oarsman on the 1886 Harvard crew, who wrote from Cambridge, April 17, 1887:

My dear Penny—

Ever since you were here last fall and expressed a desire to "get at" those Yale men once more I have felt that I would give almost anything to have you with us once more, sitting at your old place in the boat. Perhaps the subject of rowing has but little interest for you now, but I can not believe it, and so I thought you would be glad to hear how we are getting on this year, and I will pitch right in.

Knowing what an important year this was to be for Harvard boating I got the men to work in the fall and we learned a little. When foot ball was over I had every reason to expect that all the old men would begin after Christmas vacation. January 1st came and not a single old man came to back me up and help wipe out the unfortunate record of last year. But to make a long story short the only man (but he is the best one of all) that is now rowing with us is Bill Brooks. The others can do what they like now for I have no use for them. What I do want is a stroke. I have tried several men, but as yet no one has turned up who is really capable to stroke a Varsity crew. If that position could only be well filled I feel sure that we could lay most anything out at New London, for I expect to have a good starboard stroke in long Pfeiffer of last years freshman crew.

1887 promises to be a year of unusual interest in college boating. Cambridge, England, has written that they will send a crew over here this summer and row us a race, and we are expecting a formal challenge every day, which we shall accept of course.

Now how would this sound at the end of the year:—"Harvard still maintains her supremacy in boating, having beaten not only the crack crews of Columbia and Yale but also the winners of the Oxford-Cambridge race."

There seems to be but one way for us to realize this great hope, and that is to have you, old man, stroke us once more. I think I never felt worse for a fellow than I did for you last year, and I feel sure that we will have a set of men this year that would back you up in great shape. I can't bear to think of leaving off with such a record as we made last year, and I know you can't too; we must leave victorious, that is the only way to stop. With your stroke, with men on the war path to back you up, and with a good boat, we can bring joy to our own hearts and to all good sons of Harvard, who are as willing as ever to back us.

Dick Penrose as a student at Harvard

Nathaniel Southgate Shaler

You would only have to be absent from business about two months and you could probably arrange to have the work go on all right. I have had placed at my disposal "all the money I want," so let no question of finances stop you from coming.

We have *got* to have you, Penny, and you certainly can think up some scheme to get to Cambridge "to carry on some important experiments" or something of that sort.

With you we would have a team fit to row the gods; but without you things look dark, and I see before me nothing but sleepless nights and visions of defeat.

Return, Penny; win back your laurels, and you will do the greatest thing ever done by a stroke, and no one would rejoice at your success more than

Your sincere friend
H. W. Keyes

Of course, he did not go. If Keyes had known him well, he would have known that such a plea, however attractive it might have seemed, could not swerve Penrose from his job.

Even harder to decline must have been the call to adventure voiced in the following letter from another member of that 1886 crew, Arthur P. Butler, father of Arthur P. Butler, Jr., Fellow of The Geological Society of America.

"Dear Penny," wrote Butler from Jamaica Plain, Mass., on July 24, 1887, "Now that the college year is over and the races rowed, hard luck that we couldn't have beaten Yale, wasn't It? and I have a minute to contemplate how short a time it will be before I have to begin to work in earnest I can't help feeling that I want to do something or go somewhere before I settle down once and for all. This being the case I have of late thought much of the trip to Alaska across country that you and I have talked about.

"Now what I want to know is Have you at any time seriously thought about making such a trip and if you have would it in any way be possible for me to accompany you? Of course you would never undertake such a lengthy and one might say almost dangerous excursion without some definite object in view. Therefore, I assume that if you were really going it would be for some scientific purpose and consequently I think that from twelve to eighteen months spent with you working and studying under you would be of great material advantage to me, in fact I feel convinced that such an experience would be of far more value to me than the same amount of time and money spent in traveling abroad. Yes, just at present the only way in which I should care to see the world at all would be to ship before the mast and work my way around the globe. But such a scheme as that being particularly infeasible at this date in history where shipping is in such a state of decline, I have practically decided either to go to Alaska with you, if possible, or else to settle down at once in whatever business I seem to be best fitted for.

"I think I fully appreciate the character of such an expedition, the difficulties naturally attending it, the length of time it would take, etc., etc., and this is the very reason I should like to take the trip, for the greater the exertion and risk the greater the satisfaction in accomplishment. But there is no need of saying more just at present. By this you will see that I am very much in earnest about our Alaska trip and I know that you will ans. this letter in good faith and you may be sure that I shall be sorry to hear from you that you were after all 'playing me for a sucker.'

"I was pleased enough to receive your letter while at New London and all the boys were delighted to think that you remembered us and only wished that you had been among us. I am sorry for Harry [Keyes] that we did not beat Yale, much more sorry for him than for myself or anyone else in the boat, for he deserved to win. He made such a splendid captain and I am so glad he has accepted the position for next year for I think the same or nearly the same crew with another year for practice will be able to show Yale a beautiful stern chase.

"It is foolish when fairly licked to say the course or anything else did it but it really seems to me that if two crews were just matched in every particular the one having the west course would win. I do hope we have done with Columbia, for to row two such races within a week is too much to ask of a crew I think, and now having beaten the crew that they acknowledged was the best they have ever put in the water, why row them again and so lessen our chances in the great race. Besides, too many side-shows in shape of extra Varsity and Freshman races is death to the interest in the Harvard-Yale contest.

"Well, Penny, we will do them up brown in everything next year, for we have the best of material for eleven, nine and crew and if '88 can't equal '85's record I shall be mistaken, that's all. At any rate this chicken intends to do all he can to put the crimson above the blue.

"Pardon the length of this letter. I did not intend to bore you so long but shall, hope to find a favorable answer awaiting me when I return from Maine woods where J. Walter and I are to spend the month of August."

It is interesting to speculate as to why Penrose picked out Alaska. Although at that time it had been in the possession of the United States for twenty years, it was noted chiefly for its furs. Not for another decade would it become known for its mineral resources and witness the famous gold rush. At that time, too, there was still plenty of little known territory much closer at hand than Alaska, as the perusal of his subsequent adventures will show. It does show, however, that the boundaries of his possible travels were challenging, not only to himself, but to other adventurous souls.

In writing of those early days, Dr. Butler said in the fall of 1942: "Dick Penrose first loomed on my Freshman horizon on the float of the Harvard boat house in the early spring of 1885. He had graduated from the college in '84, but had returned for graduate work in geology, and having rowed at number 6 in his senior class crew, which won the class races that spring, had been picked by captain James J. Storrow, Jr., with almost uncanny perspicacity, to stroke the Varsity boat, in which he was one of six in the crew who had had no previous experience in intercollegiate rowing—a very considerable assignment for the candidate, and a long shot on the part of the captain.

"There was nothing Herculean in his physique. Six feet two inches in height, he weighed but 162 pounds in rowing trim. His was of the rangy type, with muscles flat along a powerful bone frame work; his back broad, chest deep, and, of special importance in rowing, loin muscles fully developed, He wasn't carrying any unnecessary amount of fat, and his endurance was extraordinary. He didn't know fear; his nerves were strong, his servants, not his master; and his spirit quiet but indomitable.

"At New London we youngsters didn't come much in contact with 'Varsity men, who looked to us like the gods of Olympus, but we could watch them in action and learn from their performance. One beautiful June morning our Freshman Crew, out for practice, ranged alongside of the Yale 'Varsity for the last mile or so of a four-mile time row, and to our great satisfaction found we could easily hold our position with it and actually draw away from it. This performance greatly pleased the members of the Senior crew, and Penrose, usually reticent, encouraged us mightily by his generous appreciation of it.

"A few days later Penrose stroked the Harvard Crew to a victory over the Columbia eight by a lead of nearly two minutes over the four-mile course, and then repeated the performance by a victory over the Yale crew, which was more than a minute behind at the finish. After these results, which proved him to be one of the best stroke oars Harvard has ever had, his place in Harvard rowing, and the popularity that went with it, was assured.

"Modest and retiring as he was in victory, his bearing in defeat was no less noteworthy. The following year things weren't going so well with Harvard rowing, and, too late to have time to get in thoroughly good rowing condition, he was drafted again to take his place at stroke in the '86 crew. In this year, for the first time, Harvard met defeat in a race with Columbia, and fared the same in the race with Yale. In a defeated, depleted and disillusioned group he was serene and unmoved.

"As a subsitute with the crew that year I saw more of 'Penny' than at any other time, and my admiration for him increased. He had the maturity of an older fellow; his aim in life was definitely decided, and, with determination, was set to make it a success.

"Geology was a global affair. Consequently, his mind was reaching out in every direction for the right point of departure in his quest. A trip in the Maine woods I was envisaging taking that summer with a roommate created common interests and provided plenty of topics for discussion. It was then, probably, the possibility of an Alaskan adventure was rather seriously considered, with the Lake of the Woods in Minnesota much in the foreground as a starting point to waters leading eventually to those of the Yukon. Every now and then an unexpectedly humerous touch lent incitement to our discussions, but a sense of aloofness and of an old-fashioned formality were nearly always present.

"I never got behind this. Our homes were separated and meetings grew fewer. Only twice, years later, did I see him, when I happened to be in Philadelphia. In the meantime, his goal as an eminent geologist had been reached. I shall always remember him as a heroic figure in both intellectual and physical attributes."

Penrose kept up his interest in Harvard rowing for the rest of his life. Under ate of November 20, 1923, he wrote in a letter to Earnest E. Smith of Boston, who had asked for answers to specific questions:

"I thank you for having written to me about this matter, for it is one in which I am greatly interested and about which I have thought much ... I will answer your several questions as they are presented:

"1. 'Shall the Crew captain be supreme and choose the coach?' I believe that the Crew captain should be absolutely supreme and should have the entire power and responsibility of choosing the coach. If the captain has the capacity to perform his ordinary duties he will be amply able to assume this responsibility and if he has not that capacity he has no right to be captain.

"2. 'Shall the Graduate Committee be supreme and choose the coach?' I feel that the Graduate Committee should neither be supreme nor choose the coach. I feel, however, that the Graduate Committee should continue to exist and be ready to consult with the captain of the Crew at his request, or, under particular circumstances, at their own request; but that their power should simply be that of an advisory board and that it should not be permitted to interfere with the captain in any other manner.

"3. 'Shall the captain and the Committee share responsibility, and if so, along what lines?' My answers to questions 1 and 2 largely answer question 3. In other words, I do not think that the captain and the Committee should share responsibility, but I feel that the whole responsibility should be on the captain and the Committee should exist simply as an advisory board.

"4. 'Who is your choice for coach, and why?' This problem has already been solved and I look forward with great hope to the success of our crew next year.

"I fee that the most important man connected with any crew is the captain, that his choice should be left entirely to the undergraduates and that the Graduate Rowing Committee should have nothing to do with his choice unless they are called on to give advice. The undergraduates certainly know their college mates better than any Graduate Committee, they are more in sympathy with each other, they know their various abilities better, and are therefore better qualified to pick out a captain than a committee composed of men many of whom may have long since left college, and must of necessity have lost some of their former familiarity with undergraduate affairs.

"All these points which have been brought up in connection with the Harvard Crew are important, but I feel very sure that the oarsman who wins races is the one that takes such a deep interest in this sport that he is instinctively drawn to it, that he makes a particular study of it with the result that he will in all probability row well, because he will row naturally and work every muscle in his body to its great efficiency."

On January 21, 1924, Penrose stated in a letter to John Richardson, chairman of the Harvard Advisory Rowing Committee that "my interest in rowing is as strong as it ever was, even in the days long gone by."

Two other letters, written by Penrose only three years before his death concern this interest. Both are addressed to George S. Mumford.

May 23, 1928

Dear George:—

No biographer ever wrote more truly, more eloquently, or with a keener sense of justice than you have done in your biography of Jim Storrow. You have depicted the man in his real character, and with a kindness and appreciation of his high attributes which could have been thus clearly observed only by a biographer who had so many of these qualities himself.

I congratulate you most heartily on this biographical sketch and greatly appreciate your kindness in letting me read it. When you were here last week I asked you if I could take a copy of it and you said I could, but after reading it twice I am impressed with the fact that it is more or less a purely confidential communication, written by you for his family, and that I might seem presumptuous in taking a copy of it. I have therefore not copied it, and am returning it to you herewith by registered mail, so that it will be sure to reach you safely.

I was much interested in the page or so which you devoted to the protest made by Yale against my rowing on the '85 University Crew because they declared that I had returned to Harvard simply for the purpose of rowing. Of course we all know that this was absolutely false and was done for purely strategic purposes. When I graduated in 1884 I had promised Professor Shaler to return the next fall to study for a Ph.D. degree, and this I did without any intention of rowing on any crew whatever. The idea of rowing on the University Crew at that time never entered my head, for I never had rowed on it before, and it had not occurred to me that I was qualified to do so. The first I knew about my being considered as a possible member of the crew was one evening when Jim Storrow came to my room and said he wanted to talk to me about the University Crew. This was the first time he had ever visited me, and I saw by his manner that he had something serious on his mind.

As was thoroughly characteristic of him, he lost no time in coming to the point and asked me if I would come down to the boat-house the next day and try my hand as a possible candiate for the crew. This was in March or April, 1885, about six months after I had returned to college, with no other idea than to study for a Ph.D. degree. I received this degree in June, 1886, and the thesis I presented in this connection was entitled "The Nature and Origin of Deposits of Phosphate Lime." In studying the geology of this subject I travelled all over the United States and parts of Canada. The United States Geological Survey somewhat later published my manuscript with the above-mentioned title in the form of one of its octavo volumes (Bulletin 46), composing over one hundred pages of text and original illustrations.

It was a very great pleasure to me to have seen you here last week, for it had been a long while since we met in New York twenty odd years ago, and in that time I have rarely had an opportunity to discuss Harvard rowing in the days when we both were active in it. The generation after us knows intimately only what has happened since that time.

November 30, 1928

Dear George:

I was greatly pleased to receive from you the copy of the beautiful description of the "Harvard Boathouse Memorial," including also an account of the crews of bygone years which used this historic structure.

The monument and its inscription are most dignified and impressive records of Harvard rowing, and the beautiful volume which you have prepared announcing its completion carries out in a remarkable manner the spirit of the beauty and historic value of this splendid memorial to a building of which many of us still have vivid recollections. The monument stands like a mute but watchful sentinel guarding the revered spot where for over half a century stood the boathouse from which issued year by year Harvard's men and Harvard's hopes in the great battle to assert their superiority in oarsmanship and to win the supremacy of the Thames.

In the text and illustrations of the volume I can see the mark of your accurate and comprehensive knowledge of Harvard rowing from its early days, and you have given this information in a clear and attractive style, which always characterizes your writings. I feel that every Harvard man who rowed on any of our crews owes you a debt of appreciation, both for the interest you have taken in the monument and for the splendid manner in which you have prepared the volume. I notice that while you are kind enough to mention many of us individually yet you in your modesty do not say enough of yourself, whereas we all know that you were not only one of the best oarsmen Harvard ever had, but were familiar with the theory and technique of rowing in a manner and to an extent which very few possessed. Long will we remember your unwavering devotion to Harvard rowing and your keen participation in its interests.

In the summer of 1885, Penrose was assistant to Professor Shaler on the United States Geological Survey, working at Martha's Vineyard and Mount Desert Island. Later that same summer he made a trip to Montreal, Ottawa, and through the phosphate regions of the provinces of Quebec and Ontario. The object of this trip was to do geological work and, especially in Canada, to study the phosphate deposits, it having been decided that phosphate should be the subject of his dissertation for the degree of Doctor of Philosophy. Before the year was over, he also made a trip through North and South Carolina, Georgia, and Florida, studying the Tertiary and later formations of the coastal region and especially the phosphate deposits contained in these formations.

His dissertation, entitled *The Nature and Origin of Deposits of Phospahte of Lime*, was published in 1888 by the United States Geological Survey as Bulletin No. 46, and after its publication by the Survey a part of it was republished in 1890 by the Royal Commission of Mineral Resources of the Province of Ontario.

In the introduction to Bulletin No. 46, Professor Shaler wrote:

"When I began my work in the U. S. Geological Survey, I asked permission of the Director to continue my studies on phosphatic deposits. There was at the time no money available for these studies; it was therefore necessary that they should be carried on without other expense to the Survey than that involved in the small share of my time which could be given to the supervision of the work. It was my good fortune, however, to find in one of my students of geology, Dr. R. A. F. Penrose, jr., a person who was willing at his own cost to undertake a preliminary study of the whole field as far as our knowledge extends and thus to prepare the problems concerning American phosphate deposits for detailed inquiry. This work he has pursued with great intelligence and energy during the two years in which he has been engaged in it. In this task he has examined all the known phosphate deposits of the United States and Canada and has made a careful inquiry into the literature of the subject... Dr. Penrose's studies were not designed to be encyclopedic in their scope, but rather to afford a synopsis of what is known of the deposits in this and other countries... My own as well as Dr. Penrose's acknowledgments are due to many persons who have given him aid in the prosecution of his work. To Prof. Charles U. Shepard, jr., of Charleston, S. C., Dr. Penrose is particularly indebted for much information and access to a great deal of valuable matter contained in his unpublished notes on American and foreign phosphatic deposits."

In this, the first published work of Penrose, the careful organization of material which marked all his subsequent work is in evidence. The table of contents shows that he thoughtfully worked out the proper sequence of presentation. Evidently his studies at Harvard had shown him the value of presenting facts in a form which leads the reader from the general to the specific without letting him get tangled up in irreverent details along the way.

The opening paragraphs in the first chapter, which is entitled "Importance of phosphate of lime in nature," give the keynote of straightforward presentation:

"Phosphorus is one of the most universally distributed of all the elements. It is found in all animal and vegetable matter, as well as in most eruptive and sedimentary rocks. Phosphoric acid composes over 40 per cent of the ashes of bones and in the vegetable kingdom it is especially abundant in the seeds of plants. Thus the ash of wheat contains over 49 per cent of phosphoric acid.

"It has been estimated that for each cow kept on a pasture through the summer there are carried off, in veal, butter and cheese, not less than fifty pounds of phosphate of lime. Consequently it will be seen that phosphoric acid is one of the most important elements of plant food, and no soil can be productive which is destitute of it. The necessity of restoring phosphoric acid to an exhausted soil has been acknowledged from very ancient times, though the cause of its stimulating effect was unknown until comparatively late date. In the days of the Romans the excrements of birds, from pigeon-houses and bird-cages, brought a high price, and Edrisi relates that the Arabians, as early as 1154 A.D., used the guano deposits found along their coast for agricultural purposes. Garcilaso de la Vega (*Comentarios Reales*, lib. V, 1604) says that the Peruvians, in the twelfth century, used the guano beds on their islands as fertilizers. Of such importance did they esteem the material of these beds that the penalty of death was imposed by the early Incas on any one found killing the birds that made these precious deposits. It was not, however, until the early part of this century, when Liebig and others showed the important part played by phosphoric acid in vegetable life, that artificial phosphatic manures came into use, and it is only in the last twenty years that the mining of natural phosphates with their conversion into superphosphates has assumed its present great and steadily increasing importance."

He then proceeds to the classification of deposits of phosphate of lime, following that with a discussion of mineral and rock phosphates in detail, including in his treatment the deposits of Canada, Norway, Spain, Nassau, France, England, Russia, Belgium, North Wales, and, in the United States, North and South Carolina, Alabama, Martha's Vineyard, Florida, and Kentucky. The appended bibliography lists 209 titles from the literature concerning these places.

Having thus evidenced a knowledge of the industry and its background, he quite logically was offered opportunity to put his knowledge to use, and after due consideration he accepted an appointment to engage in the mining of phosphates. Thus, at the age of 23, this gently reared young aristocrat from Philadelphia became superintendent of the Battle Lake (Canada) phosphate mines and a year later (1887) was appointed general superintendent of all the mines of the company in various parts of the provinces of Quebec and Ontario.

"In 1886 I was appointed superintendent of the phosphate mines of the Anglo-Canadian Phosphate Company, situated at various points northeast of Ottawa in the valley of the Aux Lievres River," he writes in his *Memoirs*. "The mines were reached by going north from the town of Buckingham by river boat and by horse in summer, or by sleigh in winter. The North Star Mine was our principal seat of operations at that time, and it consisted of a shaft probably less than 300 feet deep, alongside of which was our so-called boarding house; this consisted of a log cabin with two tiers of bunks around the sides and a central fireplace on the floor. A hole was cut in the roof to allow the smoke to escape, which was a very convenient device except in winter, when the snow fell so heavily that it was apt to come through the hole and put out the fire.

"We had about twenty miners at work under an excellent foreman called Bill MacIntosh, and during the first winter a large amount of phosphate was produced, which we had expected to haul to the Aux Lievres River in wagons, and shift thence in barges to Montreal, to be forwarded to England in ocean steamers. As luck would have it, however, an epidemic of diphtheria broke out the latter part of the winter and a large part of the able-bodied population of the district either died or fled, so that during the open summer only about one-half of our phosphate could be brought to the seaboard. The rest was shipped the next season.

"Buckingham in those days was the center of business and playful activity and was like many of our western mining camps fifty years ago. Everyone was making money in connection with the phosphate industry, and most of them were spending it again as rapidly as possible on the primitive joys of Buckingham, which, though a crude lumber camp, was to the suddenly enriched French Canadians or Scotchmen as much a paradise of joy as Paris is to the quick-rich of New York. Little did they know that within a few years the phosphate industry of Canada would be almost annihilated by the phosphate industries of South Carolina, and particularly by the new discoveries in Florida.

"In 1887 the Anglo-Canadian Phosphate Company made me General Manager of all their mines on the Aux Lievres River, and also of their mines one hundred miles or more to the southwest in the Province of Ontario, in the township of North Burgess. I did not care much for this addition to my duties because I had never felt much confidence in the mines of North Burgess; but as the man who had been running them for the Company had not been satisfactory to them I undertook the work, and for a year or more managed to make some profit from them for the Company.

"Our camp in North Burgess was on a beautiful body of water called Otty Lake, about six miles from the town of Perth, an old established settlement inhabited mostly by English-speaking people, and in great contrast in its quietness to the uproarious Buckingham. I had frequent occasions to go to Perth to attend to business in connection with the mines and was thrown in close contact with the Manager of the local branch of the bank of Montreal, Mr. R. J. Drummond, who was a most likeable character and who always showed me the greatest hospitality and friendship. This was over forty years ago, and we still keep up occasional correspondence. He had two sons and three daughters and they frequently came to Otty Lake to fish for the numerous bass in those waters.

"One of the principal industries of Perth was the manufacture of the famous McClaren's Perth-Malt, which, though clear and beautiful as water, was very subtle in its results, for it contained a large percentage of alcohol, which made it stronger than the strongest brandy. It was very popular, however, in Perth and throughout the adjoining Province of Ontario, and its manufacturer, Mr. McClaren, became a wealthy, popular, and prosperous citizen.

"During the time I was at Perth there was quite an anti-American feeling on account of the absurd fear which existed at that time that the United States was attempting to annex Canada. Of course, well-informed people like Mr. Drummond knew there was nothing in such reports, but the mass of ignorant people believed implicitly in them. The situation caused some trouble among the men in the mine and some antagonism towards what they called the Yankee manager, who had replaced their own particular manager. I tried to appease this feeling as much as possible, but it nevertheless seemed to grow, and the principal way it was manifested was by the miners underground doing less and less real work. Of course, this meant a great injury to the Company, and one night I decided to try to stop it. I went down into the mine alone, about 3 o'clock in the morning, when the night shift was supposed to be active, and found every one of the men sitting around on the rocks, smoking and gossiping and evidently oblivious to the passage of time. I then and there told them that they were all discharged, and gave them orders to come to the surface and get their pay checks. I expected this would cause some trouble, but it took them so suddenly that they all followed me up the ladder and came to my office, where, with the assistance of the superintendent, Barney Murphy, I made out the pay checks, and he and I closed the mine. The men scattered and everything was quiet for a few days. I notified the

Company at their headquarters in Montreal what I had done and they supported me in my position and told me to take whatever action I thought best.

"In the course of a few days the men began to return—sometimes one, sometimes two, at a time—and as I had already observed them all closely and knew their personal tendencies, I did not hesitate to take back into the employment of the Company the ones whom I knew to be least objectionable. A few men also came from the outside and filled the rest of the positions, so that within a week the night shift, as well as the day shift, was running as usual.

"After this episode there was a decided increase in the production of the mine, and there was no tendency to revert to the old condition of antagonism. Finally the last of the old employees returned for work, and we all shook hands and decided that we would let bygones be bygones. The 'Yankee Manager' who was once thought 'lazy' received an unexpected degree of respect. After all, Anglo-Saxons the whole world over respect a man who puts up a fair fight—particularly if he wins."

Thus the youngster won his spurs in the field of business leadership. It is significant, also, that he did not move until he had prepared a carefully thought-out plan of action. The whole incident and the confidence placed in his ability to manage the affair by owners of the mine speak eloquently of what manner of man he was even at twenty-four.

In the great mass of correspondence which Penrose left there was a letter from the aforementioned Mr. Drummond of Perth, dated January 26, 1894, as follows:

Dear Friend,

You used to be close to me in propria persona, but Christmas has passed (forgive the word and take the human joy of it) many times and you are changing to new duties and new dignities. My mind enquires, What is Penrose like now? and I feel justified in my rude thought, for Edith and Mrs. D. will say when a new book is laid before them (they perhaps don't understand) I tell them is your authorship, Oh, I would like to see Penrose again!

I have been reading the Chemical relations of Iron and Managanese for its clear literary descriptions, though practically I have little knowledge of their combinations. All the same, your kindness in sending your own writing is as substantial a fact by your book as by a blowpipe to Norman, whose birds' eggs delight him yet. Norman is away. He is ranching at Pincher Creek, N. W. T., and his mother's anxieties picture him with long beard and cowboy attire, running the risks of a western life.

Carrie and Jean are growing to be young ladies, and Andrew is in the Bank of Montreal, climbing the same ladder his father is climbing, in which there is good bread and butter for the workers, and the working gives the fame to directors. But the sunlight when it comes these short days is still a great pleasure to the Drummond family you saw together.

Don't fail to call at Perth when business or inclination leads you this way.

In 1886 and 1887 Penrose made numerous trips through the phosphate regions of Quebec and Ontario. As if his work as general manager of the mines was not enough to keep this energetic young man busy, the records show that he was making studies for his organization relative to further development. There is a *Report on a Mica, Feldspar, and Quartz property in Ottawa County, Canada*, by R. A. F. Penrose, Jr., dated March 26, 1888, in which he not only reports on the geological aspects of the situation, but gives detailed "estimates of revenue and expenditure" regarding its working for twelve months.

A subsequent memorandum, dated Montreal, April 3, 1888, states that "the report and memoranda attached, showing estimates, etc., have been prepared after careful investigations, extending over two months, by Dr. Penrose, of Philadelphia, chemist and mineralogist, and Mr. J. Keith Reid, of Montreal, both of whom have had several years experience in mining in Ottawa County, and if agreeable to the subscribers, arrangements can be made to have the management of the Company's business assumed by them." From his expense accounts, it is evident that Mr. Reid was his assistant.

A copy of his formal "report on lots 30 and 31, R. 1, Villeneuve," made in May, 1888, has been preserved. Here also is evidence of the careful worker, for, as will be seen in the chapter on his work in Texas, college students of that day were not trained in geological field methods as is the young Ph.D. of today. Here it is, a good straightforward report, capable of being understood by any one interested in mining ventures.

This property comprises the mining rights of lots 30 & 31, Township of Villeneuve, County of Ottawa, Province Quebec. It consists of about 200 acres of which about 150 are composed of a series of rugged and much eroded mountains of the Laurentian formation and 50 are covered by Clay Lake. The property is 3 miles east of the Aux Lievres River with which it is connected by a wagon road. The Aux Lievres is navigable down its course as far as Buckingham, which is about 23 miles south of the mine and on a branch road of the Canadian Pacific Railroad. Buckingham is 104 miles by rail from Montreal.

Mode of Occurrence of the Mica

The mica is of the pure Muscovite variety and occurs in crystals in a vein composed largely of white microcline feldspar, and transparent, smoky and flesh colored quartz, with black tourmaline, cinnamon garnets, uraninite, gummite and other rarer minerals in smaller quantities. The vein is about 90 ft. wide, strikes in a general N.E. and S.W. direction through a gray and sometimes garnetiferous gneiss and dips almost vertically with a slight inclination to the N.W.

The mica often occurs in crystals of very large size from which transparent plates varying from a few inches to a foot square can be cut. The mica is said to improve in quality at a depth and to lose the occasional red and chocolate colored spots which were sometimes found in it on the surface. A similar phenomenon is said to have been observed at the mica mines of North Carolina where the mica was often blemished near the surface but at a depth became much freer from imperfections. Compared with other micas this Villeneuve product is equal to any in the market not only in transparency but also in its power of resisting heat, and it is far superior to most micas now offered for sale. Three qualities of mica are shipped from the Villeneuve mine—divided according to their freedom from blemishes. The relative amounts of these grades produced is shown by the following figures given me by the manager of the mine:

From Feb. 4 to 22d, 1888, 400 lbs of cut mica were produced averaging $2.70 per lb. Of this 400 lbs, 286 lbs were first quality, 64 second and 50 third.

Uses of Mica

Cut mica is extensively used in the doors of stoves and the faces of lanterns and also in smaller quantities for various other purposes. The large consumption of mica is shown by the fact that though the Villeneuve mine now produces from 500 to 600 pounds of cut mica a month yet it is unable to supply even the Canadian market. By more extensive working of the deposit not only the Canadian demand could be supplied but also a large field could be found in the U. S. The present owners, however, on account of lack of capital are unable to work on a more extensive scale.

Scrap Mica

A large amount of scrap mica accumulates not only in mining the mica but also in the process of cutting it in the various sizes required for the market. This waste mineral is valuable in a ground state for many purposes, among which are lubricating purposes, fire proof paint, wall-paper, spangling and decorating. Markets in the U. S. can be found in New York, Cleveland, and other places and as much as $3\frac{1}{2}$ cents per pound is said to have been paid for this mineral in a ground state in Cleveland. The Cyclone mill has been found the best grinder for mica and it is claimed it can grind 3 tons per day.

The fact that both cut mica and scrap mica before being ground can go into the U. S. free of duty would render this Villeneuve mineral able to compete successfully against other micas in many of the American markets.

Feldspar

As mentioned above, one of the principal constituents of the mica-bearing vein is a pure white feldspar. Its great purity is shown by the following analysis by Mr. Thos M. Morgan:

Silica	64.7
Alumina	18.4
Magnesia	.3

Alkalis (potash and soda) not determined.

Iron and lime not present in determinable quantities.

The potash and soda have been determined by Prof. Donald as: Potash 11.46%, soda 4.04%.

This mineral has heretofore been considered worthless by the owners of the mine and is even yet being thrown on the dump in large quantities. Some 2000 tons have been collected in this way and though part of it has been exposed to the weather for 2 years it is still as white and free from stain as if it had just come out of the pit.

Such feldspar is extensively used in the manufacture of porcelain and chinaware—composing from 10% to 50% of the manufactured article. The amount used varies according to the character of the ware to be made. When ground to pass through a 130-mesh screen, it is worth $12 per ton at the numerous potteries in Trenton, N. J., and East Liverpool, Ohio. Samples of this spar have been shown by the writer to many of the manufacturers at these two places and its fusibility tested. Their judgment is that it is most excellent spar and suitable for use in even the finest qualities of porcelain. Some of them have made the unqualified statement that it is the finest feldspar they had ever seen and are very anxious to have it introduced in the market. The purity of feldspar is an item of very great importance in the manufacture of chinaware and this mineral on account of its great purity would have no trouble in competing with inferior articles now used and probably bringing a higher price. As Villeneuve feldspar is now a waste product, anything over the cost of grinding and freight would be profit.

Experiments are now being conducted to determine the expense of different methods of grinding and very reasonable freight rates to Trenton and East Liverpool are obtainable on account of the competition of water and rail transportation. As regards the consumption of the mineral, Trenton consumes annually about 10,000 tons, East Liverpool almost as much, and other potteries at Wheeling, W. Va., Brooklyn, St. Johns, Quebec and other places also use considerable quantities. As there is no duty on crude feldspar going into the U. S., it would—on account of its excellent quality—have many advantages over some of the poorer quality feldspars now used.

Quartz

Large quantities of very pure quartz also occur as one of the chief constituents of the mica-bearing vein, and are being continually thrown on the dump as worthless. This mineral is also extensively used in the manufacture of porcelain and chinaware and is worth only a dollar less, when ground to 130 mesh, per ton than the spar, or $11. About twice the quantity of quartz as of spar is used at the potteries of Trenton, East Liverpool and other places. The manufacturers at these places who have seen the quartz pronounce it of most excellent quality. Like feldspar and mica it can enter U. S. free. Finely ground quartz is also extensively used to harden soap. Many thousand tons are used annually for this purpose in Chicago and elsewhere and a market for the pure quartz of the Villeneuve mine might also be found with the soap makers.

Other Minerals

Besides the minerals already mentioned, other rarer ones also occur in the mica-bearing vein, which, though found in quantities far too small to pay to mine for themselves alone, might nevertheless be profitably saved. Among these are black tourmaline used as a second-grade emery and the minerals Uraninite and its de-hydrated form (Gummite) which are used in pottery, painting. $1 per lb. has been offered the owners of the mine for Uraninite.

Profits

From the above remarks it will be seen that this property differs from most mines in the fact that instead of producing only one marketable mineral, it produces three, mica, feldspar and quartz, besides the rarer minerals just mentioned. All these minerals occur in the same vein and all have to be blasted out in mining any one of them; so that instead of being dependent on one substance for profit there are three at least and the possible profit from the tourmaline, Uraninite and Gummite. This is a very important fact as in most mines large quantities of worthless rock have to be moved in order to win the ore or mineral sought after, whereas in the case in question a large part of the rock (feldspar and quartz) moved in mining the mica has a large and constantly increasing market.

The Villeneuve mine, as already mentioned, is being worked on a small scale on account of lack of capital and of the indefinite knowledge of the owners of the values of the other substances associated with the mica. I am informed by the manager of the mine that in the last $1\frac{1}{2}$ years, 7000 lbs of cut mica have been produced and this was done in simply opening the vein. Since Jan. 1, 1888, the monthly output of mica has been from 500 to 600 lbs with an average value of 2.50 to 2.75 per lb.—the price varying with the quality and size of the mica. I am also informed that the pay roll including the pay of every one connected with the mine has averaged since Jan. 1st/88, $900 monthly. Thus, calling the average output 550 pounds and average value 2.62\frac{1}{2}$ the monthly income would be $1443.75—showing a profit of $543.75 over the average pay sheet of $900. Outside of the pay sheet the running expenses of the mine are small as there is very little teaming, etc., etc., to be done. This profit was obtained from cut mica alone—neither scrap mica or by-products being sold. Of course while the mine is worked, as it is, by a small gang of men, the expense of management forms a large percentage of the pay sheet. The number of miners might be largely increased without in any way increasing the expense of management and thus the mining could be done proportionally cheaper. Now add to the profit of the cut mica, that of the ground mica, feldspar and quartz, or even let it be supposed that the cut mica only pays the running expenses of the mine, and that the profit is derived solely from the ground mica, feldspar and quartz, and it will be seen that a very handsome profit would be realized if the introduction of these last three products in the American market was energetically pushed.

Work done on Property

The only work done on the property consists of a large open pit some 60 ft. deep and 50–60 ft. in width and length. Feldspar and quartz are to be seen on all sides and in places the two minerals separate out from each other in seams and masses of great purity 10–20 ft. wide. The large crystals of mica generally occur in seams through this feldspar and quartz matrix though small crystals are found in various other parts of the vein.

Method of Work

The drilling is being done by air drills worked by a 3-drill Ingersoll air compressor and a 60 H.P. boiler. Hoisting is done by a small steam hoist. The mica after being blasted out is separated from the adhering rock and taken to the "cutting house" where it is sorted, split, separated in 3 grades and cut in sizes required for market. It is then taken to B'ham and shipped thence by rail to wherever desired.

Equipment

The property is well equipped for mining operations, though some few changes would have to be made for increased work. There is on it a boarding-house, stable, sheds, cutting house, boiler house, air compressor, boiler, hoist and all the tools necessary for mining operations. Labor is plentiful. Fuel and Timber for mining operations are abundant.

Penrose's notebooks of this period also show that he was employing his "extra" time in the study of the ores of the vicinity. One book carries a more or less detailed list of the Canadian molybdenite localities. At the back of the book, under date of September 11, 1886, is written:

"I hereby agree to allow R. A. F. Penrose, Jr., to mine molybdenite wherever found on my property in the township of Rose (West half of L7 R9) on a royalty of 3 cts. per pound for one year. I also agree to sell him the exclusive right to mine molybdenite on said property for the sum of $100, at any time during the year beginning Sept. 11, 1886."

His notebook of 1887 contains "Notes on Feldspars, etc., etc.; Renovo Clay deposits," and in the back of the book is his expense account from February 25 to October 10. This shows that he made journeys to Smiths Falls, New York, Boston, East Lancaster, Montreal, Ottawa, Brandywine, New Brunswick, and Bedford during that time. Most of the items concern carfare, pullman, meals, postage, and telegrams, for himself and Reid, although there is also brief mention of Willis and Phelan.

During his trips to Boston, he undoubtedly consulted with Shaler, for whom he ever manifested great admiration and affection and with whom he kept in close touch during the remainder of the life of the older man. With his everenduring interest in all that pertained to his sons, Dick's father shared in that regard. Among the Penrose letters is one from Mrs. Shaler to the elder Penrose, written from 13 Bow Street, Cambridge, and dated December 25th 1885. She writes:

"If I were to repeat to you half the pleasant things we said about you last night when the box of delicious candy arrived, I fear you would think it was literally a case of *taffy*, therefore rather than arouse any such suspicions, I shall only tell you that it made us very happy to be remembered by you and that we often think and talk of you in connection with the pleasant reminiscences of the past summer.

"I have been intending to write and thank Dick for the good care which he took of Gabnilla on her journey. I hope he is enjoying himself with you and has already regained some of the flesh which he lost during the autumn.

"It was very kind of you to wish Mr. Shaler and me to stop at Philadelphia on our way to Washington. This I fear will be impossible, but why cannot you join us there and encourage by your presence our wise men and patriots, as well as add to our pleasure, which I confess, is more to the point. Page and I are quite alone this Xmas, the others having wandered off in various directions. We both wish you and yours all the pleasure of the season."

After the death of Professor Shaler, Dick wrote to Mrs. Shaler in January, 1911, as follows:

"I have for a long time had a great desire to do something in honor of Professor Shaler at Harvard, and it would be a very great satisfaction to me to present to the University something to commemorate one whose memory I shall always cherish with the greatest regard and affection. They already have there a Shaler Research Fund, which probably serves a good cause, but I feel that I would like to see at Harvard a bronze bust of Professor Shaler, which future generations of students might come to see, and perhaps get some of the inspiration that those of us who worked under him got during his life.

"I would prefer to have an American artist do the work, as I think he could grasp the essential characteristics of Professor Shaler's nature better than a foreigner, but whatever his nationality, I would like to have the work done by the best artist obtainable.

"I am starting for a short trip to Europe next week, and I write now to ask if you are willing for me to go ahead in this matter if I can find a suitable artist in America or in Europe. I would not want to start the work without your consent.

"It seems a very long time since I have seen you, and I hope sometime to come to Washington to pay my respects."

Mrs. Shaler responded on January 26, 1911, that she "was very much touched by your letter in regard to the tribute you wish to pay my husband. A bronze bust I am sure would be most acceptable to the University and an appropriate testimony of your affection.

"You were very dear to Mr. Shaler and he often spoke of you with admiration and affection. . . . I wish very much you would come to Washington as it would give me great pleasure to talk over with you old times."

On January 30th, Penrose replied:

"I thank you very much for your kind letter of the 26th and am greatly pleased that you approve of the tribute I want to pay to the memory of Professor Shaler. The satisfaction that I shall take in the matter will be greatly increased by the knowledge that I have your approval of it. I will at once begin investigations to find out who is the best sculptor to make the bust. My ambition is that the work should be the very best that can be done, so that it may merit the approval of all those who had the good fortune to know Professor Shaler."

The sculptor who was eventually chosen was Robert I. Aitken, who became widely known for his work on the Supreme Court building in Washington, D. C.

Mr. Aitken made an original and three replica bronze busts of Professor Shaler, which Penrose distributed: one to Harvard, where it was placed in the Faculty Room; one to the State of Kentucky, of which Shaler was a native and where he served for a time as State Geologist; one to the Harvard Club of New York. The fourth copy Penrose kept in his office in Philadelphia, and after his death it was sent with the rest of his office equipment and library to The Geological Society of America in New York, where it now occupies a place of honor in the Society's headquarters. It was altogether fitting and proper, therefore, that the Geological Society, seeking to evidence its grateful appreciation of the magnificent gifts made to it by Penrose, should chose Robert Aitken to make the bronze bust of Penrose. Today, the companion busts—a great teacher and his successful pupil—stand side by side in the library gathered by the pupil.

In presenting the Shaler bust to the State of Kentucky, Penrose wrote:

"I greatly appreciate the privilege of being allowed to place this bust in Kentucky's beautiful Capitol, and to make this memorial, slight as it is, to one for whom I had the greatest respect, admiration, and affection. The world needs more men like him.

"If this bust serves to impart to even a few people a little of the noble spirit of the man whom it represents, I will feel that a great good has been accomplished for humanity."

In passing, it is worth noting that with his invariable modesty, Penrose refused to be present at the formal unveiling of any of these busts, contenting himself, when requested to be present and make an address, with a graceful letter proffering his gift, but apparently fearful lest attention be drawn to him at a time when he felt all attention should be focussed upon his great teacher.

John E. Wolff, who knew Penrose in his Harvard days, in a letter to Charles P. Berkey, dated February 10, 1939, remarked on that same life-long characteristic of Penrose. He said:

"It is sixty years since I first knew him at Harvard ... One or two incidents have remained in my memory. One is his modesty, unusual in one of great accomplishments in science and otherwise. This incident was at one of the G.S.A. dinners, when he made me sit next to him at the speakers' table, and as the time approached for his address turned to me in almost a panic and asked 'What am I to say?'.

"The other incident illustrates his independence and firmness in what he considered best. After Professor Shaler's death a number of his old students formed a memorial fund for research. Penrose refused to subscribe to that, saying to me that he thought it a shame to work Shaler's memory for any such project, and instead he had a bronze bust prepared by a sculptor and placed in the Harvard Faculty room, where I suppose it still is."

Years later (August 20, 1928) Penrose prepared the following statement concerning the Shaler bust:

In Re Bust of Professor N. S. Shaler

In 1906 my friend and old instructor in Geology, Professor N. S. Shaler of Harvard University, died after a short illness. Almost immediately his associate at Harvard, Professor W. M. Davis, commenced a violent raid on the old friends and other associates of Professor Shaler to raise a research fund to be named after him. This effort was nothing new but was one that had long been practised on the friends of any man who had died prominent in his profession. It was really an effort to commercialize the memory of a man who had spent his life in teaching his chosen subject.

Professor Davis wrote to me asking for a contribution to his research fund, and I promptly replied that I did not approve of commercializing the memory of a dead friend who had devoted most of his life to teaching geology. I might add here parenthetically that Davis was like most university professors in pretending to despise the acquisition of money.

I told Davis that I would be very glad to contribute to a life-size bronze bust of Professor Shaler, to be placed in the Harvard University yard, where it would stand forever as an inspiration to future generations of students in representing a man who was pre-eminently a scholar, a man of action and constructive accomplishments, and in his sympathetic attitude a remarkable source of good advice and assistance to his students. Davis replied to me that he had received many suggestions regarding the use to which the memorial fund might be put, but nothing quite so absurd as mine. I made no reply to this letter, for I thought that a man who would make such a statement was no fit person with whom to discuss such a subject. A few years later, therefore, I employed the well-known sculptor Robert Aitken, of New York, to make a bronze bust of Professor Shaler, and I did this with the consent of his wife and with the approval of his friends—except those like Davis, who wished to commercialize his memory instead of making it an inspiration to others.

The bust was in due time completed and was declared by everyone to be a most excellent likeness. I wrote to President Lowell at Harvard, offering to present it to Harvard University and he accepted it in a most gracious manner. It was immediately put in the Faculty Room in University Hall, where it has now stood for some fifteen or eighteen years.

Immediately after the completion of this bust the Governor of Kentucky expressed the desire to have a bronze replica made of it to be put in the Capitol at Frankfort, and as Professor Shaler was a native of Kentucky I thought this an especially appropriate place for his bust. I therefore had Mr. Aitken make a second replica, which now stands in the Kentucky Capitol with the busts of Henry Clay, Daniel Boone, and many other noted men of that State. It is in charge of the Kentucky Historical Society, and will be given careful attention.

Shortly after presenting a replica of the Shaler bust to the State of Kentucky, I was asked by the Harvard Club of New York to present one to them, on the plea that the Club was the largest Harvard Club in the United States, and that they thought a bust of Professor Shaler should properly be among their various Harvard collections. This thought appeared to me entirely proper, and again I had Mr. Aitken make a third bronze replica, which now stands on the mantlepiece in the Reading Room, facing 44th Street in the Harvard Club of New York.

I might say here that only a few weeks before the death of Howard Elliot, a former president of the Northern Pacific Railroad and of sundry New England railroads, and at that time president of the Harvard Club, he wrote to me expressing his gratification that this bust of Professor Shaler had been given to the Harvard Club of New York by me some years before.

At the same time as I had the bronze replica made for the Harvard Club of New York, I asked Mr. Aitken to make a fourth replica, and this now stands in my office at the Bullitt Building, Philadelphia, Pa. After this last bust was completed the model from which it and the others had been made was, at my request, destroyed, my idea being that enough copies of it had been made, and I did not want it to fall into the hands of people who might be entirely unsympathetic with the man it represented, and who might wish a copy of it simply out of idle curiosity.

It is of interest at this late date to note that in a letter to me dated November 23, 1912, Professor W. M. Davis, who had a few years previously declared that my suggestion of a bronze bust of Professor Shaler was absurd, wrote me stating that 'Not till yesterday had I chance of seeing the bust of Shaler which now stands in the Faculty Room through your kindness. It is an excellent likeness, and a fine memorial.'

In the matter of memorials, Penrose did not change his opinions greatly with the passing years, for in January, 1928, he wrote to Charles P. Berkey:

"Concerning the Kemp Memorial Fund, I would say that I had the greatest regard for Professor Kemp, and he and I even from boyhood had been close friends. I feel, however, as I have felt in other cases, that Professor Kemp after having spent such a great number of years in teaching at Columbia University, should be memorialized by something less material than a Research Fund. His long and efficient work at Columbia should exempt his memory from being commercialized for the sake of a few mere dollars which would go to the educational departments of Columbia University.

"I would gladly subscribe for a life-size bronze statue of Professor Kemp anywhere that your Committee might think proper, but it grates on my conscience to use the memory of one of my closest friends for material purposes. I think something more dignified would be more appropriate to his memory and would have a far better moral and intellectual effect on the students who saw it, than on the one student who might enjoy the small pittance received from an endowment fund.

"I have written plainly about this matter because I acted in the same way with the Shaler Memorial Fund. I refused to concur in commercializing his memory, but I suggested a full life-size bronze statue; but the advocates of a research fund would listen to nothing else. For this reason I had a bronze statue of Professor Shaler made at my own expense and presented it to Harvard University, where it now stands at the head of the Faculty Room, and is an inspiration not only to geologists who may look at it, but to those who realize the broad humanitarian instincts for which Shaler was given the degree of LL.D. at Harvard.

"I know that you and the rest of your Committee will in all probability unanimously object to my proposition as regards the monument to Professor Kemp."

Of Shaler himself, Penrose said in a letter to J. E. Spurr, dated January 13, 1921:

"I was a student under Shaler over a third of a century ago and I can well remember how many smug, self-satisfied workers in science sneered at him for daring to popularize the study of geology and take it out of the cloister of the recluse. Professor Shaler often spoke smilingly to me about this criticism, and after lighting his famous long-stemmed pipe, which reached to his knees, would tell me that the time was coming when such work as he was doing in popularizing geology would become essential in all sciences.

"Shaler was not only a student of pure science, but he was a philosopher and a far-sighted prophet of the needs of ages to come. When Harvard University bestowed on him the degree of LL.D. it was for his wonderful work as a 'humanitarian'; and so far as I know this was the first and last time that Harvard has honored a scientist for such qualifications. Shaler during his life was often ridiculed; Shaler today, a quarter of a century after his death, is highly honored, and as ages go by, he will be more and more respected as one who could clearly see the beacon light of the future when others were groping in the dark."

CHAPTER 5

Texas in the Early Days

"IN 1888 I was appointed by the State of Texas geologist in charge of the eastern section of that State and I left Canada to accept this appointment," continue the Penrose *Memoirs*. "I went first to Austin, the capital of the State, to meet Mr. E. T. Dumble, who was Director of the Survey, and to prepare for my work."

The story of how young Penrose—he was at this time twenty-five years old—got the Texas appointment, is told by Robert T. Hill, long identified with Texas geology, both as a member of the Texas Survey and as professor at the University of Texas, in a personal letter to J. Stanley-Brown,* dated March 23, 1932, as follows:

"I was intimately associated with Doctor R. A. F. Penrose, Jr., during the first undertaking of his scientific career, and was instrumental in procuring for him his first professional engagement as a geologist after his graduation from Harvard University. It came about as follows: With youthful enthusiasm and the backing of Major J. W. Powell, at that time Director of the United States Geological Survey, I undertook, in 1887, the task of trying to establish a State Geological Survey in Texas and a Chair of Geology in the University of Texas at Austin. After the lobbying vicissitudes of two stormy sessions of the Legislature the Geological Survey bill was finally passed, and Major Powell was requested to recommend a suitable person for the office of State Geologist. Through sad misfortune the request reached Washington when the Major was absent on a vacation with Dr. Alexander Graham Bell in Nova Scotia. A bad mix-up in nominations resulted and I received a telegram from the appointed power to come to Austin. To straighten matters out I hurried to Washington only to find that Major Powell was still absent as well as Doctor W J McGee, who was the Major's adjutant in the handling of such affairs. Then the happy thought occurred to me of sending a telegram to Professor Nathaniel Shaler, at Harvard, inquiring for a suitable man. His reply was that he had just the person for me, and was sending him to Washington to interview me. Promptly a fine, husky, rosy-cheeked, athletic-looking young man appeared with a letter from the Professor, and that was my first sight of R. A. F. Penrose, Jr.

"I explained to him the peculiar and now somewhat involved problem by reason of a name having been suggested by others which was not acceptable to the Texas authorities.

* Stanley-Brown, J.: *Memorial of Richard Alexander Fullerton Penrose, Jr.*, Geol. Soc. Am., Bull., vol. 43 (1932), p. 68–108.

"We decided that the best and only thing to do was for Penrose to find Major Powell in Nova Scotia and deliver a letter from me explanatory of the situation and requesting him to recommend Penrose in the place of the undesired nominee. This was accomplished as fast as a train could carry Penrose to the Major's presence and I hastened back to Austin with the new nomination for the proper authority. I was met with the statement, 'Mr. Hill, it is too late. During the interval since I last saw you, the previous nominee has worked up a sentiment that the appointee must be a resident of the State.' Accompanying his remarks he handed me a bunch of letters from 125 applicants, including men of every known profession except geologists, and requested that I study these and recommend to him the most suitable man. After looking over the papers carefully I found the name of only one applicant who seemed to have the least idea of what the office was to be or who had received a post-Civil War college education. This man, whom I recommended, was E. T. Dumble, who conducted the office for four years with ability. One of his first acts was the appointment, on my recommendation, of Doctor Penrose as his first assistant, and thus in the fall of 1888 he began his professional career in Texas.

"Coincidentally with the beginning of the Texas State Survey work and the coming of Doctor Penrose to Texas, I had accepted a position to teach geology in the University of Texas, and located with my family at Austin, where for more than a year I worked in close association with Dumble and Penrose, at the same time continuing and directing the studies of the Cretaceous formations in cooperation with the Survey.

"Doctor Penrose's work chiefly consisted of the study of the Tertiary formations of the eastern part of the State, to the knowledge of which he made valuable contributions, as testified by his publications thereon. Likewise, he made a special investigation of the iron ores of east Texas, which were derived from extensive glauconite formations. He also made several interesting and valuable cross-section reconnaissances by rowboat down the rivers of southwest Texas.

"At intervals he would come into Austin, where he always made my house his place of recreation and became a great social favorite with my wife and myself. This habit he continued when, later, we resumed our home in Washington. In this manner we learned to appreciate and love the man and his splendid, genial disposition.

"Before the invention of rapid transit by means of good roads and automobiles, east Texas, nearly fifty years ago, was anything but a happy hunting ground for the tenderfoot geologist, especially if he was from the land of Harvard College. Besides the almost unendurable discomforts of insects, heat and not always good water, facilities for travel and stopping places were poor at best. Likewise at that time, before the South commenced to recover from the war, and when fundamentalism was a little more fundamental than now, the people were prone to regard geology and geologists in a somewhat contemptuous way. Even to this day, when considering the conditions as they then were, I wonder how Doctor Penrose endured the brunt of field work in that environment. Only a man of his rare tact in getting along with all kinds and conditions of people, and one of his strong athletic microbe-resisting constitution, could have accomplished the task. Three other young men drawn from Harvard at about the same time became ill or discouraged and gave up the jobs.

"Due to his good breeding and early associations, Penrose possessed the art of self-control and the ability to avoid needless discussions and arguments to a degree greater than any man I have ever met. He certainly knew how to avoid trouble in a land where nearly every man he met was ready to start an argument against the teachings of geology, on the subjects of politics or religion, and on the still-slumbering disagreements relative to the sides engaged in the Civil war.

"His temperament was always sunny and cheerful, and, at times, almost jovial, and he greatly enjoyed playing small and harmless jokes upon his more intimate friends. One day, observing that I had a habit of wetting small rock or fossil specimens with my tongue, unknown to me, he doctored up a specimen of a fossil shell in his possession with as strong a decoction of nicotine as it would carry and passed the specimen to me with the request that I examine it. Promptly I passed it to my mouth, and tasting the nicotine, as promptly spat it out, greatly to his merriment, and to my education, for the habit was broken then and there.

"There had been a lapse of twenty years in our meetings when I last saw him at the annual dinner of the Society, at the Wardman Hotel in Washington, in December, 1930. Time, wealth and prosperity had made but little change in the man whom I had first met as a boyish college graduate some forty-five years before. God bless his memory, for he was one of the finest of a choice few of fine men whom I have known. He had naught but kind thoughts to think and kind words to say. In him were combined all the good things that the opportunities of inheritance, education, both physical and mental, and wealth and breeding could bestow. Besides all these qualifications he was devoid of any sissylike qualities and was what we term, in the free language of our Southwest, 'a man with the bark on.' "

Penrose's own version of his Texas sojourn, as set forth in his *Memoirs*, is as follows:

"The eastern part of Texas is largely a low-lying country, and near the coast of the Gulf of Mexico it is studded with immense swamps full of malarial and other mosquitoes. In such a region it is hard to see the rocks or other formations comprising the ground because they are usually covered by a dense growth of trees or low brush. Fortunately, however, this eastern part of the State is intersected by numerous large rivers, including the Red River on the north, and, farther south, the Sabine River, the Trinity River, the Brazos River, the Colorado River, and finally, on the border of Mexico, the great Rio Grande. All these rivers intersect the stratification of the rocks in a general cross direction, and hence in their bluffs are often found splendid exposures of the formations comprising the country. It was from observations in such places that I did most of my geologic work in eastern Texas.

"When I left Austin for my field of operation I knew just about nothing about making a geological survey, for though in those days we were taught a good deal of geology in the classroom, and were occasionally taken on field excursions, yet we were not trained in starting in an almost unknown region to study its geology. Eastern Texas had never been studied geologically to any important extent, and at first I wondered how in the world a geological survey was to be started. When this thought came to me I was sitting on one of the bluffs of the Brazos River with my legs hanging down toward the water, and looking over to the other side of the river to see if I could find any enlightenment as to the requirements of my job. All was in vain, however, until it suddenly occurred to me that if I was so ignorant as not to know how to make a geological survey, I might at least make a record of what composed the material on which I was sitting. It turned out to be a hard indurated glauconite and I made a note of this in my heretofore blank notebook, and made a mark on my map to indicate the place the note referred to. The stratification of the rock ran almost flat, and it occurred to me to see if the same formation could be found on the other side, and that if such was the case I could say that the river had probably cut through the formation, and that the bluffs on both sides showed the same rock. I promptly took off my clothes, put them on my head, and swam across the river, where I found to my great satisfaction that the same rock was cropping out in the opposite bluffs. I mention these facts simply because they were the first start toward my conception of what a geological survey should be, and from utter ignorance of the procedure to be followed I had suddenly, in a few minutes, grasped what had to be done.

"During the two years that I remained in Texas I navigated all the rivers of the eastern part of that State, studying the formation in the bluffs. It is needless to go through the details of all this work, which was somewhat laborious and which resulted in my getting so thoroughly saturated with malaria that I have found ever since then that I have been immune, even in the worst malarial districts of the tropics throughout various parts of the world."

A more intimate picture of that life is preserved in the letters which the young geologist wrote to his father in Philadelphia, that father who was interested in everything which concerned his boys.

Letter from Dick to his father, dated Mineola, Wood County, Texas, December 2, 1888

Your letter of Nov. 23d was forwarded to me from Austin and I was very glad to hear from you. I left Austin on Nov. 14th and have since been exploring northeastern Texas, travelling sometimes by rail but more often on horseback or in a wagon. I arrived here last night and start today for the country south of the Sabine River, where I will be for about 10 days and will then return to Austin to prepare my report for the next meeting of the legislature. This is such a big country that my first report will only be a very general one, but I will make a more detailed one later in the winter. I have already travelled over and explored the larger part of four counties, and as a county here is as big as some of the eastern states it means a good deal of work. I get along with the people here first rate. They are not such a tough outfit as they are made out to be. Of course, if a man wants to fight he can find plenty of citizens who will accommodate him. In a town I was in west of here a few days ago there was a man slit open with a knife, but he deserved it as he tried to brain the other fellow with a club. But there is rarely any necessity for a man to fight unless he tries to raise a row.

I think the geological survey will be of great service to this state as the people are more ignorant of what they have got than any I ever saw. Each man thinks he has a gold mine on his property, but beyond this they have no idea what they have. The few farmers and planters scattered through the country know how to raise cotton and nothing else. They depend entirely on this one crop for money to buy what they eat and wear, and when the cotton crop is poor—and it seems to be poor every year—they have to borrow money at 15 to 20% interest. The result of this is that all the planters are broke, their farms mortgaged for all they can get and many of them half starved. In almost every small town I go into I see some farmer's outfit of mules, wagons, etc., being sold by the sheriff. The soil is well adapted for raising all the grains, vegetables, etc., that a farmer could use, but they do not know how to raise them and are too lazy to learn, so they keep on raising only cotton and lose more money every year. They are the most obliging people to a man travelling through the country that I ever met, but they are so lazy that it often makes progress over the country very slow. Some people ascribe this laziness to fornicating niggers too much and this is a very popular act throughout the country, but some of the laziest men I have met are men who confine themselves strictly to white lady fornication or who only fornicate black ladies when they are driven to it by absolute necessity—such as when the white lady's husband is at home. So the nigger theory is no good.

The geological Survey includes not only the investigation of the mineral wealth of the state, but also an examination of soils and the determination of what crops they are best suited for, and what fertilizers they will be apt to need. Also the subject of irrigation and artesian wells. In this way the survey will be of use not only to the owner of mineral lands, but also to the farmer, the owner of arid lands and the owner of good artesian well sites.

We have had a few heavy frosts since I have been here, but the weather has at no time been cold. It is always warm in the middle of the day—just like Phila. weather in October.

I will be in Austin at the time the legislature meets to help get the appropriation. I know several of the members and state senators already and think we have a fair chance of getting it. There is a good deal of kicking among the country members who think a geologist and a raving maniac are the same thing—but I notice that even the farmers are glad to get their soils examined and to be told the best place to bore wells. However, I am cultivating the men who have a finger in the business and guess we can fix the kickers.

I was told when I passed thro' Washington on my way south that my phosphate paper would be out *sure* this month. Will you send some copies when it is out.

If you would like to travel through this state or anywhere through this country during the coming winter I will meet you any place you like. You will find this is a grand part of the country, and if the natives had not been so lazy it would have been booming long ago.

I have not yet heard from Speck about when he is going to Phila but expect to soon. Will write you when I get to Austin and let you know when I can go out to Las Cruces. Will try to go as soon as possible after my return to Austin.

There is a book I would like to get and cannot get in Texas. It is entitled "Chemical and Geological Essays" by T. Sterry Hunt. I would like to have it to refer to in writing up my reports. If it is not too much trouble for you to get it for me and send it by mail I would be very much obliged to you. You might be able to get a second-hand copy at Leary's, which would answer just as well as a new one. My address is always care of State Geological Survey, Austin, Texas. They forward my mail wherever I happen to be.

P.S. Tyler, Texas, Dec. 3/88. Arrived here last night from Mineola. Have received a letter from Reid saying that he was sick in N. Y., that he had had a row with the men who had promised to organize our company as soon as the election was over. I don't know what this means, but it seems to me like damned imbecility on Reid's part—as I understood from him before I came down here that he had everything fixed. Have written him for further particulars.

What sort of a venture he had in mind with Reid the correspondence does not show. In any event, it did not materialize, although there is further reference to it in his letters. From this experience, however, he learned a lesson which he steadfastly applied to his conduct thereafter—when he wanted a thing done, he did it himself.

His reason for going to Las Cruces (New Mexico) was that his brother Spencer was at that time in business there, in partnership with W. E. Laurence. Their letter-head bore the statement: "Mesilla Valley Fruit and Produce Co., wholesale and retail dealers in fruits, vegetables, hay, grain, coal, lime, agricultural implements, stoves, etc."

Dick obviously made the journey to see Speck, for on January 13, 1889 he wrote again to his father from Rusk, Texas, on stationery bearing the insignia, "State of Texas, Office of Commissioner of Agriculture, Insurance, Statistics, and History. L. L. Foster, Commissioner. B. B. Brewster, Chief Clerk." On this letter is written, evidently by his father, "Dick. Jan. 89. Admirable letter—kept in consequence."

"I received your letter of Dec. 31 on my arrival here today—it having been forwarded to me from Austin. I wrote to you from Corsicana several days ago and suppose you have received my letter by this time. As I told you then Cruces is a wretched hole and though Speck has got a commission business which will grow in time, I do not see how it can ever be a very big thing. Of course living in a new country such as New Mexico is, he has a chance to see opportunities, but this is a very uncertain thing to count on—especially when opportunities can be seen as well in better countries. The country around Las Cruces is absolutely dependent on irrigation for existence and the irrigation canals are in the hands of a lot of Americanized Mexicans and Jews, who let the irrigation improvements go to the devil and pocket the money. The result is that the subject of irrigation and hence the welfare of Las Cruces and all the surrounding country is in a very uncertain condition. The friends of Cruces say that all these things will rectify themselves and that people will not stand poor irrigation facilities when they pay for good ones. Perhaps these things *will* be righted, but, as I understand it, they have been going on in this way ever since New Mexico was taken from Old Mexico and the probability is that they will go on in the same way for some time to come. Last year Congress appropriated $100,000 for an investigation of the irrigation question in the Southwest—with a view to establishing a storage system for water in rainy seasons and the cutting of irrigation canals. But this work will necessarily be slow and probably even after the commission, which is under the direction of the U. S. Survey (Geol.) has made its report, it will be left to private enterprise to do the practical part. Even supposing the Rio Grande valley was well irrigated—a thing that would require a long time and a great deal of cash—I cannot see how Las Cruces would ever be a great center for anything but the fruit and produce of the surrounding farms. The products of the country to the south of it would go to El Paso, those of the country to the north would go to Santa Fe, Las Vegas, Albuquerque and other places nearer the markets. To the east and west of Las Cruces are *deserts* and mountains —many of which it would be impossible to irrigate. Consequently Cruces is shut off on the east and west by deserts and mountains and on the north and south by large railroad centers which will take all possible trade from it. Of course, the mining interests in the mountains near Cruces may sometime be important as bringing trade to the town, but these are very uncertain things to count on.*

"I should advise Speck to hold his lands at Cruces until he can get a good price for them, as they will undoubtedly sometime be far more valuable than now, and I should also advise him *not* to stay there himself but to start up in a better place. I think it would be worth both your while and his to look seriously into the cement business that I wrote you about. I feel sure there is a big thing in it. I wrote you full particulars about it in my last letter. My idea would be for Speck to raise the money in Phila if possible. I have sent him a prospectus written by Prof. Hill today. It shows the objects of the scheme and could be altered to suit promoters. You will see on the last page of it that Hill has put my name in for a share of the promoters' profits. I will give Speck my share and let his name replace mine in the prospectus if he wishes to take hold of the thing. I would like to take hold of it myself but so long as I hold my present position I have not time to do it. Besides, I have entire confidence in Speck's ability to work the thing. The nerve and energy that he has shown in working against obstacles in Las Cruces, show what he could do if he had a fair show. He has worked as hard as any man could work and has had to contend with a lot of damned suckers and Jews who would have discouraged most men from doing anything.

"I have never had any experience in the cement business and all I know about

---

* In 1940, the population of Las Cruces was still only 5811.

it is what I have heard; so, if Speck should think of taking hold of the thing, he should first investigate the business thoroughly and visit some of the places where it is made and learn all about their methods. I have thought seriously of resigning my position on the Survey and help work the scheme myslef, but I do not think it could be in better hands than Speck's and I am willing to let him have all the share of the profits for promoting the thing that I would have got if I had done it. Speck and Hill together can work it up and make a good deal out of it.

"I hope Philip has got better since he has gone home. He said he felt in wretched condition when in El Paso and he acted as if he really was, but I could not tell what was the matter with him. If he wants to come back to Texas I will be very glad to have him with me and will write to Dumble and insist on having him as my assistant. I have got a stronger foothold in the Survey than when I came here and will insist on Philip's having a position if he wants it. There are many hardships in the work and a man has to live often on very poor food. I don't know how he would like this, but if he would take any interest in the work he would be all right. I would see that he did not have any work too hard for him and with the exception of having to sleep in bed sometimes with two or three other men and of poor food, he would not have a bad time. When he was in El Paso he spent most of his time hanging about a drug store kept by a friend of his and did not seem to have any desire whatever to do anything else— except to get home to Phila. He said he felt faint if he tried to do anything and this seemed to be his principal ailment. Speck and I went to see a bull fight in Paso del Norte, on the Mexican side of the Rio Grande, on Xmas day, but Philip did not take enough interest in things even to go to that—though we tried to persuade him to go. I also tried to persuade him to stay here with me, but he would not do it. He seemed bent on going home and disgusted with the west.

"I am on the move the whole time and am rarely in one place for over two days at a time! I have been working hard to get the U. S. Survey to make some maps of eastern Texas and thus save our survey considerable money. I have got the chief geographer of the U. S. Survey interested and have left it with Dumble to settle the rest. If he works it right we will get good maps to do our geological work on for almost nothing.

"Reid writes that he expects to float our scheme in Chicago. I have lost all confidence in him since he let it fall through in N. Y., and don't know what in the devil he will do. What I do know, however, is that he will never have the working of any other scheme that I am interested in. The N. Y. men must have worked him for a complete softy—though he does not give a clear account of his row with them. He may possibly do something in Chicago and may have learned some sense, but I have no patience with such imbecility as he has shown.

"You say you want an estimate of what I spent on the New Mexico trip. Including my own expenses there and back and what I spent for Speck's and Philip's expenses from El Paso to Austin and what I gave them to get from Austin to Phila., it amounted in all to about $200. But there is no reason whatever why you should send me this money as you gave me money to go to Cruces with when

I was in Phila and I cashed at El Paso a check of yours for $100 which you gave me when I left Phila, so that all the money I used was yours.

"As I said in my last letter, I received the book you sent and am very much obliged for it. My address is, as always, Geological Survey, Austin, Texas.

"I wish you would try to take a trip out here this winter. I think you would like to see the country. I would get leave of absence from the survey and show you about the country, which I know pretty well now."

Letter from Dick to his father, dated Rusk, Cherokee Co., Texas, Jan. 28/89

I returned here today from an expedition in the marshes of the Neches River and have just received your letter of Jan. 11th with checks for $350, for which I am very much obliged to you. They more than cover all I spent.

I was glad to hear by your letter that Speck and Philip arrived safely in Phila.

As you say, there is nothing to prevent another company from starting up in opposition in the cement business as the deposits are found in several places in Texas, but then the first Co. that gets in will have the best show and there is probably no more competition in the cement business than in most others. The value of the deposits is as yet unknown except to us as they have not been explored by cement men.

I have been for the last week down in the marshes between the Neches and Angelina Rivers. It rained most of the time I was there and the country was flooded for several days—so much so that we had to swim rivers on horseback, etc. The thickets were so dense that we had to cut through the vines, etc., in many places to get on. One day it was raining so hard that I could not do my work, as my maps and notebooks would have been ruined, so I went on a deer hunt. In four hours we scared up seven deer and killed one. Fresh venison tasted first rate as we had been living on corn meal and pork. I would have sent you some deer meat, but the weather was warm and I knew it would not keep. One of the worst northers of the winter came up as I was crossing the top of a mountain separating the marsh country from here, on my way back to Rusk. I had got half way across the mt. and there was hardly a breath of wind blowing. Suddenly there was a rumbling sound, the mist shot off the mt. as if it had been blown up by dynamite, several trees fell and the wind was blowing about 55 miles an hour. I was alone, and the rain beat so hard in my horse's face that I had considerable difficulty in getting him down the slope on this side of the mt. My saddle bags, which were full of rocks, flapped about like feathers in the wind. I arrived in Rusk after a journey of about 10 miles from the top of the mt.

I am very sorry that I have forgotten to write to Jimmy Pierce about that whiskey, but will write to him at once. I hope Speck has recovered from his fever. He ought to present the New Mexico menagerie he had on his body to the Zoological Gardens.

What about Philip? If he wants to come down here I will get him on the survey. I wish you would arrange to take a trip down here yourself this winter. You would like the country and the winter is exceptionally mild so far this year.

Letter from Dick to his father, dated Palestine, Texas, March 14/89

I received your letter of Feb. 26 after writing to you last week and was very glad to hear from you.

I am going to Austin today and hope to see Speck there. I wrote him some time ago to Phila asking him to stop over there on his way to Cruces and have not yet heard from him. But I have just received a letter from Dumble, the State Geologist, saying that as he was looking for me to arrive in Austin every day he was holding my mail there for me, so I may have a letter from Speck when I get there.

I will not be sorry to get to Austin for a while, as I have a tremendous quantity of specimens which I have shipped there in the last 3 months and will have to have them arranged and classified, and have our chemists analyse many of them.

I have been for the last week in the Trinity River country and will make preparations later in the season to make a long journey down the river by canoe or row boat to the Gulf. But before doing that I have a lot of work to do along the Red River and the Rio Grande. The Trinity is usually a small river only about 100 yards in the widest part. Like most Texas rivers it is not much wider near its mouth than near its source though it is probably considerably over 1000 miles long. But just now, on account of a "little shower" that we had and that lasted four days, it is much swollen and in places is over three miles wide. I don't wonder they have the terrible floods here that you may remember occurred at Sabine Pass, the mouth of the Sabine River, a few years ago. The country for several miles on each side of the river is low and easily innundated. As it is very fertile it is in places well settled up and the settlers once in a while get a ducking. Judging from the amount of drift wood, fence rails, etc., now floating down the Trinity I guess some one has got a ducking this time too. But the hilly country back from the rivers is as fine a farming country as you ever saw and yet you can travel for many miles in some places without seeing a soul. I don't see why this region has not been settled as it is superior to the North West for farmers—at least in the way of climate. It must be due to the undeserved tough name that Texas bears. The people who are here are generally settlers from the older southern states and all they know is how to raise cotton. They know no more about farming than the man in the moon. Their chief characteristics are hospitality and laziness.

I have already written to Jimmy Pierce about that whiskey but have not yet received an answer. Perhaps there may be one waiting for me in Austin. I told him to have a barrel of the kind he gets sent to you by express, C.O.D. or otherwise, as the dealers wished. So you can expect it to come along any time. Will let you know as soon as I hear from him.

I will keep my eyes open for a horse such as you speak of. I know of one in Jacksonville that I think would suit you and the next time I go there will try him. I don't know whether he can be bought, but cash will get almost any horse in Texas and $300 or $400 is a tremendous price here. Will also look out for others. The trouble here is to get a horse of any size. Most of them are small. But the Jacksonville one is about the size of Macgoffin.

I have not seen my phosphate bulletin yet but will send you some copies soon as I get to Austin. I have 150 copies there which are more than I need. You speak of the position of the Ph.D. in it. That was the doings of the U. S. Survey as in my manuscript and in correcting proof I put it everywhere after my name. Will write from Austin.

Three days later (March 17, 1889) Penrose again wrote to his father, this time from Austin, Texas, on stationery marked "The Driskill":

I received your letters of the 6th and 9th on my arrival here Friday. I arrived Friday morning and Speck arrived Friday afternoon, a pretty close connection considering the fact that neither of us knew when the other would arrive. I was very glad to see Speck looking so much better than when he left here in December. He left here today (Sunday) for Cruces. While he was here we came to an agreement with Hill about the cement business, by which Speck is to settle his business as soon as possible in Cruces and come back here. Then he and Hill are to take a short trip up to Dallas and find the best place to locate cement works and get an option on the property. All that will be left to do then will be to write a prospectus and get the capital. I think Dallas—or near there—is the place to locate as it is the greatest R.R. center in the state, is a prosperous town of 50,000 people and growing fast. Speck did not know exactly how he would settle up at Cruces but I advised him to get out soon as he could and he seems anxious to do so. He thinks he can possibly sell out on good terms or else sell out part and take a mortgage for the rest. At any rate he seems determined to get out of the place and thinks that in the course of a month he can arrange everything.

There has been a big row in parts of eastern Texas about my report on the iron ores. Men who owned worthless iron ore properties kicked because I did not say they were sufficiently rich to warrant the erection of blast furnaces. There are many good iron ore lands in East Texas and the men who own these are well pleased because I have published a favorable report. But the owners of the poor lands are very mad. Many of the local papers publish very strong articles blaspheming me, but I have the backing of much stronger and more generally distributed papers and am therefore all right. Both the Dallas News and the Galveston News—the two most influential papers in the state—have published very favorable articles about my work. A Jefferson paper came out in a column and a half article abusing me in the strongest terms and demanding my discharge, etc., etc. The editor is interested in the development of certain iron lands. The article was so abusive and the arguments so absolutely without foundation and illogical that I knew there would be a reaction against the damned idiot and it came. He called an indignation meeting of the citizens of Jefferson to pass resolutions and demand of the legislature that I be discharged. Instead of passing such resolutions they all jumped on the editor and expressed their disapproval of his articles. I saw the state senator from Jefferson today and he said the editor was a damned fool.

Several other parties have demanded that I withdraw certain statements that I made but I have absolutely refused to do this in any case as I have not published anything that is not true and that cannot be proved. I have intimated to all of them that if they did not like what I reported they could go to Hell and that they were at liberty to prove that I was wrong if they could.

All this row has done me much more good than harm and will strengthen the survey with business men as it shows that it has not been bluffed into making statements suited to advance a lot of bottomless schemes. The state geologist of Arkansas [J. C. Branner] has had the same experience and in one place he was burned in effigy. All the same he will probably have this coming year over three times the appropriation he had last year. Our legislature is now in session and they have been several days squabbling over our survey bill. Some want to kill it altogether but I think the majority are for continuing it and we will probably get between $25,000 and $35,000 per year for the next two years.

I wrote you from Palestine on Thursday about Jimmy Pierce's whiskey. I have not yet got an answer from him though I wrote some time ago. He may be away as he generally goes to Baltimore for a week or so in the spring, but as soon as I hear from him I will let you know. In the meantime you can expect the whiskey to come along any time as I wrote him to have a barrel such as he gets sent to you by express—C.O.D. or otherwise, as the dealers wished. I will see that Jacksonville horse I wrote you about the next time I go there and will look out for one in other places also.

I have not yet determined what to do about the Arkansas Survey, but do not think I can take the job at present, as I am full of work here. My part of Texas includes 90,000 square miles—an area over twice the size of the state of Ohio—and travelling over it takes a lot of time. Though there is not quite so much money in it, it is a better position than the Arkansas one.

So many people have been asking me for copies of my phosphate bulletin that I find I am coming near the end of the pile of 150 copies that I bought. For this reason I have not sent you any of this lot but have written the U. S. Survey to send you 100 copies, as you suggest. They will not send things C.O.D. but require the money to be sent when the books are ordered. Therefore, I have sent them a post-office order for $15 which is the amount at 15 cents per copy for 100 copies. They will probably reach you in a few days. I have sent copies to most men I know where I think they would do good. If you will send some to some of the fertilizer manufacturers in Phila I would be much obliged. I have not sent any to them as I do not know their addresses but you can find them in the directory.

I am preparing to make a series of journeys down some of the principal Texas rivers by boat. I will buy boats at the heads of the rivers and sell them when I get at my destination or else set them adrift, as it would take too long to return upstream with them. I will return by horseback—or railroad when possible. If I get to the Gulf in any of the trips I can always return on a fishing boat or steamer. I will not start for about two weeks yet, as I have considerable work to do here.

Thus early in his career, Penrose had developed that fearlessness which was

Dick Penrose as a young man

Edward T. Dumble

one of his outstanding characteristics. Nevin M. Fenneman, for many years head of the department of geology at the University of Cincinnati, who knew Penrose only late in life, in connection with the Geological Society of America, said that he thought the most remarkable thing about Penrose was his poise.

"He always had something worth while to say," said Fenneman, "but he never seemed anxious to say it.

"Some one—I believe it was Salisbury—told me that he thought that Penrose was the most fearless man he had ever met," continued Fenneman, and he told the story of how in a western stage coach, years ago, bandits had held up the coach, looking for a man whom they apparently had not seen—or at least did not know very well.

"They asked Penrose who he was and he told them to go to a hot place, that it was none of their business who he was and to be off about their own business. They went," concluded Fenneman, "after much debating, saying they were sure he was the man they wanted. But he faced them down so successfully that they took off."

Letter from Dick to his brother Philip, dated Austin, Texas, March 18, 1889

My dear Philip

I received your letter of the 11th today. I also received the letter you wrote on Jan. 5th, when I arrived at the hotel here on Friday. Always address your letters to the Geological Survey and I will get them sooner than if sent to the hotel.

I am very glad you are getting all right and that you are having a good time. Speck arrived here on Friday and I was very glad to see him look so much better than when he left here last December. With the exception of a slight remnent of his complaint he appears in fine trim. He left here for Cruces on Sunday and expects to close up his business there soon as he can.

I was very glad to get back here for a while for I had been 3 months in East Texas living on bread and syrup. It rained so hard most of the time that I was wet for weeks at a time, but I am pretty hard to kill and I came out all right. The rain has now stopped and the warm weather has begun. I have a big summer's work before me as in the low country of eastern Texas geological work can be done best in summer since it is generally flooded in winter. I expect to do considerable travelling on the rivers by boat. The legislature is discussing the bill for our survey appropriation and we are not sure of getting it through, but I think the chances are that we will get something, probably between $25,000 and $35,000.

If you are not entirely well of your malaria I would not advise you to come down here this summer as it is undoubtedly a bad place for fevers—especially for a man who has already got it. But I think in the fall and winter time you would get along all right and I would be very glad to have you here any time you want to come.

Your affectionate brother
R. A. F. Penrose, Jr.

Letter from Dick to his father, dated Austin, Texas, April 27, 1889

I have just returned from the trip down the Colorado River. Have been away from any towns and have been sleeping on sand bars and river bluffs so that this accounts for my not having written to you for some time. We had a very successful trip and found out many new things about the geology of the country passed through. Dumble, Hill and I composed the party, though Hill only had time to go half way. There were lots of ducks, water hens, cranes, etc., along the river besides lots of fish, but we had not time to go after them and we shot nothing but one duck and a water hen. I wounded a very large white Texas crane but could not catch him.

Branner has agreed to wait for me till summer to undertake his work in Arkansas, so I will go there about July 1st or as soon thereafter as I can. Dumble has agreed to let me preserve a nominal connection with the Survey as geologist to Eastern Texas without pay while I am in Arkansas. In this way, I will be able to do the Arkansas work and at the same time be a member of the Texas Survey. I will have to do a lot of hard work before July in order to get through my work here. Next week I am going down the Brazos River in a boat for about 250 or 300 miles. Dumble and Hill will not go on this trip, so I will go alone with a man I will hire or possibly two of them. I did most all the rowing on the Colorado R. trip, but when a boat has two or 3 men in and is loaded to the water's edge with mineral specimens and fossils, it is no fun rowing it—especially when you have to take notes on the country passed through and the sun feels hot enough to cook by, so on all our other river trips I will take men to row. Niggers are the only men who can do this in the hot weather, except Mexicans. We tried a white man on our Colorado R. trip but he got knocked out in 24 hours and we had to discharge him and I rowed the rest of the trip.

These trips are very pleasant. We travelled stripped to an undershirt and in bare feet. This was the only way to keep cool. We got a little blistered with the sun at first but soon got used to it and our daily swim in the river was very pleasant. I find that taking quinine, going swimming and taking purges when constipated is a great preventative of malaria. I took all these things on our Colorado R. trip, but Hill who did not swim and took quinine only irregularly and allowed himself to become constipated was attacked with malaria the 3rd day out. East Texas is called an unhealthy country but I notice that all the people who get malaria are those who neglect proper precautions against it. It is not half such an unhealthy country as it is made out to be. There is always a breeze at night and though it is very hot during the day, a blanket and sometimes 2 or 3 of them are very comfortable to sleep in.

I have received a notice from the U. S. Geological Survey saying they had shipped those phosphate bulletins to you so I suppose you have got them by this time. I have received a letter from Speck saying that he expected to stay in Cruces this summer, but that he thought he could sell out to advantage in the fall.

P.S. I have been keeping my eyes open for a horse but have not yet seen anything that would suit you. Most Texas horses are small and, as a rule, not good looking. But I will keep a lookout for one.

In his *Memoirs*, Penrose writes of this Brazos River trip:

"On one occasion while navigating the Brazos River in a small boat with one man whom I had employed to go with me, we came to a spot which was designated on the map as the town of Washington, once the capital of the State of Texas. We landed at an old decayed river pier covered with brush, and apparently protruding into the river, alone, from the jungle. On landing, however, we found a small trail going inland, which we followed for about a mile, and then unexpectedly came upon a small town which had once been built mostly of brick, but was now mostly in ruins. Practically all the houses were deserted except one, which seemed to be a public store, and in front of it were three men sitting on chairs with a beer keg in their midst, and playing poker. These were the only residents of the once prosperous town of Washington that I saw on that visit, though there must have been others living among the ruins. The three men were very cordial and hospitable, and we all adjourned into the store to have a beer, and then another beer, and perhaps one or two afterwards. I then purchased a few supplies which we needed for our trip farther down the river, and returning to our boat we pushed off from shore toward the lower waters of the Brazos."

In a letter to his father, the young scientist gives a somewhat more picturesque version of this episode. He writes on letter-head of the Geological Survey of Texas, showing that E. T. Dumble is the State Geologist and that R. A. F. Penrose, Jr. is Geologist for Eastern Texas. The letter is dated Austin, Texas, May 14, 1889:

I received your letters of Apr. 25 and May 5 on my return here today from the Brazos River. I ought to have got the one of Apr. 25 before writing you last but suppose it was delayed in the post office here where they are very slow. I have had a very successful trip on the Brazos. I started with a big buck nigger to row from the town of Waco—on the upper Brazos—and went clear to the Gulf of Mexico—most of the way by boat and the rest by land, the whole distance being about 500 miles. For 300 miles down the river from Waco we did not strike a single settlement with the exception of the old town of Washington—once the capital of Texas—now a delapidated town of about 50 people. This town was marked on my map as being at the point where the Navisota River runs into the Brazos. I had been looking forward to laying in a stock of provisions when we got here. When we left Waco I had stocked the boat with enough grub to last 2 white men for 2 weeks. Never having travelled with a nigger I did not know how niggers ate and at the end of six days, and 2 days before we were to reach where Washington ought to be, we were clean out of grub. When we reached the mouth of the Navisota I looked around for Washington, but saw nothing but thickets on all sides. I ran the boat ashore and climbed up the bank to hunt for the town. About a quarter mile inland I saw two or three old houses and I made for these. They proved to be all closed up—windows nailed, doors locked and fast tumbling to pieces. There appeared to be the remains of an old main street of a town running between the houses. It was all grown up with grass and weeds, but I could make out an old curbing so I followed it on. Soon I came to several other houses—just like the first—locked and nailed and tumbling to pieces. But I heard a rooster crow and knew that some one must live nearby, so I kept on. Suddenly on turning a corner I came on four men sitting at a table in *the middle* of the once main street of Washington. Two were playing checkers and two were drinking whiskey and lemon. They invited me to have a drink with them, which I took. I then found out that one of them kept a store (?) in a shanty nearby and I got what provisions I could. I gave them a farewell drink out of my flask and parted on very good terms with the citizens of Washington. These four men, two mules, one dog and one rooster were all the citizens I saw in Washington. It was once one of the best towns in Texas, with several thousand inhabitants. The man from whom I bought my grub said that business was very dull in Washington!! I told him I thought so too.

There are several falls in the Brazos and in some places we had to unload our boat and let it down with a rope. In other places we went through the rapids and it was great sport. The nigger would get so nervous that he would sit in the bow and yell out 'Oh! my dear Jesus! we be lost sure this time! Jesus save this nigger!'

I took from 10 to 15 grains of quinine daily and was all right. The good it did was shown by the fact that the nigger, who would not take any, got malaria—though it is generally supposed that a Texas nigger can live where an alligator can.

I did not see much big game but killed one alligator with my 44 calibre pistol. There were lots of them on the river. We start on Thursday morning for Eagle Pass and thence down the Rio Grande to the Gulf—a distance of 500–600 miles. We will take two boats and there will be five men in the party. The only settlement of any size that we will strike will be Laredo—six days travel by river from Eagle Pass. We will probably land at Brownsville, at the mouth of the river, and return to Galveston by sea. Dumble and the Commissioner of Insurance are going but they may drop out of the party at Laredo. They are not used to camping. We will take two Mexicans to row and act as interpreters as most of the people living on the river are Mexicans. Will take my rifle and pistol and will have two shot guns besides. Will also have letters from the Governor of Texas so that we will not be arrested for smugglers. Will write to you on the trip if I get a chance but if you do not hear from me for three or four weeks, do not be surprised as I may not be near a postoffice. This will probably be my last trip for the Texas Survey—at least until I am done in Arkansas—as I go there the first of July. I have got a man to continue my work here. He was once a student of Shaler's and has since been on the U. S. Survey. He will be here when I get back from the Rio Grande. I will show him what to do in East Texas and will then go to Arkansas July 1st.

You had better just distribute those phosphate papers as you see chances to do so. I have sent copies to most of the people I could think of. You might send some to the fertilizer men in Phila or anywhere else—if you can get their addresses. I can't get them here. But don't put yourself to any trouble in the matter. I am very glad Mr. Lewis liked the article. There was a favorable review of it in the last number of the "American Journal of Science"—for April or May, I forget which. Also, "Science" printed the whole of the introduction several weeks ago. I wrote a short article for a local paper on the building stone of East Texas which was also copied in full by 'Science' a few weeks ago.

I will write the review of the phosphate article as soon as I get a chance and will send it to you.

He continues the story of that trip in his *Memoirs:*

In studying the geologic formations along the Rio Grande, I started with Mr. Dumble and with the Director of the State Department of Insurances, etc., in a flat-bottomed boat from Eagle Pass. We had had the boat built especially for the purpose of this trip, because the river below Eagle Pass was largely unknown, except that it contained many rapids and rocky places which required a staunch boat. We had it made of two-inch plank, and had covers built around the inside in which we stored our provisions, guns, etc., so that in case we upset we would not lose everything. The only map of the river below Eagle Pass consisted of the old boundary line made by the United States Government after the Mexican War in 1848, and this was intended simply to show the frontiers of Texas and Mexico. No geology, no topography, no rapids or waterfalls which we found later in the river were depicted on it, so that all this information was left for us to collect.

The three of us started from Eagle Pass with two half-breed Indians and Mexicans to row. The current was too swift and the boat was too heavy to steer with the ordinary rudder, so we arranged that I should stand in the stern with a long pole shaped as a paddle at the lower end and steer the boat in the same way as is done in a canoe. This method proved very efficient because it enabled us to dodge rocks and other impediments in our way. We carefully stored the lockers of our boat with a shot gun, two rifles, and two pistols, together with a store of bacon, flour and other provisions, but we depended somewhat on the game we were to find along the lower river for our meat. Our destination was about 350 miles down the river to Brownsville near where the Rio Grande flows into the Gulf of Mexico at Port Isabella [Isabel].

For three days we proceeded in a very satisfactory manner down the river, camping every night on the bank, and meeting with no unexpected difficulties. On the fourth day, however, we suddenly came in sight of a broad stretch of rapids which spread across the river for its whole width of about a mile. The rapids did not become visible until it was too late for us to reach shore, so I did the next best thing and tried to guide the boat through them. We were fairly successful in this, for after passing four or five miles of rough water we ran into the smooth river again. At this moment our two half-breed oarsmen became so delighted that they had not been drowned in the rapids that they jumped up to thank the Lord and all the saints for their safety, and in doing so upset the boat. This seemed very unfortunate, after having gone through several miles of really dangerous rapids and dodging rocks without being injured in any way. We had but little trouble in towing our boat to shore, where we bailed it out, took our supplies from the lockers and spread them out to dry.

The Commissioner had been noted as a prohibition advocate even in those early days of this false policy, but in spite of the fact that I was an employee in his department, I could not help realizing that the water had been very cold and that we were all shivering; hence, I produced two quart bottles of Mexican Mescal, which I had quietly stored in one of the lockers in case of emergency. The Commissioner apparently had forgotten his prohibition tendencies in the midst of all his distress in towing the boat to shore, and to my astonishment consumed more of the Mescal than Mr. Dumble, the two Mexicans, and I all together could drink. I congratulated him on his capacity, and his reply was that he was not used to this rough life. Two days later, as we were passing down the river, he got off at a small village* and returned to Austin, after wishing us the best of good fortune on the rest of our trip, and expressing his sincere sympathy with the object of our scientific research.

At the time we made this trip down the Rio Grande the Garcia revolution was in active operation, and the rebel Garcia was in the neighborhood of the Rio Grande. We were frequently followed all day by stray Mexicans on horseback, apparently watching our movements, so that we finally resorted to making camp at night on an island in the river rather than trusting to what we might find on the mainland, for we did not like the looks of these sporadic men on horseback.

From Roma [Eagle Pass] we proceeded to the southwest [southeast], making frequent stops to study the geologic formations along the river for several days. On the sixth day from Roma [Eagle Pass] we were rowing quietly down the river, which in that particular place was almost a mile wide, when suddenly before us we observed some hills rising in the distance, but supposed that the river would go around them or through them. To our surprise, however, when we got sufficiently close we found that the whole river was narrowed to a turbulent mass of water, probably less than fifty yards wide, and dashing wildly through a canyon. The force of the stream made it impossible to turn back or to land, and the only thing to do was to head for the canyon and hope for the best. On entering it we were raised as if by a high wave at sea, and then the nose of our boat was turned down on the other side as the water dashed into the central part of the canyon. Our Mexican oarsmen looked around, and for the first time observed in what kind of a situation we had been caught. They both threw their oars in the water and lay in the bottom of the boat, uttering various prayers, among which 'Sacre! Sacre! Sacre!' seemed to be the principal sound. Fortunately, the canyon was short, and in a few moments we had drifted out into smooth clear water, with no damage done except the loss of our oars. We spent the afternoon paddling around and recovered three of the oars, and that evening one of the Mexicans whittled a fourth oar out of a piece of wood we had cut from a tree.

* In his letter written at the time, Penrose states that the Commisioner left them at Laredo (*see* p. 129). Makes the same statement also in his reminiscences of the Survey (*see* p. 135).

The next day we landed at the Texan town of Laredo, which was quite a large settlement and was connected by a bridge across the river with Nuevo Laredo. These two settlements were the only ones of any considerable importance between Eagle Pass and our destination, Brownsville, so we stopped several days at Laredo to put in new supplies and repair our boat. As the river below this town seemed to spread out into a very broad stream, often two or three miles wide, we decided to make a sail in order to travel faster than by the slow rowing of two Mexican Indians. We made the sail in the backyard of the hotel at Laredo, much to the surprise of the natives, who had never seen a sail boat in those waters.

The following week we came to the town of Roma, which though composed mostly of Mexicans is on the Texas side of the river and is situated on a high hill. It is a most picturesque place, and if it covered seven hills instead of one it might be admired almost as a small imitation of the ancient Rome of Italy. It was an old-fashioned town fortified by walls on all sides, and commanded by a small troop of American sodiers. The officer in charge received us cordially and treated us in the kindest possible manner. He had learned from the Governor of the State about our errand in making the trip down the river and he did much to facilitate our progress.

Roma is kept up mostly by smuggling American merchandise into Mexico. A large part of the hill on which it is situated is honeycombed by old Mexican tunnels and chambers; and when the night is partly dark and the Mexican custom guards on the other side of the river seem particularly indifferent, whole lines of mules packed with merchandise may be seen issuing from one of the tunnels in the hill and crossing into Mexico by a nearby ford. The American officer in charge of Roma took no notice of these transactions, for, in fact, it was the duty of the Mexican officials and not the American officials, to stop smuggling into the country to the south.

Continuing southeastward from Roma the river widens into a much broader stream, and in the course of about 15 miles we reached Rio Grande City, a small settlement on the American side of the river, but of some commercial importance on account of being at a point where streams from both Texas and Mexico enter the Rio Grande. It is also the location of Ringold Barracks, where a number of United States troops were stationed to protect the border, and especially to prevent the American revolutionists under Garcia from landing on the American side. At Ringold Barracks we were in direct communication by telegraph with Brownsville, about 100 miles farther down the river, and from thence up the coast to Galveston. We took the opportunity to wire to Austin of our arrival at Ringold Barracks and of our accomplishments so far in studying the geology of the river from Eagle Pass downward.

We started from Rio Grande City with a new outfit of supplies, and much rested by a couple of days stay there. The river below became still wider, so that our geological studies on both sides required much time in crossing and re-crossing. Finally, however, we reached the town of Hidalgo on the American side, the principal industry of which is smuggling into Mexico, and the principal fame of which is having been the headquarters of many Mexican insurrectionists against the Diaz government. From Hidalgo the banks of the river became much flatter and spread out into the broad delta of the Rio Grande.

Finally, as we approached the mouth of the river we decided to land first at Matamoros* on the Mexican side, in order to make certain observations there, and then to cross the river to Brownsville on the American side. On running alongside of the dock with our rowboat at Matamoros, however, we were met by the customs guards, who did not seem to take much to our appearance. In fact, this was not surprising, because for over two months we had been sleeping in our clothes, and when we got wet, or upset, we had allowed our clothes to dry on us; moreover, none of us had had a chance to shave—so that they did not know exactly what to make of us at the landing.

I displayed a letter from the Governor of the State of Texas, to the effect that we were engaged on State scientific work, and I also explained the cause of our appearance, but did not seem to make much impression on the head of the customs guards. He finally saw my Winchester rifle strapped on the inside of the boat, and at once made the proposition that he would let us land if I would give him that Winchester. I had to decline this offer because I did not know what need there might be for the Winchester before we got through this particular trip; and therefore, being refused entrance into Mexico under any other terms than the forfeiture of my Winchester, we turned the bow of our boat northward and rowed two or three miles across stream to Brownsville, where we landed and were hospitably received. In spite of our crestfallen appearance, the letter from the Governor of the State did us good service at Brownsville, and we were actually taken in as guests at a very clean, neat-looking house which they called the hotel.

The trip had taken much longer than we expected and we had been traveling down the river for practically two months, so that our funds had run very short and at Brownsville we found ourselves in the predicament of staying at a very good hotel and being treated very nicely, but not knowing how we were going to pay it back. I had money in bank at Austin, and had some checks with me on the trip, but the checks had become wet from the river, and the two or three small banks at Brownsville which we approached with the proposition to cash one of the checks either did not like our looks or did not like our check, and declined to give us any cash.

I had figured that $100 would take us to Port Isabel, and then by steamer to Galveston; but I was at a loss how to get this money until I happened one day to be passing along the street and saw a very attractive-looking wholesale liquor shop. Knowing the kindly disposition of men who deal in wholesale liquor, it suddenly occurred to me to discuss our predicament with the proprietor, and I also showed him the letter from the Governor to the effect that we were respectable citizens. He finally became convinced that we were all right, but being a good trader he consented to accept the $100 check from me for $90 from him; in

---

* His memory seems to be somewhat at fault here. *See* letter written at the time, p. 129.

other words, I had to pay him 10 percent for the risk he took. I was glad to do this, however, and in order to make the trade pleasant and agreeable the liquor dealer gave us two bottles of whiskey to see us safely on board ship at Port Isabel, and thence to Galveston.

Two days later we started for Port Isabel to take a local steamer which ran up the coast for about 1000 miles to Galveston,* and the question then arose as to what we were to do with our two half-breed Mexican Indians. I had paid them off, and offered to give them funds enough to go up the river, but they realized that we had had considerable trouble coming down the river, with the stream, and that it would be much more difficult to go up the river. Moreover, they stood in mortal terror of the followers of Garcia, particularly when they were away from the restraining influence exercised on the revolutionists by American citizens.

I then offered to take them with us on the steamer to Galveston and send them back to Eagle Pass by railroad. This seemed to please them, and we all started for Port Isabel, about 20 miles from Brownsville, where the steamer coming up from the coast of Mexico, was to start that afternoon. Unfortunately, the steamer was burning coal, which made a great deal of smoke, and as it was coming into Port Isabel the Mexicans saw this great black hulk of a boat, with an immense jet of black smoke rising up into the skies from it. They had never seen anthing larger than a rowboat before, and when I pointed out the steamer and told them that that was the boat which was to take us to Galveston, they balked right then and there and began to utter their choicest variety of Sacres!. I told them that this was the only way of getting home unless they went up the river again, but after consultation between themselves they finally decided that if I would give them enough money to buy two Mexican burros, they would not risk their lives on that black thing out in the bay, but would go overland on the burros along the course of the river, until they got to Eagle Pass. I warned them of the danger of this trip, of the followers of Garcia, who had so often made us camp on the islands in the river rather than on the shores, and of the roughness of the country over which they had to travel. But they stood firm on the burros idea versus the black steamer, so I was entirely willing to grant their request. The two burros were bought, and I gave them all the supplies that we had left from our trip, including a rifle and a six-shooter, and they started up the river in good spirits.

For months afterwards on my return to Austin I made inquiries for these two men, but could not find any record of them from any point along the Rio Grande farther north than Ringold Barracks. From there up they would have met the principal bands of the followers of Garcia, and what happened to them I have never been able to discover. Every effort to locate them failed.

We had started from Eagle Pass with only a small quantity of provisions, consisting mostly of flour, salt bacon, dried vegetables, and other materials which we could use if we did not find anything better on our route. We anticipated, however, having wild turkey all along the river, and as we approached the Gulf

* In his letter to his father, written at the time (p. 130) he states that the distance is 300 miles.

of Mexico, large green turtles, sometimes three or four feet long; moreover, the peccary, or wild hog of that region, was occasionally found.

We were not disappointed in finding game along the river, which added considerably to our simple diet of bread and pork. The wild turkey was very numerous from the time we started our trip and we had no trouble shooting them with our Winchester rifles. They were splendid birds of a light buff color, with a white streak along the ends of the feathers in their tails, so that they were quite different from the northern wild turkey with its brilliant bronze plumage. We found that the peccary were scarcer than the turkeys, and in fact we came within shooting distance of only one of them, and even he escaped into the underbrush before we could get a shot at him.

As we approached the mouth of the river, however, especially below Laredo and Roma, the green turtle became very numerous and we could have collected them in both places. They usually crawled up the sandy shore of the river and laid their eggs there, so that they might hatch in the sun. When they saw us coming down the river in our boat they made a dash for the water, but there was never any trouble in intercepting them.

We collected and consumed the eggs in great quantities and found them very good. They were different from the egg of a chicken or other bird, inasmuch as the shell was soft, like rubber, and they were of such a character that a long time was required to boil them sufficiently to harden the albumen. Twenty minutes to half an hour was required to boil one of these turtle eggs to the same consistency that three or four minutes would be required to boil a chicken egg.

In addition to the turtle eggs, we frequently lived for days on the turtles themselves, but their flesh was extremely tough and had to be boiled for hours before it could be eaten. The soup made in this way was very palatable, especially when seasoned with sufficient salt and pepper. One of our half-breed companions told us when trying to eat a turtle steak that I had carefully cooked, that it was the toughest thing he had ever tasted, and that even his wife back in Eagle Pass, never dared to offer him such tough meat. He therefore did not understand why he should have left his happy home for the lower Rio Grande.

On my return to Austin I spent some months writing up some geological notes relating to the Rio Grande valley, and they were eventually printed in a volume entitled *A Preliminary Report on the Geology of the Gulf Tertiary of Texas*, being part of the *First Annual Report of the Geological Survey of Texas, 1889*. This publication embodied all the work I had done on the Tertiary and later formations in eastern Texas, from the northern boundaries of the State to the Mexican border.

His father preserved two letters covering this Rio Grande trip. The first is dated Mexico, May 25, 1889, and after the customary salutation, Dick wrote:

"We are camped on the Mexican side of the Rio Grande in a big thunderstorm and as we expect to pass the town of Carrizo [present-day Zapata] on the American side tomorrow or the day after I thought I would drop you a line and mail it there if possible. We have come almost 200 miles down river from Eagle Pass where we started from and have so far had a very successful trip. Dumble and I and two Mexicans are the only ones now in the party. The commissioner of Insurance dropped out at Laredo—the last railroad station we pass till we get to the Gulf—about 350 miles. We had our first rain today. It had been very hot and sultry and at 2 p.m. the thermometer was 108° in the shade and 126° in the sun. Suddenly we saw a storm coming up and we made for the shore and started to put up the tent. We had hardly got it up and the outfit inside when the wind struck us and laid the tent out flat. We got it raised again and by bracing the tent poles with ropes tied to trees have succeeded in keeping it up. The wind blew so hard at first that our tent stakes were all pulled out. It has now moderated and will probably soon pass over.

We have found it necessary to get letters from both the American and Mexican customs men in order not to be stopped by the customs scouts along the river. This is a great nuisance as each officer's district only extends from 100–150 miles along the river and then we have to get letters from new men. We renew our American letters at Carrizo [Zapata] and at that place have to cross into Mexico and make a journey of several miles inland to the town of Guerrero to get the Mexican letters. All the Mexican officials have been most obliging in giving us passports and all other help they can. We have 2 Mexicans to row. One can speak a little English and is very useful as an interpreter.

The river has had many rapids in it so far but we have not had much trouble. Some places the river runs through a narrow channel only a few yards wide through it is usually several hundred yards wide and in these narrow places it runs at a great rate. I do the steering in the stern with a long oar while the Mexicans row.

[Foregoing in black pencil—remainder in purple pencil]

Carrizo, May 28. Arrived here all right today and are just starting off down river.

Letter from Dick to his father, dated Austin, Texas, June 11, 1889

I have just returned from the Rio Grande and have received your letter enclosing that from Jimmy Pierce and that from Mrs. Morgan to Uncle Clem. I don't see why Jimmy did not order that whiskey himself as I asked him, but I suppose that great amount of work he talks about must occupy all his attention. I think however he might have ordered it for you.

We had a very successful trip down the Rio Grande. We travelled about 350 miles by row boat in 18 days. At Hidalgo—a small settlement at the head of the old delta of the river—we abandoned our boat as we had seen the part of the river we wanted to examine. Here we crossed over into Mexico to an old town called Reynosa which is connected with the Gulf coast at Matamoras by a rickety old narrow-gauge railroad owned by the Mexican government. We shipped ourselves and our outfit on this road and in six hours covered the 60 miles that separate Reynosa from Matamoras. The railroad officials would not let us take our shot guns and rifles in the passenger car and we had to put them in the baggage car—yet every man in the passenger car, including ourselves, carried a big six shooter in open view and one gent had so many on his person that he hung two of them up on the side of the car to have ready for use. The second in command of the Mexican army on the frontier was on board and he is one of the most villanous looking characters you ever saw. He carried a gold watch chain that must have weighed several pounds, a tremendous big six shooter that reached half way down his leg and a long black mustache like a horse's tail. We stopped for dinner at a small house composed of one room and built mostly of cane and straw. They gave us some very tough beef stewed in red pepper and rice and some coffee made of burned corn meal or some such stuff. At Matamoras the deputy collector of customs for Mexico was drunk and he was very anxious to have my rifle, which he said was just the thing he wanted. He could not speak any English and I only knew a few words of Spanish. I would not give him the rifle and he would not let us pass the customs office, so we had considerable discussion—at least as much as two gents can have who do not understand each other's language. At last we showed him a letter which we have gotten from one Mexican collector to another about 150 miles up the river and which we had never delivered. It was written in Spanish and as soon as he saw it he began bowing and getting off "senors" etc., and cleared out.

From Matamoras we crossed the Rio Grande to Brownsville on the American side. Here we found that, by a great piece of good luck, the Morgan line steamer had just arrived at Brazos Santiago—20 miles from Brownsville and on the Gulf—and would sail for Galveston in two days. We were in great luck to strike this boat as it only passes here about three times a month and if we had not struck it we would have driven or ridden about 200 miles overland to reach a railroad that would have taken us back here. We took the steamer and with a strong stern wind made a very quick passage to Galveston, over 300 miles by sea, reaching there in 26 hours after leaving Brazos Santiago. Brownsville is 20 miles above the mouth of the Rio Grande and is the most southerly settlement in Texas. Bananas, oranges, lemons and all kinds of tropical fruit and flowers grow here. The whole town is fragrant from the many gardens and people live in the greatest luxury. One of the fundamental principles of the people is to do no work. They get up at 8 or 9 o'clock, have breakfast and dinner over by noon and then they sleep until about 4 p. m. The next four hours they talk about their prosperous (?) country and the prospects of getting a long expected railroad. This makes them very hungry and they then have supper at 8 p. m., after which they smoke a cigarette rolled in a piece of corn husk and are so tired with their day's work that they go to bed. It is certainly a luxurious life for a man who doesn't want any better. All kinds of fruit grow here and the whole town smells of flowers. The little work that is done is Mexican labor, but it is so easy to live in such a climate that very little work is necessary.

The thermometer while we were on the Rio Grande ranged often from 105° to 110° in the shade and was one day 126° in the sun. This was pretty hot but we soon got used to it and though the sweat would be dripping off our chins, ears, and noses, and our clothes would be drenched with it, we did not mind it much. A swim in the river in the middle of the day was a most refreshing thing. We also had a large stock of lemons and cold tea. We would boil a lot of tea in the morning and cool it by towing it in glass flasks behind the boat. By following your good advice about quinine, calomel and boiled water, none of us had any fever. The worst trouble a man seems to have in the malarial part of the country is in suddenly getting constipated and turning bilious, followed with vomiting and purging—all sometimes coming on in a few hours. I have learned to detect the symptoms of the approach of these attacks and can always knock them out by taking calomel in time. Allowing yourself to be constipated for one day is apt to bring them on, but when a man has had one attack there is no necessity for him ever to have another as he understands how to detect its approach and can knock it out. I have noticed all summer and spring that the men who have fever and such attacks as I described above are the men who get constipated and rail against the use of calomel as "poison." I took 10 grains of quinine every day on the Rio Grande and calomel when necessary. I don't think there is any danger of a man getting fever if he follows the advice you gave me about quinine, calomel, and boiled water.

I will spend the rest of this month here and in east Texas finishing up my work and will go to Little Rock to start in on Branner's work on July 1st. I will not write up my Texas report now as I want to get access to a decent library before doing it and such a thing is unknown in this state. I hope your new horse will prove a success. I have been utterly unable to find one here that would suit you. There are many good riding horses but they are too small or else too ugly in shape. Beauty is not one of the strong points of either Texas horses or Texas women.

I was very sorry to hear of the death of Uncle Ned. I suppose it was not unexpected as he was very sick when I left Phila last fall.

If you write on or before June 25th, please address me here. After that my address will be: care of State Geological Survey, Little Rock, Arkansas.

P.S. Did you get any of that whiskey?

[If the reader at this point is annoyed by the discrepancies, in the matter of geographical names between the *Memoirs* and the letters, he should remember that the *Memoirs* were marked "rough draft" and were written more than thirty years after the events recorded. Undoubtedly, Penrose would have checked names of places before releasing the material.—*Editor's Note*]

Letter from Dick to his father, dated Austin, Texas, June 27, 1889

I received your letter of June 17th on my return here from a few days absence in East Texas where I have been to start a man who is to do some work there while I am in Arkansas. I leave here for Little Rock tomorrow and will arrive there the next day.

While in East Texas I made a trip down to a point on the Sabine River about 100 miles above Sabine Pass—where I wanted to collect some fossils. To reach the place, I had to go about 100 miles through western Louisiana and then cross into Texas. That part of Louisiana is one of the most delapidated regions I was ever in. East Texas is proverbial as a back country and yet the people of western Louisiana are so much more backward that they look on East Texas as a fine booming country and talk about its great prosperity. Deserted towns and plantations are the principal land-marks in western Louisiana, but pine forests now mark their old cities, and the only signs that people once lived there are an occasional pile of stones marking an old chimney, or a hole, covered over by blackberry bushes, which was once a town well. The rapid breeding of negroes is driving the whites out of many sections and many parts of the state bid fair to become very soon purely negro settlements. The place I was making for on the Sabine R. was called Sabinetown. It was *once* a town— but the bare walls of four or five wooden houses are all that is left. A farmer lives nearby and the main street of the town is now part of his cornfield.

The new man I took to East Texas scorned the use of quinine and calomel at first and the result was that after we had been out 4 days he was taken down with a bad attack of malaria. He is now getting all right and takes quinine regularly.

I will keep notes about my travels as you suggest—though I don't know when I will ever get time to write them up.

I had a letter from Speck a few days ago. He seems to be getting on very well and says he expects to make some money this summer.

Will write again from Little Rock. I wrote you from here about 2 weeks ago on our return from the Rio Grande and suppose you have got the letter by this time. I will address this letter to Phila as I suppose you will be there by the time it gets there. Hereafter my address is care of State Geological Survey, Little Rock, Ark.

P.S. June 29. I have just received your letter of the 24th and am very glad your Capon trip is doing you good. I hope you will have a pleasant trip to Mt. Desert.

In later years, in writing of this period of his life, Penrose said:

"When I speak of my reminiscences of the Geological Survey of Texas for almost two years, I have in mind not only the exploration and research which I personally conducted, but also the personality of that quiet, unassuming, but most eminently capable man who started the Survey, and who was State Geologist during the time that I was on it. I refer to Mr. E. T. Dumble, who was appointed State Geologist of Texas in September, 1888, and immediately proceeded with characteristic energy and breadth of vision to organize the work in the vast region over which he had suddenly been given authority. The Survey was under the Department of Agriculture, Insurance, Statistics, and History, but Mr. Dumble was given entire freedom of action in the development of the Geological Survey.

"It was no small undertaking for one man to organize a Geological Survey throughout the immense area covered by the State of Texas, but Mr. Dumble was undaunted by the task, and in pursuance of his plan of operation, different geologists were appointed to take care of different sections of the State. W. H. Streeruwitz was appointed geologist for Western Texas, W. F. Cummins was appointed geologist for Northern Texas, and I was appointed geologist for Eastern Texas. These appointments were made very shortly after Mr. Dumble's own appointment in the fall of 1888, and they reflected his promptness of action and his conception of the requirements of a broad system in his undertaking.

"Somewhat later, in 1889, Theodore B. Comstock was in charge of the work in the central mineral region of the State, while R. T. Hill, Professor of Geology at the University of Texas, did important work in some of the Cretaceous regions.

"In later years, numerous assistant geologists were taken on to the Survey from time to time as their services were needed, and it may be said to their credit and to Mr. Dumble's good judgment of men that their work was of a remarkably good character and favorably impressed not only men of science, but also those who were interested only in the mineral resources of the State. Among them were J. L. Tait, J. A. Taff, G. E. Ladd, D. W. Spence, N. F. Drake, and many other geologists, topographers, and chemists. J. H. Herndon was head chemist and did excellent work during his connection with the Survey.

"Mr. Dumble continued as State Geologist until his resignation in 1896, and the records of publications during almost ten years in which he administered its affairs speak for themselves as a monument of his sagacity, learning, and ability.

"I had accepted the appointment as geologist in charge of the work in Eastern Texas with the understanding that I was to occupy it for only one year, as I had already promised to do other geologic work in Arkansas on the expiration of my engagement in Texas. As a matter of fact, however, the area over which I had been given charge in Texas was so immense that I spent not only one year, but the better part of the next year, working on it both winter and summer. The region covered about 500 miles parallel to the coast of the Gulf of Mexico from the Red River on the northeast to the Rio Grande on the southwest; and inland from the Gulf coast for 200 miles or more. Over this vast area I could in a limited time do little more than make a general reconnaissance of the geology of the region, and my reports published by the Survey were intended to be of that character.

"The most that my time permitted was to work out the general sequence of the Tertiary formations which overlie unconformably the Cretaceous of Texas. The lowermost of these Tertiary formations was identified as Eocene and was tentatively called the Basal clays, or the Wills' Point clays, on account of their remarkable exposure at Wills' Point, in Van Zant County. They consist of clay and sandy strata with lignite and extensive beds of glauconite. Above the Basal clays were an extensive series of clay and sandy strata with lignite beds, underlying most of the great timber region of eastern Texas, and were classed as the Timber Belt beds of Eocene age. Above the Timber Belt beds were clearly identified a different series of beds, mostly composed of clay and sandy strata, of a clear white, gray or light sea-green color, often containing much salicified wood and plant impressions, and in places cemented into hard layers which, due to the erosion of softer strata, formed characteristic features in the topography. The Fayette beds, together with certain overlying sandy and calcareous strata, were classified as probably in the upper part of the Tertiary. In this the writer was corroborated by the examination of fossil remains by Professor E. D. Cope. Since that time the Fayette beds have been buffeted by various geologists from upper Tertiary to Eocene, the difference in opinion being in some cases lack of knowledge by later investigators as to what the Fayette beds as originally defined really comprised.

"Above the Fayette beds the Tertiary strata are of a softer and less prominent character, overlaid in turn by low-lying Tertiary clays of the coastal area, forming a fringe around the Gulf. The three great subdivisions of the Tertiary—that is, the Basal clays, the Timber Belt beds, and the Fayette beds—were named only tentatively, my idea being that future research would doubtless develop important subdivisions among them. My work being purely of a reconnaissance nature, I could not go further than to define these main divisions, and as my available time drew toward its end I reluctantly ceased, with the hope that detailed research by others would show the existence of still further subdivisions in the larger groups which I had described.

"My first work as a geologist in charge of Eastern Texas was to study the general geology of the northeastern section of the State, reaching from Louisiana and Arkansas borders westward through Marion, Henderson, Rusk, Cherokee, Van Zant, and other countries, together with the iron ores associated with them. This is a low-lying country and only in spots affords strata sufficiently exposed to study. In Cherokee County, where the ground was more hilly, I spent considerable time studying the lower Tertiary glauconite beds, with their accompanying iron ores, which were well exposed in some of the steeper hillsides. These results were published in the *Geological and Mineral Survey of Texas, First Report of Progress*, 1888.

"I soon found, however, that in the low country it was difficult to find good exposures of the underlying strata, and I therefore thought it best to carry on further studies along the rivers where they had cut through the strata and had often left banks of considerable height in which the stratified materials were clearly followed. This method of exploration was made still more desirable because the rivers ran in a general southeasterly direction, and the various formations dipped in the same direction toward the Gulf of Mexico, so that the rivers of Eastern Texas intersected the Tertiary formations from their lower strata, which lay unconformably on the Cretaceous, through higher and higher strata in the Tertiary until they entered the Gulf through the Pleistocene and recent sands and clays of the coast.

"In pursuance of this method of observation I began to work, first, overland along the banks of the rivers, especially in places on the Red River, and then along the Sabine River and the Trinity River still farther south. This experience taught me that still better results could be obtained by navigating the river in small boats and landing at various points to make observations. After a consultation with Mr. Dumble, we decided that this method of procedure could easily be carried out, particularly along the larger rivers, and we selected especially the Colorado River in Eastern Texas, the Brazos River, and the Rio Grande.

"The first of these expeditions was undertaken by Mr. Dumble and myself on the Colorado River. We descended in a small boat from Austin to La Grange. We were accompanied part way by R. T. Hill of the University of Texas, who left us, however, at Bastrop to attend to other work. We obtained much valuable data on our trip on the Colorado River concerning the Cretaceous formations underlying the Tertiary at, and below, Austin, and then farther down the river we began the exploration of the lower Tertiary, which was really the object of our expedition. We crossed through the Basal clays, the Timber Belt beds, and part of the Fayette beds. The Fayette beds were remarkably displayed in the county of that name through part of which we passed on our trip down the river. They were so manifestly in evidence, and so clear and distinct from the Basal clays, the Timber Belt beds, and other Tertiary formations, that we tentatively called them the Fayette beds. This name has been ever since maintained, though its exact position in the upper Tertiary has been subject to considerable dispute among paleontologists.

"On my return from La Grange and the Lower Colorado River I remained a few days in Austin to write up my notes and then started on a journey down the Brazos River from Waco toward the Gulf of Mexico. This time I went alone, except for a man whom I employed in Waco to assist in handling the boat. In the geologic sections I observed along the Brazos, often in bluffs of considerable elevation, a large number of good exposures were examined and described in the Basal clays which overlie the Cretaceous as seen in Waco, and in the Timber Belt beds which overlie the Basal clays. From there the river passed through the Fayette beds, in which a number of good exposures were found and described. A short trip inland from the bluffs of the Brazos westward to the old town of Washington showed the typical characteristic soil overlying this formation. It was rich in its agricultural possibilities and had once been a great cotton region. Farther down the river we passed through a more or less low-lying region but little cultivated, and overgrown with areas of grass and swamps.

"We eventually reached the town of Richmond, the first important settlement directly on the river that we had passed for many miles. Below this point the Tertiary beds are covered by the post-Tertiary sands and clays of the coastal region, forming a low tide water region.

"After a brief stay in Austin on returning from down the Brazos, I determined to finish my work in Texas by making a trip down the Rio Grande in a small boat to study the different formations in its bluffs, just as I had done on the Colorado and the Brazos. Mr. Dumble was kind enough to accompany me on this trip, and though we met with numerous difficulties on account of the unknown character of the country, and the fact that there were no accurate maps of the river, yet he was always cheerful, considerate, and ready to share every hardship which we might meet. Mr. L. L. Foster, the Commissioner of Agriculture, Insurance, Statistics, and History in the State Government, also accompanied us as far as Laredo, at which point he returned to Austin to attend to other duties of his office.

"We started our trip at Eagle Pass in a flat-bottom boat built especially for us and fortified with planks so as to be able to pass through the rapids which we expected to meet in certain parts of the river, without injury to the main part of the skiff. We employed two Mexicans to row the boat while Mr. Dumble and I attended to the steering and making observations from the stern. Our destination was Brownsville, near the mouth of the river as it flows into the Gulf of Mexico, a distance, as the river flows, of about 350 miles. The only maps of the region which were then available were those of the old survey of the boundary line by the United States Government after the war of 1848, or later maps based on them, and none of them showed much, as they were intended primarily simply to portray the line which separated the two countries. We were, therefore, totally in the dark regarding the nature of the river when we started to navigate it, but before we had finished the trip we knew a great deal more about it, and had mapped the rapids, water falls, and other unusual features along its course.

"As we passed down the river we went through a wide arid region mostly devoted to cattle raising, both on the American side and on the Mexican side of the river. Numerous bluffs of considerable height were exposed, and we had ample opportunity to observe the various formations extending from those of the Cretaceous age gradually to those of the Basal clays, the Timber Belt beds, and the Fayette formation of the Tertiary. The coal mines, both at Eagle Pass and lower down the river at San Tomas,* were carefully examined and their geologic relations were studied. After leaving Laredo and making careful observations along the banks of the river as we continued down, we finally reached Carrizo [Zapata] at the junction of the Rio Grande and the Rio Salada, flowing eastward out of Mexico. After a short stop here we proceeded down stream to the Texas town of Roma, picturesquely situated on the summit of a hill, and reminding one more of an ancient fortified town than of a modern desert metropolis. Both above and below Roma we found excellent exposures of what we considered to belong to the same Fayette beds, including perhaps other Tertiary beds which we had previously studied on the Colorado River, the Brazos, and elsewhere.

"Continuing down the river we reached Rio Grande City, at which is situated the United States military post of Ringgold Barracks. The town is situated on a bluff of hard white clay, rising some fifty feet above the river, and indurated into a substance of chalky consistency, though chemically only very slightly calcareous. It probably represents the light green clays of the Fayette beds or associated formations which had become indurated by exposure to the effect of a dry, hot climate.

"Below Rio Grande City we passed through low alluvial banks for a distance of over one hundred miles to a point about ten miles above the Texas town of Hidalgo, where low ledges rise a foot or more above the water and consist of what seemed to be the sands of the Fayette beds. A similar outcrop was seen at the water's edge at Reynosa, on the Mexican side of the river, directly opposite Hidalgo. Below Hidalgo the river widened into a broad estuary up from the Gulf of Mexico, with low flat country on both sides. We continued our course down

---

* North of Laredo, and connected with that city by rail.

the stream, and finally landed at Matamoras on the Mexican side where we crossed the river to Brownsville on the Texas side; thence to Port Isabel, where after a few days we boarded a small steamer bound for Galveston.

"We had thus completed a most satisfactory trip in a country which had previously been geologically and in many of its other physical aspects almost unknown. On my return to Austin I wrote a report containing my observations on the geology as shown along the Colorado, Brazos, and Rio Grande. It was entitled 'A Preliminary Report on the Geology of the Gulf Tertiary of Texas, from the Red River to the Rio Grande,' and was part of the Second [First] Annual Report of the Geological Survey of Texas in 1889.

"In July, 1890 [1889], I was obliged most reluctantly to leave the Geological Survey of Texas, as I had long promised Doctor J. C. Branner, State Geologist of Arkansas, to come to that state in order to examine and make a report on the geological relations of the manganese and iron deposits. I had been on the Texas Survey from November, 1888, to July, 1890, and during the whole of this time was closely associated with Mr. Dumble, both in much of my field work and during the periods that I remained in Austin writing up my reports. I always found him most cordial and sympathetic, and ready to assist me in every way possible in the problems I had to solve. He was learned in paleontology, mineralogy, and other branches of geology, a combination which was not often found in those days in Texas. Since that time, of course, that State has made vast strides in the matter of scientific work, and learned men abound there; but when I first met Mr. Dumble in 1888, he was among the few who received general recognition for scholarly accomplishments.

"Mr. Dumble had a personality which attracted the community to him, and during the early days at least he had but little trouble in securing appropriations for his Geological Survey from the State Legislature. He had the habit, which seems to be now obsolete, of always telling the truth and keeping his word, though in our enlightened (?) age of today such attributes are discarded as vestiges of antiquity; but these very qualities in him had a fundamental effect in his success, not only with those associated with him on the Geological Survey, but throughout the State in general."

At the time of the testimonial dinner given to Mr. Dumble on the occasion of the annual meeting of the American Association of Petroleum Geologists, in March, 1924, Penrose wrote to John R. Suman:

"I regret very much that important business matters here will deprive me of the pleasure of being at the dinner, but I am greatly pleased to send you herewith my check for ten dollars as my contribution towards the testimonial token to Mr. Dumble.

"I had the pleasure of first meeting Mr. Dumble about thirty-five years ago when I became associated with him on the Geological Survey of Texas. Mr. Dumble was at that time State Geologist and accomplished an immense amount of good for the State and for the cause of science in the work that he carried on. As one of his assistants I always found him a kind, considerate and wise chief, and my memory of my association with him and his Survey has always been among my pleasantest recollections. It is with much pleasure therefore that I join you and your friends in this testimonial to Mr. Dumble, and I wish you a most happy reunion."

A month later (April 18, 1924) he again wrote to Mr. Suman:

"I have received your very kind letter of April 8th enclosing a photograph of the memento which was presented to Mr. Dumble at the banquet given to him by his friends on March 27th, and also a copy of Mr. Dumble's address on that occasion.

"I thank you greatly for your thoughtfulness in sending me this photograph and speech and I shall preserve them as souvenirs of a man who was one of my best friends and for whom I have always had the greatest regard and respect. My only regret is that I could not be present on the occasion of the banquet."

Mr. Dumble died January 26, 1927.

In the test which time has put upon Penrose's work in Texas, it is interesting to note that two of his sections, printed in the first report (1890) are incorporated in the report of the area cited by E. H. Sellards and C. L. Baker in their *The Geology of Texas*, volume II, "Structural and Economic Geology."

Also, E. T. Dumble's *The Geology of East Texas*, published in 1918, states:

"The first publications to deal particularly with this area were those of Penrose in the First Report of Progress and First Annual Report of the Geological Survey of Texas. In these the broader features were mapped out clearly and a beginning was made in the work of securing detailed geological knowledge of East Texas. The general geologic section is given together with descriptions and analyses of the different deposits of iron, lignite, marl, oil, salt, etc.

"In the Second Annual Report of the Geological Survey of Texas the work so well begun by Penrose is continued and expanded. Under the general title 'Report on the Iron Ore Districts of East Texas' there appears as comprehensive a statement of the general geology and mineral resources as was possible under the conditions existing at that time. [page 6]

"The beds (Wilcox) here referred to this stage were described by Penrose in the First Annual Report of the Geological Survey of Texas as part of the Timber Belt or Sabine River beds. Kennedy first differentiates them in his Tertiary Section where the Timber Belt beds of Penrose are divided into the Lignitic and Marine. [p. 37-38]

"This is generalized from the many sections made between Bullard and Jacksonville and brings out in some measure the extremely ferruginous character of this portion of the Marine. This is further shown in the section three miles north of Rusk, as given by Penrose. [page 87]

"The lowest member of the Fayette beds of Penrose was a series of clays and lignites. Their inclusion in his Fayette was due to the fact that he found no marine fossils in them, and as he had made the final fossil-bearing beds of the Marine the top of his Timber Belt beds, these were excluded. When we found Claiborne fossils in this basal clay member it became necessary to separate it from the Fayette and the Yegua formation was instituted to include the series of gypseous and saliferous clays, sands and lignites overlying the Cook's Mountain greensands and underlying the Fayette white sands and clays. [page 102]

"The ore districts of this county (Cherokee) were mapped by Penrose and his general description of them was given in the First Annual Report of the Geological Survey of Texas from which the following extracts are taken:" and then follow Penrose's descriptions. [page 324–329]

Publications by Penrose relating to the geology of Texas, in addition to those already noted, were:

The Iron Ores of Eastern Texas
The Building Stones of Eastern Texas
The Tertiary-Cretaceous Parting of Arkansas and Texas, published in association with R. T. Hill.
The Tertiary Iron Ores of Arkansas and Texas

While still a member of the Texas Survey, Penrose had signified his desire to join the American Association for the Advancement of Science, and among his "treasures" was the certificate which noted that such election took place on the 27th day of August, 1889. The following year—August, 1890—he was elected a Fellow of that organization, and on October 24, 1898, "having paid to the Association the sum of fifty dollars, the income to be devoted eventually, to aid in original research," he was "hereby informed that, under the provisions of the Constitution of the Association, he is exempt from all further assessments and is enrolled as a Life Member."

CHAPTER 6

J. C. Branner and the Arkansas Survey

"DURING the two years that I had been in Texas," wrote Dick Penrose in his *Memoirs*, "I had frequently received invitations from Dr. J. C. Branner, State Geologist of Arkansas, to come to that State and take charge of the work on manganese and iron ores; but the wide and very interesting field for research in Texas had always made me decline this offer. On my return from the Rio Grande, however, I felt that I had covered practically all of eastern Texas in the way of reconnaissance, and I began to wonder whether a new field in Arkansas would not have its attractions.

"I was so uncertain about the matter that I spent one whole evening in my room in the Capitol Building in Austin, making a balance sheet as to the inducements for the two appointments. I must acknowledge that the strongest point on the Arkansas balance sheet was that I would be associated with geologists better known in their profession than those in Texas; while in Texas, on the other hand, my work lay largely in a wild country where one was constantly subjected to unexpected events, and which was correspondingly attractive on that account. Finally, however, success in my profession prevailed, and I wrote to Doctor Branner accepting his appointment. In the meanwhile I kept up a nominal connection with the Texas Survey for a year or more.

"I must acknowledge that I did not go to Arkansas with any great enthusiasm, but simply because it was in the interest of advancement in my profession. The country was hot, swampy, full of malaria, and had nothing of the active spirit of progress which characterized Texas."

But before taking over his duties with the Arkansas Survey, Penrose did another thing which became characteristic of his work—he made a trip to Toronto, Montreal, Nova Scotia, and Cape Breton, studying the geology of the manganese deposits of eastern Canada. Thence, following the same study, he went south through New England, the Middle Atlantic and Southern States, and thence to Colorado, Nevada, California, Oregon, and Arizona, studying the magnanese deposits of the United States. All this travel and study was undertaken at his own expense, for the purpose of better fitting himself for the problem.

"The redeeming feature in Arkansas was mostly my association with Dr. J. C. Branner, who in addition to being a remarkable geologist, was broad and liberal in character, and was respected by everyone who knew him," wrote Penrose in his *Memoirs*.

"The two years I spent in Arkansas were not marked by any events of particular importance," he continues. "I travelled from one end of the State to the other on horseback, and lived constantly on the state-wide diet of salt pork, commonly known as 'fry', and apple pie. It seemed to agree with me very well and I prospered in the same way as the natives. In those days in Arkansas, hotels were very few, except in the larger towns and cities, and in travelling one usually lived 'on the country', as it was expressed; that is, he countinued on his journey until he saw a likely-looking house, and then asked permission to stay there over night. This permission was uniformly granted, as travellers were expected to seek accommodations in this way. Many a time, however, I wished later in the night that I had slept under a pine tree, or on the stony side of a mountain, because I wondered whether or not the bedbugs would leave anything of me before morning. This difficulty was made still more aggravating because the people of Arkansas were extremely hospitable to strangers, and often when there was only one room in the cabin where I stopped and only one bed for the various inmates, they would insist on sleeping on the floor and make me sleep on the bed; whereas, I would have been truly grateful if I had been allowed to take the floor, and thus avoid most of the bugs. The natives of the country seemed to have gotten used to these little pests, for they never mentioned being bitten by them, and of course, out of courtesy, I always said that I had had a splendid night, with no discomfort. I always had much comfort in the belief that the Lord loves a cheerful liar. In travelling in different parts of the world in later years I have never met a class of people more kindly hospitable and self-sacrificing than the country people of Arkansas. Many ridicule them, but the same people might well copy them in many of their customs.

"During my stay in Arkansas I had occasion at one time to go from Arkansas Hot Springs westward to what was then the boundary of Indian Territory, but what is now the boundary of Oklahoma. I knew from my experience around Batesville in northern Arkansas that the country was not particularly characterized by cleanliness, and as all the baggage which I could carry was contained in two saddlebags hanging on the saddle of the horse I was riding, I could not take a very elaborate outfit. The trip was only about two hundred miles on horseback, but was to take about two months, on account of the geological observations I had to make at various points. For the sake of cleanliness I had a barber, before I started, clip my hair short, so that I could get along with the minimum of water in washing my head in some of the places where I stopped.

"My course took me westward from Arkansas Hot Springs along the line of the Ouachita Mountains, which has for many years been a region where the free and independent American citizen insisted on his right to distil corn whiskey without having to pay a tax to the Government. (I am referring here to the situation in 1889, and not to the present prohibition catastrophe* which has overtaken the country.) The question in Arkansas was not merely prohibition or not prohibition but it was whether the people of Arkansas should buy their whiskey and pay the Government the tax, or should make it themselves and pay the Government no tax. The local industries throughout the Ouachita Mountains became very active,

---

* The *Memoirs* were written in the 1920's.

and a large part of Arkansas was supplied with very good corn whiskey made there.

"Of course, the United States revenue detectives were constantly ranging the mountains in search of illicit stills, and when they were found it very often occurred that the officer or the owner of the still, or both, were shot; but sometimes both lived, and in such a case the officer took the still-owner to Fort Smith, in central western Arkansas, where he was duly tried and generally convicted. The sentence was usually for about twenty years in the penitentiary.

"I mention these details because they are connected with my unfortunately having had my hair cut short before starting on the journey across Arkansas. The first two nights I was greeted most cordially at the houses where I asked permission to stay until morning. The third night, as I got more into the mountains I was greeted still more cordially, and the owner of the house congratulated me on having returned from Fort Smith. The whole household gathered around and insisted on having a little corn whiskey, and I suddenly became a hero without having any right to be one. I did my best to explain that I was thoroughly in sympathy with the making of corn whiskey in the Ouachita Mountains, and that I was always glad to have some, but that my short hair did not indicate that I had been in Fort Smith, and that as I had started on this journey in the summer I thought I would be cooler by having my hair cut short. This story was not believed, and they assured me that I was perfectly safe under their protection and that if I every wanted any favor done, to appeal to them; that I had suffered in a good and honest cause, and that it was the duty of righteous people to help me. They were so intent on disbelieving my story and on believing that my hair was short because I had only just been dismissed from Fort Smith jail, that I thought it better to make no more argument about the matter.

"For days after that, as I travelled westward toward the Indian Territory border, I was met with the same hospitality and cordiality as at the farm just described, and my journey was thereby made very easy, for I was everywhere greeted as a long-lost friend.

"The people of the Ouachita Mountains district at the time I travelled through it were mostly far from any railroad, and the descendants of people who had come there from Alabama and other southern states a generation or two previously. The country was so isolated from any other part of the State on account of lack of transportation facilities, that the inhabitants rarely saw many outsiders, and the result was that they intermarried to such an extent that the effect of this was seen in an unusually large number of their children. In probably four households out of five, there were children or grown people with some physical deformity, either in their faces or in their bodies, and many of them were mentally unbalanced.

"I remember sleeping on the earthen floor of a cabin in which there were numerous other people, among whom was a full grown man who, I was assured, was totally harmless, but who took great amusement in walking around and among the sleepers with an arm full of cord wood. Several times during the night, when I saw him roaming about in this way, it struck me that he would cause considerable havoc if he got suddenly just a little crazier and began hitting people with his sticks of cord wood. The next day I departed, not without some gratification, and was soothed the following night at finding that I had to sleep in a cabin inhabited only by a man and his wife who were deaf and dumb and could only talk with their fingers. They seemed harmless as compared with the maniac with the cord wood.

"In another instance, I was travelling on my horse along a forest trail, as I had long since gotten beyond the sphere of wagon roads. It had been raining heavily for two or three days, and I suddenly came to a creek much swollen by the storms and rolling in foam in a threatening way over the rocks in its bed. The stream looked threatening, but I had to cross it, for to go back would have meant simply to wait perhaps several days until it went down. I consequently urged my horse, with considerable difficulty, to take the water, and the moment he did so I slid off and swam alongside of him, so as to relieve him of my weight. After much bumping among the rocks we reached the other side of the stream and were fortunate in finding nearby an humble farm house, where we were most graciously received by the inhabitants. My horse was not much hurt, except for a few slight scratches, which I dressed with some salve that I always carried for such purposes. I personally was not hurt, though I received a few bruises; but the kindness of the people at the farm house in helping me dry my clothes made me forget all about the swim across the stream. They said I had made a mistake in trying to cross the river when it was so high, and that a number of people who had done so in bygone years had never gotten across and had never been seen later. I replied meekly, however, that I did not see how I had made a mistake, because I had already crossed, and had had the good fortune in receiving such kind hospitality.

"My work in Arkansas had begun in the manganese regions of the northern part of the State in the valley of the White River, and to the north and west of the town of Batesville. Here I found numerous mines, some of them producing at a large profit. My later work took me to the Ouachita Mountains, the character of which I have just described. Here I found some manganese, but in quantities too small to work profitably. Somewhat later I spent several weeks passing through central Arkansas, studying the iron ore deposits, none of which I found of any commercial value.

"Later I published a report of the manganese, comprising something over six hundred pages, which was criticized locally very favorably by those who owned good properties, but most fiercely by those who lived in districts which I was obliged to say contained no workable ore. Only a couple of years before, Doctor Branner had been hung in effigy because he said there was no workable gold in the State, and he might have been hung in person if his natural modesty had not made him think it was unnecessary for him to be present.

"The same attack was made on me in connection with the manganese ores of the Ouachita Mountains, and as I think it is always more desirable to be hanged in effigy than in person, I also was not in the district at the time I was being criticized. In later years, when the people of Arkansas began to know more about their resources, they found that the report of Doctor Branner on the gold deposits, and that my report of the Ouachita Mountains on the manganese deposits, were true; and some of the newspapers that had the unusual quality of trying to tell the truth, came openly out with their approval of our formerly abused reports."

Here, unfortunately, the *Memoirs* end, but through letters and various memoranda which he left, it is possible to follow his subsequent movements in Arkansas and learn something of his reactions to men and conditions.

In the preface to the volume on manganese, which was published as volume 1 in the Annual Report of the Geological Survey of Arkansas for 1890, Branner says:

"The Geological Survey's work upon manganese was taken up in July, 1889, and entrusted to Dr. R. A. F. Penrose, Jr., assistant geologist, by whom all the work has been done except such aid as could be given by others in the mapping, drawing, and in making analyses. Every known manganese mine and locality in the state has been examined by him, and is here reported on in its general geologic relations and almost always in detail.

"Besides describing occurrences of ores in this state, the subject of manganese has been taken up as a whole. This has led to an investigation of the different kinds of ore and of the uses to which they are put. In order to ascertain the importance of the Arkansas deposits, it was necessary to know to what extent the other mines in the country could meet the demand for manganese. This made it essential that all the other manganese mines should be examined. But as the funds appropriated were not available for work outside the state, Dr. Penrose has himself met these expenses out of his private funds, and, in addition to doing the field work on manganese in this state, he has visited and personally examined every known manganese region in North America—those of Georgia, Tennessee, Virginia, Vermont, Texas, Arizona, Colorado, California, Oregon, Nevada, Utah, Nova Scotia, and New Brunswick; only lack of time prevented his visiting those of Cuba and Chile. The conclusions given in the report are therefore based upon direct personal observations, and it is felt that they are thoroughly trustworthy. . . . Dr. Penrose was aided in the preparation of the map of the Batesville region by Prof. J. H. Stoller, T. C. Hopkins, Prof. W. S. Blatchley, D. M. Barringer, and H. Landes. . . .

"Aside from the aid acknowledged in the body of the report, and in the preceding part of this preface, the work represented by this volume, from the collection of data in the field to the reading of proof, has all been done by Dr. Penrose in person. His unwearying industry and zeal, his enthusiastic absorption in, and devotion to, the work cannot be too highly praised, while his intelligent grasp of the subject and his clear treatment of it cannot fail of appreciation by geologists and by all who are interested in manganese."

Half a dozen letters to his father picture the life in Arkansas as this young man saw it. The first, which is dated Batesville, Arkansas, July 16, 1889, is written on the stationery of the Geological Survey of Arkansas, showing that John C. Branner is State Geologist, Arthur Winslow "Assistant Geologist in charge of coal regions," R. A. F. Penrose, Jr., "Assistant Geologist in charge of iron and manganese", and R. N. Brackett, chemist. After his customary salutation—My dear Father—he says:

"I have just returned here from several days absence in the back woods. I arrived in Little Rock on July 1st and a week later came here to start work. I have two assistants to do topographic and other detail work and will probably have another soon, and have been very busy since my arrival here arranging plans for work. I have the job of working up the manganese and iron all over the state and have begun here as this is the place where most developments have been made. There are absolutely no reliable maps of this region, nor any data to make one from, so my first job is to make a map. I am getting along well with this and have already had about 100 miles of roads and trails mapped and have profiles of many of them.

"I do most of my travelling on horseback as roads fit for a wagon do not abound in many places I have to go. It is pretty hot work as the thermometer ranges from 95° to 105° in the shade and I don't know how high it is in the sun. But I do know that after a day's travel in the sun a man has not got a dry article about his person and sweat is dripping from every point that it can drip from. But I got used to heat on the Lower Rio Grande and do not mind it—though it is almost as hot here as it was there.

"There is a temperance boom on in this state just now and prohibition laws exist in many places. The result is that the state is brimful of drunkards. I stopped for a few days last week at a railroad terminus called Cushman. The train came in once a day and as it approached the station you could see a string of natives coming down the hill back of the town—each with a whiskey jug in his hand. Each man would get a full jug out of the express car and deposit his empty one with the express agent to be taken to the nearest "wet town" and filled. Then they would start off up the hill—each man sucking his jug as he went, and often finishing it before he got home, and spending the rest of the night on his back in the woods sobering up.

"I thought that Texas was a pretty solid democratic state but Arkansas is more so. The local paper here stated last week that the Johnstown flood was a visitation of the 'wrath of God on the beastly big republican majority of Penna.' A reporter for the *St. Louis Globe Democrat*, which is a strong republican paper, was almost killed the other day at a country election. This is no place for a gent who wants to let loose republican sentiments—but he is all right as long as he keeps his mouth shut and says Grover Cleveland was a damned fine man and that Thurman never got drunk.

"I am very glad to hear that Philip got through his law examinations all right. I had a letter from Speck a short time ago. He says his prospects are fine for this summer's business and his alfalfa corner promises to be a great success. I start off tomorrow for the country west of here in the White River valley. Will go on horseback and will be gone about a week.

"My address is always, Geological Survey, Little Rock, Ark. Mail is forwarded wherever I am. I hope your Capon trip is doing you good."

Letter from Dick to his father, dated Batesville, Ark., July [August] 7/89.

Since writing to you last Sunday I have received your letter of July 30th. Will write more in full in a few days. Do not worry yourself about my health down here as I am as well as I ever was in my life, weigh 170 lbs. and have not been sick a day this summer. I take 5 grains quinine daily and only take larger doses when I think I need them—which is rarely. During the hottest weather in July I had not a touch of malaria. The weather is much cooler now and the most trying part of the summer is over. Will write more in full in a few days about the geological work here.

My train is just about to start and I must cut this short. Have just heard from Speck. He says he is well but very busy.

I am exceedingly glad you are comfortably fixed at Seal Harbor and hope your trip will do you good.

That his father did not entirely approve of his prospects in Arkansas is obvious from the context of Dick's letter of August 20th, which follows, but even in his disapproval the father must have been proud of the character development evidenced in the reply of his son. Having commenced a piece of work, Dick would not quit until it was completed.

Letter from Dick to his father, dated Batesville, Ark., Aug. 20/89

I have just returned here from an absence of some days and have received your letter of Aug. 11th. I also received your letter of July 30th in which you spoke about my giving up the work here and answered it several days ago—intending to write more fully later. But the other letters you mention as having written since I have been in Ark., I never received. This is strange, as everything is forwarded to me from Little Rock wherever I am. I will make inquiries at Little Rock and see where the trouble is. Your last two letters have come promptly to hand. The others may be at the survey office in Little Rock and I will make them be more careful in the future.

I thoroughly agree with you that the so-called "great" (?) democratic states are very low grade communities and the southwestern states are the lowest of the lot, as they are peopled by the lowest class of immigrants from the old southern states. They have neither the intelligence, the energy or the desire to improve their condition. They are perfectly contented to wallow through life in filth and poverty and all that they ask is not to have to work. All their misfortunes they blame on the North and never attribute them to their owned damned thriftlessness. They have not got half the intelligence of an Indian and in filth the Indians are away out of sight in comparison with them. Of course, I meet the lowest class of people in the backwoods and there are better ones in the towns, but it is only a difference in degree. I get along first rate with them as I never discuss politics nor the "nigger question" with them and these two things are the only questions they ever gather up energy enough to quarrel about.

As you say, my pay of $2000 per year is very insignificant, but I would like to finish my work on manganese here, as my work will be the first ever done on

American manganese ores. Though these ores are increasing very rapidly in importance, their nature and origin is absolutely unknown and my report will treat of an entirely new field. My phosphate article has done me a great deal of good in my business, but the report on manganese will be much longer and printed in better shape—and being in an unknown field will derive additional value.

I want to try to come home in the latter part of Nov. or early in Dec. I have a Texas report to write and want to have plenty of time to do it while in Phila where I can get access to libraries. We can discuss the matter of my position here then.

As I wrote you the other day, I take only about 5 grains quinine daily unless in very bad places, when I take more. Those doses of 30–40 grains daily that Boies wrote you about, I only take when necessary and that is very rarely. I have to use them much more often on other members of the party than on myself as they constantly neglect to take a daily small dose and when they don't take it they get malaria. I am as well as I ever was in my life and can ride and walk from one end of the week to the other without feeling it. But I have not much use for the South as a place to live in permanently. Texas is a much better state than Arkansas, but I am not sorry I made the change as the opportunities for doing good work are vastly superior here to what they are on the Texas survey.

I wish I could go with you on a trip as you mention when you leave Mt. Desert, but I do not see how I can get away from here until late in November. Perhaps you would like to go off somewhere between then and the time I have to come back here. I wish we could take trip together like we did last fall.

On the last day of 1889 Dick wrote to his father from the Virginia Hotel ("the best equipped hotel in the Territory") from Benson, Arizona:

"I have at last arrived here—several days later than I had expected—and will go to Tombstone tomorrow.

"I was greatly delayed in getting out of California by all the railroads being washed out by a choice combination of water-spouts, cloud-bursts, cyclones, etc. There was not a road in the state that was not greatly damaged. Hundreds of bridges, embankments, etc., were carried away and it will probably be almost a month from the time of the storm, before the Southern Pacific can run its through trains again. In places, several miles of track are gone and the embankments entirely swept away. As I wrote you from Stockton last week, I started east on the Southern Pacific, but was soon stopped by the washouts north of Los Angeles. I returned at once to San Francisco and arrived there just in time to catch a coasting steamer for San Pedro, the seaport of Los Angeles, which I reached in a little less than two days. On arriving here I found that for the first time in about a week a train would try to get to Los Angeles. We reached Los Angeles all right and there found that the road east of the town was almost completely washed away. This left me in another pickle, but as I had worked my way so far I thought I would try to get on, though the wagon roads were almost as badly washed away in the mountains as the railroads. I made arrangements with five other men to share the expense of the trip and after some trouble, succeeded in finding a man who was willing to run the risk of smashing his wagon and bogging his horses, and hired him to drive us until we came to where the railroad was solid to the eastward. This point we at last reached, though several times we got very badly bogged up. Here, to our joy, we found a train just ready to start east and what was still better, we heard that the road had not been washed away to the east and that it was clear and solid. It was a pretty tough train—made up of what old cars they could find, but we were glad to get it such as it was, and amused ourselves a large part of the night playing cards.

"About 200 belated passengers San Francisco bound for the east were on the same steamboat as I took. Out of this whole crowd—most all men—the only ones to reach the train were I and the five men with me. The others will probably have to wait for several days or a week to get through. Most of them are in San Pedro or Los Angeles. The five men with me consisted of two drummers, a post-office inspector, a spiritualist medium and his manager. We were on the train together for 24 hours and became very good friends. The medium was one of the biggest cranks I ever met, but he was a genial man and a very good card player. He and I beat his manager and a drummer very badly—much to their disgust. We have just parted—they for El Paso, I for this place.

"I expect to be in Tombstone one day and will then go at once to Austin and thence to Little Rock, which I expect to reach in about a week. The railroads from here to Austin and Little Rock are all right and have not been impaired at all, as the storm did not extend this far, so I will have no more trouble. The California storm was the culmination of a six weeks rain which lasted all the time I was in the state. The rainfall since Oct. has already been greater than it usually is for the whole winter. The valleys of the Sacramento and the San Joaquin Rivers—which are the most thickly populated parts of the state—have been flooded, the embankments of the rivers swept away, and houses and towns wrecked. In one place the Sacramento has changed its course and flows through a different part of the country than formerly.

"I am glad at last to get out of the infernal rain, and even the barren rocks and dry sandy desert at this town of Benson are an exceedingly pleasant change from riding in a pouring rain, belly-deep in mud on horseback, or creeping through slush and mud at the rate of ten miles a day in a four- or six-horse stage. The rain was the worst and most disasterous ever known in California—not only on account of its long duration, but also on account of the great winds which unroofed houses, etc., and in one case blew a man, horse and buggy off a bridge and into a river. However, I did not neglect the work I went to do and have seen everything that I needed to see.

"Hoping you are having no more trouble from gout, I remain,
"Your affectionate son,
R. A. F. Penrose, Jr."

"However, I did not neglect the work I went to do and have seen everything that I needed to see." Dick Penrose might have written that about any trip he ever took.

Branner, in his preface to the manganese volume, had spoken of D. M. Barringer as one of Penrose's assistants, and in the following letter to his father, dated Little Rock, Ark., April 22, 1890, Dick makes his first mention of Barringer, a fellow-Philadelphian with whom he must even then have been discussing their subsequent partnership:

"I received your letters of the 10th and 20th on my return here today and was very glad to know of your safe return to Phila and that your trip had done you so much good.

"Barringer left, as I believe I wrote you, early this month and has not yet got back. I have just received a telegram from him from Texas saying he will be here Saturday or Sunday. I do not suppose he will stay long, as he told me when he left that he wanted to be in Phila early in May. I started oft about ten days ago to see some manganese localities in the western part of the state and have just returned. I took along with me an ex-deputy sheriff who professed to know all the places where the ore was found and who claimed to be a terribly tough man. We started from here on horseback and he announced that he was going to show me what a tough man he was and that he would 'do me up riding.' The result was that when I got back here, I was riding and leading his horse—having had to leave him at a house on the way on his back trying to recuperate. In seven days of the time we travelled over 300 miles—often over the mts. without road or trail. One day, after a two-days storm and the streams all high, we had to swim three small rivers. This was not at all to the taste of the deputy who wanted to camp until the rivers went down, and it was not until I had got my horse across and began to laugh at him that he would try it. He now says that he may not be much on riding, but he can 'do me with the gloves' and if he turns up, we are going to have a match on Saturday. He weighs 190 lbs and is over six feet, but he is a yellow-faced, flabby native of Arkansas and I think I can lick him. I have bet him a bottle of whiskey I can do him up in three rounds. On our way back, I stopped a few hours at Hot Springs. It is a very prosperous town of eight or nine thousand people, built in a narrow ravine in the mountains. It is flooded with pox patients in all stages of poxyness and the roads leading to the town are lined with tramps heading for the springs. There are tramps without noses and tramps with noses and tramps with only pieces of noses; some on crutches, others limping on a stiff leg, and still others supporting each other to the baths.

"The springs come out of the side of a mountain and the water is led off in pipes to the various bath houses. Some of these are so elegantly arranged as any one could want and if a man wishes he can hire a bath tub for himself exclusively by the month or year. Out in the open air on the slope of the mountain is a big public bath, known as the "mud hole", which is free to gents at one time of day and free to ladies at another. Here the tramps and the whores without cash congregate. It is covered by a rough shed and is like a big swimming bath. Around on the outside can be seen tramps washing and soaking their feet and faces in little streams of hot water oozing out of the side of the mountain.

"There are several first class hotels in the town and it is not necessary for a man to see all this tramp business unless he wants to go look on. All he need see

Dick Penrose (right) as a member of the Arkansas Survey

J. C. Branner

is a fine hotel, a beautiful country and luxurious bath tubs built with tiles and kept very clean.

"I am going out to the Indian Territory border next week and will probably be there a month or more. I had hoped to be there by this time but have been delayed. Branner has been down with malaria but is better now. It is his own fault. I have tried to persuade him to take decent doses of quinine, but he won't do it. He sticks to eight grains a day and only takes that when he is sick. The result is that he has malaria all the time—whereas there is no necessity of his having it at all. It has been so remarkably cool this spring that I have not yet begun on quinine, but will do so as soon as the hot weather begins. It has been raining all spring and hot weather has not yet had a show.

"I have received a letter from Speck at San Francisco. He wrote in very good spirits and was just starting for Utah. You were all right in addressing him at Salt Lake as he wrote me that that was his address for the present—until April 25th.

"P.S. If you have any of those photographs we had taken last winter I would like to have one to hang up in my office."

Letter from Dick to his father, dated Little Rock, Ark., June 19, 1890

I received your letters of May 30th and June 12th on my arrival here from the southwest part of the state and am very much obliged to you for that newspaper clipping on South Carolina manganese. I had not heard of the locality before and will try to visit it the next time I come north. I finished up my horseback journey when I arrived at Nashville—having travelled almost 1000 miles and investigated the manganese region of that part of the state pretty thoroughly. I arrived there in good shape—though I cannot say the same for my horse, as the day before I got in I had ridden him continuously for 14 hours in a big northeast storm. I did this in order to reach a little settlement called Center Point by night. I got there a little after dark and it was lucky for me that I pushed the travelling that day, as the next morning the rivers were all rampant, had risen away out of their banks and carried away ferries, bridges, and everything else—not that there are many bridges in that region, but the few there were could not be seen.

The day before I got to Center Point, I stopped over night at a shanty in the Cossatot Mts., occupied by a man and wife and another woman. The man and wife were both deaf and dumb and the other woman was dying of dropsy. The deaf pair had three small children who did not seem to inherit the infirmities of their parents as they kept up the damnedest bawling all night that I ever heard. The dropsical woman sighed and groaned, the children screached, the deaf man said grace with his fingers over a dish of cornbread and pork and I smoked and damned. The next day when I met a man who could talk I felt like hugging him.

From Nashville I went to Magnet Cove on the Ouachita River and thence here. I have now finished up all my field work in Arkansas and would like very much to come to Phila this summer, but as I write up my report on this region I will have to make short trips to the different areas I have worked on to verify special points and for this reason I will be kept here in Little Rock most of the summer, but I hope to come to Phila the latter part of the summer or in the fall.

You speak of sending me some whiskey. If you have any handy I would be very much obliged for it, but it is not worth while going to much trouble about it.

I was very glad to hear that Philip had passed his examinations in such good shape and hope he will have as good luck in getting practice.

I have had several letters from Speck lately. He seems much encouraged about the prospects of the reservation being opened and I think he is on the track of a big thing. He deserves to succeed as he is working hard and is a man of nerve. I wish I could be in Utah with him. I would break loose from here for a few months and go, were it not for the fact that if I did, my report would not be ready for the next legislature and I have contracted to have it ready by that time.

I will be up to my eyes in work from now until next December. My report will comprise between 250 and 300 pages, including three large maps. The more I work on it, the more I find I have to do. Besides, I have to make a short trip to Texas and Cuba and have to do a little work in Missouri before I am done.

I have had two fine opportunities to make

[The rest of the letter is missing. What was it he had an opportunity to make—the change his father was obviously advocating?]

Letter from Dick to his father, dated Little Rock, Arkansas, July 9, 1890

I have at last got settled down to solid work and am getting in some big licks on my report, but I have got such a lot of material to work up that I have as yet hardly made an impression on it and I don't know whether I am going to have time to write it as fully as I want. I am trying to arrange things now so as to come to Phila the latter part of August. I have a certain amount of writing that I have to do here. After that I expect to spend a week visiting some manganese localities in Central Texas and then to go to northern Arkansas for a couple of weeks to finish a little work there. I want to finish all this in time to attend the meeting of the American Geological Society* in Indianapolis on August 19 and will go from there direct to Phila. I will not leave here for Texas until about Aug. 1st. There are no libraries here and it is therefore a very unsatisfactory place to do any work, so I will leave the larger part of it until I come home.

Branner has been away for over two weeks and I have been running the office—which has kept me busier than I would otherwise be. I had a letter from Speck a few days ago. The bill to open a part of the Ute Reservation was vetoed by Harrison so that some of his claims are not available—at least at present. But he has some good claims outside that he ought to make some money on.

The thermometer here has stood at over 100° every day but three for the last three weeks. It is very hot but a man can keep alive by wearing as little clothing as the law allows. It is impossible, however, to do half as much work

---

* Original name of Geological Society of America.

as in cooler weather. I have hired a very comfortable room which I share with a man named Brackett, a graduate of Johns Hopkins and chemist in the survey. He was married a year ago and his wife is now at her home in Atlanta because she is knocked up. Brackett was so broken up about it—her leaving or her being knocked up, I don't know which—that he went to bed for two days, after she left. I offered to send out to Indian Territory for two squaws for him, but he would not be consoled and said I was a "low brute." Every night when I go to bed he is at the table writing long letters to her, which I should think would cause her to have an abortion quicker than being kicked by a mule.

I wrote to you at Phila about three weeks ago.

Hoping you have had a pleasant trip at Capon and that it has done you good, I remain

Your affectionate son
R. A. F. Penrose, Jr.

Letter from Dick to his father, dated Little Rock, Arkansas, July 17, 1890

I received your letter of the 13th today. The whiskey has also arrived and I am exceedingly obliged to you for it. I have just sampled it and it is excellent. It is in great contrast to the stuff that is sold here. People in this country can't appreciate good whiskey so the dealers only sell rot-gut. I gave Brackett a drink and it almost made him forget that his wife was knocked up.

I am getting along pretty well with my work and have written about what will equal sixty pages of print. When I am done I will have between 250 and 300 pages.*

Branner returned from his northern trip on Sunday and is now laid up in bed with malaria, but expects to be all right soon.

I will send you tomorrow a copy of the Texas report containing my paper. I have only two copies but have written for some more and if you want them, will send you some as soon as I get them. I was unable to see a large part of the proof and the result is that some of it is poorly corrected and some of the sentences basely arranged, but it is better than I had expected as a Texas product. Dumble claimed that the printers would not wait long enough to send me the proof. He was mad at my leaving him and I guess this was the cause of it.

I had intended to go to Cuba early in the fall, but since you think it is best not to do so I will put it off until winter.

I wrote to Speck several days ago advising him to take a look at those hot springs in Colorado that I told you about last winter. I saw them when the ground was covered by snow and was in a great hurry on other work, but they impressed me as being a very valuable thing. They are on the western slope of the main range of the Rocky Mts. and in as beautiful a position as there is in Colorado. If they could be boomed as Hot Springs, Ark., have been, they ought to be a big thing.

I wrote you several days ago and as I said then, hope to come home the latter part of August.

---

* As it turned out, the book occupied 642 pages.

I am exceedingly glad to know that your Capon trip has done you so much good.

Again thanking you for the whiskey, I remain,
Your affectionate son
R. A. F. Penrose, Jr.

[Could the springs to which he refers have been those at Glenwood?]

Letter from Dick to his father, dated Indianapolis, August 19, 1890, and written on letterhead of The Bates (hotel)

I received your letter of the 12th on my return to Little Rock from Texas and have not answered it sooner as I had to rush right off again to southern Arkansas. I came on here today with Branner to attend the meeting of the Am. Geol. Society and the Am. Association. Branner wanted me to read a paper here and I have prepared one on the "Origin of the Manganese Ores of Northern Arkansas." I thought as long as I am in the business, I might as well go the whole hog and read a paper when I had a chance to write on a novel subject. I will be here for three or four days and will then return to Ark. to finish up my work before coming home.

I had a very successful trip in Texas and travelled over a thousand miles by rail and almost two hundred by horse in seven days, besides seeing all the manganese and iron localities I had expected to see. I got some very useful facts on the subject of manganese and the trip was well worth taking. I made my headquarters at a small town called Llano. The night I got there, a very fine fight took place between two leading citizens in the public square. The result was that the next day you could not see either of the eyes of one of the fighters and the other was "dry-docked for repairs."

As soon as I got back from Texas I had to go off to southern Arkansas with one of the chiefs of the U. S. Survey and just got back from there in time to catch the train for here. I stopped over a day in St. Louis to get some manganese statistics.

I am getting on fairly well with my report and hope to finish it in about a month after I get home. I have written up most of my Arkansas work and all my Texas and Nevada work. The work was scattered over such a large area that it takes me some time to work up the geology of each special area in which manganese is found, but I think I will get through it all right. I am very glad Speck has got home all right and hope that by this time he has got well of his cold and is getting fattened up after his hard trip. I will be very glad to talk to him about his Utah matters when I get home.

I hope to be in Phila before Sept. 15th. Every time I think I am going to get a start, something turns up to delay me, but I will make a break as soon as I can.

Politics are getting very hot in Ark. as the state elections come off on the 4th Sept. The prospects of our survey depend largely on the results as it is discussed considerably in the campaign.

Will write again when I get back to Ark., which I expect will be the end of this week.

The Survey chief to whom he refers may have been W J McGee, for, years later, when, as a member of the Washington Academy of Sciences, he received a letter from Gifford Pinchot, former governor of Pennsylvania and chairman of the W J McGee Commemorative Committee, stating that "it is proposed that a number of Doctor McGee's friends shall write papers or letters dealing with those sides of his character and his work with which they were most familiar. Your own association with Doctor McGee was of such a nature as to make a contribution from you most fitting and desirable." Penrose replied, under date of November 21, 1913:

"I have your letter of November 6th, asking me if I would send to you a letter or a paper relative to my recollections of Dr. W J McGee to be used at the meeting of the Washington Academy of Sciences, to be held on January 16th in commemoration of him. In reply, I would say that though I knew Dr. McGee for many years, I never knew him intimately, and therefore do not feel qualified to write in detail about him; but I consider it a privilege to be allowed to say a few words as a token of respect to the memory of one for whom I learned to have the greatest regard as a man and a scientist.

"My first recollection of Dr. McGee was when he went to Arkansas in 1891 or 1892 to study the Tertiary deposits of the southern part of that state. I was at that time assistant geologist on the Arkansas Geological Survey under Dr. J. C. Branner, who was state geologist. I met Dr. McGee in Little Rock and accompanied him for a few days on his trip through the southwestern part of the state. His wonderful energy and his quick grasp of the salient features of the geology of the region in which he was travelling left a lasting impression on me. I was at that time working on the geology of the iron ores of the same region, and the kindly interest Dr. McGee took in my work, as well as his pertinent suggestions, were a great stimulus to me in these investigations.

"This trip in Arkansas was the only time that I ever travelled with Dr. McGee, and I never had the good fortune to be associated with him in any of his other work, but I often met him afterward in Washington and at geological meetings. He was always the kind, considerate man that I had met first in Arkansas, always taking an interest in the work of the younger geologists, and encouraging them by good advice and suggestions. It was in these later years that I learned to appreciate his remarkable versatility, which enabled him to apply his strong intellectual powers to widely separated scientific subjects, so that he was a welcome member at all discussions, and a much sought advisor in many an intricate question.

"In the death of Dr. McGee, I feel that the world at large has lost an able scientist, and that those who knew him have, in addition, lost a sincere and sympathetic friend."

In writing of this period of Penrose's life, J. Stanley-Brown tells a story which he obtained through the courtesy of James W. Furness, of the U. S. Bureau of Mines, and Donnel F. Hewett, of the U. S. Geological Survey.*

"It should be noted that his many studies in manganese were to prove of value

---

* Geol. Soc. Am., Bull., vol. 43 (1932), p. 83.

years later when the United States found itself involved in the hideous turmoil of the Great War and all the resources of the National Research Council were requisitioned by the Government to determine the available manganese in the United States. In this connection an interesting story is told, illustrating not only Penrose's conservatism but the care he exercised in guarding his professional reputation. He was a member of the Research Council but when the decision was reached by it as to available manganese in this country he did not feel that he could concur in the conclusion of his colleagues, so he courteously and goodnaturedly tendered his resignation and retired from the meeting. The Council stood for 1,200,000 tons of 35% plus ore as against Penrose's estimate of 60,000 tons of 50% plus ore. It will be seen that even if the percentages were adjusted the former would still be much higher than the latter."

In his personal reminiscences of those days with Branner, which, as already noted, were the outstanding event in his memories of that work in Arkansas, Penrose wrote (December 7, 1905):

"I first met Dr. Branner in Little Rock in the fall of 1888. I had been appointed Assistant Geologist in charge of Eastern Texas on the Geological Survey of Texas, and was on the way from Philadelphia to Austin to take up the duties of my position. Dr. Branner was then State Geologist of Arkansas, having been appointed to that position by Governor Hughes in 1887. His remarkable work was already being appreciated both within and without the state, and I stopped in Little Rock to see and meet the man who was doing so much for science and for the State of Arkansas. I might add that most scientists who travelled through that part of the southwest in those days stopped in Little Rock to pay their respects to Dr. Branner. Later on, in 1889, it was my good fortune to become Dr. Branner's assistant on the Geological Survey of Arkansas.

"Governor Hughes of Arkansas, one of the wisest and best governors that that state ever had, took a deep interest in the matter of a geological survey of his state, and when the bill was passed providing for such an organization, he inquired carefully in various parts of the United States for the best man to make State Geologist. The result of his inquiries was that he offered the appointment to Dr. Branner, who, realizing the great good that could be done for the State of Arkansas, as well as for the cause of science, by a properly conducted geological survey, accepted the position. Dr. Branner was then Professor of Geology at the University of Indiana, and that institution, not wishing to lose him from the faculty, did not accept his resignation, but gave hin leave of absence, and retained him in his chair during all the years that he spent in Arkansas, though his work in the latter state prevented his giving much attention to his professorship in Indiana during that time.

"Governor Hughes' good judgment in securing Dr. Branner as State Geologist was soon apparent in the excellent results that developed from the work of the survey; and succeeding governors, regardless of political affiliations, recognizing the ability of Dr. Branner, were glad to continue his appointment from year to year during the six years that the active work of the survey lasted. The twenty odd volumes and other publications that now stand as the result of Dr. Branner's survey, are a worthy monument to the ability of a state geologist who combined the learning and scientific attainments of an eminent scholar with remarkable energy and rare executive ability.

"There were many difficulties, however, to overcome before this work was accomplished, difficulties due to lack of sufficient funds for survey work, or to the opposition of people who had an erroneous idea of the value of some of the state's resources, or of people who looked on geology as a sort of charlatanism and on geologists as quacks. Though the governors of the state were, as a rule, friendly to the survey, the same was not always true with the members of the legislature, so that it was often difficult to obtain adequate funds for the maintenance of the geological work, and but few men could have gotten the support which Dr. Branner secured. Fortunately for Arkansas, however, the people had in Dr. Branner a state geologist who commmanded the respect of all whom he met, whether they were opposed to his views or not, and many a legislator who came to Little Rock with the intention of opposing the survey appropriation bills, finished by supporting them, and often even becoming an enthusiastic champion of the bills, while many others, still inimical to the bills, relaxed considerably in their opposition. The result was that the survey was continued from year to year until 1893; and even after that, and up to the present time, isolated appropriations have been made to publish reports which, on account of lack of funds or the necessity for more time in preparation, had not previously been issued.

"Though successful in always securing some financial support from the state, yet the amounts were too small to carry on the many lines of investigation necessary in a region so little known geologically as Arkansas, and many a time Dr. Branner spent his own money to accomplish objects which should have been paid for by the state. Here again, however, Dr. Branner's personal magnetism, and the respect he commanded in his profession, did much to make up for the shortage in funds. Many young geologists jumped at the opportunity to come and work for him at very low salaries, or at no salaries at all; and a number of members of the survey thought themselves fortunate to work under, and gain experience and inspiration from, such a chief, with nothing but their travelling expenses paid in return. He inspired them with a zeal and enthusiasm which are rarely seen, and many a man labored through the hot summer months in the malarial swamps of the lowlands, often ill with fever, and with poor food, yet never once grumbling, but, on the contrary, believing himself fortunate to have such an opportunity. Many of these men were his former students in Indiana, who had followed him to Arkansas, while many were from other parts of the country.

"Dr. Branner himself was frequently with his assistants, sharing with them all their hardships, and affording them, by his own hard work, an encouragement which often carried them over many severe experiences. He himself worked harder than any man on the survey, both in the field and in the office, and when, as a result, he was taken dangerously ill in the winter of 1891, it was with the greatest difficulty that he could be induced to take enough care of himself properly to recover. If he had had his own way, he would have been up and off in the field, or at the office, when he should have been in bed.

"It is needless to say that a man of this kind accomplished an immense amount of work on comparatively little money, and well may the people of Arkansas be thankful that they had him as state geologist, for no one man ever did so much for the welfare of the state. Not only did he investigate the many geological features of scientific interest in the state, but he also studied and brought to notice its many mineral resources, showed where they were, and how to utilize them. The coal, the lead, zinc, and manganese ores, the clays, building stones, whetstones, mineral waters, and many other products were systematically studied and described in his reports.

"Among the many illustrations of his remarkable geological acumen may be mentioned the matter of natural gas. Dr. Branner saw where it could be found, and under his directions wells were bored near Fort Smith. These proved wonderfully productive, and at the present time [1905] are affording a cheap and excellent material for illuminating and other purposes at Fort Smith, and have added greatly to the prosperity of that city. These are only some of the many remarkable results of Dr. Branner's survey, which have added immensely to the material welfare of the state.

"In addition to all these economic results, Dr. Branner also accomplished scientific results of the very highest class, and it may safely be said that no state or federal geological reports in the United States are held in higher esteem than his, by the scientists of the country. Both from the standpoint of pure science, therefore, and also from the standpoint of economic results, his survey is without any superior and with very few equals, and all this was done on an amount of money ridiculously small compared with the value of the results.

"Probably nothing shows the remarkable influence of Dr. Branner over those around him so much as the effect of his example and training on his assistants in after life, long after the survey had been disbanded. An unusually large percentage of them, far larger than the average of geologists, have become successful in science, teaching, mining, and in other walks of life, and there is in my mind no doubt that this success was founded largely on the training they received under Dr. Branner. It was an inspiration given to others by his genius, courage, and zeal."

Throughout the rest of Branner's life, Penrose maintained his friendship and admiration for his former chief. At Branner's insistence, he taught for a brief period at Leland Stanford University, and he spent a short time with him in Brazil in which work he ever after maintained an interest.

In an envelope marked "Natural Objects named after R. A. F. Penrose, Jr.," was found a postcard from C. Wendler, Geneva, Switzerland, asking for a sample of "the bolivian mineral 'Penroseite,' " some correspondence with Branner, and the following memorandum, dated February 14, 1931:

"*The Eocene Mollusca of the State of Texas*", by Angelo Heilprin; Proceedings of the Academy of Natural Sciences of Philadelphia, Part III, 1890.

"Most of the material described in this paper was collected by R. A. F. Penrose, Jr., Geologist in charge of the Tertiary area of the State of Texas on the State Geological Survey of that State in 1887-89.

"Among the gasteropods described was one named "Clavella Penrosei", named by Professor Heilprin from R. A. F. Penrose, Jr., who collected most of the material which had been submitted to him for examination."

The Branner material consisted of three letters to Penrose. The first was dated Stanford University, California, October 10, 1912, and read as follows:

My dear Mr. Penrose:

Our papers giving the results of the expedition to Brazil last year are coming out as fast as they can be prepared and printed. We shall have altogether, I think, a volume of 500 pages or more.

I have encountered one difficulty that I venture, with much hesitation, to bother you about:—Professor Starks, who collected the fishes, has a fine lot of new material and he has prepared an excellent paper upon them. But he is not able to have the necessary drawings made to illustrate the new species. He tells me that the drawings will cost $180.00, and I have told him to go ahead and have them made. The photoengraving of the drawings and the publication of the paper will be otherwise paid for out of a fund we have here in the university. It seems pretty low down to come to you after all you have done for us, but you know what a poverty-stricken lot we professors are. If you can help me meet this bill for $180 for the drawings, your help will be very heartily appreciated.

Very truly yours,
J. C. Branner

The second letter is dated October 23, 1912, and is placemarked Stanford University:

My dear Dr. Penrose:

Yours of the 17th enclosing $180.00 to pay for the fish illustrations came duly. I had many compunctions about asking for it, but the fact is that only a few days ago a savings institution to which I had confided some of my precious funds went to the bow-wows and left me nearly three thousand dollars wiser than ever. If it hadn't been for that little episode I should have paid for those things myself. You did more than your share for that expedition without being bothered again. But we are all very grateful to you; that you can count on.

I hope you'll have a fine trip to Burma and Thibet. Bring us back some of the matrix of the rubies if you can conveniently. And get some more fresh materials for your book.

I'm glad to hear that Salisbury has gone to Chile, but the Lord pity him if he strikes the kind of steamer that I rode in on the Pacific coast.

Politics shakes my family to the center. Mrs. Branner was counting on voting for Mr. Taft; imagine her indignation at not being able to do so!

With kind regards.

Very truly yours,
J. C. Branner

The third letter is dated Stanford University, California, November 25, 1912.

Dear Dr. Penrose:
This is just to thank you for your kind inquiries of the 18th. My business losses wouldn't make anybody rich. That is one of the advantages of not having anything.

The drawings for Professor Starks' paper on Brazilian fishes are now done. They are splendid; and the handsomest new fish in the collection is named *Something-or-other penrosei*.

With best wishes,
Very truly yours,
J. C. Branner

On this letter is pasted a typewritten memorandum which reads as follows:
"In addition to the $180. to Dr. J. C. Branner, R. A. F. Penrose, Jr., sent him an additional check for $3500, in order to meet the expenses of the 'Stanford Expedition to Brazil, 1911.' "

Two years earlier while Penrose was in Paris, he had received a letter from Herbert C. Hoover, dated London, April 29, 1910, as follows:

Dear Penrose,
Please find enclosed letter from Dr. Branner. The old man seems to be badly in need of a couple of thousand dollars to see him through his Brazil business, and if you are inclined to join with me in putting up this money, I will be glad to contribute my part.

I am sorry I have not been able to get away from here, but things have been too complicated altogether to think of leaving for a minute.
Yours faithfully,
H. C. Hoover.

Obviously, Penrose responded in kind, for, although there is no other record of his contribution among his files, he wrote of this matter years later (January 11, 1924) to Professor Edward W. Berry, of Johns Hopkins University:

"On my return from some days absence I have received your letter of January 2nd relative to your proposition to publish your manuscript describing the Pliocene fossil plants collected in Bahia, Brazil, by Doctor Branner and his assistants. I think your plan is extremely good and that it would be an appropriate memorial to Doctor Branner if the Six hundred dollars which you say is necessary for the publication of your manuscript could be subscribed by his former students, as you suggest.

"I know well Doctor Branner's interest not only in the fossil flora but in the other geological features of Bahia, and on one of his longer trips I assisted him financially to a considerable extent. I feel therefore that I personally have done my duty in connection with his explorations. I realize, however, that he left much unfinished work which he would have completed if he had lived longer, and I think that his old students and associates could establish no more appropriate memorial to him than by publishing such manuscripts as yours and the other geological results which he left in a more or less unfinished condition.

"I might add that I have recently been writing a biographical memoir of Doctor Branner, and I fully realize how much important scientific knowledge might be made available by the publication of just such manuscripts as you mention."

On October 9, 1925, Dr. Stephen B. L. Penrose, president of Whitman College at Walla Walla, Washington, and cousin of Dick, wrote to him that he had "just listened with keen interest to the reading of your Memoir on Dr. Branner. It is admirable, and I am grateful to you for it and for your sending a copy of it to me. I met Dr. Branner in 1905, when I went to Stanford University to preach the Baccalaureate sermon, and he showed a friendly interest in me because of my name and my relationship to you. I am glad to have so careful a summary of his work and scientific accomplishments. I will place it in the College Library, in order that others may read it and gain inspiration from his remarkable scientific career. I congratulate you upon the performance of this pious duty to his memory, and upon the simple, straight-forward, impressive account of his life and work."

Penrose responded on November 2 (1925) that he "was very glad to get your letter of October 9th, for it seems a long time since I have heard from you, and I assure you that I greatly appreciate your kind remarks about my Memoir of Doctor Branner. Such an expression of opinion coming from a scholar of your standing means a great deal to me. He had left no bibliography of any length and the task fell on me to prepare it, because he wrote in so many different journals and in so many different languages that I could not find anyone whom I could employ to do the work. I was glad, however, to write the biography and prepare the bibliography on account of my great admiration for the man, and my long association with him."

Of his days at Stanford with Branner, Penrose had written to E. W. Woodruff, whom he had met in those long-ago days at Stanford, where Woodruff was the first librarian, after a visit in Ithaca, N. Y., in December, 1924, the occasion being the meeting of the Geological Society of America, that "it was surely a great pleasure to have seen you last week in Ithaca, and I was reminded of the days in Lauro Hall at Stanford when we used to discuss the affairs of the world."

Later, Penrose sent to Woodruff a copy of the Branner memorial, concerning which, Professor Woodruff replied (August, 1925): "Thank you a lot for the Memorial to Dr. Branner. I have just received it and read it at once. I am sure that in content and tone it is just exactly what would have pleased him. Of course your purpose was appreciative of his work as a scientist, and it was not your idea to discuss his personality, including his charm and humor. But not being a scientist, but just a neighbor of his, I remember him chiefly for his unpretentiousness, his great common sense and his (on proper occasion) love of the humorous. The memoir is a fine and dignified piece of work."

In reply, Penrose wrote, under date of September 7, 1925:

Dear Woodruff:

Thank you for your letter of August 29th relative to the Branner Memoir. I assure you that I appreciate your remark when you say that it is what would have pleased him. I remember well his charm of manner, his humor, his great common-sense and other admirable qualities, and nothing would have pleased me more than to have discussed these features more fully, but the Geological Society of America wants only brief memoirs, and the space allowed is cruelly short.

If the bibliography of Branner's work had not taken up so much space I could have gone further into the purely biographical part of the sketch; but after thinking the matter carefully over I thought as long as I was limited in space that it was more important to give his bibliography in full than to cut it short for the sake of further discussion in the biography. After all, is there not much truth in the saying that "by the work we know the workman"?

A copy of a letter from Penrose to Branner was preserved in the Penrose files. It is dated May 16, 1921, and in it he thanks Branner "greatly for the complimentary remarks which you make on the address which I gave at Chicago on the 'Relation of Economic Geology to the General Principles of Geology.' I always value extremely your criticism or approval, for I know that in either case it is sincere and comes from deep learning and wisdom.

"I made the address short, though I had much more to say on the subject, for I feared that if I made it too long the audience would get tired and not listen to it. I think it was for this reason—that is, my desire to be brief—that I neglected the reference which you mention to the work of T. Sterry Hunt on the anticlinal theory of oil and gas. I knew of Hunt's work published in the Canadian Naturalist and also published some years later in his 'Chemical and Geological Essays,' and I should have mentioned his name before that of White; in fact I had mentioned his work in my original draft of the address, but in my desire for brevity I inadvertently omitted it. I may have occasion shortly to write further on this subject, and if so I will certainly take the opportunity to correct my oversight.

"I am very sorry indeed to hear that you have been laid up in the house with sickness, but I sincerely hope that you will soon be all right again and will be getting around as usual. You have always been so active that it does not seem natural to think of you as sick."

Branner died March 1, 1922. In a list, dated August 20, 1928, of "Busts and portraits for which R. A. F. Penrose, Jr., contributed altogether or in part," there is included a portrait of Professor J. C. Branner.

CHAPTER 7

Cripple Creek and Other Ventures

DURING the next twelve years (1891–1903) this Harvard graduate, before he was forty, made the fortune which he kept and augmented during the remainder of his life. Leaving the Arkansas Survey in the summer of 1891, he made a trip to Montana with his brothers, who loved to "rough it" in the wilds. After journeying through Yellowstone Park with them, he continued his professional labors with observation trips to Butte, Phillipsburg, Cooke City, Leadville, and other western mining regions, for the avowed purpose of studying ore deposits.

For five years he had lived and worked under all manner of conditions, with all kinds of men, and had been able to look at his profession from many different angles. As a result, he had made up his mind that ore deposits were his metier, and to the study of ore deposits he devoted the remainder of his life. During those long trips by boat in Texas and on horseback in Arkansas, he had been enabled, not only to do an excellent piece of work for his "employers," but he had had that blessed opportunity for thinking things out that only solitude in the open can bring to all true lovers of nature.

Among his associates in Philadelphia was a young man named Daniel Moreau Barringer, who had also acted as Penrose's assistant on the Arkansas Survey. Barringer was three years older than Dick Penrose, having been born in Raleigh, North Carolina, May 25, 1860. He had been graduated from Princeton in 1879 and received the degree of Master of Arts from the same institution in 1882. He studied law at the University of Pennsylvania, receiving the degree of LL.B. in 1882, and for some time practised his profession in association with his older brother, Lewin W. Barringer, a member of the Philadelphia Bar.

"He had a picturesque personality, full of human sympathy and enthusiasm in all fields that interested him," wrote Penrose in 1930, writing the obituary notice of his friend for the Boone and Crockett Club. "From boyhood he was noted as a wonderful marksman with both rifle and shotgun, while with the six-shooter he rarely missed the bull's eye in target practise. His early hunting began mostly in the mountains of North Carolina, Virginia, and West Virginia, but his energy and ambition for adventure soon led him to the Rocky Mountains, which were then in many parts a wild country, primeval in character, abounding in game and only sparsely settled.

"His first trip there was in 1882, but he made numerous later trips in association with some of his friends, among whom the writer was one. These trips were designed and carried out for the pure delight of the chase, and in these early days we never took guides, cooks, packers, or any other employees. We acted as our own guide, because we knew the country as well as anyone else; we made our own camps, and packed and unpacked our own horses."

These two young men now entered into a partnership under the title of "Penrose & Barringer, geologists and mining engineers," and opened offices in the Bullitt Building in Philadelphia. Penrose never took his headquarters from that building. According to the letter-head used by the young firm, its services were available for "Reports made upon Mining Properties and advice given concerning the working of Mines."

The members of the firm of Penrose and Barringer had ideas and the gumption and wherewithal to carry them out. In April, 1891, they sent out the following confidential letter to a group of picked men likely to be interested in such a proposition:

"Knowing that you are thoroughly familiar with the importance of the subject, the following proposition is submitted to you for your careful consideration:

"First:—We are sure that you will appreciate as we do the fact, that before long the rapidly increasing population West of the Mississippi and extending to the Pacific Ocean must be self supporting in the matter of iron and steel manufacture, and will not consent to be dependent upon the East or upon foreign countries for these products, which they are today prevented from using to the extent which they otherwise would, by the present necessarily high freight rate.

"Second:—From our extended knowledge of the subject and of the Western country, we are confident that large and well located iron ore deposits are to be found throughout the Western States and Territories, especially the Rocky Mountains and the Pacific Coast and along the coast of Alaska; furthermore, it is only reasonable to suppose that some of these are Bessemer in quality.

"Third:—Up to the present time practically no attention has been given to the subject of Western iron ores, but the time is *certainly* rapidly approaching when they will receive the attention they deserve, and it is conceived therefore that the present is the best time to secure the most valuable among them, for it is certain that they can never be bought or secured for less money in the future.

"In view of the foregoing facts we suggest the following scheme for the acquirement of such Bessemer deposits:

"A. It is proposed that a syndicate of eight men be formed, of which number the undersigned are to constitute two; those furnishing the capital to constitute six.

"B. The undersigned propose to give their time and best abilities to finding, examining and acquiring such of these deposits as they may consider to possess the greatest value and advantages of position.

"C. The six other members of the syndicate to pay their travelling expenses and only such other expenses as are absolutely necessary to the accomplishment of the proposed scheme, for all of which the undersigned will render them an accurate itemized account. It is expected that this expense account will not amount to over $9,000 per annum, or $1,500 cash for each of those subscribing the capital; also, that the work can be completed inside of two years.

"D. In addition to this the six other members of the syndicate are to furnish the capital necessary to buy such properties as the undersigned may recommend; the purchase of each to be subject, of course, to the approval of those furnishing the money or of certain members selected from among them.

"E. The undersigned will further agree to give those furnishing the necessary capital the benefit of all knowledge or information with regard to iron ore deposits or business connected with the same, derived while engaged in the prosecution of their work, provided the other six will act in good faith by them and will not take advantage of such information except upon the terms and proportion of interest indicated in this proposition.

"F. The only compensation which the undersigned demand for this work in the above enterprise is 25 per cent, or one-quarter full-paid non-assessable interest in the ownership of any and all properties purchased under their advice. By this arrangement, each of the eight members of the syndicate will received $12\frac{1}{2}\%$ interest in all purchases.

"In case these terms are accepted by the remaining six members of the syndicate, the undersigned agree to give their best energies and abilities to the prosecution of the work of finding and securing the most desirable properties.

"G. Finally, the undersigned wish to state that they consider themselves peculiarly fitted to undertake the proposed work. They have personally visited and examined every iron ore deposit now being worked in the United States, the various provinces of Canada and the Island of Cuba; and they feel that they are thoroughly conversant with the varying peculiarities of iron ores in the different parts of this Continent. They have both carried on geological and mining investigations in every State and Territory in the United States, and can say without conceit that no one in the country is so well acquainted with the mining and other resources and also with the people of the West, as we are.

"During these extensive investigations the undersigned have for some years past, made careful records of the location of all iron ore deposits that have come to their notice and it is their intention to devote this knowledge to the furtherance of the proposed scheme.

"They would also add that the only inducement they have in taking up the laborious investigations proposed in this scheme, is the one-quarter interest which they are to receive in all purchases made, as heretofore stated. They have travelled so extensively in this country, that the journeys incident to the accomplishment of the scheme will be a labor and not a pleasure to them, and they consider that their good faith and confidence in the ultimate value of the properties acquired is proved not only by this, but also by the fact that they ask no remuneration whatever except their expenses while engaged in the work and their interest in the properties acquired. The six members of the syndicate furnishing the capital will risk at the most not over $9,000 per annum for two years or less; in other words, each of the six risks not over $1,500 per annum, or $3,000 in the whole investigation. The undersigned, on the other hand, risk their time and energies which, as they consider and can show, could be devoted to work returning a much larger profit than the amount risked by the other members of the syndicate. Their confidence in the proposed scheme, however, is such that they are willing to take this risk.

"In conclusion the undersigned would suggest that it is absolutely necessary to the success of the proposed scheme that the intentions and operations of the syndicate be as little known as possible, for were it generally rumored that a syndicate had been formed to control Bessemer Iron Ores in the West, many persons would attempt to anticipate their operations in individual districts and consequently make the properties much more difficult and expensive to acquire. It is therefore expected that those to whom this proposition is suggested, whether or not they accept the conditions offered, will consider the *whole matter strictly confidential*."

In March and April of the following year (1892) the two young men were in New Mexico, searching for likely coal and iron deposits, their report of that trip being addressed to "The Owners of the Hanover Iron Properties." The letter of transmittal tells the story in detail:

"On March 19th, while in Silver City, we received directions from you, through Mr. L. W. Barringer, to examine into and report on the coal resources of New Mexico. As this was quite an extensive piece of work, we proceeded at once to El Paso in order to obtain certain facts concerning the coal areas, which we required in mapping out our itinerary.

"On March 21st we proceeded to San Antonio, New Mexico, and thence to Carthage. From here on the morning of March 22nd, we took stage for White Oaks, a distance of ninety miles, where we arrived on the morning of March 23rd. The 23rd and 24th we spent in examining the coal near White Oaks and the 25th in visiting the Salado coal field south of White Oaks. On the 25th we started back to San Antonio, reaching there on the 27th and reaching Albuquerque on the morning of the 28th. Here we stayed until that night in order to obtain certain facts about the Cerillos and Gallup coal fields, and early on the 29th we reached Cerillos. That day we visited the Cerillos mines and on the 30th we drove to and examined the Wallace coal field. The same night we took train for Gallup, arriving there on the 31st. That day and the next (April 1st) we spent in examining the mines of the Gallup region and on the night of April 1st we took train for Magdalena, arriving there the afternoon of Apr. 2nd. On Apr. 3rd we drove to the coal fields twenty miles distant from that town, returning the next night, Apr. 4th. The same night we proceeded to Socorro and from there on the first train to Silver City, arriving there Apr. 6th.

"From here it was our intention to visit the much-talked-of coal field in the Cooney district about 100 miles north of Silver City. The one man, Capt. Cooney, who was reported to know the locality of the deposit, however, was absent at the time we reached Silver City and we were compelled to wait for him until Apr. 13th. On that day we started north, and on the 14th we reached Capt. Cooney's ranch. On the 15th we started for the settlement of Luna near which the coal was reported to exist. We reached Luna after a very difficult trip, on the night of the 16th. Here we found that a friend of Capt. Cooney whom the latter expected to guide us to the coal, had left the country for Texas. But another prospector who had been a partner of this man, informed us that the coal lay 70 or 75 miles north of Luna. From his description we at once saw that this would bring the coal within the southern extension of the Gallup field and as we had already been there we recognized that Capt. Cooney had been misinformed and we therefore refused to go any farther. On Apr. 17th we began our journey back to Silver City, arriving there on the 19th. The trip proved fruitless, but had the coal existed where we were told by the best informed people in Silver City and Socorro that it did exist, it might have been of great value to the owners of the Hanover iron deposits. It was this idea that prompted us to make a journey which was at the same time difficult and extremely tedious. On Apr. 20th, we left Silver City for the Raton coal field, arriving there on the afternoon of the 21st. The same day we visited the coal mines of Raton and Blossburg, and managed to reach Trinidad on a freight train at night. On the 22nd we visited the coal mine in the neighborhood of Trinidad and here ended our investigations.

"We would further add that this examination of the coal resources of New Mexico has taken us over a month (exactly 33 days) of uninterrupted work, accompanied by over 2000 miles of travel by rail and about 1000 miles of tedious travel by stage and on horseback. We have not lost a moment's time that could have been saved and we have devoted all our energies to the investigation entrusted to us. We hope, therefore, that the present report will satisfy the wishes which prompted you in having us make it."

The report, which covers thirty-four pages, after giving a general picture of the coal deposits in New Mexico, proceeds to describe in detail each of the areas covered in the letter of transmissal, and concludes:

"We believe that one of your objects in having this coal investigation made was the idea that it might be possible for you to locate good coal lands directly from the government or to acquire them in districts already located by others. Both these alternatives are possible, since even in the known coal fields, there are doubtless large areas of coal lands unlocated because the people on the spot do not know enough about the geology of coal to appreciate its underground extent. After our thorough study of the coal conditions of the territory, however, we do not advise you to acquire coal lands at the present time either from the government or otherwise. The reasons for this are several:

"First. In the first place the government price of coal lands is $20. per acre within 15 miles of a railroad and $10 per acre beyond that distance. Private interests, of course, would have to be bought at a still higher figure. At such prices a considerable amount of money would be required to purchase anything like a coal area worth having. Now we do not think it advisable for you to lock up this money when it is by no means clear that you will, within any reasonable time, realize enough on it to compensate you for the risks you take.

"Second. In the second place the coal trade of New Mexico is controlled by the Santa Fe system which also controls every mile of railroad in the coal area of the territory. As this system owns its own coal lands and has its own coke ovens (at Trinidad), it is to its interest to discourage other coal mining industries; and moreover, as it has it in its power not only to discourage but to actually suppress such companies by making prohibitive freight rates, these companies are absolutely at the mercy of the railroad and it is a somewhat precarious undertaking for them to start operations.

"Third. In the third place neither the coal nor the coke is entirely first class, and as eastern coke can now be bought in New Mexico almost as cheaply as the local product, it becomes a very serious question whether it would be advisable to use the New Mexico material at its present price. These prices, moreover, are not likely to be lowered as long as the Santa Fe System controls the situation."

Somewhat later the iron-ore deposits in Grant County were found, and Penrose and his partners invested with excellent monetary results. In a letter to J. Stanley-Brown, dated April 6, 1932, James W. Furness, of the U. S. Bureau of Mines, tells of that venture as follows:

"I believe it was in 1894 that Barringer, Brockman, and Penrose made an examination of the iron deposit situated some six miles east of Fort Bayard Grant County, New Mexico. Some thirty-one claims had been located by a prospector then living in Silver City. It was estimated by Penrose that these deposits contained more than 10,000,000 tons of iron ore of a grade of approximately 40 per cent iron. A deal was made with the owner and for a cash consideration of $85,000, the partnership took over the property. The thought was that money could not be better invested than in natural resources. It is believed that little consideration was given to immediate development. However, within a year negotiations were entered into with the Colorado Fuel & Iron Company, which resulted in a twenty-year lease. One of the terms of the lease was that a minimum tonnage of 200,000 tons a year should constitute the basis for royalty payment, and that the royalty should be 10 cents per ton of ore mined.

"As there were surface stains of copper in the vicinity, a clause was inserted in the lease providing that should the ore at any time contain precious ore metal value, other than iron, in excess of the then current iron ore price, that certain other conditions must be complied with and royalties increased proportionately. The occurrence of copper in these ores constituted almost from the start of development a bone of contention between the partners. Penrose maintained that the amount of copper indicated was an aggravation and an annoyance only; Barringer insisted that the deposit was of the type where oxidation had taken place and that in depth pyritic ore would be encountered. In other words, the deposit was similar in type to the Rio Tinto of Spain. Penrose maintained that the deposit was of the type of contact metamorphic; and time, of course, proved Penrose correct.

"After receiving royalties for twenty years, when the Colorado Fuel & Iron Ore Company wished to renew the lease, Barringer opposed Penrose and the result was the sale of Penrose's interest to Brockman and Barringer."

In the back of the Penrose notebooks covering that 1892 spring trip around New Mexico is the carefully kept expense account, which is extremely interesting as a picture of the man, the country and the times. Here is a sample:

Mch. 22—San Antonio to Carthage (2)	$	.80
" "—Stage, Carthage to White Oaks and return (2)		46.00
" "—Dinner (2)		1.00
" "—Brandy		1.75
" "—Supper (2)		1.00
" 26—Man at White Oaks		2.00
" "—Horse hire " "		15.00
" "—Board (2) " "		24.50
" "—Supper (2)		1.00
" 27—B'fast and l'dging		2.00
" "—Meals (Carthage)		1.00
" "—Carthage to San Antonio		2.00
" "—Meals " "		1.00
" "—San Antonio to Albuquerque		6.90
" 28—Board, Albuquerque		8.60
" "—Cigars "		2.00
" "—Albuquerque to Cerillos		2.00
" 30—Board, Cerillos		
" "—Horse hire "		16.00
" "—Meals, Wallace		1.50
" "—Fare, Wallace to Albuquerque		1.00
" "—Fares, Albuquerque to Gallup		19.00
" "—Sleeping car & porter		4.50
" "—Whiskey		1.50
" 31—Breakfast		1.50
" "—Telegram to Plume		.50
" "—Paper (Gallup)		.30
" "—Notebook		.65
Apr. 4—Team and grub to see Magdalena coal		17.40
" 7—Beer		1.00
" 11—Comforters & oil cloth		4.40
" 12—Coffee pot, plates, cups, etc.		2.55
" "—Groceries		2.75
" "—Canteen, ropes, knives, etc.		3.00
" 16—Jelly at Luna		.50

According to this expense account, Penrose returned to Philadelphia by way of Cheyenne, where he remained from April 23 to 26, doing what he could to aid his brother Charles, who had unwittingly gotten mixed up in the struggle between the great cattle owners who had used the Wyoming plains for years and the small landowners who came in at that time and began to put up fences, a struggle more familiarly known in Wyoming history as the Johnson County War.

After securing his medical degree, Charles Penrose had been resident physician at Pennsylvania Hospital from 1885 to 1886, and the following year he was out-patient surgeon at the same institution. In 1888 he was one of the founders and surgeons at Gynaecean Hospital, Philadelphia, and in 1890 was surgeon to the German Hospital. That fall he developed pulmonary tuberculosis and spent the next two years trying to regain his health. The winter of 1890 he was in Florida and the following summer and fall he spent camping in Wyoming. In November of 1891 he was in Colorado Springs, and just before Christmas he was persuaded by Dr. A. W. Barber, University of Pennsylvania medical school graduate of 1883, and acting governor of Wyoming, to move to Cheyenne. He lived at the Cheyenne Club and there met many of the owners of great cattle herds. In April, 1892, when the cattlemen planned the expedition into Johnson County which ended so disastrously, they invited the young doctor to go along as surgeon attached to the expedition. His health was apparently much better, and he probably looked upon the expedition as something of a lark.

In his story* of this adventure Charles Penrose says: "Governor Barber knew all about the expedition and advised me to go on it," and, also, "I had at least one interview with Barber and VanDeventer [afterward member of the United States Supreme Court] before going on the expedition, and we talked the matter over and either Barber or VanDeventer (I think the latter) gave me a telegraph code by which to communicate with them if I found it advisable to do so on the trip. This code I tore up and threw in the Platte River on my way to Douglas."

The story which Dick Penrose heard upon his arrival at Cheyenne as recorded in the Charles Penrose documents† was briefly as follows:

The expedition had secretly boarded cars at Cheyenne railway station the evening of April 5 and had as secretly disembarked in the early dawn of the next morning somewhat east of the then little town of Casper. Mounting their horses, which had also been on the train, the expedition rode north toward Buffalo, bent on raiding the headquarters of a band of "rustlers." Their first objective was the KC ranch, where now the village of Kaycee stands, two days hard riding from the point of leaving the railroad. There, they besieged Champion and Ray, leaders of the band, and after an all-day battle killed both of them.

Young Dr. Penrose, however, did not reach the KC, for the second morning out from Casper, he was too ill to ride and with a companion was left to make his way back. His companion took him to the ranch house of a friend 80 miles north of Douglas, which he reached April 8, and when he had sufficiently recovered, he started back alone for Cheyenne.

Meantime, the "invaders" had been stopped by the Johnson County men and were in turn besieged and might have fared badly indeed, had not Acting Governor Barber appealed to Washington for aid and the troops from Fort McKinney, 25 miles from Buffalo, arrived to stop the fight and arrest the "invaders," who were eventually taken to Cheyenne for trial. The feeling throughout the State ran high, and when young Dr. Penrose rode into Douglas he was recognized as a member of the expedition. Realizing that he might expect short shrift from the indignant citizens and noting that he was recognized and being followed, he appealed to the sheriff for protection.

* The subject of a master's thesis by Louise VanValkenburgh at the University of Wyoming, where documents have been placed on file by Charles' son, Boies Penrose II.

† These include Charles' letters to his brother Boies, his friends, Robert Halston and Owen Wister, the famous writer.

He spent the rest of the day and that night behind the bars in the little jail, hearing the waves of talk and shouts which marked the efforts of the local citizens to prevail upon the sheriff to release him for lynching, and watching with professional interest one of his cell-mates, a pervert.

The sheriff, afraid that his little stronghold might not hold out, sent word secretly to Cheyenne, and at dawn a lone engine steamed into town with Barber's representative aboard. He walked straight to the jail and before the citizens were aware of what was happening, he had demanded the custody of Penrose from the local sheriff, had whisked him aboard the engine, and was steaming south toward Cheyenne, where young Charles was again placed in protective custody for a short time and was then allowed to leave the State.

The trial of the "invaders" was held the following January, but the case was dismissed on the grounds that Johnson County refused to pay any of the expenses incident to the prosecution.

The year 1891 stands out vividly in western mining history for that spring gold was discovered in Cripple Creek and the rush to that great field began. Spencer Penrose was in Colorado Springs, having sold out his business in Las Cruces, New Mexico. He joined the rush with his friend, Charles L. Tutt, and together they secured claim to what eventually became the C.O.D. mine, one of the early productive properties, where Spencer Penrose made the foundation of his fortune, which, when he died in November of 1939, was estimated at seventeen million.

Dick Penrose, also, undoubtedly began his lifelong interest in the district at that time. In 1892, he visited Cripple Creek, and his notebook records the fact that at that time there were "15 paying mines—some mines paid for development—too soon to estimate output. Possibilities—good." Two years later, he went back to the area with Whitman Cross to make the detailed study of Cripple Creek which was published as Annual Report 16 (1898) of the United States Geological Survey, *The mining geology of the Cripple Creek district, Colorado.*

Decisions in the life of Penrose marked the year 1892. Hitherto, he had moved along from one post to another, each the outgrowth of previous associations. In 1892, however, he came to many partings of the way, and the decisions he reached were the measure of the man and his ability to judge a situation, not only in its current offerings but in its future possibilities.

On January 18, 1892, S. F. Emmons, of the United States Geological Survey, wrote to him from Washington that he was "authorized by the Director and Chief Geologist of the Survey to ask if you are willing to take charge, under my general supervision, of the field work of a geological study of the Mining District of Aspen, Colorado, on the same general plan as my monograph on the geology of Leadville. A topographical party has already been at work there during the past summer, and a grade-curve map of the most important part of the district is already completed. Maps of the underground working of the principal mines in this district have been obtained to the number of forty, and are being reduced to a common scale, preparatory to being assembled on an enlargement of the topographical map. As soon as these are completed, actual field work can be commenced, but I am not sure that a great deal of money can be devoted to the work before the next fiscal year beginning July 1, 1892. I wish, however, to assure myself of your services at once that plans may be made for the future. This district is the most interesting from a geological point of view in Colorado and in economical importance stands next to Leadville, which it may one day surpass especially if, as we may reasonably hope, our work materially aids exploration.

"I estimate that it may take two or three years to complete and publish the work, and there will be an immense amount of accurate underground observation required. My expectation is that you, with perhaps one or two assistants under you, will do the principal part of the field work, as I can only spare time myself to give you at the start the benefit of my experience as we go through some of the principal mines together, plan out the work with you and act as general advisor during its continuance. There will undoubtedly be some very complicated problems of structural geology to solve. I intend that you shall have full credit for your work, and expect, if you undertake it, you will let no outside matter interrupt it until it is completed.

"I should hope that you would be able to commence field work in May, but plans will have to be talked over after it is definitely understood that you are willing to undertake it. I shall be glad to hear from you on the subject at your earliest convenience."

Unfortunately, no copy of Penrose's reply is available. On what grounds did he decline this offer which must have seemed flattering indeed to a young man of twenty-nine? Was he already impressed with the possibilities of Cripple Creek and did he have a prescience that an offer to do that work might be forthcoming? Or was it simply that the future looked too glowing for him to tie himself up so tightly for three years—three years is a long time to any one in the twenties? In any event, he has written laconically in long hand, across the top of the letter, "I declined this offer. R. A. F. P. Jr."

That same year (1892) Branner had left the Geological Survey of Arkansas to take up his duties as professor of geology at the newly established Leland Stanford Junior University. Penrose was offered the vacated post in Arkansas, probably upon the recommendation of Branner. He refused. He was also offered the position of Assistant Professor of Geology at Stanford, which post he, likewise, refused.

Branner did, however, prevail upon him to give a series of lectures on economic geology at Stanford the following spring (1893), during the course of which he met and formed a friendship with Herbert Clark Hoover, the future president of the United States, which lasted until his death, almost forty years later.

Branner evidently never gave up the endeavor to get Penrose to Stanford, for as late as November 12, 1914, he wrote:

"Thus far I have not found any one for head geologist here. You are the one I should prefer above all others because I know we have about the same ideas about what to do and how to do it. If you can make any suggestions, I shall be glad to get them. I doubt if Salisbury would want to leave Chicago. Willis was sounded, but he is tied up in Argentina.

"I look forward eagerly to the end of this year. About the future I am not bothering much."

In the margin, Penrose has written in pencil, "Declined."

A third offer which Penrose declined in 1892 was that of the editorship of the *American Geologist.*

Instead, in the fall of 1892, Penrose became a member of the first faculty of the department of geology in the new University of Chicago, of which William R. Harper had assumed the presidency. The head of the geology department was Thomas Chrowder Chamberlin, the third great figure in American geology to influence the life of Penrose.

Writing in the Chamberlin memorial issue of the *Journal of Geology* (May–June, 1929), Penrose speaks of "the wonderful ability with which he (Chamberlin) organized his Department and the *Journal of Geology*, and the efficiency in teaching and research with which he inspired all who came in contact with him, and which will long remain a forceful and beneficient influence in the years to come."

Other notable members of that first faculty were R. D. Salisbury, professor of geographic geology; J. P. Iddings, associate professor of petrology; C. R. Van Hise, nonresident professor of Precambrian geology; W. H. Holmes, nonresident professor of archaeologic geology; George Bauer, of the biological department of the University, assistant professor of paleontology; Edmund Jüssen, docent in European stratigraphy.

In the "Program of Courses in Geology" for that first year, Associate Professor Penrose is listed to give two courses for "graduates and students of the University of Chicago," each occupying five hours a week in the second quarter of the second term. The first, Course No. 13, was "Elements of Economic Geology: The relations and contributions of geology to the various industries, constructional materials, such as building stones, bricks, cements, etc. Fertilizing materials (of geologic origin), such as marls, phosphates, gypsum, nitre, etc. The geological origin and nature of soils. Resources for water supply, as artesian wells, and similar topics." The second course was "Ore Deposits and Allied Formations: Besides ore deposits, which will be the leading topic, the course will include the discussion of non-metallic deposits of similar commercial relations and utility, as coal, mineral oils, natural gas, phosphates, sulphur, etc. The course will embrace descriptions and classifications of the deposits, the criteria for distinguishing them and determining their value, the methods of mining, the metallurgical processes used in their reduction, their chemical properties and geological relations, and the theories of their origin."

W. C. Alden, later geologist of the United States Geological Survey, was one of Penrose's students in those early days at Chicago. Of Penrose, he wrote (1932):

"He was a refined and pleasant gentleman; the classes were small, and his lectures, which were rather informal, gave us a great deal of interesting information about the occurrence of the ores and about the developments in the various mining regions, with many of which he was personally familiar."

In addition to his teaching, Penrose records that he "was intrusted with the problem of starting a mineralogical collection, and he presented his own somewhat limited personal collection to the University. At that period also the World's Columbian Exposition in Chicago was approaching the time when it would close, and the question with many of the exhibitors had arisen as to what to do with the materials they had assembled there. Many of the states of the United States and many foreign countries had brought to Chicago specimens of their minerals, ores, and other exhibits for display. The writer was successful in securing for the University some valuable gifts for the mineral collection of the Department of Geology, including many contributions from English, English Colonial, French, Swedish, and other foreign exhibits, as well as from the individual collections of many states in America. A large part of the splendid exhibit of the state of California was secured for the University."

Not only did he inaugurate the mineralogical collection, but he also took upon himself the laborious task of labeling each specimen .

Penrose became an active editor on the *Journal of Geology*, and "here again," he writes, "in the conception of the field of activity of the *Journal of Geology*, Chamberlin displayed his remarkable initiative and breadth of vision in planning a publication which would be devoted not only to the contributions of the Department, but to similar contributions from leading geologists throughout the world; and more than all, that the *Journal* would not be a medium for publishing simply local descriptions, but that it would be developed in such a way as to bear mostly upon broad conceptions of problems of fundamental importance. No geological journal, if indeed any journal in any branch of science, was ever designed with a grander ideal than that displayed in the announcement of publication of the *Journal;* and the history of the *Journal of Geology* since its foundation over thirty-six years ago has maintained this spirit and has commanded the respect not only of all geologists but also of scientists in general throughout the world."

In addition to his duties as an editor, Penrose also contributed papers to the *Journal*. Rollin T. Chamberlin, son of T. C. Chamberlin and his successor as editor of the *Journal*, wrote in his memorial tribute to Penrose* that "to the first volume of the *Journal of Geology*, which started strongly with articles on the broad, fundamental problems of geology by men of recognized standing, Penrose contributed a discussion of 'The Chemical Relation of Iron and Manganese in Sedimentary Rocks.' His thorough treatment of the many factors and principles governing solution and precipitation of these important elements made this a work of much scientific and practical value. In the second volume of the *Journal* appeared his studies on 'The Superficial Alteration of Ore Deposits.' The influence of this was widely felt, and it was, in fact, one of the studies out of which ultimately came our present ideas of secondary enrichment. Later his writings dealt more largely with selected mining districts arising from his almost unrivaled personal acquaintance with the principal mining regions of the globe."

Writing in 1941 of the man of those early days, R. T. Chamberlin declared that "he was not the sort around whom stories readily develop, being always the

* Journal of Geology, vol. 39 (1931), 756–760.

correct model gentleman and somewhat reserved in conversation. During several of the years while he was professor at this University [Chicago], he and Professor Salisbury each had a room with a privage family at 5540 Kenwood Avenue. Later a bachelor group built a large brick residence at 5730 Woodlawn Avenue, which some of us in later years dubbed 'The Nunnery.' In later years it was occupied by Salisbury, Iddings, Tarbell (Greek Department), and Freund (Law School). I am not sure, but I am rather inclined to think that the building was built in time for Penrose to be a member of the group during his last year here.

"Though I was just finishing the first year in high school when Penrose left the University, I do remember the particular enthusiasm of our family whenever he dropped around to call. Though never very talkative, he had great personal charm. As a boy, I was much impressed by his splendid athletic figure which gave the impression of very great strength."

What with his teaching, labeling of specimens, editing, writing, and the problems which constantly confronted the firm of Penrose and Barringer, Penrose found his time amply occupied.

Before assuming his duties at Chicago, he had spent considerable time in 1892 at his chosen work in Colorado. In addition to the investigations for the Hanover people and his trip to Cripple Creek, his notebooks show that he investigated and reported upon a group of mines at Cochiti, New Mexico, and at Calumet and Orient in Colorado. His expense account states that the object of his trip was to study the gold, silver, and copper mines of the southwest and the coal mines of New Mexico and Colorado.

At Cochiti, he visited and reported on the Albemarle, the Lone Star, the Iron King, and the Crown Point mines, gold mines in the Rio Grande valley, south and west of Santa Fe. The mines at Calumet and at Orient were for iron.

In the spring of 1893, Penrose gave the course of lectures on economic geology at Stanford University, to which reference has already been made. Evidently he was still looking about for his particular niche in life, if one is to judge by a letter from F. W. Woodruff, first librarian of Leland Stanford University, who wrote him under date of March 17, 1893:

Dear Dick,

The day after you left, Mrs. Comstock received a letter from Dr. Schurman* saying that he was now satisfied as to your ability as a general geologist and that there remained one other question to be discussed; namely, salary. He wants to know if you would come for $3000 a year. I infer that if you would, he would offer you the place.

Do you want my opinion? Here it is: I think you can get $3,500, and if I were you I wouldn't go for less. There are two ways to go about it. The first one is to tell them that, in view of your ten years experience and prospects elsewhere you couldn't think of accepting less than $3,500. The other way would be to modify

* Dr. Jacob Gould Schurman, president of Cornell from 1892 to 1920, and later U. S. Minister to China and Ambassador to Germany.

that somewhat by saying that while you have had ten years experience since leaving Harvard and have published considerable, yet in view of the fact that your experience as a lecturer has been limited to two courses, one course at Stanford and one course at Chicago, you feel that you would be willing to accept $3,000 the first year, upon the condition that at the end of the first year your salary be raised to $3,500.

If you are somewhat indifferent about going to Cornell, I would give the first answer; but if you really have a definite desire to go, I would give the second answer. Of one thing I am morally certain: after you have been a year at Cornell you will like it and they will like you and want to keep you; so that I do not think that with the offers you would be likely to get to go elsewhere if you were a success at Cornell, there would be any difficulty in your getting $4,000 to $5,000 within a few years. Besides, it would be a great honor for a kid of your age to be head of the Dept. of Geology at Cornell, which unquestionably is one of the three or four big universities in the country.

Now as soon as you get this letter in Philadelphia and come to a decision, write immediately to "Prof. J. H. Comstock, Cornell University, Ithaca, New York," giving him your answer to Dr. Shurman's question, and he will communicate it to Schurman. Whatever you write to Comstock let it be so that the letter may be turned over to Schurman, and don't forget to put your address at the head of it, so that if Schurman should want to telegraph to you he could reach you at once.

There has been a great big yawning void ever since you left us. What for did you go and do it? And my goodby to you was as unsatisfactory as a presidential levee, which your departure resembled. I hate to be one of a mob, and had it not been that I felt sure of seeing you again before many months, I would have soused the quadrangle with my tears at the thought of being one of a procession to file before your Highness and touch your paw remotely.

Keep me informed of yourself and believe that though I'm a slanderous brute, I am likewise

Your faithful friend
E. W. Woodruff

Here is a picture of a man of good-fellowship, the young man who made friends easily wherever he went. Why he did not pursue the Cornell project further is not evident from the material available. Perhaps it was more Woodruff's doings than his own—the tone of the letter would seem to indicate that such might be the case. Or perhaps he still had his mind fixed on that western country which was to reward him so richly for his faith in its bounty.

Penrose evidently returned to Philadelphia by way of Cripple Creek, for on April 19, 1893, from his office in the Bullitt Building, he sent to George H. Webster, of Colorado Springs, a report of the examination he had made on April 8 and 9 of the Eclipse gold mine in the Cripple Creek mining area.

"My advice to you is against putting any money into the investment," he wrote Mr. Webster. "This conclusion has been reached after having very carefully examined and sampled the mine; and my reasons for so advising you are fully stated in the present report and in the conclusions at the end of the report."

In the conclusions, he says: "I do not condemn the mine absolutely, for there is a possibility of finding another rich ore-shoot in vein No. 1, and there is also a possibility of finding better ore in future work on vein No. 2. Neither vein, however, contains at present in sight any valuable quantities of good ore, and I consider that the financial risks in searching for better ore in the Eclipse Mine are so great as compared with the chances of success, that I advise you against the purchase of the mine."

In May, in company with F. Lynwood Garrison, Philadelphia mining engineer, he made an investigation of fire-clay deposits at Renovo, Clinton County, Pennsylvania, for on June 3 the two men reported on the deposits to Henry W. Brown, of Philadelphia.

His notebooks of 1893 show that he visited mines at Globe, Bisbee, and Black Canyon, Arizona, the last-named being "gold deposits on the north side of the Phoenix and Prescott stage road, about 55 miles northwest of Phoenix and 2 miles northwest of Goddard's stage station."

That summer he spent some time in Cripple Creek, as evidenced by the assay report of J. S. Neall who, on September 26, 1893, made assays for him of ore from the C.O.D. mine, and from two reports on the situation at Cripple Creek, made to the Hon. S. W. Dorsey, of Denver, Colorado, and dated November 10 and December 8, 1893. Both reports are signed by both Penrose and Barringer.

The first report concerns the Victor mine; the second deals with the district as a whole, and calls attention to "the careful investigation we have made, occupying us a number of weeks." In the light of subsequent knowledge, it is interesting to note that "our investigations show that the great majority of the paying gold deposits are to be found in or closely adjacent to the porphyry area, and that in many, if not most, cases they owe their origin to the eruptive masses or dikes of phonolite traversing this area. This latter fact we were only able to prove after careful study, and it is not at all known by the miners because superficial decay has made the two rocks look so much alike that the miners have not been able to distinguish between them. This is notably the case on Raven Hill and Battle Mountain. In some cases, however, the gold deposits occur in the porphyry some distance from the phonolite dikes, yet it is not impossible that they may be more or less dependent on them. These facts probably explain why the best mines so far found occur in groups, the most important of which are known as Bull Mountain, Battle Mountain, Globe Hill, Raven Hill, and others. These and other facts also cause us to believe that the gold deposits as a rule will continue down to depth sufficient for all practical purposes and are not merely superficial. It will doubtless be found, however, that the gold in some of these deposits occurs in more or less irregular 'shoots' or rich bodies, with intervening barren ground . . . These alternating bodies of rich and poor ground together form the gold deposits or veins herein considered. In some cases these veins are distinct bodies of quartz occupying fissures in the porphyry, as in the Victor and other mines; in other cases the veins are impregnations with gold of the country rock along certain lines. These impregnations occur in several positions: in the granite at the contact with phonolite dikes, in the porphyry, and in the phonolite at the contact of these two rocks, and in the porphyry some distance away from the phonolite, as already mentioned. It is our opinion that by far the greatest amount of gold will be produced from the veins in the above-described porphyry area, especially in proximity to regions traversed by phonolite dikes ... It is worthy of note that the general strike of the veins is the same as the general strike of the phonolite dikes traversing the porphyry and granite. This fact still further confirms our opinion regarding the close connection of the phonolite dikes with most of the the gold deposits.

. . . .

"In conclusion, we wish to state that we have watched the progress of the camp from its beginning, and that, as a result of several visits, we have formed a favorable opinion of it, and finally that we believe that for a number of years to come it will continue to be an important producer of gold."

This report was presented before Penrose began his detailed work on the area with Whitman Cross, and when, as he states in the report, the deepest mine was 320 feet. Time has proved the correctness of his judgments and the modesty of his assertions.

That must have been a busy summer for Penrose, for at the end of August, he wrote to his father, who was then at his summer place in Seal Harbor, from the American House at Hamden Junction, Ohio, as follows:

"I have just arrived here from the southern part of this state, where I stopped on my way east to look into a proposed coal scheme which some people want us to help them with. I leave here tonight for Philadelphia and will arrive there tomorrow. I have had a very successful trip and I think it will pay me well to have taken it, for I have learned a great many new points about some new iron districts in the Lake Superior region which will help Barringer and me very greatly in our business. It has not been a pleasure trip for I have been doing a good deal of hard work and hard travelling, but I think it has paid.

"I spent a week in the new iron region of northeastern Minnesota after writing to you about two weeks ago from Duluth. Then I went to Chicago and spent three days at the International Geological Congress. I would not have made a special trip to attend this meeting, but as long as it was on my route I thought I might as well show up. From Chicago I went to southern Ohio and have now just arrived here on my return.

"I spent a few days in the Michigan copper country and I wish I had known the names of the copper company there that you once told me you had an interest in, as I might have found out something about it. I saw the country very thoroughly, however, and perhaps when I hear from you what the name of the company is, I can tell you something about it.

"Northern Michigan and Minnesota have lately been swept by forest fires* and

---

* The famous Hinckley Fire of 1893.

a number of towns have been completely swept away and nothing is left but piles of ashes, bricks, etc. I never realized how completely a town could be swept out of sight until I saw the ruins of a town called Matchwood in Michigan. I had been there a week before and the town was all right. It contained a number of brick buildings, large business blocks, etc., and was in a flourishing condition. A week later I passed where Matchwood ought to be and saw not one solitary house—only piles of ashes and brickes, a stove and other iron utensils in each pile of ashes, and little columns of smoke rising from each former site of a house, as if to tell people what had happened to Matchwood a few days before. In the forest, on the outskirts of the ruins, a man had put up a tent with a sign 'All that is left of Matchwood. Liquors and fine imported cigars for sale here.' I asked him what was the matter with Matchwood and he said he allowed hell had struck it. It looked as if he told the truth.

"I hope you are having a pleasant time at Seal Harbor."

On November 7, 1893, Penrose left Chicago for Denver, where he joined Barringer, who had been doing some investigating in Montana, and together they left Denver on the 14th for Bowie, Arizona, where they took the stage—the Sunday stage at that, for they had to pay extra fare, according to their expense account—for Globe. They spent ten days at Globe, investigating the resources of the Old Dominion Mine and the general region and preparing the answer to three questions for their client, F. E. Simpson, of Boston: i.e.,

"(1) Is it advisable for you to consolidate your interests in Globe with those of Phelps, Dodge & Co.? If so, what is the relative value of the different properties, and on what basis should this consolidation be made?

"(2) Will the ore on your own and other properties continue down indefinitely in as great abundance as it has already been found in the upper workings, or will it increase or decrease in quantity?

"(3) Will the ore at greater depths than have yet been reached continue down in the form of oxidized ores like those so far mined, or will it run into sulphides? This question has an important bearing on the commercial value of the ore, as the sulphide ores are poorer and more expensive to work than the oxidized ores."

Although they "were closely watched by the representatives of Phelps, Dodge & Co.," they managed to get enough information, "without disclosing the object of our visit," to enable them to report with confidence to their client that "we are clearly of the opinion that it is to your interest to consolidate with Phelps, Dodge & Co., on the best terms you can make, and our reasons for so thinking are as follows:

"(1) We believe that in the aggregate the properties of Phelps, Dodge & Co. contain more ore than is now left in the Old Dominion properties, as already explained.

"(2) The fact that the Old Dominion Copper Co. has been the sole ruling power in the Globe district has undoubtedly greatly facilitated your operations, for if you had had to compete with other strong operators in stores and for freight, wood, and all the other requisites of mining, you would have been at much greater expense, and your profits would have been measurably less. For reasons already given, you cannot hope to occupy much longer this advantageous position unless you absorb or consolidate with those who are in a position to operate in competion with you.

"(3) We think that the prestige of your mine, acquired by years of very successful operation and most excellent management, places you in a better position to negotiate satisfactorily to yourself with Phelps, Dodge & Co. at the present time than at any future date, especially if it should become known that the ore in your mine is not so abundant as it has been."

That they were ever watchful to do all possible for the advantage of their clients is evidenced in a paragraph of the report, which reads:

"While it is somewhat foreign to the errand on which we were sent, because the property is not controlled either by yourself or by Phelps, Dodge & Co., we think it may be of some interest and importance to you to know that we consider the Dime Mine in Copper Gulch well worth careful investigation. We found here that the geological conditions for ore are not unfavorable, and some very good ore has been disclosed in the small amount of development work already done, though to demonstrate the value of the property further development is required."

In the next to the last paragraph, there is that touch of the gracious Penrose which distinguished his relations with others throughout his life. The paragraph reads:

"Before closing, we do not think it improper to express to you our high opinion of the excellent manner in which Mr. Berray is conducting your mining operations in Globe. We consider him remarkably conversant with the occurrence of the ore and with the mining possibilities of the different claims in the district; and, for these reasons, as well as for his other many excellent qualities, we consider him admirably fitted, far more so than anyone else in Globe, to superintend operations should consolidation be effected."

Before leaving Globe, the investigators "thought it to your interest for us to visit the copper deposits in the Black Copper and Bloody Tanks districts some eight miles west of Globe, and partly controlled by Phelps, Dodge & Co. We found here some small and more or less isolated deposits of oxidized and sulphide ores, but we were not at all favorably impressed wth the quantity of the ore, and we feel confident that these districts will not become of any very great commercial importance."

This is the country of the now-famous Miami and Inspiration mines, but their development did not begin for another thirteen to sixteen years, after the beginnings of Utah Copper had shown what could be accomplished in the way of profitable mining of low-grade ore.

Leaving Globe on November 28, Penrose and Barringer returned to Bowie and then made a side trip to Bisbee and Benson, where they remained until December 11, and then returned to Philadelphia. A copy of the statement submitted to Mr. Simpson, shows that the fee for investigating the properties at Neihart, Montana, and Globe, Arizona, was three thousand dollars, plus traveling expenses. No wonder he was not excited at the prospects of a position at Cornell at three thousand a year!

Early in 1894, Penrose was studying the genesis of the red ore of the Clinton. Eugene A. Smith, State Geologist of Alabama, wrote him in this connection, as follows:

"Your letter of the 17th has been received. I am afraid I cannot give you very much information bearing upon the genesis of the red ore of the Clinton. Where our mining has penetrated the red ore stratum beyond the reach of atmospheric action, or at least where it is very inconsiderable, the ore is very generally found to be a ferruginous limestone, sometimes called hard ore, sometimes a self-fluxing ore. The iron even then is sufficiently oxidized to give the mass a red color. Near the outcrop, the ore is practically free from lime, and is rather open, or porous but not very much so, and known generally as soft ore. In much of it we find the shells, bryozoans, and other fossils ferruginized; i.e., the lime of the shell has been replaced by iron. It does not seem to me that the whole of the iron could have come from the limestone, because the leached ore is still very nearly the same bulk as the hard rock, not enough difference I think to let us explain the surface ore as merely a leached variety of the original rock. Apparently some additional iron has come in from somewhere. To go back to the deep-seated ore, I don't think any of our mines have gone so far as to discover the iron in the form of the carbonate alone; it is always at least partially oxidized.

"I have always been intending to go systematically to collecting specimens which might throw light on this subject, but have as yet very little variety among them. Red ferruginous limestone at one end of the series, and tolerably pure red ore at the other. I have not yet seen any of the Clinton ore bed in the form of a ferruginous limestone with the iron all in the form of ferrous carbonate.

"I am sorry I can't be of service to you in this matter."

Early in that same year (1894) also, Penrose received an offer which to many young men in his circumstances would have been extremely desirable, offering adventure and travel with an opportunity to practice his chosen profession. It is another tribute to his level-headedness that he refused to be turned from his determined path even by the following letter:

2013 Walnut Street
Philadelphia, March 21, 1894

Richard A. F. Penrose, Jr., Esq.,
  Assistant Professor of Geology,
    Chicago University,
      Chicago, Ill.
My dear Penrose:

At the request of Lieut. Peary* and Prof. Heilprin, I have about decided to take charge of the expedition which will start in the early summer to bring home the Peary party from their present quarters in Bowdoin Bay. The party

---

* Afterward Rear Admiral Robert E. Peary, who on April 6, 1909 reached the North Pole.

will only number five or six men, and will leave New York about June 25th, and return to Philadelphia about September 15th. Most of the time will be occupied in examining the western shore of Ellesmere Land in Jones' Sound and in locating the Iron Mountains near Cape York.

About a year ago I spoke to you of the possibility of my connection with the next Peary Relief Expedition, and expressed the hope that you would be able to joing the party as geologist. I take pleasure in again offering you the first chance to become the geologist of the outfit. Should you consider the matter favorably or desire further particulars, I will be happy to advise you further.

Kindly consider the above confidential.

Very truly yours,
Henry G. Bryant

Early in April, Penrose received another flattering offer, this time from I. C. White, at that time professor of geology at the University of West Virginia, and later, and for many years, State Geologist of West Virginia. They were evidently on excellent terms for the letter begins "My dear Penrose." White then proceeds to state that he has "recommended you for the vacant directorship of the Missouri Geological Survey.... Should you consent to take the position, I don't think there would be any trouble about your election, and I'm sure you would be sufficiently politic to keep the Survey alive and moving. X. is a good fellow and I am personally very fond of him, but he seemed to lack tact in dealing with men. You would be strong where he was weak in securing support for the Survey."

Thus early in his career he had earned a reputation for tact and administrative ability, but he had also learned to chart his own course,and again he declined an offer, which, whatever its disadvantages, must have pleased him.

Instead, on May 1, 1894, Hoke Smith, then Secretary of the Department of the Interior, signed the appointment of Richard A. F. Penrose, Jr., of Pennsylvania, as "Geologist in the Geological Survey at a salary of Ten Dollars per diem when actually employed, to take effect when he shall file the oath of office and enter on duty, 'Temporary Force.' "

This appointment was to cover his work with Whitman Cross, of the United States Geological Survey, in making the first detailed report on the gold-mining district of Cripple Creek, the results of which were published in the sixteenth annual report of the United States Geological Survey, under the title, "The mining geology of the Cripple Creek District, Colorado." It forms Part II of *The geology and mining industries of the Cripple Creek district of Colorado.*"

Of those days at Cripple Creek in the summer of 1894, Dr. Cross wrote to J. Stanley-Brown, under date of March 15, 1932, as follows:

"Penrose and I had never seen much of each other until we became associated in the work of the Geological Survey at Cripple Creek. We did not meet very often there, for I was working most of the time in the country immediately around the center of mining operations while Penrose was studying the ore deposits underground. I lived in camps and he in town.

Cripple Creek, Colorado

Boies, Charles, and Spencer Penrose

"We naturally conferred frequently in camp, in his office room, at lunch, or on the rock exposures about the mines. We had a mutual interest and became good friends very soon.

"As to Penrose's personality, he was a quiet, reserved type of man, not easy to get on intimate terms with, I imagine, even by those with whom he was thrown the most. But we were always interested in the same things—different phases of one job. We could begin at each meeting where we left off at the last one, and soon we understood each other very well.

"I never had reason to change my early impression that Penrose was one of the simplest, most straightforward, and thoroughly trustworthy men I ever met. He was simple because his interests were always in advancing the job he had on hand. There seemed fewer side issues, less distracting pleasures, than in any other acquaintance of mine. His honesty of purpose stood out and always for something worth while. One could have confidence that he would not mislead, yet he was not inclined to tell all he knew or thought, unless it was advisable. It would have been impossible to extract information he did not care to give.

"If Penrose knew how to play, I never found it out. His mind seemed always on his work.

"From his accounts of experiences with mining men and engineers at Cripple Creek I judge he usually gained their confidence quickly by straightforward approach. Only a few Cripple Creek mine owners or managers seemed loath to admit him to free inspection.

"Toward the end of his work the manager of one of the principal mines still held out, though seeming friendly enough. After several appointments broken by the manager, Penrose lost patience when once more his man failed to appear at the mine office at an appointed hour. So he picked up the telephone, got in touch with his man at the hotel in town, and something like this went over the wire:

"'You've broken another engagement. Now let me tell you something. If you want me to examine your damned mine before I leave town, you've got to be here in fifteen minutes. I won't wait any longer.'

"The office force gasped and was frightened. That was language the manager might use, but would he take it from Penrose? In less than the time named the said official dashed up the hill on a fine horse, rushed in with profuse apologies, and gave Penrose carte blanche to see everything.

"Telling me about it, Penrose remarked quietly, 'I find that's the only way to handle blasted idiots like that chump.'

"It was one of the mines he most needed to know about.

"At the close of our work at Cripple Creek, Penrose and I spent an evening together summing up our studies and estimating the future for the camp. We agreed that intelligent prospecting would develop new ore deposits in a short time, but within a limited area. I jokingly remarked that Penrose surely (and I possibly) could go out and secure abundant capital to back a thorough search for new bonanzas. We might make a fortune offhand. Taking me too seriously, he agreed to that but said he should, of course, not take up professional work in

Cripple Creek, for some years at least. It would not be fair to the Survey nor to the mine owners who had put confidence in him.

"He had many connections through which that might have been done and the Survey had not adopted at that time the policy of securing pledges from its employees not to engage in such practices, for a term of years, but Penrose had high ideals of conduct and never violated them for personal gain, I am sure.

"I think he disliked social contacts—why, I never found out. It might be easily explained with reference to Society in the fashionable or high-brow senses, but I have never known of a home circle of his refined friends where he seemed to enjoy himself.

"About three or four years ago I had quite a talk with him in Philadelphia and he seemed just as friendly and frank as of old. He told briefly of the desires he had cherished to help rejuvenate the University of Pennsylvania (from his position as trustee, I think) and the Academy of Natural Sciences of Philadelphia (of which he had been president for a time). He intimated that he was prepared to help them financially, but his efforts apparently were not appreciated and he had retired from both bodies. He was on the lookout for other opportunities. He was no doubt thinking of the Geological Society of America, but did not say so."

That same idea of Penrose—"the perfect gentleman"—seems to have been true of all who knew him. In 1938, the compiler of this work spent the summer tracking down every available clue to information, especially with regard to his work at Cripple Creek. All those interviewed had ever the same answer: "Penrose was a perfect gentleman, fine looking, a good dresser, very quiet, never said anything in a group of men he couldn't have said before a group of women. I don't remember any anecdotes about him, but he was a fine geologist and one on whose word you could rely."

In Cripple Creek, in Colorado Springs, in Denver, in New York, in Chicago, in Cincinnati, the story never changed in any respect.

Looking out over the valley of Cripple Creek from a tiny office high above the C.O.D. workings, one rainy day that summer (1938) an old-timer told how he had first met Penrose late in the nineties and later "used to meet him every afternoon at four at the Hotel Vanderbilt for a drink and a bit of gossip."

The Old-Timer had previously worked in Canada, north of Toronto.

"Do you know," he said, "that Penrose knew more about that country than I did even though I worked there for years. One day he said to me:

"'Do you know that near your workings in Canada are some of the oldest rocks in America, and the same rocks are also to be found in the Glass Mountains of Texas?'

"Some years later I was working for oil down on the Pecos and I made a trip over to the Glass Mountains to see if he was right. I had some specimens of the Canadian rocks with me, and he *was* right.

"He was interested in the Rocky Mountain Club of Cripple Creek," the Old-Timer added, "and probably was instrumental in getting its members the privileges of the Engineers Club in New York."

There was nothing of the weakling about Penrose; he was, as Joseph Stanley-

Brown* so fittingly said in his fine tribute, "essentially a man's man.... When it came to the question of judgments and decisions Penrose was like 'The cat that walked by himself' in Kipling's *Just So Stories*. He was a good listener but his conclusions were his own and no information was given out concerning them except of his own volition. He often asked his lawyer friend, John Stokes Adams— the door always stood open between their offices in the Bullitt Building in Philadelphia—many questions about wills, but his will was in his own handwriting and no one saw it until its probation. Still it is a very skillfully drawn document and doubtless embodies many of the suggestions of his cherished comrade....

"Richard Penrose possessed great capacity for making friends and as the years went by and his interests expanded, these friends grew to be a small selective army scattered over the world.... It was my good fortune to know Doctor Penrose intimately during the two years preceding his death. Few persons I have met made a stronger appeal. He was free from all pettiness of life and from those habits and vices which so frequently mar social relations. He was kindly both in attitude and spirit—even gentle. There was a quietness in his demeanor and conversation that gave him the air of a silent man. His benevolences, always thoughtfully chosen, were many but not advertised. His manner was courtly and deferential. Possessing a commanding figure and charming presence, he was nevertheless modest even to the point of shyness. Life's experiences had taught him caution but when he gave his confidence it was almost with abandon. He was a born aristocrat scientifically and personally, but without even a hint of ostentaciousness or of snobbishness. His standards in life and in science were high and unyielding—he lived his best and did his best."

Mr. Stanley-Brown wrote of the man in his sixties, but those same attributes characterized Penrose in his thirties, as well.

W. H. Leonard, a close friend of Spencer Penrose with whom he shared quarters in those early days in Cripple Creek, recalled that "Dick would gather with us frequently at the National Hotel, for a drink and a bit of talk but in the main he seemed to be engrossed with his studies of the area."

The report of Cross and Penrose was hailed with enthusiasm by the mine owners and would-be mine owners of Cripple Creek as the *sine qua non*, The Book of the area. No well-regulated mine office could afford to be without it, a condition which prevails even unto this day.

"For the first two years of the Cripple Creek era," wrote Henry Lee, Jaques Warren, and Robert Stride, in a book on Cripple Creek and Victor, published by the Union Pacific, Denver & Gulf Railway in 1897, "every would-be expert had a story of his own to account for the rock and vein formation of the camp. Rarely did two agree, and frequently some of these wise men reversed their own fiats as often as the moon changed her phases. The first account of the somewhat complicated geological structure of this region, to be accepted with a degree of confidence in its correctness, was the result of field work of the United States Geo-

* Memorial of Richard Alexander Fullerton Penrose, Jr., Geol. Soc. Am., Bull., Vol. 43 (1932), p. 87.

logical Survey, under the direction of Dr. Whitman Cross, assisted by Professor R. A. F. Penrose, Jr., of the Chicago University, who had charge of the economic geology... So far as the writer knows, Professor Penrose was the first scientist to hazard the prediction that the Cripple Creek veins would continue to considerable depths and maintain their values. Three years ago, when it was the fad for prominent mining men to assert that the death knell of the district was already being rung, he made a forecast to the contrary. It is agreeable to look back over three years and to compare prediction with fulfillment."

To those who today look back over the fifty years of productive history of Cripple Creek, with its fluctuating fortunes and ever-continued flow of the precious metal which has made it one of the world's greatest gold-mining camps, the acuteness of Richard Penrose's vision is evident.

In *The Mountain States Mineral Age* of 1924, an article by Jack F. Lawson, entitled *Cripple Creek Gold Shipments Increased by Bonanza Strikes; Prospecting at Great Depths as Well as in Near Surface Workings Rewarded Beyond Calculations*, stated that "early in December, 1923, Cripple Creek awoke after years of lethargy to find itself heir apparent to an untold store of riches in the lower levels of mines within the newly created drained area made possible by the Roosevelt tunnel, thru the discovery of rich vein drillings assaying 100 ounces gold and 65 ounces silver to the ton on the 2700-foot level of the Portland Gold Mining Company. This find followed a somewhat similar strike of the year previous on the 2600-foot level of the same mine which encouraged its owners to carry on an extensive deep-level development campaign, now fully justified.

"Since the Portland's discovery several rich strikes have been made on the eighteenth level of the Cresson Gold Mining Company of equal magnitude, also the United Gold Mines, including the Vindicator, and several other firms, bearing out a prophesy made 25 years ago by an expert geologist, Professor R. A. F. Penrose, to the effect that Cripple Creek would eventually see the return of metal mining operations on a scale unprecedented since the boom days.

"Mr. Penrose stated at the conclusion of an extensive survey made a quarter of a century ago at the request of the United States geological service that rich ore would be found in the district at as great depths as the ingenuity of man could devise in the way of machinery and equipment to take it out. How this prediction has been borne out is evident from the recent strikes which have transformed Cripple Creek from an almost deserted gold camp into a thriving mining community."

R. W. Lesley, of Philadelphia, sent the clipping to Penrose, who responded with characteristic modesty:

"My idea at the time I published the results of my investigation was that the geological conditions at Cripple Creek were such that there was a good chance that some of the veins might go to very great depths. I did not mean that all the veins at Cripple Creek would reach great depths, but I did mean that the geological evidence, so far as I could interpret it, led me to believe that some of the veins would do so. It is a pleasure, therefore, to feel that one's predictions have come true after such a long interval."

In 1902, following the growth of the Cripple Creek district, there was considerable agitation to have a re-survey made of the area. One June 14th, Charles D. Walcott, then director of the United States Geological Survey, wrote to Penrose:

"Have you returned to this country, and if so when will you show up in Washington? I shall be away a great deal during the summer, but I should like to talk with you about a re-survey of Cripple Creek. We are getting many petitions to have you bring the survey up to date so that we can publish another folio."

A week later, D. V. Donaldson, president of the Colorado Springs Mining Stock Association, wrote to Penrose on behalf of the mine owners, saying that "mine owners and citizens of Colorado are deeply interested in the re-survey by you and are anxious to have it made at the earliest possible moment... The original survey made by you has been of inestimable value to the Cripple Creek District, and all mining men in this section are desirous that you should make the re-survey."

On July 7, Donaldson again wrote, saying "that since reading your letter we have decided to recommend our people to wait for the re-survey until next year, owing to the fact that we consider it very important for you to have charge of this work."

The following October, C. M. Hayes, geologist in charge of geology of the United States Geological Survey, wrote to Penrose, asking for estimates of costs of field work and preparation of report. He also called attention to the fact that "the operators in the Cripple Creek mining district, Colorado, are exceedingly anxious to have a re-examination of that district made under the auspices of the Geological Survey, and are further particularly anxious that you should do the work."

Four days later (October 17, 1902) Penrose wrote to the Survey, definitely refusing to make the re-survey. In response to that letter, Walcott wrote:

"I very much regret that your services are not available for this re-examination, since your first survey has given so much satisfaction and the operators were particularly anxious to have you make the re-survey."

On October 28, Donaldson also wrote, regretting his decision, and adding, "I am sure your decision will disappoint a great many of the mine owners, as they have been very earnest in their expressions that the work be undertaken by you. Accept our thanks for your offer to furnish us with any information concerning your previous work in the District."

The summer of 1894 saw exciting days in Cripple Creek for labor trouble between mine owners and mine workers resulting in the blowing up of one mine and the death of several persons. State militia was called out. The mine owners organized several companies of deputies. Dick and Spencer Penrose joined Company K, recruited largely from among the members of the popular El Paso Club. Eventually, labor won its battle, which was for an eight-hour day and a three-dollar-a-day wage.

Writing to Spencer Penrose, on June 17, 1924, Dick said: "I have read with much interest the clippings you sent me about the events which led up to the Cripple Creek War of 1894. I will keep them as important records of that exciting time, for they relate to occurrences which those of us who were involved will always remember."

After completing his work in Cripple Creek in 1894, and before returning east, Penrose spent August 21 to 23 at Park City, Utah, examining the Ontario Mine; August 25 and 26, at Mercur, Utah, examining the Mercur and the Marion mines; and August 26 to 28, at Eureka, Utah, examining the Eureka, the Centennial, the Bullion Beck, and the Gemini. From Utah, he went to Idaho, examining mines at Silver City and DeLamar.

From his notebooks, it is evident that ever as he moved about the country examining mines and claims and passing judgment on ores and future possibilities, he kept in mind the possibility of forming a company. One item in this Idaho notebook discusses the "American Mining, Milling and Development Company"; the other deals with "Mt. Adams."

"It is proposed to organize a company for the purpose of acquiring, developing, operating, and selling mining properties in the western states and elsewhere," he writes under the first heading. "Capital stock shall be $500,000, of which $200,000 goes to the promoters, $200,000 is sold, and $100,000 is treasury stock—all non-assessable.

"There shall be a president, a secretary, treasurer, and general manager.

"The duties of the general manager shall be to keep thoroughly familiar with the various mining camps and their latest development; to notify the board of directors of any desirable properties which in his opinion should be acquired and on the consent of a majority of the board to acquire such properties on the most desirable possible terms. It shall also be his duty to look after the development of any properties thus acquired and to see that each is placed in the hands of a competent superintendent.

"This company does not start in without any definite field of action for after a large amount of travelling the writer has two valuable properties which he would highly recommend to the company as worthy of their attention.

"A sinking fund of 10 percent of the net profits is to be started and continued until it amounts to $200,000, when it is to be discontinued and the total net profit paid in dividends which will be declared at the discretion of the board of directors."

From the tone of the notes, it is obvious that at that time Penrose had in mind for himself the post of general manager in such an organization.

Under the heading, "Mt. Adams," Penrose is thinking in terms of the firm of Penrose and Barringer. Only the outline is given, but it is ample enough for one to reconstruct the picture:

Purchase Price—$100,000

20% comm. to promotors

12 mo. option

Work begins in May

$25,000 to be paid at or before end of option; rest to be paid out of first earnings.

Sellers allowed to hold as much stock as they like up to $25,000 in proportion to their holdings.

Property to be managed by P. and B. who are to get no salary until mine is paid for. They also to get 20% of the stock of the company formed on purchase of mine for their services.

$20,000 to be raised for development.

$25,000 to be raised to pay at the end of one year if property is taken.

If this first payment is made, then a company of $500,000 is to be formed.
    $75,000 stock to be sold to pay for rest of mine
    125,000 stock to be sold for roads, mill, and working capital
    100,000 for treasury stock
    100,000 to P. and B.
    100,000 to those who originally put up.

                    $500,000
100,000 to P. and B.
100,000 to all other promoters
100,000 treasury stock
100,000 for property
 20,000 to repay development money
 80,000 working capital

After development is done and before company is formed the ore mined during development is to be sold and proceeds to be paid to promoters and P. and B. equally.

Alternative: They to put up $20,000 for development.
    If successful, form a $500,000 company.
        They to put up $200,000 cash and take 250,000 stock
        P. and B. to take 150,000 stock
        Treasury, 100,000 stock.
    All ore mined and shipped during development to pay expenses first and then the net profit to be put to the credit of owners on account of option.

Or: They to put up $20,000 development.
    If successful, form $500,000 company.
        They put up $125,000, of which $25,000 goes for a first payment and 100,000 for working capital and equipment.
        For this they take 250,000 shares of stock
        The remaining $75,000 for mine to be paid out of first profits. The first $25,000 is to give the lessor that much interest in the property regardless of other payments.
        100,000 stock for treasury
        150,000 to P. and B.

In any mining the production is kept up only by the discovery of new mines and of new ore bodies in old mines. The present condition of the silver industry is such that no prospecting for new mines is going on and very few of the old mines are looking for new ore bodies. They are simply taking out what ore they have in sight. The greatest producers in the world, Broken Hill, is closed. The natural result of this is a fall in production and a corresponding rise in price.

Thirty years later, under date of March 31, 1924, the American Mining and Milling Co., of Portland, Oregon, wrote to Penrose that according to their records he had made an examination of the Iron Sides property near Boise, Idaho, adding that "this property is twelve miles northwest of Boise, Idaho, and is alleged in the papers of the Company this 100-ton capacity which is now on the property and intact was built upon your recommendation."

Penrose replied on April 18 that he "never made a detailed report on this property, but I examined several gold mines in the neighborhood of Boise, Idaho, thirty years or more ago and I think that possibly the Ironsides Mine may have been one of them. I did not make these examinations for any individuals or company, but I made them simply to study for my own geological information the occurrence of gold in that vicinity. I would not therefore feel justified in stating at this time anything definite about the properties in question, for my visits to all of them were short and I never considered that my observations were in a form to present to any prospective mining organization in that region."

Many years after that Idaho visit, Penrose told Charles P. Berkey, then head of the department of geology at Columbia University, that he had examined hundreds of mines and carefully weighed their prospects before he put a penny into one. That his investments were successful is, therefore, a tribute to his ability as a geologist and his refusal to be swerved from hard scientific facts by any flourish of an enthusiastic imagination. It might also be termed self-reliance, confidence in his own judgment and an ability to stand alone regardless of what the rest of the crowd might do.

Penrose made several other mine examinations in 1894. One was for F. Lynwood Garrison, of Philadelphia, and concerned rock supplied as a paving stone by the Lumberville Granite Company. Another concerned mining property at Gold Hill, Boulder County, Colorado, which he examined in November. In his report, made December 7, 1894, to Edwin A. Stevens, of Hoboken, New Jersey, he wrote:

"As a result of the small and irregular character of the ore bodies, on the one hand, and the extreme richness of the ore, on the other, the history of mining on Gold Hill has been that, with a very few exceptions, the mines operated by companies have not been successful, while the mines operated by individuals or leasees who work their ore bodies with care and mine in a slower and more cautious manner than most companies; and who, as they work themselves in the mines, keep a personal watch to prevent stealing of ore, have in a number of cases been moderately successful. In no case, however, has any very great bonanza been found on Gold Hill, notwithstanding the amount of thorough development work which has been done in the district, though some mines have produced profitably for limited periods... In view of the foregoing and all other facts that we learned concerning your properties, it is clearly our advice that for the present, at least, no more money should be put by your Company into these properties, for there is nothing to warrant it. We do advise, however, that the properties be at once advertised for lease on royalty, and that the best terms offered by reliable parties be accepted... In conclusion, we would say that whatever you do, it is distinctly our advice that at present you put no more money into the properties."

On December 20, Penrose again left Philadelphia, in company with Barringer, and went to Tucson, Arizona, where on Christmas day they set forth on a horseback trip to the Santa Catalina Mountains, a matter of someting like a hundred miles of hard riding in the round trip. There they examined a group of gold mines known as the Southern Belle. Later, they reported to their client that, although there was gold, it was of such quality and quantity and the difficulties of milling and transportation were such that they did not recommend it as an investment.

CHAPTER 8

Mining in Arizona Territory

THE year 1895 marked a climax in the Penrose career. In January he reached the peak of his academic life, when a letter from William R. Harper, president of the University of Chicago, notified him that he had been promoted to a full professorship in economic geology in that institution. In December, the partners, Penrose and Barringer, together with John M. Brockman began mining operations at what later became Pearce, Arizona, and Penrose was elected president of the company, known as the Common-Wealth Mining and Milling Company, which mined gold and silver in Cochise County, some 25 miles from the old town of Tombstone.

Barringer had known Brockman as far back as the fall of 1891, and perhaps even earlier. In a report which Barringer made for Henry C. Butcher, of Philadelphia, dated September 18, 1891, he says, "As prearranged, I met Mr. R. L. Heflin at Deming, and with him went to Silver City, eight or nine miles south east of which the mine is situated. In company with Mr. Heflin and Mr. John Brockman, I spent three days upon the property and in the immediate neighborhood of the same." He speaks of the exploratory work having been done by Heflin and Brockman, and in conclusion recommends the purchase of the property. This may, or may not, have been Barringer's introduction to Brockman. In any event, Penrose was in Silver City in March and April of the following year and undoubtedly saw Brockman at that time, if not before.

Stanley-Brown* tells the story of this great adventure thus:

"At Silver City, whither Barringer had induced Penrose to go, there lived a German banker named John Brockman who was well known to Mr. Spencer Penrose. In addition to being the owner of a large ranch at the time Richard Penrose first met him, he was president of the First National Bank in Silver City and was highly regarded. His familiarity with the business affairs of his community and his high standing made him a valuable and valued associate. . . . It led to the formation of a very capable trio which held together and soon moved on to a brilliant success in what came to be known as the Commonwealth Mine.

"An assayer had told Brockman about some good ore which was coming from the cattle ranch of a family named Pearce in Cochise County in the southwestern [southeastern] corner of Arizona. Brockman had to go to Los Angeles and it was decided that en route he should stop off at Cochise Station on the Southern Pacific and visit the Pearce mine, eighteen miles distant. The mine was only about 300 yards from the old 'Santa Fe trail,' and Penrose frequently told the

---
* Geol. Soc. Am. Bull., vol. 43 (1932), p. 84.

story of crushing in his mill the ore-bearing rocks blackened by the campfires of the overland emigrants to California. The Pearces permitted an examination of the mine by Brockman, who found the development to consist of a 50-foot shaft and a 150-foot cross cut in ore, the assays of which indicated about $100 to the ton. For every ten dollars in silver there was a dollar of gold. Brockman wired Penrose and Barringer at Silver City to come to Cochise. This they did promptly and after a careful examination of the property, Penrose decided that it had excellent possibilities and that they would proceed with the business. A 90-day option was taken on the ranch for $250,000 and on the contract being signed Penrose and Barringer hurried to Philadelphia to raise the necessary funds. The scheme they presented to their old friends was the capitalization of the mine for $1,275,000 in dollar shares—of which one million shares were to be put in the treasury. An issue of $275,000 of bonds was to be made, the collateral for which was to be 275,000 shares of stock. The bonds were to be retirable dollar for dollar in stock at the option of the Board of Directors. Although Barringer was being staked apparently by Penrose the remaining million shares of treasury stock were to be shared equally by the three promoters—if all went well. The promotion was a success. Dr. Charles Penrose subscribed $50,000 in cash, and the balance was taken by friends of the two men. This seems to have been a case of confidence in Penrose's mining knowledge plus social prestige.

"When Drexel, Morgan & Company's certified cheque for $50,000 was offered to the Pearces it was declined, and Penrose had to go to Kansas City, get $50,000 in gold, and thus make the first payment as required by the option. When the gleaming gold was offered, the Pearces exclaimed, 'We did not know that there was so much money in the world.' Barringer's aside comment to Penrose was 'Dick, we could have gotten this mine much cheaper than we did.' Incidentally the deal was nearly upset by Mrs. Pearce insisting on reserving the right to run a boarding house. Later she had to be bought out as a nuisance value.

"The three men took off their coats and went to work. Brockman, by reason of previous residence in Mexico, was made manager, as nearly all the miners were Mexicans from across the nearby border. The entire equipment at the start was a 2-horse winch. . . . Ore had to be hauled eighteen miles to Cochise and by rail to Pueblo where was located the old Philadelphia smelter. The sampling was all done and watched by Spencer Penrose, of the firm of Penrose, Tutt, and MacNeill, at Cripple Creek, where they operated a sampler.

"In eighteen months there was taken out of the mine a million dollars in net returns. The bonds were retired by stock, as provided, and the remaining million dollars of shares was divided among the three. In the next four years the Commonwealth yielded some $6,000,000 . . . a stamp mill was built and the bullion taken out by pan-amalgamation and shipped by Wells, Fargo & Co. to the San Francisco mint. . . .

"The company obtained a charter to build a short railroad line to Cochise and asked E. H. Harriman, of the Southern Pacific, to take over the charter and construct the road. He at first refused but later built the road just as the Commonwealth had completed its stamp mill, so the little piece of railroad never hauled a pound of ore from the mine.

"When the Commonwealth ceased to pay $100,000 per month, Penrose decided to get out and he sold his interest for something under a million dollars to Count Pourtales and his associates."

The resignation took place in 1903, when Penrose moved on to his next big commercial adventure—the formation of the Utah Copper Company and the beginnings of the great copper mining works at Bingham Canyon, Utah.

In the years between 1895 and 1903, Penrose had been instrumental in building up a new town at the mines, called Pearce, which at one time had several thousand inhabitants and became not only important for the mining industries surrounding it, but also, later on, an important agricultural community in the Sulphur Spring Valley, in which it is situated.

The Common Wealth was only one of a group of mines in what was known as the Turquoise Mining District in the then Territory of Arizona, the others in the group belonging to the partners being the Silver Wave, the Ocean Wave, the North Bell, the One and All, and the Silver Crown. The list of legal documents and receipts shows that the period from the date of the agreement of lease of the property between James Pearce and John Brockman (December 7, 1895) to that of the agreement of trust, signed by R. A. F. Penrose, Jr. (March 20, 1896) must have been one of great industry on the part of the three partners.

Some idea of Penrose's movements during the month of March (1896) is gleaned from four letters, written to his father. The first two were written from Chicago, where he was evidently performing his duties as a professor of economic geology. They show that despite his many pre-occupations, he found time to do graciously and promptly little things that would satisfy the wishes of his beloved father.

Letter from Dick to his father, dated Chicago, March 5, 1896

I received your letter enclosing your check for $75 for the watch and I attended to the matter at once. The Elgin watches are said to be the best. The highest grade Elgin works without a case have heretofore cost $90, but the Elgin company have found that it does not pay to make such high grade works, so they have stopped it and are selling out their stock of this grade. I managed to get one of these sets of works at the wholesale place I wrote you about, and by getting various kinds of discounts, etc., on it I paid only $47 for it. This is the finest watch made in the world. It contains 21 jewels and is adjusted for changes in temperature, elevation and everything else which can affect a watch. It is the same watch that is used by the man here who has charge of the "Western Union time" by which all the clocks of this city are regulated. He says it is the only watch he ever had that filled the bill. You said you wanted a nickel case so I got one, open face, numerals of the kind you wanted, stem winder, the best made, cost $0.75. This seems very cheap, but the reason is that the whole outfit came from a wholesale store where I got it at prices lower than most retail dealers could have got it. The whole outfit would have cost you retail about $100—as it is you get it for $47.75. You sent me $75 and I therefore enclose my check for $27.25 as the balance due you.

The watch is now at the store being regulated. I will get it this week and carry it for a while to see if it goes all right and then I will send it to you. If you prefer a gold case I can get you a very good one for about $20, but I got nickel as you said you preferred it.

I leave here for Arizona on the 19th of this month and sooner if possible. Everything seems to be going along well there, and I have got several people on the string to go into it when the time comes. I may possibly get off from here on the 13th or 14th.

P.S. If you want a gold case for the watch, it will be no trouble at all to change the nickel one, and I can get you a first class gold one.

Letter from Dick to his father, dated Chicago, March 11, 1896

I got your letters about the watch, and yesterday I got the gold case and had it engraved as you directed. The dealer has had it running for two weeks and says it is perfectly regulated; therefore I will ship it by express to you today.

When I came to look into the gold case matter I found that the best kind cost a little more than I had told you, but as you told me to get the best, I did so. If you don't like the pattern I can change it for you. It is the best made case that can be gotten anywhere. The works cost $50 but I got a discount for cash which brought them to $47. The case cost $48 but I got a discount which brought the cost of the whole outfit—works, case and all—to $92.12 as you will see by the enclosed bill. I had to buy the watch in the name of another man or otherwise the wholesale place would not have sold it to me. This is the reason the bill is made out in his name.

Speck and McNeil have been here for two or three days, but they leave tonight for Colorado Springs.

I leave for Arizona about next Tuesday. The reports from there are first rate. After I have been there again I will write you and let you know whether it is advisable for you to invest. From what Barringer and Brockman have been writing me, the mine has turned out fully up to our expectations.

I will write more in full before I leave here.

P.S. The watch has already been shipped to you from the wholesale store. They have just told me about it. I believe they paid the express but am not sure. If they did it will be marked paid.

Letter from Dick to his father, dated "On Train, March 14, 1896, Kansas"

Your letter of the 12th with some other mail was brought down to me at the train just as I was leaving Chicago tonight. Lewin Barringer had met me in Chicago by appointment and we were just starting for Arizona to fix up the legal matters at the mine. He had to be back in Phila in a few days and could not wait over for me, and yet he could not go west alone for I am trustee and had to be present. I thought over all these things and concluded that it would be best for me to go on with Lewin as a great deal depends on this trip; and if it is necessary I will come back with him in a few days and get Philip. I will have to come back soon anyhow to raise the rest of the money we need for the mine. I drop you this short line now to let you know where I am. My address will be Willcox, Arizona, till you hear from me again. I have arranged to meet Pourtales along the line of this road tomorrow and he will go with us. I have power of attorney from Tal so that all hands interested will be present. We will incorporate a Co. at once. I will write further from Willcox. Will also write Philip urging him to go west, but I am not sure it will do him much good.

Letter from Dick to his father, dated Planters Hotel, St. Louis, March 30, 1896

Lewin, Ro and I have just arrived here from the mine. The mine looks *great* and fully equals the expectations of all of us. We have incorporated under the laws of Arizona and are going to raise the rest of the money we need as a first mortgage on the property, at 10% for one year with a good bonus of stock for nothing.

I received your letters of the 13th and 17th at Willcox and am very greatly obliged to you for your offer to invest in the mine. I will explain the whole thing to you when I see you in a few days and if you want to come in I think you can make some money. We are here for a couple of days to place some of our mortgage bonds and will go from here to Chicago to do the same thing. Thence we will come to Phila and New York to place the rest. I would have stayed out in Arizona but Lewin thought it important for me to come east while the bonds are being placed as I am trustee for both the bond holders and for the mine owners, and have also been made president of the company, the incorporation papers for which we will have in a few days. As soon as all the bonds are placed I will go west again. The bonds are secured by over three times their value *in sight* in the mine, so that they are entirely safe. Moreover they get 10% interest and a good bonus in stock for nothing; while at the expiration of the mortgage the bond holders have the right to either take cash or to reinvest in the stock of the Co. I will explain all this more fully when I see you, which will be in four or five days.

One other letter from Dick to his father concerns the mining venture. It carries the new firm's letter-head, but is dated from El Paso, Texas, May 10, 1896:

"I should have written to you sooner but since we left San Francisco I have been on such an uninterrupted rush I have not had a moment to call my own.

"As I telegraphed from San Francisco, we completed the deal on our mine on April 30th. We paid a *total* amount for the mine of $240,000. This includes the $10,000 we paid last winter and the $10,000 we wired on from Philadelphia. We thus got a reduction of $35,000 from the original price of our option which, as you know, was $275,000. We got the reduction on consideration of the fact that we paid cash down three months before it was due. Our company has thus got $35,000 more in the treasury than we expected.

"From San Francisco, Brockman and I went direct to the mine to arrange for shipping ore. We have now got our freight teams to work and will make our first shipment tomorrow or the next day. We will begin by shipping ore to El Paso and may later ship also to San Francisco and Pueblo.

"Lewin and Ro left San Francisco a few days after Brockman and me, and we met again in Phoenix, the capital of Arizona. Here we held our first directors meeting and issued the mortgage of $300,000 to cover our debt to the bond holders, as well as doing other necessary business.

"I am in El Paso today arranging railroad and smelter rates and expect to have everything settled all right tomorrow. After we have begun to ship to the smelter here, I will tackle the smelters at Pueblo and San Francisco and try to cut rates still lower. At any rate, however, even if we continue to ship only to El Paso, we will have very reasonable rates from both the railroad and the smelter; but, of course, if we can cut rates still lower by getting one smelter to compete with another, it will mean just so much more money in our treasury.

"Lewin and Ro leave tomorrow for Philadelphia to attend to issuing the bonds and stock certificates. I will stay out here and at the mine, to look after the ore shipments. Brockman will stay at the mine and get out the ore as fast as we can ship it.

"Philip is at the mine and is looking very well. I have arranged to give him a job in connection with shipping the ore and he is much pleased. I am sure that if we can once get him working at something in which he takes an interest, he will be all right.

"I will write again soon. My address for the coming two months will be Willcox, Arizona."

Two other interesting letters of that period have been preserved. One is from Shaler, his old teacher; the other, from S. F. Emmons, of the U. S. Geological Survey.

Letter from N. S. Shaler, dated Cambridge, Mass., March 13, 1896

My dear Penrose:
I am much obliged to you for your kind letter and for the Cripple Creek memoir. It is not often I have a chance to congratulate a man in one letter on two successes, as I do you on the contribution and on your promotion to a full professorship. It is indeed a comfort to see the boys get on.

Come to us when you can to refresh our eyes with the sight of you, but come or not be sure that you are well remembered by us all.

Letter from S. F. Emmons, dated Washington, April 14, 1896

My dear Penrose,
Yours of the 9th was duly received, and copy of report sent as requested. Allow me to congratulate you on the good news we learned from Iddings with regard to your mining venture.

The Director desires me to make certain inquiries of you.

First, from what you have seen, what would you regard as the most promising district in New Mexico or Arizona, preferably the former, for the Survey to do economic work in. It is perhaps unnecessary to hint to you that we desire as far as possible to do work in a region that is likely to develop a considerable extent of mineral-bearing country, rather than single mines, so that the practical use of the survey work may impress itself upon the country, as in the case of Cripple Creek. We have now to pay regard also to political subdivisions, and cannot confine our work to rich regions like Colorado.

Second, We are expecting that M.C.'s from the mining states will secure an additional appropriation this year of say $25,000 for mining work; we are short, however, of men of sufficient experience to take charge of the economic work in a given district. Can you think of any such persons in private life, who would be likely to work on the survey, and whose geological knowledge you consider sufficient for such purpose.

Third, With regard to yourself. Could you probably undertake any work for the survey this summer? Say a work that would not require so much time or as exhausting treatment as Cripple Creek and which could probably be done in a couple of months. I have in mind the area covered by the Telluride atlas sheet, the areal geology of which was done by Cross last summer. The primary object would be the preparation of an economic sheet to accompany the areal sheet in the folios, and which should be accompanied by a concise characterization of the ore-deposits of the district, with some graphic representation on the map more than the mere indication of location of shafts, etc. Something on the general plan of my work on the Anthracite—Crested Butte folio, but with "all modern improvements."

Let me hear from you, as soon as convenient, what are your plans, etc.

No copy of Penrose's reply is in the files, but he did not take the offer. That summer of 1896 was spent mainly on business for the mines at Pearce. His list of trips for that year states that they consisted of "several trips from Philadelphia to Arizona, California, Colorado, and back to Philadelphia, on mining business."

In September of that year he received a letter from a young man, whom he had met during his stay at Stanford University, a young man who was destined to become world-famous, and with whom he kept up a correspondence for the remainder of his life. The letter, written in long-hand, is dated San Francisco, September 6, 1896, and is addressed to Mr. R. A. F. Penrose, Jr., at Colorado Springs. It is short and to the point:

Dear Mr. Penrose,

How did the British Columbia scheme turn out; I should be glad to hear of something.

Forwarded you $20.00 some time since to Colorado Springs and as I have heard nothing suppose you received it all O.K.

H. C. Hoover

There are no copies of the Penrose answers to the Hoover letters, but the latter indicate that those replies must have been gracious and friendly. The young mining engineer wrote again the following February (1897) from Berkeley:

Dear Mr. Penrose:

Was more than glad to get your note for I was about to start down on my own hook. Due to the encouragement of a quasi-mining engineer I know in Prescott. I am therefore indebted to you for saving my $150. Good things are rare.

Means is about to go to Randsburg and some other points and therefore his address can best be found by applying to me at Berkeley as I shall be constantly informed of his whereabouts. In case the job should develop we should like to know at once for the state of our exchequer permits of any sort of mining work. In case we were both idle it would be economy for the owners to take us both for two can do underground work in less than $\frac{1}{2}$ time one—for there is so much figuring, etc. We both have very fine instruments. So one of us or both will take it if it comes. We have both had considerable experience in all kinds of mine surveying and I have had three or four jobs involving legal questions of importance and can therefore attend to matters of title, etc.

Thanking you for your interest, I am

        Yours
        H. C. Hoover
         2225 Ellsworth St.,
         Berkeley, Cal.

Letter to Penrose at Wilcox, Arizona, from Herbert Hoover, dated San Francisco, March 1, 1897

I am about to trouble you again. I have been offered, through Mr. Janin, a situation with a strong English company in Western Australia. My duties will be the periodic inspection of their different mines and reporting on their various conditions and prospects, and the examination of new properties with view to purchase.

Mr. Janin wishes me to secure from you a letter which he can forward to the London offices in regard to myself if you would be good enough to do so. The fact that you have offered me charge of one of your properties I take as evidence of your confidence, and therefore impose upon you to this extent. The position is a very excellent one, commands a good salary with a good chance of progress. I should like to have this at the earliest possible date that it may forwarded, together with those of Janin, Mein, Pichoir, Lindgren and Branner. The letter should be addressed to Mr. Janin at the Pacific Union Club in this city. I forward you a copy of this letter to Philadelphia in order that I may catch you at the earliest possible date.

Letter from Herbert C. Hoover, dated San Francisco, March 17, 1897

My dear Mr. Penrose,

Your splendid note to Mr. Janin arrived all right and has been forwarded to England. Accept my sincere thanks for it.

The firm in England is

Bewick, Moreing & Co.,
Broad St. House, New Broad St.,
London, E.C.

They asked Mr. Janin to nominate them a man and to my surprise he nominated me. His letters will arrive in London about March 20-21 and should some contingencies arise I may accept your kind offer to cable them. Their cable address is "Bewick" London. I will telegraph you if it seems necessary. I will of course re-imburse any expense you may be put to.

As to some eastern influence I should appreciate it very much for my success depends on my outside (outside of Janin) backing largely.

The position pays $6000.00 per year and some fees which make it worth $10,000. a year with expenses. But better than that it is a strong company in a confidential position and in a new country. I am therefore anxious to secure it.

I do not want you to go to any trouble to yourself or place yourself under any obligations. Should you get some work done on them it may be addressed to them direct.

Thanking you for your many favors and kindly interest and encouragement, I am

Yours truly
H. C. Hoover
2225 Ellsworth St.
Berkeley, Cal.

Letter from Herbert C. Hoover, dated London, Hotel Cecil, Strand, April 12, 1897

My dear Mr. Penrose:

Today completed arrangements by which I go to Coolgarlie as inspector for Bewick, Moreing & Co. at a salary of $5000 per annum and some extra fees. I desire to express my great obligations to you for the various kindnesses you have so freely extended and I hope I shall be able to vindicate your good opinions.

Very sincerely yours,
H. C. Hoover

Letter from Herbert C. Hoover, dated Menzies Club, Menzies, Western Australia, November 21, 1897

Dear Dr. Penrose,

To trouble you again; I have the impression from somewhere, I cannot find where, that gold is soluble in a solution of Tellurium Oxide in H_2So_4. Can you cite me the authority if correct or any investigation on the subject?

Our library facilities are very, very limited in W. A., and I am endeavoring to prepare a paper on surficial alteration (enrichment in fact) of Westralian ore deposits.

There is without doubt an enrichment beyond any other mining region known —probably due mostly to mechanical causes. There is no rapid erosion nor has there been since late Tertiary in W. A., simply the slow attrition by wind and weather and consequent settling of gold upon or near the outcrop and its possible penetration. The strong alkaline waters acting with the accessory minerals as Te, might I fancy take the gold into solution and redeposit it in the presence of further agents or at water level. The surface being a lowering horizon through erosion the *first* line of enrichment at water level would ultimately become the surface.

The fact remains however as the dozens of wrecked English Companies witness, that there is a most wonderful enrichment above water level—generally less than 200 feet, more often 100 feet.

There are some good mines, however. And West Australia from being a general burying ground for English capital may turn out to be a *fair* vineyard.

I am

Sincerely yours
H. C. Hoover

P.S. T. A. Rickard is now with us but will probably be telling you of W. A. within next 6 months

Letter from Herbert C. Hoover, dated Octagon Chambers, Hunt Street, Coolgardie, Western Australia, 2nd April, 1898

Dear Sir,

Yours of the 15th Jan. and 2nd February to hand, for which I am greatly obligated.

Regarding Mr. Minard, changes in our staff have left us full of men for the present, but we have continual openings, and will, I hope, be able to engage him during the next few months.

I am leaving the Engineering staff of Bewick Moreing & Co. to accept the management of the "Sons of Gwalia" Gold Mines, together with the Consulting Engineership to the "East Murchison United" and several other Companies, at a much better salary.

The two mines mentioned are superb mines, and will, with the 100 stamps we are now designing, turn out I hope 20,000 ounces of gold per month.

There are some very fine mines indeed in Westralia, but not a great many. Possibly fifteen of those now known will ultimately pay dividends, and when you consider these fifteen stand on the market at a total value of over $50,000,000 you will see things are over-rated. There have been 482 mines floated in England out of West Australia with a total capitalization of over $350,000,000.00. Therefore no country in the World has witnessed such rank swindling and charlatan engineering, and the time to suffer from it is yet to arrive, for most of the "Wild Cats" are still extant.

The Geology is very complex. The valuable Mines all being impregnations, in fact the normal fissure quartz veins are so pockety and irregular that their nature is almost sufficient condemnation.

Thanking you for your many favors, I am

Sincerely yours,
H. C. Hoover

The year 1897 was like 1896 in many respects. Penrose was busy with his mining venture, but he found time to make a trip to Mexico in October, in company with Francis T. Freeland, for the purpose of examining the properties of the Kansas City Smelting and Refining Company and of Mr. Guggenheim's Sons, at Sierra Mojada. The mines examined were the San Salvador, the Encontada, and the Atalaya.

The year 1897 likewise marked the one venture of Dick Penrose into the political field. He allowed his name to be placed in candidacy for the appointive office of Governor of the territory of Arizona. Just why he permitted this to be done seems strange in a man of his temperament, but doubtless the citizens of that territory had convinced him that it was his duty, and Penrose was never one to shirk what he considered to be his duty.

A little booklet, containing the "Territorial Indorsements" of his candidacy, included a petition signed by a majority of the members of the nineteenth territorial legislature of Arizona, February 11, 1897, addressed to the President-elect of the United States (William McKinley) as follows:

"The undersigned members of the Nineteenth Legislative Assembly, of the Territory of Arizona, irrespective of politics, hereby recommend to your favorable consideration (whenever a change is made in the Governor of this Territory) the appointment of Richard A. F. Penrose, of Wilcox, Arizona, for Governor of this Territory. Mr. Penrose has been a resident of this territory for the past five years, and has extensive business interests here. He is a gentleman whose moral character and integrity are above reproach, and we confidently assure you that if he is appointed Governor of this Territory that his administration will be honest, conservative and satisfactory to our people and be a credit to your administration."

The booklet also contains letters from prominent citizens of Phoenix, Tucson, Wilcox, Tombstone, Bisbee, Benson, Prescott, Florence, Bowie, and Pearce. Penrose must have been especially touched by the petition, sent by the employees of his mines at Pearce.

"We, the undersigned, citizens and residents of Pearce," runs the petition, "in the Territory of Arizona, reposing especial trust and confidence in the honesty, ability, and integrity of R. A. F. Penrose, Jr., respectfully present this, our petition, praying for and recommending the appointment of the said R. A. F. Penrose, Jr., to the office of Governor of Arizona. He is eminently well qualified for the satisfactory performance of every duty required of him as Governor. While a partisan, R. A. F. Penrose, Jr., would perform the duties of the office satisfactorily to the people and the administration, regardless of party bias.

"We earnestly commend him to you as one worthy of the honor of such an appointment and as deserving it through service to his country, and honest and faithful public and party service."

Members of the Territorial press likewise added their praise of this geologist, just turned thirty-three, but already prominent throughout the west for his honesty of purpose, sound judgment, and amiable disposition.

"The most prominent among our candidates for Governor to-day is the Hon.

R. A. F. Penrose, Jr., of Cochise County," said the *Phoenix Herald*. "He was born in Philadelphia in the early sixties, is a graduate of Harvard University, from which institution he also received the degree of Doctor of Philosophy in Geology. He has at various times been connected with the United States Geological Survey, and the geological and mining surveys of several Western States. He has held the position of Professor of Economic Geology and Mining in the University of Chicago, and has given lectures on the same subject at Leland Stanford University, in California. His principal pursuit, however, has always been mining, in which he has been very successful. Six years ago he was consulting engineer of the Old Dominion Copper Company, and for a number of years he has been engaged in mining in this region of the country, especially in Arizona, where he is now president of the Commonwealth Mining and Milling Company, which owns the Pearce Mines in Cochise County.

"There are but few who are so thoroughly acquainted with the resources and the needs of Arizona, for he has, in his prospecting and mining operations, traversed every corner of the territory. He is equally familiar with the great mining, cattle, agricultural, lumber and other resources of the territory, and realizes most fully the great future in store for a region so richly endowed by nature, if developed on business principles. He is a large property owner himself, and has brought large sums of capital into the territory from Eastern investors, which has been judiciously invested for the benefit of those who relied on his good judgment and for the development of our resources. He is a staunch Republican, and has always been on the side of good government and the improvement of the territory. The confidence felt in him by Eastern people is shown by the large investments that have been made in Arizona through him, and his honest and prompt dealings here are appreciated by those who know him and have had business transactions with him.

"Those who know Mr. Penrose are his staunch and unswerving friends. He is a quiet, unassuming gentleman, as substantial and capable men generally are, and one, too, who though he has never sought political preferment will, in political position, be as sound and clean as he has been in every walk of his busy life. Mr. Penrose is a man in whom the people of Arizona implicitly trust, wherever he is known, and he is widely known. That the powers that make Governors may honor him and the territory is the hope of a large body of stalwart Republicans of the territory."

The *News* of Williams (Arizona) spoke of him as "a learned gentleman" whose chances were "favorable." The Phoenix *Gazette* remarked that "the new gubernatorial possibility is a young man, possibly 32 years of age, large and evidently of a jovial nature."

The *Arizona Daily Citizen*, after several paragraphs concerning "the appointment of a man whose mental and moral calibre is commensurate with the responsibility he will assume in his office," declared that "Democrats and Republicans are interested alike in good government, and the interests of neither should suffer because their political opponents are in power," and added:

"There are years of record behind Hon. R. A. F. Penrose, and on no page of his history is a single mark to his detriment. That he is capable is eminently proven by the conspicuous record he has made in his duties as a professor of geology, as a lecturer, and as a miner. That he is scrupulously honest is a fact which needs no further demonstration than the eminent confidence in which he is held by all who have the pleasure of his acquaintance.

"Mr. Penrose is not a politician in any sense. He is an unassuming, dignified gentleman of sterling qualities of head and heart, whose cause is being pushed by an admiring following of friends, regardless of any party ties, and who hope to see him assume the reins of territorial government for the good he can and will do, and for the credit which his administration will bring to our greatly maligned territory."

The Tombstone *Prospector* was equally enthusiastic:

"A number of gentlemen of more or less prominence have been mentioned as possibilities for the place of chief executive of Arizona; but few have been spoken of, so far as we have heard, that meet all the requirements of that exalted position. The first thing to be considered in this, as in all places of trust and honor, is the man's fitness for it; his knowledge of the needs of the people and of sturdy character to deal justly with the people; to ignore party hacks and in all things to be one of the people, free from narrowness and above small things. We have such a man in our midst, one we believe will meet the requirements of the office and give perfect satisfaction to the whole people.

"This gentleman has never been prominent in politics in the territory, but has large property interests here and is a bona fide citizen of the territory, is permanently and deeply identified with the industries of the country. It is the Hon. R. A. F. Penrose, president of the Commonwealth Mining Company, and one of the principal owners of the great Pearce mines in Cochise County. Mr. Penrose is a broad, liberal-minded, progressive gentleman, and would command the respect and hearty co-operation of the people."

The reason for the agitation for governor arose from the fact that a change of administration was due on March 4, the Republican McKinley following Democrat Cleveland. But despite these endorsements and despite the fact that he was a brother of Boies Penrose, then a member of the United States Senate and a prominent Republican, Penrose did not get the appointment. There is no record among his things to show whether he was glad or sorry at the outcome, but he evidently decided that one venture into politics was enough, for the following year when he was importuned to permit his name to be used as candidate for Territorial Delegate to Congress, he refused.

Charles C. Randolph, editor of *The Arizona Republican*, wrote him on August 19 (1898), "Your visit to Phoenix had the effect of starting a veritable boom for you and I can assure you that if you will say the word we can put up a winning fight."

All through August and September he was bombarded with letters from prominent citizens throughout the state, begging him to reconsider his decision not to permit his name to be used.

In November, 1899, Webster Street, chairman of the executive committee for Arizona statehood, wrote to Penrose at Pearce, on another political venture:

"The Executive Committee appointed to arrange for campaign at Washington, in the interest of statehood for Arizona, would like to be informed as soon as possible of those who expect to go to Washington on that mission.

"You having been appointed as a committeeman to visit Washington, you will kindly advise us if you will be in attendance. . . . Your services are very much needed in the work, and it is the hope of the Executive Committee that you lend your presence in Washington with the other members of the Committee."

In April, 1900, he received a letter from the governor of Arizona, N. O. Murphy, who said: "Since my return from the east I have heard considerable gossip about the make-up of the delegation to the National Convention, and from the information I have received you are slated as one of the delegates. I hope it is true, provided you want to go, and I am sure that the Territory's interests will be safe in your hands."

In July, Murphy again wrote to Penrose, this time with reference to the possibility of his being a delegate to Congress, and on September 18 (1900) he sent Penrose the following telegram:

"Irreparable dissension in the Democratic party makes Republican success certain this fall. You are recognized by all as the most satisfactory man for Congress that can be named for the sake of Arizona and Statehood, the Republican party, and yourself. I hope you will authorize me to state that you will accept the nomination of the same if tendered you. Answer quick."

But to all these offers, Penrose returned a refusal. Perhaps he thought one politician was enough for any family. More likely, it is that the position held nothing attractive for him and that his father, ever his mentor and prod—for above all things he prized that father's words of commendation and approval—was quick to see that political activities would undoubtedly interfere with his chosen profession and his mining activities.

By this time, also, he held office in several important and growing industries, and his time was altogether taken up with duties which he enjoyed and which he could pursue without any of the handshaking and lip service which the politician must give in order to maintain office, services which were ever distasteful to one of his independent thought and action.

In 1896, Penrose became a director in The Colorado-Philadelphia Reduction Company, with works at Colorado City. The officers of the company were Charles L. Tutt, president; Charles M. MacNeill, vice-president and general manager; Spencer Penrose, secretary and treasurer. Wendall P. Bowman was the other member of the board.

From 1899 to 1915, Penrose was a member of the executive committee of the Hanover Bessemer Iron Ore Association, which owned producing iron and copper mines in New Mexico. He was also a director of the Cripple Creek Sampling & Ore Company at Cripple Creek, and a director of the Gila Valley, Globe & Northern Railway Company from 1898 to 1903. In 1900, he became a director of the Philadelphia, Germantown and Norristown Railroad, a position he held until his death.

In the spring of 1899 he was in San Francisco on business and witnessed the departure of troops for Manila. From the Palace Hotel there, he wrote of it to his father, under date of May 25:

"I came up here a couple of days ago to arrange some new freight rate business with the Southern Pacific Railroad. They have been making some changes in their freight rate combinations that did not suit our plans, and rather than have an endless amount of correspondence, I came right on here, and here I am going to stay until I get what we want. I think I will have everything arranged satisfactorily to all parties this week, and I will then return to the mine, where I will stay a few days, and then start east—arriving in Phila about June 10th or sooner.

"We have arranged for our next dividend on June 4th, and I will sign the checks when I get home, which will be a few days after the date of the dividend.

"Brockman is at the mine. Everything is all right there except that just at present we are a little short of high grade shipping ore, though we may find more of it in our development work.

"San Francisco is ablaze with patriotism over the war. There are over 15,000 troops here now, ready to start for the Philippine Islands, and more are coming in from all over the country, on almost every train. Three big trans-Pacific steamers carrying about 3000 troops have just this moment left the harbor on their way to Manila. I have just come down from the roof of this hotel, which is one of the highest buildings in the city, where I have been watching the boats sail out of the bay. Almost every house has all the flags out that it can carry, every steam whistle in the city is blowing as hard as it can blow, fire-crackers and rockets are going off at every corner, the forts in the bay and at the Golden Gate are firing salutes, the war vessels and the revenue cutters in the harbor are doing the same, every tug, ferry boat and steamer is trying to make a bigger noise than its neighbor. In fact, a stranger would think the whole community had gone wild. No one talks of anything but owning the Philippines, and the only kick that is heard comes from the troops that are left behind, because they have to wait a few days until the other transport boats are ready to take them to Manila.

"P.S. May 28th. I have just finished up all my business satisfactorily with the railroad and will start for the mine this afternoon."

Two other letters concern the business at Pearce.

Letter to his father, dated Pearce, Arizona, February 2, 1901

I was very glad to get your letter of Jan. 25th, and am very much obliged to you for having answered that telegram from Shaler. I also received the letter from Shaler that you forwarded. Shaler wanted me to meet a man named Purington, who has been in Siberia, to talk about some gold mines there.*

I arrived here last Sunday night and found everything in good shape. The new mill is running full blast. The mines look fairly well, and we are having no

---

* Possibly here is the motive for his Siberian trip, which took place later that same year.

trouble supplying ore for the increased capacity of the mill. It will be a month or more, however, before all the small details about the mill are complete, as there are a number of little things yet to be done; but in the meantime we are running full capacity and the whole plant is very satisfactory.

We are striking a great deal of water in the bottom of the mine, which adds considerably to the expense of mining; but on the other hand the water is useful for the mill, and if it increases much more, we will be able to run the whole mill on the water from the mine, and can shut down the pumping plant at our well. At the present time about half or more of the water used in the mill is coming from the mine.

We have been able to introduce a few changes in the chemical treatment of our ores which, I think, will add considerably to the percentage of gold and silver that we extract. It is necessary for us to do everything of this kind that we can, as we are running on a rather close proposition anyhow, and the price of silver has begun to drop again. I cannot see any reason however for this drop being more than temporary, unless it is done by the manipulation of those controlling the silver market.

We are having a blizzard here today and it is snowing hard. This is very unusual down here in the valley, though snow is not uncommon in the mountains surrounding us. Up to the time this storm struck us we had been having as perfect weather as could be; but today our freight wagons are stuck between here and the railroad, our telegraph line is down, and it is the Hell of a day generally.

I will write more definitely about my movements in a few days. I may possibly have to go to San Francisco for a few days on some business with the Southern Pacific R. R., but I am not yet sure about this. In the meantime my address will be here at Pearce, as mail will be forwarded to me wherever I go. Brockman is well and sends regards.

Letter to his father, dated Brown Palace Hotel, Denver, Colo., February 27, 1901

I was very glad to get your letter of Feb. 11th which was forwarded here to me. I arrived here from San Francisco last Wednesday, having been almost four days on the trip instead of about two days, which is the usual time. The cause of the delay was that our train was wrecked in crossing Nevada, killing six people and injuring several others. A deep embankment had been washed out by heavy rains and our train plunged head first into a chasm. Why every one on the train was not killed is almost a miracle. The accident occurred before daylight in the morning, during a terrific deluge of rain. The train was composed only of Pullman and mail cars, and was the crack transcontinental fast express of the country. The passengers were all in bed at the time. I happened to be awake at the moment of the accident, and the whole thing happened and was over almost instantaneously. In a moment we had been transformed from one of the finest and most luxuriant trains in the world, to a chaotic mass of wreckage mixed with dead and wounded people. Those who were not hurt had their hands full for a few hours helping the injured, as we were about twenty miles from the nearest source of assistance, and it was some time before help came to us. This is the third time I have been in a railroad wreck, and the third time I have come out without a scratch, but I am not especially desirous of testing my luck too often. I cannot conceive of a much more horrible sight than a wreck like this one.

I am here for a few days looking after some matters connected with our Pearce mines and our Hanover iron business. I may possibly have to go to Pearce again before I come east, but I hope not to have to do so. If I do not go to Pearce again, I will come to Philadelphia early in March.

I hope Tal and Speck will have a good trip in Cuba. I wish I could have gone there with them.

The weather is perfect here, and it seems more like summer than winter. I will write more definitely about my movements in a few days, but in the meantime my address will be here at the Brown Palace Hotel, Denver, Colorado, as I think the chances are against my going to Pearce before I come to Philadelphia.

In 1898, in addition to several trips made from Philadelphia to Arizona, California, and Colorado, on mining business, Penrose also made a trip to the state of Washington and to British Columbia for the same purpose. The following year, in addition to his regular trips on mining business, he made one to Montreal, Ottawa, Winnipeg, Vancouver, Victoria, Seattle, Portland, and intermediate points. In 1900 his trips were strictly business ones to Arizona, California, and Colorado, and he was in Vancouver in September of that year, as he notes in his diary of the Alaskan trip (chapter 12).

By March of 1899, Penrose had joined various organizations in connection with his profession. He lists particularly the American Association for the Advancement of Science, of which he became a Fellow in October of 1898; The Geological Society of America, into whose Fellowship he was admitted in 1889; the American Institute of Mining Engineers, the American Geographical Society, the Colorado Scientific Society, the Geological Society of Washington, the Academy of Natural Sciences of Philadelphia. In June of 1900 he was elected Secretary of Section E of the American Association for the Advancement of Science, and in response to the formal notification of appointment, wrote: "I wish to express to you and to the General Committee of the Association my sincere appreciation of the honor you have done me, and to assure you that it gives me much pleasure to accept the appointment."

In November, 1899, he received a request from the director of the department of mining and metallurgy of the United States Commission to the Paris Exposition of 1900 to forward a photograph of himself to be placed upon the walls of the hall devoted to geology, mineralogy, mining, etc., among those "Americans who have distinguished themselves in some one of the departments allied to this group." His picture was also included at the World's Fair at St. Louis in 1903, as a member of the "late Geological Survey of the State of Arkansas."

In December, 1899, he received an appointment from Governor Murphy of Arizona as "a delegate to represent Arizona at the International Mining Congress to be held in Milwaukee, Wisconsin, June 21–23, 1900."

CHAPTER 9

Adventures in Eurasia

AND now this modern Alexander, still young (37 years), having proved his ability as a student, as a member of a group of field workers in the state surveys, as an independent geologist, as an explorer for precious metals, as a mining engineer, as a mining executive, and finding himself plentifully supplied with this world's goods, accumulated by his own efforts, sought new fields for conquest. Or, perhaps, it would be more accurate to say that he sought adventure in another field.

Up to 1901 he had written three important works—on phosphate deposits, on manganese, and on the economic geology of Cripple Creek—and several short papers on ore deposits. Then, for nine years (1894 to 1903) no publication came from his pen. He had been extremely busy, of course, with monetary matters which would not brook delay, but for one brought up in the tradition of Shaler, Branner, and Chamberlin—particularly the last-named—this dearth of publication must have been a source of regret.

And so began another phase in the life of this versatile gentleman and serious student. In 1901, having visited most of the important mines and workings on the North American continent, he set out to "conquer" the world of ore deposits. Between the spring of 1901 and the fall of 1912, he visited every continent and studied the ore deposits, taking careful notes and obviously making every preparation for the writing of a work which all his friends expected to come from his pen. But it never came.

"I feel sure that he planned a large work on the ore deposits of the world, and he felt that in order to present the subject adequately it was necessary for him to visit all the more important mining regions," wrote Waldemar Lindgren in his memorial tribute to Penrose, which appeared in the *Proceedings* of the American Philosophical Society for 1933. "He visited most of the outstanding mining districts, and some of them he described in papers, mostly published in the *Journal of Geology* and in *Economic Geology*. . . . But from these thirteen years of wanderings came only ten papers, the longest containing thirty-two pages. Many of these were most excellent and attracted much attention, but nevertheless Penrose himself no doubt felt the result was incommensurate with the great effort and length of time spent. . . .

"There is no doubt that Dr. Penrose obtained an excellent schooling in geology and mineralogy at Harvard. But in those days the field methods were not taught as well as they are now and like many of us Penrose had to work out some of them by himself. In some ways it is the better though more laborious proceeding. Neither were modern methods of the petrographical and mineralogical examinations of ores developed at that time. It is, therefore, in the highest degree creditable that he was able to produce, within a short time of his graduation, work like that on the phosphate deposits, the manganese deposits, and the superficial oxidation of ores. Those were researches which were standards for many years and contained a great deal of new information.

"His reading covered almost all of the ore deposits of the world and during his extensive travels he accumulated a vast fund of information. I know it was his intention to write a book on the ore deposits of the world. But when his travelling years were over many other things—public service and financial interest for instance—occupied so much time that he could never realize his ambition. Many interesting and valuable papers came from his years of travel but after all they were not what he had expected them to be.

"I think he found that he had not devoted enough time during his earlier years to general geology and petrography. And I am sure that this failure to realize his aims proved a deep disappointment to him. A man is not necessarily to be judged by the volume of his writings. I think all mining geologists agree that Dr. Penrose was one of the most brilliant students of mineral resources of his time."

J. Stanley-Brown, in his memorial tribute, which appeared in the *Bulletin* of The Geological Society of America, likewise commented upon this seemingly strange inconsistency.

"From the years spent in Texas and Arkansas, the investigations in the Cripple Creek District and indeed from all the work done up to 1901, when he began his world-wide travels, there was a reasonable expectancy that there should have come from him in monographic form splendid results that would shed lustre on his name as a geologist—especially as he was in that year only thirty-eight years of age and had shown not only masterly interpretative powers but great breadth of vision in his chosen field of work. Merit is not to be determined by numbers of papers or pages, but from these thirteen years of wanderings, between 1901 and the Great War, and from the large expenditure of physical effort and money in connection therewith, there came but ten papers, only one of which runs to as much as thirty-two pages. . . . These are all admirable studies, but when taken in connection with his familiarity with ore deposits, both actual and theoretical, one wishes that there might have been by research and compilation exhaustive monographs on this important subject."

Rollin T. Chamberlin, son of Thomas C. Chamberlin and for many years editor of the *Journal of Geology*, wrote also along the same line in his memorial tribute to Penrose which appeared in the *Journal*.

"One of his ambitions was to write a book on ore deposits and with that end in view he set out to see all the important ore deposits of the world. He was an early visitor to Rio Tinto and the South American copper districts, studied the gold placers of Tierra del Fuego when they first attracted attention, and crossed Siberia before the Trans-Siberian railway was completed. Most of the necessary traveling had already been done, though shortly before his death he was planning to go again to Burma. The great pity is that the book was never finished; with his capacity for great pains and scrupulous accuracy, it would undoubtedly have been a production of exceptional merit. Its lack of completion must be charged to the prodigality with which he gave his time and energy to the multitudinous causes in which he became interested. His helpfulness in so many different lines of endeavor was truly at the expense of his own scientific work. But therein probably lay even greater usefulness than in the more restricted field of personal research."

"His writings on ore deposits are marked by insight and clarity," declared *Mining and Metallurgy* in its memorial statement (September, 1931). "Many have regretted that business responsibilities in later years prevented his writing more, for what he did publish was always good."

All these reasons advanced for his failure to write the monograph on ore deposits were undoubtedly factors of real importance, but probably that of greatest importance was the entirely human and personal one—lack of incentive. The great incentive in the life of Dick Penrose was the father who died in December, 1908.

It is surely not without significance that among his literary effects are to be found extensive documentation concerning all his efforts until that time. It is not without significance that his travels and his observations of ore deposits are discussed in his letters to his father (all carefully preserved), his diaries, his notebooks, but that nothing is to be found concerning the trip in 1912 to Burma, beyond the bare statement in his "List of Trips," that he "went to Burma via Marseilles, Red Sea, and Ceylon. Travelled over interior in the valley of Irawaddy River, visiting Rangoon, Pegue, Mandalay, etc. Returned via Ceylon, Red Sea, Malta, Marseilles, Paris, London, and New York."

The father, in tribute to whom he always remained "junior," had been both father and mother to him ever since the untimely death of his beautiful mother when he was only sixteen—not only father and mother, but example and encouragement to the quiet, bookish, modest man. By example, precept, and constant sympathetic prodding that father of four famous and outstanding sons had quietly, and probably without any one of the sons being aware of it, urged each to be independent and a success in his chosen field. By wise counsel and ingenious implanting of ideas, he had helped each one to develop himself, for without self-development no one can be a real success. When that father died, two of his sons were married; one was an outstanding figure in American politics, with many goals still ahead. For his namesake, the son who had made his home with him, however, what goal remained? He had more money than he needed, more power than he enjoyed; he had seen the world, and he was already an outstanding success in his profession of geologist and in his career as a mining man. His written works were hailed as authority. He had shown the world that he was master; there was no need to continue the struggle and effort, for without effort, research, and real labor he could not have presented a monograph on ore deposits as his father would have wished it presented. And even if it were presented, and everyone acclaimed it, the very praise would have a hollow sound without the "Well done, my son," of the one for whom he cared most.

Probably Penrose himself never thought the matter out to this extent; undoubtedly, the book was one of the things he "meant to do" and probably his desire to return to Burma, which he confessed to many persons in the last years of his life, was due to the fact that he felt keenly the failure to provide himself with the "missing" notebooks and carefully recorded observations which had marked his trips before 1909. But the things in this life that a man *really* wants to do, he generally manages to do—particularly one as advantageously situated as was Penrose.

Other duties and many honors crowded his hours, together with an increasing anxiety to find the best possible "heir" for his wealth and his ideals. All these things kept him occupied and afforded him a degree of sublimation so that to the world he might seem thoroughly satisfied with life. Stanley-Brown said that Penrose "seemed a very lonely man but apparently was wholly unaware of it." He could not have been the sensitive person he showed himself to be throughout his life, without being aware of his "aloneness" after the death of his father. "Alone" is not the same as being "lonely," of course. One can be alone and have so many things to occupy himself that he has no time for loneliness. In order not to be "alone" in this world, one must know that he is all-important to at least one other human being—that his love, his opinions, his interests, his welfare are matters of the foremost vital concern to some one else. Man cannot live by bread alone, nor can he "live" entirely for himself—when he cannot do for others and live for others, then man is indeed "lonely"—terribly and awfully lonely.

And so Dick Penrose, after the death of his father, might have gone on, publishing book after book on his travels and observations, but that was a matter of interest to those he knew but not of vital concern to any one. Instead, he devoted his time and effort to a matter which could be, and is, of vital importance to others. Many men have written books; few have given so wholeheartedly of all the labors of his life to those not of kin as did R. A. F. Penrose, Jr.

The money left by his mother and by his father was in trust, so that Penrose, although enjoying the income from it during his life, could not dispose of it. All the millions which he gave away, during his lifetime and at his death, were his own, collected by his own knowledge and good judgment. He gave them all to others and through those gifts he has made for himself a monument, unique and lasting. Few men have achieved a greater goal or achieved it more magnificently.

But to return to 1901 and the thirty-seven-year-old geologist and mining engineer, starting forth on a new adventure, for it was an adventure in every sense of the word to travel in unknown Siberia and the Orient in 1901, only two years after the Boxer Rebellion had shown Westerners the resentment held against them by many Orientals. From his letters to his father, it is obvious that it was his first voyage abroad by himself.

The story of that year of search—from April, 1901, to April, 1902—is best told in his correspondence with his father, his notebooks, the little book, *The Last Stand of the Old Siberia*, which he published, and in the articles which resulted from those travels. The avowed object of the trip was "to study ore deposits of parts of Europe and Asia, including the iron mines of Lapland, the coal, gold and other mines of Siberia, the copper mines of Japan, the tin mines of the Malay Peninsula, the graphite and precious-stone mines of Ceylon, the sulphur mines of Sicily, the iron mines of Elba, the copper and iron mines of Spain."

Letter from Dick to his father, dated H.M.S. "Majestic," April 17, 1901

We have just started and I drop a line to you to be mailed at Sandy Hook. The day is perfect, my stateroom is first rate and everything points to a good voyage. I have not yet seen any one on board that I know, but I am used to travelling alone and can do it again. Barringer, and a fellow from Denver, and a fellow from San Francisco, who happened to be in New York, came down to the dock to see me off. I will write fully before I reach the other side.

In a cable, dated London, April 25, he reports that he has "just arrived. good passage," and signs it "Dick."

Letter to his father, dated Hotel Cecil, London, April 25, 1901

We reached Liverpool this morning about seven o'clock and arrived here about twelve o'clock by a special train that is run to take the passengers of White Star boats to London. On my arrival here I cabled you that I had just arrived and had had a good passage.

When I left Phila, you asked me to write a daily account of what happened on the boat, but I found that this involved so much repetition and uninteresting detail that I thought I had better summarize the trip in a letter after my arrival here.

I mailed a few lines to you as we passed Sandy Hook. At that time I had not seen any one on board that I knew but I found several people later on, among them a fellow named Chalfant from Pittsburg, a fellow named Sproul from the same place, a fellow named Crebbin from Denver and another man from Colorado. Later on in the voyage I met Mrs. Travis Cochran of Phila, and also Mrs. J. Parker Norris of Phila, who was going abroad with two daughters. These were all the people I knew, though I met a number of others casually. Altogether there was a very good crowd on board. There were over 270 first cabin passengers. My stateroom was one of the best on the boat, and if I crossed again on the Majestic I would pick out just the same stateroom in preference to any other on the boat.

I was not at all seasick through the whole voyage, though for a couple of days out from Sandy Hook we had strong head winds and heavy seas, which seemed to make most of the passengers sick. Contrary to my expectation however I felt first rate, never missed a meal on the whole trip and never even thought of feeling seasick.

We left New York promptly at noon on the 17th with the same accuracy in time as a transcontinental railroad train starts from Chicago to San Francisco. Barringer had come down to the dock with me, and before we left a fellow named Bogy from Denver and a fellow named Wiltsee from San Francisco, both of whom I knew and had seen in New York before starting, turned up to see the boat off. We all had a farewell drink together. The day was perfect until we got out to sea when it became cloudy and the sea rough. This continued that night and the next day. After that we had intervals of smooth or slightly rolling seas until we reached the coast of Ireland, and from there on we had very smooth water. I don't know enough about ocean travelling to say whether the trip taken as a whole was smooth or rough, but people who seemed to know said it was about medium.

Most of the passengers seemed to be Americans or of other nationalities than British, so that, though there were a good many British on board, the boat did not seem like the "Little England" that some people had told me it would. The food was good and the servants could not have been more efficient. There was a fine smoking room, library and bar room, and in fact every kind of equipment was as good as in a first class hotel.

When we arrived at Liverpool this morning it took only a short time to get the baggage through the custom house, and then we started for London and made the trip through—about 200 miles—in 4 hours without a stop. When we arrived here I got a cab and drove with my baggage to this hotel, where I have a good room and where everything seems to be very comfortable. Most every one that I talked to on the voyage spoke against this hotel because they said it was too "big" and not so comfortable as the small English hotels, but I have not found anything to find fault with yet. The hotel is something on the principle of the Waldorf in New York and is run especially for American business. I would much rather stay at a place like this, where a man is lost in the crowd, than in one of the purely English hotels which are haunted only by Englishmen and which seem to be imbued with an idea of superiority because they wont have any modern improvements. At any rate this hotel seems first class to me and I will stay here until I find out differently. The house is a magnificent building and seems to be full. It is between the Strand and the Thames River in a very convenient vicinity.

Tomorrow morning I will go down to J. S. Morgan & Co., to get my mail and will hunt up some people I know here. I want to go to Cornwall to see some tin mines soon, but I will return here from there, and this will be my headquarters for some time to come.

I don't see much difference between London and New York. Everything looks about the same, except that they do not seem here to have learned yet to speak or pronounce the English language so as to make it understandable; they will not have spittoons lying about at convenient places, which is a great inconvenience; they will not put ice in your water or other drinks unless you make a special effort for it; and all the bar-tenders seem to be women.

I will write again in a few days when I have my plans more definitely mapped out. In the meantime, if you write, you better address me care of J. S. Morgan

& Co., 22 Old Broad St., London, England, as mail will be forwarded to me wherever I am; and I think it is better to have that as my address here than this hotel, as they will forward mail more promptly, and in case I should have any reason to change hotels it would be inconvenient to have this hotel as my address.

I hope you have entirely recovered from your operation and that your face is as well as ever again.

Letter to his father, dated Hotel Cecil, London, May 2, 1901

I have been here just a week, and as I believe the next mail for America leaves here today I thought I would drop a line to you.

I am getting used to London and have done most all that I wanted to do here. The people here whom I knew, and others to whom I had letters, have all been very obliging. It is a little slow doing anything here as compared with the U. S., but it only requires a little patience. The people seem to be strong on dinners, lunches, etc., and I have been invited to several of them. They are all right, but I am not on this kind of lay just at present to any very great extent. The people are very hospitable, and Americans are certainly treated in good shape.

I have not been around to see many of the sights of London yet, but I have learned to find my way about a considerable part of the city without any trouble. For a mile or two in different directions from this hotel I can get about as easily as I could in Philadelphia, and this area includes most all the places that I care to visit.*

This hotel is very conveniently located and very well kept. The climate of London however is horrible. Today it is so dark that I have had to turn on the electric lights in my room to see to write this letter, though it is the middle of the afternoon. The air is full of smoke, dust and fog. Englishmen seem to like this, but I have not yet been educated up to that extent.

I have met several people in London whom I knew, among others a man named Hartman and a man named Capt. Hunt, both well-known iron manufacturers of Pittsburg. I also met Paul Stewart of Philadelphia a few days ago, but I think he has gone back to Paris, where he stays most of the time.

I have not been in any great hurry to leave here, as I thought it was a good place to learn a little about European customs before going on to the continent. I am going down to Cornwall in a couple of days to see some tin mines. After that I will return here, and expect to go to Paris about May 10th or 12th. From Paris I think I will go to Spain for a short time, and thence to Sweden, but I will arrange these plans more definitely when I get to Paris. I had a telegram from Pourtales† at Budapest the other day saying he had written me and asking me not to make any definite plans until I heard from him, but I have not yet got his letter. I am in communication with my friend in Sweden and I think I have that trip satisfactorily arranged. I expect to meet him there early in June.

* Area includes shopping district, Westminster Abbey, Houses of Parliament, Thames embankment, National Gallery, British Museum.

† The man to whom he sold his interest in the Common-Wealth mine two years later (*see* chapter 8, page 195).

I received my first batch of mail from the U. S. the other day, but it consisted mostly of only business letters.

When you write, you had better address me care of Morgan, Harjes & Co., No. 31, Boulevard Haussmann, Paris, France, as I will probably be in Paris before you answer this letter.

I hope you are entirely well again.

Letter from his father, dated May 6, 1901

Your letter of Apr. 25 reached me this morning, and, true to my promise, I answer it immediately. I was very glad to get it and to know that so far, your trip had been agreeable and prosperous. I received your note by the pilot from Sandy Hook, also your cablegram on your arrival in London and they were both most welcome messengers. I was glad to know you had so many acquaintances and friends with you. Mrs. Cochran and Mrs. Norris I knew from my boyhood, and the husbands of each as well, so in them you had lifelong friends. Mrs. Cochran was John Lambert's mother's first cousin and Mrs. Norris is the widow of her brother and was in her youth a great beauty and belle. She was a Wilmington girl like your Mother. I think you were most fortunate in not being seasick at all. Did the Bromo coffine cause it?

Well, here we are in "statu quo." You are the one to tell us of your adventures and all the "news." I am getting on satisfactorily. My face is "first rate" and the scar already scarcely noticeable. By the time of your return it will have practically disappeared. Philip got off last Tuesday, Aprl. 30, and I have not heard from him since (6 days).

Boies still *says* he is going to the Rockies when the legislature adjourns (about first week June). Tal will join him middle of Aug. and perhaps Spencer also at that time. Spencer and Tutt and MacNeill are now in New York, working up a "mill trust" of their own of $10,000,000. Spencer is very hopeful of success, and, if they carry out their scheme, it will give us all a great deal of money on *paper*, and, as Spencer says, no matter what the stock and bonds may sell for in New York, they will go on straight ahead and pay big dividends. Tal and Eric are still making money, but that is all right. You will make all you want after you return home and have the great benefit of your trip besides. As yet we have had no warm weather and the fires are all going. The trees are all in leaf and the Park very beautiful.

Do not neglect to write me over a week *at least* and always tell me when you receive a letter from me and its date, and I will *always* reply, even if I have nothing to write about. The Commonwealth dividend came to hand May 1, and was very acceptable. There is no mail for you at 1331, so I suppose it all goes to your office. Spencer was here on Sunday but went back in the 10 p.m. train. He and Tutt will come over on Saturday to the Rabbit* dinner.

Letter to his father, dated Hotel Cecil, London, May 11, 1901

I have just returned here from a trip of several days in Cornwall, where I went to see some of the tin mines. I spent several hours in the Dolcoath mine,

* A group of convivials who met monthly for dinner.

which is the largest tin mine in Europe, and saw a great deal that was well worth seeing. Cornwall is not a very great mining district, but it is interesting in as much as it has been worked continuously since the time of the Phoenicians, and as it is gradually being worked out, it will probably not be many years before no mining is done there at all. It was for this reason that I was anxious to see it.

I found that there are still a number of respectable people named "Penrose" in Cornwall, and though I did nothing to proclaim my origin from Cornish people, yet when my name was found out, I was treated in far better shape than if it had not begun with "Pen"; and I saw all I wanted to see, in spite of the fact that I had been told in London that Cornish people were very peculiar and might be a little slow in "loosening up." I could find no fault however with the way they treated me. All the same, I am very glad that I am an American and not a Cornishman, for the people of Cornwall are today in about the same condition as they were 100 years ago, and in about the same condition as I suppose they will be 100 years hence. They think the sun rises and sets in Cornwall, and though they have a pitying sympathy with any one who leaves Cornwall, yet they think he has had damned bad judgment.

I went to Camborne, Penzance, St. Michael's Mount and other places in Cornwall; and then, having seen all I wanted, I pulled out for London.

My friend from Sweden, whose name is Hjalmar Lundbohm, has been here on business for several days, and I have arranged with him to go to Sweden and Lapland the end of June or early in July. He has just started tonight on his return to Stockholm by sea—a trip of about two days. He was on the Swedish government commission at the World's Fair in Chicago in 1893, and I have known him since that time.

Pourtales has been telegraphing me about some mines in Servia that he wants me to see, and I have at last arranged to go there with him. I had hoped that he would go to Philadelphia to attend the annual meeting of the Common-Wealth Co. in June, but the Servian mines seem to have interested him so much that I doubt if he goes to the U. S. at present. Pourtales is at present at his place in Silesia, but he will meet me in Berlin next Wednesday. I will leave here next Tuesday night and go direct to Berlin via Flushing, where I will arrive Wednesday evening, May 15th. Then we will go to Servia and possibly travel around that part of Europe together for a while. I do not know whether Pourtales' mines are any good, but I can soon see, and the trip will be a very interesting one anyhow. After this trip, Pourtales wants me to visit him at his place at Glumbowitz in Silesia; but I do not think I will have time to do this, and besides, I do not want to be bothered with any social business in Europe.

The trip to Servia will make me postpone my trip to Spain, but if I have time, I will go there after I leave Servia and before I go to Sweden. Spain gets very hot in the summer, however, and therefore if I find that it is getting too late in the season to go there after I leave Pourtales, I will postpone the trip for another time—possibly in the fall. But I will know more definitely about all this in a couple of weeks.

I will not go to Paris on my way to Berlin, but will go there after I have been to Servia.

I have been longer in England than I had expected to be, but I do not think the time has been lost. I have seen and learned a great deal, and have arranged for most of my movements during the summer. I had at first intended to get some kind of courier here who could speak different languages, and take him to the continent with me; but it seems hard to get such a man, so I have decided to get such men locally in different countries where I need them. I will go to Berlin alone, and of course when I am with Pourtales I will not need any one; nor will I need any one in Sweden. When I go to Spain, I think I will take a courier as an interpreter.

It felt sort of strange when I first reached England, but now I have got used to things here, and I feel just as much at home, and can go about anywhere in London or elsewhere in England as easily as I could in the U. S.

When you write, you better address me in care of Morgan, Harjes & Co., 31 Boulevard Haussmann, Paris, France, as they will forward mail to me wherever I am. I will write you again after I have planned the trip with Pourtales. I have not heard from you since I left home, but as the last mail that I have received from our office in Phila was dated April 26th, I probably have not yet had time to hear from you. I wrote you last week and also the week before, and hope you have received the letters.

I hope you are entirely well again, and that your weather in Philadelphia is better than this fog and rain that seems to be perpetual here.

Letter from his father, dated Sunday, May 12, 1901

Your letter of May 2nd received last night. I was very glad to hear from you and to know that your affairs were prosperous. I wrote you a week ago, immediately on the receipt of your first letter, written on your arrival in London. Always when you write tell me which of my letters have reached you and *where* and when. I hope Pourtales will join in your Siberian expedition. Apart from the mere pleasure of his society, you will have the great advantage of his knowledge of Russian ways and usages. Be sure to tell me if you and he are to join forces.

We here are doing as usual. I am as usual, and my face improving daily. Boies is in town. He seems in fine shape and good spirits and looks first rate. He proposes starting for the Rockies the end of June, the uncertainty element being the result in the delay in the adjournment of the legislature caused by the delay in the decision of the Penna. Supreme Court on the Ripper bill. When the legislature adjourns he will be able to arrange with precision his movements.

Tal moves to Atlantic City on Tuesday of this week. Spencer and Tutt are in town today. Last night they were at the Rabbit dinner. The "Panic" in New York upset their plans greatly, since, up to then, they were carrying everything before them. It may be better this week. They go back to New York tomorrow evening. May so far has been delightful here, decidedly cool with a good deal of rain but this is vastly better than the hot dry weather we have some springs. I still am in my thickest winter flannels.

Your Aunt Lyd has gone to Carlisle for a few weeks. Nel Penrose of Germantown came here a few days ago to announce her engagement to "Mr. Hodge" the fellow who told your Uncle Clem about the Lehigh Navigation Stock, etc. Mr. Hodge is "Assistant superintendent" of the Lehigh Co. She brought him to see me a few nights ago. He is 35 years old, is a widower with one child—5 years old. He is a gentleman, comes from first class stock (he is a grandson of Prof. Charles Hodge of the Theological Seminary at Princeton who was most highly esteemed and of national celebrity and a brother of my predecessor in the University of Pennsylvania).

Letter to his father, dated Monopol Hotel, Berlin, N.W., May 16, 1901

I joined Pourtales here yesterday evening, and as we are going to start for Servia this evening, I thought I would drop a line to you before leaving.

I left London Tuesday night and went to Queensborough at the mouth of the Thames River. There I took a steamer the same night and arrived at Flushing in Holland in the morning. At Flushing I took a train for Berlin, passing through Holland and Prussia, and arriving here at 7 p.m. yesterday. The trip was very interesting. The boat was small and most of the people seemed to be seasick, but I was again fortunate enough not to be sick. The train from Flushing to Berlin was a fast express with a dining car etc., etc., and was very comfortable.

Berlin is one of the finest cities I have ever seen. It contains about 2,000,000 people and is a thoroughly modern, well-kept and very clean and beautiful place. I had expected to stay at a hotel called the "Bristol," as they make a specialty of speaking English there, but Pourtales was staying at this house, so I came here. They cannot talk much English here, but with the little they know, and the little German I know, I get along very well. Besides, I have been with Pourtales most of the time I have been here, so I don't have to talk much German.

We leave here tonight and arrive at Pourtales' place in Glumbowitz tomorrow morning. The next day we continue going south and arrive at Vienna the same evening, and get down into Servia the following day. We will probably be about five days in Servia, visiting the mines I wrote you about from London, and will then return for a few days to Vienna and to Budapesth; thence to some mines I want to see in Germany. Pourtales and I will probably be together during all these trips. After that he will probably remain in Germany and I will go to Paris. These are my plans at present. I may change some of the details as circumstances may require. Pourtales knows Servia, Austria and Hungary very well, so he is a good man to travel with. I hope to be in Paris about June 10th or 12th, and you had better address all letters to me there, care of Morgan, Harjes & Co., 31 Boulevard Haussmann, where I will receive them on my arrival. I have not heard from you since I left home, but I will get any letters you may have written, when I get to Paris.

Hoping you are entirely well again, I am

Your affectionate son
R. A. F. Penrose, Jr.

Postcard to his father, dated Basias, Hungary, May 20, 1901

Pourtales and I just arrived here. We go to Servia today. Will write when have another opportunity which may be several days. All well

R. A. F. P. Jr.

[Had signed it "Dick" and then crossed that off and used the initials instead.]

Letter from his father, dated 1331 Spruce St., Friday, May 24, 1901

Your letter just received, and I reply *promptly*. This is the *third* letter I have written you, always within 24 hours of receiving yours, so, though my letters have not as yet reached you, they have all been sent you promptly and on time. Be sure always, when you write me, to mention what letters of mine (and their dates) have reached you, etc., etc. My first letter was to London, my second to Paris and now, my *3d* also to Paris. I was glad to hear from you and to know that all your schemes were working so well.

Your visit to Cornwall must have been very interesting, and when you get back you can tell us all about our Cornwall relations. I am glad you are to have Pourtales part of your time and *I hope* all the time you are in Russia. Give him my *affectionate* regards and tell him how pleased I am that you are to have him anyhow part of your trip. As far as I can make out from your letters you are having *just about* as good a time as any fellow could wish to have—*and it is your due*—richly earned. Don't fail to write me *once a week*. I look forward with much interest to receiving news from you.

We are all the same. I heard from Philip a few days ago. He was in El Paso. Spencer and partners have concluded their deal $13,000,000. It all *sounds* very fine. Tutt and MacNeill have gone back to Colorado. Spencer and two Colorado lawyers remain East to attend to final details, Spencer in the meantime making Atlantic his headquarters and going to New York when required. He expects to be East some two weeks longer. But both he and Tutt expect to be *constantly* East as they are to have an office in New York. Of course he will write you.

Boies *says* he will go West about July 1. Spencer and Tal the middle of Aug. I expect to leave for Capon this day week, but until I get to Seal Harbor *after* July 1, you better direct your letters to me at 1331 Spruce St.

Letter from his father, dated 1331 Spruce St., Monday, May 27, 1901

Your letter of May 16 from Berlin is before me; it came on Saturday. This is my *fourth* letter to you, the third addressed to Paris. I am very glad to know you are with Pourtales and hope you will keep together all summer. How lovely it must all be for you. Do not fail to tell me which of my letters reach you— indeed, I cannot understand how any of them *can* miscarry. I go to Capon on Friday, for a three weeks stay. I don't enjoy the idea of going, but I feel that I ought to go and get out of Philadelphia. Continue to direct all your letters to 1331 until you know I am established at Seal Harbor.

The Supreme Court of Penna. decided today the Ripper bill of Pittsburg in *our* favor—4 to 3, 2 of the 3 being the democratic judges. Of course that means a great deal for our side and for Boies. Boies will now be able to make all his arrangements for his Western trip. He is in good shape. Tal is up in town tonight, to take his launch, he bought from VanRensselaer, to Atlantic. Something was wrong with the engine so he could not get off as he intended and will stay here tonight. Spencer came up from Atlantic with him to go on the launch, but when the hitch occurred he hurried off to New York to look after the final details of his deal. I am as usual. The weather still keeps cold. Today, *May 27*, I have a big fire in the library. The thermometer for the last three days has been about 52° straight along. This is very unusual.

Write regularly. I enjoy your letters much and keep them all.

Give my regards to Pourtales and *be sure* and tell him how glad I am to know you are together.

Letter to his father, dated Budapest, May 27, 1901

Pourtales and I have arrived here from our trip to Servia and Roumania, and we start for Vienna this afternoon. I drop this short line to you now and will write more fully from Vienna. We had a most interesting trip, though the mines we went to see, did not amount to very much. It was getting very hot in southern Europe when we left there, but it is much cooler here.

I will write fully in a few days. We are just starting for our train now.

Letter from Dick to his father, dated Hotel Meisel & Schadn, Vienna, May 31, 1901

The last time I wrote in full was about two weeks ago in Berlin. Since then I have written you a postal card from Basias in Hungary, and a short letter from Budapesth.

After leaving Berlin, Pourtales and I went first for one day to his place in Silesia. Thence we went south through Austria and Hungary to a small town in southern Hungary, on the Danube River, known as Basias. This was the point from which we were to start for Servia to visit the gold mines that I wrote you about. We stayed one night at Basias, and the next day we crossed the Danube and entered Servia at a place called Gradista. The change was wonderful. In the width of the Danube, we seemed to have passed from European to Oriental conditions. From Gradista we took a native wagon, a sort of four-wheeled cart without springs, and drove about 30 miles up the valley of the Pek River, into the interior of Servia, to a place called Njeresnitza. We could not understand our driver's language and he could not understand ours, but we got to Njeresnitza all right, and there we were met by a German named Bonkowsky, with whom we could talk German, and who was manager of the mines we had come to see.

We made headquarters at Njeresnitza for several days, and made trips in various directions into the mountains to see the old mines. The mines did not amount to very much, so I advised Pourtales not take hold of them unless the owners proved that they had something very much better than what they showed us. I had not at any time counted very much on the mines, so the result of our examination was not disappointing to me; and besides, I was very glad to have taken the trip, as the country was very interesting and we saw it under especially favorable circumstances.

Njeresnitza is a small Servian village of about 100 people. We lived largely on chickens, roast pigs, cheese made of sheep's milk, and a drink made of coffee ground to an impalpable powder and mixed in hot water, which is the Servian method of drinking coffee. These things together with Servian wine and a brandy made of prunes formed a very good diet. We were very well treated by everyone we met, though all our conversation had to be carried on through an interpreter. The military commander of the district in which we travelled offered to give us an escort of troops, but we did not take them.

It happened that while we were at Njeresnitza, the annual festival of the Servian peasants occurred. On this occasion they all collect at certain points throughout Servia, bringing roast pigs, chickens, sheep's-milk cheese, wine, etc., and have a grand spree for several days. Njeresnitza was one of the assembling points and a great crowd of Servians, together with Roumanians, Macedonians, Gypsies, and other races came together. The celebration went on all day and all night. When anyone got tired, he would go to sleep wherever he happened to be, and when he woke up he would begin again to eat, drink and dance. Foreigners are very rare in this part of Servia, so we were treated especially well and were looked on as a sort of strange curiosity.

From Njeresnitza we returned to Gradista, and there took a boat down the Danube to Turnu Severin, in the kingdom of Roumania. Here I had the first occasion to use my passport, as no one is allowed in Roumania without one. Usually one is required in Servia, but we were not asked for ours there. Between Gradista and Turnu Severin we passed through the cañon and the "Iron Gate" of the Danube, which were very fine sights.

From Turnu Severin we went to Budapesth in Hungary and thence returned here. Turnu Severin is a prosperous but very hot port on the lower Danube, and we were very glad to start back for Hungary after spending one day there—or rather one night.

Budapesth is a very prosperous place, and used to be a great sporting town, but with its prosperity have come many changes, including a wave of reform, that has taken away from its old reputation.

Vienna is by far the finest place I have seen in Europe. They have fine water which is brought from the mountains about 40 miles away, and it is a great comfort to get to a place where the water is good after being in countries where the water is considered poison. The streets of the city are big and wide, the buildings are often magnificent, and there are more good-looking women than I have seen in all the rest of Europe put together.

We arrived here last Monday night, and after spending three days here, we made a circuit through southern Austria, stopping on the way at Eisenertz to see one of the largest iron mines in Europe. We got back yesterday, and will start the day after tomorrow for Berlin, and thence to Paris. We will probably stop on the way to see the salt mines at Stassfurth in Germany, and the iron mines of Luxemburg, and will arrive in Paris about June 10th or 12th. Pourtales had not intended to come to Paris, but his wife is there now, so he is going on with me so as to meet her there.

I am very glad to have seen southeastern Europe and am also very glad to be back in Vienna, as it was getting very hot when we left. I remember that Abbe Huc, in his "Travels through China," says that all China smells of musk. In the same way all southeastern Europe smells of garlic. The smell does not come from the plant but from the people who eat it, and it seems to exude from every pore in their bodies. It becomes first very noticeable in Hungary, and grows stronger as you go south through that country. In Servia everything smells of it, and in Roumania the whole air is saturated with it. If we had gone a little farther southeast—into Turkey—I suppose it would have been still stronger.

I will write again when I get to Paris. I have not had my mail forwarded to me from there, as I was travelling around so rapidly that I thought it might get lost, but I will get it all when I get there. I have not heard from you since I left Phila, but will get any letters you may have written when I get to Paris. My address for the present will be care of Morgan, Harjes & Co., 31 Boulevard Haussmann, Paris, France.

I will direct this letter to you at Phila, though I suppose it will be forwarded to you at Capon, as I believe you told me you were going there about June first.

Letter from Dick to his father, dated Paris, France, June 10, 1901

I arrived here from Berlin last night, and was very glad to get your letters of May 6th, 12th, 24th, and 27th at the office of Morgan, Harjes & Co. this morning. It is needless for me to say that the thing that pleased me most was to learn that you are entirely well again.

I would have gotten several of your letters sooner, had it not been that I have been travelling about so rapidly lately that I thought it best to let my mail remain here, as they are very slow in forwarding mail in Europe. Hence your letters received today were the first I have gotten from you since I left Phila.

I have also received a letter from Speck about the mill consolidation. I think the scheme is most excellent, and Speck, Tutt and MacNeill deserve the greatest credit for the way they have carried the deal through.

I am glad to hear from you that the Common-Wealth dividend was so well received. I have a long letter from Brockman telling me of new discoveries of ore in the mine. In fact things seem to have improved greatly at Pearce since I left, and I think it will be a good thing for the stockholders if I stay away for a while, as things may then get still better.

I was very glad to hear of the favorable decision on the Ripper bill. The "insurgents" will probably now keep quiet for a while.

The last time I wrote you was last week from Vienna on our return from Hungary, Servia and Roumania. From Vienna, Pourtales and I went to his place in Silesia for a few hours while he attended to some business. Thence we went to Breslau, Germany and thence to Berlin, where we stayed a couple of days. From Berlin we went to the celebrated salt mines at Stassfurth. These are mostly owned by the German government, and Pourtales' influence enabled us to see them in good shape. These mines are the principal source of potash salts in the world, and the quantity is simply inconceivable to anyone who has not been there, so you need not fear any shortage in bicarbonate of potash for a long time. The source of potash is sufficient to cure all gout, rheumatism, boils, exema, and Bright's disease for ages to come. The potash occurs mostly in the form of chlorides and sulphates, together with other chlorides and sulphates, and is made into other salts of potash artificially. From Stassfurth we had intended to go to the iron mines of Luxemburg, but we heard that they were small and not very accessible, so we came on here.

I had intended to go to Spain from here to see the mines at Bilbao and Rio Tinto, but everyone tells me that it is so terribly hot there now, that I will postpone this trip. I had partly arranged to go with one of the owners of the mines at Bilbao, but even he has backed out on account of the heat. Even in Paris the heat is equal to a genuine "scorcher" in Chicago. I may possibly visit some places I want to see in France during the next two weeks; and about July 1st I am going to Sweden. I am trying to persuade Pourtales to go to Russia with me after I have been in Sweden. He has an idea that he ought to go back to Silesia, but he wants to go to Russia, and I think he may go. He is a fine man to travel with as he is always in a good humor, never gets discouraged by difficulties, and can put up with any hardships. Our trip through Servia and Roumania was a pretty severe test of a man, and I never saw a fellow stand up better than Pourtales did under all hardships.

I have not seen much of Paris yet. There are a good many good looking women here, and they seem to have a little more style about them than the women of Germany and Austria, but I have not yet seen in Paris the good "raw material" that exists in Vienna. If the Viennese women were dressed up the way the women are here, they would beat them all out of sight. I have not yet seen much here however, and perhaps I can tell you more later.

My address will be here, care of Morgan, Harjes & Co., 31 Boulevard Haussmann, for some time to come. I am staying at the Hotel Continental, which is a large and very comfortable house, but you had better address all mail to Morgan, Harjes & Co., as they will forward it to me when I am away.

Hoping you will have a good trip to Capon, I am

Your affectionate son
R. A. F. Penrose, Jr.

Letter from his father, dated Capon Spring, Friday, June 14, 1901

You see I am at Capon, where I came two weeks ago. The place is as lovely and beautiful as ever and, at this beginning of the season, with very few guests as yet. It suits me better than any place I ever was at. I shall leave in a week and plan to be in Seal Harbor before July 1st, so after receiving this letter you may direct your letters to Seal Harbor.

I am as usual, but Philip's death has broken me up completely. I can't suffer myself to brood over it; if I did, I think it would kill me right off. His body is expected today in Phila., and Boies and Tal have decided that it had best be buried at once. I shall not however go to Phila. to be present at the final disposition. It would be horribly painful, and, if the weather should be hot, as it always is at this season, I believe it would kill me right off, and I do not think this termination of my career necessary or desirable.

Continue to write me once a week. I look for your communications and am always relieved to receive them. Give my regards to Pourtales and tell him how glad I am to know he is your companion in so much of your trip and would be still more pleased to feel that he was to be your companion through the whole of it. Of course, the boys will keep you informed of what they have done, also Spencer doubtless has posted you on what they all think a very desirable deal—certainly, on paper, it looks very fine and gives us all *on paper* a great increase in our holdings.

Letter from his father, dated Capon, Sunday, June 16, 1901

Though I wrote you a long letter only two days ago I feel I must acknowledge your very interesting letter from Wien, May 31. I am delighted that you are having so very pleasant and profitable trip. Do try and take Pourtales along with you everywhere. I shall feel much more easy about you than if you were alone. Indeed, since Philip's death, I have been anxious about you all the time. For God's sake take *extra* good care of yourself.

You speak in your letter of the dreadful water you meet. Drink nothing but bottled water or boiled water; i.e., tea and coffee. But you know all this from your Texas travels. Your "Bill of fare" in Servia must have been very fine. Chicken and little pig ought to be wholesome diet and palatable as well. As you see I am still here. It is rainy this morning so I sit at my window, *with a great coat* on and write letters—this, the first, I am now writing. The mountain on all sides of me, profound quiet, as to be expected on a rainy Sunday morning at nine o'clock. We have not more than 20 or 25 guests in the house, the result of the cool and very wet season. When you write me, tell me of your plans, particularly of the Siberian railroad and if Pourtales is to go with you on that trip and when you write again you may direct to Seal Harbor as I told you, I believe, in my last letter.

Philip's body has not yet reached Phila; at least, it had not when Boies wrote me Friday, so I can tell you nothing on the subject of his funeral. Boies, however, wants a *conventional service*—religious services, etc., etc., and I think he is right. So I have written him to arrange everything to suit himself, not Tal, who, I am sure, will "kick" at the idea of a preacher brought in. But Boies from a wise point of view is right.

Don't fail to write me over a week *at least*.

Letter from Dick to his father, dated London, England, June 19, 1901

I was terribly shocked and grieved to hear of the death of Philip a few days ago, while I was in Paris. I heard of it indirectly through a cable of sympathy from Barringer and Brockman. I at once cabled to Tal about it, and he replied to the effect that Philip had died of pneumonia in El Paso. This is all I have as yet heard. My first impulse, as soon as I heard the news, was to come home at once, but Tal told me in his cable, not to do so. Therefore I thought I better wait until I heard something further. After hearing from Tal, I cabled to you telling you what I had heard, and that Tal had cabled me not to come home, and asking you to cable me if I could do anything. This was several days ago, and as I have not yet heard from you, I suppose you have thought you would write instead of cable. I sent my cable to you at Philadelphia, as I supposed that if you were not there, it would be forwarded to you.

The whole thing seemed so awful, that I did not feel like staying in Paris, and I came on here, after leaving instructions in Paris to forward all mail and telegrams promptly to me here.

I know no further details than those I have mentioned, but I hope to hear further when the next mail from America comes in, which is due tomorrow or the next day. If you think I had better come home, I will do so at once. If not, I will stay here for about a week and will then go to Sweden. I am ready however to come home now or any time that you say so.

Please address all letters to me hereafter to care of J. S. Morgan & Co., 22 Old Broad Street, London, England, as they will forward them to me whether I am in Sweden or elsewhere. This address will reach me a little quicker, if I go to Sweden, than my Paris address.

Letter from Dick to his father, dated London, England, June 27, 1901

I wrote you on my return here last week, but have not heard from you for a long time. The last letter that I have received from you was dated May 27th. I have been here about ten days, and am going to take a boat tomorrow for Gotenburg, Sweden, whence I will go by rail to Stockholm, where I expect to meet a man named Lundbohm, and visit some of the iron mines of Sweden and Lapland.

As I wrote you last week, however, I am ready to come home at once if you think I better do so. When you write, you better address me care of J. S. Morgan & Co., 22 Old Broad St., London, England, as they will forward both mail and telegrams promptly to me, and I find that address more convenient than my Paris address.

There is nothing new here to tell you. Pourtales went back to his place in Germany some days ago. If I do not come home this summer, I think he will go to Russia with me when I get back from Sweden—probably in August.

I will write more fully from Sweden, when I know my plans more definitely.

Letter from his father, dated Seal Harbor, July 1, 1901

Your letter of June 10 from Paris is before me. I received it after my return to Philadelphia from Capon, but deferred replying until my arrival here. I got back on Saturday, June 22. My trip to Capon would have been satisfactory enough had I not been so completely broken up by Philip's death. Though I had contemplated the possibility of such a catastrophy for years, yet when the shock came it upset me completely, and I have not yet got myself right again, and it will be a long time before I do, if I ever do. It gives me great satisfaction to know you are having such a prosperous time and I am simply delighted to learn that Pourtales most probably will accompany you to Siberia. His companionship will be invaluable to you in every way.

Your account of your visits interests me greatly. The Strassfurth salt mines must be most interesting and I am greatly pleased to know that potash salts can't be "cornered" by any combine. Your accounts of the ladies of Germany and Paris are interesting as well as very instructive, and when you shall have added to your lore a thorough knowledge of Lapish ice beds and Siberian and Manturian maids you will be as experienced as John L.—who boasted he had tried them all. I don't believe, however, you will find any finer material anywhere in the world than in Spain, but I do not remember what John said of the Spanish girls.

I got here on Friday morning, June 28, as I had planned, after a journey from Phila unprecedented for terrible heat and dirt, yet on time. But when I drove into my own place, I came into a Paradise. Everything is beautiful as possible. The place looks better than ever before. The grass, trees, flowers are all very fine, so now I am completely settled and as comfortable as it is possible for an old man to be. I am sorry you cannot see it all this year, but, if I should live to another summer, I have the satisfaction of being sure everything will look better than this summer, for so it is, each year better and better, as the things grow and grow straight along. I was much interested in your reference to Brockman's discovery of new ore in our mine, though you do not tell me of the value and nature of the strike. I asked Will to go and see Barringer about it all, but Barringer gave him very little information—indeed, nothing to base an opinion on.

I suppose the boys wrote you about Philip's funeral. The body was taken from the undertaker's (Bringhurst) and conveyed to 1331 Spruce St. The Rev. Bolton (Boies's friend) read the episcopal service and went to Laurel Hill. Nobody present but the family—Mr. Hunt, Miss Bache, Rex Shober. Everything seems to have been done with great propriety and precision and as Boies wished. I got home four days after. I felt that it would have killed me to go through it all, especially if the weather should have been very hot and depressing (as it turned out to be), so I am well satisfied that I did what I felt I ought to do in the matter.

My regards to Pourtales. Be sure and tell him how much satisfaction I have in feeling he is to be your companion in your Siberian trip. You both will have a splendid time I am sure.

Letter from Dick to his father, dated Grand Hotel, Stockholm, July 2, 1901

I wrote you from London just before I left there last week; and on my arrival here I was exceedingly glad to find your letters of June 14th and 16th which had been forwarded to me.

I left London last Friday (June 28th) in a small but very good Swedish steamship called the Thorsten, and in a little over two days arrived at Goteborg, on the southwest coast of Sweden. This is one of the largest seaports of Sweden, and is an active modern town. From Goteborg I came to Stockholm by train, a journey of about 11 hours.

The trip down the Thames and through the North Sea was very interesting. On the second day we came in sight of Denmark, and followed along this coast until we reached the Skagerak and Kattegat, which are a sort of inland seas on the coast of Norway and Sweden. Denmark is a low flat country, but when we came in sight of Goteborg the country was high and mountainous.

Our boat was small but very comfortable. The captain, a Swede named Ericsson, spoke English and was a first rate fellow. There were not many people on board and I was the only American. There were four English people, and the rest were Swedes and Norwegians. Most Americans and English come here by train from Flushing in Holland. In fact every one in London whom I consulted, advised me to come by train, as they said the sea was very rough in these waters and the boats small; but it takes over two days to come here by train, and I have found that long distance travelling by train on the continent of Europe is not very comfortable, so I decided to come by boat—rough water or not—especially as the boats are staunch and thoroughly seaworthy. As it turned out, we had a very good voyage and I was not seasick. Hereafter in travelling in Europe I shall always take boats instead of trains whenever I can, as the boats seem generally to be good, and the trains are almost invariably bad.

When I arrived in Stockholm I met my friend Lundbohm, and we expect to start for Lapland in 4 or 5 days. Our plan is to go as far north as the railroad will take us. Thence by wagon and canoe still farther north to where Lundbohm is opening some large iron mines; thence northwest overland to the Lofoden Islands on the northern coast of Norway; thence down the Norway coast by boat to Christiana* and thence back here. It is possible that Lundbohm may have to stay in Lapland, as he is carrying on some very large mining operations there, but he will come at least as far as the Lofoden Islands with me, and I will return here about the last week in July.

As I wrote you the other day, Pourtales has gone back to his place in Germany, as he had some business to attend to there, but we have agreed to go to Russia together in August. We will go to the Ural Mts., and through part of Siberia. It is doubtful if we go clear across Siberia to the Pacific Coast, as the railroad is not yet completed; but we expect to meet about Aug. 1st and then we will arrange the details of the trip. We will probably meet in St. Petersburg† or Berlin. I can go from here to St. Petersburg by sea in a day and a half. I gave Pourtales your message of greeting and he told me to give you his best regards.

I am going tomorrow to Dannemora, Sweden, to see what were once the greatest iron mines of northern Europe, and will return the next day to get ready to go to Lapland. I am going to take an interpreter with me to Dannemora, as I can't speak a word of Swedish, and Lundbohm is too busy with the preparations for Lapland to go with me. He offered to go, but I would not let him do so. He is a first rate fellow and I don't want to impose on his kindness too much. When I was in Germany and France I found that the few words of German and French that I could speak were of great help to me at times when I was alone there; but

* Now Oslo.
† Leningrad.

in Sweden I cannot speak a single word of the language, and hence an interpreter will be useful at Dannemora.

Stockholm is a beautiful town of about 400,000 people. It is built on a lot of small rocky islands connected by bridges and facing the Baltic Sea. Very few of the people speak anything but Swedish, but they are very hospitable to strangers, and I find I can get about town with very little difficulty. In fact, I have been so much recently in countries where I could not speak the language, that I am beginning to get along very well with a few words and a good many signs.

I will address this letter to you at Seal Harbor as you have told me to do so. I am very glad to know that your trip to Capon did you so much good, and I hope your summer at Seal Harbor will be equally pleasant.

I will write again before starting for Lapland.

Letter from his father, dated Seal Harbor, Maine, July 3, 1901

Yours of June 19 just received. I reply *immediately*. I have written you *twice* since Philip's death—once from Capon and then immediately on my arrival here. Though, as I have already told you, I have looked upon his premature death as *inevitable* for years, yet, when it actually happened, it was a terrible shock to me. It made me sick, broke me up completely and even now I cannot permit myself to think of it or him, it so entirely unnerves me. But, there! even as I write, I feel myself undone again, so I will stop. I wrote you a very brief account of his funeral. I received your cablegram sent to me at Capon. I did not reply to it as I knew Tal had cabled you. I realized how shocked you would be, but, it would have been needless, and foolish to the last degree, for you to have come home, or to have *changed your plans in any respect whatever*. Later in the year I hope you will return to Paris and have a good time there in *every possible way*, but be sure you do not shorten your stay abroad one minute or alter your plans. Stay in Sweden as long as you find it pleasant or profitable and in Siberia as well. It gives me no little satisfaction to think of what a nice time you have been having and may reasonably expect to have while abroad and don't think of coming back until the end of the year at any rate. I find all your letters very interesting, so please do not let them be shorter or less frequent. *I have kept them all*.

Seal Harbor is more lovely and perfect than ever before, and Sea Bench *splendid*. The weather through the country terrible, as *you know* it can be, but, with a glorious sea breeze all day and nights cool enough for a blanket, what could one ask for better in the end of June and beginnings of July. How fortunate I am to possess such a perfect refuge and the thought is very pleasant to me that I have made it myself—*out of my own head*. Your Aunt Lyd is much better since she is here, and she and Jane do all they can to make me contented.

I have not heard from home since I left, so can tell you nothing of any one save myself, but I am as comfortable and well off as any *old man* in the country.

Letter from Dick to his father, dated Grand Hotel, Christiania, Norway, July 8, 1901

We have been delayed a little in starting for Lapland, as Lundbohm had to go down unexpectedly to the southern coast of Norway on some business, but we expect to start in a few days. Our preparations are all made, and all we have to do is to start. In the meantime, I have come over here from Stockholm, as I wanted to visit some mines near the border of Sweden and Norway, and by doing it now I will save just that much time when we return from Lapland.

After writing to you last week I went to Dannemora, Sweden, to see some of the oldest mines in Europe. Thence I went to Upsala and then back to Stockholm. I took an interpreter with me and found him very useful, though it was often a nuisance to have him around. I have no interpreter here and am getting along very well. It is wonderful how much a man can do without saying much in a country where he does not speak the language. I am beginning to think that talking is largely a habit.

It takes about 13 hours by rail to come here from Stockholm, and the country is very much like the coast of Maine—a series of mountains, marshes, lakes, islands and fjords. Christiania is beautifully situated at the head of a long fjord, and is an interesting old town, but not nearly so large as Stockholm.

I will return to Stockholm tomorrow and will join Lundbohm again there. Then we expect to start for Lapland at once, or at least within a day or two. I will write again more fully in a few days, after we have started.

Letter from his father, dated Seal Harbor, July 10, 1901

Your letter of June 27 is just received and I am very glad to hear from you. I wrote you in June from Capon—I think *twice;* also, this is my second letter to you from here since July 1—all of which letters you will assuredly receive. But, my special object in writing promptly today is to tell you—what I have told you in all my other letters that you have not yet gotten—by no means think of coming home before your fully appointed time. Stay as long as you possibly can—even if it be until next summer. Your return would not help poor Philip—or *me*—and, as for me, I am getting along very satisfactorily, so, I *again repeat* stay away as long as possible and later on in the Autumn go to Paris and pay a good long visit there, and have all the fun you can come across. I am delighted at the idea of Pourtales being your travelling companion in Russia and Siberia. It relieves me of no little anxiety about you.

Do write me often even if it be a postal to let me know of your whereabouts and welfare. I am enjoying my life here in a *physical way*. Everything is lovely. My place never so beautiful. My surroundings are very fine—food, comfort, etc., etc. *Not much society* but enough (old Barr, Aunt Lyd, and, later on, Uncle Wir and old Dr. Wicoff). I don't hear or know much of Phila and the boys at home but I suppose Boies will get off this week.

Today, July 10, I have received cheques from the Phil-Coronso Company and one from the Standard Co. When does the Commonwealth declare its next dividend—the last was May 1?

Letter from Dick to his father, dated Grand Hotel, Stockholm, July 13, 1901

I wrote you only a few days ago from Christiania, but I thought I would drop this line to you now, as we start for Lapland tonight, and it may be several days before I have a chance to write again. We had intended to go from here as far as we could by railroad, but we have changed our plans and will leave here by boat going north, through the Gulf of Bothnia, for about three days, to a place called Lulea in northern Sweden. From Lulea we will go overland northwest into Lapland.

I will write again from some point along our line of travel. The weather is fine and I think we will have a good voyage. Our party consists of Lundbohm, another Swede, and me. Our boat is a very comfortable Swedish steamer.

Letter from Dick to his father, dated "On board Steamship Norra Sverige," Gulf of Bothnia, July 16, 1901

I am writing this letter on board the Steamship Norra Sverige, on our way from Stockholm to Lapland. In about three hours we will reach Lulea, at the head of the Gulf of Bothnia, and at the mouth of the Lulea River, one of the large rivers of Lapland.

I wrote to you hurriedly just before we left Stockholm. That night we started on our journey north. The weather was perfect, and this time of year, though the sun sets, yet there is no darkness all night in the latitude of Stockholm, and the trip from Stockholm through the many islands that line this part of the Swedish coast was very beautiful. But we had no sooner reached the open Baltic Sea than we ran into a dense fog, and we lost a large part of the night creeping along slowly to avoid colliding with other boats. Towards morning, however, the fog cleared off, and we turned north into the Gulf of Bothnia, which is the northern extension of the Baltic Sea, and lies between Sweden on the west, Finnland on the east, and Lapland on the north. That day and the next were as perfect as could be. We stopped at several small ports on the Swedish coast, and had a good chance to see the country. Our course lay almost due north during these two days.

The third day—that is today—is cloudy and dull, but there is no fog and no storm. We have continued north all day, and will keep on doing so until we reach Lulea tonight. The days have been becoming much longer as we have come north, until now the sun dips only a short distance below the horizon, and it is broad daylight all night. When we get to our destination in Lapland, we will probably be where the sun does not set at all this time of year.

We will stay tonight at Lulea, and in the morning will continue north overland into the interior of Lapland by a small railroad that the Swedish government has recently built to bring the ore of some iron mines to tide water at Lulea. In this way we will arrive at a place called Gelivare in Lapland and well within the Arctic Circle tomorrow afternoon. From Gelivare we will continue northwest to a place called Kurunavaara, where Lundbohm's mines are situated, and which is our destination. These mines are some of the largest iron mines in the world and I look forward with much interest to seeing them.

On this boat, most all the people are Swedes. With the exception of Lundbohm, I am the only one who speaks English, but some of the other people speak German, and I get along with them very well in that language. I am gradually getting used to the Swedish diet of raw fish, smoked fish, boiled fish, salt fish, dried fish, beer at breakfast, beer and potato-brandy at dinner, beer and lobsters at night, etc., etc. Some of these things may not seem very good to you, and they did not seem so to me at first, but I am getting used to them now, and they seem to agree very well with me.

I will mail this letter at Lulea.

Letter from his father, dated Seal Harbor, July 19, 1901

Your letter of 2d July, Stockholm, reached me Wednesday. I was much interested in all your experiences and *delighted* to know Pourtales would be with you in Russia and Siberia, a part of your trip I have dreaded to have you undertake alone.

When I passed through Phila I asked your Uncle Will to call on Barringer and ask him about the new strike of ore that you told me of in one of your letters. Barringer *made light of the strikes*. Said "Dick *was too* enthusiastic"!!! etc., etc.

When should there be another dividend? Aug. 1 or Sept. 1? Does Brockman make any more reports of new strikes? I was pleased to learn of your fine trip by sea from London to Sweden. You are right—a sea trip is, by far, preferable to a land trip when one is not easily made seasick, and I consider you now an "immune" as far as seasickness is concerned.

I want to repeat here (what I stated so carefully in my last several letters to you) not to shorten your stay abroad *one minute*, and, after your return from Siberia, go to Paris and have all the fun you can get hold of, or anywhere else, for that matter, where you can find amusement or pleasure. You, most probably, will, often, in the future, go abroad—but, I want this pioneer trip to be full of fun and profit. I am doing satisfactorily here.

Your Aunt Lyd seems better. I lead my old, regular life—my three hour drive daily, my Barr Sunday visit, my one cigar at 8 p.m., my one and a half ounces of whisky at dinner and *no more* until next day at same hour—a little monotonous doubtless but the scheme seems to suit me. Anyhow it is a becoming and dignified mode of life for an old man, who has done big work and good work for a long life.

I shall look for your Russian letters with great interest and much less anxiety now I know Pourtales is with you.

Letter from Dick to his father, dated Kuruna, Lapland (Sweden), July 20, 1901

We arrived here all right after a journey of five days northward from Stockholm. I wrote to you last on board our steamer coming up the Gulf of Bothnia. That night (July 16th) we arrived in Lulea, at the head of the Gulf. The next morning we started north by train, and that afternoon arrived in a place called Gellivare, which is some miles within the Arctic Circle. The next day we continued north, and the same afternoon we arrived here, at Kuruna. This place is a small settlement between two mountains known as the Kurunavaara and Luossavaara. There are iron mines in both mountains, and Lundbohm is the manager of them. The mine on Kurunavaara is the largest iron mine that I have ever seen, with the exception of our Hanover iron mines in New Mexico. The sole object of the railroad in Lapland is to haul the iron ores of these and other mines. It is being built by the Swedish government, but is not yet finished. We had to come part of the way here on a construction train. The road starts from the Gulf of Bothnia on the east, and runs west, with the object of coming eventually to the Atlantic coast in Norway. At present it runs only a few miles west of this settlement.

When I wrote you before leaving Stockholm I told you there was another Swede in our party besides Lundbohm. At that time I had not met him and did not know who he was. Afterwards I found that he was the Governor of the Swedish province of Dalarne, and one of the directors of the mining company here. His name is Holmquist and he is a first rate man. He cannot speak English, but we manage to talk together a little in German.

We are far within the Arctic Circle here, in the extreme northern part of Lapland and about in latitude 68°. The sun does not set here this time of year, and it is broad daylight all night. The country has all the appearance of being in the polar regions. It is mostly a vast succession of lakes, swamps and barren flats, with occasional rocky ridges, or higher mountains rising up prominently in their covering of perpetual ice and snow. To the west of here can be seen the peak of Kebnekaisa, the highest mountain in Lapland, rising up like an immense iceberg from the low country around it. The vegetation even in the lower parts of this region is poor and scattered, as the climate is too cold for it to prosper. Moss, stunted birch and pine are about all that grow, and these are often few and far between. A few reindeer, bear and foxes manage to live here. The soil is too thin to cultivate, and the summer is too short to raise crops even if the soil was good. The country is cold, bleak and desolate; and but for the mines, very little would be heard of it. A few Laplanders lead a wandering life with their herds of reindeer in the mountains. They look like the trees—small and stunted—as if they had hard work living. When I look at them, I think of the story of Afrasia that you gave me to read a couple of years ago; and I can see now that the author of that book knew the Laplanders and the Lapland scenery well.

We start on our return trip in a few days, and expect to reach Stockholm before August 1st. We will go back a different way than we came here, but we have not yet definitely decided our route. We will probably however go west from here to the Norwegian coast, and thence south by boat. The trip from here to the Norwegian coast would be mostly by wagons, and small boats on the lakes, as the railroad is not yet completed.

I will write again in a few days. I am having a very interesting trip.

Letter from his father, dated Seal Harbor, July 25, 1901

Your letter of July 13 reached me this morning. The letter from Christiania came five or six days ago. I write at once expecting you will receive this letter before going to Russia.

I am much pleased to know how satisfactorily you are progressing and what a very good time you must be having.

I have a letter from Boies this morning from Gardiner, Montana. He had been to Yancy's for several days, felt fine. Reported Yancy as young and brisk as ever, ten of the old horses still around and able to go with him. He had fine fun at Yancy's, fishing, etc., and is *exuberant* over his trip and his improved condition. Ralston is with him and Hague and Bill Leigh (Beaver Dick's son) have joined him. He is to meet Tal and Spencer at Ketchum, Idaho, Aug. 15. Spencer is now East, signing bonds of the new company in New York, and at Tal's also. I am well and very comfortable. Your Aunt Lyd is better since she came here. The peace and quiet of Sea Bench are most grateful to both of us. Now, however, as Aug is here we cannot expect to be so quiet; so many people come to Maine in Aug that I suppose we shall have visitors right along every day. Last night Lydy Robinson came out from Bar Harbor. Next week Christine comes, also your Uncle Will and Lilly Hageman and the old Doctor Wikoff and a good many other people whom we know. Tell me exactly how to write you while in Russia.

Letter from Dick to his father, dated Stockholm, Sweden, July 28, 1901

We arrived here last night from the north, after six days of almost continuous travelling—a large part of the way by boat, wagon, horseback and on foot.

On my arrival, I was very glad to find your letters of July 1st and 3d, and to know that you are so comfortable at Seal Harbor. It must be perfect at your place. I am very glad to know that Aunt Lyd is so much better, and hope that she will have no return of her sickness. I have read in the papers of the terrible heat in the U. S., but hope that you have not suffered from it in Seal Harbor. Even up here in Stockholm it is very hot, and today would be a very hot day even for Philadelphia. No such heat, it is said, has ever before been known in Sweden.

I have written you twice since we left here for the north on July 13th, once on board our steamer in the Gulf of Bothnia on July 16th and once from Kuruna in Lapland on July 20th. In the latter letter I told you that our plans were somewhat indefinite as to how we would come south, but we finally decided to go northwest overland to the Arctic Ocean, and thence south along the coast of Norway.

We left Kuruna on the morning of July 22d. Lundbohm was detained by business at the iron mines, so Governor Holmquist and I came alone. The Lapland railroad was completed for only a few miles west of Kuruna, but we went as far as we could on it, and finally came to the shore of one of the largest lakes of Lapland, known as Torne Jnö. Here a small launch, owned by the Swedish government, was waiting for us. The government officials had arranged to give us the use of it to go to the west end of the lake. We arrived there late that night, and stayed until morning at a small settlement known as Tornehamn. We had gradually passed from the low country in northeastern Lapland to a very rugged mountainous country in northwestern Lapland. Though there were snow and glaciers in all directions, yet the heat was intense, and I have rarely seen such oppresive hot weather. The mountain sides were deluged with torrents of water from the melting snow and ice.

The next morning we started over the mountains with horses. We could get only two horses and one small wagon in Tornehamn, and there was only room in the wagon for one of us, so, as Holmquist is somewhat fat and not used to riding, we arranged that I should ride one of the horses and he should take the other with the wagon. All that day we passed through a very rugged country, deluged with water from the melting of the ice and snow under the great heat that prevailed. In the afternoon we arrived at a Swedish government post on the northwest edge of Lapland, near the Norwegian border, known as Wassijaur. Here they had been notified of our coming, and the officer in charge had a fine dinner for us, including the Swedish delicacies of raw salmon and potato brandy. The Norwegian government geologist for northern Norway, named Vogt, whom I have known for some years by correspondence, but whom I had never met before, had heard of our coming and came to Wassijaur to meet us. He travelled the rest of the day with us.

Late in the afternoon we left Wassijaur, travelling part of the way in wagons and part on foot; and early in the night we came abruptly out of the mountains and down to sea level, on a fjord on the coast of the Arctic Ocean in Norway. Here again the government had put a small steamer at our disposal, and that night we went to a place called Narvik, lower down the coast. The next day we took another steamer to Svolvär, which is a small fishing town on one of the Lofoten Islands. Here we caught one of the regular mail steamers from Hammerfest, and went down the coast to Trondhjem, Norway, where we arrived after a pleasant but very hot voyage of 36 hours. From Trondhjem we came here by train.

The trip was most interesting throughout, though the great heat in the last few days that we were in the Arctic regions, was not especially pleasant. Both Lundbohm and Holmquist are first rate men to travel with, and we all got along excellently together. The whole trip since we left here has covered about 2,000 miles, and we have crossed the Scandinavian peninsula from the head of the Gulf of Bothnia to the Arctic Ocean, through one of the least known parts of Europe. I have never been treated anywhere better than in Sweden. All the people from the highest to the lowest seem to take a pride in doing all they can for foreigners —especially for Americans. Governor Holmquist is one of the best men I ever travelled with. The six days that we were alone together we had to converse in German, as he speaks no English. Neither of us spoke German very fluently, but we got along very well. He can speak much more German than I can, but by the time we got back here, we could talk together without any difficulty. He has some queer ideas of America. He told me that he had heard that one of our principal amusements in the U. S. was hunting and shooting niggers, and he was very much surprised when I told him this was not true.

On my arrival here, I have heard from Pourtales to the effect that he is not at all well, and his doctor has insisted on his going at once to Carlsbad for a course of treatment, so that he will not be able to go to Russia with me. This upsets my plans a little, and I have not yet decided what arrangements I will make about the Russian trip, but I will decide in the next few days and will then write to you further. I think very probably I will go from here to St. Petersburg by boat, a journey of only 36 hours, and there I can employ an interpreter, if necessary, to go farther with me. I will however remain here in Stockholm a few days longer to make further inquiries about the matter and will then write you fully about my plans.

You say in your letter of July 1st that you have not been able to find out anything definite about the new discoveries of ore in our mine. I do not know anything *very* definite myself, except that Brockman has written me that he has found some large bodies of new ore, which, though not of very high grade, is yet high grade enough to work, and is in very large quantities. I do not think it will increase the number of dividends per year, as it is not of high enough grade, but it ought to add considerably to the life of the mine.

I will write again in a few days—before I leave here.

Letter from his father, dated Seal Harbor, August 5, 1901

Your letter of July 16, from Lulea, reached me yesterday, and I reply at once, but, I fear, too late to catch you before leaving for Russia. I enjoyed your account of your varied and most interesting experiences greatly. Certainly you are having a most interesting and valuable trip. I keep all of your letters, which you will find an interesting history of your travels.

I am well and very comfortable. Seal Harbor is now packed with visitors, so full that not a room, or even a part of a room, can be had. Your Uncle Will and Dr. Wikoff are here, with young Bill and his wife and several other members of the family. But, I do not mix with the cottagers and after my daily drive, seldom leave my own place. I have had another letter from Boies from St. Anthony. They had come from Yancey's, there in five days, making about 30 or 35 miles daily, and were going to the head of Salmon River next day. He was to meet Tal and Spencer at Ketchum's on Aug. 15th. He reports that the trip has done him great good, etc., etc., and altogether appears to be having a magnificent time. I had a letter from Spencer last night. He had finished up his new mill work, and was starting for Colorado Springs that afternoon. He, too, seems to have had a fine visit East, notwithstanding his work. He took a trip with Eric on *his yacht*, a large schooner to Newport, etc., and had a most happy time. He and Tal are to meet at Cheyenne Aug. 13 and join Boies at Ketchum on Aug. 15. I have no news to tell. Christine and the Baird girls and "Aunt Becky" came to Bar Harbor on Saturday. I have not seen them yet. Spencer Biddle and his wife are somewhere on the Maine coast.

I close to catch this morning's mail.

Letter from Dick to his father, dated Stockholm, Sweden, August 5, 1901

I wrote you fully a few days ago on my arrival here from Lapland. Since then I have received your letter of July 10th and am very glad to know that you are so comfortably settled at Seal Harbor.

I start for St. Petersbourg tomorrow night on a steamer called the "von Dobeln". It is owned by a Finnish (Russian) company which runs a line of very good boats between here and Russia. The "von Dobeln" is said to be the best boat, and therefore I have waited here a little longer than I had expected in order to go on it. The journey from here to St. Petersbourg is only two nights and one day. We cross the end of the Baltic Sea and go up the Gulf of Finnland to St. Petersbourg.

I cannot determine exactly my movements in Russia until I get there, as I cannot get much information as to how to get about there until I reach St. Petersbourg. When I get there I will see Charlemagne Tower, the American Ambassador, who is now in St. Petersbourg, and will also see several Russians to whom I have letters. I will then be able to arrange my plans. It may be too late to go to Siberia, as things freeze up there early in the fall, but I will find out about all this in St. Petersbourg and will then write to you fully. Of course I would be glad if Pourtales were going with me, but, as I wrote you in my last letter, he cannot do so, as he has to go to Carlsbad. I am very sure however that I can get along very well alone; and I hope you will not let the fact that I am going alone worry you. I have made my plans carefully and know just what I am doing. I do not anticipate any more trouble in travelling in Russia than anywhere else in Europe. I find that a man that behaves himself properly can travel without any trouble anywhere that I have ever been, and I expect to find the same thing in Russia. If I find that it is too late in the season to go to Siberia, I will come back from St. Petersbourg through Europe, and will then visit the mines of Spain that I had intended to see last spring, before I took the trip with Pourtales to Servia. But of all this I will write you fully from St. Petersbourg. I note what you say in your letter about staying in Europe as long as I feel like it, and I will act accordingly. So far, everything has been very interesting.

I leave Sweden with regret, as it is a very attractive country, and the Swedes are excellent people. For a small place, Stockholm is one of the most beautiful cities I have seen in Europe, and the hotel where I am staying (the Grand Hotel) is the cleanest and best that I have stayed in since I left the U. S.

P.S. I enclose a few photographs which I took in Lapland, and which I thought might be of interest to you.

Letter from Dick to his father, dated St. Petersbourg, Russia, August 10, 1901

I arrived here all right on Thursday from Stockholm, and was very glad to find your letter of July 25th, which had been forwarded here from London. I also received your letter of July 19th just before I left Stockholm.

We had good weather and a pleasant voyage here from Stockholm. We stopped on the way at Hangö and Helsingfors in Finland. The latter is the capital of Finland, and is a very neat-looking little town on the north shore of the Gulf of Finland. The people on our boat were of various nationalities, and not largely Swedes and Norwegians as on most of the boats I have sailed on lately. They spoke in Russian, German, French, Swedish and Finish—and a few in English.

St. Petersbourg is a very fine and beautiful city. I am staying at the Hotel de l'Europe, which is a very comfortable house. There is very little English spoken here and not much German, so I have employed an interpreter, and with him I can get about without any difficulty. I saw Charlemagne Tower, the American

Ambassador, here for a few minutes this morning, and am to see him again tomorrow. I will then decide about my plans. Tower was very cordial and will be able to give me much information about how to see the places I want to visit. I will write you fully about my movements in a few days. I like Russia very much from the little I have seen of it so far, and I expect to have a very interesting trip here.

I note what you say about Barringer, and I do not understand his saying that I was too enthusiastic. It may have been the hot weather that affected him, or the fact that one of his children has been very ill. I will keep you notified of anything new that I hear. As I wrote you in a recent letter, my own information is meagre, but I have perfect confidence in Brockman's management and in the honesty of both him and Barringer. I suppose we will soon have another dividend, but I have not tried to dictate about this; as I knew that Brockman and Barringer, being on the spot, could decide better about dividends than I could in Europe. If there is any delay about the dividend, it is probably because some of the earnings are being put into the sinking fund with the idea of eventually getting it up to $100,000 again. I will write you as soon as I hear more definitely about this. A weekly cash statement is sent to me showing the financial condition of our Co., and in the last one that I received I notice that $25,000 more has recently been added to the sinking fund, making a total now of $75,000 in that fund. In spite of this, however, we also had on the date of this last statement (July 20th) over $70,000 in our general account, so I think that a dividend will soon be forthcoming.

Our plan is to gradually get the sinking fund up to $100,000 without interfering too much with dividends, and after it has reached that amount, all the earnings of the mine will be available for dividends, which should therefore be correspondingly more frequent.

I am exceedingly glad to hear by your letter that Boies is getting so much better in the west, and I hope that he and Tal and Speck will have a fine trip.

I will write again in a few days.

P.S. Please continue to address me care of J. S. Morgan & Co., 22 Old Broad St., London, England, as they will forward mail wherever I am.

Letter from his father, dated Seal Harbor, August 13, 1901

Your Stockholm letter of July 28 received and is before me, also your letter from Lulea and Kuruna. I suppose by now you have received more of my letters, since I have written you most regularly and faithfully. Of course, I have not the news to communicate that your letters contain, but I can tell you the small events of our experience here, and at home, and *then, after all*, it is the receiving of a letter from *home*, and the knowledge that it is all well with them there, that makes a "home" letter appreciated. I was extremely interested in the narrative of your journey up to Kuruna and back again to Stockholm. How lucky you were to have had the "Governor" as your companion. You could never have accomplished the thing alone. Your reference to the polar scenery and people is most interesting. I am glad I gave you "Afraja" to read. Its charming descriptions of Lapland scenery are unique, and, I suppose, the "maids on ice" of the inhabitants are more interesting, as also unique experience, than in any other point of view. I am distressed at your news of Pourtales. I do hope you will be able to pick up some nice fellow as companion, or that maybe, Tower can help you in this when you get to St. Petersburg. I have nothing new to tell you. Our days pass *swiftly*, but uneventfully. I am well. I have no more news about the boys. Tal left Atlantic on Saturday. They all meet on Aug. 15. I suppose I shall have letters from all the boys when they get to Ketchums before going into the wilderness. I had a long letter from Kate* today, inclosing photos of the children, which are very charming. She has invited Sally Penrose of Carlisle to stay with her during Tal's absence. Sally is so fine a girl that Kate looks forward to her visit with great pleasure.

Letter from Dick to his father, dated St. Petersbourg, Russia, August 17, 1901

I have carefully investigated the subject of going east over the Siberian Railway, and have found that it is not only a very easy matter, but also a very interesting trip; so I have decided to go. I have had several talks with Charlemagne Tower about it, and he not only thinks the trip a good one but he even advises me to go. Through his influence I have gotten a general letter from Prince Hilkoff, Minister of Ways of Communication, in Russia, directing the various officials along the road to give me any assistance that I may need. I will also have an interpreter who is the son of the chief clerk in the American Embassy. He seems to be a very reliable young fellow, and he speaks Russian, English and French. The interpreter I have had here is a good man, but he does not seem to be very healthy, and I was afraid he could not stand the journey across Siberia. Therefore I have taken this other man. He has never been in Siberia, but after all, what I need is only an interpreter to talk through; and I can do the rest.

The route that I will follow is this: I go tonight to Moscow, which is the starting point of the Siberian Railway; and Wednesday—Aug. 21st—I leave Moscow, going east over the Siberian Railway through the Ural Mountains and into Asia, passing through West Siberia via the towns of Perm, Omsk, and Krasnoyarsk to Irkutsk—a journey of nine days. Thence across Lake Baikal, a journey of half a day. Thence by railroad again to Stretensk on the Amur River, a journey of two days. Thence by steamboat on the Amur River through East Siberia to Khabarovsk, a journey of about 8 or 9 days. Thence by railroad again to Vladivostok on the Pacific Coast, a journey of a day and a half. From Vladivostok there is easy communication to various places by boat, and I will probably go to Nagasaki in Japan, and then to Yokohama. The whole trip from Moscow to Vladivostok will take me about 24 or 25 days. From Vladivostok to Nagasaki is only 3 or 4 days journey by boat.

I do not want you to worry yourself about my taking this trip without Pourtales. Of course I would be very glad if he had been able to come, but as long as he cannot, I do not see any reason for my not going. I am not acting hastily, but have studied the whole matter carefully before coming to a decision, and I can

* Tal's wife.

see no difficulties whatever in the way. In fact I cannot imagine much more favorable auspices than those under which I am going. The route is now a recognized line of travel and people go over it every day. I will write to you from different points along the route as often as possible, but it may happen that sometimes I may not be able to mail letters for several days in succession, especially on the Amur River, so do not be worried if you do not hear from me as regularly as heretofore. Remember that no news is good news, and when you do not hear from me for a longer time than usual, you may assume that I am all right but have been a little delayed in being able to mail letters. I think however that I can write fairly regularly.

St. Petersbourg is a fine city and I have taken great interest in seeing it. It contains about one and a quarter million people, and is built on a grand scale, with wide streets, beautiful buildings and palaces, and with many canals cut through the city and leading off from the Neva River. All the people whom I have met have been very kind and hospitable, and I am beginning to feel as much at home here as if I had lived here for years. The first secretary of our Embassy here under Tower is a man named Pierce, who is a brother of Prof. J. M. Pierce, of Harvard College; and the second secretary is a man named Morgan from Aurora, N. Y., who is also a Harvard graduate. They are both first rate men.

When I reach Japan I may come home across the Pacific via San Francisco, or I may go to Hong Kong and Manila, and thence back to Europe via the Suez Canal, and then home. But in all this I will be guided by circumstances when I reach Japan. When you write, you had better address me care of the Chartered Bank of India, Australia, and China, Hong Kong, China, because that is a good central point, and if I do not go direct from Japan to Hong Kong, I will have my mail forwarded from Hong Kong to me.

If at any time I have occasion to cable home giving any other address, I will cable to J. C. Jones in our office at the Bullitt Building, Phila, and I am writing him to forward you copies of any cables I may send. The reason that I have thought it best to cable to Jones instead of direct to you, is that probably in the far east they will not have Seal Harbor in their list of cable offices. Very probably, however, I will have no occasion to cable.

Have you ever heard anything from Dr. Woods about my candidacy for the Union League Club of Phila? If not, and if you are writing to him at any time, won't you please ask him how things stand? If I am elected I will be greatly obliged to you if you will ask Dr. Woods to have the bills for dues, initiation fee, etc., sent to James Collins Jones, 460 Bullitt Building, Philadelphia, who will pay them for me out of funds I left with him.

I will write to Jones to send you a check for $150 in payment of the dividend due you last month on the 200 shares of the stock of the Camden & Burlington County R.R. which I hold in the trust fund.

I hope you are having a pleasant summer at Seal Harbor. It is still very warm here, but cool weather is expected soon. I will write again before I leave Moscow.

P.S. Charlemagne Tower sends you his regards.

Letter from Dick to his father, dated Moscow, Russia, August 21, 1901

I arrived here from St. Petersbourg three days ago and will start tonight for Siberia over the new Siberian Railway. I wrote twice to you from St. Petersbourg, and in the last letter I described to you fully the Siberian route that I will follow. I have all my preparations in excellent shape, and my interpreter has so far proved very satisfactory. He seems to be intelligent and reliable. I have a very good compartment in the train for the journey to Irkutsk, which, as I wrote you in my last letter, is the first stage of the trip, and takes about nine days.

I expect to arrive in Vladivostok on the Pacific Coast in about 24 or 25 days from here, that is, about the middle of September, though of course there is always the chance of a few days delay in the steamers going down the Amur River, as they do not always make very prompt connection with the trains. From Vladivostok, it will take only four days by sea to go to Japan. The boats coming south from Vladivostok to Japan stop at some of the ports of Korea on the way, so I will probably have a chance to get a glimpse at that country.

As I wrote you in my last letter, my address for some time to come will be care of the Chartered Bank of India, Australia, and China, Hong Kong, China; and I will arrange to have mail forwarded to me from there wherever I am.

Moscow is a very attractive city. It retains many of its ancient features. The old citadel, the peculiar architecture of the houses of the town, the variously colored roofs, and the brilliantly gilded domes of the many churches, all combine to make a very interesting sight. The people all seem to be prosperous and very fond of having a good time; and there seem to be a great many very good-looking women here, which naturally makes any town look attractive.

I will write again in a few days and will mail the letter from the train on the way to Siberia.

In a manuscript concerning this Siberian trip, from which he quoted copiously for his published book, *The Last Stand of the Old Siberia,* Penrose wrote in detail of this train journey. Excerpts from the manuscript will be inserted at intervals, labeled "Manuscript."

From the Manuscript

A daily train starts from Moscow for the trans-Siberian journey, but twice a week this train is faster than on the other days, and is known as the "train de luxe". Its average speed is about twenty miles an hour from Moscow to Irkutsk, and slower from there to Stretensk. The time required is about eight days from Moscow to Lake Baikal; three days from Baikal to Stretensk; from ten to thirty days, according to the condition of the water, from Stretensk to Khabarovsk by river; and thirty odd hours from Khabarovsk to Vladivostok by rail. When the road around the south end of Lake Baikal is completed, and when the Chinese Eastern Railway is open for general travel, much more rapid time from Europe to the Pacific can be made; while with the introduction of heavier rails and with shorter stops at stations, a much faster rate of speed can be maintained. With the through railway completed and with the average speed increased to thirty miles per hour, the trip from St. Petersburg to Vladivostok could be made in about eight days. Adding three days to this as the time required to come from London to St. Petersburg, and seven days as the time from New York to London, the trip to the Pacific Coast of Siberia could be made in eleven days from London or in eighteen days from New York. The saving of time thus accomplished is shown by the fact that it now takes about forty days to go from London to Vladivostok via Suez Canal and the Indian Ocean; and it takes from twenty-five to thirty-five days to go from New York to Vladivostok via Vancouver or San Francisco and Japan, while if the different steamers on all these routes do not make good connections, these times may be considerably lengthened.

The writer crossed Siberia shortly after the railway as far as Stretensk had been opened for travel.... The large station at Moscow was a crowded place when the Siberian train was preparing to start, for even to Russians the journey is a long one, and the friends of many of the passengers were there in great numbers to see them off. Finally the regulation three bells, rung at intervals of several minutes, gave the signal to start, and promptly on schedule time, at 9.05 p.m., we pulled out of the ancient capital of the empire for its newer possessions in the far east.

The train was composed of first and second class passenger cars, with a dining car, library, bath room, barber shop and apparatus for gymnastic exercises. This last feature becomes important in such a long overland journey as across Siberia, and it might well be adopted by some of the American trans-continental trains. The passenger cars were cut up into compartments with two or four berths in each and an aisle on the side of the car; while the whole train was lit by electricity. The cars were attended by Tartar porters, who here as in most hotels and public places in Russia are the usual servants. They are said to be honest, trustworthy and fairly sober. The whole train was in charge of a Russian official. Some of the trains carry a church car in which services are held for passengers, as well as for the people at the stations at which the train stops long enough for this purpose.

We had a separate compartment in one of the cars, our neighbors on one side being a priest of the Greek Church and his family, and on the other side the family of a banker in Siberia. Several Russian officers were also on board, as well as several civilians bound for the gold districts, another bound for the far north on the Lena Valley, a Frenchman who had butter dairies in the Obi Valley, and many others. Very few were going all the way across Siberia, most being bound for intermediate points.

The train was much crowded, but every one was good humored and courteous as they filled every available corner with their many bags and bundles, including large baskets of supplies, the inevitable tea pots and boxes of cigarettes, and a great deal of bedding with mattresses, sheets and pillows. This bedding is not necessary on the train, as it can be procured there by paying extra, and it is stipulated by the railway authorities that they will have the sheets and pillow cases changed once every three days of the journey; but it is needed when the passenger leaves the train and branches off on the river boats and postroads. Bedding is also useful at many of the hotels of Siberia, because very often when a traveller rents a room, he finds in it a bare iron or wood bedstead, as he is expected to carry his own bedding. At many of the hotels, however, these articles can be procured from the proprietor at a fixed price for each sheet, pillow, pillow case, etc., so that a bill for one night's lodging and fare often includes a dozen or more items.

Our route led us first through the grain districts of eastern Russia, in the valley of that great water highway, the Volga River, past the agricultural metropolis of Samara, and thence to the Ural Mountains.

Letter from Dick to his father, dated "On Train, Siberian Railway, Russia, August 23, 1901."

I am writing to you on the train on our way to Siberia. I wrote to you fully just before we left Moscow two days ago. Today is our second day on the train, and I will mail this letter at some station this evening.

Ever since we left Moscow we have been passing through a fine agricultural country. Last night we passed the Volga River, and this afternoon we are approaching the Ural Mountains, which we will cross tonight; and tomorrow we will get into Siberia.

Everything so far has gone very comfortably with us. The train is very good and the weather has been fine, though a little warm. We will reach Irkutsk on the 29th. I will write again in a few days. I think we are going to have a good journey all the way, and a very interesting one.

Letter from his father, dated Seal Harbor, August 25, 1901

Your two last letters from Stockholm (Aug. 5) and St. Petersburg (Aug. 10) with the Lapland photos (most interesting) are before me. I am delighted to know of your successful journeys by land and sea and *sometimes almost* wish I was along with you. Ever bear in mind, in all traveling, the constant peril from typhoid fever from impure water and in every place, where you are not sure of the purity of the water, remember my old Texas and Arkansas advice that served you so well in times past, to use boiled water only; i.e., tea, coffee, etc., etc.

I hope Tower and your Russian friends will arrange to have you attended while in Russia, not only by a hired currier, but by some of your friends themselves, as well as by Russian officials. The Russians should be only too happy to welcome and do honor to a man so wise in the very knowledge they most need—mining engineering and economic geology—and should see—as I have no doubt they will see—that they give him a good time.

I am well and getting along very satisfactorily. Seal Harbor and all Mt. Desert are still overflowing with people and will be for two weeks longer, then (thank God!!) *I* will have it to myself. I have letters from Boies, Tal and Spencer from Ketchum, Idaho. They met there, as agreed upon, on Aug. 15, Boies and Ralston coming in from a camp they had established about 100 miles off. Ralston left that afternoon for home and the boys packed up and returned to Boies's camp next day. They plan to be home about Oct. 1st. Boies wrote in fine spirits and said he was in a "magnificent" condition and Tal wrote that "Boies had not been so well for years." Much obliged for your information about our mine, etc. Spencer wrote me that his affairs were all prosperous and that *very soon* the sampler would begin dividends, from which statement I infer the sampler is not to be absorbed by the mill trust.

I had a nice letter from Kate yesterday enclosing photos of her kids. Sally Penrose is staying with her during Tal's absence.

From the Manuscript

The Urals are a picturesque forest-clad range not unlike parts of the Allegheny Mountains, and they separate the plains of eastern Europe from those of western Asia. The Ural Mountains are the boundary of Europe and Asia, but the governments of Perm and Orenburg, which are included in the political limits of European Russia, overlap the Urals and extend a short distance into Asia, so that Siberia proper does not commence along the line of the railway until we reach the government of Tobolsk, 130 miles east of Cheliabinsk. Where the dividing line is crossed in the heart of the Urals, a large stone monument has been erected bearing on one side the inscription "Europe" and on the other side "Asia."

The most noticeable feature as we descended the east slope of the mountains into the plains of Asia was the great size, freshness, and succulence of the vegetation, which here shows a wonderfully luxuriant growth, while on the western slope it was dry and parched. This feature is characteristic of the whole of Siberia, and many of the shrubs and trees which are common to both regions, grow to much greater size there than in Europe. On both sides of the mountains we passed numerous iron manufacturing districts, for this part of the Urals is the great iron region of Russia; and at many of the stations some of the products of the works, such as cutlery, daggers, and small ornamental castings, were offered for sale.

We continued eastward over unbroken steppes for over 1000 miles in the governments of Tobolsk and Tomsk and the Kirgiz country, across the valleys of the Tobol, Ishim, Irtish and Obi rivers, whose courses meandering toward the north are marked by long lines of trees intersecting the plains. As far as the eye can reach are seen scattered fields of grains, separated by grasslands brilliant with wild flowers, and dotted by droves of cattle with their Kirgiz herdsmen; while occasionally caravans and emigrant wagons pass slowly along the country roads. Whole train loads of butter from the dairies of the Obi Valley are shipped thence by sea to England. Bee culture has also reached a considerable stage of development in the Tomsk Government and throughout the regions to the east, the bees seeming to prosper greatly, and immense quantities of honey are produced. Of such importance has this industry become that the Russian Government has appointed a special commissioner to look after bee culture and to study the best methods of promoting it.

The steppe regions contain numerous prosperous rural communities, and a number of towns of considerable size, with population of from ten to sixty thousand people. Along the line of the railway Cheliabinsk, Kurgan, Petropavlovsk, Omsk, Tomsk, etc., are especially noteworthy. The town of Kurgan is built on what are supposed to be the ruins of an old Tartar fort, though the native legend relates that this spot was the tomb of the daughter of a powerful Tartar chief, that robbers attacked it to obtain the treasure buried with her, and that the princess in rage rose up and drove off in a chariot drawn by two white horses. Tomsk is connected with the main line by a branch road, and is the chief town of the government of the same name, as well as the commercial center of West Siberia. Like many other Siberian towns it was started as a fort in the early days, but gradually expanded as the commercial necessities of the region required, until now it contains over 60,000 people. It has some fine buildings, telephones, telegraph lines, electric lights, churches, theatres, newspapers, hospitals, and all the equipments of a modern city. It has many schools, scientific societies, and one institution of higher learning, the Tomsk Imperial University, with a library of over 100,000 volumes.

Letter from Dick to his father, dated "On Train, Siberian Railway," Siberia, Russia, August 25, 1901

This is our fifth day on the train since leaving Moscow, and I thought I would write to you and mail the letter at a station called Ob, which we will reach this afternoon. Ob is on the River Ob, which is one of the largest rivers of Siberia, and rises in the Altai Mountains to the south of the line of this railroad.

I wrote you three days ago. After that time we crossed the Ural Mountains and came into Asia. On the European side of the Urals the weather was very hot and the country looked dry; but on the Asiatic side it was cool, and everything was green and fresh from recent rains. We are now in the interior of West Siberia, and ever since we crossed the Ural Mts. we have been going through a level alluvial country, which is a very rich agricultural region. Tomorrow we will get into a more mountainous country, as we approach the region of the Yenesei River.

We are having a very pleasant and interesting journey. It rained yesterday, but today it has cleared off and the weather is perfect—just like a summer day in Colorado.

As I wrote you in my last letter, we will reach Irkutsk on the 29th, and will then take another train and continue east. I will write again in a few days.

It is hard to write on a train, but I hope you will be able to read this letter.

From the Manuscript

To the east of Tomsk we approached the mountain region and travelled for about 1,000 miles through a rugged country, occasionally intersected by higher mountain ranges, with many fertile valleys, across the governments of Yenisei and Irkutsk to Lake Baikal. This country is abundantly watered by many streams, the most important being the Yenisei and its tributary, the Angara, and in many parts it is heavily covered with forests. Hunting is a popular occupation here among both Russians and natives, but it has been carried on so actively during the 300 years or more in which Siberia has been known to the Russians, that some of the animals, especially the sable, which is the most sought-after of all the fur animals, have been almost exterminated. Laws have been recently made, however, restricting hunting to certain times of year, and also defining the methods under which it shall be carried on, thus giving the game a chance to escape complete extermination.

The mining resources of this mountainous region are rapidly becoming prominent, especially the gold mining, which is a newer industry here than in the Urals. The gold occurs both in placer deposits and in veins, most of the production, however, coming from the placers, as vein mining has been but little developed, and even in placer mining only the richest alluvium is worked. The Ural Mountains, and the Yakutsk and Amur Territories are the chief gold producing regions of Asiatic Russia, though the governments of Tomsk, Yenisei, and Irkutsk, and the Territory of Transbaikalia produce considerable, while the Territory of Ussuri and the region of the Ohkotsk Sea and Kamchatka produce a little. The total production of all Russia in 1900, including Siberia and the Urals, was a little over $20,000,000. Taking Siberia and the rest of Asiatic Russia as a whole, its possibilities as a gold producing region are simply enormous. It is bounded on the south, west, and east by gold-bearing mountains, and an extraordinary number of the streams from these ranges show signs of gold in their alluvium, while many of them are wonderfully rich. It would seem that at no very distant time, the gold mines if properly exploited, might easily produce instead of $20,000,000 annually, many times this amount; and in these great gold possibilities surely lies enormous future wealth for the government and the people of Russia.

Coal or lignite of various geological ages, including Carboniferous, Jurassic, and Tertiary, is very generally distributed throughout the eastern part of Siberia, but wood is so cheap that coal has not been much worked except for the railway, and on the coast for ocean steamers. The beds are of considerable size, and the quality is often that of a very good bituminous coal, while elsewhere, especially in the Tertiary strata, it is in the form of brown coal or lignite. Iron ores also occur in a great many places in the Ural Mountains and in the mountains of the eastern part of Siberia. They are extensively smelted on both slopes of the Urals, but farther east they are worked to only a limited extent in the governments of Yenisei and Irkutsk, and the Territory of Transbaikalia. The abundance, however, of iron ore and fuel in Siberia offers the basis of a great iron manufacturing industry, though up to the present time, the limited markets have retarded its development.

Letter from Dick to his father dated "On Train, Siberian Railway," Siberia, Russia, August 29, 1901

I have written you twice since we left Moscow on this train on Aug. 21st;— once on Aug. 23d and once on Aug. 26th. We will arrive at Irkutsk tonight, and I write now so that I can mail the letter there.

I mailed my last letter to you at Ob on the River Ob. After leaving that station we continued east across the Yenisei River and into the more mountainous country between there and Irkutsk. This afternoon we are approaching a still more mountainous country. Our train will stay tonight at Irkutsk; and in the morning, instead of taking another train as I thought we would have to do, we will go on to Lake Baikal in the same train, arriving there tomorrow afternoon. Thence we cross Lake Baikal in a steamer, arriving on the other side tomorrow night. Thence we take another train, and in two days and a half reach Stretensk on the Shilka River. This river is one of the streams that combine to form the Amur River, and we go down it in a steamer to the Amur, and thence down the Amur to Khabarovsk, where we again take a train to Vladivostok.

We have had so far a very pleasant and interesting trip, and I think we will have the same experience for the rest of the journey. I will write again in a few days; but do not be surprised if my letters come to you a little less regularly after we get east of Lake Baikal, as I may not have as good opportunities to write as I have had up to now. I will, however, write as regularly as possible.

I hope you are well and are having a good summer at Seal Harbor.

From the Manuscript

The largest town in the mountain region is Irkutsk in the government of the same name, which we reached after eight days and nights continuous travel from Moscow. It was founded about the middle of the seventeenth century as a fort and trading post, at which the tribute of furs paid the government representatives by the native Buriat tribes was collected. It has played an important part in Siberian history, and by the census of 1897 it had 52,000 people, though it has grown considerably since then. Like Tomsk it has all the conveniences of a modern city, and the newer and finer stone buildings are in strange contrast with the older heavy one-storied log cabins, surrounded by high fences of equally heavy logs, and entered through mysterious-looking small gates or doors, recalling the days when Siberian houses were built more for security than for beauty. The activity of the town by day and night, the saloons, restaurants and hotels crowded with people, together with the dance halls running full blast, are the result of the sudden boom given by the railway, which arrived there in 1898.

Leaving the city of Irkutsk, we continued up the Angara Valley for a few miles to the station of Baikal on Lake Baikal. This lake is the largest body of fresh water on the continent of Europe and Asia, and is second only to the great lakes of America and Africa, being about 400 miles long and from 17 to 55 miles wide, with a depth sometimes reaching between 3,000 and 4,000 feet. It is fed by numerous streams, notably the Selenga, flowing from Mongolia, and has its outlet in the Angara River, a tributary of the Yenisei. It is completely surrounded by rugged mountains, and has many rocky islands and precipitous capes, eroded by the elements into fantastic forms which are believed by the natives to be the homes of different deities; hence the lake is known by them as the "Holy Sea." It is noted for the stormy weather usually prevailing, and the normal condition of the waters during a large part of the year seems to be one of turbulence. In spite of this, however, the lake is an important channel of communication and a number of boats do a lucrative business on it. The railway maintains powerful steamers for the transportation of passengers and freight pending the time when the road shall be completed around the south shores. One of these boats, the "Baikal," is a very powerful ice-breaker used in crossing the lake in winter, as the water freezes to a depth of from four to seven feet. It is also used in the summer as an ordinary transport.

On arriving at the lake we found the steamer "Baikal" waiting for the train. The weather during the morning had been clear and perfect, and we began to think that we might have a good passage, but before the boat started a heavy storm arose, and as we left the shore, the waters of this grand but inhospitable inland sea were a mass of billows and spray. On the boat could be seen better than on the railway the different races and tribes that circulate along this great interior highway. Russian soldiers and peasants from all parts of the empire, Chinese, Tartars, Tungus, Buriats, Yakuts, and various other tribes, each in their own native dress, all talking in different languages at the same time, crowd and jostle each other in their rush to cross the gang plank and board the ship. Below, in the cabin, the few first-class passengers eat, drink, smoke cigarettes, and play cards and musical instruments. The steamer continues through the fog and storm, the deck passengers become colder and wetter, the cabin passengers grumble at the slowness of the voyage, and finally, after about seven hours, the lights of the Mysovaya mole and the shrill whistles of the transport announce the arrival in port. The passengers are quickly transferred to the new train and again the land journey is resumed toward the east.

After leaving Lake Baikal we entered the Territory of Transbaikalia, which, with the exception of an area of steppe land in the southeast, in the direction of the Desert of Gobi, is almost entirely a high mountainous country, well watered by many streams; and though the climate is very severe, the subsoil being frozen both summer and winter over almost the whole of the province, many valleys are successfully cultivated in places where the soil thaws for a depth of a few inches during the summer. The Amur Territory adjoins Transbaikalia on the east and is, like it, essentially a mountainous country. It is separated from the Chinese province of Manchuria by the Amur River, which is the main artery of travel through the region.

It was in Transbaikalia, on the Onon River, that, according to the Mongol legend, their great chief of the 13th century, Jenghiz Khan, was born. In fact, the original home of the Turko-Mongolian tribes which overran Asia and eastern Europe in the middle ages, is supposed to have been in southern Transbaikalia and the adjoining parts of China. The Turks of what is now the Turkish Empire probably came originally from here, but they have become so much mixed with Caucasians since they settled in Europe and western Asia, that they are a very different people from the original Turkish stock, which is seen in its less adulterated condition in some of the Siberian tribes. It may be stated here that the natives of Siberia are mostly scattered nomadic tribes, differing considerably in different parts, but with the exception of a few tribes of uncertain ethnology in the coast provinces, they are largely of Mongolian, Turkish, or Finnish origin; and many of them, at least, are descendants of once much more numerous and more powerful people, having been driven by superior force or by the overcrowding of their original homes, to seek new lands in the unoccupied or sparsely inhabited regions of Siberia. Among the most numerous are the Kirgiz tribes of southwestern Siberia, the descendants of the Turko-Mongolian hordes whose invasions in the Middle Ages carried terror to the people of Europe; the Yakuts, a Turkish tribe, who wandered many years ago from their more southerly homes to the Arctic regions, and have now become so thoroughly acclimatized that they not only exist there, but are even among the few native tribes of Siberia that are increasing in number; the Tonguses, a Mongolian tribe, which extends in greater or less numbers from the Yenisei River to the Pacific Coast. Among other more or less numerous tribes may be mentioned the Ostiaks, Voguls, Samoyedes, Buriats, Tartars, Giliaks, Aleuts, etc.

Transbaikalia occupies a unique position among the provinces of Siberia inasmuch as it has been for ages the great channel of entry for Chinese products into Russia and for Russian products into China. This is partly because it is the shortest route to Europe from eastern China, and partly because the Selenga Valley offers a much easier passage across the frontier than any of the routes to the west, where the rugged mountains make the few passes that do exist more or less difficult. From the earliest days a large part of the tea brought to Russia from China has come over this route. The town of Kiakhta in the Selenga Valley, near the frontier, was and is still the great international market where Slav and Mongol meet and trade.

A novel industry in Transbaikalia is the catching and domesticating of the "maral," or wild deer, for the sake of its horns, which are considered a very valuable medicine by the Chinese. The maral sheds its horns once a year, and they are collected and sold at high prices to the Chinese merchants who ship them south into China. In a similar manner the Siberian finds ready purchasers among the Chinese for the bones, claws, and other parts of the northern tiger which abounds in Ussuri on the Pacific Coast. These parts when ground up and administered to a patient are supposed to have wonderful effects, and the Chinese are said to give this medicine to their soldiers to keep up their courage in war.

Letter from Dick to his father, dated "On Train, Siberian Railway," Siberia, Russia, September 2, 1901

We will arrive at Stretensk on the Shilka River this afternoon, and I write now so as to mail the letter there. I mailed my last letter to you at Irkutsk on Aug. 30th, though the letter was dated Aug. 29th.

From Irkutsk we continued east to Lake Baikal, which we crossed in a steamer in about five hours, and then we took another train for Stretensk, and have now been on it for two and a half days. At Stretensk we will take a steamer going down the Shilka and Amur Rivers towards the Pacific Coast. I have written you about this route in previous letters.

Lake Baikal, which we crossed three days ago, is the largest lake in Siberia, being over four hundred miles long, though only from forty to seventy miles wide. It is a beautiful body of water and is surrounded on all sides by high mountains. Since leaving Lake Baikal, we have been all the time in a beautiful mountainous country, known as the "Trans-Baikal."

Since leaving Moscow we have now been almost twelve days and twelve nights on the train, and I never before realized that such a long journey by train could be made so comfortably. We have had so far not only a very interesting, but also a very pleasant trip.

Do not be surprised if you do not hear from me for two or three weeks after getting this letter, as it may be that when we get on the Shilka and Amur Rivers, mail may be sent to America across the Pacific via San Francisco instead of via Europe as in my previous letters. This would cause a break in the regularity of my letters. I am not sure that this will occur, but it may do so, and I mention it so that you will not be surprised if you do not hear from me for a longer time than usual. I will keep on writing as regularly as possible.

From the Manuscript

We continued our journey eastward from Lake Baikal through the mountain country, across the Yablonoi Range which, in Transbaikalia, forms the continental divide between the waters of the Arctic and those of the Pacific, past the historic towns of Petrovsk, Chita, and Nerchinsk, to the terminus of the railway at Stretensk on the Shilka River. This town was only a short time ago a quiet Cossack village, a line of log cabins strung along the river bank, but the arrival of the railway has given it an unwonted activity, for it is here that all the transcontinental traffic has to be changed from train to boat or vice versa. On our arrival our first effort was to secure passage on a steamer down the Shilka and Amur rivers. After applying at several boats along the shore and finding that they were all full, we secured passage on a freight boat named the Vladimir Monamakh. This was a large, flat-bottomed, stern-paddle steamer loading with salt and general merchandise for the lower Amur; and as even this boat was very much crowded, we were fortunate in securing the right to sleep on the seats in the dining saloon.

Letter from Dick to his father, dated Stretensk, Siberia, Russia, September 4, 1901

I wrote to you a couple of days ago on the train coming here, and mailed the letter on my arrival. I have remained here a couple of days waiting for a boat going down the Shilka and Amur Rivers. We could have started on a boat yesterday, but we got better accommodations by waiting here until today for another boat. We start this afternoon, and go down stream to a place called

Blagoveschensk, where we take another boat for Khabarovsk further down the Amur River. Thence we go by train to Vladivostok. We will probably reach Vladivostok in about two weeks.

As I said in my last letter, do not be surprised if you do not hear from me for two or three weeks after getting this letter, because when we get down on the Amur River, it is possible that mail for America may be sent across the Pacific via San Francisco, instead of via Europe as in my previous letters, thus causing a break in the regularity with which you have probably been getting my letters heretofore. It might possibly be even over three weeks before you get my next letter after this, but I will continue to write as regularly as possible, and the letters will doubtless reach you sooner or later.

This town of Stretensk is the present terminus of this part of the railroad, and is situated on the Shilka River, which, as I have written you, is one of the streams that combine to form the Amur River.

The weather continues very fine, with cold nights and warm days, and we expect to have a very good trip down the Shilka and Amur Rivers.

P.S. Even if my next letter should be sent to you via Europe, it will reach you at least two or three weeks later than this letter, as it takes a long time for mail to come up stream by steamer on the Shilka and Amur; so in any case, do not be surprised if you do not hear from me again for a few weeks.

Letter from his father, dated Seal Harbor, September 6, 1901

Your letters of Aug. 17 and 21 (Moscow) are before me. I have been expecting the latter all week and reply at once to both.

I am greatly pleased to know that everything is working so happily with you, and feel that you are making your long journey under the most favorable circumstances, even though you have not Pourtales with you. I rather feel *now* as if your best plan would be after China and Japan, Manila, *India*, Suez Canal, Constantinople, Cairo, Rome, Venice, Spain, Paris, and Home! It all may take you a month or more longer, but the time of year will be most favorable and it seems a pity to pass any of these places. If *I* were with you I would *add* to this itinerary a trip up the Nile in a sailboat—my *only* weakness. But, as *I* am not along, we can save this for *another?* winter. If anything would tempt me to go abroad it would be Egypt and the Nile. I had a talk with Dr. Woods about the Union League business before I went to Capon, and told him to send all the bills to me. He replied it was a matter of no moment, etc., etc. But I will write him now again, and let you have his reply. I will also give him your message. I have no especial news to send you. Have not heard from the boys since they left for camp, nor from Kate.

Nel Penrose (Germantown) is to be married the middle of Oct. I may get something and send it for you. My present will be a silver tea service. If I get anything for you, most probably I will write to Kate to get it for you. I am well and getting along comfortably. I expect now to stay here until about Oct. 20th, so you had better after the receipt of this letter direct to 1331 Spruce St.

Your Aunt Lyd and Jane will remain as long as I do and this secures my comfort during the whole season. Christine, the Baird girls, Aunt Becky, Arthur Colby, Lydy Robinson and Mona, Spencer Biddle and wife are at Bar Harbor, where, however, I seldom go. Seal Harbor is so fine that I do not care for any other place.

Jones sent me the cheque for $150.

Do you intend to keep your "interpreter" until you return to Europe. It seems to me he would prove very useful and valuable as a mere traveling companion.

I look for and read your letters with great interest *and keep them all*.

From the Manuscript

The loading of the boat [at Stretensk] was all done by hand, no trucks were used and everything was carried on men's backs. Gaily attired music girls played harps and violins alongside the gang plank to encourage the men, and this, together with frequent drinks of vodka, seemed to inspire them to great activity. The more vodka they drank and the more music the girls played, the harder the men worked, until at last the boat was loaded. Then some cattle and sheep were driven aboard for the settlers on the lower Amur; and finally after waiting three days, the boat was ready and we started down the Shilka, crowded with freight and emigrants and carrying a few cabin passengers, and with a mixed crew of Russians, Manchurians, and Koreans.

The Russian Government has done much to improve navigation on the Amur and its tributary, the Shilka, as it is a most important channel of travel, not only because the Amur is on the Manchurian frontier, but because it is the gateway through the mountains to the Pacific provinces. Lighthouses from point to point indicate the course of the channel, and signal stations are established at certain intervals, indicating by means of graduated poles, visible at long distances, the depth of the water from day to day; so that the steamboat captains have only to glance at these indicators as they pass to learn the condition of the water. Steam dredges are also kept working at shallow places in the channel. In fact, the methods for assisting navigation are remarkably complete, and rarely anywhere can be seen a more thoroughly efficient system for river navigation than this one established by the Russian Government in the remote interior of Asia.

The Shilka below Stretensk flows through a high rolling country in the foot hills of the Yablonoi Mountains, until it reaches the eastern limit of Transbaikalia, where the Argun, flowing in a broad muddy stream from northern China, joins it and together they form the Amur. A short distance below is the village of Pokrovsk, a small Cossack settlement of a few hundred inhabitants, which we reached on the second evening from Stretensk. This is the first of a number of Cossack villages, which represent posts established along the left bank of the Amur by Count Muravioff, for protection of the frontier, after the treaty of Aigun with China in 1858. They are usually built in clearances in the forest on the bank of the river, and consist of rows of log cabins, above which rise the spires of the Greek churches which they almost all possess. The people live, in times of peace, by farming, hunting, fishing, and gold mining, while in times of war they are soldiers.

We arrived at Pokrovsk late in the evening, and, as at most of the Cossack villages, as soon as our boat touched shore, women and children hurried to the river bank selling milk, onions, and mushrooms to the passengers, a large flat mushroom fried in fat having a ready sale. A dense fog settled down on the river shortly afterward, so that we were compelled to anchor until it cleared the next morning. Some distance below, the river flows through the Big Khingan Mountains which extend from the Great Wall of China northward into Siberia. The country is very wild and mountainous, densely covered with forests, and with but few settlements. An occasional small village, or the isolated log house of the guardian of a river signal station, or an emigrant's raft floating slowly down stream, are all that break the primeval grandeur of the region. Large flocks of wild geese and ducks, migrating southward with the approach of winter, fly up from protected coves as our boat passes rapidly down the swift mountain current.

The next night, some distance below the Cossack village of Dzhalinda, we were again compelled to anchor on account of fog, and did not start until late in the morning. The evening was spent taking wood on board for fuel, an operation that had to be performed every day. The wood-choppers, who have camps along the river, build fires during the night to attract the attention of the steamers as they pass, and the captains of the boats bargain for fuel at different places. On this night, the fog came down thickly as the sun sank behind the mountains, and the dense forests were dimly lit up in spots by the beacons of the Russian woodchoppers, whose heavy forms in their long coats could be dimly seen through the mist, warming themselves by the fires; while the tall gaunt half-naked forms of the Manchurians and Koreans, belonging to the boat's crew, moved up and down the steep banks carrying their burden of wood

Passing down the river we continued through the mountains for three days more, occasionally reaching open areas as some large tributary emptied into the Amur. Each night we were stopped by dense fogs, but each morning it cleared off into a perfect day, cold and bright. After six days we finally reached Blagoveschensk, the capital and commercial metropolis of the Amur Territory, with a population of about 33,000 people.

Letter from Dick to his father, dated Blagoveschensk, Siberia, Russia, September 10, 1901

We arrived here all right this afternoon from Stretensk, after a very good trip of almost six days down the Shilka and Amur Rivers. We were a little longer than we had expected in getting here, as we were delayed a little in getting off from Stretensk, but when we started, our boat made very good time.

I wrote to you twice from Stretensk. We take another boat tomorrow afternoon from here, and continue down the Amur River to Khabarovsk—a journey of about three days. Thence we take a railroad train for Vladivostok on the Pacific Coast, which we will reach in about a day and a half from Khabarovsk.

We are having a most interesting and pleasant trip. The weather is perfect, and we have been very well and kindly treated wherever we have been.

I will write again in a few days, but, as I have said in several recent letters, do not be surprised if my next few letters reach you somewhat late, as I don't know from time to time when I will have a chance to write, or by just what route letters will be sent to America.

From Vladivostok I will go to Japan, but I will write you fully about all this when I get to Vladivostok, and find what steamer I can get to Japan. The steamers sail very frequently.

From the Manuscript

We arrived [at Blagoveschensk] on September 10th, 1901, and the next day the first news of the shooting of President McKinley on September 6th reached Blagoveschensk in a short telegram to the Russo-Chinese Bank, stating that the President had been shot, but that the wound might not be fatal. It was gratifying for an American to observe the universal sympathy and regret shown by the people of this remote Siberian town over the dastardly attack on the President, and their universally expressed hope that summary justice would be dealt out to the would-be assassin.

Letter from his father, dated Seal Harbor, September 17, 1901

Both of your letters (on train) are before me, the last (Aug. 25) reached me Sept. 15. By all means continue to write me very frequently as it is a great satisfaction to receive your letters and to feel that *so far* you are all right. It does not matter whether you scribble only one line with a pencil, I am *grateful* for it, and intensely interested in all you see and do.

I had a letter from Tal, dated Sept. 2nd, in camp. They were having a splendid time though not much big game—3 deer, 1 sheep, and any amount of ducks, sage hens, trout, etc., etc. They are 7200 feet elevation in a region *filled* with small glacial lakes, all full of splendid trout and ducks.

We are all terribly distressed over poor McKinley's death and the whole country is stirred to its utmost over it, as much or even more than over Mr. Lincoln's assassination.

Nellie Penrose (Germantown) is to be married Oct. 17. I have ordered for her a silver tea set similar to those I gave to her sister Bess and to Lil Blight—cost about $500. It has occurred to me that you would like to send her a wedding present, so I shall arrange to send her in *your name* something she would like to have and which shall cost about $50. I will pay for it and you can pay me when you get home.

I am getting along as usual. The season here is over, to my great satisfaction, as Seal Harbor is most pleasant before the people come and after they leave. I shall leave here Oct. 22 for Phil. Your Aunt Lyd will stay as long as I do, since Mrs. Gibson is living in New Mexico and of course not able to take her place here in October; hence, all your letters now should be directed to 1331 Spruce St.

I have just had a letter from Kate at Atlantic. She writes in fine spirits.

From the Manuscript

It was at Blagoveschensk in July, 1900,* during the Boxer troubles in China, that the Manchu-Chinese threatened to massacre the people of Blagoveschensk and the small Russian settlements along the river. It is easy to imagine the feeling of the isolated Russian communities in this vast region, where from Irkutsk to the Ussuri River, a distance of over 2,000 miles, there is only one town of any considerable size, and that is Blagoveschensk; while just to the south, separated from them only by the river, were millions of Chinese and Manchurians, whom the Chinese Government had never been able to hold much in check, waiting only for a chance for massacre. Under such conditions the civilized man must strike to kill in protection of his home and family, and that is what the Russians did. Any other course would have meant ruin for them.

The Chinese of Blagoveschensk, about 5,000 in number, had planned, in connection with Chinese and Manchurians from the outside, to massacre the people of the town on a certain day; but the Russians anticipated their plans and attacked them, killing many and driving the others into the river where most of them were drowned. The Chinese from the Manchurian side of the river, on July 16, 1900, bombarded the town, but did little damage and were finally driven away. A story is told of two Russian soldiers, each wounded in one arm, and being unable to handle their guns alone, they stood together, one holding his gun with his uninjured arm, and the other pulling the trigger with the one hand that remained to him. The fight once started was continued until the Chinese were driven far into the interior of Manchuria, and their river settlements abandoned and burned. Notable among these was the town of Aigun, 23 miles below Blagoveschensk, on the Chinese side of the river, an old and prosperous river port, made familiar by the Russo-Chinese treaty of 1858, and one of the most populous settlements of this part of Manchuria. Not a house is left standing, nothing except innumerable brick chimneys rising up from the ashes of the town like blackened tombstones in a graveyard. Nearby, on the river front, a small camp over which the Russian flag floats, indicates the dwelling of the guard left by the victors.

Russia has not abandoned Manchuria since she first invaded it at this time, and it is well for that beautiful but ill-governed country, for the Russians are rapidly restoring law and order where formerly there were riot and anarchy, and where the country was overrun by brigands. Moreover, the East Chinese Railway, which was being constructed through Manchuria under Russian direction and in accordance with a definite agreement with China, did not receive protection from the Chinese Government in the troubles of 1900, so that the Russians were forced to guard their own property.

We left the Vladimir Monomakh at Blagoveschensk, and after a short stay there secured passage on the mail steamer "John Cockerill," a fine river boat bound for Nikolaievsk near the mouth of the Amur. We had intended to stay longer in this region, but winter was coming on and we had to get to the Pacific

* The year previous to Penrose's visit.

Coast before the river froze. The "John Cockerill" was crowded with freight and passengers, including many emigrants. The cabin passengers were more numerous than on the Monomakh, and included many Russian officers going to different stations in the eastern part of Siberia.

On leaving Blagoveschensk the river widens out into a magnificent stream of from one to three miles in width, bounded on both sides by broad plains, though the mountains again closed in as we approached the Little Khingan Range, and still farther down, the Vanda and the Kendeh-a-lin ranges. Three days after leaving Blagoveschensk we reached Khabarovsk, a town of about 15,000 people, beautifully situated on the high bluffs of the Amur just below its confluence with the Ussuri River. It is named after the famous Cossack leader Khabaroff, who invaded the Amur region about the middle of the 17th century, and contains a fine monument to Count Muravioff who finally acquired this region for Russia two centuries later. Here we heard the news that an operation had been performed on President McKinley and that he was expected to recover, a hope in which at the time we greatly rejoiced, but in which we were to be sadly disappointed on our arrival at Vladivostok a few days later. We left the mail boat at Khabarovsk and took the Ussuri branch of the railway to Vladivostok, a distance of over 400 miles south through Ussuri province. The country became more and more cultivated as we proceeded south, and showed the ameliorating effects of the proximity to the Pacific in a climate much milder than that we had found in the Amur Valley. Many small settlements and villages were passed on the way, but none of them was of any considerable size except Nikolsk, with about 15,000 people, which is the point of junction with the East Chinese Railway and an important military station.

Letter from Dick to his father, dated Vladivostok, Siberia, Russia, September 17, 1901

We arrived here late yesterday afternoon, having completed the journey from Moscow to the Pacific Coast in 26 days.

I wrote to you last from Blagoveschensk. From there we continued down the Amur River by steamer to Khabarovsk, which we reached in three days. We stayed one night there, and the next morning took a train on a railroad which runs between Khabarovsk and Vladivostok, arriving here in a day and a half.

We have had a first rate trip throughout, and I shall always be glad that I took it. My interpreter has proved himself intelligent and generally useful. He will start back for St. Petersburg this week. I will leave here on Thursday for Nagasaki, Japan, on the Russian steamer Aygun, arriving there in three days. Thence I will go to Yokohama, which will take about a day and a half more. When I get to Yokohama and get my mail I will decide about my future movements. My mail has been going to Hong Kong, but I will have it forwarded to Yokohama while I am there.

I had at first thought of coming home via San Francisco from Japan, but I am now inclined, if when I get my mail I find no reason for coming home immediately, to go around via Hong Kong, Manila, India and Suez Canal to Europe again. When I leave Japan it will be just the time of year to make this trip, and there are very good steamers running along this route. But of all this I will write fully from Yokohama, and I will not make the trip if there is any need of my coming home immediately.

I was greatly grieved to hear of the death of McKinley. I have not yet heard any details about it, but hope to do so when I reach Japan and see the American newspapers.

P.S. You had better address letters to me from now on, to care of J. S. Morgan & Co., 22 Old Broad St., London, England, as I will have them forward mail to me wherever I am.

From the Manuscript

On our arrival at Vladivostok we were heartily welcomed by our efficient American commercial agent, Mr. Greener, who is the only official representative of the United States Government in all Siberia. A large American flag floating from the top of his house on a prominent hill in the city was a most grateful sight to one who had not seen this emblem for a long time, but a second glance showed it to be at half mast, and with a shock we recognized this first sad intimation we had had of the death of President McKinley, three days before. The Russian naval fleet then in the harbor showed its sympathy with the loss to our nation by firing salutes and making other naval demonstrations; and universal regret and indignation over the assassination were heard on all sides.

Vladivostok is the great Pacific Coast port of Siberia, and is situated on a narrow strip of hilly land extending into Peter the Great Bay at the head of the Japan Sea. The harbor of Vladivostok is known as the Golden Horn, and is one of the best on the coast of Asia. Its depth is great enough for any ships navigating the Pacific Ocean, while its mouth is narrow and protected from the sea by protruding tongues of land and islands. The town is in latitude 43°6'N, which is only a very little north of New York, yet the climate, owing to the cold Arctic influences along the Siberian coast, is as severe as in many places much farther north. The harbor is frozen usually from the middle of December until early in April, but the channel is successfully kept open by ice-breakers, and commerce is not interrupted at any time of the year.

Vladivostok was founded by the Russians as a military post in 1860. At that time it was of little commercial importance, but it grew rapidly, and in about ten years, it had replaced Nikolaievsk as the principal port of the Siberian coast. In 1891 the Ussuri Railway was started as the first division of the Siberian Railway, and by its completion to Khabarovsk in 1897, as well as by the completion of lines west of Stretensk, somewhat later, Vladivostok was connected directly with Europe by railway and river routes. The town now has a population of some 60,000, about half being Russians, with a few other Europeans and a few Americans, and the rest Chinese, Japanese, and Koreans. It is one of the most substantially built towns in Siberia, most of the houses being of stone and brick, and the government buildings, banks, etc., being fine modern edifices. The docks, which were formerly built of wood, are being largely replaced by massive stone structures that make the town look as if it was there to stay. It contains a number of schools, churches, charitable and scientific societies, several periodicals, hotels, and a theatre hall. The Eastern Institute, situated here, is a school where students are taught the Chinese, Manchurian, Japanese, Mongolian, Korean, and other Asiatic languages to prepare them for government service at Asiatic stations.

In the streets everything is active and noisy; carriages dash up and down with the horses galloping in a way that delights the heart of the Russian cab driver; heavy trucks loaded with merchandise move slowly back and forth from the docks; occasionally a company of Russian troops passes through the main streets, strong, healthy, powerfully built men, who look well capable of filling their task of guarding northern Asia. In the market place on the shore of the Golden Horn, Chinese and Korean junks unload and offer their goods for sale, while farther along the bay the large sea-going steamers are loading and unloading, and the Korean dock laborers in their white clothes, together with the Chinese, seem to work harder than anyone in town. Back from the bay, on the other side of the town, is the camp of the garrison of Vladivostok, and nearby is an exile settlement made of neat log cabins with gardens, and beautifully situated on the side of a hill. The exiles here are those who have finished their terms of hard labor. Farther down the hill, on the shore of the bay, is a brewery surrounded by an attractive grove of trees, where on hot days Russians go to drink beer.

Letter from Dick to his father, dated Yokohama, Japan, September 28, 1901

I arrived here yesterday after a nine days journey from Vladivostok in Siberia. If I had been able to come here direct from the Siberian coast, it would not have taken so long, but I had to change steamers at the two Japanese ports of Nagasaki and Kobe, which took up considerable time.

I wrote you from Vladivostok before I left there. I also wrote a number of times in crossing Siberia. I wrote very frequently as the mails are often slow in that country on account of the uncompleted condition of the railroad, and my idea was that by writing often, there would be a chance of at least some of my letters reaching you promptly. As I told you in many of my letters from Russia, I was treated first rate wherever I went in that country, and the whole trip was well worth taking. Many of the Russian customs and ways are different from ours, but when a man understands them and adapts himself to them, he gets along first rate. The means of travel are just as confortable as they are under similar conditions in the United States.

The journey from Moscow to the Ural Mountains was across a rich prairie country very much like Kansas and Nebraska. Then we crossed the Ural Mts., which are very much like the Green Mts. of Vermont—not very high, and covered with green grass and forests. East of the Urals we entered the region of the great "steppes" of Western Siberia, which is a vast alluvial plain in the watershed of the Tobol, Ishim, Irtish and Ob Rivers—all large rivers rising in the mountains dividing Siberia and Western China, and flowing into the Arctic Ocean. Still farther east we entered the mountain region at the headwaters of the Yenisei and Lena Rivers, which also flow into the Arctic Ocean. Lake Baikal is in this same region, and we crossed it by steamer. It is the third largest fresh water lake in the world, and is in Siberia near the border of Mongolia. It is surrounded by very high mountains, and is noted for the storms which are almost continuous there. One of them was raging while we crossed it, and I could realize why the natives held it in so much awe. It is supposed by them to be the home of all kinds of devils and gods.

When, after twelve days travel, we finally reached the present terminus of the Trans-Siberian R.R. at Stretensk, we had come to waters draining into the North Pacific Ocean instead of into the Arctic Ocean, but we were yet over 2000 miles from the Pacific Coast. The journey down the Shilka and Amur Rivers from Stretensk to the Coast, was a little slow, but not uncomfortable. The Amur forms the border between Siberia and Manchuria, and the signs of the war in this region last year between Russia and China were frequently in evidence. We finally reached Vladivostok after 26 days travel from Moscow. The whole journey from St. Petersburg had taken 30 days, but this time included almost four days that we stayed in Moscow. The distance of our route from St. Petersburg to Vladivostok was about 10,000 Russian "versts" or almost 7000 miles. Vladivostok is rapidly becoming an important seaport, as it is the only town of importance on the Siberian coast, and though the harbor freezes in the winter, it is kept open by an ice-breaker. The town already contains 30,000 Russians and about 30,000 Chinese, Japanese and Koreans.

From Vladivostok I sent my interpreter back to St. Petersburg, and I started south on the Russian steamer Aygun. There were only a few passengers on board and we had a very good voyage south along the coast of Korea, and across the Sea of Japan to Nagasaki. Thence by a Japanese steamer I came to Kobe, Japan, and thence by another Japanese steamer to Yokohama. I found the Japanese boats very comfortable and first class in every respect. On the boat from Vladivostok I met an American named Thomsen, who is president of the Centennial Mill (flour mill) Company of Seattle in the State of Washington. He ships flour all over the Orient, and he was on a tour of inspection looking over his various agencies. He is a first rate fellow, and as he also was coming to Yokohama we have been travelling together for some days. He has been out here several times before, and knows the country well—especially Japan. He sails for Seattle in a few days. I was very glad to meet in him not only a good American citizen, but also some one who could speak the English language, because in coming across Siberia I rarely met any one who could speak anything but Russian, and even my interpreter could speak only very limited English. I picked up a few words of Russian during the trip, but not enough to do much good.

I go in a few days to a place called Ashio, near the town of Nikko, in the interior of Japan, to see some celebrated copper mines. Thence I return here again. My mail will arrive here from Hong Kong on October 4th or 5th, and then I will determine my future movements. If I find there is no need of my returning home at once, I will go back to Europe via India and the Suez Canal, in which case I should get home in December or January. If there is any need of my returning home sooner, I will do so from here, via San Francisco, but of all this I will write when I get my mail.

I will address this letter to you at Seal Harbor, as it will probably reach there before November 1st, and I suppose you will not leave there until about that time. My next letter I will send to you at Philadelphia. I hope you have had a pleasant summer at Seal Harbor. I hope to hear from you when I get my mail from Hong Kong, as I have not gotten any mail from the United States since early in August. When you write please address me care of J. S. Morgan & Co., 22 Old Broad Street, London, England, as they will forward all mail to me.

Letter from his father, dated Seal Harbor, September 29, 1901

Your two last letters are before me—viz., from Irkutsk, Aug. 29, and from Stretensk, Sept. 2, the latter reaching me this morning. I cannot tell you the comfort your letters are to me, assuring me that, up to their date, you were well and having a grand time. I am as usual. I plan to leave here for Philadelphia, Oct. 22nd, so direct your letters hereafter to 1331 Spruce. I see, by the papers, Boies has returned, coming two weeks before he expected in order to attend Mr. McKinley's funeral. He must have barely made it, as he had only time to go to Canton, and was too late to be present at the ceremonies at Washington.

Don't forget in your travels, my old teaching, and your practicings when in Texas and Arkansas. Remember the Chinese can live, with impunity, in the most unwholesome localities, and the *sole* reason is they use no water, but boiled water (tea) and little or no food but cooked food (rice). Any one living thus almost necessarily escapes typhoid fever, dysentery and cholera, the great dangers in traveling in the East—an attack of which would greatly interfere with the success of your expedition. Don't forget also your quinine in malarial regions—10 to 15 grains daily straight along for weeks or months. So also your calomel and purgative. It is *so* important that you should keep in first class condition while away that I feel that I must impress all the above upon you. I can't tell you any family news. I have not heard from Tal and Spencer so I infer they are still in Idaho, though I am under the impression they planned to come out about Oct. 1st. But I suppose Jones and Barringer keep you well posted as to what goes on in *their* departments.

You won't get any of my letters for so many weeks that they most probably will have lost all their interest by the time you read them, as I suppose it takes a month or more for a letter to go from here to China.

Letter from Dick to his father, dated Yokohama, Japan, October 6, 1901

I wrote to you a few days ago on my arrival here from Vladivostok. Since then I have received your letter of Aug. 5th which was forwarded from London to Hong Kong and thence here, and which arrived with the first mail that I have received from the United States for almost two months. It is needless for me to say that I was exceedingly glad to get your letter and to know that you were all right and having a good summer at Seal Harbor.

Since writing to you last, I have been up in the interior of Japan to see some celebrated copper mines at a place called Ashio, and had a very good trip. I went first to a place called Nikko by train, and from there across a range of mountains to Ashio, in what is called a jinrikisha, which is a sort of two-wheeled sulky pulled by one, two or three men as the condition of the roads may require. Sometimes two men pull and one pushes behind. These men are trained to the business and go along at a good trot for hours at a time. In the cities the jinrikisha is generally pulled by one man and is the principal means of getting around, as horses are very little used. At first I felt a good deal like a damned fool sitting in one of these things and being pulled around by a Japanese not bigger than a jack-rabbit, but I soon got used to it.

From Ashio I returned to Nikko, where I stayed one day, and then returned here. Nikko is noted for its very ancient Buddhist temples. In one place a long line of stone statues, erected to noted Buddhas during different ages, fringes the river bank. The very old ones at the upper end of the line are gradually crumbling to pieces, but further and further down the line, they become better and better preserved, as the newer ones are approached. At certain times of year pilgrims come here and paste pieces of paper, bearing their names, on their favorite Buddhas. The result is that many of the Buddhas are covered with scraps of paper like scales on a fish. Most Japanese are Buddhists, and their religion seems to be a very respectable one. I don't wonder that they ignore the horde of American and European missionaries who are trying to pump Christianity into them, and still prefer their magnificent Buddhist temples, full of works of art and many cheerful-looking statues of their gods. Many of the temples also maintain a dancing girl, dressed in the finest clothes that Japan can supply, whose duty it is, during periods of long protracted wet weather, to go through a sort of dancing performance in order to propitiate the God of Rain and persuade him to clear the skies. This seems to be the right way to treat a god, and the result is said to be that the rains usually do stop promptly.

Since receiving my mail from Hong Kong, I find that there seems to be no need of my coming home direct from here via San Francisco, so I will return via the Suez Canal and Europe, as there are a number of places in southern Asia and Europe that I would like to see. I will leave here next week for Hong Kong, and will go thence to Singapore and Penang, where I want to stop over for a few days to see some tin mines. Thence I will go to Colombo in Ceylon, and thence through Suez Canal to Europe. I will reach Europe in about two months from the time I leave here, and the whole journey will be by sea, on good steamers, as I will not have occasion to go far into the interior at any of the ports where I stop over. I had at first felt inclined to come home directly from here via San Francisco; but when I found there was no need of it, I thought I might as well come by the longer route via Suez Canal, as I can thus stop at several places I want to see, whereas by going direct to San Francisco I would see nothing. I do not think I will stop at Manila as it takes too long to get there, and I am told that civilians are not allowed beyond the town, and that there is nothing to see there anyhow. The places that I want to stop at are all on the main lines of travel of the steamers running between here and Europe, and it would require a considerable divergence from this route to go to Manila.

I have heard from both Brockman and Barringer since I got here, but both letters were over a month old. Everything seemed to be all right at the mine, and I believe the last dividend was paid on September 10th. The cause of the long time since the previous dividend was due to the low grade of the ore milled. There are very large bodies of this low grade ore, and though they make the dividends a little less frequent than could be desired, yet they will add considerably to the length of life of the mine.

I often feel as if I ought to be home attending to my business instead of travelling, but I cannot see what I could do at the mine even if I was there, other than what is already being done by Brockman. Anyhow, I will not be sorry when I get back and see how things are going.

....

Oct. 11th—I started this letter several days ago, but as there has been no American mail leaving here since then, and will not be any until tomorrow, I have not mailed it. When you write please address me care of J. S. Morgan & Co., 22 Old Broad St., London, England, as they will forward mail promptly to me. I will write again before I leave here.

P.S. I will address this letter to you at Philadelphia as I suppose you will soon return there.

Letter from Dick to his father, dated Yokohama, Japan, October 16, 1901

I start tomorrow on the Japanese steamer "Nippon Maru" for Hong Kong, where I will arrive in about ten days. I will be there about three days, and will then take another steamer for Singapore, where, as I wrote you last week, I will stop over for a few days to visit the tin mines of Penang, etc. Thence I will continue back to Europe—arriving in London in probably two months or a little more from here.

It has been raining most of the time that I have been in Japan, but I have managed to see a good deal. It is a very interesting country and I would like to stay longer, but there is so much that I want to see on the way back to Europe that I must keep moving, especially as I have already stayed here longer than I had expected to do.

I have not heard from you since your letter of the 5th August, but I expect to get later mail at Hong Kong, and I will write more fully from there.

When you write, please address me care of J. S. Morgan & Co., 22 Old Broad St., London, England, as I will keep them posted by telegraph as to where to forward my mail.

Letter from Dick to his father, dated "SS Nippon Maru," October 18, 1901

I wrote to you before leaving Yokohama, on the 16th, but as the boat will stop today for a few hours at Kobe, Japan, I thought I would drop a line to you to mail there. We have had a first rate voyage so far, and we ought to reach

Hong Kong in 8 or 9 days from here. There are not many passengers on board, and none whom I know, but the boat is very comfortable and I have a stateroom to myself, so I look forward to a very good voyage to Hong Kong. The boat will touch at Nagasaki, Japan, and at Shanghai, China, on the way to Hong Kong.

Letter from Dick to his father, dated "SS Nippon Maru," October 21, 1901

We have just arrived tonight off the mouth of the Yangtzekiang River, China, and we are anchored out at sea, until morning, when we will go up the bay to Shanghai. I hear that the American mail will leave Shanghai in a couple of days on the steamer "China", so I thought I would drop a line to you to mail on it.

Our boat will be one day at Shanghai unloading cargo, and then we will go on to Hong Kong, where we will arrive on Oct. 26th. We have had, so far, a first rate voyage. I have written you in the last few days from both Yokohama and Kobe in Japan, and will write more fully when I get to Hong Kong. Do not be surprised, however, if my letters reach you a little irregularly, as sometimes there is an interval of several days between the sailings of boats carrying mail to the United States.

Letter from Dick to his father, dated Hong Kong, China, October 26, 1901

I arrived here yesterday and was very glad to find your letters of Aug. 13th and 25th, and of Sept. 6th and 17th. It had been a long time since I had heard any recent news, as my mail had been collecting here for several weeks. I am very much obliged to you for having sent Nellie Penrose a wedding present for me, as it is just what I would have done if I had been at home. You say in your letter that I need not pay for it until I get home, but I might just as well do it now, especially as I want to send to you also the money for my Christmas presents to Sarah Beck and others. I began this thing last Christmas so I suppose it is well to keep it up, and if it is not too much trouble for you to distribute it, I will be very greatly obliged to you. Last year I believe I sent Sarah Beck $30; Lydia Biddle of Carlisle $25; the Penrose girls of Carlisle $25; and Nannie Thomas $25. I would have sent more, but you told me not to do so. I enclose my check for $200 to pay for the present to Nellie Penrose, which you said you thought would be about $50, and also for the Christmas presents to the others, which I will be greatly obliged if you will distribute at the proper time. If you think I better send to any of them somewhat more than I did last year, please use up the amount of the check as you see fit, and if it is not enough please let me know.

I don't like to bother you about this matter, but I thought it best for you to attend to it, if you will, as I do not know the exact addresses of some of the people, and moreover I am not the expert that you are in writing letters for such occasions.

The boat on which I came from Yokohama was not due here until today, but it made very fast time and got here in 9 days instead of 10. I mailed letters to you from Kobe and from Shanghai on the voyage. We had a very good trip though a little rough. Coming down from Shanghai through the China Sea and the Formosa Channel the monsoon winds were blowing a gale, but they were in the direction we were going, and they were the cause of our steamer making such rapid time. The sea was like a mass of white foam for two days and the boat rolled about considerably. I was not seasick, and am beginning to feel that I am almost immune to that trouble. There were not many passengers on the boat and it was therefore all the more comfortable. This is the third Japanese steamer that I have travelled on recently, and they are certainly excellent boats. They are clean and have first class food, and are not overloaded with foolish restrictions like the English boats. A man can smoke where he wants, and do about as he pleases as long as he does not interfere with other passengers.

I am going tomorrow to Canton, which is one night's travel from here into the interior of China by boat. The American Consul there is a man named McWade, from Philadelphia, who is a friend of Boies, and whom I also used to know very well, and I have arranged to meet him there. From Canton I will return here, and then will go to Manila next week. This is contrary to my plans as I gave them to you in my last letter from Yokohama, but since then I have concluded that it is foolish to go through this part of the world without seeing something at least of the Philippines, so I have decided to go. I have engaged passage on a steamer that sails from here next Wednesday, and will get there in a little less than three days from here.

From Manila I will continue on to Singapore, etc., as I wrote you from Yokohama. I would like to go to all the places you suggest in your letter of Sept. 6th, and expect to go to most of them. The only trouble is that out in this country, where almost all travelling is done by boat, it takes a long time to get about. It is the most pleasant mode of travelling that I have ever struck, but it is slow, and people here think no more of a week or two than they do of an hour in the U. S.

You speak of a trip to Egypt as a thing that you would like to do. If you will come, I will meet you anywhere in Europe or elsewhere that you appoint, and at any time, or I will come back to the U. S. and start fresh with you, and make the trip with you. I am sure you would like it, and they say that the trip up the Nile that you speak of, is very fine. So all you have to do is to say the word and I will meet you and arrange all the plans so as to give you no trouble; and it is needless for me to say that nothing would give me more pleasure than to take this trip with you.

I have only recently seen the full American newspaper accounts of the assassination of McKinley, though I had heard of it a few days after it occurred. I was very greatly grieved and it seems terrible that such a thing is possible in the U. S. It has shocked the whole world as much as the people of the U. S., and wherever I have been signs of respect and sympathy have been shown. I first heard of it at Blagoveschensk in the interior of Siberia. I was at dinner at the house of the local director of the Russo-Chinese Bank, when he received a telegram from St. Petersburg saying that McKinley had been shot. A few days later, at Vladivostok, where I arrived shortly afterward, the Russian squadron then in the harbor were flying the American flag at half mast, and fired 21 guns as a sign of sympathy for McKinley's death.

Letter from his father, dated 1331 Spruce St. (Philadelphia), October 28, 1901

Your letter from Yokohama reached me Saturday, Oct. 26. I have received also *all* of your other letters, the last three via Japan and the Pacific steamers. You don't know what a comfort your letters have been to me, and, also, now I know you are in civilization again how much more easy I feel about you. I am delighted you have had so splendid a trip and that so far everything has prospered with you. I wrote you some weeks ago *not* to hurry home, but to take all the time you cared to.

Everything is getting along in the same old way, and there is not the slightest occasion for you to shorten your trip, even if it should occupy you until the *Autumn* of *1902*. You may be now having the opportunity of your life—that is, *no one sick* and your money affairs O.K. Such being the case, enjoy it while you may; *go everywhere*, stay as long as agreeable or profitable, have all the "fun" possible, wind up in Paris and have all the "fun" there until you are tired and *then* you can come back, but, *not before*.

As you see, I have left Seal Harbor. I am not sorry to be again in Philadelphia and getting settled for the winter. Boies is here, very busy with his politics, speaking every night, etc., etc. He is in fine condition, *never* looked as well. *He* says we will beat at the coming election. Tal and family come to town on Nov. 1st. Spencer writes in good spirits from Colorado Springs. Indeed, the hunting trip seems to have benefited the crowd vastly, and Boies and Tal certainly never looked better, and Tal says Spencer is equally fine. Philadelphia is all dug up by this damned new telephone company—Spruce St. from end to end horrible. I fear it will last all winter. I suppose now you will meet people you know straight along.

Tal told me on Saturday that "they" said you are now in Pekin!!!

When I see Dr. Woods I will learn how the Union League stands and will write you all about it. You have been elected a director of the Norristown R. R.

I shall look now for your letters regularly. Certainly, it is a matter of surprise to me that all of your letters so far have reached me.

Letter from Dick to his father, dated Hong Kong, China, October 30, 1901

I wrote to you fully a few days ago, but I drop a line to you now as I start for Manila tomorrow, and will not have a chance to write again until I get there. I had expected to get off today, but the boat was delayed waiting for the mail from America, and will not start until tomorrow.

I was in Canton on Monday and was very glad I went there, as it is a very interesting place. I was treated very well there by U. S. Consul McWade, about whom I wrote you in my last letter. Canton is a city of almost 3,000,000 people, and has not been phased by foreign encroachment. It is one of the dirtiest, and certainly the most bad smelling place I was ever in. It is impossible to get out of all kinds of stinks. There is a law that all streets must be at least 7 feet wide, and most of them do not much exceed this. The Canton Chinese are very much opposed to foreigners, and as one goes through the city, the people along the streets express their opinion of the "foreign devils" in a very loud way; but the viceroy seems to be a very good man, and he holds the people down, so that they do not dare molest foreigners except with words. During the Chinese troubles last year, often as many as 300 Chinamen a day were beheaded in Canton in order to suppress the disposition on the part of the people to annihilate the foreign consulates. The American Consulate is still provided with an ample supply of rifles, etc., for protection.

McWade is a fighting Irish-American, and would certainly put up a magnificent scrap if his consulate was ever attacked. It is a case where the right man is in the right place, and he seems to have more influence with the Chinese officials than any man in Canton. Boies got him appointed, and certainly made a good selection.

I have written to Jones telling him that if the invitation to subscribe to the Assemblies next winter came to me at the office, to send it to you. I do not know whether it will come to the house or the office. I told Jones to send it to you if it came to the office as I wanted you to decide what was best to do in the matter. Of course I could not, and would not, go to the Assemblies next winter even if I were home, on account of Philip's death, but I did not know whether it would be proper to subscribe and then not go, as I do not want to appear mean about not subscribing simply because I can't go. If you consider it proper to do so, my inclination would be to subscribe and then not go, but you doubtless have your own ideas about what is best to do, and I hope you will do as you see fit. If you think it well for me to subscribe, I will be greatly obliged to you if you will do so for me, and take the money out of the check I sent you last week, or if there is nothing left of that check after paying the other things out of it, I will pay you the amount of the subscription when I get home. But I hope you will use your own judgment altogether in deciding whether to subscribe or not to subscribe for me, as you know best what is proper to do.

I will write fully from Manila, where I will arrive in about $2\frac{1}{2}$ days from here. It is very hot here, but I have gotten some tropical clothes and am getting along very well. Please continue to address me care of J. S. Morgan & Co., 22 Old Broad St., London, England.

Letter from Dick to his father, dated Oriente Hotel, Manila, P.I., November 5, 1901

I drop a line to you to tell you that I arrived here all right on Monday. We had a very good passage from Hong Kong. I will return to Hong Kong in a few days, and from there will go to Singapore. I have met several people whom I know here, and it seems very good to be in the domain of the U. S. again. I will write more fully in a few days.

Letter from Dick to his father, dated Manila, P.I., November 8, 1901

I start back today for Hong Kong on the same boat as I came here on. I am very glad that I came to Manila, as not only is it a very interesting place, but

I have also gotten an idea of the conditions in the Philippines that could not be gotten without a trip here.

I have seen a good deal of the town, and have also been down to Cavite, where Dewey sunk the Spanish fleet. I went there on a U. S. government launch. Several of the old wrecks of the Spanish ships are still there—mostly submerged but sticking partly above water. The Government is now having them removed.

It feels very good to be once more where American influence is on top. There is an air of common-sense and business-like methods about it that I have not observed in the foreign countries that I have visited in the last six or seven months. The military regulations make more or less red tape necessary, but there is no more of it than is needed. I would like very much to visit some of the other islands of the Philippine Group, but the means of getting about are so slow that I have decided not to do so.

The Philippinos are small, inoffensive-looking people, but the recent fights that the American troops have been having with them show that they are not so harmless as they look. A few of them are well educated and have fine places here, but most of them are very ignorant and no better than savages. The Government is doing a great deal in the way of improving Manila and the islands in general; and it is remarkable how much has been accomplished in three years. The natural resources of the islands seem to be enormous, and I have no doubt that a great many large fortunes will be made here.

I have met a number of people whom I know here—among others Brewster Cameron, a nephew of ex-senator Don Cameron. He used to live in Arizona, where I knew him well. He is doing a big commission business here.

I had hoped to go direct from here to Singapore, but I find that I would have to wait so long for a boat, that it will be a saving of time to return to Hong Kong and go from there to Singapore, so I will do so. I should arrive in Hong Kong on the 11th, and will leave as soon as possible for Singapore—a journey of about six days by sea. I wrote to you a few days ago from here and will write again from Hong Kong, before starting for Singapore.

Letter from Dick to his father, dated Hong Kong Hotel, Hong Kong, November 12, 1901

I arrived here all right today from Manila, and will sail tomorrow on the German steamer "Kiautschou" for Singapore. The trip from here to Singapore takes about five days, and the "Kiautschou" is a magnificent big boat—one of the best that sails these waters—so I expect to have a very good voyage. The boats between here and Manila are mostly small, and as the trip across the China Sea to Manila is considered one of the roughest trips on the Pacific Ocean, they get a good deal of tossing about. I went to Manila and returned on the same boat—a small steamer called the "Diamente". It was a very sea-worthy boat, but she never stopped plunging and rolling from the time she left one port until she reached the other. From now on to the time I get back to Europe, I will be travelling in the course of big steamers and will not have to take any more small ones.

I wrote to you twice from Manila. I had a very interesting trip there and shall always be glad I went, though I was not sorry to get away as it was very hot and was raining most of the time I was there. Manila is considered one of the hottest places in this part of the world, and its position at the head of a big bay, and surrounded in three directions by low wet country, makes it easy to understand why it is so hot. At the same time it is a beautiful place and excellently situated as a sea-port; and I do not see what there is to prevent its becoming one of the greatest commercial centers of the Far East.

In the past two months I have seen a good deal of the coast of Asia and the surrounding islands in Siberia, Japan, China, the Philippines, etc.; and the thing that impresses me most strongly is the immense commercial possibilities for the future in this part of the world. If the natural resources of these regions were developed, the commerce of the Atlantic Ocean would be like a drop in the bucket compared with that of the Pacific. The greatest impediment to development, however, is undoubtedly the natives who inhabit the larger part of these regions, and their great numbers. With the exception of the Russians and the Japanese, they do not like the so-called "progress" of western people, and only want to be left alone.

I expect to be in and around Singapore for about ten days, as I want to see some tin mines in that region. I have some letters to people in Singapore, and I expect to see all I want. From Singapore I will go to Colombo on the island of Ceylon, where I will remain a few days, as I want to visit some precious stone mines not far from Colombo. From Colombo I will probably go directly to Europe via Suez Canal, but I will write to you more definitely about my plans beyond Colombo when I get through with that place and Singapore. I would like to see something of India, but I do not know whether I will have time, though I may spend a few days there. It takes some time to see India properly, and I think perhaps it might be better to reserve it for another trip. But of all this, I will write to you later. My present plans are to try to reach Europe in January, and to come home in February.

I expect to get some mail in Singapore, and I hope I will find some of your letters there. I will write again when I reach there.

The weather has been very hot wherever I have been in the past few weeks, and I suppose it will be equally hot in the places I am going to visit in the next few weeks, but by following your suggestions about boiled water, etc., I am keeping in first rate condition, and never felt better in my life.

P.S. Please continue to address me care of J. S. Morgan & Co., 22 Old Broad St., London, England, as they will forward mail to me.

Letter from Dick to his father, dated "Am Bord des Reichspostdampfers 'Kiautschou', den" 16th Nov. 1901

We expect to reach Singapore tomorrow morning, so I write to you tonight and will mail the letter when we arrive in port.

I wrote to you from Hong Kong just before sailing on this ship. We have had an excellent voyage, and I don't think I have ever travelled on such a good boat in every respect as this is. It is very large and not crowded. The food is excellent; and each stateroom has an electric fan, which is a great comfort in this tropical climate. The passengers are mostly Germans, with a few English, and three or four Americans.

The weather has been very hot ever since we left Hong Kong, but that is to be expected in this latitude. We are rapidly approaching the equator, and when we reach Singapore we will be only one degree north of it.

I will write again in a few days from Singapore, when I determine how long I will stay in that region.

Letter from Dick to his father, dated Singapore, November 19, 1901

I wrote to you three days ago on the steamer just before reaching here, and mailed the letter after landing. Since arriving here I have been busy making arrangements to see the tin mines on the west coast of the Malay peninsula. I start tomorrow up the coast by boat, and will stop at several places to see the mines.

The Malay peninsula supplies over 60% of the tin of the world, and the business is largely in control of the British. I have a letter of introduction from the Chartered Bank of India, Australia and China to their agents in some of the places I will visit, so I expect to get along very well.

In about 10 days I expect to reach the town of Penang, on the coast about 350 miles north of here; and from there I will go to Colombo, Ceylon, and thence probably on to Europe; but I will write further about my plans from Penang. It may be a week or ten days before I have a chance to write again, but I will write as often as I have opportunity.

This country is very interesting but very hot. Singapore is on an island at the south end of the Malay peninsula. The peninsula itself is a wonderfully rich country in its natural products. I have been today on a trip to Johore Bharu, the capital of the native Malay state of Johore, which is on the mainland about 15 miles from here, just across the channel from Singapore Island. It is a very interesting place. I saw the Sultan's palace, his collection of tigers and various other interesting sights. In the palace are large paintings of the Sultan and of the members of the British royal family, which shows how the British are getting in their work with the natives.

Letter from his father, dated 1331 Spruce St. (Philadelphia) November 20, 1901

Your letter of Oct. 21 on ship and mailed at Shanghai received yesterday, and I need not tell you how much pleasure it gave me to know that you are well and having a good time.

I have not written you for several weeks, because I knew you would not receive my letters regularly, and to get a bunch of *old* letters, each repeating the same thing, is not very interesting, so I have waited until you got well within reach, and now that you are so near Hong Kong, where you will receive all of your old back mail, I write again. I believe I have received all of your letters written since leaving Siberia; viz., Oct. 6, long letter, Yokohama, Oct. 16, 18, 21. It has been a great satisfaction to me to be kept in close touch with you even though the "news" comes some weeks after the transactions, so please keep on right along in the same practice of writing me not less frequently than once a week and now that you are again well within reach I will write you more regularly. In the first place, let me repeat what I have already written you *not to hurry home*. There is nothing to bring you here, and, it would be a sin to shorten your trip a day even, so take all the time you desire for business or pleasure and, if that should keep you abroad until well in 1902, it will be all right. Nothing will suffer from your absence. Your Union League membership is all right, and Woods has arranged with the committee that you are to be elected *immediately* on your return.

I am reasonably well and am just recovering from a "spell of acclimatization" to the air and environment of Philadelphia, which, after Seal Harbor, are simply poison. I begin to feel that I must live somewhere else in winter. Philadelphia is becoming almost an impossibility for me. Tal, as you know, entertains the same feeling. I feel now as if I would go to Lakewood, and Tal urges Tampa and the West Gulf Coast for me. Well, we will see. I am so extremely comfortable at home that it seems hard to be obliged to *flee* from it in cold weather as well as hot.

Boies is in Washington, arranging for the winter, so I am alone.

Letter from Dick to his father, dated Ipoh, Perak, Malay Peninsula, November 25, 1901

I wrote to you a few days ago from Singapore. Since then I have arrived here at Ipoh, which is a small town in the interior of the Malay state of Perak. I have been making this my headquarters for a few days; but will leave in a couple of days for Penang, which is on an island on the Malay coast, owned by the British. From Penang I will take a steamer for Colombo in Ceylon. I have had a most interesting trip here, and have seen many tin mines. I have been treated first rate by some English people who live here. Though this Malay region of Perak is theoretically under a sultan, it is practically controlled by the British.

I will write fully from Penang. I drop this line to you now just to let you know where I am.

P.S. Nov. 26th—I start for Penang tomorrow afternoon, and will arrive there the next day. I have seen all I want to see here, and have seen it under very favorable and very pleasant conditions.

Letter from Dick to his father, dated Penang, Straits Settlements, November 29, 1901

I arrived here yesterday from the Malay Peninsula, and will sail tomorrow for Colombo, Ceylon, on a British steamer. I wrote to you from Ipoh a few days ago and from Singapore a few days before that.

I left Singapore ten days ago, and came up the Malay Coast in a small steamer for two nights and a day, to a place called Teluk Anson. From there I went inland to a small place called Ipoh, which I made my headquarters while I was in the interior. Ipoh is the most important tin mining center on the Malay Peninsula, and I made numerous trips in various directions from it, seeing many tin mines and getting a very good idea of how it occurs and how it is mined. After leaving Ipoh, I returned to the coast and came here by steamer.

The Malay country is a most interesting region, even aside from the tin mines. It consists of a long narrow range of mountains running north and south, with lower country on both sides. The whole region is covered by a dense jungle, and no one can conceive of how hard it is to get around, without trying it. The tropical vegetation is interwoven into an almost solid mass, and every now and then there are great swamps, which are almost impassable. There are more different kinds of snakes, centipedes, scorpions and bugs and insects of every kind, than I ever saw before. The country is not healthy, and many people are laid up with malaria, dysentery and other diseases. I took quinine all the time I was there and a little calomel; and I never felt better in my life. I also drank only boiled or bottled waters, which is certainly the great secret of keeping well in any country—either in the north or south.

The country is very hot, and a man is usually wet through with sweat from head to foot. The natives hatch duck and chicken eggs by simply keeping them in baskets in their houses; and it is not uncommon to see a big flat basket containing probably a couple of hundred eggs spread over the bottom and now and then a duck or chicken appears out of one of the shells. The mosquitos are thicker and bite harder than in any country I have ever seen. This is the rainy season now, and the heavy showers that occur every day seem to encourage the mosquitos.

Part of the Malay Peninsula is owned by Siam and part is theoretically under local sultans, but practically controlled by the British. In the latter part, there are five totally different kinds of people—the aborigines, the Malays, the Chinese, the Indians, and the English. The aborigines, who inhabited the country before the Malays came, are a very wild people. They live altogether in the jungle and are rarely seen. The Malays are very numerous but very lazy. They do nothing but raise enough rice and chickens to live on, and occasionally hunt. They are small people and look like the Philippinos. Some of the women are very good looking.

The Chinese do most of the work and most of the business of the country. Some of them are very rich, and they are essentially *the* people of the Malay Peninsula. Some of the large Chinese mine owners employ Englishmen as managers, etc., and it is a strange sight to see white people working for Chinamen. I was treated finely at the house of a rich Chinaman named Foo Choo Choon, at a place called Lahat. He owns a big tin mine. When I left, he gave me his photograph.

The various Indian tribes on the Peninsula have emigrated from India. They are usually employed as laborers—especially in making roads—a job for which they seem to be especially suited. The English people are not numerous, but they practically control the country. They have built many fine wagon roads, and have done a great deal to open up the country—which only a few years ago was an almost impenetrable jungle. They have also built a few short railways. The universal language is Malay, and it is spoken alike by the Malays,

Chinese, Indians, and English. So little English is spoken that I had to have an Indian interpreter part of the time.

This town of Penang is really named Georgetown, but it is commonly known as Penang. The island is only a few miles off the Malay coast, and is a beautiful place, heavily covered with tropical forests. Across the straits separating it from the mainland, can be seen Mt. Kedah, an immense peak far off in the interior of Siam. Most of the people here are British and Chinese, and as usual, the Chinese seem to be making all the money. They have the finest houses and drive the finest horses in the city. The English play cricket and drink Scotch whiskey while the Chinese are working, and hence the result. Moreover, the Chinese dress and live more sensibly than the British. Some of the higher class Chinese wear a few thin clothes, while the others, as well as the Indians and Malays, go about almost naked. It is so hot that it is far more comfortable with no clothes, yet the British will insist on wearing their numerous layers of clothing simply because they did it in England. When an Englishman goes to an entertainment where there is dancing in this country, he carries along several extra shirts, so that he can change his clothes from time to time as he sweats through them during the evening. A Chinaman goes in sensible clothes and doesn't get hot.

As I have said, I leave here tomorrow for Colombo in Ceylon, arriving there in five or six days from here. I will stay there about a week, and will then probably go on direct to Europe. Though I do not know of any immediate necessity for my coming home, yet I begin to feel that it is getting nearly time for me to come back and attend to business. It will take almost three weeks to go from Colombo to Italy. I will probably land at Naples and go up through Italy, but I will write more definitely about this from Colombo, when I get my mail which I expect to find there. I want to try to be home sometime the latter part of February or early in March, unless I find it necessary to come sooner, in which case, of course, I would come home direct.

Please continue to address me care of J. S. Morgan & Co., 22 Old Broad St., London, England, as they forward mail to me. I have not gotten any of your letters for many weeks, but I hope to find some at Colombo, where I have had my mail forwarded from London. I thought it better to let mail collect at certain places, instead of having it scattered all over the country, as in this way it is less apt to be lost. This however doubtless accounts for my not having heard from you for so long.

I hope you are well, and that you have gotten comfortably settled at Philadelphia after your return from Seal Harbor.

Letter from his father, dated 1331 Spruce St. (Philadelphia) December 3, 1901

Your letter from Hong Kong, *Oct. 26*, was received *yesterday*. Its arrival relieved me *immensely*, since for the last two weeks I have been in a sort of *panic* about not hearing from you. I received your letter from Shanghai, as I wrote you, several weeks ago, and *then* this last long pause, of several weeks. However, now I have learned of your safety and the prosperous condition of your journey,

I am *content*. Now you are within reach of a telegraph. Hong Kong seems only a sort of Camden,* and I realize I can communicate with you if necessary.

I agree with you about Manila. It would be a pity to miss it at this time. So, too, bear in mind all I have written you about not hurrying in your journey. Take until the *Autumn* of 1902, or *even later*, if you find you can put in the time either to profit or *fun*. There is absolutely nothing to bring you home. I am as well as usual and you need have no anxiety on my account. In my last letter I wrote you about the Union League, how it had been arranged to elect you on your return to Philadelphia. So, too, I wrote you that you had been elected a director of the Phila-Germantown & Norristown R. R. I told Dick Dale when he stated the circumstance to me that I "congratulated the *company* on your election." Boies went to Washington last week for the winter, expecting, however, to return every Friday or Saturday during the session. So I am alone, which, however, is no hardship. I will deposit your cheque and when I send out *my* Christmas cheques I will send out *distinct cheques* in your behalf. The amounts we agreed upon last Christmas are all right, and I will not increase them. Nellie Penrose bought a *pair* of silver candelabras with the $50 I told her she might use for *your* present. She is delighted with them. Boies, Tal and Spencer all made her handsome presents, so she did well out of our crowd.

I don't think we can manage Egypt *this* winter, but *seriously* I might do it next.

Letter from Dick to his father, dated Galle Face Hotel, Colombo, Ceylon, December 6, 1901

On my arrival here yesterday I was very glad to find your letter of Oct. 28th, which had been forwarded from London, and to know that you had gotten back safely from Seal Harbor, and were comfortably settled again in Philadelphia. I am also very glad to know that Boies, Tal and Speck had such a good hunting trip, and that it did them so much good. I hope that Boies and his friends have won in the November elections.

I am very much obliged to you for having engineered so successfully my election as director of the Norristown R. R., and I am very glad to have become a director.

I wrote to you last from Penang, just before I sailed for this port. I arrived here all right after a very good trip of five days. On the boat I met two men from Denver whom I knew very well—one named Moore and the other Hoffman. They were making a trip around the world. They had not time to stop here, so they went on by the same boat and I stopped over.

Ceylon, from the little I have yet seen of it, seems to be a beautiful island, and this hotel at Colombo is excellent. It is the first decent hotel I have found since leaving Japan. The hotels of China, the Philippines, and the Malay Peninsula are all simply rotten. They are dirty, often full of bugs, and the grub is poor, but here in Colombo is one of the best hotels I have struck since I left the United States.

* Across the river from Philadelphia.

I will be in Ceylon, or on the adjoining mainland of India, for the next few days, and will then start direct for Europe. I would like to go through northern India and Burmah, but it would take a couple of months to do this properly, so I have decided to postpone this for another trip in the future, as I begin to think that it is nearly time to be starting toward home and attending to my business. I note what you say in your letter about my staying away as long as I like, and I expect to go to several places in Europe on my way back, so that it will probably be about three months—or almost that—before I get home. I think I will go direct from here to Naples, Italy, but I will write you fully about this when I decide just what time I will leave here and what boat I will take. I think I will leave here in about a week or less, but will write you fully before doing so.

Letter from Dick to his father, dated Galle Face Hotel, Colombo, Ceylon, December 12, 1901

I start this afternoon for Naples, Italy, by the British steamer "Omrah" of the Orient-Pacific line. I had intended to take one of the German boats, but could not make my plans fit in with their times of sailing. The "Omrah" however is a large and very fine boat; and it takes only 14 days from here to Naples, while most of the boats take from 16 to 18 days.

I wrote to you on my arrival here a few days ago. Since then I have been up to Kandy, which was the ancient capital of Ceylon, and to several other places. This island is the most beautiful place that I have ever seen. The climate is very hot, but the mountains, the tropical forests, and the general scenery are all very fine. I had wanted to see something of the precious stone mining business here but it is all in the hands of the natives, and as they are very secretive, I have not seen everything, but I have seen enough. I will write more fully from on board the ship.

Letter from Dick to his father, dated on board steamship "Omrah", Arabian Sea, December 16, 1901

I wrote to you just before leaving Colombo on the 12th. We sailed that night, and today is now the fourth day out. We have had fine weather; a little hot but getting cooler every day, as we get farther north.

I was sorry to give up going to northern India and seeing something of Cashmere, Burmah and those countries, but this trip would have taken several weeks, and would have made it necessary for me to start again towards the East, so I thought I would postpone it for another time. Having crossed Asia by the extreme northern route, through Siberia, and by the extreme southern route, through Hong Kong, the Malay Peninsula, Ceylon, etc., I thought I had better leave the intermediate route through northern India, Cashmere and Burmah for another time.

This boat is a large steamer built especially for comfort in the tropics, and is one of the most comfortable boats I have ever travelled on. It is intended to carry almost two hundred first class passengers, and there are only fifteen on board, so there is lots of room. It has come from Australia and is bound for

England, and its stop at Colombo, where I got aboard, was only for the purposes of coaling and taking on mail.

We are now crossing the Arabian Sea, and sometime tomorrow we are due to reach Cape Guardafin, on the east coast of Africa. Thence we go up the Red Sea to the Suez Canal, which we should reach on the 22d or 23d. Then it takes a day to pass through the canal to Port Said on the Egyptian coast, and from there it takes about three days to reach Naples, so we ought to arrive there about Dec. 27th. I will probably not have a chance to mail this letter until we reach Port Said, so I will keep it open until then.

Dec. 22d

We are approaching the Suez Canal this afternoon, and will reach Port Said tomorrow morning. I will probably mail this letter there. We have had a first rate voyage so far. The weather has been fine, and it is rapidly getting cooler. I am the only American on this boat. The rest are all English, or English colonists from Australia, Ceylon, and other places in the East.

I will write further from Naples, where I expect to get some mail again. We arrive there Dec. 27th.

Letter from his father, dated 1331 Spruce St. (Philadelphia) December 18, 1901

Your letter from Hong Kong, of Nov. 12th reached me today, and I reply by *return mail*. I have, also, before me your previous Hong Kong letter of Oct. 30th, as well as your two Manila letters, of Nov. 5 and Nov. 8, so I have received them all. I don't reply to every one, since you will receive my letters in lots of several, and each individual letter, in each lot of several, resembles the rest. Hence, I write only after the receipt of two or three from you. Each letter you write me is a great pleasure to me, since I not only have an idea of what you are doing and how you are prospering but am assured of your welfare as far as you have got. In your last letter, now before me, of Nov. 12, you say you plan to get back in February. Now I advise you not to attempt it. Winter and Spring are the season for southern Europe and I would do up Rome, Naples, Venice, North Africa, Spain, Paris, before thinking of returning. Everything is running along so well here, and *I* am well, that there is nothing to hasten your return, so stay, anyhow until the hot weather of *next summer*. So, too, thus early let me insist that you do not undertake to bring home any souvenirs to *any one*, not excepting me even, *but I do not include* one or several "best girls" in this suggestion. The custom regulations are so *strict* that you may have much trouble and some expenses in New York, so avoid it all by bringing in nothing to anybody but the "best girls." These, of course, must be exceptions. Tal and I concluded it would be best for you to subscribe to the Assemblies, so that is all right. On Sunday, I shall send your Christmas cheques as you requested, paying out of the $200 you sent me. I shall not increase the amounts, so you will, after sending them and paying for Nellie Penrose's wedding present, have $70 to your credit.

I am sorry to write that our good dentist, Dr. Essig, died of pneumonia a few days ago.

I have a letter from Spencer. He expects to come East by Jan. 1. We are *all* well. Tal just at present is at Sand Bridge with Kate.

Letter from Dick to his father, dated Naples, Italy, December 28, 1901

I arrived here all right yesterday after a very good voyage of fifteen days from Ceylon. We had fine weather and smooth seas all the way, until the last night before reaching here, when it got a little rough.

The trip through the Arabian Sea, the Red Sea, the Suez Canal and the Mediterranean was very interesting. I had expected to see a great piece of engineering work in the Suez Canal, but it is nothing extraordinary. It is simply a very cheap-looking ditch, 87 miles long, cut through a sandy neck of land which is only a few feet above water level. The finest thing about it is a colossal bronze statue of De Lesseps at the north entrance of the canal. The engineering difficulties to be met building the canal amounted to nothing as compared with the difficulties to be met in building the Nicaragua or Panama Canals. All the Suez Canal required was a lot of steam dredges working for a few years—and the job was done.

We came through the Straits of Messina the day before we arrived here, and during the night we passed the volcanic island of Stromboli. It happened to be in eruption at the time, and was a very fine sight.

My mail has not yet arrived from London, but I expect it in a few days, and I will then decide how long I will stay in Italy. I want to see some of the sulphur mines here before leaving.

It is cold here, and Mt. Vesuvius is covered with snow—which is said to be a very unusual thing. It feels very good however to get into a cold climate again after the heat of the tropics, though it seems very tame to be back in Europe again as compared with travelling in Asia.

I will write more in full when I get my mail and arrange my plans definitely. In the meantime my address will be as usual care of J. S. Morgan & Co., 22 Old Broad St., London, England, as they will continue to forward mail to me wherever I am. I wrote to you twice from Ceylon, and once on board ship, mailing the last etter at Port Said, Egypt.

Letter from Dick to his father, dated Hotel Villa Acradina, Syracuse, Sicily, January 4, 1902

I came to Sicily from Naples three days ago to see some of the sulphur mines, as this island is the chief sulphur-producing place of the world. I have seen some of the mines, which are mostly in the vicinity of Girgenti, and have also been to Mt. Aetna, but did not go to the top, as it was covered with snow. I arrived here at Syracuse last night, and am just starting back today for Naples. I will write to you fully from Naples. Will arrive there tomorrow morning. I drop this hasty line to you now just to let you know what I am doing.

The day I left Naples I received my mail from London, and among it were your letters of Sept. 29th, Nov. 20th, and Dec. 3d, all of which I was exceedingly glad to get, as it had been a long time since I had heard from you. Your letter of Sept. 29th had gone to Hong Kong, thence had been forwarded to London and thence to Naples. I will answer them all fully when I get to Naples. I have to cut this letter short now, as I have to get ready to start for Naples.

Letter from Dick to his brother Boies, dated Naples, Italy, January 4, 1902

Dear Boies

I have been intending for a long time to write to you, but a man does not have much chance to write when he is travelling around from place to place. Tal wrote me of your success in the November elections in Phila. I was very glad to hear of it and I congratulate you most heartily on it.

I travelled through central Europe last spring, and in the summer I went up to Sweden and Lapland. In August I went to Russia and thence across Siberia to the Pacific Coast at Vladivostok. I had a fine trip in Russia and was never treated anywhere in the world better than I was there. The Russians are very fine people, and no one who travels through their country can help having great respect for them. I saw Charlemagne Tower in St. Petersburg, and he was very polite in helping me in my arrangements to cross Siberia. The U. S. government certainly has a splendid man in him as Ambassador. He has a magnificent house in St. Petersburg.

From Vladivostok I went to Japan, China, Manila, the Malay Peninsula, Ceylon, and thence here. I saw Bob McWade in Canton, China, and he treated me first rate. Here again the right man seems to be in the right place, and you did a very good thing when you got him appointed. He seems to have a great influence with the Chinese officials. Canton is the dirtiest place I have ever seen. You can smell it for miles before you reach it. There are 3,000,000 Chinese there and they hate the "foreign devils." When a white man passes through the streets they express their opinion of him in very choice language. Bob McWade has no easy job there but he holds it down in splendid shape.

I was very glad that I went to the Philippines, as they are a very interesting country. Manila is a fine place and seems sure to become one of the great commercial centers of the Orient. In fact it is so already. I met a number of people I knew there.

From Manila I went back to Hong Kong and thence to the Malay Peninsula to see the tin mines there, which supply 75% of the tin of the world. Thence I went to Ceylon and thence through the Suez Canal to this place.

I expect to be in Europe for some weeks more as I want to visit some of the mining regions that I missed when I was in Europe last summer. I have been visiting the principal mining regions in the countries in which I have been travelling, as a matter of scientific interest, and also to get an idea of the mining resources of Europe and Asia.

I hope to get home in March, and in the meantime my address will be care of J. S. Morgan & Co., 22 Old Broad St., London, England, as they forward mail to me wherever I am.

Your affectionate brother
R. A. F. Penrose, Jr.

(Across this letter is written in pencil "Dr. Penrose" and it is enclosed in a Boies Penrose envelope addressed to his father in Philadelphia.)

Letter from Dick to his father, dated Naples, Italy, January 7, 1902

I wrote to you from here on Dec. 28th and also a short letter from Syracuse, Sicily, a few days later. I arrived here again yesterday and will leave for Rome tomorrow or the next day.

Just before I went to Sicily, I received from London your letters of Sept. 29th, Nov. 20th, and Dec. 3d, all of which I was very glad to get, as it had been a long time since I had heard from you. You say that the news you give me must be very stale by the time I get your letters, but I assure you it is not, and there is nothing that I look forward to with so great pleasure at each place where I expect mail, as finding your letters.

I am very greatly obliged to you for distributing the Christmas money that I sent you; and also for all that you have done for me about the Union League, and the directorship in the Norristown Railroad. I hope you will thank Dr. Woods for his kindness to me in the Union League matter. I appreciate it very greatly. If there is any chance of there being any slip in the matter of my election by my long delay in coming home, I hope you will let me know, as I am more than ever anxious to become a member of the Union League, and I would willingly cut my trip short and come home at once if it were desirable to do so for the Union League matter. If therefore Dr. Woods thinks there is any such necessity, please let me know and I will return at once. If you should think it necessary to cable me about it, you can always reach me at my address in London (J. S. Morgan & Co., 22 Old Broad St.) as they open telegrams and repeat them to me.

I note what you say about the use of boiled water, quinine, calomel, etc., and I have followed this advice as strictly as possible. I realize fully its benefits. I have been in many unhealthy places, where most people were either sick, or getting sick, or just getting over sickness, and I have been entirely well.

I am sorry you were worried, as you say in your letter of Dec. 3d, about not hearing from me for two weeks previous to that date, but you will notice that it was the fault of the mail, as my letters to you of Oct. 22d and 26th were written only four days apart, and yet you received them two weeks apart. You may be assured that I write to you regularly, and if any delay occurs, you can put it down to delay in the mail, and not be worried. In fact I am surprised that you have received my letters so regularly as you have, as the mail service in Europe and Asia is not up to ours, and in the Far East especially it is often very bad.

I had a very interesting trip in Sicily, where, as I wrote you, I went to see the sulphur mines. I went from here to Palermo, Sicily, by steamer, thence to the south coast of the island by railroad, to a place called Girgenti; thence to Catania and up Mt. Aetna, but not to the top, as the snow prevented it; thence to Syracuse; thence to Messina and across the Straits of Messina to Reggio, on the mainland of Italy, and thence back here by railroad. I was not only very glad to see the sulphur mines, but also to see Sicily in general, as it is a very interesting country, especially the old Greek ruins at Syracuse and at Girgenti. The latter place was the Acragas of the Greeks and the Agrigentum of the Romans. Syracuse is one of the most interesting places I ever saw. The old Greek walls and part of the old town still remain. The farmers' carts in the country districts of Sicily are painted all over with gayly colored pictures representing scenes in Sicilian history.

My plans now are to go to Rome this week, thence to the Island of Elba where I want to visit the iron mines that supply Italy with most of its iron; thence possibly to a couple of mining regions that I want to see in Spain; thence up to Paris, and from there to London, and thence home. I think I should get to London about March 15th, and to New York shortly before the end of that month. I am not a bit tired of travelling, and I would like to keep on and visit Australia, etc., but I think I had better come home at this time, to look after the mine and other business.

I have several letters from Brockman. He had a little trouble with the men, but the strike is all over and the mine is running again. The recent fall in the price of silver has cut a big hole in our profits, and will necessarily make dividends less frequent; but we have very large bodies of ore still in the mine, and silver will have to drop very much lower before we would have to close down. In fact, I do not think it will ever drop so low that we cannot work it—at least while we have no further expenses than those we are now incurring.

Letter from his father, dated January 8, 1902

I received your Ipoh letter (Nov. 25 and 26) yesterday, your Penang letter (Nov. 29) two days *before*. I also have your Singapore letter (Nov. 19). I was much relieved by your Penang letter, the first for almost two weeks. You must be having a most lovely time in spite of the heat and the vermin. I am sorry you did not provide yourself with mosquito netting to guard you against that, the *only cause* of malaria, yellow fever and doubtless many more afflications of which as yet we do not know. I believe, now, that not only mosquito but bedbugs, fleas, flies, etc., etc., cause many painful, dangerous and even fatal diseases, and I shall be very glad when you have reached regions where they are less numerous and less harmful. Your quinine, calomel, etc., etc., are, of course, of inestimable value, but mosquito netting equally so. But you will not receive this letter until you are out of all these annoyances and dangers and *next time* you go to Asia you will be well provided with netting as well as drugs. I am so glad that you are so well and that all my suggestive safeguards have proved so valuable to you.

Now about coming home. *Take your time*, don't hurry, everything is going on in a most satisfactory way. You *will never* be able to be away with less care or trouble than now, so make your return mid summer, rather than March or April. It seems a sin to leave southern Europe at the time of year most pleasant to be there. How I wish *now* I was along with you, and *we* will talk over *my* Nile trip after your return. I grieve to have to write you that Tal has lost his baby, Tal, Jr. It has broken us *all* up. Tal seems as if he could not get over it.

The child died most unexpectedly the day before Christmas, after a convulsion of over three hours, due, *apparently* to its teeth. It was well and going out the *day before*. Tal and Kate and Sarah go to Florida next week for some weeks, a course I approve of highly.

I sent your Christmas cheques and have had replies from *all* the beneficiaries, which replies I have put in your map case to keep for you.

It will be a comfort to hear from you that you are again in Europe. It seems then as if you were really home again.

Letter from Dick to his father, dated Rome, January 13, 1902

I was very glad to get your letter of Dec. 18th a few days ago.

I wrote to you last on Jan. 7th from Naples, on my return there from Sicily. The next day I went up Mt. Vesuvius, as I wanted to see the crater. The railroad up the mountain was not running, so I went on foot, but it was not a hard climb. I have climbed many a harder mountain in the United States. The volcano was not in active eruption, but dense clouds of smoke were coming out, and on looking over the edge of the crater, the molten lava could be seen, heaving up and down, and every now and then spurting upwards with a loud explosion, but not coming high enough to run over the side of the crater.

From Naples I came up here, and for the last few days have been seeing some of the sights of Rome. The ancient Roman things have been greatly mutilated by the people who came after them, and it is hard to tell whether the inroads of the mediaeval barbarians from the north, or the Christians, did most to destroy them. The marble column of the Roman emperor Trajan still stands, but the bronze statue of Trajan which once surmounted it has been taken down, melted and re-cast into a statue of St. Peter, which has been replaced on the column. Trajan would probably feel a good deal of a shock if he knew this.

I expect to be in Italy for a week or so more, and then take a boat from Genoa to Gibraltar, and go up through Spain. I note what you say about not hurrying home and I will not do so, but, as I wrote you before, I cannot help feeling as if I ought to come home before very long and look after my business a little.

I also note what you say about not bringing home any presents. The only places where I have bought any such things were Japan and Ceylon, and these things I have sent on by freight, complying with all the custom-house regulations, and will pay the duty when they arrive. I have arranged to have them stored on their arrival, until I return. I did not get many things, but only a few which I thought were worth buying, mostly for presents.

You said in one of your letters that you might like to go to Egypt next winter, and I am very glad to hear this. I would be very glad to go with you whenever you get ready, and I am sure you would find the trip interesting. On my present trip I have seen Suez, Port Said, Damietta, and the Suez Canal in Egypt, but I reserved Cairo and the Nile for another trip, so whenever you want to go, I am your man.

I will write again in a few days, before I sail for Gibraltar.

Letter from his father, dated 1331 Spruce St. (Philadelphia), January 20, 1902

Your letter from Naples, Jan. 7, reached me Saturday, Jan. 18th, as also I have received your first Naples letter, as well as your letters from Syracuse. Indeed, as you say, it is very pleasant to reflect that I have received, I believe, every single letter you have written me since you left home, even that Malay letter from the interior before you wrote your Penang letter—a very fortunate circumstance for me, since I am always imagining some catastrophy happening, and then a letter from you relieves my mind and my anxiety is for a moment relieved.

In your letter you talk about getting home before the end of March. Now let me beg you not to hurry. Everything is going on most satisfactorily. I am well, as is all the crowd, so have your "fling". A few weeks in Paris at this season *ought* to furnish a great deal of fun. If you come back by mid summer it will be plenty soon enough. Your affairs are in a most satisfactory condition. You will be put into the Union League just as soon as you return; *that is assured*. And I understand that everything at your mine is running satisfactorily. Tal left yesterday (Sunday) with Kate and Sarah for Tampa, for a stay of two months or more. I was very glad to have them go. They have been completely crushed by baby's death, and it seems impossible for them to rally. They both look badly indeed. I felt as if I was almost as bad. I had no conception *I* should feel it so much, but I have done so most keenly, and it has been an overwhelming grief to me. The child was so splendid and died so unexpectedly that no one was prepared for the result. Spencer is here, is a good deal in New York in connection with his mill business, seems to be having a good time and also seems to be well satisfied with the condition of all of his affairs. I don't pretend to understand half but will bide my time until you return to explain it all to me.

Boies is now most of his time in W.

I have written you a very long letter. I hope you can read it.

Letter from Dick to his father, dated Venice, Italy, January 20, 1902

I wrote to you last from Rome a few days ago. From Rome, I went to see the iron mines on the Island of Elba, off the coast of Italy. Here I was treated very well by the manager of the Italian Company that owns the mines. He put a steam launch at my disposal, and I went to various places along the coast of the island, seeing most of the important mines, and getting a very good idea of the island in general.

From Elba, I came back to the mainland of Italy, and went to Pisa and Florence, and then came here. Venice is the most attractive place I have seen in Italy, and I would like to stay longer, but I have to leave tonight to catch a boat at Genoa for Gibraltar. I will arrive at Genoa tomorrow, and go thence by a North German Lloyd boat to Gibraltar, and thence up through Spain overland. It will take about 4 days from Genoa to Gibraltar. I will write fully from the latter place. I have to cut short this letter now, so as to get ready to start from here, and I just drop this hasty line to you to let you know about my movements. I have not heard from you since your letter of Dec. 18th, but I hope to hear again when I get my next mail in Spain.

Letter from Dick to his father, dated Grand Hotel Madrid, Seville, Spain, January 29, 1902

I wrote to you last from Gibraltar on Jan. 25th. From there I went to the neighboring town of Algeciras, in Spain, by boat, and there took a train for this place, where I arrived the same night. The next morning I went to the Rio Tinto copper mines, which are about seven hours travel by train from here. I was treated very well there by the manager of the English company that owns the mines, and saw everything very satisfactorily.

The Rio Tinto mines are the largest copper mines in Europe, and I was very much interested in seeing them. I stayed over night at Rio Tinto, and the next day returned here.

The city of Seville is one of the largest cities of Spain, and is a very interesting place. It was once one of the centres of Moorish power, and some of the old Moorish buildings still remain.

I will start tomorrow for Madrid, but as I want to stop at one or two places on the way, I will probably not get there for about four days.

I will write more fully in a few days. I have not yet received any of my mail since I left Italy. I expect to reach Paris about Feb. 15th.

Letter from Dick to his father, dated Grand Hotel Suisse, Cordova, Spain, February 3, 1902

I leave here this evening for Madrid, and I thought I would drop a line to you before starting. I wrote to you last from Seville on Jan. 29th. From there I came on here, and the next day went to Granada, which is a most interesting and beautiful place. The Alhambra, or palace of the old Moorish kings, is still well preserved, and is a wonderful building. When I first came to Spain, I had not planned to go to Granada, but I am now very glad that I went, as it is well worth seeing.

From Granada I returned here, so as to catch the fast train which runs three times a week from Southern Spain to Madrid. I will reach Madrid tomorrow, and will stay there two or three days. Thence I will go to see the iron mines of Bilbao, in northern Spain, and thence on to Paris, where I expect to arrive on or before Feb. 15th. I have not yet received any of my mail since leaving Italy, but I hope to find some in Madrid. Will write again in a few days.

Letter from his father, dated 1331 Spruce St. (Philadelphia), February 5, 1902

Your last two letters are before me—Rome and Venice (the last came yesterday). Each letter is a great pleasure, and, at the same time, a great relief to me. I am glad you have taken, anyhow, a little time to see Rome, Florence, Naples, and Venice. It would have been simply a sin to have passed them by without a visit. Now, at any rate, you have "been there" and have seen them. Vesuvius must have been most interesting. About forty years ago, young Edward Bayard, a lieut. in the U. S. Navy, son of Mr. Ed. Bayard of Philadelphia, made the ascent, as you have done, on foot, with a few naval officers. There was no active eruption at the time, but one of those sudden spurts which you refer to in your letter occurred while the party was on the rim of the crater. A falling stone broke Bayard's arm and a few days after *he died* from lockjaw. He was a very fine fellow and all Philadelphia was greatly shocked. So, *you* have accomplished a feat, not without its real perils. We are all very well. Tal is at Tampa in Florida, but does not like the place and will leave for Fort Myer, about 150 miles farther south, where he proposes to remain for a couple of weeks and then to come home. Christine was here this morning. She purposes to join Kate in Florida and then go to Aiken in Carolina to be with Liddy Robinson (who has a cottage there). Mrs. Van Rennselaer invited you to a supper (after the opera) tomorrow, Thursday, evening. I answered the note "Not in the city, would regret greatly" etc., and signed the reply merely with "P"—. Boies is in town tonight; he came at 6 p.m. and returns at midnight. He is doubly busy, as Quay has gone to Florida for the winter. He is, however, "first class", which affords *me* unbounded satisfaction. Spencer is still in New York and expects to be at least another month, watching and *nursing* his stock, which has been listed on the New York stock exchange. So far our winter has been by no means a pleasant one, and for the last two weeks has been simply *atrocious*. Now—8 p.m.—as I write this letter the thermometer out of the library window is 14° and it is entirely too cold for me to take my evening walk—not, however, a cause for just regret.

Letter from Dick to his father, dated Grand Hotel de la Paix, Madrid, Spain, February 5, 1902

On my arrival here yesterday, I received the first lot of mail that I have gotten for several weeks, and among it I was very glad to find your letter of Jan. 20th. The last letter that I had received from you before that, was dated Dec. 18th. If you wrote between those dates, the letter was probably among the mail that had not reached Gibraltar when I left there, and which was forwarded to Paris, where I will get it on my arrival there.

I was terribly grieved and shocked to hear by your letter of the death of Tal's child. I have today written to Tal, extending my sympathy to him and Kate. It seemed a long time afterwards to be writing to him, but I felt that I ought to do so, and I hope I did right. I cannot tell you how sorry I am to hear of the loss of the child. Of course the loss is greatest to Tal and Kate, but I feel that it is a most sad loss to all of us.

I will leave here tomorrow night for Bilbao, in northern Spain, to see some large iron mines there, that have been famous for many centuries. Thence I will go to Paris—possibly stopping on the way for a day at San Sebastian, in Spain, and a day at Bordeaux. At any rate, I expect to reach Paris on or before Feb. 15th. When I get there, I will arrange my plans for the immediate future. As the time approaches at which I had planned to come home, I feel more like following your suggestion and not hurrying.

I have been travelling so rapidly for the last few months, that I would like to get to some good place like Paris, and just stay there for a few weeks. I am not tired of travelling, but I have a lot of notes, etc., on different mining regions that I have visited, which I would like to write up for future reference. Moreover, I expect to get in Paris a lot of information that I want about the mining resources of Europe in general, and all this will take more or less time. In view of all this, I thought I would decide to stay in Paris for at least a few weeks, and then be guided by circumstances as to my movements.

Madrid is a beautiful and very interesting city, and I am very glad that I stopped over here. I will write again in a few days. In the meantime, it will probably be best for you to continue to address me care of J. S. Morgan & Co., 22 Old Broad St., London, England, until I write further.

Letter from Dick to his father, dated Grand Hotel Continental, St. Sebastian, February 10, 1902

I arrived here yesterday afternoon from Bilbao, and will leave today for Paris. I could have gone on from here to Paris last night, but by waiting until this morning, I catch the fast train running between Madrid and Paris. I will reach Paris late this evening.

I had at first thought of stopping for a day at Bordeaux on the way to Paris, but the weather is bad, and it has been raining for several days, so I have determined to go on direct to Paris.

I had a very good trip to Bilbao, and was much interested in seeing the iron mines there, which are among the largest in the world. I had letters of introduction to some of the mine managers and was very hospitably treated.

This town of San Sebastian is a great Spanish summer resort, but just now, in the winter, there are but few visitors here. The town is beautifully situated on the shore of the Bay of Biscay, with the mountains rising up immediately behind it.

I will write again in a few days from Paris. I wrote you last from Madrid on Feb. 5th, and from Cordova shortly before that.

Letter from his father, dated 1331 Spruce St. (Philadelphia), February 15, 1902

Both your Gibraltar and Seville letters are before me. Though I have little in the way of news to tell you, yet I write to keep in close "touch" with you, since by now (Feb. 15) you are or expected to be in Paris and therefore next door to Philadelphia. Your letters interest me greatly. I feel that from what you say about Venice I should move there to live. Truly it is the very reverse of Philadelphia—noisy, dirty, dusty, horrible! Philadelphia has become a place so abominable that were I not so *very old* I would move, perhaps to Washington. The only great advantage it gives *me* is that my personality is lost in the crowd and rush and I am able to be a recluse with the minimum amount of observation and comment.

We are all well—everything going on as when I last wrote. Tal and Kate are still at Tampa. Tal wrote me that the place would not suit me so I have abandoned all idea of going to join them there, if I ever had any real idea of going, which I begin to doubt exceedingly. When you get to Paris, I want you to take plenty of time to see all there is to be seen and have all the fun you care about. Spencer Biddle should be there or in Switzerland, but, of course, you will meet plenty of people there whom you know. There is so much to see and do in Paris and London that one could readily pass months in either and always find fresh subjects. I suppose if you go to Brussels and Belgium you will come across or see Pourtales. I hope he is well again. How he must regret his lost opportunity in failing to make the Siberian connection with you. I wish I were now with you in Paris. I could spend hours every day, as we did in 81, going to the Louvre, but you have had such a surfit of "art" in Italy that perhaps you will never care to look again at an "old master" and his "chromos."

Letter from Dick to his father, dated Paris, France, February 16, 1902

I arrived here a few days ago from San Sebastian, Spain, and was very glad to find your letter of Jan. 8th, which had been forwarded from London to Gibraltar, and thence here. I received your letter of Jan. 20th in Madrid, and answered it from there. I also wrote you a few days later from San Sebastian.

Spain is a very interesting country, and in its natural features it is very beautiful, but it is not a comfortable country to travel in, especially in winter. Some of the hotels are good, but the railroads and other means of travel are mostly very bad, and the winter weather is cold and stormy. Almost every one is constantly coughing; and pneumonia in many places is very prevalent, and very fatal. The houses are rarely heated, and people in the hotels have to sit and shiver in their overcoats. But few of the trains run over 15 or 17 miles an hour, and many of them not over 10 or 12 miles. They could easily be beaten by a good horse. A train that runs over 20 miles an hour is a fast express in Spain.

In spite of all these things, I am very glad I went to Spain, as it is very interesting and very different from the rest of Europe. I found the Spaniards universally polite and considerate wherever I went.

I have met a number of people that I knew since I arrived here, among them several fellows from Colorado and Utah; also Paul Stewart from Philadelphia. Stewart went to London a few days ago on his way back to the United States. I expect Lundbohm, who is the Swede with whom I went to Lapland last summer, here in a few days; and I may possibly go with him to see some iron mines in Luxemburg, Belgium, but I will not make any plans about this until he arrives. At any rate, I expect to be in or around Paris for a few weeks, as the Luxemburg trip will only take two or three days. It is cold here, but I am at an excellent hotel, called the "Hotel Ritz" which is the newest and best hotel in Paris, so that the cold is not troublesome, as it was in Spain. Paris is certainly the most comfortable city that I have struck anywhere since leaving the United States.

In my letter to you from Madrid, I told you how terribly grieved I was to learn by your letter of Jan. 20th of the death of Tal's Baby. That was the first I had heard of it, as your previous letter (Jan. 8th) did not reach me until I arrived here. I hope Tal and Kate will be benefitted by their trip to Florida.

I will write again in a few days. In the meantime you had better continue to address your letters to me as usual care of J. S. Morgan & Co., 22 Old Broad St., London, as they will forward mail here as long as I stay.

Letter from Dick to his father, dated Hotel Ritz, Paris, France, February 24, 1902

I wrote to you from here last week. I had expected to go this week to see some iron mines in Belgium with Lundbohm, from Sweden, with whom I went to Lapland last summer, but he has not yet arrived here, so I have waited for him. The weather has been very bad anyhow, so I did not object to postponing the trip.

I have met a great many people I know here, and it seems almost like being back in the United States again. Paris is certainly the most attractive city I have seen in either Europe or Asia; and it seems especially attractive now that I have seen most of the large cities on this continent, and know how superior Paris is to all of them. The best hotels, the best-looking girls, and the best comforts for living, in general, are certainly centered here.

I had a letter a short time ago from Pourtales, saying that he thought of going to the United States this spring, and asking me when I was going, so we may be able to arrange to go together. I would like to follow your advice and stay in Europe until next summer, but there are a number of things that I ought to attend to at home, so I think I will sail for New York in a month or so. Everything seems to be going all right at the Common-Wealth mine, but I can't help feeling that after almost a year's absence, I ought to be on the spot for a while and see how things are running. You will doubtless receive the Common-Wealth dividend, declared in February, before you get this letter.

I see by the weekly letter that I get from my office, that the dividend of the U. S. Reduction & Refining Co., on the stock held by me as trustee and by me personally, has been received. The dividend on the stock held by me as trustee belongs to you. I also owe you the dividend of January on the 200 shares of Camden & Burlington County R. R. stock held by me as trustee; but as I expect to be home so soon, I can probably settle up all these things best with you when I get there.

I will write again in a few days. I see by the papers that you have been having bad storms at Philadelphia, but I hope you have not suffered from them.

Letter from his father, dated 1331 Spruce St. (Philadelphia), February 25, 1902

Your St. Sebastian letter reached me several days ago, and I have also received your Cordova letter. The Madrid letter came at last, but was delayed several days after the receipt of the St. Sebastian letter. I am glad you wrote Tal about his baby's death. The shock was *terrible* to us all. Tal and Kate and I were very much broken up by it. The child was buried in my father's lot in Laurel Hill, by the side of *my* baby (Boies primus). I did not go to the funeral. I really felt as if I could not bear the trial, and Tal and Kate agreed with me, so nobody went but Tal and Kate and Boies and your Uncle Will and the *clergyman*—Boies's friend, the Rev. Bolton, who officiated at Philip's funeral in June. Tal and Kate and Sarah are now in Florida, but I think they will return by middle of March. They needed to go somewhere to break up their sad associations, and I have no doubt the change will be of the greatest benefit to them.

You are wise to take a rest in Paris. In making your plans, you might determine not to return at the soonest before the end of your year of absence. You left April 17, 1901—*and* as *long after* as you can put in the time *pleasantly* to yourself, since there is absolutely nothing to make your immediate return necessary, and I am well, so go slow, have a good time, enjoy all that Paris offers, and you should meet many people whom you know there and who can help you in the racket. At home we are all as heretofore. Spencer spends a large portion of his time in New York, looking after his stock and bonds, coming home for Saturday and Sunday. Boies is exceedingly busy. The weather for the past month has been most trying and I have not been able to drive at all, a great privation since I am compelled to walk until my legs and feet give out. Our friend, Dr. Wood, 15 and Spruce, *is to be married* next weeks, March 5, to a New York lady (Miss Mary Husbands), a friend of his daughters and all of his children are "delighted"?. I fancy she is an exceedingly nice person, since she has many warm friends. One friend, Mrs. Clark of New York, a very rich woman, $30,000,000 (sewing machines) gave her as a present a very fine house and a cheque for $25,000 and insisted, as Miss H's mother was dead, that the wedding should take place at her house, etc., etc.

I am expecting every day your first Paris letter. Up to now I have your letter from Cordova, Feb. 3d, Madrid, Feb. 5, St. Sebastian, Feb. 10, and today is Feb. 25.

I hope you will have an awfully nice time in Paris.

Letter from Dick to his father, dated Hotel Ritz, Paris, France, March 4, 1902

I was very glad to get your letter of Feb. 15th a few days ago. I wrote to you last week telling you that perhaps Pourtales would come to the United States at the same time as I come, as he had written me that he wanted to go this spring. But in reply to my last letter to him, he has written that his health has compelled him to go to Carlsbad again, also that family matters make it difficult for him to leave at present, so I will come without him. I have not decided yet just what boat I will take, as there are several fellows here whom I know, who are going to the U. S. in the next few weeks, and I may arrange to come with some of them.

My Swedish friend, Lundbohm, has not yet turned up, nor can I hear from him. He wrote me last some weeks ago from northern Lapland, and spoke of the immense snow storms there. He may be snowed up somewhere, as he should have been here two weeks ago. If he don't come soon, I will give up the trip to the iron mines of Belgium, as it was largely because he wanted me to see them with him that I thought of going.

I have been on several automobile trips in the country around here, with a man from New York whom I know, named Guggenheim, who has two of the best automobiles in Paris. The French automobiles are wonderful things. They can go 40 and 50 miles an hour up hill and down hill, without any difficulty, and with no discomfort to the people in them.

As I wrote to you last week, Paris is certainly the finest city in Europe, and I will be sorry to leave here, but by the time I go, I will have been here over a month, and that seems a good while to stay in any one place. I don't know of any place in Europe except Paris, where I would care to stay that long, but here a month seems like two days. I have learned to speak enough French to get along very well wherever I go.

You say in your letter that you wish you were here, and could see the Louvre again. I wish very much that you *were* here, for I am sure you would like it. I don't believe that Paris can be beaten anywhere in the world as an attractive and comfortable place to live, and if you were here, I would be very glad to stay much longer. I have been to the Louvre twice since I have been here—more simply because I remembered it from our trip here in '81 than for any other reason. I have not been able to cultivate any appreciation for the productions of the old artists, and I can see more to admire in modern French pictures and in modern France in general, then I can in ancient France, and in the dreary-looking paintings of crucifixes and martyrs, which people call "works of art" by "old masters."

I will write again in a few days when I decide just when I will sail for New York. I think I will start sometime in the next three or four weeks, but I will leave here some days before sailing, as I would like to have a week or ten days in London before I leave Europe.

Letter from Dick to his father, dated Hotel Ritz, Paris, France, March 11, 1902

I was very glad to get your letter of Feb. 25th a few days ago. I am sorry to hear that you have suffered so much from bad weather in Phila., but I hope you have had the same change to better weather that has occurred here. After weeks of stormy weather, it is now clear and bright, and like spring.

I have about decided to sail for New York on the North German Lloyd steamer Kronprinz Wilhelm, which leaves Southampton on Mch. 26th and arrives in New York about Apr. 2d or 3d. I will decide in a few days and then write to you definitely about it. I will have been in Paris about a month and a half by the time I leave, and though I am not in any way tired of it, yet I think I had better be starting home, and looking after my business for a while.

The longer I stay in Paris the better I like it. When I first arrived here I thought I would be ready to leave in a couple of weeks, but at the end of that time I found that I had only just begun to know Paris, and now at the end of a month here, I have concluded that it is about the finest place I have ever struck for a man to spend a few weeks in. I have met a number of mining men and others, whom I know, from California and Colorado, so I have not lacked companions. I also met Tony Drexel here. He had come from England with his wife. I have not seen or heard of Spencer Biddle, so I suppose he is probably not in town.

I hope Tal and Kate are all right again, and that their trip to Florida did them good.

If I sail on the 26th, I will go to London about the 20th, so as to have a few days there before sailing, but of all this, I will write you definitely in a few days.

I was much surprised to hear, by your letter, of Dr. Woods' marriage. I wish I had known it in time to send him a wedding present. I have however something for him which I bought in Japan last fall, in recognition of all he did for me in the Union League matter. I sent it home from Japan with other things by freight, and will give it to him when I arrive.

I will write further in a few days, when I decide definitely about which boat I will come on.

Letter from his father, dated 1331 Spruce St. (Philadelphia), March 12, 1902

Both your Paris letters are received (Feb. 16 and 24); the latter came yesterday. I reply to it promptly. I am happy to know that you are "resting" after all your fatigue and hardships (change means "rest") and, especially, after all you suffered in Spain. I have always had a horror of Spain and Spaniards, and now, when you describe the cold and dismal hotels and wretched trains I am confirmed in my opinion. A Spanish woman may be splendid as a "chere ami" but "hell" as the mother of one's children, so don't fall in love with dark eyes and mantillas of Spain.

Tal and Kate got back yesterday from Florida, both much improved for their change. Tal will go for snipe next week to Sandbridge. Kate will stay at home to attend to her household affairs. Spencer is still East but expects to start to Colorado next week. He refers to the affairs of the mills as being in very flourishing condition. The Commonwealth dividend reached me last week. With regard to the Colorado mills dividends as well as the Burlington R. R., make yourself entirely easy. We can fix them up in short order after your return, even if you should not come back for *a year*—but, seriously, do not make any effort to return until *after* your year is up; say until end of April or May.

I do hope you can arrange with Pourtales to come with you, but tell him that you do not intend to hurry, and if he wants to get off before you are completely ready, let him go by himself. In returning, take the finest boat and the best rooms, and wait for your boat and rooms rather than accept anything to make time. I am well and getting along at home very satisfactorily. I shall be very very happy to have you back again.

Letter from Dick to his father, dated Hotel Cecil, London, England, March 20, 1902

I arrived here last night from Paris. I have decided definitely to sail for New York on the Kronprinz Wilhelm, of the North German Lloyd line, which leaves Southampton on Mch. 26th and arrives in New York on April 1st or 2d. I have gotten a very good stateroom on this boat, and as it is a fine ship I think we ought to have a good voyage. I have been on a few of the German boats in the far east and in the Mediterranean, and as they were all good, I decided to come home on one of them.

I was very sorry to leave Paris, but I had been there for some time, and as all good things must have an end, I thought I might just as well start home now as later, especially as I want to have a chance to go to Arizona and look around a little before the annual meeting of the Common-Wealth Co. this spring.

My whole trip, from the time I left home almost a year ago, up to the present time, has been most pleasant and interesting, and I shall always be glad that I took it, for I have seen and learned more than I have ever done in twice that time at any other period of my life. The winding up of my trip at Paris has doubtless been the most pleasant, and probably not the least instructive part of my trip. I do not believe that there is a place on earth where a man can have such a good time as in Paris, and I have learned to respect the French people much more than I used to do. In spite of what people may say about their degeneracy, their methods of running cities and other crowded communities cannot be beaten anywhere. In an almost six weeks stay in Paris, in which I saw almost everything, both respectable and disreputable, I saw only two drunken men, and never saw a row or dispute of any kind. Everyone was polite and happy. I don't know of any Anglo-Saxon community that can boast of the same thing.

I will be very glad to get home again, for the chief thing that I have learned on my trip is, that, as a permanent thing, there is no place equal to the United States to live in.

CHAPTER 10

A Harvard Alumnus

IN the spring of 1901, before he left for his year's trip to Europe and Asia, Penrose resigned as secretary of Section E of the American Association for the Advancement of Science, a post to which he had been elected in June, 1900, notifying the permanent secretary of that organization, L. O. Howard, that he would not be able to be present at the Denver meeting which was scheduled for August 24 to 31, 1901. On April 18, 1901, Howard replied that "your resignation as Secretary of Section E was laid before the Council at its meeting held yesterday afternoon and was accepted with regret."

While he was still abroad, he received a notice from the Board of Overseers of Harvard College, signed by Winthrop H. Wade, secretary, announcing that he had "been appointed by the Board of Overseers a member of the Committee on Mining and Metallurgy for the year 1902, and to request that you will accept said appointment."

On it, a penciled notation in his father's handwriting states that he "notified Mr. Wade that you are abroad and will return in February, when the matter will receive attention." Penrose accepted the position, which he maintained from 1902 to 1923. He also served as a member of the Visiting Committee to the Department of Geology, Mineralogy and Petrography in that institution from 1915 to 1923, and again from 1925 until his death. During the same periods he was also a member of the Visiting Committee to the School of Engineering.

The School of Mining and Practical Geology was founded at Harvard in 1865, with J. D. Whitney as head and a distinguished faculty in geology, mining, and metallurgy, drawn partly from the outside and partly from professors already serving, either in Harvard College or in the Lawrence Scientific School.

The dates (1902–1923) for his participation on the Committee to visit the Department of Mining and Metallurgy are taken from Penrose's own list of positions held, but that he was a member prior to 1902 is shown by a report made by the committee to the Board of Overseers in November, 1901, which is signed by Penrose as chairman. The statement, prepared with his usual meticulous attention to the preparation of a well-organized report, includes background, findings, and recommendations. His discussion of the education of a mining engineer is worthy of widespread circulation and emulation, for he speaks with the voice of experience.

"*The Committee appointed to visit the Department of Mining and Metallurgy at Harvard University inspected the Department on March 29th, and beg to submit the following report:*

"The course of instruction [as given in 1901] in mining and metallurgy was first planned in connection with the Lawrence Scientific School in the academic year of 1895–96, but only preliminary instruction was given until the year, 1896–97. In that year certain courses on mining and metallurgy were given by the Department of Geology and Geography, it being considered desirable to carry on the instruction in this manner until the plans for the new department were matured. These courses increased, and were given in more or less close connection with the Department of Geology and Geography until 1900, when they had become so prominent a feature in themselves that the Faculty constituted a separate Department of Mining and Metallurgy in the Division of Geology. The Department of Mining and Metallurgy, however, always has been, and very properly still remains, in close relationship with the Department of Geology and Geography.

"The work from 1896 to 1898 was carried on mostly in the University Museum, while the course in metallurgical chemistry was carried on in Boylston Hall. In 1898–99, the Corporation gave the Carey Athletic Building for the instruction in mining and metallurgy; and in the same year a bequest of $5,000 by Mrs. Rotch to the Lawrence Scientific School was used in making necessary alterations in the building and in partially equipping it. In 1899 the sum of $20,000 was donated by the brothers and sisters of John Simpkins, of the Class of 1885, for the equipment of additional laboratories as a memorial to their brother. The Rotch and Simpkins funds have made it possible partially to adapt the old Carey Building to the needs of the new department. Out of the same funds a wing has been added to the east end of the building, for assaying and smelting work; some of the laboratories have been equipped and some of the more essential apparatus and machinery have been bought. The building is, of course, not as good for the Department of Mining and Metallurgy as one constructed especially for that use, but in the absence of funds necessary for a new building, it can, with the expenditure of a few thousand dollars more, be made to meet the present wants. The work of remodelling and equipping the building has been done by Professor Smyth with admirable judgment, and the money used has been spent to the best possible advantage; but many things requiring further funds yet remain to be done.

"The course of instruction in the Department covers four years, and consists of lectures, laboratory work, reading, and field work. The courses for the first two years are closely related to those of the first two years in the Department of Engineering, with slight changes designed to lead the student up to the courses relating more purely to mining and metallurgy in the third and fourth years. Most of the subjects essential to the education of the mining and metallurgical engineer are treated, but lack of sufficient funds for laboratory equipment has curtailed the full development of certain most important branches, especially metallography, electro-metallurgy, lixiviation of ores, coal mining, and the designing of metallurgical plants.

"From 1896 to 1899, there were two instructors directly connected with the work on mining and metallurgy; in 1899 a third, and in 1900 a fourth, were added.

"In 1895 to 1896, seven students took courses in mining and metallurgy. This number has steadily increased until now the Department includes 46 students and facilities for instruction, especially in the chemical laboratory, are already far too small for the number of students.

"The Department has prospered from its inception, and already includes nine per cent. of the students of the Lawrence Scientific School, having more students than the whole school contained ten years ago. It has progressed much more rapidly than most newly formed technical departments, in spite of the fact that until last year it was without a building, and had to do its work where it could find a chance. The instructors are all active, capable men, devoted to their specialties, and thoroughly equipped to manage their respective parts of the work of the Department.

"After a careful study of the conditions and needs of the Department, we find that the most pressing wants at present are as follows:

"1. An expansion of the instruction.

"2. A more complete equipment of the chemical laboratory, which has already been greatly outgrown, and is in no way commensurate with the requirements of the instruction given in it. The Department cannot do its chemical work in Boylston Hall, where the regular chemical instruction of Harvard University is carried on, as that building is already over-crowded, and, moreover, it is not the place for purely technical work of the laboratory of a Department of Mining and Metallurgy.

"3. Laboratories for metallography, electro-metallurgy and lixiviation of ores (chlorination, cyaniding, etc.).

"4. A fund for maintenance. The Department has already acquired a considerable quantity of mining and metallurgical apparatus and machinery, which requires the attention and care of a skilled mechanic, while attendants for other purposes in the building are required. Moreover, the expenses of water, power and other requisites of the different laboratories have to be met. The Department has had an appropriation of $250 a year from the Corporation for the last two years, as well as a special appropriation of $500 for metallurgy. The laboratory fees have this year amounted to $800. The expenses of the different laboratories have been so far paid from these three sources, but with the increased amount of apparatus and machinery, additional funds will be required for maintenance. With the growing number of students, the laboratory fees will increase, but this addition will not be enough to meet the increased expenses. It has been estimated by those in charge of the Department that a fund which would yield an income of $1,000 yearly, in addition to the laboratory fees and the yearly appropriation from the Corporation, would be enough to cover the running expenses of the whole Department.

"5. More space should be provided in the building for drafting, making models, and for increasing the lecture room facilities. It is estimated by those in charge of the Department that $3,500 will be required properly to equip the chemical laboratory; $2,000 to furnish and equip a drafting room; $10,000 to $12,000 to build an addition to the west end of the building for increased lecture room facilities, to make a basement for a model-making room, and to equip both these additions.

"It is the opinion of your Committee, now that the Department of Mining and Metallurgy has been started and is working on a successful basis, that it should receive the necessary support. Your Committee therefore recommend that an effort be made to secure the above mentioned funds for the Department. They will add greatly to the efficiency of the instruction, and will also enable the Department to handle a largely increased number of students.

"The education of a mining engineer involves the study of probably more different subjects than almost any other technical course. He must be familiar with geology, chemistry, mathematics, physics, electricity, civil engineering, mechanics, metallurgy and assaying, besides other technical subjects. Moreover, he should have a good idea of business matters, and should have a thorough general education in sciences and arts. The life of a mining engineer is often spent in remote regions—far from civilization—in which he has to meet technical, political and business difficulties of all kinds. A man surrounded by these conditions should not only have a technical education, but also the general education necessary to cope with the problems by which he is sure to be confronted. He should be a man capable of becoming a dictator in an isolated community, where he must depend on his own resources to overcome all obstacles and to meet all emergencies, where he is the sole ruler, and where he must know not only how to conduct the purely technical parts of his work, but also how to handle his men, maintain or even initiate a practical organization of the community in which his mine is situated, and make large business transactions. It is an easy matter to educate a man to take charge of a mine or of metallurgical works in the midst of civilization, where he can get assistance and advice at all times, and where most of the business parts of the operation are carried on by others; but to educate a man to take charge of properties in remote regions is a far more difficult problem. With the vast development of mining now going on in western America, Africa, and Asia, the latter class of man is needed, and the demand for his services is rapidly increasing. Many good mining operations to-day are injured or even ruined by the want of such a man. No field of employment to-day offers the same inducements in salary and other opportunities as this does. We believe that with a thoroughly equipped mining department Harvard University can produce a graduate whose capabilities for handling large mining matters will be of a very superior grade, as the instruction in mining can be so interwoven with the general education that a student can obtain not only the necessary technical learning, but also the general education indispensable to a man who is to handle large mining operations.

"Before closing this report your Committee would like to refer to the excellent work done by the instructors in the Department of Mining and Metallurgy. The conception of forming such a department originated with Professor Shaler, Dean of the Lawrence Scientific School, many years ago, but it was not until 1895 that he was able to start it. Since then his advice and assistance have been most important factors in the development of the new Department.

"Professor H. L. Smyth, the head of the Department and Chairman of the Committee of the Faculty in charge, has been most successful in gradually increasing and improving the different courses of instruction, and his administration of the department, in re-arranging the old Carey Building, equipping the different laboratories and making the best out of the limited funds at his command, has been excellent.

"Mr. Sauveur, whose work in metallography has given him a high position in that very important branch of science, has done excellent service in the Department. Mr. White, in charge of the chemical work of the Department, and Mr. Raymer, in charge of the metallurgical work, are deserving of great credit in accomplishing much work with limited facilities."

Penrose's relations with his alma mater were always close. From 1903 to 1906, he was an Associate of the University Museum, concerning which William Morris Davis, professor of Geology at Harvard, wrote him on November 30, 1903 as follows:

My dear Penrose—
When I wrote you recently about your relations to Chicago, it was with the object of seeing if you would come under the definition of an Associate of the University Museum, an honorary appointment, of persons "qualified for and engaged in research or exploration, independent of other scientific institutions." You so clearly did come under that class that our Department recommended your nomination to the Museum Committee, and the Committee has today voted to nominate you for appointment by the Corporation as "Associate in Geology" for three years.

This does not impose any duty on you—it is rather an expression of our interest in and appreciation of your high-class work, and of our hope that, should the Museum contain materials that would aid you, you should make use of them. We like to think of you still as one of us, or one with us.

Few appointments have thus far been made, the position of Associate having been established only last year. The other associate nearest to geology is Springer, in paleontology, author with Wachsmuth of monograph on crinoids.

Will you kindly send me word at your early convenience if you will accept this appointment. I trust your decision will be favorable.

Have you yet learned anything of Furness of Borneo?

Penrose accepted the appointment for a single term, 1903 to 1906.

In 1915–1916 Penrose was a member of the Committee on the Mining School of Harvard, under the chairmanship of Edgar C. Felton, other members being John Hays Hammond, Charles P. Perin, Benjamin B. Thayer, Robert M. Catlin, and Pope Yeatman. Together with the Committee on the School of Engineering of Harvard, also under the chairmanship of Felton, the committee made a report to the Board of Overseers of Harvard College concerning the newly instituted cooperative arrangement with the Massachusetts Institute of Technology and the future of engineering and mining at Harvard.

Penrose's gifts to Harvard for geology and its various fields were generous and long continued. On September 25, 1916, the President and Fellows of Harvard College in Boston voted their "desire to express their gratitude to Mr. Richard A. F. Penrose, Jr., for his generous gift of two hundred and fifty dollars for assistance in Economic Geology." Ten years later, on November 10, 1925, he wrote to Charles F. Adams, treasurer of Harvard University:

Dear Charley:—

Another year has rolled around since I last sent a small contribution for the Geological Department at Harvard University, and I am now taking great pleasure in enclosing my check again for two hundred and fifty dollars ($250.00), to be used for the benefit of the Geological Department in such manner as you may see fit.

I hope you will acept this contribution with my best wishes for the Department for which it is intended and for Harvard University in general. It is always a great pleasure to me to be at least of some little service to the old college from which I graduated over forty years ago.

On November 13, Mr. Adams replied:

My dear Dick:

The College is duly grateful for your welcome gift for the Department of Geology. I like to think that your days in that department contributed something to the success which has come to you.

It is always a pleasure to hear from you, though I must confess to something in the nature of sadness at the thought that it was forty years ago when you were a University stroke and I was a freshman.

In a letter to L. C. Graton, dated June 1, 1923, Penrose said:

"I thank you very much for your letter of May 25th telling me what had been done by the assistance of the Special Fund for Economic Geology.

"I have read the letter with the greatest interest and I feel that no fund of that comparatively small amount could have been spent more advantageously or more to the benfit of the science and of the University than the particular fund in question.

"I realize in saying this that the results of course are due to your excellent management, your thorough familiarity with every detail of the subject, and the broad vision which you take of it. I wish you every success in the continuance of this work, and I will always be interested in its results."

Besides serving on the committee on geology, mineralogy, and petrography, and the one on engineering and mining for many years, contributing freely of his funds to the department of geology and to the various projects put forth by his class, Penrose maintained active relationship with the Harvard Club of Philadelphia and the Harvard Club of New York, where he was a Life Member.

On April 9, 1924, the secretary of the Harvard Club of Philadelphia wrote: "Your kindness in sending your check to help toward the success of the Harvard Club dinner is acknowledged very gratefully. I am sorry you could not be here."

The month following (May 19, 1924) he wrote to Thomas K. Cummins, secretary of the class of 1884 at Harvard:

Dear Tom:—

I have received your notice of May 15th relative to our Class Dinner on July 18th [June 18th] and I am enclosing the return post-card stating that I expect to be present on that occasion.

Some months ago, in reply to your previous circular, I sent you my check for one hundred dollars for the Class Fund. I suppose you have received it, though I have not heard anything to this effect. The only reason I bring up the subject is to say that if the Class Fund is still a little short I will be glad to contribute something more to help it along.

Ten days later, Cummins replied, apologizing for his failure to acknowledge the check and looking forward to seeing him on June 18th. Fate, however, interposed so that instead of being present on the 18th, Penrose sent a telegram of regret on the 16th saying he would be unable to attend. Cummins promptly replied:

"You know that the fortieth anniversary only comes once, so if you can manage to sidetrack other matters, even at the expense of neglecting your duty, try to come on and give us all the pleasure of seeing you."

Penrose could not, of course, "sidetrack" any duty and did not go, but on June 19th he wrote to Cummins that he regretted his inability to go and added, "I regret this all the more because I had been looking forward with pleasure to being present at the celebration of our Fortieth Anniversary.

"I hope, however, that you had a most enjoyable reunion and that no one made any of those speeches about our becoming old men. We have not yet reached the age to think that we are old, and most of us have too much to do even to consider the matter. I personally am beginning to feel that fortieth anniversary is simply one of the early celebrations in the history of a class at Harvard."

Under date of August 19, 1924, Nathan Pereles, secretary of the Associated Harvard Clubs, wrote of the continuation of the Penrose appointment to the Committee on the Shaler Memorial, other members including William Morris Davis and A. J. Garceau.

In October of that year (1924) Penrose wrote to the *Harvard Graduates' Magazine* that he had "received your recent communication regarding subscribing to the *Harvard Graduates Magazine* and I beg to enclose my check for four dollars ($4.00) in payment of this subscription.

"I am a graduate of the Class of 1884, and though I regularly get the *Harvard*

Alumni Bulletin yet through some oversight I have in all these years neglected to subscribe to the *Harvard Graduates' Magazine*. I suppose it is never too late to begin, however, and I shall look forward with pleasure to reading the numbers for this year when they arrive."

That year (1924) Penrose was president of the Academy of Natural Sciences of Philadelphia, as he notes in a letter to Professor Thomas Barbour of the Biological Department of Harvard, to whom he wrote December 19, to "thank you greatly for your papers on 'Biology at Harvard' and 'More about Harvard Biology' which you have so kindly sent me and which I have read with the greatest interest.

"I am glad you have brought out so forcefully not only the needs of the scientific departments at Harvard but also your very timely remarks concerning the service rendered by the collections in a research museum in which specimens are loaned to other workers in the same field. In many ways we are in the same difficulties at The Academy of Natural Sciences of Philadelphia as you are at Harvard, but we live in hopes and in spite of our troubles the Academy is making rapid advancement."

The following March (March 19, 1925) Penrose wrote to Dr. A. G. Kollock, at Darlington, S. C., thanking him for "your kind letter of March 6th and for your expressions of sympathy at the loss of my brother Charley. I know how close you and he were in comparatively recent years when he went south shooting, and he always came back with a pleasant recollection of his having met you again. His loss was a great shock to all of us and I cannot yet get used to what has happened.

"It seems ages since I have seen you but I remember the old days at Harvard when things seemed gayer and brighter and when we were not suppressed by so many iniquitous laws as we are at present.

"Many thanks for your kind inquiries regarding the rest of us. Speck is married and is at present on a trip through the Far East. My brother Philip died many years ago in El Paso, Texas; and I am still the old bachelor that I have always been."

The following month (April) he sent his regrets at being unable to attend the luncheon given the Harvard Glee Club, but also enclosed his check to purchase five tickets for the concert that evening as a token of his interest in the success of the concert.

In May, the Harvard Varsity Club's eleventh annual dinner called for his regrets at not being present, but, he added: "I know, however, that such meetings usually cost somewhat more than is charged for them," so he sent the money to pay for his dinner ticket anyway.

In June, Henry G. Brengle wrote him that "it has been suggested that the Harvard Club of Philadelphia make up a fund to be used as contribution toward the drive for $45,000,000 now under way by the University of Pennsylvania.

"If one hundred members of the Harvard Club would give $100 each, this would create a fund of $10,000, which, as citizens of Philadelphia, would be a graceful evidence of our regard, and a fitting compliment to a sister university.

"Will you be kind enough to let me know if you agree in this and will be willing to contribute $100 to such a fund. If not, do not bother to answer this letter."

Penrose's characteristic reply, addressed to "Dear Brengle" and dated July 1, 1925, was as follows:

"On my return from a few days absence I have received your letter of June 17th and I see clearly that the germ of raiding the already over-burdened City of Philadelphia for funds has even entered your level-headed brain. The conception of the Harvard Club of Philadelphia driving for a fund to help the drive of the University of Pennsylvania is a double inquisition, but has some points of merit, because if the system is followed Philadelphia will soon be drained of all it owns and its sorrows will then be over.

"I often feel like the man who cried out that because 'he would not sell all he had and go out and beg or borrow money to give away he was cussed, discussed, boycotted, talked to, talked about, hung up, robbed and nearly ruined, and that the only reason he was clinging to life was to see what in Hell was coming next.'

"In spite of all these cynical remarks, however, it gives me much pleasure to enclose my check for one hundred dollars ($100.00) as a contribution which you ask for the Harvard Club's Fund for the University of Pennsylvania."

The other "hundred men" were evidently not quite so generous as Penrose, for the sum finally turned over to the University of Pennsylvania for its drive was $8,200. In response to a letter from Nathan Hayward, president of the Harvard Club of Philadelphia, thanking him for his help in the drive, Penrose answered under date of August 31, 1925:

"I am greatly pleased that this action on the part of the Harvard Club of Philadelphia has been so thoroughly appreciated by the University of Pennsylvania, and I think that it was a most excellent move by our Club. I am very glad indeed to have been one of the contributors to the fund, and I feel that you deserve the thanks of all the members of the Harvard Club for having consummated the conception of this gift."

Perhaps his budget for Harvard that year was exhausted by these contributions, perhaps he did not wish to contribute to the particular cause; at any rate on November 16 (1925) he wrote to Charles Palache that he was unable to contribute to the purchase of the Woodworth library for Harvard, although he had "heard of the death of our most worthy friend Professor Woodworth, last summer and was greatly grieved, for I had known him since the time that I was in Harvard and I always had the greatest regard for him as a geologist and a teacher." And then he added: "I regret this (inability to contribute) because, as you know, I have always felt the deepest interest and sympathy with the Department of Geology at Harvard, and I have on different occasions made contributions to it. I hope that you may be able to raise the money you need from some other source, and that in the future I may be able to contribute for some other worthy purpose in your Department."

During the summer of 1902, the list of Penrose journeys shows that he "made several trips to Arizona, California, and Colorado, on mining business."

During that summer, also, he obviously had a visit with Herbert Hoover, for, on October 17, 1902, Penrose wrote to Hoover, who had returned to England, as follows:

My dear Hoover:—

When you were here during the summer, you were looking for men that might be useful to you in your foreign mining operations. There is a young fellow whom I have known since he was a boy, a graduate of the mining school of McGill College of Montreal, who might be of some use to you. He has had several years experience in British Columbia, both in managing small properties and in reporting on others. He has also had some experience in Arizona where he acted for some time as assayer for our Company. His father was an American and his mother was English. He is very intelligent and hard working, and understands his profession thoroughly. He is probably about 30 years old, and I personally would have a great deal of confidence in his ability, though he has not had as wide an experience as some other men. He probably would not as yet do for one of the larger positions which you wanted to fill, but he may be of considerable service to you in a subordinate position. If you should ever be in need of such a man I will be glad to put you in communication with him.

I hope you are meeting with success in your mining operations, and that we will see you in this country again before long.

Sincerely yours,
R. A. F. Penrose, Jr.

The Hoover reply, written on the letterhead of the firm of Bewick, Moreing & Co., "Mining Engineers and Mine Managers," shows that Herbert C. Hoover is now a member of the firm, the other members being C. Algernon Moreing, A. Stanley Rowe, and Thomas W. Wellsted, and that the scene of their operations includes Johannesburg, Transvaal Colony; Kalgoorlie, Western Australia; Auckland, New Zealand; Tientsin, China; and Tarkwa, Gold Coast Colony. The letter is dated October 28, 1902, from 20 Copthall Avenue, London, and reads as follows:

My dear Penrose,

I am in receipt of yours of the 17th October, and I shall be wanting some men pretty soon, but I have not as yet settled for a partner in Western Australia and until then I do not feel like engaging anybody to work under him.

In regard to the process for treating telluride ores, of which I spoke to you and which is so successful in Western Australia, I enclose you, herewith, an article read before the Institute of Mining & Metallurgy here upon the matter.
....

Since the pamphlet which I send you was written, we have reduced the expense of working this process, on the Lake View Mine, where a monthly tonnage of 6,000 tons is handled, to 19/- per ton, excluding the General Management of the Company. This figure includes all treatment and metallurgical salaries, assaying, etc., and power of £ 5 per h.p. per month, and only excludes the salary of the General Manager of the Company and his office staff.

I find on reference to the Hannan's Brownhill that the power item amounts to about 28% of the total expenditure, and as at Cripple Creek this cost of power could be reduced by fully 80%, you will see that the working costs at Cripple Creek could be brought down to close on 15/– per ton, especially in view of the fact that we also have to pay for water out of this 15/–, and also have inferior labour to that at Cripple Creek. This would, in round terms, amount to about $3.75 per ton. I, therefore, believe that this is a process which will sooner or later be introduced into Cripple Creek.

Letter from Penrose to H. C. Hoover, Esq., % Bewick, Moreing & Company, 20 Copthall Avenue, London, E.C., England, dated January 14, 1903

My dear Hoover:—

Your letter of October 28th was forwarded to me in the west, and I have submitted the pamphlet which you sent me to the milling company controlled by my brother and his friends. Your process certainly seems to have some good features, but I do not think that the cost in Cripple Creek would be as low as you estimate. Though as I have had very little experience in Cripple Creek in this direction myself, I do not feel able to form an accurate opinion. I will write to you further after I have heard from the people to whom I submitted the pamphlet.

With best regards, and wishing you all the good wishes of the New Year, I am,

Sincerely yours,

R. A. F. Penrose, Jr.

CHAPTER 11

Beginnings of Utah Copper

OF 1903 with its momentous changes in his life, Penrose with his accustomed modesty wrote (in a sketch of his life, dated December 27, 1928) that he "resigned as President of the Commonwealth Mining and Milling Company, and proceeded to Utah, where he became one of the founders, together with his brother Spencer Penrose, D. C. Jackling and Charles M. MacNeill, of the Utah Copper Company, which has since become a very important organization."

Today, one of the great sights of the world is Bingham Canyon, Utah, where the great open-pit mines of the Utah Copper Company represent the largest individual movement of material of any kind made by man in world history. It is famous in mining history as the first great mine to prove that the theory, advanced by a young metallurgist named Daniel C. Jackling, for the utilization of low-grade copper ore was workable and eminently profitable.

In 1903, however, Bingham was just another mining community near Salt Lake City, its fabulous future undreamed of, even by its promoters. To be sure, it was one of the oldest of the Utah mining districts, having been worked since 1864, but its early history centered upon its production of silicious gold ore and silver-bearing lead ores. Today, it is famous as the largest single producer of copper in the world, the first shipment of copper ore having been made from the Highland Boy mine in December, 1896.

Jackling, whose story is as romantic as that of any Alger hero—a poor farmer boy who worked his way through the Missouri School of Mines, walked to Cripple Creek in its early boom days because he did not have the fare necessary to ride the stage which connected Cripple Creek with Divide, a station on the Colorado-Midland Railroad, twenty miles away, and became one of the most famous among famous American mining men—had been consulting engineer with MacNeill and Spencer Penrose. They knew his ability to work and had confidence in his judgments, but before they invested the money needed for the development of the Bingham mines, they consulted Dick Penrose. When he decided that Jackling's concept and the geological lay of the land warranted the venture, the die was cast and Utah Copper Company began its spectacular career.

According to Jackling,* the only member of the quartet living when this book was compiled, "neither he (Penrose) or others of his Colorado associates had ever heard of that prospect prior to January 1903, when, after a matter of four years of continuous and mostwise active interest in the deposit, I presented it to

* Letter from D. C. Jackling to H. R. Fairbanks, dated March 25, 1942.

Charles M. MacNeill for consideration in the early part of 1903. The data embodied in this presentation included my favorable report on the property rendered to my then employer, Joseph R. DeLamar, in September, 1899.* There is nothing in my recollection or records to indicate that Mr. Penrose ever visited Bingham until June, 1903, when he accompanied MacNeill, Spencer Penrose and myself to Bingham. . . . Charles M. MacNeill was the dominating spirit and influence in the small group which achieved its initial success in mining industry in the early days of development of the Cripple Creek District, where and when, beginning in 1893, I first became acquainted and, in a limited way, associated with the original MacNeill-Penrose group."

Of that beginning, Dick wrote to his father from Salt Lake City, under date of June 15, 1903:

"I expect to start for San Francisco tomorrow, and I thought I would drop a line to you from here before going.

"I wrote you last from Colorado Springs. From there, Speck, MacNeill, Tutt and I came here, where we have been working for the last few days perfecting the details of our copper deal. We have organized a company called the Utah Copper Company, and will carry on our operations in this way instead of as individuals. Speck and MacNeill wanted me to be president of the Co., but I did not accept, as I did not want to be tied down too much, and I can be just as much use to the Co. without being an officer, so they elected me a director. They elected MacNeill president, and Speck secretary and treasurer, and an excellent man named Jackling, general manager. Tutt will probably be vice president.

"We are gradually getting in shape here to go to work, and by the time we leave we hope to have made satisfactory preliminary arrangements. Our idea is to erect as soon as possible a mill with a capacity of about 500 tons of ore daily. It will take several months to finish this, and MacNeill and Jackling will look after the construction while Speck is on his hunting trip and I am in Alaska.

"We have spent a lot of time in making arrangements with the principal owner of the copper mine for the interests that we have options on from him, but this matter is now settled, and the papers are in the bank ready to be taken up by us if, after our mill is built, we decide that it is wise to put up the remaining money due on the property.

"We are today trying to get a suitable place to locate the mill, and as we need a lot of water for the mill, it is necessary to be very careful in the selection of a location, but we hope to get one.

"Speck and MacNeill return to Colorado Springs tomorrow, and from there Speck goes to join Boies in British Columbia. I will send this letter to you at Phila., as you said you expected to return there on your way to Seal Harbor about the 20th. I have not heard from you since I left Philadelphia, but if you have written, I suppose I will get the letter in San Francisco, as I believe I gave

---

* For the full story of the development of Bingham Canyon, *see* A. B. Parsons: *The Porphyry Coppers*, 1933. Published by A. I. M. & M. E.

that to you as my address. I will write fully from there about my Alaska plans. We are all well. Speck is in good shape, and I never felt better.

"I hope you will have a good summer in Seal Harbor, and that you will find the place as attractive as ever.

"P.S. Until I write further, my address will be Palace Hotel, San Francisco, Cal."

Concerning the matter, Jackling himself said* that "they invested for themselves and quite a number of associates and friends the modest amount of $500,000.00, which was all the money made available to me for developing the mine and building the commercial scale experimental plant at Copperton. $500,000.00 was the full authorized capital of the original Utah Copper Company, a Colorado corporation. It was not until after this original development corporation had been supplanted by the New Jersey company of higher capitalization that the Messrs. Guggenheim bought $3,000,000.00 of convertible bonds of the New Jersey corporation of the same name, viz.: Utah Copper Company."

Of his own participation, Jackling wrote in the same letter that "in the early days of the Utah Copper Mine I had very little money with which to acquire and retain a financial interest in the enterprise, and such security-owning interest as I had was paid for in money at exactly the same price per share as that paid by MacNeill, the Penrose brothers, or anyone else."

That the faith of these men in Jackling and the venture was more than justified has long been known. According to the "Approximate Balance Sheet of the Utah Copper Mine, showing disposition of 'new' capital and operating profits up to December 31, 1931,"† the total net income up to that time had been $296,565,000.00.

According to Jackling, "the gross value of production from the beginning to December 31, 1941 was $931,034,368.44, this being the gross proceeds of the sale of all metals produced to that date. The net income derived from such production was $434,186,454.76 (before depreciation and federal taxes were deducted) or $323,348,118.04 (after deducting depreciation and taxes). The gross value of production for the year 1941 was $78,698,765.75, and the net income for that year was $44,936,093.08 (before depreciation and federal taxes were deducted) or $23,892,908.30 (after deducting depreciation and taxes)."‡

Of this association, Jackling wrote to Charles P. Berkey on April 12, 1939:

"You doubtless know that by far the major part of Mr. Penrose's fortune came from the several mining and metallurgical industries conceived, developed and operated by me, beginning with the Utah Copper enterprise in 1903. Prior to that time my acquaintance with Dr. Penrose had been scarcely more than casual.

........Our later association developed into not only a very warm mutual

---
* Letter from D. C. Jackling to H. R. Fairbanks, dated March 25, 1942
† A. B. Parsons: *The Porphyry Coppers* (1933) p. 93
‡ Letter of D. C. Jackling to H. R. Fairbanks, dated March 25, 1942

friendship, but an equally genuine mutual admiration from both personal and professional standpoints. Penrose's counsel and support, financially and otherwise, were of inestimable value to me in creating the Utah enterprise and other similar ones that followed it, which at their inception were subject to derision by mining engineers and engineering publications, and, in fact, characterized by some as reprehensible schemes of a get-rich-quick order, the promoters of which should be subjected to punishment.

"As regards my business and professional association with Penrose, my files are outstanding as evidencing his continuing encouragement and commendation. That characteristic was one of the prime elements of this great man's nature. He was not only kindly in disposition, but generous in lending his great abilities in support of either person or cause that appealed to him as worthy.

"When he, his brothers, and their associates decided to lend financial aid to the Utah enterprise, they had no thought, any more than I had conception, of the vastness of its potentialities. These gentlemen knew me as a former employee in some of their early Colorado enterprises. They had faith in my integrity and confidence in my technical ability. They were all somewhat skeptical about the possibilities of the Utah undertaking as I represented them, but they knew my statements and prognostications were sincere. Penrose and his associates had witnessed other undreamed of, almost inconceivable, occurrences in the creation and advancement of mineral industries of the intermountain region of the United States. Their decision to support me in what appeared to be an adventurous undertaking to say the least was based more on personal sentiment than upon business reason—in other words, upon the reflection of human interest rather than upon the assurance of material gain. For all the long years of my association with Dick, his brothers and their friends, no one was more ardent in continuing declarations of commendation, or could have been, than was Dick Penrose in recognition of an achievement that was beyond comprehension at the outset and in large measure so up to the time of Penrose's death.

"My association with Penrose in a strictly speaking social way was never especially close. I was busy in my own field and he in his, and our meetings were all too rare; but when it was my pleasure to be with him, I enjoyed his companionship as much as that of any friend I have known. His friendship was of genuine, lasting, wholehearted order rarely experienced. He enjoyed the lighter occupations of life as thoroughly as he recognized its weightier obligations. The rod and the gun, in company with out-of-the-way places to use them, inspired him to heights of almost boyish enthusiasm.

"I cannot recall any specific occurrences that would serve as subjects of interesting anecdote. The man's simple and kindly greatness of nature was so ever-expressive that incidental evidences of it which might otherwise be employed as the basis of anecdote became matters of course.

"I have no expectation that you would care to or could use anything that I have said in terms; but, if I have been able to convey some measure of my conception of my friend's majesty as man and scientist that you can frame in words of your own, I will have achieved an end deeply gratifying to me. I thank you for affording me the opportunity to make the effort."

Surely no man ever received a finer tribute from a fellow worker. Jackling graciously loaned his files for use in the preparation of this book, and from it the following excerpts are taken:

Letter from Penrose to Jackling, dated December 13, 1910

It seems a long time since I have seen you. Do you never intend to come east again? I hope we will see you here before very long. I was west during the summer, and had intended to stop in at Salt Lake City to see you, but found that you had gone to Arizona, so I did not stop over there. I hope everything is going well with you, and that your mining propositions are prospering.

Letter from Jackling to Penrose, dated December 26, 1910

I also hope the next time you come west you will let me know so that I can make arrangements to meet you. I am traveling so much that I could see you in California most any time, either going to or returning from our southwestern properties. Everything is moving along very nicely with me and I am consequently in a mood to enjoy to the full the existing season.

Letter from Penrose to Jackling, dated November 9, 1911

I drop a line to you to congratulate you on the most excellent quarterly report of the Utah Copper Company as of September 30, 1911. The reduction in cost per pound of copper from 8.02¢ to 7.56¢ as against the previous quarter certainly shows excellent work; and when it is considered that this was done in spite of having to treat lower grade ore in the last quarter than in the previous quarter, the result is remarkable. I think that every stockholder ought to appreciate greatly your excellent management of the property, and I wish you every success in your future operations.

I hope you have had a good trip in your round of the copper mines and that you found everything to your satisfaction.

I hope it will not be long before we see you in the east again.

Letter from Jackling, dated "enroute, Denver to Salt Lake City, Utah, November 15, 1911

My dear Dick,—

I thank you heartily for your kind letter of November ninth which I have just received as I am returning from a trip to Ray and Chino. I think we are doing very well in Utah, under the circumstances, but we won't really begin to show the results that I have been striving for until we are operating at full tonnage which I hope will be not later than this time next year. We will then produce results that I believe will be very gratifying to all concerned in the property and very astonishing to those who have not believed in it.

Things are working out in a fairly satisfactory way at the other properties.

They have been a little slow at both, but big things usually are slow, and while the delays in accomplishing just what we have expected are more or less disappointing, they should not be considered in any sense discouraging.

We had a very pleasant trip. Left Spec at Colorado Springs this morning and Charley at Denver this afternoon. So far as I now know, I will not be East until our annual meetings in the spring, although it may be that I will take a short trip to New York about the first of the year.

A month later, Penrose wrote to Jackling that he had sent him cigars "which I hope you will smoke with my best wishes for a Merry Christmas and a Happy New Year," and then he adds, a bit wistfully perhaps, "I wish I could be in Salt Lake on Christmas and have a smoke with you."

"I too wish that it were possible for us to spend a Christmas together," replied Jackling on December 22 (1911). "I had expected that I might go east this year for New Year's, but it is impossible for me to do so. It is of course gratifying for me to be able to report that things are moving along nicely with all the properties now. We have had the same sort of delays and disappointments at Ray that always occur with new propositions and doubtless we will have some of the same thing at Chino, although the plant is starting off in a good deal better form than applied to the early operations at Ray. These things, however, are only temporary and ere long they will have been forgotten and the properties be operating just like Utah is. I possibly may be a little self-satisfied in doing so, but I cannot help but agree with you that Utah is doing splendidly. Before you receive this you will doubtless have heard from the other boys that Utah's earnings for the month of November were nearly $600,000 including railroad earnings. We cannot expect during the cold weather that will apply for the next two months, to do quite as well as we would do otherwise, but Utah will come out in the spring and summer in a way that will more nearly indicate its possibilities, and I have no hesitation at all in predicting that by this time next year we will be accomplishing things that will not only please the stockholders, but will greatly surprise the copper-producing world."

"I was sorry not to have seen you in New York last week" Penrose wrote to Jackling under date of June 5, 1916. "John Montgomery and I called on you at the Ritz-Carlton Hotel about four o'clock Saturday afternoon, but were told that you were out. We left a card for you. I hope to have better luck the next time I am in New York, and in the meanwhile, I am very glad indeed to know that you are safely back in the United States after your long voyage. I hope you had a pleasant and successful trip in every way."

In December of that same year (1916) in the course of his annual letter of transmittal of his Christmas-gift cigars, Penrose wrote to Jackling, "I was very glad to have seen you in New York last week... I congratulate you most heartily on the splendid results you are producing at the Utah, Chino and Ray properties, and on the wonderful ability you have shown in their management."

In August (20th) 1919, Penrose wrote enthusiastically to Jackling:

My dear Jack:

I feel that I must drop a line to you to congratulate you on the wonderful increase in the percentage of saving in copper metal as shown in the recent quarterly reports of the Utah, Chino and Ray Copper Companies. It is splendid; and I can see in it the result of the long and careful study you have given to this subject. It is a result I always felt that you, with your wonderful genius for such matters, would eventually work out."

In reply, Jackling wrote from San Francisco, August 26 (1919) as follows:

My dear Dick:—

I am very appreciative of the contents of your letter of August 20th. It is true that the improvement in results at the Arthur plant are little less than remarkable, but we have been sustaining them now for a sufficiently long period to be sure that we cannot only maintain them at Arthur, but duplicate them at Magna when the latter plant is similarly provided with flotation equipment. It has been a very long pull to develop satisfactory flotation methods for application to Utah ores, which we find have been more difficult to treat by this method than the ores at any of the other properties. You will recall that we only began experimenting with flotation about the time the war commenced, and thereafter for the better part of two years we were trying to devise something that would meet the requirements in Utah without the use of acid. After the acid plant at Garfield Smelter, in which we own an interest, was constructed, we determined that an acid state was necessary in order to accomplish good recoveries, and at the same time make an acceptable grade of concentrates, and up to date we have never been able to get away from this. All the time we were endeavoring to develop the process, we were hampered by the perplexing legal questions constantly arising in the Butte & Superior litigation, and lost a great deal of time in an endeavor to avoid using something upon which the Minerals Separation Company could exact contracts that would mean millions of dollars. We are now operating with more than twenty pounds of oil, and presumably are clear of the Minerals Separation process, but it is an expensive proceeding, and I hope before too long something will develop to clear the atmosphere and permit us to use a more economical process as regards quantities of oil and other re-agents. We have not begun the installation of a flotation plant at Magna yet, or at least have only barely begun it, partly because we have been uncertain as to the type of plant we ought to build to operate at the least cost. One other reason for not having gotten further with the application of flotation at Magna was that the Arthur plant was not finished until early this year, and it was impossible during the wartime to get enough workmen to carry along construction at both plants even if we had felt warranted in doing so in the face of the high cost of everything. Since the Magna plant has been closed on account of curtailment of production, the situation has not changed much. Workmen are scarce, costs of everything are just as high as they were during the war period, and we have felt therefore that it would be best to use our limited forces in the completion of other improvements, particularly in the fine grinding department of the Magna plant, which were already in progress, and let construction on flotation rest until the atmosphere both from an industrial viewpoint and that of litigation cleared somewhat. All of the work necessary in the Magna plant to bring it up to a capacity of about 24,000 tons per day has been practically completed, so that when we can operate that plant again, it will be just as efficient as the Arthur plant is now, with the exception of the flotation feature, and this can be applied very rapidly.

I suppose you know pretty much all about the troubles we are having at Nevada. It seems that there is no means of keeping peace in the family at that point and now would appear to be as good a time for a shutdown as any other time. On the whole I presume that we should consider ourselves fortunate that we have not had more labor troubles at our properties during and since the war. Our wages have not been any higher than elsewhere, and in most cases not as high, but still we have been freer from disturbances of this kind than any of the other copper mines that I know about.

With kind regards, I am,

Sincerely yours,
D. C. Jackling

In thanking Penrose for his Christmas cigars that year (1919) Jackling added, "More than all, however, I value the personal friendship which prompts you to remember me at each holiday time."

The following year (December 10, 1920) in his annual Christmas letter, Penrose declared that "I know that it seems like sending coals to New Castle to send cigars to San Francisco, where probably the best cigars in the world can be gotten, but this small gift which I am sending you means more than the cigars, for it is an expression of my deep appreciation of your friendship and the wonderful manner in which you are managing the companies under your control."

In his reply (December 27, 1920), Jackling added: "Mr. Herrin was in for a toddy with us Christmas afternoon and spoke about how much he enjoyed his recent visit with you here. He tells me he is trying to figure out some way to take a vacation trip with you. I can understand how he would like to do this. Nothing would please me so much as to be able to do it myself."

Letter from Penrose to Jackling, dated Philadelphia, December 5, 1921

My dear Jack:—

I sent you by express a couple of days ago from New York some cigars of the brand Romeo and Juliet Seleccion de Lux, with my best wishes for a Merry Christmas. I wrote a letter about them to you the next day. The letter was written hastily by the stenographer in the hotel and she inadvertently spelled your name wrong by omitting the "k".

I write now to apologize most sincerely for this unintentional mistake, and I cannot yet understand how the letter slipped through without my noticing the error, but I hope that you will excuse it.

With kindest regards, I am,

Sincerely yours,
R. A. F. Penrose, Jr.

In his reply, Jackling said: "I regret that you were not at the Directors' meetings as the atmosphere was quite a little more reassuring than it has been for some time in the past. It looks now like another two or three months at the most would see the worst of our troubles over and such a prospect is about as good a Christmas present as either one of us could wish from a material standpoint. I am hoping that next Christmas will bring conditions that will justify real and mutual congratulation."

On January 10, 1922, Penrose again wrote to Jackling, saying: "I have received your very kind note of the 5th inst., with clipping from the San Francisco Chronicle of January 4th, containing your interview concerning my brother, Senator Penrose.

"I cannot tell you how much I appreciate your kind words concerning my brother, for I know that but few people knew him better than you did and the picture you have drawn of him in your interview is so absolutely true that I do not think that even a member of his family could portray his character better.

"His life was spent in public service and the subject of gain or profit never entered his head. In fact, he died a comparatively poor man. His only ambition seemed to be to carry out the duties of his office in a loyal and self-sacrificing manner. I believe that the unremitting manner in which he stuck to his post was one of the causes which hastened his death."

A year later (January 2, 1923) Jackling wrote that "You have been one of my staunchest friends and supporters for a very long time, and I believe you know that my appreciation and reciprocation of all this is most genuine."

On December 17 (his birthday), 1923, Penrose wrote in his annual letter to "Jack" that "I only wish that I could be in San Francisco at Christmas time to have a smoke with you. I remember well my visit with you there about a year ago and I hope to repeat it again if I have a chance to come to the Pacific Coast during the coming year."

A year later he was still looking forward to that pleasure, for in his letter of December 10, 1924, he says, "It has been a long time since I have seen you in San Francisco, but I hope to be there some time next year and I am looking forward to the pleasure of seeing you there."

On December 15, 1925, he again wrote to Jackling, again sending cigars and wishing him a Merry Christmas, and adding, "I have as yet no plans for coming to California, but I expect to resign my work as President of The Academy of Natural Sciences of Philadelphia this coming winter, and I will then have a freer foot to travel. I will look forward then with pleasure to coming to the Pacific Coast."

In a letter, dated October 14, 1926, Jackling wrote to Penrose that "the principal purpose of this note is to tell you that I have recently created a President's Gold Medal for employees and officers of the Utah Copper Company who have been affiliated with its operations and business for twenty years. There are only four of the old official list who will be entitled to this medal, viz: yourself, Spec, Hayden and myself. By the end of this year there will be nineteen employees who will qualify in length of service. The medals to be awarded up to the end of 1926 are ready for engraving, and I request that you tell me how you want your name to appear, that is whether R. A. F. Penrose or R. A. F. Penrose, Jr.

"These medals are beautifully designed, the size of a $20 gold piece and containing $20 in gold value. They are distinctly a President's medal. I have not made them a Utah Copper Company medal for the reason that I did not want to establish a precedent that some future administration might not wish to perpetuate."

In his reply (October 15, 1926) Penrose declared that he had "read with much interest your plan to present the President's Gold Medal to those who have been affiliated with the operation and business of Utah Copper Company for twenty years; and I feel much honored that you should consider me worthy of one of these medals.

"You ask me if I would like my name to appear simply as R. A. F. Penrose or R. A. F. Penrose, Jr. I would suggest that you let it appear as 'R. A. F. Penrose, Jr.' I retain the 'Jr.' not out of any affectation but as a business necessity, in order to avoid complications in matters in which my father was connected."

In his annual Christmas letter that year (1926) Penrose said: "I was sorry to have seen so little of you when you were in New York, but somehow everyone seemed to be after you and I had not much chance to see you. I hope, however, that you and those of us who represent the Old Guard may get together some time soon."

Another interesting letter to Penrose of that same period is from C. M. McNeill, president of Utah Copper Company and is dated New York, November 8, 1917. After addressing him as "My dear Dick," McNeill says, with an almost audible chuckle: "Played a rather good trick on you today. At a meeting of the Board of Directors of Utah Copper today Mr. Eugene Meyer, Jr., resigned, and at my suggestion—which was backed by Hayden, and in fact all of the directors—you were elected to fill the vacancy thus occurring.

"I hope very much indeed that you will find it convenient and desirable to serve, as your advice and counsel, particularly now when things are more or less strenuous, will be more than ever valued. As a matter of fact, my reason for suggesting this, which has always been in my mind and I know it has been in the minds of some of the other directors, was occasioned by your own remark at lunch last Saturday, and therefore I assumed upon our old acquaintance and friendship to this extent. I can heartily congratulate the Utah Copper Company.

"Am sending this to you by Spec, as he says he is to see you later in the day."

Another letter from McNeill, this time as president of the Chino Copper Company and dated New York, April 16, 1920, is similar.

"Dear Dick," he says, "just as a formality, and to let you know that formal action has been taken concerning the matter I have talked to you about several times, it gives me pleasure to now advise you that you have been elected a member of the Board of Directors of Chino Copper Company at the stockholders' meeting held in Portland today. I think the Company is to be congratulated on your consenting to become a member of the Board."

But to return to 1903 and its changes. It is a tribute to Penrose, the man and his methods, that although he parted business ways with his partners of many years' standing—Brockman and Barringer—he remained on the best of terms with them until death intervened.

When he became convinced of the possibilities in Utah Copper, he made it a matter of honor to point out these possibilities to his old friends and partners, as is shown by Brockman's letter to him, which follows, and an undated and unsigned letter in Penrose's handwriting—presumably his own copy of his reply.

Letter from Brockman to Penrose, dated Pearce, Arizona, June 4, 1903

Dear Mr. Penrose:

I have received your favor of the 25th ulto.

In regard to the Utah copper proposition, the amount of stock mentioned, namely one or two thousand shares is entirely too small to bother with; I am looking for larger fish. I know of course that there are more or less chances to be taken in any mining venture and always invest accordingly.

I hope the meeting went off smoothly on June 1st. I was sorry not to be there, but owing to our $25,000.00 damage suit it was impossible to get away. I expect Mr. Goodrich out here in a few days to look over the ground. I feel very confident of winning the case, it all depends however on the jury we secure. Miners will stay with one another regardless of the testimony in a damage suit, and if there are any miners on the jury we may be forced to carry our case to the Supreme Court.

I just received a letter from W. J. Smith enclosing release duly signed by Mrs. Harrison Smith, widow of the pumpman killed while you were here. That case is therefore closed.

Everything here continues about the same as usual. I have discontinued work in the 7th level winze. We crosscut to the footwall and drifted along the footwall 35 feet without finding any values.

I want your opinion as well as Mr. Barringer's about sinking another hundred feet. I do not care to take the responsibility of sinking without your opinion. I do not want you to leave it to my judgement, but want your candid opinion.

If you both decide to sink we will do so; otherwise I will take no steps toward doing so.

I hope you have a pleasant trip in the north and find some good mines. Be careful however, that you don't get froze in before you start back. I prefer to remain in Arizona where it is warm.

Kindly thank your Father for his invitation to stop with him in Philadelphia and express my sincere regrets at not being able to see him again.

With best regards, I am

Sincerely yours,
John Brockman

Letter from Penrose to Brockman, undated, but written on Palace Hotel, San Francisco, stationery, obviously just before sailing for Alaska in 1903

My dear Brockman

Your letter of June 4th has been forwarded to me here and only just received here. Hence my delay in replying. I note what you say about the copper proposition and I fear I did not make myself clear to you in my letter of May 25th. You say 1000 or 2000 shares are too small to bother with. I did not mean that this was all you could get, but only suggested it to you as a flyer. Barringer would not take any of it. He said he had no money to spare, but whether this was really his reason, or whether he did not like the proposition, I don't know. When Barringer would not come in, I did not like to urge you too hard, and this is the reason I suggested only a small amount, especially as the whole thing is a good deal of an experiment.

[crossed out:—I can get more stock if you want it, but again I want to impress on you that I am not urging it on you. If you want to come into the company please let]

If you do not want to come into the deal because you do not like the scheme, of course that is all right, and perhaps you are wise as the ore is very low grade. But if you are keeping out because you thought you could not get enough stock, please let me know how much you would like, and I will at once see what can be done. But please bear in mind that I am not urging you to come into the scheme. All I want to do is to find out what your wishes are.

My boat sails for Alaska in a few days, so I will be greatly obliged if you will wire me here on receipt of this letter and let me know your wishes in this copper matter.

Etc., etc., etc.

Years later (December 26, 1923) Brockman, then a retired millionaire, wrote to Penrose from the Brockman Building in Los Angeles: "It was a great pleasure to receive your package of Coronas and I have already enjoyed several fine smokes which I sincerely wish you might have shared. You never forget the pleasure I take in a good smoke and counting back yesterday, as I comfortably puffed one of your fine cigars, I realized that for more than twenty years you have given me this pleasure at Christmas time. I assure you your remembrance of me is greatly appreciated and while I smoke I recall many of the good days we spent together and wish we might live them over again."

In a letter from Cuba, dated two months later (February 14, 1924) Brockman again makes mention of the old days, saying, "I find I have come to Cuba some years too late. If I were a few years younger I would sail into the gambling and drinking with the best of them, as in the old days in New Mexico, but now I find I must give my years their due."

In April (1924) Brockman again wrote to Penrose, saying that he had contracted pneumonia on his way home from Cuba, but was getting along, although "it is tedious business recovering my strength but it is impossible to keep a tough old specimen like myself down for long so I hope to be about and able to complete my travels by a trip to our old resort, Apache Tajo, pretty soon."

Penrose replied on May 5 (1924): "I hope you will have no further return of this ailment, for I remember the very bad time you had years ago in Silver City when you had a former attack of pneumonia and when it was only by Coal Oil Johnny keeping you filled up with good stout milk punches that you pulled through the crisis. Remember that there are not many Coal Oil Johnnies around these days, so please be careful of your health."

In June (1924) Brockman wrote once more, recalling Coal Oil Johnny, and saying that he had had "a very pleasant visit from Barringer last week. He was in Arizona on business and came on to Southern California for a few days. He looks very well and has not changed much since I last saw him."

According to the clipping which Brockman enclosed in his letter, Barringer had been visiting at Meteor Crater, Arizona, which he and a group of associates had owned for some years and had spent considerable money trying to find the meteor which had caused the crater. At that time he was considering the sinking of a 1509-foot shaft at some distance from the rim, thinking that perhaps the meteor had plunged into the earth at an angle. It was subsequently found in such a position.

Penrose, in his reply of July 16(1924) says: "We have had a fairly good summer so far, though the last week or two have been a little hot. I am getting a little tired of staying in one place, for I am not used to this sort of confinement and I hope next fall to have a freer foot and possibly to come out to Los Angeles by way of the Panama Canal to see you. The modern railroads of to-day going west are not what they used to be when you and I traveled east and west so much. They are always fearfully crowded with people and the new steel cars become so hot in the summer that they are almost intolerable. There is no longer any such comfort as you and I used to find when we got the fast California Express to stop at our station at Cochise, Arizona, and take us on board into a good, cool, old-fashioned pullman car. They say that the iron cars are safer than the wooden ones, but I would prefer to be smashed up comfortably in a wooden car than to be roasted to death in a broiling hot iron car."

On December 27 (1924), Brockman again wrote to thank Penrose for the cigars, saying, "for twenty-five or thirty years I have smoked your good Christmas cigars and although I do not need them to remind me of our friendship of long standing, I very much appreciate your kind rememberance of me each year, and take much pleasure in the many good smokes I have from your box."

In his reply (January 15, 1925), Penrose said: "It was a very great pleasure to me to hear from you... and to know that those small cigars which I sent you have reached you all right. I do not know whether or not you have yet switched to a large cigar, but the ones I sent you are the small ones like you and I used to smoke together in the old days. I only wish that I was in Los Angeles to have a good old-time smoke with you and see how we would stand on a game of dominoes."

On February 27 (1925) Brockman wrote that he was "being taken into the city of Glendale, much against my will. If things keep building up around me I am going to hunt a hole in the desert and crawl into it, but will try to notify you when I change my address to Apache Tajo, for you might like to visit me there sometime... I hope that Dr. Penrose [Charles B. Penrose] is enjoying his stay in the South, and will return much improved in health, and that you and Spencer are very well... I have just had an interesting letter from the curator of the Peabody Museum, of Cambridge, in which he describes some excavations which have been made on the Mimbres River, near the site of my old mill, where a very complete Indian pueblo has been uncovered. I am glad that responsible people are taking an interest in these relics at last so that some of them will be saved."

On March 11 (1925) Brockman once more wrote to Penrose, this time a letter of sympathy on the death of his brother Tal [Dr. Charles Penrose], the news of which had been sent him by Barringer. Then on March 30, Penrose received a telegram saying that Brockman had died that night of pneumonia.

In writing to Brockman's daughter, Margaret Brockman Thompson, Penrose, addressing her as "Dear Margaret," said: "I shall always remember with the greatest pleasure the many years in which your father and I were associated in mining in New Mexico and Arizona, and still later our continued friendship after he moved to California. The times are vivid in my memory when I used to visit your father and mother at your house in Los Angeles, and many an agreeable time we had there.

"I shall always treasure the memory of your father as that of a broad, liberal, kind and sympathetic friend, loyal in both good times and bad, and one of the few men in this world on whom one could always rely."

Of Barringer, the remaining member of this triumvirate, Penrose wrote, in 1930, in an obituary notice for the Boone and Crockett Club, that "he had a picturesque personality, full of human sympathy and enthusiasm in all fields that interested him. As a Trustee of the Jefferson Hospital in Philadelphia he took the same interest in saving human life as he took in hunting big game in the West, or in quail shooting in the South, or in duck shooting on the Atlantic Seaboard. As game in the West became scarce he was as enthusiastic an advocate of its conservation as he was in his interest in human conservation in the Jefferson Hospital.

"He never sought game in Africa, Asia, or South America, not because he disliked those countries but because in the time of his active career the western part of the United States, particularly the Rocky Mountains, the Sawtooth range, the Salmon river valley and innumerable other sections, swarmed with game.

"These regions were the huntsman's paradise; no blight of civilization had yet arrived; game wardens were unknown; the real huntsman was in fact his own game warden, for he learned to shoot only when meat was needed in camp, or when a bull elk displayed an especially large head of horns. It was not the real sportsman that created the necessity of game wardens, but it was the hide hunters who destroyed game for the commercial value of their skins, and still later it was the amateur huntsman who sought game purely for the sake of killing.

"Aside from Barringer's wide hunting experiences, he was also interested in mining and in natural history, and he did much work in what is known as the Meteor Crater in northern Arizona, in order to demonstrate his theory that it was not due to a subterranean outbreak, but to an impact from a meteoric mass."

In the Penrose files are two letters other than the one to Jackling in which he discusses the retention of the "junior" after his name. The first is dated June 9, 1925, and is addressed to George L. Harrison, of Philadelphia, member of the Board of Trustees of the Academy of Natural Sciences of Philadelphia.

"Dear Harrison," writes Penrose, "I have finally decided to retain the word 'Jr.' after my name in the Academy publications. My name with the 'Jr.' is already on certificates and other documents and therefore I feel that there would be a constant source of error if I used the name with the Jr. and without the Jr. After consulting men of financial and literary prominence I find that they advise me to retain the Jr. My strongest reason, however, is that my father wrote considerably and I also have written somewhat. Both what he wrote and what I wrote have been occasionally quoted, and unless there was some means of distinguishing our names there would be a sad mix-up.

"I am writing this to you so that the matter will be clear in considering the 'Jr.' on my name. You told me yesterday that you intended to leave it off. I do not think it makes any difference to the Academy whatever whether you or I leave 'Jr.' on or take it off. It is purely a personal consideration and I would advise you to do just as you personally wish."

The second letter was addressed to Sydney H. Ball and dated January 25, 1926. In it, Penrose states that "in looking over the Minutes of the Council meeting of the Society of Economic Geologists held December 29, 1925, I notice that my name is referred to as 'R. A. F. Penrose.'

"I regret that for business reasons it is necessary for me still to retain the 'Jr.' after my name, and for this reason I have always used this troublesome appendage in connection with the Society of Economic Geologists and other organizations in which my name has appeared. If you find no objection therefore I would be very greatly obliged to you if you would record my name as 'R. A. F. Penrose, Jr.' I assure you that it is not my fault that I have such a long name. It was given to me when I had nothing to say about it, and I offer this explanation as a palliating circumstance in making the above request."

CHAPTER 12

Alaska in 1903

THAT summer of 1903 was a busy one for Dick Penrose for in addition to his mining ventures, he went to Alaska to study ore deposits. From his letters to his father and from the diary he kept, the Alaskan trip can be reconstructed in considerable detail.

Letter from Dick, dated Palace Hotel, San Francisco, Calif., June 28, 1903

I was very glad to find your letters of June 6th and 10th on my arrival here a few days ago, and to know that you had been so comfortable at Carlisle. I don't wonder that the president of Dickinson College wanted you to make a speech at commencement, as you are undoubtedly their most illustrious graduate.

I have been considerably delayed in getting started for Alaska, but I will get off next week. I wrote to you last week from Salt Lake before starting here. On my arrival here I found that Brockman had been having trouble arranging express and freight rates over the new railroad to Pearce, which has just been completed, and he was telegraphing me to try and settle matters satisfactorily. This took me several days, and then I had to go down to Los Angeles to see Brockman and decide about certain matters connected with the mine. I have just returned here, and our railroad matters are all fixed up, so I can leave without further delay.

I had expected that a man named Montgomery from Denver would go to Alaska with me, but he has backed out, so I will go alone. I have no doubt, however, that I will find plenty of people in Alaska whom I know, and after all I would rather go alone than with a fellow who might be always kicking on a few hardships.

I leave here on the 27th by rail for Seattle, and will sail from there on July 2nd, on the steamer "City of Seattle" for Skagway, on the coast of Alaska, where I will arrive about the 6th or 7th. Thence I will go inland to Dawson City, arriving there in 2 or 3 days from the coast. I will probably stay at Dawson some days, as it is the headquarters of mining in the interior. I expect to leave there about the 20th of July, and go down the Yukon by boat for about 1600 miles to the mouth of the river at St. Michael's on Bering Sea. There I will take another steamer for Cape Nome, to the north of St. Michael's, which is the chief mining region of northern Alaska. I ought to get to Cape Nome early in August, and may stay there a couple of weeks. Then my plan is to take a steamer direct back to Seattle or San Francisco, a journey of between 2 and 3 weeks, passing from northern Alaska down through the Aleutian Islands, which reach between Alaska and the

Siberian Coast, and thence down the coast of southern Alaska to Seattle or San Francisco, where I ought to arrive sometime in September.

These are my general plans, but of course, I may have to change them from time to time as occasion demands.

I will write frequently whenever I have a chance, but I hope you will remember that mails in Alaska are very uncertain and often far between, so if by any chance you should not hear from me for several weeks at a time, do not be worried, as such lack of news is bound to occur sometimes when a man is in such a remote region. I will write frequently, so that even if some of the letters never reach you, others will do so.

If you write before July 15th and address the letter to me care of Golden Gate Hotel, Cape Nome, Alaska, I will probably get it before I leave there. I expect to reach there before the 15th of August and to leave before the 30th of August. It ought to take between three and four weeks for mail to get from Seal Harbor to Cape Nome.

I hope you have reached Seal Harbor by this time, and that you are comfortably settled there. I will address this letter there, as I suppose you have started by this time.

Letter from Dick, dated The Washington, Seattle, Wash., July 2, 1903

I wrote to you a few days ago from San Francisco, and I drop a line to you again now to tell you that I am sailing for Alaska tonight on the steamer "City of Seattle." I expect to arrive at Skagway on the coast of Alaska in less than a week, and to get to Dawson City on the Yukon a few days later. The weather is perfect and I am sailing on one of the best of the Alaska boats.

I have met several people I know here, among others a man named Thomsen, who lives here. I met him two years ago in Vladivostok, Siberia, and travelled through Japan with him. He has done a great deal for me in helping me arrange my Alaska trip.

I will write again from some point along the way.

From the diary

July 2—Sailed from Seattle on S.S. "City of Seattle" [for] Skagway. Boat due to leave at 8 p.m., but did not get off till 9.15 p.m. Weather cloudy but not cold. M. Thomsen came down to dock to see me off. Have been treated very politely by all the officials of the Pacific Coast S. S. Co., as well as by everyone else I met at Seattle.

On board are Prof. Barnett, of Stanford University; Lieut. Roome, of U. S. Navy, and probably 60 other passengers. Boat not crowded and fairly comfortable.

July 3—Arrived at Vancouver about 9 a.m. Were due to leave at noon, but did not get off until 2.15. Walked about town and found it much improved since my last visit in September, 1900. Streets have been well paved with wood blocks or asphalt, and the town looks busy and prosperous.

Passed up the Straits of Georgia during afternoon and evening. Weather cloudy and cool. Some little snow on mountains. High peaks are in plain view on the mainland and lower hills on Vancouver Island, to the west.

July 4—It rained hard last night but today it cleared off into perfect weather, clear and bright. Have not stopped all day and will not do so until reaching Ketchikan tomorrow a.m. Have been passing through Queen Charlotte Sound all day. Some mountainous scenery. Some of the passengers celebrated the 4th with fireworks.

July 5—Reached Ketchikan, the chief port of entry of southern Alaska about 10 a.m., and walked about town. The town is built at foot of a small mountain in a clearance in the forest and contains a few hundred people; log and frame houses; plank pavements on sidewalks and streets as the ground is boggy and wet. Later in afternoon we reached the old Russian town of Wrangel, beyond which the rugged peak of Mt. Wrangel raises its snow-capped peak. The town is beautifully situated and, like Ketchikan, contains numerous totem poles, many Indians, few hundred whites. Streets, like Ketchikan, are all paved with planks.

J. J. Coyle joined our boat at Ketchikan to go to Skagway. He is U. S. fish commissioner.

Letter from Dick, dated on Board S.S. "City of Seattle," Alaska Coast, July 6, 1903

We will reach Skagway on the coast of Alaska tonight or tomorrow morning, and I thought I would drop a line to you, and mail it when we reach there. We have had a very good voyage all the way up from Seattle. The first two days it rained a little, and the second night it poured so hard that the boat had to stop for a while, while we were passing through a narrow channel among some islands. But the last two days have been perfect. We have stopped at several ports since starting, among them Ketchikan, Wrangel and Douglas Island, and we have just left the port of Juneau, where we stopped three hours. All these places are small coast settlements of from a few hundred to a couple of thousand people, maintained mostly by mining and salmon fishing. There are many salmon canning establishments along the coast, and a large part of the canned salmon of the world comes from Alaska.

The coast is very much like that on the other side of the Pacific, in Siberia and Korea, and is very rough and mountainous, with glaciers and snow-capped mountains in all directions. Mt. Wrangel, which we passed last night, looks like a solid mass of snow, and yet the climate on the shore and at sea is as mild as that of Maine. I visited this afternoon the Treadwell mine on Douglas Island, one of the largest gold mines in the U. S.

This boat, though small, is as comfortable as could be expected under the circumstances, and it has the great advantage of not being crowded, as the rush of miners has already gone north.

When I leave Skagway tomorrow I will go direct north to Dawson City, where I will arrive in three days. I will go the first 110 miles by a short piece of railroad which has been built over White Pass, and thence will go down the Lewes River by boat to the Yukon and down the Yukon to Dawson. I will write further from there.

I hope you are well, and that you find everything all right and comfortable at Seal Harbor.

From the diary

July 6th—Arrived at Juneau about 10 a.m. and stayed three hours. The town contains about 2000 people and is beautifully situated at the foot of a mountain. It has many stores, a good hotel, and is a very prosperous looking place. The Treadwell mine on Douglas Island, across a narrow channel from Juneau, has $6,000,000 invested in plant and property, and employs many men. The boat stopped there 1½ hours after leaving Juneau.

Proceeding north from Juneau, we passed through a beautiful country with high mountains heavily covered with snow and glaciers, and up Lynn Canal to Skagway, where we arrived about 11 p.m. Went to the "5th Avenue Hotel," a very comfortable place. Skagway is a neat town of about 2000 people, the head of navigation for large boats in the Lynn Canal, and the terminus of the White Pass & Yukon Railway, which runs northward from Skagway for 111 miles across White Pass, along Lake Bennett, to White Horse.

July 7—At 9.30 a.m., started for White Horse on railway. The railway passes up a creek toward White Pass, 2500 feet high, in about 20 miles. The ascent is not very steep and the railway is well built along the granite hills. Thence the railway passes along Lake Lindermann and Bennett Lake, through a hilly country sparsely covered with stunted pine and spruce and some cottonwood. The terminus of the railway is at White Horse on river of same name. Here we arrived at 4.30 p.m., and sailed at 9 p.m. on S. S. Selkirk for Dawson. Below White Horse we passed through a number of lakes connected by channels, until came out on Lewis River. Followed this to mouth of Pelly River, below which the stream is known as the Yukon. The country is wild and rugged but not so much snow nor so many glaciers seen as on coast, as this interior region has not nearly so much rainfall. Timber mostly small pine and spruce, with some birch and cottonwood.

July 8—On S. S. Selkirk in country described above. Boat very crowded.

July 9th—Arrived Dawson at 12 noon. Found good room reserved for me at Regina Hotel. No boat ready to go down river, but one expected (The Sarah) daily from St. Michaels.

Dawson is a very substantial little town of about 4000 people, though once there were about 40,000 here. It is on the banks of the Yukon, just below the confluence of the Klondike River, and it is well laid out in streets parallel to and at right angles to the river. Jewelry stores and bar rooms are numerous. The upper part of the town, on the upper side of Klondike River, is known as Lousetown and is the home of the sporting element. The town is very orderly and looks more like an old settled country village than one of the great mining camps of the world. The many jewelry stores offer for sale rings, pins, and other ornaments made of Klondike gold and Klondike nuggets. Immense warehouses line the river where the Northern Commercial Company and the North American Transport and Trading Company store goods brought up the Yukon from St. Michaels, by the steamers that both those companies own.

The barracks of the Northwest Mounted Police are in the town, and the order that they maintain in the wild and unsettled country of Yukon Territory is wonderful. Miners bring in their gold, alone, without guards, from the most remote parts of the district without fear of robbery. Such dangers are unknown, and a few hundred of the mounted police maintain this perfect security all over the territory.

There are quite a lot of Indians here, but they are of a superior class and try to emulate the white man in industry. In fact, the Klondike District was discovered by an Indian—Skukum Jim.

The town being isolated from the rest of the world has to look solely to its own talent for amusement. There are several baseball clubs here, which have almost daily games in the barrack grounds. There is a stock company for theatrical performances. There is a social club known as the Zero Club, and an Athletic Club with one of the largest arenas for sparring that I ever saw. Sparring is a favorite amusement and many big fights occur. Choinski and Slavin are both in the district. Choinski was knocked out in $1\frac{1}{2}$ rounds a short time ago in a fierce battle by a local star. The organization of Yukon Pioneers includes those who were on the river before the rush of 1898, and the Artic Brotherhood includes those who have seen the ice form and break on the Yukon.

Many people become insane in Dawson. Last year 15 were sent out, and already this year there are 10 to go. There are also many suicides.

A person who has been here a year or more is called a sour-dough, and a newcomer is a cheechak.

Letter from Dick, dated Regina Hotel, Dawson, Y.T., July 10, 1903

I arrived here all right yesterday in a little less than three days from the coast. This was unusually quick time, as I was lucky in catching a good boat down the Lewes River to the Yukon.

This town is situated on the banks of the Yukon River, in Canadian territory, and about 100 miles east of the American boundary in Alaska. It contains about 4000 people and is a very active place. Though it is a Canadian town, most all the people are Americans, and most all the mines are owned by Americans. They celebrate the 4th of July here the same as in the U. S. The town is the headquarters of the Klondike region, and has the record of being the most isolated place of its size on the North American continent. It is almost 2000 miles from any other town of any size, and during the winter it is completely isolated, so that all the supplies are brought in during the summer, either overland from Skagway or up the Yukon from St. Michael's on Bering Sea, and are stored in large warehouses to supply the people during the winter.

Every one here has been very polite and hospitable, and I am going to start today on a three days trip with horses through the mining districts. I am going with a mine-owner named Wills, and with a man named Hartman, who is the postmaster of Dawson. I was invited to dinner today by the Governor, locally known as the "Commissioner" of the Yukon Territory, in which Dawson is situated, but I cannot go, on account of the trip to the mines.

They have a club here called the "Zero Club," but the name applies more to winter climate than summer. The weather now is very warm, and though the sun dips slightly below the horizon at night, there is no such thing as darkness. People do not go to bed much during the summer. They make up for it in the winter. A common amusement in the summer is to have a baseball game after dinner, a theatrical show in a dance hall after that, and horse races on the main street until morning.

I expect to start down the Yukon for St. Michael's next week, but I will write again before leaving here.

From his diary

July 10–12—Started on a trip through the Klondike and Indian River districts in a team with Dr. E. A. Wills, Mr. Hartman, and Mr. Tyrrell. Drove most of the night and at 3.30 a.m. arrived at Gold Run. The long daylight lasted all night. During the three days, we visited the mines of the principal creeks of the district, and returned to Dawson on the night of the 12th. The Dominion government has built between 200 and 300 miles of excellent roads through the districts, which have greatly facilitated and cheaped mining. Excellent road houses are found at short intervals along the roads, where good cigars, beer and whisky can be gotten.

July 13—Remained in Dawson. No sign yet of any boat from below. Until one comes, we cannot start for St. Michaels.

July 14—Visited the Larson-Fuller-Norwood mine on Bonanza Creek, with Mr. Fuller and party. No boat yet in sight.

July 15—In Dawson. No boat yet.

July 17—In Dawson.

July 18—Visited the Violet quartz mine on west side of El Dorado with Mr. Tyrell and Mr. McConnell of the Canadian Geological Survey.

Letter from Dick, dated Regina Hotel, Dawson, Y.T., July 18, 1903

I wrote to you a few days ago on my arrival here, and had expected before now to have started down the Yukon for the coast, but no boat has yet arrived. In the meantime, however, I have put in the time travelling all over the Yukon mining region in this vicinity, including the Klondike District and parts of the valley of the Indian River. I have seen a great deal of interest, and have been treated first rate wherever I have gone.

The boats that go down the Yukon spend the winter at the mouth of the river, at a place called St. Michael's, an old Russian post. When the ice breaks up in the spring, they come up the Yukon with supplies for the river settlements, and then return for another cargo. It is one of these boats that I expect to take, but none of them have yet arrived. As there is no telegraph communication between here and St. Michael's, no one can tell how far up the river the boats have gotten; and as it is over 1600 miles from here to the coast, their whereabouts is indefinite. Some of them are already overdue, and the only explanation for their non-appearance is that the ice was late in leaving the lower river, or that they were heavily loaded and may have stuck in the bottom. It is probable, however, that one of them may reach here in a few days, and then I will start at once down river. The trip down stream is much more rapid than up stream, and as the boats going down are not heavily loaded, there is not much danger of sticking in the bottom of the river. There are a number of other people who want to go down the river, and their principal occupation just now is looking down stream to catch the first glimpse of the smoke of a steamer coming up the Yukon. I personally am not bothering a bit about it, as I am making good use of my time seeing the country. Moreover, there is a very good hotel here, and I consider myself very lucky in not being delayed in a more uncomfortable place.

The country around here is bleak and barren. The timber is small and scattered, and often stunted and dwarfed, as in Lapland and Northern Siberia. The ground is covered with a deep growth of moss and peat, and is very boggy, so that it is very difficult to get about except where trails or roads have been made. From some of the higher hills, can be seen the main range of the Rocky Mts., forming a high divide between the waters of the Yukon and the McKenzie Rivers, and extending northward to the Arctic Ocean. Dawson is the only town of any size within many hundreds of miles, and as it is almost completely isolated in winter, the people are dependent on their own resources for almost everything. Not much in the way of agriculture can be carried on here, on account of the length and severity of the winters, so different trading companies maintain large warehouses, which they keep filled with supplies brought up the river in the summer. Two years of supplies are kept constantly on hand, so that if anything should delay the new supplies coming up river, the town cannot be starved out. At the different trading stores here can be found almost everything that anyone could want, from the cheapest to the best, including as fine liquors and cigars as could be found anywhere. A stock company has theatrical performances almost every night, and the usual number of saloons and dance halls enliven the town. The upper end of Dawson is known as "Lousetown" and is the resort of the sporting element. Everything, however, is perfectly orderly, and I have never been in a mining town where such good order and personal safety existed. The police system is the best I have ever seen.

I will write again before leaving here, which I hope will be in a few days. I hope you are having a good summer at Seal Harbor.

From his diary

July 18–21—In Dawson. No boat yet in sight. Many passengers want to go down river but cannot do so. Much grumbling. The S. S. "Sarah" is 10 days overdue; the "Hannah" 5 days; and the "Isom" 2 days. River very low, and it is supposed they may be stuck in bottom. There is no telegraph communication down river and no one knows where they are.

July 22–24—Waiting in Dawson for boat. No news of any boat yet, except the Kerr, a refrigerator boat which was reported at Eagle, 110 miles below Dawson, on the 23rd.

July 25—The S. S. "Sarah" was reported at Eagle last night. She will arrive tonight or next a.m. There is much rejoicing in town, especially among the 70 or more people who want to go down river. I have for the past week been trying to get someone to go down river with me in a canoe—about a 20-day trip—but no one seems to want to undergo the hardships.

July 26—"Sarah" arrived at 10 a.m. She is being quickly unloaded and is scheduled to sail for down-river points at 12 p.m.

1 p.m.—We are just leaving Dawson, weather fine, and about 75 passengers. The boat is a little crowded but I have a stateroom alone for at least the first day.

July 27—Passed "40-Mile" at about 4 a.m., and arrived at Eagle at 9 a.m. Eagle is a small town just beyond the Canadian border, in Alaska. Said to contain 200 civilians, 100 soldiers, and 300 dogs—the latter used mostly in sleighs in winter. There is a small military post here; also some good vegetable gardens with potatoes, beets, cabbages, etc. Radishes and beets grow especially luxuriously here and in the Klondike.

I should have mentioned above that before leaving Dawson, there was a personal examination of passengers for gold, as a royalty of $2\frac{1}{2}\%$ is charged by the Canadian government, and much is smuggled. For some reason unknown to me, I was not examined.

At Eagle our baggage was examined by the U. S. customs collectors, and after a stay of three hours we continued down river. The "Sarah" burns oil as a fuel, which is said to be cheaper than the wood sold along the river at $5 to $10 per cord. At Dawson, wood is $15 per cord.

At about 8 p.m., we arrived at Circle City, so named from a large bend in the river—a small town something like Eagle and supported by gold-mining interests in the neighboring creeks.

So many people got on board at Eagle and Circle that the staterooms became crowded, and to avoid being in a room with three people, I was moved into room with Senator Dietrich.

July 28—Arrived at Fort Yukon on north side of river in morning and stopped only a few minutes. There are only a few whites and Indians here, and we stopped only a few minutes. Fort Yukon is an old post, but is now of little importance. A Catholic mission is situated here.

We passed several boats going up river last night and this morning.

Just below Fort Yukon the river passes within the Arctic Circle, but comes below it again a few miles below. About 10 miles below Fort Yukon, we stopped $3\frac{1}{2}$ hours to take oil from a scow with four wood tanks of oil, containing about 650 gallons each.

July 29—About 8 a.m., arrived at Rampart on the south bank, a small town apparently about the size of Eagle. Court is now being held here, and many of our passengers got off at this point, though others came on board to go to lower-river points. The Northern Commerical Company and the North American Transport and Trading Company have stores here as well as at Circle, Eagle, and all important points on the Yukon below Dawson. The "Sarah" is one of the N. C. packets. Gold mining near Rampart.

In the p.m., we arrived at Tanana, at the mouth of the Tanana River, about 100 miles below Rampart. Here is a small town probably about the same as Circle, and also a military post with one company of soldiers.

During the day we passed many Indian camps. The Indians this time of year are busy catching and drying salmon for food for themselves and dogs. They open the fish and hang them on poles and frames to dry. There are only a few Indians in each camp. The Alaska Indians are very friendly to Americans, though they are said to have disliked their old Russian masters. Many dogs hang about their camps, eating and sleeping and barking. The Indians are rapidly dying of white man's diseases. Rain all this p.m.

July 30—Arrived in morning at the station at the mouth of the Kayukut River, up which a steamer was preparing to run to mining districts 600 miles above the Yukon. Some of the passengers got off here to take the boat.

A short distance below here we arrived at the small station of Nulato on the north bank. In the afternoon we arrived at the small station of Kaltag. Here the telegraph line leaves the river and makes a short cut to the coast—90 miles off. The line was just completed to Dawson, but burned partly down a few weeks ago. Now there is telegraphic communication between Dawson and Eagle, and between Rampart and St. Michaels, but not between Rampart and Eagle.

July 31—During the night and early a.m., we passed Anvik, Koserefski, and other small stations, and in morning arrived at "Russian Mission" on north shore, between Koserefski and Andreofski. Here is a red Greek church with green roof and a few Indian hangers-on. The Greek churches here, as well as at St. Michaels, Sitka, and elsewhere in Alaska, are the remains of Russian occupation and are governed by a Greek bishop in San Francisco. There are but a few real Russians left in Alaska. Most have left or died, though there are many Russian half breeds.

The hills begin to be lower and greener, indicating proximity to coast. In the evening we reached the Andreafski River and went up it to the small station of the same name, which is the winter headquarters of the N.C.Co's steamers. Rain all day.

Below Andreafski we gradually entered the delta of the Yukon—a great extent of flat marshes covered with a coarse rank grass.

August 1—The river meanders through the delta in several channels. We took the most northerly one, and about 5 a.m. passed out into Bering Sea, which was as smooth and placid as a mill pond. We continued up the coast for about 80 miles to St. Michael Island on the north shore of which is the station of same name—a U. S. military reservation. Here we arrived at 12 noon and 2 p.m. sailed on the side-wheel tug "Sadic" for Nome. St. Michaels was an old Russian post before the U. S. got Alaska, and the old wooden blockhouse, with small iron cannons, is still there. It looks like a miniature fortress and is not large enough for more than 5 or 6 men.

Many ducks and geese seen on Yukon; no large game.

August 2—Arrived Nome 2 a.m. Had very smooth passage and very crowded boat. Went to Lawrence Hotel, as the Golden Gate Hotel, to which I had intended to go, had burned down a few weeks ago.

Letter from Dick, dated Cape Nome, Alaska, August 3, 1903

I arrived here yesterday morning at 2 a.m. on a small steamer from the mouth of the Yukon River, and was very glad to get your letters of July 1st and 9th. I am very sorry to hear of the trouble you have been having with rheumatism. It is certainly very hard on you, after all the trouble you had with colds last spring, to be now laid up again. I most earnestly hope that you will soon be all right, and that the summer at Seal Harbor will put you in first-class condition again.

I wrote to you hurriedly a few days ago, just before leaving Dawson. I sailed that night on the steamer "Sarah" for the mouth of the Yukon. The boat had just arrived from the lower river, and it was unloaded quickly and sent back the following night. It had been almost two weeks late in reaching Dawson, as it had been stuck on a sand bar down the river for some days.

We left Dawson about 1 a.m. with about 70 passengers, composed mostly of miners, traders, and a few government officials. The boat was a large stern paddle steamer like a Mississippi River boat, and was very comfortable. Many of the passengers were kicking on the food, etc., but it all seemed very good to me under the circumstances, as a man cannot expect a Waldorf Hotel on a Yukon River steamer; and if he does, he had better not come to the Yukon. We came rapidly down the river, and had the good luck to miss all the sand bars, and to reach the sea in six days—a distance of over 1600 miles without being stuck anywhere. Part of the time we were within the Arctic Circle. The country is mostly mountainous, and only sparsely inhabited by Indians and Esquimaux. At some points the remains of the old Russian occupation of Alaska are seen in small Greek church missions. There are but few Russians in Alaska, but there are many half breeds, and the Greek Church of Russia still maintains several missions. I do not think, however, that they get many converts, as the Indians do not like the Russians, though they are very friendly with the Americans, and take a great pride in calling themselves "American citizens" and in flying the American flag.

The Yukon empties into Bering Sea by several channels meandering through a very large delta, and on arriving at the mouth of the river, we passed up the coast to the island of St. Michael's, where there is a U. S. government post, and where the old Russian blockhouse, with small iron cannons, can still be seen. From there to Cape Nome is about 120 miles by sea, and as our river boat was not safe for sea travelling, we secured a small side-wheel steamer, which was said to be sea-worthy, and in about twelve hours, being fortunately favored by a fair wind and a smooth sea, the latter a very unusual occurrence in these parts, we reached Nome. We landed in a row boat, as there is no harbor here, and all vessels have to anchor offshore.

The principal hotel here, the Golden Gate, has recently burned down, but I managed to get a room in another house, though Nome is so crowded with people that it is no easy job to get a place to sleep. Fortunately your letters arrived after the Golden Gate Hotel had burned, so they were not lost. The town of Nome consists of two or three rows of houses strung along the beach. There is very little space to build on, as the boggy tundra begins directly back of the beach, and the immediate water's edge is the only solid ground. Some day a storm is likely to wash the whole place away. The town looks out on Bering Straits, which connect Bering Sea and the Arctic Ocean. To the south is Norton Sound, a part of Bering Sea, and to the north and east for hundreds of miles are immense areas of Arctic tundra, low, boggy, moss-covered flats, devoid of trees, and at a depth of a few inches frozen solid the whole year. A more bleak or inhospitable place for a town could scarcely be found, but the wonderful richness of some of the gold mines has been inducement enough for about 7000 people to collect here. It is raining here now, and has been raining for several weeks, and this seems to be the normal summer weather here.

I will probably be here and in the vicinity for a couple of weeks or so, and will then take a boat direct to Seattle or San Francisco, where I expect to arrive the end of August or early in September. Possibly, however, I may stay here a little longer, as there is a good deal to see around here. I am in first class shape and never felt better.

I hope that you have entirely recovered from your rheumatism, and will have no further return of it. From now on, until I write further, you had better address me at Palace Hotel, San Francisco, as that will probably be the surest place to reach me on my return south.

From his diary

August 3rd—In Nome. Rainy. Moved to Sheldon Hotel as had some friends there. Stormy. Two vessels washed ashore.

August 4—Visited mines on Anvil Creek. Went there on the "Nome & Arctic Ry", which is about 9 miles long and built over the tundra. The train runs 6 miles an hour. Roadbed very bad. Stormy.

August 5—Visited mines of Anvil, Dexter, and other creeks. Stormy.

August 6—In Nome, waiting for S.S. Oregon to sail for Seattle. Clear.

August 7—Sailed for Seattle at 9.30 p.m. on S. S. Oregon. Sea quiet, weather perfect, boat very comfortable.

Nome is town of about 7000 people—closely built and narrow streets—on beach facing Bering Strait. The tide rises only 2 feet here, but probably sometime in a storm the town will be washed away. Back of it are many miles of tundra, offering no foundation for houses. Storms are of very common occurrence here. Large amounts of drift wood from the Yukon are seen along the coast, having been brought up by the current that flows north through Bering Sea in the summer and south in winter. This drift wood was a godsend in the early days in Nome, before lumber was brought in.

August 8—Foggy. Are approaching Aleutian Islands and running very slowly to avoid running on rocks.

August 9—Fog lifted for a few moments this morning and we passed the Aleutians successfully, going between Unimak Island and the Alaska Peninsula. High snow-capped peaks visible in the distance. We passed S.S. Ohio about 8 a.m., going north, and then the fog settled down again for the day.

August 10—In North Pacific. Foggy, sea choppy, many passengers seasick.

August 11—In North Pacific. Foggy, smooth sea.
August 12—Same as 11th.
August 14—Same.
August 15—Arrived Seattle at 1.30. A small crowd was on the dock to meet the returning passengers.

Letter from Dick, dated Palace Hotel, San Francisco, Calif., August 24, 1903

I have just arrived here from the north, and I drop a line to you to let you know that I have gotten back. I received your letter of July 20th just before leaving Cape Nome, and I was very glad to get it. If you have sent any letters since that date to me at Nome, I have not yet gotten them, but they will be forwarded to me. As I wrote you from Nome, I also received your two letters previous to that of the 20th.

I have returned here about a week sooner than I had expected, as I found that I could see all that I wanted of the Cape Nome country in less time than I thought.

I came down from Bering Straits on the steamer "Oregon," an old boat which had been recently repaired. It is one of the best of the Bering Sea fleet—which, however, is not saying very much, as most of them are old vessels cast off from other routes, and some of them have a very bad reputation for safety. The "Oregon" arrived off Cape Nome in a storm, which was so severe that she had to put to sea again without making a landing. The same day two other vessels were driven ashore on the Nome beach. On the third day, however, the Oregon succeeded in landing her passengers and freight in small boats, as the water is too shallow for steamers to come up to shore.

Storms are so frequent in Bering Sea, that we expected a stormy trip south, but by the time the "Oregon" was ready to start, the weather had cleared, and we had a fairly good passage across Bering Sea and the north Pacific to Seattle, which we reached in a little less than eight days from Cape Nome. The only disagreeable feature was the dense fog, which enveloped us for almost the whole voyage. There are not many boats in those northern waters, and not much chance of a collision in a fog, so we did not slow down, but went full steam ahead, fog or no fog. We had about 140 passengers on board, many of whom were seasick, as the "Oregon" is a small boat, and having no cargo coming south, it rolled considerably.

I feel well repaid for having taken this trip to Alaska, as I have been able to become familiar with the mining possibilities, not only of Alaska, but also of the adjoining Yukon Territory of the Canadian Northwest.

From Seattle I came here overland, where I will remain for two or three days, as I have some business with the Southern Pacific Railroad. Then I will join Brockman in Arizona, and from there go to Denver, and from there go east, arriving in Phila about Sept. 15th. At least these are my plans at present, if I am not detained in Arizona, and I know of nothing to detain me there beyond a few days.

When I get to Phila., I thought that if convenient to you, I would come directly to Seal Harbor to see you for a few days, arriving there between Sept. 15th to 20th. But if it is not convenient to you for me to come at that time, I hope you will not hesitate to say so. If you will drop a line to me at Pearce, Arizona, when you get this letter, and let me know about this, I will probably get your letter before I leave there.

You do not say anything in your last letter about your rheumatism, but I hope that it is entirely well again.

Here is another example of the unfailing Penrose courtesy. How many sons would have written to ask if it would be convenient for them to come to their father's house? Most of them would have just appeared, sure that the warmth of the welcome would overlook any inconvenience to the housekeeping arrangements.

One other letter in the files for 1903 obviously concerns an errand which he undertook for his father in October. It is dated the 22nd.

"I visited the Bayard Taylor place at Kennett Square yesterday in company with Mr. Samuel Sinclair who lives at Kennett.

"The town of Kennett Square is on one of the branches of the Phila., Wilmington and Washington Railroad, $33\frac{1}{2}$ miles from Philadelphia, and 12 miles from Wilmington. West Chester is 12 miles distant by wagon road. The town is three miles from the state line of Delaware, and has a population of about 1700—originally mostly quakers, now mixed. There is a considerable sprinkling of niggers. The town is a neat-looking agricultural place.

"The Bayard Taylor place is one mile north of town. A trolley line is being built from Kennett Square to West Chester, which will pass within about 200 yards or less of the house. The property comprises 120 acres of high rolling land, partly under cultivation, with some good areas of woods—especially near the house—consisting of maple, poplar, oak, chestnut, hickory, pine, cedar, etc. Two fairly good apple orchards are on the place.

"The house is a red brick structure, of a general square shape, with a tower in front, two stories and an attic high; the whole thing containing probably a little more room than your house at Seal Harbor. It was built in 1859 and is very delapidated. The woodwork is rotting in many places and considerable repairs are badly needed. The house is on the edge of a clump of trees, and commands a good view of a very beautiful country. It lays about 200 yards off the main township road, and is reached by a private road entering through a stone gateway—old and broken down. A small house is at the gateway; also a small frame house for a farmer is near the main mansion; also numerous barns, wagon houses, hay lofts, etc.—all originally good but now very delapidated. The main house is now inhabited by a farmer and his family. One of the children has scarlet fever and the doctor had told them to let no one in the house, so I could not see the inside, in spite of the fact that I told the people that I was not afraid of the fever. But from what I could see through the windows from the outside, the rooms are large and capacious with high ceilings—but like the outside—much delapidated and badly in need of repair. The whole place reminded me very much of some of the old ante-bellum mansions in the south, which still reflect their former grandeur through a mantle of squalor and decay.

"The people who at present live on the place get water from a well; but Dr. Levis used to pump it from a spring on the property, and he is said to have considered it very fine water.

"The neighbors are numerous, but none very close. The township road which passes the property is, as I have said, about 200 yards or less from the house; and along this road one is rarely out of sight of farmers' houses. Many of Bayard Taylor's relatives seem to live in the vicinity. The neighbors are apparently all very respectable farmers. There is a considerable sprinkling of niggers, about as many as are usually found near the border of Delaware.

"I am told that the owners want $16,000 for the place. Perhaps it could be gotten for less. I think that at least $10,000 more would be required to put the house in shape. There are several trains a day, which go from Phila to Kennett in from $1\frac{1}{4}$ hours to $1\frac{1}{2}$ hours.

"The place is secluded, but it is also somewhat tedious getting there, as the trains are crowded and stop at a great many stations. It could be made into a very attractive place, but this would require a good deal of time, labor and expense. I think you would be pleased with it if it was put in shape, but it is a question in my mind whether you would not be just as much pleased with some other place already in good shape, and easier to get to.

"If you want me to do anything further in this matter, I will be very glad to do so.

"I hope you are having a good trip at Atlantic City, and that it is doing your health much good."

CHAPTER 13

Trip to the Antipodes

BUSY with his many interests, Penrose spent the first half of 1904 in the United States, making several trips to Arizona, California, and Colorado on mining business. In July he set forth once more on his travels to see the ore deposits of the world. This time he selected for his field of study the Sandwich [Hawaiian] Islands, the Samoan Islands, New Zealand, Australia, and Tasmania, returning to New York in the spring of 1905 by way of Ceylon, the Suez Canal, and Europe.

While he was away, he received the following letter from J. A. Holmes, chief of the Department of Mines and Metallurgy in the Division of Exhibits at the St. Louis Exposition of 1904:

My dear Penrose:—

I am extremely anxious to have you serve on the International Jury of Awards in the Gold Section of the Department of Mines and Metallurgy, between September 1st and 10th, and I sincerely trust that you will not fail of accepting the appointment which is hereby sent to you.

You will meet a delightful party of men, representing mining and metallurgical industries of this and some foreign countries, and you will not find the work either long drawn out or tedious; your railroad fare, including sleeper to and from St. Louis will be paid, and there will be an allotment of $7.00 per day to cover your expenses while you are engaged in this work in St. Louis.

Hoping to receive a favorable and prompt response from you, I beg to remain,

Yours sincerely,
J. A. Holmes

Of course, he could not accept.

Judging from the manner in which he made his reports to others and from the well-rounded background which his office library offers, it is obvious that Dick Penrose never set forth on a trip to foreign lands without giving himself adequate preparation. Among those to whom he wrote concerning his projected trip to the Antipodes was Herbert Hoover, who knew that country from his own experience.

Letter from Penrose to H. C. Hoover in London, dated May 18, 1904

My dear Hoover:—

I expect possibly to take a trip to Australia this summer, and may sail the latter part of June or in July. I think I will go via San Francisco and the Oceanic

Steamship Line. I am not yet entirely certain that I can go, but I am trying to shape things in that direction; and therefore thought I had better write to you to ask you if you could find time to drop me a line and let me know what are the most interesting points to visit in West Australia. If you can do this, I will be very greatly obliged to you.

Hoping you are well, and with best regards, I am,

Sincerely yours,
R. A. F. Penrose, Jr.

Letter from H. C. Hoover, dated 20, Copthall Ave., London, England, May 31, 1904

My dear Penrose:

If I were going to Australia to take a look round at the mines, I should go first to New Zealand, and there look at the Waihi Mine, in particular. You might also look at a mine which we have there, called the Talisman, of which Mr. H. A. Stansfield is in charge. He would be able to introduce you at the Waihi which is but a few miles distant and on the road.

From thence, I would go to Sydney, and from Sydney to Queensland, in order to see Gympie, and possibly Charters Towers. The latter is not of so much interest, but the same journey would embrace the Mt. Morgan. I have no personal friends in that region to whom I can introduce you, but you will have no difficulty in seeing whatever you wish to see there.

In New South Wales there is the Cobar District, if you wish to visit copper. The copper mines there are very much of the same order as all the rest in the world and are not of much interest.

In Melbourne, you will find two of our staff—Mr. D. P. Mitchell and Mr. C. S. Herzig, and they would hand you round over that Colony. The main things to see are Bendigo and the Deep Leads. They will probably be able to give you introductions into Broken Hill and Tasmania, if you wish to go there.

I would certainly go to Western Australia, where you will find Mr. W. J. Loring and Mr. W. A. Prichard in charge of our business, and a great many American mine managers, some of whom you may know already. We have about 25 mines there. They will be delighted to entertain you, and will show you everything in the Colony.

Our offices in Australia are at the following addresses:

C/o The Talisman Mine, Karangahake via Auckland, New Zealand
Equitable Building, Collins Street, Melbourne, Victoria
Mouatt Street, Fremantle, Western Australia
Macdonald Street, Kalgoorlie, Western Australia.

I send you letters of introduction, but I have written to them each, telling them that you contemplate taking a journey into their country, and that they are to extend to you every courtesy that they possibly can.

Very sincerely yours,
H. C. Hoover

Letter from Penrose to H. C. Hoover in London, dated June 11, 1904

My dear Hoover:—
Many thanks for your letter of May 31st, with letters of introduction for Australia. I am sure they will be of great use to me in finding out what to see and where to go in that country, and I appreciate your kindness very greatly. I hope that I will be able to visit some, if not all, the places you mention in your letter, and I should be very glad indeed if I should happen to meet you out there. I do not yet know just when I will start, but may be able to get off sometime this summer. Before I leave I will drop a line to you again, and let you know my address out there, so that if you should happen to come that way we might be able to meet.
With best regards, and wishing you every success, I am,
Sincerely yours,
R. A. F. Penrose, Jr.

Letter from Penrose to H. C. Hoover in London, dated June 24, 1904

My dear Hoover:—
I leave here Sunday for San Francisco, and will sail from there on July 7th for Aukland, New Zealand, and from there to Australia. If you happen to be in that part of the world during the summer, I hope you will let me know. My address, care of Union Bank of Australia, Sydney, Australia, will reach me until about the end of August, and after that my address will be care of J. S. Morgan & Company, 22 Old Broad Street, London, as they will forward my mail to me in the far east. Besides going to New Zealand and Australia, I hope also to go to Tasmania, and if my time permits I will also try to go to South Africa, and come up thence along the west coast of Africa to Europe. If I do not see you on one of your trips to Australia, I hope to do so on my arrival in London sometime next fall or next winter.
I want to thank you again for the letters of introduction which you so kindly sent me; and with best regards, and wishing you every success, I remain
Sincerely yours,
R. A. F. Penrose, Jr.

The story of this trip is well covered in his letters to his father, his diary, and his notebooks, and these sources will be indicated.

Before sailing from San Francisco on July 8, he sent the following telegram to his brother Spencer at Colorado Springs:

"Many thanks for telegram. Am staying at Palace Hotel. Am sailing July eighth. Goodbye and good luck."

Letter from Dick, dated Palace Hotel, San Francisco, Calif., July 7, 1904

I was exceedingly glad to get your letter of July 1st and to know of your safe arrival at Seal Harbor. I appreciate very much the trouble you took to write so soon after your arrival there, as it is a great pleasure for me to know before I sail that you had gotten to Seal Harbor so comfortably and pleasantly.

I sail tomorrow on the steamship Sierra of the Oceanic Steamship Line. The boat was scheduled to sail today, but has been delayed waiting for the English mail for New Zealand, which goes by way of New York and San Francisco, though the English mail for Australia goes by way of Suez Canal. We will get off tomorrow, however, sure.

Col. Bowman telegraphed me that he could not go on the trip, so I go alone. I am sorry not to have him along, but much prefer to have no companion than one who went reluctantly. In fact, I have travelled so much alone that I am used to it.

I will write to you frequently, just as I did on my last long trip, and whenever possible will do as you suggest, and write once a week. But if you do not hear from me for much longer intervals, do not be surprised. Mail service in foreign countries is not so prompt and not so reliable as ours; and often letters are lost or are unaccountably delayed, so that you may sometimes get several letters at once and then perhaps none for several weeks, though they may have been written and mailed at regular intervals.

In crossing the Pacific Ocean especially, mail will be slow in reaching you, as it has to come back again over the Pacific to reach this country. Our boat calls en route at Honolulu and at the Samoan Islands. I do not know whether or not I will have a chance to mail letters at either place, but if I do, I will write from there. If not, I will write on my arrival in Auckland, New Zealand, on about July 26th or 27th. I will be there a few days before going over to Australia. At best, it will be several weeks or more after I sail from here before a letter from me can reach you. Always remember, however, that no news is good news. Nothing is going to happen to me, so don't worry.

I have registered a cable address for J. C. Jones at our office in Philadelphia, so that if I have occasion to cable, I will do so to him; and I have written him asking him that in case I cable anything of importance, to communicate it to you. I do not expect, however, to have occasion to cable.

I hope that you and Aunt Lyd are now comfortably settled at Seal Harbor, and that you will have a pleasant summer there.

P.S. July 8th. I sail at 2 p.m. this afternoon. The weather is fine and I think we will have a good voyage.

From the Diary

July 7th—San Francisco. I was to have sailed today for New Zealand on the S.S. Sierra, but the ship was held to wait for the English mail which was late. I did not object to the delay, as I had a number of matters to attend to, and a lot of mail to answer.

July 8th—We sailed promptly at 2 p.m. Mr. J. O'B. Gunn and Col. Draper came down to the boat to see me off. When one is starting on a long trip alone, he surely appreciates very much his friends coming to see him off. Though I am alone on this trip, yet I find that among the passengers on the ship are Mr. Bissell, attorney for the Santa Fe Railway, whom I believe I once met in Chicago.

Dr. Nicholas Senn, the Chicago surgeon, is also a passenger. Mr. Gunn and Col. Draper introduced me to Captain Houdlette of the Sierra and he seems like a very pleasant fellow. He comes from Maine.

There are only 53 first-class passengers and the boat is not at all crowded as it can hold several times this number. Most of them are bound for Honolulu; most of the rest for Sydney, with a few for Pago Pago and Aukland. A large proportion of them are English. Another passenger is Prince "Cupid" or Prince Kalanianole, the Hawaiian delegate to U. S. Congress. He is a native Hawaiian, and seems like a very pleasant fellow.

The weather is perfect, and as we passed out of the "Golden Gate," I thought California never looked so beautiful. In fact, I must acknowledge to suddenly having a great feeling of regret at leaving my country for so long a trip. Nothing that I can ever see in foreign countries can ever equal that last view of the Golden Gate as it gradually faded in the distance. I watched it until the shoreline became indistinct and gradually faded away as we steamed westward. The old Cliff House on the south side of the Golden Gate was the last habitation that I could discern on the coast. Then we passed the Farallones Islands, a few rocky peaks some 30 odd miles from San Francisco, and then as we went farther west these, too, disappeared, and the next land we will see will be the Hawaiian Islands, some 2000 miles to the westward, which we are due to reach in about six days.

A stiff westerly wind is blowing and the sea is a little rough. The boat is rolling considerably and very few passengers turned up for dinner tonight. I myself do not feel at all sick. I had a long talk with Mr. Bissell in the evening and turned into a very comfortable bunk about 10.30 p.m. I have the whole stateroom to myself, and it is certainly a comfort to have the whole space and not be crowded with other passengers.

Bissell has been sick and is on a trip to Hawaii with his wife, son, and niece, for his health.

July 9th—At sea. Weather cloudy and wet; sea still a little rough, and many people seasick. This is a good boat and the food is excellent; the captain and all the officers seem to be first-rate men and always agreeable. That feeling of vast loneliness that I had as I saw the American coast fading away yesterday has gone. Now I look forward to the next shores we shall reach.

I have walked the deck, slept, and eaten all day.

July 10th—At sea. This is Sunday and a clergyman held services in the "Social Hall" of the ship. I did not attend. Weather still wet and cloudy. Sea much smoother.

July 11th—Weather perfect; sea quiet. We passed south of latitude 30° N about noon today, and the weather is becoming much warmer. In fact, the hot sun, the balmy air, and the occasional showers seen in the distance, all show our approach to the tropics.

July 12—At sea. One of the seamen went crazy today and raised a slight row before he could be put in irons.

Letter from Dick, dated S.S. Sierra, at sea, July 13, 1904

We will reach Honolulu in the morning, and I drop a line to you to mail there, as we will have a chance to go ashore for a short time before we start off again. This is the sixth day out from San Francisco and we have so far had a first rate voyage.

I mailed a letter to you the day we sailed from San Francisco (July 8th). We got away prompt at 2 p.m. A couple of fellows that I knew in San Francisco came down to the boat to see me off. The weather was perfect, with a stiff northwest wind blowing; and when we steamed out of the harbor and off to the west, I thought I had never seen California look so beautiful, as it gradually faded in the distance. There are certainly but few places on earth, where the scenery can equal that of the Bay of San Francisco.

The sea was a little rough for the first two days after leaving San Francisco, but since then it has been smooth and the weather fine. We are now approaching the tropics, and though it is hot, the weather is not oppressive and the occasional tropical showers that we have during the day, do much to cool things off. The only person that I found I knew when the ship sailed, was a man named Bissell, an attorney of the Santa Fe Railway, whom I had once met in Chicago. He has been sick and is on a trip for his health to the Sandwich Islands with his family. He is a first rate fellow, and I will be sorry when he leaves the ship at Honolulu. Dr. Nicholas Senn, the Chicago surgeon, is also a passenger, but he has been sick in his stateroom ever since we started, and I have not yet seen him. I do not know him except by reputation.

There are only about 50 first class passengers in all, and the boat is not at all crowded, as it could carry several times this number. Most of them are Americans bound for Honolulu; most of the rest are Australians bound for Sydney. There is an American army [navy] surgeon on his way to join his ship in the South Pacific, an Australian horse racer, a native Hawaiian so-called "prince," a coal mine owner of New South Wales, several plantation owners of the Sandwich Islands, and others.

This ship is a very good boat. It is not so big as the large Atlantic liners, but it is very comfortable, the grub is first class, and the boat makes 15 or 16 knots per hour. We have been coming directly southwest from San Francisco, and the Sandwich Islands will be the first land that we have sighted since leaving the coast. From Honolulu we change our course to almost due south, and cross the equator into the South Pacific. In about a week from Honolulu we should reach "Pago Pago" in the Samoan Islands; and if we stop there long enough to send mail ashore, I will write to you from there; if not, I will write from Auckland, New Zealand, where we will arrive about the end of this month.

From the Diary

July 13—The crazy seaman escaped tonight but was caught again and put in irons. We will reach Honolulu in the morning and he will be put ashore there. It is very hot.

July 14—Arrived at Honolulu quarantine station about 6.30 a.m. Quarantine officer came aboard at 7 and we landed about 8 a.m.

The town of Honolulu is a neat pretty little place with a narrow harbor cut artificially out of the coral rock. It is well protected by coral reefs. The town looks much like a town in southern California, with its fine lawns, palms, etc. The business part of the town is built mostly of brick, with some stone, streets macadamized and kept well watered; white and native policemen; good hotels and stores with American prices; people very polite and obliging, but indolent as a necessary result of the climate. The town is well supplied with water from a lake up in the mountains. Town lies on foothills of mountains rising 2000 feet or more above the sea. Most of the people are natives, Japanese, and Chinese; white people not very numerous. Town said to have about 50,000 people. There is a very fine aquarium almost as large as that in New York or Naples.

Was struck by lack of forests on the hills. They are bare or covered with only brush and grass, which gives them a fine green appearance. Some timber in the valleys. The general character of the country is much like that of the coast ranges of California.

The weather is hot but not oppressive. This a.m. the thermometer was 74° and this p.m. it was 85°, with a somewhat high humidity.

Dr. Abeken, U. S. Navy surgeon going to Pago Pago, and I took lunch at the Hawaiian Hotel, on the open porch where the tables were set. We had poi cocktails, a milky-looking extract from a native plant; taro, edible root of a soapy consistency and not much taste, etc.

(A few days ago, one of our passengers was bitten by a centipede in his bunk. The wound made a bad sore and the ship's doctor put antiphlogiston on it with apparently very good results in drawing out the poison.)

They say at Honolulu that the changed conditions since the annexation of the islands to the U. S., they have been much less prosperous. The prohibition of contract labor from Japan has raised the price of wages, much to the distress of sugar growers, from $9 to $18 per month.

At about 7 p.m., we had finished taking coal on the ship and unloading the 900 tons of freight for Honolulu, and we set sail to the south, a fresh west wind making a rather rough sea during the evening.

Dr. Abeken, one of the passengers on the ship, has a love letter from a Spanish girl which he cannot read as it is written in Spanish. He asked me to help him decipher it, but I could not do so.

July 15—At sea. Fine smooth sea and east wind. Passed latitude 16° N this p.m.
July 16—Ditto. Passed latitude 11°N this p.m.
July 17—Ditto. Passed latitude 6°N today. The weather, though hot, is much relieved by the brisk east winds. The thermometer ranges from 78° to 82°. We saw a number of gulls and other tropical birds today, which probably came from Palmyra Island, which we passed on the West, though not in sight of it. This and other neighboring islands are the beginning of the South Sea Islands and Polynesia.

There are a couple of Samoan girls on board in the second-class cabin, bound from Honolulu to Samoa. One of them is very pretty, and several of the boys are running after her; so far, without success.

Letter from his father, dated Seal Harbor, July 17, 1904

Your letter from San Francisco is before me, received a few days since, and, as the latest date for a letter to you in *Australia* is July 20, I write this on July 17. My next letter shall be about Aug. 1, and shall be directed care of J. S. Morgan & Co., etc.

I felt disappointed at Bowman's failure to join you, but, after all, as you say, you have travelled so much alone that you are used to it, and prefer it, and, then, you are going to places in direct communication with England and the United States and not to Siberia and other out of the way places.

I shall look with great interest for your next letter, etc., etc. I am now settled for the summer and everything working smoothly and pleasantly. My new man is a great success, an excellent house servant, quite industrious, efficient. He has but *one* defect—he *stammers*, and, I do not perfectly take in all he wishes to say. Should I get accustomed to this and should he be able to run the place at 1331, I think he will prove a *treasure*.

Before leaving home I engaged a successor to poor Mary—a friend of Jane's—who was housekeeper for the Douglasses—the Lake Superior promoter—for 17 years. I liked her *looks* and talk. She seems about 40, and I hope as good as she *seems* and talks. This is a great point gained—feel sure of some reliable person to take charge.

Seal Harbor never was more beautiful than it is this summer and Sea Bench never more attractive. I never tire of admiring it—mountain, sea, forest, lawn, garden, all in one. *You* will see many and varied beautiful and grand things during your travels, but not one combining so much as the one I enjoy at this minute as I write at my window looking north on Mt. Sargent. I hope I shall hear from Tal before I close this letter, so as to give you the latest news from Atlantic City. I had a letter from Boies, "Butte, Montana," yesterday. So far they (he and Arthur E. Brown, of the Zoo) had a very prosperous and pleasant time. They planned ultimately to "go over to the Idaho side of the Teton Mountains" and camp out, expecting to return early in Sept. I am delighted Boies is off and hope he will stay late and do *nothing* in the presidential campaign. His trip, if long enough, ought to do him much good.

I have just had a letter from Spencer. He says they have settled everything satisfactorily with Col. Wall and all the rest, etc., etc. He also says he has been confined to *his bed* and "tea and toast" for several days with a severe attack of *gout*!!! in his foot, but is now better and intends to visit the mill *next* day. As I have had no letter from Tal by today's mail I must close without any account of his doings.

From the Diary

July 18—We crossed the equator today at 3.25 p.m. The weather is perfect and a fresh east wind keeps things cool, so that it is hard to realize that we are in the hottest latitude of the earth. The air is moist, however, and a slight exertion produces profuse sweating.

There is an old custom among sailors that if a person has never been across the equator before, he must be ducked in the sea when he first crosses that line. There was some talk in fun among the passengers of ducking two or three of us on board who had never been across, but no effort was made. I think they feared we would make a fight and possibly duck some of the other fellows. The passengers are becoming well acquainted and most of them are a very good crowd. There are only about twenty of us, as the rest got off at Honolulu. Captain Houdlette is a fine man and is liked by all.

Letter from Dick, dated on board S.S. Sierra, South Pacific Ocean, July 19, 1904

We crossed the equator today and are now passing through the South Sea Islands, though we have not come within sight of any of them, and will not do so until we reach the Samoan Group in a couple of days from now. But the occasional appearance of sea gulls and albatross show that islands are not far distant, on one side or the other of our course. The weather is very hot, as might be expected on the equator, but the prevailing easterly winds of these seas make it bearable.

I mailed a letter to you at Honolulu on July 14th. We arrived there in the morning, and after unloading freight and taking on coal we proceeded south. Honolulu is a prosperous-looking town of about 50,000 people, mostly natives and Japanese, with fewer Americans and Europeans. Dr. Abeken of the U. S. Navy, who is a passenger on this ship, and I took in the sights of the town while we stopped there. It is in latitude 20°N, and has a fine climate, though hot. The natives seem to spend most of their time bathing in the sea, eating and sleeping; and I think that if the white people stay in that climate long enough, they also will soon be doing the same thing.

There is not much going on, on board ship. The weather has mostly been fine, with only one night of bad weather the day after leaving Honolulu. Most of the passengers got off at Honolulu, and there are only about 20 left. Dr. Abeken leaves the ship at the Samoan Islands. Dr. Senn of Chicago, about whom I wrote you in my last letter, is going to Australia and thence north to India. I believe he is investigating the conditions of some of the hospitals in the tropical countries. There is an American machinery manufacturer from Boston on board, who is going to Australia to try to open a market for his products, but if the talk I hear on board is true, I don't believe he will do much business. There are only eight Americans on board altogether. The rest are mostly Australians.

July 21st

We are just approaching Pago Pago, on Tutuila Island, one of the Samoan Group, in latitude about 10°S. This is an American possession occupied by a few hundred troops. The English and the Germans own other islands in the same group. We will stop at Pago Pago to put off mail and supplies, and I will take the opportunity to mail this letter there. We have now been two weeks out from San Francisco, and the only land that we have seen up until today was when we stopped at Honolulu. The weather is still very hot, but not especially disagreeable, as we have a constant breeze.

We will arrive at Auckland about July 28th and I will write further from there.

From the diary

July 21—It rained torrents last night and today cleared off into a hot sweltering day. We entered Pago Pago harbor about 6.30 a.m. This is an almost completely enclosed harbor—small, only about 1 mile long in some places and half a mile wide, but deep and safe—possibly an old crater—completely surrounded by high peaks, rugged, and, so far as seen, of a much decomposed volcanic rock. Peaks rise perhaps 1000 feet or more above sea, densely covered with tropical verdure to top—a veritable jungle, with many cocoanut and bread-fruit trees. Many natives live about the harbor—light brown, fat, good-natured people, well and symmetrically built, half naked, girls very good looking. Leprosy said to be unknown among them; much elephantiasis.

Natives live in their picturesque round houses open on all sides and with thatched roofs. They sell all kinds of trinkets to steamship passengers, especially a mat made of the bark of tree beaten out thin and looking like thin leather and painted in various patterns. The native women are said to be the best looking in the South Pacific and in great demand as kept women among white people in Fiji and elsewhere. All the natives do much tatooing. The men mostly have their legs tatooed down to their knees looking as if they wore light blue trunks. The women also have their arms, bellies, etc., tatooed. The face is not tatooed. The women also paint their bellies brilliant colors.

The U. S. government maintains one ship—the old Adams—a wooden training ship at Tutuila, and a small naval force. The commander's house is on a bluff near the dock and is a large comfortable structure of wood. The government is building roads and improving the settlement and the harbor.

The weather is sweltering hot on land.

We left Pago Pago at 12 noon and continued south. The air is becoming much cooler this evening.

July 22—At sea. Much cooler. Thermometer 72°.

July 23—Same.

July 24—At sea. Thermometer 63°.

July 25—We crossed the 180° W. longitude and therefore skipped a day, so that instead of this being Sunday, it is Monday, July 25th. A fierce southeast wind is blowing. The boat is rolling very much and most of the passengers are sick. The weather has turned quite cold, about 50° to 55° or at least it seems cold after coming out of the tropics. We expect to reach Aukland sometime tomorrow.

July 26—The sea moderated this morning and we arrived in Aukland about 2.30 p.m. Aukland is picturesquely situated on the east side of the north island of New Zealand and has a beautiful harbor enclosed by islands and peninsulas. Town built mostly of wood on account of earthquakes, though some stone buildings have been erected. The most striking feature of the town is the light coffee-color that most all the houses are painted. The streets are wide and well paved, some with asphalt; good trolley lines and buses. The stores good and full of American goods. In fact, the whole surroundings look very like a prosperous American town.

I stopped at the Star Hotel, a stone structure with very good food and fair rooms. Everything is neat and clean, but cold. People here, as in Europe, don't seem to heat their houses. They hug a small fire in the sitting-room or elsewhere, and suffer with cold and dampness in bedrooms. Many of them have colds, chill blains, etc., as a result. In America, we may perhaps overheat things, but elsewhere they underheat.

In the evening, some of the Sierra passengers came to the hotel for dinner. Among them were Messrs. Brown, Warren, Mayor, Schirmer, Collins, etc. We all had dinner together, and afterwards I went down to the boat to see them off for Sydney, for which port they started about midnight. I took down to the boat a box of Havana cigars for Captain Houdlette, for he is a first-rate man and had treated me well.

Letter from Dick, dated Star Hotel, Auckland, N. Z., July 27, 1904

I arrived here all right today, after a voyage of a little less than three weeks from San Francisco. I never had a more pleasant voyage anywhere. With the exception of one or two days, the weather was perfect; and as the boat was not crowded and the staterooms and grub were good, everything was very satisfactory.

I mailed a letter to you from Honolulu and one from Pago Pago, on Tutuila Island, in the Samoan Group, and I suppose they will reach you in due time.

We stopped several hours at Pago Pago and had a chance to see a good deal of the island and the natives. The island is a cluster of volcanic peaks covered with a dense tropical foliage; and the harbor of Pago Pago, which is almost entirely enclosed by hills, looks very much as if it was a submerged volcanic crater. The natives live mostly on bread-fruit, cocoanuts, bananas and fish. Leprosy, which is so common among the Hawaiian Islanders, is said to be almost unknown among the Samoans, though elephantiasis is very prevalent. The Samoan women have the reputation of being the most beautiful of all the South Sea natives, and from what I saw of them I think they fully deserve this reputation. I do not know where any better looking women could be found anywhere.

After leaving Pago Pago, the weather became rapidly cooler, and in less than two days after leaving the tropical heat of the Samoan Islands, we were in the mid-winter weather of this southern hemisphere. Here in Auckland, which is in latitude about 38°S, the weather is about as cold as at Atlantic City in the winter.

This town of Auckland is a small place of about 40,000 people, though counting in the outlying districts, there are about 80,000 people. It is the commercial metropolis of New Zealand and is a well-kept, prosperous town. I start tomorrow by railway to visit the Waihi gold mine about 100 miles south of here. As it is one of the largest gold mines in the world, I have a curiosity to see it. Then I will visit the New Zealand geysers, and then return here. From here I will then go to Sydney, Australia, where I will arrive about the middle of August. It is only a four days voyage from here to Sydney.

I will write further before leaving here.

From the Diary

July 27—Stayed around Auckland to sort of get my bearings. Arranged for trip to Waihi gold mines and to geysers at Rotorua.

July 28—Went to Paeroa by train—six hours—arrived 4 p.m. Took stage at station for Waihi, 14 miles up the valley of the Ohinemuri River, a very beautiful trip through a rugged mountainous country. Arrived about 7 p.m., and stopped at Meyer's Hotel, a very comfortable place for a mining town hotel, consisting mostly of bar rooms and billiard rooms downstairs and bedrooms on the second (top) floor. Presented letter of introduction from T. A. Rickard to Percy Morgan, director of Waihi School of Mines, and arranged to go through the mines tomorrow.

July 29—Went through the mine with Mr. Morgan and a foreman. Saw the mill and other works. Took stage to Paeroa in the afternoon, pouring rain all the way. Took afternoon train from Paeora to Te Aroha, where I will stop overnight.

July 30—Still raining. There is a very good hotel here, the Hot Springs Hotel, and there are a number of hot springs comprised in a government reservation, and said to be very good for rheumatism.

Took 11.40 a.m. train for Rotorua, arriving there 5.50 p.m. Still raining hard. Took stage for Whakarewarewa, 2 miles, where I stopped at the Geyser Hotel.

There are a number of geysers about Whakarewarewa, depositing siliceous sinter just as in Yellowstone Park. At the time of my visit none of them were going up more than 4 or 5 feet. One of them is said to go up 60 feet or more every few days, but though I stayed there four days, it did not "spout." The largest geyser in N.Z. is at Waimangu* 18 miles from Whakarewarewa, but it was not spouting at the time of my visit so I did not go to it. Previously it is said to have spouted every 2 or 3 days, but when I was in the region it had not spouted for over 2 weeks, and people feared that there might come a volcanic eruption as a result of the stopping of this safety valve.

Ten miles from Whakarewarewa (southeast) is the old Maori town of Wairoa, which in 1886 was destroyed by an outburst of volcanic ashes from a mountain† some miles distant. I visited this town. The ashes cover almost everything, though the upper parts of some of the higher houses can still be seen. In some places the ashes were 15 or 16 feet deep; in others, 1 or 2 feet. They fell in the form of a bluish gray wet mud full of steam and with some coarser rock. Several hundred Maoris were killed at Wairoa; and at another town nearer the volcano, many more were killed and the town completely obliterated by many feet of ash.

The drive from Whakarewarewa to Wairoa is through a volcanic country, full of small lakes occupying volcanic cones and very picturesque. They have been stocked with trout by the government.

* [Park says (*Geology of New Zealand*, p. 172) that water is projected to height of 1200 feet.]
† Mt. Tarawera

At the time of my visit, no geysers of any size were spouting in the district, though near (70 miles) Lake Taupo, between 50 and 60 miles south of Whakarewarewa there are said to be a number of smaller geysers like those at Whakarewarewa. The three principal geyser localities are Whakarewarewa, Waimangu, and [Wairoa].

When a geyser ceases spouting, it can often be started up by putting soap in it. But this method seems to exhaust the geyser and has been stopped.

There is a small Maori settlement of about 100 at Whakarewarewa, living in wooden huts, sometimes ornamented with Maori carvings. The children and some of the adults soak in the geysers in the cold weather to keep warm. Often at night when they get cold they throw off their blankets, run to the geysers to warm, and return to bed.

They are good-looking people and well built. I saw a Maori dance at Whakarewarewa by 8 or 10 girls, called a "Poy Dance," because they swing in their hands small bell-shaped balls made of reeds and hung to a string. The girls are wonderful in the way they could work their hips and bellies. The Samoan women do the same thing in dancing. They move their hips and bellies to keep time with the music of the dance.

The Maoris were originally cannibals, but have given up the practise. In olden days they preferred eating other Maoris rather than white people, whom they considered too salt. The Maoris never use salt.

The Maoris are bright intelligent people, are represented by 3 or 4 members in the Colonial parliament, and are shrewd in business. They often intermarry with the whites, and the whites are not lowered in their own estimation thereby. They have been rapidly decreasing in recent years, but are said now to be holding their own. They number about 40,000 in all. They are supposed to be of Malay origin and came to New Zealand about 600 years ago, when they exterminated the aborigines whom they found there.

August 3—I stayed in the geyser region until today, and it has been raining almost all the time. Came back to Auckland today. Raining and snowing all the way.

Letter from Dick, dated Auckland, New Zealand, August 4, 1904

I wrote to you on my arrival here last week. Since then I have been on a trip through the north part of New Zealand and have just returned here. I travelled partly by railway and partly by stage or buggy, and had a very interesting trip. I went first through the Waihi gold mining region, and thence south to the region of the New Zealand geysers, which are much like those of our own Yellowstone Park. I have also visited several of the New Zealand volcanoes, some of which have been active in recent years. It has been raining or snowing most of the time on this trip, but it is now midwinter in this region, and such weather is to be expected.

I saw a good deal of the native Maori tribes in the interior. They were once cannibals, but are said now to have given up the habit of eating each other. When the practice was in vogue, however, they always preferred to eat their own people rather than white people, as they complained that white meat was too salty. The Maoris never eat salt.

There were a number of Maoris in the geyser region when I was there, and they seemed to spend a large part of the time soaking in the hot water of the geysers to keep warm. Frequently during the night, the Maoris would get up out of their blankets and run to the geyser to get warmed, and then return to bed again.

New Zealand is a beautiful country and full of natural resources. It supplies large quantities of cattle, sheep and grain to England, Australia and South Africa; and also has rich mines of coal, gold, etc. The northern part of New Zealand is largely volcanic, and numerous high volcanic peaks are scattered over the island. In fact in the immediate vicinity of Auckland, a number of volcanic peaks are to be seen. The decomposition of the volcanic rocks makes a very rich soil, and hence the great productiveness of many New Zealand lands. I visited a place about 150 miles south of here, where, in 1886, a volcano [Tarawera] had become active and had shot out great quantities of steam, hot mud, and volcanic ashes, burying several Maori settlements and killing many people, under conditions very much resembling those which overwhelmed Pompeii. I could still see some of the remains of the Maori huts in one of these buried villages.

The New Zealand people are very friendly to Americans, and I have never been better treated anywhere in a foreign country than here.

I sail from here on August 8th for Sydney, Australia, and will arrive there on the 12th or 13th. I will write further from there.

From the Diary

August 4—In Auckland. Went to top of Mt. Eden, a hill probably 500 feet high on the outskirts of town. It is an extinct volcano and a well-defined crater is in the center. A beautiful view of the country is had from the summit.
August 5—In Auckland. The rain has stopped and the weather is perfect. I have engaged passage to sail on S.S. Moana of the Union Steamship Company, for Sydney, Australia, on August 8.
August 6—In Auckland. Saw football game between Auckland and Wellington. Latter won. Great excitement and about 8000 people present.
August 7—In Auckland. This is Sunday and very quiet, more so than Philadelphia. Took ferry boat to Devonport and carriage to a lake about 5 miles, a beautiful little body of water occupying an old crater and not very much above level of sea. Took this trip with a Mr. Butcher from Wellington.

Yesterday I called on Mr. Wallace, whom I had met at Whakarewarewa and who asked me to call on him here. He is a very pleasant fellow.

There are large herds of wild horses in New Zealand. They are domestic horses gone wild and are so numerous that the settlers shoot them to keep them from eating up their grass.

The New Zealand domestic horse is descended from the English horse, but is small, much like our broncho. He is very tough and strong, and has wonderful endurance. The stage coaches go just about as fast uphill as downhill and at a good gait. The New Zealanders have a queer habit of clipping their horses' bellies and not their backs. The idea is to keep the mud from sticking to them.

August 8—Was to have sailed on S.S. Moana for Sydney, but she has been delayed by stormy weather on the coast and has not yet arrived from Dunedin, her starting point. She will probably sail tomorrow.

This town of Auckland is very quiet, and the saloons all close at 10 p.m. The hotels also close at 10 p.m., and if one comes in later than that, he has to ring a bell, and the night porter looks at him through a little hole in the wall, and if satisfied with his appearance, lets him in.

New Zealand is a beautiful country, and one of the richest in natural resources that I have ever seen. If it were in America it would be one of our richest districts. It supplies large quantities of cattle, sheep and grain to England, South Africa, and, in times of drought, to Australia. Its soil is very rich, and they say that in parts as many as 8 sheep can be fattened to the acre. The country has also productive coal, gold, and other mines.

The government is purely socialistic. The government owns almost everything—railways, telegraph lines, street-car lines, health resorts, many kinds of insurance companies, and some coal mines. The system may have its advantages but I have not seen many of them. Everything is orderly and respectable; no poverty or squalor is noticeable, but an absolute lack of progressiveness and individual enterprise is noticeable everywhere.

No inducement is offered for any man to do better than any one else. A large part of the people are government employees among whom superior personal qualifications count for nothing, as promotion depends entirely on length of service. No inducement is offered any one to work any harder than the law absolutely compels him, and that is not very hard. Holidays are very numerous, and people seem to pay more attention to horse racing, football, cricket, bridge whist and other games than they do to their business. There is nothing especially bad in the conditions of living in New Zealand, and yet nothing especially good. Everything is sort of mediocre, and every person seems to be satisfied with mediocrity in his pursuits. No one seems to have any ambition to get ahead of the other fellow.

A large manufacturer of binding twine in New Zealand told me one day that they (the New Zealanders) did not want to see any one get very rich and that he approved the idea. The same idea pervades all classes. Mediocrity in wealth, ability, progress, and everything else is what they want and what they come very near getting. The result is a commonplace, cheap sort of condition in everything.

If this is the result of socialism, New Zealand with all its natural resources will never become an America.

Another feature of New Zealand customs, whether the result of socialism or not, is the smallness of everything. The railroad cars are very small and the seats in many of them are just about broad enough for a rabbit to sit on. The rooms in the hotels are very small, and the beds are short and narrow, and it is often hard to keep from rolling out. When they build a fire they do it with about a handful of coal, though coal is very cheap. The trolley cars are very small and the seats are so little as to be ridiculous, looking as if they were made for Lilliputians. The bottled waters are put up only in little half-pint bottles, and a thirsty man wants a dozen of them. Even the horses are small, and the ideas of the people on general subjects are similar. One man said to me that the geyser region was the best-known resort for rheumatism in the world, though I saw only about six people taking "the cure" there.

August 9—Sailed at 11 a.m., on S.S. Moana for Sydney. Weather rainy, but sea smooth. Have very comfortable stateroom on top deck. There are about 50 or 60 passengers on board, mostly Australians or New Zealanders. I am the only American on the ship. Americans do not seem to be very numerous in these parts, and when they do appear, they seem to be looked on as a sort of curiosity, though they are treated with the greatest courtesy.

The Moana is a fine little ship of about 3800 tons. Food very good.

August 10—At sea. The Tasman Sea, as the body of water between New Zealand and Australia is called, has the reputation of being very rough and stormy but so far on this voyage it has not been so. There is a gentle swell on the sea and many of the passengers are sick, but it is not rough.

Have been playing "Napoleon" all evening with Sir John See, ex-premier of New South Wales. He was made a "Sir" at the time of the federation of the Australian states. He has risen from the ranks and is a very bright man.

August 11—At sea. Fine weather, becoming warmer as we approach Australia.

August 12—At sea. We expect to reach Sydney this evening about 11 p.m.

Letter from Dick, dated on board S.S. Moana, Coast of Australia, August 12, 1904

We are approaching Sydney, Australia, and will land there tonight, so I drop a line to you to mail when I get ashore. I left Auckland, New Zealand, on this ship four days ago, and have had a very good voyage across what is known as the Tasman Sea, which is the part of the Pacific Ocean between New Zealand and Australia.

This ship, the Moana, is much smaller than the one on which I came from San Francisco, but she is an excellent vessel. There are some 50 or 60 passengers on board, most of them Australians and New Zealanders. So far as I know, I am the only American on the ship. Americans do not seem to travel much in these parts, though they are certainly treated very well when they do so.

I expect probably to be some six weeks or more in different parts of Australia, but I will write more fully after I have gotten to Sydney and made my plans about getting around in different parts of the country.

I wrote to you twice while I was in New Zealand, and though the American mail does not leave there at very frequent intervals, yet you will probably receive those letters before you receive this one.

From the Diary

August 13—We reached Sydney at 11 p.m. last night, and I came up at once to the Australia Hotel. This a.m. I started to find out about going to the tin mines of New South Wales and to Mt. Morgan, but it is Saturday today, and no one seemed to like to talk business much, so I am waiting over until Monday. Cricket teams, getting ready for Saturday on Friday; getting ready for business on Monday.

August 14—This is Sunday and very quiet. It is clear and warm, and I have taken a long walk in the park. Last night I put on a dress suit at dinner as I was told it was the custom. Most of the other people were dressed the same way. Tonight I did the same, but found that with one exception I was the only man in the dining room with it on. I suppose the idea is that going to church on Sunday so purifies the soul that the body needs no purification, and one can come dirty to dinner. I think it all perfect nonsense to have to wear a dress suit at a public hotel at any time, but if it is done on week days I don't see why it should not be done on Sundays, unless for the above-mentioned reason.

Letter from Dick, dated The Australia Hotel, Sydney, August 15, 1904

I wrote to you hurriedly on the steamer just before landing here three days ago, and as I learn that the mail for the United States leaves here tomorrow, I write again so as to catch it.

My stay in New Zealand was very interesting and I saw a great deal. The New Zealand system of government is very socialistic. The government owns railroads, street car lines, telegraph lines, insurance companies, coal mines, health resorts, etc., etc. In fact there is but little chance for individual effort. A large part of the population are simply government employees, and they are no more ambitious than most government clerks in other countries. They don't work any harder than they have to, because there is no inducement; and promotion on account of superior individual merit seems to be unknown.

The effect of all this seems to be to suppress all personal ambition. Everything and every one seems to be sort of mediocre in character. Nothing seems very bad in the conditions of New Zealand, but nothing seems extraordinarily good. No new inventions or ambitious undertakings ever startle the community. Everything is commonplace. There is no great poverty or squalor in the cities, nor on the other hand is there any great wealth. The government seems to object to any one becoming either rich or poor. A monotonous and commoplace mediocrity seems to characterize the country. The people adopt what they think best from the rest of the world, but produce nothing new themselves. They slumber under the flattering illusion that they have solved all the problems of living.

I start tonight by railroad for Brisbane and Rockhampton, in the state of Queensland, which is in the northeast part of Australia and just north of this state of New South Wales. At Rockhampton I will visit the Mt. Morgan gold mine. This is a very celebrated mine, and is supposed to occupy the site of an extinct geyser. As this is an unusual phenomenon, I thought I would like to see the conditions under which it occurs, as the information might be useful in other regions.

Sydney is a large place of about 400,000 people and seems to be a prosperous place. I am staying at a hotel called "The Australia" and it is very comfortable. I will return here in about ten days, from Queensland.

I have not yet received any mail from the United States since I left San Francisco, but some will probably arrive before my return here. Please continue to address me care of J. S. Morgan & Co., 22 Old Broad St., London, England, as they will forward mail promptly.

From the Diary

August 15—Today I called on the government geologist; also at the office of Mr. J. Brown, whom I had met on the Sierra. He was not there, but his chief clerk secured a letter of introduction for me to Mt. Morgan from one of the directors.

I had intended to go to Mt. Morgan by train tonight via Brisbane and Rockhampton, but several people have told me that by sea was more comfortable, so I will sail tomorrow afternoon on the Aramac of the Australia United Steam Navigation Company.

August 16—Sailed at 6 p.m., on the Aramac, a comfortable little steamer of about 2100 tons, carrying about 40 passengers and a cargo of chickens, geese, horses, cows, and general merchandise for "northern ports." This is a coasting steamer and her first port is Brisbane. The food is very good, and I have a large stateroom to myself. The night is fine and clear.

August 17—At sea. Weather, perfect; sea, smooth. Temperature probably about 60°. The captain of the Aramac had travelled with Alexander Agassiz on two of his deep-sea dredging expeditions on the coast of Australia and in the South Seas. Had a long talk with him this morning.

The rolling hilly country of the Australian coast has been in sight all the way up from Sydney, a green forest-clad country.

August 18—Arrived at the mouth of the Brisbane River about 9 a.m., and went up the river 14 miles to the town of Brisbane. This is the capital of Queensland and a neat town of about 50,000 people, in a rolling country, green and very picturesque. Another passenger and I took lunch at the Gresham Hotel, and it was very good. Our ship does not leave here until Saturday afternoon—i.e., August 20—so I have been putting in the time seeing the town, though there is really not much to see. The government buildings are good and substantial, built of a sort of yellowish sandstone. Went to the office and got a copy of Dr. Jack's report on Mt. Morgan, to read before visiting that mine.

August 19—At Brisbane. Slept last night on board ship. Walked about town most of the day with other passengers; had several "scotch and sodas" and took lunch at the hotel (this time Glennon's Hotel) which was very good. In fact, most Australian and New Zealand hotels seem to have very good food, and excellent butter, but they pay less attention to their sleeping rooms, which, though clean, are small and cramped, badly furnished and often lit with bad gaslights or only candles. Since leaving America I have not been in a hotel where I could read in my bedroom with any comfort at night. The sheets of the beds are always clean and neat, but the mattresses are old fashioned and often too soft.

The weather in Brisbane is warm—almost hot—as this is the beginning of summer here and the town is about in latitude 28°S. It is said to be very hot here in summer, and I can well imagine it.

Letter from his father, dated Seal Harbor, August 20, 1904

Your letter postmarked "Pago Pago" July 22, received last Monday. I write today and direct to care of J. S. Morgan & Co., realizing you will not receive my letter for a long time, but, at same time, I fulfil my promise of writing you regularly; hence, about first week in Sept. I will write you whether I receive a letter from you in the meantime or not. I am very glad to know that, so far, your trip certainly is a success, that you are having sufficient companionship, that you appear to have *good* doctors about, etc., etc. I do trust, and I also believe, that your future experience will be like your present until you get home again. I am still doing satisfactorily up here and hope that I shall meet no drawbacks. Everything about me, as heretofore, is charming. I had a visit yesterday from "Mr. Thomas J. Bush" Bar Harbor, whom you knew at Bar Harbor, with Spencer and Philip. He called, as he told me to see "the father of his friends, Dick, Speck and Philip." I was gratified by his call, and I told him when Spencer came to Bar Harbor to pay Christine a visit I would invite the girls over here to lunch and would *now* invite him to join the party. He seemed much pleased with my invitation, etc., etc. So he shall have the peculiar institutions of Sea Bench as a reward for his courtesy; viz., barbecued chicken and blue berry pie!!!

Spencer expects to be up here early in Sept. He intends a day or two for Seal Harbor, and the rest of his visit to Christine and the gayeties of Bar Harbor. I have a letter from Boies still in camp, Aug. 8, in Idaho or it may be Wyoming, "Buffalo Fork of Snake River camp."

Letter from Dick, dated Brisbane, Australia, August 20, 1904

I wrote to you a few days ago from Sydney. From there I had intended to come here by railroad, but I found that a very good little coasting steamer was about to come this way, so I came here on it by sea. The same boat leaves tomorrow for the north, and I will continue on it as far as Rockhampton, about 250 miles farther up the coast, and will return from there to Sydney next week.

On the way back to Sydney I may stop over at Newcastle, which is the great coal mining district of Australia. I met one of the owners of the largest mines there on the ship coming from San Francisco to New Zealand, and since my arrival in Australia, he has been urging me to come see his mines, and stay with him for a week or so. I will not stay that long, but I may stay part of a day.

This town of Brisbane is the capital and commercial metropolis of the Australian state of Queensland. It is in latitude 28°S. and much warmer than southern Australia, which is in latitude 35° to 39°S.; but the summer heat has not yet started. The coral islands of the south Pacific begin off the coast of Queensland and extend north up into the East India Islands. Extensive pearl fisheries are carried on, to the north of Queensland, and the northern part of the state is also rapidly becoming a great sugar producing country.

On my return to Sydney, I will continue on my main line of travel westward along the southern coast of Australia, stopping first at Melbourne, in the Australian state of Victoria; but I will write further before I leave Sydney.

From the Diary

August 20—We sailed at 2 p.m. today for the north, with a lot of sheep on the deck and a general cargo below. Weather perfect and sea quiet.

August 21 and 22—At sea. Weather fine and sea smooth. About noon we passed Lady Elliot Island, which is a small coral (?) island once noted for the guano it produced. We arrived at the mouth of the river on which Rockhampton is situated about 9 p.m. Rockhampton is about 40 miles up the river. We were met by a steam tender which took passengers and freight aboard for Rockhampton, while the Aramac proceeded north. It took till about 1 a.m., to get all the freight on the tender, and in the meantime the passengers had gone to bed in the cabin. About 6 a.m., we arrived in Rockhampton, had a very good breakfast at the "Commercial Hotel" and left at 8.40 a.m. by train for Rockhampton [Mt. Morgan]. The distance is only 24 miles but we did not arrive there until 10.30. Went immediately to the office of the Mt. Morgan gold mining company, met Capt. Richards, to whom I had a letter of introduction, and also his assistant, Mr. Seale, and arranged to go through the mine in the p.m.

Spent the afternoon in the mine, got dinner at the Imperial Hotel, and took train for Rockhampton at 6.40 p.m. Typhoid fever is very prevalent at Mt. Morgan.

August 23—In Rockhampton. I am waiting for the train for Sydney, which leaves here every Monday, Wednesday, and Friday; and as this is Tuesday, I have to wait until tomorrow. This town has a population of about 10,000 people and [is] almost exactly on the Tropic of Capricorn. The spring is just commencing, and it is very hot, the air also being full of moisture, though the weather is clear.

The government buildings here, as elsewhere in Australia, are substantial and artistic, built of a yellowish gray sandstone. In fact, here, as elsewhere in Australia, the number of fine substantial buildings in proportion to the population is remarkable. Though this looks well, I fear that it is what has caused part at least of the enormous debt of the Australian states. A town of 10,000 people really does not need public buildings that would do credit to a city of a million people. In America we begin with small and cheap public buildings and as the town grows, we replace these with better ones, but here, as soon as a town is started, it must have magnificent public buildings, as if they were to last hundreds of years and as if the town would surely become a metropolis. In America, the town has become such before it gets its fine buildings; in Australia it gets them to start with, and often becomes of no importance. The Australian method is good, and the cheapest in the long run, provided the town does grow to a large city, but as most towns do not do so, their method must be an immense expense for comparatively little benefit. There is more practical common sense in the American method.

The Commercial Hotel here is very comfortable. The people here, as elsewhere in Australia, are great tea drinkers. They drink it when they get out of bed in the morning, the maid bringing it to the rooms about 7 a.m. At breakfast they drink tea again. At about 11 a.m., the maid again brings tea to the rooms. At lunch they again serve tea. At 4 p.m., the maid again brings tea to the rooms;

and at dinner more tea is served; while in the evening it is often drunk again. In fact, tea is shoved at a man at every turn, and the maid looks at you in amazement if you tell her that you don't want it. She can't comprehend one not drinking tea at every opportunity. In this country, both men and women drink tea with equal diligence. In fact, in many of the bar rooms, arrangements are made for serving tea in the same way as whisky or beer; and at the railway stations it is also served. Most of the important railroad stations have bar rooms, and as many people drink tea as alcoholic drinks. The Chinaman is not in it for a moment with the Australian, as a tea drinker.

August 24—Started south by train at noon. Will reach Brisbane tomorrow a.m., about 6 o'clock. The railways in Queensland have a 3-foot 6-inch gauge, and the cars are small, narrow, and not very comfortable—speed of train about 20 miles per hour. There is a sleeping car on this train, which is known as the "fast" train. The berths run longwise with the sides of the car, and are, in fact, narrow benches with an arrangement for letting down another narrow bench from above, making an upper berth. During the day the upper berth is hung up and the people sit on the long narrow lower berths. The train stops at eating stations for meals, which are fairly good. The men are all put at one end of the sleeping car and the women at the other, a curtain being swung between. The car is not very crowded and is therefore not especially uncomfortable. The porter is a very obliging sort of man and looks after the passengers very well.

The different states of Australia have different gauged railroads, thus requiring transshipment of passengers and freight at each frontier. Queensland has a 3-foot 6-inch gauge; New South Wales, 4-foot $8\frac{1}{2}$-inch; Victoria 5-foot 3-inch; South Australia 5-foot 3-inch and 3-foot 6-inch; and West Australia 3-foot 6-inch.

The cause of this difference is said to have been due to state jealousy. When one state (formerly "colony," now "state" since the federation) started a certain gauge the other state had to have a different gauge so as to show its independence!! The result is great additional expense and loss of time in transshipping.

August 25—Arrived Brisbane about 6 a.m., got breakfast at Gresham Hotel, and left by train a little after seven for the south. Arrived at the New South Wales border about 4.30 p.m., and changed into a N.S.W. train. Here I found a comfortable sleeping car—exactly like a pullman car. In fact, I believe it was a pullman, though some of the passengers claimed that it was made in Australia.

August 26—Arrived Newcastle about 7.30 a.m., and stopped over here at the invitation of Mr. John Brown, of J. & A. Brown, coal mine owners, whom I had met on the boat from San Francisco. I took breakfast and lunch with Brown, and he sent me on a trip on one of his tug boats around the harbor. He treated me most hospitably and kindly in every way. Left for Sydney in the afternoon, arriving there about 6.30 p.m.

Letter from Dick, dated The Australia Hotel, Sydney, August 27, 1904

On my return here from the northern part of Australia, I was very glad to find your letter of July 17th and to know that you found everything so satisfactory at

Seal Harbor. As you say, I do not think there is any place of its kind that can equal it; and the best thing about it is that it suits you so well.

I am very glad to hear that Tal expects to have an addition to his family, and I hope Kate is getting along all right. Our family seems to be a little short on populating the next generation; and I think we owe Tal and Kate a debt of gratitude for making up for this negligence.

I was very sorry to hear that Speck has been laid up with gout, but hope that the attack will not last long, and that he will soon be on his feet again.

I wrote to you last week from Brisbane, on the Pacific Coast of Queensland. From there I continued north by sea to Rockhampton, and thence went inland to visit the Mt. Morgan mine, which is considered one of the great gold mines of the world. I had a letter of introduction there, and was very well treated. From Mt. Morgan I returned to Rockhampton, and thence south by railroad for almost 48 hours to Newcastle. Here I stopped over for a few hours at the invitation of a man named John Brown, who is the largest coal mine owner in Australia; and thence I came on here. I believe I wrote to you that I had met Brown on the ship coming from San Francisco. He is a first rate fellow and more like an American than an Australian.

I arrived here last night, and will leave tomorrow by train for Melbourne, on the southern coast of Australia, about 18 hours journey. Brown is also going there on some coal business, so we will go together. He will come down here from Newcastle tonight.

I was glad to have seen the northern part of Australia, but also glad to get away from it, as it was very hot, and the mosquitoes were very bad. I was well supplied with mosquito nets, however, and was not troubled much. Northern Australia is becoming a great sugar and cotton country; but the Australian parliament has passed a bill against the importation of black labor, because they say they want to maintain a "white Australia" and the sugar and cotton planters are in great trouble because white labor can't work in that climate and the government won't let them have black labor.

From Melbourne, I expect to go to the island of Tasmania, off the southern coast of Australia, but I will write further about my movements after reaching Melbourne.

From the Diary

August 28—Left Sydney at 7.50 p.m. by train for Melbourne. John Brown came down from Newcastle last night and is going to Melbourne on the same train. The train has two good sleeping cars of a rather antiquated pullman car style, but very comfortable. It is crowded with people, as this is "Fair" week in Melbourne and also the Federal Parliament is in session.

August 29—Arrived Alford Junction on the Victoria frontier about 7.30 a.m. Got breakfast at a "20 minute" eating station and shifted to a Victoria train for Melbourne. Passed through a fine agricultural country with the "Australian Alps" to the south—a low range of mountains rising a few thousand feet in height. Passed numerous old placer gold workings, now abandoned and grown up with grass. Even the Chinaman can rarely make these old placers pay—so thoroughly has the gravel been worked over.

Arrived Melbourne about 1.30 p.m., and went to the Grand Hotel. Had intended to go to Menzies Hotel, but Brown was going to the Grand, so I went to have company. It is a very comfortable place and I pay 9 shillings per day for a room and breakfast, getting other meals where I like.

Melbourne is about the same size place as Sydney but is a much finer-looking city, with wide streets and fine buildings. The government buildings are simply magnificent. In fact, all over Australia the government buildings are very fine structures. The Australians have spent great sums of money even in small towns on public buildings, far better buildings than necessary. The result is that they are head over heels in debt and can't borrow any more money from England, which up to date has been their source of ready money. In fact, they seem to think that is what England is for—that is, to lend them money. They pay about £ 200,000 annually to the English government to help support a few war vessels for their protection, but so far as I can learn this is all Australia pays to England. The English government has certainly been very liberal and indulgent to these colonies, and they get very little in return. The colonies did send troops to help in the Boer war and they did good service; but the colonies also boycott English mail ships because they have black Laskers for stokers and have protested against the importation of Chinese labor into South Africa. The Australians believe in a "white" Australia and will not permit the importation of black or Chinese labor for the sugar and cotton plantations of Queensland—much to the disgust of the planters.

August 30—Went to Bendigo in the afternoon train, arriving there about 9.30 p.m. Stayed at a most excellent little hotel called the Shamrock, kept by a Canadian named McMartin. The hotel was built by a rich man and is a beautiful building with white marble steps inside, fine bedrooms, bathrooms, etc. It never paid the owner and has now changed hands, having been bought by an American named Crawford, who is the agent of the Dr. McLaughlin medicines. As a matter of fact, the Australians pay much more attention to their food than we do in America, and even in the small towns one finds excellent food. In America we have far better bedrooms and sanitary arrangements than in Australasia, but the Australasians have on the average better food. I have not yet had a bad meal in Australia or New Zealand.

August 31—Visited the Hustlers No. 1 mine at Bendigo and drove over the district with Mr. Crawford, owner of the Shamrock Hotel. Also called on Mr. George Lansell, to whom I had a letter. He is a very rich man, made it in mining at Bendigo. He is 80 years old but very active. He treated me very politely and insisted on opening a bottle of champagne.

Returned to Melbourne this evening, arriving 11 p.m.

September 1—Went to Ballarat on the early morning train, arriving there about 11 a.m. Went around the district to see the old placer mines with Mr. Bryant of Ballarat.

Ballarat is a beautiful little town of about 40,000 people with the usual fine government buildings, wide streets ornamented with many statues, a fine public park, a fish hatchery and a fine lake kept stocked with trout for the sport of the people of the town. Ballarat is the only town I have ever heard of that has its own trout lake within its borders, where everyone can get plenty of fish. I should say that the lake covers probably 100 acres or more, and many row boats and small yachts are on it.

Returned to Melbourne tonight—arriving about 10.15 p.m.
September 2—In Melbourne.

Letter from Dick, dated Grand Hotel, Melbourne, September 3, 1904

I wrote to you last week from Sydney, on my return from the northern part of Australia. From Sydney I came on here by train, a distance of about 600 miles to the southwest. Melbourne is about the same sized place as Sydney, that is, it has a population of about 400,000 people; and it is the metropolis of the southern part of Australia, just as Sydney is the metropolis of the eastern part of Australia.

After arriving here I went up into the interior, to visit the gold mines of Ballarat and Bendigo, which were the scenes of the early gold discoveries of Australia. I had letters of introduction there and saw the country very satisfactorily.

I sail from here tonight for the island of Tasmania, about 200 miles south of here and will arrive there tomorrow afternoon. I want to see a celebrated tin mine at Mt. Bischof in Tasmania, and will return here to Melbourne the latter part of next week. The following week I expect to go to West Australia, which comprises the extreme western part of Australia. I will go there by sea, a journey of about 5 or 6 days, as west Australia is not yet connected with this part of Australia by railroad.

It is much colder here than at Sydney, as it is much farther south, and the winter weather is still in full swing here. But I much prefer the cold to the heat of the northern part of Australia.

I have met here a fellow named Mitchell, who used to be one of my students at Stanford University, in California, when I gave a course of lectures there in 1893. He is now in charge of the mining operations of a large English company in this region, and has been very obliging in assisting me to see all I wanted to see in this part of the country.

I will write further before I start for West Australia.

P.S. I will address this letter to you at Philadelphia, as it will probably not reach there until October, by which time you will probably have returned from Seal Harbor. I hope you have had a good summer there.

From the Diary

September 3 and 4—Sailed at 5 p.m. for Launceston, Tasmania, on the S.S. Coogee of Huddard, Parker & Co. S.S. Line, a 750-ton boat. A heavy wind was blowing and we looked for a rough passage across Bass Strait, 250 miles or more, to our destination. We reached "the heads" about 8 p.m., in a gale. Of two other ships that were to have sailed for Tasmania, the same day, one never started at all, and the other reached the heads and then put back, but the Coogee went on, and I do not think I ever had such a night at sea. First she seemed to be under water and then clear out of water. Most of the 30 or 40 passengers were sick and not a soul on board slept that night. I must acknowledge that for the second time since I first crossed the Atlantic in 1881 I was seasick. The other time was crossing the China Sea from Hong Kong to Manila in 1901. Last night I ate dinner but it came up again very soon afterwards.

The next morning it was still rough and the sea did not moderate until we entered the mouth of the river, 40 miles below Launceston. From there upstream to the town was through a beautiful rolling country. Launceston is a picturesque little place of probably 25,000 people. It was Sunday, when I arrived, and as Tasmanians are very religious the town was "shut" tight. Even the curtains were drawn in the shop windows, so I did the next best thing to seeing the town—i.e., went to sleep until dinner.

September 5—Took train at 8 a.m. for Burnie on Emu Bay, 111 miles; arrived at 2.30 p.m. Passed through a beautiful rolling agricultural country. High mountain peaks capped with snow were occasionally seen in the distance. The train was very slow, and the cars small as the gauge is only 3 feet 6 inches. In one of the compartments a small water closet was partitioned off. This was the only one on the train and it was looked on as a great luxury; and most every one patronized it, some of them many times, thus showing their appreciation of this great novelty! In fact, the door of the closet seemed to be the favorite place to meet and gossip, as all Tasmanians seem to know each other, and most of them are said to be related, as there is very little new immigration. There are about 125,000 people in Tasmania.

It is still winter in Tasmania now, and it is cold and bleak, the winds coming unobstructed from the south polar regions; but even in winter the country is beautiful. It is a mass of mountain peaks and short ranges, with many streams and fertile valleys. The prize sheep of Australasia come from Tasmania, and some of the rams sell for breeding purposes for $1000 or more. The island much resembles Mount Desert, but the foliage is very different, consisting of eucalyptus, box, and other gum trees.

Furness Hotel at Burnie is an excellent place, considering that it is in a country village, and very glad I was to get there as it had been very cold on the train, the only heat being the so-called foot-"warmers" which were about as warm as an iceberg.

September 6—Started at 7.10 a.m. by train for Warratah, where the Mt. Bischoff tin mine is located, and arrived there at 10.30 a.m.—about 50 miles through a mountain country and a rise of about 2000 feet above sea. The mountains of Tasmania are not the sharp rugged kind, but are gentle sloping and heavily covered with soil as this is a very rainy region, and the rocks have disintegrated to considerable depths, forming a heavy soil.

Warratah is a small mining town, just at present heavily afflicted with an epidemic of influenza. About one-sixth of the men at the mine and a large part of the people of the town were laid up.

Saw the mine and left by train again at 4.40 p.m., arriving at Burnie about 8 p.m. This is a fearfully slow train and it did not even have foot warmers.

September 7—In Burnie. The weather, which has been wet and rainy for the last few days, has cleared off and today is beautiful. Sailed at 8.30 p.m. for Melbourne on the S.S. Flora of the Union S.S. Co. She is a 1260-ton boat and very comfortable. The sea is smooth as a mill pond and we are having a very comfortable voyage, in great contrast to the trip over.

September 8—Arrived Melbourne about 3.30 p.m., after a very smooth passage across Bass Strait. I find that Brown has returned to Sydney as he has a horse entered in the races there for the 10th.

September 9—In Melbourne. Went automobile riding with Mr. Mitchell of Bewick, Moreing & Co., but the wind was blowing so hard that it was not very pleasant. We were, of course, stopped by a policeman. I say "of course," because this seems to be part of automobiling the world over.

Melbourne is a beautiful city, but it seems to be always either raining or blowing, and when it blows the dust from the interior comes in and envelopes the city like a storm in a desert.

September 10—In Melbourne. There are two football games going on this afternoon and the town is deserted. Everyone has gone to the games—40,000 people are said to have gone to one of the games. Football and horse-racing are the great amusements in Australia, but above all, horse-racing is the national sport. I have not yet seen a town in Australasia, however small, that did not have a race track. One day in New Zealand our train stopped at a small siding where there was a railroad shed and about two houses, but all the same there was a fine race track with a grandstand. But few people seem too poor to own a horse in Australasia and most of them are race horses. With us in America, race horses are a luxury but out here they are a necessity like Scotch whisky.

Left Melbourne at 4.50 p.m. for Adelaide.

Letter from Dick, dated South Australian Hotel, Adelaide, September 11, 1904

I arrived here this morning from Melbourne, about 500 miles travel by railway. The last time I wrote to you was from Melbourne, about a week ago, just as I was starting to sail for Tasmania. I had a very good trip in Tasmania, and on returning to Melbourne I came on here.

Adelaide is the capital of the state of South Australia, and looks like a clean well-kept city with fine wide streets and numerous parks. Australia is divided into five states: Queensland, with its capital at Brisbane; New South Wales with its capital at Sydney; Victoria with its capital at Melbourne; South Australia with its capital at Adelaide; and West Australia with its capital at Perth. Though Sydney and Melbourne are the two largest commerical centers of the country yet Adelaide is a very important point.

I had a very interesting trip in Tasmania, and saw the tin mines of Mt. Bischoff, which are totally different from those of the Malay Peninsula, which I visited three years ago. Tasmania is a very mountainous island, over 200 miles long and about 150 miles wide. It lies about 200 miles off the south coast of Australia, from which it is separated by what are known as Bass Straits. It is still winter there now and the mountains are covered with snow. The climate this time of year is cold and bleak, as the island is exposed to the full effect of the cold winds that come unobstructed from the south polar seas. In summer, however, the climate is said to be very fine; and even now in the winter the scenery is very beautiful.

I landed on the island at a town called Launceston, and went thence to Emu Bay by train, over 100 miles to the west; then south for about 50 miles into the mountains, to the Mt. Bischoff tin mines, and back to Emu Bay, from where I took a steamer back to Melbourne. The Tasmanian cars are very small and the trains run very slowly. The cars are cut up into small compartments, and in one of these compartments on the train from Launceston, there was a small water closet partitioned off on one side. This was looked on as a great luxury, and most of the passengers showed their appreciation of it by patronizing it, many of them very frequently; and during the day the door of the closet was the favorite point for passengers to meet and gossip.

I go from here tomorrow by train to visit a celebrated gold mine known as the "Broken Hill Mine" and will return the next day. The end of this week, I will sail from here for West Australia; where I will land in about five days voyage. Adelaide is near the western limit of the railroads of Australia, and West Australia has to be reached by sea, though there are some isolated lines of railroads in West Australia itself. I have engaged passage on a very good ship, and when I land in West Australia, I will go inland on one of these western railways to visit the gold mines of a district called Kalgoorlie. This will finish up all I want to see in Australia, and I will be ready to sail for Europe from West Australia some time in October. I can take either of two routes to Europe; one via Suez Canal and the other via South Africa. If I should take the latter, I would stop over in South Africa for a few weeks, and arrive in Europe probably in December. But of all this I will write more fully when I get ready to leave Australia, and see what ships are sailing about that time.

When I get to West Australia, I expect to get some mail which has been forwarded from London, and I will probably find some of your letters among it. The last letter I got from you was the one you wrote me at Sydney dated July 17th. The letters you addressed to London will be forwarded to me from place to place, and I expect to get the first ones in West Australia. Please continue to address me care of J. S. Morgan & Co., 22 Old Broad St., London, England, as I find that this is the quickest way to get mail out in these parts, on account of the greater number of ships sailing from England than from America to here.

From the Diary

September 11—Arrived Adelaide at about 10 a.m., after a very good trip from Melbourne (482 miles) in a comfortable compartment sleeping car. Went to the South Australian Hotel, where I got a good room and found things very comfortable.

Adelaide is a beautiful town of about sixty odd thousand people, well laid out with wide streets, many parks and public squares, fine government buildings, clean, and with an air of health and comfort rarely seen in a city. It is far and away the prettiest place I have seen in Australasia. The people also look healthy and well, and the women are by far the best looking that I have seen in the country. The weather this time of year is perfect, fine, clear days with thermometer 60° to 70° and cool nights. The air is much drier than in Melbourne and Sydney. Like all Australian cities, however, the side walks are paved with asphalt, which even now is hot on the feet, and in summer must be painfully hot. The streets are macadamized and kept well watered. In Melbourne and Sydney, also, the side walks are mostly asphalt and the streets are macadam or asphalt.

Both Adelaide and Melbourne are very dusty in dry weather—a fine impalpable dust that seems to penetrate everything. It is said to blow in from the interior.

September 12—Took train at 4.50 p.m., from Adelaide to Broken Hill—334 miles. The railway is part broad gauge (5 feet 3 inches) and part narrow gauge (3 feet 6 inches). Late in the evening we got a small sleeping car, something like the one from Rockhampton to Brisbane.

September 13—Arrived Broken Hill at 8.10 a.m. The country here is typical of the interior of Australia, a dry sandy desert, with a scattered growth of small bushes like sagebrush, no trees, isolated mountain peaks, not very high, in various directions, and in fact just like a portion of Arizona or New Mexico, with the same dry clear air, fine sky, and the inevitable sand storms. Today there is a very severe sand storm blowing, and people are going about holding their hands to their faces, so cutting is the sand and fine gravel in the air.

I put up at the "Freemasons Hotel" and later in the day visited the celebrated Broken Hill silver mine, where I was very cordially treated by Mr. Delprat, the general manager. Took lunch with Mr. Delprat and started back for Adelaide by the 7.10 p.m. train. The sleeping car was not crowded and had a very comfortable night, though we had to get up about 5 a.m. to change from the narrow gauge to the broad gauge cars.

September 14—Arrived Adelaide about 11 a.m. Spent the day in Adelaide.

September 15—In Adelaide.

Letter from his father, dated Seal Harbor, September 15, 1904

I have received both of your New Zealand letters (July 27, Aug. 4) by the *same mail*, early in Sept. I have written you already three letters, this being the fourth, and I shall again write by middle of Oct. whether I get a letter from you in the meantime or not from Australia.

I was much pleased and much relieved to get your letters and to know that you were having such a fine time. Your letters, moreover, are exceedingly interesting and I have preserved them carefully, as I did your letters from Europe and Asia in 1901 and also those in 1903 from Alaska. I am getting along most satisfactorily.

How different from last summer. Sea Bench is perfect! I plan to leave on Oct. 5 and shall go *most reluctantly*, but I shall remain only for a few days at home and shall go to Atlantic for the Autumn. I begin to feel that it is foolish for me to be in Philadelphia more than I can help, the conditions are so extremely undesirable. Spencer has been here for *four* days, and has just left for a visit of a few days to

Christine in Bar Harbor. He seemed to really enjoy the peace and quiet of Sea Bench. He goes West about Oct. 1, stopping a few days at St. Louis. Boies is back and hard at work in politics. Tal leaves Ventnor Oct. 1 for his place at St. Davids.

Indeed everything running along very much as when you left. The summer has been unusually cool; indeed, here we have not had one bad day and fires almost every night since we arrived on July 1.

Spencer tells me that Pourtales is not doing anything with or for our Commonwealth Mine, that the leased mine proved worthless, etc., etc. We were certainly lucky in getting out at 7 cents per share.

From the Diary

September 16—In Adelaide. Will sail tomorrow for Fremantle on the Yongola of the Adelaide Steamship Company.

Letter from Dick, dated South Australian Hotel, Adelaide, September 17, 1904

I wote to you from here last Sunday. Since then I have been to Broken Hill, a mining town about 334 miles into the interior from here, and have returned again. I sail today by steamer for West Australia and will arrive there in about five days. The weather is fine, and I think spring is beginning to appear in these parts. The trees are beginning to bud, and things look like they do in May in the United States.

Broken Hill is well in the interior of Australia, in the desert region that comprises most of the central part of this island—or, as the Australians prefer to call it, this continent. The interior country is very much like Arizona and New Mexico with the same dry climate, fine clear weather, and occasional sand storms. While I was at Broken Hill a sand storm occurred that was equal to most of the Arizona brand.

Australia has not many rivers and but few mountain ranges. Tasmania and New Zealand are very mountainous, but most of Australia is more or less flat. In the southeastern part there are a few low mountain ranges, but these are the only ones of any importance. The country is fertile in many places along the coast, where it gets a certain amount of rainfall, but most of the interior is an utterly barren desert. As a natural result of the absence of mountains, there are no large rivers in Australia, so that there is but little chance for irrigation, such as there is in the American arid regions. The largest river in all Australia is the Murray, which is about half the width of the Schuylkill. In fact, Australia is more devoid of conspicuous natural features than any country that I have ever seen.

I will land in West Australia at a place called Fremantle, or possibly I may land at a place called Albany, a short distance south of Fremantle. In either case, I will go inland by railroad for about 300 miles to Kalgoorlie, which is now the principal gold mining region of Australia. This railroad to Kalgoorlie, is not connected with the railroads in this part of Australia, but is an isolated line in the western extremity of the country.

I will write further from West Australia.

From the Diary

September 17—Sailed from Port Adelaide, about 10 miles from Adelaide, at 4 p.m., on the Yongola. The weather is fine and the sea very smooth. The Yongola is a new ship—about 4000 tons—and very comfortable. I have a deck stateroom and have paid extra to have it all to myself. Prof. Gregory [John W. Gregory], ex-government geologist of Victoria, is a passenger. He is on his way to Scotland where he has recently been appointed professor of geology at the University of Glasgow. I have met him before in Melbourne. He intends to get off this ship at Albany and visit the Kalgoorlie gold region, and as I also am going to Kalgoorlie I will get off with him at Albany, instead of going on to Fremantle, one day's further sail. I had intended at first to go to Fremantle, as the railway trip from there to the gold fields is shorter than from Albany, but Gregory wants to see the country by rail.

September 18—At sea. We are crossing the "Great Australian Bight" on the south coast of Australia, and there is a heavy swell on the sea that has made many passengers sick. No land in sight.

September 19—At sea. Heavy swell. Most passengers sick. No land in sight. I have not felt at all sick since starting on the voyage.

September 20—At sea. Water much smoother. We sighted land at about 2 p.m., and at 6 p.m., we entered Albany harbor, a small picturesque place surrounded by low green hills and fairly well protected from the sea. The town which probably contains 5000 people, is nestled along the shore at the foot of the hills.

We disembarked in a drizzling rain and went to the Freemasons Hotel.

September 21—Gregory and I started at 7 a.m., by train for the north, passed through a low but picturesque country, partly grass land and partly timber, sparsely settled, until 10.30 p.m., when we reached Spencer's Brook, 287 miles from Albany. We had had a compartment to ourselves all day and were very comfortable.

At Spencer's Brook we changed to the Kalgoorlie train and got into a good sleeping car of the compartment type, with a corridor on one side of the car. We fortunately got a four-berth compartment to ourselves. Gregory has been working (writing) all day. He is a most industrious man. He never seems to mind being interrupted and is always in a good humor, but when you don't talk to him, he starts writing again.

The railroads of West Australia have a 3-foot 6-inch gauge, but the cars are comfortable and lavatories numerous. It is the most comfortable narrow gauge road I ever travelled on.

Here, unfortunately, the diary ends abruptly.

Letter from Dick, dated the Palace Hotel, Kalgoorlie, W.A., September 23, 1904

I arrived here at Kalgoorlie yesterday, about 300 miles inland by railroad from the coast of West Australia.

I wrote to you last week from Adelaide in South Australia, and the same day I sailed on a very good steamer, called the Yongola, for West Australia. The boat was a new one of about 4000 tons, and it was one of the most comfortable steamers that I ever travelled in. The newer steamers, built in the last few years, are certainly a great improvement over the older ones in their arrangements for passengers.

I landed at a town called Albany on the southwest corner of Australia, and came up the west coast for about 300 miles by land, and thence into the interior for about the same distance to this place.

Kalgoorlie is one of the newest, and the most important of the gold mining regions of Australia; and it is one of the great gold regions of the world, ranking as it does with Cripple Creek and South Africa. I will stay here for a few days to have a look at what is going on in the gold mining way, and will then go to Perth, the capital of West Australia. Perth is a few miles inland from Fremantle, which is the chief Australian port on the west coast. When I reach Perth, I will go over to Fremantle, where I expect to find some mail which has been forwarded to me from London, and I will probably find some of your letters among it.

I have met a number of Americans here, who are interested in one way or another in the gold mining industry of this region, and I am having no trouble seeing all that I want.

I will write again in a few days.

Letter from Dick, dated the Palace Hotel, Perth, W. A., 1904

I was very glad to get your letter of Aug. 1st, and to know that you are so well. It is certainly very fortunate that you have two places that agree with you so perfectly as Seal Harbor and Capon. Your letter has been forwarded from London and came in the first lot of mail that I had received since leaving Sydney over a month ago.

I wrote to you last week from Kalgoorlie, in the interior of West Australia. From there I came down here to Perth, which is the capital of West Australia, and which is only a few miles inland from the shores of the Indian Ocean. The seaport for Perth is Fremantle, twelve miles west of here, on the immediate coast.

I had intended to sail from West Australia for South Africa, and thence from Capetown up the west coast of Africa to Europe. In fact I had already engaged passage by that route, and was waiting here until the steamer came along, but a telegram has just reached the agent of the steamer here, stating that it ran on the rocks in Sydney harbor as it was coming this way, and is, for the present at least, out of commission. There are but few boats going by this route, and the next one on which I could get passage does not sail for a long time, so I will not wait for it, but will go on to Europe via the Red Sea and Suez Canal.

I had been hurrying through Australia so as to get to South Africa before the hot weather began there, but now that I cannot go that way, I am not in so much of a hurry, and will try to see a little more of West Australia before I leave. I will probably sail from Fremantle for Europe sometime in October. There are plenty of boats going at frequent intervals to Europe from there via Suez Canal, so that I will not be subject to the same delay as by trying to go via South Africa (Capetown). I will determine in the next few days what boat I will take, and will then write further about my plans.

I had a very satisfactory, and a very interesting trip to Kalgoorlie; and saw a number of the principal gold mines. There are a number of Americans at Kalgoorlie, and I had no difficulty getting into any mine that I wanted to see.

Letter from his father, dated Seal Harbor, October 3, 1904

I received all your Australian letters, which came in a sort of bunch, that is all received within two days of each other. The first—your letter while still on board of your steamer, Aug. 12; your last, Sydney, Aug. 27. I preserve all your letters, which are not only very interesting but very valuable. It gives me a great deal of pleasure to realize that you are having so successful a trip. I only wish you had with you a steady regular companion from now on until your return, though Mr. John Brown, of course, is very good as far as he goes.

I plan to leave here on Wednesday, October 5, and shall leave with great reluctance. Spencer writes me he got back to Ventnor from here and Bar Harbor all right, stopping over a day or two in New York to hold the annual meeting of the U.S.R. &. R. He writes the stockholders meeting was most *"harmonious"*, etc., etc. He also sends much good news about the Co. Firstly, the rival mill "has *busted* and is now in the hands of sherif." Secondly, the output of ore has greatly increased, so that the Standard mill is running *full time*, etc., and they have started the Florence mill (idle for months past) to *its* full Capacity. It seems to promise a return to our old prosperity, etc., etc.

Tal's hoped for "boy" was born so prematurely that it survived only a few days! *I* was greatly disappointed. Of course, he will keep right along trying, but the time necessarily must be short, so I see nothing left but for *you* to help in the good work and after your return home we will pick out for you a *desirable* party. I have written you regularly and no doubt you will receive all my letters in a lump and I shall continue to write you whether I receive any from you or not.

Letter from Dick, dated Perth, West Australia, October 8, 1904

I will sail on Oct. 10th from Fremantle, 12 miles west of here, on a British mail steamer which goes first to Columbo in Ceylon, thence to Aden in Arabia, thence through the Red Sea and the Suez Canal to Port Said in Egypt, thence to ports in southern Europe and on to England. The boat is called the India. There are a number of boats called the India in these eastern waters, but this special ship the India is a large 8000 ton steamer belonging to what is known as the Peninsula and Oriental Steamship Co.

I should have preferred to have gone to Europe via South Africa, so as to have seen the latter country, but as I told you in my letter of last week, the ship on which I had taken passage to go that way, had run on the rocks and was out of commission; and no other available boat goes by that route for a long time.

The boat on which I sail on the 10th is a fine steamer and faster than the average. It will reach Marseilles in about four weeks and England in about five weeks. I may possibly stop off at some of the ports on the route, but unless I change my present plans, I will probably continue on the same ship at least to Marseilles, and possibly on to England; but I thought that perhaps I would land at Marseilles and see a little of that part of Europe. But of all this I will write later on. In any case, I expect to get home the latter part of December or in January.

I have seen Australia from one end to the other, and though it has taken somewhat longer than I had expected, I do not think the time has been misspent. The trains move slowly in Australia and the people take many holidays, so that it is difficult to get around very rapidly. In New Zealand and Tasmania I found the same difficulty, but as they are smaller countries, it did not matter so much. I think the Australian people are without exception the laziest outfit of white people that I have seen in many a long day. Nothing terrifies them so much as the word "work"; and the ingenuity they display in killing time, and making every one else kill time in travelling over their country surpasses all belief. A large part of their time is consumed in holidays; and most of their attention is taken up by cricket, football, and horse racing. Business and other matters are secondary considerations; and in them they do not want any one to excel the rest of the community. They are content with, and seem to strive for, a cheap mediocrity in everything, in much the same way as appears to be the case in New Zealand.

The so-called "Labor Party" is largely in control in Australian politics, and they spend most of their time legislating against working—an entirely unnecessary thing to do, as the people would not work anyhow.

The Australians are in fact the spoiled children of the British nation. All they ask for is not to have to work, and they trust to their mother England to take care of them.

This town of Perth is the capital of West Australia and is a very picturesque place. It has about 60,000 people and is situated on a small stream known as the Swan River, a few miles above where the river flows into the Indian Ocean. The town is in latitude 32° South, and the weather is beginning to get warm, as the Australian summer is just coming on. The climate here, however, surpasses that of any part of Australia that I have seen. Since I have been here the weather has been almost perfect, with warm days and cool nights.

I will write regularly on the voyage from here to Europe.

Letter from Dick, dated On board S.S. India, Indian Ocean, October 19, 1904

I wrote to you last from Perth, Australia, on Oct. 8th. On Oct. 10th I sailed on this ship from Fremantle, near Perth. We have been following a northwest course through the Indian Ocean, and today will reach Columbo, on the south coast of Ceylon. This will be the first land we have seen since leaving the Australian coast, and I will take the opportunity to mail this letter there.

Soon after leaving the coast of Australia we got into the tropics, and the weather has been very hot. We are now just north of the equator, having crossed the line into the northern hemisphere. The atmosphere in these parts is so saturated with moisture that the heat feels much worse than it really is. The thermometer hangs around 90°, and does not vary much at night or day. The intense humidity keeps everything damp and wet. But this ship is a very good boat, built for the tropics, and is very comfortable. The officers are white men, and the sailors are Indians (from India), Arabians, and niggers. A large ice machine on board supplies an abundance of ice, which is a very useful thing in a climate like this. The food is first class and the boat is not crowded. There are only about 40 first class passengers, mostly English and Australians, with some Germans. A man named Pomeroy and his wife, from California, and I are the only Americans. Americans don't travel much in Australian waters. Australia, with its socialism and its class legislation, always in favor of the so-called working man, who, in that country don't work, but who wants to make the man who does work divide up, offers but little inducement in a business way to a man of any enterprise.

Our boat stops about 48 hours at Columbo to put off and take on cargo, and to take coal. Then we will continue on westward towards Europe, our next stop being Aden, on the coast of Arabia, where we will arrive towards the end of October. From there we will go north through the Red Sea towards the Mediterranean. If we stop at Aden long enough to go ashore, I will mail my next letter from there; if not, I will write from the next port at which we can go ashore.

I have not seen any American papers since leaving San Francisco almost four months ago. Australia is the only white man's country, that I have ever seen, where American papers cannot be found. They keep only their own papers which have no news. I look forward to getting some American newspapers in Columbo, as it is a sort of meeting place for steamers from all over the world, a sort of ocean cross-roads station. I was there for several days on my return from the Malay Peninsula three years ago.

Letter from Dick, dated On Board S.S. India, Coast of Arabia, October 28, 1904

I wrote to you last just before we arrived at Colombo in Ceylon. Our ship stopped there two days, and as it was very hot on board ship, several other passengers and I went ashore and stayed at the "Galle Face Hotel" until the boat was ready to sail. This hotel is the best that I have ever stayed at anywhere in the east. It is in a grove of cocoanut trees on the beach facing the Indian Ocean.

The Sengalese, as the natives of Ceylon are called, are small people, but the best looking Asiatics that I know of. The women, though a little dark in color, are often very attractive, and it was a cheerful sight to see some good looking women again after being in Australia, where they are as scarce as hen's teeth.

From Ceylon we went north west for four days to the coast of Arabia, and thence along that coast. We will arrive tomorrow at Aden on the southwestern corner of Arabia. I may be able to mail this letter there. If not, I will do so at Port Said in Egypt. The weather has been very hot, the thermometer hanging around 90° and the humidity amounting almost to complete saturation of the air.

October 31st—I did not mail this letter at Aden, as I found that it would go to America sooner if I held it and mailed it at Port Said, where we will arrive tonight. From Aden we entered the Red Sea and sailed directly north for three days and a half, when we reached Suez, at the head of the Red Sea and at the south end of the Suez Canal. We entered the canal last night and are now in it. We will reach Port Said, at the north end of the canal, tonight, and I will mail this letter there.

From Port Said we go direct to Marseilles and thence to London. I may get off the boat at the former place and go up to Paris for a few days, or I may stay at Marseilles a few days to see that part of the country. I will write more fully about my plans when we reach there. The weather has cooled off very much and we are now in a very comfortable climate. Several people who have been suffering from various heat troubles on board are now getting all right. I have felt first class all along. This is a fine ship and I have never had a more pleasant voyage anywhere. I have been on it now for three weeks today, and it will be about a week more before we reach Europe.

Letter from Dick, dated Hotel Continental, Paris, France, November 14, 1904

On my arrival here from the east, I was very glad to find your letters of Aug. 20th, Sept. 15th, Oct. 3rd, and Oct. 17th, which had been forwarded here from London. It had been a long time since I had received your other letters in Australia, and I was very glad to know that you were so well and had such a good summer at Seal Harbor. I hope you will have an equally good trip at Atlantic City, and I think you are very wise to go there, as it is certainly far better than the smoke and dirt of Philadelphia.

The last letter that I wrote to you, I mailed at Port Said, Egypt, and the previous one in Ceylon. I suppose you will get them both before this reaches you.

I arrived at Marseilles on the steamer India a few days ago, and after a short stay there, came on here by train, a journey of about 14 hours. It took just a month to come from Fremantle in Australia to Marseilles. I have never had a better voyage, and was sorry to leave the ship at Marseilles. There were neither too many nor too few people on board. The weather was fine most all the way except in the tropics, where it was very hot. On the last voyage of the ship, two people died of the heat, but on this voyage no one died. Several were laid up with various heat troubles, but recovered promptly when we got into cooler weather. I was in first class shape all the trip. At Ceylon we took on board a number of people being sent back to Europe sick with tropical diseases—mostly malarial troubles—and some of them looked as if they would never live to get to Europe, but they all seemed to improve on board ship.

In coming through the Mediterranean we passed through the Straits of Messina, between Sicily and Italy, and by the volcano of Stromboli, on an island north of the Straits. The volcano was in full eruption, and a stream of lava was flowing down into the sea. Thence we skirted along the islands of Corsica and Sardinia to the coast of France.

Paris seems like a very good place after Australia. I have met Paul Stewart from Philadelphia here, also several other people whom I know. I will probably stay here for a short time, and will then go to London and thence home, but I will write more definitely about my movements when I decide what boat I will take home.

I am staying here at the Hotel Continental. I had intended to stay at the Ritz, where I stayed the last time I was here, but it was so crowded that I could not get a room. This hotel (the Continental), however, is very good and a thoroughly first class house.

When you write, please continue to address me care of J. S. Morgan & Co., 22 Old Broad St., London, as they will forward mail if I am here, or will hold it for me when I go to London.

Letter from Dick, dated Paris, France, November 25, 1904

I was very glad to get your letter of Oct. 31st a few days ago.

I wrote to you last on November 14th, after my arrival here from Marseilles. Paris seems much the same as when I was here three years ago. I have met a number of people whom I know from Colorado, California and elsewhere; also a man from Stockholm, a Swede, whom I met when I was there on the way to Lapland some years ago. He is a member of the Swedish Parliament and treated me very politely when I was in Stockholm. I met Mrs. Moncure Robinson and her daughter in the street a few days ago. I believe they expect to sail for home early in December.

There is a man here from Colorado who has a fine twenty-four horse power automobile, and I have been making a number of trips with him, sometimes for considerable distances from Paris. There are a great many places of interest in this part of France, and we have gone to many of them on his automobile. It is certainly a very good way to see the country, as the automobile goes faster than most trains, and it enables a man to be independent of railway connections.

There are a number of other places that I would like to see in this part of the country, and as long as there seems to be no special reason for me to hurry home, I thought I would take your advice and stay here for a while. I will probably come home the end of December or in January, but as I may not be home before Christmas, I enclose my check for $300., and will be greatly obliged to you if you will send my usual Christmas presents to the Carlisle people and to Nanny Thomas, etc. I forget exactly how much I sent each one last year, as you sent it for me; but you probably have a record of it, and I have made my check for $300, so as to be sure to cover the amount. I hope this matter will not be too much trouble to you.

The weather here is fine, cool and clear, with frost almost every night. I hope you have had a good trip at Atlantic City, and that it has done you much good.

Please continue to address your letters to me care of J. S. Morgan & Co., 22 Old Broad St., London.

Letter from Dick, dated Paris, France, December 10, 1904

I was very glad to get your letter of Nov. 13th a few days ago. I wrote to you some days ago, enclosing my check for Christmas presents to the Carlisle people, etc., and I suppose you have received it by this time.

The weather here has been wet and stormy for the last few days, but now it has cleared off, and is very fine. I took dinner with Mrs. Moncure Robinson a few days ago. Spencer Biddle and his wife were there.

An American named Reed, who now lives near Nantes in France, where he has leased a so-called "chateau" has been here for some days. I used to know him in Colorado, and as he seems to know Paris very well, I have seen a number of things here that I never saw before.

Paris is one of the most interesting places that I have ever seen. I thought I had learned something about it the last time I was here, but have seen very much more this time. It is amusing, however, to see the conceit of these Europeans about their antiquities. They point with pride to something a few hundreds or a thousand years old, when, compared with what is seen in Japan and China, it has not even begun to get old yet.

There are a good many Americans here, and almost every day I see some one new that I know.

The mail for the United States leaves today, so I drop this line to you to wish you a Merry Christmas and Happy New Year.

Letter from Dick, dated Paris, France, December 23, 1904

I was very glad to get your letter of Dec. 5th a few days ago, and also to know that everything was all right at home, and that there was no reason for me to be in a hurry to get back.

I fully appreciate the importance of the good advice you have given me in your letter about not drinking Paris water. I do not drink any of it. The only water that I do drink is bottled water of one kind or another. In fact in travelling anywhere outside of the United States, I never think of drinking any but bottled waters, unless I happen to be in some place where I have reason to know that the water is especially good. Even in Australia the local water is usually bad, and I drank only bottled waters there. The Australians will tell you that their water is very fine, but I noticed that typhoid is very prevalent, and in some places that I visited it was epidemic.

Ordinary water and fresh milk are two things that I try to avoid, and in doing this I feel that I eliminate a large part of the risk of sickness in travelling. When I was in Tasmania last September one of the cattle inspectors told me that the inspection of cattle had only recently been started there, and that, though the people had believed their cattle to be perfectly healthy, yet as a matter of fact, almost every cow on the island had been found to have tuberculosis.

I am very glad to hear that the Atlantic City deal is going through. Tal wrote me fully about it, and I think it is excellent. It not only preserves the chief advantages to be derived from holding the property for an increase in value, but also provides more than enough income to pay the taxes on the meadows, which will be a great relief to you. I cannot imagine a more satisfactory deal, and it proves your wisdom in holding on to the property for all these years. I think, your proposition about the disposition of the income is very liberal on your part.

The weather here is fine and clear, with frost almost every night, though last night we had considerable rain. I was at a dinner the other day at which Henry Watterson, the Kentucky newspaper editor, was present. He is over here recovering from the Democratic defeat in November.

I have been doing a good deal of automobiling, and have a number of places yet to see. Will write further shortly.

Letter from his father, dated Friday, December 25, 1904

Your letter of Dec. 10th reached me two days ago and I was very glad to get it. We are all doing well at home. Tal returned from his Western shooting trip two days ago. He reports his trip a complete success in every way and *highly* interesting, with many new experiences!

Boies is now home for a few days. He goes to Harrisburg the end of the week to be there at the opening of the legislature on Tuesday, Jan. 3rd. Spencer is still west but expects to be home in January early. We have had a dismal December, cold, snowy, etc., etc.

I am very glad you are having a good time in Paris. You are fully entitled to it, after all of your discomforts in your trip, *so do not hurry home*. Take all the time you can put in satisfactorily, even if it cause you to remain in Paris until next summer or even later. Your present experiences are an education to you in many things, while at the same time they are agreeable. It must be delightful to meet so many nice people whom you know. The snow and ice have been so bad that I have sent my horse back to the country. It seems a sin to keep the poor animal shut up all winter (as I *did* last winter). Now this winter I just put him back in the barnyard, where, anyhow, he has good air, etc., etc., and the result is that I am compelled to walk some three hours daily, which I hate and which tires me greatly.

You are missing many parties, balls, etc., etc., but this, I fancy, will not cause you much grief. Boies, as you know, never attends any, and Spencer, whose *courage is undoubted*, has not yet arrived.

[*Postscript*]

The French bonne [picture postcard] arrived in time to give your Christmas greetings. Poor thing! her legs *are* awful thin!

Letter from his father, dated Tuesday, January 3, 1905

Your letter of Dec. 23rd received yesterday. I was very glad to receive it and reply at once!

We are all well, and all of our affairs are going on smoothly. It is a blessed relief to have the holidays over. The hysteria incident to Christmas; the tumult and commotion and imbecility of New Year are most trying to *me*. I am sure there is nothing like it abroad! Though you do not *say* so in your letter, yet I infer you are enjoying yourself, and just so long as you can have a "good time" in Paris, or anywhere else abroad, don't come home, even it it takes you until next summer to get through with your fun. Moreover you are receiving an education in *worldly* matters that cannot fail to be useful to you. It is a good deal like going to dancing school; that is, you are pursuing your "education", and, at the same time, you are having an awful lot of fun in doing so. I am glad you are so prudent in regard to water, milk, etc., etc. My old lectures to you when in Texas and Arkansas have not been forgotten! Uncooked foods of all kinds are to be looked after. In France, "salads" are popular—lettuce, water cress, etc., etc.; unless you are sure of them (and you can't be sure at any hotel or public place) should be avoided. For this reason *I* never eat such things away from home. I should consider myself *poisoned* if I ate such (*uncooked*) foods at any hotel *even at* the Belleview. I expect Spencer tomorrow. He is to be one of Reed's groomsmen I believe on Saturday, and the first Assembly is to be on Friday, so he comes to enjoy a little gaiety. Tal also will go to New York to assist at the wedding.

I look for a letter from you *once a week*.

Letter from Dick, dated Paris, France, January 6, 1905

I wrote to you some days ago, and since then I have been most of the time in Paris, as the weather has been so bad that there was not much comfort in travelling about. It has been raining and snowing most of the time for the past ten days, and the winter is said to be unusually severe for these parts.

I had expected to go to the Hartz Mts. of Germany this week, to see some of the ancient German mining regions there, but they have had such unusual snow storms, that I was told that it would be impossible to get around with any satisfaction, and I have given up the trip, at least for the present.

It is no hardship anyhow to stay in Paris for a while, though I would not care to be one of those Americans who live here. Paris is a most excellent place for a short time, especially after a long trip, but as a permanent thing, no place can equal the United States.

I will write more fully later. I had thought that the mail for the United States did not leave until tomorrow, but I have just heard that it leaves tonight, so I will have to cut this letter short.

Letter from his father, dated January 20, 1905

Your letter of Jan. 6 reached me on Monday. I was very glad to receive it and to know that you were all right, etc. Of course, you *must* be having a pleasant time but your letter does not reveal anything you are doing to secure such results. I believe you are doing a very wise, as well as a very agreeable thing, in remaining in Paris for a good long visit. There is absolutely nothing to bring you home and you are not wasting time where you are, but you are seeing and learning many things that are pleasant and may be useful to you, while here you would be doing really nothing. So take your time and get all the milk out of the Paris cocoanut or, as that might not be possible, get a good lot of it out.

We are all well and everything is going on as usual. Spencer reports his Western interests as very satisfactory. The copper stock and bonds have gone up greatly and he plans big projects. I am doing well. The weather here has been abominable, so I have not had my horse in town since early in Dec. It is something of a deprivation to have no horse and my legs often ache from too long walks, but actually there has been no driving possible up to now, so I plan not to have my horse brought to town again until end of Feb. or in March. Spencer tells me Pourtales and wife have gone back to Germany, where perhaps you may meet them.

I fancy by now he will think we were wise to "get out" on the seven cents basis. I tell Spencer the wisdom on my and Tal's parts consisted in following *your* advice in the matter. Boies is very busy, looks well, but is getting *awful* fat. It is dreadful to be *built* so. Still, he does a tremendous amount of hard work and doing it well; only an *over*-fed man can do such work and not break down.

Letter from Dick, dated Paris, France, January 20, 1905

I wrote to you a few days ago. The next day I received your letter of Dec. 25th, and today I have received your letter of Jan. 3rd, both of which I was very glad to get. I am sorry that you have been having such a bad winter in Philadelphia, and that you have not been able to use your horse. I hope, however, that you will have better weather from now on. The weather here for the last month has also been very bad, with much snow, rain and fog, though the thermometer has not often gotten below 20° here in Paris. To the south, however, in Switzerland, the papers report much colder weather, and many people have been frozen, including a number of Trappist monks in a Swiss monastery. It seems to have been a very cold winter all over the northern hemisphere.

You speak of the noise and uproar at Christmas. It is much the same here, except not so noisy. Most of the French Christmas seems to be the night before Christmas, when they have what they call "Reveillon," in which all hands collect in cafes and restaurants after midnight, and celebrate until the next morning. The whole city seems to turn out, and they have a very good time. The next day they sleep; and after that they get down to business again.

Many thanks for your advice about not eating uncooked food. I appreciate the importance of it, and have been following it. I note what you say about staying here long—even until next summer. I would like to go to South Africa next summer, but I think it would be a little long to wait here until then, and I think perhaps I better come home for a few months, and make a fresh start later. My present idea is to go to London about, or before, the middle of February, stay there a few days, and then take a steamer for New York the latter part of February. I will write further about this in a few days, when I have arranged my plans.

Paris is a very good town, in fact I do not know of any better place to have a good time in; and until the bad weather of the past few weeks, I also travelled around a good deal outside of Paris, and saw much that was of interest. The weather is now much improved, and from what people say, it ought to continue good at this time of year.

Until I write further, my address will be, as usual, care of J. S. Morgan & Co., 22 Old Broad St., London, England.

Letter from Dick, dated Paris, France, February 3, 1905

I was very glad to get your letter of Jan. 20th yesterday. Paris is a very pleasant place, and it would be no hardship for me to follow your advice and stay longer, but I think I better be moving, as I have already been here for a good while. The only reason that I have stayed here as long as I have, was because I happened to meet a number of people that I knew, and because Paris seemed like a very attractive place after Australia. I have done a good deal of automobiling, as I happened to know several people who had automobiles; and I had expected to go on an automobile with a man here to the Hartz Mts. of Germany, but the weather was so stormy and the roads so bad, that we had to abandon the trip. I have, however, seen most of the sights of Paris, and many outside of Paris, more, in fact, than I had ever expected to see. I have not learned much French, but can speak enough to get about without any trouble, and I can read the French newspapers as easily as if they were in English.

I have not seen or heard of Pourtales here, and suppose he is probably in Germany. I have had a couple of letters from Brockman, in which he did not speak very hopefully of the prospects of finding a new mine for the Commonwealth Co. So far as I can see at present, I don't think we made much of a mistake in selling out.

There was considerable excitement here a few days ago on the occasion of the riots in St. Petersbourg, and a guard was placed around the Russian Embassy to protect it, but everything now seems to have quieted down.

Paul Stewart is going to the south of France, and wants me to go with him, and to return with him to the United States the end of March, but I do not care much for the fashionable winter resorts, and so will not go. I expect to leave here about the middle of February for London, and will probably stay about a week there, and then sail for New York the latter part of February. I have not engaged passage on any particular boat, and will not do so until I get to London, as there are several good boats sailing about that time, and there is so little travel across the Atlantic this time of year, that there is no difficulty getting staterooms. I will write further when I decide what ship I will take.

Cablegram from Dick to his father, dated London, February 22, 1905

Sailing today Kaiser Wilhelm der Grosse. Arrive New York twenty eighth
                                                                   Dick

Telegram from Dick to his father, dated Hoboken, N. J., March 1, 1905

Just arrived. Will come Philadelphia this afternoon
                                                R. A. F. Penrose, Jr.

CHAPTER 14

Africa and its Gold Fields

AFTER his return to the United States from Australia, Penrose spent the remainder of 1905 in his native country, making several trips from Philadelphia to California and other western States on his mining business. Data concerning 1905 are meager but show that he was carefully following up his investments, making mining reports, actively occupying himself with matters educational and scientific, and enjoying a western camping and hunting trip with his brothers Charles and Spencer.

Early that spring (May 17, 1905) he received the following telegram from H. C. Hoover, then at Monterey, California:

DO YOU KNOW ANYTHING ABOUT GOLD DYKE MINE BOULDER COUNTY COLO   IS IT WORTH EXAMINATION   REPLY COLLECT

Judging from his previous report on gold mining in Boulder County, already noted, and from the tone of the Hoover reply, which follows, his report must have been in the negative:

My dear Penrose:—
I troubled you the other day in the matter of Colorado Mines, as I had been asked from London to find something about them. I did not anticipate that there is anything in that district that could be of any value, but I felt obliged to trouble somebody to find out.

You have my sincere thanks for the trouble you took, and you should answer such telegrams "collect."

Yours faithfully
H. C. Hoover

That same month (May, 1905) he received word from Allen Danforth, Comptroller of Harvard, thanking him for a gift of fifty dollars and stating that "at a meeting of the President and Fellows of Harvard College in Boston, May 22, 1905, it was *Voted*, That the thanks of the President and Fellows be sent to each giver towards the expenses and salary of an instructor to accompany the Class in Mining 12 on an excursion through the South, and for the general use of the department of Mining and Metallurgy, and that the name of each giver be entered in the donation book of the College."

The following year a similar letter from Howard L. Blackwell, comptroller, thanked him for a gift of one hundred and fifty dollars for "aiding Instructors and Assistants in the department of Mining and Metallurgy to visit mines and metallurgical establishments, and for defraying the expense of lectures in special subjects in the same department during the academic year 1906–'07."

At the end of May (1905) a letter from Edward J. Nolan, recording secretary of the Academy of Natural Sciences of Philadelphia, to which he had been elected a member on July 25, 1899, stated that he had been appointed a member of the Committee on the Hayden Memorial Award, the other members being Professor Henry Fairfield Osborn, of Columbia College; Professor Frederick Prime, of Girard College; Professor Amos P. Brown, of the University of Pennsylvania; and Dr. S. G. Dixon, president of the Academy. This was not his first appointment to this committee, for under date of May 27, 1902, he had been sent the following letter from Council of the Academy:

"You have been appointed by the Academy a member of the Committee to decide as to who shall be this year the recipient of the Hayden Memorial Geological Award. The fund on which the award is founded was given by Mrs. Emma W. Hayden in commemoration of her husband, the late Prof. Ferdinand V. Hayden. According to the revised terms of the trust, a gold medal is to be awarded every third year for the best publication, exploration, discovery or research in the science of geology and paleontology, or in such particular branches thereof as may be designated. The award and all matters connected therewith are to be determined by the Committee appointed by the Council of the Academy.

"The other members of the Committee this year are: Theodore D. Rand, Benjamin Smith Lyman, Henry F. Osborn and Amos P. Brown. Mr. Rand has been requested to act as temporary chairman. I have no doubt the selection can be made, partially at least, by correspondence.

"The award up to 1899 was made every year and consisted of a bronze medal and the balance of interest on the fund. It has since been modified as stated. The recipients have been as follows:

    1890   James Hall
    1891   Edward D. Cope
    1892   Edward Quess
    1893   Thomas H. Huxley
    1894   Gabriel Auguste Daubell
    1895   Karl A. Von Zittel
    1896   Giovanni Capellini
    1897   A. Karpinski
    1898   Otto Torel
    1899   Gilles Joseph Gustave Dewalque"

By 1905 he had for two years been a member of the Publication Committee of the American Philosophical Society, a post which he continued to fill for twenty-five years—until 1927.

The end of June, he was off on a camping and hunting trip into his beloved western wilderness, as the following telegrams show:

From Spencer Penrose at Colorado Springs to Dick at Philadelphia, June 28, 1905

Please telegraph me definitely what time you reach Cheyenne will meet you there

From Dick at Philadelphia to Spencer at Colorado Springs

Tal and I leave here tomorrow Friday afternoon reaching Cheyenne ten twenty Monday morning leaving Cheyenne ten fifty five Monday morning. Try meet us on train. Outfit meet us at Ketcham. Boies not coming. His gun is in Idaho and you can use it instead of yours if you wish.

From Spencer at Colorado Springs to Dick at Philadelphia, June 29, 1905

Will meet you Monday morning Cheyenne. We have just telegraphed Babbitt fully in regard to Utah company.

From Dick at Philadelphia to Spencer at Colorado Springs

Telegram received. We will expect you on train Cheyenne Monday morning. Tal will be there sure and I will come unless detained in New York by copper matter. I think terms in your telegrams to Babbitt very liberal and do not see how New York people can consistently refuse them.

From K. R. Babbitt at Hollywood Hotel, West End, New Jersey, to Dick at Annex Hotel, Chicago, July 1, 1905

Received wire late yesterday instructing me one third cash balance thirty and sixty days agree you and Beatty determine sinking fund think can close Monday

From Dick to Babbitt at Hotel Wolcott, New York

Telegram to Chicago received. Please substitute some one instead of me to determine ore in sight as I expect to be out of country at time in question. Have wired MacNeill suggesting F. H. Minard of Denver. Answer Ketchum Idaho.

From Dick to C. M. MacNeill, Colorado Springs

Babbitt wires he hopes close Utah matter on terms satisfactory to you Monday. He says you desire me determine ore in sight when time comes in connection with Beatty. Please wire Babbitt and name some one instead of me as I expect to be out of the country at time in question. Minard is good man.

From Dick to Western Union Operator at Ketchum, Idaho

Please hold telegrams which come in name of Penrose. Will arrive Tuesday or Wednesday.

From C. M. MacNeill, at Colorado Springs, to Dick at Ketchum, Idaho, July 3, 1905

Telegram received. Speck will explain everything suggested to Babbitt by wire your name be used and that if you could not act you could name substitute probably Minard. Best wishes you all for pleasant trip.

From K. R. Babbitt at New York, to Dick at Ketchum, Idaho, July 3, 1905
Will arrange as you suggest either proving you or your nominee or name Minard

Although the date of this proving is not noted, it is obvious that Dick was even then planning his trip to the Africa he had been compelled to pass by on his return from the Antipodes. According to his own list of "Positions Declined," Penrose had in 1904 refused the post of "manager of mines in the Transvaal shown after war $50,000 value," and he naturally felt a desire to look over the possibilities on that continent.

Before going, however, in cleaning up his affairs at home, he evidently wrote to Professor William Morris Davis, of Harvard, regarding his status as an Associate in the Museum at Harvard, for the Davis reply is preserved, and reads as follows:

Letter from William Morris Davis, dated Harvard Travellers Club, Cambridge, January 28, 1906

My dear Penrose,

As your letter of the 27th indicates that I have still time for another to you, let me write a few lines about the position that you have as Associate in the Museum. The story is as follows:—

Four years ago, I suggested to the Museum committee that we should ask the Corporation to establish the position of Associate, my feeling being that it was extremely desirable to bring into relation with our resources here as many investigators, explorers, original students as possible; to get them if we could in the way of coming here for parts of the year to work; to aid them as far as we could, and thus to give ground for hope that they would in turn aid us, not only by allowing their names to stand on our list of Associates, but by giving us specimens, by reporting their progress here, in the way of lectures, and in the distant future by leaving us their collections, and so on. I believe some such plan is very desirable, for the Museum is a fearfully heavy responsibility for us to carry; it is a rather lonesome place in its bigness; and it is not nearly enough resorted to by investigators. Why indeed shd it be; we take no pains to attract them; we just stand and wait. The scheme of Associates, then, was to try to overcome this isolation; as far as such a scheme could contribute to overcoming it. Well, the committee adopted the plan unanimously; the Corporation approved it, and a form of announcement was prepared for the Catalog. A few names were proposed; yours I think among the first lot. And then the thing fell practically dead. At the following year, the committee showed no interest in it whatever; I tried to brace it up; but to no avail. I believe we did make two new appointments; but since then it has not even been talked about in Committee—because the Com. has not met! There has been no committee meeting this year. And so an excellent plan (as I still believe it to be), a plan that recommended itself to our astute Corporation, and was well spoken of by our wise President, is likely to go for naught. I measure the usefulness of such a plan, not by its value at the beginning; but by looking forward twenty or thirty years, and seeing then a long and high-class list of Associates, a list in which any man might be proud to find his name; a list that would do us great credit, and from which we shd have all sorts of pleasant and profitable relations. Such a list was entirely within our reach; but so peculiar is Harvard indifference (perhaps I shd say, in this case, Agassiz' indifference) to the future, that the whole thing is apparently going to vanish into thin air. It strikes me as rather absurd to adopt such a plan unanimously, to go to the point of asking formal action by the Corporation (rather a ponderous body to move) to announce the thing publicly in the Catalog; and then to let it drop and fall into desuetude, innocuous, I hope; but certainly not deserved. It makes me rather frantic, this sort of thing; but I am not able to improve it. I have done my very best to keep it going; but to no avail. You are just the sort of man to be on such a list. Pumpelly is another; Barrett a third; Springer, of corals, a fourth, and so on; we should have made it a splendid list in a few years; and now it is going to run out, according to all appearances. It is a great disappointment to me.

I feel that this explanation is due to you; for your name was put on the list at my suggestion. I still believe fully in the plan; and regret immensely that no one else seems to care anything for it; not eno at least to carry it forward.

Best wishes for your journey. Should you wish to meet a bright live Africander at Cape Town, look up Louis Serrurier; his home address is High Level Road, Sea Point, about two miles out from Cape Town; but he is in business in the city. A very bright fellow; and I think he would welcome you if you called yourself a friend of

Yours sincerely
W. M. Davis

Early in February, Penrose set forth for Africa, the record of that journey being carefully preserved in his correspondence, his diaries, and his notebooks.

Letter from Dick, dated Dampfer Kaiser Wilhelm der Grosse, February 6, 1906

I drop a short line to you to mail at Sandy Hook when we pass there. We got down to the boat in good time this morning, and sailed promptly at 10:30 a.m. The thermometer was only three degrees above zero in New York this morning, but the day is clear and bright, and we have fine weather for starting. There are probably over two hundred first class passengers on board, but the boat is not very crowded.

From the Diary

February 6—Am starting today on a trip to South Africa via England. Sailed at 10 a.m., from New York on the North German Lloyd S.S. Kaiser Wilhelm der Grosse. My brother Speck and Dr. Keely are on board. They are going to Cherbourg and then to Paris. I get off the boat at Plymouth.

The weather today is clear and cold, with a brisk northwest wind blowing. The thermometer was only 3° above zero this morning in New York. The boat is fairly well filled—an unusual thing this time of year. There are probably over

300 first-cabin passengers out of a possible capacity of 450. There are also a good many second and third class passengers, the latter showing that all the immigrants to the U. S. do not stay there—a very fortunate thing for the U. S.

The sea is a little choppy outside of Sandy Hook and many people are getting sick.

February 7—The sea is rough and a high wind blowing from the northwest. Probably 90 percent of the passengers are sick—including Speck and Keely. I am not sick but do not feel very chipper. Towards midnight the sea has begun to moderate. Run of vessel, 482 knots.

February 8—Clear, bright day, smooth sea, and warm weather. The effect of the Gulf Stream is now very noticeable. Almost everyone seems to have recovered from seasickness. Run of vessel, 486 knots. Light south winds.

February 9—The day opened clear, bright and warm, with smooth sea, but became more windy later on, with heavy swell from northwest. Run of ship, 515 knots.

February 10—Heavy swell from northwest all day. Boat rolling heavily. Many people sick. Run of ship, 505 knots.

February 11—Same weather as yesterday. Run of ship, 495 knots.

February 12—Fine clear day with smooth sea. About 11 a.m., we sighted the Scilly Islands, and shortly afterwards "The Lizard." Thence we proceeded along the coast of Cornwall, arriving at Plymouth about 3 p.m., almost exactly 6 days from New York (i.e., allowing for difference in time). We were delayed about two hours before landing at Plymouth as we were taken ashore in a tender and a lot of bullion and specie had to be unloaded on the tender before it could proceed. On landing we passed through the custom house and boarded a special train at the dock, which finally started for London about 7 p.m. The distance is about 250 miles and we covered it in a little over 4 hours—very good time. The train was very comfortable and had a good dining car.

Speck and Keely stayed on the ship and proceeded thence to Cherbourg; from there they were to go to Paris on Speck's automobile which was to meet them there.

On my arrival in London, I went to the Savoy Hotel, to which I had previously written to hold a room for me. I found that they expected me, and had a good room with a comfortable fire ready for me.

Letter from Dick, dated Savoy Hotel, London, February 13, 1906

Our boat arrived at Plymouth late yesterday afternoon, and I came on here by train, arriving late at night. Speck and Keely stayed on the ship and went to Cherbourg, whence they will go to Paris.

We had a first rate voyage, and it took us almost exactly six days from New York to Plymouth, allowing for the difference in time between the two places. The sea was a little rough most of the time, but we had no fogs and but little rain. The boat was fairly well filled, but as most of the people were seasick a large part of the time, it did not seem crowded as people were in their staterooms.

I will get around today and make my arrangements to go to South Africa. I drop this line to you now before starting out this morning, and will write more fully in a few days. I may possibly join Speck and Keely in Paris for a few days before going to Africa, but will decide this when I find what boat I will take.

My address for the next few months will be care of J. S. Morgan & Co., 22 Old Broad St., London, England. They will forward mail to me wherever I go from here.

I hope that you are well, and that your ear is entirely cured.

From the Diary

February 13—In London, arranging for my trip to South Africa.
February 14—Same. Called on Hoover and we took lunch together.
February 15—Same. Took dinner with F. Roudebush.
February 16—In London, arranging for African trip. The weather is wet and rainy, and has been so ever since my arrival, with the exception of one day. The Savoy Hotel is one of the best houses I ever stayed at. The food is excellent, and I have changed the room that I first had for a very comfortable room with a bath and all modern appliances, telephone, etc., and even steam heat in the bathroom—a rare thing in a European hotel.
February 17—In London. Raining all day.
February 18—In London. Raining most all day. This is Sunday and a very quiet day here.
February 19 to 21—It has been raining almost continuously since the 18th. The weather is dismal. I have engaged passage for Cape Town on March 10th on the Walmer Castle. I will go to Paris tomorrow to seek better weather and to see Speck and Keely.

Letter from Dick, dated Savoy Hotel, London, February 21, 1906

I wrote to you about a week or so ago, on my arrival here. I have had to postpone sailing for South Africa until March 10th, as there seems to be a scarcity of good boats going there just now, and most of them are very crowded. But I have finally gotten a first rate stateroom on a first rate boat sailing from Southampton on March 10th, by way of the west coast of Africa to Cape Town.

In the meantime, as I have finished all my business in London in connection with this trip, I think I will go to Paris tomorrow, where I will remain until a few days before my boat sails, and then return here.

I had a letter from Speck a couple of days ago. He and Keely got to Paris all right with his automobile, and he seems much pleased with it. I believe that they expect to start off on a trip to the south of France in it before long, but I will probably see them in Paris before they start.

Today is a fine clear day here, but most of the time since I arrived it has been raining or sleeting, or so foggy that it was often hard to see across the street. I cannot understand how people can live all the time in such a climate, and yet the people I see look healthy and well.

I will write again before sailing for Africa.

From the Diary

February 22—Started for Paris on the 11 a.m. train from London. The rain has gone and weather perfect. The train to Dover is very crowded because, in addition to the regular number of passengers for France, there are many more on the way to Marseilles to take the P. & O. steamer for the East. I believe it is the Bombay steamer. The crossing the channel was like a mill pond. The boat that took us was the Invicta, one of the new turbine boats, and a wonderfully smoothly running little ship. We went from Dover to Calais in just one hour, boarded the train at Calais in a great commotion and rush for seats on the train. The French train was excellent and ran very fast, reaching Paris in about 4 hours from Calais.

Dr. Keely met me at the station, which was very kind in him as I had no reason to expect him to take the trouble to do so. We drove to the Regina Hotel, where I found an excellent room with a bath engaged for me. I had telegraphed ahead to them to reserve a room with bath for me.

Got dinner with Speck and Keely, and went to bed about midnight.

February 23 to 26—In Paris with Speck and Keely.

February 27—Speck and Keely started south on Speck's new automobile. The day was fine and beautiful, but it seemed very lonely after having been running about with Speck and Keely. I hunted up Paul Stewart, Knapp, and others at Williams'.

February 28 to March 5—In Paris. The Regina is an excellent hotel, clean and well run. I will go back to London tomorrow (March 5) preparatory to sailing for Africa.

Letter from Dick, dated Paris, France, March 3, 1906

I wrote to you last week from London, just before coming here. I found Speck and Keely here and was with them for three or four days, when they started for the south of France in Speck's automobile. I will stay here until the middle of next week, when I will return to London preparatory to sailing for Africa on March 10th. I was much tempted to go with Speck and Keely to the south of France, but after making all arrangements to start for Africa on the 10th I did not want to defer the trip.

Speck has asked me to write to you about a matter, concerning which he said he was going to write to you himself. A couple of ladies from Colorado Springs, friends of Speck's, came over from New York on the same boat with us three weeks ago; and they have, at Speck's invitation, gone south with him on his automobile. One of them is a widow named Mrs. McMillan. Her husband was a son of ex-U. S. Senator McMillan of Michigan. He (her husband) enlisted in the U. S. Army at the beginning of the war with Spain in 1898, contracted fever in Cuba, and later, in his weakened condition, contracted consumption, from which he died. Mrs. McMillan is a very good looking and a very agreeable woman of about 35 years old, a blonde of medium size. She has one child, a girl of 14 years old. She comes originally from Detroit, Michigan, and Speck says that she is of one of the best families there. He says he has known her well for several years. She came here to put her child to school in Switzerland, and the other lady who came with her seems to have come as a sort of companion. I understand that Mrs. McMillan is fairly well off financially and wants to educate her daughter abroad.

Speck seems very much devoted to Mrs. McMillan, and she equally so to him. He has talked to me about proposing marriage to her, and has asked me to write to you about it, and pave the way for him to write to you. Mrs. McMillan seems to understand Speck thoroughly, and the impression I have gotten of her is that she is a thoroughly sensible woman, whom a man ought to get along with if he can get along with any woman whatever. The fact that she is a widow has given her an experience with her first husband that lets her know what men are; and her 35 years of age has probably removed all the obnoxious ambitions of many modern women, that she might have had. I doubt, however, if she ever had any, as she seems very sensible.

Speck tells me that for two years, he has carefully considered the proposition of marrying her, and feels that he is not now deciding on a snap judgment, but after due consideration. He seems to have been with her a great deal and to know her thoroughly. Speck is peculiarly situated. He can't read much on account of his eye, and, as he himself says, he is not interested in any particular subject that would lead him to seek amusement from literary or scientific sources. He is, therefore, peculiarly dependent on social intercourse. As he himself said to me the other day, he "cannot sit down at 8 o'clock in the evening and read until bed time," nor can he go on forever drinking rum at clubs. Therefore he seems to think his only refuge is to get married.

I do not claim to have any wisdom on matrimonial subjects, and I fully realize that I am a damned poor hand to give any advice on such subjects, but I cannot help feeling that Speck would be very much better off if happily married than in his present condition, for reasons which I have just mentioned and which Speck himself gives.

Speck talked to me a good deal about this matter before he left here, though he had never mentioned it to me before we met in Paris. I could of course see, however, that he was very devoted to the lady coming across the ocean. I did not try to influence him one way or the other in his matrimonial desires, but I did advise him strongly, before taking any definite action, to go home when Keely goes, in a few weeks, and see what effect a change of air and surroundings would have on his feelings in the matter. I also told him that if he was bent on getting married, it would be more dignified to go home first and to consummate the deal there, rather than to do it here in a foreign land. He said that he had tried going away from the lady for months at a time, but that the separation had no effect on his affection for her. My advice to him, however, to go home first; and if he still wanted to marry the lady, to do so there rather than here, seemed to appeal to him; and when he left here he gave me the impression that he would do so. He will then have a chance to talk to you about the matter. It seems very hard for him to get courage to write to you, because he fears you may think him foolish, but I told him you would do no such thing, and would only give him such advice as you thought best for his own happiness, and he promised me to write to you.

Since he left here on his automobile, I have had a letter saying that he would write to you, and asking me again to be sure and do the same. Hence the cause of this long letter. I hope you will approve of my advice to Speck. As I have said, I am anything but a specialist on matrimony, and it seems comical for any one to consult me on it, but I have tried to give Speck the best judgment I could.

I will drop a line to you from London before sailing for Africa. My address will, during my absence in Africa, be care of J. S. Morgan & Co., 22 Old Broad St., London, England.

From the Diary

March 6—Left Paris on the noon train and went to London via Calais. The train was not crowded and the channel was as smooth as a pond. Arrived in London promptly at 7.05 p.m., and went to the Savoy Hotel.

March 7 to 9—In London. Weather mostly good. Only one day of those three was rainy. I have met my old friend, J. H. Means,* in London. He has been pretty much all over the earth, doing mining work, since I last saw him about nine or ten years ago.

March 10—Left London at 11.35 a.m., for Southampton, to go on board R.M.S. Walmer Castle for Cape Town. Frank Roudebush came to the hotel to say goodbye before I left, and at the station I found Means and Dickinson waiting for the same purpose. I felt very lonely this morning, and it was a most pleasant surprise to have these friends see me off.

It was raining hard at Southampton and we did not get off until about 4 p.m. Just before starting, my steward handed me three farewell telegrams, one from Speck at Nice, one from Mrs. McC and Mrs. F., and one signed jointly "MacNeill, Cooks, Hamlins, Reeds." It was a very great pleasure to receive these telegrams.

We at last sailed in a pouring rain. As soon as we got out of the harbor the sea became rough, and very few people turned up for dinner at 6.30 p.m. At the present moment the sea is heavy and rain falling.

March 11—A dark rainy gloomy day, and a heavy sea. We are crossing the Bay of Biscay and this condition of affairs is said to be normal in these parts. If so, I am very glad I don't have to pass these parts very often. Probably three-fourths of the people on board are seasick. I myself have not yet felt the slightest sickness. Thermometer in stateroom, 52° at 8 a.m.

March 13—The same. The temperature gradually rising; about 60° F at 8 a.m. There are about 80 first-class passengers, mostly English and a few Germans; largely men but a few women. About 20 passengers are bound for Madeira; the rest seem mostly to be going to Cape Town and thence to other points in South Africa. Many of them are young men, looking as if they might be going to Africa to fill positions; some of them are army officers; some, mining men, etc.

The food on this boat is first rate and the staterooms excellent. I have a large stateroom on the promenade deck, all to myself. The officers all seem very courteous.

* Means had been on Arkansas Survey with Penrose.

Letter from Dick, dated Union-Castle Line, R.M.S. "Walmer Castle," March 13, 1906

This ship will stop for a short time tomorrow morning at the Portugese town of Funchal, in the Madeira Islands, and I will take the opportunity to mail this letter there.

We left Southampton in a heavy rainstorm on the 10th. The first day out was rough and stormy, and most of the passengers were more or less seasick. It continued rough across the Bay of Biscay, but after passing Cape Finisterre in Spain, the sea grew much smoother, the sun came out, and ever since then we have had perfect weather.

This is a fine ship. The staterooms are comfortable and the grub is very good. There are about eighty first class passengers, but no one that I had ever met before. They all seem to be English and a few Germans.

After leaving the Madeira Islands tomorrow, we pass through the Canary Islands and down the coast of Africa, but do not stop anywhere until we reach Cape Town, in about two weeks or so. I will write next from Cape Town, which will be the first place that I have a chance to mail a letter after the present one; and, as I said in my last letter from London, my next letter, that is my first one from Cape Town, will not reach you for some time, as it takes about two weeks for me to go from Here to Cape Town, and it takes almost three weeks for a letter to get back to England, and then a week or more for it to get from England to Philadelphia. There may even be still further delays if the letter has to wait at one place or another for a steamer; so that it may be a couple of months or so before you next hear from me. But as I have said before, I will write regularly and eventually the letters will reach you.

As I said in my last letter, my address while in Africa, will be care of J. S. Morgan & Co., 22 Old Broad St., London, England, who will forward mail to me just as they have done in previous trips.

P.S. According to the postal regulations, the mail sent on shore from this ship at Madeira must carry Cape Town stamps. Hence the Cape Town stamps on this letter, though it is mailed at Madeira.

From the Diary

March 14—We arrived at Funchal in the Madeira Islands at about 6 a.m., and left at 11.45 a.m. We had a chance to go on shore and see the old Portuguese town, which lies in a little bay with high green hills rising abruptly behind it to a height of probably 1500 feet. It is a beautiful situation, and the hillsides covered with gardens and vineyards are very picturesque.

Making wine (including madeira wine), growing fruits, early vegetables, etc., and the tourist business are the chief industries of the island. In the town, which is a small place of probably few thousand people, the narrow crooked streets, paved with small cobble stones collected on the beach and turned on end, the white houses, the little gardens, cafes, etc., all have a very Portuguese appearance. Instead of wagons, the people have low sleighs shod with iron and pulled by oxen. These glide with comparative ease over the well-polished cobble stones. The flower girls with beautiful white roses and other flowers are everywhere and give a great quantity of flowers for a few cents. The madeira wine, which all visitors are expected to sample, is not bad, though probably very new. Thermometer 62° at 8 a.m., in my stateroom. Later in day, warmer but not hot.

March 15—At 3.30 a.m. we passed the island of Teneriffe in the Canary Islands, and I got up to see it. The moon was shining brightly and the high peaks of the island were plainly discernable, surrounded by clouds in upper parts. We passed on the west side of the island and almost within stone's throw of it. The light of the Spanish lighthouse was shining clearly, as was also the light on a small island just west of Teneriffe. We passed through a channel between the two islands.

Thermometer 65° in stateroom at 8 a.m.

March 16—A fine clear day, warm and balmy. It begins to feel like the tropics. People are beginning to appear in thin clothes, and deck games are becoming popular.

Thermometer at 8 a.m., in my stateroom 69°.

March 17—Fine, clear and warmer. At 5 a.m., we passed in sight of Cape Verde, the extreme western point of Africa. It is a low flat region covered with trees and owned by the French. It is known as the "white man's grave" on account of the fearful mortality from fevers. As I walked the deck in the clear moonlight (the sun was not yet up), I could not but reflect on how many pathetic and tragic scenes must have occurred at Cape Verde! How many a poor fellow had laid down his life in that fearful coast of West Africa. There is on this ship a man from West Africa, and he is looked on as a sort of freak of nature because he is still alive and apparently well after many years in that country. At Cape Verde now a high lighthouse throws its warning rays 27 miles out to sea—as if to warn the mariner alike of the dangers of the rocky coast and of the fever-ridden land.

After passing the Cape, I returned to bed, glad that I was on a fine mail ship, 6 miles from the coast, and not on the land.

Yesterday, Captain Rendall, of this ship, a fine man and noted sea captain, invited me up to his room, and in the course of our conversation he told me that the temperature of the sea that day at a depth equal of the keel of the boat, was 64° F. At Southampton on the 10th, it was 48°. He said that on the equator it would be about 85°.

The weather is now getting hot. Up to now we have had a good northeast wind which has made the voyage cooler than usual, but today is really tropical. At noon we were in latitude about 12° N. At 8 a.m. in my stateroom the thermometer was 72° F. The sun is intensely hot, but I notice what I have always observed in the tropics—i.e., I feel wonderfully well. Wind, light northeast.

Tomorrow we will pass down the coast of Liberia, the settlement founded by negroes (freed slaves) sent over from America by some philanthropists some 75 or 100 years ago. There is a man on board who has often been there. The country is supposed to be a sort of a republic, but badly governed. He tells me they used to own two very small gunboats which were the pride of the nation, and the principal occupation of which was to fire salutes on all occasions. As they were usually short of coal, they had to go to some merchant ship and borrow a few sacks of coal when they wanted to get up steam. One was called the "Gonnorrhoe" They have both since sunk. This man told me that the principal source of income of the country was selling postage stamps to collectors. As not many people go there, the stamps are rare and bring good prices. To keep them constantly interesting the country every year or so is said to get out a new issue.

We were about on latitude 12° at noon.

March 18—Clear and very hot and sultry. Thermometer in my cabin at 8 a.m. was 83°. We are in the region of calms, lying between the northeast and the southeast trade winds on the Africa coast. Tomorrow they say we will reach the region of the southeast trade winds and it will be cooler. Last night as we entered the region of calms there was an intense smell of rotten seaweed and dead vegetation generally. This is said to be due to the accumulation of these materials in this region.

We were on latitude 7° N at noon.

March 19—Last night was intensely hot and sultry. It was very hard to sleep. Thermometer at 8 a.m. in my cabin was 84°. Humidity, intense. Toward afternoon a slight breeze from the south sprang up and made things a little more tolerable. People on ship seem to be becoming very active in deck sports and all kinds of games are constantly going on in spite of the heat.

We were just south of latitude 2° N at noon today. Crossed the equator about 9 p.m.

March 20—A cool fresh breeze from the southeast is blowing and the air feels considerably fresher than yesterday. Sky bright and clear; sun very hot. The thermometer in my cabin at 8 a.m., was $81\frac{1}{2}$. We were about in latitude 2° S at noon.

March 21—Much cooler, with fresh wind from south. Thermometer at 79 at 8 a.m. We were in latitude 7° S at noon. The whole ship has gone mad over "sports," including all kinds of deck games. They have a committee of nine with a president, chairman, two secretaries, a treasurer, judge, clerk, of course, started, and various sub-committees. In organization they are a wonder to behold. Long and serious are the discussions in committee regarding such serious topics as potato races, egg and spoon races, chalking the pig's eye, bun and whistling race, etc., etc. The ponderous sports organization carries through the details of the various events with due seriousness and dignity. The sports started with the first and second class passengers in combination. Then a coolness occurred between the two classes because the gate separating the parts of the deck occupied by the two classes happened to be closed by accident during a dance. The second class took offense at this and refused to consider all apologies. At last they reconsidered their position, made friends again with the first, and today everything seems to be harmonious again.

March 22—Fine clear day. Thermometer at 8 a.m. 76°.

March 23—Same. Thermometer about same.
March 24—Fine, clear day—slight rolling sea. Some people sick. Thermometer at 8 a.m. about 73.
March 25—Beautiful clear day. Smooth sea. Thermometer 71°. Most people have abandoned thin clothes and put on thick ones again.
March 26—Same. Thermometer 68°.

Letter from Dick, dated Union-Castle Line, R.M.S. "Walmer Castle," Southwest Coast of Africa, March 26, 1906

We are due to land at Cape Town tomorrow morning, and I drop a line to mail to you as soon as I get there, as the mail steamer for England leaves the next day, and this letter will go on it.

We have had a first rate voyage throughout, and will land at Cape Town in 17 days from Southampton, which is considered a very good trip. The weather was a little hot for about a week while we were crossing the equator and the tropics, but now as we are approaching the Cape of Good Hope, it has cooled down, and no one could want better weather than we have had for the last few days.

A good many of our passengers got off at Madeira, and we now have only about forty in the first class department. I am the only American among them. The rest are British, Germans, and Boers.

I wrote to you last on Mch. 13th, the day before we stopped at Madeira. Madeira is a very interesting place, and as the ship stopped there some hours, I had a chance to see a good deal of it. From Madeira we passed south through the Canary Islands and down the coast of Africa to Cape Verde; thence across the Gulf of Guinea and direct to the Cape of Good Hope. We have not landed, however, since we left Madeira, almost two weeks ago.

I will write again in a few days, after I have got on shore and have made plans for my trip in Africa.

P.S. Cape Town, March 27th—We reached Cape Town this morning at daylight.

From the Diary

March 27—Arrived at Cape Town at 6 a.m. Fine clear day. Left ship at 8 a.m., passed baggage through custom house and went to Mount Nelson Hotel. Later in day went about the town with some fellow passengers. Cape Town is beautifully situated in a picturesque little bay surrounded by high hills. A flat plateau, said to be 4000 (?) feet high,* rises abruptly back of the town and is known as Table Mountain. The town contains about 70,000 people, English, Dutch, and black. It was captured from the Dutch by the English in 1806, but even yet many old Dutch buildings remain. The Dutch and English do not intermarry very much. Many of the people seen in the streets have Dutch features, and many of the names on the signboards are Dutch. There were a few Dutch people in the steamer coming here, and they seemed quiet well-behaved people.

* 3500 feet.

The Mt. Nelson hotel is situated on a hillside overlooking the town and is beautifully located. It is a fairly comfortable hotel.

I had intended to go overland from here to the interior, but have changed my plans since coming on shore and will return to the Walmer Castle tomorrow and go on her to Durban, and thence into the interior. The boat is due to sail at 4 p.m. tomorrow.

Letter from Dick, dated Mount Nelson Hotel, Cape Town, March 28, 1906

I wrote to you a couple of days ago, just before landing here from the steamer, and mailed the letter when I got on shore. The same steamer on which I came here, leaves today to go up the east coast of Africa to Durban, about four days sail from here. I have decided to go on it to Durban, as it will not only give me a chance to see some of the southeast coast of Africa, but also when I get to Durban, I will be nearer to Johannesburg and the South African gold fields, which I want to visit, than I am here. It takes two days by railroad from here to Johannesburg, and only one day from Durban to Johannesburg, Therefore after spending a couple of days or so in Durban, I will start inland to Johannesburg.

This place, Cape Town, is a very picturesque town, beautifully situated at the head of a bay surrounded by high hills. It has about 70,000 inhabitants, and seems like a prosperous well kept town. It seems very good to get on land for a couple of days after a 17 days voyage from Southampton.

From the Diary

March 28—Went to the railroad station to see the passengers from our boat off on the train for Johannesburg and the train for Rhodesia. It is two days travel to the former place, and 4 days to the latter. The cars look clean and neat. The sleeping cars have compartments for four persons and a corridor on the side.

At 3 p.m., I was again on board the Walmer Castle, and at 4 p.m., we sailed. The weather at Cape Town had been perfect, though a little warm, and as we steamed out of the bay, the town looked very picturesque, nestled in among the hills. Still farther back, higher and more rugged mountains rose in the distance. The town has a neat well-kept appearance, though business is said to be very dull, due probably to the reaction from the extreme activity during the war, and also to the dullness of the gold-mining industry. The diamond mining, however, at Kimberley, begun some 40 years ago, is the main support of Cape Town. Many of the buildings are fine and substantial. The postoffice, the railroad station, and some of the banks are fine modern stone structures. The railroad station is well arranged and would be a credit to any town. The Standard Bank of South Africa is a beautiful building, with fine stone columns in front, and the postoffice is large, substantial and well arranged. The streets are well paved and the stores good. The suburbs are pretty and neat, with many shade trees (many of them eucalyptus from Australia) along the streets. The suburbs extend around the bay on both sides of the town. Back of the town the ground rises too rapidly for suburbs. Most of the town is modern, but in the suburbs many old Dutch houses are seen. A mile or two from the center of the town, to the west, is what is known as Sea Point, where there is a hotel and fine sea bathing. The town of Wynberg, to the east of Cape Town, is one of the chief suburbs.

There are many negroes in Cape Town, giving the appearance of a southern town in America. They look much like the American negro and show various admixtures with the whites in their color.

The surrounding country looks very arid, though it is said to be cultivated in places, mostly by Dutch farmers. The English are mostly in the city.

Cape Town is one of the great ports of entry and ports of shipment for Cape Colony. Considerable wool is shipped from here. The other chief ports are Port Elizabeth and East London.

The wind is blowing hard this evening as we round Cape of Good Hope. It is said to be generally rough here. The sea is very choppy and many people seem sick. Most of our passengers left the ship at Cape Town, but we took on few new ones. There are probably some 25 or 30 in the first class.

March 29—Beautiful clear day with strong east wind and choppy sea. We passed Cape Aguilhas, the most southerly point of Africa, at about 4 a.m. We are now going along the southeast coast, within sight of land. The shore looks dry and arid, with high mountains rising up some miles back from the coast.

Letter from Dick, dated Grand Hotel, Port Elizabeth, South Africa, March 30, 1906

I wrote to you a couple of days ago from Cape Town, just before sailing from there. The boat stops here for a few hours, and I take the opportunity to drop a line to you. We leave here again this afternoon for Durban.

This town of Port Elizabeth is on the southeast coast of Africa, and is a shipping point for wool and ostrich feathers from the interior.

We will arrive in Durban the day after tomorrow, and from there I will go inland to visit Johannesburg and the South African gold fields. I will write further in a few days.

From the Diary

March 20—We arrived at Port Elizabeth about daylight today, and after breakfast went ashore on a tug. The country has become green and fertile-looking, with rolling hills reaching to the shore. Port Elizabeth is said to be the chief exporting and importing port of Cape Colony. It is a town of about 40,000 people, and is a shipping point for wool, hides, ostrich feathers, etc. It is warm here today and the cool shade of a pleasant little hotel called Grand Hotel, is not bad. We sailed at about 7 p.m., for East London.

March 31—Reached East London about daylight. Did not go ashore as the sea was very rough and we were anchored about 2 miles out, and there was a chance of not getting back to the ship again if we went ashore. The town seems to be much the same character of place as Port Elizabeth. The day is hot and moist. We sailed for Durban at 4 p.m.

April 1—Arrived Durban about 2.30 p.m. There is a breakwater here, composed of two parallel jetties between which ships pass into a large salt-water lagoon, which makes a very good harbor. The town is situated around this lagoon and on the hills sloping up from the water's edge. The higher part of the town is called the Berea.

I stayed at the Marine Hotel, which faces the lagoon, and is a very comfortable place, with the wide porches, etc., of oriental hotels. The only fault I find with it is that there are bedbugs in my bed. It is the first time for years that I have had to use my little bottle of oil of cedar, but I find that a few drops of this on the bed drives away the bugs for the night.

This town faces the Indian Ocean and partakes of the general character of many Indian Ocean towns. The climate is very hot and moist. The least effort throws one in a violent perspiration, though the latitude is as far south as about $29\frac{1}{2}°$ S. The waiters at the hotel are Indians and Singalese; the room servants are white chambermaids, and Zulus to do the hard work, so that several races are represented. The Zulus also run rickashas in the town and dress up in all kinds of grotesque garbs, with feathers on their heads, pieces of wild animals' skins hanging loosely on their bodies, and, most popular of all, two cow horns are fitted to each side of the head. Almost all rickasha men have these horns, even if they have little or no other clothes.

There are about 40,000 people in this town, and it is the metropolis as well as the chief seaport of Natal. Being near Zululand, many Zulus are here. They are fine big strong-looking people, and always in a good humor—singing, dancing, etc.

The Indian corn of America is grown extensively here by both natives and whites. It is the only place that I have ever seen it growing outside of the U. S. It is said also to be raised very extensively in the Transvaal. It is the chief food with many natives, who are said to be very fond of it and among whom it is known as "mealie cobs."

April 2—In Durban. There are some mosquitoes here, but they are not as bad as the bedbugs. I think that one great trouble with Africa is that the equator runs through the center of it. All kinds of bugs and "varmint" as well as diseases seem to originate there and spread north and south. There are more different kinds of small bugs, ants, etc., here than I ever saw. The great rindepest scourge which a few years ago devastated the cattle and sheep of South Africa, began in the tropics and spread south, killing all cattle in its route. Now they claim to know how to innoculate against this special scourage, but a new one in the form of some deadly tick, which kills cattle, has come down from the tropics. The people blame these scourges on Rhodesia. Before the advent of the white man, these pests did not spread in the same way, as there was less intercourse between the different parts of the continent, but now with European means of communication, railways, etc., the diseases spread.

After the rindepest scourge, came the war, when most of the cattle and sheep that had escaped the disease, were killed. Then came the tick scourge, so that now people hestitate to raise more cattle, and a large part of the meat of South Africa today is imported from South America and Australasia. Still the splendid grass-covered prairies of Natal and the Transvaal must eventually encourage people to the cattle business again.

April 3—In Durban. It is very hot and sultry, and we have had a shower each night I have been here. I have today taken passage on the S.S. Africa to sail from Durban on May 2nd, up the east coast of Africa to Europe. In the meantime I will go inland to Johannesburg and Kimberley, and return here to take the boat.

There is little or no native timber in this region, though the eucalyptus tree from Australia has been transplanted and grows luxuriously. Most of the country, however, is a rolling hilly region, rising quite rapidly from the coast and covered with a fine growth of grass.

Letter from Dick, dated Marine Hotel, Durban, South Africa, April 4, 1906

I arrived here all right by sea from Cape Town on April 1st. I wrote to you from Cape Town and also from Port Elizabeth, a small place where our ship stopped for a short time on the way up here. We had a very good voyage from Cape Town, though the sea was a little rough coming around the Cape of Good Hope, at the south end of Africa. It is said to be almost always rough there, as it is where the waters of the Atlantic and the Pacific meet, and windy weather seems generally to prevail.

This town of Durban is on the east coast of Africa, facing the Indian Ocean, and is the principal white settlement in the British colony of Natal. It is near the border of Zululand, and there are many Zulus in the town. They are big strong people and are physically the best built race I ever saw. Almost every man looks like an athlete in perfect training. The women are not much on looks, but seem to be as well built as the men. There are also many Indians from Madras, and Singalese from Ceylon here, and these, as well as the Zulus, seem to be the servants, and to do the hard work for the white men.

Durban is in latitude between 29° and 30° south of the equator, and this is just the beginning of fall in this southern hemisphere. It is still a little warm here, though it is getting cooler every day, and a fresh breeze from the Indian Ocean makes things very comfortable. The coast of Africa here looks like a garden as it rises up from the sea in green rolling hills, covered with a dense growth of semi-tropical vegetation. Durban is one of the few good harbors on this part of the African coast, and therefore it attracts a good deal of shipping, which has made it a very prosperous place, with probably a population of thirty or forty thousand people.

I leave today for Johannesburg in the Transvaal, about 24 hours travel from here by railway. Johannesburg has an altitude of over 5000 feet and is much dryer and cooler than here on the coast. I will stay there several days to take a look at the gold mines, and will then go to Kimberley, about one day's travel from Johannesburg, to see the diamond mines there. I will write further from Johannesburg.

I hope you are well and that you will not have any further trouble with your ear.

From the Diary

April 4—I will start at 5.50 p.m. today by train for Johannesburg. I found that I had to have a permit to go to the Transvaal. I only found this out today. It usually takes several days to get them, but after several interviews with the "permit clerk" and the American consul, Mr. Rennie, I succeeded in getting a special temporary permit, allowing me to stay in the Transvaal 40 days. This permit business is a remnant of the war. It is not much enforced now, but is best to have one.

April 5—I left Durban last night at 5.50 p.m., in a little bit of a compartment with two other men, one a Jew drummer and one a man who seemed to be in great pain with diarrhoea. The compartment was hardly big enough for one man; for three it was unbearable. It was not over 6 by 6 feet and was really meant for 4 men to sleep in. The whole train was made up of these so-called sleeping cars. The cars are little corridor cars with separate compartments. The railroad here, as everywhere else in South Africa, is only a 3-foot 6-inch gauge, so the cars are necessarily small. When a train starts, the name of each person and his place in the compartment is written on a card and stuck up on the outside of the train until it starts. Then the conductor keeps it as a memorandum.

Rather than endure a night in the little compartment in which I had been put with two other people, I interviewed the conductor and finally secured a two-berth compartment to myself. This was very comfortable and had an individual wash basin. Most of the other compartments had to use the wash rooms at the ends of the compartments.

There was a very fair dining car on the train, where they served a very fair dinner. As we started inland, we rose rapidly and were soon at an elevation of several hundred, then several thousand feet. Pietermaritzburg was reached in about 4 hours. It was the scene of much fighting during the war. Like many Boer towns, it is situated in a low hollow, such situations being chosen, it is said, on account of getting water.

About 8 a.m. the train stopped and it was reported that we would be delayed a few minutes, as a car was off the track ahead of us. We were delayed almost five hours before we started again. The delay was at Ingogo, near Majuba Hill, which is of great historic interest, as the place where the Boers defeated the English in 1881 and where the English defeated the Boers in 1901. We arrived at Johannesburg about 11 p.m., and I went to the Carlton Hotel, a new and very comfortable house.

April 6—In Johannesburg. This is a fine-looking town, with about 100,000 people and fine substantial buildings. I looked up several people I knew, among others Stark and W. L. Honnold. Both were very cordial. Stark has an automobile and promises to take me over the district and show me everything. He lunched with me and I took dinner with him at his house. He has a wife and three children.*

---

* J. Stanley-Brown in his memorial to Penrose for the *Bulletin of the Geological Society of America*, tells how "when attending, by mere chance, the 'Easter egg rolling' ceremony at the White House in 1932, it was my good fortune to meet a young lady named Mrs. Stark McMullin, a protege and friend of Mrs. Hoover. In some curious way which now escapes my memory, the name Penrose was mentioned and to my amazement Mrs. McMullin quickly said 'Oh, yes, I knew him; when I was a little girl of about 8 he visited my father in Johannesburg, and he used to tell us children the most interesting stories.' How incredible. Easter eggs in Washington and bedtime stories in Johannesburg, but it is very revealing as to one phase of his character and another bit of unexpected testimony as to the kindliness and friendliness of this man's nature."

April 7—Visited the mill of the Village Deep mine in the morning and in the afternoon visited the South Geldenhuis Deep mine, underground and on the surface.

April 8—This is Sunday and therefore cannot do much, people are away from their place of business. Took lunch with Honnold and took dinner with Mr. H. H. Webb, of the Consolidated Goldfields Company.

April 9—Visited the East Rand Proprietary property, about 15 miles east of town, with Stark in his automobile, and went underground in their Angels mine.

In afternoon went underground in the Robinson mine near town, and also visited the Crown Reef mine.

April 10—Went with Stark and Mr. Cullinan, one of the chief owners of the Premier diamond mine, in the latter's Napier automobile, to see this mine.* We first went to Pretoria, 45 miles, and thence to the mine, 24 miles more. Covered the total distance in about $2\frac{1}{2}$ hours. We started at 6 a.m., got breakfast at Pretoria, and lunch at the mine. Mr. Cullinan was very hospitable and showed us everything. We returned to Johannesburg by train in the evening, taking about $5\frac{1}{2}$ hours.

April 11—In Johannesburg.

Letter from Dick, dated Carlton Hotel, Johannesburg, South Africa, April 12, 1906

On my arrival here a few days ago, I was very glad to find your letter of March 3d, and to know that you were so much better. Your letter had been forwarded from London to Cape Town and thence here. I am delighted to hear that your ear is entirely well again, and I hope you will have no further trouble with it.

I wrote to you last week from Durban, on the west coast of Africa. I stayed there three days after landing from the steamer from Cape Town, and then came on here to Johannesburg. This town is at an altitude of almost 6000 feet above the sea, and is much cooler and dryer than Durban. The climate is very much like that of parts of New Mexico, with cool nights and clear bright days. Johannesburg is the center of the gold mining industry of the Transvaal, and is a very prosperous town, of about a hundred thousand people. The mines extend both east and west of the town, for a distance of some 250 miles or more in either direction. During the past week I have visited a large number of the mines, and have gotten a very fair idea of the district. There are many Americans here connected with the gold mining industry in one way or another, and some of them I knew before I came here, so that I have had no trouble seeing all that I wanted to see.

The Transvaal is a far better country than I had expected to see. It is partly mountainous and partly prairie country, covered with a rich growth of grass, but with very little native timber, though the eucalyptus tree from Australia has been successfully transplanted here, and grows very luxuriantly. The country has great mining resources in the way of gold, coal and other products, and it has a fine climate and a rich soil. I don't wonder that the Boers fought hard before

---

* It was at the Premier Mine that the famous Cullinan diamond, weighing $3025\frac{3}{4}$ carats, was discovered in 1907.

giving it up. There are still many remnants of the war in the way of block houses, forts on hill tops, armored railroad cars, etc., now of course all out of use. The Boers and English seem now to live very peaceably together, though I believe if the Boers had any other place in South Africa to which they could go and found a new South African Republic, they would do so. Unfortunately for them, however, South Africa is now pretty well occupied by the English, Germans, Portuguese and native tribes, and the Boers have not much show to move. I must say, however, that they are very well treated by the English, and have equal rights with any other white people here.

I go from here to Pretoria, the capital of the Transvaal, tomorrow; and after that will go to Kimberley, about seventeen hours travel by railway from Pretoria, to see the diamond mines there.

After I have visited Johannesburg and Kimberley, I will have seen most of what I came to Africa to see, but I may visit a few other places as long as I am on this continent, and I may possibly take a boat up the east coast of Africa, but of all this I will write further, when I have finished at Kimberley and have arranged my plans more definitely.

I will write again in a few days.

From the Diary

April 12—Visited Lancaster West mine at Krugersdorph, 25 miles west of J'burg, with the consulting engineer, Mr. Hoffmann. It is remarkable how many Americans there are on the Rand, all in leading positions in the management of mines. There are probably several hundred in all. All seem discontented and wish they were home. But many realize that they have been in Africa so long that they have lost connection with affairs at home, and they fear to leave a good salary in Africa, to a possibility in America—and a possibility which with every year's absence grows less and less; for affairs move quickly in America, and if a man stays away long he loses touch with things, returns to his own land ignorant of what has been occurring and forgotten by his old associates. I think it is a great mistake for any American to stay away from home, that is to stay in a foreign country, for over a few months at a time. If he does, he risks losing or seriously impairing the benefits of that greatest of all blessings conferred on a human being—that is, American citizenship.

April 13—In Johannesburg. This is quite a town for a mining camp. They claim a population of 100,000, but may have 70,000 or 75,000. The streets are wide and macadamized or asphalted; there are some very creditable business blocks, some eight or nine stories and of steel a la Americaine. The stores are good, and the Carlton Hotel is excellent. It is the best town for a mining camp that I have ever seen.

There is but little native timber in the Transvaal. The country is a wide, open, rolling plain, 4000 to 6000 feet above sea, covered with a rich growth of grass and sparsely watered by a few small streams. The Vaal River between the Transvaal and the Orange River Colony is hardly more than a small muddy creek. Water is scarce in South Africa. The eucalyptus tree has been successfully transplanted from Australia and on the outskirts of J'burg there is quite a forest (artificial) of this timber, called the Saxonwalk. It is of several thousand acres, was planted by an old resident, and recently given to the city as a park.

Eucalyptus is used somewhat for mining timbers, but the best timber is brought from Oregon and other northern regions. I am told that in West Africa there is lots of timber that looks very good when cut, but that it rots quickly underground. Therefore they have to use Oregon and Norwegian timber. Some is also brought from Australia.

April 14—In Johannesburg. Yesterday was Good Friday and therefore a very close holiday. Today is practically a whole holiday because yesterday was Good Friday; tomorrow is a holiday because it is Sunday, and the next day, Monday, will be a holiday because it is "Easter Monday." Wednesday afternoons and Saturday afternoons are always holidays, as are also any other days that these people have any possible excuse to make a holiday. The British African is like the Australasian, always looking for a holiday and always paying much more attention to cricket and football and tennis than to his business. Yet they are always crying out that the negro will not work, he is lazy, etc. In all the time I have been in Africa, I have not seen a white man do any hard work. The negro and Chinaman does it all, and yet the Englishman is always howling for more work from the negro and complaining that the British imperial government will not allow him to *make* the negro work. At the same time, if a white man keeps his store open beyond a certain hour in the afternoon, or on Wednesday or Saturday afternoon at all, he may be arrested and fined; for, they argue, one man (white) should not be allowed to work while the others are playing. This would be taking an unfair advantage of the man who wanted to play, and such a thing is an unpardonable sin in the eyes of a British colonial. Play, including what they call sports, cricket, tennis, football, etc., seems to be their main object for living; work is a minor consideration and to be relegated to the black man. "It is a black man's country," once said an Afrikander to me, when I had irritated him by suggesting that it might be better for the white man if some of them work, "no white man can work here, it would be below his dignity, he can only direct others (negroes) in *their* work." But, unfortunately, the Afrikander (meaning the white man in Africa) has not even time to spare from play to superintend the work of others. Hence, the numerous Americans in positions of responsibility in Africa. The Britisher won't work; the American will. The Americans are as a rule bright, energetic and effective, though in some of them I could see that love of play and that willingness to lead a lazy, unambitious life that characterizes the British colonist. The force of example is too great for the weaker ones. The British colonist is spoiled by having too many black servants. Their chief occupation is resting.

April 15—This is Sunday, and everything in town is closed as tight as if the whole community had done some great wrong and were off trying to atone for it.

For the last few days there have been great swarms of what are called locusts, but which look like simply large grasshoppers. The Kaffirs catch them by holding a coat or blanket against the on-coming swarm and enveloping them. They consider them a great delicacy. They are so numerous that they look like a cloud in the sky and even obscure the sun. I saw an immense number of them a few days ago near Krugersdorp. In a few hours they often devastate a farm of grain, grass, etc.

April 16—Again another holiday—"Easter Monday." What this term means, I don't know, but the people seem to observe the day as religiously as they do Sunday. The British Colonial idea of the chief object in life is to devise excuses for resting.

There was a dust storm in Jonannesburg today, which looked like the same thing in El Paso, except that the dust is brick red instead of brown, and leaves a red color on everything.

The climate here is fine, dry and clear, not unlike that of Deming, New Mexico. In summer (November to March) it is said to be wet and hot; in winter (April to October) cool and dry. The town is supplied with good water from a well in a limestone formation about 12 miles away. The water used to be very bad, gotten from local sources near town.

The labor on the Rand is Kaffir and Chinese. The Kaffirs were very plentiful before the war, but during the war they made money and now they prefer to live at home with their wives. Hence the importation of Chinese on limited time contracts, the men to be sent back to China at the expiration of their time. There are 50,000 already in the Transvaal and 10,000 more coming. The imperial government has forbidden the importation of any more.

The Kaffir wants many wives, not only for the pleasure and the standing in his tribe that it gives him, but also because any daughters that he gets by them have a market value for so and so many cows, as wives for younger men. Hence, daughters are greatly welcomed by the parents. They are a source of income, just as are cattle and sheep.

The British colonial complains that the Kaffir will not work for him; he (the colonial) will not even work for himself. The colonial wants to get money so as to buy wine, midnight suppers, and actresses, finally winding up with a "liver" and Bright's disease. The Kaffir gets a little money, takes himself off to the wilds, buys a few wives, builds a hut for each, lives lazily, happily, and frugally, preserving his liver and kidneys and living to a great age. Many African negroes live to 100 years and more. I think the African idea of enjoyment is better than the colonials. No wonder he objects to being charged each year with a "hut tax" (£1 in Natal) for the so-called protection that British give him.

April 17—I started at 9:30 a.m., for Kimberley over the newly opened direct line via the Vaal River valley and Fourteen Streams. The latter place is so called because here the Vaal River splits up into 14 little rivulets. The whole river at its best is not more than a creek.

Mr. Symondton, whom I met on the boat from Southampton to Cape Town, is also going on the same train, bound for Cape Town, so we will travel together to Kimberley. He is a Scotchman and a first-rate fellow, and I am glad to have company.

The day has been beautiful and even the "tin houses" look cheerful in the bright sun. Wood is so expensive in this interior region, that most of the houses are built of corrugated iron and are commonly known as "tin houses." It is not a pretty material for a house, but when painted and grown over with vines it is not so bad as it would seem. Some few houses are of stone, brick, or adobe, but most are of "tin."

Most of the South African railroads have been built by contract at so much per mile, and hence they zig-zag all over the country to make mileage. It is the same with this new road to Kimberley, and a very tiresome feature it is to any one who wants to get anywhere. I could not get any time table of the line. The railroad officials, with that negligence of passengers' comfort which characterizes all government railroads in all lands, do not have any for distribution or for sale at the stations. At one station where I inquired for a time table, they told me I could get one at a bookstore uptown, but as the train stopped only two minutes I could not go uptown. What makes the lack of time tables still worse is that the officials themselves do not seem to know when trains get anywhere, so that one has just to sit there in a dirty, dingy, little place like a horse's stall, on a train called "train de luxe" until he gets there.

Finally, we reached Kimberley about 12:30 midnight, and I bid farewell to Symondton and went up to what I was told was the best hotel in town, the "Sanitorium," a comfortable old ramshackle sort of a place, which is not, as its name suggests, a sort of asylum or hospital, but a house erected by the De Beers Company for visitors to stop at. It pretends to be very swell and people are looked over very carefully before being admitted. I got a room and went to bed, and was glad to be off the train.

April 18—Called on Mr. Alpheus Williams, manager of the DeBeers Consolidated Mines, Ltd., who is an American, and who was very polite in sending me around to see the diamond mines. Here, as in Johannesburg, most of the men in responsible positions seem to be Americans. I took dinner with Mr. Henrotin, manager of "The Kimberley Mine," at the Kimberley Club.

April 19—In Kimberley, examining the mines. It has been raining hard all afternoon. Will leave tonight at 6:30 p.m. for Johannesburg.

April 20—Arrived at Jonannesburg this morning about 10:30 a.m., from Kimberley. The Central South African Railway, as this line—or, rather, the system to which this line belongs—terms itself, run the dirtiest sleeping cars I have ever seen in the world. They charge 5 shillings a night for what they call "bedding." This charge is small, but what is given for it is worse than nothing. I would rather pay 100 shillings not to have it. The sheets are filthy—old sheets used many times over and wrapped up after each using so as to make them look new. The blankets are coarser than any they would even put on a horse, and far dirtier. They look like dirty old rag carpets. The wash rooms in the sleeping cars are simply filthy—worse than any I have ever seen in Siberia or other remote places.

Letter from Dick, dated Carlton Hotel, Johannesburg, South Africa, April 20, 1906

I wrote to you from here last week. Since then I have been doing a good deal of travelling about this part of the country. I went first to Pretoria, the capital of the Transvaal, and then returned here. I left here again the beginning of this week and went to Kimberley, a great diamond mining region, about 300 miles southwest of here.

Kimberley is the largest diamond mining center in Africa, and in fact the largest in the world. I saw several of the mines and the methods of working them, all of which was very interesting. The diamonds occur in the solid rock, which is mined and exposed to the air on the open ground until it disintegrates, when the diamonds are sorted out, partly by machinery and partly by hand. Most of the mines are controlled by one company, which employs about 30,000 natives, known as Kaffirs, and over 3000 white people. It is said that about two thirds of the diamonds are sold in the United States.

I left Kimberley last night and arrived here about noon today. I have found Johannesburg a very good central point from which to make these trips to other places, and therefore have been making it a sort of headquarters since I have been in the interior of Africa. Besides visiting the Kimberley mines, I also visited, some days ago, a large diamond mine known as the Premier Mine, about 75 miles northeast of here, where about a year or so ago a diamond weighing over 3000 carats, and several times the weight of the Kohinoor diamond,* was found.

I will stay here in Johannesburg a few days, and then I am thinking of going back to Durban, on the east coast of Africa, and up the east coast by steamer, visiting Zanzibar and other places, and thence passing north through the Red Sea and the Suez Canal to Europe. There are many places of interest on the east coast, and this is a good time of year to go there.

I will write more fully in a few days.

[Notation on the letter: "Received May 22 and answered June 11"]

From the Diary

April 21—In Johannesburg.

April 22—In Johannesburg. This again is Sunday and a very dull day, but fortunately Honnold had invited me out to his house to spend the day and it passed very pleasantly. I stayed there for lunch and dinner and came back in the evening. He has a nice place about 2 miles from the center of town.

April 23—In Johannesburg. I had Stark and Hoffman to lunch with me at the hotel.

April 24—In Johannesburg. Took lunch with Hoffman at the hotel.

April 25—In Johannesburg. Took lunch with William Mein at the Rand Club. Will leave tonight at 8:30 p.m., for Durban. This time I have been able to secure a two-berth sleeping car compartment on the so-called train de luxe, entirely to myself by paying two first-class railroad fares. The fare is about six

---

* Original weight of Kohinoor was 800 carats; present weight, 108.9 carats.

cents per mile, and I paid twelve cents. These are excessive charges, but the privacy and comfort of a compartment alone is worth it, and it saved me the trouble of having to coddle up to the conductor and try to persuade him to give me a compartment alone. This graft of the conductor is publicly recognized. The officials of the railway will tell you to bribe the conductor if you want a compartment alone. This is one of the fine moral results of government ownership of railways.

In America the railways and other corporations and those representing them try to help foreigners; in South Africa they simply try to rob them. The hotels add fictitious items to their bills; the railway officials pass off dirty bedding, napkins, etc., so as to charge the government for the washing and put the change in their pockets. The freight and passenger charges are simply outrageously exorbitant. So great are they that the net profit of the Transvaal Railways last year was £1,500,000 sterling.

Washing napkins, sheets, and all such things goes against the grain of South Africa. They dread having it done. They howl for their "tub" in the morning, which is often in a filthy slopping bath tub, but they do not mind using a napkin that looks as if it had wiped the excess egg off the mouths of a hundred different people before it reached the present users.

What has built America has been the individual efforts, unhampered by paying royalty to products of mines, etc. (10% in Australia, 60% on diamonds, $2\frac{1}{2}$% in Canada). In Africa and Australia, big companies owned in England have done the work. The individuals were only hirelings—the money went to England. In America the owners were there and the money stayed there. The term "home," used in Canada, Australia, and Africa as applied to England, is most pernicious, inasmuch as it constantly reminds the people that where they are is not home. They take less interest in the country, want only to make money and go home.

The original idea of the American settlers was not to make money, but to have freedom of thought. For this they left Europe (they had ideals) and as soon as they landed in America that soil became their home. The people of Australia and Africa went there, not with any ideals, but simply to make money and return "home." Hence, Americans have developed a continent and built up an empire, while the Australians and Afrikanders have only made a makeshift of their country for the sordid purpose of getting money. In America, money-making was an incident and a recent one; in Australia and Africa, it was the whole incentive.

April 26—Arrived in Durban at 7:30 p.m. in a pouring rain, went to the Marine Hotel, where I got a very good room.

April 27—In Durban. Still raining hard, and cool. The Marine Hotel, however, is a very comfortable hotel, the best I have struck in Africa, and I am perfectly contented to stop here until May 2nd, on which day I will sail up the east coast of Africa for Europe on the Austrian Lloyd steamer "Africa."

Letter from Dick, dated Marine Hotel, Durban, Natal, South Africa, April 27, 1906

I arrived here last night from Johannesburg, a journey of about 24 hours by train. South African sleeping cars are much inferior to American cars, and a journey is not made in the same luxury and comfort as in the United States; but at the same time the cars here compare well with those of Europe.

I wrote to you last week from Johannesburg. I have not heard from you since your letter of March 3d, which I received in Johannesburg a couple of weeks or so ago. I fear that some of my mail may have gone astray, but it will probably catch up with me eventually.

I was terribly sorry to hear of the earthquake and fire at San Francisco. Only very vague reports of the occurrence have reached here, but I hope that the catastrophy has not been so great as it has been represented here.

I have now travelled over a good part of South Africa, and have seen all the chief mining districts. I have returned here to Durban to take a steamer up the east coast of Africa. I will sail on May 2d, on one of the Austrian Lloyd boats known as the "Africa." The ship is now in port here, and I went aboard to look it over today. It is a fine ship of about 5000 tons and comparatively new. I have one of the best cabins on it. Our route will be up the east coast, stopping at ports in Portugese East Africa, thence along the coast of German East Africa to Zanzibar, thence northward around Cape Guardafui, at the east extremity of Africa, thence through the Red Sea and Suez Canal to the Mediterranean, where I will land at some port in southern Europe. I may go directly through to Europe with the ship, or I may stop over at some of the ports. I will be guided by circumstances in this matter. If the boat stops long enough at ports for me to see all I want, I will stick to it; if it don't, I will land and take the next boat. I will write regularly whenever I have the opportunity to mail letters during the voyage.

When you write, please continue to address me care of J. S. Morgan & Co., 22 Old Broad St., London, England, as I keep them notified of my address by cable from time to time, and they forward mail promptly.

From the Diary

April 28—In Durban. Still raining, though it looks like clearing tonight.
April 29—In Durban. Sunday and very quiet; but then Durban is always unique and interesting, *even on Sunday*, and the hotel is very comfortable. I would much rather spend Sunday here than in Johannesburg. The weather has cleared and the day is fine, clear and cool.
April 30—In Durban. I bought two fur rugs (golden jackal) today and shipped them home by Thomas Cook & Son. They cost £10 and £10:10 respectively, and I thought they would make nice presents to some one at home. They are beautiful rugs, and the ones most popular in Africa.
May 1—In Durban. A fine, clear, cool day.

Letter from Dick, dated Durban, Natal, South Africa, May 1, 1906

I wrote to you from here on April 27th. Since then I have received your letter of March 20th, and I was very glad to hear from you again, and to know that your ear was giving you no further trouble.

I am glad you feel so favorably about Speck's matrimonial matters. Since my arrival here, I have received a cablegram from him telling me of his marriage in London, and I have replied by cable sending my congratulations to him and his wife. I hope he is going to be happy. As he himself said to me in Paris, he has not gone into this matter hastily, but after over two years acquaintance with the lady, so they ought both to know their own minds.

If I had known Speck was going to be married so soon, and in London, I would have delayed my trip to Africa to help him out at his marriage, but I thought I would probably be back before it occurred.

In my last letter I told you that I would start in a few days up the east coast of Africa. I am off in the morning on this journey. The weather is perfect, though a little warm, but when the ship gets out to sea on the Indian Ocean, it will be cool enough, at least until we approach the equator. I will write regularly when I have a chance to mail letters.

Durban is the most attractive place I have seen in Africa. It is beautifully situated on the slopes of green hills rising up from the shores of the Indian Ocean, and extending inland until they blend into the high uplands of central Africa.

From the Diary

May 2—Sailed at 9 a.m., on the S.S. "Africa" bound up the east coast of Africa for Europe. This is an Austrian ship, but many of the stewards, etc., are Italians. The signs about the ship are in Italian or in Italian and English, and some also in French and German. It is a beautiful little ship of about 5000 tons, built with every convenience for the tropics, with electric fans, etc., etc. I think it is the coolest hot-weather boat I ever saw, and a very excellent feature is the dining saloon on the promenade deck. The grub is good, and everyone very courteous. There are probably 50 passengers in the first-class department, but more are expected at Delagoa Bay and Beira.

May 3—Arrived at Lorenzo Marques about 3 p.m. Went on shore with three Americans who are on board, Messrs Knight, Swift and Woltmann. This town is in Delagoa Bay and a very good harbor. It is an old Portuguese settlement, with narrow crooked streets, white houses, streets paved with little rough blocks of stone, and dirt and filth galore. It is supposed to be a very gay place, and many of the boys come here from the Transvaal for a little spree. There are probably 10,000 people or less in the town. It was once very unhealthy and is still a bad place for fevers. The mortality in some years has been as high as 400 per 1000 per year. But the town is now more healthy on account of drainage, etc.

May 4—We stayed last night on the ship at Delagoa Bay and sailed for the north about noon. Last evening, one of our passengers, a woman, died of malarial fever. She had been at Victoria Falls and had contracted malaria and had started with her daughter to go back to England. She was fairly well on leaving Durban, but had a relapse at Lorenzo Marques and died. Some say it was Black Water fever—a severe form of malaria. The body was put ashore last night and will be buried this morning. It is said that the daughter will go on with the ship.

There were a great many mosquitoes on the ship last night and it will be a wonder if some of the passengers do not get malaria.

May 5—The weather has been perfect ever since we left Durban, warm with light head winds which kept things cool. We have been in sight of land ever since starting, running 4 to 6 miles from a low, sandy shore, with sand dunes covered with a scant growth of salt grass.

Letter from Dick, dated on board S.S. Africa, Mozambique Channel, East Coast of Africa, May 5, 1906

I wrote to you on May 1st from Durban. On the next day I sailed on this ship, which is an Austrian steamer, bound up the east coast of Africa.

The first port we stopped at was Lorenzo Marques, in the Portugese possessions in East Africa. It is a very old town founded by the early Portugese explorers. We stayed part of a day and a night there, unloading and taking on cargo, and the next day we continued north.

We are now passing up the Mozambique channel, which separates the island of Madagascar from the African mainland; and tomorrow we will reach the Portuguese town of Beira, which is on the mainland of Africa just south of the mouth of the Zambesi River, one of the largest rivers of Africa. I will mail this letter at Beira.

The weather has been fine and the voyage first rate so far. It is a little warm, as we are approaching the tropics, but we have had light head winds ever since starting, and these have made the heat much less noticeable.

This boat is very comfortable and the grub is good. It is fairly well filled, but not crowded, with passengers of various nationalities; and many languages are spoken on board, including German, Italian, English, French and Portuguese, etc.

I will write further when I get a chance to mail letters on the way up the coast.

From the Diary

May 6—We reached the Portuguese settlement of Beira about 3 p.m. today. It was the captain's plan to leave again at 5 p.m., but as soon as we came into the harbor, the ship and all on board were put under arrest by the Portuguese authorities. It seems that some man in Lorenzo Marques had committed murder and theft and had escaped on the Africa when she sailed. The Lorenzo Marquez authorities telegraphed to Beira to stop the ship until the man was found. A thorough search was made, but no trace of him could be found. Finally, suspicion fell on a solemn-looking priest assiduously reading his Bible on a corner of the third-class deck. He had large flowing skirts, and when accosted and asked to move, it was found that a man was concealed under his skirts. The man was the one they were looking for; the pseudo-priest was not a priest at all, but a confederate of the other man, who had dressed as a priest so as to conceal his pal under his skirts. Both men were arrested, and we then expected to sail, but during this time the tide had fallen (the tide rises and falls 11 feet here) and the water is too shallow to let us out of the harbor. We must wait until morning, persecuted by mosquitoes, and very hot.

Beira is a small place, not so large as Delagoa Bay (Lorenzo Marquez) and situated at the confluence of two rivers. The muddy water of these streams fills the small bay on which the town is situated and discolors the water for miles out to sea, though the rivers are not large.

While we were held at Beira, police were put at the head of the gangway to keep people from leaving the ship. Several of us wanted very much to go ashore, but for a long time were not allowed to do so. Finally, one of our passengers, Senor Morelli, a Portuguese gentleman, explained the police chief that we were Americanos and were all right, so we were allowed to go on shore. No one else was permitted to leave the ship that evening.

The streets of Beira are very sandy, and all travel is done on little narrow-gauge tracks laid in the sand. Street cars run on this; also a sort of hand car like a rickasha on wheels, pushed by niggers.

May 7—Left Beira about 11 a.m., and sailed north. Weather, fine; light head winds; sea smooth. We have taken on a good many passengers at Lorenzo Marques and Beira, and now have probably 70 out of a possible 82 in the first class. The boat seems full, but not crowded. Most of the passengers—probably over half—are English. Four of us are Americans—i.e., Knight, Swift, Woltmann, and I—a few are Portuguese, and perhaps a few are Italian, French, and German.

It is a free and easy sort of boat, but everything is very comfortable, and it is refreshing to escape from the strict and rigid rules of British boats. We are not compelled to go to church on Sunday (there is no Sunday service as on British boats); we do not have tea stuffed into us on all occasions, as on British boats; do not have a steward look at us in contempt if we don't take a morning bath, etc.

May 8—At sea. Occasionally in sight of land; occasionally, not.

May 9—At sea. We passed the promontory of Mozambique last night, but did not stop. The wind is partly in our stern and the day clear and hot. Yesterday afternoon a man was taken with a sort of fit, probably due to heat, in the smoking room. He kicked and fought, but was finally brought to by the doctor and several sailors. We have had fine weather with light head winds ever since starting. Winds most on the starboard bow.

Letter from Dick, dated on board S.S. Africa, East Coast of Africa, May 10, 1906

We will reach Zanzibar tonight, and I write a line to you to mail there. I wrote to you last, just as we were coming into Beira, in Portuguese East Africa, on May 6th, and had intended to mail the letter there, but I thought that the letter would reach you sooner, if mailed on the ship, so I did so. We stayed almost a day at Beira, which, like Lorenzo Marquez, where we had stopped a few days previous, is an old Portuguese post on the African coast.

We have now passed north of the Portuguese territory, and are off the coast of equatorial Africa. The shore has been in sight more or less every day since we left Beira. It is a low flat country covered with a dense jungle. We are now only six or seven degrees south of the equator, and it is a little hot, but the weather is clear and fine, and a good breeze tempers the effect of the heat, so that as long as a man keeps out of the sun, he can be very comfortable. All the cabins on this ship have electric fans, which are a wonderful comfort in the tropics.

P.S. This ship will stop a day or two in Zanzibar, and I will proceed north on the same boat.

From the Diary

May 10—Fine and clear. We got into Zanzibar harbor about 10:20 p.m., but will not go on shore until morning.

May 11—In Zanzibar. We landed early in the morning with small boats, and went to "Africa Hotel," where several of us ordered a table for lunch to be ready at 12:30 p.m. The old town of Zanzibar is a most interesting and unique place, with its little narrow streets, sometimes not over 4 or 5 feet wide—winding in and out in every conceivable direction. The Sultan's palace is a large square modern structure, but his harem is an old walled castle from which all visitors are excluded. The Sultan has only four wives, as his religion forbids him more, but he has a large harem.

The town is built mostly of coral rock cemented in mud, one-storied houses being most common, while a few have two stories, with queer little upper porches and blue shutters. It was from one of these porches that Emin Pasha, after being rescued by Stanley, fell and injured himself while a little full. The gardens and the home of the famous slave trader, Tippoo Tib, are also in Zanzibar, and though Tippoo himself has died, his place is still held in awe and respect by the people, for slavery still exists in Zanzibar, and men and women slaves are common. The smell of the town is strong of cocoanut oil, and when this is mixed with a smell of dried fish and humanity, it is very strong. Every house that one passes seems to give out a new smell, and every smell seems to be worse than the last, until many people get sick.

When we landed on the beach many guides accosted us who wanted to conduct us through the town. One of them said: "My name is George Washington. I never tell a lie." He was black as ink and pock-marked. I did not insult the memory of the real George by engaging him. But I mention the incident to show the shrewdness of these people in guessing at the nationality of strangers. The people are mostly Arabs and Swahilis, the latter native tribes. There are also many Indians. The plague broke out in the postoffice the other day and instead of disinfecting the place they simply moved the postoffice.

Came on board at 5:30 p.m., and sailed for Mombasa at about 7 o'clock this evening.

P.S. The Sultan of Zanzibar is under British influence. He is very friendly with the English and spends much time in London. He is on way there now.

May 12—Arrived at Mombasa at daybreak this morning—about 11 hours' sail from Zanzibar. This town was an old Portuguese settlement when a fort was built about 1570, called "Fort Jesus." The Portuguese lost and retook the place several times in wars with Arabs and other natives. In 1895 the place was "annexed" by England. It is now the outlet of the Uganda Railroad which runs from Mombasa to Nirobe on Lake Uganda, 24 hours travel. The old fort still stands.

There is a native population of probably several thousand, apparently the same kind of people as at Zanzibar, and a white population of probably a hundred people. The town is only about 4° south of the equator, but a brisk breeze has made the day very comfortable.

May 13—We left Mombasa at 5:30 p.m., yesterday, with a cool breeze off the bow, but during today the wind has come around to our stern. The heat is great. Thermometer 89° in my cabin. Humidity intense.

May 14—At sea. Very hot following wind. Thermometer at 8 a.m. in my cabin 90°.

May 15—We rounded Cape Guardafui about 9 a.m. today, and turned our course northwest up the Gulf of Aden. Heat intense, with light following wind. Thermometer 91° at 8 a.m. At Mombasa several monkeys were taken aboard by passengers. They are now tied to the masts and spars, and the deck looks like a menagerie. There are also several other wild animals, wild cats, wild boars, etc., etc., in cages. These, with the negroes, Indians, and various dark races in the steerage, give a strong smell to the boat.

Cape Guardafui is a bleak, barren, dry rocky point, rising several hundred feet above the sea, and blending into still higher flat-topped peaks farther inland. It looks like a piece of Arizona.

May 16—The heat today has been intense. The wind, which is very light, is in our stern. The thermometer tonight at 10 p.m. was 104° and the humidity very great.

I find that in this very hot weather the use of a little bicarbonate of potash as a diuretic does one much good. A little Eno's salts in the morning and one grain of calomel in the evening, also help. I am covered with prickly heat, as are most of the other passengers. I find that avoiding salt baths and washing with fresh water and soap is the best treatment for this.

May 17—Heat still intense, winds in stern. Arrived Aden about 5 p.m., and sailed again at 1 a.m. Swift and Knight left the ship here to take a boat for Bombay. I went ashore for an hour or so with several other passengers, but Aden is a very unattractive place. Our ship took on a great quantity of gum arabic here, which seems to be the only important product of the country. The natives are thin, sickly looking people, with a peculiar sort of exema on many of their scalps, and very dirty. They are mostly Somalis from the other side of the Gulf of Aden.

May 18—In Red Sea. Following wind. Heat intense.

May 19—Same. For about a week the thermometer in my cabin has not been below 90°. This would not be much in a dry climate, but the intense humidity makes it very oppressive. At night the people cannot stay in their cabins, and they lie about the deck in all kinds of undress garbs.

May 20—In Red Sea. The heat was intense this morning, but about 11 a.m., the wind shifted to the northwest and is now blowing stiff in our bow. It is wonderfully refreshing, and every one is beginning to revive. One woman has been very ill with the heat. She had a temperature of 104° a couple of days ago, and the doctor gave her the cheering news that if it went any higher she would die. She seems better today.

I think, taking it all in all, this voyage from Mombasa to here has been the hottest I ever took anywhere. As I am writing now, at 4 p.m., the thermometer is down to 88°, which is so much cooler than it has been that it seems very comfortable. Probably we can sleep tonight. It has been hard to sleep at all for a week or more.

May 21—In Red Sea. Little cooler. Light puffs of head wind.

Letter from Dick, dated on board S.S. Africa, Red Sea, May 22, 1906

I wrote to you last on May 10th, and mailed the letter at Zanzibar. I have not written since then, as any letters would have had to go on the same ship as I am travelling on, and hence letters written any time before I leave the ship would reach you as soon as if written earlier on the voyage.

Zanzibar is one of the most interesting, but one of the dirtiest places that I have ever seen. An old Arab town, it has been the center of the East African slave trade from very remote ages, and even yet slavery flourishes there. The Sultan of Zanzibar is a good deal of a sport and maintains a large harem. It is closely guarded and I could only see the outside, though I would have liked very much to have looked over the ladies inside.

The streets of the town consist of a labyrinth of narrow alleys, often not over 4 or 5 feet wide, running in all directions, and crowded with a lot of half naked Arabs, who look at a white man in anything but a friendly manner.

The stink that comes from the houses is the worst that I have ever met anywhere in the world. I thought that Canton, in China, stunk, but it is not in it with Zanzibar. The combination of rancid cocoanut oil, dried fish, and human sweat, makes a smell the like of which I have never before experienced.

From Zanzibar, we continued north to Mombasa, on the African coast, about 4 degrees south of the equator. This used to be an old Portuguese post, known as "Fort Jesus." Now it belongs to the English. It is somewhat similar to Zanzibar, but not so dirty.

From Mombasa, we kept on northward to Cape Guardafui, which is the eastern extremity of Africa, and is a high, barren, rocky promontory reaching out into the Indian Ocean. Here we changed our course to the northwest, up the Gulf of Aden, which lies between Somaliland (in Africa) and Arabia, and finally reached the port of Aden, on the coast of Arabia, after six days sail from Zanzibar. Aden is a British coaling station at the south end of the Red Sea. It is also a shipping point for large quantities of gum arabic.

From Aden we started up the Red Sea and will reach Port Suez, at the north end of it, today. The heat for the last eight or nine days has been intense, the thermometer frequently ranging over 100° and the humidity always high. The thermometer in my cabin had not been below 90°, night or day, for 8 days, until yesterday, when it fell to 88°. It was 104° by the ship's thermometer on the upper deck at ten o'clock at night, a couple of days ago. This would not be very bad in a dry country like Arizona, but with the humidity at almost 100, it is very bad. We are now through the worst of it, however, and the weather is cooling down as we get farther north.

We will reach Port Suez this afternoon, and this ship will then go through the Suez Canal to Port Said, at the north end of the canal. I will go ashore at Port Suez and take a train to Cairo, stay there a short time and then go to Port Said by train, where I will again join this same ship, and go on to Europe. I have never been in Cairo, and I thought I would take this opportunity to drop in there for a day or two. From Port Said this ship goes to Brindisi and Venice in Italy, and thence to Trieste in Austria. I will get off at one of these ports—which one I will decide later—and will go thence to Paris and then to London. But I will write further later on, when I have made more definite plans.

P.S. I will mail this letter either at Port Suez or Cairo.

From the Diary

May 22—Arrived Port Suez about 12:30 p.m. Weather slightly cooler. Went ashore on company's launch, and five of us took 7 p.m. train for Cairo, arriving there about 11:30 p.m. We went to the Continental Hotel, as Savoy was not open, got good supper, and went about town, saw dance, etc. Went to bed about 2:30 a.m.

May 23—Got up at 5 a.m. today and took 6 a.m. tram car to pyramids. Got breakfast there, saw pyramids and sphinx, went back to Cairo, drove to Citadel, returned to hotel and took 11 a.m. train for Port Said, where we joined the S.S. Africa again at 4 p.m. We had a splendid and most interesting trip, and it was well worth taking. It was a little hot from Suez to Cairo, but nowhere else. In the early morning at Cairo it was really cold, and we were buttoning up our coats.

Cairo is a town of over 500,000 people, situated on the Red Nile, and a queer combination of ancient Egypt and a modern city. The native quarter has little narrow, crowded streets, and is a good deal like Zanzibar on a big scale; the newer part of the town has fine boulevards, good stores, hotels, etc., and might be mistaken for a bit of Paris or Vienna.

May 24—We sailed at 7 p.m. last night from Port Said. As soon as we got out into the Mediterranean the weather cooled, and the thermometer fell to 72°

in my cabin. Surely the Suez Canal separates the Orient from the Occident, not only in people but in climate.

May 25—At sea in the Mediterranean. We passed close in along the shore of Crete today. It is very mountainous and picturesque island, with snow on some of the higher peaks and small settlements nestled away in the valleys.

May 26—At sea. We passed up the west coast of Greece today, but the land was only dimly visible, as there is considerable haziness.

Have been going up the Adriatic Sea all day. Stopped for about an hour at Brindisi tonight, to put off mail and a few passengers.

May 27—At sea.

Letter from Dick, dated on board S.S. Africa, Adriatic Sea, May 27, 1906

I wrote to you from on board this ship on May 22d, and mailed the letter at Cairo the next day. I got to Cairo by leaving the ship at Port Suez, at the head of the Red Sea, and going overland by train. From Cairo I came to Port Said by train and joined the same ship again. We are now in a much cooler climate, which is a great relief from the fearful hot weather we have been having.

From Port Said we came out into the Mediterranean and went northward to the island of Crete, thence up the west coast of Greece, and over to the coast of Italy, where we touched at Brindisi last night. We are now passing up the Adriatic Sea and will reach Venice in the morning. I will land there and go on to Paris by train, though I may stop a day or two in Venice before starting. I drop this line to you now to mail at Venice, and will write more fully from Paris. The voyage from Durban, in Africa, to Venice will have taken just four weeks, less one day, and though at times very hot, yet it has been very interesting, and I am glad I made it.

From the Diary

May 28—Arrived at Venice early in forenoon. We passed up the Grand Canal and anchored opposite St. Mark's Square. Went to the Grand Hotel, which has very good food, but very bad rooms. Weather very hot. Saw a few of the sights of the town in afternoon and evening. As I had been here in January, 1902, the place was not new to me. St. Mark's Square looked a little bare with its tower tumbled down.

May 29—Merison and I started at 2 p.m., for Paris, going direct via Milan, Turin, Lyons, and Dijon. We got a wagon-lit sleeping car at Turin, which, like all European cars of this kind, was very hot and uncomfortable. We were allowed ten minutes at Milan for dinner. The Europeans talk about the hasty meals of Americans, but often theirs are much worse.

May 30—Arrived in Paris a little after 2 p.m., the train being a little late. We had a very good breakfast and lunch on the dining car. We went to the Hotel Continental, where we had wired from Venice for rooms, and got fairly good ones. This is Grand Prix week and there is a very great crowd in town.

May 31—My bed at the hotel has a good many bedbugs in it, but as the city is simply jammed with people I think I will keep it as being less bad than some other I might get.

I found today that Speck and his wife were in Paris at Hotel Princess, and I called on them this evening. They both looked first rate.

June 1 to 8—In Paris.

Letter from Dick, dated Paris, France, June 4, 1906

I have arrived here from Venice, where I landed from the steamer on which I came from Africa, and it seems very good to get back here again.

Speck and his wife are here and seem to be very happy. They are staying at the Hotel Princess, where they have very good apartments. I am staying at the Hotel Continental, as I have stayed here often before and feel more at home here than anywhere else in Paris. Speck and his wife both look first rate and seem to be having a good time. I took dinner with them the day before yesterday, and they took dinner with me last evening. They are starting today on a several weeks trip to Tours and Vichy, in France, on their automobile. They asked me to go with them, but I thought that perhaps people on a honeymoon were more happy alone, so I am not going.

I wrote to you several times during the voyage from Africa, but most of the time it was so terribly hot that I could not write very fully. My last letter was written just before landing at Venice, and was mailed there. The trip from Africa was one of the most interesting that I have ever had, though it was at times intensely hot, and there was a good deal of sickness on board, due to the heat and the unhealthy climate of the ports at which we called. One passenger died of some acute form of malarial fever while we were at Lorenzo Marquez. Later on another went crazy and another developed fits. Many were sick with malaria and dysentery, and we had a good deal of trouble getting through the quarantines in Egypt and Italy. When we reached Venice our ship was surrounded by ambulance gondolas, which had been called for, to take the sick to the hospitals.

This year seems to have been an especially unhealthy one on the east coast of Africa, though it is always an unhealthy region. At Lorenzo Marquez the death rate has been as much as 400 people per 1000 of population per year! Night after night it was too hot to sleep until 2 or 3 o'clock a.m. No one could stay in a cabin with the thermometer 104° or 105° and most people wandered about the deck in their night clothes until towards morning, when it was possible to get a little sleep.

When we reached Beira in Portuguese east Africa, we were all put under arrest by the Portuguese authorities, because it was suspected that there was an escaped murderer on board from Lorenzo Marquez, and the Portuguese authorities said they were going to hold the ship and its officers and passengers until the man was produced. Soldiers were put on board to guard us. The ship was searched from stem to stern, but the man was not found. At last, after we had been under arrest for about a day, suspicion rested on a Portuguese priest, with a long flowing robe, who sat in a corner of the deck, never moving and apparently greatly interested in his bible. The priest was questioned; he said he knew nothing of the murderer. Then he was told to move out of his corner; he refused, and they pushed him out. Then from beneath the skirts of the priest's robe appeared a man who made a dash to jump overboard, but was caught. He was the murderer, and his friend the priest was trying to conceal him under his robe. Both men were taken ashore, the rest of us were freed from arrest, and we set sail at once for Zanzibar, everyone greatly pleased, not only being free from the Portuguese officials who held us prisoners, but also at getting away from Beira, which, situated at the confluence of two large tropical rivers, is a most unhealthy place, and is infested by mosquitos.

Aside from all these troubles, however, the voyage was a pleasant one. There was a very agreeable crowd on board, composed of various nationalities, and I shall always be glad I took the trip. The voyage took four weeks less one day, and the country I saw is absolutely unique and different from any part of the world I have ever visited. I am in good shape and never felt better.

I have gotten here sooner than I had expected and am ahead of my mail, but I expect it will all be here in a few days. When I get it and hear how things are going at home, I will decide on my future movements, and will then write further. For the moment, Paris seems very good after Africa, and I don't mind staying here a little while, but I think that perhaps I will come home before long.

My address is still care J. S. Morgan & Co., 22 Old Broad St., London, England.

From the Diary

June 9—Went to Tours to see Speck and his wife, who had gone there on their automobile. I wanted to take to them some wedding presents that I had gotten for them. I have just returned to Paris again this evening.
June 10 to 16—In Paris.
June 17—Went to London via Calais with Ralf Preston, Joe Harriman, and Mr. Mitchell. Had very smooth passage. Found good room reserved for me at Savoy Hotel, London. I had wired ahead for it. I took dinner this evening with Preston at the new Ritz Hotel.
June 18 to 26—In London.

While Penrose was in London, he saw and talked with Herbert Hoover, evidently discussing the possibility of making another trip to New South Wales, for the latter wrote to him on June 26, addressing his letter to "Dear Penrose" at the Savoy Hotel and saying that if Penrose were to go to Broken Hill he would have no difficulty in securing access to all the mines.

From the Diary

June 27—Sailed for New York on the Kaiser Wilhelm der Grosse. I had the same stateroom that I had last February coming to Europe, and the same that I had when I went home from Europe in February, 1905.

June 28 to July 4—Had a very smooth and uneventful passage to New York. Arrived at quarantine on the night of July 3rd, anchored, and went up the bay in the morning, arriving at Hoboken docks about 9 a.m. The weather is fearfully hot and sultry today. After passing the customs I drove over to Jersey City and went direct to Philadelphia.

Later in 1906, Penrose made a trip to California, Utah, Colorado, and other western States, on mining business.

Another Hoover letter belongs to this period. It is dated July 31, 1906, and after thanking Penrose for his letter of July 19, and discussing various matters, he added "I am leaving for New York on the 'Kaiserin Augusta Victoria' on the 3rd August and am spending a month's vacation in the States and hope to see you there."

CHAPTER 15

Around South America in 1907

ONE MORE continent remained to be visited, and in the spring of 1907 Penrose set forth to study the ore deposits of South America, a trip which occupied him from March until November. Again, the record is complete, with letters to his father, diary, and notebooks.

Before he started, he again wrote to Hoover.

Letter from Penrose to H. C. Hoover, ℅ Bewick, Moreing and Company, 20 Copthall Avenue, London, dated March 11, 1907

Dear Hoover:—

I drop a line to you to say that I expect to be in London the end of March or the first week of April, on my way to South America, to take a look at some of the mining industries there. I want especially to see the nitrate fields of Chile and some of the iron districts of Brazil. I do not know whether you are in London, but if so I hope to have the pleasure of seeing you.

I hope everything is going well with you, and that all your Australian and other interests are prospering.

With best regards, I am,

Sincerely yours,
R. A. F. Penrose, Jr.

Letter from Dick, dated on board S. S. Cedric, March 22, 1907

I never saw a much finer day to get started on a trip. The weather is perfect.

I took dinner with Cobb and John Montgomery last night. This morning I got down to the boat at 11 a.m., and it sailed promptly on schedule time at 11:30.

There are very few passengers on this boat, and there is no one on board that I know. I do not think that there are a hundred passengers in the first class, and this number seems lost in a big boat like this. I have an excellent stateroom, on the top deck and very large.

Will write further from London.

From the Diary

March 22—Sailed from New York for Liverpool on the White Star Steamer Cedric. We left promptly on time at 11.30 a.m. The weather is fine and clear, and as we passed out of Sandy Hook at about 2 p.m. the sea was as smooth as a pond. Light Northwest wind.

This is an immense boat (21,000 tons) and has been all winter on the run between New York and the Mediterranean. It is now returning to England to prepare for the summer run on the North Atlantic. There are only about 60 first class passengers and these seem lost on an immense ship like this. I have a large roomy stateroom on the upper promenade deck. This is a slow boat, 8 days from New York to Liverpool, but it is so big and comfortable that it makes up for its slowness.

The sea has been smooth all day, and tonight is beautiful. I am glad it is, for this business of going away alone is a dreary proposition at best, for the first few days, and unless the weather is good the dreariness is intensified. I dined with Cobb last evening. He invited John Montgomery and me, and we had a very pleasant evening.

March 23—Weather fine and sunny—sea smooth. The food on this boat is first rate and the general equipment in all parts of the boat are excellent. Wind light from N.W.

March 24—The weather was warm and sunny in the morning but clouded up and looked threatening in evening. Sea rougher. They held services on board the ship today, as it is Sunday, and the church goers were treated to a sermon of 45 minutes by a clergyman on board. Wind N.W.

March 25—Cloudy, wet and flurries of snow. Sea somewhat rough. Many of the passengers are sick, though such an immense boat as this is not affected much by the ordinary rough weather. Wind N.W.

March 26—Fine clear sunny day. A stiff northwest wind makes quite a swell, but the day is perfect and warm as summer.

March 27—Cloudy and drizzling. Light south wind but smooth sea. Warm and sultry. Southerly winds.

March 28—Today is as bright and cheerful as yesterday was gloomy—clear sky, bright sun and stiff N.W. winds. I have never seen a finer day on the North Atlantic.

March 29—Morning cloudy but clear by noon, and the afternoon and evening were perfect. Light N.W. winds.

Letter from Dick, dated on board S. S. Cedric, March 30, 1907

We came in sight of the coast of Ireland today, and are due to reach Liverpool tomorrow morning, so I am writing a line now to mail when I get on shore.

The voyage has been a first rate one, and the weather has been good most of the way. A stiff northwest wind has been blowing most of the time since we left New York, and this has sometimes made the sea a little rough, but not uncomfortably so. In fact, this boat is so big (21,000 tons) that a very heavy sea would be required to affect it much. It will be almost a day late in arriving at Liverpool, and the reason they give is that the boat has not been in dry dock for some months, so that its bottom is covered with sea-weed and barnacles. I believe it goes into dry dock when it gets to Liverpool. The grub and the staterooms, however, are first rate, and it is a very comfortable boat to travel on.

When I reach Liverpool, I will go direct to London and make arrangements about sailing for South America, and will write further as soon as I decide on what boat I will go. The first boat that I know of that I can take, sails on April 11th, and if I find it all right, I may take it, but I will write further about this in a few days.

From the Diary

March 30—Came in sight of first light on coast of Ireland about 3 a.m. and went along coast all day. Weather perfect—clear, bright and warm. The sea is as smooth as a mill pond, a rare thing in these parts. We stopped at Queenstown about 2 p.m. to let off a few passengers and the mail, and thence proceeded towards Liverpool. The night was clear and quiet.
March 31—Arrived Liverpool about 3 a.m. and went up to landing stage at 8.30 a.m. At 9.30 a.m. special train started for London, arriving at 1.15 p.m., with no stops.

The voyage has been a good one with far more than the average of good weather for the North Atlantic—especially at this time of year. The boat was comfortable, grub good and passengers few. I was put at the purser's table opposite some ladies, though I usually prefer to be off in some quiet corner where I do not have to talk. A very loquacious drummer, however, on the opposite side from me kept up such a continuous line of conversation that I was not troubled by having to keep it up.
March 31 to April 9—In London. Have been stopping at Savoy Hotel where I had a very good room. I met J. H. Means in London. He used to be on the old geological survey of Arkansas and has travelled much in remote places since then. I suggested to him that he come to South America with me and he has agreed to do so. I am very glad of it, as he is a good companion and an agreeable fellow.

I have met Frank Roudebush, H. K. Scott, A. L. Pearce, and several other people I knew here. Have had fine sunny weather most of the time and a very pleasant visit to London. Means and I have taken passage on the steamer Oriana of the Pacific Steam Navigation Co. for Valparaiso. We are to sail from Liverpool on April 11th.

Letter from Dick, dated Savoy Hotel, London, April 8, 1907

I arrived here all right on March 31st after a very good voyage. I mailed a short letter to you when I landed at Liverpool and suppose that you have received it by this time.

I have arranged to sail for South America from Liverpool on April 11th. I go on the steamer Oriana of the Pacific Steam Navigation Co. It is a fine ship of about 8000 tons, and I think I am fortunate to find it going just at this time, as there are not many boats of this size going to South America. It goes from England down the coast of France, Spain, and Portugal, thence across to Brazil and down the east coast of South America, through the Straits of Magellan, and up the west coast to Valparaiso in Chile, which is the end of the voyage, and which takes about five or six weeks from here. The ship stops at a good many ports, so that there are chances to go ashore occasionally on the voyage.

When I arrived here last week, I met a man named J. H. Means, whom I used to know on the Geological Survey of Arkansas. He was on that Survey when I was on it. I knew him well then and have known him ever since, having run across him in various parts of the world at different times. For many years since he left Arkansas, he has been travelling in all kinds of remote parts of the globe, making exploration for British mining corporations. From Arkansas he drifted up to northern China and Japan, then to the west coast of Africa, to South America and many other places. A few years ago he led an exploring expedition into Abyssinia. When I met him this time, it occurred to me that he would be just the fellow to come to South America with me, if I could get him to do so. I suggested it to him, and he at once jumped at the idea, as a number of the places to which I am going, he has never seen. He is not very well off financially, so I will help him out in the expenses of the trip. He is a native of the state of Indiana, is about 50 years old, and has travelled enough to know how to get along under all circumstances. Moreover, he is strong and healthy, and is not liable to get sick, which is a great advantage. There are not many men that I would pick out for a trip like this one to South America, but I have known Means for 17 years, and I do not think I am making any mistake in taking him along.

We will leave here together on the 10th of April for Liverpool, and will sail from there on the morning of the 11th. We will go direct to Valparaiso, and from there will probably take another boat farther up the coast; and then we may return to Valparaiso and come across the Andes and up to Brazil. But we will not be able to decide on the details of the trip beyond Valparaiso until we get there. I will write you fully about our plans from Valparaiso, and in the meantime, of course, I will write regularly during the voyage, when I get a chance to mail letters at ports at which we stop. My address, until I come home, will be care of J. S. Morgan & Co., 22 Old Broad St., London, England, as they will forward mail promptly to me. It seems ridiculous to send mail from the United States to South America by way of England, but I am told that this is the quickest way for most of the places to which I am going, so I have decided that it is best to have all my mail come here, and to have it forwarded from here to me. I will keep J. S. Morgan & Co. informed from time to time as to just where to forward it.

I hope you are well and that your rheumatism is cured. I will write again before long from some port that we stop at.

From the Diary

April 10—Means and I went on to Liverpool on the 12.10 (noon) train, arriving at 4:05 p.m. Went to Great Western Hotel as it is at the railway station, though not as good a place as the Adelphi. We got fair rooms and very good food.

April 11—We sailed on the Oriana promptly on schedule time at noon. This ship is of about 8000 tons and seems comfortable. We each have a cabin to ourselves, for which we paid $1\frac{1}{2}$ fares apiece. My cabin is on the top deck, but Means took his on the main deck as he prefers it.

The day is dark and rainy but the sea is smooth.

April 12—At sea. Day rainy in morning but clear in afternoon. Sea smooth. There are about 60 first class passengers on board so that we are not at all crowded. Means and I seem to be the only two Americans, the rest being mostly English, Portuguese and South Americans.

Letter from Dick dated R.M.S. "Oriana," April 12, 1907

I wrote you a long letter a few days ago from London, telling you about my plans for the present voyage, and also about my having, by chance, in London, run across a man named Means, who used to be on the Geological Survey of Arkansas when I was on it, and who has come on this trip with me.

We sailed from Liverpool yesterday at noon, with smooth sea and a drizzling rain. Today we are off the coast of France. The sea is still smooth, and the sun is coming out, which is very acceptable, as it has been cold and wet since starting. We will stop tomorrow at the port of La Rochelle-Pallice, on the coast of France, and I drop this line to you to mail there.

This is a comfortable boat and not crowded, there being only about 60 first class passengers. The grub is good and the cabins comfortable, so the prospects for a good voyage are favorable. So far as I know, Means and I are the only two Americans on board. The rest are English, Germans, Spanish and Portuguese.

I will write again from some port farther on.

From the Diary

April 13—Arrived at 6:30 a.m. at La Rochelle-Pallice which is the port of La Rochelle, about 4 miles off. After breakfast Means and I went to La Rochelle on a steam tram road. The town is an interesting old French seaport. Parts of the old walls, gates and forts are left. The fleet of small fishing boats is very picturesque. This coast used to be a great sardine fishing region but these fish seem now to have moved south to the coasts of Spain and Portugal, much to the loss of the French fishermen and to the gain of the Spanish and Portuguese, who now carry on the industry.

We got a very good lunch at the Hotel de France and walked back to the boat in the afternoon. When we left the ship in the morning we had expected to sail early next day, but the overland mail was late and we are now told that it may be late tomorrow morning when we sail.

April 14—Sailed at about noon. The weather is clear but a stiff breeze blowing which kicks up a little sea. Many people are seasick. We are crossing the Bay of Biscay, so a little rough weather is to be expected.

April 15—Weather clear and cool. Sea smoother. We arrived at Coruna on the north coast of Spain about 2 p.m. The town is situated at the head of a beautiful little land-locked harbor. It is an old Spanish fishing town. Means and I went ashore and walked about for an hour or so, but had to return to the ship soon as we were to sail at 4 p.m. We took on many Spanish emigrants here, bound for Brazil and Argentine. They are not a bad looking crowd, and look much better than many that come to New York. There are now several hundred emigrants on board, mostly Spanish. We sailed from Coruna at 4 p.m.

Letter from Dick, dated R.M.S. "Oriana," April 16, 1907

I wrote to you on April 12th, and mailed the letter at La Rochelle, on the coast of France. The ship remained over 24 hours there, discharging and taking on cargo, so we had a good chance to see the town. It is a very interesting old French seaport, with much of its mediaeval walls and fortresses still left.

From La Rochelle, the harbor of which seems to be known as La Rochelle-Pallice, we came across the Bay of Biscay to Coruna in Spain. This took about 24 hours, and as the water was a little rough, many people were seasick, but when we got to Coruna, which has a beautiful land-locked harbor, they soon revived. Coruna is a small seaport, and we stopped only long enough to take on a lot of Spanish emigrants for Brazil and Argentine.

From Coruna, we came around Cape Finisterre, at the northwest point of Spain; and last night we reached the Spanish port of Carril. Here again we took on more emigrants, and started away early this morning. There are about 1000 emigrants on the ship now, and we are to take on more at Lisbon. They are not a bad looking crowd, and look a lot better than many of the emigrants that arrive on the ships coming into New York from Europe.

We are now passing down the coast of Portugal, a very picturesque mountainous country. The sea is a little rough again, and many people are sea sick. This afternoon we will stop for a few minutes at Oporto in Portugal, and early tomorrow we will arrive at Lisbon. I will mail this letter at Lisbon, as we will not be at Oporto long enough to go ashore.

After leaving Lisbon, the next port at which we stop will be St. Vincent, in the Cape Verde Islands, 5 days sail from Lisbon. I will write from there if we stop long enough to mail letters. From St. Vincent, we go direct to Rio Janeiro, about eight days sail from St. Vincent. My letters from St. Vincent and Rio Janeiro will probably not get to you for some time after this one, as the mails there, especially at St. Vincent, are slow and far between, but they will probably reach you in the course of time. We have, so far, had a first rate voyage.

From the Diary

April 16—All yesterday afternoon we coasted along the Spanish shore, a high rocky coast studded with little villages in the hollows and valleys. At about 10 p.m. we passed the Cape Finisterre light, the northwestern point of Spain, and about 11 p.m. we dropped anchor in the beautiful little harbor of Carril. Here we remained until 10 a.m. this morning when we sailed again. We took on some more emigrants at Carril and now have about 1000 on board.

We have sailed most of the day close in to the shore of Spain and then of Portugal. It is a very picturesque mountainous coast, with an almost continuous line of villages along the water edge. At 4 p.m. we reached Leixoes, which is the port of Oporto, four miles inland. Oporto is the headquarters of the port wine industry. Leixoes faces the open sea, and a breakwater makes an artificial harbor for ships. It is in the form of a semicircle with the curved part facing seaward, and an opening cut into it to admit ships. It is small but seems efficient.

We are to take on some more emigrants here and to sail tonight for Lisbon. The weather is clear, cool and beautiful. A brisk breeze stirs up a little swell on the sea, which makes some of the passengers sick.

April 17—We reached the mouth of the Tagus about 9 a.m. and arrived at Lisbon about 10 a.m. This city is situated on the north side of the river some 7 or 8 miles from its mouth. The river here is really a wide estuary of the sea, which runs a long distance about Lisbon and into which the Tagus empties. The harbor of Lisbon is very beautiful with high hills on both sides, and water deep enough for any ships. The city is built on rolling hills, and is a neat clean place, with fine houses, some beautiful avenues and good hotels. The palace at Cintra, some ten or twelve miles away, is built on the top of one of the highest hills in the region. The summer palace is near the town.

We drove about the town for an hour or so, and got lunch at the Hotel Aviendre. Lunch was very good but very slowly served. We had a bottle of some white Portuguese wine which was very good but very strong. The day was perfect and I was most agreeably surprised at the beauty, prosperity and progressiveness of the town.

We saw the King of Portugal driving in the street.

We took on more emigrants at Lisbon and sailed at 4 p.m. in fine, cool, brisk weather. There are now considerably over 1000 emigrants in the steerage, and though they are very crowded they seem contented and happy, dancing and singing a large part of the time.

We also took on a large quantity of wine at Lisbon. We had taken similar large quantities of wine into the ship at all the ports we had stopped at in France, Spain and Portugal, so that there is now a big cargo of it. In fact the chief cargo of the ship seems to be emigrants and wine.

April 18—At sea; a fine clear day with N.W. wind. We are headed now almost due south and the weather is warmer and the sun much hotter than it has been. In fact, ever since we left Liverpool up to today it has been cold and raw, though generally clear.

April 19—At sea; fine clear weather with brisk N.E. wind. This is the "Trade Wind" that blows almost all the time from the N.E. in this region of the globe. It tempers the air and makes it very pleasant. At about 5 p.m. we came in sight of Palma Island, the most westerly of the Canary Islands. To the east are Tenerife and Los Palmas Islands.

Palma Island is a hilly island covered with small white houses and a luxuriant growth of grass. Many vineyards seem to be cultivated, though we were not near enough to land to see the nature of the plants in the cultivated fields. The hills are not as high as on Tenerife, probably not over a couple of thousand feet, if that much, and covered with vegetation to the top. We passed along the S.E. side of the island for a couple of hours. At about 10 p.m. we passed Ferro Island, a small member of the Canary group.

The ship's doctor, Dr. Letchmore, was very sick today with malaria. He has recently come from the west coast of Africa, where he contracted malaria, and this is his first voyage on this run. He has a high fever. A clergyman on board took care of him, gave him a pint of champagne and put him to bed.

The fourth officer, Mr. Whall, is also laid up with a broken toe and a bad throat.

There was dancing on the deck tonight for the first time during the voyage and things begin to take on a tropical air.

April 20—At sea; splendid weather, warm but with a cool N.E. breeze. For the last few days I have been walking hard for 1 hour daily on deck, and feel much better for it. Today is the second day on which we have had a sweepstake on the run of the ship, and I have won both times, though the amount was small—£1 each time. This system is for each passenger to put in a shilling and draw for numbers, no auctioning, etc.

April 21—At sea; fine, clear and cool weather; thermometer 75° in my cabin. Winds N.E.

Letter from Dick, dated R.M.S. "Oriana," April 21, 1907

We will arrive tonight or early tomorrow at St. Vincent, in the Cape Verde Islands. I will mail this letter there if we stop long enough to go on shore; but if we do not, I will mail it on the ship, and it will go on shore in the ship's mail bag, which will be forwarded to England by the next boat of this line that goes that way; in which case it may be somewhat late in reaching you. If I can mail it on land, it will go to Europe, and thence to the U. S., by the first ship of any line that carries mail from St. Vincent.

I wrote to you last on the 16th, just before reaching Lisbon. The next morning we arrived off the mouth of the Tagus, and went up that river to Lisbon. We remained there most of the day, and had a good chance to see the city. It is finely situated on the banks of the Tagus, and is a very clean, well-kept, prosperous-looking town. Means and I drove about the city during the morning, got lunch at a very good Portuguese hotel, and returned to the ship in the afternoon. We sailed from there early in the evening.

After 48 hours at sea from Lisbon, we passed through the Canary Islands, but did not stop. The Canaries are a group of mountainous islands, much cultivated by the Spaniards, who own them. One of the islands, named Tenerife, rises over 12,000 feet above the sea.

We have been sailing south for almost four days from Lisbon, and are now less than ten degrees north of the equator. The weather is getting hot as we approach the equator, but it is fine and clear, and the northeast trade winds, which blow almost continuously in this part of the world, greatly relieve the oppressiveness of the heat. I am glad that Means came along with me on the present trip. He is always in a good humor, and knows how to take care of himself without being looked after.

The next port at which we touch after leaving St. Vincent will be Rio Janeiro in Brazil, eight or nine days sail from St. Vincent. I will write further from Rio Janeiro.

From the Diary

April 22—We arrived at St. Vincent on the island of St. Vincent, Cape Verde Islands, at midnight last night. Anchored till morning, then took on 600 tons of coal and sailed at 2.30 p.m. We went ashore for a few hours and the cricket team from the ship played a game with the St. Vincent team, in which the latter won.

The town of St. Vincent is simply a small place of no special interest, noted especially as the central cable station from which cables radiate to all parts of the world. The town, and in fact all the Cape Verde islands, are owned by the Portuguese, but the cables seem to be run by the English and English seems to be the language spoken by the white people. There are many negroes who have been brought in the early days from Africa, and there is also the usual number of mixed white and black.

The island of St. Vincent is mountainous and rugged, with little or no vegetation and with a dry parched appearance. I was surprised at this, as the islands in the tropics are usually very luxuriant in their vegetation. It is explained, however, by the small rainfall, some years there being none at all. At one time it is said that there was no rain for 7 years. The ordinary rainfall is said to be from 1–15 inches yearly. In the hollows and dry cañons sometimes a few shrubs and stunted trees grow, but the higher ground is almost barren. The water used at St. Vincent is distilled from sea water. There are no running streams, though a little water has been gotten in wells.

The rocks of the island seem, so far as seen, to have been of igneous origin, in alternating layers of dark massive basic material, breccia, etc. These strata are more or less disturbed from the horizontal and are much cut in all directions by dikes. They (the strata) seem to dip off in several directions from the Bay of St. Vincent, and it seems possible that the latter may represent an old crater. Near the bay, the dikes are large and numerous; away from it, fewer and thinner. The eruptives often seem to be a mass of blackish material, probably augite or amphibole.

The general surface of the ground much resembles Arizona, with its dry pebbly surface, arid mountains, and waterless cañons.

April 23—At sea; fine, clear, and not hot. N.E. winds; thermometer 79° at 8 a.m. in my cabin; latitude 12° 6′ N. at noon.

April 24—At sea; fine, clear, and not very hot; light N.E. winds; thermometer at 8 a.m. in my cabin 82°. Latitude at 12 (noon) 6° 56′.

April 25—At sea; occasional showers during day; hot and sultry; light N.E. winds. Crossed equator in a shower about 4.30 p.m. Thermometer in my room at 8 a.m. 86°. This is the first really hot day we have had, and even this is not very oppressive.

April 26—At sea; showery, and hot sultry weather. We have passed from the region of the N.E. trade winds to that of the S.E. trades, and a cool stiff breeze makes the heat very endurable when on the deck, but out of the wind, in the cabins, it is fearfully hot. Thermometer 8 a.m. 83°. This morning at 8 a.m. we passed the island of Fernando Noronha, about 600 miles off the mouth of the Amazon. It is a small eruptive island, densely covered with vegetation with a steep cliff on one end and high sugar-loaf peak at the other, rising perhaps 800–1000 feet above the sea. This island used to be a penal settlement of the Brazilian government, but now convicts are no longer sent there, and there is only a signal station on the island, and no cable.

During the earthquake last year in Chile, the report was spread that the island had disappeared. The Brazilian government sent war ships to investigate and they reported that the island had disappeared. As a matter of fact it had not disappeared, but they had not been able to find it.

April 27—At sea; mostly clear but hot and sultry. Thermometer at 8 a.m. 84°. Same all the previous night. In fact the temperature in these parts drops very little at night, possibly because the wind is not so strong at night as in day. Several slight showers.

April 28—At sea; clear and hot, with showers in distance but none on us. Thermometer at 8 a.m. 84°. We are only about 50 miles off the coast of Brazil and are going S.W. along it, so that probably much of the sultriness is due to proximity of a great tropical land area. Yesterday we passed Cape St. Roque but did not go in sight of it.

The trade winds are said to extend to about latitude 18° S. and as we are today (noon) in 15° 26′ S these winds are becoming variable. This afternoon for the first time on the voyage the wind is on our starboard side, and is very refreshing to those of us who have cabins there. In this voyage one should always try to have a cabin on the port side going south, and on the starboard side going north, so as to get the effect of the cool trade winds.

This is Sunday, and they have had three services on board, one at 8 a.m., one at 10.45 a.m. and one at 8.30 p.m. Surely these people should be very good. Their fanaticism amounts to religious persecution to those of the passengers who are not so religious, for during the whole of Sunday one cannot get out of the sound of doleful hymns and religious music. We have a dean of the Church of England on board, and he, backed up by a few women, is the leader in the ceremonies.

Letter from Dick, dated R.M.S. "Oriana," April 29, 1907

We will touch at Rio Janeiro, in Brazil, in the morning, and I drop a line to mail to you there. I wrote last on April 21st, the day before we reached St. Vincent, and mailed the letter on the ship, so that it will go back with the ship's mail from St. Vincent to England by the next ship of this line that goes that way, and will be mailed to you from England.

St. Vincent is a small barren island in the Cape Verde group, and would be but little known were it not a crossing point for many oceanic cable lines. Cable lines to Europe, North and South America, Asia and Africa all come up out of the ocean and meet or cross at St. Vincent. It is a sort of ocean-cable crossroads, and the white population of the small town of St. Vincent consists mostly of telegraph operators, and enough negroes from the west coast of Africa to act as servants.

About four days after leaving St. Vincent, we passed a small isolated island called Fernando Noronha, which belongs to Brazil, and which was once used as a penal colony. No convicts are now sent there, and only a small signal station is maintained on it. It seems to be a volcanic island, and is heavily covered with a tropical growth.

When we reach Rio Janeiro, we will have been 20 days out from Liverpool, and 8 days from St. Vincent. We have had nothing but fine weather, and not very hot, in crossing the tropics. The trade winds are wonderful in the way they relieve the effects of the heat. The highest the thermometer has been in my cabin is 86°, and now that we are approaching Rio Janeiro, which is about 23° south of the equator, it is getting much cooler. The trade winds in the tropics are helped out considerably in their cooling effect by tropical showers, which come down with great force, and deluge everything on the deck. They rarely last, however, over 15 or 20 minutes, and do a great deal towards cooling the air, so that they are always welcome. Sometimes they occur several times a day. We crossed the equator in a heavy shower of this kind on April 24th.

We have about 1000 or more emigrants in the steerage, and some of them will leave the ship at Rio Janeiro, for which we will all be very glad, as the tropical heat, though it has not been very bad, has been enough to bring out a great variety of smells and stinks from them, which had previously been dormant, and the ship's doctor keeps their quarters drenched with some sort of disinfectant which smells about as bad as the people. There is no disease among them, but I suppose the disinfecting is a good preventive.

We will stop only part of a day at Rio Janeiro, and will then proceed south to MonteVideo in Uruguay, where we will arrive in the first week of May. I will write further from there.

From the Diary

April 29—At sea; a brisk cool wind blowing from S., clear and bright; thermometer 8 a.m. 80°. There is a Brazilian Mr. Pereira de Sousa on board with his mother. They are evidently gentleman and lady, and old-time Brazilians. They live at Petropolis near Rio Janeiro and are most enthusiastic about the future of Brazil, and very proud of Rio as a great and beautiful city. They got on board at Lisbon and were introduced to me by Mr. Boerg, whom, with his wife, I met in Lisbon. I had met Mr. and Mrs. B. previously in N. Y. at a dinner given by Mr. J. C. Montgomery. At this same time in Lisbon, I also met Mr. Brien, now minister of U. S. in Portugal, and formerly minister of U. S. in Brazil, where he was very much liked.

DeSousa suffered a sunstroke in New York some time ago and is only just beginning to recover, after a long illness.

We also have an old Chilean colonel on board, named Reves. He has his wife and two daughters with him. He is a genial old fellow, but seems to object to the attentions of a young Irishman who is on board to his daughters, and a large part of his time is spent running about the deck breaking up little tete-a-tetes. The old colonel has been Chilean minister to Switzerland and is returning home.

There is also on board a member of an English mercantile house in Valparaiso, named Naylor, with his wife and three young boys; also an English broker of Valparaiso named Cumming, with his wife and a small girl child and a boy baby. Naylor, Cumming and the Dean seem to be great pals.

We also had on board when we started a number of young English clerks bound for different places in South America to work in English mercantile houses, and other operations. Some get off at Rio, some at Montevideo and some are going to Chile.

April 30—We arrived off the Bay of Rio de Janeiro during the night and at daylight came into the harbor. I never saw such a beautiful sight. The morning was clear and warm, and as the sun rose up over the hills surrounding the harbor it revealed in a mass of golden rays a sight of beauty such as I have never seen in any other land. The harbor, large enough for any great city, but not too large to permit all its surroundings to be seen from any point, is surrounded by high rolling hills, covered with that wonderfully luxuriant and dense verdure for which Brazil is celebrated above all other lands. The entrance is narrow—probably some 300 yards wide—and protected on each side by a fort. It is said that during a revolution once in Brazil, the two opposing factions both held possession of one of these forts. They fired at each other for about a week, but not being able to hit each other, they settled their dispute by a peaceable agreement.

On one side of the entrance to the harbor a conical peak of granite rises up like a sugar loaf to a height of some 1200 feet. Within the harbor, the many little bays, islands, the meandering shore line and the background of the city and behind it the wonderful tropical growth make a picture more like fairyland than anything of this earth. On a high peak back of the city, called Corcovado, is a pavilion reached by a cog-wheel railway, from which a wonderful view is said to be obtained.

The city, nestled along the shore between the bay and the hills, is picturesque in the extreme. It was once very unhealthy, and most of the leading hotels are on the hills, where they were built to avoid the fevers of the lower town, but of late the city has been wonderfully improved both in sanitary arrangements and in beauty; new drainage, cleaned streets and strict sanitary arrangements have converted Rio from one of the most unhealthy to one of the most healthy cities of the world. Most of the streets have been paved with asphalt; fine street car lines intersect the city in all directions; a wide avenue, probably 100 feet wide, called Avenida Central, has been cut through the heart of the city regardless of homes and everything else, and is several miles long; a beautiful boulevard runs along the front of the city and far out into the suburbs along the bay; a wonderfully good electric light system makes the city brilliant by night; many new and beautiful houses have been built or are under construction; and the whole city presents an air of prosperity and activity surprising to anyone who has not known of the great improvements that have gone on in Rio in the last few years.

The city is a strange combination of the new and the old. The fine wide new streets are in strange contrast with the old narrow winding ways with narrow roadways and still narrower sidewalks. The fine new business blocks on the Avenida Central obscure the little old yet picturesque buildings of a by-gone age. The stores are good; the streets crowded with people; the docks piled high with coffee and other Brazilian products; the harbor full of ships of various nations, among them English, German and Brazilian ships. The people are mostly of a black swarthy color and seem to look on the stranger as their natural prey in all matters of trade.

The houses are substantial and are built of stone and concrete, often painted on the outside with bright colors.

We heard at Rio the news that several new earthquake shocks had occurred on the west coast of S. America. We sailed about 6 p.m. in a beautiful clear night.

The weather was fine, clear and bright all day, with the thermometer about 80° in my cabin. Tonight it is much cooler and the thermometer is 76°.

Rio de Janeiro is said to have a population of some six or seven hundred thousand people, while all Brazil has about 20,000,000 people.

May 1—At sea; clear and bright; stiff south wind; rough sea; many people seasick. Thermometer at 8 a.m. 70°.

May 2—At sea; clear and bright; rough sea; S. wind; many people seasick. Occasionally we see glimpses of the rolling hilly coast of Brazil. We are passing the coast of the Brazilian state of Santa Catarina, where the sea is said usually to be rough. Thermometer at 8 a.m. 67°.

Letter from Dick, dated R.M.S. "Oriana," May 3, 1907

We will touch at Monte Video in Uruguay tomorrow, and I will mail this letter there. I wrote to you last on April 29th and mailed the letter at Rio Janeiro the next day.

We stopped at Rio Janeiro almost a day and had a good chance to see the town. The harbor is supposed by most people to be the most beautiful in the world, and so far as I have seen harbors, I do not think that this reputation is far wrong. It is entered by a narrow channel and widens out inside into a large basin, surrounded by high forest-covered hills. A wave of improvement has gone over Rio in recent years, and the new buildings, streets etc., under construction give things an active appearance. One large street, about as wide as Broad St., in Phila., has been cut for several miles through the heart of the city, regardless of houses or anything else; and it is in great contrast with the older streets, which are mostly narrow alleys. The town is much cleaner, and the houses are much better than I had expected to see. Many of the streets are paved with asphalt, and the street cars are thoroughly up to date.

Rio is not only the capital of Brazil, but it is also its chief shipping point. It has about 500,000 people. Many boats of different nations are in the harbor loading with coffee and other tropical products, and the whole place has an air of activity and prosperity.

As soon as we left Rio Janeiro, we got into a much cooler climate, and today the thermometer in my cabin is 65°. The winter weather of this southern hemisphere is just beginning, and it is a good deal like Phila in October. For the last two days the sea has been rough, as we have been passing a part of the Brazilian coast called Santa Catarina, where it is almost always rough, but the weather overhead is fine and clear. We are today about 35° south of the equator, and therefore well out of the tropics.

We will stop long enough tomorrow at Monte Video to take on coal, and will then continue south, reaching, in five or six days, the Falkland Islands, which lie just east of Terra del Fuego and the Straits of Magellan, at the south end of South America. I will write further from the Falkland Islands, though as the mails do not leave there very often, the letter may be somewhat late in reaching you.

From the Falkland Islands, we will go through the Straits of Magellan and up the coast of Chile.

From the Diary

May 3—At sea—off coast of Uruguay. Occasionally a low sandy dry coast is seen. Sea smooth and often streaked yellow by the immense number of small vegetable or animal matter. S. winds; sea smooth. Thermometer at 8 a.m. 67°.

May 4—Arrived off the harbor of Montevideo at 4 a.m. and came into the bay at 7 a.m. The bay is partly natural, but being more or less open and exposed to the sea, two breakwaters from either side have been built, thus securing a capacious and safe harbor.

The city of Montevideo has about 300,000 people and is the chief city of Uruguay. It is an active prosperous place, with many small parks and squares; street cars run by both electricity and horses. Narrow but well paved streets, and very good stores. The people also are very good looking—both men and women—and very polite. Uruguay is a very rich agricultural and cattle country, and Montevideo, being the chief city, reflects its prosperity. The courtesy of the people is most marked as soon as one enters the city, and in fact even the boatmen who row one ashore show it. I went into a hotel where I was totally unknown and asked where the postoffice was. The proprietor was most polite and sent a man with me to show me where it was. There was a desk in the postoffice for strangers to write at. Above it was a sign to the effect that if any writing facilities were wanted, to ask for them and they would be furnished. As soon as I sat down to address some letters a very polite official stepped up and asked me if I had everything I wanted and if he could be of any service to me. There were wet sponges in glass jars to wet stamps instead of licking them, and when one mails a letter he takes it to an offical who cancels the stamp and then you drop it in the box. Such courtesy and facilities in a postoffice I have never seen anywhere. We in the United States might well take some lessons from Uruguay in these respects.

Uruguay is a small country with no very strong army, but it, as well as Paraguay, are a soft of buffer between Brazil and Argentine, and though both the latter countries would like to grab them, they each prevent the other from doing so, and hence the independence of the two small countries is religiously maintained.

May 5—We were taking on coal all day yesterday and all last night until 4 a.m. We sailed at 7 a.m. for the south. The day is dull and cloudy and raw but not cold. Thermometer at 8 a.m. 65°. Montevideo is situated on the north side of the estuary of the Rio de la Plata, so called because the early explorers thought it led up to the silver mines of Peru. The Plata is really a large brackish water estuary where the Parana and the Uruguay rivers flow into the sea. Across its mouth at Montevideo is about 80 miles, and up towards its head is Buenos Aires, about 150 miles west of Montevideo. Fine side-wheel steamers like those on Long Island Sound, with 3 or 4 decks of cabins and brilliantly lighted up, ply between the two cities, some starting in the morning and arriving at night, and others starting in the evening and arriving in the morning. The water of the Plata is very muddy from the material brought down by its tributaries.

Today is Sunday and very quiet on board. No morning church because the boat is being cleaned up from the dirt of coaling yesterday.

There is great rivalry between the cities of Rio de Janeiro, Montevideo and Buenos Aires, each one claiming to be the most beautiful.

A baby was born of Spanish parents in the steerage on May 3rd, and today it was christened Arina Oriana Christina, the name Oriana being taken from this ship. It is a girl. £ 2.12/6 were collected for it at the christening.

May 6—At sea; cloudy, raw weather, S. wind, smooth sea. Thermometer at 8 a.m. 55°.

I forgot to mention in speaking of Montevideo that the town was named from a small hill about 450 feet high on the opposite side of the bay. The country is mostly very flat, and this low hill is so prominent that it gave the name to the town—i.e., Montevideo, or "I see a hill."

We left quite a number of steerage passengers at Rio Janeiro and also at Montevideo, which is a great relief, as they stunk considerably. Their quarters are disinfected daily by burning sulphur. Many of them would stay in bed all the time, day after day, if not driven out by this disinfecting.

May 7—At sea; beautiful clear day, smooth sea, light N.W. wind; thermometer at 8 a.m. in my cabin 51°. Latitude at noon 47° 26' S.

This evening the wind is beginning to blow hard from N.W., the sea is becoming rough.

Letter from Dick, dated on board S.S. "Oriana," South Atlantic Ocean, May 7, 1907

I wrote to you last on May 3rd and mailed the letter at Montevideo on May 4th.

Montevideo is a town of perhaps 250,000 people, the capital and chief city of Uruguay. In fact it is the only large town in Uruguay; and the saying that "Montevideo is Uruguay" is in many ways true. The town is a propsperous up-to-date place from the standpoint of Latin-American towns, that is, the houses are good and of Spanish style, the streets are good but small, the people work a little in the morning up to about 11 a.m., then eat and sleep until 4 p.m., and then work a little more, but not enough to be very noticeable. The people are of Spanish origin and very different from those of Portuguese origin in Brazil. I noticed many very fine looking women in the streets.

The Uruguayans are the most polite people I ever met. I walked into a hotel in Montevideo and asked the proprietor where the postoffice was. He sent a man six blocks with me to show me the way. At the postoffice I sat down at a public desk to address some letters, and an official came up to me to ask if I had all the writing material that I wanted, adding that if I did not have it, he would get it for me. It is rare that a man meets such politeness in any land.

The official name of Uruguay is "The Oriental Republic of Uruguay," the term "oriental" referring to the position of the country in the eastern part of South America. It is a very rich agricultural country, but very small; and they say that the only reason that it can remain independent is that Brazil on the north, and Argentine on the south, both want it, and neither will let the other grab it, so they both jealously maintain its independence. The same thing may be said of Paraguay, a small republic lying farther inland than Uruguay. A few years ago Paraguay had a very bloody war with Brazil, in which most of the men of Paraguay were killed. Now that peace has been restored, the chief industry of the country is said to be breeding male children, so as to be ready for a new fight; and it is said to be wonderful how the women are turning out kids.

We sailed from Montevideo on May 5th, heading south, towards the Falkland Islands, which lie in the South Atlantic, about 350 miles east of the Straits of Magellan. We are now approaching latitude 50° South, and the weather is much cooler, though it still remains clear and bright. This morning the thermometer was 51° in my cabin. The Falkland Islands belong to England, and we stop there for a few hours. We will arrive there tomorrow and I will mail this letter when I go on shore.

From the Falkland Islands, we will go west again to the South American coast, and our next stop will be Punta Arenas, in the Straits of Magellan, a small port in the extreme southern part of Chile. I will write further from there.

P.S. May 9th—I found when we arrived at the Falkland Islands that the mail left there at such long intervals that I did not mail this letter there, but will mail it at Punta Arenas, in southern Chile, in the Straits of Magellan, where we will arrive tomorrow.

From the Diary

May 8—We arrived at Port Stanley in the Falkland Islands about 10 a.m. Last night a fierce gale blew. My cabin was flooded with water, and things generally about the boat were thrown around. We were all glad to anchor this morning in the quiet harbor of Port Stanley. The thermometer in my cabin at 8 a.m. was 43°.

The quarantine doctor at Stanley has forbidden any one to land, except the three passengers who were going to stay there, because there was a child with measles in the 2nd class part of the ship. The child has been isolated and every precaution taken, but the quarantine was nevertheless enforced. We remained here all day, putting off and taking on cargo, and are to sail in the morning.

Stanley is a small settlement on the eastern side of the eastern island of the Falklands. There are two main islands and many small ones. The town has about 1000 people, mostly dependent on the sheep industry, which is the chief industry of the island. The sheep were brought here from New Zealand and do very well. From the Falklands many sheep have been taken over to Patagonia and to Punta Arenas, etc., which also has turned out [to be] a good region for them, and most of the sheep men there have come from the Falklands, so that these islands have come to be known as the "sheep paddock of the South Atlantic."

The town is inhabited mostly by Scotch of various Christian sects, so that each sect has to have its church. The town is comparatively new and shows nothing of special interest. A few years ago the British Government started to make a naval station near Stanley—just across the bay—about a mile away—and are said to have spent £ 80,000 on it, but work seems to have been for the time being, suspended.

We put three passengers ashore here—one of them the Very Reverend Dean, Bishop of Christ Church, Falkland Islands, whose duty it is to circulate along the E. and W. coasts of S. America to look after his flock. He seemed to be an intelligent man for one of his kind, but most of us are relieved at his leaving the ship on account of the strenuous Sundays that he and his female supporters enforced.

The Falklands are a barren desolate group of islands, destitute of trees, but covered with grass and low shrubs. They have tried to grow imported trees, but they don't grow. Possibly this is due to the wind, but some claim it is due to shallow soil. Trees grow in Terra del Fuego still farther south. The islands are between latitude 52° and 54° S. The climate is cold, bleak and generally windy—much like northern Scotland. A man who had lived in the Falklands 20 years told me that the climate was very like that of the Shetland Islands. Snow falls in winter but does not remain very long and sometimes the ponds freeze. The rainfall is usually abundant. Today we have had several showers, separated by periods of sunshine.

No wheat, oats or other grain will grow; there is said not to be enough sun to mature it. The plant grows but the grains don't mature. Garden vegetables, cabbage, pease, etc., do well.

The islands from a distance are rocky and hilly, the hills probably rarely over a few hundred feet high and often very rocky, or cut by rocky ridges. The rock appears to be stratified, to be highly tilted at various angles, of a white or light gray color, and probably harder in some places than in others, as ridges of harder strata often protrude above the surrounding ground. I did not see the rock close enough to identify it, but it all looked the same at a distance and from the description given me I should think it may be quartzite. No mineral deposits are known. No limestone is known. The rocks all dip steeply and some almost vertically. The country in general looks like a thin layer of poor soil underlaid by this rock, which protrudes through it in many ridges, peaks and isolated boulders.

Many good and well protected harbors are found along the coast of the islands. Whalers and seal fishers often come here, the latter to ship their seal skins to England. Seals are abundant in the seas of southern Patagonia and are killed almost altogether at sea—not on land. They are said to be killed while asleep at sea. They are not often seen in the Falklands, though they are found on a group of small islands called the "Volunteer Islands," just west of Stanley. The seals are said to have excellent fur. Formerly the Falkland authorites levied a tax of one shilling per seal on all seal skins shipped from Stanley. This was cheerfully paid, and the sealers came there to have a good time, often spending £ 2000 per year there. Then the authorities raised the tax to 10 shillings per seal. The sealers would not stand for this and ceased coming to Stanley, and the Stanley people ceased getting the money the sealers used to blow in there. Now the authorities are trying to reduce the tax to one shilling again.

The climate of the Falklands is very healthy and there is but little sickness —probably because the Scotch who people them are used to this sort of climate.

There is a great quantity of peat on the islands. It is generally at or near the hill tops, and less on the slopes and in hollows. It is said to be a wonderfully good fuel—far better than Scotland peat and peat elsewhere in the north, and the people luxuriate in a cheap and good fuel. It is said even sometimes to burn and form clinkers, a rare thing in peat. It is said to seem to be formed not of moss but of grass and shrubs and is sometimes in beds 20 feet thick of solid peat. It is dug with a spade in large lumps and dried—generally dug in spring or summer so as not to freeze, for if it freezes before drying it is apt to disintegrate. If dried properly it dries in a few weeks and does not disintegrate. The beds of peat are so thick that sometimes they slide down the hills, causing a regular land slide. Such once occurred on the hill back of Stanley, and 3 people were killed.

There are many wild ducks about Stanley, and they are said to stay there all the year round and not to migrate.

The horses of the Falklands are small but very strong. They are the descendants of horses brought over by the French long ago. New stock is being bred in with them to enlarge and improve the breed.

Wild ducks stay in the Falklands all the year round. Teals, canvas backs, red ducks and black ducks said to be common. There are no large wild animals on the islands. There were once foxes but they have been exterminated. (A gray fox found in Terra del Fuego and Patagonia is much sought by many people for fur. It is different from the silver fox of the north.)

There are about 2000 people in the Falklands, about 1000 in Port Stanley and about 200 in Port Darwin on the same island. These are the only two towns of any size. The rest of the people are scattered on sheep farms, and communication carried on by schooner. There are so many good harbors that the saying goes: "Every household has its own harbor."

The tide in the bay at Stanley rises about 15 feet; outside the bay, about 7 feet.

May 9—We sailed from Stanley at 6.30 a.m. Every one was very angry that the quarantine authorities did not let us go on shore, and this feeling was aggravated by a rather rude guard being put on the ship to see that no one did go ashore.

As soon as we got out of the harbor the wind came up from the south and the sea became rough, and has been getting rougher all day. Tonight a gale is blowing from the south; the ship is floundering about in a heavy sea; the spray is going clear over the bridge; sleet, snow, rain, and hail are falling alternately and sometimes all at once. About 7.30 p.m. the deck was 2 inches deep with hail stones. The south wind, direct from Antarctic regions, is cold and piercing; the thermometer 42° in my cabin, and considerably lower on the bridge. Altogether it is as rotten and disagreeable a night as I ever saw at sea. It is now 11.30 p.m., and the ship is rolling so that I can hardly write. A flock of wild ducks has been following the ship all day. It is the first time I ever saw ducks follow a ship, but they say it is not uncommon in these parts. It is said to be a duck called a "shag," not good to eat because too fishy. It is black on its back and has a white breast —a very pretty bird and of good size.

Though the thermometer is not very low the cold is very penetrating. I have three flannel undershirts and am still cold. I think I will go to bed to keep warm.

May 10—We had a fearful night—a furious sea, a gale, snow, hail, and sleet. We have passed around the south side of the Falklands and are heading towards the Straits of Magellan. The sea had moderated a little this morning. Thermometer 40° in my cabin at 8 a.m.

All the life boats were taken well in on the deck before leaving Stanley, to prevent their being carried away. Today several of the ship's compartments which are usually kept open have been closed, on account of the dangerous navigation of the Straits, which we are approaching. At about 2 p.m. we sighted Cape Virgenes at the north side of the entrance to the Straits. It is a low promontory in the S. part of Argentine. A short distance farther S., and at the very entrance to the Straits, is the flat sandy Cape Dungeness in Chile. Both capes mark the north side of the entrance to the Straits and both have good lighthouses. Far to the south can be seen the other side of the Straits in Terra del Fuego, which here is low and flat.

We entered the Straits at about 4 p.m. At that hour it was beginning to get dark. The days are short in these far south latitudes in winter. The sun is seen even during the day only far in the north where it traverses a low arc from east to west.

Within the Straits the sea became smooth. We passed westward, through the "Narrows" and into a large bay where, about 10 p.m., we anchored in front of the Chilean town of Punta Arenas. The narrows are the first narrows encountered coming from the east. After leaving P. Arenas, there are another narrows, then a long straight channel called "long reach," then another narrows, and then another long wide stretch called "sea reach" and extending to the western end of the straits at Cape Pilar. The eastern entrance to the straits is bordered on both sides by a low flat country—really the pampas of Patagonia intersected; but to the west the country becomes higher and higher as the straits intersects the Cordillera, and the rocky Cape Pilar is in great contrast in its wild grandeur to the low sandy Cape Virgenes.

May 11—At Punta Arenas. The early morning was wet and snowy, and when day broke the town and the surrounding hills were covered with fresh snow. Later in the day the sun came out and the snow mostly disappeared.

We went ashore on a launch. Punta Arenas is said to have about 12,000 inhabitants, connected mostly with the sheep industry, and partly with mining. The streets were wet and sloppy from melting snow; the houses mostly of corrugated iron, wood, and a few of stone. It looks very much like a prosperous mining town in western U. S. It is the most southerly civilization, at least as far as towns go, in the world, being in latitude 53°+S. It was once a Chilean penal settlement, then it languished and almost was deserted, but with the growth of the sheep industry in Patagonia and Terra del Fuego, it took a new lease of life and is now a very active progressive place. The gold mining which has started up in the past few years has also lent to its prosperity. It is well lit up with electric lights.

On the front street as soon as one lands he is confronted with two prominent signs, "American Bar" over one place and "Florida Hotel" over another, both names suggestive of warmer things than are usually found on the most southerly street of the most southerly city in the world.

We got a fairly good lunch at a fair one-storey frame hotel, composed of a bar, dining room and kitchen, and then started to go back to our ship. The launch was not to be found and no one at the S.S. Co's office could tell us when it would go to the ship. The wind was coming up strong and we knew the reputation of this country for sudden wind storms which often render it impossible to reach a ship in the harbor, so, fearing that one of these might be coming up, we chartered a small sail boat, and finally got safely on to our ship, about a mile distant, after a good wetting.

The ship has been unloading cargo all day, but we expect to sail some time tonight.

Another baby was born in the steerage today. This makes the third baby born on this voyage. I mentioned the first one born; later on a second was born, and now a third. Our ship's doctor has his hands full.

There is an old Austrian living at P. Arenas and following the trade of blacking shoes. Once he had a rich gold mine in Terra del Fuego where he went every season and got enough gold to live in luxury and drink only champagne the rest of the year. But one year the mine, which was a placer, slide off the hill into the sea, and there was no more gold. Now the Austrian blackens shoes and drinks beer for a beverage.

During the mining boom in Terra del Fuego in 1904, one of the men who drew up the legal papers for the miners is said to have become so rich that he regretted that he only had ten fingers to wear rings on.

Most of the natives of Terra del Fuego have been killed off by the sheep men. The sheep men say they steal sheep and kill the natives; the poor natives say the sheep men kill them (the natives) and in revenge kill more sheep, so the natives are fast disappearing. They were once numerous, and wore but little clothes even in winter. A canoe once came up to a ship in the straits to trade hides for tobacco, etc. They disposed of all their hides except one, which an old woman had on her back. An officer offered a plug of tobacco for it, the woman refused, but one of the Indian men seized it and gave it up for the tobacco, leaving the squaw naked.

May 12—The day dawned foggy and with a mixture of snow and hail falling. Thermometer in my cabin at 8 a.m. 40°; on the bridge 35°. We had left P. Arenas at 2 a.m., and at daylight were in the narrows to the west of the bay on which the town is situated. In some places the channel is only about ¾ mile wide, but beyond it widens out into a long straight stretch called "long reach" probably fifty miles long and from a mile or two to many miles wide.

Towards noon, the fog cleared and though it was still cloudy, we had a good view of the country.

The land on both sides of the straits has become much more rugged than east of P. Arenas. Before reaching there, it was mostly flat or low-hilly. At P. Arenas it was beginning to become mountainous on both sides, while still farther west, it becomes very rugged, wild and weird. The country is mostly covered with the fresh snow of the approaching winter and occasionally some great glacier extends down the mountain side and into the sea. These glaciers are easily distinguishable from the fresh snow by their watery greenish or blueish hue and their icy character, and by the great fissures that intersect them. They are there winter and summer and represent the gradual flow of frozen water to the sea, just as a cataract represents the flow of melted water. On the north side of "long reach" about 11.30 a.m. we saw two great glaciers, watery green in color, coming from near the mountain tops to the water of one of the arms of the straits on the south, or Terra del Fuego, side. They were about a mile apart—one filling a wide valley and one filling a more confined cañon.

About noon we passed the celebrated "Glacier Bay" on the Patagonia side, on the side of which an immense glacier filling a valley perhaps half a mile wide came in a meandering form to the sea. The glacier was of a watery blue color. It began near the top of the mountain, which was perhaps 3000 or 4000 feet high, and possibly more, and which stuck its peak above the ice, though even the peak was covered with white snow. In the other two glaciers, the mountains were probably about the same height. Other larger glaciers are said to be seen elsewhere in Terra del Fuego.

The mountains of Terra del Fuego are not high, 6000 to 7000 feet being the highest (Roberts), but the cold climate and great precipitation cause many glaciers. "Glacier Bay" is noted as an anchoring place for small steamers, though large steamers cannot go there. The straits in most places are too deep to anchor in, and herein lies one of the great dangers of navigation, for in foggy weather steamers may run ashore as there are almost no lighthouses, and yet they cannot anchor on account of the great depth of the water. Moreover, there are many side channels to the straits, some of them as wide as the straits themselves, and a ship is apt to get into the wrong channel and be lost or wrecked. All these various dangers have caused many wrecks, and insurance on ships going through the straits is very heavy. Once a ship enters the straits it must keep going till it gets out, watching for rocks, sounding all the time with the rope and weight, and feeling its way along.

The side channels mentioned above, and in fact Terra del Fuego and southern Patagonia, are a mass of islands separated by these channels, often called "canals." Even Cape Horn is a small island, and something like 60 or 80 miles south of it are some other small islands, much dreaded by navigators as there are no lights on them or on Cape Horn. It would be hard to maintain a light on Cape Horn for sometimes for months at a time ships cannot land there on account of the weather. The side channels, bordered by bleak snow-covered mountains leading off into the bleak, foggy darkness of the south, are a weird but fascinating sight. One finds himself wondering what is behind the next bend in their meandering courses, and to what tumultuous sea they may lead, what lands border their dim and mysterious shores. They are an uncanny but a most impressive sight, even more so than the mountains and the glaciers.

The mountain sides are covered with streams and cataracts of water rushing down to the sea, and the impression of wetness is everywhere in evidence.

The climate of the Straits is one of the rainiest in the world. Rain or snow is said to fall on an average of 12 hours in each 24 hours. In winter there is less precipitation, less wind than summer. The southwest coast of Chile is rainier, because it gets the wet winds direct from the Antarctic; whereas these winds have dropped some of their moisture in Terra del Fuego before reaching the straits.

The Terra del Fuego summer differs from that of the far north in that it does not even have the few weeks of hot sunny weather that the far north has. The rain and wind prevent this. For the same reason, probably, the winters in Terra del Fuego are not so cold as in the far north. The summers in Terra del Fuego are a little bit warmer than the winter—that is the best that can be said of it.

Oats and other grain will grow but won't mature (Roberts). Some of the gold miners plant oats and cut them for hay without trying to mature them. Continuous rain and continuous wind are too much for it to mature.

There is very little timber along the straits, except in some of the valleys, where a stunted growth occurs. Farther south in Terra del Fuego there is more timber, especially in sheltered places, but along the straits the mountains rise up bare, bleak, and black. There is, however, great quantities of peat which is said to be an excellent fuel here. Roberts says that it will generate half as much gas (for fuel) as ordinary bituminous coal.

During the afternoon of today (i.e., May 12) we passed from "long reach" into "sea reach" and about 4 p.m., we passed Cape Pilar on the south side of the

Straits and were in the open Pacific. The scenery has been glorious during the afternoon as the fog has lifted and occasionally even the sun has peeped out for a few moments at a time, making beautiful rainbows during the occasional short showers that have fallen. As we have come west, the mountains have become higher, more rugged, and more snow-capped. We have really been passing through the heart of the southern Cordillera. Ever since this morning the high rugged mountains coming down like precipices to the sea and rising high into the sky with their snowy peaks, have been a most wonderful sight. The straits remind me of the scenery along the Saguenay River in eastern Canada, and on the coast of Norway, except on an infinitely grander scale. Towards the western end of the straits the mountains are covered from top to bottom with snow.

Cape Pilar, on the south side of the western end of the Straits, is an abrupt mountain, almost a precipice, rising several thousand feet above the sea, and at its foot is a low rocky beach from which rise two steep conical-shaped masses of black rock, probably one or two hundred feet high, like great sentinels at the door of this great canal. They suggest the pillars of Hercules.

A few miles farther north we passed a lighthouse on a group of rocky islands known as the "Four Evangelists." This light, one in the "sea reach," and two at the eastern entrance of the harbor, are all that I saw in this part of the world.

The sea tonight is rough and boisterous; the weather rainy, and a fierce southwest wind is blowing from the Antarctic regions. The temperature, however, has risen and the thermometer in my cabin tonight is 54°, which as compared with what we have had, seems almost tropical!

Terra del Fuego bears all the evidence of being a partly submerged land area. The numerous channels or "canals" resemble old river valleys completely submerged, while the many steep-sided bays and fjords are partly submerged valleys just as in Norway. The rocks, at least in the western part of the straits, so far as could be seen from the ship, are weathered and rounded like granite, showing great dark—almost black—oval surfaces, which may be due to glaciation, or which may be simply weathering. (Branner doesn't know whether there has been glaciation in the Straits, but suspects it from the fact that glaciers still exist.)

May 13—At sea; off the southern coast of Chile. The weather seemed to make an attempt to clear off this morning and the clouds raised a little, but they quickly settled down again, and it has been wet and drizzling day, with a stiff northwest wind that has kicked up a rough sea. The weather is much warmer. Thermometer at 8 a.m. in my cabin 55° and there is a balminess in the air that was not noticeable in the straits or on the Atlantic side.

Occasionally we have caught a distant view of the shore, which seems very rugged and mountainous, but with less snow than in the straits.

May 14—The day opened dark and cloudy, but cleared a little about noon and during the afternoon the sun shown at short intervals. Thermometer 60° at 8 p.m. in cabin. Light northwest wind; fairly smooth sea. We have not seen the land during the day. We are now north of Chiloe Island, which is a rainy, bleak, heavily timbered island. We have not seen any land today.

Letter from Dick, dated R.M.S. "Oriana," May 15, 1907

I wrote to you last on May 7th and had intended to mail the letter at the Falkland Islands, but I found that the mail left there at such rare intervals that I kept the letter until we arrived at Punta Arenas, in the Straits of Magellan, and mailed it there, from which point the mails go more often than from the Falklands.

We have now passed though the Straits and are going up the coast of Chile. We will stop for a few hours at Coronel, a Chilean seaport, this afternoon, and I write a line to mail to you there. The trip through the Straits was very interesting, though we had stormy weather most of the time. I will write more fully about that part of the trip and will mail a longer letter to you from Valparaiso. I write now simply to let you know that we are getting on all right, and having a good voyage. We will arrive in Valparaiso the end of this week. The weather is now fine and clear, and a great improvement over what we had in the Straits of Magellan and along the southern coast of Chile.

From the Diary

May 15—The day opened a little cloudy, but the sun has come out at intervals, and the weather is warmer. Thermometer in cabin at 8 a.m. 62°. Last night from about 11 p.m. to 1 a.m. there was fog, the first we had had on the voyage, and the fog whistle was kept actively going. After 1 p.m. [a.m.] the fog cleared.

About 2 p.m. we came in sight of land, and at 4 p.m. we anchored at Coronel, a coaling station on the Chilean coast. Coal mines are near here, and in fact this region is the chief source of coal in Chile. The mines extend from Coronel southward along the coast for a few miles to Lota. The region from Coronel to Lota is the chief coal mining center of Chile.

May 16—We left Coronel about 11.30 a.m. today, and about 3 p.m. arrived at Talcahuana, forty odd miles to the north. This is the station at which emigrants to Chile must disembark and as we have almost 500 in the steerage we stopped here to land them. It has been raining all day, and this afternoon it is raining so hard that the disembarking has to be postponed until tomorrow, so here we stay tonight. The town is a small place of probably a few thousand people.

May 17—Weather clear, bright and warm, a great relief after all the stormy weather we have had. The emigrants are being landed today. I went ashore for a short time today. Talcahuana is the port for Conception, the third town in size in Chile, and is a busy town of a few thousand people.

I forgot to mention before that some weeks ago, on this ship, an English lady told me that she had read some of Owen Wister's books and liked them very much. She said that she had heard that Owen Wister* and President Roosevelt were one and the same person, and she was much surprised when I told her that they were different people.

May 18—We finally sailed for the north at 1.30 p.m. today. We took on a cargo of beans, etc., before starting. The weather is fine and clear, and the sea smooth.

---

* Author of *The Virginian*, and a friend of the Penrose men.

Letter from Dick, dated On Board S.S. "Oriana," Coast of Chile, May 18, 1907

We will arrive tomorrow morning in Valparaiso, Chile, and this will finish a voyage of five weeks and a half from Liverpool. This ship does not go farther than Valparaiso but returns from there to England.

I wrote to you last on May 7th and mailed the letter at Punta Areans, in the Straits of Magellan; and on the 15th I dropped a short line to you intending to mail it at Coronel, on the coast of Chile, but we did not stop there long enough to go ashore, so I mailed it a couple of days later, at a port at which we stopped called Talcahuano.

The trip through the Straits of Magellan was interesting but stormy. From the time we approached the Falkland Islands, which are off the eastern, or Atlantic, entrance to the Straits, until we had passed through the Straits to the Pacific Ocean, and had got well up the coast of Chile, we had rough boisterous weather, with the thermometer hovering around freezing point, high winds, snow, hail and sleet most of the way. This is winter time in the southern hemisphere, and the Straits of Magellan are in latitude 52° and 53° south of the equator, so that the weather is severe, and the cold winds come up unobstructed from the south pole, usually blowing a gale.

For absolute bleakness and desolation I have never seen the like of the Falkland Islands and the Straits of Magellan in winter. The days are very short, and the sun appears only for a few hours far in the north, and even then it rises only slightly above the horizon, when it sinks again below the surrounding ice and snow. The winds howl around in a continuous gale, lashing the sea into a mass of foam and spray; snow and hail cover the deck of the ship, only to be carried away again by the waves that wash over it. In the Straits the rough seas are not felt, but on the Atlantic and the Pacific sides, the ocean is in a constant turbulance.

The scenery in the Straits of Magellan is wonderful. The mountains of Terra del Fuego, on the south, and Patagonia, on the north, rise abruptly from the sea for 6000 and 7000 feet, and are covered with snow; while immense glaciers fill up whole valleys and reach down to the water's edge. Numerous fjords and side channels run off from the Straits in all directions, intersecting Terra del Fuego into many islands, and reaching down to Cape Horn. Little or nothing can grow in Terra del Fuego. A few stunted trees grow in protected places, but the never ceasing gales and the cold keep down most all vegetation, and where the mountains are not covered with ice and snow, they rise up as bare black peaks of rock. It is said to rain or snow in Terra del Fuego for 12 hours out of every 24 hours the year round.

Punta Arenas, on the north side of the Straits, is the most southerly town in the world, being about in latitude 53° South. We anchored near there for part of a day, and Means and I went ashore in a small boat to see the town. It had been snowing the night before and the place looked very wintery; but on the front street facing the Straits, we saw two signs which we recognized. One was "Florida Hotel" and the other was "American Bar." These familiar names made Punta Arenas seem very home-like to us. The wind came on to blow, however, and we hastened back to the ship, as another gale was coming on, and we feared that we might not be able to get aboard if we waited too long.

We entered the Straits on the Atlantic side on May 10th; and on May 12th we passed out on the Pacific side, at what is known as Cape Pilar, an immense peak of rock rising up bleak and black from the Pacific, and too steep even for the snow to lie on. Thence we proceeded north up the coast of Chile. The sea was stormy and rough as we entered the Pacific; but in a few days we got into a milder climate, the sea subsided, the sun came out, and now we are in the warm sunny climate of central Chile.

As soon as we get to Valparaiso, we will make plans for seeing other parts of this western coast, and then I will write to you further. I expect to get in Valparaiso my mail, which has been forwarded from London and this will be the first mail that I have received since leaving London. The mail was to have been forwarded via Panama, and should reach Valparaiso before I get there.

From the Diary

May 19—Arrived at Valparaiso about daylight, got breakfast at 9 a.m., and went ashore shortly afterwards. The port authorities do not allow the S.S. Co. to have a launch to land passengers, so the latter must go ashore on the small row boats that come out for them, and each passenger must make his own special bargain with them. The result is that one arriving there for the first time and not speaking the language often pays a very high fare. The usual price for a passenger is 50 cents (Chilean), but many a passenger pays from 10 to 20 dollars, and sometimes $100 or more for himself and baggage. The S.S. officers will give you no advice or information as to what to pay. Means and I got ashore for $10 with all our baggage, and this was considered cheap. The man first asked us $20 and we compromised on $10.

We finally got ashore and had our things taken to the railroad station to go to the Gran Hotel, Vina del Mar, about 5 miles from Valparaiso, a residence suburb of the city. The hotels in town were said to be so crowded that this decided us to go to Vina. We found the Gran Hotel very comfortable. I had written to them from Montevideo to reserve rooms for us, and we found that they had two of the best for us. The building is a large square block with an open space in the center containing fountains, flowers, etc. The Chileans prefer the rooms on the ground floor so as to be able to run out quickly in case of earthquake. There is not much danger from an earthquake if one is not in a house, the main danger being in the falling walls.

In the afternoon we went to the city in a trolley car to see the effect of the earthquake.[*] The town is built largely on the slopes of the hills rising up from 100 to 200 feet above the bay, at least the residence section is so situated, while the business section is on a narrow strip of flat ground running around the water front. Much of this flat ground is "made ground" filled in by man from the material of the hills and by refuse. It was on this made ground that the earthquake of August 15th, 1906, did the most damage, while the houses on the

---

[*] The great Chilean earthquake of August 15, 1906.

hills were hardly hurt at all. The chief damage on the hills was done in a large cemetery where graves were thrown open and coffins thrown out and even cast down the hill, which is probably 100 feet or more high. The walls of the graveyard had recesses where bodies were put in addition to the bodies regularly buried within the enclosure. The bodies and coffins in the walls were hurled in great numbers down into the streets below, causing great fear among the people, who thought the time of resurrection had come. The keeper of the cemetery is said to have gone insane at the sight. It was raining hard at the time, with much thunder and lightning, which are almost unknown in this vicinity, so that the scene was indeed a terrifying one to everyone, and even today but few people like to discuss the earthquake; it is rather a taboo subject; and many people yet have nervous troubles as the result of it. It must indeed have been a frightful time; pouring rain, the most unusual thunder and lightning, the graves opening and throwing out their dead, houses falling, fires breaking out everywhere, and the ground shaking so that it was almost impossible to stand up. In the lower town, where the business section is, and where some of the poorer residences are, the damage was fearful. Houses with solid brick walls, two and three feet thick, were laid low like piles of shingles, an occasional piece of wall, an iron framework, or a chimney being all that is left of many of them; others were only cracked and shattered; others still less hurt; but almost every house on the made ground was more or less hurt; though the greatest damage was in spots—not along certain lines. Most of the damage was done by the earthquake and not by the subsequent fires as in San Francisco. The fires did some damage, but only a small part of the total. Many of the fires were of incendiary origin, and many people were very summarily shot who were caught setting houses on fire and looting. The principal theatre of the town was utterly demolished.

There was no tidal wave. This is said to be due to the great depth of the bay, which is not so much influenced by a tidal wave as shallow water. No open fissures were formed and no main line of fault, as in San Francisco, was discernable. The coast is said to have risen about one foot. This was determined at some large structures which were being built on the shore between the city and Vina del Mar. Here it is said that the engineers surveying the ground found this one-foot rise to have occurred. Other people have observed sea weed and fresh sea shells a foot or so higher than high tide now rises.

The estimates of people killed varies from 4000 to 7000, mostly killed by falling houses.

The Gran Hotel at Vina was almost shaken down, but has since been put in shape again at a cost of about $100,000 (Chilean). Many other houses in Vina were ruined or injured; and as this is the fashionable suburb of the city, many fine residences were ruined. The sight of them, with pieces of gilded walls occasionally protruding through the debris, fine furniture and carved wood mixed with fallen bricks and mortar, remind me much of some of the sights at Pompeii in Italy. The wealth and beauty of Vina were on that fateful night suddenly rendered as poor and homeless as the most humble laborer in the poorer quarters.

May 20—In Valparaiso. Called on several people to whom I had letters and was very kindly and hospitably received. I met Granville Moore, who happened to be here on a short trip. He is going to Coquimbo tonight and thence on to Iquique, where I will meet him in a week or two. Took lunch with Moore.

The dust from the ruined houses fills the air of the city, so that it was very pleasant to get out to our comfortable hotel at Vina del Mar tonight.

May 21—In Valparaiso. Many cattle are seen in the streets. These have been mostly driven over from Argentine via the same pass that travellers use. They are used in Valparaiso and also shipped extensively to the northern towns of Chile via coast steamers. These northern towns are in the arid region and are supplied with cattle and vegetables, etc., from Valparaiso and southern Chile, much of that from Valparaiso coming from Argentine. Cattle are also driven from Argentine direct to Antofagasta.

The fish of Chile are most excellent wherever I have seen them, a variety known as Congrio being apparently the most popular. We began to get good fish, on the voyage south, at Montevideo and got them all through the Straits and up the west coast. The flesh is firm and flavor excellent. I should think that fish canneries on the Straits would pay. There are none at present, though the fish are very abundant.

May 22—In Valparaiso. We took lunch with Mr. Bush of Wessel Duval & Co., who has treated us very kindly and hospitably. I had a letter of introduction to him.

A striking feature in Valparaiso is the system of having three horses hitched to the carriages. Two horses are on the sides of the pole, and a third horse with one trace on the left-hand side of the team.

May 23—Means and I started at 8.15 a.m., for Santiago with Mr. Bush, who happened to have business there and came along with us. The route leads across the coast ranges and thence up the valley which usually intravenes between the coast ranges and the main Cordillera, for about 180 kilometers to Santiago. The railway is very good and the cars are on the same system as in the U. S., not with the compartments as in Europe. The train carried a pullman car, of rather old-fashioned model, made in the U. S., and very comfortable. There was also a very good dining car, where we got breakfast at 9.30 a.m. The trip took about $4\frac{1}{2}$ hours. Everywhere along the line were signs of the earthquake. We passed numerous small towns kept up by farming and cattle raising; they had most all suffered more or less. A town about half way between Valparaiso and Santiago had been almost entirely ruined, but is rapidly being rebuilt.

Santiago is beautifully situated in a broad valley many miles wide and very fertile and much cultivated. The low green coast ranges are seen to the west and the main range of the Andes, snow-capped and rugged, rises up in all its grandeur to the east. The city itself is regularly laid out, with straight streets and a magnificent main avenue, known as the Alameda. The city being the capital receives liberal appropriations for improvements, etc., and is indeed a beautiful place. Some of the residences, in fact very many of them, are veritable palaces, with their white columns in front and their luxurious patios inside. The people are polite and cordial, and the whole place has an air of prosperity and elegance.

Mr. Swinburn had kindly put us up at the Union Club and had engaged rooms for us at "Anexo B" of the Oddo Hotel, which is the best place to stay. Means and Bush dined with me at the Club, where we were given an excellent dinner. The club is very comfortable and one of the best I know of.

May 24—In Santiago. There is a beautiful park here and well kept up. We took a drive in it and then went up a small hill in the town to look at the scenery. A wonderful view of the city and surrounding country is had from it.

Santiago was not so much hurt by the earthquake of last year as Valparaiso. A few houses were shaken down, a number considerably damaged, and many slightly injured, but they were too few to be especially noticeable in going about the town, and are rapidly being repaired. The water here is said to be very fine, being piped in from the mountains, but typhoid is very bad most of the time. This, however, is said not to be due to the water but to the open sewers that run through the city and through the houses. The sewers are sometimes, but not always, covered in the streets so as not to impede traffic, but as they pass under each house they are open, and the drainage of the house is dumped in. Hence the typhoid spreads from house to house. Much the same system prevails in Valparaiso. In Santiago the sewers are rapidly being put underground as in other cities, and probably public health will much improve. At present the town has a bad name for sickness and in the streets many people are in mourning.

We took breakfast with Mr. Swinburn at 12.30 p.m., and he gave us a splendid meal, with good Chilean wines, etc.

Santiago has about 250,000 people.

May 25—We left Santiago at 8 a.m., and arrived at Valparaiso about 12.30 p.m. We came away with a most pleasant recollection of the beautiful capital of Chile.

May 26—Sunday. We took lunch with Mr. Bush at a sort of country club about a mile from Vina.

Letter from Dick, dated Valparaiso, Chile, May 26, 1907

I wrote to you about a week ago from on board the steamer "Oriana", and mailed the letter when we reached here on the 19th.

The hotels in Valparaiso that had not been ruined during the earthquake last year, were so crowded on our arrival, that we went out to a suburb of Valparaiso, known as Vina del Mar, about five miles from the city, and there we found a very comfortable hotel. We can reach the city by railway or trolley line in about half an hour from Vina del Mar. Moreover, it is better to be out of the city just at present, for the dust and dirt rising from the ruins is not very pleasant.

Only a part of Valparaiso was destroyed, but in that part almost everything was laid flat, and houses with masonry walls three or four feet thick, were shaken down as if they were a loose pile of shingles. The hotel in which we are staying at Vina del Mar was also almost shaken to pieces, but has since been rebuilt. The scene of desolation in the part of Valparaiso which was most affected, can hardly be realized without seeing it. While in San Francisco most of the damage was done by fire, in Valparaiso most of the damage was done by the earthquake; and whole blocks of fine stone and brick buildings, are simply piles of ruins, with here and there the part of a wall, an iron framework or a chimney left standing. The work of rebuilding is going on, but the scarcity of labor is greatly delaying matters.

A couple of days ago Means and I went up to Santiago, which is the capital of Chile, and which is about 110 miles east of here, at the foot of the Andes Mts. It is a fine city of about 300,000 people, with good streets and well built houses. It was but little affected by the earthquake last year, only a few buildings being thrown down. But along the railway from here to Santiago, we passed a number of small villages which had been almost annihilated by the earthquake.

We sail from here tomorrow for Iquique in northern Chile, and will make that our headquarters for a couple of weeks or so, while we are in that part of the country. Our plan is to spend the next month or so along this western coast, then to come back to Buenos Ayres in Argentine, on the east coast, and to travel around that country for a few weeks. Then about the end of July we expect to go to Rio Janeiro, and join J. C. Branner for a short tip in Brazil. Branner, as you may remember, is professor of geology in Stanford University, California, and expects to come to Brazil in June or July.

The above plans are our general arrangement for the present, though we may change them from time to time as circumstances require. In the meantime, we are having a very satisfactory trip. We will arrive in Iquique in about a week from here, and I will write further from there.

P.S. I have not yet received any of the mail that has been forwarded to me here from London, but it should arrive before long.

From the Diary

May 27—Sailed at 11.30 p.m. on S.S. California of P.S.N.Co., for Iquique. This is a ship of about 5500 tons and Means and I each have a good cabin to ourselves. The ship is a sort of travelling passenger, freight and trading boat. Its cargo is composed of flour, grain, wine and general cargo, with many cattle, mules and some horses and dogs; among the passengers are about 100 Chileans, 4 Americans, and about 10 English. There is a circus and a theatrical troupe on board. The rear end of the ship is taken up by a travelling market, where cabbages, onions, lettuce, corn, peppers, potatoes, turnips, pumpkins, apples, peaches, pears, chickens, canary birds, monkeys, turkeys, ducks, geese, poodle dogs, and many other animals, vegetables, and fruits are sold by hucksters to the people who come aboard at the different ports in the arid regions to the north, where these things do not grow and where the ships are looked on as market places to buy such materials. The cabins are all on the upper deck forward, the market on the upper deck astern, the cargo and cattle, etc., below. The boat is really a freight with passenger and market equipment on the upper deck. The smell from the market, horses and mules is very strong. The officers are mostly English, and the stewards Chilean.

May 28—Arrived at Coquimbo about 5 p.m., after smooth run from Valparaiso. Put off and took on cargo in the afternoon and are still doing it now, with much noise and uproar. Coquimbo is a small port of probably 1000 or 2000 people, but 5 miles inland and connected by railway is the town of Serena, a prosperous settlement in a good agricultural country. Around Coquimbo are bare rocks and dry arid sandy stretches.

Coquimbo is 198 miles from Valparaiso.

May 29—We were kept awake most of the night by the handling of cargo, but finally sailed about 6.30 a.m. During the day we have been coasting along in sight of the shore, a rugged mountainous region, where sometimes only the low coast ranges can be seen; at other times the high Cordillera, capped with its perpetual snow, rising up behind the coast ranges. Numerous "benches" are observable along the shore, from 100 or less feet to several hundred feet above each other, and clearly represent successive stages of elevation. Many small islands as well as rocky points on the shore are coated white with guano, which looks like a capping of snow. Some guano has been mined along this coast, but most of the guano islands are farther north, on the Peruvian coast.

The coastal region here is settled by scattered ranches. Weather today cool and mostly cloudy.

May 30—We arrived early this a.m., at Caldera, which is the port of Copiapo, about 2 hours travel inland by train. Copiapo was once an important silver mining district; but is now not much worked. It is said to be noted for its beautiful women.

Caldera is a small place on a very dry barren sandy shore, with low barren coast ranges rising up behind. It is made mostly of frame houses and probably has a population of a few hundred people.

Caldera is 192 miles from Coquimbo.

We left Caldera in the forenoon and about 4 p.m. arrived at Chanaral, a small town at which are situated two copper smelters, one run by a French company and one by Woodgate and Sons of Valparaiso. The mines are 18 to 20 miles inland and are reached by a government railway that runs three times a week. It is an old mining district recently come into activity. The old mine is about 1700 feet deep, and the newer mines shallower. The ore is oxidized down to about 150 feet, and below that is sulphide. The ore is said to occur in igneous rocks, and the ore that is smelted at Chanaral is said to run about 10 percent Cu. About 90 tons metallic copper are said to be shipped monthly from Chanaral, which is 47 miles from Caldera.

While we were stopping at Chanaral Mr. Hall, the American manager of the Las Animas copper mines in this district, and Mr. Woodgate, who is in charge of the Woodgate smelter, came aboard to call on us. Mr. Woodgate's brother, whom we had met in Valparaiso, had cabled that we were coming.

The main deck on this ship is devoted to cattle, sheep, mules, and third-class passengers. They all sleep together amid all kinds of filth. The cattle and sheep, ducks, geese, etc., are also butchered here for food for the people on the ship, and the refuse rarely washed away. The deck is a putrid mass of blood and guts of animals, refuse of all kinds; and no one takes the trouble to wash it up.

May 31—We sailed from Chanaral about 11 p.m. last night and about daylight today reached Taltal, quite an important town, 65 miles north of Chanaral. It is the seat of a newly developing southern nitrate industry and has probably 8000 to 10,000 people. It is an old town recently become active, and is built mostly of frame and corrugated iron houses, on a dry sandy shore, with bare desert hills rising up behind. It is at the head of a small open bay.

Means and I went ashore for an hour or so, and then returned to the ship. The town is built largely on a brown sandy clay alluvium formed from the detritus from the hills, which rise several hundred feet high. Shales, sandstones seem to form most of the hills here. At Chanaral the hills also come close to the water and seem to be composed of shales and sandstones cut by many dark-colored dikes.

The country ever since leaving Coquimbo has been bleak and barren, as desert as Lower California and the Yuma Desert, in most places no vegetation whatever. This condition is said to reach from Coquimbo to Guyaquil, beyond which the tropical verdure comes in. The beaches are sandy and narrow, the coast range mountains rising up from the very shore for from a few hundred to a few thousand feet, while sometimes in the far distance inland the snow-capped peaks of the Andes rise up.

The weather has been perfect since we left Valparaiso, with warm sunny days and cool nights, the thermometer about 70° in the day and about 55° to 60° at night.

Last night a Chilean woman on board went crazy and became very violent. It required several people to restrain her. She is travelling with her husband and has fourteen children. Her cries kept us awake the latter part of the night. Today the doctor gave her an injection of morphine which quieted her. In the meantime, while we were at Taltal, the Captain had gone ashore to try to get a straight jacket to put her in, but could not find one.

June 1—We sailed from Taltal about 6 p.m., last night and arrived at Antofagasta about 6 a.m. today—a distance of 111 miles. Antofagasta is situated at the head of a small indentation in the coast and is exposed to the full force of the westerly winds, hence the harbor has a reputation for roughness which makes the steamship companies charge high rates for this port, as the boats often have to wait many days before they can unload. Today the water is not very rough, but a heavy swell is rolling in, and two rowboats taking passengers ashore with trunks, etc., have upset. But we have been putting off cargo, etc., all day. Means and I went ashore for a short time in the morning. The town contains probably 15,000 people living mostly in small frame or corrugated iron houses, and is very prosperous on account of the growing nitrate business in the pampa to the east. Like most other coast towns in Chile, it is built on a narrow strip of low ground on the water's edge, and back of it rises the bare, barren, brown hills of the coast ranges. The old sea beaches are well seen here. One about 200 feet high and the other represented by a very level top of the hills, several hundred feet higher.

A railroad here runs northwest up into Bolivia, to a place called Oruro, and it is being extended to La Paz, where it is expected to arrive in October of this year. The tin and other products from Oruro, the copper of CoroCoro, and the nitrate make this road very profitable.

There is said to be so much stealing going on, on these coast boats, that everything has to be under lock and key. The cabins are covered with locks and bolts and signs telling the passengers to use them. It is impossible to keep matches in the smoking room, as they are stolen, so that everyone must bring his own matches.

June 2—We were to have sailed last night but did not finish unloading freight, and as the water was a little rough the men would not work on the barges, so we had to wait over until today. The unloading was finished this morning, and we sailed for the north at 7 p.m. The day has been perfect, clear, dry, and warm.

June 3—Arrived at Tocopilla about 6.30 a.m., and anchored close in shore, in a quiet indentation in the coast. This town is, like most of the small coast towns, built of wood and corrugated iron. It contains probably 1000 or more people and is dependent on the nitrate industry and on copper mining done some miles inland.

This harbor, like most of the harbors on this coast, is open to the sea, but today the sea is calm and smooth, with a clear sky and bright warm sun overhead. A small island capped white with guano and frequented by many gulls lies directly off the town.

Tocopilla is 106 miles from Antofagasta. A small railway runs inland from here. It is owned by the Anglo-Chilean Nitrate Co., a British company, which has nitrate properties in the pampa to the east and is a very prosperous and profitable company now, though not formerly. There is also a large German company in the pampa to the east. The Germans in recent years have become very active in the nitrate industry as well as in most every other industry on the west coast. Many German boats are seen along the coast. Most of the ships seen in the various harbors along the coast, and there are many ships in all the harbors, are Chilean, English and German. Occasionally a French boat is seen. I have not yet seen an American boat anywhere on either the west or the east coast. Surely our blindness to the importance of this South American trade is losing us some very valuable business. The American firms on the West have some chartered English boats, but not their own.

Letter from Dick, dated On Board S.S. "California", Coast of Chile, June 3, 1907

I wrote to you last on May 26th, just before sailing from Valparaiso for Iquique, in northern Chile. We sailed on the night of the 27th on a steamer called the "California", and have been stopping at various ports along the coast, unloading and taking on cargo. The trip has been very interesting, and as we have been able to go ashore at many of the ports, we have seen a good deal of the coast of northern Chile.

We are now passing along that part of Chile known as the Desert of Atacama, which is a very mountainous but very barren country, much like parts of Arizona, but with even less vegetation. Sometimes it does not rain for several years at a stretch in this region. The chief industries are copper and nitrate mining. The nitrate industry is the largest mining business in Chile. It occurs as nitrate of soda, and about 2,000,000 tons yearly are exported. It is used chiefly as a fertilizer, and of course in smaller quantities in making the various nitrates of commerce.

The coast range mountains rise directly up from the sea all along the coast of Chile, and behind them is the main range of the Andes, rising 15,000 and 20,000 feet above the sea and covered with perpetual snow. The scenery is very beautiful, but the lack of water and vegetation makes it difficult to travel in the interior without an elaborate outfit.

This ship is fairly comfortable. The passengers are mostly Chilians. It is loaded with cattle, mules, vegetables and general supplies for the desert towns. The rear part of the ship is devoted to a sort of travelling market, where travelling peddlers have stocks of supplies, and where people from the shore come to buy. They can purchase here all kinds of vegetables, fruits, chickens, turkeys, ducks, geese, canary birds, poodle dogs, cats and monkeys; in fact, they can get almost everything that goes to make a household happy. Tons of cabbages, onions, turnips, etc., are heaped up on the decks, and are eagerly bought by people who come out in small boats when the ship arrives in port. We also had on board for some days a local theatrical troupe and a travelling circus, which were going to one of the ports up the coast.

We arrive tomorrow at Iquique, where we will leave the ship and remain a few days. Iquique is the chief center of the nitrate industry, and we want to see something of it. I will mail this letter at Iquique, and will write further from there in a few days.

I have not yet received any of my mail which was forwarded from London, so that I have not yet gotten any letters which you may have written since I left home; but probably mail will come along before very long. In the meantime please continue to address me care of J. S. Morgan & Co., 22 Old Broad St., London, England, as they forward mail promptly. The reason that I have not gotten my mail yet, is probably due to the fact that the boats run on very irregular schedules along this coast.

From the Diary

June 4—Arrived Iquique about daylight—got breakfast, and found a boatman from G. Moore had sent on board with a note to me saying that he (the man) was reliable and would row us and our things to shore. The man did not look as reliable as he was represented to be, but he proved so. I think he had a little jag on and that was all. Anyhow he took us and our things safely on shore and up to the Phoenix Hotel where Moore, to whom I had cabled that we were coming, had kindly engaged rooms for us. But before we went ashore, Moore himself came out to the ship and came ashore with us.

The Phoenix hotel is the best in town. It is a dingy, two-storey house with a big barroom and a dining room as an annex. But we found that we got used to the dinginess of the rooms. We were put up at the English Club and the Unicorn Club by Mr. C. N. Clarke to whom we had letters and who treated us very kindly. G. Moore was also up at these clubs, but being only a guest he could not put us up.

Iquique is a prosperous little place of about 30,000 people, the third city in size in Chile (Santiago and Valparaiso being larger) and the chief seaport of northern Chile. It owes its importance to the nitrate industry.

There is only one American living in Iquique. His name is Landsborough, and as he knows the nitrate district well, he is going up there with us.

Iquique, like most of the towns on the coast of Chile, is built on a narrow strip of low ground behind which rise up abruptly the coast ranges for some 2000 feet or more. Immense moving sand dunes line the coast just south of the town, and are also found filling hollows in the mountains near the coast. The big dune just out of Iquique is much feared by the people, who think that sometime in a fierce wind it will overwhelm the town.

Iquique is built mostly of wood and the houses are one or two stories. Fear of earthquakes prevents the use of brick or stone. There is a street car line run with horses or mules intersecting several of the chief streets, and it is said to pay well. The town water comes from Pica, about 80 miles southeast, at the foot of the Andes, and is piped in by an English company. The water is said to be good. The nitrate railways companies run a line from Iquique eastward onto the pampa, where it forks, one branch going to Pisaqua, 125 miles from Iquique, and one going to Lagunas, about 85 miles from Iquique. These lines tap all the chief nitrate localities in the Tarapaca district. Iquique is the chief town of the province of Tarapaca.

There is quite a large English colony in Iquique, and more English is spoken here than any place in which I have been in South America.

June 5—In Iquique. We have made arrangements to go up to the pampa tomorrow to see the nitrate fields. Mr. Landsborough goes with us. Moore had expected to go but is detained by business.

There is said to be considerable bubonic plague in Iquique and still more in Pisaqua, a port a short distance to the north. In fact, there is also said to be some in Valparaiso. It is said that we had a case on board coming up on the California and that the patient died and was put over.

The fish here as well as elsewhere on the west coast are most excellent, the Congrio and the Pegeray being said to be the best; both are excellent. Congrio is a large eel-shaped fish. Pegeray is about the size of our smelts and tastes much the same. A fish known as corbina is also excellent.

There are some immense sand dunes just outside of Iquique, several hundred feet high and covering about a square mile or so. They are steadily moving towards the town and fears are entertained that they may sometime cover it. It might pay to try the Australian (West Australian) method of planting vegetation on them to keep them from moving.

June 6—We left Iquique at 10.45 a.m., today to see the nitrate fields of the Tarapaca district. Our party consisted of Means and me, together with Mr. Landsborough and Mr. Comber, the latter the manager of the North Lagunas Nitrate Company. We went direct from Iquique up a steep grade into the coast range mountains, and in about 30 miles reached Estacion Central, in the Tarapaca pampa or desert, about 3000 feet above the sea. Thence south through this desert region for some 60 miles, to the terminus of the railway at Lagunas. Here we stayed over night at the house of Mr. Comber, who gave us a very good dinner and treated us most hospitably. It was good to find a fine bath tub and plenty of water here—a rare thing in these parts.

June 7—Started at 6 a.m., on horseback and rode over the property of several nitrate companies, returning to Lagunas station to catch the 9 a.m. train for the north. Had coffee at 5.30 a.m. at North Lagunas and breakfast at 8 a.m. at South Lagunas. When we got back to the station we found a lunch basket well stocked with food, whisky and bottled water by the thoughtfulness of Mr. Comber, for our railway trip. Got back to Estacion Central about 1 p.m., and continued north to Negreiros, where we went to the Agua Santa oficina for the night, and were treated very politely by the manager, Mr. Humberstone.

June 8—We looked over the Agua Santa nitrate property yesterday afternoon and this morning, and at 11 a.m. took train for Iquique, arriving here about 4 p.m. The weather has been very hot in the day and very cold at night on the pampa, also very dusty, and the railway train very bad and crowded. It is an English company and should be run better. On the other hand, the people of the pampa and the nitrate industry in general are most hospitable, and we got the best they had wherever we went. The people seem very fond of their little tipple; gin and ginger ale on awakening, a cocktail or so before breakfast, whisky and water during the day, champagne at dinner, and more whisky and water at night, not to forget several cocktails before dinner. They are mostly English and are about the most hospitable lot of people I ever saw in an English community.

Last night at Agua Santa we listened to a phonograph until almost one a.m. Phonographs are very popular in these parts, being sold by an American firm, and the agent for them is said to travel about in great style, with special servants, etc., etc. If there ever was a man who deserved a special place in Hell, it is the phonograph man, for he puts in the hands of people an instrument of persecution to their friends which rivals the Inquisition in cruelty. At least, I thought all this after listening to old Humberstone's phonograph till 1 a.m.

June 9—Was very glad to get back to Iquique last night. The pampa is most interesting and the people most hospitable, but I prefer to stay at a hotel where I can pay my way than to be forced to accept people's hospitality, as one is forced to do in the pampa, as there are no hotels. Balls and dances seem to be all the rage in the pampa. There was to have been one last night at Agua Santa, another the next night at a neighboring oficina, another next night at another oficina, etc., etc., indefinitely. How they stand it, I don't know. Probably the climate helps them, for it is more like the Arizona climate than any place I ever saw.

June 10—In Iquique. Collected a few maps, photos, and specimens relating to nitrate industry.

Letter from Dick, dated Iquique, Chile, June 11, 1907

I wrote to you last on June 3d, on the steamer on which we came from Valparaiso, and mailed the letter when we came ashore here. We left the ship here and went into the interior, into what is known as the Tarapaca pampa or the Tamarugal Desert. The nitrate deposits of northern Chile are situated in that region, and we spent some days travelling through the country examining them. They are an unique geological occurrence, and it was well worth a trip to see them.

The Tamarugal Desert is an elevated desert region lying between the Andes Mts., on the east and the lower Coast Range Mts., on the west. It is as barren as the Desert of Sahara, and generally enveloped in a cloud of fine impalpable dust, which goes through clothes, hats and almost everything else. We had a very interesting trip and have just got back here again. There is only one American living in Iquique, and he went on the trip with us. As he has lived in this country 17 years, he knew the desert well, and it was a great advantage to us to have him along.

Means and I leave here this afternoon by steamer for Valparaiso, where we will arrive in about a week. We will probably stay there a few days and then go south again, passing around through the Straits of Magellan, and up the coast of Argentine to Buenos Ayres. We had hoped to go from Valparaiso across the Andes to Buenos Ayres, but the snows have been so heavy lately in the mountains, that this route is absolutely impassable, so we will have to go through the Straits again. When we get to Valparaiso and decide on what ship we will take through the Straits, I will write further and tell you more definitely about our plans.

Iquique is a very prosperous little town of about 30,000 people, and is the chief seaport of northern Chile. It is built mostly of wood, as people fear to build brick or stone houses on account of earthquakes. It was not hurt in the earthquake last year, but on two previous occasions it was almost wiped out by earthquakes and tidal waves.

I have not yet gotten any of my mail which was forwarded from London, but may find some when I get back to Valparaiso.

I hope you are well and that you will have a good summer at Seal Harbor.

From the Diary

June 11—Took lunch, or what they call here, breakfast, with Mr. J. Lockett, at 12 o'clock noon. Sailed for Valparaiso at 8 p.m. on S. S. Victoria of the P.S.N. Co. This ship is very much cleaner and better kept than the California, on which we came up to Iquique. We were fortunate in getting two good cabins, and the captain seated us at his table. As a rule on steamships I avoid the captain's table, as it is too popular; but on these coast boats one gets much better, or rather much less bad, food than at the other tables. It is all bad enough and dirty. There are more English officers and fewer native officers on this ship than on the California, as well as more English passengers and fewer natives. The ship is better managed, much cleaner, and much more orderly than the California.

June 12—Arrived at Tocopilla early this a.m. Sailed about 6 p.m. These ships going south have not much freight to unload at ports in Chile. Most of the freight is coming north.

Weather fine, clear and warm.

June 13—Arrived Antofagasta about 11 a.m. and sailed about 2 p.m. today.

We were very glad to stay only so short a time at this dismal and depressing place, with its dusty, dirty, stinking streets, dingy houses and big gray graveyard on the hillside above. It is the most foul-smelling town I have seen in Chile.

June 14—Arrived Caldera about 11 a.m. and sailed about 2.30 p.m. The sea is becoming rough from a stiff south wind but weather clear and fine.

June 15—We had a rough night last night, with high seas and a fierce gale from the south. Many people were sick. Usually the bad storms on the Chile coast are from the northwest, and the dreaded "norther", as they are called, is the terror of sea-faring men along this coast. Last night, however, we had no storm, only a fierce south wind, with clear sky and no rain.

We reached Coquimbo about 1.30 p.m., and were to leave in about an hour but we found that there was a "strike" on among the local boatmen, "floteros," and there was no one to row passengers ashore or take off the little cargo we had on board. There were some Chilean warships in the harbor, and they sent off rowboats which took ashore such people who had to land, and also some freight, and then we sailed, with the rest of the freight still on board.

June 16—Arrived Valparaiso about 11 a.m., were met by some men whom Mr. Bush had kindly sent to take our things ashore, and went to the Gran Hotel, Vina del Mar, where they had rooms reserved for us. Very, very glad to get back and especially to get off the coast steamer. None of them are any too good.

June 17—In Valparaiso. A general labor strike has been proclaimed today and everything is at a standstill. The streets are full of troops who maintain excellent order and are a very fine efficient-looking lot of men. No ships can load or unload, so we do not know when we can sail. We want to go around the Straits of Magellan to Buenos Aires. We would go by the Transandine route but snow is too deep and the route impassable.

June 18—Same conditions exist today as yesterday. There is a general standstill in all business. It has rained hard all afternoon and tonight is pouring deluges, with a fierce "norther" blowing from the northwest.

Letter from Dick, dated Valparaiso, Chile, June 18, 1907

I wrote to you last week from Iquique in northern Chile. That same day we sailed for Valparaiso, arriving here all right a couple of days ago.

As I wrote you in my last letter, we have had to give up the trip from here across the Andes, on account of the great amount of snow that has fallen in the last few weeks, completely blocking the mountain passes, and making the route impassable. The guides who usually conduct travellers through by this route, now absolutely refuse to attempt it. We have tried to get other guides, but cannot do so, and, therefore, we have decided that it is best to abide by the opinion of every one who knows the Andes route, and not attempt it under present conditions.

We will, therefore, go by sea around through the Straits of Magellan, and up the coast of Argentine to Buenos Aires. We will have to wait here for about a week for a boat going that way, but we will get a very good one at that time, and will arrive in Buenos Aires before, or about, the middle of July. We will not stop at the Falkland Islands on the way, but will come up the coast of Argentine, so that we will have a change from the route that we took coming to Chile in May.

I have received some mail here, which was forwarded from London on April 23d. It is the first and only mail that I have received since sailing from Liverpool on April 11th. There were no letters from you in it, but I may possibly get some more mail before leaving here, and will then get any letters that you may have sent to London to me up to the time of forwarding from there.

We have had a first rate trip so far, and have seen a great deal of this west coast of South America.

P.S. I enclose a picture showing how parts of Valparaiso still look as the result of last year's earthquake.

From the Diary

June 19—Strike still on, but some of the men have gone to work. There was a fierce earthquake shock at Valdivia last night which threw down many buildings and seriously injured the city. A number of people were killed.

June 20—The weather cleared off yesterday, but today it clouded up again and tonight it is pouring torrents and blowing a gale. The strike is about over and the men are going to work.

June 21—Still in Valparaiso. Weather clear again today and sun bright. Stayed about the hotel most of the day writing letters. It is cold and raw in spite of the sun, and as there are no fires in the hotel, we have to sit in our rooms with overcoats and hats on. No houses in this city have any arrangements for heating. Hence, people have colds, rheumatism, and much consumption.

June 22—In Valparaiso. Weather clear and cool. The thermometer in my room has not been over 58° since we have been here. The hotel at Vina del Mar uses electricity and gas for lighting, as the electricity frequently does not work, and then the gas is used. By keeping the gas lit in my room most of the day I can raise the temperature from 52° to 56° or 58°. People dine with their overcoats on and complain of the climate, when it is really a glorious climate if people would only warm their houses a little. Most of the people I know are going about with colds.

June 23—This is Sunday and a quiet day in Valparaiso. Means and I took a long walk around Vina del Mar.

June 24—The S. S. Ortega is advertised to sail on the 29th for Buenos Aires via the Straits and we have taken passage on it.

June 24—Still in Valparaiso. We wanted to go to Santiago, but the labor troubles make travel so uncertain that we do not know whether we would be able to get back in time for our boat, so we have decided not to go.

The news has just reached here of the foundering at sea somewhere south of here and north of Corral, of the Pacific Steam Navigation boat the Santiago. This was one of their "coast boats"—that is, was used only on the west coast. She was the sister ship of the Arequipa which foundered in Valparaiso harbor in a fearful storm some years ago. The Santiago was an old boat and its machinery was said to be out of order. About 90 people, including crew, are said to have been on board, of whom only one was saved.

June 25—Still here in Valparaiso. The sailing of the Ortega has been postponed to Tuesday, July 2nd. This is very provoking as it means a great loss of time to us, but it cannot be helped. There is no other way of getting to Buenos Aires. A German boat, the Tanis of the Cosmos line, sails this week but it is filled up and we cannot get passage.

June 26—In Valparaiso. Much indignation is being shown against the Pacific Steam Navigation Co., on account of the Santiago disaster. The boat is said not to have been seaworthy. The one survivor was one of twenty who got away on a life boat. Six died of exposure and were thrown overboard. Then the life boat upset and all were drowned but this one man, who was either the third or fourth officer, and he got ashore. He was picked up on the beach in an almost dead condition by the people at a nearby lighthouse.

There is said to have been a severe earthquake shock in Valparaiso about 2 a.m., yesterday and that our hotel was considerably shaken, but I did not feel it. The people are in such a highly nervous and almost hysterical condition that I think they often believe they feel earthquakes when there really are none, though doubtless many do occur.

Letter from Dick, dated Valparaiso, Chile, June 26, 1907

I have just received some mail forwarded from London, and was very glad to find among it your letters of April 13th and 19th, and to know that you were well. I am also very glad to know that Tal looks so well after his winter in the west.

As I wrote you last week, Means and I will sail from here for Argentine via the Straits of Magellan, as the route across the Andes is impassable on account of the unusually heavy snow storms. The Andes railways have had to stop running, and the guides who conduct people over the pass on the summit, where the railway has not yet been built, absolutely refuse to make the trip.

We had expected to sail today, but our ship has been delayed in unloading the cargo that it brought here, and taking on new cargo, but we will probably get away in a few days. In the meantime, we have been taking the opportunity to see a little of the country around Valparaiso, a thing that we did not have much time to do when we were here a month ago. Valparaiso itself is in a dilapidated state on account of the earthquake, but the country around it is very beautiful. The city is built on the edge of a small bay on the coast, and immediately back of the town, the green coast range mountains rise up abruptly, while still farther inland, the main range of the Andes, at this time of year heavily covered with snow, towers up like an immense white wall, culminating in Mount Aconcagua, over 24,000 [22,834] feet high, and the highest peak in either North or South America. Mount Aconcagua is considerably over 100 miles from the town, and I think that the view looking towards it on a clear day, is one of the finest sights I have ever seen. Surely it is in great contrast with the view looking the other way, down into the town, where desolation and ruin are everywhere apparent. But little has yet been done towards rebuilding Valparaiso except to put up temporary structures of corrugated iron and boards, and even these are seen only occasionally amidst the surrounding mass of ruins. People seem to hesitate to put up more substantial buildings as they fear that other earthquakes will simply knock them down again.

From the Diary

June 27—Still in Valparaiso.
June 28—Same.
June 29—Same. The sailing of the Ortega has again been postponed until July 5th. This is very aggravating. It is raw and cold and beginning to rain again. It is hard to get the thermometer over 49° or 50° in my room. Means has a bad cold. He is taking quinine and I think will be all right again soon. Almost everyone in the hotel is coughing and spitting and going on as if the house was a consumptive hospital. They say the Chileans do not like fires and will run away from them, saying they are unhealthy, but I think that if they had more of them in their houses they would be healthier. Every night people are pacing around the patio of this hotel trying to keep warm and cussing the climate, whereas the climate is really almost perfect if the people only warmed their houses a little. The days are clear, bright, warm, and perfect, just like in Arizona, but the nights get cool and sometimes water freezes. Consumption is fearfully frequent in Chile and is doubtless due to this habit of not keeping warm. This and smallpox, together with the bubonic plague, are the chief diseases in Chile. It is said that annually 10,000 people die in Chile of smallpox, and there is a move on now to make vaccination compulsory.
June 30—In Valparaiso.
July 1—Same.
July 2—Same.
July 3—Same.
July 4—Same. The time of sailing of our ship has been again postponed to the 6th. Was there ever such a liar as a steamship agent. From day to day they keep telling us that the boat will go, and then it doesn't go. Means has had a bad time with his cold, but is now much better.

Letter from Dick, dated Valparaiso, Chile, July 5, 1907

We had expected before now to have started for the Straits of Magellan on our way to Buenos Aires, but our ship has been delayed from day to day in getting loaded, so we are still here. But the loading is now about completed, and we are to sail tomorrow. There are not many ships on this route, and hence we have had to wait for this one, but it is a fine big steamer, and it will be very comfortable when we get started.

There have been labor strikes in Valparaiso, and these have been the cause of the long delay in loading the ship. The city has been full of troops, sent down here from the capital, Santiago, to preserve the peace; and they have certainly shown themselves a very efficient lot of men in maintaining order. The troubles are now all over; both sides have made peace and the men have gone to work.

It will probably take us about two weeks to get from here to Buenos Aires, and as I may not have a chance to mail another letter to you until I get there, there may be an interval longer than usual between this present letter and my next one, but I will write again as soon as I get to Buenos Aires. It also takes longer for a letter to get from Buenos Aires to Philadelphia than from here to Philadelphia, so do not be surprised if my next letter is a little late in reaching you.

We have had a most interesting trip on this west coast of South America, and I am very glad that we came here. After we reach Buenos Aires, we will travel about Argentine for a week or two; and will then go on to Brazil, where Means and I are to meet Branner, and spend a few weeks in that country. I will write further about our plans for Argentine and Brazil when we get to Buenos Aires and have fixed more definitely on our arrangements.

P.S. I have been addressing all my letters to you at Philadelphia instead of Seal Harbor, and suppose they will be forwarded to you during the summer. I have not addressed them to Seal Harbor, because mails from here to the U. S. are so slow and irregular that a letter may take anywhere from a few weeks to several months to get there, and in the meantime you might be back again from Seal Harbor before some of my letters reached there. Therefore I am addressing everything to you at Philadelphia.

From the Diary

July 5—In Valaparaiso. This evening about 7.30 p.m., while we were at dinner, a rumbling was heard and in a moment the whole house was sharply shaken by an earthquake. It felt like the feeling when a heavy sea in a storm strikes the ship and makes it shiver from stem to stern, a sort of twisting, jarring motion. Plates and tables jumped about, waiters and guests yelled "terremoto" and dashed for the doors. One old gentleman who was sitting at a table alone made a bound that one would have thought his age altogether incapable of. It only shows how the rudimentary habits of the race will crop out under trying circumstances. There was no second shock and we all soon resumed dinner.

July 6—There was another sharp earthquake shock about 1 a.m. last night. People ran to their bedroom doors, and for a few moments there was considerable excitement but it passed off without further incident.

We went on board the Ortega this morning as she was to sail at 2 p.m., but I have just been informed that she will not sail until tomorrow. Anyhow we are on the ship and will stay until it does sail.

July 7—We sailed at last at about 6 p.m. today. This is Sunday and a large part of Valparaiso seemed to come aboard, some to see their friends off, some to loaf and drink at the bar. The custom of coming on ships, whether one has friends there or not, is a popular one in Chile. At every port, people pile on a ship when it comes into port—Europeans as well as Chileans—and loaf, drink, and gossip.

They get better and cheaper drinks than on shore, while the steamship people do not object as they make a profit off selling them drinks and charging for meals. Many of the coast boats are simply floating bar rooms, and it is said that many of them stay in port so as to make the bar-room profit.

This ship is almost two weeks late in starting and we have been waiting for it since June 16th. Even when it did get away, it was with an accident. A rope, twisted taut around a capstan, broke and, flying around, knocked down a sailor, breaking his arm and leg.

Tonight is fine, clear, and sea smooth.

July 8—Arrived about noon at Coronal, spent about three hours trying to get coal for the ship, and then got a few small barge loads. Sailed about 7 p.m., for Punta Arenas. There seems to be a constant strife for coal at Coronal. There is not enough to go round and the harbor is full of boats waiting for it.

July 9—Cloudy and drizzly. Sea becoming rougher all day. Tonight it is very rough and most passengers are seasick. Wind from north.

July 10—Wet and rough—a bleak dismal day. Even in the north Atlantic this sea would be considered rough. But this ship is very staunch and strong, built for such weather. It is all iron and steel, and is really a floating fortress. It needs to be such, for the seas that are dashing over it tonight are enough to tear many ships to pieces.

I forgot to mention that yesterday we passed a lot of carcasses of cattle which are supposed to be from the wrecked steamer "Santiago." The one man saved from that wreck is said to have been for the third time the sole survivor of wrecks. He was fourth officer of the Santiago.

July 11—Wet, rough, raining, and bleak. High seas and high north winds. Most of the passengers are seasick but Means and I are all right. There are about sixty first-class passengers, probably half English, with three Americans, several Germans and French, and a few Chileans. The whole ship seems quiet and subdued, probably on account of the bad weather.

At 3 p.m., we passed the Evangelists Islands, a group of small rocky islands, one of them surmounted by a lighthouse, lying just north of the mouth of the Straits of Magellan. They were partly covered by a fog and presented a most bleak and dreary sight. About 4 p.m., we entered the Straits, Cape Pilar being faintly visible through the fog. It is drizzling rain and sleet tonight, and blowing a gale. The ship has stopped and is floating about until daylight. It is too dangerous to navigate the Straits in this stormy weather at night as there are only two or three lighthouses along its whole course. (Darkness came on tonight at 4.30 p.m.) One of the lighthouses—St. Felix—is on the shore of the straits, just opposite to where we are now floating. We stopped here so as to have this light as a point to determine our position. Smyth Channel also branches off from the Straits opposite this light and runs north up the coast of Chile, separating the mainland from the archipelago of islands lining the southern part of Chile.

Other light houses on the coast are one on the Evangelists Islands, one just northeast of Cape Froward, and one at Cape Virgenes.

July 12—The day broke wet, foggy, and bleak. Still floating in front of St. Felix light. At 7.30 a.m. we started. There was no anchor to pull up as the water had been too deep to anchor, so we have just drifted about all night.

We passed all morning and until about 3.30 p.m., through the same kind of country as described in last trip (May of this year) through the Straits. A rugged mountainous country now encroaching on the Straits, now receding, heavily covered with snow almost to the water's edge, the snow being more abundant than in May, with few scattered trees in valleys and on slopes. But generally the country is too rugged even for trees to find a footing. Torrents flow down some of the hillsides and huge glaciers fill some of the valleys and reach down to the sea. Great flocks of gulls and other sea birds swarm the waters of the Straits.

About 2 p.m., the clouds cleared and we had a beautiful afternoon. About 3.30 p.m., we rounded Cape Froward, the extreme southern point of the South American mainland, in latitude about 54°S. We had been going southeast all morning, but on rounding Cape Froward, we turned northeast towards Punta Arenas, which is some 40 odd miles distant. Cape Froward is a dark bluff of stratified rocks rising abruptly a few hundred (200 or 300 feet) feet above the sea, followed immediately on the inland side by a high snow-capped peak, probably 1500 or 2000 feet high. The front of the Cape, as well as could be seen from the ship, is composed of stratified rocks, much twisted and contorted, looking much like Tertiary sandstones such as are seen in many places along the southern coast of Chile.

Right up to Cape Froward the mountains had been very rugged and the channel narrow and deep, often over 100 fathoms, and almost always too deep to anchor. But on rounding the Cape to the northeast the whole aspect of things changes. The country rapidly drops off in altitude, the mountains become lower and more rounded, and finally blend into a flat pampa-like country with scattered hills. The Straits widen to many times their former width and the water becomes shallower, until at Punta Arenas—or, rather, just beyond it, to the northeast—the water becomes quite shallow and offers good anchorage everywhere. The shores become low and sandy and covered with coarse grass and shrubbery, with less snow than to the west.

Far off to the east can be seen the low shores of the main island of Terra del Fuego and the region where the miners of Porvenir now are working for gold.

In other words, Cape Froward marks the eastern foot hills of the Cordillera, which a short distance still farther east blend into the plains of eastern Patagonia. Some 5 or 6 miles northeast of the Cape is the lighthouse on the Patagonian side of the Straits. In a small cove nearby is a small whaling camp, where a few small ships are gathered. To the south of Cape Froward, the snow-capped mountains can be seen running off south through the archipelago of small islands which form the western part of Terra del Fuego, and which stand like grim sentinels guarding the "Ultima Thule" of the South American continent, and culminating in the bleak rocky island of Cape Horn.

We arrived at Punta Arenas at 6.30 p.m., just in time to get the ship received by the port authorities. We are to sail again at 5.30 a.m., tomorrow.

July 13—We took on about 30 passengers last night, mostly English, with some French, Germans, and Chileans. As at most Chilean ports, they were followed on board by innumerable "friends"—about ten to each passenger—and they kept up a noisy time on the ship until after midnight, the bar room being the center of attraction.

We sailed at about 6 a.m. The day has been clear and bright, with only a light north wind, but very cold, the thermometer below freezing. The country on both sides of the Straits east of Punta Arenas becomes lower and lower until it stretches out into wide plains, with slightly undulating surface and occasionally a low rounded hill. It looks just like Kansas or Nebraska in winter, and is really the southern extension of the great plains of eastern Argentine, partially submerged. The country along the Straits rises perhaps from 10 to 100 feet, and occasionally higher, above the sea. It is grass covered and not so much cut up into islands as the more mountainous country to the west.

At about 3 p.m., we passed out of the Straits, rounding Cape Dungeness and Cape Virgenes in Argentine, both close together, and bearing north into the Atlantic. The boundary of Chile and Argentine passes between these two capes. Chile put a lighthouse on Dungeness and Argentine one at Virgenes, about a mile or two to the north. Far off to the south we could see the low shore of the main island of Terra del Fuego, covered with snow and looking cold, bleak and dreary.

East of Punta Arenas one sees much more signs of civilization than in the rugged country to the west of it, for here there is room for the great herds of sheep raised on both sides of the Straits, both in Patagonia and in the main island of Terra del Fuego. The latter is rapidly becoming a great sheep country as well as the former. Occasional small settlements of a few houses are seen along the shores, the homes of the sheep men, and some little farming is done at some of them. Small steamers of a few hundred tons are occasionally met, which ply the Straits collecting wool at the different ranches and taking it to Punta Arenas, which is the center of the wool industry and the shipping point for it. These small steamers are said to do a very lucrative business.

A few cattle were seen at one place on the Patagonia side, but sheep are the main livestock of "Magallanes", as the region of the Straits is known to the Chileans. In addition to the sheep, the chief industries of Magallanes are sealing, whaling, fishing, placer gold washing, and coal mining, the last just north of Punta Arenas, but all the industries together are small as compared with the sheep industry, which is par excellence the business of Magallanes. Quite a business is done in sealing and whaling, but the fishing is small. I could hear of no canneries or drying or salting industries, and in fact no one seems to know whether the fish are so very abundant or whether they are good for canning, salting or drying. My own observation leads me to believe that the fish are quite abundant, though perhaps not so much so as in the far north of the northern hemisphere, and that many of them would be good for salting and drying, if not for canning. They are of the same variety as those [previously] described—i.e., paggerey, congrio, corbina, and a flat fish probably the same as our flounders. The paggerey is considered the best fish on the Chilean coast.

The sun set tonight about 4.30 p.m., just as we were passing out of sight of the low flat coast of Argentine, and as it sunk down below that great stretch of plains and deserts, I had a sense of relaxation at getting away from those endless mountains and gorges through which we had been passing. I think this feeling is one of relief at getting away from the narrow field of vision in any mountainous country. I have felt the same thing in coming out of the Rocky Mountains, the Sierra Madra of Mexico, Norway and other rugged countries. One is glad to get there and also glad to get away.

We are on the open Atlantic tonight. A gentle north wind is blowing and the sea is as smooth as a pond.

We have now left Chile, at least for the present trip, and I cannot help feeling a sense of relief. This is not because the country lacks in beauty or interest—on the contrary, it is most beautiful and interesting, and the people are far superior intellectually to many races that I have met—but there seems to be a difficulty in getting about and in accomplishing anything. Every effort seems like working against a great opposing weight, nothing goes smoothly or easily, no sympathetic movement is exerted in one's behalf.

I give here a few observations and remarks about Chile and Chileans.

The Chilean people are mostly a mixture in varying proportions of Spanish and American Indian. There were originally three principal tribes of Indians in what is now Chile: one in the north, one in the central part, and one in the south. The tribe in the central part was by far the most powerful and numerous. They were the Araucanians and during Spanish rule they were never completely conquered. Chile as a republic claims to have conquered them, and though they did win some fights with them, yet the conquest was largely one of interbreeding and hence mutual. The Spanish people of Chile came out of their conflicts with the Indians a race of halfbreeds, and today most of the Chileans are more or less dark, with Indian features, etc. Some pure Spanish blood doubtless still exists, but it is rare, and seen mostly in Santiago and some of the other larger cities.

No negro blood is in the Chileans, as in the Brazilians, for no slaves were brought there from Africa.

Some of the early English and American settlers in Chile married Chilean women, and hence there is quite a class of partly English or American and partly Chilean population, all of whom, however, seem proud to be Chileans. An American or nglish doing business in Chile is said to have greatly increased his influence with the people by marrying one of them.

The admixture of Anglo-Saxon, however, is small, or practically nothing, as compared with the admixture of Indian. The latter has given the Chilean of today his chief characteristics, which are fierceness, cruelty, bravery in war, pride, independence, great physical strength, and above all a sullen moroseness which is anything but attractive to the stranger.

The Chileans seem to fear no nation but America (U. S. A.) because they realize that the U. S. will defend them from the aggression of other nations, but that no nation will defend them from the aggression of the U. S. Throughout Chile foreigners disgusted with Chilean methods are constantly suggesting to Americans that their government seize Chile. Every American knows that his government could not be persuaded by any means to do such a thing, but still the Chileans fear it. To such an extent is this foolish fear carried that it is hard for an American to get concessions or own real estate in Chile, though other foreigners can do so without any trouble.

The Chileans are most patriotic people. Viva Chile! is heard from one end of the country to the other, and their flag is always in evidence.

The usual taxes in Chile are very low, as they get such an enormous income from export tax on nitrate that they live mostly on that—some twenty or thirty million dollars (Amer.) yearly. The effect is said to have been bad on the people, who are said to have become lazy and demoralized since Chile took the nitrate fields from Peru and Bolivia.

The common Chilean is a thief by nature, as are also some of his neighbors. On the west coast steamers the cabins are fortified with numerous locks and bolts and with signs to be sure to use them, and wonderful stories of thefts are told. In Peru it is said that the merchants count on losing one-third of their goods on pack mules going from Moliendo to La Paz. It seems to be part of the nature of a Chilean to be a thief, and he steals whether he wants what he steals or not; the Peruvians may be the same.

The Chileans are very strong physically. A man will sling a sack of ore or other material weighing 200 pounds or more on his shoulder as if it were nothing.

The Chilean national weapon is a sort of small sickle, in the form of the arc of a circle, perhaps 8 or 10 inches long and with a handle. It is very sharp on the point and it is intended as a convenient implement to disembowel an antagonist. Most Chileans are said to carry them about their persons.

The Chileans are rude and brusque, and in spite of what they may say, they hate all "gringos". They simply tolerate them when they think they can make money out of them, and they look on all foreigners as their natural and legitimate prey. The first impression one gets on landing at Valparaiso, where hundreds of boatmen pounce on him to row him ashore, and then rob him, in payment for their services, of all they think he can stand, is anything but agreeable. The Chilean government will not let the steamship lines take passengers ashore on their launches, as they want the boatmen with small rowboats to get the jobs. The steamship authorities are to blame, however, for not advising and helping the passengers to deal with the boatmen. They simply tell them that there is the shore and to get there as best they can. The result is that the person arriving there the first time and not knowing the language or the people, gets robbed, loses his good nature, and cusses the natives, the steamship company and all its officers, and what is more, they all deserve it.

I was one day in a bar at Valparaiso having a drink with another man. In the midst of serving us, a Chilean walked up and the bartender, also a Chilean, at once stopping waiting on us and waited on the Chilean, serving us later on. I was surprised to notice that the man, an American, who had invited me into the bar, did not resent this. Afterwards I questioned him about it and he told me that such things were common and that a foreigner could not expect other treatment. My friend was one of the most prominent and respected foreigners in Chile, and I frankly told him that I could not understand why he would remain in a country where he could not even assert his just rights.

The Chileans must have been born tired. They are about as lazy as any people I ever met. If you ask a Chilean to do anything, he at once seems overcome with fatigue and his face grows long, but if you add to your request the words "pauco mas tarde" (a little later) he will beam with joy at the prospect of being able to put off the fearful hour of action. The earthquake of August 15, 1906, has afforded more Chileans with more excuses for procrastination than anything else in the world. They pity themselves, which is a most dangerous condition of mind for anyone to get into, and their everlasting excuse for every shortcoming is the "terremoto" or earthquake. They have sewers that not only run open through the streets of Valparaiso and Santiago, but are also open in each house, and yet they pity themselves because they die of typhoid fever. Their priests keep them from being vaccinated, and 10,000 Chileans are said to die of smallpox in an average year. They pity themselves for that, and connect it as well as the typhoid in some mysterious way with the "terremoto."

As a matter of fact, they are simply too lazy to do anything and are simply always hunting excuses for idleness. Almost all the great things done in Chile have been done by foreigners, chiefly Americans and English, and rarely is a Chilean name connected with any great works or deeds; while the names Pratt, Wheelwright, Cochrane, Edwards, O'Higgins, Clark, etc., are connected with important matters in Chile's history, and their names are found in the names of streets in Chilean towns, on statues, etc.

Every now and then the Chileans get a fit of reform and pass a number of very good laws, but they are never enforced, and there the matter drops. The virtuous legislators have made a record and are content to lie back on their virtuous laurels, so that though the statute books of Chile are full of good laws, very few of them are ever seen in operation unless they are dug up to get some "gringo" into trouble, or to squeeze something out of him.

An industrial boom seems to have come over Chile shortly before the great earthquake of 1906, but nothing much has been done since then. As a result of the boom, labor became very scarce, and the government is even now importing labor from Spain and offering all kinds of inducements in the way of land grants, etc., to immigrants. But the latter do not seem to remain in Chile when they once get there. They cross the mountains into Argentine, where they like the climate, country and government better. No one seems to like Chile but the Chileans. There are some few manufacturing industries in Chile, such as breweries, sugar refineries, as at Vina del Mar, where sugar from Peru is refined, flour mills, etc., etc.; but mining, agriculture and cattle (the last only to a small extent) are the chief industries. The nitrate mining in the north, the copper and silver and coal in the central part, and the gold in Magallanes, are the chief mining industries.

Chile was once the one great copper producer of the world, but in recent years its production has fallen off on account of the exhaustion of the mines. Most of the old mines were discovered in the old days when Chile was a colony of Spain. Since Chile has become free but few new mines have been opened. The people seem to have used up what they seized from the crown of Spain in the way of mines, but not to have looked for any new ones. Hence the gradual falling off in production as the old mines became exhausted

The harbors of Chile are mostly very deep, but very badly protected from storms In fact, they are only dents in the coast line, and the winds howl in unobstructed. An exception to this is Talcabuena and a few other harbors that are partly protected, but Valparaiso, Antofagasta, Taltal, Iquique, etc., etc., are notoriously bad. The whole coast of Chile has very deep water right up to the shore, so that in quiet weather large ships can come close in almost anywhere.

The railways of Chile belong partly to the government and partly to private companies, and all of them are very bad, so far as I have seen them. They are mostly very dirty, poor cars and worse road beds. There are many wrecks but as the trains don't go very fast, not many people are hurt. On the "expresso" from Valparaiso to Santiago there is a fairly good though very old-fashioned Pullman chair car, also a fair dining car. The ordinary cars are on the plan of American cars. At a certain point on the Valparaiso-Santiago Railway, where a number of wrecks have occurred, an undertaker has put up his sign in a conspicuous place.

All Chileans, men, women, and children, use "perfume" and powder, and the women also paint. The powder is so thick on some of the women that they look as if they had been newly whitewashed, and the whole town smells of perfume on men and women, often rotten sweaty perfume that has accumulated without being washed off for months.

The people of Valparaiso are in a condition approaching nervous hysterics as a result of the constantly recurring earthquakes. There seems to be something very unnerving in earthquakes. Perhaps it is that people lose confidence in the stability of the earth and feel that there is no longer anything solid in this world to cling to. They have been used to look on the ground, with its rocks and massive mountains as something solid, something that cannot be shaken, something to "tie to." But when they see and feel it shake like a tree in the wind, their faith in the stability of the world is destroyed. They look about wildly for something to cling to, but cannot find it. Hence, hysteria and panic.

Valparaiso has from its first founding been most unfortunate. Twice it has been almost annihilated by earthquakes, once it was almost ruined by floods from a broken dam above the city; it has been devastated by storms from the sea, has been the scene of labor riots and many other troubles. People are losing confidence in it, and in no respect is this shown so much as in the kind of houses that are being put up to replace the ones shaken down by the earthquake. Instead of the massive masonry structures that formerly existed, corrugated iron is now being used, even for two or more storied buildings. The town will probably grow up again as a "tin city" (i.e., a city of corrugated iron) in place of the fine brick and stone city that it once was. Corrugated iron construction resists earthquakes very well, and even if it is shaken down, the pecuniary loss is not so great as if a masonry building were thrown down.

Chilean money is mostly paper with smaller coins of silver and some sort of white alloy. No gold is seen in circulation, though there is Chilean gold, but it is held in banks, by the government, etc. The government insists that all tariffs on goods imported be paid in Chilean gold, and as this gradually brings most of the gold into the hands of the government, people have to buy it back from the government in order to pay their tariffs. To help them do this, the government, whenever it accumulates considerable gold, sells it at auction, where it goes at about 140, and thus the government makes a profit of 40 per cent bonus on the discredit of its own paper money with which the gold is bought.

British gold is accepted everywhere in Chile in ordinary transactions, and in fact it is accepted everywhere in South America that I have yet been. It is the only money universally taken without question on the South American continent.

A notable feature of the scenery about Santiago are the many Lombardy poplars, which were imported here and grow with great luxuriance. They make the valley about Santiago look very much like the country about Salt Lake City, Utah.

There was once an industry in Peru of capturing Indians, cutting off their heads, and taking all the bone from the inside, leaving only the skin and flesh, which soon shrunk up and dried in the arid air, leaving a miniature head with all the features shrunk evenly, probably 3 inches in diameter and with the original hair still adhering. These heads were valued as great curios, and Indians were hunted like wild beasts to procure their heads. This "industry" is said now to have been stopped by the Peruvian government.

Mr. Swinburn, agent of the P.S.N. Co. in Santiago, and the son of Don Carlos Swinburn, a pioneer Englishman in Chile, tells the following story:

Returning home one night he saw a man lying face down by a creek, insensible. He naturally went up to him, saw he had fallen and hurt himself, and began splashing water on his face. The man came to, looked up and began to yell. A policeman ran up; the man declared that Swinburn had been with him all evening, had knocked him down and beaten him. Swinburn, of course, denied it, but the policeman said that under the circumstances he would arrest them both. Swinburn then declared that the man did not even know his name. The man declared he did, but mentioned some name other than Swinburn.

"No," said Swinburn, "my name is Swinburn, and I am the son of Don Carlos Swinburn."

Then the man broke into tears, and the policeman asked the cause.

"Why," he said, "Don Carlos Swinburn is my oldest friend, and I cannot but weep to find that he has a son who is such a rascal as to assault me."

The policeman soon saw that the man was making false charges against Swinburn and set the latter free.

July 14—As we passed out of the Straits of Magellan and up the east coast last night, the sea was smooth, but it did not remain so. A furious gale from the north broke on us during the night and ship heaved and pitched most violently The storm has lasted all today and tonight is blowing harder than ever We have cut down our speed and are simply crawling along. The boat is behaving well, though necessarily pitching and rolling greatly. Most everyone is seasick. The ocean is a mass of spray and foam, and the night is black as ink. Surely the Atlantic and Pacific on the coasts of South America are turbulent seas.

July 15—The gale continued all night and was worse than ever during the early morning hours. About 3 p.m. it began to moderate. Tonight at 10 p.m., it has moderated considerably. Curiously enough, ever since this storm began on the night of the 13th, there has been little or no rain, though the sky has been heavily overcast with clouds.

July 16—The gale has passed; the sea is smooth, but sky still cloudy. We have not seen land since leaving Cape Virgenes, but are due to arrive at Montevideo tomorrow.

July 17—We were due at Montevideo this morning, but a dense fog came up and the captain anchored the ship. We have not picked up land for several days, and as the water is a little turbid it looks as if we were in or near the estuary of La Plata, where the channel is crooked and shallow, and very difficult to navigate in a fog.

July 18—About 7 p.m., last night the fog lifted a little and we pulled up anchor and moved until 9.30 p.m., when the fog again settled down, and we anchored. Started again about midnight when the fog lifted a little, but had to anchor again in short time. In morning about 10 a.m., the fog lifted enough for us to see Montevideo about 7 miles away, and we reached the breakwater about 11 a.m. We transferred to the river boat "Venus," got a good cabin, and sailed for Buenos Aires at 6.15 p.m. Today has been the anniversary of their independence in Uruguay, and it is a public holiday. All Montevideo is out in celebration, and the streets, buildings and boats in the harbor are gay with flags, but no firecrackers are heard. At about 6 p.m., just before we sailed, a bugle at the Barracks and a cannon from the fort on the hill announced the setting of the sun—a daily proceeding in this gay and beautiful city of Montevideo

July 19—The night was beautiful with a clear bright moon last night, and we had a very good trip up La Plata to Buenos Aires. These river boats are like the Long Island Sound boats from New York to Fall River, but smaller. They are very comfortable and food good; and they are very swift, going the 150 miles, or so, from Montevideo to Buenos Aires in 10 hours.

We arrived in Buenos Aires at 4 a m. today, and about 8 a.m. we left the boat, passed through the customs house, and drove up to the Grand Hotel, where we got good rooms and are very comfortable. Surely the east coast of South America is as much ahead of the west coast as the U. S. is ahead of Mexico. Here in Buenos Aires, as well as in Montevideo, one feels as if he were in civilization of a high class.

July 20—In Buenos Aires. This is a beautiful city and would be a credit to any country in the world. Many of the streets are magnificent wide boulevards, the main one, known as Avenida Mayo, is made like one of the Paris boulevards and the imitation is almost perfect, not only in the avenue itself, with its trees, newsstands, etc., but even in the architecture of the houses along it. Many of the residences here are veritable palaces. Everything is on a big, grand substantial scale, nothing cheap or shoddy. The stores are fine and full of rich and costly goods. There must be great wealth here, and it has all been made out of cattle, sheep and the boom in land values. Many of the old Spaniards who owned large tracts of land have become immensely rich from its sale, and many of the finest houses here are owned by these old Argentinos; but the architecture, the style and grandeur of everything shows the hand of the French and Italians. This is a part of Latin America that can surely rival any country in grandeur. Even the blowing of the automobile horns, usually so much complained of, is a joyous and pleasant sound to us after coming from Chile where they are almost unknown.

The saloons, theatres, and all places of amusement are open Sundays as well as any other day; yet there is no drunkeness or disorder. Surely we Anglo-Saxons could learn many things about governing towns and cities from the Latins, if we only would do it.

The people here go about looking happy and pleasant, and are always polite, much in contrast with the more sullen disposition seen on the west coast.

July 21—In Buenos Aires. This is Sunday. There is a horse race going on and everyone is going to it. Means and I went to the Zoological Garden, which is a large and most creditable display, arranged in an artistic and beautiful manner.

The city is more like a little Paris than any place I have ever seen. The style and dress of the women could not be surpassed anywhere.

Letter from Dick, dated Grand Hotel, Calle Florida 25, Buenos Aires, July 21, 1907

I wrote to you last just before we left Valparaiso, and have not written since then, as we did not have a chance to land and mail letters anywhere on the way. As I said in my last letter, we were considerably delayed in getting away from Valparaiso on account of the delay in loading the ship, but we finally started on July 7th. We sailed out of the bay on a fine clear night, but this weather did not last long, and the next day we were in a storm that lasted most of the voyage, down the Pacific coast and up the Atlantic coast with only one day's respite while we were in the Straits of Magellan. Those Antarctic seas around Terra del Fuego and southern Patagonia are about as stormy a proposition as I have ever seen. The storms never seem to end, and the ships that navigate those waters are built especially strong so that they will not be battered to pieces. The ship that we came on was a new one, only a year old, and it was more like a floating iron fortress than anything else. When day after day, and night after night, the storms and waves kept pounding at it, there was a good deal of comfort in feeling that it *was* built like a fortress.

As we came farther north we got into smoother seas, and two days ago we reached the estuary of the River Plata, and anchored off Montevideo. There we transferred to a river boat, and the next day arrived here at Buenos Aires.

I have not yet had much chance to see much of Buenos Aires, but it seems to be a fine city, and it has an air of cheerfulness and brightness that is in great contrast with the gloom which pervades Valparaiso. The people of Valparaiso are in a very depressed condition. They seem sort of dazed by a constantly accumulating series of misfortunes, earthquakes, epidemics of disease, disastrous storms, labor strikes, etc., etc. People hesitate to rebuild their houses because they fear that they will just be shaken down again, for earthquakes of greater or less force are of almost daily occurrence. Two days before we left Valparaiso, there was a severe shock which sent people dashing wildly out of their houses; and a few days before that, the town of Valdivia, south of Valparaiso, was shaken and many houses demolished. The local "earthquake prophets" are predicting still worse shocks for Chile, and this keeps the people, already on the verge of a sort of hysterical panic, in constant terror. They seem to have lost courage, and stand about in groups waiting their fate. Many of them have taken to drink for comfort, and I have never seen any people in the world who can stow away the quantity of liquor that the people of Chile can consume today.

To add to the general demoralization of Valparaiso, they have been having very bad labor strikes, the city has been full of troops, the houses and stores that were left standing by the earthquakes have been barricaded as a protection against mobs. In addition to this; there is much sickness in the town, which is daily adding many more to the list of several thousand who were killed in the earthquake.

If you will imagine a city shaken to a mass of ruins by earthquakes and several thousand people killed, with disease carrying off more people every day, with an almost continuous line of funerals passing through the streets, with almost every man, woman and child dressed in mourning for dead friends, with new earthquakes almost every day, with mobs threatening the safety of those still living and with the houses barricaded for the protection of those within, you will understand the condition of Valparaiso as it is today.

After spending several weeks there, it seems a great contrast to come here, where everything is bright and attractive, and the people are very polite. We are staying at the Grand Hotel, which is an excellent place, and about the best in the city. We will remain here until July 26th, when we will sail for Rio Janeiro, Brazil, to meet Branner. The voyage from here to Rio Janeiro takes only 4 or 5 days.

Means and I are both well, and our trip so far has been in every way successful.

I hope you are well, and that you are having a good summer at Seal Harbor.

From the Diary

July 22—In Buenos Aires.
July 23—In Buenos Aires. Everything is on a big scale and thoroughly good in this town. The hotel is excellent. It has an open central part like the Brown Palace of Denver, with a movable glass roof to the rotunda. This is an excellent scheme for ventilation. It is closed at night and opened by day. The Casino theatre here has the same thing. We took dinner tonight at a very good restaurant

with G. D. Hughes, a very nice fellow in the cattle business, whom we met on the Oriana coming from England last spring.

July 24—Means and I went today to La Plata, about 20 odd miles east of here, by train, and returned tonight. It is the capital of the state of Buenos Aires, while the city of Buenos Aires is the capital of Argentina. We went especially to have a look at the country. It is a beautiful level prairie exactly like eastern Kansas, covered with a dense growth of very green grass, a rich dark brown or black soil, highly cultivated and studded with groves of eucalyptus trees imported from Australia. One of the most beautiful avenues of trees I have ever seen in the world is the one leading up to the Museum de La Plata and lined with eucalyptus. This is surely a beautiful and wonderful tree and seems to grow almost everywhere. Starting from Australia it has been transplanted and grows luxuriantly in North and South America, Africa, and other places. I think that we in North America have the least attractive form of eucalyptus—i.e., the tall straight kind with thin foliage. The branching kind is much more beautiful. The tree is always green and therefore good in winter.

The railway to La Plata is excellent, with large and very comfortable cars of the American plan, but better than any I have ever seen at home. The seats are larger and there is more room for one's legs. They are as good as most pullman cars.

July 25—In Buenos Aires. This city contains about 1,000,000 people, and the whole of Argentine contains about 4,500,000 people. Both are growing fast, mostly by additions from Italy, Spain and other Latin countries, and most excellent settlers many of them make. There are only about 25,000 English in Argentine, and only a few hundred Americans. South America will always be a Latin country in its civilization and its sympathies. It is already and is becoming more so all the time. Perhaps it is a good thing.

July 26—We left Buenos Aires promptly on time at 10 a.m., on the steamer Avon of the Royal Mail Steam Packet Co. It is the largest ship that ever came to this town and is a great curiosity to the people. They collected in thousands on the dock to see her off this morning, most of them also going through the ship. It is a ship of about 12,000 tons, and fitted with every modern improvement—no upper berths, small tables in dining room, and everything first class. We passed down the muddy La Plata and arrived at Montevideo about 9.30 p.m., and anchored outside the breakwater. The water of the river is so thick with mud that it is almost like passing through molasses. When we consider that the river is over 20 miles wide at Buenos Aires and over 60 at Montevideo, we can conceive of the enormous quantity of sediment carried down. It is not very deep —20 feet or so near Buenos Aires, except where dredges deepen for ships, and 30 to 40 feet lower down. The muddy (coffee colored) waters emptying into the ocean, discolor the sea water for many miles out from land.

We did not land at Montevideo because we were anchored 3 or 4 miles out at sea. Montevideo is said to contain over 300,000 people, and all Uruguay to contain a little over 1,000,000.

July 27—We sailed from Montevideo at 2.30 p.m., passing up the low sandy coast of Uruguay, with green patches farther inland, until dark.
July 28—At sea. A chill northeast wind makes the ship roll considerably and most people are seasick. The ship is not half full.
July 29—At sea. Fine clear warm weather, sea smooth.

For an hour or so we were in sight of the broken mountainous coast of southern Brazil.

Letter from Dick, dated R.M.S.P. "Avon", Coast of Brazil, July 29, 1907

I wrote to you last on July 21st from Buenos Aires. We sailed from there on the 27th on this ship, the "Avon," which is a new and a very good steamer. We came down the Rio Plata from Buenos Aires to Montevideo, and proceeded thence north, up the coasts of Uruguay and Brazil. We are due to arrive at Santos, on the coast of Brazil, tomorrow, and I will mail this letter there. From Santos we will continue on this same ship to Rio Janeiro, where we expect to meet Branner, and take a short trip through Brazil.

We were about a week in Buenos Aires and found it a very fine town. It contains about a million people and is the largest city in the southern hemisphere. It would be a good city in any part of the world, and creditable to any country.

We are now again approaching the tropics as we continue northward up the east coast of South America; and the warm sun and smooth seas are in great contrast with the rough stormy seas and snowy weather that we were in only a few days ago, coming around the Straits of Magellan.

I will write further from Rio Janeiro.

From the Diary

July 30—Arrived early this morning at Santos, which is a short distance up the Santos River. It is the port for the city of Sao Paulo, and is quite a town itself, being said to be, with Rio Janeiro, one of the two largest coffee-shipping ports in the world. It is a neat clean town, with some very good buildings and pretty parks and squares. Back of the town rises up some low hills of gray gneissic rock, covered with a dense growth of tropical verdure. Slight tropical showers fell during the day. The people are great coffee drinkers. Almost every other house seems to be a coffee saloon, and the whole town smells of coffee.

July 31—Arrived at Rio Janeiro early this morning. Branner and Derby came out on a tug to meet us and we landed promptly and went to the Hotel dos Etrangeiros where they had engaged rooms for us. The hotel is fairly comfortable but very crowded. Good hotels are scarce in Rio and most of them are out of the town—up on the hills—where they were originally built to get away from the fevers of the lower city. In recent years a wave of sanitary reform has gone over Rio and the lower town is very healthy, so that most people want to stop there, but find only few hotels. The Estrangeiros is in the lower town, but on the outer edge of it.

Branner and Derby are going to accompany us on a 10 or 12 days trip up into the state of Minas Geraes to see some of the manganese and iron regions, and the old gold districts. This is a great opportunity for us, for they both speak Portuguese and know the country. We will start the day after tomorrow.

I spent some hours in the customs house today getting baggage through. The trouble was not with inspecting the stuff, as no trouble was made over that, but it was the long wait to get it inspected. All baggage, including that of immigrants, is put together and there are only two men to go through it. No one has any preference, but must wait hours until his turn comes. It is a trying ordeal and a most damnable arrangement.

Derby had Dr. Lisboa, a noted Brazilian mining engineer, to meet us at dinner tonight.

August 1—In Rio. Saw something of the town with Branner and went to the Botanical Gardens, which are noted for their many tropical plants. The finest thing I saw was an avenue of beautiful palms. The people are very courteous here, but slow, slower than any I have seen yet in South America. I feel like apologizing to the Chileans for ever thinking they were slow. They are the personification of strenuousness compared with Brazilians. The Brazilians rise early in the morning, but that is the only thing they do promptly, and I doubt if they would do that, were it not for the coffee they get as soon as they rise. They seem to need coffee every few hours during the 24. They take it in small cups which they fill almost to the top with fine sugar, and then pour in enough coffee to melt the sugar, making a sort of syrup with a coffee flavor. This is taken often 8 or 10 times a day.

Branner says he was once criticized as reckless by a Brazilian for washing his face in cold water, the Brazilian explaining that cold water on the face after getting out of a warm bed was dangerous to the health.

We took dinner tonight with Mr. McKenzie, manager of the Light and Power Company of Rio, a Canadian, and a very nice fellow. He had in his house many old ornaments that once belonged to the ex-emperor. It seems that after the emperor was dethroned, his bric-a-brac and furniture, etc., were sold at auction.

There are many fine old residences in Rio, surrounded by beautiful tropical gardens. They are usually massive square buildings of attractive architecture and with a great air of comfort. Sometimes they are elaborately decorated in different bright colors, especially blue, pink, buff, etc., and sometimes figures of persons are painted on them or small statues stowed away in little recesses.

Rio is well supplied with electric lines and some horse lines, but the main ones are electric and are very well operated. It is told that in the early days of the street car lines, it was hard to sell the bonds to build them, and they were hawked about everywhere. So common did they become that the name "bond" was given to the cars, and even today, when a man takes a car, he says he is going to go on board a "bond."

The number of drug stores in Rio is tremendous. They all seem to be prosperous and do not speak well of the much boasted health of the city. Along some streets they are as frequent as saloons in a Colorado mining camp. Their frequency may in part be due to the great sale of perfume and powder to both women and men. Everyone seems to use perfume, and the men are as strong of it as the women. The whole town smells of it. Abbe Huc says all China smells of musk; so also all Rio smells of perfume. It is remarkable how perfume on a man or a homely woman seems very offensive, but on a good-looking woman the same perfume is often attractive. I have often observed this fact, but could never entirely understand it. Almost every woman in the streets in Rio is also heavily covered with powder. I should think that the powder and perfume business in Rio would be a very profitable one. Most Brazilians have a dash of the tar brush in them and perhaps they wish to cover this up with white powder.

Perfume and powder, however, are not confined to Brazil. In Chile it is the same, and in Argentina and Uruguay it is not far different. In Chile the women put on powder like plaster.

In Rio, as in many other South American towns, lottery tickets are sold everywhere, though I believe lotteries are forbidden by law. Here is another case of South Americans making good laws but never enforcing them.

Letter from Dick, dated Rio de Janeiro, Brazil, August 1, 1907

I wrote to you a few days ago from on board ship, and mailed the letter at Santos, in southern Brazil. From there we came on here to Rio Janeiro, where we found Branner waiting for us. I also received a lot of mail here that had been forwarded to me, and among it I was very glad to find your three letters of May 28th, June 18th, and July 1st. It was a great pleasure to me to hear from you again, and especially to know that you are well, and had had such a good trip to Capon, and that you are now comfortably settled for the summer at Seal Harbor.

Means, Branner and I, together with a man named O. A. Derby, an American, who is at present the head of the Brazilian government geological survey, start for the interior of Brazil tomorrow morning, for a trip of a couple of weeks or so. I have known Derby for many years, and as he and Branner know Brazil well and speak Portuguese, I think we are going to have a very interesting trip. We are working hard tonight getting our outfit ready to start at 5 o'clock in the morning. I may not have much chance to mail letters in the interior, so I may not be able to write again for a couple of weeks or so, but if not, I will write as soon as we get back here again.

The bay of Rio Janeiro and the surrounding country are certainly one of the most beautiful regions I have ever seen. The only other place that I know of as equalling it in natural beauty, is the island of Ceylon in the Indian Ocean. When to this is added perfect weather, neither hot nor cold, it makes a combination that is hard to beat. I will write more fully later on.

I hope you and Aunt Lyd will have a good summer at Seal Harbor. If Mr. Barr is there I hope you will give him my regards.

From the Diary

August 2—We started today from Rio for the north, to visit some of the mining regions of the state of Minas Geraes. We began with an accident. The carriage horses, waiting at the hotel for us to take us to the station for the 5 a.m. train, ran off, dashed into an iron fence surrounding a fine residence near the hotel, broke the fence and raised the devil generally. The driver was arrested, and it took so much time to get the policeman to release him long enough to drive us to the station, that we missed our train and had to take a later one. Derby also lost his umbrella, map, and his "batea." We certainly did not begin the trip well, but may end it better.

Our route took us north over the mountains back of Rio and down into the valley of the Parahuila River; thence across another divide and down on to the headwaters of the San Francisco River. At about 9 p.m. we reached our first stopping place, Queluz, a small town, also known as Lafayette, a name given by the railway authorities to this place to distinguish it from another place called Queluz farther south But the real name is Queluz and the people call it that. We came here from Rio via Barra, Entre Rios, and Barbacena, all small interior towns.

The country passed through is a high rolling region, partly open and partly forest covered, rising from 2000 to 3000 feet, and in places more, above the sea. For many miles north of Rio the country was once a great coffee-producing region, but coffee seems to be so much more cheaply raised in Sao Paulo that the plantations have been almost entirely abandoned. A coffee tree is productive for 30 or 40 years, and then seems to die a natural death. A coffee tree, if abandoned, does not reproduce itself by the dropping of the beans in the soil, and an old plantation dies out without leaving new saplings.

The chief products of Brazil are coffee, rubber, lumber, and a few smaller things. They import wheat and flour, and most of their meats, etc., all of which they could probably raise themselves were they not too "tired."

A very noticeable feature of the country traversed today was the "fences." These are not fences of wood, wire or stone, but they are trenches, some 6 to 8 feet deep, dug in the ground, and everywhere the hillsides are marked by deep cuts defining the boundaries of different people's land.

This town of Queluz is about 300 miles, as we have come, from Rio. We are stopping at the "chief" hotel, a small frame shack called "Hotel Thuller". The food seems fair, but the rooms are very dirty.

Coming up on the train we stopped once for lunch, or breakfast, as they call it here, and once for another meal about 4 p.m. Both meals were plain but very good, and only 20 minutes was allowed to eat them Then the train started An article of food which was new to me was "farina." This looks like white corn meal, but is made from some root, a tuber, which is dried, ground up, and then partially roasted. It is used as a substitute for bread by the poorer people and was once used by everyone. They sprinkle it on the top of various dishes, especially beans. It is very good and one becomes attached to it. They also have some very good native vegetables which were new to me, among others "chu chu," which is a kind of squash.

All along the road we noticed many ant hills, some six or seven feet high. They are hard and indurated and stand up often like towers. Branner says these are made by the white ant, which eats earth and passes it out as excrement from which the ant hills are built. This accounts for the cemented condition of the ant hills, as if the earth were mixed with a sort of glue to hold it together. It is on account of this cemented condition that the ant hills stand up abruptly, instead of sloping off gradually, as other ant hills. The common ant hill of loose earth is also seen in many places here, but is less conspicuous and less high than the other. They are built by the black ants. The white ant hills are generally in groups of several or many to the acre, and look like stacks of corn or wheat on an open hillside. Sometimes, though rarely, they are isolated.

August 3—We visited the manganese mines some 5 or 6 miles east of Queluz, returning to Queluz tonight. The weather has been perfect ever since we left Rio, neither hot nor cold, and clear.

August 4—Visited the manganese mines northwest of Queluz and returned again tonight. Have been all day on horseback.

August 5—Started at 7 a.m. from Queluz for Miguel Bernier, on the railway, about 20 miles north. Here was once an iron foundry started by a man named Wigg. It is now closed, but Wigg has a big manganese mine about 3 miles east of Miguel Bernier, on the railway running from the latter place to Ouro Preto, and this mine we visited today. We were most cordially treated and given a very elaborate lunch, which really consumed much of the time that we should have been examining the mine. Branner and Derby met some of their old friends here, and Means and I were treated correspondingly well. It is a ludicrous sight to see a big man like Branner locked in the embrace of a little Brazilian man and patting each other on the back, which is the customary method of salutation.

We slept at Miguel Bernier tonight in one of the old houses of the Wigg foundry, but before going to bed we were given a very elaborate dinner by Sr. Dr. de Campos, at the local inn, a little board shanty, looking dingy and dirty, but which produced an excellent meal, soup, fish, eggs, steak, turkey, chicken, rice pudding, etc , etc. The Brazilians, like the Chileans, seem to be great people for meat. We washed the dinner down with beer. They make an excellent light beer in Brazil. We also had some native rum made from sugar cane, which was not bad. This is the national drink, just as rye whisky is our national drink.

August 6—We went by train for about 40 miles north of Miguel Bernier to Honorio Bicalho. Here we took to mules and rode some five miles west to Villa Nova da Lima, where is situated the famous and very old gold mine of Morro Velho, owned by the St. John del Rei Mining Company. Here we were very politely entertained by Mr. Chalmers, the manager of the mine, and a friend of Derby. It is a high rolling country here and there is evidence of much old mining. Chalmers is a great fancier of dogs and animals and has a regular little zoological garden of Brazilian animals.

August 7—At Morro Velho. Raining all day.

August 8—Derby and I started on mules today from Morro Velho to the Rio de Peixe, about 20 miles over a very rough but very interesting country. Branner is sick with diarrhea and Means has a bad cold, so they have both gone on to Ouro Preto by train and we will meet them there in a few days. Derby and I have had a very interesting ride through a high rolling country, with the peaks of Itabira and Itacolumy rising up prominently in the distant landscape.

On the Rio de Peixe the St. John del Rey Mining Company have an electric power station, from which they carry power to Morro Velho to work their machinery. We will stay tonight at the company's house here. The Rio de Peixe at this spot runs through a beautiful rocky canon, as a roaring torrent.

August 9—We left Rio de Peixe early today for Itabira Peak, some 8 or 9 miles away, to see the iron ore there. We are still travelling by muleback and using the same animals that we used coming from Morro Velho. They were lent to us by Chalmers. We also have a pack mule and two servents accompanying us on mules. The man who drives the pack mule walks. Sr. Dr. de Campos has been with us from Morro Velho.

We examined the iron peak of Itabira and then started eastward out of the mountains and down into the valley of the Rio das Velhao or "River of the Old Women." Just about dark we arrived at Esperanca, on the Central Railway of Brazil. Here there is a small iron furnace, the owner of which received us very politely and has put us up for the night at his house, where we now are. He gave us a very good dinner. He is married and has two children, and all the family were very gracious and polite, which we appreciated, as we were dirty and dusty and hungry.

August 10—We disbanded our mule outfit at Esperanca, and Derby and I started this morning by train for Ouro Preto. De Campos came with us as far as Miguel Bernier. Branner and Means met us at the station at Ouro Preto and took us up to the hotel Martinelli, the only stopping place in the town, of any account, and itself as filthy a hole as I have ever stopped in. Branner and Means both seem to be all right again.

In the afternoon we took mules and rode out to the Passagau gold mine, about six miles distant, where we were treated very politely by the manager, Mr. Bensusan. We returned to Ouro Preto tonight. The town is a quaint old place, founded about 1695 and then known as Villa Rica de Ouro Preto.* It was once the center of an active placer gold mining industry. Now the mines are mostly exhausted and only a few old negroes still wash a little gold. But the old workings, now overgrown with bush and forest, attest to a once great industry. The soft clay of the region is excavated in many places which were once the abode of the slaves that worked in the mines. Thousands of negroes in the early days were crowded into small ships and rushed over to the coast of Brazil, where they were driven in herds up to Ouro Preto to work in the mines. Many died on the ships, many more on the road to the interior, and many in the mines. The old "slave road" ran up from Petropolis to Ouro Preto and it is still used but not so much as formerly, on account of the now existing railway. Near Ouro Preto it is partly grown up in forest, but the old holes in the ground, in which the slaves lived, and in which the bones of many of them still lie, are yet to be seen. It is said that more tragedies have occurred along this route than on any highway in South America, and that is saying a good deal. The people still associate al-

---

* Ouro Preto means black gold.

most every mile of it with some awful tragedy, and the cruelty and barbarity with which the slaves were treated is still ripe in people's minds, though it was several generations ago. Along the same road, slaves were also driven from Petropolis, through Ouro Preto, and up to Diamantina to work in the gold and diamond mines there.

The white people (Portuguese) imported the slaves and ill treated them, but the negro has finally conquered the white man, not by force, but by amalgamation. They have bred in so much with the whites, not only at Ouro Preto, but all over Brazil, to such an extent that the Brazilians of today are largely a race of mulattoes. The "tar brush" has extended throughout the land and almost everyone seen seems to have negro blood. Others have Indian blood, as shown by their coarse straight black hair and their features; while still others have both negro and Indian blood. This is seen not only in the country but in the cities like Rio, Santos, Bahia, etc. It is rare to see Caucasian features or Caucasian color anywhere in Brazil. The negro has conquered the country by a peaceful process of breeding with the whites, and the mulatto and negro go everywhere and are received at hotels and restaurants on a social equality with any white people. Brazil is today as much a negro country as is Hayti or Santo Domingo, the only difference being that in the latter places the people on the average have a larger percentage of black blood in them than in Brazil, but it is only a difference of degree.

The only instance that I heard of in Brazil where a distinction is made between pure white and mulatto is by the Catholic Church, where no one with negro blood in him is allowed to become a priest. Perhaps, also, if a really black negro came to a first-class hotel in a large city, he might not be received very graciously, but if he is of a lighter color he is received without hesitation. The Brazilians have solved the negro problem by becoming negroes themselves.

The black blood in the Brazilians have given to the people a joyous, cheerful disposition, characteristic of the negro, and in great contrast with the moroseness of the Chileans. The Chileans have no negro blood in them, but they have Araucanian Indian blood to the same extent as the Brazilians have negro blood, and it is probably this that gives them their morose, fierce character, as well as their physical strength.

But to return to Ouro Preto. The town is a quaint old place with narrow streets paved with small stones and often very steep and slippery. In the central plaza is a statue of a martyr of Brazilian freedom called "Terre Dents," a dentist who in the early days preached rebellion so much that he was caught in Rio and drawn and quartered; and his head was sent up to Ouro Preto, where it was stuck on a pole in the same spot where now his statue stands. A later generation erected the statue to commemorate the champion of the freedom they now enjoy.

The old castle of the town is now the Escola da Minas de Ouro Preto, where a very creditable little mining school is located. We were treated very courteously by the president and some of the professors of the school, who were friends of Branner and Derby.

The hotel at Ouro Preto is one of the foulest I ever stayed at. The food is fairly good, as, in fact, it is everywhere that we have been in Brazil, but the whole house stinks and is filthy. If a man ever wants to be cured of being a prig, of being afraid of germs, and of a dislike to foul dirty sheets and blankets, he should take a trip in Brazil. He will be either killed or cured.

Off to the south of Ouro Preto, perhaps 40 or 50 miles, is a range of hills or mountains, the road over which was formerly known as "Deos Te Lelore" (Lord deliver you) pass, on account of the difficulty of the route.

August 11—We stayed at Ouro Preto last night, and left at 6 a.m. today by train for Rio de Janeiro, arriving there about 8 p.m.

August 12—In Rio It seems good to get back here again, though it is raining hard and the weather is thick and mucky. This is early spring in Brazil and the trees are beginning to blossom. Up in the country we saw peach trees just starting to blossom. I also saw a number of eucalyptus trees imported from Australia. This wonderful tree seems to grow everywhere that it is planted.

While we were up in Minas Geraes we saw a lot of the famously bad roads of Brazil. Many of them were once good roads in the times of the Colonies and the Empire, but now they are uncared for, washed out and generally absolutely impassable for wagons. Almost all the travel off the railway has to be done on muleback, and goods are transported in the same way, though sometimes ox teams, composed of 12 to 20 oxen drawing a two-wheeled cart, can pass along The wheels of the cart are made of solid wood, and never greased, so that the creaking and screeching of the wheels can be heard long distances away.

Some of the old roads were once paved even in the mountains. In crossing a range of hills from Morro Velho to Rio de Peixe such a road was seen. The road was once paved with stone slabs, which have now become so turned and twisted out of place by lack of care that they are worse than no paving. Here in Brazil, as in Chile, things seem to have degenerated since their so-called freedom was gained. They have used up the good things left them from the days when they were governed by kings and have not initiated any new ones themselves. This is true of their roads, mines, and many other institutions. It is a notorious fact that new mines in Minas Geraes have not been discovered for almost 200 years, and yet many must exist were the people not too "tired" to look for them.

With all their laziness, however, the Brazilians are a most courteous and hospitable people, and I have rarely been treated better in any country I have ever visited. Strangers passing on the road take off their hats to each other; the children of a household come up to a stranger to ask his blessing; no man is too busy to stop and talk with a stranger, or to go with him for hours or even days to show him some place he wants to visit; the best in the house is, in the opinion of the Brazilian, none too good for the stranger under his roof. When one has experienced such courtesy from the Brazilians, he cannot help but like them, though he may see their shortcomings in other respects. The impression left is that of a kindly, hospitable, gentle people, cheerful, merry, and lazy.

August 13—Derby took us today to call on President Pena, of Brazil, who treated us very cordially. He occupies a fine large square mansion between the Hotel Estrangeiros and the city, with beautiful gardens. In the room in which we were received were several bronze busts, among others those of George Washington and the Goddess of Liberty close beside each other. After we had been there a few moments, a small bare-footed negro boy brought a plate with a bottle of milk for the President, and we left. The President is a small man, probably 5 feet 3 or 4 inches, dark complexion, gray hair, genial manners, and a shrewd keen eye.

Letter from Dick, dated Rio de Janeiro, August 14, 1907

We have got back here from the interior, and I drop a line to you to mail by a steamer that sails for the north today. We have had a very fine trip through a most interesting part of the interior of Brazil, and have seen a great deal of the country. We will remain here at Rio Janeiro for a few days, and may then perhaps sail for Bahia in northern Brazil, but I will write more fully about our plans in a few days. I only drop this line to you now by today's steamer, so as to let you know that we have got back here all right.

From the Diary

August 15—In Rio. It has been raining most of the time since we got back from the country.
August 16—In Rio. Raining.
August 17—In Rio. Raining. The fashionable shopping street of Rio is known as Ouvidor, which is a small narrow thoroughfare about 20 feet wide, and so crowded that no wagons are allowed in it during the day. Since the grand Avenida Central was finished it has taken some of the fashionable stores from Ouvidor, but the latter still maintains its supremacy.
August 18—This is Sunday, and a beautiful clear day. Derby, Means and I went up to the top of Corcovado Peak, which is reached partly by electric street line and partly by a cog-wheel steam line to the top of the peak. A most grand and wonderful view is had from the summit. Words cannot describe it. The peak is something over 2000 feet high (about 2300 feet). We had a very good breakfast at 10.30 a.m. at a restaurant near the summit.
August 19—In Rio. Raining again.

Letter from Dick, dated Rio de Janeiro, August 20, 1907

I wrote to you a short letter a few days ago, on our return here from the interior of Brazil, and said that I would write more fully later. We had one of the most interesting trips I ever took. Our party consisted of Branner, Derby, Means and me. We started from here by train, and after reaching a small place in the interior called Queluz, we took to mules, and from then on travelled mostly by mule back. We covered altogether about 1000 miles and saw a great deal of country. Our route took us first across the range of mountains which borders the coast in this part of Brazil, and then down into the valley of the Parahiba River; thence across another divide and down on the headwaters of the San Francisco River, which is one of the largest streams of Brazil, and which empties into the Atlantic south of the Amazon.

The country we were in was a wild mountainous region, only sparsely inhabited, but known for over 200 years, on account of the gold and diamond mining of the old days. These industries have now mostly closed, but a few mines are left, and the ruins of former workings can still be dimly seen through the tropical foliage which is rapidly covering them.

The only town of any size that we stopped at was Ouro Preto, and this is now only a small place, though once it was a city of 50,000 people, and the center of the gold mining industry when Brazil was a colony of Portugal. It was founded about 1695 and was a great slave center, where slaves were driven up in herds from the coast and put to work in the mines. The old "slave road" still remains, and more tragedies are said to have occurred along that route than along any highway in South America. At present the road is not so much used as formerly, and is partly grown up in forests, but the old graves, some of them marked by crosses, which line the road, testify to things that happened there, and the traditions among the people associate every mile of it with some sort of tragedy.

The interior of Brazil is a difficult country to travel in unless one goes, as we did, with people who know the language and customs of the country, for not many strangers travel there and the methods of getting about are not easy. Most of the travelling, after leaving the railways, is done on mules. Most of the so-called roads are simply trails, impassable for wagons, and commerce is carried on with pack mules. The way a Brazilian mule can walk along the edge of a precipice, which makes the rider dizzy to look down, or can climb from rock to rock on the top of a mountain range is wonderful. It would make an Arizona jackrabbit envious.

We stopped at a number of native inns, and also stayed at some private houses on our trip, for in many places there were no inns; but wherever we went we were treated with the greatest courtesy and hospitality, and I never travelled among a more kindly people. The best in the house, in their opinion, is none too good for the stranger, and they seemed to take pleasure in assisting us in our journey in every way. The children of a household come up to a stranger to ask his blessing, and a man is never too busy to stop and talk to a stranger, or to go with him for hours, or even days, to help him see a place he wants to visit. One man went with us during a very hard day's travel, and then insisted on giving us a regular feast at a native inn, with many native dishes. All of the dishes tasted first rate, and we ate them, though we could not tell what many of them were made of. We washed them down with native wine, and a native rum made of sugar-cane. The next morning we bid him goodbye, and went on our way; but in a few days he appeared again, on a mule, and travelled two days with us, just to be sociable. That is a sort of courtesy that I have not observed outside of Brazil.

We have now visited all the places in South America that we started out to see last spring, and we will sail for the north tomorrow. We will stop at Bahia and at Pernambuco, in northern Brazil, on the coast, and will then sail for England, where we should arrive in the course of a month or so. Branner goes with us as far as Bahia, but will leave us there, as he will remain in that region to finish up some geological work that he is engaged in.

I will write again shortly.

From the Diary

August 20—We ordered some photographic views from a local photographer on August 12, and he has been promising them to us every day since then. They were views of the harbor, etc. Every day we have called for them, and every day he has had some excuse for not finishing them. Today we managed to get about half of them, and as we sail tomorrow for the north, we cancelled the rest of the order. This is just one instance of the everlasting procrastination of these people.

We dined tonight with Mr. Rodriguez, owner of the Journal do Commercio, the chief daily paper in Rio, and a very excellent paper, too. He was most cordial and gave us an excellent dinner. He is a rich man and has a very fine house, not far from our hotel, where he has collected many interesting things, pictures, wood carvings, etc. Back of his house is a beautiful garden, and looking over it can be seen what he called his two pets—i.e., Corcovado Peak and Tijuca Peak.

Rodriguez told a story of the French actor Coquelin, who is now in Rio. Coquelin wanted to start some sort of a lottery, but Rodriguez told him it was against the law of Brazil to operate any lottery. Thereupon, Coquelin went to the Minister of Interior and explained to him what he wanted to do. The minister assented, and said he would "wink" at it. Rodriguez told this as a great joke.

August 21—Means and I sailed today on the S. S. Oriba, of the P.S.N. Co., for Liverpool. We had to pay, in addition to our regular fare, a tax of 30 milreis each to be allowed to leave the country, and we had to have a special permit for our baggage taken away. This latter is done so as to prevent people exporting goods without paying the export tax. Branner has come with us and is going as far as Bahia, where he is doing some geological work. With him is his assistant, Sr. Dr. Alfredo Carvalho. The weather was beautiful as we left the harbor and went up the coast.

August 22—At sea. Got occasional glimpses of the coast, a low, rolling hilly country, covered with rich vegetation. Fine weather.

August 23—We reached Bahia this afternoon about 5 p.m., and here Branner and Carvalho left us. It has been raining hard in squalls ever since we got into Bahia Bay. Branner and Carvalho had the usual difficulties experienced at a South American port in landing, fighting with boatmen about rates, getting baggage examined, etc., etc. They do here as they do in Rio, examine small baggage on ship and big baggage on shore. Though the constitution of Brazil forbids inter-state tariff, yet it is still enforced by some of the states.

August 24—Means and I did not go ashore at Bahia as we only stayed in port a short time and it was raining hard. We sailed at 9.30 p.m. Today we are at sea. We have been having hard showers all day. Thermometer about 78° in cabin. We are in latitude about 14°S and it is beginning to feel tropical.

August 25—Sunday. We arrived at Pernambuco at 6 a.m., and left at 8.30 a.m., not having a chance to go on shore. The town is spread along a flat beach, much lower than Bahia, which runs from the beach up on to a terrace, probably about 200 feet high. The day has been wet and squally. There are only about 25 or 30 first-class passengers on this boat, and as it is a ship of 9500 tons, that number does not make much showing. They are mostly west coast people—Chileans and English from Chile. In the second-class there are forty survivors of a schooner wrecked near Cape Horn.

We had no Sunday service on board today, and were thus relieved of that form of religious persecution.

August 26—At sea. Still raining, but not so bad as yesterday. For a while yesterday after leaving Pernambuco we kept within sight of the low flat coast, but gradually we turned off eastward and Brazil faded from sight, not be seen again this trip.

August 27—At sea. Thermometer 80° in my cabin at 8 a.m. We crossed the equator last night about midnight. The weather has not been hot at all so far. I never crossed the tropics before in such cool weather. The thermometer has not been over 80° in my cabin at any time. The cool easterly trade winds have been blowing ever since we left Rio.

August 28—It rained last night, and is cool and pleasant today. Thermometer 78° in my cabin. This morning it cleared off bright and sunny with a west wind, a very unusual wind in this region of easterly trade winds. This afternoon it is raining again.

August 29—Raining most all day. Cleared off in evening. Reached St. Vincent about 10 p.m., and spent all night there, taking on coal. It was hot and the ship had to be closed up tight to keep out the coal dust, so that we have had a very noisy, hot, and disagreeable night. It is now about 5 a.m., on the 30th, and we are just sailing.

August 30—Sailed from St. Vincent about 5 a.m. Everyone a little tired and sleepy from bad weather last night. Fine weather—cooler in the morning, but hot later on.

August 31—At sea. Fine weather, though a little hot because we seem to be in a belt of absolute calm. Thermometer 82° in my cabin at 8 a.m., which is the hottest yet on this voyage. Towards evening a stiff north wind came up, causing a heavy sea and some pitching. Many passengers are seasick tonight.

Letter from Dick, dated "On Board Ship," South Atlantic Ocean, September 1, 1907

I wrote to you a long letter some days ago, just before we left Rio de Janeiro, and gave you an account of our trip in the interior of Brazil. Since then we have been making rapid progress in our journey.

From Rio de Janeiro we went to Bahia, in northern Brazil. Branner and a friend of his named Dr. Carvalho, came along with us that far, and remained there to do some geological work. Means and I continued on alone to Pernambuco, near Cape St. Rogue, on the eastern point of Brazil; and from there we left the shores of Brazil altogether, and are now on the way to Lisbon.

We crossed the equator last week in the middle of the South Atlantic Ocean, and are now in the northern hemisphere again. It was not at all hot coming through the tropics, as we had a good breeze most of the way, and many heavy showers, which kept things cooled off.

We are on a British ship called the "Oriba" and as we are having very favorable weather, it will come very close to making a record run from the Brazilian coast to Lisbon. I will mail this letter on the ship and it will be put ashore either in Lisbon or England, and forwarded thence to the U. S.

From Lisbon, Means and I will go by sea to Liverpool and thence to London. I will write further from there.

From the Diary

September 1—At sea Clear, cool and not so rough as last evening. North wind.
September 2—Same as yesterday.
September 3—Same weather. North winds. Much cooler. We reached Lisbon at about 8.30 p.m., too late to be received, so we will have to wait until tomorrow.
September 4—Took on some coal and a few passengers this morning, and sailed for Coruna at 11.30 a.m. Weather fine and clear. North wind.

I forgot to mention on September 1st that we passed through the Canary Islands that afternoon, passing on the east side of Palma Island, with its small town of Santa Cruz at the northeast corner. This is the same route that we took through the Canaries in S. S. Oriana in April.

September 5—Expected to reach Coruna at 10.30 a.m. today, but about 3 a.m. a dense fog came up and we have had to simply creep along, or float about without going at all, most all day. We are in the route of many steamers, and this is a dangerous neighborhood to be in a thick fog. We have been passing ships, or they have been passing us, all day—rarely in sight of each other on account of the thick fog, but nearby, as indicated by the fog whistles.

Towards evening the fog lifted and about 10.30 p.m. we anchored off Coruna. We will remain here tonight.

September 6—We sailed from Coruna for LaPalice—Rochelle at 7.15 a.m., after having landed several passengers and taken on about 60 more, most of the latter are going to America via Liverpool, as emigrants. The day is fine, clear and perfect, with a smooth sea, a rare thing in these waters of the Bay of Biscay.

September 7—Arrived at La Palice at 9 a.m. Landed a few passengers and took on a few others, sailing again at 10 a.m. The weather is fine, clear and warm; the sea smooth. During the afternoon we passed the French seaport of Brest, on the western point of France, and then turned to the northwest out of the Bay of Biscay and into the open ocean again.

The coast of France from La Palice to Brest is low and sandy, with occasional low rolling hills.

September 8—We passed the southwest corner of England about 9 a.m. and turned north up the coast of England and Wales. The sea is smooth, and a little fog prevails, but not enough to make us slow down.

September 9—Arrived in Liverpool early this a.m., landed and took the train for London. Went to Savoy Hotel, where I found a very comfortable room reserved for me in response to a cable that I had sent from Rochelle. It seems good to get into a clean hotel after all the filth of Brazil, for among the good features of that land, cleanliness, outside of Rio de Janeiro, cannot be numbered.

September 10—In London. Have seen several people I know and have ordered a number of books on South America that I wanted.

September 11–23—In London.

Letter from Dick, dated London, September 20, 1907

We have arrived here all right from Lisbon, and I have found your letters of July 8th and 23d, Aug. 5th and 15th, and Sept. 7th. I was very glad to get them, as it is always a great pleasure to get your letters; and it had been a long time since the date of your last letter than I received in Rio de Janeiro. I am very glad that you are having such a satisfactory summer at Seal Harbor and that you are so well. That climate surely seems to suit you well. I am also very glad to hear that Tal is all right again, and I hope that his present trip in the west will put him in better shape than ever. That must be a fine hunting region in Montana that Boies, Tal and Speck have found this summer, and I hope to go with them there on some future trip.

I wrote to you last at sea on the way from Rio to Lisbon and mailed the letter on the ship. We arrived at Lisbon all right, and from there, Means and I came on here by sea. We arrived here just five months from the time we started last spring. We have had a first rate trip throughout, with no difficulties and no hitches, and have seen all, and even more, than we had expected. We have covered about 30,000 miles of distance and have seen a large part of South America.

It was a strange sensation to get into a clean hotel when we got here; for South America, and especially Chile and Brazil and the boats on the coast, are none too clean. If you ever want to cure a man of being a prig, or of being too particular about dirt, germs, etc., you ought to send him to Brazil. He will find that people live and grow fat there in a filth greater than he ever dreamed existed.

I note what you say about keeping Means in my employ as a secretary. I had at one time thought of the same thing, but he is not cut out for a secretary, and though I think he might accept the position, yet I do not think he would be long contented with it, so I have not suggested it to him. Moreover, he has a business as a consulting engineer here, which, though not big, is yet sufficient to enable him to be independent. He is a first rate man on a trip, and I would be very glad to take him along another time; and I think he would be glad to go. We got along on our South American trip first rate, and never had a dispute of any kind.

I think I will go over to Paris this week for a while before coming home. There are several fellows whom I know there just now, and one of them is interested in some iron mines in the northern part of France, which he has often asked me to visit with him. I may go there and may also take a trip up into some of the mining regions of Belgium. Speck writes me that he and Julie* are coming to Europe in October, and has suggested that I join them for a short trip in Ger-

---

* Mrs. Spencer Penrose.

many. He says that they are going to stay only a very short time and are then going to return home. I would like very much to do this; but have not yet decided definitely about it. If I should wait for Speck, I would probably get home the latter part of November, and if I should not wait, I would probably get home the end of October or early in November. I know of no special reason to hurry home, but I do not want to stay away too long.

I will write further shortly. In the meantime my address will be as usual care of J. S. Morgan & Co., 22 Old Broad St., London, England, as they will forward mail to me.

From the Diary

September 24—Started for Paris on the 11 a.m. train, arriving about 7 p.m. Went to the Hotel Meurice, an old hotel recently renovated. I found a very good room reserved for me in response to a telegram I had sent from London. It has a good bathroom and all modern improvements. This hotel is about the best I have ever seen in Paris.

September 25–October 29—In Paris.

Letter from Dick, dated Paris, October 7, 1907

I wrote to you last the latter part of September, on my arrival in London from Brazil. When I came here to Paris, I learned for the first time of Tal's accident with a bear in the west, and I was terribly sorry to hear of it. I knew nothing about it until I arrived here, and then I heard of it from several people. I did not know where Tal was, so I cabled to Speck to find out how Tal was getting along, and I was told that he had been very badly hurt. I was greatly relieved to get Speck's reply by cable saying that he was getting all right. I hope he is entirely well again now, and that he will have no serious trouble with his wounds. From what I have heard, it was about as narrow an escape as ever I heard of a man having.

It has been raining most of the time I have been here, but today it seems to be clearing and there is a prospect of better weather. There are a number of people here that I know both from Phila and from the west, so I have not been short of people to go about with. I expect to make a short trip to Belgium when the rain stops. After that I will return here, and go from here to London and thence home. Speck writes me that he is not coming over here in October as he had intended, so I think I will come home a little sooner than I had expected, and will probably get there early in November. I have not yet decided just what boat I will take, but will write to you before I start and let you know.

I am staying here at the Hotel Meurice, which is an old hotel that has been recently renovated, and is about the best place I ever struck in Paris. It is on the Rue de Rivoli, facing the Tuileries Gardens.

I hope you will get back safely from Seal Harbor, and that you will find everything all right in Phila. My address will be care of J. S. Morgan & Co., 22 Old Broad St., London, England, until I return home.

Letter from Dick, dated Paris, October 28, 1907

I have just received your letter of Oct. 16th and am very glad to know that you have gotten back safely to Phila, and that you find everything all right there. I am also very glad to know that Tal is getting all right. He surely had a miraculous escape. I hope he will not have any lasting bad effects from his wounds. When I think how much worse the accident might have been, I think Tal is to be congratulated on having gotten off without worse results.

I note what you say about remaining in Europe, and I have certainly had a very pleasant time since I have been here, but as I have nothing whatever to keep me here longer, I think I will come home the latter part of November. I do not know any place where time seems to pass so fast as in Paris, and at the same time always pleasantly, but as I have been here several weeks, I think I might as well be moving along.

I am going to London with Paul Stewart in a few days, and I may sail from there for home sometime in November, or I may return here and sail from Cherbourg with Dr. Keely of Phila, who arrived here a few days ago, and is going home in November. Whichever route I take, I expect to sail sometime in the latter part of November, and I will write later on and let you know what boat I will take.

Some days ago I took an automobile trip up to the northern part of France with Paul Stewart and two other fellows, and we had a very good time, and saw some interesting ancient Roman iron workings. I had intended to go also to Belgium, but it has been raining so much that I have not done so.

I will write again in a few days, and let you know definitely when I will sail for home.

From the Diary

October 30—Left Paris at noon today for London with Paul Stewart, and arrived in London about 7.20 p.m. We had a very rough crossing, and I was very seasick, the first time on an ocean steamer for some years.

October 31-November 14—In London. Weather mostly fine—a very rare thing this time of year. Bought many books that have been wanting for years and sent them home by U. S. Express.

Letter from Dick, dated Savoy Hotel, London, November 9, 1907

I have about decided to sail for New York next week. Dr. Keely and some other people that I know are going to sail on the Kaiserin Augusta Victoria of the Hamburg-American line on Nov. 15th. It is not a fast boat, but it is new, large and very comfortable, and if I can get a good stateroom on it, I will probably go on this ship so as to have company. Today is Saturday, and I cannot find out until Monday if I can get a good stateroom, but if I cannot, I will anyhow sail on some boat next week, as there are several very good ones going to New York at that time. I will cable to you before I sail as to what boat I will take.

I have seriously considered your advice to stay here longer, but as I have done all I set out to do on this trip, and as I have nothing especially to keep me here longer, I think I might as well come home, even if I should come back again when Speck comes in the winter.

I have been busy here for the last few days getting a lot of books, especially on South America, which I have been trying to get for several years, but which I could not get because most of them were out of print. It is wonderful the facilities a man finds here for getting books that are hard to get elsewhere.

Letter from Dick, dated London, November 12, 1907

I have definitely decided to sail for home on the steamer Kaiserin Augusta Victoria, of the Hamburg-American Line, which leaves Southampton on Nov. 15th, and is due to arrive in New York on Nov. 23d. Dr. Keely of Phila is going to sail on the same boat. It is not very fast, but is one of the best ships afloat, and has all the newest equipments.

I drop this line to you now because there is a mail leaving for the United States tomorrow. I do not write more in full, as I will see you in a very few days after you get this letter.

From the Diary

November 15—Sailed from Southampton for New York on the Hamburg-American Line steamer, Kaiserin Augusta Victoria, an immense boat of 25,000 tons, about two thirds full of passengers. It was a clear day at Southampton, the first one I have ever seen in the many times I have sailed from that port. We had to go out to the ship on a tender, which is not as comfortable as going on board from the dock. The boat has the regular dining room, a "Ritz Hotel Restaurant," a "Vienna Cafe," and a large smoking room; also a gymnasium and practically everything that one could want. It is not a fast ship, its time to New York being $7\frac{1}{2}$ to 8 days.

Dr. R. N. Keely got on board at Cherbourg, where we arrived about 8 p.m., and then the ship turned west in a beautiful clear moonlit night, headed for home.

November 16—Clear day—rolling sea. Many seasick.

November 17—Cloudy; rough sea; heavy storm from southwest. Ship slowed down; most of the passengers seasick.

November 18—Cloudy and rough sea, but not so bad as yesterday.

November 19—Fine clear beautiful sunny day; smooth sea, and everyone feeling good. I forget to mention that yesterday the great new Cunard ship, the largest steamer in the world, 32,000 tons, on her maiden voyage to New York, caught up with us and passed us. Her name is the Mauretania. Today we caught up with and passed the North German Lloyd steamer Barbarossa and the Atlantic Transport Company's steamer Minnehaha.

November 20–22—Same fine clear weather and smooth seas.

And thus another expedition was over with Penrose's landing in New York.

From this South American trip came two papers—"The gold regions of the Strait of Magellan and Tierra del Fuego" and "The nitrate deposits of Chile"—both of them published in the *Journal of Geology*, the first in 1908 and the second in 1910. In his list of subjects to be discussed, Penrose noted these and five other titles—"Where Two Oceans Meet," "The Falkland Islands," "The Tarapaca Desert," "Valparaiso after the Earthquake," and "Islands that America has lost." On a separate sheet, under the last-named title, he had listed: "St. Thomas—bought in 1867 (*see* Fiske); Falklands; islands in South Pacific; almost lost Hawaii; Isle of Pines; Fanning Islands." A sheaf of notes shows that he intended to pursue the subject further, but apparently he never did.

He did, however, prepare a manuscript covering his first-named topic, as follows:

WHERE TWO OCEANS MEET

The Pacific coast of North and South America, including Central America, is comprised in a great mountain zone known as the Cordillera. This name is a comprehensive term applied to the several mountain ranges which occupy the western parts of the two continents, including the Rocky Mountains and the ranges lying to the west in the United States and Canada, the Sierra Madra of Mexico, with its southerly extension into Central America, and the great Andes range of South America.

The Cordillera in its western part forms a great barrier along the Pacific coast from Alaska to Cape Horn, terminating on the north in the Arctic Ocean and on the south in the Antarctic. The length of this great range is some ten thousand miles, or over a third of the circumference of the globe, and its general course varies from northwest and southeast to north and south, with local variations in other directions.

In former geological times this barrier was cut through perhaps in several places by arms of the sea, which connected the Pacific and Atlantic; but at the present time it presents an unbroken wall from its northern extremity to Cape Froward in Patagonia, which is the most southerly point of the American mainland. At this point the sea, as if finally conquering the great barrier which has resisted its course through the larger part of two hemispheres, penetrates it from west to east, forming the Strait of Magellan. Still farther south, numerous other channels are found intersecting the land and forming many islands which constitute the archipeligo of Terra Del Fuego.

A few years before Columbus discovered America, the Portuguese explorer, Bartholomew Diaz, had discovered the southern end of Africa and had passed a short distance around what is now Cape of Good Hope. Some ten years later, Vasco de Gama went still farther on the same route and finally reached India. He was the first European, at least so far as we have definite records, to reach India by way of South Africa. Subsequently, however, many other voyagers, especially the Portuguese, passed that way, and the latter rapidly spread their influence and acquired territory in the far east. Among the most notable of the Portuguese explorers in these regions was Fernao de Magalhaes, better known among English-speaking people as Ferdinand Magellan, who by his knowledge of navigation and his untiring energy and bravery performed very great services for his country.

The Portuguese soon began to reap great profit from their trade with the

Orient, and it was not long before Spain and the rest of Europe began to realize this. The route via Cape of Good Hope was long and fraught with many dangers, and many navigators believed that shorter and safer route might be obtained by going westward rather than eastward. They supposed that the intervening space was all open ocean, and they did not know that the vast land areas of the Americas intervened between Europe and the Indies. Even when America was discovered, it was believed to be Asia, and Columbus died in this belief.

When, however, it became apparent that the newly discovered shores were not Asia, but a great new continent which hindered ships from sailing to the latter country [continent], efforts were early directed to finding a way to overcome the difficulty. The people of Europe in their avarice, at that time, hungered for the gold and ivory and spices of the East. It was not until somewhat later that the great scramble for territories in America began; America just then barred their way to the oriental treasures and they must get around it or through it; hence, the voyages of Hudson and others to find a northwest passage, and, hence, Magellan's voyage to find a southwest passage. But none of the early navigators had any conception of the enormous extent of the barrier that blocked their way to their eldorado. Both the northwest passage and the southwest passage were eventually discovered, but the former has proved too dangerous and too far north, and the latter too far south, if not also too dangerous, to offer any advantages over the old eastward route.

So rapidly did exploration go on in the almost frantic rush for a westward passage to the East, that in less than twenty-five years from the time of Columbus' first voyage, a large part of the coast of North America, and the whole of the coast of Central and South America, from the Gulf of Mexico to Patagonia, had become known; and yet no passage had been discovered. The idea was beginning to arise in the minds of many European navigators that there was no passage through the Americas, and that the land extended in an unbroken barrier from the frozen oceans of the north to the unknown and mysterious seas of the Antarctic regions. Some map-makers had, to be sure, shown channels at both the north and the south ends, but these were largely, if not wholly, imaginary. No definite knowledge of a passage existed. So strong had this impression become that in 1534, Charles the Fifth of Spain ordered an investigation into the possibility of cutting a canal through the Isthmus of Panama, that region having already become known as the narrowest part of the American continent.*

There were a few, however, who still believed that a natural passage could be found, and among these was Magellan. He had made a number of voyages to the Orient by way of Cape of Good Hope, and knowing the difficulties of this route he fully realized the advantages that suitable westward route would offer. He believed that he could find a southwest passage through America, though it is not clear whether he had some definite data on which to base this idea, or whether he believed simply that the American coast had not yet been sufficiently explored

---

* As far as the author [Penrose] can learn, this was the first suggestion of a canal across Panama.

to say absolutely that there was no such passage, or whether, in his enthusiasm to find another route than that via Africa, his wish was father to the thought; but whatever were his reasons, his persistence in his belief brought upon him the ridicule of many skeptical people, and the King of Portugal, to whom he made frequent appeals for assistance to carry out his project, finally dismissed him in anger. Magellan, thereupon, went to Spain, became an adopted son of that country, was treated kindly by many interested in exploration, and finally secured the support of the King and others to make his efforts to find the long-sought passage. He was fitted out with five ships, almost three hundred men and ample stores, as well as large supplies of trinkets for trade with the natives.

Magellan's past history in the Orient had already stamped him as a man of great courage and determination, with a record for daring accomplishments which challenged the wonder of a nation and a generation in which these qualities were being exhibited with unusual frequency. It required a man of this character to make a voyage of the kind contemplated, for it was difficult to get a good class of sailors or officers to enlist in such an uncertain enterprise, and as was the case with most of the early explorers, many of the men that he did get were desperate villians, who had been pirates or other criminals, often with records that made it desirable for them to get out of sight for the good of themselves, their friends, and their country. Many a scoundrel, however, who had enlisted thinking that he and his associates could override Magellan after the fleet got underway, found the Commander was more than a match for them.

Magellan sailed from Spain on September 10th, 1519, and reaching the coast of Brazil in safety, began to pass southward, examining carefully all the indentations on the coast, in hopes of finding a passage westward, but they all proved to be bays or rivers. As he progressed farther and farther south along the coast of southern Brazil, past the mouth of the river La Plata and then down the coast of Patagonia, the weather became worse and worse, discontent among his men grew rapidly, and it was with the greatest difficulty that he prevented his officers and men from forcing him to turn back from what they considered a hopeless effort. At one time, four out of his five ships mutinied, but by prompt and daring action he suppressed the disturbance without the loss of a ship. A little later, however, one ship was wrecked in a storm. Finally, on October 21st, 1520, on passing a high sandy cliff, he found that the shore line turned abruptly westward. He had entered the mouth of the strait, and the high cliff marked the north side of its eastern entrance. The day being St. Ursula's day, and Magellan being a religious man, he named the point the Cape of the Eleven Thousand Virgins, a name now abbreviated to Cape Virgines in Spanish or Cape Virgins in English. Opposite this Point to the south, some twenty miles distant, was another prominant sandy cliff. Later on this proved to be the south side of the entrance to the strait.

As soon as Magellan rounded Cape Virgins, he seems to have believed that he had at last found the long-sought southwest passage, but his officers and crew, accustomed to many disappointments in following up the many other indentations in the coast farther north, all of which had so far proved to be false clues, refused to believe him, and it was not until he had passed through the strait and out into the open Pacific, that they became convinced. Even when he had gone half way through the strait, one of his largest ships, still skeptical and frightened by bad weather and the bleak country, disgracefully deserted and fled back to Spain.

Magellan seems to have believed that the region immediately to the south of the channel which he had discovered, was composed mostly of islands, for he saw numerous tide-water channels running into it, but it is doubtful whether he realized that he was so near the extreme southerly end of the archipelago and that only a couple of hundred miles of islands intervened between him and Cape Horn. At any rate, many geographers in Europe still maintained that the strait was only a narrow pass through America, and that to the south, the land still continued on in the great Antarctic Continent which was vaguely supposed to exist. Magellan, however, had started out to find a route, not to explore a continent, and having accomplished his great ambition, he did not explore farther south, but continued on westward. He probably realized, however, that the passage he had discovered was too far south to have any advantage over the route via Africa in reaching the Orient. Magellan passed out into the Pacific under two barren bleak peaks comprising what is known now as Cape Pilar, rising abruptly over one thousand feet above the men, like grim giants guarding this long-hidden channel. He had been thirty-eight days* in the strait and had passed through without accident. To-day a steamer can make the passage in a day, and a sailing boat in a few days, if it has good luck, but if it meets adverse weather, as much time may be required as Magellan took. Magellan's time, in view of the facts that it was the first passage through these dangerous waters, that he had no charts, that he spent much time in exploring side channels and hunting deserters, was really remarkable. He had the reputation of being one of the best navigators of his time, and probably nothing proves it better than this great achievement.

On emerging from the strait, Magellan decided to continue on to the Orient instead of turning back to Spain. As he passed northward, the weather became milder and the seas quieter, a condition that made such an impression on him and his crew, after the boisterous weather of the south, that he named the sea "the Pacific," and hence our present name for it. In those days, the means of determining latitude were accurate enough, but the means of determining longitude were almost valueless, and Magellan, like all the other early navigators, greatly underestimated the east and west distance from Europe to the Orient. He realized that he had already come a great distance westward in hunting the southwest passage, and he thought that he must already be near his goal. He little realized when he left the strait that he had covered less than half the distance from Europe to the Orient, and that over three long months must elapse before he would sight the first of the East Indies. His provisions ran out, scurvy decimated his crews, and it was in a pitiable condition that the little fleet staggered into a

* The Life of Ferdinand Magellan, F. H. H. Guillemard, 1890, p. 218.

tropical island which was probably what is now known as the island of Guam, in the Ladrone Islands. Soon afterward he discovered the southern islands of the Philippine group, and here, in a battle with the natives, the great explorer was killed, dying, as he had lived, in action to the finish.

In addition to having discovered the southwest passage, Magellan may justly be said to have been the first to circumnavigate the globe, for on previous voyages via Africa, he had travelled to the Moluccas, which are still farther east than the Philippines. His fleet, after his death, returned to Spain, without their commander, but proud in the great accomplishment of which he had been the leading spirit.

Though the Strait of Magellan was too far south to be desirable as a trade route to the East, yet it was followed by a number of the early explorers of the Pacific. Spain did her best to conceal from other nations the existence of the strait, for she did not want them to learn this route to her possessions in the Pacific. Spanish vessels, to be sure, not infrequently passed that way, but they were ordered to carry only Spanish sailors. So quiet was the knowledge kept for many years, that one Spanish writer even asserted that the strait had been lost. In 1578, however, in spite of this secrecy the English explorer Drake passed through the strait on his voyage around the world. At the western end of the strait a fierce storm drove him south and east to the neighborhood of Cape Horn before he could regain his headway and continue on across the Pacific; in fact, one of his ships was driven completely around the Horn and returned to England. Thus accidently another route between the Pacific and the Atlantic was discovered, but information gained under such strenuous circumstances could not be very definite and it was not until 1615 that Cape Horn was clearly established as the southernmost point of the Americas. In that year the Dutch explorers Lemaire and Schouten sailed through the channel that separates what is now known as Staten Island from the east coast of Terra del Fuego, thence around the Horn and thence to the Orient. They gave the name Cape Hoorn, abbreviated in English to Cape Horn, to what they recognized as the most southerly point of the continent. They made the mistake, however, of believing that Staten Island was a part of the great imaginary Antarctic Continent that Europe seemed to have so much trouble getting out of her mind, and that the channel, now known as the Strait of Lemaire, separating it from Terra del Fuego was only an arm of the sea through this great land area.

In the meantime, in 1584, Sarmiento de Gamboa had been sent out by Spain to found colonies in the Strait of Magellan for the protection of Spanish rights. Spain feared a repetition of the buccaneering exploits along the west coast of South America a few years before by Drake, who was characterized as "a man of low condition, but a skilful seaman and a valiant pirate." Sarmiento started one settlement called Nombre de Jesus near Cape Virgins, and another called San Felipe south of where Punta Arenas now stands. Both colonies ended disasterously and most of the settlers died of hunger and exposure.

The English explorer, Cavendish, found the sad remains of the San Felipe colony a few years after it was founded, and called the place Point Famine, a name which it still bears. Later came more English, Dutch, and even Portuguese expeditions, masquerading under the guise of "explorers," but in fact mostly bent on making piratical raids on the Spanish possessions on the west coast of South America and elsewhere in the Pacific.

After Sarmiento's effort at colonization, Spain made still other efforts to check the growing tide of travel around the continent and even sent out an expedition to study the feasibility of fortifying the route, but without success. None of those sent there, however, remained very long. They appear to have been content with taking a hasty glance and then returning home or proceeding westward. The stormy climate and the bleak inhospitable land offered them no inducement to remain long, and Sarmiento's effort at colonization was the only serious one attempted until modern times (1843) when the Chilean government founded Punta Arenas.

In the meantime the knowledge about the southern part of Tierra del Fuego and what lay still farther south, was of the vaguest possible nature, and remained so until 1826, when the British Government sent out an exploring expedition under King, and later on another under Fitzroy. The latter was accompanied by Charles Darwin, the naturalist, whose description of the regions has made the voyage of this ship, the Beagle, famous. These two expeditions cleared up most of the doubtful points in the geography of the region, and demonstrated that there was a wide sea and not simply a narrow channel between the south end of America and the Antarctic land. Still later, in 1842–1848, the United States exploring expedition under Captain Wilkes, threw more light on the seas bordering Tierra del Fuego and the Antarctic Continent. The voyages of King and Fitzroy, however, may be said to mark the first definite and concise information that was had of Tierra del Fuego, and their investigations are still the standard sources of information concerning it. The charts that they made are still the basis of all the charts used to-day by navigators in those waters, though minor details have been filled in from the results of a later French expedition and by other researches into the various local features of the region.

Even to-day, however, much of Tierra del Fuego and southern Patagonia is a veritable terra incognita. The various modern expeditions have prepared good charts of the strait and surrounding waters, with accurate measurements of the depth of water and other nautical data most valuable to the navigator. The out lines of the land areas have also been fairly accurately mapped and some of the mountains have been plotted and measured, but there are still vast areas almost unknown beyond their shore lines. The advent of the sheep raiser and the miner are rapidly giving us knowledge of some of these regions, but such information, though better than nothing, is necessarily vague. The Brunswick Peninsula, at the south end of Patagonia, covering an area of some 400 square miles, is, beyond its shores, almost a complete blank on the maps of to-day, and the same may be said of a large part of the main island of Tierra del Fuego and many of the smaller ones.

CHAPTER 16

T.C. Chamberlin and the University of Chicago

LATE in January, 1908, in company with his brother "Tal," who had retired from active practice in 1899, Penrose set out for a month's cruise in the Caribbean. As usual, he kept his father well posted concerning his movements. His first letter is dated "Am Bord des Dampfers Oceana den" Jan. 25, 1908, and reads:

"We are now passing down the harbor towards Sandy Hook, and I drop this line to you to mail with the pilot boat. Tal arrived in New York all right yesterday afternoon, and we came on board the ship shortly after nine this morning. The storm of yesterday has cleared off, and today the weather is fine, with a light southwest wind. This ship, the Oceana, seems very comfortable and our cabins are very good. The boat seems fairly well filled but not crowded. Neither Tal nor I have yet seen anyone we know on board.

"The first port at which we stop will be Kingston, in Jamaica, where we will arrive in about five days, and I will write further from there."

Letter from Dick to his father, dated "On Board S.S. Oceana," West Indies, Jan. 28, 08

I wrote to you the day we sailed from New York and mailed the letter with the pilot boat when it left us at Sandy Hook. Today is our fourth day out, and we are due to reach Jamaica tomorrow. We had rough weather for the first two days, and most of the people on board were very seasick. They were lying about all over the ship groaning and vomiting and wondering why they ever came on such a voyage. Yesterday the sea became much quieter, and today it is as smooth as a pond, and the people are wondering why they ever kicked on the voyage.

There are about 270 passengers on board, mostly Americans and a few Germans. The boat itself is very comfortable and an excellent sea boat. The grub is first class.

We came in sight of some of the Bahama Islands today, and will pass the Island of Hayti this evening. We will arrive at Kingston, Jamaica, tomorrow, and I will mail this letter there. We are both in good shape. Tal seems to like the trip, and I am very glad of it, as I was not sure how he would take to it. I wish you were with us, as I think you would like the voyage.

If you happen to see Boies any time soon, will you please ask him, if convenient, to have Tal and me put on the "courtesy" list when we arrive in New York on our return on February 22d. We will have nothing dutiable with us, but it will hasten our getting through the custom house. Please be careful to tell Boies that our boat is the *Oceana* of the Hamburg-American Line, and not the *Oceanic* of the White Star Line, with which our boat is often mixed up.

I will write further in a few days from some other port after leaving Jamaica.

Letter from Dick to his father, dated "On Board S.S. Oceana," Caribbean Sea, Jan. 31st, 1908

I wrote to you on January 28th from on board ship and mailed the letter at Kingston, Jamaica.

We remained at Kingston the better part of two days and saw a good deal of the town, or rather of what is left of it, and then of the surrounding country. I was interested in the effects of the earthquake at Kingston as compared with that at Valparaiso. At the latter place the earthquake was severe in spots and mild in spots, so that comparatively uninjured houses often stood in the midst of ruined districts. But at Kingston, almost the whole town was laid flat. Some rebuilding is going on, but it is slow. I doubt if Kingston, so long as Jamaica remains a British colony, will ever be what it was once, as it was originally the product of the prosperous days of Jamaica, before the abolition of slavery. Since the abolition, all Jamaica has retrograded industrially and commercially, so that Kingston at the time of the earthquake was probably a larger place than the business of the island warranted; and the Kingston that will be rebuilt will be in proportion to the requirements of its trade.

It would be well for the people of Kingston if they would build their town in another spot, for the last earthquake was not the only one that has occurred at that locality. Over 200 years ago, before Kingston was built, the town of Port Royal flourished near the same spot. It was ruined by an earthquake and partly submerged beneath the sea; and for many years afterwards the houses could be seen, through the clear water, at the bottom of the sea. Kingston was then built to replace Port Royal. Now Kingston has been destroyed and another Kingston is being built.

Both Kingston and Port Royal were on spots that are fatal in the earthquake country, that is, on soft sandy soil. It has been found in the recent earthquakes at San Francisco, Valparaiso and Kingston, as well as at other places, that the greatest damage was done in the parts of the towns built on loose ground, such as sand, gravel or clay, or on places that had been filled up with ashes and other refuse. The parts built on solid rock were much less injured and often not hurt at all. This is a different result than many people would expect, but it is the case.

We are today crossing the Caribbean Sea, going south. It is hot but not oppressive, as a good east breeze is blowing. We reach Colon, on the Isthmus of Panama, tomorrow. Thence Tal and I will go across the Isthmus to the city of Panama, on the Pacific Coast, so as to see the canal. From Panama we will return to Colon and continue on this same boat along the coast of Colombia and Venezuela. This boat stays long enough at all the ports to let us see all we want, so there is no inducement to wait over anywhere, and it is very satisfactory to stick to the same boat and to return with it to New York. As I said in my last letter, we will arrive in New York on Feb. 22d.

I will mail this letter in Colon, and will write again soon.

Letter from his father to Dick, dated "Tuesday, Feb. 4"

To insure this letter reaching you by Feb. 12, I write this morning. My next will be to Havana on Feb. 9.

I received your Pilot's letter and was rejoiced to know that you *started* with favorable weather and conditions. Later, Kate received a notice of your ship's arrival at Kingston, and, by now, must have also learned of your arrival at Colon. But I have not seen her since Sunday, so do not know.

I have missed you greatly, and days pass without my opening *my mouth* save to eat my meals, brush my teeth, and order Daniel to keep his furnace as [hot] as he can safely have it.

It has been very cold. Thermometer more or less about zero, just straight along. So I got my horse out of town in good time.

Kate was here on Sunday with the children. I gave her the directions for Porto Rico and Cuba, carefully written out with the dates for writing, etc., etc. So, I infer she has written to Tal to-day and sent him the newspapers as well. She and the children were fine on Sunday. Boies was up on Saturday and left on Sunday evening. I scarcely saw him. There seems to be nothing new at home—things just as when you left. Spencer sailed as he had planned on the 30th. I had a pilot letter from him. He said the boat was the finest and best he had ever been on. Up to now, no new thing about the Copper Co.—to-day stock at 27.

I am as well as usual, and take my daily walk, but without *enthusiasm*. I hope you are having a lovely time and look for your letters with much interest. Love to Tal. This letter is meant for both of you.

Letter from Dick to his father, dated "Coast of Venezuela, den" 5th Feb., 1908

I wrote to you last on Jan. 31st and mailed the letter at Panama. We crossed the Isthmus of Panama by railway along the line of the canal, and it was a very interesting trip. I have no doubt that the canal will eventually be built, but I do not think it will ever be completed in the 8 or 9 years that they have been figuring on.*

From the Isthmus at Colon, we sailed east along the coast of Colombia and Venezuela, to La Guaira, in the latter country, where we arrived yesterday morning. From there we went by train to Caracas, the capital of Venezuela, which is 21 miles from the coast at La Guaira and 3000 feet above the sea. The railway is one of the best pieces of engineering I ever saw. It passes through a very rough and mountainous region, and is built largely along the faces of steep precipices as it worms its way up from the coast to Caracas. It was built and is operated by an English corporation.

Caracas is a neat, clean, well-paved town of about 90,000 people, and has an

---

* Panama Canal opened to traffic August 15, 1914.

air of prosperity which is not noticeable in all South American towns. We got an excellent lunch at a restaurant there and returned to La Guaira in the afternoon.

Today about 10 a.m. we sailed for Porto Cabello, Venezuela, where we are due to arrive this afternoon. We had expected to stop at the Island of Trinidad after leaving the coast of Venezuela, but yellow fever has broken out there (at Trinidad), and if we stopped, we would be quarantined at other ports, so Trinidad has been cut out of our itinerary, and we go direct from Porto Cabello to Barbados and other West India Islands.

If I have a chance to mail this letter at Porto Cabello I will do so. If not, I will mail it at Barbados, where we will arrive in two or three days.

Letter from his father to Dick, dated "Sunday, Feb. 9th"

To-day is Feb. 9th, and I will write and mail this letter so as to be sure and meet you in Havana next week. I can hardly realize that you will be home again in two more weeks, and this is to be my last letter to you.

I received your Kingston letter a few days ago and was very much pleased that your trip up until then had been so successful. I may receive some of your other letters before Feb. 22, but up to now—Feb. 9th—only the Jamaica letter has reached me. Boies took your letter and said he would attend to your request about the customs-house men. I have only seen him for *half a minute*, but in that time had given him your message and letter, etc., etc.

There is nothing to tell you. "Happy the people whose records are tame and without incident"!!! The weather has been bitter cold straight along. We *all* keep well however and I am getting along satisfactorily. The thermometer this morning was 9°. I am able however to keep the house comfortable. Kate and the children were here for over an hour this morning. They were all splendid and all as rosy and fat and bright as possible. So Tal may feel very happy at this good report. Have heard nothing yet as to the copper allottment. Boies says "politics" are fine; he seems very busy. He goes to Pittsburg on Tuesday to some banquet. When you arrive in New York be sure to telegraph me, also state at what time you plan to arrive at home. Love to Tal.

Letter from Dick to his father, dated "Coast of Hayti, Feb. 13, '08"

We are today passing along the north coast of the Island of Hayti; and will reach Santiago, Cuba, tomorrow.

I wrote to you last on Feb. 5th and mailed the letter at Porto Cabello, Venezuela. From there we started north again, stopping at the British Island of Barbados, the French Island of Martinique, the Danish Island of St. Thomas, and the American Island of Porto Rico. All these places were very interesting, not only on account of their natural features, but also because of the different kinds of civilization represented by the different nationalities on the islands.

There is, I believe, more enterprise and hustle on the American Island of Porto Rico than in all the other islands we have so far visited put together. Some people may say that Americans do not know how to run colonies, but they are certainly producing more activity in the West Indies than the English, French, Dutch or Danish.

We had some difficulty in getting permission to land at Porto Rico, as the island was quarantined against boats coming from Venezuela, but after a good deal of talk and cabling to Washington, we got "shore leave", that is permission to go ashore for 24 hours. The port doctor knew Tal and lent him an automobile, on which we went for about 20 miles into the interior of the island, and saw a good deal of the country.

I will mail this letter at Santiago, Cuba, tomorrow. From there we go to Havana, then to Nassau, and then direct to New York, where we will arrive Feb. 22d. We are both well and have been having a first-rate trip. I think the trip has done Tal much good. His hand that was hurt by the bear last summer is much better.

The trip ended on February 22 as scheduled, and a telegram from Dick to his father on that date, sent from Hoboken, New Jersey, declared that they had "just landed. Will arrive before six this evening."

Not a hint is there in any of these letters of a possible romance, but Tal's son, writing of his uncle years later, says that the only "near love affair in which he was involved" as far as the family knew took place on this Caribbean trip. According to his nephew there was on board a "young widow" who was "very attractive and very much of a lady. Richard was quite smitten and the lady seemed willing to be serious, and my father was all for the match, but Richard refused to pop the question."

Tal's son may be right, but he also admits that Tal himself was very anxious for Richard to marry, so possibly in his anxiety he read more into Richard's attitude than was actually present. After all, he was always courteous and did everything he could to please others. Besides, on a cruise he could not pursue his usual course, excuse himself and leave the scene. In any event, he obviously did not care enough for the lady to change his way of life. He was then more than forty.

March and April of 1908 were spent in Philadelphia. In March he was elected a non-resident member of the Washington Academy of Sciences, of which Charles D. Walcott was at that time president.

Before leaving on his Caribbean cruise, Penrose had received word from I. Minis Hays, secretary of the American Philosophical Society, to the membership of which he had been elected in April, 1905, that on January 17th he had been "chosen a Councillor to fill the unexpired term of Prof. Ernest W. Brown, resigned." That same day he had also been chosen a member of the committee on publications of the Philosophical Society.

A few days later he received another communication from the secretary of the Society, thanking him for the gift of "a silver medal commemorative of Benjamin Franklin, designed by Dupre."

Already a member of the Committee on Hayden Memorial Award of the Academy of Natural Sciences of Philadelphia and a conscientious worker on the

Visiting Committee to the Department of Mining at Harvard, Penrose undoubtedly found his time well occupied with these duties in addition to his investment studies and his work as a member of the board of various commercial concerns.

From 1908 to 1910, he was also a member of the board of advisory engineers invited to inspect and advise about the holding up of the surface ground above the old coal mines under the city of Scranton, Pennsylvania.

In June (1908), he received a telegram from his old friend, Charles P. Perin, chief marshal for Harvard commencement of that year, asking him to act as marshal, but by that time he had left for the West (May 5th) on mining business which took him to New Mexico, California, Utah, and Colorado, and from which he did not return to the east until August 6. Not all his time was spent in business worries, however, for he found opportunity to visit Lower California, making the trip on board the yacht of C. L. Tutt, business partner of his brother Spencer, and sailing from San Diego.

Under date of November 17 (1908), George Otis Smith, director of the United States Geological Survey, wrote that "By the direction of the President, I have the honor to advise you that you have been designated by him a delegate-at-large to the American Mining Congress which meets at Pittsburgh, December 2–5 inclusive."

In December (1908) he sent in his resignation as a geologist with the United States Geological Survey, which was accepted by James E. Wilson, Assistant Secretary of the Department of the Interior, to take effect from and after November 30, 1908.

Undoubtedly, much of his spare time in 1908 was devoted to the careful research and preparation which he always felt it necessary to give to his writings. In his tribute to Penrose, J. Stanley-Brown, for forty years, editor of the *Bulletin of the Geological Society of America*, declared that "his manuscripts were composed with meticulous care and he welcomed any criticisms which would improve them. His esthetic sense was keen."

In the November–December (1908) issue of the *Journal of Geology* appeared his article on "The Gold Regions of the Strait of Magellan and Tierra del Fuego," with the accompanying notation by the author:

"During the year 1907 the writer twice visited the Strait of Magellan and had an opportunity to learn something of the gold-mining industry of that region. Other researches in South America prevented his making a special study of the deposits on which this industry has been built up, but it is hoped that the following general account of the occurrence and environment of the gold in this little-known region may be of some interest."

It was in 1908, also, when, according to his list of "Positions declined," he was approached by officers of the Girard Trust Company with the offer to suggest his name for the next vacancy which should occur on the board of directors of that institution.

Then in December of 1908 occurred the death of his father, counselor, and guide. This was the blow from which he never recovered.

In 1924, writing to one who had known his father and who, wishing to rent the house at Seal Harbor, had sent him a letter from that father, he said:

"I recognize in the letter of my father to you that same kind, broad and wise spirit which always characterized him in giving advice to younger men.... Regarding the cottage at Seal Harbor which you would like to occupy during the coming summer, I would say that I have in past years been lending it to a member of my family; but as you say, for the last two or three years it has not been occupied and has only occasionally been visited by me. I am looking forward however, to the time when I will either occupy it myself or perhaps some other member of my family may want to use it. If this does not occur shortly I think I may sell it, though I would do so with great reluctance on account of my memory of my father's association with it. Several people want to buy it, but I have not yet been able to bring myself to parting with it."

In 1925, under date of March 19, he wrote to William MacNaughton at Seal Harbor: "I was glad to receive your recent letter for it seems a long time since I have heard from you. I thank you greatly for your kind sympathy at the death of my brother Doctor Charles B. Penrose. It was a great shock to all of us, and even yet I can hardly realize what has happened.

"In reply to your inquiry as to whether I want things at 'Sea Bench' fixed up the same as in other seasons, I would say that of course I want it done and that I always count on your doing it for me. Whatever you do is always done well, and I feel that as long as you are looking after the place it is sure to be kept in the best of shape.

"I think I also owe you something for looking after the place at intervals during the winter, and I would be glad to hear from you as to what you think proper payment for this attention.

"I was sorry to hear that you again had bad luck in hunting last fall, but perhaps next fall will bring better things. It might be well to get a rabbit's foot and rub it on the barrel of that new gun so as to bring a little luck to it. In the old days this used to be a common custom, but I do not know whether or not it still exists at Seal Harbor.

Penrose sold the property in August, 1927 to Roscoe B. Jackson. According to John Stokes Adams, he had previously offered it to the Wistar Institute. "I think he keenly regretted the declination of his offer," Mr. Adams wrote (September 3, 1942). "I also think the Trustees of the Institute made a great mistake; had they accepted this property I am quite sure they would have received further benefactions."

Penrose's own statement of his movements for the next three years is laconic in the extreme: "In 1909, 1910, and 1911, went to Europe in the winter and went west in the summer."

His files for 1909 show an equal dearth of information. On January 25th he became a life member of the American Philosophical Society and on November 20th, Samuel Dickson wrote him that "at the annual meeting of the Wistar Association, held upon the 18th instant, you were unanimously elected a member of the Club."

Two letters to Herbert Hoover belong to this period.

Letter from Penrose to H. C. Hoover, C/o Professor J. C. Branner, Stanford University, California, Jan. 14, 1909

My dear Hoover:

I was away when your letter arrived here, and when I tried to hunt you up in New York on January 10, I was told at your Hotel that you had left. Professor Kemp tells me that he thinks you have gone to California, and that you are expected back shortly. I will probably be here in Philadelphia and in New York until the end of this month or the early part of February, and if you get around this way by that time, I would be very glad indeed to see you. I was very much disappointed in missing you in New York.

With best regards, I am,

Sincerely yours,
R. A. F. Penrose, Jr.

Letter from Penrose to H. C. Hoover, Esq., 62 London Wall, London, E. C., England, dated April 27, 1909

Dear Hoover:

I have to-day received a copy of your "Principles of Mining," which I suppose has been sent to me at your direction, and I thank you very much indeed for it. I became much interested in this work of yours when you allowed me to glance over the manuscript in New York some weeks ago, but I shall now read it carefully in print. I congratulate you most heartily on your thorough treatise of the subject. Your book is a most important addition to literature on mining, and will be useful, not only to the man interested in the practical development of mines, but also to those interested in financing them.

With best regards, and hoping you are well, I am,

Sincerely yours,
R. A. F. Penrose, Jr.

In 1909, also, he became a director of the Ridge Avenue Passenger Railway Company of Philadelphia.

His only publication of that year was an abstract which he had made of his paper, published late in 1908, concerning the gold region in the Strait of Magellan, for the *Mining and Scientific Press* of San Francisco.

The following year, however, he did somewhat better, publishing an article on "The Nitrate Deposits of Chile" in the *Journal of Geology*, "Memoir of Persifor Frazer" in the *Bulletin of the Geological Society of America*, and "Some Causes of Ore-shoots" in *Economic Geology*.

In April, 1910, he was in Paris, stopping at the Hotel Meurice, and of his summer in the west, he wrote on December 13 (1910) to Jackling:

"My dear Jack:

"I have sent you by registered mail some cigars, which I beg you will smoke with my best wishes for a Merry Christmas and a Happy New Year.

"It seems a long time since I have seen you. Do you never intend to come east again? I hope we will see you here before very long. I was west during the summer, and had intended to stop in at Salt Lake City to see you, but found that you had gone to Arizona, so I did not stop over there. I hope everything is going well with you, and that your mining propositions are prospering."

In August of 1910 he was a delegate to the Eleventh International Geological Congress, held in Stockholm, Sweden, where he represented the American Philosophical Society and The Academy of Natural Sciences of Philadelphia.

Since 1892, Penrose had been connected with the University of Chicago, although he had not given any lectures for years. In February, 1907, Harry Pratt Judson, then president of the University, had written to him:

"My dear Mr. Penrose:
"Your kind favor of the 25th inst. is received. I thank you very much for your good wishes. I am only sorry that in the last few years you have not been with us, and hope that the busy occupations of the capitalist and patron of industry may perhaps sometime so far lighten up that you may be able to revert to academic life at least for a short interval. Everything here seems promising as I am sure that your colleagues in the Department of Geology will tell you."

In December (1910), Penrose brought the entire matter of his continued position as a member of the University of Chicago faculty to a head in a letter addressed to Professor T. C. Chamberlin as head of the Department of Geology:

"Dear Professor Chamberlin:
"On my return from a couple of days absence, I have received your letter of December 17th, and I fully appreciate the desirability of your suggestions concerning the editorial staff of The Journal of Geology. The whole work of the Journal has from the beginning fallen on you and Professor Salisbury, perhaps in some cases not because the other editors were unwilling to do their share of the work, but because they were away most of the time, or, for other reasons, were unable to keep in touch with the work. I think, therefore, that it is highly desirable to do as you suggest, and to transfer to the list of associates those inactive editors whom you still wish to retain on the editorial staff, and thus make room for others who will be of more active service. I cannot see how any one could object to this change, and, in fact, I feel that any present editor who is not taking an active part in the work of editing the Journal, would be pleased to be put among the associate editors, as he would thus be relieved of occupying a position where he ought to do some active work, yet in which he was in fact doing nothing.

"In my own case, I have for years felt that I should not occupy a position of an active editor, when I do not do any of the work of getting out the Journal. Since 1896, I have done nothing for the Journal, except to write an occasional article, and I would feel much more comfortable if I was allowed to resign from a position on the active staff. Several times in recent years, I have suggested this to you, but you seemed to prefer not to make changes at those times. If now you will allow me to resign in favor of some one who can do more active work than present circumstances permit me to do, I will consider it a favor.

"While on this subject, I would like also to bring up the question of my connection with the University as Professor of Economic Geology. Since 1896, I have given no lectures, and however much I would like to resume this work, I can see no prospect of my being able to do so. In spite of my efforts to arrange business matters so that I could return to the University, I have found that year by year, it becomes more and more difficult to do so. Many business matters in which I have become interested in recent years seem to demand more and more of my time, instead of less and less, as I had hoped, and though I might be willing, so far as I personally am concerned, to make them subordinate to University work, yet out of consideration for those who are in these enterprises with me, I could not justify such action. As you know, I have on several occasions sent you my resignation as Professor of Economic Geology, but each time you have thought best not to accept it. Now, however, as it becomes every year more evident that I am not likely to be able to get back to University work, I will consider it a favor if you will accept my resignation.

"I shall always cherish among the pleasantest memories of my life the recollection of the years I was at the University and my association with you and the inspiration I derived from you. If it were possible for me to retain some nominal connection with the University, without being on the teaching staff, it would be a great pleasure to me, but I feel that I ought not to retain an active Professorship when I do not do the work of it. Whatever action you may take as regards my connection with the University or with the Journal of Geology, it is needless to say that my sympathies will always be with both of them, and I shall always be glad to do what I can to be of service to them."

Letter from Penrose to T. C. Chamberlin, dated January 12, 1911

Dear Professor Chamberlin:—

About three weeks ago I wrote to you in reply to your very kind letter of December 17th; and in the same letter I suggested incidentally the acceptance of my resignation as professor of Economic Geology at the University of Chicago, a resignation which I had sent you on several previous occasions to be accepted when convenient to you. As I have not yet heard from you in reply, and as I expect shortly to leave for an absence of some weeks and perhaps months, I thought I would write to you again about the matter.

If you decide to accept my resignation, do you not think it would be well for me to send a formal letter of resignation to President Judson, so that the matter may be properly recorded in his office? When Professor Judson was made President some years ago, I wrote to him a short note congratulating him, and he wrote back in a very friendly way, expressing the hope that I would return to the University. On account of this, and my very friendly relations with him when I was at the University, as well as on account of my own desire to have

Dick Penrose as a member of the University of Chicago faculty

Thomas Chrowder Chamberlin

my resignation properly recorded, I thought that it might be well for me to write to him, in case it is agreeable to you to accept my resignation. I would not, however, want to write to him unless you consider it entirely proper for me to do so.

If my resignation can be accepted at the present time as well as some time in the future, I think it might be well for it to be accepted now, but I do not want to insist on its being accepted at present if such action would in any way embarrass the Geological Department, or if you find it more convenient to postpone decision on the matter. I offer my resignation, as I have done on several previous occasions, because I feel that business matters will always prevent my coming back to the University; and I assure you that not only do I greatly regret having to give up my work there, but I also greatly regret the loss of the daily association with you, which I always greatly valued in the years I was at the University.

Letter from T. C. Chamberlin, to Penrose, dated Chicago, January 14, 1911

My dear Penrose:

Your letter of the 12th is at hand. You must set down my delay in action on your previous letter to my extreme reluctance to sever even my official relations with you. I am none the less compelled to realize that you are perfectly right, in view of the fact that business matters are likely to permanently prevent you from further work here. I appreciate more than I can tell you the pleasure and the benefit of your friendship and association with us and the gratification, stimulus and inspiration that your frequent calls have brought when longer stays were impracticable. However reluctantly I must yield on the main point, I shall not consent to your resignation from these frequent calls; you must keep these up anyhow.

I cannot urge any very substantial reasons for not yielding to your wish relative to resignation, other than the sentimental ones that are so strong. The work of the department is going on in fine shape, and you can at least join us in the satisfaction that you have helped us thru to a declared success. If it must be, I think you are quite right in feeling that it is best to close our official relations in a formal way that shall register our mutual regard and fill out the departmental and university records. I think President Judson would be pleased to have it done in this way.

And so, reluctant as I am, I concur in your good judgment and in your wish, and regretfully consent to the acceptance of your resignation.

I shall always be your debtor beyond what I can fully express for your association with us and for your personal friendship.

Letter from Penrose to T. C. Chamberlin, dated January 20, 1911

I have received your very kind letter of the 14th inst., and I find it hard to express adequately my deep appreciation of your very kind remarks relative to my resignation as Professor of Economic Geology at the University of Chicago. It has been with the deepest regret and reluctance that I have urged the acceptance of my resignation, and I did so only because I did not think it right to hold a professorship and not do the work of it. I hope, however, to have the pleasure of visiting you often at the University, and it will be a great privilege to me, when passing east and west, to look forward to a stop in Chicago to pay my respects to you.

I want to tell you again how greatly I appreciate all the encouragement and inspiration which I received from you during my years at the University, and this, together with all your kindness and consideration, I shall never forget.

He never did. In March, 1915, he went to Chicago, expressly for the purpose of attending the dedication of the new building in which the department of geology was to be housed.*

Letter from Rollin D. Salisbury to Penrose, dated Chicago, February 16, 1915

My dear Penrose:

We are planning to dedicate our new building on the 16th of March, and I am writing for Professor Chamberlin as well as myself to express the hope that you can be here at that time. It will be a very great pleasure to both of us and to all others in the Department if you can come. We should also be very glad if you are willing to say a few words on that occasion, but we shall not make this a condition of the invitation. Professor Chamberlin wants to have several of the Ph.D.'s of the University speak, and there may be the laying of the cornerstone of another building on the same day, so that we are obliged to keep our program rather short and all the speeches therefore will be very brief. If you feel like doing this we shall be delighted, but we shall be delighted to have you come without it.

I am planning to be away most of the time from now until the 16th of March, but I expect to be back for that date.

I have been very sorry to note from the papers that your brother, the Senator, is ill or has been. I hope his illness has not been so serious as the papers have indicated, and that it is now a thing of the past.

Very truly yours,
Rollin D. Salisbury

Letter from T. C. Chamberlin to Penrose, dated Chicago, February 26, 1915

Mr dear Penrose:

Professor Salisbury is off on his vacation and so it falls as a pleasure to me to tell you how delighted we are that you are to be with us at our Dedication. While we would dearly love to have you speak, we appreciate your feelings and will respect your wishes in that regard, so you may feel comfortable on that point.

Our building is certain to prove very satisfactory. In many respects it is beyond our best expectations. As we still regard you as one of the family, it will not be immodest to quote the statement of the business manager to the trustees

---

* Rosenwald Hall.

the other day to the effect that the University never put up a building on which the changes and extras were so small, nor one in which the adaptations to the purposes of the building were so complete.

Anticipating great pleasure in meeting you, I am,

Very truly yours,
T. C. Chamberlin

Come direct to the Hyde Park Hotel and be my guest while here. Mrs. C. and Rollin will be delighted to have a chance to chat with you.

C.

Letter from Harry Pratt Judson to Penrose, dated Chicago, March 19, 1915

My dear Mr. Penrose:—

I was extremely gratified at your kindness in coming all the way to Chicago for the dedication. It was an interesting occasion to us who have been so long connected with the work, and I hope that you found it worth while. It may not be a gracious return to you now to propose something else, and yet I think that you will be interested in it. We have a very good plaster cast of a bust of Professor Chamberlin made some years ago by Lorado Taft. It seems to me that it ought to be put in bronze. This can be done for $150. It occurred to me that the nicest way to have that handled would be not for it to be given by any one person but by a group of possibly half a dozen gentlemen, of whom I should be glad to be one, and I was wondering whether you would care to join. We would have it done next month, and put in some proper place in the Rosenwald Hall. I am sorry to miss your name from our faculty list.

Cordially yours,
Harry Pratt Judson

Letter from Harry Pratt Judson, to Penrose, dated Chicago, April 3, 1915

My dear Mr. Penrose:—

Thank you very much for your kind favor of the 26th of March with enclosed check for $25. I thought that six of us at $25 apiece would cover the ground, and thank you very much for your kindness in joining the group. No doubt the bust to which you refer is that of which you were one of the contributors. I think the plaster bust is very good, and that the bronze will be an excellent thing.

May I repeat what I have said before, that your visit to us was greatly appreciated by all, and I hope that you will always remember the University with which for so many years you were in one way or other connected.

With cordial regards and best wishes, I am,

Very truly yours,
Harry Pratt Judson

Letter from T. C. Chamberlin, to Penrose, dated Chicago, July 9, 1918

My dear Professor Penrose,

I want to thank you very sincerely for your kind words relative to the unveiling of my portrait. The kind expressions of intimate friends are among the most precious joys of life, and you have often warmed the cockles of my heart by your generous words. You will be glad to know that the portrait is very satisfactory to all friends here and that by some who are good judges of these things it is regarded as a rather unusual work of art. At any rate, it is much better than I had reason to expect, in view of the unpromising nature of the subject.

I hope you will not forget that it is always your habit to call when you are passing thru Chicago, if it is possible to do so. We have also gotten quite in the habit of expecting it, and it will be a sore disappointment if you do not give us the pleasure of seeing you as often as you can.

Very sincerely yours,
T. C. Chamberlin

Letter from Penrose to T. C. Chamberlin, dated Philadelphia, May 5, 1924

Dear Professor Chamberlin:—

I thank you greatly for the articles you have so kindly sent me on "A Venerable Climatic Fallacy," "Significant Ameliorations of Present Arctic Climates," and a review of "British (Terra Nova) Antarctic Expedition, 1910–1915. Glaciology. By C. S. Wright and R. E. Priestley."

I have read these papers with the greatest interest and profit, for I see in all of them the profound learning, the broad vision and the philosophical conception of the subject displayed by the master mind of the author. I feel that all geologists and especially those of us who are particularly interested in geoclimatic research owe a debt of gratitude to you for having so clearly discussed the subjects in question.

I hope that you are well and that everything is going satisfactorily at the University of Chicago. I admire greatly the high standard which you maintain in the Journal of Geology, and I look forward to beginning again before long to make contributions for your consideration. For two years past I have been so overwhelmed with work in trying to re-organize the activities of the Academy of Natural Sciences of Philadelphia that I have had but small chance to write, but I think I now see daylight through this task and I hope before long to have time to write up geologic notes which should have received my attention sooner.

With best regards to Mrs. Chamberlin and to Rollin, I am,

Sincerely yours,
R. A. F. Penrose, Jr.

Letter from T. C. Chamberlin to Penrose, dated Chicago, May 17, 1924

My dear Professor Penrose:

I want to express my appreciation of your very kind letter of May 5th. Your generous words do me a world of good.

I am sending you two additional papers, one in geo-climatic lines and one intended to sweep away a lot of fog regarding my view of the origin of the earth.

These and the ones I sent you recently belong to a series with a common purpose, viz.: to clear up outpost positions and to lay groundwork for the more systematic expositions of our revised Geology. The papers I send complete what I have felt was needful and I hope now to go ahead uninterruptedly with the rewriting of Volumes I, II, and III. It is a great task to rewrite the essentials of all these, but I hope to see it through. I am in better health than I was and hope to keep so till I get nearer to a reasonable stopping place.

We are delighted with the prospect that you will again be giving us of your very wide and fruitful observations.

You will be interested to know that the flood of matter for the Journal, diverted during the war and for a good while after, has again set in. But there will always be a place for you.

You will be grieved to learn that Mrs. Chamberlin passed away last summer after a short illness. I think you were away at the time.

Very truly yours,
T. C. Chamberlin

On November 21, 1924, Penrose again wrote to Chamberlin, saying that "in recent years I have been contributing five hundred dollars yearly to assist the Journal of Geology to publish its full eight numbers annually, and I am now again enclosing my check for five hundred dollars ($500.00) for a similar purpose in the issues of the Journal during 1925.

"I assure you that it gives me the greatest pleasure to make this small contribution, and I beg that you will accept it as a token of my admiration of the splendid standard being maintained by the Journal."

On December 17, 1924, Penrose again wrote, this time to R. T. Chamberlin:

Dear Rollin:

I thank you very much for your letter of December 15th relative to my contribution of $500 to the Journal of Geology. I assure you that it gave me the greatest pleasure to be of some little service in this way to a journal which is doing such remarkable work.

On the same day (December 17, 1924—which, incidentally, was his sixty-first birthday), Penrose wrote to T. C. Chamberlin:

"At a meeting of the Council and Executive Committee of The Society of Economic Geologists held on December 12th, the medal of that Society, which had been endowed for recognition of original research in the earth sciences, was unanimously awarded to you, and I am writing to you to tell you how greatly pleased I am that this action was taken.

"There is no one, either in this country or abroad, whose research work has covered such important and diversified fields as yours, and I feel that it will be doing great honor to The Society of Economic Geologists if you will accept this medal in the spirit of true recognition of scientific research with which it was awarded."

Letter from T. C. Chamberlin to Penrose, dated Chicago, December 26, 1924

My dear Prof. Penrose:

I cannot tell you how deeply gratifying your letter relative to the medal which the Society of Economic Geologists is to bestow has been to me. It has been a peculiarly precious thot to me that it is the Penrose Gold Medal—that gives it a peculiar value to me. And to know that the bestowal has your fullest approval adds to its value to me. I cannot thank you as I would like. You must do your best to imagine it.

I am planning to go to Ithaca to receive it.

Most gratefully yours,
T. C. Chamberlin

Professor Chamberlin received the medal at Ithaca, where the Society of Economic Geologists met with the Geological Society of America at Christmastime in 1924. Unhappily, the joy of the occasion was tempered by the fall of the distinguished scientist on the icy pavement at Ithaca which resulted in his being removed to a hospital and subsequently taken to a hospital in Chicago, where he remained for several weeks.

Penrose was much upset by the accident to his friend and mentor, as he wrote in a letter to Chamberlin's son, dated January 5, 1925:

Dear Rollin:—

I was dreadfully sorry about the accident to your father at Ithaca last week. I understand that Professor Weller [J. Stuart Weller] has communicated to you the circumstances. I remained in Ithaca a day longer than I had expected so as to feel sure that your father was comfortable and was being well taken care of. Professor Weller acted splendidly and remained at the hospital with your father most of the time. I admired greatly his devotion and his efficiency in handling the situation.

I am dropping a line to you now to say that I hope your father has by this time arrived safely in Chicago and that he will soon be all right again. Everyone at the meetings in Ithaca regretted his absence and expressed their deepest sympathy with him in his injury. When you have time won't you please drop me a line and let me know how he is, for I cannot help feeling anxious about him until I know he is well.

I am very sorry to hear from Professor Weller that you also have had considerable trouble with an injured foot, but I hope that you are all right again by this time. We missed you at Ithaca.

Letter from T. C. Chamberlin to Penrose, dated "Illinois Central Hospital, Chicago," January 5, 1925

Dear Dr. Penrose:

I think that Miss Heath dropped you a note telling you of my safe arrival here, and that my condition was fairly favorable. I am glad to add now that the diagnosis based on the X-ray examination here is a notch better than that at Ithaca. The experts here *do not find any crack at all.* They think that three or four weeks in bed is about the extent of the personal disaster, and that I do not think is a very great affliction, since I am expecting that it will serve the purpose of a vacation that I had not the moral courage to take of myself. But I think that whipped up by a necessity of this sort probably I will take a month's vacation and that may be about the best thing that could happen to me. At any rate, I want you to feel, my dear Penrose, that this has been an event, but not a disaster.

Weller was kindness and faithfulness itself, and he fully convinced me that if he hadn't been loaded with so much paleontology he would have made a first-class nurse.

I am not expecting to remain here at the hospital more than a very short time. My physician is arranging for a big, stout man nurse that can handle an ugly customer of this kind to take charge of me at my rooms at the hotel, and I expect to go there as soon as he can make this arrangement—in two days, perhaps, more or less.

Quite on my own initiative and without regard to instructions from the powers that be, I have been practicing movements with my left leg, first, to see what was approved and what was forbidden by the conscious powers that run down in my left thigh, and they have told me I could do and I could not do a lot of things, but I find that I can do a lot more things than I imagined would be possible for two or three weeks, when I left Ithaca. That is a little general, but it will save a lot of detail. So now, Penrose, rejoice with me that it is an event that is likely to have some good outcome, and we will let the debit side take care of itself.

I am obliged beyond measure to you for your special kindness in this matter, and I cannot tell you how much I shall rejoice in the possession of that elegant medal which bears your name and my name together.

Letter from Penrose to T. C. Chamberlin, dated January 9, 1925

Dear Doctor Chamberlin:—

The best news that I have had for many a long day was your letter telling me that you had arrived safely in Chicago and that the doctors there cannot find any fracture at all in your thigh. I am greatly rejoiced therefore to feel that your injury is probably only muscular and that you will soon be entirely well again. I have often found that X-ray examinations lead to unhappy and misleading determinations, such as occurred in your accident in Ithaca when the expert thought he had found a slight crack in the bone.

I have always admired you for your many great accomplishments, but now I have an opportunity to admire another great accomplishment in the philosophical way in which you took an accident that might have been serious, and for your feeling that it has been an event, but not a disaster; and that probably the enforced rest may be a blessing in disguise to you.

I agree with you entirely in what you say about Weller's kindness and loyalty. I saw at once in Ithaca that he had complete control of the situation, and he is a man who might become a leader in any emergency.

As I have said in a previous letter, it will always be a source of very great pleasure to me to realize that the first award of the medal of the Society of Economic Geologists has gone to you, and that you have so graciously accepted it in the spirit in which it was given as a recognition of your wonderful research in terrestrial and extra-terrestrial geology.

Three years later (December, 1927) the first award of the Penrose Medal of The Geological Society of America was made, also to Professor Chamberlin, an award which met with the whole-hearted approval of its donor.

Letter from Arthur Keith (then president of The Geological Society of America) to Penrose, dated Washington, December 21, 1927

Dear Doctor Penrose:

As you doubtless know, we plan to make the presentation of the Penrose Medal an important feature of the Geological Society of America dinner this year. Naturally, the thing would not be complete unless we again hear from you.

I am counting on you, therefore, to speak a few words of any kind or on any topic, as long as it is connected somehow with the medal and the presentation. Naturally one thinks of your early association with Chamberlin in Chicago, and the roots of your idea in founding the medal may perhaps go back to that time. I trust that you will not need any urging to speak for us, but if you do I am going to begin right here with the urging. We will all be delighted to hear from you then.

Letter from Penrose to Arthur Keith, dated December 24, 1927

My dear Keith:—

I cannot tell you how greatly I appreciate your kind letter of December 21st, asking me to make some remarks at the presentation to Professor Chamberlin of the medal of The Geological Society of America.

I assure you I am simply delighted that the first presentation of the medal is to go to Professor Chamberlin, for his record as a leader in geology, not only terrestrial but extra-terrestrial in the United States, has made him celebrated the world over. I had the good fortune of being associated with him at the University of Chicago during its first years of existence, and I learned to have an affection and regard for him which has ever increased since those early days.

Nothing therefore would give me greater pleasure than to be with you at the presentation of the medal to Professor Chamberlin, and I had expected that I would certainly be there, but at the present time I have illness in my family and I am also laid up with such a cold that it would be impossible for me to make a speech, even if I had the ability to meet this auspicious occasion.

I beg therefore that you will extend to Professor Chamberlin my most cordial good wishes and my hopes that he will approve of the design of the medal. In his broad and great conception of the different branches of geology, his approval would be a most valuable treasure.

Aside from my physical inability to be present at the meeting, I feel absolutely confident that you personally, as President of the Society, can make the proper remarks, and doubtless in a far more efficient manner than I could.

Letter from Penrose to T. C. Chamberlin, dated January 3, 1928

Dear Professor Chamberlin:—

It was a great pleasure to me to receive your kind and cordial telegram of December 31st. Your description of the meeting which showed such brilliant enthusiasm made me regret all the more that circumstances made it impossible for me to be present.

I was indeed delighted by the fact that the Committee on the Medal selected you as their nominee with entire unanimity. You can well understand how glad I was when I heard this news, for it brought me a feeling that to a great and good friend for whom I had always had the deepest respect and affection, there had come still another recognition from the geologists of the country.

What also pleased me greatly in your telegram were your most gracious and kind remarks about the medal, and your approval of its design and inscription. You of all geologists, with your great experience and your remarkable studies into geological objects beyond the earth, make your opinion of inestimable value, and I shall always keep your message as a word of kindness and encouragement from one who stands so pre-eminently capable in the geological world to form such an opinion.

Letter from T. C. Chamberlin to Penrose, dated January 9, 1927 [1928]

My dear Professor Penrose:

I cannot tell you how much I appreciate your exceedingly kind and cordial letter of the 3rd inst. I appreciate it all the more because I have yearned to write you and express my deep gratitude for all that you have done for me directly and through the good offices of others, but I felt somewhat hesitant to speak freely and fully of our deep friendship while decisions of such moment as the awarding of your medals were pending. Now that all occasion for restraint is lifted, I want to tell you that you have been a benediction to me ever since I first knew you and in so many ways. Through the start you gave me and the good influence of your careful ways, I am on "easy street" in just that little modest way that is about the right thing for a man who wants to be free at once from the burden of too much and of too little.

Your steadfast friendship for the Journal of Geology has encouraged us beyond anything we can tell you, for the diversions of the war went sorely against the kind of production we wished to cultivate through our magazine.

The two medals you established and which have come to me as first recipient, have given me not only great comfort but a degree and kind of encouragement I much needed to keep working at my vein, and to keep faith in it, till I come to the cross-feeder and the pay-bulge. I would not say so to anyone else, but I now have in the publisher's hands, a book that, I think, in time, perhaps not at once, will justify my simile. Strangely enough, I have found in the last year, that the phenomena of comets, meteors and meteorites cut across the planetary phenomena in such a way as to make them both unexpectedly rich in their mutual contributions. It already makes me happy to think how much I shall enjoy sending you a copy as soon as it comes from the press. And one of the pleasantest thoughts is that I shall have, in some degree, justified the confidence you have so steadfastly reposed in me, for, though I ought not to say it, I feel the utmost confidence that so far as the genesis of our planetary and cometary systems are concerned, I have reached a true set of cross feeders and the main "pay bulge" on both veins. I feel that we will now have a sound basis to start from in geology and that the growth of the Earth cannot have swung far from certain lines well introduced by preceding events.

I am therefore very happy in my work, as well as in the great honors that have come to me through the two Penrose Medals. I am also happy to tell you that I am in better health and working condition than for some years, and that I have produced more manuscript in the past year than in any previous year of my life and have made my highest day's record.

Again let me say that I am deeply, very deeply, your debtor. May your reward come to you in due measure in the way that will give you the highest satisfaction.

Letter from Penrose to T. C. Chamberlin, dated February 20, 1928

Dear Professor Chamberlin:—

I was so greatly pleased with your kind and cordial letter of January 9th that I have read it frequently and have every time been more and more impressed by your spirit of friendship, which I value more than I can tell you. I assure you that what little use I was to you in the early days gave me a keen pleasure, which I shall always cherish; and my friendship for the Journal of Geology has been many times repaid by the splendid manner in which you and Rollin have managed it and brought it up to its present pre-eminent position in the world of science. I hope that I will be able to continue such assistance as I can give it, and if it happens that I am able to contribute more than at present I will be very glad to do so.

I feel that you, as the first recipient of the medal of The Geological Society of America and of the Society of Economic Geologists, have pleased the whole geological profession and have added a dignity in your record of accomplishments to these tokens of admiration and regard from your fellow-workers.

I am much interested in what you say about having found that the phenomena of comets, meteors and meteorites, cut across the planetary phenomena in a manner that makes them both unexpectedly rich in their mutual contributions. Your conception is wonderful and I can readily see the wide field that it has opened for your forthcoming book. I will greatly enjoy reading it when it appears, not only as a brilliant expression of your long experience in research in this subject, but as a book that will live indefinitely and show that from the mind of the greatest American geologist has emanated this remarkable astronomical conception.

I am greatly pleased to know that you are in much better health than you have been for years, and I sincerely hope that you may long continue so. I look on my long association with you as one of the brightest spots in my memory, and now in receiving your wonderfully kind letter I feel that I have a token which I shall always preserve as expressing your cordial and hearty friendship.

Chamberlin died that same year—November 15, 1928—but not before he had seen his book published under the title, *The Two Solar Families*.

CHAPTER 17

Era of World War I

IN THE decade between 1910 and 1920, Penrose set definitely the pattern of life which he followed for the remainder of his days. His mining interests and his investments, his duties as member of many boards of direction and of scientific and professional societies, occupied most of his time. Although he kept the house at 1331 Spruce Street open and fully staffed, he maintained a suite at the Bellevue-Stratford in Philadelphia, where he lived and where he died, and also kept permanent quarters at various places in New York—Hotel Wolcott, the University Club, the Harvard Club—so that he might occupy his own room whenever he went to the metropolis, which was frequently. In all organizations and clubs where it was possible to do so, he became a life member. He attended the meetings of organizations to which he belonged, the list including various International Geological Congresses—Toronto in 1913, Brussels in 1922, Madrid in 1926.

In 1911 he went to Europe in the winter and spent the summer in western United States. That he also intended to go into the Hudson Bay country of Canada is evident from the following correspondence with Herbert Hoover:

Letter from Penrose to H. C. Hoover, dated Savoy Hotel, London, May 11, 1911
Dear Hoover

Many thanks for your telegram telling me that you have managed to get the Hudson Bay Co. to give me a letter to their posts. Such a letter would be of great assistance to me, and I appreciate greatly the trouble you have taken.

I sail on Saturday on the Mauretania. Will try to see you at your office tomorrow.

Sincerely yours,
R. A. F. Penrose, Jr.

Under date of May 22, 1911, Hoover wrote from London:

"I send you herewith a letter to the Hudson Bay Company's manager at Winnipeg. I am not certain that the working of this letter is going to carry you very far. However, you had better acknowledge it and also I would be obliged if you would address a letter to Mr. Leonard Govett, 6, Throgmorton Street, London, E.C., and say you have received it."

Letter from Penrose to H. C. Hoover, Esq., No. 1 Londonwall Building, London, E.C., England, dated Philadelphia, June 12, 1911
My dear Hoover:—

I have received your letter of May 24th, and also your letter of May 22d, the latter having been sent out to San Francisco and returned here to me. I thank you very much for the trouble you have taken in the matter of securing the letter to the Hudson's Bay Company, which you sent me in yours of the 22d inst. I am not certain that I shall get in that part of the Hudson Bay sphere of influence this summer, as I may possibly only be in the eastern part of Canada, but if I get near Winnepeg, I am sure the letter you have sent me will be very useful.

As you request in your letter of the 22d ult., I am acknowledging the letter of introduction to T. C. Ingrams, Esq., who has signed it, and also, as you request, to Leonard Govett, Esq., 6 Throgmorton Street, London.

Again thanking you, and with best regards, I am,

Sincerely yours,
R. A. F. Penrose, Jr.

Letter from Penrose to H. C. Hoover, Esq., ⁂ 1 Londonwall Buildings, London, E.C., England, dated Philadelphia, September 14, 1911

Dear Hoover:—

I have been receiving in recent months several volumes of the Hakluyt Society publications, but I have not received any bill for them. It has occurred to me that perhaps some one has put me up for membership, and yet I have not paid any dues or received any bill. Knowing that you are a member of the Hakluyt Society, I write to ask if you can give me any information on the matter.

I am sorry that I could not get away long enough this summer to go to Hudson's Bay, but I hope to do so some other time. I may possibly go to Burma on a short trip this winter, and if so, I hope to see you on my way through London. I wish I could go to Burma some time when you were going in that direction.

With best regards, and hoping you and your family are all well, I am,

Sincerely yours,
R. A. F. Penrose, Jr.

Letter from Penrose to H. C. Hoover, Esq., 1 Londonwall Buildings, London, E.C., England, dated Philadelphia, October 5, 1911

My dear Hoover:—

I have just received your letter of September 26th, stating that you had paid to the Hakluyt Society the sum of $5.00 as my dues for the first year, and I beg to enclose herewith a post-office order for that amount to refund you for the same. I hope you will pardon my delay in sending you this, as I did not know until I received your letter that you had paid it for me.

I hope everything is going well with you in London. I saw Jack Means in New York a few days ago and he looked very well. He was going farther west, I believe. Things are a little quiet here in a business way on account of the manner in which the Government has been getting after some of the trusts, but I think that people will some time realize that the Government has no intention of trying to ruin our industries, and then perhaps things will begin to look up again.

With best regards, I am,

Sincerely yours,
R. A. F. Penrose, Jr.

It is perhaps significant that for this middle period of his life, Penrose apparently kept no carbon copies of his own letters, only those from others being in his files. (The letters to Hoover were supplied from the Hoover files.) Both before and after this period, Penrose kept complete files with meticulous care. But he does not even give the dates of his trip to Burma in 1912. The record simply says: "Went to Burma via Marseilles, Red Sea and Ceylon. Travelled over interior in the valley of Irrawaddy River, visiting Rangoon, Pegue, Mandalay, etc. Returned via Ceylon, Red Sea, Malta, Marseilles, Paris, London and New York."

As already stated, there are no letters, no diary, no notebooks of this Burma trip, and only three other sources concerning it are preserved in his files. One is a reference in a letter written to him by his cousin, Ellen Penrose, of Carlisle, in 1925, in which she says: "I remember your telling me after one of your trips about giving the Grand Lama of Tibet a banana when you paid him a visit on the top of his high mountain and how he ate it with great enjoyment."

The second reference is in a manuscript concerning himself, evidently prepared in response to a request for a biographical outline of his life, and dated December 27, 1928, in which he says: "He went again to Asia to study the southern extension of the great plateau of Thibet, which runs southward through the eastern part of Upper Burma, returning again to Europe by way of Ceylon, the Suez Canal and Malta."

An envelope marked "In re Burma," in his files contained some slight additional information. Ships' passenger lists show that he sailed from New York to Southampton on January 13, 1912, aboard the S.S. "Oceanic"; from Marseilles to Rangoon on February 16, aboard the "Herefordshire"; from Rangoon to Colombo, Ceylon, on March 20, aboard the "Herefordshire"; and from Liverpool to New York on May 18, aboard the "Lusitania," reaching the latter city on May 24. Apparently, he continued on the "Herefordshire" to Marseilles at least, for under date of March 24, 1912, the Port Surgeon of Colombo issued a permit to him to go ashore and return to the Herefordshire "in quarantine."

The reason for "quarantine" may have been the "plague," for his embarkation notice from Rangoon, dated March 13, states that "in compliance with Plague Regulations passengers are requested to be at Barr Street No. 2 Jetty promptly at 2 p.m. on the 20th March 1912 for plague inspection prior to embarkation."

For the rest, the envelope contained a clipping from the *Mining and Scientific Press* of May 13, 1911, of an article on "Ruby Mines of Burma" by John L. Cowan; a clipping from the *Ceylon Observer* of March 5, concerning the voyage of the "Herefordshire"; a small map of Burma; a clipping from *The Burma Critic* of February 22, 1912, concerning "Crabs and the Formation of Land"; a clipping from an undesignated paper on "pagoda festivals"; a sheet of notepaper from Minto Mansions Hotel at Rangoon with the name C. Paul Ratmann written on both sides; and a sheet of lined paper with three notations written across the lines, in pencil in Penrose's handwriting.

These notations are:

"Ruby are Mogok tract, 60 m.E of the Irrawaddy & 90 m. NNW of Mandalay. Burman Ruby Mines Co.

"Also at Nanyaseik in the Myitkyina Dist & at Sagyin in the Mandalay Dist.

"Jade mines are beyond Kamaing, north of Mogaung in the Myitkyina Dist. Only supply in world dark green."

The item in the *Ceylon Observer* occupies an entire column and is mainly concerned with the report of the ships met, games played, concerts, etc., but one notation is of special interest.

"Going down the Gulf of Suez on Friday 23rd," reads the item," the dazzling white patches (utterly unlike the white sand) on the hills towards the Sinai range elicited some discussion; and a veteran Scottish passenger for Rangoon, Mr. W. Connal, who had travelled in the Peninsula, gave a verdict in favour of those who held that it *was* snow; he had himself been overtaken by a heavy snowstorm on the slopes of Sinai (at no higher elevation than we looked at) as late as April 15th one year—and the way the natives of his party laid hands on it, giving 'thanks to Allah for this food,' and ate it with their repast, left him no doubt as to the theory that the Manna of the Israelites was snow."

A railroad timetable for Burma and the fact that he could not have been in Burma more than about ten days, together with the absence of any recorded observations, would explain why those who knew him in the last years of his life heard him repeatedly express the desire to return to Burma.

In June, he was evidently still in Philadelphia, for Jackling wrote to him there on June 3rd, with the news that things were well with Utah Copper and that "for the month just closing, for instance, we made over ten million pounds of copper, which means at current prices for copper, not very much short of a million dollars profit. I hope to duplicate or improve this result as an average matter for the balance of the year. . . . I am going to Alaska early in July so that if you come west during that month I will probably miss you, but if you are on the Coast after the first of August I will arrange to see you somewhere."

Later that same month (June 25), Jackling again wrote: "When I returned here a few days ago I found a copy of your history of *Gold Mining in the United States*. I have been pretty well covered up with work since I got back and have not had a chance to read it carefully, but have glanced through it to a sufficient extent to find it exceedingly interesting. Please accept my best thanks for your courtesy and thoughtfulness exerted in my direction in this and many previous instances.

"Charley and Spec are going to be over here the end of the week. I will be here until the 3rd of July, then to Butte for a couple of days and then to Alaska. Expect to return here about the 25th or 26th of July and during the month of August I am figuring on taking an outing somewhere. I wonder if we could not get together and have a fishing trip? I have been thinking some that I might go up into the Jackson's Hole country. The Short Line is just completing a branch that will put that country pretty close to transportation, and I have thought it might be a good time to go in there and look for a place to buy as a permanent fishing and hunting ground. All this is 'air castle' to a certain extent as I don't know yet that I can even get away in August at all, but would be glad to have you write me your plans for that month anyhow."

Penrose did not reply until July 9 (1912), when he wrote (and these letters were preserved in the Jackling files):

My dear Jack:—

I was very glad to get your letter of the 25th ult. a few days ago, and would have replied sooner, but I knew that as you started for Alaska, you would not get my letter until your return.

I would like very much to do as you suggest and go on a fishing trip to Jackson's Hole in August, but I have been delayed here so much that I am afraid that I will not be able to do so. Even now, I do not know just when I will get away, but I hope to start west before the first of August. I expect to go to Denver first, where I will have to remain for a few days, and then to Los Angeles to see Mr. Brockman. If you get time in August, why don't you run down to Los Angeles, and if the Revolution in Mexico has quieted down enough, we can slip down the coast of Lower California and get some good fishing there I have been there before, and I know that the fishing is good On the other hand, I am afraid you will find Jackson's Hole simply overrun with tourists, and I should have my doubts as to how good the fishing there was. In the old days, twenty or twenty-five years ago, it was almost a paradise for hunting and fishing, but since the tourists have discovered it, it has been more or less worked out.

I will write again before I leave here, and I hope we can meet somewhere in the west, as you suggest, for a little trip.

I hope you are having a successful trip in Alaska.

Letter from Dick, dated San Francisco, Calif., August 12, 1912

My dear Jack:—

I heard a few days ago that you had returned from Alaska, and I have been hoping that you might be possibly coming this way to take that fishing trip we were discussing some time ago; but I have not heard from you and I suppose you have been very busy since your return to Salt Lake.

I came here from Denver some days ago, and would have stopped over in Salt Lake to see you, but at that time you had not yet returned.

I hope you had a pleasant and successful trip in Alaska and accomplished all you went after. I expect to be here until the latter part of this week, and then to go to Los Angeles. My address in Los Angeles will be c/o John Brockman, Esq., 206 Security Bldg., and I will probably stop at the Alexandria Hotel, so if you come that way I hope to see you.

Letter from Jackling, dated New York, August 21, 1912

My dear Dick:—

I have just received your letter of August 12th written from the Hotel St. Francis, San Francisco. After my return from Alaska I found it necessary to come down here for a few days but will be back in Utah a little before the first of the month. I then have to take a trip to Butte for a few days and will expect to reach Los Angeles some time from the 10th to the 15th of September on my way to the Ray and Chino properties. I shall be very glad to see you if you happen to be in California at that time.

I had a very successful trip to Alaska and with all a very pleasant one. We have taken up the Alaska properties and I expect will make a very good showing from them.

Letter from Dick, dated Los Angeles, September 3, 1912

Dear Jack:—

I was very glad to get your letter of August 21st and to know that your trip to Alaska had been a success and that you had found such valuable property.

I am sorry you have not gotten here sooner for a little fishing, as it has been exceptionally good all along the coast this year. I hope another year we can arrange to get together on a fishing trip, down south of here. I am not sure that I will be here when you pass through on your way to Arizona, but if not I hope to see you later on in the east. I must be going that way soon.

A few days ago I took the liberty of giving a letter of introduction to you to Mr. A. Y. Smith. Mr. Smith was formerly of Arizona, but is now interested in a silver-lead mine near Pioche, Nevada, and in it he finds a gangue material that he thinks would be useful for lining converters in copper smelting. He was anxious to be put in touch with the people at the Garfield smelter to discuss the matter, as he has had experience in supplying somewhat similar materials from elsewhere to the smelters at Bisbee. I did not know any of the people at the Garfield smelter, so I took the liberty of giving Mr. Smith a letter to you.

Telegram from Dick to Jackling, dated Denver, September 25, 1912

Just arrived here. Let me know if I can be of any service to you here or in Utah. Answer Brown Palace Hotel.

Telegram from Jackling to Dick, dated Salt Lake City, September 25, 1912

Thanks for your wire. I believe there is nothing that you can do just now. Spec is here and has gone over situation fully. He agrees with my plan of action which up to date appears to have been a little slow but which I believe will bring satisfactory results in a very short time.

The occasion for these two telegrams appears to have been labor troubles, for on November 5 of that same year (1912), Penrose again wrote to Jackling, saying, "I drop a line to you to congratulate you on the excellent manner in which you have handled the labor troubles at Bingham and the rapidity with which you have settled them. Many such troubles have lasted months and years, but you have cleared up the whole situation in a few weeks.

"Every stockholder in the Company owes you a debt of gratitude for what you have accomplished, and I personally wish to express to you, not only my thanks, but my admiration of the way in which you have handled the matter."

Letter from Jackling, dated "On Southern Pacific," November 10, 1912

Dear Dick:—

Many thanks for your complimentary letter of November 5th. I think we have gotten out of the strike difficulty rather fortunately, and as long as one always has to have this sort of thing to contend with in the building up of a new industry, I am just as well satisfied that it came when it did. We are building up our organization slowly in Utah but I think we will be in fair shape by the end of the month. The strike isn't bothering us so much now as the general shortage of labor coupled with the fact that a great many of the class of foreigners we use are returning to Europe on account of the Balkan War. Moyer and his bunch have been using every effort to cause us trouble at Ray, but I don't think they are going to succeed. I am now on my way down there, going to Globe first, however, where I will meet MacNeill. Will then return to Ray and afterwards double back to Chino.

Early in 1913 (January 16), Penrose attended a dinner given by Henry G. Bryant at the Bellevue-Stratford in honor of three great Polar explorers—Capt, Roald Amundsen, Rear Admiral R. E. Peary, U.S.N., and Sir Ernest H. Shackleton, C.V.O. The other guests at this notable affair were Cyrus C. Adams, Rudolph Blankenburg, Herbert L. Bridgman, A. H. Burnett Buckenham, Eckley B. Coxe, Jr., Samuel J. Entrikin, William K. Haupt, A. H. Hetherington, H. LaBarre Jayne, Alba B. Johnson, W. W. Keen, Robert N. Keely, William Libbey, John H. McFadden, Christian Moe, P. F. Rothermel, Jr., Frank C. Roberts, and Paul J. Sartain. Among Penrose's "treasures" is the engraved souvenir of this occasion, with the autographs of the three guests of honor inscribed thereon

Letter from Penrose to H. C. Hoover, Esq., San Francisco, Calif., dated Philadelphia, January 4, 1913.

My dear Hoover:—

I have heard of your election as a Trustee of Stanford University, and I drop a line to you to congratulate you. I also congratulate the University, for I am sure that your services to them will be most valuable, and I wish you every possible success in guiding the destiny of your institution.

I hope it will not be long before you come east again, and that I will see you when you get this way.

With best regards to you and to Mrs. Hoover and the children, and wishing you all the good wishes of the New Year, I am,

Sincerely yours,
R. A. F. Penrose, Jr.

P.S. Since writing this letter I have heard that you are expected in New York this week, so I will mail this to your office there. Hope to see you in New York soon.

P.

To this letter, Hoover replied on January 9, 1913, as follows:

My dear Penrose:—

Many thanks for yours of the 4th of January. I appreciate very much your congratulations and believe I can be of some service to that institution.

I am sorry I have got to rush over to London straight-away, and am leaving on the "Carmania" on the 11th, but expect to be back again in the course of another two months and hope to have an opportunity of seeing you again.

Letter from Edward V. d'Invilliers, dated Philadelphia, June 26, 1913.

My dear Penrose:—

Of all the congratulations extended to me in connection with the recent action of the University of Pennsylvania none has been more truly appreciated than your own, feeling as I do both the sincerity of your action and the significance of a commendation from such a source.

Personally I have always been brought up with such a holy reverence for the title "Doctor of Science" that I can in no way conceive the propriety of bestowing it upon me; nevertheless, coming from my Alma Mater, I can truthfully state that I have greatly appreciated the honor, however difficult it may be to live up to its requirements.

Penrose's own record for 1913 says: "Went to Europe in winter and west in summer. Attended twelfth International Geological Congress in Toronto in August."

At that congress, Penrose, together with Henry G. Bryant and W. B. Scott, was a delegate of the American Philosophical Society. He was also a delegate of the Franklin Institute, of the State of Pennsylvania, of the University of Pennsylvania, and of The Academy of Natural Sciences of Philadelphia. His report of this congress meeting was published in the *Journal* of the Franklin Institute, November, 1913, to which organization he had been elected a Resident Member in July (1913). In December of that year, he declined membership on the Board of that institution.

Of his movements from 1914 to 1920, very little information can be obtained from the records he left. Under "Regions Traveled for Exploration and Geological Research," he lists visits to Lower California in 1914, 1915, and 1916," and to "various other parts of America, 1917, 1918, 1919, 1920, and 1921."

In January, 1914, his paper on "Certain phases of superficial diffusion in ore deposits" appeared in *Economic Geology*, and the following year the same journal carried his "The Pitchblende of Cornwall, England."

His 1914 notebook shows that he was interested and studying the question of radium, and that he visited Green River, Table Mountain, and the Henry Mountains in Utah.

"Went by automobile from Grand Junction, Colo., to Placerville, via Delta, Montrose and Ridgway (about 117 miles) on Sept. 18," he records in his 1914 notebook; "thence on Sept. 19 via Norwood, Naturita, Coke Ovens to East Paradox valley and ascended the southern escarpment to the carnotite mining district known as Long Park (56 miles); thence back to Delta via the same route on Sept. 20, and thence into Grand Junction on Sept. 21st. (Total distance, including an additional 16 miles on account of a mistake in roads in Paradox Valley, 375 miles.)"

According to the same notebook, he then went to Central City, Colorado, to study the pitchblende of that district. It was not until 1917, however, that his paper on *Radium and uranium, their uses and occurrence; their political and commercial control*, prepared for the United States Department of the Interior, appeared as document number 13.

In October (October 29, 1914), Penrose received the following letter from Rudolph Blankenburg, at that time mayor of Philadelphia:

"I enclose copy of a communication received from the Assistant Secretary of the American Mining Congress, inviting me to appoint delegates to their Seventeenth Annual Convention, which will be held at Phoenix, Arizona, December 7-8-9-10-11, 1914.

"As the City itself is not directly interested in this Convention, I would ask whether you would be willing to go as its representative.

"If you can do so, will you kindly let me know. The City has no appropriation to pay expenses of such a trip; the expenses would have to be borne by the delegate himself. By giving this matter your attention, you will oblige."

In the communication from the Assistant Secretary to which the mayor refers, is the statement that "this meeting will be one of the most important ever held by this organization, and in order that it may be of the greatest value to the Mining Industry, it is essential that every section be represented."

That same December, Penrose was in Philadelphia at Christmas time, as witness the following:

Letter from R. S. Bassler, secretary of The Paleontological Society, dated U. S. National Museum, Washington, D. C., January 7, 1915

My dear Doctor Penrose:—

I am instructed by the Paleontological Society to extend to you and your associates Messrs D'Invilliers, Brown and Spurr, our grateful thanks for your whole-souled and in every way successful efforts to render the Philadelphia meeting of the Society just concluded a more than ordinarily memorable one. Let me add also that the Society particularly recognized our great indebtedness to you personally for your unstinted liberality and unflagging efforts to make us all feel as though we owned the place. Of course in a case like this, the mere knowledge of having done your best is no small reward. But the assurance conveyed by this official acknowledgment of the unqualified success of your efforts in our behalf may we trust render your satisfaction in a measure complete.

With kindest regards, in which I am joined by our President, Dr. E. O. Ulrich, I am,

Very sincerely yours,
R. S. Bassler

Several Hoover letters are included in this period of Penrose's life.

Letter from Penrose, dated October 28, 1915, addressed to Hoover in London

My dear Hoover:—

On my return from a long absence in the West I received your letter of September 7th and the reports of "The Commission for Relief in Belgium" which you have kindly sent me. I have read these reports through with the greatest interest and with the deepest sympathy for the noble cause in which you are so earnestly and efficiently working. What you have done is simply wonderful; and the executive ability and the originality of resource which you have displayed will always command the respect and admiration of all who read the history of the present war.

I thank you very much for your message to my brother Spencer, telling him that his step-daughter was well, and I have communicated the news to him.

Wishing you every success, and with kindest regards, I am

Sincerely yours,
R. A. F. Penrose, Jr.

Penrose evidenced his approbation in more than words, contributing not only directly to the fund, but also to the Stanford Belgian relief fund. In December of 1916, Penrose wrote to Dr. Alonzo E. Taylor, of Philadelphia:

"On my return from a few days absence I have received your letter of December 8th, and I thank you very much for the news you sent me of my friend Herbert C. Hoover. I have known Hoover for many years and have always recognized in him a man of very remarkable ability. It is a great pleasure to me to see now this ability being manifested in such a splendid way for the cause of humanity. No words of praise are too great for him, and it is a pleasure to know a man who is doing so much good for so many people, and doing it in such an entirely unselfish and efficient manner.

"I hope your trip to Europe has been satisfactory to you. I am sure that you also have done much good on a continent distracted by war, and I am glad to welcome you home again."

That Hoover felt for Penrose an equally high regard is evidenced in the following statement prepared by him especially for incorporation in this volume:

"Early in 1917 I came to the United States from Europe to reorganize and refinance the Belgian Relief Commission which was then requiring some $25,000,000 per month to furnish food to the 10,000,000 people occupied by the German armies in Belgium and northern France. I badly needed a strong man to take over the second in command in the commission in charge of our American offices from whence we were buying, shipping and hoping to finance our supplies. He needed to be a volunteer who would give up all other interests and devote his entire time to the work.

"I approached Mr. Penrose to take the job, and without hesitation he accepted. It was proposed he take on the work as soon as he could settle his affairs, late in April. Before we got started the unlimited submarine war began, America was in the war, and the Relief Commission became a part of inter-governmental activities."

Letter from Dick to his brother Senator Boies Penrose, dated January 27, 1917

Dear Boies:—

Mr. H. C. Hoover, who is chairman of the Belgian Relief Committee, is now in New York and is going to Washington in a few days on some official business which he has there in connection with his Belgian Relief affairs. He asked me for a card of introduction to you and I gave it to him. I do not know exactly what he wants to see you about, but he is engaged in a most worthy work, and anything you can consistently do for him will be greatly appreciated by both him and me.

Your affectionate brother,
R. A. F. Penrose, Jr.

Letter from Dick, dated January 27, 1917

My dear Mr. Hoover:—

I have not yet had a chance to see my brother, Senator Penrose, since I gave you a card of introduction to him, but I have written to him telling him that you would probably call on him. I hope he will be able to be of some assistance to you.

It was a great pleasure to have seen you again the other day in New York, and I wish you every success in the noble work you are carrying on in your Belgian Relief Committee.

With best regards to Mrs. Hoover and the children, I am,

Sincerely yours,
R. A. F. Penrose, Jr.

Letter from Senator Boies Penrose, dated Washington, D. C., February 5, 1917

Dear Dick:

I have yours of January 27th, advising that you have given Mr. H. C. Hoover a card of introduction to me.

If Mr. Hoover calls I shall be glad to see him.

Your affectionate brother
Boies Penrose

Telegram to Richard Penrose from H. C. Hoover, dated Washington, May 19, 1917

YOUR BROTHER HAS DEVELOPED A CONSIDERABLE VEIN OF PERSONAL OPPOSITION TO ME WHICH I THINK IS ENTIRELY UNJUST AND MUST BE BASED ON SOME MISREPRESENTATION OR SOME MISUNDERSTANDING   I WONDER IF IT WOULD BE POSSIBLE TO HAVE YOUR COOPERATION IN STRAIGHTENING OUT THIS MATTER   I AM NOT UNDERTAKING THIS SERVICE BECAUSE I LIKE IT OR BECAUSE I WANT TO BUT BECAUSE I CONSIDER EACH MAN MUST DO HIS DUTY LIKE A GOOD SOLDIER NO MATTER WHAT THE PERSONAL SACRIFICE IS AND THIS IS A GOOD DEAL ON MY PART

HOOVER

Letter from Senator Boies Penrose, dated Washington, D.C., May 24, 1917

Dear Dick:

I have yours of May 21st.

I am not opposed to Mr. Hoover and I have never met anyone who did not speak in the highest terms of him. I am, however, opposed as are a good many Senators to the demands of the present administration for certain dictatorial and arbitrary powers, particularly in connection with the production and conservation of food. It seems to me there is a good deal of hysteria on this subject. The proposition involves general principles and not Mr. Hoover personally.

I shall be glad to explain the situation to you more fully when I see you. Just now I am closely tied up in Washington with daily sessions of the Senate and Finance Committee, including Saturdays, and I do not expect to be in Philadelphia for several weeks.

Your affectionate brother
Boies Penrose

That same day (May 24, 1917) Bradley Stoughton, secretary of the American Institute of Mining Engineers, wrote to Penrose that he desired to send him for his signature "an engrossed nomination to honorary membership of Herbert C. Hoover. He was nominated by more than the required number of members of the Institute and elected an Honorary Member, but some of his friends have expressed a desire that his nomination should be signed by many of the prominent members of the Institute in order that he may have the document for framing, together with his certificate of honorary membership."

Meantime, Penrose had received other letters from Hoover.

Letter from H. C. Hoover, dated New York, February 2, 1917

My dear Penrose:—

Thanks for your check. I can quite appreciate that you have generously met the many demands for funds for the relief of Belgium, and these all eventually come through our Commission. Of course, we prefer to receive donations direct as we are quite sure then that nothing will be deducted for expenses.

Thanks for your congratulations. I am hoping that we have been able, in addition to relieving the suffering of Belgium, to advance the interests of our country abroad.

Hope to have another opportunity of seeing you before I return.

Yours very truly,
Herbert Hoover

[The word "Chairman" beneath his name is crossed out in ink.]

Letter from H. C. Hoover, dated New York, February 10, 1917

My dear Penrose,

I did not tell you I was coming to Philadelphia because I did not want any of my friends to hear my sputtering efforts in public and besides, you needed no missionary work in connection with Belgian Relief and therefore are not compelled to be bored.

I am afraid I will be stuck in this country for some weeks from the outlook, and I will no doubt have more time and be able to meet you later on.

Yours faithfully
H. C. Hoover

Letter from Herbert Hoover, dated New York, February 14, 1917
My dear Penrose:—

I am sorry that you have been annoyed concerning Belgian Kiddies. When I received your check I turned it over to them as they are desirous of making this fund, which is truly representative of the mining fraternity, as large as possible, and they are dear, good fellows whose only purpose is to express some sort of appreciation of the work which I have been doing. There was no intention on their part of making the fund in any way undignified. There is no expense attached to their organization, and they hand the money back to us dollar for dollar. At any rate, I have asked them not to worry you about certificates.

Yours very truly,
Herbert Hoover

[The word "Chairman" beneath his name is crossed off in ink.]

Later that same month (February, 1917), Penrose received an invitation from George Wharton Pepper, stating that "Mr. Herbert Hoover, chairman of the Commission for Belgian Relief, will be in Philadelphia on Thursday, the twenty-second. He has promised to meet a few gentlemen who are deeply interested in the work he is doing. You are invited to meet him at three o'clock, Thursday afternoon, February twenty-second, at 1524 Walnut Street."

The remaining letter for this period in the Hoover file is from Mrs. Hoover. It is written on stationery of Lindon W. Bates, 111 Broadway, New York, from 14 East 60th Street, and is dated March 15 (no year).

"Dear Mr Penrose," she writes, "May I trouble you a few minutes about the back of the cover of Mr. Hoover's mining book—Because I know how highly he values your opinion.

"Before he went away he gave the publisher as the title "Principles of Mining"—with "Valuation, Organization, Administration," as sub heads.

"This is the sketch sent me by the Publisher for approval.

"It seems to me the name is too close to the title to be 'good-for-looking.' And that *I* might like 'HOOVER' *on the back* better than the initials. Do you think there is any other mining Hoover that might feel he would be arrogating too much to himself to have the initials on the front only?

"Also the publisher has slipped an 'and' in, between the subheads. Is that an advantage?

"But more important than any of these—as he was leaving he suddenly said, 'I think "Investment" ought to be included amongst those titles, but four would be too many. Arrange them in as many ways as you can, and see if "Investment" should be substituted for one of the others.'

"And that is what I can not tell. The three as they are certainly are more euphonious. But do *you* think that 'Investment' will be better in, and if so, how would you arrange the three?

"And other suggestions would be most gratefully received.

"I am sure you will not mind my troubling you?

"Yours sincerely

"Lou Henry Hoover"

There is no copy of the Penrose reply, but the book was published under the title and sub-title: *Principles of Mining; valuation, organization, and administration.*

Stephen B. L. Penrose, Dick's cousin who for many years was president of Whitman College at Walla Walla, Washington, writing in 1940, recalled that during a visit to Philadelphia in the winter of 1917–1918, "I called on Dick at his office in the Bullitt Building and he asked me if I could come to a Wistar Party at his house, 1331 Spruce Street. A day or two later the big engraved invitation arrived and in due time I went to the gathering. It included many of the most distinguished men of Philadelphia and I think that we listened to a paper by somebody, but mainly I recall talking with a lot of strangers and eating an elaborate supper served buffet fashion in the dining room on the half landing above the main floor. As Dick was the host, I had hardly a word with him.

"On this same visit I think it was that Dick's brother Charley invited the Penrose men of our generation to a dinner at his house on Walnut Street and there I met Dick, Boies, Charley, Dr. Clement A. Penrose from Baltimore whom Dr. Osler regarded as the ideal general practitioner of the United States, and Col. George H. Penrose, Commandant of the U. S. Army in Philadelphia. Spencer Penrose was in Colorado Springs and could not attend. It was a pleasant occasion for me, for I had not seen Clem Penrose since he was a small boy and I met George for the first time, which developed into a long and affectionate friendship, but nothing of the conversation lingers in my mind and I chiefly remember the epicurean dinner, which was, I think, the finest in quality I ever ate. I had seen Boies oftener than any of the others, for on my short visits home I used to look him up at the Republican headquarters in Philadelphia or call on him in Washington, where he was very friendly and willing to render me such service as I might need. After this dinner I may have seen Dick once or twice either in New York or in Philadelphia, but nothing happened that I can remember.

"Although my cousin and I were on excellent terms, I do not suppose that I actually saw him more than a dozen times in all my life.

"My uncle, Dr. R. A. F. Penrose, lived in Philadelphia at 1331 Spruce Street and sent his boys to the Episcopal Academy, while my father, Judge Clement Biddle Penrose, lived in Germantown, a remote suburb in days before the automobile, and sent me to attend the William Penn Charter School in town.

"One summer when my brother and I were visiting other cousins in Atlantic City, we were all invited to dinner at Uncle Aleck's, where all his boys were. Boies and Charley were studying to enter Harvard that fall, which will serve to date the event. We ate a Gargantuan meal, which ended with huge slices of watermelon, four inches thick, and I can still recall my hopeless admiration for the ability of the others to get away with it. I did not see any of them again for at least ten years.

"It must have been in the early nineties, when he was back in Philadelphia at the end of his work as State Geologist for Arkansas and Eastern Texas, that I ran across him at his father's house where I happened to be calling. He told me that he had been obliged to live on quinine and whiskey while at his work on account of the fever and ague.

"The next time I saw him was in Chicago in 1895 or 1896 where he was lecturing at the University of Chicago. We took lunch together and I remember two incidents of our long talk: he asked me to go with him to explore the least known portion of the globe, which he said was the region between southwestern China and Burma...Then we got to talking about social conditions and presently we had organized between us the P.E S., the Painless Elimination Society, for relieving the world of its incapables; he was elected president and I secretary-treasurer. There were no funds and no other members and no other meeting was ever held but it would have been worth keeping alive."

When the National Research Council was organized in 1917, Penrose became one of its working members in the Geology and Paleontology Committee, of which John M. Clarke was chairman. Under the direction of that committee, Penrose wrote for the Army a short resume of the possible services to be rendered by the geologist in wartime, under the title *What a Geologist can do in War*. Today his remarks might not make news, but the value of geology along such lines was not common knowledge in those days of World War I.

"This brochure has been prepared for the purpose of stating succinctly and clearly the competency of the geologist in war service," declared Dr. Clarke in the introduction. "It is commended to the attention of commanding officers."

In these days, when practical application of geological knowledge is becoming more and more taken for granted, it is well to remember that this acceptance is comparatively recent, and if geologists are today reaping the benefit of this wider knowledge and fuller acceptance on the part of the general public it is because of the efforts of earlier workers who patiently explained those benefits to the uninitiated, not once but many times.

"A knowledge of geology can be made of use in many ways in time of war, not only to the army in camp but to the army on the march and the army in battle," wrote Penrose. "The ground on which an army camps, the ground which it traverses, the rocks on which heavy guns are placed, and the roads over which these heavy guns must be hauled, the ground in which trenches, tunnels and other openings for protection or storage are dug, the water supply for the army, and many other subjects are important matters in determining the success of military operations, and in most of them the geologist has a special knowledge which can be of use to army officers.

"The distribution and character of the rocks, their stratified or unstratified nature, their porosity, strength, elasticity, composition and other physical and chemical properties, all have a bearing on the welfare of an army and are all familiar to the geologist, but are outside the knowledge of most army officers. In the education of the army officer, the numerous matters of a military nature that demand his attention necessarily prevent him from studying these geological subjects, and yet a knowledge of them is of importance to the success of military operations.

"The drainage of the camp and the sanitary arrangements are matters of great importance, and here the geologist, by his knowledge of the structure of the ground, can be of assistance. Dry and sufficiently high ground is, of course, desirable from a sanitary point of view, though from a strategic point of view perhaps it cannot always be occupied; and in places where military necessity requires a camp in a low, swampy place, there may be spots that are better drained than others, or where the character of the water is less objectionable and less infested with mosquitoes and other insects. A knowledge of the geology of a swamp is, therefore, as important to the welfare of an army camp as a knowledge of mountains and plains.

"A true comprehension of the topography and geology of arid regions, such as are found in the southwest, is often necessary for the safety of a camp, for many attractive-looking meadows are really the bottoms of dry creek beds, and before morning, storms in the mountains above may convert them into roaring torrents, sweeping everything before them. Hundreds of pioneers and others in our southwest have lost their lives in this way. Many of them knew the danger of camping in dry creek beds, but they did not grasp the topography of the country sufficiently to realize that the convenient flat spots which they chose for camp were really in line of drainage channels, and hence in line of danger.

"The geologist, when circumstances permit, can locate the more easily worked and dryer formations for digging trenches and tunnels, and can thus often save not only unnecessary time and labor, but the calamity of wet trenches with the resulting rheumatism, pneumonia, tuberculosis and other diseases. He cannot always perform this service, for trenches must be dug where strategic necessity requires them, and, moreover, an army often cannot wait until the geologist makes his examination; but when opportunity permits, the geologist, more than anyone else, can be useful in this matter. An instance of how tunnels and underground openings can be kept dry, even among formations that are mostly wet, is shown remarkably in the case of the underground railways in London. The old original underground railways were dug near the surface, often in porous water-bearing materials, and were damp and uncomfortable. The new underground railways, commonly known as the tube-railways, were made largely in the 'London Clay,' which formation, though underlaid and overlaid by wet strata, is itself so impervious to moisture that excavations made in it are comparatively dry. The result is that the tube-railways are dry and healthy passages. This instance is mentioned to illustrate how a knowledge of geology can affect the character of underground work.

"The ground on which heavy artillery is to be stationed is of the utmost importance, for on its firmness, elasticity and other qualities depends to a large extent the accuracy of a gun's work. Here again the knowledge of the geologist is of importance, for to him the structure and the physical and chemical character of rocks have been a life study, while they are unknown quantities to men of most other professions.

"The roads on which heavy artillery is to be moved must be far stronger than most roads. In fact, in America there are to-day probably few roads that could bear without damage the heavy artillery used now on the western front in Europe. In case of war, our wagon roads, and perhaps some of our railways would have to be greatly strengthened to be serviceable. The selection of the rock and other materials to accomplish this result, the location of the quarries, their extent and their capacity for production, are all within the province of the geologist.

"The geologist in his comprehension of the meaning of topographic, geologic and other maps, in other words in his ability to 'read maps,' can be of much service to army officers. All army officers of course are supposed to be able to understand topographic maps, but to them the contour lines mean only elevations and depressions on the surface of the country, in some places abrupt and in others more or less gently sloping. To the army officer ground is ground, hills are hills, and hollows are hollows. To the geologist, however, ground, hills and hollows have a varying significance. The character of the contour lines on the topographic map may often give him a suggestion of the geological structure of the region and even of the probable nature of the rocks. In fact, if a geologist has even only a very general knowledge of the geology of a region, a contour map may give him a very definite idea of the character of the rocks or other formations comprising any certain district in that region; and if he has in addition a geologic map, his interpretation of conditions is still more accurate. This knowledge indicates to him the character of the mountains, hills and valleys, enables him to judge whether a valley probably consists of low swamps or dry meadows; whether the rivers are deep and difficult to ford, or shallow and easy to ford; whether they are swift and full of rapids, or slow and moving sluggishly.

"The special knowledge of the geologist enables him even without topographic, geologic or any other maps to see many things at a distance not apparent to others. Through his field-glasses he can look far ahead on the line of march, and can observe geological conditions and identify the most available passes over ridges or through mountain ranges; he can determine whether the slopes indicate underlying rocks which might make the passes smooth and easily traversed, or whether they indicate rocks which might offer abrupt and difficult impediments to the passage of an army; he can predict whether the slope on the other side of the range is probably steeper or has a more gradual incline than on the near side, whether it is likely to be an open country or timbered, as well as many other features of practical importance to an army. Many a mountain pass might look desirable to one not familiar with its geology, while another pass, apparently more difficult, could be seen by the geologist to be much more available.

"The geologist can often be of much service to an army in the question of water supply. In regions where surface waters are abundant and suitable for use, the geologist may not be needed, but where underground water has to be sought, his services become of importance. A study of the circulation of underground waters is as much a part of the education of a geologist as the study of the nature of rocks and minerals, of geological formations, of topographic and geologic maps, and the various other matters already mentioned.

"The surface of the ground in many regions, especially in the arid parts of our west and southwest, looks like a dry and barren waste, but often at a depth of from a few feet to a few hundred feet, underground waters are circulating. The discovery of such waters would be of great value to an army, not only in giving them a local supply of clear, fresh water, independent of outside sources, but in saving the expense and the time of men and mules or motor trucks in hauling water from a distance, which, even after it reaches camp, may be hot, muddy and insipid. Underground waters of course cannot always be found, and even where they exist they are often too limited in quantity, or too great in depth, to be available under the circumstances of immediate necessity; but in many places they do exist and could be reached by some form of portable boring machine. The knowledge of the geologist is essential in locating them.

"The problems of landslides and snowslides in mountainous regions, due to vibrations caused by heavy cannonading, the possibility of the use of the seismograph in determining the distance of artillery fire, and many other allied subjects, are important matters for the geologist in studying his sphere of usefulness in the field of battle.

"In addition to the matters already mentioned, the geologist whose work has been in the more newly settled parts of the world, and not in the older settled region where he has lived in civilization, is an efficient scout. His training has been in the wilds among mountains, hills and plains; often without trails, where he has had to take his course by the blazes on the trees or from the stars, the moon or his compass, and often surrounded by hostile natives. He can fight, cook, withstand bad weather and discomfort, and still keep on with his scientific work; he has acquired the woodcraft of the old trapper together with the education of a scientist. Few other men possess this unique combination of accomplishments."

Penrose's war-time service on the National Research Council also included membership in several committees on war work of the Division of Geology, among them the committee on water supply for military camps, of which he was chairman, the committee on the utilization of peat as fuel, and the committee on materials for rapid highway construction. After the establishment of the Research Council as a permanent agency of the government in 1919, Penrose continued as a member of the Division of Geology and Geography until 1923, serving from 1920 to 1923 as a member of the executive committee of the Division.

Among the professional organizations to which he belonged at this period and to which he devoted special attention were the National Academy of Sciences, the Geological Society of America, the American Philosophical Society, the American Association for the Advancement of Science, the Colorado Scientific Society, the Academy of Natural Sciences of Philadelphia, the Mining and Metallurgical Society of America, the American Institute of Mining and Metallurgical Engineers, American Museum of Natural History, the Washington Academy of Sciences, the Geological Society of Washington, the Royal Geographical Society of London, American Geographical Society, the Franklin Institute of Philadelphia. He also belonged to the Zoological Society of Philadelphia, the University Museum of Philadelphia, the Historical Society of Philadelphia, the Hakluyt Society of England, and the Wistar Institute of Anatomy and Biology.

On October 7, 1911, the secretary of the American Philosophical Society, I. Minis Hays, wrote, thanking him in the name of the Society for his "gift of a bronze medal struck by the Republic of France, in memory of the San Francisco earthquake, 1906."

In 1911 he was elected a trustee of the University of Pennsylvania, to fill the post made vacant by the death of Bishop Ozi W. Whitaker, a position which he held for the next sixteen years. In 1920 he declined an offer to become Provost of the University, to succeed Dr. Edgar F. Smith. Through this period, therefore, he actively maintained his interests with the four universities with which he was identified during his life—Harvard, Stanford, Chicago, and Pennsylvania. To each he gave not only service but money.

His resignation in 1927 from the trusteeship of Pennsylvania is typical of the man. Not being in accord with the findings of the committee on administrative re-organization of the University, he felt that the easiest solution of the difficulty was for him to resign. And resign he did despite the protests of the other members of the board and the officers of the University.

For the most part he had given up the active pursuit of his profession, one of his last commissions being as a member of the board of advisory engineers which served from 1908 to 1910 as the result of the invitation to inspect and advise about the holding up of the surface ground above the old coal mines under the city of Scranton, Pennsylvania.

That Penrose, however, ever maintained an active interest in the various problems of his profession is shown by his correspondence. The following excerpts from the correspondence he had with Professor Alfred C. Lane, of Tufts College, concerning radium, are examples:

Letter from Lane, dated Washington, D.C., December 19, 1923

My dear Mr. Penrose:—

I find that Mr. H. V. Ellsworth of the Canadian Geological Survey is working on a pegmatite within which are large crystals both of Uraninite (with U) and Allanite (with Th) both radio active. I hope you will take a chance to see it if you can, and will drop me a line telling me what you have published, and if you will also what U. deposits you have visited, and have unpublished notes on. In studying the Pu:U ratio we shall hope to cooperate with one so well informed as you and certainly give all credit for whatever help you find it practicable to give.

Yours truly
Alfred C. Lane

Letter from Penrose, dated January 23, 1924

Dear Professor Lane:—

On my return from a short absence I have received your letter written from the Cosmos Club of Washington some time ago concerning the matter of the studies of you and your associates in fields in which uranium and radium take an active part. In accordance with your request I will send you as soon as I can get it up a list of what I have published on the subject of uranium, radium and their disintegration products. Most of my work in this connection has been done on the geologic occurrence of these materials.

I note what you say about the pegmatite dike in Canada containing crystals of uraninite and allenite being studied by Ellsworth. I do not know the location of the occurrence which you describe, but I have some old notes relating to certain geologic observations made by me some forty or fifty miles north of Ottawa on a dike containing quite numerous nodules of gummite. I collected some specimens of gummite and the associated feldspar and quartz. I think I have given away all the gummite specimens, but I have some notes on them and will look them up as soon as I can get a little relief from the work that seems to be forced on everyone at the first of the year.

Late in February, Penrose again wrote to Lane, sending him three publications on pitchblende in Cornwall, radium and uranium, and saying that he had "also written several other articles on the subject of uranium, radium and their decomposition products, but the above publications cover the ground referred to in the others. Among the latter was one written for the United States Department of the Interior during the recent war.

"I have personally visited and examined the pitchblende deposits of Cornwall, of Gilpin county in Colorado, and elsewhere; also the carnotite deposits of Colorado and Utah and other localities producing these and other uranium minerals. Many years ago I found nodules from the size of a pea to the size of a hickory nut of the mineral gummite in a pegmatite dike at the old Villeneuve mica mine, situated in Range I of the township of Villeneuve, Ottawa county, Province of Quebec, on the east bank of the Du Lievre River. The dike is composed of feldspar, quartz and muscovite mica and intersects granitic and gneissic rocks. The gummite, though present, was of rare occurrence and possibly it is an alteration product of uraninite as the specimens found were from superficial openings. The mine was long ago worked for white mica (muscovite), but as it was almost forty years ago when I visited it I do not know whether it is now open."

Letter from Lane, dated Cambridge, Massachusetts, February 29, 1924

My dear Mr. Penrose:—

Many thanks for your letter of February 26th and the valuable information enclosed, which is not only of use to me personally but I will also turn it over to Wells of the U. S. Survey, who probably has it but I want to make sure that he does not overlook it.

It would be a wonderful thing if we could get a lead uranium ratio so that we could depend upon it to date minerals, and in that case we might be able to tell which of two veins were the older, and it would be a fine thing for someone to take as a special subject of research, or back up the research of some institution, in which they were interested.

T. W. Richards is already interested. If we could have a man at work all the time in his Lab! Two things we want—a systematic test of the various products of concentration to see which are most radio active and a test for 1 pu 1,000,000 of lead.

Letter from Penrose, dated March 26, 1924

Dear Professor Lane:—

I was very glad to get your letter of February 29th concerning what you are doing in the way of seeking a lead uranium ratio, and I agree with you that such an accomplishment would be a most desirable thing and would undoubtedly throw much light on the relative ages of certain mineral veins. I feel sure that this line of research is a very desirable one and I would be glad to know how you are progressing in it.

I have always been much interested in the geological occurrence of uranium minerals and other materials carrying radium or its decomposition products, and though I have only published the three or more articles which I mentioned to you in my last letter on the subject, yet I have a considerable amount of material in my notes, which some time I would be glad to discuss with you.

The following June, Lane again wrote to Penrose, saying that "the committee has just acquired three or four pounds of pitchblende from Central City, Colorado." He adds: "I am going to England this summer and your notes on the Cornish pitchblende will be very helpful. And I shall appreciate anything further as to what and whom I should see."

Letter from Penrose, dated July 14, 1924

Dear Professor Lane:—

On my return from a short absence I have received your letter sending me a brief copy of what you expect to be the basis of your committee report on Radium, and I feel that you are starting along the right lines. I will observe your request that the report is "not for publication."

If you go to England this summer I hope that my article on The Pitchblende of Cornwall may be of use to you. I described in it some of the more important localities where uranium minerals occur, but there are many others which I did not visit.

You might find it interesting when you are in London to visit the mineral collection of the British Museum at South Kensington, where they have a large and beautiful collection of uranium minerals from Cornwall.

Hoping that you will have a pleasant trip, and wishing you every success in your research, I am,

Sincerely yours,
R. A. F. Penrose, Jr.

Letter from Lane, dated London, July 31, 1924

My dear Mr. Penrose:—

As you see, I am in London and have found your articles of use especially in getting me in touch. But I am not going down to Cornwall as nothing is running and the 30 or 40 dollars that the trip would cost can better be spent in buying pitchblende. The So. Jemas mine which you mentioned is the only one now active and that finds that mining five months a year is enough to supply the demand, and this does not happen to be the five months. I hope I have done something here to stir up people so that they will determine the PU:U ratio right here. I have talked with people who are interested in the mine and I saw Flett, head of the Geological Survey. He is going to Toronto and will be in the U. S. until about Oct. 1st. I hope you will chance to see him and if so put in a word for a report on British ores, and also for (incidental thereto) a good analysis of the Pitchblende.

In November, 1924, Lane again wrote to Penrose, in part as follows:

"I was able to get a number of analyses of the Katanga deposits, and the lead uranium ratio there figures about .08 which would make the age something like twice that of the carboniferous granites; i.e., about that of the Taconic uplift.

"There is some interesting work described in a recent Canadian report, where they have tried to concentrate a pegmatite and didn't find much radio active material, not appreciably more in fact than in an average granite. The interesting thing is that they have concentrated practically all the radio active material from 20 pounds into .03 of a pound. Now if we can do that, and I think we might be able to do a little better, it should be possible to get the lead uranium ratio of granites and determine their age thereby.

"Don't you want to investigate that problem yourself, collecting material from some granites the age of which is of interest and importance, possibly from the part disintegrated by frost, and then get people at Harvard and Tech to concentrate and analyze it? I think for about $3,000 we should get epoch making results."

Letter from Penrose, dated January 12, 1925

My dear Lane:—

I was glad to know by your recent letter that you have returned from Europe and I hope that you saw enough in Cornwall to make your trip worth while. I am not surprised that you were not able to get any good analysis of the Cornish pitchblende showing the ratio of lead, thorium and uranium. I fear that the lack of commercial importance of the Cornish pitchblende at the present time has been responsible for this lack of scientific data concerning its composition.

I am much interested to know that in the Katanga deposits the lead uranium ratio figures about .08. Would it not be possible to get someone at Tufts College or at Harvard chemical laboratory to make analyses of Cornish or Colorado pitchblende in order to get at the ratio in that particular material? I feel moreover there is no doubt that you could get the lead uranium ratio of certain granites in the same method as the Canadians have used on pegmatite, and I do not think this would be a very expensive or elaborate experiment.

I thank you greatly for your kind suggestion that I should undertake the investigation of this problem myself. Nothing would please me more than to join you in this, for I have always been deeply interested in the chemical and physical properties of radium, and especially in their relation to geologic age of rocks I have, however, so many other matters on my hands at present that I feel that I would not be justified in undertaking this additional problem. I might feel inclined to contribute towards it if it is being done by you and your friends as a permanent research and not by a temporary committee.

Similar correspondence with Professor Edson S. Bastin, of the University of Chicago, offers evidence of his interest in such problems.

Letter from Penrose, dated April 10, 1924

Dear Doctor Bastin:—

I thank you greatly for your Bulletin of the United States Geological Survey on "Origin of Certain Rich Silver Ores Near Chloride and Kingman, Arizona," which you have so kindly sent me.

I have read this paper carefully and with the greatest interest and I feel that you have very clearly established the fact that at least in the region you have discussed the mineral proustite is of hypogene origin. Your arguments are excellent, and I can say that the observations I have made on the same subject in the southern part of Arizona would seem to corroborate all you have said in the matter.

As regards the argentite mentioned in the region you have described, I am interested in knowing that you find it partly hypogene and partly supergene. I have had in past years numerous occasions to study deposits in which argentite was more or less abundant, and though in some cases it was supergene yet in many others it seemed to be undoubtedly hypogene. The region in which I studied these deposits was to the south and the north of the line of the Southern Pacific Railway through southern Arizona.

A year or more ago you spoke to me about wanting a specimen of cassiterite from the Malay Peninsula for microscopic examination. At that time my collection of the few specimens I had of cassiterite from this region had been mislaid and I have only recently been able to locate it. All the specimens are rather small, for when I went through that region I was travelling as lightly as possible and had no facilities for making large collections; but if you desire a small specimen I will be very glad to send it to you.

Letter from Bastin, dated Chicago, April 23, 1924

My dear Dr. Penrose:

I thank you very much for your kind letter of April 10th, in which you refer appreciatively to my report on the ore deposits of the Kingman-Chloride district in Arizona, and compare the results with your own observations. I am very much interested to learn that you have reached similar conclusions from the study of neighboring deposits. Ransome, I think, when the paper was submitted to him, felt that I was somewhat rash in introducing a note of encouragement for further exploration of the deposits into the report; but, in view of the microscopic evidence that most of the silver minerals were primary, I felt that those interested in mining in the district were entitled to whatever encouragement these observations implied, although at the same time I tried to be cautious by indicating that other factors were also concerned in the matter of persistence of the deposits in depth.

I am now engaged in writing up the results of rather extensive microscopic studies of the ores at the mines at South Lorrain near Cobalt, with some considerations of the ores at Cobalt proper and it may interest you to know that some of these ores show distinct skeleton crystals of silver unquestionably primary and surrounded by cobalt and nickel arsenides.

Thanks for your kind offer to forward a specimen of cassiterite I should be delighted to have such a specimen if you can conveniently send it, but I would not want to inconvenience you in view of the many duties which I know are pressing upon you.

I am delighted to note that the Academy of Natural Sciences of Philadelphia has elected you its President.

Letter from Penrose, dated May 7, 1924

My dear Professor Bastin:—

I have received you letter of April 23rd and I am much interested in what you say concerning your microscopic studies of ores at South Lorrain and at Cobalt, and in your discovery that some of them show distinct skeleton crystals of native silver, unquestionably primary. I think these observations are very important.

In regard to the specimen of cassiterite from the Malay Peninsula which I promised to give you, I would say that I am sending to you today by registered mail a specimen from what was known at the time of my visit there in 1901 as the Tronoh Mine, not far from Ipoh in the Malay State of Perak. I collected it myself at that mine. The specimen is not large, but it is the only one which shows fairly well the tetragonal crystalline structure of the mineral.

Letter from Penrose, dated November 14, 1924

Dear Doctor Bastin:—

I thank you greatly for your Bulletin 750-C on "Observations on the Rich Silver Ores of Aspen, Colorado," which you have so kindly sent me and which I have read with the greatest interest. I am very glad indeed that you are following out these researches on silver minerals. Your present paper supplements in a very wonderful way your papers of some months ago concerning the Arizona localities which you had studied, and I think some time you ought to bring your results together in a general treatise on the subject.

From 1909 to 1911 and from 1913 to 1915, Penrose served as Councillor for the American Philosophical Society, of which he became a member in April, 1905.

In 1913, 1914, and 1915 he was vice-chairman of the Committee on Mining Geology, of the American Institute of Mining and Metallurgical Engineers, which he had joined in 1889, and of which he was a member for forty-two years. On March 27, 1916, Bradley Stoughton, secretary of the Institute, wrote him that "on recommendation of President L. D. Ricketts, the Board of Directors of the Institute have appointed you Chairman of the Committee on Mining Geology."

Evidently Penrose felt some hesitancy about accepting this chairmanship, for on April 3 (1916) Stoughton again wrote to him, acknowledging his letter of March 28, and noting "with great regret that you are reluctant to accept the Chairmanship of the Committee on Mining Geology. Our Board of Directors believe that with you at its head this Committee might continue its past usefulness to the Institute and also enlarge its activities.

"As far as residence in New York City is concerned, we really think there is a misunderstanding on your part in this regard. In looking over the various committees we find that there is not a Chairman of any one of them who is resident in New York, and some of the very best Chairmen are resident a long distance away. We have only one Chairman of a Sub-Committee resident in New York. If this reason alone impelled you to hesitate accepting the Chairmanship, we hope that you will consent to withdraw your declination.

"The writer of this letter will be in Philadelphia for an engagement on the afternoon of Wednesday, April 5th, and would gladly spend the night in Philadelphia if it would be convenient for you to give me a short interview on Thursday morning to talk this matter over. I think that I can convince you that your residence outside of New York is no handicap in the work, and that, furthermore, the exercise of executive ability at rare intervals and without occupying much of your time, will be all that is required for the position of Chairman of the Committee on Mining Geology."

Evidently Stoughton was successful, for the records show that Penrose served as chairman of the committee that year. From 1927 to 1930, he again served as a member of the committee.

An engraved card, dated January 31, 1915, and bearing the signatures of B. B. Thayer, president; G. C. Stone, treasurer; and Bradley Stoughton, secretary, conveys the information that "The Board of Directors of the American Institute of Mining Engineers desire to express to Mr. R. A. F. Penrose their sincere thanks for his generous contribution toward the Institute's share of the cost of the land on which the Engineers' Building stands, and to report that sufficient subscriptions having been received their final payment has been made."

Although Penrose was not a charter member of the Mining and Metallurgical Society of America, which was formed in April, 1908, he was elected the following year, March 5, 1909. In 1913, he became a member of the Council of the society, a position which he held for nearly twenty years, until his death in 1931. In October, 1918, he declined the presidency of that society.

Percy E. Barbour, secretary of the society, writing in 1940, declared that "he took a very deep interest in the Society generally, and in the details of its operation. For example, he followed very closely the monthly financial statements which we issue and very frequently wrote complimentary notes about them."

He also contributed three items to the society's *Bulletin*.

Penrose also served as a member of the Committee on Ethics, to which he was appointed by J. Parke Channing during his term as president of the society. On April 10, 1924, writing to Louis D. Huntoon, then secretary of the New York Section of the society, Penrose said:

"I have received your letter of April 5th stating that the subject of 'Professional Ethics' will be discussed at the next meeting of the New York Section of the Mining and Metallurgical Society of America on April 16th.

"I am very sorry indeed that a previous engagement here on that day will prevent my being present, and I regret this all the more because, as you may possibly remember, the subject of professional ethics was in the early days of the Mining and Metallurgical Society taken up and carefully studied by a Committee of which I was a member. The report of this Committee was sent to the Society and I suppose it is still on file. Of course this report was prepared some years ago, and perhaps many new features of the subject may have arisen since that time which should be included in a more elaborate report.

"As I am still a member of the Committee on Professional Ethics I am very much disappointed that I cannot be with you on the 16th, but I wish you every success at the meeting, and I hope the subject will be fully discussed by those present, for the Committee thereby may receive important suggestions."

In October of that year (1924), asked to contribute two dollars or more to the expenses of the New York Section, Penrose sent a check for ten dollars, adding, "I think the meetings of your New York Section are very important and I only regret that as I live in Philadelphia I do not have a chance to attend many of them."

In July of that same year, asked by Thomas H. Leggett, then president of the society, to nominate five or six men "who have rendered the Mining Industry most distinguished service. Individual success should not be considered but rather service to the industry or to mankind. Mining Industry is to be taken in the broad sense to include Metallurgy and Economic Geology," Penrose replied that he felt "better qualified to mention names connected with economic geology than with metallurgy. I therefore suggest the names of J. E. Spurr, H. Foster Bain, David White and Millard K. Shaler, all of whom are well known for their accomplishments for the general welfare of mankind in their particular profession."

A week later (July 14, 1924) Penrose again wrote to Leggett:

"On my return from a short absence I have received your recent letters concerning the awarding of the gold medal of the Society of Economic Geologists.

"I have always felt that a medal of this kind which does not have to be given at any specific intervals should only be given when a case appears where the man is so pre-eminently deserving of it that there can be no doubt in any one's mind of the propriety of awarding it to him.

"Under such conditions the medal is a real recognition of merit; but under conditions which require that the medal shall be awarded at certain intervals the man generally has to be sought among many, and this very action is apt to create jealousies and hard feelings which of all things are most lamentable in the recognition of merit."

On March 10, 1913, Penrose became a Fellow of the Royal Geographic Society of London, on nomination of Henry G. Bryant, president of the Philadelphia Geographical Society. On the formal notification of his election, Penrose has written in pencil: "Have paid for Life membership."

He evidently followed the policy of becoming a life member of any organization or club having that class of membership, possibly because the very number of those organizations made the payment of annual dues a time-consuming task. Obviously, also, he had a deeply ingrained feeling that all dues and obligations should be promptly met, for, as Charles W. Henderson, of the United States Bureau of Mines, president of the Colorado Scientific Society in 1938, noted, "Penrose was notable with the Society because he always sent his check for dues before the bill could be mailed to him, so all we ever sent him were receipts. He kept up his membership to the end and aways made the folks out here feel that he was standing by us through all difficulties."

Henderson also recalled that one day he had happened to be in the Bullitt Building of Philadelphia on an errand, and happening to notice Penrose's name on the directory board, had called upon him at Room 460. He said he was astonished to find it such a dark office and went away with the impression that it looked out upon a brick wall. It did. The other permanent impression made upon him by that visit was the size of the big table desk, a desk which now occupies a place of honor at the headquarters house of the Geological Society of America, at 419 West 117 Street, New York

Although he was nominated to Phi Beta Kappa in 1884, it was not until forty years later (November 5, 1924) that he received a letter from Joseph M. Jameson, professor at Girard College and president of the Phi Beta Kappa Association of

Philadelphia, noting "that you are living within easy reach of our meetings, and I am wondering whether our Philadelphia Association of Phi Beta Kappa has been brought to your attention."

Penrose joined the organization the following April, saying in the letter enclosing filled-out application card and check for dues that he had "known of the Philadelphia Association but in the rush of other affairs I have not had a chance to ask much about it and therefore I appreciate your cordial letter."

In addition to his duties as an active director of Utah Copper Company, Penrose was until 1915 a member of the executive committee of the Hanover Bessemer Iron Ore Association, a post which he accepted in 1899; a director of the Philadelphia, Germantown and Norristown Railroad, from 1900 until his death; a director of the Ridge Avenue Passenger Railway Company of Philadelphia, from 1909 until his death.

At the close of 1911, he received word from C. Stuart Patterson, president of The Western Saving Fund Society of Philadelphia, that "greatly to my gratification, the President Judges of the Courts of Common Pleas have today appointed you a Manager of this Society. You will receive from the Secretary the official announcement. I earnestly hope that you will accept, and that we will have the pleasure of seeing you at this office at our annual meeting on Tuesday, 2d January next."

Across the face of this letter, Penrose has written in pencil, "Declined." Patterson refused to take "NO" for an answer the first time, and wrote again on January 2, noting that "the Treasurer has received your formal declination of membership in our Board, and I have received your personal note to me, for which I thank you.

"We had our annual meeting today, but I did not present, nor say anything about your declination, for the reason that I earnestly hope that you will reconsider your conclusion. I really want you in our Board. If you will talk to any of the members of our Board, they will tell you that we do not expect constant attendance at all our meetings. Indeed, if we did have that expectation, it would be impossible for us to secure the strong and representative men whom we have. I know that you will find your personal associations here agreeable, and I know that you will also find that the demands upon your time and attention are comparatively slight. What is more important, you will see that our organization is so thorough and our guards against wrong-doing on the part of any officer so complete that the Managers do not incur either an onerous or a dangerous degree of responsibility."

Penrose had made his decision, however, and could not be moved. This did not imply stubbornness on his part, for he could be convinced, as witness the correspondence with Stephen Birch, president of Kennecott Copper Corporation, relative to Penrose becoming a director in that organization.

Birch wrote to Penrose, under date of April 8, 1924, stating that "the annual meeting of Kennecott is on May 6th and I would like very much to have you as one of our Directors." In his reply of April 12, Penrose said that he greatly appreciated the "kind suggestion that you would like me to be one of the Directors of the Kennecott Copper Corporation, but I feel that there are many other men who know much more about the affairs of your Company than I do and that therefore it would not be consistent for me to become a Director. I assure you, however, that I greatly appreciate your kind thoughtfulness in this matter and I wish you every possible success in the management of the Company of which you so ably act as President."

That same fall (October 9, 1924) Birch again wrote to Penrose, the "owing to the death of Mr. Elliot C. Bacon there is a vacancy on the Kennecott board and I wish that you would come on the board."

This time, in his reply, Penrose explained his position in detail.

"I assure you that I greatly appreciate your offer to nominate me to fill the vacancy created by the death of Mr. Elliot C. Bacon on the Board of Directors of the Kennecott Copper Corporation. I highly appreciate the honor of being on such an important Board, and if I was a holder of any considerable amount of Kennecott Copper stock I would take very great pleasure in accepting your kind proposition. As I still hold my Utah Copper stock, however, I would seem to be in a somewhat ambiguous position as a Director of the Kennecott Copper Corporation.

"As you are aware, the reason I have been holding my Utah Copper stock is that I was one of the original founders in the development of the mine, and I felt reluctant to part with it. I realize, however, that sentiment cannot stand in the way of modern progress, and yet, if my continued ownership of Utah Copper stock does not interfere with the plans and projects of the Kennecott Copper Corporation I would still prefer to retain it. In such a position, do you not think it would be somewhat inappropriate for me to become a Director of the Kennecott Copper Corporation?

"I had hoped to hunt you up in New York this week but I have been detained in Philadelphia. I expect, however, to be in New York next week and will make a point of trying to get in touch with you and will be very glad if we can have lunch together."

A month later (November 7, 1924) Birch wrote again to "Dear Dick," informing him that "To-day we elected you a Director of Kennecott Copper Corporation, and I cannot tell you how much it pleases me to have you on our board."

In his acknowledgment, addressed to "Dear Stephen" under date of November 22 (1924) Penrose, after noting his appreciation of the honor, adds: "As I have written to you before, however, I do not want to go on the Board with any feeling on your or its part that I am thereby expected to turn in my Utah Copper stock for Kennecott Copper Corporation stock, because, for reasons that I have given you before, I prefer to hold the Utah Copper stock."

Then he adds, "I want to assure you that my sympathies of course are with the Kennecott Copper Corporation, and if I should become a Director I would naturally work for its interests; but I thought that the situation should be clearly presented to you so that there may not be any misunderstanding in the future."

Two days later (November 24, 1924) Birch reassured him on that point, declaring that "I do not feel, nor does anybody else, that there is any obligation on your part to turn in your Utah stock. That is your own personal affair and I understand your reasons."

That same year (1924), Penrose became a member of the board of directors of the Nevada Consolidated Copper Company, and in 1927 a director of the Braden Copper Company of Chile. His positions in these three copper companies he held until his death in 1931.

In writing to John H. MacGowan, vice-president, and subsequently president, of Braden, November 25, 1924, Penrose thanks "Dear Jack" for his "kind words about my having been elected a Director of the Kennecott Copper Corporation. I still hold my Utah Copper stock because I have held it from the beginning and would feel like parting with an old friend to give it up. My sympathies are with the Kennecott and I will always take pleasure in serving it; though in the past few years I have been trying to dodge new jobs, with the result that I find I am accumulating more and more."

The following year, however, he decided to dispose of his Utah holdings, and in that final moment of that long relationship, he did a typical Penrose act. He wrote to D. A. Crockett, transfer agent of the Utah Copper Company (July 22 1925):

"Now that I have disposed of all of my Utah Copper stock which I have held for so many years, but which I thought it well to sell, I am writing to you to thank you for your always gracious and efficient treatment of the various transfers which I have made through you.

"The promptness, accuracy and courtesy with which you have handled the business of your office during these many years past will always be remembered by us who were associated with you."

Penrose closed the letter "with kindest regards and hoping perhaps to have business with you again in the future."

Crockett replied on July 27, having "just returned from a two weeks vacation" to "find on my desk what is undoubtedly the finest and most welcome letter that has ever come to me from the outside business world during my entire career...It is difficult to express the real measure of my appreciation but I wish to assure you that I shall retain that letter and hold it in as high regard as I have always held your acquaintance."

Penrose would probably not have considered himself as a "club" man, but the list which he prepared a few years before his death shows eleven in Philadelphia, five in New York, two in Chicago, three in Denver, one in Colorado Springs, one in Salt Lake City, and one in San Francisco. Many of these clubs maintain not only general social rooms, but bedrooms, so that his membership in organizations in cities which he frequently visited made it possible for him to feel a certain amount of "at-homeness" wherever he went.

Reference has already been made (in his letters to his father during that long trip to Siberia and the Orient in 1901–1902) to his joining of the Union League of Philadelphia, of which his brother Boies was already a member. The other members of the family followed in due time, Spencer being elected in 1905 and Charles in 1909. Richard became a life member in August, 1919.

In 1892, in company with Spencer he had become a member of The Philadelphia Club, membership in which is limited to five hundred. As originally organized in 1834, the club had comprised a group of men who met to play cards at "Mrs. Rubicam's Coffee House" on the northwest corner of Fifth and Minor streets. Subsequently, it moved to the old Adelphi Building and changed its name to the Adelphi Club. In 1850 it was incorporated under the title "The Philadelphia Association and Reading Room," but changed that designation in 1859 to its present title. A note of thanks to Richard, dated 1902, shows that he had contributed one hundred dollars "for the purpose of having portraits of former presidents of the clubs painted."

On June 6, 1930, he wrote to Gouverneur Cadwalader, secretary of the club:

Dear Gouverneur:—

I have received the official notice to the members of The Philadelphia Club relative to the action taken at the annual meeting on May 12, 1930, to establish a class of Life Membership which any resident member may enter upon application to and approval by the Board; also that the life membership will cost $4,000, and will relieve the member from the payment of further annual dues.

I think this is an admirable plan, and I beg that you will enter my application for life membership. In doing this I feel that it will not only be a deep gratification to me to become a life member, but also a great pleasure to realize that in so doing I am expressing my loyalty to the Club and its traditions, as well as helping to promote the object of all of us to put the Club on a sound financial basis.

I hope you will let me know when my application for life membership has been acted on by the Board, as I would be glad to send the remittance promptly.

On June 26 (1930) he sent his remittance to the treasurer, the board in the meantime having acted upon the application.

Frequent reference has been made in these pages to "The Rabbit," a social club of Philadelphia to which his brothers also belonged, the members meeting twice during each winter month to do their own cooking.

"He was an expert in cooking fish," wrote M. L. Parrish, of the Philadelphia firm of Parrish and Company, in 1940 of Dick, "but rarely would stay to eat his own production. Just before dinner was served, he would invariably take his departure. The little clubhouse is about eight miles from the city. Quite often on Rabbit days some of us—he and I and occasionally others—would walk out to the little clubhouse in Fairmount Park.

"He would often take drives in his motor through the surrounding country, especially New Jersey," continued Mr. Parrish. "While he was a member of the Philadelphia Club and other clubs, he seldom visited them," adding that "he had few friends, but many acquaintances. He was not a mixer and one might almost say that he was a recluse."

On June 12, 1924, in a letter to the secretary of The Rabbit, T. Charlton

Henry, Penrose wrote that although he had already taken out two of the $400 certificates to one of which each member of the organization had been asked to subscribe, "I realize fully the importance of having no debt overhanging 'The Rabbit' property, and therefore it gives me much pleasure to enclose my check for four hundred dollars as a third contribution to a participating certificate." On June 19 (1924) he wrote further, "I assure you that it gives me great pleasure to assist in this way in a place which plays such an agreeable and pleasant part in the lives of its members."

When The Midday Club of Philadelphia was organized in July, 1929, Penrose was among those who became original members by invitation. Sponsors of the club included W. W. Atterbury, Robert K. Cassatt, Thomas S. Gates, George Wharton Pepper, Edward T. Stotesbury, and Samuel M. Vauclain.

Another limited membership (500) organization to which he belonged was the Rittenhouse Club of Philadelphia, his election having been in 1902. Organized in 1875 as the "Social Art Club," its organizers including S. Weir Mitchell and Caspar Wister, the club was admittedly "A permanent social club for promotion of literary, artistic, and antiquarian tastes among the citizens of Philadelphia, and such kindred purposes as the Club may, from time to time, determine, by establishing and maintaining a library and reading room, and a collection of works of art and antiquities, either by loan or otherwise." Barringer was also a member of the Rittenhouse, having been elected in 1883.

In 1912, Penrose became an Associate Member of the Pen and Pencil Club of Phildelphia, an organization of newspaper men, to which he also contributed gifts as well as his regular membership dues.

In 1905, in company with his brother Spencer, Penrose was elected a member of The Racquet Club, a Philadelphia organization "for the purpose of maintaining racquet courts and facilities for playing the games of racquets, court tennis, hand ball and facilities for other like athletic sports and for gymnastic exercise."

Reminiscent of his college activities was his life membership in the University Barge Club of Philadelphia, to which he was elected April 29, 1886. Although a third of the active membership of the club, which was organized "for the purpose of instruction and improvement in, and enjoyment of, the art of rowing, and the cultivation of a friendly feeling in all who participate in this amusement and exercise" is confined to "graduates or undergraduates of the University of Pennsylvania," three Penrose boys—Boies and Charles (1882) and Richard—became life members, another (Spencer) became an honorary member in 1890, and a fifth (Philip) was also a member. This was another organization in which Barringer was also a life member, having been elected in 1882.

Penrose was also a member of the University Club of Philadelphia and the Harvard Club of Philadelphia.

In the spring of 1918 (May 8) the secretary and treasurer of the Automobile Club of Philadelphia, wrote that "in accordance with your request, I have proposed you for membership in the Automobile Club. Your name will be acted upon at the next meeting of the Board of Directors. Meanwhile, I shall be glad to have you avail yourself of the Club's facilities."

His unfailing desire to do the right thing is shown by a letter which Penrose wrote (March 22, 1924) to the secretary of the Philadelphia Country Club, which he had joined in 1902:

"I have long been a non-resident member of the Philadelphia Country Club because for many years I lived in the west and was but little in Philadelphia. I am now here, however, more and more, and I think it is only proper if I am to keep up my membership in the Club I should pay resident dues. I have not had an occasion to use the Club for many years, but I would be very glad to be transferred from the non-resident to the resident list if this is feasible."

Penrose was a life member of the Harvard Club of New York and of the University Club there, to which he was elected non-resident member February 6, 1918. According to the University Club records he maintained a residence at the club from January, 1919, until his death, having a particular room which he rented by the year. Spencer had been elected a member on January 6, 1904.

On April 10, 1918, Penrose became a member of the Union Club in New York, his sponsor being Edmund Waterman Dwight.

Other New York organizations to which he belonged were the Boone and Crockett Club (a sportsman's organization), the Down Town Association (an organization maintaining a restaurant for a group of business men in the Wall Street neighborhood), and the Explorers Club to which he was elected an active non-resident member in May, 1929. At one time he was a member of the City Lunch Club of New York, but resigned in December, 1916.

His Chicago clubs recall his association with the University of Chicago, being the University and the Quadrangle Club.

In November and December, 1925, there was considerable correspondence between Penrose and the Quadrangle Club, concerning a lost check which should have paid Penrose's dues for that year. The matter was finally straightened out, and on December 9 (1925) Penrose wrote to the manager of the club, noting that he had become "a member of the Quadrangle Club during the early years of the University of Chicago when I was Professor of Economic Geology there, and though I resigned this position some twelve or fourteen years ago, yet I have kept up my membership in the Club for old times' sake, in recollection of my cordial relationships at the University.

"For this reason I wrote to you about my dues, for I am always careful to be prompt in such matters. I regret giving you all this trouble, but will be greatly obliged to you if you will let me know if this remittance covers my obligation to the Club until the dues for the next current year are payable."

Penrose was proposed for membership in the University Club of Chicago in June of 1908 by Rollin D. Salisbury, professor at the University, and William Franc Anderson, vice-president of the Harris Trust and Savings Bank. He was elected a non-resident member on October 30, 1908, and remained a member until his death.

"As you know, every Club has its officers elected at the annual meeting; but there is always an office force which holds over, and I was fortunate enough to be able to become acquainted with Mr. Penrose through the Secretary's work," wrote Harriette E. Hills in July, 1940. "He knew the names of the employees, asked for them when he came to the Club and was very appreciative of every service. One thing he did every year was to write a letter to the Club the first of November, enclosing a check for the Christmas Fund, and wishing each and every employee a 'Very Merry Christmas.' He took the time in his busy life, to think of our Christmas, and that letter was sent to every department every year for each employee to read. It was such a pleasure to have him come—he was so gracious and kindly, and left us all with the feeling that a great man had been among us."

His three Denver clubs were the The Denver Club, to which he was elected in 1896 and of which he became a life member in 1918; the University Club of Denver, and the Denver Country Club.

He was also a life member of El Paso Club of Colorado Springs, a class of membership he entered in the summer of 1918, after inquiring how this could be done. He sent the requisite check, in acknowledging which the secretary of the club wrote:

"The Board highly appreciates the kindly sentiments you express and trusts that the future may permit more frequent and extended use of the club for the greater pleasure of all concerned."

Then he added, "I am pleased to add that it was ordered that the war tax imposed on members dues be assumed in this instance by the club."

But Penrose would not have it that way, and on August 2 (1918) the secretary again wrote, acknowledging receipt of dues and war tax and adding, "Your generous act and kind sentiments are highly appreciated."

In Salt Lake City, he belonged to the Alta Club, which had been organized and incorporated in March, 1883, with membership limited to 350. Richard was elected September 8, 1909, his brother Spencer and D. C. Jackling having become members in 1904. Other well-known mining men who were members were Walter Aldridge, Lewis S. Cates, Karl Eilers, Sidney Jennings, and Pope Yeatman.

Penrose was also a non-resident member of the Pacific-Union Club in San Francisco, having been elected April 17, 1905. On July 31, 1922, the president of the Club, K. R. Kingsbury wrote that "The Board of Directors in accepting the valuable gift which you made to the Club of a medal struck off by the French Government in commemoration of the bravery and efficiency of the people of San Francisco in rebuilding their city after the fire, wish to extend its thanks and assure you that this gift is much appreciated by the members of the Club."

That Penrose availed himself of the club privileges when he visited San Francisco is shown in a letter which he sent in November, 1924 to F. A. Humphrey, assistant secretary of the club, in the course of which he remarked that he "was very glad to hear from you again and hope that everything is going satisfactorily at the Pacific-Union Club. It has been almost two years since I have been in San Francisco, but I have been detained here by many matters, though I look forward to a trip to the Pacific Coast some time before long. It is always a pleasure to me to come to the Pacific-Union Club, and I well remember your cordial welcome when I was last there."

In addition to his regularly maintained rooms at the University Club in New York, Penrose also rented a room at the Hotel Wolcott in the same city, also by the year. Of this habit of living in hotels, which he continued to the end of his life, Penrose wrote in a letter to F. B. Loomis (December 9, 1921) in connection with arrangements for the annual meeting of the Geological Society of America, "I think that Amherst College has certainly been most liberal in opening its own buildings to the geologists, and I think we all appreciate this greatly. As far as I personally am concerned, however, I have lived most of my life in hotels and I suppose that I had better continue to do so, as it is hard to teach an old dog new tricks."

Again, in writing to his brother Charles (January 22, 1924) then at Aiken, S. C., he says: "I think you are wise to stay at the hotel instead of opening your cottage, for though a hotel is often lonesome enough, yet a cottage is more so; and after all one can get many comforts at a hotel that he could not find in a rented cottage.

"Let me know if I can do anything for you here. I will write to you about the allocation of the copper dividends when the information is worked out by the bookkeepers in New York."

That same wistful note is evident in several letters, among them one to Professor W. H. Emmons, of the University of Minnesota, to whom he wrote on October 17, 1921:

"It gives me great pleasure to welcome you home from the far off land of China. I have been there myself and I know how far away and lonesome it seems, especially when you have no companions."

Again, in a letter to his brother Speck, dated March 22, 1924:

"Please give my kindest regards to my friend in the Post-Office Department of Morgan, Harjes & Company, whom you say inquired after me and tell him that I appreciate his remembering me and that I hope to see him the next time I have the good luck to come to Paris.

"I hope you will drop me a line when you get this letter and let me know how you are getting along. In the meanwhile let me know if I can do anything for you, and if you are not feeling a good deal better I will be glad to come over to Paris to see you."

Later that same year (October 28, 1924) he writes again to Speck that he is "sorry you cannot stay east more than a day or two but I suppose your other plans, as you describe them, will prevent your doing so. I hope, however, that you and Julie will always remember that a most cordial welcome awaits you here whenever you come this way."

In this connection it is noteworthy that in all his correspondence, which bears every indication of a meticulous attention to all the forms of polite social intercourse, he sends only one letter of thanks for a gift to himself. Many are the letters from others acknowledging gifts from him and he acknowledged Christmas cards. Does that mean that no one ever sent him anything? Perhaps those who might have done so felt that he had everything he needed or wanted. Even in the matter of books, there is frequent recommendation from various correspondents that he read this or that, but only one writer said he was sending the book for his attention.

Such a condition could not have failed to make an impression upon even a less sensitive man than Richard Penrose, and may very well have been a contributing factor in the "reserve" which every one who knew him remarked as increasing in strength as he grew older.

That one letter of thanks was to his cousin, Ellen Penrose of Carlisle. It is dated January 24, 1925, and reads as follows:

Dear Nellie:—

I thank you greatly for your letter of January 18th and for the beautiful little penknife which has just arrived. You and your sisters were very kind to send it to me, and I shall keep it not only because you have sent it to me but because it is so artistic and useful.

CHAPTER 18

Beginnings of the Society of Economic Geologists

UNDER date of April 5, 1920, eight prominent geologists, particularly interested in the economic aspects of that science, sent out a suggested constitution and by-laws for the formation of a society for "the advancement of the science of geology in its application to mining and other industries; the diffusion of knowledge concerning such application; the advancement and the protection of the status of the profession; the definition and maintenance of an adequate professional standard; and the formulation and maintenance of a code of professional ethics."

The eight men were James F. Kemp, head of the Department of Geology at Columbia University; Louis C. Graton, professor of mining geology at Harvard University; Alfred H. Brooks, geologist in charge of the Division of Alaskan Mineral Resources, United States Geological Survey; E. W. Shaw and Ralph Arnold, members of the United States Geological Survey; Josiah E. Spurr, editor of the *Engineering and Mining Journal;* George H. Ashley, State Geologist of Pennsylvania; and Waldemar Lindgren, professor of economic geology, Massachusetts Institute of Technology.

To a picked list of sixty names, the small group also submitted the question of a name for the new society and a ballot of officers, the sixty thus chosen to become members of the Organizing Committee of the new organization.

The constitution and by-laws were ultimately adopted with some changes. Of the three names submitted—Society of Economic Geologists, Society of Geological Engineers, Society of Applied Geology—the first was finally chosen. The ballot for officers resulted in the choice of R. A. F. Penrose, Jr., as the first president of the new society. Other officers chosen were: vice-president, E. S. Bastin, professor of economic geology at the University of Chicago: directors: W. H. Emmons, head of the Department of Geology at the University of Minnesota and director of the Minnesota Geological Survey; Hoyt S. Gale, in charge of the section of non-metallic deposits of the United States Geological Survey; A. C. Veatch, geologist with the Sinclair Consolidated Oil Company; H. V. Winchell, prominent consulting mining engineer and geologist; and Professor Lindgren.

Formal announcement of name and officers was made on June 3, 1920 by Sydney H. Ball, prominent mining geologist, who had been acting as secretary for the Committee of Eight.

Of the propriety of such a move, Penrose had apparently in the beginning some question, but having satisfied himself of the worthwhileness of such a venture, he set about giving of his best to the organization and the proper development of such a society. The years 1920 and 1921 saw him with this work as his first care, and again and again in his correspondence, particularly in the opening months is there evidence of his far-seeing vision and careful judgment in the efforts made to have the organization established on sound, dignified, and long-enduring foundations.

The story of that formative period is best told in the correspondence which Penrose carried on with those who were its active participants.

Letter from Penrose to S. H. Ball, dated April 16, 1920

On my return from a short absence I have received your letter of April 5th with enclosures relative to the formation of a society for economic geologists and I have read them with the greatest interest. I have known for some time that such an organization was contemplated, but I did not know that it had progressed so far as I now learn from your communication.

I highly approve of the organization of such a society and it will give me much pleasure to become a member of the "Organizing Committee of Sixty" who will form the nucleus of the new organization.

As regards the name of the society, I should strongly prefer the title "Society of Economic Geologists" in preference to either of the other names which have been suggested in your communication to me.

As regards the copy of the proposed Constitution and By-Laws which you have sent me, I would say that I think in many respects they are excellent; but I have often wondered whether a society of this kind could not have some advantages as a section of the Geological Society of America rather than as an entirely distinct organization. I have no doubt that you and your associates have discussed this matter fully, but I personally would feel that a very close relationship to the Geological Society of America would be extremely desirable.

Letter from Penrose to S. H. Ball, dated April 20, 1920

I wrote to you some days ago concerning the organization of the new society of economic geologists and I expressed to you my pleasure in accepting your kind invitation to become a member of the Organizing Committee.

Since that time I have been thinking seriously about this matter and I called at your office in New York yesterday to discuss it, but I was told you were out of town. I am therefore writing to you again.

I feel that my first allegiance among geological organizations is to the Geological Society of America, and I do not want to be put in the position of having a divided allegiance. I would be very glad to join a society of economic geologists which would represent a section of the Geological Society of America, or I would be very glad to join a similar organization which would be entirely independent of either the Geological Society of America or of any other organization. The difficulty I feel in the present situation, however, is that you and your associates have put into the Constitution of the new society of economic geologists a statement to the effect that it shall meet yearly with the Geological Society of America and yearly with the American Institute of Mining Engineers. I feel that the new society cannot serve two masters, and that it should either be closely affiliated to the Geological Society of America as a section, or else be absolutely independent of both the Geological Society and the American Institute.

I can readily understand that perhaps for the present it may be desirable to meet with the two other societies as indicated in your Constitution, but I do not think that such regulations should form part of the Constitution. I feel that meeting places should be arranged from time to time by the Council or other governing body, according to change in circumstances; but absolutely to bind up the new society with a contract to meet at certain times with two other societies seems to me a matter that has no place in a Constitution. Conditions may change from year to year and may make it undesirable at times to follow this part of the Constitution, and yet it is difficult to change a constitutional clause. Why, therefore, cannot this clause be omitted from the Constitution?

I have written to you thus fully about this matter because I feel so strongly about it that I now think I would be reluctant to join an organization which commits itself so absolutely to a policy which might in the future prove to be very embarrassing and unwise. For this reason I beg that you will for the present keep in abeyance my former letter in which I accepted your very kind offer to become a member of the Organizing Committee of the new society.

Letter from Penrose to James F. Kemp, dated April 22, 1920

Dear Jim:—

It was indeed a great pleasure to receive your very cordial and kind letter of April 18th. I feel as you do that no new friends are like one's old friends, and I constantly find that I am always hanging closer to those with whom I have gone through the early years of my life.

I have read with the greatest interest what you say concerning your connection with the proposed new society for economic geologists and I have also read the correspondence between you and Spurr, Leith and Winchell, which you enclosed. I find that I feel very much as you do about this matter. I have yet to be convinced that there is any necessity for a new society. We are all overwhelmed with work connected with already existing societies, and one more means simply that much added to the burden. Moreover, I feel that I cannot approve of the Constitution as offered in a circular which Mr. Ball has sent to us. In this connection I enclose herewith to you a copy of a letter which I have written Mr. Ball on this subject, and you will notice at the end of it that I have asked him to keep in abeyance for the present my former letter in which I accepted the offer to become a member of the Organizing Committee of the new society.

I have no doubt that if the few who are ambitious for it push it hard enough they will find that many geologists will become members simply because it is a geological organization, and they will think that they have to belong to it, but not because they enthuse over it. I still feel that the Geological Society of America has for the last couple of years or so given more and more recognition to economic geologists, and if this tendency continues will not economic geologists finally come into their full rights in the parent society without having to form a new one? After all, it seems to me impossible to draw the line between pure geology and applied geology. One blends into the other, and purely scientific research can be carried on in both.

Would it not be well for some of us to meet some time in New York and discuss this matter before committing ourselves definitely to it? It is a serious step to organize a new society unless it is backed up by enthusiasm and by numbers.

Letter from J. E. Spurr to Penrose, dated April 29, 1920

Ball has shown me copy of your letter regarding the proposed Society of Economic Geologists. I hope you will join in with us and that questions of provisions of the Constitution may be taken up by the Council in due course of time.

The Society offers the promise of uniting all economic geologists in one group; I found, on discussing it, that many prominent geologists never attended the Geological Society meetings, and that as a rule these were much attached to the Geological activities of the Institute of Mining Engineers. All, however, recognized the advantages of unity.

There was a general understanding among the original committee that the new society would cooperate in a close and loyal way with the Geological Society of America, but it was not thought fitting to put into the Constitution anything that spoke for another Society. The effect of the new society would be, however, to bring to the meetings of the G.S.A. a far larger number of mining geologists than ever before, and would, therefore, greatly improve the tone and activity of this parent Society.

Letter from Penrose to J. E. Spurr, dated May 1, 1920

My dear Spurr:—

I thank you for your letter of April 29th, and for your remarks about the proposed Society of Economic Geologists. I fear you have misunderstood my letter concerning this matter to Mr. Ball. What I meant to state in that letter was that if the Society was to be an independent one, instead of a section of the Geological Society of America, I thought that it should not state in its constitution that it should necessarily meet with any other society. The time might come when we might want to meet independently, and though at the present time, I entirely approved of the proposed meetings with the G.S.A. and with the American Institute, yet we cannot tell what the future may bring forth in this matter.

I think therefore that the meetings with these two Societies ought not be written into the constitution, but should from time to time be provided for by resolution of the Council. It is difficult to change the constitution, but a resolution of the Council may be changed from year to year.

Of course my preference would have been to have seen the new society formed as a section of the G.S.A., but I find that this is not a popular idea, and if, therefore, the society is to be independent, I feel very strongly, as I have said above, that no provision as regards the other societies with which it should meet should be put into the constitution, but that they should from time to time be determined by the Council.

I would be greatly pleased to have your opinion on this matter, for I think it is most important.

Letter from Penrose to S. H. Ball, dated May 6, 1920

Dear Mr. Ball:—

On my return from a short absence in Washington where I was attending the meeting of the Division of Geology and Geography of the National Research Council, I have received your recent letter relative to the proposed Society of Economic Geologists. While in Washington I had a chance to talk to several geologists about this organization and there seemed to be a very general impression that it was a necessary and desirable one. I personally fully agree with this sentiment.

I feel, however, like some others with whom I have talked, that the Organizing Committee of Sixty ought to have the right to discuss and, if necessary, change the articles of the Constitution. I would be very glad to know if such is going to be the case. I mean no reflection on the Constitution as drawn up by the first Committee, but as I wrote you some days ago, I think that there are some details which might be amended to advantage. If the Organizing Committee is to have the power to do this I would be very glad indeed to become one of them, as you so kindly suggested in your letter of April 24th.

Letter from Penrose to J. E. Spurr, dated May 6, 1920

My dear Spurr:—

I thank you greatly for your letter of May 4th concerning the proposed "Society of Economic Geologists" and I fully appreciate the attitude of those who formed the Constitution in wishing to make permanent the feature of meeting with certain other organizations. Of course I am entirely willing to agree with the majority, but I have wondered whether this same provision had not better be made by an act of the Council of the Society rather than by a clause in the Constitution. It is hard to influence posterity, and it might be found some time in the future that it would be desirable to meet in other ways. Under such circumstances the Society might have a great deal more difficulty in amending the Constitution than in changing a resolution of the Council.

All this, however, I hope to be able to discuss with you in New York next week. I will call you on the telephone when I get there, and would be greatly pleased if you could take lunch with me so that we could go over the matter together.

Letter from J. E. Spurr to Penrose, dated May 22, 1920

My dear Penrose:—

The polls for the new society were opened yesterday by a quorum of the original committee consisting of Lindgren, Graton, Ball and myself. The outcome is as follows:

    Name of Society—Society of Economic Geologists
    President—Penrose
    Vice-President—Bastin
    Councillors—Lindgren, Emmons, Winchell, Veatch and Gale

There was a very gratifying response to the invitation sent. Out of the sixty selected, fifty votes were received, and of the other ten practically all can be accounted for as being out of the country and otherwise unable to respond.

In view of your opinion on the subject, to which, as a matter of fact, our opinions all agree, arrangements were made to switch the clause regarding the meetings with the G.S.A. and the A.I.M.M.E., from the constitution to the bylaws, and inserting a further proviso that this arrangement would last until otherwise decided. This will be done by a letter sent out to the fifty voters, and the matter will be put in such a way that there is no doubt that it will be agreed to.

Regarding the affiliation with the Geological Society of America—that, as I advised you, is already thoroughly understood and needs only to be put into effect by agreement between the two societies, when the formation of our society is announced.

I was requested by the committee to advise you of the outcome of the election, as above.

If you will advise me of your acceptance of the presidency, the organization of the society can be published; it will then be, I understand, in order, at your convenience, to summon the council for its first meeting.

Letter from Penrose to J. E. Spurr, dated May 27, 1920

My dear Mr. Spurr:—

On my return from a few days absence I have received your letter of May 22nd notifying me of the outcome of the polls for the new Society of Economic Geologists, which were opened yesterday, and that I was reported as being elected President.

I appreciate greatly the very high honor which this election means, but at the same time I feel that there are many geologists in the country who could fill the position of President far more efficiently than I could, and for this reason I really regret that one of them was not elected, for the Society would, I frankly believe, thus be more capably served. In my present condition of uncertainty, therefore, I beg that you will allow me two or three days to consider this matter so that I will be able to determine whether or not I can arrange my affairs to accept the election; and also whether or not I feel that in view of the importance of the new Society I can conscientiously do so.

Do you not think that the publication of the Constitution and By-Laws of the Society had better be delayed until we can have a meeting of the Directors to discuss the change in the features which you mention?

Letter from Penrose to J. E. Spurr, dated May 31, 1920

My dear Spur:—

I have carefully considered your letter of May 22nd in which you tell me that I have been elected by the Organizing Committee of Sixty as President of the Society of Economic Geologists.

My delay in replying to you definitely about this matter has not been due to any reluctance to accept such an honorable position, but to my hesitation as to whether or not I am worthy of it. My conclusion, however, is that if the Organizing Committee has seen fit to elect me I should not go against their wishes; and though I know full well that there are many economic geologists who could fill the position far better than I can, yet it gives me much pleasure to accept the election.

I assure you and our associates that during my term of office it will be my ambition to help establish on a firm and efficient basis a Society which I predict will be a guiding light in the field of geology as applied to the welfare of mankind.

Letter from J. E. Spurr to Penrose, dated June 1, 1920

My dear Penrose:—

I have yours of May 27 regarding your election as president of the Society of Economic Geologists.

I hope very much that you will decide to accept this position, since I feel that you are eminently qualified for it, and I know that this is the opinion of the principal economic geologists of the country, as is evidenced by the vote that you received.

Should you still have any further doubt on the subject, I hope that you will give me the opportunity of talking the matter over with you.

Letter from J. E. Spurr to Penrose, dated June 2, 1920

My dear Penrose:—

Since writing you yesterday, I have received your welcome letter telling me that you have accepted the presidency of the Society. I think I may congratulate the Society upon your acceptance. On the other hand, however, I feel that you will find this is a very worthy position, as I anticipate that the Society will be a great one.

I will transmit your suggestion in your letter of May 27 regarding postponing the change concerning the meeting place from the Constitution to the By-laws until the thing can be discussed at a meeting of the directors. In view of your preference, I have no doubt this matter will be postponed.

I am advising Mr. Ball of your acceptance of the office and he will at once advise the committee of 60 of the outcome of the election and send a special letter to each of the other officers advising them of their election. As soon as these letters have been sent out and have been received, the matter will, I take it, have passed out of the hands of the original committees and be entirely in the hands of the elected officers, and the next move would appear to be for you to call a meeting of the board of directors.

I plan to announce the formation of the Society in our issue* of June 12, unless you see some reason for further postponing this notice.

Telegram from Penrose to J. E. Spurr, dated June 7, 1920

Letter June second just received. I beg that you will not announce the formation of the new Society in your issue of the twelfth. I have ample reason to think that the organization has been forced too rapidly. More deliberate procedure will insure greater final success. Will write.

Letter from J. E. Spurr to Penrose, dated June 8, 1920

My dear Penrose:—

I have your telegram of June 8 and shall postpone the announcement of the formation of the new society until you think it advisable to make it.

Letter from Penrose to J. E. Spurr, dated June 8, 1920

My dear Spurr:—

I had been trying to get you on the long distance telephone all morning but failing to do so I had just begun to dictate a letter to you when I finally succeeded in getting you at your office, and therefore from our conversation over the telephone you are aware how I feel in regard to postponing the announcement of the formation of the new Society in your issue of June 12th. I sent you a telegram briefly explaining my arguments for this postponement last night, and I think that our conversation over the telephone to-day made them clearer.

I am very glad indeed that we are to meet for lunch at the Harvard Club in New York at 12:30 next Friday and I am looking forward with much pleasure to discussing this matter further with you at that time.

In the meanwhile I want to thank you greatly for your letter of June 2nd, which I received on my return from New York, and also for your letter of June 7th, which I received this morning. I appreciate your very complimentary remarks about my election as President of the Society, but I assure you that I am still in very great doubt whether someone else could not fill the position very much better than I can.

Excerpts from letter from Penrose to S. H. Ball, dated June 7, 1920

I was greatly interested in the details concerning the Society which you gave me last Friday, and our conversation threw much more light on the subject than I had had before. I believe that there is a great field for a society of economic geologists, but I cannot help feeling that we have been going rather rapidly in this matter and that we ought to be very careful about the details of the organization, and that we should also try to avoid injuring the feeling of anyone

---

* Spurr was editor of *Engineering and Mining Journal.*

eligible for the Society who has not yet been approached. In looking over the list of the Committee of Sixty it seems to me that several very desirable men have been omitted from it. For these and other reasons I telegraphed to Mr. Spurr last evening, suggesting that it might be well for him not to announce the formation of the new Society in his issue of the 12th as he intended to do, but to delay the matter until we could proceed more deliberately in the preliminaries.

Of course any slight changes in the Constitution or in the By-Laws might possibly be made more easily before declaring the organization complete than afterwards, and we might also find among those not mentioned in the Committee of Sixty someone who might be more suitable than I am for President.

I hope that I will have an opportunity to discuss this matter further with you in a few days, in New York.

In the month between June 7 and July 6, there was much correspondence between Penrose and Spurr and between Penrose and Ball concerning the matter of changes in the Constitution and By-Laws being confirmed by the original committee of eight, who should in turn submit them to the Organizing Committee of Sixty for ratification before any formal announcement or further steps should be taken by the elected officers. On this matter of procedure, Penrose seems to have been courteous but obdurate. Finally, an agreement was reached.

Letter from Penrose to J. E. Spurr, dated July 6, 1920

Many thanks for your letter of July 2nd. I am very glad to know that the two changes in the Constitution which were submitted to the Committee of Eight have been satisfactorily agreed on by the majority of that Committee. . . .

As soon as we hear from a considerable number of the Committee of Sixty concerning the notice of the change in the Constitution which Mr. Ball was to send out last week I suppose we had better try to get together as many of the Board of Directors as possible and proceed to elect a secretary. In the meanwhile, however, I hope to be in New York some time in the next few days, and if you are there it would give me great pleasure if you would take lunch with me and we can discuss these matters at that time.

In the meantime, Penrose had written to Ball and to Graton concerning the affairs of the new organization.

Letter from Penrose to S. H. Ball, dated June 25, 1920

My dear Mr. Ball:—

I have received your letter of June 23d, enclosing paragraphs from letters which you have recently received from Messrs. Winchell and Bastin.

As regards Winchell's remarks about when to start in getting more closely together in the matter of the Society of Economic Geologists, I would say that I have already heard the same expression from two other sources. I have delayed calling a meeting on account of matters which Mr. Spurr has doubtless already communicated to you and which I think are extremely important for the original committee of eight or nine to attend to before the committee of sixty takes over the control of the new society. Mr. Spurr, I believe, has discussed these matters with you and I feel that prompt action by the original committee is very necessary. Mr. Spurr has doubtless told you why it seems extremely important to have the original committee send out their supplemental notice, instead of leaving it to the committee of sixty. For this reason, I have delayed calling a meeting until the communication has been sent out.

Regarding the communication which you sent me from Bastin, I would say that I also have received a very kind letter from him, expressing about the same ideas as he has expressed to you, and offering to cooperate with me in any way possible. I have only gotten it on my return here to-day, but will answer it at once. I do not think that Bastin's plan of holding a meeting with the American Institute in August is feasible, for it is not going to be possible to get together a proper organization by that time. I think that our first meeting had better be held with the Geological Society of America in Chicago next December. By that time, we ought to be thoroughly organized and can carry on a systematic, well-ordered meeting, whereas an impromptu affair in Michigan with the American Institute in August would not show the society in its best light. In matters of this kind, I always feel that it is better to go a little slower at first and get started right than to try to rush things headlong and then to find that it requires many years to get straightened out.

Letter from Penrose to L. C. Graton, dated June 28, 1920

Dear Professor Graton:—

Many thanks for your letter of June 21st and for your very kind remarks regarding my election as President of the Society of Economic Geologists. I greatly appreciate the confidence you express in me, but I still feel that there are many others who could fill the position far better than I could. I hesitated for some time to accept it, but after consultation with Spurr and Ball I concluded that it might obviate various complications if I did accept it, and hence I find myself in an office which I would much prefer to see someone else in.

The whole matter came to me so suddenly that it has taken me some time to realize just where we stand. It seems impossible to get anything but a very meager meeting of the Directors or of the Committee of Sixty at this time of year, as they are mostly scattered in every quarter of the country. There are features in both the Constitution and By-Laws that need careful consideration, and I will try to call some sort of meeting in the early fall. If this proves impossible I do not see what else we can do than to wait until the meeting of the Geological Society of America in Chicago next December, when we can surely get enough members together to take some effective action. In the meanwhile I will be working upon such details as I can, and I would be very glad to have any suggestions that you may have in mind, for I value greatly your good judgment and common sense. My feeling is that it is all-important to get started right, even if this means a little delay, for by so doing we may avoid many future difficulties.

Letter from Penrose to L. C. Graton, dated July 6, 1920

Mr. Spurr has forwarded to me your letter of June 28th to him. I think you misunderstand my suggestion of a more elastic provision for the meetings of the Society of Economic Geologists. I agree with you entirely that it is most desirable to meet with both the Geological Society of America and the American Institute of Mining Engineers. I have been a member of both Societies for over thirty years and my loyalty to both of them has never been questioned. I may have been more active in the work of the G.S.A. than in that of the A.I.M.E., but I have always taken an active interest in the A.I.M.E. It was my loyalty to the G.S.A. that made me hesitate to take office in the new Society, for I feared that the latter might detract from the influence of the former; but after talking to Spurr, Ball and others, it seemed that I had better go along in the capacity to which I had been elected.

I think, however, that arrangements for meetings should be made by a resolution of the Directors, and not be put in the Constitution. No man can predict what the future may bring forth; it is futile to try to influence posterity; and therefore I think that the question of meetings should be more elastic than a constitutional provision permits. I would most heartily favor a provision by the Board of Directors to the effect that the annual business meeting of the new Society should be held at the same time and at the same place as the general meeting of the G.S.A, and I would also be glad if we could become affiliated with the G.S.A. under the new provision that that Society now has in contemplation. I can see no objection to holding one meeting in a year with the A.I.M.E., and even affiliate with it if our Society so desires. But why should we shut out all other societies with whom from time to time it might be desirable to affiliate either in the United States or in foreign countries? Yet the original constitution was strongly suggestive of restricting affiliation to the two Societies in question.

As soon as we can get a meeting of the Directors together I would be glad to support any suggestion that for the present we have the two meetings yearly, the annual business meeting at the same time and place as the annual meeting of the G.S.A., and the other meeting at the same time and place as one of the meetings of the A.I.M.E. I judge from your letter that this would be satisfactory to you.

I note what you say about dues and I agree with you in much that you say; but do you not think that for the present at least most of our members will be members of one or both of the other Societies we have discussed, and hence practically all members will be paying $5.00 yearly, and very few, if any, $10.00 yearly? Moreover, suppose members of other well known societies who might be eligible to membership in the Society of Economic Geologists should become candidates, why should they also not have the right to the same reduction in dues as the members of the G.S.A. and the A.I.M.E.? They could justly claim it, and hence as most of our members will doubtless be derived from the membership of other societies, why put in the provision of $10.00 a year simply to catch the very rare exception? It would be but little help to the Society financially and would rather suggest a sort of "class legislation," which is rather offensive.

I will be very glad indeed if you can find time to let me hear how you feel about these matters.

Letter from L. C. Graton to Penrose, dated Calumet, Michigan, July 12, 1920

My dear Mr. Penrose:—

Many thanks for your letter of July 6th. You persuade me to agree with you entirely with regard to both the dues and the places of meeting. I am sorry to have caused you this trouble, but am glad to have been brought into accord.

Letter from Penrose to L. C. Graton, dated July 22, 1920

My dear Professor Graton:—

I was very glad indeed to get your letter of the 12th on my return from some days absence, and to know that we are both of the same opinion with regard to the dues and the places of meeting of the Society of Economic Geologists. I assure you that it was a pleasure to me to have been able to answer the questions you asked in your previous letter, for it shows you are taking a deep interest in the affairs of the Society, and such men as you are the kind that we need to make the Society a success.

Letter from Penrose to S. H. Ball, dated July 22, 1920

Dear Mr. Ball:—

I have received your letter dated Leeds, Utah, July 16th, relative to the position of secretaryship of the Society of Economic Geologists. Of course we all greatly regret that you feel that you cannot accept the position permanently, for I am sure that you would fill it with the greatest dignity, efficiency, and honor. I am very glad to know, however, that you will temporarily retain the secretaryship until the Board of Directors can appoint your successor.

We are going to try to have a meeting of the Directors of the Society in New York on July 29th. I am not sure yet whether or not we can get a quorum, but if we can do so we will be able to transact some of the more important business matters. As yet no one has been agreed on as permanent secretary, and I hope therefore that you will do as you say, and act temporarily as secretary at such times as you are in New York, until we can appoint another member of the Society.

Letter from Penrose to S. H. Ball, dated August 13, 1920

I have received your letter of August 10th and am very glad to know that you are home again.

I was very sorry that you could not have been present at the meeting of the Directors of the Society of Economic Geologists on July 29th, but Spurr kindly consented to act as "Secretary for the meeting." We voted to hold an organization meeting at Chicago on December 28–30, 1920, at the same time and place as the Geological Society of America. We also elected J. Volney Lewis Secretary and Treasurer of the Society, but he is in the west and will not return until

November 1st. I therefore sincerely hope that you will still continue to act as Secretary pro.tem. until he gets back. In the mean time, if you have occasion to take another trip, either Spurr or I will try to keep things going.

I expect to be in New York some time next week and will call on you in the hope of finding you still there.

If you need any further details about the proceedings of our meeting on July 29th, Spurr can give them to you.

The meeting had been held at the Harvard Club in New York, where Penrose had invited the members of the Council to be his guests at luncheon and to discuss, in addition to the points made in his letter to Ball, "the question of directors and officers for next year; and the question of additions to our membership, which is a very important matter and which I [Penrose] think should be given attention as soon as possible in order not to give offense to those who were not included in the Committee of Sixty."

As he wrote later to W. H. Emmons, professor at the University of Minnesota (October 17, 1920), Penrose found that "the first year or two in organizing a new society of this kind is surrounded with innumerable difficulties. I think, however, that we will be able to make a very good showing at our meeting in December."

He wrote innumerable letters during those summer months, many of them for the secretary, Mr. Ball, who was away from his office, and many of them in his official capacity as president. Having decided to accept the appointment as president, he devoted his time to that task, even to working out the various forms for letter-head, nomination blanks, and insisting that the various steps be made with due regard to parliamentary procedure. Not until October did he finally get away from Philadelphia and the East in order to make a hurried trip to Utah, Arizona, and California, on his personal business errands.

Letter from Penrose to E. S. Bastin, dated August 9, 1920

My dear Professor Bastin:—

I was greatly pleased to get your letter accepting the appointment for the arrangements for the December meeting of the Society of Economic Geologists. When the Committee was appointed no definite mention was made of a Chairman, but everyone seemed to take it as a matter of course that you as Vice-President of the Society and living in Chicago, would naturally be Chairman of the Committee. I beg therefore that you will accept the Chairmanship at my request.

I have read with interest what you say about affiliating with the Geological Society of America under the new terms of affiliation which are now being voted on by the Fellows of the G.S.A. I personally highly approve of the amendment permitting this kind of affiliation and have voted in favor of it. If the amendment passes, I understand that, as you say, it provides that an affiliated Society may choose from its own membership a Vice-President of the G.S.A. I would highly approve of our Society adopting affiliation under these terms.

Regarding the question you bring up concerning "Economic Geology" as the official organ of our Society, I would say I am most friendly to *Economic Geology* and have always done what I could to help it. I have, however, discussed the subject in question with several people and there seems to be a difference of opinion. They all feel friendly to *Economic Geology*, but many of them seem to think that other journals should not be cut off from papers on economic subjects. I think this subject should be carefully discussed at our Chicago meeting next winter.

I think that at that meeting there will also be a great many other matters of importance concerning the organization and future policies of the Society of Economic Geologists which will need discussion. It has occurred to me, therefore, that if you think proper, a good deal of time ought to be allowed for this purpose. This would necessarily restrict the time allowable for the reading of papers. I suppose perhaps we ought to have some few papers, but I should think that they ought to be of the highest class and rather brief. All this, however, is up to you as Chairman of the Committee on Arrangements.

Letter from Penrose to E. S. Bastin, dated August 24, 1920

Dear Doctor Bastin:

I suppose at some time during the coming fall it will be desirable to send a notice to the members of the Society of Economic Geologists regarding our meeting in Chicago next December. Of course this procedure will be largely a duplication of the notice sent out by the Geological Society of America, because most of the members of the new Society at the present time are probably members of the G.S.A., but at the same time a notice sent directly to the members of the new Society would probably tend to show that it intends to be an active, live organization.

I am writing to you now about this matter to ask you whether you think it would be better simply to send an announcement to each member of the Society of Economic Geologists to the effect that we would meet with the G.S.A. in Chicago on December 28th to 30th, 1920, or whether we should go into more elaborate detail as to what we intended to do there. As there is still a great deal of vagueness about what we really intend to do at that meeting, I should think simply a plain statement of where and when the meeting would occur would be the more desirable course to follow. I would like very much, however, to have your opinion on this matter.

I have received a letter from Lewis, from Salt Lake, saying that he expects to be East about the first of November, and will be able to take hold of the work of Secretary of the new Society. I think, however, that if we had some of the above mentioned details already arranged for him when he returns East considerable time might be saved. I also think that perhaps it might be well to have some sort of letter head printed, giving the name of the Society in plain and simple type, and the names of the officers and members of the board of directors. If you think well of this matter I will try to look after it.

Letter from Penrose to E. S. Bastin, dated August 30, 1920

My dear Professor Bastin:

I thank you greatly for your letter of August 26th, which I have read with much interest.

I agree with you in thinking that at the meeting of the Society of Economic Geologists in Chicago in December there will be time enough for a certain number of papers and that there may be many members in attendance who would prefer to listen to papers than to attend to organization matters. Your plan, therefore, would allow any one to exercise his own taste at the meeting.

. . . .

At the meeting of the Board of Directors held in New York on July 29th, it was decided not to ask for any dues before 1921 but that the regular dues should become payable at the beginning of that year. I suppose that any small expenses that may be incurred between now and that time can be collected out of the dues for 1921. I, personally, will be glad to stand the expenses which I incur up until that time but there is no reason why the other officers of the Society should do so if they do not wish it.

I am having some stationery printed for the Society here in Philadelphia and will send you some as soon as I can get the work done. I would have had it sooner but I wanted to get the arrangement of the letter-heads properly made and I wanted to get good paper. This has delayed me a few days.

A few days later (September 2, 1920) Penrose again wrote to Bastin that he hoped "in a few days to have properly headed stationery printed and I will send you some as soon as I can get it. There seems to be endless delays in printing and in getting paper, but I hope that it will only be a few days when I can send you at least the first instalment of the stationery." Five days later (September 7), he again wrote to Bastin concerning the stationery:

"I have had some stationery printed and three sets of envelopes, one bearing your name, one bearing Lewis's, and one bearing mine. The letter-heads are the same in all three cases. After discussing the matter of the letter-head with Spurr and others, we decided that it should be made as simple as possible and therefore we used only the initials of officers and directors in all cases except where there was only one initial, and then we spelled out that name. We also left out the addresses of everyone except the Secretary. Of course his address was essential. In cases where you or I use the paper we can put our addresses at the head of it. We all seemed to think that by leaving out all addresses except that of the Secretary, the name of the Society at the head of the paper would become correspondingly more prominent."

In that same letter of September 7, Penrose said that "to each member of the Committee of Sixty I expect to write an individual letter accompanying the above-mentioned enclosures [Constitution and By-Laws and names of the Committee of Sixty], stating the date of the meeting, the names of the Committee on the local programme for the Chicago meeting and other details." He also said that he had "discussed the question of nominations in detail with Mr. Spurr and we both agree that if anyone really wants to send in a nomination it is all right for him to do it, but that perhaps it is not well to force this matter until the meeting in Chicago, because some of the Committee of Sixty, though they will have in their possession the Constitution and the By-Laws, might not fully appreciate the qualifications required for a new member and might inadvertently recommend a man who might not be elected, thus hurting the feelings of both the candidate and the proposer."

About this same time, he also wrote to Bastin that "I neglected to express my appreciation of your remarks about your desire to continue our close affiliation with the Geological Society of America. I personally feel the same way. The new Society is an outgrowth of the G.S.A., and I feel that we should always maintain the closest relationship with the parent organization. We can, of course, when it seems desirable, meet with other organizations, but I cannot help feeling that our annual meeting should be with the G.S.A. I hope some time soon to have the pleasure of discussing this matter with you in person."

The matter of nominations to membership in the new Society occupied much of his time and thought during September. On the 13th, he wrote to J. Volney Lewis, concerning a proposed nomination: "I would suggest that we go a little slowly about nominating anyone unless he has a very good chance of being elected, for if a man is defeated, his feelings are hurt, his proposer is hurt, and the Society is apt to be charged with too much discrimination." On the 27th, he wrote to Bastin, "I expect to send out this week a letter to the members of the committee of sixty relative to the matter of electing new members, and I am having a blank form printed for nominations. I am not at present sending out these blank forms, but am stating in the letter which you will receive in a few days that they can be received by application to the Secretary. Spurr and I and several others thought that this method of distributing the blanks would be better than sending them broadcast to the committee of sixty—a process which might be construed as working a propaganda to increase our membership."

Circulars and nomination blanks kept Penrose much occupied until he left for the West, but when he did go, he could write to Spurr, under date of September 30, "I think that for the present I have done everything in my power to help along the organization of the Society of Economic Geologists. My final act has been to send a batch of nomination blanks to you, to Lewis, and to Ball. . . . I feel now that the Society is a going concern and that all the officers are active on their jobs; but if you think of anything else that can be done before I return, November first, I hope you will let me know."

But no sooner had he gone west, than Penrose remembered other details, for he wrote to J. Volney Lewis on October 9, from San Francisco: "When I left Philadelphia some days ago I thought that I had already in printed or mimeograph form all the documents which we would need at our meeting next winter. It has occurred to me since, however, that we will require some printed registration cards and some blank form of receipt for dues. I will attend to having both of these printed when I get back East in November. We also ought to have a program stating the proceedings on different days and perhaps giving the abstracts of papers to be read at the meeting. I have written to Bastin, asking him to let me have a copy of the program he has arranged when he has completed his plans. I will then have it either printed or mimeographed. I am writing to you now simply to let you know that I have these various matters in mind, for you may also have thought of them yourself."

Up until the meeting in Chicago, Penrose continued to busy himself with matters of printing and other endless details concerning the first meeting of the organization. On December 13 he wrote to Lewis: "On my return from a couple of days absence I have received your letter of December 11th and I greatly appreciate the kind remarks which you have made about the printed matter which I have been getting out from time to time for the Society of Economic Geologists. I assure you it is a great pleasure to me to feel that you approve of it. Many times I tried many different patterns before settling on what seemed the most dignified for the Society."

But printed forms were not his only worry. On September 15, Myron L. Fuller wrote to Penrose that he took "pleasure in acknowledging your letter of September 8, which I find awaiting me on my return from a summer in the Mackenzie and Arctic districts of Canada.

"I note with much interest the constitution and details of organization of the Society of Economic Geology, together with its able list of officers. I appreciate the inclusion of my name on the Committee of Sixty.

"I may say, however, that my interests have of late years been entirely in petroleum, while your society will naturally devote itself largely to metalliferous matters.

"This fact, and the further fact that I have practically retired from economic work of any sort, makes it seem undesirable for me to maintain membership in any but the few societies in which I am especially interested.

"I feel, nevertheless, that your society will fill a long felt want, and I wish you every success in organizing and putting it in position among the large and strong societies."

To this, Penrose replied on September 20, thanking him "for your cordial remarks concerning the Society of Economic Geologists. It is a matter of great regret to me that you hesitate to remain as one of the original Committee of Sixty. You know your own interests, however, and the matter is for you to determine. I hope sincerely, however, that you will reconsider your decision, as you will add strength to the organization."

Penrose did not accept the matter as mildly as his letter might sound, for he immediately wrote to Ball and to Frederick G. Clapp, asking them to use their influence to get Fuller to reconsider. "I have written to him asking him if he would not reconsider his resignation but I thought it would be well also to write to you to ask you to use your influence on him not to resign," he wrote to Clapp, and added, "So far as I know, he is the only one in the whole organization who has definitely resigned up to date."

His procedure proved effective, for October 5, Fuller again wrote to Penrose, saying that "since writing you some two weeks ago that it did not seem expedient for me to accept membership in the new Society of Economic Geology, several friends have taken the matter up with me and urged me to reconsider. Under the conditions I shall be glad to follow their wishes and will accept membership and help in any way I can."

Penrose had already departed for the west, but he wrote to Fuller from Los Angeles, on October 14, saying that he was "very greatly pleased that you have decided to retain your membership in the Society of Economic Geologists. I assure you that so far as I have been able to observe there has been no discrimination in the organization of this Society against oil geologists. I think that an inspection of the list of the Committe of Sixty will show that oil geologists are fairly represented, as they certainly should be.

"My conception of the sphere of the Society," continued Penrose, "is that it should be open to all geologists who are eligible to become members on account of their accomplishments in oil, metallic products, or any geologic occurrences. Unless we take this broad vision of the organization and of its membership I should feel that there was no use in continuing with it at all. I think therefore, that anyone who joins it will find that a spirit of fair play to all those engaged in applied geology of any kind is the prevailing feeling."

Penrose had already written to Clapp on September 30, much along the same lines, saying, "I personally should feel that the Society was making a great mistake if it did not represent every branch of economic geology; in fact, I should immediately resign as an officer if I thought it was going to confine itself either to metallic or non-metallic substances. I think that it should include every phase of applied geology, and I look forward to the time when it may have sections representing different kinds of applied geology. I feel the greatest interest in the future of this organization, but I fully realize that its success will depend on the breadth of vision that its officers and directors take in their recognition of all branches of the profession."

He also found time from his personal business in the West to promote the cause of the new society. Under date of October 21, he wrote from San Francisco to Spurr that "since coming to California, I have made a point of getting in touch with the various members of the Society of Economic Geologists who live on the coast, so as to tell them what we have been doing and let them feel that they are in touch with the progress of the organization."

On his return to Philadelphia, Penrose once more plunged into the plans for the Chicago meeting of the society. On November 3, he wrote to Edward B. Mathews, treasurer of The Geological Society of America, thanking him "for sending me the copy of the form of receipt of The Geological Society of America for annual dues. The reason I wanted it was that I am getting up a form of receipt for dues for the Society of Economic Geologists and I knew that I could follow no better example than the form gotten up by The Geological Society of America.

"You will probably be surprised at my being President of this Organization," he continued. "The reason is that I was elected without being consulted, and though I was inclined to decline the position, considerable pressure was brought on me to retain it, so that I finally concluded that it would probably be best for me to accept it for the short time which I would have to serve. One of my principal reasons in accepting it was that I am very anxious to see the new Society closely affiliated with the Geological Society of America and I think that we are going to succeed in accomplishing this result. Our first meeting will be held at the same time and place as the Geological Society of America in Chicago next December and I hope by that time we can formally become affiliated with the parent Society, that is, the G.S.A."

During this period, also, Penrose was continuously being requested to sign nominations for the new organization, but, as he wrote in a letter to Benjamin L. Miller, professor at Lehigh University, "there seems to be an impression in some quarters that the president of the Society, on account of his official position, should not make nominations, as such action on his part might be interpreted by some of the members as an effort to use his official position in urging special nominations," and he added with justifiable pride, that "the affairs of the new Society are progressing very satisfactorily, and I cannot help feeling that it is going to fill an important position in the field of applied science."

Some of these nominations worried him. He feared lest things being too precipitate should involve the society in misunderstandings or change the objectives for which the organization was formed. In writing about a distinguished engineer, whom some one had proposed, Waldemar Lindgren in a letter to Penrose, said that when the matter had been presented to him to make the nomination it was "rather embarrassing to me because although I would be very glad to have [him] in the Society, yet I can not see that he is to be regarded as an economic geologist, however distinguished his contributions have been in related fields." Penrose replied that he agreed "in believing that no one should be nominated unless he can be regarded as clearly within the class of economic geologists as distinguished from men in other professions."

On December 7, Penrose also took up the matter of "a list of men from foreign countries who might be eligible as members of the Society of Economic Geologists," sending Spurr a list of those who might be considered.

The question of the best possible form of Constitution continued to fill his thoughts, and in a letter to J. Volney Lewis, Penrose wrote under date of November 30, that "I think that it is not altogether desirable to spread broadcast copies of the Constitution as it now exists, because quite a number of changes will have to made in it at our coming meeting, and I believe that it would be better to wait until we make these changes before giving too much publicity to the Constitution. I would suggest therefore that the present Constitution should be given out only when especially necessary. One of my reasons for this suggestion is that it is desirable to eliminate altogether from the Constitution the class of 'Associates' and to have only members. You may remember we discussed this matter in New York, and in talking with Spurr a few days later he approved of the idea. Lindgren is strongly in favor of the change."

Penrose also found time for many little acts of courtesy, which throughout his life were characteristic of the man, like the following letter to George Otis Smith, director of the United States Geological Survey, dated November 2, 1920:

Dear Doctor Smith:—

I have received a letter from Professor Bastin, of the University of Chicago, saying that you had kindly promised to attend a meeting of the Society of Economic Geologists next December and to present a paper. I drop a line to you now simply to thank you very much indeed for the interest you are taking in this organization and for your kindness in offering a paper for the meeting. Your interest in the Society will of course add greatly to its dignity and standing and your paper will doubtless be one of the most important events in our first meeting next December.

One of the last things he did before going to Chicago to attend that eventful meeting, for the success of which he had labored so long, was to write to Secretary-Treasurer Lewis (December 21):

"I beg to enclose herewith my check for five dollars ($5.00) in payment of my annual dues to the Society of Economic Geologists for 1921. I assure you it gives me much pleasure to begin my dues to our new organization."

Lewis acknowledge the receipt the following day, and added: "The Society is under tremendous obligation to you for the time, labor, and money you have expended so freely upon it and the splendid manner in which you have infused it with vigor. This will gradually be realized by the members after the Society gets well under way as a dignified functioning organization, commanding universal respect, as it surely will.

"I look forward with great pleasure to the privilege of working with you at Chicago—and afterward."

In the midst of all these details of organization—and it must be remembered that at this same period he was a member of the Visiting Committee to the Department of Mining, of the Visiting Committee to the Department of Geology, Mineralogy and Petrography, and of the Visiting Committee to the School of Engineering, at Harvard; a trustee of the University of Pennsylvania; a member of the publication committee of the American Philosophical Society; member of the Council of the Mining and Metallurgical Society of America; member of the Board of Directors of The Wistar Institute of Anatomy and Biology; member of the Executive Committee of the Division of Geology and Geography of the National Research Council; as well as the director in various commerical companies and railroads, in addition to his investment studies—Penrose found time to write his first presidential address for the Society of Economic Geologists. Short and to the point, as he had promised Bastin in a letter written some time before the meeting, the address was delivered December 28, 1920, in Rosenwald Hall at that same University of Chicago which had been the scene of his first attempts as a lecturer, nearly thirty years before.

Penrose chose as his title *The Relation of Economic Geology to the General*

Principles of Geology, and the address itself might well serve as the introduction of the new organization to the geological profession.*

"The term economic geology is used to indicate the application of the general principles of geology, that is, purely philosophic or theoretic geology, to material uses," Penrose said. "Scientific research is possible in both these branches of geology. Research in purely theoretic geology consists in an effort to unveil the as yet undiscovered secrets of the earth; research in applied or economic geology consists of making useful to mankind the various facts that purely theoretic geology has disclosed; but economic geology may go further and disclose some of these facts itself. Both fields may attract the highest degree of intellectual and scientific talent.

"The investigator in purely theoretic geology, whether in the field or in his laboratory, is absorbed in seeking only new truths in the earth sciences; he works in an atmosphere of seclusion entirely removed from the affairs of man, and wholly in communion with pure science; while the economic gelogist is in active touch with the affairs of man and is quick to study the best methods to apply to material uses the scientific discoveries produced by his more seclusive ally or by himself.

"Many geologic phenomena have been utilized by mankind long before their scientific significance was known. Thus prehistoric man often lived in caves of splendid proportions without having any conception of how these abodes were formed, until geology many centuries or even hundreds of centuries later demonstrated their origin. The discovery of flowing Artesian water in Artois, France, was made centuries before its geologic cause was known, but when this cause was found the discovery of similar wells was vastly increased by economic geologists. The discovery of oil for the first time in a boring was made in Pennsylvania in 1859, and was simply a wild venture, but when some thirty years later Dr. I. C. White developed his epoch-making theory that oil was to be found where certain structural features of the rocks favored its accumulation, the search at once became an intelligent and successful exploration.

"Thus many geologic phenomena have been used for practical purposes by man before geology has made their causes known. On the other hand, the causes of many geologic phenomena have been discovered long before their usefulness has become apparent; but in years or perhaps generations later this knowledge has become of great value to the human race. A striking instance of this is the careful petrographic study of rocks, which has been wonderfully developed in recent years and which at first was apparently a purely unpractical study. It has now, however, become of very great practical importance in deciding the resistance of different rocks to atmospheric and other conditions. If such knowledge had been available in by-gone ages many ancient stone structures now crumbling in ruins might still be standing, because they would have been built of more durable rocks. Even in recent times the brown sandstone in some of the splendid buildings of New York, now crumbling in premature decay, might also

* Printed in *Economic Geology*, volume 16, no. 1, January, 1921.

have been substituted by more resisting materials; and many of our highways, quickly torn in ruins by the automobile, might have been made durable for ages. The minerals pitchblende and carnotite (sources of radium), and many other occurrences were all once studied simply as matters of purely scientific interest, representing a part of the unravelling of the secrets of the earth, but their economic value has since been discovered.

"Where research in theoretic geology ends and that in economic geology begins is indefinable. The work in one is the supplement of the other, and no distinctive line can be drawn between them. Both strive for the truth, whether that be simply scientific or economic. Likewise among economic geologists no sharp line can be drawn. Many of the latter specialize in particular subjects, but they are all geologists and they are all devoting their attention to the application of geology to useful purposes. There should therefore be no distinction between those geologists who devote themselves to iron, copper, oil, clay products, saline deposits, and other metallic or non-metallic materials. The only difference between the oil, the iron, and other economic geologists, is in the matter of detail. There may be a disposition of one class or another to assert its superior importance over the others. Such a feeling seems out of place in the broad conception of the grand work of geology applied to the great industries of the world, and any envious distinction as to the special object to which economic geologists are applying their talents is unworthy of the greatness of their work. No class of economic geologists should vie with another for importance or notoriety, but they should all work together in the great effort for the benefit of industry, science and mankind.

"Through all the relationship of work in economic geology to that of work in purely theoretic geology one great feature stands out, and that is that the success of economic geology started originally from discoveries in theoretic geology. Geologic actions during all time have been in operation, for the laws of nature, discovered or not discovered, are always in effect; but the economic geologist after the discovery of the laws governing these actions may guide or hasten their utility. When Isaac Newton discovered the law of gravitation he found what had not before been explained to man, but the force which he described had been in operation from the remotest times of which we can conceive. Newton's discovery simply made this force intelligible and more applicable to the purposes of man. So also have the purely scientific studies of minerals, of rock structure, of igneous magmas, and of the vast chemical and physical changes in the earth's history disclosed what has been going on for gelogic ages, and after their discovery by the student of purely theoretic geology, have supplied the data for further research by the economic geologist. Economic geology therefore cannot progress faster than the new discoveries in geologic science. The latter must always be in the lead, just as the pathfinder in the forests must precede the highway.

"The application of economic geology is of such inestimable value to mankind that its study needs no stimulus, but geologic research, whether by purely theoretic or economic gelogists, is less familiar to the general public, and is often forgotten in the wild scramble for direct material results; yet it is the basis on which all benefits to mankind from economic geology have been derived. During the recent war many geologists, both economic and purely theoretic, nobly gave their services in one way or another entirely to their country, and research departments were largely depleted of their workers. With the termination of the war some of the research workers have returned to their old pursuits, but many have been weaned away by more worldly ambitions in economic geology. The limit of elasticity has been strained; the rebound has not been complete. The progress of economic geology cannot be maintained unless the trend of discoveries of new truths in the earth's secrets progresses. No house can be built to a height greater than the foundation can support.

"I believe that now more than ever the world is in need of work in geologic research. Cannot the economic geologist increase his assistance in this matter by drawing scientific conclusions, and publishing them, from the vast practical experience in commercial work that comes to him? Sometimes business difficulties prevent this, but often these can be honorably adjusted. In many cases this has been done, but vastly more can be accomplished, and the economic geologist in so doing can raise himself from the position of one who simply applies the ideas of others, to one who is in himself productive of both research and economic results, thus rendering him both the originator of scientific conceptions and the fabricator of their useful applications, the discoverer of new constructive ideas as well as one who uses ideas already formulated. In the conception of such an ideal I look forward with unwavering confidence to the future power for good to mankind and usefulness to science which will be exerted by the Society of Economic Geologists, not only as a national but as an international organization."

At the constituting meeting the officers for 1920 were continued by appropriate ballot for the year 1921.

"The attendance at each session was about sixty, and the interest is attested by the fact that the seating capacity of the room was exceeded and several people stood throughout the sessions," reported Secretary Lewis to the members of the Society in his report of the occasion. "A fine spirit pervaded these first meetings. There was widespread interest in the new Society and it was accorded a hearty welcome on every hand. It begins its career with an asset in the general good-will that should materially facilitate its development into a useful and fruitful organization."

The president of the Society was equally delighted with the way things had gone.

"We all missed you personally very much," he wrote to George Otis Smith on his return to Philadelphia. "Dr. P. S. Smith read your article in an admirable way and it was greatly appreciated. As an officer of the Society, I beg to thank you personally for having taken the trouble to write this article and have it read because anything from you always adds to the success of a meeting of this kind.

"The meeting of the Society of Economic Geologists was in every way a great success," he continued. "In fact, it was more successful than any of us had even dured to hope. There was a great deal of enthusiasm and a large attendance. The hall in which we met was packed with members and others from the outside. I mention this simply to show you that there seems to be a real place for this new Society and I think that every one now realizes that we are thoroughly on our feet and are a going organization."

Penrose started right in with his continuing duties at the beginning of the new year, among his letters of January 1, 1921, being one to A. C. Veatch, in which he said, after commenting upon the general enthusiasm which marked the meeting, "Before the meeting the Council amended the Constitution in some respects and in the open meeting the amended Constitution was unanimously accepted. In addition to a number of minor changes the principal changes which we made in the Council were to change the name of 'Board of Directors' to 'Council' and to eliminate totally the class of 'associates'. Our idea in this was that an associate would be looked on by the public in general as a member, whereas the members themselves would know that he was an associate because he was not qualified to be a member. We thought it best, therefore, to have but one class and to let that consist of members, so that anyone who was not qualified to become a member could not belong to the Society at all."

Letter from Penrose to James F. Kemp, dated January 2, 1921

My dear Jim:—

I write to tell you how greatly I appreciated your wonderful ability as a toastmaster at the dinner of the Geological Society of America last week. Your kindness made it impossible for anyone to decline to speak when you called on them.

Just before the dinner broke up I left the room with Leith, Spurr and others at our table, not because we were tired but because the heat in that particular corner was becoming so intense that we had to seek some air. I understand that after we had left, you again referred to me in a very kindly manner and made some remark to the effect that I did not often get on my feet to speak.

I cannot tell you how I appreciated all this kindness on your part, and I want to assure you that, as I look back, I realize that what made me speak at the dinner last week was the marvellous expression of good fellowship and kindness which beamed forth from your own wonderful personality. I am glad that I spoke, for otherwise I would always have felt that I had shirked my duty as President of the Society of Economic Geologists; and for your insistence in this matter I thank you.

I hope that your efforts at the meeting of the Geological Society did not tire you too much, and I look forward with pleasure to listening to your Presidential Address next December. In the meantime I beg to extend to you and to Mrs. Kemp the best of all good wishes for the coming year.

That same day (January 2) Penrose also wrote to Bastin saying that "as a member of the Society of Economic Geologists I want to thank you most sincerely for the admirable manner in which you, as Chairman of the Programme Committee, carried out your plans at Chicago at our first meeting last week. I feel that our Society made an excellent start and that a very large part of its success was due to your wise and efficient management."

Two days later, he again wrote to Bastin, that "since writing to you a couple of days ago it has occurred to me that it is important for the Society of Economic Geologists to clean up the debts that it incurred in 1920. These are not great, but certain sums are due you, Ball and Lewis for incidental expenses. I talked to Lewis about this over the long distance telephone yesterday and he said he would write to you for your account.

"What I personally have spent I consider a contribution to the Society," he continued, "and will not collect, but no such action is necessary on the part of others; and when the Society has settled up the accounts of you, Ball and Lewis, we can start the new year clear of debt."

On January 5, he wrote to Lewis that he had "talked to the printer about the most desirable form in which to issue our printed constitution and by-laws. He suggests that we put it in the shape of a small pamphlet with a stiff paper cover which will fit into an ordinary sized envelope. It occurred to me that perhaps this form would be very desirable. If you approve of this method I will go ahead, and you may be sure that I will select good paper and a good cover."

Lewis, however, thought that a larger size would be more suitable for filing, so Penrose had both sizes printed and sent to Lewis for distribution. During January, Penrose also had new nomination blanks printed and new letter-head made up in which he "spelled out the first or second names of all the officers and councillors, except my own. I thought that probably you [he was writing to Bastin] and the others would prefer this method. I did not spell out my own first name because my full name is already too long, though I feel that I am not responsible for this as I did not name myself."

Concerning the booklet, Lewis wrote Penrose on January 23 that "the booklet containing the Constitution and By-Laws is a very handsome piece of work, and the Society is again greatly indebted to you, both for your generosity and for the high standard you have established and so consistently maintained in its stationery and printing. The booklet is a delight to the eye and to the touch—a splendid combination of good materials and good taste."

Two other special matters engaged Penrose's attention and filled his correspondence that January—one was the matter of getting the nominating committee at work because of the long time necessary to elapse between nominations and elections, and the other was the matter of preparing a list and working out the form by which foreign economic geologists might become members of the new society.

Late in January (the 29th) he wrote to A. C. Veatch, chairman of the nominating committee, as follows:

"I feel that it is presumptuous in me to decline a nomination before it is made, but I have heard from more than one source that certain members of the Society of Economic Geologists may suggest that my name be put on the ballot for one position or another for next year, and I am writing to you to beg that you will not put my name on the ballot for any position whatever.

"I feel that we should establish the precedent of having all officers, except the Secretary and Treasurer, serve only one year, and I beg therefore that you will not consider my name either for any office or for the Council.

"I assure you that I greatly appreciate the honor I have already received from the Society, and my sympathies and efforts will always be freely given towards its advancement and welfare."

In replying to this letter, Veatch wrote (February 4, 1921) that "The Nominating Committee has unanimously decided to request you to reconsider the decision, communicated in your letter of January 29th to each of us, not to permit your name to be proposed for President of the Society for 1922.

"We regard the present year as a somewhat irregular one," he continued, "and, while we all share your views with regard to the desirability of single terms, we feel that this is one of those justifiable exceptions which sustains the rule.

"We are all of the opinion that in this formative period the Society will be much benefited by your being President for 1922, and we have included your name in the three nominations for the Presidency which under the By-Laws the Nominating Committee is required to make.

"We all hope we can win you to our way of thinking, and will not make our report till we hear from you."

But Penrose was not to be moved, although not insensible to their praise and duly appreciative of the honor intended. A month later he was equally concerned that the name of Josiah E. Spurr be included on the nomination blank.

Letter from Penrose to J. Volney Lewis, dated March 4, 1921

Dear Professor Lewis:—

I have received your letter of March 3rd and also the ballot for new members of the Society. I congratulate you heartily on the way you have gotten up this ballot and on your brochure relating to the work of the individual candidates. Both documents are excellent and reflect credit on your good taste and good management. I appreciate greatly the amount of good work you have expended in getting up the details relative to each particular candidate.

I am greatly surprised and disappointed to hear that Spurr has requested you to remove his name from the list of nominees for President of the Society for 1922. I received a letter from him at the same time that I received your letter and he enclosed a copy of what he had written to you. I feel there must certainly be some misunderstanding in this matter, and I at once sent Spurr a long telegram requesting that he should reconsider his decision, and stating that I would consider it a disaster to the Society to have him withdraw his name.

I note that in the copy of his letter to you which he sent me he said he would explain his reasons, if you wished. I cannot conceive of what these reaons are and I am sure he must be laboring under some misunderstanding. I will be in New York next week and will make a point of seeing him. I would go there tomorrow to see him, but he is rarely in town on Saturday. In the meanwhile I hope that if you write to him again you will express yourself just as strongly as you possibly can in trying to make him reconsider his decision. If he should send you his reasons for wanting to withdraw I would be greatly obliged to you if you would let me know what they are, so that I can act intelligently in trying to persuade him to let his name remain in nomination.

I hope you will not send out the nominations for officers until this matter is definitely decided. There is plenty of time to send out this ballot, even if we waited for a month or so longer, and I feel strongly in wanting Spurr to remain on it, so I think we should delay the ballot until we have made every effort to make him reconsider his action.

Two days later, Lewis replied that he fully shared with Penrose "the great disappointment at Spurr's decision. We must, if possible, induce him to withdraw his request for the removal of his name from the ballot; for I feel that the Society must have his leadership to follow up most effectively your excellent work. Inevitably it will suffer, it seems to me, if it falls into less sympathetic and less able hands. There is plenty of ability in the Society, but there are few who have the zeal for the organization and the grasp of its ideals and its possibilities that Spurr has, and I should like to impress him with our moral right to draft him into service. I shall let you know at once about any communication that I may get from him. In the meantime I wish you the fullest measure of success in your efforts to win him over to your point of view."

Meantime, Penrose had already written to Spurr.

Letter from Penrose to J. E. Spurr, dated March 4, 1921

My dear Spurr:—

I am putting it mildly when I say that I was dreadfully shocked and grieved to learn by your letter of March 2nd that you intended to have your name removed from the list of nominees for officers of the Society of Economic Geologists for 1922. I cannot conceive of anything more disastrous to this Society in which we have both taken such deep interest than to see your name left off the ballot. You are the logical man for President and there is no one in the whole list of members who can fill the position so well as you. I personally would not have taken anything like the interest I do in the Society this year, and that I did in the Society last year, had I not been always looking forward to you as being our next President, for I know that under your control the Society would thrive in a manner which otherwise would be impossible.

In your letter of March 2nd you enclosed a copy of your letter of that date to Lewis in which you intimated that you would be glad to explain your reasons, if desired, for this action. I feel very sure that there must be some most unfortunate misunderstanding that has made you withdraw, and I beg that you will let me know what it is, for after talking with a large part of our membership I have found that they practically all expect you to be the next President and will all be disappointed if you withdraw your name. They all realize that you were the one who conceived of the possibilities and the necessity for the Society and many of them have wondered why you were not put on the ballot for President at the first election. I believe that the general impression was that it was your own modesty that kept you from accepting any nomination in the beginning, and now I beg that you will not disappoint the membership again.

I feel so strongly on this point that I would come over to New York to see you about the matter tomorrow—Saturday—but as I understand that you are usually not in town on Saturday I will put off the trip until as soon as possible next week; and in the meantime I sincerely hope that you will do me the favor of not definitely declining the nomination until I have at least had a chance to discuss the matter with you.

Three days later (March 7) Spurr wrote to Penrose about the matter, declaring that he "felt, as you know, during the first year of the Society that the fact that I had taken the lead in organizing the Society was of itself sufficient reason why I should not be elected an officer. I believed that this was for the good of the Society, in at once dropping any influence which I naturally assumed at the beginning. I am also inclined strongly to believe that this holds good for 1922, for I would not like to feel that any one had grounds for believing that I pushed the organization of the Society on account of some personal benefit or honor which might come to me thereby. I think I can help the Society about as well as a member as I could as an officer.

"Another consideration," he added, "is that of the Mining and Metallurgical Society. Although I am quite determined not to serve more than one year as president of this Society, and am, moreover, quite sure that there is no danger of being pressed to do so, nevertheless, my work in this Society is taking a great deal of my time and thought, and I think it would be a very good plan to get rid of one obligation which involves so much service, and have an interval, before taking up another which will also mean work, because I should hope to carry it on with the same serious care which you have given it."

Letter from Penrose to J. E. Spurr, dated March 9, 1921

My dear Spurr:—

I have just received your letter of March 7th, and though I am counting on seeing you at lunch tomorrow I am dropping a brief line to you now to express my feelings regarding what you say in your letter about wishing to withdraw from the candidacy for President of the Society of Economic Geologists.

Regarding your first point, that you have always felt that you had taken so active a part in the early stages of the Society that you ought not to seek an official position for fear that your earlier efforts might be construed as efforts to form a position for yourself, I can assure you that no one on this earth who knows you would ever have such an idea. You have always been so modest, liberal and unselfish in all such matters that the only regret we have about your various actions of this kind is that you have refrained only too often from taking an official position when the members of the organization and the cause which it might represent both would have been greatly benefited by your leadership.

I fully realize what you say about the work involved in such a position but I assure you that by January, 1922, the Society will be running along so smoothly that the President will not have so much to do as he has had in the past.

Lewis is making a splendid Secretary and will be able to handle the affairs that come to him as efficiently as Hovey is doing for the G.S.A. today.

....

I beg that you will for the sake of the science of applied geology and for the sake of all your friends that you will accept the nomination for our leader.

In the end, Penrose's arguments prevailed and Spurr reconsidered his decision, allowing his name to be placed on the ballot.

That same March, Penrose took up with the National Research Council the matter of representation of the Society of Economic Geologists in the Division of Geology and Geography, which matter was accomplished in June with the naming of two representatives—F. L. Ransome and Horace V. Winchell.

In those first days of the organization, before it was firmly established financially, Penrose had been caring for the many matters involving money. In this, as in his every disposition of money, he did it with a nicety of feeling concerning the whole procedure which betokened the man ever thoughtful of others, their feelings and their reputation. For example, he wrote to Lewis, under date of April 16, 1921, that he had "received your letter of April 15th, enclosing bill for $36.25 for printing for the Society of Economic Geologists, and I beg to enclose my check for that amount drawn to you in payment of it.

"I am sending the check to you personally," he continued, "instead of to the printer, as I thought it might look better for the Society of Economic Geologists and make a better impression on the printer if payment came directly through you as Treasurer of the Society, instead of through me, whom the printer does not know. My idea would be, if agreeable to you, for you to deposit the check in the checking account of you as Treasurer, and for you to send your check as Treasurer to the printer. If however you prefer some other method of procedure please use your own good judgment.

"I assure you that it gives me much pleasure to be of service to our Society occasionally in this manner until it is firmly established financially on its feet."

In early April, Penrose, Spurr, and Lewis worked out a form of cooperative relationship with The Geological Society of America, whereby the Council of each organization appointed a member to represent it on the Council of the other organization. When the matter had been duly approved by the Council of The Geological Society of America, Penrose appointed Lewis as delegate, May 23, 1921, and early in June the Society of Economic Geologists received word that The Geological Society of America delegate to their Council would be George H. Ashley.

Each month brought its problem to the conscientious president of the Society of Economic Geologists, and each problem was solved only after thorough consideration of all its aspects, its future application, and a thorough discussion with other members of the Council.

In a letter to Spurr, dated May 9, 1921, Penrose wrote that "after discussing with you last week the question of whether or not it is proper for the Society of Economic Geologists to recommend oil geologists or other geologists for special work, I read again the letter from Mr. Goodwin of Georgia, which you had forwarded to Lewis concerning the special case under discussion. I observed that Mr. Goodwin said he wanted a geologist who would examine the property and who would also become interested in its development. Apparently he wanted a promoter as well as an expert, and this seemed to complicate the situation more than before. I therefore advised Lewis in a conversation over the telephone that it might be well simply to refer Mr. Goodwin to the Employment Bureau of the American Institute of Mining and Metallurgical Engineers. In the meanwhile perhaps we will have time to decide definitely on the question of recommending geologists for particular work; but under any circumstances, I should think that it would be well for our Society to refrain from recommending promoters.

"I sincerely hope that this solution of the question is satisfactory to you," he concluded, "and if not, I would be greatly obliged to you if you would let me know whether you have come to any firm opinion relating to the subject."

That solution was apparently satisfactory, for there is no further mention of the matter in his correspondence.

His letters of June show that he spent the time in Philadelphia, occupied in large measure with routine matters of membership, programs, printers, in connection with the Society of Economic Geologists and that on the 24th he attended a meeting of the Council held in New York.

In July, he concerned himself with the question raised in a letter from S. H. Ball, dated July 12, who wrote that it had occurred to him "that the Society of Economic Geologists might well, through its Executive Committee, call to the attention of those in charge of the tariff bill, now before Congress, the fact that

1st the reserves of oil in the United States are strictly limited;

2nd that the United States must import oil since its needs are greater than the oil production of the country and

3rd that American financiers should be encouraged to invest in oil lands outside the United States so that the country may have the first call on the reserves of oil developed by them.

In view of the above, the proposed duty on crude oil impresses me as one of the most foolish propositions ever made by a legislative body."

In his reply, Penrose remarked (July 15, 1921) that he thought "that a great many people in Washington are already familiar with these situations and that they particularly realize that American financiers should be encouraged to get control of foreign oil fields.

"As regards the Executive Committee of the Society of Economic Geologists taking up this matter," he added, "I would be very glad to see it do so if we could get a sufficiently large number of the Executive Committee and Council to represent the sentiment of the Society. How would it do for you to consult with the members of the Executive Committee and the Council in New York and sound their feelings in this matter? You are close to those who live in New York and can get them on the telephone. I think the matter is important."

Three days later (July 18) after having thought more concerning the matter, Penrose again wrote to Ball, saying that it had "occurred to me since writing you last that perhaps this matter might properly be handled by our Committee on Political Geology. This Committee was formed for that particular kind of purpose and is composed of Leith, Spurr and any one else whom they may select as a third member. I do not know whether or not the third member has ever been appointed.

"I have received to-day," he continued, "a letter from Professor Lewis, on the general subject which you have brought up and he suggests either taking it up with the Committee on Political Geology or with the membership at large. He seems to feel that an expression of opinion from the membership at large would be much stronger than an expression of opinion from a smaller body of the Society; but he seems to feel that a recommendation from the Committee on Political Geology would be desirable. I feel that he is right in this respect and have advised him to communicate with the Committee on Political Geology, and after getting their approval, to communicate, if possible, with the membership at large or to have the Committee on Political Geology do so.

"Of course the question of time in this matter is important because we are all anxious to see legislation concerning the oil properly handled. I may see Spurr in New York in the next day or two and will ask him if the Committee on Political Geology cannot take this matter up immediately."

A few days later (July 22) he wrote again to Ball that "now that Congress has settled the threat of a tariff on petroleum there is no need of our taking any action; but I was glad you brought up the matter, for it shows how we can be useful in crises of this kind, and we have the necessary committees, etc., to handle such matters promptly in the future. I sincerely hope that you will not hesitate at any time to offer suggestions of a similar nature for I feel that one of the functions of our Society is to take up such subjects."

Under that same date, Penrose wrote to Spurr that "these numerous meetings of the Council and Executive Committee this year may seem to you to have been rather tedious, but they have been necessary on account of having promised that any members elected during the present year should be charter members. By the end of the year this will really have caused us to hold three meetings for the primary consideration of candidates, thus making six meetings to act on the question of membership alone. Moreover, there are unusual matters necessarily incident to a new Society which had to be considered at these meetings."

Four days later (July 26, 1921) Penrose again wrote to Spurr that he had "received the copy of your letter to Leith concerning the co-operation of the Committee of the Society of Economic Geologists on Political Geology and the Committee of the Mining and Metallurgical Society of America on Domestic and Foreign Mining Policy.

"Your suggestion of co-operation is excellent and will certainly avoid much duplication of effort, thereby helping to remove one of the almost hopeless difficulties which one sees in the various scientific organizations in Washington. I believe also that the co-operation of these two Committees will doubtless produce important results in guiding the Government in Washington on the question of tariff and in other matters."

Concerning the Society at that period, Penrose wrote in a letter to P. G. Morgan, director of the Geological Survey of New Zealand, that "the Society of Economic Geologists already numbers something over one hundred and twenty, and before the year is over I think we will have over one hundred and fifty. We could of course get a vastly greater number, but all of us feel that in a Society of this kind it must be quality and not quantity that counts. For this reason we probably will never be very numerous; but at the same time when our list of members is seen to contain such men as you, and others noted in our science, it will doubtless be an important factor in geologic work. . . . I sincerely hope that you will some time honor us with a trip to this country. I remember well and always with great appreciation your kindness and hospitality to me when I travelled through New Zealand many years ago."

All through the hot summer of 1921, Penrose remained at Philadelphia and made repeated trips to New York, chiefly on business in connection with the Society.

"I have just received the package from the printer containing a supply (presumably 200) of the new printing of your address at the Chicago meeting," Lewis wrote to Penrose on July 28, "In its new form it is very attractive in typography, paper, and cover—a delight to the eye and the touch.

"I congratulate you on your excellent taste and also on your good judgment in selecting a printer who has the skill and will take the pains to turn out first class work. Again the Society of Economic Geologists is indebted to you for setting a high standard, which I trust it may profit by in the years to come."

Each month that summer there was at least one meeting of the Executive Committee or the Council to attend and some months there were more, and then in August, Lewis wrote to Penrose that he felt he must resign as secretary of the organization in order to undertake some work in Mexico. This was a matter of deep regret to Penrose who had enjoyed his relationship with Lewis, as is shown by his correspondence.

Letter from Penrose to J. E. Spurr, dated August 24, 1921

My dear Spurr:—

Lewis has gone on a short trip to the Lake Superior region, but expects to be back in time for the Wilkes Barre meeting of the Society of Economic Geologists.

On the train going out to Lake Superior he wrote me a letter saying that he had made plans which would keep him most of the coming year in the neighborhood of Tampico, Mexico, adding, however, that he would probably not leave before October 1st.

Lewis has been a most admirable Secretary for the Society and I think his departure from this country just before the annual meeting in December would be a distinct loss, not only to the Society but to the cause of Economic Geology. I have written him urging him in the strongest terms to defer his departure until after the winter meeting at Amherst and I sincerely hope he will do so.

Possibly when he wrote to me he may have been a little tired, in fact he looked tired to me at the last meeting of the Council and Executive Committee in New York on August 4th and I told him then that he had better be careful and not work too hard. I acted myself both as President and Secretary during those long eight months from April to December, 1920, in which time Lewis was in the

West and could not be of much assistance. From this experience I know what amount of work is envoloved in running such an organization, especially in the early stages of its development. Since Lewis returned from the West and assumed the duties of Secretary and Treasurer, he has worked almost continuously for nine or ten months, and from my experience I am not at all surprised that he is worn out. I think, however, his Lake Superior trip will do him good and he may return with more ambition to continue in his position.

I am writing to you now because I thought that if you also would write to him at Lake Superior and urge him to continue as Secretary and Treasuer at least until after the Amherst meeting in December, you would have great influence over him.

Penrose spent the remainder of August and the greater part of September on the problem of a new secretary, writing many letters and discussing the matter with other members of the Society. His first choice was evidently Charles P. Berkey, professor of geology at Columbia University, for he wrote to Spurr on September 2, that "after seeing you yesterday I talked to Veatch personally about the matter of the secretaryship of the Society of Economic Geologists, and I talked to Ball about the same matter over the telephone.... They both highly approved of Berkey, and as you and I also highly approve of him, we thus have an informal vote of three members of the Executive Committee and four members of the combined Council and Executive Committee. I would therefore feel no hesitancy in this emergency in asking Berkey to fill the expiring term of Lewis. Berkey could then be re-elected for the coming year at our winter meeting.

"I tried to get Lewis on the telephone but he had not yet returned from Lake Superior. I will call him on the telephone on Sunday night, when he is expected home, and will try to find out his ideas about this matter. In the meanwhile I have not approached Berkey on this subject, for I felt that he is a man of too high standing in his profession to offer an appointment with a string on it, so I have deferred seeing him until I have talked with Lewis."

On September 9, Penrose again wrote to Spurr that "after seeing you (yesterday) I went up to see Berkey at his house for he was too sick to be at the University, but said over the telephone that he was not too sick to receive visitors. I told him that we all wanted him to accept the position of secretary and treasurer of the Society of Economic Geologists. He was very kindly in his expressions of appreciation at the offer but said that he intended shortly to start for an absence of almost a year in Mongolia, and as he considered that a secretary should be a man who was more or less constantly on the job he could not consistently accept our offer.

"It may be of interest to you also," Penrose added, "to note that the G.S.A. had offered Berkey the position of secretary to succeed Hovey, but that he had declined for the same reason that he felt compelled to decline our offer. He expressed much interest in our Society."

At length, S. H. Ball was persuaded to assume the role once more—at least until the meeting in December. He assented with much reluctance, and when the annual meeting came and he was still in Nevada on some field work, he wrote to Penrose (December 19, 1921) that he was "most disappointed and embarrassed to find I will not return East prior to Jan 1st, and hence will miss the Amherst meeting.... My feeling that I should not have accepted the secretaryship is thus sadly proven correct."

The Penrose correspondence files of this period show more vividly than would be possible in any other manner how seriously he took his position as president of the Society of Economic Geologists and how truly he was its leader in that early period. He wrote fully and almost daily regarding the organization, his letters concerning themselves with details of meetings—Executive Committee, Council, Society at Wilkes Barre with the A.I.M.E., annual meeting at Amherst with the G.S.A.—the printing of every conceivable form necessary for the conduct of the Society's business, new members to be invited and letters of welcome to new members personally, printing of annual program and requests for papers for that program, stationery, co-operation with other organizations, mailing of printed matter to the membership and the most suitable times for that mailing. He personally designed and supervised all the printed matter prepared, and paid for it by sending the secretary-treasurer the amount due, which that officer then paid as coming from the funds of the society. He showed ever that same attention to minute detail which marked his work as a geologist and was certainly a contributing factor in his professional and financial success. His letters are models of polite usage, and his correspondence shows him to have been a master in the art of diplomatically discharging difficult tasks which in the hands of less urbane leaders would have spelled disaster. Ever that unfailing courtesy and lack of unseemly haste which would permit him to take time in the rush of attending to every detail concerning the annual meeting at Amherst to write at length to Ball's secretary, explaining why he had set the place of the executive meeting for Williston Hall rather than Appleton Cabinet.

He always had time for the gracious things of life, as witness, for example, his letter to Lewis, dated July 8, 1921, in which he said: "I want to congratulate you on the accuracy and speed with which you have done the great mass of work which came about from our last Council meeting, and I beg to thank your daughter for the splendid assistance which she has given you. The electric fan to which you refer may have been of assistance, but it was the spirit of you and her that made the work accurate and rapid."

And every once in a while, by a turn of phrase he lightened his correspondence with a remark, gravely but nonetheless humorously put. Writing to Lindgren in August, 1921, concerning the program for the annual meeting at Amherst in December, he says: "When I make this request [for papers] I do not mean that the papers are for the more or less joint meeting which is to be held with the American Institute in the middle of September, but I mean them for the real annual meeting in connection with the Geological Society of America in December." And again, referring to the printing of the same program, he wrote to E. O. Hovey on December 11, "Lindgren's programme is now in the hands of the printer, but as the principal man is laid up with tonsilitis and most of his employees are laid up with inertia I am not quite sure when I will get this proof. ... This dreadful business of being rushed at the last moment by the programme committee of the Society of Economic Geologists is, I suppose, very similar to what you have been tolerating for the last fifteen years as Secretary of the G.S.A., and I now do not wonder that you have taken a house in the country and are beginning to withdraw from the den of torment where you are persecuted in New York."

In addition to the multitudinous tasks which were his in connection with the Amherst meeting, Penrose found time to design a new emblem for the letterhead of the Society and a pin for the members.

"You will notice," he wrote to A. C. Veatch on November 8, 1921, "that I have inserted a new emblem to indicate the international character of our Society. I thought that such a method would be the most effective way of indicating the world-wide scope of our membership. I would be very glad to know if you have any suggestions to make concerning it, for I have only inserted it at the present time to give our membership a chance to criticise it."

Concerning the pin, he wrote to Lewis on December 4, that he had "thought for a long time of some emblem which would indicate the international character of our Society without having to state this in actual words, and finally I concluded that the two hemispheres would accomplish this object."

And ever, back of all this work and care for detail, was the thought that through the efforts of the society might be promoted a greater effectiveness through international relations with other geologists.

"I feel that all scientific societies, especially geological societies, should keep closely in touch with each other," he wrote to Elwood S. Moore, at that time secretary of Section E of the American Association for the Advancement of Science, in connection with the Toronto meeting of that organization.

To complete the tasks he had set for himself that year, he found that, as he wrote to Waldemar Lindgren, chairman of the program committee, on November 15, "Mr. Ball tells me that you expect me to give some sort of Presidential address at the meeting of the Society of Economic Geologists in December. I never seek opportunities to make talks, but at the same time I try never to shirk a responsibility when it is required of me; and therefore it will give me great pleasure to write a short paper which will probably take not over ten or, at the outside, fifteen minutes to deliver. ... I am preparing this paper now and in a very few days will send you the title and a brief abstract. I am dropping this line to you now simply to tell you that I am conforming with your wishes as conveyed to me by Mr. Ball."

Of his activities on Thanksgiving Day in 1921, Penrose told in a letter to Ball, dated November 25.

"I spent Thanksgiving Day reading your paper on 'The Geologic and Geographic Occurrence of Precious Stones,' and I can assure you that I do not think I ever spent a more interesting and instructive Thanksgiving. It was certainly better than freezing to death at a football game and than gorging one's self with turkey. I did neither of these things, but I feel that I have reason to give thanks for the privilege of reading your article.... I have gone carefully over the article to see if I could add any material or make any criticism concerning what you have said, but I cannot do so. My own experience in regions of precious stones has been in the Kimberley region and the region of the Premier Mine in South Africa, in Burma, Ceylon, and sundry places in the United States. The sapphires of Montana, the turquoises of New Mexico, and the garnets of Arizona have always interested me very much. In all of these places, both in our country and in foreign lands, my observations entirely agree with yours."

And the last moment before leaving for Amherst, Penrose wrote to Frances E. Stamm, secretary to Ball, "When I was in New York last week I told you that I would send you not later than tomorrow a copy of the members of the Society of Economic Geologists, with their academic titles such as 'Doctor,' 'Professor,' etc.

"I am still working on this list but have found it is taking a little more time than I had anticipated, but I expect to finish it by tomorrow; and as I will be in New York probably on Thursday I will bring it with me and give it to you at that time.

"I am dropping this line to you simply to let you know that I have not forgotten the matter and to explain why you will not receive the list tomorrow."

At the Amherst meeting Penrose spoke on *The Society of Economic Geologists: Its Sphere and Its Future*, not only giving the statement of the status of the organization, but making a plea for co-operation between geologists and geological societies.

"For many years a feeling has existed among certain geologists who were applying their science to practical purposes that the men who adhered purely to research were so engrossed in their work that they found scant time to call attention to the material usefulness of their discoveries," said Penrose. "About two years ago this feeling took form in the organization of the Society of Economic Geologists. This action was not due to any controversy with any other society; on the other hand, the new Society started out with the encouragement and best of good wishes of all allied socieites. They all thought that there was a place for it and that they would collaborate with it.

"The Society of Economic Geologists has rapidly gotten together, has found itself, and has developed in a remarkable and totally unexpected manner. It has displayed its sphere of usefulness by the papers that have been read at its meetings, by the activities of its committees, by the character of its membership, and by an indescribable educational influence.

"Today this Society contains one hundred and forty-three members. Though it was started in the United States, an important portion of our membership has come from foreign countries—England, Canada, Mexico, Australia, New Zealand, Norway, Sweden, France, Belgium and Japan—and all of these members realize, as do our own members from the United States, that a Society of Economic Geologists has long since been needed the world over, and could work independently but in thorough harmony with the older geologic societies. The Society of Economic Geologists has therefore automatically become an international organization. The badge and the seal which we use today, indicating the two hemispheres, is a token of recognition of this world-wide membership.

"We have passed the experimental stage; we are a working organization with a rapidly growing influence for good for our members and for industry. We do not seek numbers in our membership; we seek efficiency; we do not seek those who have attained an evanescent notoriety, but we seek only those who have given true and honest work in the application of the principles of geology to the welfare of industry and mankind. We seek friendly relations and meetings where we can come together in the same camp and tent with others whose interests lie in allied directions. Throughout the last two years we have met on different occasions the geologists of other societies. We know that the contact has been beneficial to ourselves and we hope that it has not lacked benefit to those we met.

"Economic geology is simply the application of the numerous parts which make up the science of geology. Thus, paleontology, stratigraphy, petrology, chemical geology, as well as other phases of the earth sciences, are all connected and inseparable in making up one grand whole, and economic geology uses them all. The specialist in one branch in his intense enthusiasm for his own work may forget and even look down on the work of other specialists, but this is due only to ignorance of what the others are doing, and the fact remains that we are all working in one great field, the earth sciences.

"The application of geologic principles in economic problems, however, requires a temperament and education as essential as does the study of the most abstruse problems in any science. No matter how learned a geologist may be, if the ability to apply his science to economic problems is not born in him, or else acquired by long and tedious knocks, he will fail miserably. I have seen many most pathetic cases of this sad result, where theoretic geologists eminent in their profession as instructors or scientific workers, have been gravely humiliated by utter failure in attempting to do economic work, and have brought disaster both to their employers and themselves; while in the sphere of theoretic science they have received the world's recognition of their splendid work. Moreover, there is an intellectual, intangible, almost a spiritual side to any purely theoretic feature of the science of geology which must not be ignored and is ennobling in any liberal education.

"All branches of geology are so closely related that whether they are studied for theoretic, economic, or for educational purposes, the difference is purely a detail. The theoretic geologist develops facts on which the economic geologist works out material good, and the latter brings data useful to the former; the work of both helps towards that knowledge of the earth priceless in a liberal education. The economic geologist travels widely and continuously from one end of the world to the other; his time is spent in travelling and observing; he sees geologic objects, which the purely theoretic geologist often cannot see, for the latter is mostly occupied in teaching, in laboratory research, and in limited periods of field work. Hence many of the papers published by economic geologists have afforded new material for the theoretic geologist. On the other hand, the economic geologist profits by the work of the theoretic geologist in the latter's development of new truths. The study of fossils by the paleontologist is as necessary in following out certain economic problems as is the work of the economic geologist in applying them.

"Thus both the theoretic geologist and the economic geologist become the collaborators of each other. We must admit, however, that certain professional economic geologists, active in industrial work, do not give their fair share to this collaboration. They think that their employer might not like them to do so, or that they have not the time to write. As far as the employer's consent to allow the economic geologist to publish conclusions from specific reports goes, I beg to say that after extended inquiry I know of but few employers who would not grant this permission provided the business details were not divulged. As regards the time that the economic geologist has to write for scientific journals, the matter is entirely his own concern; but I know of very few such geologists who are so busy that they cannot find time occasionally to write and give the information that they owe to the theoretic geologist, who makes none of the economic profits and works for his science alone.

"If the proper equilibrium can be established, neither the economic geologist nor the theoretic geologist will be the debtor; neither will be the creditor; but both will work to their mutual good and self-respect. If such an ideal can be accomplished, and I have no doubt that it will eventually be so, then will the purely theoretic, the purely economic, and the educational feature of the science, progress side by side and to the welfare of all mankind.

"We all rejoice that for the second year of the existence of the Society of Economic Geologists we have the pleasure of meeting with The Geological Society of America, and especially in the environment of this great College of Amherst, made famous, among others, by Hitchcock, Emerson, and that honored pioneer in mineralogy, C. U. Shepard. These great men have aided the later work of all geologists, whether purely theoretic or economic, and I am sure that all of us feel it a privilege to meet in the halls where they once taught and where their worthy successor, Professor B. F. Loomis, now presides."

The meeting at Amherst ended about noon on December 30, and Penrose left immediately for New York, where he spent the night, returning to Philadelphia the morning of December 31. That day his brother Boies died suddenly in Washington.

"No man ever worked more truly, honorably, and in a more disinterested manner than he did," Penrose wrote to E. S. Bastin, on January 13, 1922, "and I feel that it was his continuous hard work that brought on the illness which resulted in his death."

Now Richard alone was left to call the old house at 1331 Spruce Street home. He kept it open and fully staffed until his own death, ten years later, but he lived most of the time in a suite which he took at the Bellevue-Stratford Hotel.

But even with the completion of his two years of continuous and arduous service for the Society of Economic Geologists, Penrose found that his task was not finished. All during that January of 1922, there were questions concerning the minutiae of administration detail to be turned over and discussed with the new president and with the secretary. And all this was in addition to the infinite details connected with the death of his brother and the settlement of that estate. So quietly and efficiently did Dick Penrose conduct his affairs that on January 5, he wrote a long letter to Ball, enclosing his dues for the year 1922, discussing the matter of dues for foreign members, and in conclusions, said: "This and a large number of other matters I would like to discuss with you, for though I am no longer connected officially with the Society I still feel a deep interest in it and would like to tell you fully everything that happened from the time you went until you returned."

At the Amherst meeting, Penrose had presented members of the Society with the gold emblem of the organization, which he had designed.

"I neglected to ask you one question when you were here," wrote Ball, as secretary, on January 14th, "and that is regarding the distribution of the gold emblem of the Society of Economic Geologists which you so generously donated to the Society. Undoubtedly they were given to the members who attended the Amherst meeting and also members with whom you came in contact from time to time, which leaves the out-of-town members, excluding those who attended Amherst, without emblems. Will you kindly give me your opinion in this matter? I would suggest that if you had a good number made up originally, you send same to the out-of-town members with your compliments. If, however, you prefer, this office will be glad to send same."

Penrose replied that he entirely agreed with Ball regarding the desirability of sending each member an emblem, and added, "I think that it would be more appropriate for you than for me to send them to our members because I am now out of office and such action on my part might seem presumptuous. I think that you as Secretary are the proper person to send them.

"As you express your willingness to do this, I will send to you as soon as possible by parcel post, special delivery, about a couple of hundred of these emblems. I think that in New York I have some additional ones and if you need more than I am sending I will be glad to turn them all over to you at once.

"I have not forgotten the matter of an engraved block for our emblem for letter-heads. I have been talking to the engraver this morning and he says he can make the emblem in the form of a small block which can be set in between two columns of names, just as we have been using the old electrotype block in the past. I will send it to you as soon as it is finished and I think it will look much better on the paper than simply the electrotype emblem. The names of officers and councilors of course can easily be put on either side of the emblem in ordinary type, in such way as you see fit."

But that was not the end of the matter of the emblems, for January 24, he again wrote to Ball, "I cannot find any very satisfactory form of container which will take in the emblem and the box containing it, such as you desire. The nearest I can come to it would be a small manila envelope, which I know is made and which I believe is about $4\frac{1}{2}$ inches long by $2\frac{1}{2}$ inches wide. I should think that perhaps the emblem and the box enclosing it could be put in this, and stamped with pre-cancelled stamps so that it would not be mashed by the cancelling apparatus. I believe pre-cancelled stamps can be gotten from the postoffice.

"I simply mention this matter as a suggestion, but your own good judgment will probably guide you better than anything I can suggest with the information I have been able to obtain."

Waldemar Lindgren, the new president of the Society, had urged Penrose to remain actively connected with the administration as a member of the Executive Committee, but Penrose wrote him (January 21, 1922), saying "I have considered this subject carefully ever since you mentioned it to me last Thursday when I met you in New York, but I do not see how I can consistently accept the appointment.

"I highly appreciate the honor of such a position and your kind thoughtfulness in offering it to me, but I will be away a large part of the present year; and I am very anxious if possible to take up again some research work in the Far East which I began several years ago and which I have not yet completed. Such work means several months absence at a time, and for that reason I do not think it would be fair to the Society to accept an executive position which requires strict attention.

"I will, however, whenever possible and when desired by you, be glad to attend meetings in which you think I could be of any use, without however having any official connection with the Society.

"My interests are wholly in the Society and I assure you that my efforts will always be to help forward its welfare and efficiency."

Even then his duties were not completed, for on February 10, Ball again wrote that "after several attempts I find that it is hopeless for me to attempt to write up the minutes of the Amherst Meeting, particularly as I was not there. I know you took notes on the various meetings and request that you do me and the Society the great favor of re-writing same."

Penrose answered on February 12, that he was "sorry you have had so much trouble with the minutes of the Amherst Meeting, and I can readily understand that you find it almost hopeless to attempt to write them up, as you were not there. I assure you that it will give me much pleasure to write them over or to amend them so that they will give a more comprehensive history of the events of the Amherst Meeting. I can do this all the more easily as I observed during the meeting that the acting secretary was extremely busy with many matters and I, therefore, made a few memoranda at different times in case they should be needed by him. He did not, however, call for them and I will use them in the present task you have asked me to undertake."

Penrose evidently set about his task at once, for on that same day he wrote to Alan M. Bateman:

"Mr. Ball has written to me asking me to help round out the minutes of the Amherst Meeting of the Society of Economic Geologists so that they will fully represent all that occurred at that time. You may remember that we discussed the subject of these minutes when we met in New York on February 3rd.

"I think I can round out the minutes properly from various memoranda that

I took during the meeting, but there is one thing about which I would like to ask you. You may remember that you and Graton made a very kind and considerate resolution concerning me and called for its adoption and for its incorporation in the minutes of the meeting. This motion was passed but it does not appear in the minutes of the secretary pro tem. I assure you that I am not seeking flattery, but I feel that no man can be indifferent to the expression of goodwill from his friends and fellow-workers, and, therefore, it occurred to me that if the minutes are to cover everything that was done at the meeting, this resolution should be incorporated. If, therefore, you have any memoranda about the resolution that you could send me, I will incorporate it in the revised minutes together with other additional data."

On March 1, Ball wrote to Penrose from Coffman, Missouri, thanking him for the completed minutes, and on the 9th, Penrose replied, adding that "if there is anything I can do to assist in the affairs of the Society of Economic Geologists, I beg that you will call on me."

At the Amherst meeting occurred one of those unfortunate incidents which grows out of misunderstandings and increases the resulting ill feeling until it bursts of its own weight and lack of real foundation. It all grew out of the matter of places at the annual banquet of the Geological Society of America. Various versions of the affair can be gleaned from the correspondence.

One member of the Society of Economic Geologists voiced his indignation in a letter to E. O. Hovey, secretary of the Geological Society of America, a copy of which he sent to Penrose.

"As a member of the Society of Economic Geologists," he wrote "I desire to express my personal feelings regarding what I consider a deliberate affront to the said Society made either by yourself or by the local Committee at Amherst when you failed to find places at the Speakers' Table for Dr. R. A. F. Penrose the retiring President, and Dr. Waldemar Lindgren, the newly elected President of the Society of Economic Geologists.

"As I happen to have definite information that these gentlmen were advised that places had been reserved for them at the Speakers' table, and then were later notified that a mistake had been made and that there were no seats for them there, I cannot reconcile this information with the fact that just before the dinner started I saw you pass just in front of these two gentlemen while you were diligently seeking several persons of lesser importance to fill vacant seats at the head table. The occurrence is especially hard to explain in view of the fact that Professor Lindgren had been asked to respond to a toast and had returned to Amherst for that special purpose after he had been called to Boston on business.

"It is unexplainable how sometimes persons honored to high positions in large Societies cannot be big enough to overcome their personal feelings for the good of the Society or Societies they are supposed to serve. I intend to use what influence I have to see that in the future the Society of Economic Geologists when it holds joint meetings, either holds them with Societies which offer it the common courtesies or else that it holds separate meetings of its own."

Copies of this letter were sent to Dr. Lindgren, Charles Schuchert, and James F. Kemp, as well as to Penrose.

In reply, Hovey wrote (January 5, 1922):

"Your favor of the 3d instant is at hand and I beg to say that no affront was intended to the Society of Economic Geologists in connection with the annual dinner of the Geological Society of America, and I am sorry to hear that any umbrage was taken by the members of the former Society.

"I did not have the final say with regard to the seating at the Head Table, but as I had something to do with reference to it I am willing to take whatever blame there is attached thereto.

"The intention was to have the incoming presidents of the affiliated societies at the table. In place of Doctor W. D. Matthew, President of the Paleontological Society, his father was taken instead of himself; Professor T. L. Walker was there and a place was reserved for Professor Lindgren. Professor Lindgren, however, could not be found even after the dinner was begun, and therefore his place was filled by someone else. It is not true that he was advised that a place had been reserved for him and then he was later notified that a mistake had been made and there was no seat for him there. Whatever happened between Doctor Penrose and myself lies wholly between us.

"At least one half of the people who sat at the Head Table did so of their own volition and not by invitation of the Local Committee or the Officers.

"Professor Lindgren was not the only one who was scheduled to speak that evening, but unfortunately had to be sidetracked on account of the unexpected length of the programme. The term "Speaker's Table" as used in your letter is a misnomer, because the men whom Professor Kemp had expected to call upon were scattered about in various parts of the room and were not gathered together at one table. Our dinners have always been of informal character, but little importance is to be attached to a man's sitting at one table or another at them."

In the meantime, Penrose had replied to his champion, under date of January 9, thanking him "for your communication of January 3rd representing a copy of your letter to Doctor Hovey concerning his actions at the banquet at Amherst in Christmas week.

"I think that your letter is admirable," he continued. "It is thoroughly dignified and straight to the point, and I sincerely hope that it will have the good effect which it deserves. I assure you that I greatly admire your courage in speaking out your thoughts in the matter.

"I hope that some time when you are in Philadelphia you will let me know so that we can get together and discuss this and other matters concerning the Society of Economic Geologists. I will call you on the telephone from time to time in hopes of trying to find you in Philadelphia, though I know that you are such a busy man that you are rarely here."

Kemp wrote to Penrose on January 11 (1922) and in the course of his letter noted that he had received "the letter of which you have a copy, which relates to the unfortunate incidents of the dinner. I greatly deplore any infelicity and have written ——— a long letter about the arrangements as I knew about them. I saw him last evening at the M. and M. Society's annual dinner and presentation of the medal to Charlie Goodale and am relieved to know that my letter was taken in the best of spirit."

Whatever annoyance Penrose had felt at the dinner and at the time when he answered the letter had, at least on the surface, vanished by January 13, when he replied to Kemp that he had seen a copy of the letter in question.

"Of course those little difficulties must occur at any large meeting," he added. "As far as I was concerned, I was delighted to be relieved of having to make an after-dinner speech and I appreciated greatly being finally allowed to sit elsewhere than at the speakers' table. I thought that dinner was not only excellent, but very interesting, and the meeting between Professor Emerson and his two illustrious students, you and Dr. John M. Clarke, was certainly most touching to all of us."

But in spite of the ease with which the difficulty had seemingly been repaired, the wound still rankled in the minds of members of the young society who felt that their organization had been insulted. And as such things have a way of doing, matters otherwise unnoted began to assume a suspicious aspect.

On January 19th (1922), J. E. Spurr wrote to E. O. Hovey, secretary of the Geological Society of America, as follows:

Dear Sir:

I am moved to write you as a member of the Geological Society of America, and also of the Society of Economic Geologists, but without any official position in either society, concerning one or two suggestions which I believe represent a widespread opinion.

The first is concerning real elections of the officers of the Geological Society of America, such as are conducted successfully in the Mining and Metallurgical Society of America and the Society of Economic Geologists. I am fully convinced of the advisability, and even necessity, of having the members of the society control the society, rather than a self-appointed group. In saying this, I am not thinking about the council or officers of the Geological Society of America, but simply about a system, which system also is practised by the American Institute of Mining and Metallurgical Engineers, and I think, with equally unfavorable results, for the system rests unfavorably on the members and, therefore, eventually upon the society.

If I can furnish assistance in any way in crystallizing the opinion of the members of the Society upon this point, I shall be glad to do it in accordance with the constitution and by-laws of the Society. If it is not too much trouble, I shall be glad if you will indicate to me the course to be pursued.

The other point which I have to take up is of minor importance, but we are often influenced by petty things. It is that the annual banquets of the Geological Society should be more systematically and diplomatically planned, and should be regarded as joint banquets of the G.S.A. and the other geological societies which meet with it.

Spurr sent a copy of this letter to Penrose, and in response, Penrose wrote on January 23 that he had "read the letter with the greatest interest and think that it is most timely. I hope Hovey and the Council of the G.S.A. will take serious consideration of your advice and I congratulate you on the clear and diplomatic manner in which you have presented your suggestions."

Hovey replied to Spurr (January 24, 1922) that he was "glad to have your opinion with regard to the matters mentioned, although I do not agree with you. I am writing now merely as a Fellow of the Geological Society of America and not as the Secretary.

"Regarding the election of officers of the Geological Society of America I would say that the method can be changed by amending the By-Laws, if the Society desires; and of course the Secretary must carry out any instructions that the Society gives him. When the G.S.A. was first organized in 1888, three nominations were made for each office, but this plan was given up after four or five years, and the present plan in its broad provisions adopted. The Council is in no sense of the word a 'self-appointed group.' It is an elected body, with the exception of the past presidents who remain on the Council for three years after their year of active service. At present there are seventeen men on the body, seven of whom must go off every year. This insures a continuous supply of new blood, since the Secretary, Treasurer and Editor are the only members who can be re-elected indefinitely.

"To amend the By-Laws requires a majority vote of the Fellows present and voting at any annual meeting, provided that printed notice of the proposed amendment of By-Laws shall have been given to all Fellows at least three months before the meeting, hence, if you wish to change the By-Laws regarding the election of officers it is advisable to prepare your proposed amendment and thrash it out with the Council in sufficient time to give this three months notice. There will be a meeting of the Council in April and you will not find any antagonism, beyond the settled conviction that the present method of procedure is the best for our Society. The Council is always open to convictoin, but it is interesting to note how each successive Council, after discussion, settles down to the form of procedure already in vogue.

"Annual banquets of the G.S.A. have always been regarded as very informal affairs. At the recent one in Amherst it was the intention to have seated at the head table the incoming presidents of the affiliated societies, and a place was reserved for Professor Lindgren, but he was late and could not be found in time to put him where he belonged. He and several others were omitted from the list of speakers, because Professor Kemp thought that the earlier speakers had used up so much time that it was too late to call upon the others. One half of the diners who sat at the so-called head table did so of their own volition, and it was not a speakers table in any sense of the word."

When Penrose received a copy of the Hovey letter, he hastily wrote to Spurr (January 30, 1922), saying "Hovey's letter brings out several points which I had not known before, especially the fact that the plan of making three nominations for each office had been tried for four or five years in the early history of the

G.S.A. I had thought that this plan had been tried for only one year and that that year had been more recently than at the beginning of the existence of the Society.

"I feel that these facts deserve serious consideration and that we should not act too hastily in the matter," he concluded. "For this reason I would prefer that you do not use my letter to you of January 23rd relating to this subject at the present time, for I can see the situation more clearly now than when I wrote that letter."

No copy of "that" letter is in the Penrose files, but in his letter of the 30th Penrose showed, as always, his ability to judge a situation on its merits and not to be ruled by his personal feelings, however keenly he may have felt the prick at the time.

Meantime, he had written with his accustomed courtesy, to Professor F. B. Loomis, local chairman at Amherst (January 7, 1922):

"Now that I have returned to Philadelphia from Amherst I am writing to tell you with what great pleasure I look back on all your cordiality and kindness to the members of The Geological Society of America and the Society of Economic Geologists while at Amherst during Christmas week. I do not think that anyone, even with the greatest scrutiny, could think of anything that you had not thought of and provided for, and I assure you that we all most sincerely appreciated your cordiality and kindness during the meeting.

"The machine-like accuracy and the personal consideration with which you carried through every detail of all the arrangements are simply admirable, and I am sure that we will all long remember your kind consideration and hospitality."

For the rest of his life, Penrose continued his interest in the Society of Economic Geologists and remembered it in his will. In October of 1921, he had considerable correspondence with Bateman concerning the method of reproducing the emblem of the Society on the covers of reprints. He took the matter up with the firm of Philadelphia jewelers who had made the original steel engraving, and found that an electro-plate would probably serve the purpose best. "If, however, you still desire the steel plate," Penrose wrote to Bateman, "I will be extremely glad to have it made and present it with my compliments."

Bateman did "still desire the steel plate," for in a letter from Penrose to S. H. Ball, secretary of the Society, dated April 10, 1922, he thanks Ball "greatly for your letter of the 8th notifying me of the vote taken at the meeting of the Council and Executive Committee of the Society of Economic Geologists on April 7th, thanking me for the engraved steel plate of the Society which I had the pleasure of presenting on that occasion. I assure you that it gave me the greatest pleasure to make this slight contribution to the Society and I appreciate deeply the kind and thoughtful action taken by the Council and Executive Committee.

"I also thank you greatly for the copy of the Minutes of the Annual Meeting of the Society of Economic Geologists held at Amherst last December. I have read it with the greatest interest, and think that your presentation of the Minutes covers all the important features of the meeting. I beg especially to express my appreciation of the motion of thanks concerning me by L. C. Graton and A. M. Bateman. I assure you that it is one of the greatest pleasures of my life to receive this complimentary notice from the members of our Society and I shall always treasure it as one of the greatest honors that I have ever received from my fellow geologists.

"I have today ordered one thousand sheets of the new paper printed with the new emblem and the names of the present officers and councilors, just as they stand on your present paper. I have also ordered one thousand envelopes of the ordinary size with your address in the corner, and five hundred long envelopes inscribed in the same way. I have directed that on the envelopes the emblem shall be put on the flap."

Penrose forwarded the stationery to Ball on April 26, and in his accompanying letter wrote that he hoped they would "reach you safely and that the Society of Economic Geologists will accept them from me as a present, with my compliments."

The following year (1923) Penrose presented the Society of Economic Geologists with an endowment fund, from which a gold medal would be awarded as a mark of distinction for work in economic geology. The medal is now known as the Penrose Medal.

First hint of his thought in this matter is found in a letter to J. E. Spurr, dated January 6, 1923, in which he says that he has "often thought of what you suggest, that is, that the Society should establish a Gold Medal for extraordinary advance in the knowledge of economic geology. I should think that this Medal need not necessarily be given at any stated periods, but that it should be given when some remarkable case of efficiency occurs. In the M. & M. Society, as you know, the Medal is given yearly; in the Academy of Natural Sciences of Philadelphia the Medal is given every three years."

On January 21, he again wrote to Spurr, assuring him that "I have not forgotten our talk about the medal and endowment some days ago. Shortly after I had received your letter I received from Ball a copy of the minutes of the meeting of the council and executive committee on January 10th in which the medal committee as mentioned consists of: J. F. Kemp, chairman, R. A. F. Penrose, Jr., A. C. Veatch. I should think therefore that it was the place of Kemp to call this meeting, as he is chairman. I also think, however, that as he has not yet called it and as at the January meeting of the council considerable difference of opinion as to the character of the medal was expressed, it might be better for you and me to meet together before the committee meets so as to formulate some definite form of medal and terms of bestowal to present to the committee. I think this would save much time, especially as you may remember that Veatch was in favor of a medal of one of the commoner metals, while Kemp did not express himself strongly on the matter at all.

"Personally I feel that the medal should be first class or not given at all and to be first class from the modern standpoint means that it should be made of gold. I have collected a good deal of information from the Philadelphia Mint and from others about the matter of medals and the dies for them, all of which I shall be glad to submit to you when I see you.

"I am much interested in this medal business," he adds, "and think that it ought to be pushed to a finish instead of being left to an uncertain fate."

By the 27th of March, when Penrose again mentioned the matter to Spurr, the making of the medal was well advanced.

"I have been after the man who is making it every few days," Penrose wrote, "and I think he will soon have it ready, certainly after the first of April. The work seems to be excellent and in some respects even remarkable. I have had to make a few suggestions to him regarding the relief work on the two hemispheres. As I told you, the two hemispheres are not flat, but are oval, and the relief work is engrossed on these oval surfaces. This is a complicated and unusual proposition. The engraver says this is the first time he ever tried it, but he is much interested in it, and I think we are going to get a most excellent result. I will get one or two copies of it in bronze as soon as possible, and then we can decide whether or not any change is necessary before having one cast in gold. I think it would be well to have one cast in gold and kept in the treasurer's office to be presented when the occasion arises."

In the meantime, he had written to Kemp (February 15), thanking him for "your letter of February 9th containing the report of your Committee of the Society of Economic Geologists on the Society's medal. The report is most kind and considerate and I beg to express to you and to your Committee my deepest appreciation and thanks for it.

"I have already started to have the die for the medal made, and I think that the artist is going to make a good product," he continues.

"I have carefully thought over what you say about the provision which we adopted at our Committee meeting, allowing the medal to be awarded to all scholars in earth science regardless of whether or not they are members of the Society of Economic Geologists. You refer to the Geological Society of America as a proper Society to award world-wide medals. It seems to me that there is ample room for two medals in the great field of geology. I am a member of both Societies and my sympathies are with both. I would be glad to contribute to a medal to be given by the Geological Society of America, in addition to what I have already done for the Society of Economic Geologists, but I really could not tolerate depriving the Society of Economic Geologists of the time-established customs of awarding their medal to anyone they please, whether in this country or in a foreign country."

The die was finished in May and Penrose then set about attending to the case in which it should be presented and to the repository for the endowment fund. On May 9th he wrote to Ball:

"After our conversation yesterday I have thought carefully about the question of the repository of the funds for our Medal, and I must say that I now believe that they should be held in New York.

"I have come to this conclusion because New York will probably always be the centre of our Society, and it would seem natural that at least the funds contributed for such purposes as the Medal should be held near headquarters, where they may be easily accessible to the officers of the Society. The funds are as safe in New York as here, and this will avoid the many petty difficulties of dealing with banks outside of New York.

"With this belief, I am enclosing to you herewith a draft on New York for two thousand dollars ($2,000.00) as a Medal Fund to make the Medal and its accessories at times when it may be needed."

Then he added, "I will also either send you, or bring to you at our meeting next week, the gold and bronze copies of our Medal. I took them back here with me last night so as to try and get the white lined boxes which you prefer to the colored one that I had with me.

"I sincerely hope that you will look on the matter of holding the Funds in New York as I do, for I assure you I will feel much better if you do so."

The following day (May 10, 1923) Penrose wrote to Spurr, as follows:

"I have received your letter of May 9th stating that you agree with the suggestion of Ball that on the inside of the cover of the case which contains the Medal of the Society of Economic Geologists there should be stamped the inscription 'Medal Founded 1923 by R. A. F. Penrose, Jr.'

"I assure you that I appreciate this suggestion on the part of you and Ball, and it gives me the greatest pleasure to accept it in the same spirit of graciousness in which you made it.

"When I founded the Medal I did not do so for the sake of personal notoriety, but because I thought such an award by such a society as the Society of Economic Geologists would be an encouragement for great and original work.

"After thinking over our conversation on Tuesday about where the two thousand dollar Endowment Fund should be placed, whether in New York or in Philadelphia, I finally came firmly to the conclusion that it should be in New York, so as to have it near the headquarters of the Society and free from all the difficulties which sometimes occur in checks on outside banks.... I feel that the funds are just as safe in a New York bank as they would be in a Philadelphia bank, and that they more properly should be in New York. I sincerely hope that you agree with me on this matter."

Conditions governing the award of the Penrose Medal by the Society of Economic Geologists were formulated by the founder, endorsed by the Council, and adopted at a meeting of the Council and Executive Committee, held at the Harvard Club in New York, November 2, 1923. They are as follows:

"1. The Society of Economic Geologists shall present a gold medal in recognition of unusually original work in the earth sciences.

"2. The recipient of the medal need not be a member of the Society of Economic Geologists, but if he has done any geologic or other work remarkable in the earth sciences, he may be awarded the medal regardless of whether or not he belongs to any society.

"3. The medal shall not be presented at any particular time or at any particular interval. The first presentation may be begun at any time not exceeding three years from date, and under no circumstances shall the second or succeeding presentations be made in less than three years or longer intervals. Possibly these intervals might at times amount to four, five, six, ten or more years, as those in control of the presentation decide what geologist or other worker in the earth sciences shall show the extraordinary merit required for the medal.

"4. The granting of the medal to any particular person shall be decided by those representatives of the Society who are elected by the general vote of the Society, such representatives being the President and Vice-President, together with five members of the Council, creating in all a body of seven members, of which six shall be required for a majority.

"5. The medal shall bear on one side the two hemispheres, representing the insignia of the Society, the other side being reserved for the presentation inscription."

The first award of the medal was made in December, 1924, to Thomas Chrowder Chamberlin.

Before the first presentation, in a letter dated December 16, 1924, Kemp wrote to Penrose: "We broke up so hastily the other afternoon, that I forgot to ask you if you would not like to make the presentation speech, or address, at that time. It would give us all great pleasure if you would do so, and as prospective toastmaster, I can easily arrange it without consulting with anybody else."

To this, Penrose responded, in the fashion almost anyone could have predicted, saying "I assure you that I greatly appreciate your kind suggestion that you would like me to make the presentation speech at that time. I feel, however, that the medal endowment is now entirely the property of the Society of Economic Geologists, and that simply because I had the privilege of presenting it to the Society it would be presumptuous in me to make the speech when the medal is presented to the recipient. For this reason I think that you as President of the Society of Economic Geologists are the appropriate one to make the speech, and I am sure that we would all be greatly pleased to have you do so. I hope, however, to have the pleasure of hearing your address.

"I want to tell you again how much I appreciated the award of this medal to Chamberlin. It is a recognition of his pre-eminent research work in the earth sciences and will show that the Society of Economic Geologists seeks for its medal a man of such wonderful accomplishments."

That as he grew older, Penrose evidently decided that it was good for men while still alive to hear the praise which is all too often reserved for their obituary notices, is evident from a letter written to his friend, E. W. Woodruff, of Cornell, concerning that presentation of the S.E.G. medal to Chamberlin. He wrote to Woodruff on January 6, 1925 that "the medal that was given to Professor Chamberlin by the Society of Economic Geologists last week was one that I had endowed, to be given periodically in recognition of original research work. I thought that money spent for this purpose was better than establishing the hackneyed endowment of a fellowship to give an education to someone who perhaps did not need it, or who might be injured by it. The principle I followed was somewhat the same as that in having the bronze bust of Professor Shaler made."

Subsequent awards of the S.E.G. Medal have been made as follows:

1927—Waldemar Lindgren
1929—J. H. L. Vogt
1931—David White
1933—Louis DeLaunay
1935—Charles K. Leith
1939—Reno H. Sales
1942—William H. Emmons
1944—Walter C. Mendenhall
1947—Bert F. Butler
1950—L. C. Graton

CHAPTER 19

Philadelphia in the Nineteen-Twenties

THE FINAL decade in the life of Richard Penrose, from 1922 to 1931, was spent in Philadelphia, the home of his childhood, engrossed in caring for the many threads of interest he had spun for himself around his world. These were years full of honors well earned, gracefully accepted, and graciously acknowledged. Despite this, however, there is a wistful note in his correspondence, a nostalgia for the old days of purposeful endeavor and acknowledged goals to be won. It was fine to have won the goals he had set for himself, but it was also sad to have no more great goals toward which to work.

He seems to have been drawn particularly close to his brother Charles in those days. Charles' wife had died in the spring of 1918, and the two brothers seem to have been drawn together in their sense of loss, the one of his father, the other of his wife. "Tal" died in February, 1925, and then Richard was lonely indeed. He occupied a suite at the Bellevue-Stratford Hotel in Philadelphia, and spent less and less time at 1331 Spruce Street, the house of many memories.

Miss Marion Ivens, who had been Tal's secretary, continued to occupy the same post for Dick until his death. She had her office in the Spruce Street house. In a letter to J. Stanley-Brown, written a year after Richard's death, Miss Ivens told how, after she had finished the letters and other work for "Mr. Richard," she would take it "to the Bullitt Building for filing. The Doctor was so systematic that he could lay his hands on anything he wanted, and frequently brought up certain papers which he needed when dictating to me. When he was through with them they were returned to the office at the Bullitt Building. Of course I did not work there and know nothing about the system the Doctor used at that office."

Three outstanding events marked those final years of his life—his four years (1922 to 1926) as president of the Academy of Natural Sciences of Philadelphia, his year (1930) as president of The Geological Society of America, and his illness in 1923.

This was the first serious illness of Penrose's life, and coming, as it did, when he had spent sixty vigorous years unaware of the toll which illness places upon one's physical and mental powers, Penrose found it difficult to adjust himself to a different tempo. John Stokes Adams, the friend with whom he shared a general office in the Bullitt Building—each having also his private offices—said, after Penrose's death in 1931, that it had seemed to him that Penrose never fully recovered from that illness. More and more he withdrew from social intercourse until he became "the quiet lonely figure" which those who knew him only in those last years considered to be the man. True it is that throughout, his life showed characteristics of the introvert, but until that illness, which taught him the bitter lesson of physical limitations, he had found a nice balance in strenuous physical exertion.

In a letter to his brother Spencer, dated January 1, 1924, he notes that "in medicine, just as in many other pursuits, a man as he gets older is apt to get more or less set in his ways and less in sympathy with modern progress." Again and again, one finds in his letters the nostalgia for the good old days. That he still kept up with old friends in the same old spirit of camaraderie is shown in the series of letters which passed between him and John C. Montgomery in 1924 and 1925.

On March 20, 1924, Penrose wrote to "Dear John" from Philadelphia, saying "It seems a long time since I have seen or heard from you, but this is not altogether my fault because when I am occasionally in New York and call up your office you are generally out. I was very sorry, however, last week to learn that the reason you were out was that you were not well and had stayed at home, and I am dropping a line to you to tell you how sorry I was to hear this and that I hope you will take good care of yourself and soon be on your feet again. It does not seem natural to go through 165 Broadway without stopping in to see you and therefore I hope that you occasionally put in an appearance there.

"I happened to meet Frank Roudebusch in the street the other day and he said he had recently seen you. He looked in first-class shape and I was glad to see him so well. He told me he was going up to Canada but would be in New York again before returning to London.

"Please drop me a line when you have a chance and let me know how you are."

That same autumn (October 16, 1924) Penrose again wrote to Montgomery, then in Denver, that he had been in New York "a few days ago and saw some of your friends. They are most all doing the same old thing, that is, watching the ticker and wondering what stocks or bonds are going up or down the next morning. Your office seems to be going along all right, but I miss the cheery greeting of the head chief and I hope that it will not be long before you report there again for duty.

"I hope you will give my kindest regards to my friends in Denver. It has been some years since I have been there, but my recollection of their always kind and cordial greeting is just as fresh in my mind as it was years ago."

The day after Christmas (December 26, 1924), Penrose again wrote to Montgomery that "we miss you in New York, though I am not much there myself. Your friends constantly ask after you, and the only news I can give them is that I occasionally get about two lines written along an immense sheet of Denver Club paper giving me a sort of phantom message from you; but it is always welcome because I know it means that you are getting better and are willing to indicate to a man that if he does not care to receive a couple of lines from you, he knows where he can go to."

The following summer (June 11, 1925), Penrose acknowledged that "it was a very great pleasure to get your recent letter and to know that you had entirely recovered. It was the first intimation I had that you were sick, and it is a sad commentary on the fact that in the old days I used to hear about almost everything that was going on in Denver, and now no one writes me anything.... I am glad to hear that you are on your feet, for the old ranks must stand together....

"I miss you in New York. I was there yesterday and hunted up your old office to find if some of the other inmates could tell me anything about you, but they were all gone. I am sure they left because they were lonesome for the old chief who used to dictate to them terms and conditions on which they were allowed to exist in those rooms of yours at 165 Broadway.

"Please let me hear from you soon."

The Montgomery reply to this letter, written at The Denver Club and dated June 15, 1925, is addressed to "My dear Dick."

"I was very glad to see your old familiar phist again," he writes. "I had made up my mind that you had gone abroad.... This week died Tom Odonnel, John Mitchell and Vidler. The latter had a beautiful home on Lookout Mt.—all members of this Club. I am treated like a Prince and am enjoying myself immensely. I made a few important changes in the menu, which probably accounts for it. Denver is a wonderful city—full of pep.... I often wonder why I hanker for Little 'ol N. Y. Last week Marjorie Reed passed away and last night Andy Hughes fell down and sprained his hips badly. There are few left in the club that you knew—Dr. Jayne and Bill Stapleton who also is ill. Jayne has no beard and looks like a young man. Oh, yes, Tom Stearns who is the same merry old soul. The rest are either younger sons or new members.

"I am in good health again, eat three good meals a day and an occasional cocktail, when I can get it. I am mortally afraid of this bootlegger stuff. My legs—d--m 'em—are not very strong, but ... Now drop me a line occasionally, if not oftener."

Dick's answer, dated Philadelphia, June 29, 1925, declares that "it was a pleasure to get your letter of June 15th and to see that your old snap and ginger had returned. It is surely hard to keep the Irish down and I hope that you will long continue to live up to that good old tradition.

"Your long list of people who have died in Denver in the last few weeks is grievous and astonishing news. I suppose you must spend a large part of your time keeping an obituary list of your friends who have departed this life. In that beautiful climate of Denver there ought to be no such cause for people acting in this way and I hope you will see that it ceases, for I expect to come to Denver soon and want to find at least some of my old friends alive.

"It has been very hot here for the last two or three weeks but I suppose it might be hotter. I am glad to know that you occasionally get a cocktail even in Denver, in spite of your dread that the bootlegger gin may be bad. I thought that in your virtuous state of Colorado such people as bootleggers did not exist and that it was only along the vicious coast of this effete eastern country that the good Lord has allowed such friends to come to the relief of the thirsty, the weary and the worn."

Another letter from Montgomery, undated, thanks Penrose for "the paper on John Casper Branner. I enjoyed it ever so much, so much that I gave it to John Finch.... I remember with much pleasure our many walks from Wall Street to 42nd. I often find myself wondering who in Hell you walk with these days. If now in your sere and scientific leaf you ever think of anything besides Relativity and Logarithms, you read Little Ships, the best novel I have read in years; all about the Irish whom you love."

Obviously in answer to this letter, Penrose wrote (October 20, 1925) that "it was a great pleasure to get your letter a few days ago for I had not heard from you for so long a time that I began to think you were like the proverbial clam and were always going to keep shut up; but your letter shows that you have come to your old self again and I am delighted to know that you are so much better and can walk around as in the old days. Why do you not practise your old stunt of running at full speed from Arapahoe Street up to your house like you used to do when you rushed from Tartoni's restaurant, kept by your friends Phil Golding and Cavanaux, after you had consumed a ruddy duck and a bottle of wine? I fear, however, that Denver cannot now show times like those.

"I have just returned from New York, but I find that most of our old friends have scattered, and I have no one with whom to walk up town, as you and I used to do. Sometimes the English language is heard in the streets of that city, but Greek, Italian, Slavonic languages, and almost anything except our own, is predominant in many quarters.

"I have been reading the Irish novel which you recommended to me called 'Little Ships.' I have not yet had time to get far into it, but surely the scraps and rows at its start do credit to the race which it portrays. You ought really to be proud of your people, for they say in New York that the Jews own the town and the Irish run it for them."

For four years, from his election to the presidency at the end of 1922 until his resignation at the end of 1926, Penrose devoted his first attention to The Academy of Natural Sciences of Philadelphia. [His relations with the Geological Society of America will be considered in Chapter 20.]

As far back as 1918, he had been opportuned to accept that position. The first mention of it in the available files is in a letter (October 18, 1918) to him from Edward J. Nolan, recording secretary and librarian of the Academy, in which he says:

"I am sure I am not violating confidence in sending you the inclosed. I wish I could add in any way to its force but I endorse cordially every word that Mr. Morris writes and I hope they will have the desired effect not only in putting the right man in office but in keeping out the wrong one.

"The salaried officers, I would say heartily if I were not one myself, are all good men, but the President of the Academy should belong to a different class, and I know of no one who could supply the requirements in such full measure as yourself.

"I hope you will not decide adversely except on the full conviction that an acceptance of office is quite impossible."

The "inclosed" letter to which Nolan refers is from Effingham B. Morris, president of the Girard Trust Company, who had written to Dr. Nolan, under date of October 17, 1918 that he had had "two talks with Dr. R. A. F. Penrose, Jr., in the past two days, and although I know that at first he declined to take the presidency of the Academy hoping to induce his brother, Dr. Charles B. Penrose, to take it, I think if he is asked again he will accept it; as Dr. Penrose has decided that his other engagements prevent his doing so.

"I venture to think it would be greatly to the advantage of the Academy to have a scientist of Dr. Penrose's standing at its head; particularly as there would thus be the chance of increasing the interest of the public in the work of the Academy in geology. If I am not mistaken, interest in geology in this country practically had its inception in the Academy of Natural Sciences; and that branch of science has perhaps not been pushed strongly by the Academy in recent years, owing to the claims of other equally important parts of its work. I hope you will put the matter before Dr. Penrose again as promptly as possible."

In his reply to Nolan, Penrose said (October 23, 1918) that he had "been absent in Washington and in New York for some days past, and only yesterday afternoon received your letter of October 18th; hence my delay in replying, for which I hope you will pardon me.

"I have read with deep appreciation your kind words about me as a possible candidate for the Presidency of the Academy of Natural Sciences, and I have also carefully read the letter to you which you enclosed from Mr. Effingham B. Morris concerning the same matter. It is needless for me to say that nothing would please me more than to feel that I could consistently accept this nomination, and I have again carefully considered the matter in hopes that I could find my way to do so, but I am always forced back to my previous conclusion that my time is being so much occupied with other matters, and will probably for some years be so continuously occupied in the same way, that I cannot consistently accept this nomination. I feel that if I did so, it would be unjust to the Academy of Natural Sciences, for I realize that it would be impossible for me to give sufficient time to the position properly to perform the duties of President."

That same day (October 23, 1918), Milton J. Greenman, director of The Wistar Institute of Anatomy and Biology, wrote to Penrose:

"Since you were here on last Wednesday I have been thinking of the good results which might be accomplished should you find it possible to accept the Presidency of the Academy.

"In addition to the decided gain for the Academy there lurks in my mind a thought that, working from the Academy, the special institute in which you are interested, could be brought into existence somewhat more easily without sacrificing in the least degree its independence.

"I hope you may be able to accept this important position, because with your ideals of research and your knowledge of the workings of the institution you can give the Academy an enormous boost. Then too while this is going on, the Geological Institute would come into existence in a place equipped with all the connections and associations for the development of such a research institute."

Thus, more than a dozen years before his death, Penrose had begun to think of the establishment of a geological endowment for research, to which he refers again and again in subsequent years. (This phase will be discussed more fully in Chapter 20.)

Three other letters dated 1918 concern this proffer of the presidency. On October 25, Witmer Stone, editor of *The Auk*, a quarterly journal of ornithology, published by The American Ornithologists' Union, said in the course of a letter of thanks for the Penrose memorial to Amos Brown, "I wish also to express my regret that neither you nor your brother find yourselves able to accept the nomination for the presidency of the Academy. At the same time I feel that we owe you a great deal for the earnest consideration that you have given the matter in what I fear may have seemed *too* persistent efforts on our part to change your attitude. I can assure you however that it was due to our conviction as to your eminent fitness for the office."

That same day (October 25, 1918) Nolan had again written him:

"I appreciate highly your letter of yesterday received this morning. Of course I regret your decision all the more as it seems to be out of the question to induce your brother to be our candidate. If Conklin lived in Philadelphia I think the solution of the difficulty would be easy."

The following day (October 26) Morris wrote to Penrose:

"I have yours of the 25th this morning, and regret exceedingly that you have been forced to come to the conclusion which you indicate in regard to the presidency of the Academy of Natural Sciences.

"In my judgment, it is lamentable that neither you nor your brother, Dr. Charles B. Penrose, can see your way clear to undertake these duties, as either one of you would be ideal men to take this position; and I am sure you would not only maintain the traditions, but increase the prestige of the Academy if either one of you could see your way clear to undertake the duties."

In the years that followed, this matter was brought more than once to Penrose's attention. And ever in his thoughts was the idea of a "research institute in geology" that would be for "pure geologic research."

In an article entitled *Postbellum Reflections on the Place of Paleontology among the Sciences*, presented before the Paleontological Society at Washington in December 1918, John M. Clarke quoted a passage "emanating from a practical geologist whose career has been marked by eminent attainment. The comment is on broad lines of geological science, all the more applicable to use because of this." On the margin of his copy, Penrose had put the initials "RAFP," evidently signifying that he was the practical geologist so designated. The quotation is as follows:

"Applied geology is of such inestimable value to mankind that its study needs no stimulus, but pure geology is often, and now more than ever, forgotten in the wild scramble for material results; and yet it is the basis on which all benefits to mankind from applied geology have been derived. During the war many geologists have given their services in one way or another entirely to the country and research departments have been permanently weaned away by mere worldly ambitions in applied geology. The limit of elasticity has been strained; the rebound will not be complete. These ambitions, however, can not be realized unless the trend of discoveries of new truths in the Earth's secrets can be maintained. A house can not be built to a height greater than the foundation will support. I believe now, more than ever, the world is in need of work in pure geologic research."

That the words of Greenman had remained in his thoughts—"there lurks in my mind a thought that, working from the Academy, the special institute in which you are interested could be brought into existence somewhat more easily without sacrificing in the least degree its independence"—and that it was with this in mind that he finally yielded to the importunities that he become President of the Academy is shown by his letter to John M. Clarke, when, under date of May 6, 1924, he said:

"Regarding the establishment of a department of geology at the Academy of Natural Sciences of Philadelphia, you know from our previous talks and correspondence that my main object in accepting the presidency of that institution was to establish a geological department there.... After almost two years experience I have found that the institution is not receptive and I now realize the futility of such an effort. At the same time I do not like to leave the Academy without doing something to improve it in some way, and hence my present attempt to make changes in its organization which will enable it to function better than now in scientific research along the lines—all purely biological—which it now cherishes so fondly. If I succeed in this I will feel satisfied to resign as president, knowing that I have at least contributed something to the welfare of the Academy."

That he did succeed in accomplishing that something which he had set out to do is shown in the reports in the Year Book of the Academy for the year ending December 31, 1924, published in Philadelphia in 1925.

"Changes of a fundamental character have been made in the administrative organization of the Academy during the past year," says Penrose in his report as President, "and it therefore seems proper to give a brief summary of the causes that required them.

"In the year 1812 a small group of men in Philadelphia who were interested in the natural sciences formed a society to pursue their investigations and discussions. In 1817 this society was incorporated under the laws of the State of Pennsylvania as The Academy of Natural Sciences of Philadelphia. In the following year a document containing the act of incorporation and what was called a 'constitution' was published, the latter being only a few very brief rules to guide the new society and really representing a small code of by-laws.

"In later years documents relating to the management of the Academy were entitled 'act of incorporation and by-laws,' and they became its sole organization. No form of a more or less elaborate constitution, separate and distinct from the act of incorporation and by-laws, such as exists in many other scientific societies, was ever adopted by the Academy. The by-laws therefore have always been more important than in other societies, because they have been the main instrument controlling its operations.

"The act of incorporation of the Academy has been amended twice in the history of the society in order to adapt it to changing conditions. The by-laws have been amended in many and various ways from generation to generation, with the result that some of the clauses became contradictory or impossible of enforcement because they conflicted with the older rules. The Academy functioned under these by-laws by precedent and mutual understanding, not by any rigid interpretation of them.

"The early management of the Academy was in the hands of the officers, among whom were included four curators. The latter under the by-laws acted as a board in conducting some of the administrative affairs of the society. In later years as the Academy increased its activities in different branches of science a larger administrative body known as the council was formed, and the board of curators was retained to co-operate with it. The Academy, however, still continued to grow and to become more intricate in its operations, until even with the best efforts of the council and the curators it was rapidly failing to function in an efficient manner, thus interfering seriously with the original research and thought which had made it renowned both in America and in all other parts of the civilized world.

"On account of these difficulties the council determined early in 1924 to amend the charter and totally to revise the by-laws, in hopes of accomplishing better results. The form of administration by the council and curators was abolished. A new governing body known as the board of trustees was created, and a new council, corresponding to the museum board in other scientific societies, was established. The board of trustees was to have charge of all the administrative and financial affairs of the society, while the council was to act in matters relating directly to the pursuits of the scientific staff. A new position of director of the museum was also created.

"The work on these changes began in March, 1924, and the legal and other details required to put them into effect consumed the rest of that year. Many meetings of the general membership of the Academy, representing the corporation, had to be called to act in accordance with the tedious methods of procedure prescribed in the old by-laws regulating amendments. The revised by-laws of today are practically a new code and were finally accepted by the Academy in November, 1924.

"On February 17, 1925, the first annual meeting under the new by-laws was held and the officers and the board of trustees were duly elected. On the same day the board of trustees met to appoint members of the scientific staff and to make provision for the proper co-operation between the board and the council. This general change of organization is now in full force and has operated up to the present time for the greater efficiency and more active progress of the Academy. All the different steps taken in accomplishing it are given in detail in the carefully prepared report of the recording secretary, and need not be repeated here."

The report of the recording secretary, James A. G. Rehn, opened with the statement that "the year 1924 marked an epoch in the history of the Academy, as during that period imperatively needed changes in the organization of the institution were made possible. These involved a change in the Charter and a complete revision of the By-Laws."

After discussing the steps in the revision, the report recorded the meetings of the organization, loss and gain in membership, and under the section concerning gifts, stated that "during the year the President, Dr. R. A. F. Penrose, Jr., presented to the Academy a most commodious and modern safe for the protection of records, important papers, the corporate seal, etc., as well as a number of beautiful rugs and pictures for the Central Office and that of the Recording Secretary. In addition he supplied rugs and furnishings for the Office of the President. The Council of the Academy has placed upon record its appreciation of these most welcome gifts."

In addition to these gifts, the report of the Treasurer, S. Raymond Roberts, shows that Penrose, who at that time was listed as one of the two "benefactors" of the Academy—a benefactor being one who had made "a contribution to the Academy of ten thousand dollars"—had also given to various funds of the institution as follows:

Joseph Leidy Commemoration Meeting Publication Fund	$ 400.00
Contributions for Vertebrate Zoology	$ 100.00
Zoological Record fund	$ 25.00
Contribution for Union List of Serials	$ 200.00
Contributions for 1924 Botanical Expedition	$ 100.00
Contributions for Building Maintenance	$3,600.00

In the Report of the Curators, signed by Witmer Stone, executive curator, two paragraphs concerns Penrose. The first is in the general statement:

"Through the generosity of Dr. R. A. F. Penrose, Jr., it was possible to make important and necessary repairs to the building. All of the outside woodwork was painted and the smoke stack repointed, while corrugated glass has been substituted for the clear panes throughout the main Museum halls, giving better diffusion of light, and protecting the specimens from the direct rays of the sun. New window shades were also provided for the Library and the lower Museum floor, and the old Museum in the north wing which has been closed for several years was thoroughly cleaned and the collections stored there rearranged. Much local field work in the various departments has been carried on and valuable additions to the collections secured."

The other paragraph, under the heading "Minerals and Rocks," states that "Dr. R. A. F. Penrose, Jr., presented a large polished section of a pegmatite pipe in riebeckite-granite from West Quincy, Mass., which is now exhibited in the Mineral Hall."

In the first six months of 1925 he spent even more, having, among other things contributed five thousand dollars "for deficit in 1925 legitimate expenses," thirteen hundred dollars for insurance, and one hundred dollars as contribution to the expenses of a trip by Henry A. Pilsbry, curator of the Department of Mollusks and Invertebrates other than Insects.

In acknowledging the five-thousand-dollar gift, James A. G. Rehn, secretary of the Academy, wrote (March 19, 1925):

"I wish to extend to you the earnest thanks of the institution for your continued interest and support, which has always been tendered with a full appreciation of our needs and aspirations.... As a representative of the scientific staff I feel privileged to assure you of the moral support and cooperation of that body, in the often wearisome and perplexing task of directing the policy and work of the Academy. That it has always been done by you with entire single-mindedness of purpose and full realization of the true needs of the institution, enables us to take up our duties day by day in the confidence that the one at the helm appreciates our problems, and works with us toward their solution."

In his reply (March 23, 1925) Penrose said, in closing:

"I assure you that I deeply appreciate your kind and cordial remarks about the work I have been trying to do for the Academy and I feel that whatever success may attend my efforts will always be the greatest reward that I could receive."

One suspects that Penrose may have been secretly as pleased with the little typewritten notes which were attached to several letters from the office of the treasurer. One of them is signed E. J. Bryan, and doubtless the others had the same source. At any rate, he carefully preserved these little slips of paper, two and a half by four and a half inches. One says: "I am afraid our childhood fairy tales deal too much with good genii in the feminine gender; for the enlightenment of modern youth I shall have to see that 'Cinderella' has a sequel, 'Ansop' with a fairy *godfather*."

Another of these notes declares that "it truly is good of you to put so much of your personality into The Academy and time will surely show the benefit derived by everyone. It does sometimes seem as though kindness and generosity were not appreciated, and it becomes discouraging, but if one's ideals are finally accomplished it is a great joy and satisfaction, isn't it? And after all, the things we are able to do, and get done in spite of obstacles, for our fellow-men brings its reward in an inward glow of love and satisfaction."

Although Penrose declined to serve further as president, he kept up his affiliation with The Academy until his death. There was nothing remarkable about this continuing interest so far as Penrose was concerned. It is indicative of the caliber of the man that he never associated himself with a project or a person until he was convinced that the interest would be directed toward a worthwhile object. And once that hurdle was overcome, he remained loyal. In his long list of active positions held and affiliations made, it is significant that these terminated only when the association had completed its avowed task or conditions had so changed that different adjustments were in order. The man was like a magnet which held only the worthwhile projects and held these with a tenacity which was untiring.

At the time of his breakdown in 1923, he was not only president of The Academy of Natural Sciences of Philadelphia but was giving of his time and energy and thought in the same wholehearted manner to his work as a Trustee of the University of Pennsylvania (1911–1927), member of the Board of Directors of The Wistar Institute of Anatomy and Biology (1915–1931), member of the publication committee of the American Philosophical Society (1903–1927), member of the Executive Committee of the Division of Geology and Geography of the National Research Council (1920–1923), member of the Executive Committee of the Society of Economic Geologists (1922–1925), member of Committee on Economic Geology of the American Institute of Mining and Metalurgical Engineers (1913–1931), member of the Council of the Mining and Metalurgical Society of America (1913–1931), member of Visiting Committee to Department of Mining, Harvard University (1902–1923), member of Visiting Committee to Department of Geology, Mineralogy and Petrography, Harvard University (1915–1923, 1925–1931), member of Visiting Committee to School of Engineering, Harvard University (1915–1923, 1925–1931), director of Utah Copper Company (1903–1904, 1909, 1917–1931), director of Philadelphia, Germantown and Norristown Railroad (1900–1931), director of Ridge Avenue Passenger Railway Company of Philadelphia (1909–1931).

And all this in addition to his careful attention to investments, a task which would be more than sufficient to keep most persons fully occupied. After his illness he was compelled to reduce the number of his interests somewhat, although the reduction was practically negligible, for new relationships took the place of those he discarded.

Concerning Penrose's relations with the Wistar Institute of Anatomy and Biology, Edmond J. Farris, executive director of the Institute, wrote to Edward W. Mumford, secretary of the University of Pennsylvania, under date of January 29, 1940, as follows:

"Dr. Richard A. F. Penrose, Jr., was elected a member of the Board of Managers of The Wistar Institute of Anatomy and Biology at a regular meeting of the Board on June 28, 1915, to succeed the late Mr. Samuel Dickson. His death was announced at the meeting of the Board held on Oct. 15, 1931, as representing the Academy of Natural Sciences. He attended 33 out of 47 meetings of the Board during his incumbency.

"There is no mention made in the minutes of his representing the Academy of Natural Sciences at the time of his election to the Board in 1915. However, at the meeting of the Board Jan. 6, 1928, a letter was presented from T. Chalkley Palmer, President of the Academy of Natural Sciences, that Dr. Penrose with Col. William Procter are nominated as representatives of the Academy.

"Dr. Penrose in 1928 presented to the Institute, in collaboration with Mr. Samuel S. Fels, a collection of Esquimaux skeletons collected by Mr. W. B. VanVelin from near Point Barrow, Alaska, in 1917–19. In addition he gave the Institute a gift of $1,000 in 1930 and the same amount in 1931.

"From the memory of Miss C. N. Perrine, who remembered Dr. Penrose, she stated he was very loyal to The Wistar Institute and offered his Bar Harbor estate for the Institute's use. It was refused because of lack of funds to manage the same. His first generosity was definitely for geology."

The 1924-1925 files of the Institute in the Penrose material opens with a letter (January 24, 1924) addressed to Dr. M. J. Greenman, director of the Institute, in which Penrose declares that "the book by you and Miss Duhring on 'Breeding and Care of the Albino Rat for Research Purposes,' is a most remarkable and valuable volume. I started to read it last night and never put it down until I had finished it, for I found it full of most instructive and interesting material.

"You have surely developed the matter of breeding and caring for the white rat to a remarkable extent and your present methods have been so carefully developed that they seem to me perfect. The volume is another manifestation of that wonderful constructive genius which you have so long displayed in all your fields of work at the Wistar Institute."

In a letter (May 30, 1924) to Effingham B. Morris, president of the Board of Managers of the Institute, Penrose wrote: "I entirely agree with you that a comprehensive account of the work of The Wistar Institute, issued at intervals of several years, would be both desirable and instructive.

"I feel that The Wistar Institute under the admirable directorship of Doctor Greenman has developed along lines on which General Wistar would have been pleased to see it grow. Of course, many new discoveries in zoology made in later years have led to work in fields of research far beyond the conception of scientists at the time General Wistar lived, but this work seems to me to be in accord with the spirit of the deed of trust, and to be the logical result of the conception of the Institute.

"I feel that no one would be more pleased than the General himself if he could see the wonderful research work which is being done at the foundation which he established. The kind of report, therefore, that you suggest would serve the double purpose of showing the relation of the work now being done at the Institute to the wishes of General Wistar, and also showing the wonderful progress made under the inspiration of the ideals of the Institute."

The following winter, Penrose wrote concerning a Board meeting scheduled for December 12, 1924, "I regret very greatly that I have a meeting of a geological organization in New York that same afternoon, and as I have promised to attend it on account of some important business which will be considered, I will not be able to have the pleasure of attending your Wistar Institute meeting. I assure you I regret this very much indeed, but I have definitely committed myself to attend the meeting in New York, so that I cannot be absent from it."

Penrose went to the annual meeting of the various "geological organizations" held at Ithaca in 1924, at which time the medal of the Society of Economic Geologists was presented to Chamberlin. On January 6, 1925, he wrote to Hampton L. Carson (a leader of the Philadelphia Bar and at one time President of the American Bar Association, who was frequently addressed as "General" because he had served a term as Attorney General for the Commonwealth of Pennsylvania):

Dear General:

"I telegraphed to you from Ithaca last week telling you how sorry I was that I would not be able to attend your Wistar Party on Saturday evening. I was at Ithaca attending a meeting of The Geological Society of America and was delayed there longer* than I had expected, so that I telegraphed instead of writing in order that you might hear from me promptly.

"I want to tell you how greatly disappointed I felt that I could not be present on that occasion, for I had looked forward with much pleasure to being there and it was only the unexpected delay at Ithaca that prevented my doing so."

Penrose's records show that at the beginning of 1925, the Board of Managers of The Wistar Institute consisted, besides himself, of Caspar W. Haines, Dr. Morris J. Lewis, Effingham B. Morris, Samuel S. Fels, Arthur L. Church, George Vaux, Jr., John Cadwaladar, and Charles E. Ingersoll. Vacancies in the Board were filled, according to Dr. Greenman, by selecting "such men as were interested in the promotion of research anatomy and willing to take active part in the Institute's management. This is an essential factor in the Institute's success."

On February 11, 1925, Penrose wrote to Dr. Greenman, stating that he would be present at the Board meeting of February 19, and adding "I have also read with much interest the copy of the organization, deed of trust and by-laws of The Wistar Institute as printed in 1894, which you so kindly sent me. This is the first opportunity I have had to possess a printed copy of these documents and I am very glad indeed to have them."

As will be shown in the following chapter (Chapter 20) Penrose was even then studying the question of trust funds, and, as is shown by his letter to Morris (already noted) he felt that the Wistar Institute fulfilled the wishes of its donor, he doubtless studied "these documents" with special interest.

On February 26, 1925, Hampton L. Carson wrote him concerning the qualifications as a college president of a certain professor. Penrose responded on March 6, apologizing for the delay as due to "death in my family" (his brother Charles), saying that he knew the professor by name but knew nothing of his administrative abilities or his capacity for dealing with people outside academic circles, but adding that "it will give me much pleasure to inquire promptly into this matter, and I will write you again as soon as I can get the information you desire."

He made the effort and on March 14 was able to report to Carson, "I have inquired, as you requested, concerning the suitability of the gentleman to whom you refer for a position as president of one of our smaller colleges. I have been told that he is not only a man very efficient in his profession, but has had sufficient experience in administrative and worldly matters to be qualified to fill such a post as you described in your letter.

"I have never met the gentleman personally, but the information I have given to you comes from one who tells me that he knows him very well."

* He had stayed because of the accident which befell Professor Chamberlin, as already noted in Chapter 16.

In this same connection, another letter in the Penrose files is of special interest. It shows that if he felt the occasion warranted it, Penrose was never niggardly in his praise of a fellow scientist. The letter is written in response to a request for confidential information concerning the qualifications of Dr. Isaiah Bowman (then president of the American Geographical Society) for the presidency of a state university, a position, according to the questioner, "more difficult than that of the presidency of the United States. There are the following relations (1) to the undergraduates, (2) to the Alumni, (3) to the Trustees and Regents, and in all three relations there are always potentialities of trouble."

Penrose replied that he had "never known Doctor Bowman intimately, but I have known him fairly well for some years and have frequently had occasion to meet him. Both of us once served as members of the Division of Geology and Geography of the National Research Council in Washington.

"I feel that Doctor Bowman would be a most capable man as president of such an institution as you mention. He is a learned scholar, a man of wide breadth of vision, diplomatic in his intercourse with other men, and always gives one the impression of efficiency. His executive ability in scientific matters has been shown by his remarkable success in the management of the American Geographical Society in New York, which he has developed into one of the leading geographical organizations of the United States and Europe.... I do not know whether Doctor Bowman* could be induced to leave his work in New York, but if the university you have in mind succeeds in getting him, I think they would be very fortunate."

Toward the end of that year (December 21, 1925) Carson again wrote to Penrose, saying that he had "been appointed by the American Philosophical Society to prepare an Address commemorative of the late Dr. I. Minis Hays for the February meeting.

"As you were in close touch with Dr. Hays for many years and have personal knowledge of the character of his work, particularly in arranging for the annual Programme of Exercises of The American Philosophical Society, and his correspondence with gentlemen invited to deliver Addresses, it would gratify me very much if you will assist me by writing me your impressions of his work, with a brief description of his methods of action."

Two days later (December 23, 1925) Penrose replied that "I will be very glad to gather together what information I can concerning these matters. Dr. Hays did so much of his work on the strength of his own initiative and his ability to manage the affairs of The American Philosophical Society that I am not yet quite certain how much detail I can give you, but I will do my best. I have always felt that it was through his efforts, his diplomacy and his ability to get along with scientific men that The American Philosophical Society owes much of its present high standing in the world of Science, literature, and other fields of activity."

The Penrose correspondence shows that ever he was ready to answer such

---

* In 1935, Dr. Bowman left New York to become president of The Johns Hopkins University.

requests to the limit of his ability, regardless of how much effort and research was entailed. Requests for money seldom met with the same reception, unless it was a cause with which he felt himself in sympathy, and then he gave generously.

As one reads the correspondence of 1924 and 1925, for example, the impression of request after request grows. Every writer seems to want something of Penrose —his money, his time, his name, his association. It must certainly have seemed to him that very few, except his old and familiar friends, cared for him and not for what he could do. Through it all, however, he retained a gracious attitude toward his fellowman, when he might easily have fallen into cynical distrust, as though he understood the peculiarities of others and liked them despite their faults.

He apparently kept no list of his charities, but in the files for a single year are records of gifts to the Historical Society of Pennsylvania, contribution to a scholarship trophy of Phi Beta Kappa alpha chapter of Massachusetts, the Philadelphia Police Beneficiary Association, the Public Baths Association of Philadelphia, the Fairmount Park Guard Pension Fund Association, the San Cristoforo Day Nursery, the Children's Seashore House at Atlantic City, St. Mary's Hospital at Philadelphia, the Bedford Street Mission, the Volunteers of America, the Lankenau Hospital at Philadelphia, the Jewish Hospital at Philadelphia, the Calvary Settlement House, and innumerable special requests for memorials, special-occasion gifts, and all the other requests that would in the natural course of events come to his hand.

In general, Penrose replied to requests for money by sending exactly the sum asked for, evidently thinking that if the asker had wanted more he would have asked for it, but again and again he followed up his first letter with an offer of more if more were needed.

For example, in December, 1921, he wrote to Professor F. B. Loomis, of Amherst: "In the circular which you sent around to the members of the Geological Society of America on November 1st asking for a contribution of one dollar apiece from the members for a loving cup for Professor Emerson, and also suggesting that letters of appreciation and congratulation would be in order, I would say that at that time I sent my dollar, and offered to send more if necessary.

"If you find that your fund is too small I hope you will let me know and I will be glad to 'chip in' more."

Penrose's good works were many and most of them were unknown except to the recipient, and sometimes even he did not know. The following letter is characteristic of this situation. It is addressed to the treasurer of one of the prominent organizations in which Penrose was much interested.

"In talking to H---- last Saturday," he writes, "I found that A---- has not paid his annual dues to that society for several years, and that he was liable to be dropped from membership on this account. I asked H---- if he would not consult with you as to giving me, as a fellow member of the society, permission to pay these back dues for A----. H---- called me on the telephone this morning and said that you had consented to do so, and that the amount due was fifty dollars. I am therefore enclosing my check for this amount in payment for these dues; and I assure you that I greatly appreciate your kindness in allowing me to do so. . . . I feel very sure that his neglect to pay his dues was entirely unintentional and for that reason I am very glad to have the privilege of paying them. He is one of the best known scientists in America and I feel that it is a credit to maintain him in our membership."

To one of his employees who had been ill, Penrose wrote: "I am enclosing to you my check for one hundred and twenty dollars as your salary for the month of April. I hope you are getting very much better and that you will soon be entirely recovered from your injuries." The letter was written on the 29th, so that presumably it would reach the man on the last day of the month. There is also a receipted bill for two hundred dollars for medical services rendered to another of his employees.

To a man in one of the trust companies who had helped him with his income tax returns, Penrose wrote, "I thank you very much for your kind attention to this matter and I assure you that I greatly appreciate all the time and assistance which you gave me yesterday in making up my income tax return for 1923."

That summer (June 12, 1924) he again wrote: "I want to assure you how greatly I appreciate all the trouble you have taken in connection with my recent income tax report and with the transmission of the Chino Copper Company certificates to New York.

"Now that these matters have become things of the past I am sending you a few cigars, which I beg you will smoke with my best wishes and sincere thanks."

In thanking him for the cigars, his correspondent wrote that "you must not however get it in your head that it is any bother for me to take care of anything you want done. On the contrary it is always a pleasure."

The following summer (July, 1925) the same correspondent wrote to Penrose that he had been "waiting some time in the hope you might stop in my office so that I could talk over with you a certain proposition I have in mind. Briefly it is this. Owing to sundry reasons, one of them being the approaching marriage of my daughter, I find I am in need of funds. I want to place a mortgage of $15,000 on my house at C———. I believe and am so informed by real estate men that the property is worth at least $25,000, although I did not pay anything like that for it some 23 years ago. At present there is a mortgage of 10,000 which would, of course be paid off. If you could take such a mortgage, it would be a very real accommodation and I think there is ample security back of it.

"I have hesitated quite a lot about making you this proposition and am afraid I have been somewhat brutally frank in presenting it. However it is intended as a business proposition and I trust you will be equally frank in your decision."

There is no copy of the Penrose reply—perhaps he did not write one, for at the bottom of the letter he has written in pencil: "I took no mortgage but gave him a loan, to be paid when he got ready, of $5000. He is never to be urged for it; and on my death the loan is to be cancelled. R. A. F. Penrose, Jr."

Only twice in this last decade of his life did Penrose journey abroad, and both times he went because of professional interests. In the summer of 1922, he attended the International Geological Congress, held at Brussels, Belgium, as (to quote his own words in his list of journeys) " representative of the United States Government, the University of Pennsylvania, American Philosophical Society, The Franklin Institute, Academy of Natural Sciences of Philadelphia, Society of Economic Geologist, Mining and Metallurgical Society of America."

In 1926 he was a "delegate to International Geological Congress, Madrid, Spain, from various scientific organizations."

In June, 1922, he wrote to Sydney H. Ball, acknowledging his letter "enclosing letters of introduction to Mr. Shaler and to Professor Cornet in Brussels. I thank you greatly for your kind thoughtfulness in sending me these letters and I am sure that it will be a pleasure to call on them during the time I am in Brussels.

"I hope of course to see you in New York before I sail, as I will not start before the latter part of July; and I would also like to discuss with you certain features as to what might be accomplished in the way of economic geology during the Congress."

In another letter to Ball (July 10, 1922) he acknowledges receipt of the "announcement of the Fall Meeting of the Society of Economic Geologists with the American Institute of Mining and Metallurgical Engineers to be held in San Francisco in September of 1922. I think that this meeting should be a most successful one and I only wish that I could be there. I assure you I would much prefer to go to San Francisco than attend the Belgium Congress, but as the winds seem set for the latter I am definitely determined to go and have my tickets in my pockets. I hope to see you in New York before I sail, which will be on July 22d."

On July 19 (1922) he wrote to Spurr that he regretted "greatly that you still feel that you cannot go to Brussels, but perhaps at the last moment you may change your mind. I am leaving tomorrow for New York and will sail on the Lapland for Antwerp on the 22d."

That he also spent some time in London is clear from a letter written December 22, 1924, to F. H. Praed, of the firm of Sifton, Praed and Company of London, (booksellers) for he says:

"It seems a long time since I have seen you or Mr. Sifton but I have not been in London since my last trip there in August and September, 1922. I have been so busy with the reorganization of The Academy of Natural Sciences of Philadelphia that I have had no chance to do much travelling since I last saw you; but I still have in mind my proposed trip to the eastward from the upper waters of the Irrawaddy River, and if at any time any new maps or new literature relating to that particular part of the world appear I will be very glad if you will let me know about them. I might add that when I was in London in 1922 I think I got from you about everything that had been issued up to that time. My work at The Academy of Natural Sciences will soon be much less exacting than it is at present, and then I hope to get away on a long trip. I expect to come to London probably some time next spring, and if so I will look forward with pleasure to seeing you and Mr. Sifton."

By September 18 (1922) he was back in Philadelphia for he wrote to Ball on that date that he would "probably be in New York later in the week." Two days later (September 20, 1922) he again wrote to Ball that he was "unexpectedly called to Seal Harbor, Maine, next Friday afternoon to attend to some business matters in connection with a small property which I own there, but I will return to New York some time next week and will make a point of seeing you then. In the meantime, I will work while traveling on the summary for Economic Geology."

Victor Emanuel III, king of Italy, twice decorated Richard Penrose "in recognition of your scientific merits and of the value of your achievements in the field of geology." In 1922 he was made a Cavaliere in the Order of Saint Maurizio and Saint Lazzaro, and in 1928 he had conferred upon him the decoration of Commendatore of the Crown of Italy. That same year (June 29, 1928) he also received a medal from the Italian government in commemoration of the dedication of the Fountain of the Sea Horses in Philadelphia, commonly known as the Italian fountain, a gift which Penrose made to the City of Philadelphia, where it was placed in Fairmount Park.

In a letter (September 21, 1922) to Carlo Schanzer, Senator of the Kingdom and Royal Minister of Foreign Affairs at Rome, Penrose wrote: "I assure you that I appreciate most highly this very great honor, and I take the greatest pleasure in the knowledge that the privilege of such an illustrious and noble Order has been granted to me. It will always be a most precious treasure to me, and it will be a stimulus constantly to accomplish more and more in the science to which I have devoted my life."

The following day (September 22, 1922) he wrote to Commandatore Francisco Quattrone, Italian Minister Plenipotentiary at 44 Whitehall Street, New York: "I highly appreciate the great honor of the appointment to this ancient and distinguished Order, and I beg to thank you personally for the great interest you have so freely manifested in this matter.

"I hope some time that it may be my good fortune to meet you personally in New York. I have heard so much about you from my friends, and about the deep interest that you take in many industrial and scientific matters, that I assure you I would be very happy indeed to have the honor of expressing my thanks to you in person."

In his reply, Quattrone spoke of "our common friend Mr. Viti."

It was not until a year later, however, that Penrose received the official statement of this award from Prince Gelasio Caetani, at that time Italian Ambassador to the United States, who wrote to him from Washington (September 28, 1923), saying:

"It gives me particular pleasure to send you herewith the diploma of the decoration of Knight of the Order of the Saints Mauritius and Lazarus which

His Majesty the King of Italy conferred upon you by Decree of June 18th, 1922 in recognition of your scientific merits and of the value of your achievements in the field of geology.

"Accept at the same time my cordial congratulations for the distinction by which you have thus been honored."

In his reply, Penrose, after acknowledging the honor and the pleasure its conferring had given him, added:

"Your own great accomplishments in science and its related fields are so well known that I feel deeply gratified that the diploma has come to me through your hands. I take this occasion to express to your Excellency my compliments and my highest esteem."

On September 21, 1928, Count Vittore Siciliani di Morreale, then "Minister Plenipotentiary of H. M. the King of Italy," wrote to Penrose:

"I have the most pleasant duty of informing you that His Excellency the Royal Italy Ambassador at Washington has just communicated to me that by Decree of June 25th, 1928, His Majesty the King of Italy has conferred upon you the decoration of Commendatore of the Crown of Italy.

"I avail myself of this opportunity to renew to you my most sincere and heartiest congratulations for the well deserved distinction conferred upon you by my Government, as a recognition of your friendly sentiments toward Italy and the Italians."

Replying on September 26 (1928), Penrose said:

"I assure you that I deeply appreciate the very high honor of this Decoration which has been conferred upon me, and I shall always look on it as one of my most valued possessions, and above all, as a token of that sincere friendship and admiration which I have always had for the Kingdom of Italy and its people."

On October 5 (1928), The Royal Consul General of Italy, Mario Orsini Ratto, notified Penrose that he had "just received the insignia of the decoration conferred upon you by His Majesty the King of Italy.

"As the 1st of November the Italian Community of Philadelphia will celebrate the tenth anniversary of the great victory of 1918 at the Elks Club with a reception and a dance, I have the intention to deliver personally the decoration to you and other gentlemen with the attendance of several prominent American men.

"I would, therefore, ask if you could kindly be present at the ceremony in question at 10 p.m. of that day."

On October 16 (1928), Penrose replied to Dr. Ratto:

"I assure you that I am greatly touched by the high distinction of the honor of this decoration, and I would be sincerely pleased to receive it at the time of the commemoration of this great and glorious event in the history of the brave Italian Armies. I am, however, obliged to leave Philadelphia next week on some matters of much importance, and will not be able to return until after November first, so that I regret extremely that I will be deprived of the pleasure of being present on this most auspicious occasion; but I shall feel greatly honored to receive the Insignia of the decoration at your convenience, and I shall always hold it as a very high distinction and as a most gracious token of that sincere friendship and admiration which I have always had for the Kingdom of Italy and its people."

Under date of November 27 (1928), Dr. Ratto sent Penrose the insignia, which was duly acknowledged on December 3. Early the following year (February 18, 1929), Dr. Ratto sent Penrose the diploma, with a courteous note of congratulation, to which Penrose as courteously replied on February 25.

But this was one time when Penrose's absence was not to be passed over lightly, and evidently he had not been the only one of those thus honored who had been conspicuous by his absence. On March 28, C. C. A. Baldi, editor and publisher of *L'Opinione*, "the principal Italian daily and Sunday family newspaper" in Philadelphia, wrote to him:

"I trust I am in order in writing you, and asking that you forward me your photograph, as I would like to use the photograph in L'Opinione. I am anxious to correct a false impression existing in the minds of some regarding the decorations recently bestowed on you and others by His Majesty, The King of Italy, at which time none of the recipients were present. I am satisfied the decorations were appreciated and I do not want to leave a bad impression in the minds of some of our people."

Penrose wrote (April 10, 1929) to Chevalier Baldi, protesting against any such interpretation being put on his action.

"I beg to assure you, as I have already assured Doctor Ratto, of my deep appreciation of the very high distinction of this Decoration, which I shall always preserve as a most valued possession," he wrote, "and above all, as indicating the admiration and friendship that I have always had for Italy and the Italian people."

In his perturbation that anyone should interpret his actions as discourteous, Penrose evidently overlooked the fact that Baldi had requested his photograph, for on April 15th, Baldi again wrote, calling his attention to the matter. On April 24th, Penrose, having just returned "from a short absence," sent the desired photograph with another letter protesting his esteem for the decoration. Chevalier Baldi acknowledged receipt of the picture on April 29th, and there, presumably, the matter was dropped.

In the spring of 1923, Penrose was ill for several weeks, but had recovered sufficiently by the middle of May to attend a meeting of the Society of Economic Geologists council in New York on the 18th and 19th. On the 25th of June, he wrote to Sydney H. Ball:

"I have just received your letter of June 23d, stating that Horace Winchell told you that he had been in Philadelphia last Thursday and that he had tried three or four times to get in touch with me and was greatly disappointed in not being able to get me on the phone. I assure you that I am very sorry indeed that I missed Horace, for he and I have always been on the closest and most friendly terms and it is a great pleasure for me whenever I can see him.... I have not been over to New York for a couple of weeks or so, for I knew you would probably be away, and I thought that probably, just as in Philadelphia, no one was doing anything more than he really had to do during that frightfully hot weather."

On July 19 (1923) Penrose wrote to Spurr that he planned to "start early in August for a short trip by sea up the Northern Coast of Canada in the neighborhood of Prince Edward Island and Labrador, and I expect to return here again early in September."

Five days later, Penrose again wrote to Spurr: "I expect to start for Canada next week, but I will write to you more definitely about my movements before I go. This is the fourth time I have tried to take a trip this summer, but each time before now I have been prevented from doing so by one thing or another. I hope, however, to get started this time."

In a letter to Ball (July 25, 1923) Penrose discloses that his trip will not only include "the eastern provinces of Canada, passing Nova Scotia, Prince Edward's Island and other points," but that he will continue "up the St. Lawrence to Quebec" and expects to be back the end of August.

Two days later (July 27, 1923) he again wrote to Ball, thanking him for his good wishes for a pleasant vacation, and extending "the same wishes to you wherever you may go to get a little relief from all the hard work you have been doing. Personally I would rather stay here and work on the many things that I have on hand to finish, but I suppose I can do them better after a short vacation." Evidently the trip was taken under doctor's orders.

In another letter to Ball (November 14, 1923), he acknowledges that he "was greatly pleased to get your postal card from Portugal a few days ago and to know that you are having a pleasant and satisfactory trip. I agree with you that Portugal has much to show strangers in the way of wonderful buildings. I have traveled in that country somewhat and have been more than once at Lisbon and I have often thought that Portugal was one of the least appreciated countries I have ever visited.

"Mr. Shaler was at my office today and I was very glad indeed to see him again. I will always remember with much appreciation his kindness to me when I was in Brussels in 1922."

In December (1923) the celebration of the hundredth anniversary of the birth of Joseph Leidy at the Academy of Natural Sciences of Philadelphia, of which Penrose was at that time president, occupied most of his time, although he found opportunity to attend the meetings of the Society of Economic Geologists and the Geological Society of America in Washington at Christmas time.

The year 1924 found him sticking closely to his work in Philadelphia, work which he found very confining, as he complained again and again in his correspondence, but which he had not the faintest idea of shirking. Here, as in all other tasks he had set for himself in life, he did not stop until the work was finished—if not to his entire satisfaction, at least to the best of his ability. Apparently, he spent almost the entire year either in Philadelphia or in New York, with the exception of a trip in August to Toronto, where he represented the Academy of Natural Sciences at the meeting of the British Association for the Advancement of Science, held that year in Canada.

Two interesting letters in his files concern that Toronto meeting. One is from the head of the department of geology in a prominent university; the other is Penrose's reply.

"There is a possibility that Doctor J.---- may stay in South America until the first of January," begins the former, "and if so it might be possible for us to arrange to have some man give a course of lectures on economic geology during his absence. I had in mind the possibility of getting some man who might be attending the British Association at Toronto but as I think it over the scope widens and it occurs to me that there might be some other European, preferably not a German, whom it would be interesting to invite over for a short course of lectures. I think I might possibly scrape up $1500 to $2000 for this object.

"I am writing you now because of your wide acquaintance with the economic geologists here and abroad for suggestions. Do you know whether de Launay speaks good English? I would like to get hold of some outstanding figure whom we as Americans would like to have over here to treat with prominence. If such a man is not available I am inclined to think of some young Englishman of prominence who is making good in economic geology."

In his reply (June 27, 1924) Penrose said: "I think that perhaps some good American economic geologist might be better than most foreign men in this profession, because the American takes a somewhat different view of the subject than the European; though the geologists in Australia and New Zealand seem to lean more towards the American conception of their subject. For this reason I would suggest that you either get someone from the United States, or perhaps someone from Australia or New Zealand in case the latter should happen to be in this country at the meeting of the British Association at Toronto.

"I could highly recommend Percy G. Morgan, Director of the Geological Survey of New Zealand, Wellington, New Zealand, to give a good course on this subject. Willet G. Miller, Toronto, Ontario, would also be an excellent man. Among our own economic geologists you can doubtless make a choice as well as I can. I think that J. E. Spurr could fill the place admirably if he would accept it. Of course C. K. Leith could also give an admirable series of lectures on economic geology. Another man from the Far East whom I have not mentioned above but who might possibly be at the Toronto meeting, is Lewis F. Fermor, Director of the Geological Survey of India, Calcutta. I have met him on several occasions and consider him an excellent geologist, and he has been in touch with many of the large economic problems in India."

Less than a year later (March 13, 1925) Penrose wrote again of Professor Miller; this time, to Duncan Chisholm of Toronto, whom he addresses as "Dear Duncan."

"On my return from a short absence," Penrose wrote, "I have received your letter telling me of the sad news of the death of Doctor Miller, and enclosing a newspaper clipping concerning his great accomplishments.

"I was greatly shocked and grieved to hear of his loss, for he was one of my best friends, and I always enjoyed meeting him at the various geological congresses that we held in Canada and the United States. He was a good friend of all of us and his death is a loss both to science and mankind in general.

"I do not know whether Doctor Miller left any family, but if so I beg that you will extend to them my deepest sympathy.

"I sincerely hope that you are well, and that some time if you ever come here or to New York you will give me the pleasure of a visit."

To the head of another geology department—William H. Hobbs, at the University of Michigan, of whom Penrose had written to Ball (November 28, 1922) "he is a man full of energy and initiative"—Penrose wrote (January 8, 1924):

"On investigation I find that the notice which was sent to members of the American Philosophical Society who were particularly interested in different branches of science asking them to nominate a certain number of those eligible for membership, was intended to carry no particular recommendation for any special number of nominees. I find that different committees similar to the Geological Committee have nominated all the way from one or two to five or six persons. Many of the committees have taken no action whatever. In one case three were nominated with the recommendation that one of them be favorably considered for membership immediately, and that the other two be allowed to wait over for future consideration.

"I personally feel that it is not fair to nominate, without their consent, several prospective candidates when consideration of the names of most of them will obviously be deferred; and yet it is against the rules of the Society to consult such candidates concerning the matter.

"In view of what I have said I would suggest that we select one man and recommend him for favorable consideration at the next election and in this way have a reasonable chance for getting him elected, instead of recommending several men with the almost certainty of having their consideration for membership postponed.

"If the Geological Committee and the Paleontological Committee would both follow this plan we would probably be able to elect one of each profession, thus making really two geologists."

On March 27 (1924) Penrose wrote to Dr. Charles C. Harrison, asking whether he, as president of the University Museum, Philadelphia, "would think it proper for me to become a Life Member of the University Museum. I understand that it is possible to become a Life Member by the payment of five hundred dollars, without assuming any other financial obligations.

"In recent visits to the Museum I have been greatly impressed by the wonderful work which is being accomplished there under your direction and the excellence of the lectures and the Museum displays. For this reason I would greatly value my membership in this institution."

Dr. Harrison replied in the affirmative, thanking Penrose for his words of encouragement. Thus, Penrose again manifested his adherence to the old adage, "whatever is worth doing at all, is worth doing well," for as president of the Academy of Natural Sciences, his interest in lectures and exhibits led him to investigate the work being done along these lines in other similar institutions.

Penrose also devoted some thought to the matter of the proper presentation of scientific matter, from the point of view of physical appearance rather than content, as two letters of this period show. The first was a letter to Ball (April 18, 1924) in which he says:

"I cannot help feeling that if the Society [Society of Economic Geologists] can afford it, its publications would look much better and convey a much better impression if they had covers than if they had not. I have in recent months received several separates from geological societies without covers, and though of course the importance of an article depends on what is contained in the printed matter, yet an appropriate cover adds not only to its dignity, but also to the facility of preserving what it encloses."

A year later (April 21, 1925) he wrote to Gellert Alleman, of Swarthmore College, that "all scientific articles are of course primarily important in accordance with what they contain, but a good looking exterior and binding adds much to the appearance and attraction, and undoubtedly leads many people to read them who might otherwise not do so. All of the articles which you have sent me [in connection with the centenary celebration of The Franklin Institute] are important contributions to either pure or applied science, and the excellent manner in which they have been issued is a great credit to you who have cared for it."

On June 4 (1924) Penrose wrote to James F. Kemp: "I want to tell you how sorry I was that I could not have attended the dinner of the Society of Economic Geologists on May 23rd. My absence was not due, as you suggest, to fear of being called on to speak, for as the years go by I am really afraid I may become garrulous on such occasions."

Kemp had consulted him regarding Snake River gold mines—the only occasion, so far as his correspondence shows, when he was consulted professionally by a fellow-geologist—and the letter of June 4th continues:

"I have read carefully the two letters you handed to me in New York concerning the Snake River mine, and I readily can understand them after the hasty look that I had of the maps when I was with you last Monday. The proposition is certainly an interesting one, but do you not think that a great many more samples should be taken and assays made in order to establish the real average values of the ore at different spots?

"I think that the work you have done on the property in the construction of your maps and in the admirable explanation of your ideas concerning the locality, could not be better. I do not know exactly what your idea is regarding your future action in this matter, and I am therefore returning herewith the letters which you gave me to read."

The end of October (1924) Penrose wrote to Ball, evidently in response to a call for help, saying that he could "deeply sympathize with the troubles of a long-suffering secretary of the Society of Economic Geologists in securing sufficient 'separates' to complete the seven volumes of the publications of the Society of Economic Geologists, and I assure you it will give me much pleasure to help in any way I can.

"I would have replied to your previous letter about Bateman's paper on Primary Chalcocite: Bristol Copper Mine, Connecticut, but I was hoping that you would be able to secure it from someone else. I judge, however, that you have found this impossible and therefore I am sending to you my copy of the paper. It is with regret that I part with it, for I consider it a most valuable and important treatise on the subject; but as I have it of course in Volume XVIII of Economic Geology it seems to me rather selfish to refuse to give up a separate when you need it for your particular purposes. I am sending it to you therefore today under separate cover."

Bateman later sent Penrose another copy.

The following month (November 4, 1924) Penrose wrote to his old friend, John Brockman, that he had "just returned from voting for Mr. Coolidge," and was wondering whether Brockman was about to set forth on a projected trip to Spain and Italy.

"If you sail by way of New York," Penrose continued, "I sincerely hope you will let me know so that I can come over and see you.

"My earnest desire to come out to California this fall has been prevented by the amount of work I had to attend to here, especially in connection with The Academy of Natural Sciences. Next year, however, I hope to be freer and then I can move around as I used to do in the old days when you and I traveled together. I do not think much of this business of being compelled to stay in one place month after month. It does not seem natural or right to have to do so when one has been used to roaming over the west."

To the *Proceedings of The Academy of Natural Sciences of Philadelphia* for 1924, Penrose contributed a tribute to Robert G. LeConte.

"Last summer, when all nature was in its most glorious bloom," he wrote, "a great shock befell The Academy of Natural Sciences of Philadelphia in the loss of Doctor Robert C. LeConte. He had for many years been a member of the Council of the Academy and was always in thorough sympathy with its activities.

"His work in life covered many fields and was undertaken with an unselfish energy and interest peculiar to the man. From his boyhood he had been ever buoyant and happy, full of the very joy of living, and radiating good nature and kindliness to all with whom he came in contact.

"A graduate of the University of Pennsylvania, he later became one of its Trustees; as a surgeon in the Pennsylvania Hospital and other hospitals of Philadelphia he acquired a national reputation in his chosen profession; as a sympathetic patron of biological research he was a member of the boards of many scientific institutions.

"As a soldier he showed great efficiency and loyalty in the National Guard of Pennsylvania for many years and in the Spanish War in 1898; while later as an officer in the American Navy, in the recent war in Europe, he dispayed such brilliancy of accomplishment that he was rewarded with many decorations and insignia of merit.

"His achievements were great and diversified. He was at once a scholar, a soldier and an altruist, and when the end came a sad void was left in the hearts and the lives of his friends."

At this same period, Penrose was also actively concerned with affairs connected with the University of Pennsylvania, of which he was a Trustee from 1911 to 1927. As such he did his duty toward the institution as he saw it, with all the thoroughness and attention which were his wont under similar circumstances. In 1915, he also became a Manager of The Wistar Institute of Anatomy and Biology, which is affiliated with the University, as noted elsewhere in this chapter.

During his term as Trustee, he made gifts to the University totaling nine thousand dollars, none of it apparently earmarked for the Department of Geology. Dr. Frederick Ehrenfeld, of that department, writing of Penrose under date of February 5, 1940, states that "he was always very sympathetic to the needs of the Department of Geology and Mineralogy, and to the members of the staff, so far as he was able to help by words and voice.

"During his term of years Dr. Penrose was understood to have endeavored to bring to the Department a more adequate equipment both in physical needs and increase of staff. He wished to present to the Department from time to time valuable ores and mineral specimens but there was no adequate way in which to display them, and Dr. Penrose did not feel himself in the position of supplying the needed cases and room space in which to house the above sorts of material.

"Dr. Penrose made efforts to interest other persons in the building up of a strong department here but for various reasons these efforts were fruitless of practical result.

"The members of the staff in Geology and Mineralogy were always able to consult with Dr. Penrose freely as to their needs and interests. Dr. Penrose was invariably sympathetic, interested, and his encouragement in times of discouragement and of need of support was a very real thing."

The Penrose files for 1924 and 1925 show that despite his preoccupation with affairs at the Academy, he found time to give earnest thought to the problems of the University.

Early in the summer of 1924, he received a letter from Randal Morgan, stating that the Trustees of the University were prepared to meet $100,000 expenses in connection with a campaign for "the creation of a permanent organization which would function from year to year and continuously in an effort to interest the entire community of Philadelphia and those interests in the State of Pennsylvania outside of Philadelphia whom the University might perhaps feel it was naturally entitled to apply to for assistance, and also the Alumni of the University, in forwarding the interests of the University and particularly in assisting it in the provision of funds, both for capital and operating purposes, from year to year and when needed."

In his reply (June 6, 1924), Penrose declared that he was "willing to make a contribution towards this fund for I had fully intended to contribute to the endowment at a later date, but I would like to say that I highly disapprove of the principle of assessing trustees. I have seen the same action taken in other boards in educational and scientific institutions and it has always produced unfortunate results. The plan does not seem right to me; it seems like drafting a soldier before he has had a chance to enlist. Moreover, I think the effect will be to prevent certain men who might be desired as new trustees from accepting, because though they could give of their time and services to the University they might not be able to afford an assessment.

"I have been hoping for a long time that an organized drive on the public for funds might be averted, particularly in view of the fact that bequests and gifts to the University have been coming in rather rapidly recently; and I fear that the proposed drive will not only be unpopular in the community but may curtail the flow of unsolicited donations.

"If, however, you approve of the action of the Board of Trustees as of May 19th, I will be glad to send you immediately my check for $5,000. as a contribution to the Trustees' fund above mentioned."

On June 12, Penrose again wrote to Morgan, thanking him for his detailed reply to his previous letter, and adding:

"I understand fully your explanation of the situation and I am very sure that with your broad knowledge of the conditions at the University and your wisdom as a man of large affairs, any plan which meets your approval is necessarily good.

"I might add that my absence from the last two meetings of the Trustees was due to the fact that for several months I have been working uninterruptedly on the reorganization of the Academy of Natural Sciences, and I therefore was not able to be at these meetings. I hope to attend more regularly before long."

A week later (June 19, 1924) Penrose again wrote to Morgan, thanking him for a letter and noting that "Mr. Gates has been kind enough to send me a copy of the 'Suggested plan of procedure in connection with the University of Pennsylvania.' I have read it carefully several times, and though I realize that it is intended to be somewhat different from the ordinary form of drive, yet I cannot see much difference in it except that the community will be subject to solicitation over a period of several years instead of all at once.

"Of course the University has gone so far in this matter that further discussion of its desirability is unnecessary. I suppose it is bound to try its own experiment in the solicitation of funds by a general campaign. I often wonder why colleges and universities before making organized campaigns for funds do not study the discouraging results that have come to other institutions in similar experiments."

Penrose paid the promised five thousand dollars and the following April received another letter, saying that the ante had been raised to $150,000, and asking for a further contribution. He replied, after formally acknowledging the subject of the letter:

"In a later letter from Mr. G.— I was requested to make contributions to the General Fund which was being raised, and I replied to him that I had already contributed $5000. to the amount necessary to start the campaign, and that I was contributing considerably to The Academy of Natural Sciences of Philadelphia and other institutions in which I have long been interested, that I could not at present contribute any more to the University of Pennsylvania. I regret that I still feel in this matter as I did when I wrote to Mr. G.—."

And there, apparently, the matter rested.

The previous winter (February 25, 1924), in a letter to the Hon. John C. Bell, whom he addressed as "Dear John", Penrose acknowledged his appointment to the committee to discuss the budget to the Graduate School of Medicine of the University, and notes that the committee is scheduled to meet on March 4th, at which time" there is to be an important meeting of the Council of the Academy of Natural Sciences and I regret greatly that this will prevent my attending."

Penrose's unfailing efforts to remain inconspicuous are obvious in his letter of February 16, 1924, addressed to J. Hartley Merrick, Vice-Provost of the University, replying to an invitation "at the request of President Penniman, to act as one of the 'Trustee Sponsors' for two recipients of honorary degrees at the 'University Day' ceremonies at the Academy of Music on February 22nd.

"I am very sorry indeed that an important engagement on February 22nd will prevent my being present at the 'University Day' ceremonies and that this will deprive me of the honor of being one of the sponsors. I regret this all the more because I highly approve of the award to the candidates in question. Their professional accomplishments amply justify the recognition that has been given them by the University of Pennsylvania."

The following summer (July 3, 1924) Penrose wrote to E. W. Mumford, secretary of the University, regretting his inability to attend a Trustees' meeting, as he had "an appointment with the solicitor of the Academy of Natural Sciences to go to court in connection with securing an amended charter for the Academy of Natural Sciences, but if I get through this work in time I hope to attend the meeting of the Board of Trustees."

At the bottom of a carbon copy of his letter to Mumford, acknowledging notice of a meeting of the Board of Trustees to be held September 15, 1924, Penrose has written in pencil:

"I nominated Dr. G. E. deSchweinitz for trustee to succeed Dr. R. G. LeConte at this meeting. Mr. Louis C. Madeira seconded the nomination, and the board unanimously approved it. R.A.F.P. Jr., Sept. 15, 1924."

His correspondence shows that this was by no means an unpremediated action, but that he had carefully paved the way by letters to several members of the Board before the event took place. To several he wrote:

"I beg to suggest for your consideration the name of Doctor George E. de Schweinitz to fill the place of our poor friend Doctor LeConte on the Board of Trustees of the University of Pennsylvania. You know Doctor de Schweinitz so well that it is needless for me to enlarge on his pre-eminent qualifications for the position.

"I feel that his appointment would not only be a gracious recognition of his past services to the University but would also open a field in which he could continue his activities in guiding the administrative development of his profession."

His correspondence also shows that he acknowledged notice and promised to attend board meetings on October 20 and December 15, 1924. On October 27, 1924, Penrose wrote in reply to Dr. J. H. Penniman, president of the University:

"I regret greatly that I am called out of town today and will not be able to attend the meeting of the Board of Trustees this afternoon.

"I am writing now simply to express my regret that you are preparing for a drive for funds for the University of Pennsylvania at a time when the whole country has been overburdened by such afflictions.

"We hear elaborate statements of what drives for funds have done for other universities and smaller institutions, but when we get at the innermost facts we find that the results have generally been greatly exaggerated.

"I confidently believe from my personal experience in such matters that these organized drives seriously interfere with the normal flow of gifts and bequests which might otherwise come to the University in a dignified and unsolicited manner, and which might aggregate more than the amount derived from drives."

Dr. Penniman replied in detail (October 31, 1924) and on November 4, Penrose again wrote to him, saying in part:

"I thank you greatly for your letter explaining your ideals in the suggested procedure for beginning an endowment campaign for the University of Pennsylvania. I regret that you were put to the trouble of writing such a long letter to explain this matter, but I assure you that I deeply appreciate the trouble you have taken.

"As I am not an alumnus of the University of Pennsylvania I often hesitate to speak out what I think at the meetings of the Board because I fear that they may be interpreted as the utterances of an outsider. When, however, I see a situation which is obviously inadvisable for the University I feel that it is my duty, as long as I am a Trustee, to say something about it."

Penniman replied (November 6, 1924) that he appreciated Penrose's "feeling, in regard to Board meetings, but at the same time regret that you do not speak more freely on every subject that interests you, because your training gives an authority to what you say, such as much of the discussion in the Board meetings does not possess."

Penrose, in acknowledging this letter (November 12, 1924) declared that he appreciated "greatly your kind remarks about my speaking more freely at the meetings of the Board of Trustees on subjects in which I am interested and I will hereafter try to do so, though I always hesitate unduly to prolong meetings at which so many important matters have to receive attention."

The following spring (March 2, 1925) Penniman again wrote to Penrose, stating that "at the last meeting of the Board, I raised the question of modifying the retiring age from 68 years to 70 years, in the case of members of the University Faculty, who are eligible for Carnegie pensions. The Carnegie Foundation provides the stipend, beginning with the year in which a man attains the age of 70. Our Statute requires a man to retire at the age of 68. Unless the University continues the man to the age of 70, or retires him at the age of 68 and pays him a pension, he will lose two years of pension or two years of salary as the case may be, because of the discrepancy of our retiring age, and that of the Carnegie Foundation. The Board directed me to appoint a Committee to consider and report on the matter, and I am writing to ask whether you will not serve as Chairman of the Committee, the other members being Judge [John M.] Gest and Dr. [Charles J.] Hatfield. If you have not a copy of the Carnegie rules, I will have one sent to you."

Penrose replied on March 7, accepting the appointment, and adding: "I feel that it must be a great hardship on certain men of advanced years to be obliged to struggle through the period between 68 and 70 for their living. It will, therefore, give me much pleasure, to accept your appointment as chairman of the committee... I, personally, feel that many a professor at 70 is as good as many others at 50, and sometimes far better."

The committee met in due course, and, according to the letter written (April 18, 1925) by Penrose to Dr. Penniman, "the matter was discussed in all its aspects and a resolution was unanimously adopted by your committee suggesting to the Board of Trustees the desirability of increasing the retiring age at the University from sixty-eight years to seventy years.

"I am sending this report to you because I may possibly not be able to attend the meeting of the Board of Trustees on Monday afternoon, April 20th, and in such event I would be greatly obliged to you if you would communicate it to the Board at that time."

The files show that he did not attend the meeting. Instead, he sent a telegram from New York to Penniman, saying that he was "unavoidably detained" and asking Penniman, if he approved of the report, to present it at the meeting.

An undated manuscript in his files, "prepared at the request of Wharton Barker, Esq., a Trustee of the University of Pennsylvania," shows that Penrose had given consideration to *Geology* and its *Scope in University Education*, as the title reads. After defining geology and giving details concerning its various branches of study, Penrose states; under the heading, "Importance of a Knowledge of Geology,":

"A knowledge of at least the principles of geology is an important part of any liberal education, and in many scientific and other pursuits a thorough knowledge of geology is absolutely essential. From the earth come the metals we use, the coal we burn, the water we drink, the soils of our fields, the food we eat, and in fact almost everything that man uses or meets in his daily career. To many people the nature of the earth and its products remain throughout their lives one vast mystery. They know that there are mountains, valleys, and oceans on the earth's surface, but have never thought to inquire how they came there. They know that the mines produce metals and coal, the springs produce water, and the soils produce plants; but why, and how this happens, is all unknown to them.

"Those who have even only a superficial knowledge of geology have a vast advantage over those who have none, for to them every river, mountain, valley, even every creek, field, or mud-bank, has a meaning which not only increases their enjoyment of nature and travel, but makes their lives much more useful to themselves and others.

"Relation of Geology to Other Sciences and Pursuits

"From the earth springs the animal and vegetable life that inhabits it, and the sciences that treat of these subjects must recognize the importance to them of the science which treats of the source of all the objects of their inquiry. Some knowledge of geology, therefore, should be a preliminary or an accompaniment to the study of zoology, botany, and other allied fields of investigation. For the same reason the study of mining, agriculture, sanitation and many other pursuits likewise require a previous knowledge of geology, for the mines, soils, and other materials and conditions with which they deal cannot be properly approached without it.

"Relation of Geology to Mining

"A department of geology need not include a department of mining engineering. It might seem unnecessary to mention this fact, but in the minds of many, geology and mining are so closely associated that it seems desirable to point out this distinction here.

"Though geology as a science can be pursued without any knowledge of the technicalities of mining, yet the study of mining engineering requires a knowledge of geology. A department of geology, therefore, should give the prospective student of mining engineering the necessary geological training, but should stop there, and leave the practical application of this geological knowledge to a course at a mining school. It does not seem, at least for the present, either necessary or desirable to establish a mining school at the University of Pennsylvania. Such an institution involves great expense, requires much ground, many buildings, and a large amount of apparatus, and there are already many good mining schools throughout the country which are ample to take care of all the students who desire to make use of them. The University of Pennsylvania could do much better than establishing a mining department by building up a first-class department of pure geology, which would prepare students not only for mining engineering but for other pursuits in which such knowledge was desirable.

"Extent of Geological Instructions

"The study of geology should be adapted to three classes of students:

"1. Those who want only a general knowledge of geology in relation to the composition, structure, and history of the earth, as a part of a general education.

"2. Those who want a deeper knowledge of geology as a basis for the study of other sciences, such as zoology, botany, etc., or as a preliminary to the study of mining engineering, agriculture, and other pursuits.

"3. Those who want a thorough knowledge of geology as a basis for teaching, or for a career of original geological research.

"The Teaching Staff

"The number of professors and assistants necessary properly to carry on a department of geology depends largely on the character of the professors. The writer is firmly of the belief that a few well paid men are far better than numerous under-paid men. High salaries secure the best men, keep them contented, and let them live with the dignity due their positions. The work and utterances of such men redound to the credit of the institution they represent, and their instruction and personal influence is of great service to the students. Low salaries are apt to bring an inferior grade of men and poor teachers, whose work is of but little value to the student, and whose irresponsible utterances in public bring discredit and ridicule to the institution with which they are connected. Three or four high-class, well paid professors with good assistant professors and instructors, could carry on a most creditable department of pure geology."

Another letter to Penniman at this time, shows that Penrose was ever ready to help, if he thought the matter worthy of his aid. Under date of October 6, 1925, he wrote that "a young man named M. K. has been in the Wharton School on a free scholarship, but having failed in a recent examination in French, his scholarship thereby automatically lapsed. I have been asked to inquire if it would be possible for the young man to have another examination in French, as he feels that he can now pass it, and thus regain his free scholarship. His parents are poor and he needs this help.

"I do not know the young man personally, but I am told that he is a worthy and industrious student, and as I do not know to whom else to inquire about the matter I am writing to you."

Penniman replied the following day, saying that he had investigated the matter and that "Mr. K. must have had a re-examination in his subject this fall, unless his failure was such as not to entitle him to a re-examination. If he had a re-examination and did not pass it, he has already failed twice in the subject, and must repeat it in class. The most that we can do for him will be to allow him a deferred payment privilege... There are probably a hundred other boys in exactly the same situation."

In his reply, (October 8, 1925) Penrose says:

"I thank you very much for having taken the trouble to write me about the case. From what you say, I was obviously misinformed about the qualifications of the young man, and I will so notify those who asked me to intercede in his behalf. I will of course decline to go any further in the matter of this student, and I regret greatly to have unintentionally given you this unnecessary trouble."

Between the lines the reader cannot help but feel that Penrose then and there resolved never again to interfere in similar matters.

A letter from William Pepper, dean of the School of Medicine at the University, dated April 1, 1924, also caused Penrose some perturbation, as his reply shows.

"The enclosed advertisement appeared in the Evening Bulletin a few days ago," wrote Dr. Pepper, "and you will note that your father is quoted as having recommended Capon Springs Water. It also calls him Dean of the Medical School, although I do not believe he was ever burdened with this job.

"Following the appearance of the advertisement, letters arrived here at the University addressed to Doctors Gibson and Agnes, similar to the one that you received. It is a good example how misleading such advertisements are. One might think that all these men were still alive and had made the statements about Capon Springs Water quite recently. It is easy enough to say that men who have been dead for some years made such statements, but it is not so easy to disprove such supposed quotations. We are having a fine example of this same sort of thing down in the United States Senate at present."

In the advertisement in question, which occupied full four columns, Dr. Penrose was quoted as saying that "Capon Springs Water cures almost everything. For infants, as well as older children, for used-up, overworked men and women, Capon is simply perfect." Penrose replied concerning the "alleged statement" that "my father frequently visited Capon Springs and felt that his trips did him a great deal of good, but my impression was he considered that he got the benefit chiefly from the mountain air. At any rate, I do not feel that he could have made any such absurd statement as appeared in the newspaper clipping.

"This is surely a period of muck racking and of abusing the memories of people long since dead. It seems even to be the fashion just now to hunt up people who say that someone who has died said something else against someone else who had also died. I often think that if the dead could get up and speak there would surely be a greater row raised than is now going on even in Washington."

Several other letters of this period are interesting as indicative of Penrose's philosophy of life and his attitude toward old friends and ideas of duty.

Letter from Penrose to Lucius W. Mayer, dated Philadelphia, August 4, 1924

Dear Mr. Mayer:—

I have read with much interest your article on "The Engineer's Relation to Finance" which you gave me some days ago in your office.

I agree with you entirely regarding the fact that the engineer does not get the recognition he deserves. I feel that one reason for this is that the term "engineer" is unfortunately applied to too many kinds of pursuits, instead of being confined to the larger and more important callings to which it should refer.

The wide gap you mention as existing between the engineer and the financier is I believe not altogether the fault of the latter. The engineer is usually wrapped up in his own pursuits and voluntarily leaves the financial matters to others. Moreover, many scientific and technical men make the grave mistake of believing the financial side of their problems to be unworthy of their attention. Of course many men make fortunes without having much education, but the financial development of the great engineering problems of the world require just as much education, ability and intellectuality as do the engineering problems.

My own experience has been mostly in scientific work, but I have had several occasions to observe the wonderful ability with which an enterprise, thoroughly good from an engineering standpoint, but thoroughly bad from the standpoint of a profitable investment, has been saved by some financial genius.

I think that the two professions should work in harmony and that one should supplement the other. If such a condition could be produced, both the financier and the engineer would partake of the credit, the fame and the profits resulting from the legitimate enterprises conducted by their joint efforts.

In a letter to Dr. Robert N. Keely, whom he addresses as "Dear Bob," Penrose wrote under date of March 10, 1924:

"I was very glad to get your postal cards from Algiers and from Nice and to know that you are having a good trip. I hope everthing is going well with you and Watson and I only wish I was with you, for I have always looked on Algiers as a most attractive place; and of course Nice is always good.

"Everything is going along as usual here. I occasionally see Judge Mellors and John Huniker and Upton White. Upton's knee is getting better and he walks around almost as usual, but he does not seem to come to Philadelphia as often as he did last year. Huniker and I have been talking of going down by automobile to see him, and I suppose we will probably do it some time soon when the weather gets a little warmer. We have had a very fine winter here, with no very cold weather and many beautiful days. Of course, the weather has not been like that of Algiers and of Nice, but it is good enough."

In a letter to Dr. Alexander Macalister at Los Angeles, Penrose wrote to "My dear Mac" on April 18, 1924:

"I hope that you will have time to see the Grand Canyon of Colorado on your way out, for it is well worth a visit. . . .

"I am glad that you met some of my good old friends in Los Angeles and I hope you will give my best regards to Billy Bayly and to the others whom you have met there. Billy Bayly is a good old sport, and in fact you will find that he is not so very old either when he gets started.

"Everything is about as usual in Philadelphia. I am getting a little tired of having been here almost continuously since last fall and I am apt to start on a trip somewhere some time soon, though I have not yet made any definite arrangements. . . .

"I hope that you will have a pleasant time in California, and please do not get misled with all the gaieties of Los Angeles and surrounding surburbs. I expect to hear a report of reasonably good behavior from you on your return here, though no such report from anyone perhaps could be expected to be perfect."

That same summer, Macalister wrote to "My dear Dick," from a steamer en route to Europe that he certainly had "enjoyed very much the donation you presented me with a few days before leaving. There is of course a bar aboard but the comparison is nil with your wet goods."

An interesting sidelight on this period is furnished by his friend, John Wagner. In a letter to the compiler of this work, he wrote (August 21, 1940):

"One habit he had which I often remember was that on a hot day, he would call me up about noon and ask 'What about a trip across the bridge for a few hours of Jersey air?' My answer was generally yes, depending entirely upon whether I could get away from work or not. He would arrive at my office with the car at 2:00 sharp, when we would start out, cross the bridge to New Jersey, and each time take a different trip, the selection of which was left to his chauffeur. We enjoyed the air in the open car and talked about the various interests we had in common, with virtually never anything serious or unpleasant included, thus affording us both an afternoon of real relaxation. The trip invariably ended at

4:00 P.M. at my office, giving me an opportunity to sign letters and clean up the day's work. On a trip of this kind to him two was a company, and three would have been a crowd.

"The fact that he had a motor and a regular chauffeur gave him some concern as he was very fond of walking. Often in walking to his office he would shun the larger streets, fearing perchance he might come across his chauffeur and hurt his feeling by not having ordered the car.

"Dr. Penrose was an active member of The Rabbit, one of the old cooking clubs of this city, and, incidentally, a member of its Board of Governors, and well known as the 'fish cook', an art of which he was an expert. A little occurrence in this connection, which often comes to my mind, was when the Board decided to hold a meeting at the clubhouse with dinner afterward. There being nothing but water in the clubhouse, it was considered advisable that a risk should be taken in transporting necessary stimulants for the small party. None of us apparently had any rye easily accessible, which, incidentally, each and all preferred.

"Dick was not present when this was talked over. I suddenly remembered that I was to meet him at his house and proceed by his 'open air route' as he called it (his car with the top down) to the meeting. When I arrived he invited me to have a little of his fine old rye before starting out. While enjoying this, in his bashful way, he said, 'John, I have a bottle of brandy in my overcoat pocket. Do you think it would come in well after the dinner?' This being my opportunity, I said, 'Dick, frankly, I am sure the boys would prefer rye whiskey.' To which he replied, 'I have two of them in the other pocket.'

"As a result, the party was a perfect success.

"I fear no one will ever know of his charities, which were far from few, as he preferred giving direct rather than through the various charitable institutions."

Writing to B. Dawson Coleman on April 22, 1924, Penrose declared that "I cannot tell you how sorry I am that I am not going to be able to be at the 'Rabbit' on your day next Saturday. Something always seems to have turned up recently on the days that I wanted to go to the 'Rabbit' and I particularly wanted to be there on your day on Saturday, but there is an important meeting of the American Philosophical Society here on Saturday afternoon and a dinner of the same organization in the evening.

"As a number of geologists from out of town usually attend this event, and do not come here other times in the year, I feel that I ought to be on hand to meet them."

To another old friend of Cripple Creek days, Clarence C. Hamlin, of Colorado Springs, Penrose wrote (October 4, 1924) that he "was extremely sorry to have missed you when you called here yesterday. I did not receive your telegram until towards one o'clock, and as I was absolutely obliged to go out of town before three, I left the office a little after two.

"I was particularly disappointed in missing you, not only because it is always a great pleasure to see you, but also because there were a number of things about which I would have liked to have talked to you.

"I am addressing this letter to you at Colorado Springs, as I suppose you are on only one of your rapid trips to New York; but I will be in New York next week, and if you are still there I will surely hunt you up. In the meanwhile, if you should come this way again, I hope you will let me know so that I can make a point of being here."

In reply to Hamlin's letter, Penrose wrote again to "Dear Clarence," acknowledging its receipt and adding that, as he had previously noted, "I was greatly disappointed to have missed you here, but business which deeply concerned others besides myself compelled me to be away the afternoon you were in town. . . . Won't you please let me know when you arrive in New York and I will either come over there or will of course at any time be delighted to see you in Philadelphia."

Macalister had spoken of the gift of liquor from Penrose. That was during the days of prohibition, a subject on which Penrose felt strongly and to which he made frequent reference in his letters.

Letter from Dick to his brother in the U.S. Senate at Washington, dated Philadelphia, October 29, 1919

Dear Boies:—

I want to congratulate you on being one of the few Republicans who voted to sustain the President's veto of the prohibition enforcement act. This iniquitous act passed Congress under shamefully strong Republican support; it is a pompous and verbose document of over fifty pages, written in such a puerile, hysterical and intolerant manner that of necessity it disgusts every normal minded person. Inquisitions of the Middle Ages could not have been drawn up in a more vindictive document.

Will the Republican Party never come to its senses? You must look beyond the boundaries of the narrow intellects of a few prejudiced leaders to feel the pulse of the American people, and if the Republican Party cannot acquire this broader vision they are courting defeat.

I travel considerably and meet different classes of people, so that I know that prohibition to-day, outside of a small but very well organized minority, is disgusting and repellent to the vast majority of the American people. What we need is less infringement on the rights of man and more of the liberty and freedom for which the Republican Party once stood. If this party is going to try to crush the people to the level of what was once the status of Russian serfs under the pretense of establishing a modern Utopia, I believe they will have hard sledding at the next election. To-day they are receiving the blame for prohibition, and the Democrats are laughing up their sleeves.

Your affectionate brother
R. A. F. Penrose, Jr.

This was a subject concerning which all four Penrose brothers felt alike. Charles, the medical doctor, wrote to D. M. Findlay, president of the Moderate League of New Zealand, on September 19, 1922, that "at the request of Mr. Charles S.

Wood, manager of the Pennsylvania Division of the Association Against the Prohibition Amendment, I send you the result of my observations on the effect of prohibition in this country.

"Drunkenness has increased, and it is of a kind more dangerous to health and to the safety of society.

"Prohibition is creating a race of liars, hypocrites and law-breakers.

"The infringement of personal liberty, and the unfair and illegal methods used by those who enforce prohibition have brought about a disgust for legal authority, and have gone far towards diminishing patriotism.

"Prohibition has impaired the health and diminished the happiness of the millions of people in this country who had formerly enjoyed the temperate use of alcohol.

"The sick who require alcohol are harmed by their inability to get a sufficient amount and to obtain a good quality. 'Drug store whiskey' has long been a name for inferior grades.

"In many cases of disease the doctor's therapeutic means are handicapped by the restrictions in prescribing alcohol.

"Addicts to morphia and its products, cocaine and many kinds of depressing drugs, have greatly increased throughout the country.

"Prohibition has added to the discontent among workmen and has therefore favored strikes.

"Posterity will curse those who have brought about this blight on the happiness and welfare of the people of this country; viz., the cowardly politicians, the hired propagandists, and the sinister financial interests that have controlled them."

On April 22, 1925, Mr. Findlay wrote again to Dr. Penrose, noting that "three years ago, just prior to our 1922 triennial struggle to preserve our social liberty in this country and to bring sanity to bear on our liquor question, we had the honour of receiving a communication from you setting forth your views in regard to the operation of the Eighteenth Amendment in the United States.

"We venture to address you again with a request for your matured opinion of the so-called Prohibition Law after five years of actual experience."

Charles Penrose had died in the early months of 1925, and Dick replied (October 6, 1925) that "My brother and I had the same opinion regarding the prohibition movement. We both considered that it was a dreadful mistake and that it was accompanied by innumerable harmful and dangerous results, such as were enumerated in the letter of my bother to you some two or three years ago. The sad consequences which he anticipated have gradually been becoming true in this country, and very many people are beginning to appreciate that some change must be made.

"The custom of using alcohol in the form of wines, beers, and liquors, seems to have begun almost with the beginning of the human race. It dates at least back to the commencement of accurate history, and certainly no effort to prevent in a short time a custom which people have practised from time immemorial can be a success. We in the United States are looking forward to the repeal in the near future of this iniquitous effort of well-meaning but ignorant people to prohibit the use of alcohol in any form. I wish you every success in your campaign against this movement in New Zealand."

In the summer of 1924 (June 11) Penrose had written to Charles S. Wood, manager of The Association Against Prohibition, acknowledging receipt of his letter of June 5th and "would have replied sooner but I have been waiting to discuss the matter with my brother Doctor Penrose.

"I entirely agree with you that we have had enough hypocrisy on the part of many members of Congress on the liquor question, and it is time that there was a show-down and that the wishes of the vast majority of the people were considered rather than the interests of individual members of Congress, who think that they may get votes by at least pretending to be dry."

That Penrose continued to feel this way about the matter to the end of his life is shown in letters to two other correspondents. The first was C.C. Hinckley, national secretary of the Association Against the Prohibition Amendment, to whom he wrote (February 8, 1926) acknowledging "your favor of January 29th regarding the admirable progress made by the Association Against the Prohibition Amendment through your National Headquarters in Washington, and asking me for a contribution in addition to those that I have been regularly making ever since prohibition was put into effect. Some of my contributions have been sent to your Washington headquarters, but most of them have been sent to the local headquarters here in Philadelphia.

"I never make any pledge about any money contributions for the future, as I never know what the future may bring forth; but I enclose my check for fifty dollars which I hope you will accept as a token of my continued sympathy with your cause."

The record shows that in September of that same year he also contributed one hundred dollars to the Pennsylvania division of the organization.

Letter from Penrose to Edward Lowber Stokes, of Philadelphia, dated December 3, 1928

Dear Mr. Stokes:—

On my return from a few days absence I have received your letter of November 27th relative to a contribution towards the monument to be erected at Verdun as a tribute to the sodiers who fell defending that historic fortress. I have read carefully the circular concerning this memorial which you so kindly left at my office the other day, and as I feel entirely sympathetic with the erection of the monument I take great pleasure in enclosing you my check for one hundred dollars as a contribution to that cause. In accordance with your request I have made the check payable to the order of the Bank of New York and Trust Company.

I am glad to learn by your letter that you thought enough of my recent article in the Inquirer (September 13), entitled "Some Aspects of the Prohibition Problem" to want a copy of it, and I assure you that it gives me much pleasure to enclose one to you. With it I am also sending you an editorial which appeared in the Evening Bulletin a few days later concerning this article.

My article in the Inquirer was not intended as a literary effort, but simply as a brief and plain statement of facts as I saw them, and was written in a rather colloquial manner so that anyone could understand it. I had a number of letters from Republican voters referring to this article and saying that it had been useful to them in showing that a good Republican voter could adhere to the regular Republican ticket in the election of last November, and rely on his own party for modification of the prohibition laws.

I have in preparation a much more comprehensive article on voluntary temperance brought about by a campaign of education, as opposed to absolute prohibition brought about by force. I do not know, however, whether or not I will publish the article.

With kindest regards, I am

Sincerely yours,
R. A. F. Penrose, Jr.

Letter from Penrose to Edward Lowber Stokes, dated December 26, 1928

Many thanks for your letter of December 21st, with the quotation from Gladstone's speech of April 8, 1886, which so clearly sets forth that people cannot be regenerated by force, but if given a principle of freedom they will by a process of self-education be guided more correctly than by the exercise of undue authority.

I agree with you entirely on this subject, and hope before long to have the pleasure of discussing it further with you.

Letter from Dick to his brother Spencer, dated Philadelphia, February 6, 1920

My dear Speck:—

I have received your letter of February 1st and am sorry that you are not going to be here at my Wistar Party next Saturday. You were present at the first one I ever gave many years ago and I only wish that you could be present at this one.

Boies expects to go to Florida in perhaps a couple of weeks and to return in the early spring. I understand from what you tell me that you also expect to be here in the early spring.

I am glad to find the weather in Colorado so perfect. I agree with you that it is a climate which people do not know as well as they should, but it is only a question of time when they will realize the advantages that state possesses. At the present time, however, this oppressive and destructive prohibition law is discouraging everyone from travelling much in this country. I believe that it should be the duty of every good citizen to have it modified, at least to the extent of letting people have wines and liquors in reason.

Letter from Dick, dated Philadelphia, February 25, 1920

My dear Speck:—

I have received your letter of February 10th. Boies and Tal went to Florida last Monday and expect to be back early in April. I expect to go west, probably to California, about the 10th of March. I have stayed around here for over three years and feel tired and stale. I think I will come back from California early in April.

Letter from Dick, dated Philadelphia, February 27, 1920

My dear Speck:—

I was very glad to get your letter of the 23rd and I thank you very much for the information you have given me about the copper companies. I had already received the circulars concerning the allocation of copper distribution and dividend from New York, so that I was familiar with the conditions; but I appreciate all the same your kindness in writing me about the matter. If the advice contained in the circulars holds good we will all surely save a great deal of income tax by the parts of the distribution credited to capital.

I note that you say that you expect to come here the end of March, and perhaps sail for Bermuda the first week of April. I expect to go west in March and will probably not be back until towards the middle of April.

Spencer wrote (September 28, 1925) to Dick that he had "no objection to having the Spruce Street house painted on the outside if you desire to have it done, but I do not think it will make much improvement in the looks of the building as Spruce Street is an exceedingly dusty and dirty street, and I believe a month after the house is painted it will look the same as it did before. However, do whatever you want as whatever you do will be entirely satisfactory to me.

On October 7 (1925) Dick replied, noting "what you say about your having no objection to the Spruce Street house being painted on the outside. I assure you that I will try to run the house as safely and conservatively as possible, but as it is the old home of the family, and is a well-known residence in the City, I feel that it is the duty of you and me as trustees to keep it in a presentable shape. As you say, the neighborhood is very dusty, and any building rapidly looks badly even if it has been painted only recently. For this reason I have often wondered whether or not it was worth while to keep this house open so completely as we do now, and if we should ever conclude that it was not a desirable place to spend our time I will be glad to close it up and put a watchman in charge. I hope, however, that this necessity will not arise any time in the near future, and that you and I can maintain the house in the condition that it should be kept, as the birthplace of all of us brothers and as the residence of our mother and father."

Two years earlier, the question of what to do with the house at 1331 Spruce Street had occupied considerable correspondence between Dick and Spencer. The day after Christmas (1923) Spencer wrote that he had been "thinking the other day about the house at 1331 Spruce St. I believe I understood from you that perhaps it would be necessary to get out of it on account of the big buildings going up on all sides. I do not see any reason for selling, or getting out of the house notwithstanding how many large buildings are built around it. I am more than willing to put up my share of all running expenses, as I get considerable use out of it. For that matter, if you and Tal ever think it is necessary to sell it, I wish you would give me first chance to buy it, as I would not like to see it get out of the hands of the family."

Dick replied on New Year's Day, 1924 that he (Spencer) was "mistaken when you thought that either Tal or I were anxious to sell it. I personally would be strongly against selling it and I am sure that Tal feels the same way, for he has often expressed himself to that effect. I think it is very important that we should keep the house among ourselves for it is useful to all three of us, and it is the one place now where we can all get together and meet and in which we have a mutual interest. I do not think it matters at all how many big buildings are going up on all sides of us. In fact in some ways it is an advantage, for it tends to improve the neighborhood. In any event, neither Tal nor I would ever think of suggesting the sale of the house without your entire approval and consent."

On October 20, 1925, Dick wrote to Speck from Philadelphia that he had seen "Jackling in New York yesterday and he seemed to be in very good shape, but so many of our old friends have left there since prohibition converted it from a great metropolis to a town with more or less a country atmosphere, that it is sometimes a lonesome place to go to."

Two days later, he wrote again, acknowledging receipt of "your letter of October 15th telling me that you are making a collection of old wine and whisky bottles with their original labels, and asking me to keep for you any which I may have and which I think may not be in your collection. I assure you that I will be very glad to do this, and I think I can help out your exhibit with a few odd specimens.

"Your large collection of these relics of times when the American people were not burdened with legislation passed under the influence of idealists, fanatics and other narrow-minded and undesirable persons, will always be of great interest in recalling the times when the blight of prohibition had not yet involved a free country."

In these years Speck evidently tried to induce his brother to do more traveling, for on more than one occasion Dick declines an invitation to accompany Spencer on a trip. On the first of January 1924, he wrote that he was "glad to hear about your trip to Paris and the north coast of Africa. I am sure that it will be a splendid and most enjoyable one. I only wish I could go along with you, but for this winter at least I will be pretty closely tied up here by the Academy of Natural Sciences. Next year I may have a freer foot. Our celebration at the Academy went off in good shape on December 6th. There was a very large crowd and everyone seemed pleased. I am enclosing to you a programme of the meeting as I thought it might be of interest to you."

Later that same month (January 17, 1924) he again wrote to Speck, "I hope to see you here before long and I suppose of course you will come to Philadelphia before you sail for Europe. All the boys are asking after you and would be glad to see you at the Philadelphia Club as well as at The Rabbit. The 'Rabbits' have been fairly active this year, but once every two weeks is a little too frequent for me; and moreover I have been so much tied down with the endless work of the Academy of Natural Sciences that I have not had a chance to run around as much as I would have liked."

On March 4th (1924) he again wrote, hoping "that you will have a good trip in Morocco, and I am sure that it will be a very interesting country. I am sorry that I could not have gone there with you. I have been in Philadelphia or New York all winter and am getting very tired of sticking around in one place. It does not seem natural to me to do so and I have never done it before, so I think before long I will take up my old habits of travelling around a little. The Academy of Natural Sciences has taken up much more time than I had anticipated, and as I do not want to retain my position as President there unless I can give sufficient time to it to run it in a proper manner I think I may resign next year.

"If you see Paul Stewart or Spencer Biddle or Louis Biddle in Paris, please give them my kindest regards. I may possibly get around that way some time before the year is out."

A few days later, Dick wrote to his doctor-brother Charles (Tal) who was spending the winter at Aiken, S. C., that he understood "that Miss Ivens sent to you a few days ago a letter from Speck saying that a French doctor claimed to have discovered that he [Spencer] had an internal ulcer. I do not know how you feel about this matter, but if Speck needs attention for any such ailment I think he ought to come home and be looked after here. Those foreign doctors may be all right, but I think Speck would get better care in the United States. If Speck does not come home I will be very glad to go over to Paris and see him; but I think his best plan is to come home. Perhaps after all he may have no ulcer whatever."

But not a hint of this concern is found in his letter to Speck four days later (March 22, 1924), when he notes that "everything is as usual here. I have been kept very busy by the Academy of Natural Sciences all winter. The position as President is a very exacting one and I do not know how long I can stand it."

Spencer had returned to the States by May 14, for on that day Dick wrote to him at Colorado Springs, asking him to "give my regards to all the boys in Colorado Springs. I am looking forward to coming out there some time later in the year."

A month later (June 6, 1924), however, he is not so optimistic about the prospects, for he writes to Speck that "Colorado Springs must be beginning to look beautiful and I wish I could run out there for a short trip, but just at present my particular job at the Academy of Natural Sciences keeps my nose so close to the grindstone that I do not think I will be able to get away until September. Next year, however, I intend to resign, and then I will have more freedom."

The following month (July 23, 1924) he wrote to Speck that he did "not care for short trips and am willing to wait until I get a chance to disappear for several months." Accordingly, Speck wrote him (September 22, 1924) concerning a trip he was contemplating to India, giving his itinerary, his temporary plans, and asking various questions: "Do you think this time of year is too late to go to Burma? . . . I thought perhaps you might want to take a trip and meet us some place on the way. Why don't you think the matter over and meet us in India, and we can all come back to London together?"

Letter from Dick, dated Philadelphia, October 7, 1924

Dear Speck

I was very glad to get your letter of September 22nd and I am much interested in the plan that you propose of going to India by way of the Pacific about the middle of January.

I think you are wise in taking one of the Japanese boats from San Francisco, for all of them on which I have sailed have been clean and well kept and are not "dry." I think that you will find one day in Honolulu about as much as you want. It is now much like a town in southern California. The most interesting feature of the Hawaiian Islands is the volcanoes, but you would probably not have time to visit them, and as the principal one is now more or less in eruption you probably could not see much of it.

I think your plan of five or six days in Japan seems a little short, but perhaps under the present conditions, when the Japanese are probably not particularly anxious to see Americans, the time may be sufficient. One day in Shanghai is all you want, and the six days you mention in Hong Kong are far more than enough to see that place, unless you take the night boat that runs up to Canton. The present conditions in China would make it inadvisable to go farther up the river than Canton, and perhaps it would not be desirable to go even there. I went to Canton just after the Boxer revolution twenty-three years ago, and the people threw stones at us in the streets.

Of course you will have a good time in Manila, as you know General Wood so well. The trip from Manila to Burma, however, could not in the old days be made in the same ship, if you wanted a good one. Possibly today there are better ships running in that direction but I still think that your best way to go to Burma and India would be to take a first-class steamer from Manila to Singapore, and then take one of several very good local lines which run from Singapore to Rangoon in Burma, and thence to Calcutta in India. Singapore is a sort of ocean crossroads and ships pass there from all directions. In Burma you will doubtless land at Rangoon, where you possibly might see all of that country you wanted, but if you desire to go farther inland you could go up the Irrawaddy River to Mandalay and Bahmo. As you are going to have a great deal of that southern Asia country, however, in your trip, you will probably see enough of Burma at Rangoon and will be glad to go on to Calcutta, where you will find good hotels and where you can take a good overland railroad to Bombay.

At Bombay you will of course find plenty of boats to Europe. The P. & O. Line is excellent, but the Orient Line is just as good. I have travelled to and from India on both lines and would as soon take one as the other.

If you want to go to Java, as you suggest in your letter, you can find a good line of boats from Holland running out to the east and stopping at Batavia. You could catch one of these boats at Singapore.

You asked me about the best time of year to go to Burma. Of course the winter time is best, but it is a hot country at any time of year, and so far as my experience goes, it is not much worse in the early spring—when you expect to get there—than in the middle of winter. It is a low country, however, except in the Far East part of it, which is mountainous, and the climate in Rangoon is apt to be very hot and sultry.

If I can let you know anything more about all these matters please write to me and any information I can give you is always at your command.

I thank you greatly for your suggestion that I might meet you at some place on the way. Nothing would please me more than to meet you in India or Burma and come back to Europe with you, but until next spring I will be closely tied down with my work at The Academy of Natural Sciences. After that I will be free and will be glad to take any trip you suggest; though by that time you will have returned from the particular trip you have in contemplation for this winter.

Your affectionate brother
R. A. F. Penrose, Jr.

While Spencer was away on this trip, his brother Charles died. Dick had written to Spencer on December 27 that "Tal has gone to Aiken, South Carolina. He was in bad shape when he left here. Doctor MacAlister and a nurse went with him. MacAlister returned a few days ago and the nurse remained. MacAlister thinks that Tal is a sick man, but he hopes that the climate in Aiken may help him. I am writing to you about this matter because I think you ought to know about it before you go away on a long trip."

Speck replied on January 3, saying that he regretted "very much to hear that Tal was in bad shape when he left Philadelphia and consequently I do not like going away at the present time, but the Doctors tell me that it is the best thing to do for Julie [Mrs. Penrose] and for this reason we are leaving next week. I sincerely hope that the climate of Aiken will benefit Tal and I really think that it will do so, because when he is in Philadelphia or Devon he has too much to do."

"Tal" died at six a.m., February 27 (1925) on board the train enroute from Aiken to Philadelphia. The funeral was held March 2. Four days later (March 6, 1925), Dick wrote to J. A. Hull at Colorado Springs:

"I thank you greatly for your recent telegrams and assistance in trying to reach Spencer Penrose so as to notify him of the death of my brother Doctor Charles B. Penrose. Spencer's answer to you and to me obviously indicate that he cannot come here much sooner than he had originally expected to do before he left on his trip. I regret this, as there are several matters of family importance which ought to be acted on, but I will do my best to hold any important action back until he returns.

"The death of my brother Doctor Charles B. Penrose came very unexpectedly. As you know, he had been more or less ill for several years but none of us expected any such sudden and fatal result. I assure you that I greatly appreciate your kind telegram of sympathy."

Just a year before (March 4, 1924) Dick had written to Speck that "there is nothing particularly new here. Tal is still in Aiken and seems to be getting along in first-rate shape. I think it has suited him this winter better than any other place he could have visited. He walks two or three miles a day and goes around to entertainments, so you can imagine that he must be in a cheerful mood."

The following Christmastide (December 24, 1924) after receiving two letters from Dr. Alexander MacAlister, the doctor who had accompanied the sick man to Aiken, who had written that Tal was not in good shape but that from present appearances he thought that he (Tal) would be "very comfortable for the winter, and I firmly believe this is the best place for him," Dick wrote to Tal at Aiken:

"Miss Ivens showed me your telegram to her saying that you had arrived safely in Aiken, and I was very glad to hear it. I am sure that the climate there will be better for you than here. You just missed a cold and wet spell which has lasted over a week here.

"MacAlister wrote to me on his arrival in Aiken telling me that you and he had gotten there all right, and I sent him a letter in reply; but I had no sooner mailed it than he called me on the telephone from Camden to tell me the same thing, so he evidently did not stay down there very long. I hope, however, that everything is going all right with you and that a few weeks of clear warm weather in South Carolina will soon put you on your feet.

"Everything is going along as usual here. Boies [Charles' son] and Sarah [Charles' daughter] were here for a few minutes a couple of days ago and they both looked first-rate. Boies had just come from Cambridge and was going to Sand Bridge with a friend. He started last night.

"If I can do anything for you in Philadelphia please let me know."

On the fifteenth of January (1925) Dick again wrote to his brother, noting that "it has been just a month since you left here so I thought I would drop a line to you. You left just about the right time for it has been a cold stormy month since the middle of December. We are now having some fine clear days, and possibly the rest of the winter may be good enough.

"I went up to Ithaca in New York to attend the meeting of The Geological Society of America the last week of December. There was a good deal of snow and the weather was very cold, but we had a good meeting.

"Boies has been laid up with a slight attack of jaundice, but he is now out and around again and looks as well as ever. I believe he expects to go back to Cambridge the end of this week. I went up to see him at 1720 Spruce Street several times while he was sick. He was in bed a few days, but was up and moving around the house some days later, without going out. He now seems in first-rate shape and came to see me yesterday. Doctor Stengel treated him, and Miss Devennie took most admirable care of him and looked after him carefully until he was entirely well.

"There is nothing particularly new here. Everything is going along in its usual routine. The 'Rabbits' have been given as usual and I have been to several of them but I do not stay very late and usually get away soon after dinner is served."

Letter from "Tal", dated Aiken, January 25, 1925

Dear Dick—

I have not written since I came here because I have not been well and have been confined to my rooms and porch for the past three weeks. Had a severe asthmatic attack three weeks ago that nearly put me out of business. I hope to improve and will write you further how things progress. Have received your two letters.

Your affectionate brother
C. B. Penrose

Dick wrote again on February 12 (1925):

"I was very glad to receive your letter of January 25 and to hear about you, for it was the first word I had had from you since you went south. You must surely have had some bad weather in Aiken, but the same kind of weather seems to have spread all along the Atlantic Coast this year. From Philadelphia north it has been snow, and with you in the south it has been rain. The weather report of snowfall in Philadelphia is that it has been greater this year than for thirty years past. I hope that when the better weather begins you will improve and that you will be able to move around a little more than you have been able to do during the winter.

"I saw Boies on his way back to Cambridge a couple of days ago. He seemed to have had a very good time at Aiken, and told me that he thought you looked much better. I was talking to Miss Devennie on the telephone after her return from Aiken and she also reported you in much better shape, so I think you went to the right place this winter.

"Everything is going along all right at The Academy of Natural Sciences. I have been renominated for the third time as President, and you have been nominated as a member of the Board of Trustees instead of as a member of the Council. The Council under the new organization becomes practically a museum board, while the Board of Trustees takes over the administration of the institution. The election occurs February 17th, and immediately after that the Board of Trustees will meet to appoint the members of the scientific staff and of the Council. This will be purely a form, as the Council will be composed practically of the same members as formerly, with the exception of one or two additions and of a few that have been taken from it for the Board of Trustees. You will probably get notices from the Secretary about this matter, and therefore I thought I had better explain it to you. There is no need at the present time for your giving it any more attention than you have previously given the ordinary notices of the Council meetings.

"I was at 'The Rabbit' given by Edward Beale a few days ago and it went off very well. The Rabbit seems to have taken a new lease of life, and the attendance on the regular days is often over thirty. Many of your friends were asking for you, particularly Beale, who asked me to send you his best regards.

"Bob Keely has gone on another trip to the West Indies with a friend of his called Abercrombie, but he expects to be back the end of this month. The trip includes stopping at a number of unusual islands, and I would have liked very much to have gone with him but the final details of this reorganization at the Academy have held me more or less to the grindstone all winter. Next year I hope to have more freedom.

"I hope that everything is going all right with you in Aiken and that you will some time drop me a line and let me know how you are getting along."

Five days later (February 17, 1925) Dick wrote again to Tal:

"Since writing to you a couple of days ago Miss Ivens has shown me the circular sent out by the Kennecott Copper Corporation regarding the allocation of distributions for 1924. You will see by this circular that the Company considers all their distributions as capital, except 58 cents per share, which must be considered as dividend and must be enumerated among your other income from dividends.

"I am sure that the circular will be perfectly clear to you, but I thought I would drop you this line so as to let you know that in making up your income tax return you should include as dividend from the Kennecott Copper Corporation only 58 cents on each share of the stock which you own. I wrote you a few days ago and will write again shortly, but I am dropping this line simply because I knew that you would probably have the matter of the tax on the Kennecott Copper Corporation stock on your mind.

"I hope that everything is going well with you and that you will continue to get better. It has been a very long time since I have had a word from you, and I would be very glad if you would drop me a line when you have a chance and let me know how things are going."

Dick was continually advising his brothers about financial matters, and in most cases they evidently followed his advice, to their advantage. The previous year (January 22, 1924) Dick had written to Tal at Aiken:

"I was very glad to get your letter of December 29th some days ago and would have answered it sooner but I have been waiting to find out something about the proposed merger of the Ray and Chino Copper companies so that I could tell you about it. I knew nothing about the matter until it was sprung on me at a Directors' meeting of the Chino Company some days ago. Since then I have looked carefully into it and as yet I can see no particular objection to the merger from the standpoint of the interest of either the Chino or the Ray Company. Neither company is paying dividends and perhaps something in the way of overhead expenses, supplies, marketing of copper, etc., may be saved by the merger.

"Just at this time the copper market is suffering not so much on account of lack of buyers as it is on account of the tremendous flood of copper, coming not only from the American mines but from the mines of South America and the Congo region of Africa. The Cerro de Pasco mine, the Chile Copper mine and the Braden mine, all in South America, are producing an enormous tonnage of copper; while the copper mines in the Congo region of West Africa are also producing likewise. Before the war these foreign mines were not producing anything like what they are producing now, and America had a good deal of a monopoly in the European market. Ten years, however, have changed the situation and

Chile, Peru and Africa are cutting deeply into the American market in Europe. The hope therefore of our domestic production is in increased consumption in the United States. At the present time the rate of domestic consumption is increasing enormously, so that there is a chance that the loss in foreign markets may be at least partly compensated.

"I have received a telegram from Speck asking me what I thought about the merger and I have written him something along the lines that I am writing you. I have also told him that the merger may possibly be the basis of a still further merger of other copper properties in the southwest, and if this should be the case some people think that the Ray and Chino combined into one would get better treatment in such a future merger than if existing as separate units."

A fortnight later (February 15, 1924) Dick wrote again to Tal, giving details of Utah Copper matters, Kennecott Copper distributions, federal income tax returns, adding that "the annual meetings of the Chino and Ray Copper companies to take action on the merger occur today, but I do not intend to be present at either of them. If the merger is consummated it will mean that the Chino Company will disappear as a separate organization and its assets will be taken over by the Ray Company. In this respect the merger will be something different from the attempted merger of the Utah and Kennecott last spring, for in the latter case it consisted only of an offer by Kennecott to buy Utah stock from individuals; whereas the present situation between Chino and Ray is an offer from Ray to buy all the property of Chino and close up the organization of the latter company.

"Personally, I am getting rather tired of these everlasting attempts at mergers, but the Chino and Ray deal may have some advantages in forming a basis for future enlargements and consolidations with other companies.

"I fear that you will think I have been very long-winded in discussing all these matters, but I realize that when a man is away from home he often likes information about things in which he is interested, and for that reason I have written fully, and will write further later on regarding the Chino and Ray merger in case it is consummated."

The day before (February 14, 1924) Dick had written to Tal, acknowledging receipt of his letter of February 6th and declaring that "I agree with you entirely that it is an infernal nuisance converting copper stocks or any other stocks into stocks of a new or modifying corporation, for it is apt to cause considerable complication when the securities are eventually sold. I understand, however, that such matters have received considerable attention from people skillful in these computations and I believe that one would therefore not find so much difficulty in figuring out loss or gain as he might anticipate. Of course a man actively engaged in speculating and buying and selling stocks every day must probably give a much more lengthy report than one who buys and sells only occasionally for purposes of investment or of policy.

"I am very glad to know that things are going so well with you at Aiken, and it surely speaks well of that place when you say that the climate is equal to the best climate of Colorado."

A day or two later (February 19, 1924), he again wrote to Tal that "Mr. J. R. Carpenter, Jr., of The Pennsylvania Company, told me today over the telephone that he was sending you a form of Claim for refund of the 1918 Federal taxes on the estates of S. H. B. Penrose and R. A. F. Penrose.... It seems absurd to me to think that the Supreme Court will uphold any such procedure, for if it did, the beneficiaries of many of the vast trust estates in this country could claim exemption from taxation on their incomes for 1918. For this reason I wonder whether it is worth while resurrecting old returns in order to make a claim which may be turned down by the Supreme Court, and even if not turned down would probably involve a good deal of time, trouble, legal expense and other costs in securing it.

"After you have received Carpenter's letter I would be very glad if you could find time to drop me a line and let me know how you feel about this matter."

Two days later (February 21, 1924), he again wrote to Tal:

"I have just received your letter of February 18th on my return here from a couple of days absence in New York. The Ray-Chino merger went through with a considerable majority vote and eventually the Chino Copper Company will go out of existence.... I told them that you were in the south and probably would not return until after the first of April, and they said that you could dismiss the matter from your mind and transfer your certificates any time you return in that month. Probably even later than April would also be early enough; so you will see that you can attend to the matter when you get good and ready."

Dick also wired to Tal to that effect the same day and again on February 28.

The middle of the following month (March 18, 1924) Dick again wrote that he "was very glad to get your letter of March 3rd a few days ago and to know that everything is going satisfactorily with you at Aiken.

"I was in New York for a couple of days last week and I find that the Ray-Chino merger is gradually being carried through by the transfer of certificates of Chino stock for Ray stock, but the matter does not seem to excite any great general interest. I suppose this is because both of them are non-dividend paying stock and are therefore not of such general interest as if they were active in cash distributions. I see by your letter that you are in some doubt as to what to do in this matter, and I will be very glad to talk it over with you when you return here. I myself have not yet taken any actions.

"Boies was here on Sunday and Monday and I was very glad to see him. He looks in first-rate condition, and said he had been passing his recent examinations very successfully. He went back to Cambridge last night."

A week later (March 25, 1924) Dick again wrote to Tal, this time concerning another matter:

"I have received from Mr. J. A. Hull a copy of a letter to him from a man named McKay asking if your house in Silver City was for sale, and also a copy of Hull's reply to McKay.... As I was very sure that you are anxious to sell this property I wrote immediately to Hull telling him that the property belonged to you and not to the estate of Senator Penrose, as McKay seemed to think, and that I understood that it was for sale. I did this so that Hull could keep in touch with McKay in case you wanted to do business. Hull is a very capable man and might be a suitable person to make this sale for you.

"I received your letter a few days ago saying that you would be here on April 1st and I will be very glad to see you home again."

Even after his brother returned to Philadelphia, Dick continued to write him in detail concerning business matters, evidently in order that matters might be set down in proper order for consideration. For example, on November 3, 1924, Dick wrote that "Miss Ivens has shown me the statement of the present condition of the Estate of R. A. F. Penrose which you asked her to give me.

"I think a distribution from income of $10,000 to each of the beneficiaries would be entirely proper.

"As regards the investment of principal of $5399., I would suggest that we invest $5,000. of it in Philadelphia City 4's registered bonds, and let the $399. remain in bank for future investment. I suggest Philadelphia City bonds, registered, for the $5,000. because in recent years most funds in the Estate of R. A. F. Penrose which we have had to invest have been put in these same securities, so that by investing again in them we would simplify bookkeeping and other accounts."

The following day (November 4, 1924) he again addressed Tal at "1331 Spruce Street, Philadelphia, Pa.," saying that he had "been thinking about the matter of Sand Bridge, which we discussed yesterday. I believe that if a new house was built there with the idea of renting it to sportsmen, the executive management of the property would be greatly increased, for tenants for each season would have to be sought and approved by someone. From what you said, I judge O'Conor does not want to assume much more work at Sand Bridge, and yet this new house would require a good deal more.

"Under the present situation none of us are using Sand Bridge much, and yet constant improvements are going on which make it a very desirable place for anyone who would use it. I would be in favor of letting in some new and active members, one of whom might take over the management of the place when O'Conor gets tired of it, and the rest of whom might acquire interests in the property.

"I am simply dropping this line to you as a memorandum, for I am going to New York tomorrow afternoon and will not be back until Friday."

Sand Bridge was a shooting place near Sigma, Virginia, held by the Sand Bridge Syndicate, which on November 23, 1922, had for its members the three Penrose brothers—Charles, Richard, and Spencer—Alexander Van Rensselaer, and J. C. O'Conor. After the death of Charles Penrose, his son Boies was admitted to membership in his place, and subsequently William Proctor and Leroy Frost were admitted to membership in July, 1925. The yearly assessments were in the neighborhood of fifteen hundred dollars and the shooting season, says O'Conor, in a letter dated October 29, 1925, "in accordance with custom, for wild fowl will open on the 10th of November and remain open until the first of February."

In his report concerning the place, dated New York, August 14, 1924, O'Conor declared that "there are over twelve hundred pheasants in thriving condition and the greater part of them are so well grown that a goodly number will be brought to the guns for next season and it is hoped that all the members will take advantage of this shooting. It is believed more birds will be killed if the shooting is limited to two days a week, say Wednesdays and Saturdays on which days wild fowl cannot be shot.

"I am unable to state how the first brood of quail have thriven through the very wet season. Now the season is dry undoubtedly there will be a second brood and there must be a number of quail about as their whistle could be heard on every side.

"Unfortunately the wild turkeys have failed. They did very well until they got to be quite a fair size when suddenly a pestilence apparently removed them. We still have a few of pure wild stock with which to carry on."

Earlier that same year (May 14, 1924) Dick had written to Speck who had returned from Europe but had missed a Sand Bridge luncheon fixed on a day presumably to suit his convenience, but the boat was delayed and he had missed it. He had, however, stopped at Philadelphia and had seen Dick.

"I fully understand the Sand Bridge mix-up as you explained it," wrote Dick. "After all, I think that the Sand Bridge meeting could much better be held in some one's office and be finished promptly without dinner or lunches or other sorts of celebration. I would be very glad if in the future they could simply be held in O'Conor's office in New York, and then the members could scatter where they desired after it was over."

Dick had joined the Philadelphia Rifle Association November 1, 1898.

The death of his brother Charles left Dick with many estate matters to settle. He had cabled to Spencer at the time, and on April 4 (1925) he wrote that "when you get home there are quite a number of family matters which I think we ought to discuss."

Three weeks later (April 25, 1925) he again wrote, somewhat impatiently, to Spencer in Paris that "things are moving along here, and I regret to say that many family matters which should be acted on by you and me jointly are either waiting your arrival, or if necessary, will have to be attended to by me personally or in some other way. I have had a tough time for the last two months, with no member of the family to consult about what was best in our affairs, but I am trying to do what seems proper, in lack of any assistance."

Spencer had returned by June 4 (1925) for on that day, Dick wrote to him at Colorado Springs that "in estimating the items of principal in our father's estate I find that the value of the Utah Copper Company stock is somewhere around half the total value of the estate. You and I are the only two surviving trustees of this estate, and a trustee is supposed to be more conservative than if acting for himself, and also to have the interests of future generations in his mind. For this reason, you and I might often take a chance in our personal affairs which we would not have a moral right to take in a trust estate, even though that estate does permit us to invest the money in other than so-called legal securities. I am writing to you therefore to ask you definitely what you want to do in this matter. ... I will be greatly obliged to you if you will let me know definitely your attitude in this matter so that I can act accordingly."

That fall (October 9, 1925) Dick wrote to Speck, saying:

"Our father's own property started as a trust fund with our generation, and the generation of Boies Penrose, 2d and Mrs. Van Pelt [Sarah Penrose] is only the second generation of beneficiaries, so that it cannot be distributed until their children become beneficiaries; hence the somewhat awkward situation which now exists of having partly to divide the estate of Sarah H. B. Penrose and yet to hold the whole of the estate of Richard A. F. Penrose in trust."

A week later (October 16, 1925) he again wrote to Spencer concerning trusts:

"In a letter which I received from you some days ago, you asked me why the same Court ruling which ordered the division of the securities of the Estate of Sarah H. B. Penrose, so that Boies Penrose, 2nd, and Mrs. Van Pelt would received their shares, did not also apply to our father's estate. The question of the division of the Estate of Sarah H. B. Penrose was in doubt in the minds of all of us until it was finally decided by the Court that it should be done.

"It is hard for me to figure out all the legal details in this question, but I think that the basis of it was that our father had held the Estate of Sarah H. B. Penrose during his generation, and that we brothers have held it as trustees since our father's death. Therefore if the generation after us, as represented by Boies Penrose, 2nd and Mrs. Van Pelt, become beneficiaries, the part of the estate representing the share as it might be called of their father, would have to be divided among them, as they seem to represent the third generation in the matter. Not being a lawyer, I am not certain of these details.

"All these complications about the division of estates seems to me to show the absolute absurdity of anyone trying to influence posterity by making rigid trusts. If the trusts are made at all, they should be more or less elastic so that they can be adapted to the changes in conditions as time passes. The results of most trusts always seem to me to work a hardship and inconvenience on the descendants of the person who creates them.

"In order not to add further to this complication at the time of my death, I have made a clause in my will leaving all my right, title and interest in the estates of our father and mother to you personally. This, I hope, will avoid further difficulties of the kind we are having now."

In addition to his other duties, Dick also found time to answer courteously a mass of letters of condolence. Several of them are cited because of the background of the writer shown in the replies:

Letter to Mrs. J. W. Carter at Silver City, New Mexico, dated March 30, 1925

Dear Mrs. Carter:—

I deeply appreciate the very kind message of sympathy which you sent me from you and Colonel Carter. The letter you wrote in my care to my niece Sarah was forwarded to her, and you may have heard from her before now.

My brother had not been well for several years but he had not been seriously sick. He had spent the winter in South Carolina and was returning apparently much improved when he passed away on the train. His loss was a dreadful shock to all of us.

I remember well the good old days in Silver City when we were all together, and I hope that some day I may be able to come there again.

With kindest regards to you and the Colonel and hoping he will soon be as well as ever again, I am,

Sincerely yours,
R. A. F. Penrose, Jr.

Letter to Dr. Henry H. Koons, Brockman Building, Los Angeles, dated April 14, 1925

My dear Doctor:—

I thank you greatly for your kind letter of March 16th and I deeply appreciate your words of sympathy in connection with the death of my brother. He had not been well for several years but was not considered seriously sick, so that his loss came to us as a great shock and grief.

Since the date of your letter I have also heard from Margaret (Mrs. Thompson) about the death of her father Mr. Brockman. This again came as a great grief to me, for we had been associated so many years in New Mexico and Arizona that I always felt the greatest regard and respect for him. Our later acquaintance after he moved to Los Angeles was a great pleasure to me, and my recollection of those old days will always be vivid in my memory.

With kindest regards, I am,

Sincerely yours,
R. A. F. Penrose, Jr.

In a letter addressed to "Dear Dick," Dr. Edward Martin, of Philadelphia, wrote (May 13, 1925), thanking him "for your sketch of Charley's college career. I got a lot from your talk about him. Perhaps my memory is deficient, but I gathered that Boies, the elder, was 6 ft. $4\frac{1}{2}$; you, the second, 6 ft. $2\frac{1}{2}$; Charley, the third, 6 ft., and that Philip and Spencer trailed down to mere dwarfs of 5 ft. 11."

In his reply (May 15, 1925) Dick declared that "your estimates of the various heights of him and his brothers is about correct." And then he added: "Our ancestors on both sides have tried to be respectable, law-abiding people."

Tal's son, Boies Penrose 2nd, was graduated from Harvard University that year (1925), and on May 19, Dick wrote to his nephew:

"It was a great pleasure to me to receive your letter of May 12th on my return from a few days in New York, and I greatly appreciate your kindness in asking me to come to Cambridge at the time of your class day and commencement. Nothing would please me more than to do so, for I would like very much to see you go through the final performance of your four years' study at Harvard, but I am so overwhelmed with work, not only that which I have been attending to regularly but also with many new matters that have been thrown on me in the last two months, that I fear I will not be able to be present. Moreover, I feel about worn out and I think that as soon as I see an opportunity I will get away for a week or two.

"I hope, however, to see you here before you start back for Cambridge, and you may be sure that my best wishes will be with you on class day and commencement. I always look forward with interest and sympathy to the work you are doing and I hope you will let me know whenever I can be of any service to you. I hope you will also let me know when you come this way, for a cordial welcome will always await you."

The letter is signed "your affectionate uncle" and across the face of it, Penrose has written in pencil "Wire greetings 16th and 18th".

Young Boies spent that summer abroad, and on September 3, Penrose again wrote to him, addressing the letter to 1720 Spruce Street:

"I hear that you are expected back soon and I am dropping a line to you to welcome you home and to say that I hope to see you before long.

"Sarah has told me that you intended to enter the Law School here in Philadelphia, and if there is anything that I can do to help you in arranging your entrance matters I hope you will call on me, for I will be very glad to lend you such assistance as I can. The whole affair, however, is very simple. I believe that all you have to do is to go over to the Law School and see the Registrar, or someone else in control, and announce your intention of taking up your Law courses this year. If there is any hitch, however, please let me know.

"I hope you have had a splendid trip abroad and have seen much that interested you.

"Hoping soon to see you, I am, your affectionate uncle, R. A. F. Penrose, Jr."

Two months later, Penrose again wrote to young Boies at Devon, Pennsylvania, saying that "it seems a long time since I have seen or heard from you and I have been wondering why you did not once in a while drop in at 1331 Spruce Street. Sarah comes in occasionally, but it has been some time since I have seen you, and I am always anxious for you to know that I will be glad if you will let me know whenever I can be of service to you in any way.

"I hear occasionally indirectly about you at the Law School and that you are getting along there first rate. I have no doubt that at the start the lines of thought which are involved in the study of law are somewhat new to you, and therefore require more concentration than may be necessary later on. I think, however, that you will never regret having taken up the study of your profession, and whether you ever practise it or not, the knowledge and splendid training which it will give you will always be a pleasure and a benefit to you.

"It has just occurred to me to write to you this morning, because in looking over some books in my library in the Bullitt Building I found a small volume written a few years ago by the Dean of the Law School at Cornell University, who is an old-time friend of mine, and which bears the title 'Introduction to the Study of Law.' I thought you might be interested in looking at it some time when you are here."

Several other letters from the mass of family correspondence are included for the insight they give into the character of Richard.

Letter to his cousin, Miss Valeria F. Penrose, of Germantown, Pa., dated Philadelphia, March 28, 1924

Dear Vallie,

I thank you greatly for your letter of March 22nd enclosing that most interesting copy of a letter from Mrs. V. F. Penrose to her children and dated November 27, 1836. I am glad you found it, because so many old letters of this kind are apt to be mislaid and neglected and often lost forever. I shall preserve it as an interesting record in the family history.

I had a long letter from your brother Stephen some time ago telling me about his new plans for seeking an endowment for Whitman College and holding down the number of students, so that those who were allowed to attend could get a proper education. I think his ideas are excellent and I wish him every success.

I hope that you will have a very enjoyable trip if you finally decide to go to Chile. You will find Valparaiso a very interesting seaport, and Santiago, which is the capital of Chile and only a few hours travel by train from Valparaiso, a really beautiful and attractive city.

Again thanking you, I am,

Your affectionate cousin,
R. A. F. Penrose, Jr.

In a letter (April 11, 1924) to the same correspondent, Penrose said:

"I thank you very much for the old memorandum relating to the Medical School of the University of Pennsylvania in the years 1847 to 1848, and I shall preserve it as an interesting souvenir of the years just preceding the time when my father became professor at the University.

"When I saw you yesterday you seemed anxious to know how to address me and I had not an opportunity to explain that I did not know any better way for you to do so than simply to address me with my own name. I was never much of a hand on insisting on the use of titles.

"I hope to see you before you leave for Chile and if there is any information I can give you about that country before your departure I will be very glad to do so."

A month later (May 12, 1924) he wrote to her again:

"I thank you greatly for your note enclosing the humorous 'Valentine to Doctor Penrose, 1857.' I have read it with much interest and shall preserve it among my records of my father.

"I hope to see you soon and go over some of the other papers you told me about. I assure you that my inability to get out to Germantown recently has not been due to any intention on my part, but simply to the fact that I have been away so much lately that I have had to neglect temporarily many things which should have been attended to sooner."

The following day (May 15, 1924), he wrote to her again:

"My brother Charley tells me that he does not feel inclined to go to the meeting which you have called at Aunt Lyd's house on May 21st to go over the personal belongings which she left. I also feel somewhat the same way, for such affairs are always painful to me, especially after the death of a near relative [his father's sister] like Aunt Lyd, and I find so many painful experiences of every-day life without seeking more of them, that I hope you will pardon me for not attending the meeting.

"I had hoped that we might have been able to turn over some of the property that would come to us from our grandmother's estate to our Carlisle cousins, but I am told that this cannot be done."

Later that year (November 12, 1924) he once more wrote to her, this time addressing his letter to Valparaiso, Chile:

"I was very glad to get your letter some weeks ago and to learn that you had arrived safely in Chile and were enjoying your trip. There are many places of interest there and you have doubtless already seen some of them, but Chile is a very extensive country, at least in length, and there are many places well worth visiting.

"You refer to Vina del Mar, and this brings up some recollection of the place many years ago, just after the great earthquake in Valparaiso in 1896 [1906]. The town was almost destroyed at that time, but the hotel at Vina del Mar was left, and I made my headquarters there for some weeks while I was in Chile [1907].

"Everything seems to be about as usual here, and I hope that you will not become so fond of South America that you will remain there, for after all in the long run the United States is a very good country to belong to."

The "Stephen" referred to in the letter of March 28 was Dr. Stephen B. L. Penrose,[*] for many years president of Whitman College at Walla Walla, Washington. To him, on March 11 (1924), Dick had written:

"I have been much interested in what you said in your letter of January 21st concerning your ideas of the proper development at Whitman College and I think your attitude is entirely correct. I hope you will have every success in raising the endowment you need, for Whitman College has surely taken a high place in the education of the west. You have developed it along such broad and wise lines that I am looking forward to your making it an institution second to none in the country with a similar endowment, and probably far ahead of many institutions with great endowments.

"I am glad you did not seek State aid for Whitman College. I firmly believe that it tends to lower the independence, the dignity and the efficiency of any college or university. The University of Pennsylvania has for years received State aid, but I have always regretted this fact. It is only now starting a campaign for a large endowment and may eventually be able to reduce or eliminate the aid received from the State. I do not think that Harvard has ever received State aid.

[*] *See* letter from him, Chapter 17.

"I am greatly pleased with what you say about restricting your number of students so that they may receive proper education from the members of a strong efficient faculty instead of being only a vast crowd, as at many larger institutions, who never get nearer to their instructors than to hear them lecture from a distant platform. State aid generally means an unlimited study body while endowment permits the curtailment of the student body, and hence I am sure that you are on the right track at Whitman College by seeking endowment and holding down the student body to five hundred.

"I believe that Amherst admits only five hundred students and cares for them by the income from their endowments, with no State aid. On a visit there a few years ago I was greatly impressed by the atmosphere of dignity, efficiency and independence. I suppose Williams College is a somewhat similar institution but I have never had a chance to visit it. Stanford University, the University of Chicago and some other endowed institutions in the west and middle west have made decided restrictions in the number of students and have thereby added greatly to the efficiency of instruction; while the University of California, the University of Michigan and other state-aided institutions still struggle under the yoke of vast numbers.

"I congratulate you on your policy and on your efforts for an endowment, and I wish you every success in both."

Penrose did not, however, send anything more substantial to help in the creation of the endowment. Two months later (May 5, 1924) he wrote to Stephen's wife that he fully appreciated "the importance of Whitman College to the northwest and to the country at large, for Stephen has built up a remarkable institution there which reflects the greatest credit on his wisdom and his executive ability. However much I would like to assist in this project I regret to say that I am so overwhelmed with similar requests that it is now out of the question for me to do anything in this matter. My sympathies are with the project and with Stephen's effort to make Whitman College a self-supporting endowed institution of the first class, and I am sorry that I cannot take part in it."

In July of that same year (1924) President Penrose, in the course of a letter to Dick, said:

"Last week, when I was in Victoria, B. C., I met President Nicholas Murray Butler of Columbia University in the lobby of the Hotel Empress. He greeted me very cordially and then took my breath away by saying that he had written to President Coolidge only a few days before and had recommended me for appointment as Ambassador to Japan. He said that he had told the President that it was imperative that a man from the Pacific Coast should be appointed to the position in view of the feeling of the Pacific Coast towards the Japanese and that I was the best man for the position.

"It was an amazing compliment which naturally pleased me greatly, although I realize that nothing whatever may come of the suggestion."

To this, Dick replied on July 28 (1924):

"I have read with interest what you say about the appointment to Japan and I am very sure that no better man than you could be found to fill it. It would be a very great honor and the experience would be interesting to you and of great importance to your country.

"I wonder, however, in reading your letter whether you really want to leave Whitman College. You took hold of it many years ago as a small institution and you have built it up into a great college of much more than national fame. If you should leave Whitman College it might continue to grow but would not continue to do so in the way that it would prosper under your control. A high diplomatic appointment is always flattering and the work is of national importance, but the position is temporary, and the incumbent is often subject to somewhat onerous and embarrassing orders from those under whose instructions he works. A college president, on the other hand is largely his own master, and particularly in your case he is practically independent of anyone else."

Late in the following year (November 28, 1925) President Penrose again wrote to Dick, thanking him for an invitation to attend a Wistar Party at his house on December 5, and enclosing a "little leaflet which contains a speech which I made last winter before the State Legislature of Washington, and which was said to have considerably influenced the vote of the Legislature against the Child Labor Amendment."

In acknowledging its receipt, Dick wrote (December 22, 1925) that he had read the speech "with the greatest interest and I am very glad that you have put in such clear and convincing language the objection to the Federal Government assuming autocratic power in this particular subject.

"I have long thought about the question of child labor and I feel that the people of the United States, though they may have become somewhat erratic and fanatical on other subjects, can be safely relied upon to look after their children, and that the matter, as you say, is one peculiarly the business of the family and the individual states. The statistics which you show to the effect that every one of the forty-eight states has laws prohibiting child labor before the age of fourteen will enlighten many people who are prone to give too much power to our central Government."

Letter from Ellen W. Penrose, dated Carlisle, April 15, 1924

My dear Dick

Ever since I have been at home from my trip to Phila I have had it in mind to write you but so very varied and numerous are my different occupations there has not been a minute.

What I wanted when I was in Philadelphia was to hand you in person a small bottle with some home made grape wine which I had brought down for you. It is made by a very ancient recipe said to have been handed down from Old Noah. It is considered very fine. Indeed, in fact, when I opened my bag in the train there was such a whiff all the men turned round to see what was doing, so I was afraid of being arrested as a Bootlegger if I gave it to any one else at your door.

Jennie and I decided to drink it up when we could not give it to you. We felt rather blue considering the circumstances. I was so sorry as I wanted you to test it and see what you thought of our feeble efforts to break the Volstead Act.

Vallie Penrose tells me you are collecting Family Records. I have some in which you may be interested, relating to our Great Grandmother Biddle. I will bring them down next time I come and shall hope to see you, but if I am not able to will leave them for you. I bought them from a woman who had found them in the attic of Cousin Beckie's old house on High Street where Auntie Baird lived for many years during the life time of her mother Gran Biddle and her own.

The old papers had slipped in under the boards of the old floor. When the boards were moved there they lay having been there many many years.

When I have another chance will try the little stunt again of taking you a bottle of our home brew and shall hope to be more successful in giving it to you.

Sincerely and affectionately
Nellie

In a letter addressed to "Dear Nellie" and dated May 29 (1924) Penrose thanked her "for the old family papers which Jennie gave me the other day and said they were from you. I shall go over them with a great deal of interest and will keep them among other similar documents which I have and which may some time in the future be useful in further compilations regarding the family."

The following month (June 17, 1924) he wrote again to "Dear Nellie," thanking her "for the old newspaper which you and Jennie found in your attic, giving an account of the death of our grandfather Charles B. Penrose, and including a sketch of his life.

"I do not know exactly in what part of Philadelphia he was born but I will try to look into this matter, as well as the matter of where he went to school in Kentucky. All these records are interesting in connection with the family and I greatly appreciate your sending the paper to me. It will keep it carefully with the other papers you sent me and will investigate it further as soon as I have an opportunity."

Letter from Dick, dated Philadelphia, July 29, 1924

Dear Nellie:—

Since the time you sent me some weeks ago an old newspaper containing a short sketch of our grandfather I have been trying to look up the two points about which you inquired, namely, where he was born in Philadelphia, and where he went to school in Kentucky.

As regards his birthplace, I find that he was born at his father's country place near Frankford, Philadelphia, in 1798. At that time of course the neighborhood of what is now Frankford was open country, and I suppose that his father probably owned a large place there.

I cannot find any record to the effect that our grandfather attended school in Kentucky, but I do find a record to the effect that he probably attended school at St. Louis, Missouri, which for a number of years was the residence of his father, who had been appointed by President Jefferson as a commissioner of the Louisiana Territory.

All the papers you have sent me recently are very interesting and I think will be of much importance if some of us should get around to writing a new edition of the "Penrose Book."

Affectionately yours,

Letter from Ellen W. Penrose, dated Carlisle, December 27, 1924

Dear Dick

Many many thanks for your Christmas present which Jennie gave me on Christmas day. I often wonder what we would really do without you and Charlie and Spencer to send us such wonderful presents and just sending a little letter of thanks seems very meager in comparison with what I think about you all. But will you please thank them for me, too.

I wonder if you have gotten any more Family records lately.

I picked up a curious old print of one of the first engines on the Cumberland Valley Railroad the other day which is very interesting to me on account of the part which our Grandfather Penrose took in the beginning of the road. I think he started it. Well, many old men have come to see it and tell me it is a picture of the first engine. I am making a collection of different things which would interest those who are coming after us and I shall hope to have them for Sarah's children. I wonder whether they will really care as much as we do for to me it is so interesting. I am told our Grandfather at one time owned quite a number of houses here and one day I went into the house at the corner of this street and the woman who owns it took me into the room where your Father and mine were born. It was the house Grandfather first lived in after his marriage, when the tale goes he only had $500.00 a year.

I am sorry that I have been taken off of this letter so often while writing. It is very much broken up but so many people have rung the front door bell this afternoon I am sorry I had it mended. It has been broken for a month. Next time I shall wait.

Thanking you again for your thought of us, I am,

Affectionately
Nellie

On January 24, 1925, Penrose wrote to her, thanking her for her letter of January 18th "and for the beautiful little penknife which has just arrived. You and your sisters were very kind to send it to me, and I shall keep it not only because you have sent it to me but because it is so artistic and useful.

"I have been so busy lately with The Academy of Natural Sciences that I have not had time to look up further family records, but I have found some, and I have preserved carefully those which you sent me. When you and Jennie come to Philadelphia I will be very glad to talk this matter over with you, for I think among us we have a good deal of new material relating to the family."

On March 5 (1925) Ellen Penrose wrote to Dick that "when I was with you yesterday I entirely forgot something I wanted to tell you very much. I was thinking so hard of the days that are past, when I used to visit your father,

Uncle Alex, in the room where we sat, every thing just as it used to be when he was here, it just put all out of my mind.

"On Monday I got a sweet little note from Miss Aggie Mahon who you may know was a great friend of your Mother's. The old lady wrote having seen Charlie's death in the paper to ask me to tell you of her sorrow for his brothers that are left.

"She is almost a hundred years old and almost blind so it was really a wonderful letter."

Penrose replied (March 20, 1925) that "it was a great pleasure to have seen you and Jennie here a few days ago, and I hope you will drop in at the house whenever you have an opportunity for a cordial welcome will always await you.

"You refer to the note you have received from Miss Agnes Mahon, whom I remember well as a friend of my mother's many years ago. It was certainly very good in her to have written to you about Charley's death and I greatly appreciate her kind thoughtfulness. I do not know her address or I would write to her directly, but when you write to her again won't you please express my deep appreciation of her remembrance of the old days. She used to come here frequently to dinner during my mother's lifetime, and also often visited her at our cottage at Atlantic City."

Evidently Ellen Penrose sent the address, for on March 30 (1925), Dick wrote to Miss Mahon at Kingston, N. Y.:

"My cousin, Miss Nellie Penrose of Carlisle, has told me that she had heard from you expressing your sympathy at the sad loss of my brother Charley, and I write to tell you how deeply I appreciate your kind thoughtfulness in doing so.

"When Nellie Penrose wrote to me about your letter it brought up vividly memories of the old days when you and my mother were such good friends, and how she and all of us were happy when you came to visit her in Philadelphia and at the old cottage in Atlantic City. This was all many years ago, but it is still as fresh in my mind as if it were yesterday and I have always cherished the remembrance.

"I hope that you are well and that the world has been treating you with the kindness that you deserve."

A fortnight later (April 16, 1925) Dick wrote again to Miss Mahon:

"I was very glad indeed to receive your recent letter of April 1st and I thank you greatly for the beautiful Easter card which you sent me.

"It seemed good to hear from you after all these many years which have intervened since the times when you used to visit my mother here. There are not many of us left at present. My brothers Boies and Charley and my youngest brother Philip, have all died, and Spencer and I are left. Spencer is at present on a trip around the world but I expect that he will return here in the course of a few weeks. He lives most of the time in Colorado Springs, but comes to Philadelphia occasionally.

"Your impression that I lived in the west was correct inasmuch as I did live there for over thirty years, but just at present I am living in Philadelphia. I am not a physician, as you have been told, but I am a geologist and am interested in mining in the west.

"It is a great pleasure to me to know that you are so comfortably settled and I hope that you will continue so. All your good and kindly acts to others in bygone years entitle you to any comfort and happiness that can come to you."

Letter from Ellen W. Penrose, dated Carlisle, June 9, 1925

My dear Dick

Thank you many times for your great kindness and thought for us, making life for us so much easier. I was much touched by your letter to Jennie. It has always been one of the things I most loved to do when I am in Phila to go to your home. I loved to see Uncle Alex and have him tell me about his brothers and himself, the life they lived up here in Carlisle when they were all boys together, the house they had at Middlesex where they hunted and fished, then of the interesting books he had been reading. I always went after these talks and got something to read he had told me of. I think he was one of the most interesting people I ever knew. Now I love to come and see you. You make me think of Uncle Alex. Then I just think that house of yours most wonderful; it gives me all sorts of pleasure to go into it.

Miss Aggie wrote me she had had such a lovely letter from you. It gave the old lady much pleasure.

Cousin Minnie Biddle is very poorly but she is almost ninety. She is, in fact, this month.

In looking over some old letters the other day I found one from Charlie written two summers ago just before he went West. I felt as I read it over how much you brothers had been to us these years. What would we have done without you. Thank you, dear Dick, for it all.

I am looking forward to seeing you up here. You know you promised to come up this month and see us. Please come.

Affectionately
Nellie

On January 2, 1925, Penrose received a letter from another Charles Penrose, who said:

"I thoroughly enjoyed our conversation over the 'phone the other afternoon. Perhaps you will remember being very kind to a small boy of about twelve who was then interested in electrical engineering and to whom you gave a vision of what engineering means. That small boy was me.

"Possibly one member of the family is interested in what another member does. On the chance that you may be, a copy is being sent you with the author's compliments of an address on 'New England's Power Resources,' delivered two years ago at Boston before the Cotton Association. With it go my warm personal regards.

"At San Francisco, Dr. Terrill said many good things about you and I was glad of the chance to give you his message the other day."

To this, Penrose replied on January 7, 1925:

"I was very glad indeed to receive your letter of January 2nd. I remember well when you and I talked about engineering many years ago that you appeared to take an unusual interest in it. Your later experience has surely shown that you had an innate ability for that profession.

"I have also received your paper on 'New England's Power Resources' which you have so kindly sent me and which I have read with great interest. It is full of valuable material and many of the statistics which you give are very important.

"Doctor Terrill of San Francisco, to whom you refer, is a very good and close friend of mine. He studied medicine a long time ago under my father at the University of Pennsylvania, but later moved to the west."

An envelope in the Penrose files marked "Fairmount Park Commission" contained the certificate of appointment of his brother, Charles B. Penrose, "for the term of five years from the first Monday in June, 1917." As these appointments were for five years and as Charles died in 1925, during his second term of appointment, Richard was asked to complete the unexpired term. Under date of March 4, 1927, he received his appointment as "a Commissioner of Fairmount Park, for the term of five years, beginning the First Monday of June, 1927."

Letter to Major Thomas Martin, secretary of the Commissioners of Fairmount Park, dated Philadelphia, December 7, 1925

Dear Major Martin:—

I have received your very kind letter of December 1st telling me that the President of the Commissioners of Fairmount Park has asked you to notify me that he has appointed me a member of the Committee on the Guard; and in reply I beg to say that it gives me much pleasure to accept this appointment.

Very truly yours,
R. A. F. Penrose, Jr.

According to "The Book of Rules" of the Commission, this meant "a committee on the guard, of five members, to have charge of the appointment, discipline and discharge of the Park Guards."

Another civic project with which Penrose was identified in these last years was the Free Library of Philadelphia to the Board of Trustees of which he was appointed by the Philadelphia City Council on June 25, 1928. On October 4 of the following year (1929) he was unanimously elected vice-president of that board. That he had been a frequent contributor to the library even before that time is shown by various gifts acknowledged, particularly in August, 1919, when he received word of thanks for almost two hundred books and pamphlets. In October, 1929, the librarian thanked him for the presentation to the library of the extremely valuable four-volume set by Mary Vaux Walcott of "North American Wild Flowers."

In 1929, Penrose became first an active and then a life member of the Geographical Society of Philadelphia.

"As I am sometimes away from Philadelphia for long intervals," he wrote on November 20 (1929), "it would be a convenience to me to become a Life Member of the Society rather than a member who pays simply yearly dues. If this procedure is proper I would be very glad to send my check for Life Membership."

In December of the previous year (1928) he had been elected a Fellow of the American Geographical Society.

Penrose was also a life member of the Historical Society of Pennsylvania (1920) and in 1927 was elected a Deputy Governor of the Pennsylvania Society of Colonial Governors.

In 1925, he declined the presidency of the Mining and Metallurgical Society, and in 1929 the presidency of the Society of Economic Geologists, but the following year he was elected president of the Geological Society of America, the last post of this kind which he held.

Early in 1929, Penrose received a letter from W. C. Wilson, dated King of Prussia, Pa., January 28, to the effect that "shortly before father's death in 1905 he had me get in communication with your brother, the Senator, with the view of having you elected President of the Germantown & Norristown Railroad Company; he being conscious of the fact at that time that his days were numbered.

"Senator Penrose reported to me that you could not accept on account of your absences from the city. Have the conditions changed and would you consider accepting the presidency at this time? I know nothing of the composition of the Board of Directors but I thought it well to call this to your attention.

"I trust you will consider the matter very seriously as father had a very high regard for your ability."

Penrose replied two days later (January 30, 1929):

"I have received your very kind letter of January 28th regarding a successor to your good brother, Mr. C. C. Wilson, as President of the Philadelphia, Germantown & Norristown Railroad Company. I was greatly shocked and grieved at the loss of your brother, for he had made for many years an active, efficient and loyal President of the Company, and I looked on him as a worthy son of that great and good man, your father, who was President of the Company when I first became a member of the Board of Managers.

"After the death of your father in 1905 Mr. C. C. Wilson told me just what you have told me in your letter, that is, that it had been his expressed wish that I should be his successor. At that time I was so overwhelmed with other work that it was impossible for me to accept the position, though I understood that arrangements had been made to elect me. Of course, I would have gone very far to have acceded to a request from your father, but in view of the fact that I would not have been able to give the proper time to the position, I felt that out of loyalty to his memory and to the Company, I should not accept it when I knew that I could not give it the time which it should have.

"Now again I am deeply touched by your reference to your father's wishes almost twenty-five years ago, and your suggestion that I should again consider the Presidency of the Company. I have thought the matter over carefully, but

I am again forced to the same conclusion as that which I found necessary in 1905. I am so much occupied with other matters that I can rarely find an hour to attend to my own affairs from early morning until late at night. My work is not of a selfish nature, and most of my activities are in connection with more or less public institutions of an administrative, educational or scientific character. I am therefore, though most reluctantly, forced again to give up any consideration of the Presidency of the Philadelphia, Germantown & Norristown Railroad Company, for I feel that the position is an important one and that the incumbent should be a man who can devote the proper time to its duties."

During this period of his life he did very little writing. Two memorial biographies of John Casper Branner—one for the *Bulletin of the Geological Society of America* and the other for the *Memoirs of the National Academy of Sciences*—and the article on *The early days of the Department of Geology at the University of Chicago*, in the *Journal of Geology* (already quoted) were all, except for his address, *Geology as an agent in human welfare*, as retiring president of The Geological Society of America (1930) and the accompanying presidential report.

He did, however, contribute to the *Proceedings of The Academy of Natural Sciences of Philadelphia** the following tribute to "The Honorable John Cadwalader, 1843–1925":

"John Cadwalader was connected with The Academy of Natural Sciences of Philadelphia in various capacities, as a member of the Council, as vice-president, as president, and at the time of his death as a member of the Board of Trustees. He was not by profession a scientist, yet his intellectual perception and kindly interest enabled him to grasp the importance of scientific work as indispensable to human progress, and he was always deeply interested in the ideals and accomplishments of the Academy.

"His family since early Colonial days in Pennsylvania has been active in public affairs, and the spirit of loyalty, honor and patriotism for their country was always strong among them, with the result that from generation to generation they were eminent among their fellowmen. The Honorable John Cadwalader was a worthy descendant from such ancestry. He was by profession a lawyer and occupied many important legal positions, but with his great breadth of vision he took part in many other spheres of activity in the City, the State and the Nation. He was prominent not only in his profession but as a statesman, an educator, a financier, and a publicist in many fields. His altruistic nature led him ever to work for others and to think but little of his own welfare and health, until in his eighty-second year he collapsed at the very time that he was performing an important public service.

"Mr. Cadwalader, in addition to his ability in a remarkable diversity of public affairs was noted for his courteous and considerate manner in dealing with all classes of people. He recognized the amenities as opposed to the crudities of life, and had that rare combination of ability and refinement which is fast disappearing in the mad rush of modern materialism. The Academy and the whole community have lost a true and loyal friend, a survivor of a passing type of gentle-

* Vol. 77 (1925), p. 378.

man which was once the spirit and the controlling element in the brilliant days of generations that have passed."

The previous year (December 4, 1924) Penrose had written to another Cadwalader (Charles M. B. Cadwalader) at the Hampton Gunning Lodge, Waterlily, N. C.:

"Those wonderful canvasback ducks which you so kindly sent to me through Wharton Huber were splendid. I never saw such magnificent specimens, and I wondered whether their skins in the Academy would not have been of more scientific use than to eat them; but Huber said that you sent them to be eaten, and therefore with the accompaniment of a little wine your orders were fulfilled, and a most cordial recollection of your kind thoughtfulness was the effect."

Another letter of gastronomical interest was addressed to J. Franklin ("Dear Frank") McFadden of Philadelphia and dated December 25, 1925:

"I cannot tell you how greatly I appreciate your kind letter and the copy of that most important and valuable volume entitled 'Les Meilleures Recettes Culinaires pour Poissons, Crustaces et Coquillages' which you have been so kind as to import from Paris for me. When you lent me your other copy I read it with the greatest interest and profit, but I am now very glad indeed to have this copy you have given me lest I forget some of the important details which it contains when it becomes my duty to cook fish [at the Rabbit].

"This book surely teaches one how to cook any kind of 'poissons' and allied creatures in any form agreeable to the connoisseur, and the information given in it, if generally studied and known, would make many homes happier and divorce courts fewer."

Two other letters concern books. On June 25, 1924, he wrote to "Dear John" T. Huneker, of Philadelphia:

"I know the book just published *Across the Great Crater Land of the Congo* and though I have not yet received it I have put in an order for it. When it arrives I will read it with much interest, and now that I know it has your approval, I am sure that my time will be well spent in perusing it."

The other letter (May 29, 1924) is addressed to Dr. W. A. Jayne of Denver:

"You ask me what I think of a book published a year or so ago called *Beasts, Men and Gods*. I have read it with wonder and astonishment. Poor old Siberia seems for ages to have been the victim of fabulous stories and has been saddled with many of the horrors of European Russia for which it was not responsible. I have not been in Siberia for over twenty years, but no such fantastic events as are portrayed in this volume were apparent at that time. Of course, since my visit to Siberia numerous revolutions have occurred, and I have no doubt that there have been stirring times; but the book reminds me so much of the fabulous adventures of Baron Munchausen that I cannot take it seriously.

"I hope you are well. I often think of Denver and the good times we used to have there in the old days."

The final Hoover letter also belongs to this period. After his nomination for the Presidency of the United States, in June, 1928, the candidate wrote:

My dear Mr. Penrose:

I was glad to have your telegram of congratulation. From a friend of so many years standing it comes with much increased value.

Yours faithfully,
Herbert Hoover

In connection with the Hoover campaign for election that fall, Penrose wrote to Nelson B. Gaskill, of The Hoover Business League, in Washington:

"On my return from a short absence I have received your very interesting letter of October 10th calling my attention to the extremely important work that Mr. Hoover has done as Secretary of Commerce for American business.

"I have known Mr. Hoover for a great many years and have always had the greatest regard and respect for him as a man of wonderful initiative and executive ability. I have always been a staunch Republican, and at the present time I am more than ever pleased that I have such excellent cause to remain loyal to the good old Republican party. I shall take much pleasure in voting for Mr. Hoover, Mr. Curtis, and the rest of the Republican ticket on November 6th.

"I thank you for the enclosures which you have sent me concerning Mr. Hoover and his accomplishments. I have for years been familiar with them and have admired them, and in accordance with your suggestion, I would be glad to have a few copies of such of this material as you can spare, so that I may distribute it where it will do the most good for Mr. Hoover."

In March, 1924, Penrose was invited to be one of the one hundred members of the Organizing Committee of the then-forming National Museum of Engineering, but he declined on the grounds of his many duties. In June, of the same year, he was asked to be an Associate Member with "no obligations whatever except the payment of $10.00 annual dues." He again declined, saying "I assure you that it was with regret that my various other duties prevented my joining your Organizing Committee at the time you were so kind as to offer me membership on it. For the same resaon I feel that I cannot at present consistently accept your very kind offer to become an associate member."

In this connection he wrote to George Iles, a member of the Organizing Committee, whom he knew:

"I already belong to so many organizations connected more directly with my own profession of geology that I hesitate to join new ones, because I always find that joining a new society means doing endless work on some committee or in some official capacity, so that in these modern days it really becomes necessary to confine one's activities to a certain class of such organizations."

In response to Iles' letter of explanation, Penrose wrote again, under date of July 14:

"I think that the idea is excellent but it will require a great deal of organizing and also large funds to put it on a suitable basis.

"My profession is that of a geologist and the work of most of my life has been connected more or less directly with that subject. In recent years I was one of those who formed the new Society of Economic Geologists of which I was president for two years. I am now engaged in trying to do what I can for the old Academy of Natural Sciences of Philadelphia, which was founded over one hundred and twelve years ago, and if I can bring it up to a condition where it will function properly along modern lines of science I will feel amply rewarded.

"I have mentioned these facts simply to show that my hands are full of work, and, however much I might wish to do so, I really could not take over any new work at present."

Another example of his reticence is shown in the correspondence between him and Andrew C. Lawson in 1923 and 1924 concerning the establishment of an "Abstract Journal of Geology." Lawson, then chairman of the Division of Geology and Geography of the National Research Council, wrote to Penrose (October 22, 1923):

"In my letter of September 20 I called attention to the pressing need of founding an Abstract Journal of Geology. Since then the National Research Council has endorsed the project of raising funds for this purpose; and the Division of Geology and Geography is moving in that direction. The Division after mature consideration decided that an Abstract Journal would be one of the most effective instrumentalities of advancing the science of geology. The literature of geology is so immense that no one can hope to familiarize himself with its content from month to month, as it appears, and have time for anything else. To meet this situation it is proposed to do what some other sciences, notably chemistry, have successfully done, namely, to establish a journal with salaried editors whose function it shall be to summarize or abstract the essential features of papers on geology published in any and all countries, and to publish such abstracts, properly classified and indexed, periodically. The working geologist will then, as a subscriber to the abstract journal, have before him the literature of his day in condensed form; and by glancing over this he may see what papers he must read *in extenso*, and get suggestions from the new ideas that are appearing in his own and allied fields. The subscription to such a journal would, it is hoped, pay for paper and printing. We need in addition to this an assured income of $10,000 per year for editorial and clerical services. To secure this it is proposed to raise the sum of $200,000 to be vested in the National Research Council as Trustee, and by the Council funded to secure the income desired. Another agency will have to be found to undertake the direction and management of the publication with the funds thus provided. It has been suggested that the Geological Society of America would be an appropriate agency, and might be willing to assume this function.

"There are four sources from which contributions to the proposed foundation may reasonably be expected: 1. Geologists. 2. Wealthy patrons of the science of geology. 3. Universities and societies. 4. The industries that are concerned with the exploitation of the natural resources of the earth's crust and are to some extent appreciative of the practical value of geology. Steps are being taken to invite contributions from mining and petroleum corporations, and this letter is intended to afford a similar opportunity to geologists themselves. Subscriptions may be made upon the enclosed blank either for a lump sum, or for a certain sum annually for five years. The money thus pledged will not be called for until the whole $200,000 had been subscribed.

"The Division will be very grateful for the active cooperation of individual geologists in securing subscriptions from patrons of science and from mining or petroleum corporations. This may be best done where several geologists are in touch by organizing a local committee to canvass the field. The subscription blank may be copied wherever necessary."

Evidently hearing nothing from Penrose, Lawson wrote to him again early the following year (January 4, 1924):

"In a few weeks I intend to take the road for the purpose of personally interviewing the management of mining and oil companies to solicit contributions to our fund for an Abstract Journal of Geology. In doing this it would be of very great assistance to me to have as large a contribution from geologists as is possible, and, knowing your sympathetic interest in the project, I am taking the liberty of asking whether you would not at this time be willing to give us a subscription that would swell somewhat the amount now in hand?

"The enclosed endorsements from all parts of the country will show you how very generally the project is approved. Everyone with whom I have corresponded or spoken regards the success of the project as of prime importance to geology, and I have heard of no objections. There is nothing that I know of in the way of financial assistance to our science that you could do that would be more heartily appreciated by the geologists of the country. You are aware, of course, from my circular letter that subscriptions will not be called for until the entire sum is raised, and that subscriptions may be of a single sum or may be spread over five annual payments.

"Trusting that you will appreciate the motive for my again appealing to you at this time, and that you will not take the appeal amiss, I am, with kind regards, sincerely yours, Andrew C. Lawson."

This time, Penrose answered (January 15, 1924):

My dear Lawson:—

I have received your letter of January 4th with enclosures showing the expressions of approval of your plan to create an Abstract Journal of Geology. I personally think your plan a most excellent one and would like to see it realized. I think that the Journal could properly be supported as you say by the large corporations engaged in mining or otherwise operating the mineral resources of the country, for it is through a knowledge of geology on the part of at least some of their employees that their prospect of success largely depends.

Regarding your suggestion that I personally might make a large contribution, I would say that nothing would give me more pleasure than to do so if possible, for I fully realize the great importance of your project to the science of geology; but I am contributing to so may other different causes, both in geology and other branches of natural science, that I simply cannot make any large contribution to the proposed Journal at present. If you happen to come this way at any time I would be very glad to show you what I am doing and I think I can convince you that I am not in any way selfish, but that there is a limit to one's means.

I would be glad to talk over this matter further with you some time, and in the meanwhile with kindest regards and wishing you every success in the enterprise. I am

Sincerely yours,
R. A. F. Penrose, Jr.

Letter from Lawson, dated Washington, January 16, 1924

My dear Penrose:

Many thanks for your very kind and frank letter of January 15. I am very glad you wrote to me so frankly about the matter so that I shall not be laboring under any misapprehension. I am coming up to Philadelphia before long to try and find Parker and thru him to get in touch with some of the coal mining companies, and on that occasion I will be very glad indeed to drop in and see you.

With much appreciation of your kind and sympathetic interest in the project for an Abstract Journal of Geology, I am

Yours sincerely
Andrew C. Lawson

One other reference is made to this project. On July 14th of that year (1924) Penrose again wrote to Lawson:

"I have received your Bulletin of the National Research Council entitled 'The Continental Shelf off the Coast of California' and I have read it with the greatest interest and profit. Your description of the region of the Continental Shelf and the different segments of the Shelf are all most important and they seem to me to have a direct connection with the studies in earth movements which you have been making in past years on the Pacific Coast.

"I was sorry not to have seen you before you left Washington, for I have often wondered what you have done concerning your plan for an abstract journal of geologic literature. I have heard that certain universities have been more or less interested in the matter, but it occurs to me that such a journal could perhaps be more properly handled by the Geological Society of America, which is national in its character, than by any local organization."*

As a rule, Penrose was extremely punctilious about answering letters promptly; even frankly begging letters received his courteous refusal. Only those from obviously chronic beggars are marked "not answered" across the face.

Among the few letters to women in his correspondence is one to Mrs. Mary B. Ponting, of Berkeley, California, who had written him in 1925 concerning copper stocks, and who closed her letter: "If I am asking too much of you, just say so and put this in the waste basket and I will love you just the same. Devotedly, Mary B. Ponting."

* The Geological Society of America now publishes annually *Bibliography and Index of Geology Exclusive of North America.*

To "Dear Mary" he replied (September 3, 1925):

"Oh my return from some days absence I have received your letter concerning your tribulations about your copper stocks.

"I think your best plan is to consult some reliable Trust Company or banker with whom you may have dealings. The opinions here on the matter of copper stocks are many and varied, and it is very difficult therefore to get at all the facts.

"I was very sorry to have missed you when you were in the east, but you always make such hasty trips that it is difficult to know where you are. I do not blame you for preferring that beautiful climate of the Berkeley Hills to the hot, wet climate of Philadelphia in the summer."

As was natural, Penrose received many wedding invitations, and he had evidently decided that silver was always acceptable, for there are many notes of thanks for silver baskets, silver pitchers, and silver candlesticks. Apparently, he very seldom went to the weddings, for most of the invitations carry across the face the word "regretted."

In thanking him for a gift, one bride-to-be wrote:

"Father tells me that it may be hard to persuade you, but I do hope you will come to my wedding. I would so like to really meet you and thank you in person for your kind thought of me."

The correspondence does not show whether or not he went to the wedding, but the chances are even that he did not.

When the daughter of his friend, J. Volney Lewis, announced her marriage, he wrote:

"I have received the announcement of your marriage on October 4th and I beg to extend to you and to Mr. Cook my most hearty congratulations.

"I am sending to you a small gift which I beg you will accept as a present I would have sent sooner if I had known of the time of your wedding. I remember with much pleasure the days several years ago when you so earnestly and unselfishly assisted your father, and through him assisted the rest of us in establishing the Society of Economic Geologists on such a firm and substantial basis."

In a letter to Wallace W. Atwood, president of Clark University, who had extended an invitation for him to be a member of the advisory council of the soon-to-be-established journal of *Economic Geography*, Penrose wrote under date of December 18, 1924:

"I have received your letter of November 22nd relative to the new quarterly journal which you are starting at Clark University, called Economic Geography. I admire the broad sphere which you intend to cover and I am sure that it will be most useful, both from an economic and a scientific standpoint. I feel that the time is coming, both in geography and in geology, when those on the purely research side and those on the economic side will wake up to find that there is no sharp separation between the two lines of work. The one supplements the other and they are interdependent. I think that your conception of the new journal recognizes this fact.

"I greatly appreciate your kind invitation to join the Advisory Council connected with the editorial board of which you are chief. I fully recognize the honor of such a connection, and nothing would please me more than to accept your proposal if it were not that I am already overloaded with other work. Of course, many people join advisory boards and rarely do much work connected with them. I personally, however, feel that when I am on such a board I should do work connected with it, and just at present I feel that it would be impossible for me to undertake it."

Penrose's statement concerning his participation in any activity to which he lent his name is confirmed by Charles P. Berkey, for many years secretary of the Geological Society of America, who said that more than any other president of that society, Penrose exercised an active and sympathetic participation in every detail of its successful functioning.

In November, 1925, Penrose again wrote to Atwood:

"I have recently been reading the two copies of your publication 'Economic Geography' which you so kindly sent to me some little time ago, and I am greatly impressed with the broad scope and originality manifested in these publications as the result of your splendid conception of the possibilities of the subject.

"I would have written you sooner, but I have only recently been able to read the two copies you sent me, and after I had begun them I found that every article was so well worth careful attention that I have read all of them.

"I wish you every possible success in this new and unique work, and I am sure that Economic Geography will play a wide part in both the scientific and economic development of the world."

The Penrose correspondence is crowded with evidence of his words of praise and encouragement for others. That he was proud of his native state and took a practical interest in its betterment is shown in the following excerpts from his his correspondence with George H. Ashley, State Geologist of Pennsylvania. They are dated May 15, 1924, March 24, 1925, and November 23, 1925, respectively.

My dear Ashley:-

I thank you greatly for your Bulletins Nos. 81 to 85, which I have received on my return from a few days absence and which I shall read with the greatest interest. They surely show a remarkable activity and accuracy in the work you are conducting so admirably in Pennsylvania.

I have also received the bound copy of Volume I on 'Oil and Gas' and a similar copy on 'Oil Resources in Coals and Carbonaceous Shales.' I congratulate you heartily on having at least been able to get some of your reports actually printed and bound. It seems a pity that all of the work that you are now doing and which you have done since you have been in office should not be published in the same way. I am particularly glad to notice that you have adopted the quarto size in the two bound publications which you have sent me.

Dear Ashley:-

I thank you greatly for your Bulletin C.1 on the Soil Survey of Adams County, Pennsylvania, by Messrs. Patrick and Bennett.

I intend to read this Bulletin with the greatest interest and I am sure with much profit, for I am greatly pleased that you are giving this attention to the subject of soil surveys in this State. People in the west are altogether too prone to think that there are no good soils in Pennsylvania, and a little advertising such as you have given the subject in Adams County, together with the splendid map which accompanies the Bulletin, will work for the good of the State.

My dear Ashley:-
I thank you very much for your two Bulletins on 'Limestones of Pennsylvania' and 'Bituminous Coal Fields of Pennsylvania—Coal Analyses', which I have received to-day and have been looking over with much interest and profit. I shall read them more carefully during the week, but I hasten to write to you now to congratulate you most heartily on their comprehensive character and on the admirable way in which they have been prepared and printed.

It seems splendid to me, after your long and strenuous efforts, that you have at last been able to start a regular series of published volumes, which are a credit to you, to the State and to those who have prepared them under your able direction. I look forward with much hope and interest to the future bulletins of your Topographic and Geologic Survey of a similar character to those you have sent me.

That Penrose hated shoddy things and unbusinesslike ways is obvious from his punctilious care of his own records and correspondence. That he was equally inclined to forgive and excuse any one who was sincerely penitent, is shown by the following correspondence with the publisher of a scientific "Directory."

"Dear Sir," wrote Penrose, under date of May 12, 1924. "I have received the copy of your 'Directory' published April, 1924, and asking me to send you the price ($2.00) and the amount of postage of the parcel as soon as possible.

"I beg to say that when you notified me of the forthcoming publication of this Directory I sent to you my check in payment for a copy of it when issued. This was some time early in September, 1923, and I think if you will look up your records you will see that I have already paid for the copy you have sent me.

"As regards the postage which you ask me to send you on the parcel, I enclose herewith six cents in stamps, which I suppose will cover that item.

"I will be obliged to you if you will look up your records and let me know whether or not you have ever received my check for $2.00 which I sent you last September, for if you have not received it I will remit that amount again to you."

The publisher replied (May 15, 1924) that "the printed slip asking for payment was sent you through carelessness. The payment was made by you in September and was credited."

In the summer of the following year (June 3, 1925) Penrose again wrote to the publisher:

"I have received a notice from you stating that it is the fourth one you have sent to me concerning the Directory. I must say that I had somewhat lost interest in this publication, for it has frequently in the past been far behindtime in being issued, and to me it is often disappointing in not containing names which I would expect to be there. Moreover in the case of your last edition I sent you my prepayment and I received a receipt from you, and yet when the book came to me I received a bill for it.

"Of course I realize that this was simply an oversight, but it is annoying to have to remember the details of such matters. Though I make no promise whatever about subscribing to your forthcoming volume, yet if when it is published you will let me know I will consider whether or not to take a copy of it.

"I might add that my address, etc., as published in your last Directory is correct."

Two months later (August 25, 1925), Penrose again wrote:

"I have received the copy of the Directory which you sent me and enclose herewith my check for two dollars and ten cents in payment for it.

"I observe that you left my name out of your Catalogue, but I suppose this was by accident.

Very truly yours,
R. A. F. Penrose, Jr.

"P.S. I find your directory very interesting."

The publisher replied immediately (August 28, 1925), saying that he was "very sorry your name was not included in the Directory. I can't see how it occurred, and I am especially sorry because I think we had a misunderstanding in regard to the last edition.

"I hope I shall be able to get things correct in the next edition.

"I am returning your check and trust you will accept the copy sent you."

Whereupon, Penrose replied (August 31, 1925):

"I have received your letter of August 28th returning my check for $2.10 which I had sent as my contribution to your Directory because you had found that my name had been unintentionally omitted. This omission was of no importance, and I consider your little volume a very valuable and useful book. I have done more or less editing myself, and I know how often certain clauses are unintentionally omitted. I am therefore returning the check, and ask that you will accept it just the same as if my name had appeared."

Another letter, interesting because it is indicative of the character of the man, is addressed to Hayden, Stone & Co. (March 30, 1925):

"I have received your communication asking whether I wish you to continue sending me your Weekly Market Letter. You state that you are glad to send it for a reasonable time to those whom you do not number among your clientele, but that you are naturally not interested in offering this service indefinitely.

"In reply I would say that for many years I have had an account with Messrs Hayden, Stone & Co., and though it has not been an active account it has always contained a surplus of cash over and above the securities in it. You can see the situation by looking up the matter in your books.

"Your letter indicates to me that I am receiving you Weekly Market Letter as a favor. I assure you that I appreciate the importance of this publication, but I do not wish to ask any favors and if you find it undesirable to send it to me I will be obliged reluctantly to concur with you in your opinion."

Penrose smoked cigars and, like most smokers, was particularly fond of certain brands. In October, 1925, he wrote to a firm in Broad Street, New York:

"I am writing to you at 60 Broad Street, New York, though I know that you have moved somewhere else, but not knowing your exact address I thought that this letter might be forwarded to you.

"I am writing to ask whether or not you still deal in those little Hamlet cigars which I have gotten from you for many years. Please do not consider this letter an order, as I am simply asking for information.

"If I knew your present address I would call on you some time when I am in New York."

The letter was forwarded, and by return mail he learned that the business had been consolidated with another firm and that the matter of the Hamlet cigars was being investigated. A second letter reassured him that the new firm could order the required cigar from Havana, but it would probably take a month for delivery. In the end, Penrose decided that "I doubt whether the manufactures of Hamlet cigar are still making just the brand and quality of this article that you used to have, but perhaps some time I can run across a substitute for it." He courteously wished the firm success, and there, apparently, the matter was dropped.

Except for fishing and, possibly, shooting, Penrose does not seem to have been much interested in sports. In a letter to J. Volney Lewis (July 5, 1921) he said, seemingly facetiously, "Now that the holidays are over and James Dempsey has won the prize fight, I suppose we can get back to work."

To Spurr, he wrote (May 31, 1923): "I have been ill for a few days and the doctors want me to change my habits and take up golf, but as I understand golf, it gets to be a question between sacrificing your work or the game, and so I am hesitating."

Less than a week later (June 5, 1923) he again wrote to Spurr that "I agree with you in not taking too much to golf. It is very good for people who have nothing else to do or who watch the daylight saving clock until 3 or 4 o'clock and then dash wildly off to chase a little white ball across a field. I think what will cure you quicker than anything else when you get on your feet will be to go fishing and do plenty, but not too much, walking. Fishing is really a wonderful diversion and to me a cure for many things. It takes your mind absolutely from your work, for otherwise the fish will escape, and it does not take an endless amount of time. . . . Don't forget going [to go] fishing. There is a cheerful and psychological element about it that few people recognize."

Also worthy of note is the fact that nowhere in his letters, diaries, or records is there mention of the theatre or opera or concert.

Another interesting side-light is indicated in a letter to Lewis (October 3, 1921) when Penrose says:

"I think you are right in delaying your departure for a few days, for I know by experience that there are not many things so disturbing as to start on a long journey and after your departure to remember many things that should have been done before going. The plan I usually follow is to fix a certain day for going, with the knowledge before hand that it is going to be about two weeks later before I get off."

"There is nothing like the high seas for a rest and for good fellowship," he wrote to another correspondent (May 29, 1925). "I suppose now, since your association with the French professor in Philadelphia for several months, that you will be talking French to everyone you meet in the streets of Paris; but I always found in the old days that your French was very good, when you wanted to use it. Perhaps Upton White would like a nice letter written by you in French, so that he can still further turn up the corners of that dictionary of his.

"Speck arrived here last week, and as usual, dashed wildly off to the west a few days later."

"I only wish that I was with you," he writes to a friend in Paris (June 9, 1925) "and could sit under some of those awnings on the boulevards looking at the city, which, as you say, is worth a visit at any time and at any age. The good old Hotel Continental which you mention reminds me of many pleasant visits I have had there myself.

"I hear that you have been having some hot weather in Paris. We have also been having it here in Philadelphia. For the past week the thermometer has risen considerably above 90, and for two days it was above 100. A cool highball under a Paris awning on a boulevard in Paris would have been a very pleasant addition to Philadelphia, but sad to say, it may be a long time before we can reach that stage of civilization. Perhaps some of those philosophical thoughts of yours with which you regale Judge Mellors and Doctor Baldy and other interested people, may throw some enlightenment on why a French city is always happy and an American city is so generally unhappy. In France you see the smiles and gaiety and in America you see the grouches and despondency. Can't you throw some light on this very difficult subject?"

In a letter to Dr. Robert N. Keely that same summer (July 13, 1925) Penrose states that he is "delighted to know that you are still enjoying what you most properly call 'the centre of civilization.' I wish I was with you so that I would have a little change from the centre of inquisition and ignorance.

"You will be interested to know that at the present time there is a wild legal fight going on in Tennessee as to the merits or failing of the theory of evolution, and particularly the descent of man. Your friend Mr. William J. Bryan, and many other eminent people of his kind have arrayed themselves against a remnant of common sense in Tennessee and in many other middle west and northwest states. I think before long they will probably hang Darwin in effigy.

"Many old ladies' clubs are very indignant to think that they should have come from monkeys; and many old men's clubs claim that they have not hair enough on them to show any origin of monkey parentage. Mr. Bryan I understand even points to the top of his head to show how impossible it would be for him to have had any kinship with a hairy-headed beast. If you were here your deep philosophical thought would undoubtedly help them unravel this problem; and that shaggy hair of yours might make you a valuable witness for the evolutionists. I do not, however, think that either the ladies or gentlemen in Paris are bothering very much as to whether they came from monkeys or not. There are many worse animals than monkeys to have come from and I have seen some people who call themselves human beings who would be less desirable as ancestors than monkeys—all of which goes to show that as soon as you quit this land of the free some freak discussion arises which needs your wisdom for its solution.

"Doctor Macalister sails for Europe some time soon, and perhaps you will meet him. I am glad you met Bill Brevoort and if you see him again I hope you will give him my best regards. Write when you have a chance, for it is always a pleasure to hear from you."

In an age apparently too rushed to be courteous, Penrose's unfailing and gracious courtesy toward all was outstanding. Whether he was thanking a fellow geologist for sending him a reprint of an article or sending his check in payment of a duly authorized expense, he managed to give to each letter an individual appreciation which must have pleased the heart of the recipient. Letter after letter among his files show this gift of individual courtesy. The following are chosen as representative:

Letter to Col. J. W. Carter, Silver City, New Mexico, dated January 23, 1925

My dear Colonel:—

On my return from a short absence I have found the very kind and cordial Christmas card from you and Mrs. Carter; and though I am late in acknowledging it I assure you that my expression of appreciation is none the less sincere.

I hope that everything is going well with you and that Silver City and its climate are as attractive as ever.

We have been having some genuine old-fashioned cold weather in the east, but we have many fine clear days, which often remind me of the days when we used to drive around Silver City in the winter time when the thermometer was hovering around zero. I hope some time to have the pleasure of coming there again.

With kindest regards to you and Mrs. Carter, and wishing you all the good wishes for the New Year, I am

Sincerely yours
R. A. F. Penrose, Jr.

Letter to Dr. Samuel N. Rhoads, Franklin Book Shop, Philadelphia, dated January 6, 1925

Dear Doctor Rhoads:—

I enclose my check for twenty-four dollars ($24.00) in payment for the accompanying bill for a set of Roger's Geological Survey of Pennsylvania in three volumes, and for the binding of them in buckram.

I thank you greatly for the trouble you have taken in this matter and I think the binding is excellent. It is strong and thoroughly in keeping with the volume.

I have been hoping to have the pleasure of dropping in to see you at 920 Walnut Street, but I have been so busy at The Academy of Natural Sciences that I have not yet had an opportunity to do so. I hope, however, to see you soon, for there are several other books about which I would like to consult you.

With best regards, I am,

Sincerely yours,
R. A. F. Penrose, Jr.

Letter to B. Dawson Coleman, of Philadelphia, dated December 26, 1924

Dear Dawson

This seems to be the time of year when people are sending around congratulations and best wishes that each other may live and prosper. I am therefore writing to you to tell you how greatly pleased I am that you have been elected President of "The Rabbit" and I also congratulate the members of "The Rabbit" on having you as their head. I am now sure that it has very many happy and successful years before it.

Sincerely yours,
R. A. F. Penrose, Jr.

Letter to Oscar Hecker, of Philadelphia, dated December 31, 1925

Dear Mr. Hecker:—

Again I have received your kind and thoughtful Christmas remembrance in the form of that extremely useful little calendar pad which you have sent me. It is surely the most useful little desk arrangement that I have ever seen for the purpose of keeping records of dates and it is also a constant reminder of your good will and graciousness.

With the compliments of the Season and wishing you the best of all good wishes for the New Year, I am,

Sincerely yours,
R. A. F. Penrose, Jr.

Letter to Professor W. O. Hotchkiss, University of Wisconsin, dated March 27, 1924

Dear Professor Hotchkiss:—

I thank you greatly for the reprint of your paper on "The Lake Superior Geosyncline" which you have so kindly sent me. I have read it with the greatest profit and interest and I congratulate you on the original manner in which you have treated this subject and the important points in geologic structure which you have brought out. Your paper certainly represents an important advance in the study of the Lake Superior region and I hope to see further publications by you on the same subject.

With kindest regards, I am,

Sincerely yours,
R. A. F. Penrose, Jr.

Letter to Dr. George A. Hoadley, editor, Journal of The Franklin Institute, dated April 11, 1925

Dear Sir:—

I am writing to thank you for the beautifully prepared "separates" of the addresses by Dr. Little on "The Fifth Estate" and by Professor Rutherford on "The Natural and Artificial Disintegration of the Elements."

I heard these addresses when they were delivered at the time of the Centenary of The Franklin Institute in September, 1924, and they struck me as being remarkable in their originality and comprehensiveness. I shall keep them as a record of the two subjects discussed and of the noted men who spoke on them.

I beg to congratulate you upon the excellent manner in which these papers have been printed and bound.

With kindest regards, I am,

Sincerely yours,
R. A. F. Penrose, Jr.

Letter to John W. Brock, Philadelphia, dated March 31, 1925

Dear Mr. Brock:

I have received the notice that you have moved your offices from the Bullitt Building to 1607 Walnut Street, and I am dropping a line to you to wish you every success and gratification in your new quarters.

We will miss you sadly in the Bullitt Building, for you have for so many years been identified with it that we have all considered you as one of the permanent tenants. I fully realize, however, that the trend of business in Philadelphia is westward, and though perhaps this does not make much difference to you, yet on upper Walnut Street you will be nearer to your home and to your other interests.

I hope to have the honor of dropping in soon to pay my respects to you in person.

With best regards, I am

Sincerely yours,
R. A. F. Penrose, Jr.

Letter to Messrs. Petzelt & Keyser, Philadelphia, dated August 14, 1925

Dear Sirs:—

I have just received the accompanying bill for $350.00 for painting and repairing my Marmon automobile, and I enclose herewith my check for three hundred and fifty dollars ($350.00) in payment of your bill.

I used the car for a short time this afternoon and I want to tell you how beautifully it looks and how well and carefully you have fixed it up.

Very truly yours,
R. A. F. Penrose, Jr.

Letter to John F. Lewis, Philadelphia, dated December 11, 1924

Dear Mr. Lewis:—

I thank you greatly for the copy of the Thirteenth Annual Report of the Art Jury which you so kindly sent to me. I have read it with much interest and profit; and parts of it I have gone over more than once so as to get a thorough conception of the deeds and the ideals of the Art Jury.

I admire greatly what you have already done and what you contemplate for the future. The Memorial Fountain in Logan Square representing "the Wissahickon and the Schuylkill" is very beautiful, and reminds me of the painting representing "The Nymphs of the Seine, the Marne and the l'Oise" by the artist La Lyre.

Your contemplated improvements in the Parkway, along the Schuylkill and elsewhere in the city, are all efforts for the public good, which I sincerely hope will soon be on their way towards accomplishment. I congratulate you most heartily and wish you every success in this great work.

With kindest regards, I am,

Sincerely yours,
R. A. F. Penrose, Jr.

Letter to Clare Walker Banta, Wells Fargo-Nevada National Bank, San Francisco, dated December 26, 1924

Dear Mr. Banta:—

Many thanks for the beautiful and unique Christmas card and especially for the cordial greeting which it carries. I greatly appreciate your kind thoughtfulness, and beg to extend to you the compliments of the season and the best of all good wishes for the New Year.

The picture on your card particularly interests me as showing steps in the development of the great Wells Fargo banking and express corporations. The phantom figure of the old pony express, indicating the beginnings of these activities, and the final clear-cut figures of the aeroplane indicating their most modern accomplishment, are extremely interesting. The old Wells Fargo express stages, and later the railroad trains, always carrying a Wells Fargo express car, were intermediate stages. Surely the name Wells Fargo & Company has from the earliest days stood for progress and fair treatment to all with whom it has come in contact.

Again thanking you, and with kindest regards, I am

Sincerely yours,
R. A. F. Penrose, Jr.

Letter to Thomas Willing Balch, Philadelphia, dated November 1, 1924

My dear Balch:—

On my return from a short absence I have received your very interesting book on Legal and Political Questions Between Nations which you so kindly sent me, and though my acknowledgement of it is somewhat late I assure you it is none the less sincere.

I read the book yesterday with the greatest pleasure and profit, and I think that you have set forth your subject in a wonderfully comprehensive manner. So many books of this kind are written in such deep and profound legal language that we laymen cannot understand them; but your book, on the contrary, is written in such good and clear English that even a mere geologist can read it and grasp your ideas.

The work is a worthy sequel to the other books on related subjects which you have previously written.

Again thanking you, and with kindest regards, I am

Sincerely yours,
R. A. F. Penrose, Jr.

Letter to The Editor, The Evening Bulletin, Philadelphia, dated March 13, 1925
Dear Sir:—

I thank you sincerely for the copy of The Evening Bulletin as of March 2nd containing a very kind and comprehensive account of my late brother Doctor Charles B. Penrose and the rest of our family, including myself.

I read the article when it first appeared with the greatest interest. I do not know who was its author but he was obviously a man who knew most of us well and who seemed to take a kindly pleasure in telling about the family. I beg that you will extend to him my deep appreciation of the article he has written.

With best regards, I am,

Sincerely yours,
R. A. F. Penrose, Jr.

Letter to Dr. J. Hall Allen, Philadelphia, dated October 21, 1924
Dear Doctor Allen:—

I have received your card announcing the removal of your offices to 515 South 15th Street and I am dropping a line to you to wish you every possible success in your new quarters. I remember well the great good you did me when I was suffering from rheumatism many years ago and I shall always appreciate your kindly treatment of that affliction.

With best regards, I am,

Sincerely yours,
R. A. F. Penrose, Jr.

Letter to Hugh D. Miser, State Geologist, Tennessee, dated September 16, 1925
Dear Mr. Miser:—

I have received the announcement of your appointment as State Geologist of Tennessee, and I am writing to extend both to you and to the State my most hearty congratulations.

Your wide experience on the United States Geological Survey and the excellent work which you have done for it render you particularly qualified to fill this position, and I assure you that I wish you every possible success in your future work in that State.

With kindest regards, I am,

Sincerely yours,
R. A. F. Penrose, Jr.

Letter to A. E. Carlton, Colorado Springs, dated July 13, 1925

Dear Bert:—

I thank you greatly for the annual report of the Holly Sugar Corporation which you have so kindly sent me. I have read it with the greatest interest and it has given me much information about the sugar industry in the particular districts to which it refers.

It seems a long time since I have seen you in the east, but I hope you will always remember that Philadelphia is still on the map and that a cordial welcome will always await you when you come this way.

With kindest regards, I am,

Sincerely yours,
R. A. F. Penrose, Jr.

Letter to J. McKeen Cattell, New York, dated January 3, 1924

Dear Doctor Cattell:—

I beg to extend to both you and to the American Association for the Advancement of Science my most hearty congratulations on your election as President of that organization. The American Association is most fortunate to have as its head you who have always been so prominent and active in the advancement of most of the subjects of human knowledge which it so efficiently promotes.

With best regards and wishing you every success in the continuance of your great and unselfish work in science, I am,

Sincerely yours
R. A. F. Penrose, Jr.

Letter to Dr. Herbert B. Carpenter, Philadelphia, dated June 5, 1925

Dear Doctor Carpenter:—

It gives me much pleasure to enclose my check for twenty-nine dollars ($29.00) for your kind professional services. This whole household felt a sense of satisfaction and relief after they had been vaccinated by such a skilful and efficient doctor.

With best regards, I am,

Sincerely yours,
R. A. F. Penrose, Jr.

Letter to the Proprietors of the Bullitt Building, Philadelphia, dated July 11, 1925

Dear Sirs:—

Last spring I was desirous of obtaining a little more space in the Bullitt Building and I was seriously considering the rooms left vacant last April by Mr. John W. Brock in the southeast corner of the fifth floor.

I spoke to Mr. William McMullan about this matter and he said he would hold them until I decided what I wanted to do. In the meanwhile, I have found that I will not need them, but I feel that I should make some payment to the Proprietors of the Bullitt Building for the time that Mr. McMullen has held these rooms awaiting my decision. I will be very glad therefore if you will send me such a bill as you think proper for my option on these rooms.

Very truly yours,
R. A. F. Penrose, Jr.

To this the proprietors replied that they "very greatly appreciate your attitude as therein expressed" but add that they "could not think of making any charge in the matter for so old and valued a tenant."

Letter to W. F. Ogburn, professor of sociology at Columbia University, who had sent Penrose a form letter requesting statistics concerning his family to be used in a study then being made, dated January 12, 1925

Dear Professor Ogburn:—

I have received your letter of December 29th enclosing a card for me to fill out concerning the dates of birth of my brothers and sisters and the dates of death of those who are not living.

I beg to say that there has never been a sister in our family, but that there have been several brothers, and I enclose herewith your card duly filled with the statistics for which you ask.

Wishing you every success, I am,

Sincerely yours,
R. A. F. Penrose, Jr.

Letter to LeRoy A. Owen, of Thomas Cook & Son, Philadelphia, dated March 6, 1925

Dear Mr. Owen:—

I have received your letter of March 5th enclosing bill for $40.50, covering cost of cable to Spencer Penrose via your Singapore office and the reply from that office to you that the cable had been communicated to him.

I enclose my check for forty dollars and fifty cents ($40.50) in payment of this bill and I beg to thank you extremely for the trouble you have taken in this matter. You rendered me valuable assistance in getting in touch with my brother at that time.

Sincerely yours,
R. A. F. Penrose, Jr.

Letter to Charles Penrose Keith, of Philadelphia, dated May 21, 1924

Dear Mr. Keith:—

When I met you in the street car a few days ago you asked me if I would find out at the Academy of Natural Sciences whether or not the large whale which is on exhibition there was the one which was caught in the Delaware River near Kensington about the middle of the last century.

I have investigated this matter and find that the whale which is on exhibition on the first floor of the Academy was one which was stranded off Ocean City, New Jersey, in 1911, and was presented to the Academy.

The skeleton of the whale to which you referred as having been caught at Kensington about 1855 or 1857 was presented to the Academy and the bones are still there, but it has never been mounted. I hope that when our present efforts at reorganization in the Academy are completed we may be able to have this second skeleton mounted and put on exhibition.

With best regards, and thanking you for the interest you have taken in this matter at the Academy, I am,

Sincerely yours,
R. A. F. Penrose, Jr.

Letter to Mrs. Arthur Clement, Seal Harbor, Maine, dated March 17, 1925

Dear Mrs. Clement:—

Your Christmas postalcard, addressed to Miss Jane Wallace, and sent to my office in care of me, was received some time ago, and I have been trying to find Miss Wallace, but without success. She was with my Aunt, Miss Lydia Penrose for many years, but she left years ago, and my Aunt died last spring, so that I can get no trace of her. I am therefore returning the postal card so that you may know that it reached Philadelphia but that I could not find Miss Wallace.

Hoping that everything is going well with you at Seal Harbor, I am,

Sincerely yours,
R. A. F. Penrose, Jr.

Letter to Miss Florence M. Braker, Philadelphia, dated May 13, 1925

Dear Miss Braker:—

I am sending to you today from Messrs. Caldwell & Company of Philadelphia a small gift which I hope you will accept as a wedding present in memory of your coming marriage, and with it I beg to extend to you the best of all good wishes for your future happiness and success.

It is an additional pleasure to make this small present, for not only I but the rest of us at the Academy greatly appreciate your loyalty and the efficiency of your work during the whole period in which you were connected with it.

Sincerely yours,
R. A. F. Penrose, Jr.

Even the renewal of his subscription to *The Pennsylvania Gasette* (October 15, 1924) called for something special:

"I enclose my check for $4.00 as my contribution to The Pennsylvania Gazette for the coming year; and with it I send to you my congratualtions on the excellent manner in which the Gazette is being maintained, as well as my best wishes for its future."

CHAPTER 20

Relations with the Geological Society

PENROSE'S relations with The Geological Society of America were of long standing. He was elected to the Fellowship in May, 1889, while a member of the Geological Survey of Texas, having been proposed by R. T. Hill, Alpheus Hyatt, and J. J. Stevenson. He is number 151 on the roll books of the organization, so that he was a member practically from its beginning (the preliminary organisation meeting having been held in December, 1888).

As already noted (chapter 6) he went with Branner to Indianapolis in the summer of 1891, where he read one of the two papers which he presented to the society, that one being on *The Tertiary Iron Ores of Arkansas and Texas*. The other paper was his presidential addres of 1930. He did make three other contributions to the *Bulletin* of the society, however, but they were all memorials—to Persifer Fraser, to Amos P. Brown, and to John C. Branner.

According to the records, he attended fourteen annual meetings in those forty-one years, those of 1899, 1900, 1902, 1906, 1909, 1920, 1921, 1922, 1923, 1924, 1925, 1926, 1929, and 1930. He recommended only four men for membership—he may have signed other nominations, but only four were elected. They were James Perrin Smith, of Palo Alto, Calif., recommended by Branner and Penrose, and elected in December, 1893; Thomas C. Hopkins, of Chicago, recommended by Branner, James Perrin Smith, and Penrose, and elected December, 1894; Noah F. Drake, of Tientsin, China, recommended by Branner, R. T. Hill, Penrose, and F. W. Simonds, and elected December, 1898; and John F. Newsom, of Stanford University, recommended by Branner, Penrose, George H. Ashley, and T. C. Chamberlin, and elected December, 1899.

Except for his attendance at five annual meetings, Penrose seems to have had no special interest in the society until he was elected Councilor at the annual meeting of 1913. In that capacity he served for three years—1914, 1915, and 1916. According to the record, he attended the Council meetings called for 1914—in January and December—and the only meetings called in 1915 and 1916, those of December.

The official record of that period of his service carries three entries. He was asked to form the local committee for the annual meeting held in Philadelphia in 1914. *Council Minutes* for December 28, 1914, carry this item:

"In view of the satisfactory financial condition of the Society and on account of the necessarily increased labor of administration, the Council voted, on motion of R. A. F. Penrose, Jr., to place the Secretary's annual salary[*] at one thousand

---

[*] This was not used as salary by the Secretary but for office expenses in connection with the Society.

dollars, beginning December 1, 1914. For the same reasons it was voted to increase the Treasurer's allowance for clerical hire to one hundred dollars per annum, beginning December 1, 1914."

At the same Council meeting, Penrose was a member of a committee composed of himself, Wallace W. Atwood, and Harry Fielding Reid, to consider the question of relationship to the American Association for the Advancement of Science. The committee recommended that "the G.S.A. meet with the A.A.A.S. and take complete control of the Section for four years, including the Chicago meeting of 1920, providing the officers of the Society become the officers of Section E and provided also that Section E be confined to Geology and a separate section be created for Geography." Evidently, nothing came of this recommendation, for the *Council Minutes* record that "there was a great deal of discussion and finally no conclusive action in the matter, the chief difference of opinion arising from an uncertainty as to the precise relations intended between the two organizations and the unwillingness on the part of some of the members to favor joint meetings with any considerable frequency."

In 1916, the minutes also show that "Dr. Penrose presented the matter of publication of a map of Brazil, prepared by Dr. J. C. Branner. Professor Atwood suggested that it be accompanied by a suitable explanatory paper." The map and paper were published in 1919, part of the edition in English and part in Portuguese.

In 1916, Penrose was a member of the Publication Committee.

In 1917, when William Bullock Clark, of Johns Hopkins University, died, considerable pressure was put on Penrose to accept the position of treasurer in the society, held by Clark since 1907. On October 5, John M. Clarke wrote:

My dear Doctor Penrose:

I regret very much your letter of October 1st, in which you express reluctance to accept the position of Treasurer of the Geological Society. There is no man as competent, and I really think that it would be a fine thing if you could, in such a capacity as this, get into a controlling touch with the organization. The only thing I can do in view of your statement is to send it on to the Secretary, Dr. Hovey, with a suggestion that you be asked to reconsider your decision.

I hardly know what to say about your enclosure for the expenses of this Committee*—cheque for $100. It is really needed, but I am most reluctant to let the work of this Committee impose upon your personal generosity and bigness of heart. Suppose I keep it temporarily until I can find out just what the Research Council is willing to do or able to do in regard to meeting these expenses? I have just returned from Baltimore and Washington and find that Mathews is much in need of help in getting his bulky but important Report on the Roads into shape, and I must in some way help him out. I think perhaps, so far as his need is concerned, the Executive Committee will respond. I am most appreciative of your extremely helpful disposition and act.

Very sincerely yours,
John M. Clarke

* Not a G. S. A. committee.

Clarke evidently wrote to Hovey that same day, for the next day (October 6, 1917) Hovey replied, thanking Clarke for Penrose's letter, and adding: "I hope to see him within a few days myself and lay the case before him from the standpoint of the council vote as it is coming in. Thus far I have received ten ballots nine of which are for Penrose."

Although Penrose was seemingly adamant on this subject, Clarke wired him on October 24 (1917): "You have twelve out of thirteen votes. Will you not change your decision." But Penrose would not change.

Because Penrose and Clarke were outstanding men in geology of their day and because the correspondence between the two men reveals interesting sidelights on the character of each, it is, perhaps, not amiss to insert at this juncture, some letters written during the last year of that friendship (Dr. Clarke died in May, 1925).

Letter from Clarke, dated Albany, N. Y. January 7, 1924

My dear Dr. Penrose:

Under another cover I am sending to you a photostat copy of an original letter of C. S. Rafinesque, written in 1853 while he was living at Philadelphia.

I do not know how many of Rafinesque's letters are extant, but I think very few indeed, and when I ran across this in a collection of letters which were addressed to Dr. Lewis C. Beck, Mineralogist of the old Natural History Survey of New York, 1836–1842, I felt that a copy of it should go to the botanical archives of your Academy.

Rafinesque, as you doubtless know, was an extraordinary genius and I am inclined to think that American botanists would like to have this letter published in full, perhaps photographically. The comments at the bottom of the letter were made by Beck himself. These do not appear in full as it would have been necessary to turn the page in order to get the rest of them.

With best wishes

Very sincerely yours,
John M. Clarke

Letter from Penrose, dated Philadelphia, January 17, 1924

Dear Doctor Clarke:—

I received some days ago your letter of January 7th telling me that you were sending me a photostat copy of an original letter of C. S. Rafinesque written in Philadelphia in 1853. The copy of this letter has not yet arrived but I am looking forward with much interest to seeing it when it comes.

I do not think there are very many Rafinesque letters extant and I am sure that the copy of the one you speak of will be very interesting. I greatly appreciate your kind thoughtfulness and will write to you further when the letter arrives.

With kindest regards, I am,

Sincerely yours,
R. A. F. Penrose, Jr.

Letter from Clarke, dated Albany, N. Y., January 21, 1924

My dear Dr. Penrose:

The photostat of the Rafinesque letter was sent to you in your official capacity as President of the Academy and it is probably in your office. Perhaps I should have sent it to Dr. Stone or you may decide that Dr. Stone should add it to his archives.

Very sincerely yours,
John M. Clarke

Letter from Penrose, dated Philadelphia, January 23, 1924

Dear Doctor Clarke:—

I have just received your letter of January 21st. Your most interesting photostat of the Rafinesque letter arrived only the day before yesterday. You were right in sending it to me at the Academy of Natural Sciences as I am there almost every day, and I am often in communication with it several times a day.

I have already handed the Rafinesque letter to the Academy as a gift to it from you, for I supposed from your previous letter that as a matter of course you sent it for this purpose. I assure you we all greatly appreciate it, not only for its interest and historic importance but also as a gift from a most illustrious member.

With kindest regards and again thanking you, I am,

Sincerely yours,
R. A. F. Penrose, Jr.

Letter from Clarke, dated Albany, N. Y., April 21, 1924

My dear Dr. Penrose:

Fate seems now to forbid my breaking soup and fish with you this year in honor of Benjamin Franklin. We get a flat tire once in a while for overspeeding. There is a chance of my meeting you in Washington, whither I ought to go for the occasion of the consecration of the new building and in order to pay my respects to the President of the United States, who is going to pontificate.

If I am unable to go to either place, I shall be sure to miss a lot of information about the atom which no home can be perfect without.

I left you feeling glad that I had not missed the chance to see you, but I presume if we had talked still later into the night we should not have gotten much further forward with that very important and appealing problem of substantial help to geological science.

You still cherish, I think, the hope that your Academy will now approach you in such a manner as to make it possible for you to carry out the splendid proposal you made to your Board of Trustees. In the passing phases of conversation I said something about a scientific exploring expedition into the heart of Gaspe, intimating that it might be done to the credit of your Academy and of yourself. Scientific explorations afford a never ceasing supply of important information and they have to be carried out under the auspices or through the agency of some well funded institution. It was quite obvious to me that you were not thinking along just such lines as I then suggested and I have, since seeing you, been pondering as to the way in which geologic science in this country could be served best.

Out of all the phases of geology, the one that has beyond question the most important bearing on the welfare of mankind is paleontology—the study of the evolution of life. The whole plan and doctrine of evolution would be a mere chip on the waves if it were not anchored by the evidence from paleontology. We have scratched the surface of the earth here and there and have run across some very tangible lines of evidence which cannot be discounted. Somehow, in my experience I have found nothing in science that inculcates so broad and complete a conception of the problem of human life as the data of paleontology and if I were king I should turn over all the revenues of my kingdom into the promulgation of this science.

Some years ago I made my will and left all that I have or might ever have to the support of students in this science. It was the expression of a good intention, but its execution would have been an injustice to others, so that will is dead and buried, even though the thought and purpose survive. Many years ago, too, I talked this matter over with Doctor R. S. Woodward, then secretary of the Carnegie Institution at Washington, as a proper subject for a Carnegie man. Doctor Woodward was sympathetic, has always been sympathetic with the project, even though his angle was, by training, different from mine. I discussed the matter before that with Mr. Carnegie, who was interested enough to see that it came to Doctor Woodward's attention, but there we are. These are among my failures. They are, however, ideas which have not been born in vain and I am sure the benefit which is to accrue to mankind from this science of ours can be measured best in terms of the life which has preceded us on this earth.

When you have reached this point in this letter you probably will be dancing around on one toe and wishing that it had rained too hard the other night for me to go out, but take the suggestion in good part and perhaps there may be something in it that will be worth your thought.

Very sincerely yours,
John M. Clarke

Letter from Penrose, dated Philadelphia, May 6, 1924

Dear Doctor Clarke:—

I must apologize for not having answered sooner your letter of April 21st, but between attending the meeting of the Philosophical Society here and the dedication of your new building at Washington and other meetings demanding immediate attention, I have been sadly delayed in my correspondence.

Regarding the establishment of a department of geology at the Academy of Natural Sciences of Philadelphia, you know from our previous talks and correspondence that my main object in accepting the presidency of that institution was to establish a geological department there. After almost two years experience I have found that the institution is not receptive and I now realize the futility of such an effort. At the same time I do not like to leave the Academy without doing something to improve it in some way, and hence my present attempt to make changes in its organization which will enable it to function better than now in scientific research along the lines—all purely biological—which it now cherishes so fondly. If I succeed in this I will feel satisfied to resign as president, knowing that I have at least contributed something to the welfare of the Academy.

I fully appreciate what you say about the importance of paleontology. I feel that it is the connecting link between life as it at present exists back through geologic times until it becomes more and more obscure and finally disappears in rocks which, so far as we know, carry no remnants of life. As paleontology necessarily involves a study of almost every other branch of geology, it seems to me the most comprehensive of all the earth sciences. When I get through the press of work at the Academy, and this will be soon, I hope to discuss this matter further with you.

Your remark in our conversation a few days ago about a scientific exploring expedition in Gaspe did not go over my head, as you think, but I stored the thought up for consideration at an opportune time.

It was a great pleasure to have seen you here even if only for a short time, and we missed you at the meeting of the Philosophical Society as well as in Washington.

With best regards, I am,

Sincerely yours,
R. A. F. Penrose, Jr.

Letter from Penrose, dated Philadelphia, August 27, 1924

Dear Dr. Clarke:

The volume on the "Devonian Crinoids of the State of New York" by Miss Winifred Goldring is most interesting and of very great importance. The presentation of the subject, the illustrations, and the general character of the volume are splendid. I thank you greatly for it and especially for your kind inscription, sending it to me as a "buttonhole bouquet."

The "lilies of the sea" were never treated with greater care or more beautifully than in this publication, and throughout it I can see the years of thought you have given to the subject and the master-hand of your genius. If you publish many more books like this I fear you will force me to become a paleontologist instead of a mere geologist.

Again thanking you and with kindest regards, I am

Sincerely yours,
R. A. F. Penrose, Jr.

Letter from Penrose, dated Philadelphia, September 5, 1924

Dear Doctor Clarke:—

I was very glad to get your letter of September 2nd and to know that you are coming this way at the time of the meeting of The Franklin Institute as a delegate from the University of the State of New York. It will be a great honor to the Institute for you to act as the representative of your great organization in Albany during the centenary celebration.

I expect to be here part of the time of the celebration, but as it lasts three long days I am not sure that I can follow out the whole programme because I have to be out of town part of the time.

I have been working hard all summer on the new organization for the Academy of Natural Sciences and this has been one of the hardest jobs I ever undertook, for it has been very difficult to reconcile conflicting opinions and prejudices and overcome the precedents from bygone generations. The task is at last completed, however, and has now only to go through the tedious process of formal adoption by the Academy. Unless unexpected oppostion appears the new system ought to be in thorough working order next winter. I feel a little worn out after spending all summer at this work, and for that reason it was my intention to go away for a few days about the middle of this month. This is what may prevent my being here at the whole of The Franklin Institute celebration. I am looking forward with pleasure, however, to seeing you some time during that event.

With kindest regards, I am,

Sincerely yours,
R. A. F. Penrose, Jr.

Letter from Clarke, dated Albany, September 10, 1924

My dear Dr. Penrose:

My plans have been considerably torn apart and I shall have to satisfy myself by coming down to represent my University for the colorful function Wednesday morning (it will probably rain!), take a little time on Pine St. to find a china cow and beat it for home, as my renewed and continuous fight for a new museum begins Thursday morning. Can we not arrange for luncheon together on Wednesday?

Sincerely yours,
John M. Clarke

Letter from Penrose, dated Philadelphia, September 11, 1924

My dear Doctor Clarke:—

I have just received your letter of September 10th and I assure you that it will give me the greatest pleasure to meet you here next Wednesday morning at what you cheerfully designate the "colorful function." I cannot understand why this particular kind of function should suggest academic costume, and in a "questionnaire" that I have received from The Franklin Institute we are asked to state whether we will be in academic costume or not, evidently suggesting that some people do not expect to be in this dress. I have a perfectly good academic gown, but I hope not to wear it.

I hope you will let me know as soon as you arrive here and that you will have lunch with me on Wednesday; and we can also try to find that china cow in the afternoon that you are looking for on Pine Street.

Late in the afternoon I am obliged to go out of town, but I have a number of things that I would like to talk over with you before you disappear again to take up your strenuous work for a new museum at Albany.

With kindest regards, I am,

Sincerely yours,
R. A. F. Penrose, Jr.

Letter from Penrose, dated Philadelphia, January 3, 1925

Dear Doctor Clarke:—

I was very glad indeed to have seen you in Ithaca and hope that you have arrived safely in Albany.

I have not forgotten your suggestion that I contribute $25.00 to a portrait of Doctor C. D. Walcott. He has always been a good friend of mine, and I assure you that it gives me much pleasure to enclose my check for fifty dollars ($50.00) instead of $25.00 as a contribution for this purpose. I sincerely hope that you will see fit to give the portrait to Doctor Walcott personally, and not to any particular institution. He will thus be able, if he wishes, to give it to any institution that he sees fit.

I have not yet heard from Professor Chamberlin since leaving Ithaca, but I am expecting some word from him on his arrival in Chicago. I saw him just before he left Ithaca and he did not think that he was seriously injured.

With kindest regards, I am,

Sincerely yours,
R. A. F. Penrose, Jr.

Letter from Clarke, dated Albany, N. Y., January 6, 1925

My dear Doctor Penrose:

You certainly do rise with the sun!

I have your letter enclosing your cheque for $50. for the Walcott portrait, but I have not yet got my Committee to agree to putting this project through. Perhaps your generous gift will be just the thing needed to help it to its conclusion. Some folks' eyes bulge so with important projects which may or may not get anywhere, that they are likely to forget the appropriate and timely thoughtfulness of one's neighbors.

If I fall down in this undertaking, the cheque will be duly returned to its master.

Very sincerely yours,
John M. Clarke

In a letter to Clarke dated January 15, 1925, Penrose says:

"The scientists of the State of New York surely live to good old age. James Hall, Mr. Luther [D. Dana Luther] and many others manifest the effect of righteous living and your salubrious climate. I hope that you as the peer of all of them may correspondingly exceed them in longevity."

Letter from Penrose, dated Philadelphia, February 9, 1925

Dear Doctor Clarke:—

I have received your letter of January 28th and regret greatly that you found it necessary to return the check for fifty dollars which I had contributed to the proposed portrait of Doctor Walcott because you found that other people were not responsive.

In these days when almost everyone is on such a mad selfish rush it is difficult to accomplish a kindly deed such as you contemplated. It is often surprising to me to find that certain scientific men believe that by some sort of Divine right the world owes them everything and that they owe the world nothing.

With kindest regards and hoping that eventually you may be able to carry out your ideas of a portrait of Doctor Walcott, I am,
Sincerely yours,
R. A. F. Penrose, Jr.

Letter from Penrose, dated Philadelphia, February 13, 1925
Dear Doctor Clarke:—

I thank you greatly for the cordial invitation, which doubtless came from you, to attend the private view of The Reconstruction and Restoration of the Ancient Fossil Forest of Gilboa, New York.

I only wish that I could be present on this occasion, not only to see the fossil kings of the ancient forests, but also to see the very live king of New York's geology; but a previous engagement here will prevent me from having the pleasure of accepting this kind invitation.

Hoping you are well, and with best regards, I am,
Sincerely yours,
R. A. F. Penrose, Jr.

That spring, Clarke returned to the thought of the Paleontological Institute. Under date of May 6 (1925) he wrote to Penrose that "The Paleontological Institute is the thing the world needs most. Like the Wistar Institute, it would sit above the noise and dust, and get right down to brass tacks. This earth is an apple and only such an Institute can squeeze the real juice out of it."

Penrose replied the following day (May 7, 1925):

"I agree with you that the Paleontological Institute is the thing the world needs most in scientific research today, but where can we get the men to work in it? Most geologists are digging for oil, coal, iron or other similar things, and I regret that in spite of numerous efforts I have not been able to get track of some one with sufficient scientific spirit to ignore these more material subjects. Even your friend, Dr. N. M. Fenneman, who once thought so little of economic geology, has now written a paper in Science on "A Classification of Natural Resources"! What are you going to do when such outspoken opponents of economic resources, and one of whom we trusted absolutely for pure research, begins to write on such subjects?"

A week later (May 14, 1925) Clarke wrote to Penrose that "when I got home I found that Professor Kemp had been here during my absence, as a messenger from the National Academy, carrying in his pocket the Thompson Medal. I feel rather queer about this award. I have no doubt it was given with the best heart on the part of my colleagues in the Academy, but I still entertain somewhat mixed feelings as to the propriety of awarding it to me."

To which, Penrose replied (May 16, 1925) that "it gives me the greatest pleasure to congratulate you as the recipient of the Thompson Medal. I can well understand that a man of your sensitive nature may have his doubts about the propriety of the award, in view of the fact that you were one of those who helped to inaugurate it, but I am very sure that those who gave it to you, and all your other friends in the geological profession, realize that you received it purely from your own merit and would really feel hurt if they thought you felt that there was any impropriety in your accepting it. I only hope that all the future recipients of this medal may approach at least to some degree the splendid standard of accomplishment which you have set."

Two days later (May 18, 1925) Clarke wrote his last letter to Penrose:
My dear Dr. Penrose

That was a very nice letter, which just came in. I shall put it away in lavender while I go off to the hospital for the summer. My performances in Philadelphia and before got me into serious trouble. Wish me good luck.

Sincerely yours,
John M. Clarke

On May 30, 1925, Frank P. Graves sent Penrose a telegram from Albany. It read:

Regret to inform you that Dr. Clarke passed away last night. Funeral Monday two thirty p.m. Will you act as honorary pallbearer.

Undoubtedly, Clarke helped Penrose in the crystallizing of his ideas with regard to a research institute, but however much he may have been impressed with the superior claims of paleontology, he still clung to the mother science which had been his for so long, to geology.

At the annual meeting in December, 1918, Penrose was elected first Vice-President of the Geological Society, and as such attended Council meetings in December, 1918, April 1919, and December 1919. On December, 29, 1919, together with H. E. Gregory and E. B. Mathews, he was a member of a special committee to prepare and submit to the Council a resolution or letter to the government authorities regarding the reported overcrowding of scientific departments at Washington. The committee's resolution was adopted.

In 1923, Penrose was a delegate of the Society to the Joseph Leidy commemoration meeting held in Philadelphia and the following year (1924) he performed a similar function for the Society at the centenary celebration of The Franklin Institute, reference to which was made in the foregoing Clarke correspondence.

Beginning with 1924, Penrose was a member of the Finance Committee of the Society until he became President in 1930. In 1928 he was a member also of the Special Finance Committee and the following year was a member of the Committee on By-Laws. It was at that time (1929) that the Society underwent its change of form to enable it to become a properly functioning body to receive trust benefits. Undoubtedly, Penrose worked so tirelessly and so enthusiastically for this change, because he saw here at last an opportunity to fulfill his dream of establishing a research institute in geology. None of this, however, did he breathe to his confreres, working always, so he said, that the Society might be established on "a better business basis."

E. B. Mathews, who was then treasurer of the Society and a fellow member of the Finance Committee, frequently consulted Penrose regarding investments. Indicative of his considered judgment is the letter he wrote to Mathews (October 27, 1924) in which he says:

"I have received your letter of October 24th relative to the suggested investment of some of the funds of the Geological Society of America in 'French External 8% bonds.' I feel that a scientific society should seek safety rather than high interest, and therefore I would strongly advise good American securities rather than foreign ones. All Europe is still in a ferment, and interest obligations to America there might be hard to get in a general disturbance. Moreover, our own Government is not particularly noted for protecting the financial investments of its citizens abroad. I would advise you therefore to avoid foreign bonds at present."

As already noted (Chapter 18) Penrose had established a medal for the Geological Society, similar to that of the Society of Economic Geologists. Its first recipient, as in the case of the other society, had been T. C. Chamberlin, and this award was made in December, 1927.

Correspondence concerning this medal of the Geological Society had begun immediately after the award of the S.E.G. medal in 1924, for on January 11, 1925, William H. Hobbs, head of the department of geology at the University of Michigan, wrote:

Dear Penrose:

I have meant ere this to tell you of my great satisfaction in your decision to found a medal for achievement in geology to be awarded by the Geological Society of America. It is a fine thing to have done and will, I believe, have excellent results.

With best regards,

Very sincerely yours,
Wm. H. Hobbs

Penrose replied (January 16, 1925):

Dear Hobbs:—

I was very glad to hear from you by your letter of the 11th. I had hoped to see you at the meeting of the G.S.A. in Ithaca in December, but was disappointed in not finding you there.

I think that perhaps the medal foundation to which you refer as having been made by me was an endowment for a gold medal which I gave to the Society of Economic Geologists a couple of years ago. By the terms of the gift it was to be awarded for pure research in earth sciences, so that the economic geologist might express his appreciation of the importance of research in his work in applied geology. The first award was made to Professor T. C. Chamberlin at Ithaca last December.

You speak of my having founded a medal for the G.S.A., and I assure you that though I have not yet done this I would take great pleasure in doing so, if they wish it. I have often thought of offering such an endowment to the G.S.A., because it is the mother Society of all similar organizations now active in the United States. Some time when I see Doctor Berkey I will talk the matter over with him.

With kindest regards, and hoping you are well, I am,

Sincerely yours,
R. A. F. Penrose, Jr.

Hobbs replied (January 22, 1925) that he was "delighted to learn from your letter that you would take great pleasure in founding a medal to be regularly awarded by the Geological Society of America. I think there is no question but Fellows of the Society would without exception welcome such a foundation. It is a very fine thing on your part, and it would be so recognized."

In his reply (January 26, 1925) Penrose stated emphatically that "I would like to have it very definitely understood that the work would be solely in pure geology and not in any kind of applied geology. In this connection, I might add that the medal which I founded for the Society of Economic Geologists was given with the understanding that it was to be given only for research in pure geology, my idea being that the award would manifest the recognition of the economic geologist to his associates engaged in research."

A few days later (January 28, 1925) Hobbs wrote again to Penrose, declaring once more that he was "much delighted at your willingness to found a medal in pure geology for the Geological Society of America. I have taken the liberty of forwarding your letter to Dr. Berkey so that the matter may be considered in regular form by the Council.

That same day (January 28, 1925) Hobbs wrote to Berkey:

Dear Berkey:

I enclose a letter from Dr. Penrose in which he promises to found a medal for research in pure geology if agreeable to the Geological Society of America. In previous correspondence I ventured to assure him that there was little doubt the Society would welcome such a foundation. I forward his letter to you for consideration by the Council.

With regards,

Very sincerely yours,
Wm. H. Hobbs

Berkey answered this letter; whereupon Hobbs wrote once more to Penrose (February 6, 1925) that "as I wrote you, I took the liberty of forwarding your

John M. Clarke

Penrose Medal of The Geological Society of America

letter of January 26th to Secretary Berkey. In his reply, just received, he says: 'It is hardly appropriate, perhaps, for me to raise the question with him until I hear directly from him. It would be eminently appropriate, however, for you to urge him to go ahead with it.' He adds, 'Am glad to know about it and we would undoubtedly welcome any move of that kind that Penrose would care to make.'

"The whole matter, then, is one of procedure, and I hope you will take the matter up directly with Dr. Berkey."

Letter from Penrose, dated Philadelphia, February 14, 1925

My dear Hobbs:—

Many thanks for your letter of February 6th. I note what you say about Doctor Berkey's remarks concerning a medal for the Geological Society of America and I will communicate with him on the matter. My idea for the medal would be that it should be made of gold and that it should not be given too often—perhaps once in three years. I would like to see it of a design which showed some originality and did not display the bust or name of any geologist of present or past times. I would also like to see it represent some allegorical subject which would be at the same time beautiful and dignified and which would be eminently symbolical of the activities and ideals of geologists in general, and of The Geological Society of America in particular.

Of course all these details would have to be decided upon by the Geological Society of America, and I have mentioned them simply to let you know what I had in mind; but I would like to provide that the medal should be given only for research in pure geology.

With kindest regards, I am,

Sincerely yours,
R. A. F. Penrose, Jr.

Letter from Penrose, dated Philadelphia, February 18, 1925

Dear Doctor Berkey:—

I hear that you are leaving New York on Saturday, February 21st, and I am dropping a line to you to wish you a pleasant and profitable trip to Mongolia and a safe return. We will all miss you during your absence but I can well understand the attraction of the wonderful field of research which you have in prospect.

In some recent correspondence with Professor Hobbs of the University of Michigan relative to the question of medals, I suggested one for the Geological Society of America to be given in recognition of pure scientific geology. My idea of such a medal would be that it should be of gold and should not be the ordinary commonplace representation of the bust or name of any particular person prominent in our profession in past or present generations, but that it should represent some allegorical subject which would be both dignified and beautiful and yet symbolical of geology.

I simply mention this subject now for your consideration, and we can probably take it up on your return.

With kindest regards, and again wishing you a most successful trip, I am,

Sincerely yours,

R. A. F. Penrose, Jr.

Berkey replied the following day (February 19) expressing his appreciation "of the offer that you have made to the Geological Society. Professor Hobbs had intimated that you had this mind, but I felt that it was not appropriate for me to take the matter up until it had first been broached by you.

"I can assure you, I think, that a foundation of this kind would be considered a great service by the members of the Society and the awards would be looked forward to as marks of real distinction.... Had you in mind that it should be awarded every year, or only for occasional, very distinguished services? These are matters of administration that you have thought of, no doubt, for you must have considered the whole question, also, in connection with the medal of the Economic Geologists.

"There is absolutely no question in my mind of the acceptance of the proposition by the Council, and I would appreciate it very much if you would work out a plan of administration that you think would fit the needs, that might be presented as a working basis at the same time that the general foundation is to be discussed."

Letter from Penrose, dated Philadelphia, December 22, 1925

Dear Doctor Berkey:—

On my return from a few days absence I have received your letter of December 15th and I am delighted to know that you have returned safely from your trip in Asia. I hope you had a successful journey and accomplished all that you planned to do.

I have read carefully what you say about my suggestion to you early in the year regarding the foundation of a medal for The Geological Society of America to be awarded for distinguished services in purely scientific geologic work. During your absence I have been thinking considerably about this matter and I assure you that I will be very glad to make the foundation for the medal if I can do it to the satisfaction of the Geological Society. My idea would be that the medal should be made of gold and that it should not be given at definite intervals, but that the Society should present it when it was pre-eminently deserved by some geologist who had accomplished remarkable work. This would give the medal more meaning and greater scientific importance than if awarded at specified intervals.

My idea of the design of the medal would be that it should not be the ordinary commonplace token displaying the bust or name of any geologist of present or former times, but that it should show some originality and should represent some more or less allegorical subject which would be symbolical of the ideals of those engaged in research in the earth sciences.

I am not yet sure whether I can come to New Haven at the time of the meeting of the Geological Society next week, but at any rate I will not be able to be there at the time of the first Council meeting on December 27th. It is possible that I may be able to come to New Haven on December 28th or 29th for a day or two, and if so I shall hope to see you and talk further about the matter of the medal. I am writing now so that, if you think proper, you may discuss the matter with the officers and members of the Council when you have an opportunity. If they approve of my offer I will be glad to submit one or more designs for their consideration.

With kindest regards, I am,

Sincerely yours,
R. A. F. Penrose, Jr.

Penrose wrote again to Berkey on January 15 (1926), saying that he "was sorry that I had only such a brief talk with you at the meeting of the G.S.A. at New Haven in December concerning the endowment of the medal of the Society.

"I knew from what you told me that the Council had accepted my offer to endow a medal, but I was not quite sure whether they desired me to suggest a design or whether they would prefer to attend to this matter themselves. Either course would be entirely satisfactory to me. My only wish is to do what the Council thinks best for the Society.

"I have one or two conceptions for what seems to me a dignified and at the same time symbolical medal which I would be very glad to offer, but I do not want either you or the Council to feel that it is a condition of my offer, for if the Council prefers, I would be glad for them to suggest the design.

"Some time when you have an opportunity I hope you will drop me a line and let me know what was the general feeling of the Council when the matter was discussed. Of course it is needless for me to add that in making the endowment I would expect to present the die to the Society, and also a sufficient fund to pay for the making of the medal in gold at such times as it should properly be given."

Berkey replied (January 20, 1926) that "the Council accepted your offer to endow a medal for the Society, and generously left the detail in the hands of yourself and the Secretary. Their only additional action involved the question of adequate endowment to make the medal permanent. The matter of design was referred to in your letter that was submitted to the Council, and was accepted in principle. Your ideas, therefore, are to be worked out with no limitation whatever.

"I note that you have worked already on the design, and when you are ready to go over this matter in more detail I will meet you at your convenience and we can talk it over. As you know, I am enthusiastic about the whole project, and am quite anxious that we have something fine to present. I suppose that we should work out the whole scheme in a definite form for formal presentation and acceptance by the Council at one of its meetings this year. I should think, then, that the proper step would be to have a standing committee appointed to make recommendations to the Council. I see no way to distribute the responsibility of administration outside of the Council itself. They should be held responsible, but the whole detail of administration ought to be worked out as a part of the report that we should make when the die is presented.

"Any time that you want to go over any part of the project I shall be glad to meet you."

Penrose replied on January 22, in practically the same vein as in his previous letters. On February 13 (1926) he wrote again to Berkey, reassuring him that he had "not forgotten about the medal for the Geological Society of America, and for the last two or three weeks I have been working with an artist to get the design in proper shape.

"My idea of the medal is to make it representative of geologic science in its broadest scope and to have it partake of the great natural features of nature rather than of anything small or local. I already have had prepared two or three designs along these lines, and when I arrive at something satisfactory I hope to come over to New York and show it to you."

Some time during the next six weeks the designs were completed and Penrose took them to New York to show Berkey, for on April 1 (1926) he again wrote to Berkey that "the preliminary work for the die for the medal of which I showed you the design in New York has been started and I hope it will be ready some time this summer.

"I have showed a plan of the medal to two astronomers, both of whom approved of it from an astronomical point of view. One of these was Doctor Miller, [John Anthony Miller] who has charge of the observatory at Swarthmore and is well known for his astronomical observations in different parts of the world. He spoke highly of the design and approved of the way in which the astronomical features had been handled.

"I would like some time soon to create the endowment for the making of this medal. As I told you some days ago in New York, the medal will contain approximately three ounces of gold, and I find that it can be made, including the cost of the gold and the inscription, for about one hundred dollars. I would like, however, to provide for more than this amount in case it might be needed in the future.

"Of course the medal may often not be given for intervals of several years; but my idea would be to provide a fund, the interest of which would permit the making of a medal once every year, and that if the medal should not be presented for a period of several years the income of the endowment fund should be allowed to increase in its own interest until a sufficient amount has accrued to permit the making of three gold medals. After that time I think the income of the fund, in excess of the amount required to keep up a reserve for at least three medals, might properly be used for the general purposes of the Society.

"I think that an endowment fund of somewhere around four thousand dollars ($4,000.) would considerably more than meet all costs, and I am writing to you now to ask whether you think the Council would prefer to have this money in safe securities, or to have it in cash and invest it themselves. If I send the cash in form of a check or draft I would like it to be deposited and invested promptly, so that the whole matter might become a closed incident.

"In transmitting the endowment I will be glad to send a formal letter presenting it to the Society and mentioning the conditions which we have discussed. At the end of such a letter my idea would be to insert a clause giving a great deal of latitude to the Council in changing these conditions as may seem desirable from time to time."

Tentative terms of endowment of the medal were drawn up and signed by Penrose on May 17, 1926, and, with only minor changes, were approved by the Council, and the donor gave his final consent on March 4, 1927. According to these terms, "Nominees for the medal shall be selected by the Council of The Geological Society of America, and may or may not be members of the said Society. Nominees for the medal may be selected from any nation or any race of people" In the final clause, Penrose states that "the sole object of the donor in making the gift is to encourage original work in purely scientific geology, and the one feature which he desires to emphasize is that the income from this fund shall be used only for this purpose."

In his letter transmitting the tentative terms of endowment, Penrose wrote to Berkey (May 19, 1926) that he would "follow the suggestion made in your letter of April 12th, that it will be better for me to invest it for the Society instead of giving the cash. I had at first intended to limit the amount of the fund to $4,000. in cash or securities, but I have thought that in the future the cost of producing the medal may increase, and therefore I think I had better enlarge the endowment fund by presenting $5,000. par value City of Philadelphia 4% bonds maturing in 1953. These bonds are legal securities for trust funds in this State, and would seem to me a suitable investment for the endowment fund of the medal. On the market today they vary in price from 99 to 100, so that the endowment will represent practically $5,000., the interest on which will be $200. yearly."

That there were additional costs in this procedure is shown by a letter which Penrose wrote (June 21, 1926) to John Ray Sinnock at the United States Mint at Philadelphia, and in which he says:

"I am enclosing my check for three hundred and seventy-five dollars ($375.00) as the final payment for your skilful and admirable work on the geological medal which you have just completed for me. You will remember that I sent you the first check of $375.00 a few weeks ago, so that this second one completes the payment.

"I also still owe the Mint their charges for making the gold medal and six bronze medals from the die, and also for their last copper plaque, for which I shall pay as soon as I get the bill. In addition to this I owe you for the six cases for medals which you have made for me, and for the engraving by Mr. Miller on the two old medals which he was so kind as to do for me."

Concerning the design of the medal, Penrose wrote Berkey (October 26, 1926) that he was "particularly pleased that they (the Council) approved of the design which I had worked up for the medal. The details of this design had been more or less in my mind for almost two years; but the problem I had to solve was to represent them in their proper degree of importance as geologic features. After many months of experimenting in different ways with the assembling of the material I wished to present, I found that the final design as shown in the medal seemed to accomplish my object."

What that object was he had already noted in his letter to Berkey of August 27, 1926:

"In the face, or obverse side, of the medal I have attempted to show what one might see if standing off in space and looking at the earth and the moon, with the earth so turned that it shows North and South America. The sun of course is used simply symbolically, because it is so far from the earth as compared with the moon that it would not be possible to put it in its proper astronomical position in a small space. The moon, however, is correct, as to the view which would come to one standing off in space.

"The idea of the medal is to show the gradual extension of the study of geology to the moon, and possibly to other planets; hence the title 'Geology, Terrestrial and Extra-Terrestrial.' I have tried to depict on the moon some slight concave spots, to represent the supposed volanic (?) vents and other topographic features.

"Surrounding the medal on the front side are a series of well-known fossils, which I selected as a border because they seemed appropriate to a geological medal, and also relieved the impression that the medal was an astronomical one. On the reverse side of the medal I have made the chief feature two volcanic cones, with the fumes coming from one of them as a recognition of physical and chemical geology, just as the border on the front recognizes astronomical geology and paleontology."

In a subsequent letter (February 3, 1927) Penrose adds:

"I note what you say about the geologic age of some of the fossils in the border of the medal. They are indeed mostly Mesozoic or Tertiary, but I had no special predilection for these forms over older ones. I found, however, that if I tried to represent a great diversity of geologic fauna I was going to get a somewhat bizarre and awkward looking border. In fact the most difficult matter which I had to decide in the design of the medal was this paleontological border, and I made many drawings before having reached the one which is now represented on the border. I regretted greatly to have had to leave out the poor old trilobites, but though I tried them in one of my drawings they did not work in well with the other fossils, such as I have used. My desire was simply to give recognition to paleontology as a part of geology, but not to trace life continuously in its long course from the oldest fossiliferous rocks, and out of consideration for the looks of the medal and the proper balance of the border I found myself forced to the fauna I adopted. This meant no disrespect for the older forms of life, but was simply an effort to design a medal dressed in presentable yet truthful clothes."

As already noted in Chapter 16, Penrose was delighted that Chamberlin was made the first recipient of the medal in 1927. He was equally pleased at the designation made in 1931, for, in a letter written a month before his death on July 31, 1931, he wrote to Berkey:

"I have received your communication sent to the members of the Council of The Geological Society of America formally announcing the award of the Penrose Medal by a unanimous vote to Doctor William Morris Davis. It is needless for me to say that I am greatly pleased at the selection of the nominee by the Committee on the Award.

"Professor Davis is one of the world's leading geographers and geologists and his researches have exerted influences of great importance on both these sciences. His creative mind and wonderful ability for research have led to his being considered the greatest worker in geomorphology, and his numerous published works illustrate not only his activity in geomorphology, but in geology, meteorology and pedagogy. I personally have known Doctor Davis for over fifty years; and year by year my admiration for him and for his constantly growing versatility increases. I think the Committee on the Award is to be congratulated."

This medal, designed and endowed by him in 1927, has become known as the Penrose Medal of The Geological Society of America. It is available, but not necessarily given, each year. In the twenty-three years which have elapsed since its endowment, the medal has been awarded twenty times, to men who head the Honor Roll of the Geological Society:

1927—Thomas Chrowder Chamberlin
1928—Jakob Johannes Sederholm
1930—François Alfred Antoine Lacroix
1931—William Morris Davis
1932—Edward Oscar Ulrich
1933—Waldemar Lindgren
1934—Charles Schuchert
1935—Reginald Aldworth Daly
1936—Arthur Philemon Coleman
1938—Andrew Cowper Lawson
1939—William Berryman Scott
1940—Nelson Horatio Darton
1941—Norman Levi Bowen
1942—Charles Kenneth Leith
1944—Bailey Willis
1945—Felix Andries Vening Meinesz
1946—Thomas Wayland Vaughan
1947—Arthur Louis Day
1948—Hans Cloos
1949—Wendell Phillips Woodring

On January 6, 1930, Penrose wrote to Berkey, acknowledging receipt of the formal notification that he had been "elected President of the Society for the year 1930.

"It gives me much pleasure to accept this election," he continued, "and I beg to assure you and the other Fellows of the Society of my deep appreciation of the honor thus conferred. I shall endeavor to maintain the high standard of this office set by the long list of illustrious geologists who have preceded me since the foundation of the Society.

"I thank you for your kind offer of co-operation and I assure you that I will be greatly pleased to avail myself of your efficient and always wise advice in the administration of the affairs of the Society."

That he did so fully, is shown in the letter which Berkey wrote him on September 4, 1930 that "no one in my time has shown so great practical interest in the welfare of the Society or has given so much careful thought to its plans for the future as you have. Any organization is fortunate if it has men who are willing to give so much of themselves to its welfare. Perhaps a larger number might do so if they did not become too easily overwhelmed with the responsibilities that belong to their various tasks in making a living or a place for themselves. I know, myself, how difficult it is to keep one's mind perfectly clear on any such interest in the midst of a variety of over-lapping and conflicting duties.... I am immensely concerned with the problem of the welfare of the organization. Except for that fact, I should have dropped most of my responsibilities in it long ago."

As he had done since 1928, Penrose contributed generously from his own funds for the conduct of the Secretary's office. He instructed the Secretary to investigate the possibilities and costs of a permanent and separate home for the Society in New York, and continually, throughout his year as president and in the six months that followed before his death, expressed his ideas concerning the Society and its future welfare. But never did he commit himself as to that future.

In view of the terms of his will, which was admitted to probate on August 6, 1931, it is interesting to note that on June 25th of that same year (1931) he wrote to Berkey that he thought "that the question of endowment might some time be considered. I have had this matter in mind ever since I began years ago to present small sums to the Society to help out the work of the departments of the secretary, the editor and such other offices as may require it. I have no doubt it would be a convenience to you to know sometime ahead, perhaps a year or two, how much you are likely to get during any current period. This is always a difficulty, unless the organization has an endowment of which it uses only the interest instead of the total capital of the gift.

"I think the special needs of the Society are in the departments of the secretary and the editor. Perhaps the treasurer may also require funds. The fact, however, that until the last three or four years the Society has been able to run fairly satisfactorily indicates to me that it is not at present in a desperate condition financially, but could be assisted to advantage by a further endowment.

"In regard to your suggestion about using an endowment fund for investigation, I would say that I have always understood that the Society has never made any special point of carrying out research investigations. Its objects have always seemed to me to be the meetings where members read papers and discuss with

The Aitken bust of Penrose

each other the relative merits of the subjects involved; also the publication of the results announced in the papers read at the meetings. I have always felt that the question of research and investigation is the work of members of other institutions which may report them to the Society at any of its meetings, and which may secure a dignified and lasting form of publication in the Bulletins of The Geological Society of America.

"Regardless of the uses to which the income of an endowment fund might be put, I do not see any possibility of raising such an endowment fund at the present time, as you suggest. Most people who would like to give to it are not able to do so, on account of the financial condition which exists today. Later on, however, it might be found well to start a small endowment fund, to which might be added gifts from time to time so that it would eventually become a power in the activities and efficiency of the Society. I beg, however, that you will understand that at the present time I am personally making no offer for any endowment fund. I will try from time to time to make small contributions to the Society, but it would be very unbusinesslike to attempt any endowment worthy of consideration under the present financial conditions of the country."

That same meticulous care for detail and sympathetic understanding for the exigencies attendant upon the successful conduct of a scientific society which Penrose showed as president of the Society of Economic Geologists, and which have been treated at length in that chapter, marked his year as president of the Geological Society of America.

Letters written in the six months between the close of his presidential year (December, 1930) and his death (July 31, 1931) manifest that continuing interest. On January 26, he wrote to Mrs. Miriam F. Howells, administrative assistant to Secretary Berkey, acknowledging receipt of a progress report by Herman L. Fairchild who was at that time engaged in writing a history of the Geological Society.

"I have read Professor Fairchild's communication with much pleasure," wrote Penrose, "and I am greatly pleased to know that he is taking so much interest in the matter. He is better qualified than anyone else to write this history, and I judge from his letter that he will keep actively at work on it until it is finished."

Later that year (May 28, 1931) he wrote that he would go to New York for a meeting with Fairchild concerning the book, saying "I can stay in New York all Monday afternoon, and also Tuesday if Professor Fairchild desires it. . . . It will save rushing Professor Fairchild too much in his work also. He has shown wonderful interest and activity in it and we do not want to work him too hard."

On the 25th of June (1931) he wrote to Berkey about the Fairchild book:

"As regards the final type and general style of the volume, I agree with you that Hobbs' book on 'The North Pole of the Winds' seems very satisfactory. The size of the volume I suppose should conform to the size of the Bulletin of the Society, but the type might be better, the margins more generous, and the paper of all things should be good. I think the highly glazed paper, such as is used by Holt & Company and in some of Putnam's books, often detracts greatly from the volume. Many publishers will tell you that illustrations can be printed only on highly glazed paper, and hence they make their whole text of that kind of paper; but it is a known fact that a dull paper of high quality can take the impressions of illustrations just as well as the glazed paper. In the case of Fairchild's volume, I do not suppose there will be any illustrations outside of the plates which may be inserted.

"I think that Fairchild's history of the Society will be a very valuable publication and will become a constant reference book in libraries and scientific institutions. The Society is fortunate in having such a man who has lived throughout the life of the Society to date and knows all its experiences; while we are also fortunate that it was your thought to ask him to write the history. I will be very glad to hear further from you as the development of this work progresses."

A fortnight later (July 8, 1931), Penrose wrote again concerning this matter:

"I have been thinking of the binding, the paper and the type to be used in the make-up of Professor Fairchild's book on the History of The Geological Society of America. If there is any shortage of funds in order to publish this volume I hope you will let me know, for I am much interested in it and will be glad to help out with its publication, after it has eventually passed the inspection of you and Mr. Stanley-Brown."

Again and again in those letters of 1931, Penrose refers to the fact he has "been suffering from an attack of grippe from which I am gradually recovering, but I find that the after-effects seem to be about as annoying as the acute attack." This sentence is in a letter dated February 12. On March 9, he wrote to Berkey that he was "still out of commission on account of the after-effects of the grippe, which I do not yet seem able to shake off.

"I have also received the copy of the Minutes of the various Council meetings held at Toronto in December, 1930," he continues. "The final meetings of the 1930 Council and the 'advanced' meetings of the 1931 Council were so much mixed up that I find a good deal of information with which I was not previously familiar, especially in the Minutes of the two meetings of the 1931 Council. Two resolutions on page 10 of the Minutes seem to me to be somewhat extraordinary, though as I was not present at the particular meeting of the 1931 Council at which these resolutions were passed, I of course do not appreciate the motive behind them. I refer specifically to the resolutions on 'Editorial and Publication Policy' and on 'Committee on Making Geology More Useful.'

"The resolution on 'Editorial and Publication Policy' providing that 'the president be empowered to appoint a committee to investigate the editorial and publication policy of the procedure of the Council' seems to me a somewhat revolutionary and unnecessary action. The editing and publishing of the Bulletins of the Society ever since Mr. Stanley-Brown has been Editor have been so admirable that they have commanded the respect not only of the members of the Society, but of all others who have had occasion to refer to the Bulletin. I cannot therefore understand why it is necessary to interfere with one of the departments of the Society which can be well left alone. There are certainly many other matters which could be given attention with more reason."

He makes no further reference to the other resolution, but in an earlier letter to Berkey (February 12, 1931), he wrote that he had "had a couple of letters from Doctor Lane telling me that he thought it would be well to appoint a committee 'to make geology more useful to the country' and suggesting that I become chairman of it. I felt that such an activity was one that was hardly within the sphere of The Geological Society of America, and moreover if the committee was appointed, its field would be so comprehensive that I would not for the present be able to give it the time it would require."

Not to many men is given the privilege of reaching the peak of their career at the very end of life. That Penrose considered the honor accorded him by the members of his profession in electing him president of The Geological Society of America the supreme one of his life is abundantly evident. Geology was not only his profession, but his first and only love. For that science he had worked in Canada, in Texas, in Arkansas, in Colorado, and he had been richly rewarded not only in published works but in the achievement of wealth from natural resources, especially in Arizona and Utah. Granted that Penrose had the advantage of social background and prestige, it was through his own efforts that he and the other members of his family acquired wealth from the mines of the west.

But always Penrose spoke of himself as a geologist, not as a mining man or a mining engineer or any of a number of ways he might truthfully have designated. Always he was a geologist.

He was interested not only in geology, but in his fellow man—man, not a family of his own, occupied his attention. One cannot have thoughtfully followed his comments in his letters and his diaries as recorded in this book without being impressed with this fact, seemingly so at variance with his retiring nature, but obviously so attractive to his thinking.

And so it was particularly fitting that his last published work, his most carefully prepared contribution, for it was to be presented to his peers at the greatest moment of his life—when he read his presidential address at Toronto, on December 29, 1930, seven months before his death—should deal with his two most absorbing interests:

GEOLOGY AS AN AGENT OF HUMAN WELFARE

From the earliest times in human history the economic and industrial activities of man have been changing the natural features of the earth's surface in many different ways, such as by constructing dams, by diverting the courses of rivers, by connecting oceans and seas with canals, by tunnels, by mining, by draining oil from the rocks containing it, and in many other ways modifying the natural course of geologic processes.

Much has been written concerning this material influence of man on the earth, but the opposite effect, that is, the influence of the earth on man, has received much less attention; and yet from primitive times it has been active. It seems proper therefore to note the action of geologic phenomena on man throughout the ages in which he has existed. These influences may be either beneficial or detrimental to man's welfare; they may advance his physical and mental development and his grasp on life, or they may form obstacles in his progress, and at times threaten his very existence. Though periods of slow development and even times of retrogression have occurred in human history, yet throughout the ages as a whole the change, especially in mentality, has been forward, and indicates that man has been able to adapt himself to such geologic surroundings as he has had to meet.

The earliest well authenticated remains of human life as yet known are in late geologic times, in the Pleistocene Epoch, during the last Great Ice Age, and in what is known in prehistoric archaeology as the Paleolithic Period of the Stone Age; but man or his predecessors may have been active among the animal life of the earth before those times.* The Paleolithic Period was characterized by the use of flint, chert, jasper and other materials of a flinty character, susceptible of being chipped into sharp-edged weapons or fashioned into other utensils. Ivory and bone were also used in a similar way, while various hard rocks, such as granitic materials, were often used for axes and heavy weapons.

Paleolithic man was a dweller in caves and other shelters formed by geologic action and is often referred to as the cave man. Had it not been for these retreats together with his flint and stone weapons, he might not have found protection from the elements and from his enemies in the form of other animals; and hence some of the early human races might have disappeared on account of the lack of assistance offered by geologic agencies.

In the caves together with the remains of Paleolithic man occur in different places those of the reindeer, the mammoth, the cave bear, the fox, the wild horse, the bison and other animals, mostly of forms now extinct. Drawings and paintings on the walls of caverns, as well as ivory carvings, indicate a degree of art among these primitive men which suggests an advance from a possible former less developed condition.

Previous to the Paleolithic times, in the Prepaleolithic or Eolithic Period, flint and other fragments chipped in a manner to suggest a crude handicraft, are often found in alluvial or subaerial deposits. Such materials frequently occur in formations much older than the Pleistocene and even in the Pliocene Epoch or earlier times. Many archeologists doubt their connection with mankind, while others believe that some of them at least are true artifacts. However this may be, it is a recognized fact that some undoubted artifacts occur in older geologic environments than those in which human bones have yet been found, and this suggests that the bones of remote primitive man who made them have decayed and disappeared, while his more resistant flint and stone implements remain intact.

Among the oldest human remains as yet known is a fragment of a lower jaw found in an alluvial deposit at Mauer near Heidelberg, Germany (*Homo heidelbergensis*) and supposed to belong to the beginning of the Pleistocene Epoch. This fragment as well as parts of a human skull found near Piltdown in Sussex, England (*Eoanthropus dawsoni*), are usually accepted as the two most ancient

---

* The present discussion relates to only distinctly human primates, as distinguished from what in remote times may have partaken of the character of both the anthropoid ape and man, such as the remains of the so-called ape-man (*Pithecanthropus erectus*) found near Trinil in Java.

evidences of human life as yet discovered. A more complete skull, but of vastly later date in the Pleistocene Epoch, was discovered in a cave in the valley of Neanderthal near Düsseldorf, Germany, and represents what is known as the Neanderthal man (*Homo neanderthalensis*). Somewhat later a complete skeleton of a similar human being was found in a cave near Le Moustier, France.

Human remains and implements resembling those found with the Neanderthal or Mousterian man, have also been discovered in many other places in Europe, North Africa, Arabia, Asia Minor, China and elsewhere. He seems to have thrived particularly during periods of recession in the several alternating advances and retreats of the Glacial Period, when the milder climate favored his development. He did not make pottery and did not use metals; he had no cattle or other domestic herds; he was a hunter living by the chase.

The Neanderthal man was succeeded in the latter part of the Paleolithic Period and the beginning of the Neolithic Period of the archaeologist by other races among whom the flint and other stone implements derived from geologic sources were more carefully finished and polished than in the preceding period. The Aurignacian, Solutréan and Magdalenian man thrived in these times. Copper implements made their appearance. Man began to emerge from caves, except where convenience made them desirable, he built shelters in the open, made pottery, and gathered together herds of cattle. Signs of civilization began to appear, and with it came the more and more modern races of man (*Homo sapiens*).

The caves which gave protection to primitive man depended largely on the character of the geologic formations which permitted the creation of these and other shelters. They were formed in many ways, but mostly in calcareous rocks through which surface waters impregnated with carbonic acid gas from the decay of vegetation percolated into cracks in the rocks, and by their solvent action created openings varying from small cavities to large caves, and frequently to great caverns. They are common throughout the world wherever limestone or other calcareous rocks exist. They often provided the early man not only with shelter but with water, for many such caves have springs or running streams within them; and sometimes they supplied him with food in the form of other animals which also had sought refuge there.

Caves which may at times have afforded shelter have also been formed by the beating of the sea on the rocks adjacent to the coast. This has occurred not only in limestone but in sandstone, granite, basalt and other materials which during the ages have succumbed in spots to the constant wear of the waters. In later times some of these coastal areas have been elevated, and the caves are found high up on the land. Other less frequent geologic influences may also have provided similar refuges for primitive man.

In North America caves and great caverns occur in many places, but they do not seem to have been used permanently as dwellings to the same extent as in Europe and Asia. The human remains sometimes found in them seem to be there as a result of accident or temporary necessity throughout bygone ages but do not show signs of permanent habitation. This may be due to the fact that the ancestors of the American Indian when they migrated to this continent had reached a stage in civilization that enabled them to construct their own habitations without resorting to the primitive shelters of caves.

The cliff dwellers in the southwestern part of the United States and in Mexico represented in a certain way a class of cave man, inasmuch as their habitat was in the rocky cliffs of canyons, but they were of comparatively recent date, and in no way connected with the cave man of the Stone Age of Europe and Asia. Many archeologists believe that they date back only from several hundred to a few thousand years. They seem to have been an early part of the great family of Pueblo tribes which now inhabit the open country in the same neighborhood as are found the remnants of the old cliff dwellings.

These dwellings were sometimes caves in the faces of the cliffs, or were artificial structures built by man on shelves of rock in similar localities, or were combinations of both. Some of the caves were enlarged by man into capacious dwellings or even underground villages. Flint instrumets and utensils are numerous, as well as bows and arrows, pottery, baskets, personal ornaments and other decorations, many of them not unlike those made by the modern Pueblo tribes.

The cliff dwellings were used not only as shelters, but also for the storage of corn and other products of the field, as well as for religious ceremonies and for burial places. They are mostly high up on the cliffs, several hundred or a thousand feet above the lowlands, though some are down near the water level. The cliffs themselves consist of a great variety of rocks, including sandstone, various calcareous materials, shale, basalt and eruptive tufa.

Though we thus see that the cliff man had no relationship with the cave man of primitive times, yet his preservation, or at least his protection, was due to similar geologic conditions of environment, which supplied not only shelter but flint and other materials for his utensils, and rock for the buttressing of his habitation.

Volcanic action has always had a marked effect on man and his destiny. It has generally been of a tragic character, due to the sudden upheaval of volcanic materials and the destruction of human life and property, but often its aftereffects have been beneficial to human welfare in returning desirable materials from great depths to the surface of the earth.

Volcanoes occur in many parts of the world, being particularly abundant in the regions of the Pacific Ocean. In the Malay Archipelago they are so numerous and enormous that it has often been called "the rookery of volcanoes," while elsewhere through the Pacific regions they are abundant not only on the land, but especially on the sea bottom. In Mexico, Central and South America, in the West Indies, in Iceland, Europe and many other parts of the world they are among nature's most spectacular manifestations of unrest.

Mount Vesuvius has been studied in its eruptions for almost 2,000 years, and hence its history gives us more enlightenment on the effect of volcanic action on man than other regions where eruptions have only been investigated in later periods. Until the first century of the Christian era Mount Vesuvius had been considered an extinct volcano and had been inactive during historic times, so that the neighborhood with its salubrious climate and wonderful soil had become thickly populated.

About the year 63 A.D. numerous slight earthquake shocks were felt in the vicinity of Mount Vesuvius and these gradually increased until without warning, in the year 79 A.D., Mount Vesuvius itself broke out in a more violent eruption than it has ever developed in later times. The materials thrown out consisted mostly of volcanic ashes and dense clouds of steam and gases. The ashes overwhelmed the cities of Pompeii and Herculaneum and other places, and so sudden was the upheaval that many of the inhabitants were suffocated and buried in the volcanic materials. It is probable, however, that the loss of life was not so great as at first believed, and we know from the letters of Pliny the Younger, that a large part of the population fled to the sea at the first dreadful shock of the outburst, and thus escaped the annihilation which befell those who were more tardy.

The uncle of Pliny, known as Pliny the Elder, a noted naturalist of his time, was then in command of the Roman fleet in the waters of that region. As soon as the volcanic outburst began he put into shore to rescue the refugees, but was overcome by fumes and ashes and died like many of his countrymen. The younger Pliny describes the occurrence in a letter to the Roman historian Tacitus, and tells how he himself refused at first to leave the shore because he wished to save his uncle, but when convinced that this was impossible, he led his mother and others out of the danger zone.

In other regions than Mount Vesuvius even greater catastrophes have befallen humanity as the result of volcanic action. In Iceland, in the year 1783, a tremendous eruption of the volcano Skaptar is said to have destroyed about one-fifth of the population of the island by the direct results of the outbreak and the famine which ensued. Even more loss of life and property has occurred in the great volcanic eruptions in the Malay Archipelago and other places, but their historic records are less definite than in countries which have been longer studied.

In 1772 the volcano Papandayang in the Malay Archipelago broke out with such force that the upper 4,000 feet of the cone are said to have been blown off and thrown broadcast, destroying over 40 villages. The most enormous eruption known, however, was that of the volcano Tamboro on Sambowa Island, near Java, in 1815, when actually many cubic miles of material are estimated to have been thrown into the air, destroying life and property throughout the region, while the clouds of ashes and gases obscured the sky for hundreds of miles distant. In 1883 the volcano Krakatoa in the Strait of Sunda, between Sumatra and Java, broke out in an enormous eruption throwing ashes to great heights and over vast areas. The atmospheric disturbance was felt around the whole world, and the seismic waves accompanying the eruption overwhelmed the coasts of Java and Sumatra, causing great loss of life. The volcanoes of the Hawaiian Islands are frequently in active eruption, and the spectacular outbreak of Kilauea in 1924 is well known to all of us, while Mauna Loa, the greatest of all Hawaiian volcanoes in size, is noted for the frequency and vastness of its lava flows.

The foregoing remarks have described only the disastrous effects of volcanic action on mankind; but there is another and more cheerful side to the problem, and that is, the beneficial effects. It has often been asked why the agricultural populations around Mount Vesuvius and Mount Etna, after being driven from their abodes and after their villages and vineyards had been destroyed, have almost always returned when an eruption subsided. One reason for this is the natural reluctance of people, particularly in Europe, to forsake the salubrious climate and rich soil which have in previous days rendered them prosperous and happy; but a particular reason is that the materials composing volcanic ash and lava are remarkably rich in fertilizing substances, such as phosphates and various other salts of calcium, sodium, potassium, iron and other elements important to vigorous plant growth. In the warm, moist climate of southern Italy and Sicily the volcanic ash and lava rapidly disintegrate and the fertilizing constituents are set free, thus creating a soil often far richer than the one that had preceded it, which may have been more or less exhausted by the continuous cultivation for generations.

The disintegration of lava on Mount Etna is often artificially assisted by encouraging the growth of a large native cactus which rapidly takes root in the cracks and fissures of the rock and by its expansive power tends to disintegrate it and hasten its decay. On both Mount Etna and Mount Vesuvius the stone quarries worked in the hard lava form an additional source of income to the owners of the surrounding vineyards. Hence we find that the inhabitants of these volcanic regions flee in terror when eruptions occur and destroy all they own, but respond to the lure of the old home and return full of hope, with a knowledge that future prosperity awaits them.

Volcanic eruptions also restore enormous quantities of carbonic gas to the atmosphere, and thus replace that which has been absorbed by plant life and certain animal organisms. They also raise from deep-seated sources large quantities of water, often in the form of vapor, and thus return it to the surface.

In early historic times volcanic eruptions were regarded as something mysterious and uncanny, suggesting that the end of the world was approaching, or that the gods were angry, or that something altogether mysterious had occurred. In the flight of the population from Pompeii during the eruption of 79 A.D., the general outcry of the people was that there were no more gods, for they and the earth and its inhabitants were headed direct for everlasting ruin. In later times, however, man began to investigate volcanic eruptions in a more self-composed manner, and the modern scientist who has devoted himself to volcanism has shown that they are purely local manifestations which can even in some cases be anticipated.

The influence of earthquakes as a geologic agent affecting man is very marked, not only by the great destruction of life and property, but by the mental effect of shock and terror which often deeply impresses itself on the minds of those who escape with their lives.

They occur in many parts of the world, in Europe, Asia, Africa, America and elsewhere, but are most notable in the region of the Pacific Ocean. Though they attract particular attention on the land, yet a far larger number occur on the sea-floors, especially in the Pacific, the West Indies region of the Atlantic and elsewhere. These submarine earthquakes often give rise to immense waves, popularly known as tidal waves, which, however, have no connection with tides. They are caused by sudden changes in the level of the sea-bottom, which either force vast volumes of water upward, or let similar quantities downward, in either case transmitting their motion to the surface and thus creating immense waves. The so-called tidal waves there are well termed seismic waves, as indicating their origin in seismic disturbances. They often roll onto the adjacent land, causing as much devastation as if the earthquake had occurred on shore, and sometimes more.

The destructive aspect of earthquakes has been manifested in many great seismic movements which have become records of horror in the history of human fatality. Among some of those familiar to most of us may be mentioned the great earthquake at Lisbon in Portugal in 1755 followed by an overwhelming seismic wave whereby the city was reduced to ruins, with the loss of 30,000 or 40,000 people. In Japan numerous earthquakes have occurred, and in fact most of that country is in a constant condition of greater or less vibration. The last of its great outbreaks was the terrible catastrophe of 1923 at Tokyo and Yokohama, in which 100,000 lives are supposed to have been lost. Almost equally disastrous earthquakes have occurred in many other places.

In regions closer to our home may be mentioned the series of earthquakes in 1811 in the Mississippi Valley, about 50 miles below where the Ohio River enters the Mississippi. The principal disturbances were near New Madrid, Missouri, but others also occurred on the east side of the river in Kentucky and Tennessee. In places the land sunk many feet, and for brief periods the Mississippi River actually flowed backward in its course as a result of the collapse of its bed. The disastrous earthquake at Charleston, South Carolina, in 1886, is well known to many of us, and both it and the Mississippi earthquake were in regions where earth movements of such magnitude did not seem probable.

The great earthquake in California on April 18, 1906, was of all others in America in historic times preeminently notable in its extent. The movement followed for some 270 miles or more a great fracture zone extending along the coast. It was mostly horizontal and the displacement varied from a few inches to over 20 feet. Fence, fields and roads were thrown out of line. In San Francisco the water mains were broken, and a large part of the city was burned from lack of water to quell the fires which started in many different places. Here, as often in other earthquake disasters, the loss of life and property was due not so much to the earth movements as to the fires which were started as a result of them.

It has generally been found that the greatest destruction by earthquakes occurs in soft ground, either of an alluvial character, or such as is made in cities by filling up hollows with debris of various kinds, and known as made ground; while on the higher land, particularly on the rocky parts, catastrophes are much less severe. This is doubtless due to the fact that the amplitude of vibration in an earthquake movement is much less in solid rock than in loose material, so that a structure built on a mountainside may be only damaged, while one built below on soft material may be reduced to ruins. This feature was particularly noticeable in the earthquake at San Francisco in 1906. The principal destruction was on the water front along the Bay of San Francisco, while higher up on the hills where residences were built on rocky foundations the earthquake itself produced much less damage, but the fire which followed the earthquake spread death and destruction in both the lower and the upper parts of the city.

The earthquake at Valparaiso, Chile, on August 16, 1906, only a few months after the California disaster, extended along the coast for some miles; and as in San Francisco, the greatest destruction was caused in the soft or made ground along the water front of the bay, while the structures on the hills back from the lower city were much less injured. The lower city was almost completely destroyed, and when the speaker visited it shortly after the earthquake, efforts to restore it had only begun. The estimate of the people killed varied from 4,000 to 7,000.

On a hill but little above the lower city in Valparaiso, a large cemetery was located where graves were thrown open and great numbers of coffins hurled down the hillsides into the streets below, causing fear and panic among the people, who thought the time of resurrection had come. The keeper of the cemetery is said to have gone insane at the sight. Rain was falling in deluges at the time, with much thunder and lightning, so that the scene was indeed terrifying to everyone, and even at the time of the visit of the speaker but few people would discuss the situation which had left such a lasting impression on their memories.

Mention might be made of many other earthquakes which have taken their toll of life and property, and have had a lasting and painful mental effect on those who survived; but just as in volcanic eruptions, the scientific study of their nature has to some extent abated the feeling of terror and helplessness which they inspire. In earthquake regions man is learning to reduce the danger by selecting proper locations for buildings, suitable materials for their construction, and above all, by endeavoring to provide water supplies that may survive earthquake shocks and thus be used to quell the fires which cause more loss of life and property than the seismic disturbances themselves.

The erosion by rivers has a twofold effect on man, one beneficial because it creates vast areas of alluvial soil available for agricultural purposes, and the other harmful because it creates floods, often accompanied by great destruction of life and property.

In the upper course of a river the current may be swift enough to keep the channel clear of the lighter sediments, but in its lower parts the waters may move more sluggishly as they pass through a lower country before they enter the sea; and hence the sediments instead of being entirely carried on sink partly to the bottom of the river. This constant accumulation of silt gradually raises the level of the river bed and the waters overflow, often spreading over vast areas and depositing a rich alluvial soil wonderfully adapted to agricultural purposes.

Hence from prehistoric times large communities have grown up along the lower parts of many rivers, especially on the broad deltas at their mouths, and thus these alluvial regions have often been important geologic influences in the early migrations of man. Among such regions in Europe may be mentioned the thickly inhabited deltas of the River Po, the Danube, the Rhone and other streams, while the enormous delta lands in Africa and Asia are preeminent in size and historic interest, notably those of the Nile in Africa, and of the Euphrates, the Tigris, the Indus, the Ganges and the Brahmaputra in India. The great alluvial region in ancient Mesopotamia and Babylonia, lying between the Euphrates and the Tigris rivers, was once so widely populated that it was known as the cradle of civilization. It supported many ancient cities, such as Ninevah, Babylon, Nippur, Ur, Bagdad, and numerous other once prosperous communities.

One of the greatest delta lands in the world is that of the Yellow River, Hoang-ho, in eastern China, which from remote ages has supported a vast population.

Though the streams which have formed great alluvial plains have at times brought happiness and prosperity to the inhabitants, yet they have only too often also brought great loss of life and property. Where agricultural communities and other settlements have grown up, embankments have been made to restrain the river floods; but as the sediments continue to settle and the river beds continue to rise, the embankments have to be built higher and higher. Ultimately in time of high water the embankments may be broken down and the surrounding lowlands may be subjected to great floods. Hence the efforts of man to confine rivers to definite channels and thus to reclaim for agricultural purposes the fertile floodplains which were nature's provision to accommodate the excess water when the rivers rose, have often been accompanied by great catastrophes.

When the floods subside, however, the breaches in the embankments are often repaired, the people return and agriculture proceeds as formerly. This process of reconstruction is often repeated time after time as new breaches occur, and thus a somewhat precarious but highly lucrative agriculture is continued often for ages.

The frequent floods in the lower Mississippi River illustrate such occurrences. The first embankments or levees near New Orleans, about 150 years ago, were some 4 feet in height, but as the river bottom rose they had to be built up several times that high. The levees have been extended northward up the Mississippi River for many hundreds of miles and throughout this great distance numerous breaks frequently occur. Hence the disastrous floods and loss of life and property in the Mississippi Valley which shock the country at frequent intervals.

In other lands many similar results have attended attempts to confine rivers to narrow channels and prevent them from overflowing their natural floodplains. The River Po in Italy has been embanked for so many centuries that its bottom is many feet higher than the surrounding lowlands, and disastrous floods have at times followed breaks along its course. In China the Hoang-ho has often broken through its embankments with enormous loss of life, and many of us can remember the great flood of 1887 along this river, in which more than a million, perhaps several millions, of people were lost.

In ancient times in other parts of the world, many of the old embankments were abandoned and are now found only in a condition of decay. Their history of disaster is lost in the vagueness of bygone ages.

The mineral products of the earth have probably been of more material benefit to mankind than any other single geologic influence. Even the men of the Stone Age were careful to open quarries where the best flints for their implements could be found. The character of different flints was closely inspected, and in fact this material was in many ways to primitive man what iron and steel are to modern man.

During the latter part of the Stone Age and following it, weapons and utensils of copper made their appearance among prehistoric man. Still later came the use of bronze and this was followed by the Iron Age, in which a greater impetus to human welfare than in all previous times started and still continues to be a dominant factor in man's progress.

The beginning of the use of copper, bronze and even iron is involved in greater or less obscurity in different localities, and doubtless the use of each was dominant at different times in different parts of the world. In fact, flint or stone implements were often used by backward races after others had long since begun to make implements of metals. In Neolithic times copper began to be used before flint was discarded. The advent of the use of metals, however, has always supplied the necessary element for rapid human progress; more things, greater things and quicker things were accomplished by the use of metals than by the flint and stone implements of primitive man.

The modern age includes both the use of iron and of many other metals, so that we exist in a time which though preeminently one of iron, is also marked by the extensive use of copper, lead, zinc, gold, silver, nickel, aluminum, tin and many other metals, while to these must be added the numerous alloys, such as brass and bronze, which are made from them. Hence the present times are characterized more by human handicraft in fabricating metals than by the use of any one of them, and may well be termed preeminently the age of manufacture.

To the metals now used must be added other materials of a geologic character which have advanced human welfare, such as natural fuels, including coal, petroleum and gas, without which the efforts of modern man and his accomplishments would have been much retarded. We must also consider the stone for structural and ornamental purposes, and many other geologic materials which have affected human welfare, such as soils, springs and water supply, and the rapidly increasing and enormously important use of waterfalls and other moving waters in generating power.

Space does not permit a full description of the mode of occurrence of these geologic products nor of the details of many other similar subjects that come close to man, but well can it be said that while the man of primitive ages developed only slowly in great periods of time, yet through the utilization of metals and other geologic products and geologic conditions, mankind in a vastly shorter time changed from a savage living solely by the hunt to the civilization of ancient historic times, and thence to that of the present day. In the Stone Age his efforts were engrossed in a struggle for existence against the elements and the wild beasts that surrounded him; today, with his actual existence assured against these dangers, his efforts are devoted to constructive endeavors and to defending himself not against the beasts of the forests, but against the ferocious attacks of the hostile elements of his fellow man.

A knowledge of at least the general principles of geology is an important part of any liberal education and is essential in many scientific, literary, artistic, engineering and other pursuits of the present day. Nevertheless geology was the last of the great fields of research in natural history to receive scientific attention. Biology was well developed before the basis of geology on which it was founded received recognition. This was doubtless due to the fact that animal and plant life were more immediately noticeable to the casual observer than the nature of the rocks below, and thus scientific study began on the surface objects which attracted most attention; but as the spirit for research increased it tended to seek deeper and deeper below purely superficial manifestations, and thus revealed geology. Until the beginning of the last century the science of geology in its modern interpretation was hardly recognized as more than the vague conception of a few dreamers; today it demands the attention of the world as the basis of all human knowledge of natural history.

Those who have a knowledge of geology have a vast educational advantage over those who have none, for to them every continent, ocean, river, mountain, valley and even every creek, field or sand bank, has a meaning, which greatly increases their interest in the observation of nature. To the man who has no geologic knowledge, continents and oceans mean only land and water, valleys and mountains mean only hollows or elevated spots on the ground, and the various minor details of the earth's surface are looked on indifferently as things that occur as a matter of course, and may be convenient or objectionable, according to his line of thought.

The geologist interprets his science in a form that makes clear the dependence upon the earth of man and his best attainments in civilization, and he realizes the fact that the problems of human life and living are bound up with the problems of geology. Geologic history and the great records of evolutionary processes which it embodies not only in physical and biological aspects, but in psychological, social and economic lines, carries a wealth of instruction unequaled in any other field of learning. As geology becomes rounded out to a still greater fulness it will teach the world profound lessons in the evolution of the highest products of life and thus will have surpassing value in the education of mankind.

CHAPTER 21

Relations with the American Philosophical Society

THE story of Dr. Penrose's relations with the American Philosophical Society was prepared by Edwin Grant Conklin, Secretary of the American Philosophical Society from 1901 to 1908, Executive Officer from 1936 to 1942, and President from April 1942 to April 1945, and again from April 1948 to date.

His contribution is as follows:

In the same year in which Dr. Richard Alexander Fullerton Penrose, Jr., was born (1863), his father, R. A. F. Penrose, M.D., Professor of Obstetrics and Diseases of Women and Children, University of Pennsylvania, was elected a member of the American Philosophical Society, and he continued to be a member for forty-five years until his death in 1908.

The minutes of the meetings of the Society contain no record of his active participation in those meetings, but it is safe to assume that he prized the honor of membership in America's premier learned society and in common with other Philadelphia members contributed to the entertainment of non-resident members and guests at the more notable meetings and celebrations of the Society.

Among these celebrations during the period of the elder Penrose's membership was the one-hundredth anniversary of the granting of the Charter of the Society, held in 1880; the one-hundredth anniversary of the death of Franklin, 1890; and the one-hundred and fiftieth anniversary of the founding of the Society, held in 1893. Other notable meetings that called out all local members of the Society were held at intervals, whenever distinguished foreign members, such as Lord Kelvin or Sir Archibald Geikie, were present. And when the Annual General Meetings were established in 1903, with their large attendance, the local members provided the lavish entertainment offered.

There can be no doubt that the son and namesake of Dr. Penrose knew much of the American Philosophical Society during these years of his father's membership, and that, in common with scholars in general and Philadelphians in particular, he looked upon membership in this Society as a most distinguished honor. His older brother, Charles B. Penrose, M.D., Ph.D., LL.D., Professor of Gynecology in the University of Pennsylvania, was elected to membership in the Society in 1909 and continued in membership until his death in 1925, but there is no record in the minutes of the Society of his having taken any active part in the business or meetings of the Society.

Dr. Richard A. F. Penrose, Jr., was elected a member of the Society in 1905, the second year after the establishment of the Annual General Meeting in April, when election to membership was given additional significance by its being held only during the Annual General Meeting and also by the limitation of the number of persons who could be elected in any one year to fifteen. He formally accepted membership and signed the Laws a short time after his election, thus promptly indicating his gratification at this recognition of his scientific standing. He had at that time been assistant geologist on the geological surveys of Arkansas and Texas, geologist in charge of mining on the United States Geological Survey, Professor of Economic Geology at the University of Chicago, an editor of the *Journal of Geology*, officer in several mining companies, and author of approximately sixty scientific articles and books.

In the year following his election the two-hundredth anniversary of the birth of Benjamin Franklin was celebrated at the Annual General Meeting of the Society, with the active cooperation of the United States government, the Commonwealth of Pennsylvania, and leading learned societies, scientific institutions, and universities throughout the world. This was in many ways the most colorful meeting ever held by the Society, and there can be no doubt that the volumes and published report of this meeting left a lasting impression on the new member, as they did upon all members and guests of the Society.*

Although he read no papers at the meetings, Dr. Penrose took an active part in the business of the Society. He was an active member of the Committee on Publications from 1906 to 1926, and during this long period of service he read and reported upon the acceptability of certain papers offered for publication. He was elected a member of the Council for the term 1908–1911, and again for 1913–1915. He was also a member of an informal but very important Committee on Policy which formulated plans for the future of the Society and especially for a proposed new building on the Benjamin Franklin Parkway. During the active campaign for funds for the new building he made a small contribution for this purpose. But it is reported that he was so much annoyed by persistent appeals of representatives of the company which was employed to raise funds that he warned one of the solicitors that he would give nothing if he were further annoyed. However, his interest in the larger plans of the Society, if not specifically in a new building, is indicated by his letters to President Francis X. Dercum, congratulating him on the publication, "Mankind Advancing," which was used in that campaign.

In 1909, Dr. Penrose was elected to membership in the Wistar Association, that innermost social organization of members of the American Philosophical Society, to which his brother Charles was also elected in 1915. This Association had its origin in 1799 or 1800 in the Sunday evening parties for distinguished scientists and literati held at the home of Dr. Caspar Wistar, at Fourth and Lo-

---

* Penrose did not attend this meeting, for that spring of 1906 was the period of his trip to Africa, from February 6 to July 4. *See* Chapter 14.

cust Streets, Philadelphia. Dr. Wistar succeeded Thomas Jefferson as President of the American Philosophical Society in 1815, and the Wistar parties were held on Saturday evenings from 1811 until the death of Dr. Wistar in 1818. Thereafter, the Wistar Association was formally organized, consisting of twenty-four members of the American Philosophical Society, and their successors elected by the Association to fill vacancies caused by death or resignation. Each member, in turn, gave a Wistar Party for other members and invited guests. At first these parties were held on Saturday evenings, from October to May; later, they were reduced to one in each of these months, and the time was shifted to Friday evenings. The centenary of the Wistar Association was celebrated by a notable party in the Hall of the American Philosophical Society on May 4, 1918, and both Penrose brothers were among the hosts on that occasion. There is reason to think that the cordial social association of the Wistar Parties left a lasting impression on Dr. Penrose. He prized his membership in the Society and was proud of his family's connection with it, but there's no real evidence that he contemplated making the Society one of the chief beneficiaries under his will. It is said that he consulted no one with regard to the drafting of that will, which was dated June 12, 1930, slightly more than one year before his death on July 31, 1931.

By the terms of that will, after making certain minor bequests, he left the bulk of his estate to the American Philosophical Society and the Geological Society of America, in equal parts, with only one restrictive clause: "Both of these gifts shall be considered endowment funds, the income of which only to be used and the capital to be properly invested."

Both the size of his estate and its allocation to these two societies came as a great surprise. His relations with the Geological Society of America had been close and helpful, as has been recorded in the preceding chapter of this book. He had given the officers of that Society many intimations of his desire to establish a Geological Institute, but there were no similar intimations of his intention to endow the American Philosophical Society. However, he was thoroughly familiar with the past history and present work of the Society and especially with its general meetings, with the annual assembly of scholars and the presentation of papers from every field of science and art. It seems not unlikely that in making his will the broad character of the work of the Philosophical Society appealed to him as complementary to the specialized field of the geological sciences, which represented his own field of research.

Everyone who knew Dr. Penrose was aware of the fact that he disliked show and publicity and that he held high ideals of genuine research work. Consequently, the Committee on Policy of the American Philosophical Society decided that the income of the Penrose Fund should be devoted largely to the promotion of knowledge through investigation. As a result of several meetings of this Committee, the following recommendations were made to the Society:

"Any memorial to Dr. Penrose should consist of evidence of major advances in knowledge made possible by use of the Penrose Fund. It is suggested that decision regarding the actual form of this memorial be made later in the light of experience gained during the first few years of operation of the fund. Such a specific suggestion is found in the minutes of the Committee on Policies of January 14, 1933, as follows:

" 'USE OF FUNDS FOR ADVANCEMENT OF KNOWLEDGE THROUGH INVESTIGATION

" 'Advancement of knowledge through investigation should be built upon present plans of the Society through development of researches naturally arising in relation to reports and discussions presented in connection with meetings of the Society. The Committee therefore recommends that funds set aside for the advancement of knowledge through investigation be applied to continue development of meetings by the Society on the highest possible level through selection of outstanding topics which may represent the interests of both science and the humanities. The Committee suggests development of these meetings by securing the ablest speakers and investigators to be obtained and the use of adequate funds for expenses of such persons invited. It further suggests use of funds for aid in investigation on studies or questions to be presented through carefully arranged programs of the Society. The Committee therefore recommends specifically:

> " 'That there be set aside from the funds of the Society such a sum as may be required for the handling of the meetings, with the expectation that this amount would not be less than $5000 per year.
> " 'That there be set aside from the funds of the Society an amount not less than $20,000 per year to accumulate as a fund for use in advancement of knowledge through investigation, with the assumption that plans for development of the meetings and work of the Society as described above would be considered in the use of this fund.

"In order that the funds appropriated for the advancement of knowledge through investigation shall be administered with that wisdom which requires a background of experience, a continuity of policy, and an objective consideration of proposals, the Committee recommends that:

"A standing committee of at least five members, preferably with at least one representative from each of the four Sections (Classes), shall be appointed by the Council to make final recommendations to the Society in regard to appropriations for the advancement of knowledge through investigation. It is suggested that these members be appointed for overlapping terms of three years with possibility of reappointment.

"*Character and Cost of the New Society Building.* With realization of the advantages which will accrue from a new and adequate building, and with careful consideration of the relative values and obligations involved in such a building and in the activities of the Society, the Committee recommends:

> That the cost of the proposed new building for the Society be kept within the amount actually available in the building fund. That if the funds above specified are inadequate the building be reduced to fit the fund, or the building program be deferred until adequate funds are available.
> That the income from the Penrose Fund may be used in the building pro-

gram only for the furnishing of the building and to an amount not to exceed $100,000.

"*Publications of the Society.* Since publications form a vital part of the Society's policy and program and a part in which the Society has unique opportunities, the Committee recommends:

That funds be set aside from the income of the Penrose Fund for support of publications.

"*Library of the Society.* It is suggested that under this heading there be included the specific recommendations of the Library Committee, with such modification, if any, as the Committee on Policies shall prescribe."

Thus, it is apparent that the Society decided at once that while the income of the Penrose Fund should be used to support all the regular work of the Society its principal use was to be for the "advancement of knowledge through investigation." A new standing committee, representing many fields of learning, was authorized to administer this function. This committee is now incorporated in the revised Laws as the Committee on Research.

In the distribution of the Penrose estate to the principal beneficiaries, his library, documents, letters, and memorabilia were allocated to the Geological Society of America, as being more specifically of geological value and therefore more useful there than at the American Philosophical Society. Consequently, the latter society has only a small amount of his correspondence and manuscripts, as well as the records of his official connections with the Society. Under these circumstances, it seems necessary and desirable to confine this chapter to the uses which the American Philosophical Society has made of the Penrose Fund.

Report of the Principal Uses of the Penrose Fund by the American Philosophical Society

Every phase of the life and work of the Society has been improved and stimulated by the use of the income from the Penrose Fund. First of all, it enabled the Society to take possession of the whole of its building, much of which had been rented for necessary income before the receipt of this bequest.

From the time when "Philosophical Hall" was completed in 1789 until 1932, the whole of the first floor and parts of the basement had been rented to various civic and commercial enterprises. In the earlier years, even the meeting rooms of the Society on the second floor were shared with other scientific or learned societies. A third story was added to the building in 1890 for the accommodation of the Library, but this was soon greatly overcrowded and many of the books had to be stored in safe-deposit vaults. It was, in large part, this overcrowding of the Society's rooms while other portions of the building were rented for income that gave point to the drive for a new building. The general membership of the Society, recognizing the unique character of "Philosophical Hall" and its location on Independence Square, dreaded the proposal to abandon this shrine of science and learning for a marble palace on the Parkway. The resolution, quoted above, not to spend more than $100,000 of the income of the Penrose Fund for the new building, and that only for furnishings, and the fact that the estimates for the new building were well above the funds pledged for that purpose, joined with legal difficulties as to title to some of the land on the Parkway, led the officers and members of the Society to vote at the General Meeting in April 1935 to abandon the projected new building, to remain in our historic home, and to find new quarters for the Library in its vicinity. Fortunately, the latter was made possible by renting space in the Drexel Building, immediately opposite "Philosophical Hall" on Fifth Street. The recovered rooms in the first floor and basement of the Hall have been appropriately restored and equipped for lecture hall and executive offices, and practically all the contributors to the fund for a new building consented to the transfer of their gifts to the general funds or to the research funds of the Society. Thus, these funds have been increased by approximately one million dollars.

The Penrose bequest thus came in the nick of time to enable the Society to decide to devote its resources 'to the promotion of useful knowledge' rather than to the glory of the Parkway. There can be no doubt that this decision would have met with the hearty approval of Dr. Penrose, who cared more for genuine research work than for vain show. While the Penrose bequest marks the turning point in this policy of the Society, it is only fair to record that the leader in the many and difficult adjustments made necessary by this change of plan was the President of the American Philosophical Society at that time, the Hon. Roland S. Morris.

All the work of the Society has been stimulated and enlarged by the Penrose Fund, for, while it was wisely determined that the major portion of the income from that fund should be used for the "advancement of knowledge through investigation," it was also decided that that income might be available for the meetings, publications, and library, which also contribute to the advancement of knowledge.

Meetings. The meetings of the American Philosophical Society are now among the most interesting and important assemblies of scholars in America. In the early days, attendance at meetings was confined almost entirely to local members and occasional guests. Members from a distance rarely were present in person, their participation in meetings usually consisting of letters or 'communications'. Under these circumstances it was possible for local members to meet frequently in small numbers. Until the present century, meetings were held regularly on alternate Friday evenings, from September to June, but with the removal of residence of most of the local members from the center of Philadelphia it became more and more difficult to get a quorum of members present at the meetings.

Early in the present century the plan was adopted of having monthly meetings instead of fortnightly ones, and in 1902 the Annual General Meeting at the end of April each year was instituted. These general meetings at once became a great success, but the stated monthly meetings languished. At the General Meetings it was the custom of local members to provide luncheons and dinners, and sometimes accomodations at homes or hotels, for members and guests from a distance.

But the greatly increased attendance of out-of-town members and guests at the General Meetings made this delightful hospitality a burden on local members. Therefore, it was voted by the Society in 1934 to provide such entertainment from the funds of the Society, and this unique feature of our meetings has contributed greatly to their popularity.

The former unequal burden of entertainment placed upon Philadelphia members as compared with those from a distance was also reflected in the membership dues of the two groups. During the last decade of the nineteenth century and the first three of the twentieth all members who resided within thirty miles of Philadelphia's City Hall were assessed ten dollars; other resident members, five dollars; while foreign members paid no dues. When it became no longer necessary to collect the relatively small sum derived from annual dues, the Society decided to cancel, at least for the present, all membership dues, and thus to enhance the honor of membership by divorcing it completely from financial contributions. No other learned society in America is so completely and exclusively an honor society as the American Philosophical Society. However, it is expected that all members will recognize the increased obligation which this honor places upon them to render some valuable service to the society which has so signally honored them.

In place of stated monthly meetings of the Society, each limited to a single evening and drawing members from only a small area, it was decided in 1936 to hold two general meetings a year, each extending over two or more days, with original communications, lectures, and symposia, together with receptions, luncheons, dinners, and, hotel accommodations for members from a distance. The Annual General Meeting, held toward the end of April, extends over three days and is the principal meeting of the year. At this meeting the annual election of officers and members is held and the chief busines of the Society is transacted. The principal evening lecture at this meeting is the R. A. F. PENROSE, JR. Memorial Lecture, which carries an honorarium of two hundred fifty dollars. These lectures have been given by leading scientists, scholars, and publicists of this and other countries. At these general meetings, there is usually held a symposium on some timely topic.

The Autumn General Meeting is usually held in November and, in addition to communications, lectures, and symposia, gives opportunity to recipients of grants to present in person the results of their work. Important business of the Society at this meeting includes the consideration of the budget for the following calendar year and the canvassing of the four classes for candidates for membership, together with actual meetings of the Committee on Membership.

In addition to these two general meetings of the Society, a midwinter meeting is frequently held in the month of February, at which representatives of various societies, educational, and scientific institutions, and other organizations are brought together to exchange opinions and, if possible, to formulate conclusions regarding specific problems.

The first of these midwinter conferences were held in February 1937, at which representatives of thirty-five organizations met to discuss "Methods and Results of Grants in Aid of Research." The consensus of opinion of this meeting was favorable to the plans adopted by the Research Committee of the American Philosophical Society, and valuable methods for cooperation among organizations which make grants in aid of research were established. The midwinter meeting of 1938 was devoted to problems of the "Publication of Research." In 1939 there was a joint meeting with the Franklin Institute, devoted to "Progress in Astrophysics" and in memory of Elihu Thompson. In 1940 the centennial celebration of the "Wilkes Exploring Expedition" was held, and in 1941 the centenary of "Geomagnetism in America" under the leadership of Alexander Dallas Bache was celebrated. In 1942 the first of two important meetings on "The Early History of Science and Learning in America" was the topic, and that of 1943 was a discussion of "Post-War Problems." In 1944 a symposium on "Taxation and the Social Structure" was held and in 1948 the theme was "Frontiers in Human Relations."

Publications. In the field of publication the Penrose Fund has greatly enlarged and improved the work of the Society. In addition to the increased volume of work published in the *Proceedings* (23 volumes, 1933-1950) and *Transactions* (18 volumes, 1933 to 1950), a new series, the *Memoirs*, was started in 1935 for the publication of monographs of book length, which are generally too extensive for publication in periodical journals. In the course of fifteen years, twenty-seven of these volumes of *Memoirs* have been issued.

The annual *Year Book* of the Society was started in 1937, to contain the Charter and Laws, lists of officers, committees, and members, minutes of the meetings of the Society, reports of standing committees, lists of representatives at celebrations, awards of prizes, obituaries, etc. In previous years many of these items had been included in the *Proceedings*, usually under roman pagination, and the Charter, Laws, and lists of members were issued in separate pamphlets from time to time. The increased activities of the Society made necessary much longer reports of committees, and the desirability of separating this business of the Society from the scientific and learned articles in the *Proceedings* led to the establishing of the *Year Book* series. A large part of each issue is taken up with brief reports from recipients of grants from the Penrose Fund, every such recipient being expected to present for publication in the *Year Book* an abstract of the work accomplished with the aid of his grant. The thirteen volumes issued to 1949 contained from 398 to 494 pages each, and the general usefulness and importance of the *Year Book* have been abundantly demonstrated. The annual budget provides from $20,000 to $30,000 for all these publications, drawn in considerable part from the income of the Penrose Fund.

The Library. The Library of the American Philosophical Society is especially rich in records of the early history of science and learning in America, in long series of the proceedings and transactions of other learned societies, and in a unique collection of historically valuable documents, manuscripts, letters, etc. Among the latter the archives contain more than eighty percent of all the known writings of Benjamin Franklin, as well as many letters and manuscripts of other scholars, scientists, and statesmen in the early history of this country. In addition to these unique features the Library for many years collected current monographs and journals in all fields of learning, even though these were found also in other libraries in Philadelphia.

In the general reorganization of the Society following the Penrose bequest, it was decided to avoid as far as possible useless duplications with other libraries and to strengthen and enlarge the unique features of the Library. In accordance with this policy, many letters, manuscripts, and publications bearing on the early history of science and learning in America have been and are being acquired. Largely by means of the Penrose Fund the Society has been able to add to its already universal collection of Franklin letters and documents, his correspondence with Richard Jackson in London before and during the War for Independence, and his more personal and intimate correspondence with his favorite sister Jane Mecom, and with Catherine Ray Greene, whom he met through his sister and with whom he corresponded throughout his long life. The archives of the Society now include an unrivaled collection of the writings of Benjamin Franklin.

A notable collection of letters bearing on the origin of species and the general theory of evolution has recently been acquired, including 177 autograph letters of Charles Darwin to Sir Charles Lyell and 277 letters to Lyell from 26 other scientists; also a microfilm of the Darwin letters and papers at Down House, Kent, acquired through the courtesy of the British Association for the Advancement of Science. Other important collections of Darwin letters are being considered, all of this made possible by means of the Penrose Fund.

The *Library Bulletin* of the American Philosophical Society is now printed in the *Proceedings* while the report of the Committee on Library appears in the *Year Book*. These call attention of scholars to the unique or rare collections in the Library, thus making them better known to investigators. This new library policy, as well as the more commodious location of the library in its present quarters, has been aided in part by the Penrose Fund.

Research. The largest expenditure from the income of the Penrose Fund has been for the "advancement of knowledge through investigation." The budget has appropriated for this purpose from seventy-five to eighty-five thousand dollars and, in addition to this, the incomes of the Johnson Fund, amounting at present to twenty-eight thousand dollars, and of the Daland Fund, of thirteen thousand dollars, have been made available to the Committee on Research for the support of research in special fields.

The Committee on Research now consists of fourteen members, representing that number of different fields of research. They are nominated by the President and elected by the Council for a term of three years. All serve without compensation other than for their actual expenses in attending meetings. Five meetings are held each year, and from twenty to sixty applications for grants are considered at each meeting.

The following general principles have been adopted by the Committee:

1. Grants are made only for the promotion of research in the fields of scholarship.
2. Grants are not made toward the payment of salaries of members of the staff

of an educational or scientific institution. It is expected that such institutions will cooperate by furnishing for the investigation at least necessary general laboratory, library, office facilities, and secretarial assistance.

3. Grants are not made for professorships, fellowships, scholarships, or in general for work on doctoral theses. They are not given for usual or permanent equipment of the institution involved. Special apparatus of lasting value purchased by means of a grant shall become the property of the Society; to be returned to the Society when the project for which it was purchased has been completed.

4. Projects, methods of procedure, places where the work is to be done, and cooperation of the institution where the research is to be conducted and of other institutions or agencies should be clearly stated.

5. Projects requiring long continued support are not in general assisted.

6. Any publication of work supported in whole or in part by a grant from this fund shall state in connection with the title that the work was supported by a grant from the particular fund of the American Philosophical Society from which the grant was made, and a copy of such publication shall be sent to the Society.

7. As a general policy the funds allocated to each project are disbursed quarterly by the Society to those in charge, unless the nature of the work requires a different arrangement.

8. Reports of expenditures from grants are expected semi-annually, and a report of progress shall be made by the grantee to the Committee on Research annually. A summary of the results accomplished shall be presented to the Society for publication in its YEAR BOOK when the research for which the grant was made is completed.

9. No recipient of a grant shall thereby become an employee of the Society.

These principles and limitations have grown out of the experience of the Research Committee of the American Philosophical Society and have been approved by other organizations that make similar grants in aid of research. The proposal has been made that fellowships or professorships be established, but to do this equitably in an organization covering so large a field as does the American Philosophical Society would require a great deal more money than is available; besides, other serious difficulties are involved in such a proposal. The question of a few large grants instead of many small ones has also been carefully considered and the conclusion reached that more good can be accomplished with less risk of serious loss by making many grants of moderate size rather than a few large ones. No absolute limit has been placed on the size of any grant, but, in general, it is understood that it should not exceed five thousand dollars, and grants of this amount are rare. Grants may be repeated in worthy cases, but no long-continuing support of a project can be undertaken.

Every recipient of a grant is required to report upon the work which has been accomplished with the aid of his grant, and abstracts of these reports have been published in the *Year Book* since 1936. It is not possible to assess critically the value of all the work done by grantees, but it is the judgment of persons who have

TABLE I
Summary of Grants awarded from the Penrose Fund from July 31, 1933 to December 31, 1950

Class	Subject	Grants	Amounts
I	Mathematics	10	$ 5,936.00
	Astronomy and Astrophysics	52	47,340.00
	Meteorology	5	3,232.00
	Physics	83	83,132.53
	Geophysics	3	4,200.00
	Chemistry and Geochemistry	62	52,450.00
	Engineering	1	75.00
	Total	216	$196,365.53
II	Geology	12	$ 6,805.00
	Paleontology	21	11,875.00
	Geography and Physiography	3	1,200.00
	Zoology	149	102,375.53
	Genetics and Cytology	69	59,519.00
	Ecology, Limnology, and Oceanography	21	13,662.50
	Botany	103	78,273.71
	Dendrochronology	1	500.00
	Bacteriology	8	3,900.00
	Anthropology	30	34,685.00
	Psychology	39	28,570.00
	Anatomy	20	10,855.00
	Physiology	77	62,782.00
	Biochemistry	10	7,165.00
	Pathology, Medicine, and Immunology	15	10,900.00
	Total	578	$433,067.74
III	History, American and Modern	110	$ 94,928.00
	Political Science and Government	19	26,310.00
	Economics	13	13,725.00
	Sociology	13	10,950.00
	Jurisprudence	11	12,900.00
	Statistics	1	200.00
	Total	167	$159,013.00
IV	Philosophy and Education	11	$ 9,000.00
	History, Ancient, Medieval and Cultural	125	90,159.25
	History of Science	9	4,810.00
	Archaeology	58	65,857.00
	Ethnology	17	14,600.00
	Philology and Languages	51	48,845.00
	Literature	20	25,586.00
	Drama	2	1,000.00
	Music	17	11,570.00
	Art	15	13,600.00
	History of Art	2	1,500.00
	Architecture	5	4,180.00
	Total	332	290,707.25
MISCELLANEOUS		21	43,750.00
	Grand total	1,314	$1,122,903.52

had much experience in handling funds for the promotion of research that the methods employed and the results attained by the American Philosophical Society in this work compare favorably with similar work of other institutions.

During the first seventeen years (1933–1950), one thousand three hundred and fourteen grants from the Penrose Fund were made for a total amount of about one million, one hundred and twenty-three thousand dollars, or an average of a little more than nine hundred dollars each. The distribution of these grants in various fields of learning is shown in Table I.

The number of grants in geology, geophysics, and geochemistry have been relatively few, and these were made only after consultation with the officers of the Geological Society of America showed that the projects concerned lay outside their field. Paleontology has fared somewhat better, but again only when the projects were not included in the Geological Society's program.

If it was in the thought of Penrose when he made his will that the promotion of geology and the earth sciences would be cared for by the Geological Society of America and the remaining fields of knowledge by the American Philosophical Society, the table showing the distribution of grants to various subjects indicates how well the American Philosophical Society has fulfilled this function.

CHAPTER 22

Search for an Heir

THROUGHOUT the last years of his life, Richard Penrose was seeking an heir for the great fortune he had accumulated by his own efforts—not for the money which he had inherited, for he had actually inherited very little, the estate of both his mother and his father having been in the form of a trust fund, the principal of which he could not touch. But the fortune which he had made was his to dispose as he pleased, and he searched, as every man seeks to do, for a means which would best fulfill his own objectives.

The late Charles Schuchert, emeritus professor of invertebrate paleontology at Yale University, who knew something of that search, wrote the story thus:

Schuchert's Recollections concerning Penrose's High Ideals for the Betterment of Geological Research

It is not clear in my mind exactly when and where I first met the late Richard Alexander Fullerton Penrose, except that it was about 1910, and that the introduction was made by my intimate friend, John M. Clarke. At later meetings of the G.S.A. we often shook hands and commented on the doings at these gatherings. My first letter came from him in middle March, 1929, when, as chairman of the Committee on the Hayden Medal awarded every third year by the Academy of Natural Sciences in Philadelphia, he notified me that I was to be the recipient of the medal the following month. After the short ceremony, Penrose asked me to dine with him at the Bellevue-Stratford Hotel, and here we spent the rest of the evening in his large apartment, chatting about things geological and paleontological.

Early in this conversation, he began to unfold to me what he had been trying to do for Geology in the city of his birth, saying that for over a decade he had been wanting to found a research institute there for Geology and Paleontology.* We discussed this subject for more than two hours, and returned to it next morning.

I shall never forget this evening of April 16, 1929, in the Penrose apartment, because it stands out in my memory as one of the most astonishing events in my life. Penrose began by telling me how he had been trying for several years to induce Clarke, first, to accept a professorship of Geology at the University of Pennsylvania, and, failing in this, to have him assume the directorship of a research institute for Paleontology and Geology which he hoped to endow in

* Note reference to such an idea in letter of M. J. Greenman to him, October 23, 1918—*see* Chapter 19.

Philadelphia; in neither case, however, was he able to persuade Clarke to leave his beloved Albany, where he was master of his own environment.

Luckily, I have been able, through Clarke's son, Noah H. Clarke, to find the written offer made by Penrose to Clarke regarding the professorship at the University of Pennsylvania. The letter from Penrose is dated October 14, 1919, and it is of further importance in showing that Penrose had even at an earlier time been speaking to Clarke about founding "an institute of geologic research."

Dear Doctor Clarke:

I have received your letter of October 10th and am greatly pleased that you do not absolutely turn down the idea of the professorship of geology at the University of Pennsylvania, but I am disappointed that you still hold aloof. There never was a time when the University needed such a man as you more than at present. The Provost and several of the trustees to whom I have spoken about the matter are just as anxious as I am to have you with us.

I fully realize the innumerable and old associations that bind you to Albany, but here also you will find a receptive community ready and anxious to see your genius revive the leadership in geology and paleontology, once so strongly represented here by Rogers, Lesley, Cope, Leidy and others. As regards the institute of geologic research, I am still hoping that it will be forthcoming after an extravagant Government relieves us of its destructive taxation. I am not, however, under present conditions certain enough about this matter to feel that I can conscientiously ask you to count it in any way a determining factor in your consideration of the professorship. The professorship must stand alone in its inducement for you to come here.

Hoping that you will finally decide favorably towards us in the University matter, I am

Sincerely yours,
R. A. F. Penrose, Jr.

A new vista came to Penrose in 1922, when he was elected president of the Philadelphia Academy, an office which he held for four years.* This election soon revived his idea of founding an institute of research, and on May 2, 1922, he wrote to Clarke:

"I am not forgetting the Institution of Geology, and I hope now to take more active steps in the matter than I did when I first suggested it to you several years ago. I am still in doubt whether to try to make the Academy of Natural Sciences essentially a geological institute for research without any students, but with well paid professors, or whether to start a totally new institute. I think that the Academy would easily lend itself to such a proposition, and of course there are some men there who would be strong additions to a research institute.... I will write you further after I have crystallized this matter more. In the meanwhile I am going over the forms of endowment in somewhat similar institutions."

From the above we see that Penrose began to think of endowing a research

* *See* chapter 19.

institute in Paleontology and Geology before 1919, and from what follows it seems apparent that he never gave up this ambition of his, even after learning during his presidency of the Academy that that body was not willing to allow the earth sciences to dominate its activities. It appears that he kept on hoping that eventually he would be able to induce Clarke to head a separate institute in Philadelphia, but to this the latter never consented. However, Clarke wanted to help in another way, and he tried to influence Penrose—according to information given me by Ruedemann* at Albany on June 19, 1929—to found such an institute in the capital city of New York, with an endowment rumored to be about one million dollars. This plan did not appear to meet Penrose's desires, since he wanted the institute to be in Philadelphia. Noah Clarke says† that his father mentioned the Philadelphia plan to him on several occasions, "but he always seemed doubtful about accepting such a position because of his great desire to continue in his work here in Albany. I know that the two men often discussed the idea and father worked out a tentative organization for it at one time." Unfortunately, all this planning came to an end with the death of Clarke in May, 1925, and in the following year Penrose stepped out of the presidency of the Philadelphia Academy.

Returning now to the above-mentioned memorable evening in 1929, Penrose continued to unfold to me his ideas of what he wanted to do, chiefly for Paleontology, and several times he expressed his great disappointment at not getting Clarke to come to Philadelphia—his wife, Mrs. Fannie V. Bosler, had been born in Philadelphia and lived there until their marriage—and build up his long-desired institute for research. It was, of course, a great surprise to me to note that Penrose nearly always spoke of an institute for Paleontology and Historical Geology, and only incidentally of Geology. Expressing this surprise, I remarked to him, "Penrose, you were a life-long geologist, and chiefly an economic geologist, why do you want to build up chiefly an institute for Paleontology and Historical Geology?" He answered that it is these sciences that bring out most of the philosophy of the earth sciences, since they have the vistas throughout geologic time. Naturally, his reply thrilled me, and I could not help telling him that I was both pleased and astonished at his attitude. Since then I have often wondered if he had read Clarke's statement that Paleontology "is the most far reaching of all the sciences. In it lies the root of all truth, out of it must come the solution of the complex enigmas of human society." Finally, I said, "Penrose, do you want me to help you?" He replied, "I wish you to consider the matter." The thought came to me—and I expressed it to him—that as I was then about seventy years of age, I could not personally undertake to develop such a research institute, and I asked whether he wished me to find a young man who could be depended upon to build such a one. He answered in the affirmative, but in the weeks following, after much hard thought, I had to admit that to find a man with the necessary qualifications for the task would be most impossible at that time.

I had to make plans for the research institute of which Penrose was talking,

* Rudolf Ruedemann, Clarke's assistant, and later State Paleontologist of New York.
† In a letter to Schuchert, dated March 17, 1939.

with one handicap—lack of information about the amount of endowment he had in mind. In our conversations he gave me the impression that he might be a millionaire—but not a multimillionaire—and when later on I put the question to several geologists who were well acquainted with him, they thought he mght have something like a half-million dollars. Since then we have all learned how well he kept the amount of his wealth to himself; but according to one of his acquaintances, it appears that his fortune had increased by leaps and bounds during the last ten years of his life, while he was selling all his mining interests at the inflated values of those years.

After my discussion with Penrose I returned to New Haven, and on April 23 I wrote him a letter of thanks for his marked kindness to me in Philadelphia, and said that I would write him later about the matter of the research institute. This I did on April 30 (1929) as follows:

My dear Doctor Penrose:

Ever since our two conversations in Philadelphia about your good intentions toward invertebrate paleontology, I have been thinking over what you said, and shortly after my return to my desk I wrote out a long plan of some things that could be done. I then handed this plan to two of my counsellors, when it became evident that I was in all probability overshooting the mark. Furthermore, to carry out a grand plan one must be able above all to point out the man who can put the plan into execution. Such a person does not appear to be present among the older paleontologists, and the young men have not had enough responsibility put upon them to stand out and show what they can do.

My greatest difficulty in formulating plans lies in the fact that I do not know how much money you wish to put into the foundation, nor how large a research institute you think desirable. Like all ideals, the sky is the limit, but to bring them down to earth and make them practicable one is dependent not only on means but even more on suitable men. Of course, men will grow with their duties, but then an institute can not shine at once even though it may do so with time.

Some years ago I gave an address on the status of American paleontologists, and it has value at present in helping to stimulate ideas. Will you please read the the copy I am sending you? In this address of ten years ago I said:

> "We all know that paleontology is the biology of all time, while botany and zoology are but the studies of the organic terminals of some of the life that has lived through a thousand million years. The theory of evolution was made possible through the chronogenetic record as discerned by the paleontologists and through the phylogenies of living plants and animals. Nor can the distribution of modern floras and faunas be determined without a study of the life of the past, or the rate or speed of evolution and the origin of many organic trends be understood without a knowledge of the climates of the past. The fact that American invertebratists and paleobotanists are doing so little along these lines is a blot on our science—all the more so because of the good example set us by Hyatt and his school, and by the vertebratists.

There is no continent with a better array of well preserved fossils, or a longer geologic sequence of them."

From the above you will see that I then thought the most desirable trend to take up was the biologic side and not the chronogenetic one of invertebrate paleontology. I am still of this opinion, and so are my counsellors. The Institute for Paleontologic Research, even when restricted to the study of invertebrate fossils and adequate publication, can easily be developed into a project consuming up to $25,000 a year, and extended as much more as a patron chooses. It is this conclusion that frightens me, and here is where I need to know your wishes.

Probably the most stimulating help in invertebrate paleontology would be endowment for adequate publication. Such an 'institute' could easily be attached to your Philadelphia Academy, and would not require the finding of the exceptional man or men, the making of collections, or their preserval and husbanding in a museum. All that is required for this plan is a good editorial board (anyone would serve without pay), and paid editor (part or full time) with financial help in having the necessary illustrations made by draughtsmen or photographers. Such a publishing institute to print only quarto memoirs and monographs, while the smaller papers would be taken care of, as at present, by the established periodicals. This institute to give precedence (1) to the biology of North American fossil invertebrates, (2) the biology of fossil plants, and (3) to the biology of fossil vertebrates. So long as there is help demanded for the first category of publications, there would be no money for the second and third types. I put plants ahead of vertebrates since the latter studies are so dramatically attractive that they probably will always find it easy to get means for publication.

This second plan could be made atractive with an income of around ten thousand dollars per annum.

A third plan for you to consider is the present move of the Paleontological Society, which is closely affiliated with the G.S.A., to start a journal of its own. Such a medium could be administered through the G.S.A., the Philadelphia Academy, or one of the university presses. In this case five thousand dollars per year would greatly stimulate paleontology in general.

Will you, my dear Penrose, think these things over, and then express your wishes either by letter or in further conversation? I will meet you anywhere, either at Philadelphia, New York, or New Haven.

Yours truly
Charles Schuchert

To this, Penrose replied, May 11, 1929:

Dear Doctor Schuchert:—

I hope you will pardon me for my delay in answering your letter of April 30th, which enclosed your letter of April 23rd, and also the copy of your article on "American Paleontologists and the Immediate Future of Paleontology," which you have so kindly sent me and which I have read with much interest and profit.

I appreciate deeply the kind words you say in your letter of April 23rd about your visit to Philadelphia, and I assure you that all of us were greatly pleased to see you here on that occasion. I personally was particularly glad to greet you, for geologists are few and far between in this city, and I was delighted to have an opportunity to talk with you, as the great exponent of paleontology, which, as you so truthfully say, is the biology of all time, while botany and zoology are but the studies of the organic terminals of some of the life since its early appearance on the earth. I feel that no branch of the study of the earth's history comprises so wide a field of truly scientific and philosophical research as paleontology, and particularly invertebrate paleontology from which other phases of this science have developed.

I thank you for your suggestions as to the different ways in which I could be of service to paleontology, and it will give me much pleasure again to take this matter into careful consideration. During the lifetime of our good friend John M. Clarke I often discussed it with him, and at one time thought that I might be able to persuade him to undertake the administration of a paleontological institute here in Philadelphia, but his attachments to Albany were too strong.

I appreciate greatly your cordial remarks about my having been nominated for President of The Geological Society of America for 1930. The nomination came as a complete surprise to me, for I had never even dreamed of such an honor. I have in past years served on the Council, and once as first vice-president. I never sought personally for any official position, but if the Fellows see fit to confirm my nomination at the next annual meeting I will feel that their action is a very high compliment which I shall always treasure among my happiest recollections.

I hope to write before so very long again concerning your extremely kind suggestions about the encouragement of work in paleontology, and in the meantime I beg to thank you greatly for the trouble you have taken in communicating with me about the matter. I assure you I deeply appreciate your interest.

With kindest regards, I am,

Sincerely yours,
R. A. F. Penrose, Jr.

Not hearing from Penrose further during the summer, I wrote him on September 11, 1929, as follows:

My dear Doctor Penrose:

Since I got your good letter of May 11, I have often thought about your wishes to found a Paleontologic Institute in Philadelphia, and had hopes that you would call me to New York or to your hotel to talk over this matter. During the summer while up in Gaspesia, the land Clarke loved so well, the thought often came to me and I wondered if you, too, were thinking out some plan. In the meantime came the disastrous turn of affairs in the Philadelphia Academy, where I had half hoped we might find some way to make connection, but now I wonder if there is any one of the old institutions which might be gathered into your plan.

I can not say that I have evolved anything positive, because there are many ways in which you could help paleontology, but you may have arrived at some plan. If you are to be in New York during the next month, please send me a letter or a telegram telling me where I can have an evening's chat with you. With both of us feeling out the other, we should arrive at some scheme or hook on which to begin to hang our cherished hopes and so build on toward the institute that you have in mind. Will you let me know?

Trusting that you had a pleasant summer, I am

Yours truly
Charles Schuchert

Penrose's reply to this, dated September 19, 1929, was as follows:

Dear Doctor Schuchert:—

On my return here from a short absence I have received your very kind letter of September 11th and am greatly pleased to realize that you have not forgotten our conversation here last spring concerning a paleontological and geological institute. As I told you when you were here, I have had this ambition in mind for many years, and I had hoped to start such an organization in connection with one of the old scientific foundations in this city, but I have found no sympathy or encouragement to make this effort. Interest in scientific subjects in different places goes by cycles, and surely in Philadelphia today, in spite of old traditions, paleontology and geology in general may be considered almost lost sciences.

After years of study of old individual scientific institutions in Philadelphia and elsewhere in the eastern states, I find that most of them seem to have outlived their usefulness. They filled a sphere one or two hundred years ago, but their activities have been largely replaced by the scientific departments in the great universities of today, which were never dreamed of at the time that the small individual institutions of former generations were active. The American Philosophical Society is perhaps an exception.

When I became President of The Academy of Natural Sciences of Philadelphia in 1922, I still had the ambition to build up a geological institution in connection with it, but I found after a few years that such a project would not be desirable, and as I did not care to continue to hold a position which was purely an administrative one in connection with branches of science other than those in which I was particularly interested, I resigned. Moreover the recent unfortunate and ill-advised action of the Academy in selling their archeologic collections makes me wonder whether other collections might not also be sold when those who had been active in creating them had passed over the Divide.

I have recently begun to think that perhaps the work of an institute such as we discussed might be carried on through the agency of The Geological Society of America, which, being a national organization, ought to encourage this work at such places as would from time to time seem desirable. Of course, such a plan would make me relinquish the idea of an institute in Philadelphia, yet as there exists but little interest in such a project in this city at the present time, perhaps it would be wise to leave the enterprise in hands which might function wisely in future generations.

I hope some time to run up to New Haven to talk this matter over with you, or perhaps we might meet in New York during this fall; but in the meanwhile I would be glad if you would give a little thought to the suggestion regarding The Geological Society of America.

I am greatly pleased to hear that you have had such a pleasant summer in the good old Gaspe country, rendered famous by many travellers but pre-eminently so by John M. Clarke in his admirable volume. I hope some time that you also will add something to our knowledge of this unique region.

With kindest regards, I am,

Sincerely yours,
R. A. F. Penrose, Jr.

My next missive to Penrose was written on October 2, 1929, and a week later I sent him a printed article on Endowments. My letter read:

My dear Doctor Penrose:—

I have been thinking over further the matter of the Paleontologic Institute, and have much to talk over with you about it; and as I said in my last letter, let us get together for a good long talk, 'feeling out each other' along the lines of your letter dated September 19. I could readily see you some week end, say Saturday, October 12 or 19, leaving here on the through Washington train at 11 A.M. and getting to West Philadelphia about 5:30 P.M. I could put up at your hotel and then after dinner we could talk out this matter in your room; maybe we would want to renew it next morning, and then I could return home on an afternoon train.

I agree with you that since your ideas do not fit in with present Philadelphia institutions, you could, as you suggest, have them carried out through the Geological Society of America, but in this event the Society would have to transform its constitution, and I rather think it also is not properly equipped as a trust-holding corporation. On the other hand, a few of our American universities have strong paleontologic departments and are well equipped to husband just such trust funds as you propose to give, and probably at no expense to you. Furthermore, research institutes along the lines of your wishes would prosper best in a university environment (on this point I will send you some enlightening literature as soon as I can get it), and it is probable that one of them would furnish, free of upkeep, the necessary home to house the staff of the institute.

The most pressing needs of American paleontology at present are means of adequate publication, and a beginning could be made at once in getting out a journal under the auspices of the Paleontological Society which is now casting about to get such a journal started. We paleontologists very much need an octavo journal appearing, say, six times a year, for short papers, discussions, news, and proceedings of the Society. From three to five thousand dollars annually would establish this journal, and later on subscriptions and sales would help toward enlarging it as the need grew.

Teaching in the proposed institute should be reduced to a minimum, although teaching also clarifies and widens every researcher.

Beginning in a small way, and while you are at hand to counsel with the rest of us, I am sure we can find the men to do the research, building them up and casting out those found wanting. The leader should be of middle age, but most of the staff would be young people with some years of paleontologic research behind them.

The institute you will make possible should not be too restricted, and we must counsel with one another where to lay the stress of our endeavors. The institute can not, of course, do everything, and moreover, would not want in the least to interfere with present conditions. It would be to give additional help and stimulus to paleontology along the higher ideals, and act as a sort of clearing house to harmonize the efforts of all American paleontologists.

Good luck to you, and advise me when I can visit you.

Yours truly
Charles Schuchert

To this, Penrose replied October 19, 1929, as follows:

Dear Doctor Schuchert:—

On my return from a short absence I have received your letters of October 2nd and 9th, as well as the printed account which you so kindly sent me of the symposium organized by Doctor Cattell on "How can endowments be used most efficiently for scientific research?" comprising articles by Chamberlin, Boas, Wheeler, McMillan and Münsterberg.

I have thought seriously about your remarks in your letter of October 2nd. I read in Science the articles which you sent me when they came out. They all contain suggestions well worthy of consideration, but I feel that every endowment of any kind must be considered from its own particular standpoint and not from an "average" of information and experience derived from other endowments.

In looking over the changes that have occurred in different departments of learning at the larger universities and other institutions, even during my lifetime, I am strongly impressed with the fact that activity in paleontologic and other geologic research shifts at intervals from one institution to another and that no one center of learning ever has a pre-eminent monopoly of any one branch of science for any great length of time. My own personal knowledge of the history of geology in Philadelphia, which seventy-five or eighty years ago was a center of geologic knowledge, and in which now the study of geology plays but a small part, has done much to lead me to the above-mentioned belief.

I am gradually coming to the conclusion that a national organization like The Geological Society of America, which is not bound to any particular institution but is on terms of friendship and good will with all of them, might be the best source through which to distribute the funds of a paleontologic or other geologic endowment. The very fact that the Society is national in character gives it from time to time a broad knowledge of the distribution of talent in the branches of geology which it represents, and hence would permit it intelligently to use funds to assist where for the time being certain researches are being pre-eminently pursued.

An individual investigator may do brilliant work, but it ceases when he passes away; a geologic institution may likewise do brilliant work, but when those who have created this efficiency no longer exist the institution loses its luster; but a scientific subject never dies and the more it is studied the greater and greater stands out its comprehensive importance in nature.

With best regards, I am,

Sincerely yours,
R. A. F. Penrose, Jr.

P.S.—I am returning under separate cover the pages from Science which you so kindly sent me, as I thought you might like to retain them. I personally have also put my own copy of them on file for future reference on the subject of Endowment.

P.

As this letter called for no answer, I wrote none. After this letter of October 19, 1929, I did not hear again from Penrose, and did not see him until the year of his presidency of the G.S.A., at the meeting in Washington in late December, 1930. He assured me then that he was still favorably inclined toward Paleontology, and that he was thinking of backing up with financial assistance the proposed Journal of Paleontology, then under discussion between students of fossils in the two geological societies. I had no further communications from him, nor did I see him again before his death in July, 1931.

In forwarding his manuscript for inclusion in this work, Schuchert wrote to Charles P. Berkey, secretary of the Geological Society of America, that he had long hoped that it might be used in such a volume, adding that "the proof of his wishes I now send you, so that it may go into the memorial volume for future Councillors and Secretaries of the G.S.A. to read and to remember.

"This does not mean that I am disappointed with the outcome and present management of the Penrose Fund. On the contrary, I am greatly pleased with the liberality shown by our Society toward Stratigraphy, Paleontology, and Historical Geology, and in sending you the enclosed documents my hope is that the Society will ever keep on as it is now going; that the geologists will never forget the paleontologists; and that the latter will ever remember that in the unity of the earth sciences there will be mighty geological strength."

In thanking Schuchert for his contribution, Berkey noted that "your experience with Penrose is of great interest to me. There are many similarities with my own experience. I never knew quite what to count on and probably no one was more taken by surprise than I was myself when the real facts came out, after his death. He had a most peculiar dislike for publicity and an even more violent dislike for any urging, yet if one failed to follow up he was almost as touchy about the assumed lack of interest in his suggestions. I never knew quite how much to say or whether to say anything. It would be interesting to know, if we could know, more of the intimate operations of his mind on these matters. This is a thing, however, that he probably did not reveal to a living person. Surely, he did not to me."

Nor were Schuchert and Berkey the only ones who felt that way, for Waldemar Lindgren in his memorial* to Penrose says:

"When his geological work and his mining work were drawing to a close, he found himself a wealthy man; a wealth obtained legitimately, extracted from the treasures of the rocks not acquired from others by manipulation and trickery. Any one would be justified in feeling proud of such an attainment. And now, the question would begin to take form: What to do with the money? He could not take it along; he had no immediate family. I am sure he appreciated it only as a trust, as something to be put to work for the benefit of science and posterity. His private benefactions were many, but most carefully chosen.

"Knowing of his wealth many professional gold hunters, emissaries of diverse institutions, tried to turn his mind towards their own objects, but all such attempts were failures from the moment his keen intelligence divined their intentions. He would give freely, generously, but only for purposes selected by himself.

"I was one of those gold hunters myself. It was for a projected bibliography of economic geology, sponsored by the National Research Council.† I came to Penrose, explained the matter and told him that we were all 'chipping in' and said I would like to have his name on the list, for anything he would choose to give; anything would be welcome. And I was astounded, in fact quite overwhelmed by his generous response.

"But as to the disposal of his wealth he took no one into his confidence, except that we all knew of his deep interest in the American Philosophical Society. And, of course, we also knew that he would like to do something for his own beloved science and for the Geological Society of America.

"Nevertheless his magnificent gifts to these two organizations, gifts unencumbered by hedges and restrictions came as a complete surprise. Penrose revealed himself in the character of the unselfish benefactor aiming only at the promotion and progress of science. He said in substance: 'Here is the money: take it and use it wisely and well. There are many things I would have liked to do but could not; life was too short. You try to accomplish them! Carry on!'"

The person who was in intimate contact with the rest of this search was Dr. Charles P. Berkey, who, for twenty years, in addition to his duties as executive officer and teacher in the Department of Geology at Columbia University, was secretary of the Geological Society of America. He tells the story thus:

Secretary Berkey's Recollections

For many years after Penrose was elected to Fellowship in the Geological Society in 1889, he was a frequent attendant at the annual meetings, but he seldom took any part other than to present himself and re-establish friendship

---

* Printed in the Proceedings of the American Philosophical Society, vol. 72, no. 3, 1933.

† Now being published with the aid of funds advanced by the Geological Society of America from the Penrose Bequest.

with the elders of the organization. As time passed, not many came in that class, and he made virtually no effort to expand its range. He almost always was missing by the morning of the second day of meetings. Whether a bit bored by the proceedings or too busy to stay or simply through with his visiting, no one could tell.

Despite his distinguished personal appearance he took no advantage of that fact to attract attention or to impress the younger generation. He came and went without particular notice except from the few who were admitted to his circle. He was graciousness itself if any one were fortunate enough to be brought into touch with him, for he was a born gentleman with the breeding and poise that belong. But he shrank from every appearance of display or any form of publicity. Even the ordinary social events of the meetings that have become fixed and simplified out of the custom of past years, such as the presidential address and the annual dinner with its few simple ceremonies, were a nightmare to him. He seldom attended any of these functions except the smoker, and when in the course of time it came his turn to preside he evidently passed through one of the trying experiences of his life.

It was a curious turn of the wheel of fate, therefore, that in later years made him the chief sponsor of one of our most formal ceremonies—the bestowal of the medal of the Geological Society to the person judged to have attained highest distinction in furthering research in geologic science.

Penrose had shown interest in the Society years before, but had not come into close touch with its administrative affairs. Now, however, in the twenties, he began to take a larger part. He was elected to the Council; he more frequently had a word to say about the conduct of its affairs, and passed with some hesitation from one advisory post to another, giving special attention to the committee on finance. Ultimately, he became President of the Society in the year preceding his death. His interest in the organization increased steadily throughout that period, and his concern with the conduct of its affairs became increasingly marked.

As early as 1926, Penrose's interest in the Society began to take concrete form. At that time he began the measures to relieve the growing pressure on the Secretary's office caused by a rapidly expanding membership by making contributions to the allowance for stenographic assistance. These contributions became more and more frequent during the remaining five years of his life. Although such interest was unusual from the members, it came so naturally from him as to cause no great ripple of expectancy. To those directly involved, however, it gave greatly needed support, for, with his gifts, it became possible to secure and pay for clerical services that hitherto had been simply absorbed in the burden of the day. With Penrose's help a full-time assistant became at last a reality. Mrs. Miriam F. Howells' valuable service to the organization dates from 1923, but before Penrose made a full-time assistant possible, she was giving only part time. She thus was the first person in the history of the Society to devote all her working time to the organization.

In the first written reference to the secretarial burden, which had by that time become excessive, Penrose had this to say (in a letter to Berkey January 18, 1928):

"I thank you for your letter of January 10th relative to the meeting at Cleveland, and I appreciate your writing to me so promptly, for I know that you must be overwhelmed with work connected with the meeting. What you need is a permanent assistant secretary, who receives a good enough salary to devote his time entirely to the work of the Society, thus relieving you of a large part of the drudgery. I think such a man could be gotten if the Council would give sufficient time and attention to the matter."

Two years later (January 6, 1930) he expressed a willingness to assist personally in paying the price of such relief: "I hope you have gotten rested up after all the work you did at The Geological Society of America meeting at Washington. Some time in the next week or two I am coming to New York and if you are there I would like to discuss the matter of giving you more assistance in the details of your office as Secretary. Your controlling influence is absolutely essential to the welfare of the Society, but I feel that there are many details which you might wish to hand over to someone else who was capable of doing the work. Year by year your burden as Secretary of The Geological Society of America is increasing and it is proper that you should ask such assistance. I feel that some steps should be taken immediately towards accomplishing this object, and I personally would be willing to help out in the matter."

This was something entirely new, for, although he had been making occasional contributions, this was the first time he had declared that he was willing to assume such obligation and make it an issue.

A few weeks later (February 19, 1930) he wrote:

"I beg to enclose my check for Five hundred dollars ($500.00) as a contribution to The Geological Society of America, to be used for the work in your office as Secretary, until other arrangements can be made. I am doing this because I fully realize from our conversation in New York a few weeks ago, and also from my previous knowledge of the situation, that much work is being thrown on you personally which might be done by others, and I hope therefore you will accept my contribution with my best wishes that it may be of some service in the great work you are doing for the Society."

In replying to a letter from Penrose (September 24, 1930) enclosing another check for five hundred dollars, the Secretary wrote (September 28):

"I will put it to as good use as I know how. I don't suppose you can fully realize how much I appreciate your very practical helpfulness and the backing that you are giving in so many ways toward improvement of The Geological Society."

In that letter of September 24th Penrose had said:

"I thank you for the details you have given me about the administrative operations of The Geological Society of America, and particularly in connection with your office. As I have already said, I think that your Department, as Secretary, is the mainspring of the whole administration of the Society, and I feel that it is there that assistance should first be given. I also realize that everything cannot be done in a day and that we had better begin a little slowly and progress toward the ideals we have already discussed. I beg to enclose my check for Five hundred dollars, which I hope you will accept on behalf of the Society as a contribution from me, with the request that it be devoted to the assistance of the Department of the Secretary.

"I am glad to know that you can get the cooperation of Mrs. Howells on full time instead of part time, as of course was necessary during the past year. Her remarkable efficiency as your assistant secretary, and her broad knowledge of the affairs of the Society, will relieve you of much work. I feel that after you get some relief in your office we can better discuss further matters in connection with the Society by personal interviews, which are much more satisfactory in enabling us mutually to understand the requirements of the Society than by letter."

It was a long step in improvement of secretarial service when Mrs Howells was induced to come on full time as my assistant in the administrative work of the Society. Her gift for remembering persons and their numerous questions furnished better contact with our membership and greatly eased the former burdens of the Secretary. Her knowledge of the routine and of Council action and reaction was now of great help in the frequent discussions with Penrose. In no small measure her efficient help in those days must have furthered materially the interests of the organization, for he often referred to it in appreciative terms.

By this time, suggestions or comments or questions were coming from Penrose every few days. We took for granted that his increased interest was due to his feeling of responsibility as president of the Society. No one seems to have discerned the other reason, to the effect that he already had begun to feel a sort of partnership relation or part ownership and responsibility for its conduct. One other reference to the Secretary's office is pertinent. On September 12, 1930, he wrote:

"I think you are the one to sketch out some programme by which the assistance you desire in your office might be accomplished, for it is you that understand most intimately all its details and intricate requirements. I would be greatly pleased if sometime soon we could have another meeting on this subject. Meanwhile I would be very glad if you could find an opportunity to sketch out your ideas on the re-organization of your department, with you as its guiding spirit."

These requests for conferences had been another feature which marked the Penrose presidency. They began almost at once, for on February 21, 1930, he wrote:

"Your letter has given me much information which I did not have before.... I am sorry to hear that you have been suffering with a cold, but I hope you are all right by this time. You ought to take good care of yourself. Why don't you run over here to Philadelphia some morning and take lunch with me, and, if you are obliged to return the same day you can take an afternoon train back. It would do you good to get away from your office a while, and it is needless to say that I would be delighted to see you. If you find it impossible to do this, I hope to see you in New York in the next week or so.... In the meanwhile, please let me know if I can be of any further service to you."

Each conference gradually developed into a discussion of some specific need of the Society. Not only was he concerned with the needs of the Secretary, he looked forward to the future of the organization and to its proper setting as a scientific society with adequate support. On October 7, 1930, he wrote:

"I was very glad to get your letter of October 3rd and to know that you are making such satisfactory arrangements for handling your office routine. I happened to be in New York for part of the day Saturday and I took a chance of going up to the University in hopes of finding you there, but you were away. Your assistant, however, showed me your new offices on the second floor, and I think they are very good. The storage room for the supply of back Bulletins is admirable, for it will be easy to keep clean and amply capacious for present needs.

"I suppose you will still be able to use your rooms on the first floor for some of the purposes of the Society and thus temporarily matters must be much more satisfactory to you than formerly."

The "new quarters" to which he refers were made possible through an adjustment of the space allotted to the Department of Geology at Columbia. A small room in Schermerhorn Hall had been set aside for the Society. In addition, a small, inside, wholly dark room became temporarily available, and this was fitted up with shelving on which, for the first time, the whole reserve of published material issued by the Society could be arranged. These improvements for our special use were paid for out of Penrose gifts to the Secretary's office; the remainder of the money went to pay for assistance, equipment, and supplies.

A week later, (October 15, 1930), Penrose again referred to the new quarters:

"I think that everyone was greatly pleased with your new quarters, or rather your additional quarters, at Columbia, and your conception of a 'Presidential Gallery' is most interesting. It recalls many an old associate with whom we worked in years gone by. I think that we should also have a gallery of pictures of Secretaries and Treasurers, so as to make your collection representative of those who have occupied active official positions in the Society since its beginning."

The "gallery" to which he refers is now a permanent part of the Secretary's office, and is on view at the headquarters of the Society.

It was during a conference at this time that Penrose expressed the conviction that the Society should have its own home and authorized the Secretary to inquire into the availability of a suitable location. Upon being reminded that the Society was not at all prepared for such greatly expanded expenses as this seemed to contemplate, Penrose gave the only direct promise that came from him in all the years of my contact with him. But it could mean much or little. No one then knew what his fortune measured, so when he said, "I have provided for The Geological Society in my will," the promise was still almost as vague as though it had not been spoken. Not until the will was read was there any adequate appreciation of what those words signified.

This preliminary statement was followed in due course with written expression of the same thought. Under date of September 12, 1930, he wrote:

"I think that eventually the Society should have its own building, and that this should be in New York. It need not be an elaborate establishment, but it should be in a dignified neighborhood, and the Society should be in a position to keep it up. Before considering such a project, however, I feel that the Society should be put on a little better working basis and that the duties which are piling up year by year more heavily in your department, should first receive consideration and relief, so that you might feel justified in giving more time to the affairs of the Society without being subjected to the physical and mental strain of doing too much outside work."

In another latter, dated March 23, 1931, he again discussed the matter as follows:

"I note what you say about the importance of establishing the Society in a permanent home of its own, and I agree with you that this is desirable if it can be accomplished on some practical basis. At the present time, with the fanatical tendency towards ruthless changes in all things which have heretofore had the confidence of the country, I think it would be well to go a little slowly in the matter. Perhaps it would be better to rent quarters in the beginning so as to see how the plan works out, and to find whether sufficient funds may be available.

"The innumerable details regarding a permanent headquarters, its location, its characters, its managements and its uses, would have to be thought out. You are the only one who can do this, for your long experience as Secretary puts you in a position to realize better than all of us put together the many matters that would demand attention in such an enterprise. It seems to me that the first thing that should be done would be for you to prepare a concrete plan for a headquarters, and also a preliminary estimate of the cost of the project.

"If eventually it is found possible for the Society to have a home of its own, I will be sympathetic and may be able to contribute to some extent, though I must make a point of not committing myself in such matters at present, and not until I know what kind of a proposition is suggested, because we are living in an age in which no one can tell what may happen from year to year."

Early in the spring of 1931, the urge to see some move made toward either a permanent home or separate hired accommodations seemed to take Penrose's chief attention, and culminated in authorization to look around for a suitable place. That search was begun and followed far enough to furnish comparative figures on the cost of properties in four different localities in New York: (a) Gramercy Park and vicinity; (b) the Murray Hill district; (c) the American Geographical Society locality; and (d) Morningside Heights and the Columbia University neighborhood.

I was engaged on that investigation at the beginning of the summer of 1931 and gave considerable time to it between other duties. After several places had been selected for comparison, Stanley-Brown accompanied me on a tour of inspection. As a result of that investigation, we became convinced that the Columbia University locality was the most promising. We reported our progress in a letter to which Penrose made the following response (May 18, 1931):

"I have received your letter of May 13th with enclosures relative to the locations of properties which might be desirable for a future home of The Geological Society of America.

"The growth of the Society has increased in recent years to such an extent that today you are crowded into very small and inadequate quarters at Columbia University. We have discussed the desirability of having an entirely separate building as headquarters of the Society and thus relieving the strain on the University and on you.

"I have recently been coming to the conclusion, however, that if we bought or erected an entirely separate building in New York, you would still be obliged to spend a large part of your time at Columbia University in connection with your duties there, and the probable result would be that you would naturally attend to a large part of your business as Secretary of the Society in the same office at Columbia. Hence a second office somewhere else in the city would become simply an annex to your office at Columbia, thus creating a situation which I do not think desirable. The governing center of any organization should be in one place, and members of the Society who want to see you would naturally go to the office which you occupy instead of that of an assistant.

"I think therefore that the best plan would be to persuade Columbia University to grant or rent to the Society more space than at present. In this manner you, as the active spirit of the Society, would be absolutely in control at one center instead of being in real control at your office and having an assistant represent you in a separate building."

Progress had been made with the commission to search for a house or location at Columbia, and it was while this was in process, but before any definite commitments had been made, that his wholly unexpected death was announced. In the meantime, also, still another approach had been taking form.

Housing, whether of the Society or of the members, interested Penrose. Six months before the annual meeting held at Toronto, he wrote (June 27, 1930):

"Relative to the meeting of The Geological Society of America in Toronto next December and the question of housing the members of the Society who may attend the meeting, I would like to recall to you my suggestion that there be no effort to persuade members of the Society to occupy quarters at the University of Toronto, but that they should be given a free opportunity to stay at a hotel if some of them should wish to do so.

"Doubtless many of the younger members would like to stay at the University dormitories not only because the charge would probably be somewhat less than at the hotel, but also because they themselves have only recently come from college dormitories elsewhere and are used to them. I am very sure, however, that quite a number of the older members would prefer to stay at the hotel, not only for the greater freedom that it gives them, but also because it relieves them of the feeling of occupying some one else's quarters."

This was virtually the turning point in the manner of housing the annual meetings of the Society, which are now held in hotels of sufficient size to accommodate as many of the members as may wish to attend.

Another matter concerning the Society on which Penrose had decided ideas was the qualifications for Fellowship. He was a firm advocate of a severely limited membership based strictly on maturity and accomplishment. He had no enthusiasm for numbers and regarded large expansion with decided disfavor. To him, membership in the Geological Society was a seal of attainment that was not to be grabbed, but was to come in due time to those who proved themselves worthy. Penrose had no love for the commonplace and no confidence in the untried. He was a born aristocrat and a confirmed conservative. No one in the Society was more insistent on maintaining high standards.

More than once he proposed to offer an amendment designed to limit the number of Fellows, and was induced with some difficulty to accept the *status quo* as a fair compromise.

Undoubtedly, something of the same attitude was held by most members of the Council with which Penrose was closely associated. Under date of January 14, 1930, Edward B. Mathews, Treasurer of the Society, wrote to Penrose:

"I agree with you that the Society could do much more in the way of promoting geological science if we had an adequate financial support. We could do much in the way of publishing monographic studies which now are published with great difficulty. Such a series would, I feel confident, add much to the prestige of the organization but I do not see how we can finance anything of that sort or the organization of a full-time secretariat without increasing of dues or an increase in membership. Since I am conservative and prefer an arrangement of officers such as we have at the present time, which retains something of the gentlemanly fraternal atmosphere, I am not in favor of increasing dues or lowering standards for membership in order to get more revenue for this purpose."

In reply to Mathews, Penrose laid further emphasis on this matter of form of organization and membership qualifications. After stating that the finances had been efficiently handled by the Treasurer, Penrose said (January 18, 1930):

"I agree with you that the income of the Society is not in any way adequate to support what it might accomplish in the way of publishing monographic works and rendering proper clerical assistance to the Secretary and to the Treasurer, who of course carry on the brunt of the work of the Society. I think it only proper, as you suggest, to retain the arrangement of officers such as we have at the present time, and I would be much opposed to increasing the dues for the purpose of acquiring greater revenue, and even still more strongly opposed to lowering in any way whatever the standards for membership. As I wrote to you in my last letter, I personally would be glad to do something in the way of helping the constantly increasing expenses of the Society, and I hope before long to have an opportunity of discussing this matter with you and Dr. Berkey."

All during the year 1930 while Penrose was president of the Society, he was studying the structure of the organization with a view to its future possibilities. That is all clear now; at the time, the Secretary was delighted to have as President of the Society a man whose business experience and excellent judgment enabled him to offer constructive measures for consideration. The previous year he had led the investigation and criticism of the original constitution and by-laws, based particularly on the lack of adequate provision for the administration of possible endowments or other large funds, which finally led to the incorporation of the Society. This move, made in 1929, involved considerable change in the organic structure of the organization. The following year, during the Penrose presidency, additional corrections were made in the by-laws.

In a letter, dated May 8, 1930, Penrose wrote:

"I feel that for many years past the exact sphere of activity of the Finance Committee has been somewhat vague, for the By-Laws do not provide for any such Committee, and yet a brief amendment could solve the difficulty.

"Until recent years the Society has functioned under rules which were formed when it was a small organization, but since that time it has grown greatly and will doubtless grow still more; hence I think that the By-Laws which were efficient in the early days should be adapted to meet later-day necessities. This feature is particularly important in regard to gifts and bequests which may be made to the Society, and which should be handled in a business-like manner."

This was the first written reference to possible bequests, but it was in such a form that surely no one would become much excited about it. That it was a key subject in his mind, however, is now clear.

It is a common, and indeed a usual thing, for a new member of the Council or one returning to it from a period of other interests to bring in a new point of view or to propose an improvement reflecting to some extent his personal angle and experience. It was accepted, therefore, as a normal result when Penrose entered upon active service in the Council of the Society that there should be revival of critical study of the operating methods and especially the financial structu e of the organization. Such development would have been expected, and it came. But in this instance obviously there was more than the usual amount of personal design back of the general form. He was planning to use the formula himself. These moves, we now know, preceded the writing of his final will by only a month or two.

That was of a piece with his intellectual aristocracy and general reserve. His thinking was direct and his language simple. As a matter of fact, he gave the bequest, not with the purpose of booming the Society, but in the belief that the Geological Society of America had existed long enough to have become stabilized. In that belief he rested his faith in the Society—and charged it with great responsibility. He thought it would last. He thought it could resist both dry rot and pointless enthusiasm. He banked on the average judgment and performance of the mature and experienced, well-meaning men of his own time. The fact that he sat in successive Councils, with critical, searching mind for several years and still had enough faith to establish a great trust to serve geological science forever, was itself a mark of outstanding confidence that surely should never be violated.

How Penrose came to his decisions surely no one ever knew. Probably the instrument disposing of his fortune, which was dated only a short time before his death and was written by his own hand, was a kind of "end stage reaction product," after a long line of primary crystallizations, deuteric replacements and mature metamorphic changes genetically in principle not very unlike the life stories of certain ancient rocks familiar to him as a specialist in petrology.

Attempts to plant the idea of a bequest in favor of some educational institution or specialistic organization clearly did not satisfy his purpose, although there were numerous deserving opportunities. Evidently he was searching for something else, and the reasons were not far to seek. He was quick to detect a lead to his assumed financial competence—perhaps over-quick where there was no impropriety whatever. He particularly loathed "beggars" who presumed upon his friendship. Yet after a promise had come into the open from him, he was inclined to be offended if it were left over-long without at least a gleam of interest or appreciation.

He was not inclined to take advice, although he always considered suggestions. He was as cautious in this search for an heir as he had been in selecting the few mineral prospects that had made him rich. Probably John M. Clarke, of Albany, came as near persuading him to finance a specialistic adventure as any one ever did. Dr. Clarke and Professor Schuchert together almost closed a well-conceived scientific adventure, as already outlined in an earlier section of this chapter. It may be that the urgings of Clarke were too pressing, or the suggestions of Schuchert were too difficult to organize, or that the project was not of close enough personal interest or not broad enough, or that he was not then ready to finance so large an adventure, or any one of a number of cross leads which finally left him wholly free from these and all other promises. But of all proposals known to have pressed claims upon him, this one by Clarke and Schuchert seems to have come nearest to success. It made a deep impression and was always referred to with great consideration. These men were his friends; he never seemed to resent their urgent advice. Clearly he wanted to help this enterprise along.

In this connection, attention is called to a paragraph in the Penrose letter of October 19, 1929, to Schuchert, which has special significance here:

"I am gradually coming to the conclusion that a national organization like the Geological Society of America, which is not bound to any particular institution but is on terms of friendship and good will with all of them, might be the best source through which to distribute the funds of a paleontologic or other geologic endowment. The very fact that the Society is national in character gives it from time to time a broad knowledge of the distribution of talent in the branches of geology which it represents and hence would permit it intelligently to use funds to assist where for the time being certain researches are being pre-eminently pursued."

It is clear that the trend for some time had been away from sharply delimited objectives and specialistic interests to the broad aspects of science. Accepting that choice as reasonable and wise, it is not difficult to discover adequate excuse for his deliberation and his final acceptance of the Geological Society of America, covering the whole of geologic science, and of the American Philosophical Society, whose province is all useful human knowledge.

The financing of these two societies is an amazing adventure, the full importance of which for the future no one is sufficiently wise to measure.

Looking back, as we have just now over the period of his closing years, one can readily discover a rapidly growing interest in the operation of The Geological Society, until there came a time when it simply took possession of him. He had become a Councilor, and in that period established the Society's medal. He became a close observer of trends as successive Councils came to power. He developed definite ideas on policy and administration and bemoaned the scant support furnished for its operation. Upon assurance that our thin stream of resources did not warrant further drain for this purpose, he thereafter gave the Secretary, for addition to equipment and to the paid service of the central office, a few hundred dollars whenever it appeared to be needed. We never made the mistake of asking for money. We never admitted that the funds were entirely gone. We never gave occasion, either, for embarrassment or suspicion by solicitation or complaint.

Finally, he became President of the Society. With this honor, marking as it does the approval of a large number of competent representatives from his own field, he was highly pleased. He gave much time to the administrative affairs of the Society—more time, in fact, than any other officer within my long experience as Secretary.

It was his custom to come to New York weekly on business, and he usually closed the day by telephoning the Secretary. If the Secretary was in the city, Penrose came to the university as promptly as a taxi would bring him. On these occasions usually some phase of the work or some element of policy or some plan for improvement was discussed for a while, never over-long.

In looking back now, I can discern the progress of implications then unnoted. For instance, he wrote (July 5, 1930):

"I would like to send you at the present time another check for $500.00 to help in your Geological Society of America work. Some months ago when I spoke to you about this matter, I recollect that you told me the money was not needed at that time, but if you can make use of it now I assure you that it will give me great pleasure to send it to you promptly."

I replied that it could be used, and promptly, under date of July 9, came the following:

"It gives me much pleasure to enclose my check for Five Hundred dollars ($500.00) drawn to the order of The Geological Society of America in the same way as I have made former contributions, and I ask that it be used to assist in your work as Secretary. I assure you that I am greatly gratified to feel that I am of some service to the Society in this matter and to know that my contribution will help relieve some of the burden you are carrying in connection with your rapidly increasing duties. I hope later on to do more for the Society, and the next time we meet I would like to discuss this matter further with you."

The implication in this letter went entirely over my head. I had become accustomed, through many long years, to doing everything myself, and virtually paying for it in extra time, worry, and drudgery. So I could not believe in the seriousness of such a promise, and I do not recall that it caused the slightest ripple of expectation. The gift was used in lightening the personal load and in paying better for our clerical service. There it ended for the time, and the topic would never have been raised again if it had not been kept alive by him.

It was about this time that an urgent invitation was received from Penrose to visit him in Philadelphia for conference. Those invited were Stanley-Brown, Lindgren, Berry, Mathews, and myself.

The time set was midday, September 9, 1930, and the place was his office in the Bullitt Building. Upon arrival we found that one of the rooms of his suite had been set for luncheon. With little loss of time, after welcoming everyone, he led the party to the well-supplied table with the remark that we should find it equally comfortable to carry on our discussion there.

None of us knew why the conference was called but we took it for granted that his immediate concern was to discuss current matters connected with his own responsibilities as President of the Society. It developed, however, that his special interest on this occasion was the financial structure of the Society.

As previously noted, he was not wholly satisfied with the procedure established for handling finances and he questioned the adequacy of the system in case of possible large bequests. It was at this meeting that he urged that Stanley-Brown, who had had wide experience in financial affairs, should assume the responsibility for any securities that might come to the Society or for the investment of funds. To this, everyone was ready to agree, not only because of the known competence of Stanley-Brown, but also because it was evident that Penrose trusted his judgment.

One of the fruits of that conference was a revision of the By-Laws relating to investment procedure.

The afternoon was spent talking over the affairs of the Society. Whether or not Penrose got what he wanted out of the conference, no one could tell. Perhaps he did, for he expressed himself as gratified with the visit. But when we turned homeward, toward evening, we were little wiser than when we came. We had to admit that the conference was probably not intended for our benefit. It was his conference. We agreed to his proposals, and for the time this satisfied him.

It is just possible, however, that this was one of the relatively few occasions when long strides were made in satisfying his mind. We now know that he had already written the will, but it may have needed support. Perhaps the conference was called in part to satisfy himself on matters that were not at any time brought into the open or emphasized. It probably was a very important day in the life history of the Geological Society.

Three days after that conference a letter with the following comment on the Society's future was received:

"It was a great pleasure to me to have seen you and Mr. Stanley-Brown here a few days ago, and was only sorry that you could not have stayed longer and have discussed the various matters of The Geological Society of America in which we are interested.

"I personally have always hesitated up until now to say too much about constructive improvements to lighten the increasing burden on the officers of the Society, because I have learned by experience that it is a difficult and often a thankless undertaking to try to guide methods established almost a half century ago into lines of greater efficiency with less burden.

"Since our talk here on September 9th and also in view of your letter of September 4th, I feel that perhaps you will not misunderstand me if I write briefly concerning some of my thoughts on the subject of the Society. I can see clearly that the main part of its organization which needs further assistance is your department, as Secretary. It is really the hub of the activities of the Society, and with proper assistance given to you it will function not only more strongly itself, but indirectly will extend this strength also to the departments of the Editor and the Treasurer. Your own broad knowledge of the affairs of the Society, and your personality as an influence on those assisting you, are essential to its success. I would like to see you relieved of the details to the extent of having the whole time of an assistant secretary, instead of part time. Part time in any activity never brings the same result as full time."

On November 13th (1930) came another call for conference, which ostensibly was to be a discussion of the Toronto meeting to be held the following month, but which turned out to be another hour of pondering on Geological Society affairs, as is obvious from the following quotation from his letter of November 14th:

"It was a pleasure to have seen you in New York yesterday and to have had a further talk with you about the affairs of The Geological Society of America. What is most on my mind at the present moment is that the Toronto meeting should be a success, and after that event is over I hope we will be able to take up the discussion of matters relating to the future welfare of the Society."

About this time the following still more direct semi-promise concerning the Society's future came in a letter, dated October 7, 1930:

"I have hopes, however, for larger things for the Society, if they wish them, in the years following my retirement from my present official position. You are already starting the ground work on which much larger creations for the welfare of the Society may be based."

Another letter of this same period (September 24, 1930) contained the following paragraph:

"Of course my term of office expires very shortly, but I assure you that for many years, even before I was officially connected with the Society in any capacity, I have been thinking of methods by which its condition could be improved and made easier for the officers; and even after I retire next December I will still continue to be interested in its affairs."

In a letter written about a month (June 25, 1931) before his death a paragraph sums up the matter well and emphasizes his thought of an endowment, indicating that this problem had been uppermost in his mind for a long time:

"I think that the question of an endowment might some time be considered. I have had this matter in mind ever since I began years ago to present small sums to the Society to help out the work of the Department of the Secretary. I have no doubt it would be a convenience for you to know some time ahead, perhaps a year or two, how much you are likely to get during any current period. This is always a difficulty, unless the organization has an endowment of which it uses only the interest instead of the total capital of the gift."

Thus it appears that his last forward-looking concern was to insure liberal financial support to the two organizations that seemed to him to satisfy in somewhat differing measure the ambition of his youth, when the whole world became his field and all things were possible: the goal of one, The Geological Society, to cover the whole range of geologic science, his own chosen professional field; the goal of the other to sweep a still wider range, for on the American Philosophical Society, established by Benjamin Franklin, was imposed the task of covering all useful human knowledge.

The morning that Penrose's unexpected death on July 31, 1931, was chronicled in the news of the day I unexpectedly met W. C. Mendenhall, then director of the United States Geological Survey, as I turned into a busy street in the city of Los Angeles. We spoke with regret of his untimely passing, and wondered, quite naturally, if the suddenness of his death had found his plans uncompleted. We should have known better; throughout his lifetime, Penrose was ever ready for whatever situation presented itself; in the great adventure of death, he would not be caught unprepared.

Then on September 9, 1931—a year exactly from that before-mentioned Philadelphia conference—a letter came to the Secretary at his office at Columbia University, a letter from the Pennsylvania Company for Insurance on Lives and Granting Annuities, advising that the Geological Society was named in the Penrose will, which had been deposited in the safekeeping of that company, and requesting that properly designated officers be present at a meeting in Philadelphia to discuss the matter.

Stanley-Brown and I made the trip to Philadelphia on the designated day. There, together with representatives of the American Philosophical Society, we heard Mr. David, Trust Officer of the Pennsylvania Company, read the will.

Last Will and Testament of Richard A. F. Penrose, Jr.

Be it remembered that I, Richard A. F. Penrose, Jr., of the City of Philadelphia and the State of Pennsylvania, do make and declare this as and for my last will and testament in the manner and form following, to wit:

First: I give, devise and bequeath to my brother, Spencer Penrose, all my right, title and interest in the property over which I have the power of appointment conferred on me by the will of my father, Richard A. F. Penrose. I also give, devise and bequeath to my said brother Spencer Penrose all my right, title, interest and estate in the property known as 1331 Spruce Street in the City of Philadelphia and the State of Pennsylvania.

Second: I give and bequeath to each of my three first cousins in Carlisle, Pennsylvania, namely Miss Sarah M. Penrose, Miss Ellen W. Penrose, and Miss Virginia A. M. Penrose twenty thousand dollars ($20,000).

Third: I give and bequeath to my Secretary, Miss Marion L. Ivens, twenty-five thousand dollars ($25,000) provided she is in my employ at the time of my death. I give and bequeath to my assistant Secretary, Miss A. M. Feeney, three thousand dollars ($3,000) provided she is in my employ at the time of my death, and I also give and bequeath to the assistant or clerk who may be helping her with my work at the time of my death five hundred dollars ($500).

Fourth: I give and bequeath to Thomas Tobin who was once in charge of our old stable on Juniper Street, Philadelphia, and who is now employed at 1331 Spruce Street, Philadelphia, five thousand dollars ($5,000). To any other household servants at 1331 Spruce Street who may have been in my service for two years or more and are still in my service at the time of my death, I give and bequeath the amount of two years' wages on the scale in force at the time of my death.

Fifth: I give and bequeath to the club known as "The Rabbit" near Church Lane and Belmont Avenue, Philadelphia, ten thousand dollars ($10,000) to be used as they may see fit. I also give and bequeath to "The Rabbit" all of the so-called "Certificates of Equitable Property Interest in The Rabbit" which may be held by me at the time of my death.

Sixth: I give and bequeath to the University of Chicago, Chicago, Illinois, to be used for the benefit of the Journal of Geology, of which I have had the honor of being one of the editors and associate editors for many years, fifty thousand dollars ($50,000).

Seventh: I give and bequeath to the Economic Geology Publishing Company (incorporated under the laws of the District of Columbia) to be used for the benefit of the Journal known as "Economic Geology" twenty-five thousand dollars ($25,000).

Eighth: I give and bequeath all the rest, remainder and residue of my estate, real and personal, of which I shall be seized or possessed at the time of my death, in two equal parts, one of these parts to the American Philosophical Society held at Philadelphia for Promoting Useful Knowledge, and the other of these parts to the Geological Society of America (incorporated under the laws of the State of New York). Both of these gifts shall be considered endowment funds the income of which only to be used and the capital to be properly invested.

Ninth: I nominate, constitute and appoint my brother, Spencer Penrose, John Stokes Adams, and the Pennsylvania Company for Insurance on Lives and Granting Annuities to be the executors of this my last will and testament.

Tenth: I order and direct my executors herein named to pay all inheritance taxes on my estate and on all legacies contained herein out of the principal of my estate so that all such taxes may and shall be charged out of the principal of my residual estate.

Lastly, I hereby revoke and make void any and all other wills by me at any time heretofore made.

IN WITNESS WHEREOF I have hereunto set my hand and seal this twelfth day of June Anno Domini one thousand nine hundred and thirty.

Richard A. F. Penrose, Jr. (Seal)

Signed, sealed, published and declared by the testator above named as and for his last will and testament in the presence of who at his request and in his presence and in the presence of each other have hereunto subscribed our names in witness thereto.

Wm. S. Andes
Edward C. Lukens

Thus had the breath of his life gone out and his own work was ended. But Fortune had favored and good judgment had increased the rewards of successful effort. With fine discrimination he had weighed, in what seemed to him to be the true proportion, the amount that belonged by right to his family and to each dependent, until every recognized obligation was cancelled. Then, with the original account balanced with meticulous regard for its sources, he gave the residue —measured in millions—to the perpetuation of human knowledge and the unraveling of the history of the Earth. The vision that he could not reach himself he commissioned to younger men and yet younger men, from generation to generation, to continue as long as there still are hidden secrets in the Earth and men have the urge to search for them.

A TWENTY-YEAR SUMMARY

BY H. R. ALDRICH

Secretary of The Geological Society of America

The appearance of this volume, at a time after the Society has completed 20 years of operations under the benefaction of Doctor Penrose, cannot fail to prompt many questions in the minds of the variety of readers from many walks of life—geologists and other scientists, lay folks from the professions and world of business, students of biography and genealogy, officers of other scientific organizations, patrons of other sciences, possibly some potential patrons, and citizens of many lands.

All sorts of questions must arise from a situation so unique from every possible angle! A little-known profession interests a member of a prominent family best known for its political connections. He rises to the heights of the profession as a practitioner, professor, investor. He is recognized by the small but oldest and principal geological society in the United States, serves as its president, and a few months later bequeaths to it his half estate, that the income therefrom may be utilized in the pursuit of purposes to which he had given his professional years. Probably no other small organization in a relatively obscure science was ever so richly endowed.

Comprehensive coverage of the area of inquiry would require a second volume. For this neither time nor space is here available. In fact, it would require deeper insight into the future than we possess. It would amount to a "biography" of the Society with parts, chapters, and paragraphs setting forth the devotion and loyalties of many Fellows, and closing with at least a word of prophesy.

Some who inquire how purposes have been served and what has been accomplished will look not alone for the tangible results that can be counted out or otherwise measured. They will look for the intangibles, the stimulus to research and publication, and to lay appreciation of geologic science, its economic and utilitarian values, as well as its cultural values, its contribution to the ultimate of all purposes—a better way of life.

Many absorbing questions now anticipated must await other treatment. One good reason for this is that since the beginning of these two decades geologic science has witnessed a tremendous rebirth, an almost explosive evolution, phenomenal growth in every essential aspect. Thus, the Penrose Bequest came at a most opportune time, at the very depth of the most devastating economic depression. It would be difficult if not impossible to determine the role played by the Society in the developing science through the injection of the income from the Bequest. The two forces have been acting concurrently, but cause and effect relations cannot now be distinguished. At least the Bequest revolutionized the Society. It opened new vistas, bolstered courage, relieved frustrations, supplied sorely needed support, provoked constructive discussion and planning, and enabled earth scientists to take their rightful places in the rehabilitation of the endless frontier of scientific research. At the close of these decades geology is in a position of promise and responsibility not expected at their beginning. If it may not claim an essential part in these developments, at least we may say that the generous gift added momentum to the independent movement.

Stated most simply, the basic question is: "What income has flowed from the Penrose Bequest and what has been done with it?" In most condensed form the answer is given in the following table of rounded figures:

		Per cent	Annual average
Income Derived	$3,930,000		
Expenditures:			
1. For publication	$1,360,000	39.82	$68,000
2. For grants in aid of research	833,000	24.39	41,650
3. For Secretary's office	533,000	15.61	26,650
4. For Treasurer's office	281,000	8.23	14,050
5. For Council and Committees	181,000	5.30	9,050
6. For miscellaneous purposes	137,000	4.01	6,850
7. For International Geological Congress	90,000	2.64	
TOTAL	$3,415,000	100.0	

These seven channels of expenditure lead directly or indirectly to the fostering of investigation of geologic problems and the printing and distribution of the results. It might have been otherwise of course. In fact some readers will be particularly interested to observe what the Society has not done. It has not entered upon a building program. It has not accumulated a library. It has not established professorships, fellowships, or scholarships. It has not engaged in subvention of areal surveys and expeditions, or in the sub-endowment of other institutions. It has not in any way mortgaged the future years other than to continue to provide minimum facilities and competent staff for the central office. Each new Council taking over at the close of the fiscal period finds itself free and responsible for the allocation of the prospective income of the succeeding period.

Let us examine each of these seven channels to see something of their tangible as well as their intangible product.

1. PUBLICATIONS: In the first four decades of the life of the Society, prior to 1931, publication outlets had been none too adequate. The establishment of the *Bulletin* was a prime reason for organization in 1888. But it was financed wholly from annual dues and subscriptions and could be produced only four times a year. Each first annual number contained the official records of the preceding year of this Society and, for several years, of one or more of the associated societies, the abstracts of papers presented at the Annual Meetings, and the memorials to departed Fellows. The three succeeding numbers carried geologic papers and without restrictions upon fields of specialization. The four issues were limited in volume and illustration largely by the element of economy, serviced by labor-loving editors, and nursed by friendly printers.

Consequently as the founding fathers had established the Bulletin as a primary objective, so the Council of 1931 resolved that a first use of the Penrose income should be to provide more adequate publication outlets.

The Bulletin of 1933 and 1934 appeared in six issues. Editorial services were provided on a continuing professional basis. The official material for 1933 was segregated and printed in 1934 as the first of a series of separate volumes of Proceedings. By January 1935 the need for twelve issues of the Bulletin had been recognized. Photographs were reproduced by the more effective collotype or full-tone process. Folded charts and maps, either in black and white or in color were permitted. Throughout succeeding years the ruling policy has been adequacy of presentation within reasonable expenditure. Many efficiencies of format and their attendant economies have been introduced. Furthermore the expansion of the membership, and of the number of subscribers, and the wise establishment of more than 350 free depositories throughout the world not only extended the service of the Bulletin but permitted the write off of rising first costs over a steadily increasing edition. Because of increase in pages each annual volume since 1935 is organized in two parts, each with its table of contents and half-year index. While the mortality among manuscripts runs 25–30 per cent, the files are wide open to authors regardless of their membership, field of geologic interest, or nationality.

Despite this overall expansion of the Bulletin it failed, however, to provide outlet for those manuscripts of length and/or character too long or otherwise unsuited to publication in a journal.

The *Special Papers* series was created in 1934 as an outlet for long papers, largely bibliographies and compilations of reference material. They were issued in paper covers and when discontinued and merged with the Memoir series in 1946, in response to a demand for hard binding, had reached Number 60! Many of the manuscripts had been completed privately and laid aside because of lack of publication facilities. Many others were initiated privately under the assumption that when completed they would be fairly well assured of printing. Others were aided by grants from the Society. Some were prepared by committees of the National Research Council. Many are long since out of print. One has been re-printed by photographic off-set processes, and others no doubt will be accorded similar treatment when demand justifies, since the character of the material is in the category of basic reference materials or tools for research and hence of more than passing value and interest.

Memoir 1 was issued in 1934. This series had been authorized to carry outstanding, longer manuscripts of a nonbibliographic character. Several are presentations in English of special field and laboratory methods and techniques developed abroad. They are bound in library buckram. They proved to be highly popular and several to date have been reprinted to meet high continuing demand. In 1946 a comparison of Special Papers and Memoirs disclosed a distinction without essential difference other than the desirable hard bindings of the Memoirs. The Special Papers were therefore discontinued. Within this twenty-year summary 47 Memoirs and two special volumes of identical appearance are included.

As is true with the Bulletin and Special Papers, so with the Memoirs—authors are not required to hold membership in the Society. Their manuscripts are received for approval and processing solely on the basis of scientific merit.

The *Bibliography and Index of Geology Exclusive of North America* was authorized early in 1932 as a service to research and to supplement the Bibliography of North American Geology published by the United States Geological Survey. The two provide fairly complete bibliographic coverage of world literature of geology. Both are prepared in the Library of the U. S. Geological Survey by independent yet co-operating groups of bibliographers. The Society maintains its staff of three who are trained in geology and bibliography and have a reading knowledge of every foreign language. The source material is found in one or another of several libraries of which the Library of Congress is quite important. Each volume carries an invitation to authors in other lands to send reprints of their papers in order that they may be incorporated and given the wide and useful distribution of this unique volume. More than 300 serials are examined and their important papers in earth science briefly abstracted and indexed. The volumes have been printed annually, except for the war period. They are bound in service buckram and have won highest commendation. Fifteen volumes have appeared up to this date.

Wall Maps. The two decades have witnessed growing interest in the syntheses of accumulating field data, and their stimulus of further analysis and research. The funds available through the Penrose Bequest permitted the issue of small large-scale maps as illustrations of individual papers in the Bulletin, Special Papers, and Memoirs. Many geologists hold to the view that accurate maps are more to be desired than long descriptive texts. In extension of these views the Society has allocated funds to the use of committees organized for the compilation and synthesis of many small maps upon large small-scale wall maps. Five of these have appeared to date and another is in process.

Geologic Map of North America was prepared under a grant, printed and issued in 1946. The lithographic plates have survived several reprintings and a special committee is now engaged in a total revision. Canadian and Mexican authorities have agreed to co-operate and the United States Geological Survey will do the printing.

Geologic Map of South America was prepared under a committee which operated through the Department of State to assure the co-operation of the proper authorities in each of the thirteen nations of the southern continent. The American Geographical Society was a prime mover in this project as well as an important contributor. A first trial edition in black and white was issued (in 1945) with an invitation to criticize and contribute information. The colored edition was issued in 1950.

Glacial Map of North America was compiled by a committee organized under the National Research Council of the United States but including Canadian representatives; it was drafted in the offices of the Geological Survey of Canada. This, a first compilation of accumulated data, has promoted many field researches organized to fill blank areas and restudy problems in strategic localities. A revision is in prospect for the not far distant future.

Tectonic Map of Canada. Under a special grant from the Society, a committee of the Geological Association of Canada searched the geologic literature and synthesized a wall map to represent the major structural elements of Canadian geology. The map is printed on the projection and scale of the geologic map of Canada and, although differing in scale and projection, complements the tectonic map of the United States issued some years ago by the American Association of Petroleum Geologists.

Geologic and Tectonic Map of Venezuela was prepared by Professor Walter H. Bucher following a protracted visit as guest of the government of Venezuela. Many of the commercial companies operating in the oil and mining fields of Venezuela contributed both information and the services of their professional staffs.

The Associated Societies will surely sanction mention of annual contributions to enable them to join in the aim to provide adequate outlets in their special fields of geologic science. Without presuming to enumerate numbers of additional pages and volumes, or to specify improvements in quality of text and illustration, it is fair to note here that the American Mineralogist, the Journal of Paleontology, and the Bulletin of the Seismological Society of America have enjoyed the use of essential sums over the two decades.

Concurrently, distributions have multiplied over widening areas through increase in membership and subscriptions. Moreover, from lesser numbers of Bulletin "Exchanges" a number of Depositories have been established by mutual agreement with around 350 libraries at universities, institutes, surveys, and other institutions throughout the world which receive all publications without obligation to return their material. Each depository functions as an outpost or agency for the further dissemination of these results of research. Many readers thereby discover that they may purchase private copies. Prices have been maintained at average manufacturing cost plus 20 per cent for handling and shipping.

One heartening, tangible, direct result of this increase in distribution is that over this short period of time dues paid and money receipts from sales and subscriptions have increased from $4,870 and $3,587 respectively in 1932 to $27,000 and $35,000 in 1951; and to an overall total of $426,000. The total of miscellaneous income from sources other than securities which, of course, is returned to the general fund, is approximately equal to the expenditures for administrative and fiscal purposes. In other words, the income from securities is now available for the scientific purposes of the Society—Grants in aid of research, publications, and meetings.

These then are the first and most tangible results which the Society can show for 20 years of operation under the Penrose Bequest:

Total rounded sum expended for publications.................................. $1,360,000
   1. For the expanded Bulletin..................... $480,000 or 35.3%
   2. For editorial and bibliographic salaries.......... 237,000   17.4
   3. For 47 Memoirs............................. 180,000   13.2
   4. For aiding associated societies with their journals 132,000   9.7
   5. For 60 Special Papers........................ 109,000   8.0

6. For 15 issues of Foreign Bibliography	69,000	5.1	
7. For 5 Wall Maps	65,000	4.8	
8. For 18 volumes of Proceedings (plus Interim Proceedings)	57,000	4.2	
9. For miscellaneous items*	31,000	2.3	
	$1,360,000	100.0%	$1,360,000

* Includes reprinting of Bulletin articles, Special Papers, and Memoirs; two 10-year Indexes to the Bulletin; Rock Color Charts; Special Color Plates for Economic Geology; Redrafting and many other items of preparation, manufacturing, and distribution cost.

2. GRANTS IN AID OF RESEARCH were begun in 1932 and at the end of our 20-year period 649 have been authorized of which, however, 49 were wholly cancelled, while many others have proved to be somewhat excessive, and resulting

TABLE 1.—DISTRIBUTION OF PROJECTS SUBMITTED AND AUTHORIZED IN FISCAL YEARS

Fiscal year	Number submitted	Number authorized	Total amount granted	Amount of average grant	Fiscal year	Number submitted	Number authorized	Total amount granted	Amount of average grant
1933	150	40	$47,600.00	$1,190	1946	60	40	$136,214.00	$3,405
1934	109	58	55,478.35	956	1947	50	40	78,346.00	1,959
1935	66	43	33,964.00	790	1948	27	21	93,372.00	4,446
1936	66	45	60,874.00	1,353	1949	40	24	56,543.00	2,356
1937	49	35	48,107.05	1,375	1950	33	18	37,275.00	2,071
1938	47	37	36,926.50	998	1951	24	20	61,330.00	3,066
1939	66	46	40,260.00	875					
1940	55	47	41,570.00	884	Total	992	649	989,488.17	1,525
1941	58	51	40,060.90	786					
1942	25	23	18,487.24	804	Less 49 grants completely cancelled (600 effective)			92,631.24	
1943	17	16	15,541.00	978					
1944	14	12	10,462.00	872					
1945	36	33	77,077.13	2,336				$896,856.93	

in refunds. Several grantees have had more than one grant, but between 500 and 600 individuals have been assisted with their investigations by amounts averaging approximately $1,500. The maximum grant to date has been $54,000, the minimum, $40.

A few simple tables from printed records will adequately amplify these simple summary statements.

Table 1 gives answer to the expected question whether all applications are granted. They are not all granted of course, and the record suggests a ratio of two grants out of three applications. This table shows other things of interest. For example it shows how the amounts, numbers, and averages have varied through the years. In opening years a great many applications were received, and the mortality was high. The maximum appropriation was in 1946 immediately following the cessation of hostilities in World War II and the release of talent, inspiration, and energy from military service to science.

Table 2 shows the distribution of grants with respect to the fields of specialization, their number, amounts, and averages. No segment of the geologic frontier has been excluded.

Table 3 gives the distribution by amounts. Clearly the grants have been mainly aids to research rather than complete subsidies. Salaries to grantees have been looked upon with disfavor, and this has proven to be not too harsh a policy since the overwhelming majority of those having free time to devote to research have been salaried members of the teaching profession.

It will be noted, too, that of the total amount authorized, some $90,000 less became effective on account of total cancellations, while partial cancellations and sums appropriated but not expended up to the close of the fiscal year ending July 31, 1951 account for another $60,000.

TABLE 2.—DISTRIBUTION OF EFFECTIVE GRANTS IN MAJOR FIELDS OF GEOLOGY

Field	Number	Amount granted	Approximate average
Economic	18	$35,090.00	$1,949
Geophysics and Geochemistry	69	226,130.00	3,263
Mineralogy	25	70,299.00	2,812
Paleontology	158	188,300.90	1,192
Petrology	92	117,566.60	1,278
Vulcanology	19	23,740.00	1,249
General (Structural, Physiographic, Stratigraphic, Glacial, Sedimentation)	219	235,730.43	1,076
Total	600	$896,856.93	$1,494

TABLE 3.—DISTRIBUTION OF GRANTS BY THE AMOUNT OF GRANT

Amount	Total number	Percentage of total number
Over $10,000	10	1.6
$5,000–10,000	17	2.8
4,500– 4,999	5	0.8
4,000– 4,499	9	1.5
3,500– 3,999	11	1.8
3,000– 3,499	21	3.5
2,500– 2,999	26	4.3
2,000– 2,499	28	4.7
1,500– 1,999	42	7.0
1,000– 1,499	60	10.0
500– 999	183	30.5
Under $500	188	31.5
Total	600	100.0

This then is a concise summary of accomplishment under the program of aid for research.

3. The SECRETARY'S OFFICE accounts for about 16 per cent of the total sum expended during these two decades. While we may not point to it as an achievement in the advancement of geology on a par with publications or even with the research grants, perhaps it is not entirely irrelevant to point out accomplishments of organization and function.

Physically the office is a house, a one-time city dwelling, now included as a part of the campus of Columbia University, hence within the appropriate environment and atmosphere of research and teaching. Arrangements for its use were made in 1932 by Doctor Berkey, at that time Secretary of The Society, upon learning from President Butler that this house at 419 could be made available. Physically the office contains the official accounts, records, and archives of the Society. Here too is the furniture, equipment, and other physical property of the Society other than the stock of publications which is stored within the air-conditioned stacks of the near-by Butler Library. The house establishes the official corporate address of the Society. Here the Board of Directors, or Council, convenes, and official committees meet, if efficiency of operation, convenience, and economy factors so recommend.

Columbia University joined in the spirit of generosity and as a co-patron of geologic science made the building available to meet the needs for the imminent expansion of the Society. There are no documents of any sort. There are no official visitations. The Society enjoys absolute freedom in the use of the building and is responsible for the interior, the housekeeping and decoration, and the utilities, while the University cares for the structure and exterior and places its service department on call. Granted that this is no accomplishment in narrow sense, the role that the Society was to play and is playing in the advancement of geologic science by the administration of the Penrose Bequest engendered this expression of generous co-operation. The Society expresses its appreciation in the form of an annual appropriation to the research funds of the University.

The top floor of the building is arranged to provide simple sleeping accommodations for four people. Here Officers of the Society and others in line of duty may be served. Here we have accommodated scientists from other lands who find that on account of exchange problems official travel allowances must be most carefully husbanded. Our guest book is coming to be an imposing roster of world figures in the geologic sciences. A good will throughout the geological profession and a free exchange of ideas are being fostered in this simple accomplishment made possible by the University.

The secretariat should be regarded as but one, though perhaps the largest single integrated unit in the Society. It is a central point but in no sense a center of directorate. The staff has been kept small, and the turnover above the rank of temporary juniors is negligible. Every effort is made to find better ways to meet increasing demands for service by better and more efficient methods. Operations have been mechanized at every opportunity. The morale of the staff is maintained at high level by the feeling that we, too, are a part of the larger team dedicated to the advancement of science, and by confidence in the integrity of the governing body not only as expressed in salaries but in provision for retirement.

Thus the Secretary's office houses a staff alert to the ever-changing demands of geology as interpreted by an ever-changing membership in Council and Committees and eager to discern and execute the wishes of Fellows, Committees, and Councils.

4. TREASURER'S OFFICE in the physical sense has long been one and the same as the Secretary's office. The $281,000 has been expended largely for the safe keeping and managing of the securities. Salary of the Assistant Treasurer (security adviser), honorarium of the Treasurer, custodian, auditing, and bonding fees are the only major items of expense.

Again, while in ordinary sense this cannot be classified as a tangible accomplishment, from the point of view of safety of investment and success in deriving a satisfactory income from the funds of the Bequest, the appointment of Mr. J. Stanley-Brown, a Fellow of the Society who served without salary as Editor 1892–1932, Councilor 1933–1940, and as Chairman of the Finance Committee 1923–1941, and the acceptance of his judgment in securing the services of Miss Beatrice E. Carr as Assistant Treasurer were indeed very real accomplishments, and they have guaranteed the financial security of the Society throughout these 20 years. As resident "watch dog" of the securities of the Endowment and other Funds and in finest advisory co-operation with the members of the Committee on Finance, Miss Carr must be called upon to hold forth her proud twenty-year record as a prime exhibit of accomplishment.

5. COUNCIL AND COMMITTEES have served loyally, at sacrifice of time and energy otherwise to be invested in private research or gainful practice, without pay and with but modest remission of travel expenses. Honor, distinction, or glory in administration do not add up as rapidly in the minds of men of science as do study, judgment, and advice, in loyal service to a democratic organization devoted to the promotion of their science. When the query may be worded "What has the Society to show for this minor (5%) expenditure?" the answer must be, "We have the Society as it is today strengthened by experiences of the past for meeting the challenges of the future."

6. "MISCELLANEOUS PURPOSES" must be a channel in the braided stream of every account of this kind. On analysis we find that they represent largely the intangibles. Here are comprised the expenditures for meetings, including those of the several regional Sections but particularly the Annual Meetings of the Society and the five members of the family of Associated Societies. Can we measure the accomplishments of meetings? By any definition their results are intangible. They must include the exchange of ideas, the discussions and debates, the renewal of courage, determination, and ambition. They are open to any one interested and as such provide a means for the younger people and new comers from abroad to become acquainted. Above all they prompt good fellowship and good teamwork. The expenditure of $137,000, or a minor 4 per cent, represents largely the support of the central Meetings, the cost of which in earlier days had had to be parcelled out and borne by the Fellows of the Local Committee.

"Miscellaneous Purposes" include other important intangibles. Here is recorded the first of the official Penrose benefactions—the Penrose Medal. In strict sense it does not draw upon the income from the Bequest for it was endowed separately in 1927. It is of minor consequence in dollars and cents but nevertheless of major importance among intangibles. The Penrose Medal is highly prized among the list of awards to which geologists of the world are eligible regardless of nationality or specialized interests.

Here too among miscellany are expenditures authorized by Council which should be exhibited especially as evidence of "co-operation in action" with sister societies in geology and as investments for the common good of all scientists. First we cite contributions to the Office of Scientific Personnel of the National

Research Council and more recently to the American Geological Institute now housed within the Division of Geology and Geography of the Council in Washington.

7. INTERNATIONAL GEOLOGIC CONGRESS met in the United States in 1932. Field excursions crossing the continent and visiting important places of special interest were organized, and guide books were written and printed. Geologists of distinction residing in foreign lands were invited guests. Toward the cost of all these the Society expended a round sum of $90,000 as further evidence of good will and co-operation in the advancement of the science.

What has been accomplished with the income from the Penrose Bequest during these first twenty years?
1. The Endowment Fund, originally appraised at $3,884,345 in 1931 has attained a value of $4,540,235 in 1951. It has produced an income of $3,929,419 or slightly more than the original valuation. It has enabled the establishment of a Reserve Fund valued at $860,407, held in readiness for unusual projects.
2. Expenditures for publication have produced upwards of 160 volumes and distributed these to lists of individuals and institutions increasing in number from approximately 1000 to more than 3500.
3. Financial aid has been given to nearly 600 people engaged in research, in amounts averaging approximately $1500 per project.
4. The benefaction has enabled the establishment of an agency serving Fellows, Members, Committees, and Council, the geological fraternity at home and abroad, and accumulating a body of experience, policy, method upon which to build for the future.
5. The financial management has accumulated an experience, a portfolio, and an understanding of the problems of investment in conserving principal and producing income, commensurate with the safety of that principal.
6. The Council's acceptance of responsibility and the success in the management of the Society and particularly in the allocating and expending of the income for prescribed purposes at a cost of 5 per cent has developed a loyalty and a confidence in unstinting teamwork with which to face the challenge of the future.
7. The sharing of the income with other members of the family of five Associated Societies and with the combined group of all eleven geological societies now associated in the American Geological Institute, has kept alive the generous spirit of co-operation in efforts for the common good of science and a better life through better science.

Forces at work since the turning point of national economy in 1932 and which are still advancing the service of geology have been paralleled by the expanding activities of the Society made possible by the Penrose Bequest. Given a continuation of the favoring economy and government, the wisdom to profit from the accumulated experience, and the judgment in the selection of men of vision and integrity to accept stewardship, the Society cannot fail to play its full part in the future development of the science by magnifying and projecting the benefactions of the Penrose Bequest.